Baseball america

DIRECTORY

2005

Your Definitive Guide To The Game

**Detailed Information On Baseball
In All Leagues At All Levels!**

Majors
Minors
Independent
International
College
Amateur

**Published By Baseball America Inc.
Durham, North Carolina**

BaseBall america
DIRECTORY
2005

EDITOR
Allan Simpson
ASSOCIATE EDITORS
Aaron Fitt
Chris Kline
ASSISTANT EDITORS
J.J. Cooper
Will Kimmey
Will Lingo
John Manuel
Alan Matthews
Matthew Meyers
EDITORIAL ASSISTANTS
Mike Groopman
Jeffrey Simpson
PRODUCTION DIRECTOR
Phillip Daquila
PRODUCTION ASSISTANTS
Matthew Eddy
Linwood Webb
DIRECTOR, DISPLAY ADVERTISING
Keith Dangel
DIRECTOR, BUSINESS DEVELOPMENT AND CONSUMER MARKETING
Cliff Gardner
COVER DESIGN
Linwood Webb

Baseball America Inc.
PRESIDENT/CEO
Catherine Silver
VICE PRESIDENT/PUBLISHER
Lee Folger
EDITOR IN CHIEF
Allan Simpson
MANAGING EDITOR
Will Lingo
DESIGN & PRODUCTION DIRECTOR
Phillip Daquila

COVER PHOTOS
Ramon Nivar by John Williamson; John Schuerholz by Tom Priddy;
Fifth Third Field, Dayton, by Biel Photographic

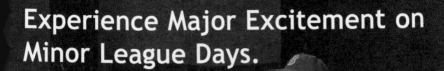

TABLE OF CONTENTS

2005–2006
CALENDAR

March

Sun	Mon	Tue	Wed	Thu	Fri	Sat
		1	2	3	4	5
6	7	8	9	10	11	12
13	14	15	16	17	18	19
20	21	22	23	24	25	26
27	28	29	30	31		

April

Sun	Mon	Tue	Wed	Thu	Fri	Sat
					1	2
3	4	5	6	7	8	9
10	11	12	13	14	15	16
17	18	19	20	21	22	23
24	25	26	27	28	29	30

May

Sun	Mon	Tue	Wed	Thu	Fri	Sat
1	2	3	4	5	6	7
8	9	10	11	12	13	14
15	16	17	18	19	20	21
22	23	24	25	26	27	28
29	30	31				

June

Sun	Mon	Tue	Wed	Thu	Fri	Sat
			1	2	3	4
5	6	7	8	9	10	11
12	13	14	15	16	17	18
19	20	21	22	23	24	25
26	27	28	29	30		

July

Sun	Mon	Tues	Wed	Thur	Fri	Sat
					1	2
3	4	5	6	7	8	9
10	11	12	13	14	15	16
17	18	19	20	21	22	23
24	25	26	27	28	29	30
31						

August

Sun	Mon	Tue	Wed	Thu	Fri	Sat
	1	2	3	4	5	6
7	8	9	10	11	12	13
14	15	16	17	18	19	20
21	22	23	24	25	26	27
28	29	30	31			

September

Sun	Mon	Tue	Wed	Thu	Fri	Sat
				1	2	3
4	5	6	7	8	9	10
11	12	13	14	15	16	17
18	19	20	21	22	23	24
25	26	27	28	29	30	

October

Sun	Mon	Tue	Wed	Thu	Fri	Sat
						1
2	3	4	5	6	7	8
9	10	11	12	13	14	15
16	17	18	19	20	21	22
23	24	25	26	27	28	29
30	31					

November

Sun	Mon	Tue	Wed	Thu	Fri	Sat
		1	2	3	4	5
6	7	8	9	10	11	12
13	14	15	16	17	18	19
20	21	22	23	24	25	26
27	28	29	30			

December

Sun	Mon	Tue	Wed	Thu	Fri	Sat
				1	2	3
4	5	6	7	8	9	10
11	12	13	14	15	16	17
18	19	20	21	22	23	24
25	26	27	28	29	30	31

January

Sun	Mon	Tue	Wed	Thu	Fri	Sat
1	2	3	4	5	6	7
8	9	10	11	12	13	14
15	16	17	18	19	20	21
22	23	24	25	26	27	28
29	30	31				

February

Sun	Mon	Tue	Wed	Thu	Fri	Sat
			1	2	3	4
5	6	7	8	9	10	11
12	13	14	15	16	17	18
19	20	21	22	23	24	25
26	27	28				

March

Sun	Mon	Tue	Wed	Thu	Fri	Sat
			1	2	3	4
5	6	7	8	9	10	11
12	13	14	15	16	17	18
19	20	21	22	23	24	25
26	27	28	29	30	31	

April

Sun	Mon	Tue	Wed	Thu	Fri	Sat
						1
2	3	4	5	6	7	8
9	10	11	12	13	14	15
16	17	18	19	20	21	22
23	24	25	26	27	28	29
30						

THE GREATEST NAMES IN BASEBALL HAVE ONE NAME IN COMMON.

SINCE
1884

Whether you're swinging wood or aluminum—or just want a commemorative bat to hang on the wall—reach for the name that's turned players into legends since 1884: Louisville Slugger. When it comes to bats, it's the only name you'll ever need to know.

TPX

Louisville Slugger®

125 Powerized
Louisville Slugger®

Louisville Slugger®
Powerized

GENUINE C271
CINCINNATI REDS

GENUINE
Rick Geddes
WRIGLEY FIELD

CUBS

Louisville Slugger®
THE OFFICIAL BAT OF MAJOR LEAGUE BASEBALL.®
www.slugger.com

EVENTS
CALENDAR
February 2005 – January 2006

FEBRUARY

28—Opening Day: Chinese Professional Baseball League.

MARCH

2—Major league teams may renew contracts of unsigned players (through March 11).
19—Opening Day: Mexican League.
26—Opening Day: Japan Pacific League.
26—National Classic High School Tournament at Fullerton, Calif. (through March 31).

APRIL

1—Opening Day: China Baseball Association.
1—Opening Day: Japan Central League.
3—Opening Day: American League (Boston at New York).
4—Opening Day: American League (Cleveland at Chicago, Kansas City at Detroit, Minnesota at Seattle, Oakland at Baltimore, Toronto at Tampa Bay).
4—Opening Day: National League (Chicago at Arizona, Milwaukee at Pittsburgh, New York at Cincinnati, San Diego at Colorado, Washington at Philadelphia).
5—Opening Day: American League (Texas at Anaheim).
5—Opening Day: National League (Atlanta at Florida, Los Angeles at San Francisco, St. Louis at Houston).
7—Opening Day: International League, Pacific Coast League, Eastern League, Southern League, Texas League, California League, Carolina League, Florida State League, Midwest League, South Atlantic League.
12—Opening Day: Korean Baseball Organization.
14—Arizona Diamondbacks at Washington Nationals; first game for Major League Baseball back in Washington, D.C.
27—Opening Day: Atlantic League.

MAY

1—Earliest date major league clubs may re-sign free agents who were not offered arbitration.
5—Opening Day: Central League.
16—Opening Day: Venezuelan Summer League.
20—First interleague games.
20—Opening Day: Northern League.
21—Junior College Division III World Series at Glens Falls, N.Y. (through May 27).
23—Hall of Fame Game at Cooperstown (Boston vs. Detroit).
25—Opening Day: Frontier League.
26—Opening Day: Can-Am League, Golden League.
27—NCAA Division III World Series at Appleton, Wis. (through May 31).
27—NAIA World Series at Lewiston, Idaho (through June 3).
28—NCAA Division II World Series at Montgomery, Ala. (through June 4).

Comerica Park, site of the 2005 All-Star Game

28—Junior College World Series at Grand Junction, Colo. (through June 4).
28—Junior College Division II World Series at Millington, Tenn. (through June 3).
31—Start of closed period for amateur draft.

JUNE

1—Opening Day: California Collegiate League, Northwoods League, Southern Collegiate League.
2—Opening Day: Coastal Plain League.
3—Opening Day: Clark Griffith Collegiate League, Pacific International League, Valley League.
3—NCAA Division I Regionals at campus sites (through June 6).
4—Opening Day: Atlantic Collegiate League, Texas Collegiate League.
4—Opening Day: Dominican Summer League.
6—Opening Day: Florida Collegiate Summer League.
7—Amateur draft (through June 8).
7—Opening Day: Mountain Collegiate League, Northeast Collegiate League.
8—Opening Day: Alaska League.
10—NCAA Division I Super-Regionals at campus sites (through June 13).
10—Opening Day: Cal Ripken Sr. Collegiate League, Jayhawk League, New York Collegiate League.
11—Opening Day: Great Lakes League.
18—Florida State League all-star game at Clearwater, Fla.
14—Opening Day: Central Illinois Collegiate League, West Coast Collegiate League.
15—Opening Day: Florida Collegiate Instructional League.
16—Opening Day: Cape Cod League.
17—59th College World Series at Omaha (through June 26/27).
17—USA Baseball Junior Olympic Championships at Jupiter, Fla., and Peoria/Surprise, Ariz. (through June 25).

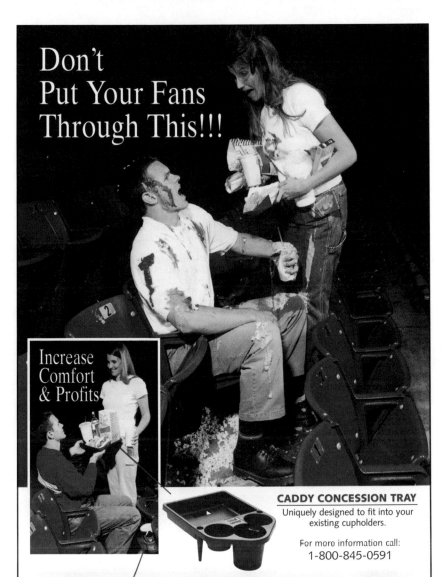

17—Perfect Game National Showcase, site unavailable. (through June 19).

20—Sunbelt Baseball Classic Series at Norman, Okla. (through June 26).

20—USA Baseball junior Tournament of Stars at Joplin, Mo. (through June 27).

21—Opening Day: New York-Penn League, Northwest League, Appalachian League, Pioneer League.

21—Texas League all-star game at Frisco, Texas; Midwest League all-star game at Peoria, Ill.

22—Opening Day: Arizona League.

24—Opening Day: Gulf Coast League.

26—USA Baseball college team trials at Raleigh, N.C. (through June 30).

28—California League/Carolina League all-star game at Frederick, Md.; South Atlantic League all-star game at Augusta, Ga.

JULY

10—7th annual All-Star Futures Game at Comerica Park, Detroit.

12—76th Major League All-Star Game at Comerica Park, Detroit.

13—Triple-A all-star game at Sacramento; Eastern League all-star game at Portland, Maine; Southern League all-star game at Mobile, Ala.

13—Atlantic League all-star game at Atlantic City, N.J.; Frontier League all-star game at Washington, Pa.

19—Central League/Northeast League all-star game at Brockton, Mass.; Northern League all-star game at Gary, Ind.

22—Japan All-Star Game I at Seibu Dome.

23—Japan All-Star Game II at Koshien Stadium.

30—Cape Cod League all-star game at Hyannis, Mass.

31—Hall of Fame induction ceremonies, Cooperstown.

31—National Baseball Congress World Series at Wichita (through Aug. 14).

AUGUST

1—End of major league trading period without waivers.

1—East Coast Professional Baseball Showcase at Wilmington, N.C. (through Aug. 4).

6—Area Code Games at Long Beach (through Aug. 10).

6—Connie Mack World Series at Farmington, N.M. (through Aug. 12).

10—AFLAC High School Classic at Aberdeen, Md. (through Aug. 13)

13—Babe Ruth 16-18 World Series at Newark, Ohio (through Aug. 20).

13—Babe Ruth 13-15 World Series at Abbeville, La. (through Aug. 20).

13—Pony League World Series at Washington, Pa. (through Aug. 20).

19—World Youth Championship at Monterrey, Mexico (through Aug. 30).

19—Little League World Series at Williamsport, Pa. (through Aug. 28).

19—American Legion World Series at Rapid City, S.D. (through Aug. 23).

23—New York-Penn League all-star game at Brooklyn.

31—Postseason major league roster eligibility frozen.

SEPTEMBER

1—Major league roster limits expanded from 25 to 40.

3—World Cup at Amsterdam, Netherlands (through Sept. 17).

OCTOBER

2—Major league season ends.

3—Opening Day: Arizona Fall League.

3—Beginning of major league trading period without waivers.

4—Major league Division Series begin.

7—Baseball America/Perfect Game 16 and under Wood Bat Championship at Fort Myers, Fla. (through Oct. 10).

11—League Championship Series begin.

22—World Series begins.

22—Japan Series begins at home of Pacific League champion.

28—Baseball America/Perfect Game World Wood Bat Championship at Jupiter, Fla. (through Oct. 31).

NOVEMBER

18—Filing date, 40-man major league winter rosters.

DECEMBER

1—National High School Baseball Coaches Association convention at Louisville. (through Dec. 4).

5—103rd annual Winter Meetings at Dallas (through Dec. 8).

7—Deadline for major league clubs to offer eligible players salary arbitration.

8—Rule 5 major league/minor league drafts.

19—Deadline for players offered arbitration to accept.

20—Last date for major league clubs to tender contracts.

JANUARY 2006

5—American Baseball Coaches Association convention at Chicago (through Jan. 8).

6—NCAA National Convention at Indianapolis (through Jan. 10).

CRAFTED FROM SELECT MAPLE.

BORN OF PURE HERITAGE.

Start with America's finest rock-hard maple. Put it in the hands of America's most experienced bat makers, and you have the unbeatable line of maple bats from Louisville Slugger.

For the powerful per-formance that comes

from premium maple, reach for maple bats from Louisville Slugger. Because when you swing Louisville Slugger, you're swinging the best there is.

THE OFFICIAL BAT OF MAJOR LEAGUE BASEBALL™
www.slugger.com

BASEBALL AMERICA

ESTABLISHED 1981

PRESIDENT/CEO: Catherine Silver

VICE PRESIDENT/PUBLISHER: Lee Folger

EDITOR IN CHIEF: Allan Simpson

MANAGING EDITOR: Will Lingo
EXECUTIVE EDITOR: Jim Callis
ASSISTANT MANAGING EDITOR: John Manuel
NEWS EDITOR: J.J. Cooper
SENIOR WRITER: Alan Schwarz
NATIONAL WRITER: Will Kimmey
ASSOCIATE EDITOR: Alan Matthews
ASSISTANT EDITORS: Aaron Fitt, Chris Kline, Matthew Meyers

GENERAL MANAGER, BASEBALLAMERICA.COM: Kevin Goldstein

DESIGN AND PRODUCTION DIRECTOR: Phillip Daquila
PRODUCTION ASSISTANTS: Matthew Eddy, Linwood Webb

CUSTOMER SERVICE: Ronnie McCabe, Jessica Ross
customerservice@baseballamerica.com

ADVERTISING SALES
DIRECTOR, DISPLAY ADVERTISING: Keith Dangel
DIRECTOR, BUSINESS DEVELOPMENT AND CONSUMER MARKETING: Cliff Gardner
P.O. Box 2089, Durham, NC 27702
Telephone: (800) 845-2726; **FAX:** (919) 682-2880

BUSINESS STAFF
ECONOMIST: Bill Porter
MANAGER, FINANCE: Cara Callanan
FINANCIAL ADMINISTRATOR: Leon Lashway
LEGAL COUNSEL: Mike Ring

BASEBALL AMERICA INC.

Mailing Address: P.O. Box 2089, Durham, NC 27702
Street Address: 201 West Main Street, Suite 201, Durham, NC 27701
Telephone: (919) 682-9635 • **Toll-Free:** (800) 845-2726
FAX: (919) 682-2880
Website: BaseballAmerica.com

BASEBALL AMERICA, the nation's most complete all-baseball magazine, publishes 26 issues a year. Subscription rates are US $76.95 for one year, $114.90 for two years. Call or write for non-U.S. addresses.

BASEBALL AMERICA PUBLICATIONS

2005 Almanac: A comprehensive look at the 2004 season, featuring major and minor league statistics and commentary; 472 pages. **$17.95** ($20.95 spiral bound)

2005 Prospect Handbook: Detailed scouting reports and biographical sketches on 900 of the top prospects in the minor leagues; 512 pages. **$25.95**

2005 Super Register: A complete record, with biographical information, of every player who played professional baseball in 2004; 720 pages. **$69.95**

2005 Directory: Names, addresses, phone numbers, major and minor league schedules—vital to baseball insiders and fans; 392 pages. **$21.95** ($24.95 spiral bound)

2005 Great Parks: The Baseball America Calendar. **$14.95**

All prices in US funds. Add $6 for shipping and handling plus $2 for each item. Allow four weeks for delivery.

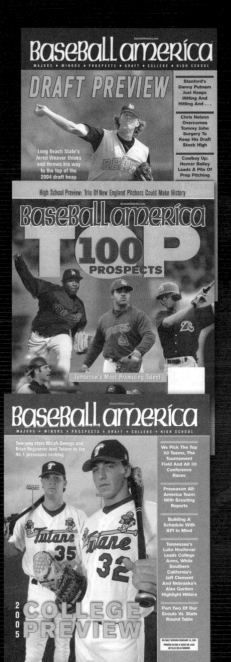

BASEBALL AMERICA
2004 AWARD WINNERS

MAJOR LEAGUES

Player of the Year
Barry Bonds, of, Giants
Executive of the Year
Terry Ryan, Twins
Rookie of the Year
Khalil Greene, ss, Padres
Roland Hemond Award (Contributions to Scouting and Player Development)
Roger Jongewaard
Lifetime Achievement Award
John Schuerholz
Vin Scully

MINOR LEAGUES

Organization of the Year
Minnesota Twins
Player of the Year
Jeff Francis, lhp, Rockies (Tulsa/Texas, Colorado Springs/Pacific Coast)
Manager of the Year
Marty Brown, Indians (Buffalo/International)
Executive of the Year
Chris Kemple, Wilmington Blue Rocks (Carolina)
Team of the Year
Lancaster Jethawks, California/Diamondbacks
Bob Freitas Awards (Best Minor League Operations)
Triple-A: Sacramento River Cats (Pacific Coast)
Double-A: Round Rock Express (Texas)
Class A: Dayton Dragons (Midwest)
Short-season: Burlington Indians (Appalachian)
Classification Players of the Year
Triple-A: Jason Kubel, of, Twins (Rochester/International)
Double-A: Jeff Francis, lhp, Rockies (Tulsa/Texas)
High Class A: Erick Aybar, ss, Angels (Rancho Cucamonga/California)
Low Class A: Delmon Young, of, Devil Rays

Baseball America's Rookie of the Year
Padres shortstop Khalil Greene

(Charleston, S.C./South Atlantic)
Short-season: Javier Herrera, of, Athletics (Vancouver/Northwest)
Rookie: Mitch Einertson, of, Astros (Greeneville/Appalachian)

INDEPENDENT LEAGUES

Player of the Year
Victor Rodriguez, ss, Somerset (Atlantic)

WINTER LEAGUES

2004-2005 Player of the Year
Johnny Gomes, of, Mexicali (Mexico/Devil Rays)

COLLEGES

Player of the Year
Jered Weaver, rhp, Long Beach State
Coach of the Year
David Perno, Georgia
Freshman of the Year
Wade LeBlanc, lhp, Alabama

AMATEUR/YOUTH LEAGUES

Summer Player of the Year (College players)
Daniel Carte, of, Falmouth (Cape Cod)
Youth Player of the Year (High school and younger)
Cameron Maybin, of, Asheville, N.C.
Ripken Baseball Youth Coach of the Year
Tony Saragas, Harlan, Ky.

HIGH SCHOOLS

Player of the Year
Homer Bailey, rhp, LaGrange (Texas) HS.
Baseball America/National High School Baseball Coaches Association Champion
Chatsworth (Calif.) HS

Baseball America's Minor League Player of the Year
Rockies pitching prospect Jeff Francis

Baseball America's
4th Annual Awards Gala

Winter Meetings • Anaheim • December 11, 2004

Another who's who of the baseball industry gathered as Baseball America honored a year's worth of winners, as well as handing out Lifetime Achievement Awards to John Schuerholz and Vin Scully.

Braves general manager John Schuerholz and longtime voice of the Dodgers Vin Scully highlighted the list of winners at the 2004 Awards Gala

Another distinguished panel of baseball's best and brightest took home the hardware at the Baseball America Awards Gala. The Gala supported youth baseball initiatives.

TRAVEL INFO
TOLL-FREE NUMBERS & WEBSITES

AIRLINES

Aeromexico	aeromexico.com	800-237-6639
Air Canada	aircanada.com	800-361-2159
Airtran Airways	airtran.com	800-247-8726
Alaska Airlines	alaskaair.com	800-426-0333
Aloha Airlines	alohaairlines.com	800-227-4900
America West	americawest.com	800-235-9292
American Airlines	aa.com	800-433-7300
Continental Airlines	continental.com	800-525-0280
Delta Air Lines	delta.com	800-221-1212
Japan Air Lines	jal.co.jp/en/	800-525-3663
Korean Air	koreanair.com	800-438-5000
Northwest Airlines	nwa.com	800-225-2525
Olympic Airways	olympic-airways.gr	800-223-1226
Qantas Airways	qantas.com	800-227-4500
Southwest Airlines	southwest.com	800-435-9792
United Airlines	ual.com	800-864-8331
U.S. Airways	usairways.com	800-428-4322

CAR RENTALS

Alamo	goalamo.com	800-732-3232
Avis	avis.com	800-331-1212
Budget	budget.com	800-527-0700
Dollar	dollar.com	800-800-4000
Enterprise	enterprise.com	800-325-8007
Hertz	hertz.com	800-654-3131
National	nationalcar.com	800-227-7368
Thrifty	thrifty.com	800-367-2277

HOTELS/MOTELS

Best Western	bestwestern.com	800-528-1234
Choice Hotels	choicehotels.com	800-424-6423
Clarion	choicehotels.com	800-221-2222
Comfort Inn	choicehotels.com	800-221-2222
Courtyard by Marriott	marriott.com	800-321-2211
Days Inn	daysinn.com	800-325-2525
Doubletree Hotels	doubletree.com	800-424-2900
Econo Lodge	choicehotels.com	800-424-4777
Embassy Suites	embassy-suites.com	800-362-2779
Fairfield (Marriott)	fairfieldinn.com	800-228-2800
Hampton Inn	hampton-inn.com	800-426-7866
Hilton Hotels	hilton.com	800-445-8667
Holiday Inn/ Holiday Inn Express	sixcontinentshotels.com	800-465-4329
Howard Johnson	hojo.com	800-654-2000
Hyatt Hotels	hyatt.com	800-228-9000
La Quinta	laquinta.com	800-531-5900
Marriott Hotels	marriott.com	800-228-9290
Omni Hotels	omnihotels.com	800-843-6664
Quality Inn	choicehotels.com	800-221-2222
Radisson Hotels	radisson.com	800-333-3333
Ramada Inns	ramada.com	800-228-2828
Red Lion	redlion.com	800-547-8010
Red Roof Inns	redroof.com	800-843-7663
Renaissance Hotels	renaissancehotels.com	800-468-3571
Residence Inn	marriott.com	800-331-3131
Rodeway Inn	choicehotels.com	800-228-2000
Sheraton Hotels	sheraton.com	800-325-3535
Sleep Inn	choicehotels.com	800-221-2222
Super 8 Motels	super8.com	800-800-8000
TraveLodge	travelodge.com	800-578-7878
Westin Hotels	starwood.com/westin	800-228-3000
Wyndham Hotels	wyndham.com	800-996-3426

RAIL

Amtrak	amtrak.com	800-872-7245

WHAT'S NEW
IN 2005

MAJOR LEAGUES

Montreal Expos move to Washington, D.C.; now known as Washington Nationals.

■ BALLPARK NAMES

Florida: Pro Player Stadium becomes Dolphins Stadium.
Texas: Ballpark in Arlington becomes Ameriquest Field in Arlington.
Toronto: Skydome becomes Rogers Centre.

MINOR LEAGUES

Triple-A

Edmonton (Pacific Coast) moves to Round Rock, Texas; now known as Round Rock Express

■ AFFILIATION CHANGES

Astros go from New Orleans (Pacific Coast) to Round Rock.
Expos/Nationals go from Edmonton/Round Rock to New Orleans.
Brewers go from Indianapolis (International) to Nashville (Pacific Coast).
Pirates go from Nashville to Indianapolis.

Double-A

Round Rock (Texas) moves to Corpus Christi, Texas; now known as Corpus Christi Hooks.
El Paso (Texas) moves to Springfield, Mo.; now known as Springfield Cardinals.
Greenville (Southern) moves to Pearl, Miss.; now known as Mississippi Braves.

■ BALLPARKS

Corpus Christi: Whataburger Field.
Mississippi: Mississippi Braves Stadium.
New Hampshire (Eastern): Name unavailable.

■ AFFILIATION CHANGES

Cardinals go from Tennessee (Southern) to Springfield.
Diamondbacks go from El Paso/Springfield to Tennessee.

Class A

Capital City (South Atlantic) moves to Greenville, S.C.; now known as Greenville Bombers.

■ NAME CHANGES

Battle Creek Yankees (Midwest) become Southwest Michigan Devil Rays.
Charleston Alley Cats (South Atlantic) become West Virginia Power.
Greensboro Bats (South Atlantic) become Greensboro Grasshoppers.
Modesto A's (California) become Modesto Nuts.
Potomac Cannons (Carolina) become Potomac Nationals.
Sarasota Red Sox (Florida State) become Sarasota Reds.

■ BALLPARKS

Greensboro: First Horizon Park.
West Virginia: Name unavailable.

■ AFFILIATION CHANGES

Athletics go from Modesto to Stockton (California).
Blue Jays go from Charleston, W.Va., to Lansing (Midwest).
Brewers go from High Desert (California) to Brevard County (Florida State), and from Beloit (Midwest) to West Virginia.
Cardinals go from Peoria (Midwest) to Quad Cities (Midwest).
Cubs go from Lansing (Midwest) to Peoria.
Devil Rays go from Bakersfield (California) to Visalia (California), and from Charleston, S.C., (South Atlantic) to Southwest Michigan.
Expos/Nationals go from Brevard County to Potomac.
Giants go from Hagerstown (South Atlantic) to Augusta (South Atlantic).
Mets go from Capital City to Hagerstown.
Rangers go from Stockton to Bakersfield.
Reds go from Potomac to Sarasota.
Red Sox go from Sarasota to Wilmington (Carolina), and from Augusta to Greenville.
Rockies go from Visalia to Modesto.
Royals go from Wilmington to High Desert.
Twins go from Quad Cities to Beloit.
Yankees go from Battle Creek to Charleston, S.C.

Short-Season

Provo (Pioneer) moves to Orem, Utah; now known as Orem Owlz.

■ BALLPARK

Orem (Pioneer): Parkway Crossing Stadium.

■ ALL-STAR GAME

New York-Penn League will hold its first all-star game at Brooklyn.

INDEPENDENT LEAGUES

Atlantic League: Pennsylvania moves to Lancaster, Pa.; now known as Lancaster Barnstomers.
Can-Am League becomes new name for Northeast League; league's Aces franchise moves to Worcester, Mass.
Central League: Amarillo moves to El Paso, Texas; now known as El Paso Diablos.
Frontier League: Springfield-Ozark becomes travel team; now known as Ohio Valley.
Northern: Calgary Vipers and Edmonton Cracker Cats join league as expansion franchises.
Golden League begins play.

COLLEGE

Four new summer college leagues—Cal Ripken Sr. Collegiate League, Florida Collegiate Summer League, Mountain Collegiate League and West Coast Collegiate League—begin play.

New plant for the Power
West Virginia will open an as-yet-unnamed ballpark in 2005

2005 DRAFT ORDER

The World Series champion Boston Red Sox will forfeit their first-, second- and third-round picks in the June first-year player draft for signing free agents Matt Clement, Edgar Renteria and David Wells during the offseason, but they'll still be the most active team in the early rounds.

Boston will have six of the first 59 picks, getting two picks apiece for losing Type A free agents Orlando Cabrera to the Angels, Derek Lowe to the Dodgers and Pedro Martinez to the Mets.

The St. Louis Cardinals and Florida Marlins will also make six selections before the start of the third round, while the San Francisco Giants won't make their first selection until the fourth round (134th overall). The Giants forfeited their picks in the first three rounds after signing free agents Armando Benitez, Mike Matheny and Omar Vizquel.

Teams will pick in descending order of 2004 record this year, without regard to league for the first time in draft history. In the past, selections alternated from one league to the other with the National League drafting first in even-numbered years. By virtue of their .315 winning percentage, the Diamondbacks will pick first—marking the second year in a row that a National League team has the first pick.

The order in the second half of the first round (picks 16-30) was set when all Type A and B free agents who were offered salary arbitration signed with new clubs. Compensation is offered to teams losing ranked free agents in the form of draft picks. A team losing a Type A free agent gets the first-round pick of the team that signs the player, as well as a supplemental pick. A team losing a Type B free agent receives only the signing team's top pick. In both cases, a team selecting in the top half of the draft rotation cannot lose its first-round pick. The loss of a Type C free agent provides a team a pick between the second and third rounds.

Following is the order of selection for the first round and supplemental rounds of this year's draft, which is scheduled for June 7-8. Adjustments in the second and third rounds and compensation for free agents lost is also noted.

FIRST ROUND

Club	Pick From	For (Type)
1. Diamondbacks		
2. Royals		
3. Mariners		
4. Nationals		
5. Brewers		
6. Blue Jays		
7. Rockies		
8. Devil Rays		
9. Mets		
10. Tigers		
11. Pirates		
12. Reds		
13. Orioles		
14. Indians		
15. White Sox		
16. Marlins		
17. Yankees	Phillies	Jon Lieber (B)
18. Padres		
19. Rangers		
20. Cubs		
21. Athletics		
22. Marlins	Giants	Armando Benitez (A)
23. Red Sox	Angels	Orlando Cabrera (A)
24. Astros		
25. Twins		
26. Red Sox	Dodgers	Derek Lowe (A)
27. Braves		
28. Cardinals	Red Sox	Edgar Renteria (A)
29. Marlins	Yankees	Carl Pavano (A)
30. Cardinals		

SUPPLEMENTAL FIRST ROUND

31. Diamondbacks		Richie Sexson (A)
32. Rockies		Vinny Castilla (A)
33. Indians		Omar Vizquel (A)
34. Marlins		Benitez
35. Padres		David Wells (A)
36. Athletics		Damian Miller (A)
37. Angels		Troy Percival (A)
38. Astros		Carlos Beltran (A)
39. Twins		Corey Koskie (A)
40. Dodgers		Adrian Beltre (A)
41. Braves		Jaret Wright (A)
42. Red Sox		Pedro Martinez (A)
43. Cardinals		Renteria
44. Marlins		Pavano
45. Red Sox		Cabrera
46. Cardinals		Mike Matheny (A)
47. Red Sox		Lowe
48. #Diamondbacks		Stephen Drew
49. Orioles		*Wade Townsend
50. #Angels		Jered Weaver

SECOND ROUND

53. Dodgers	Mariners	Beltre
54. Rockies	Nationals	Castilla
55. Athletics	Brewers	Miller
56. Twins	Blue Jays	Koskie
59. Red Sox	Mets	Martinez
60. Angels	Tigers	Percival
65. Yankees	White Sox	Orlando Hernandez (B)
72. Cardinals	Giants	Matheny
78. Padres	Red Sox	Wells
79. Braves	Yankees	Wright

SUPPLEMENTAL SECOND ROUND

81. Marlins	Mike Redmond (C)
82. Twins	Henry Blanco (C)

THIRD ROUND

85. Diamondbacks	Mariners	Sexson
86. Twins	Nationals	Christian Guzman (B)
91. Astros	Mets	Beltran
104. Indians	Giants	Vizquel
110. Cubs	Red Sox	Matt Clement (B)

Provisional selection if team fails to sign first-round pick
* Supplemental selection for unsigned first-round pick

BASEBALL
INFORMATION

BASEBALL TERMINOLOGY

■ Roster Limits
Major league rosters may include 40 players until Opening Day, when the number must be reduced to 25. The number returns to 40 on Sept. 1. The minimum number of active players maintained by each club throughout the season is 24.

■ Trading Regulations
The trading deadline is July 31. Trades may be made with any other major league club in the period from the end of the season through July 31 (midnight) without waivers.

■ Disabled Lists
There are two disabled lists, 15-day and 60-day. Players may be disabled retroactively, up to a maximum of 10 days, beginning with the day after the last day they played. A player on the 15-day DL may be shifted to the 60-day DL at any time. Players may be assigned to a minor league club for injury rehabilitation for a maximum of 20 days (30 days for pitchers).

15-day. There is no limit on the number of players per club.

60-day. There is no limit on the number of players per club, but it may be used only when a club is at the maximum of 40 players. Players carried on this list do not count against a club's control limit of 40 players. If a player is transferred to this list after Aug. 1, he must remain through the end of the season and postseason.

■ Options
When a player is on a major league club's 40-man roster and in the minor leagues, he is on "optional assignment." Players have three options and may be sent up and down as many times as the club chooses within those seasons but will only be charged with one option per season. When a player is "out of options," it means he's been on a 40-man roster during at least three different seasons and in his fourth pro season or later, he will have to clear irrevocable waivers in order to be sent down.

■ Waivers
If a player placed on major league waivers is not claimed by another team within two business days after waivers have been requested, then the player has "cleared waivers," and the team has secured waivers for the remainder of the waiver period. The team then can do one of two things:

1. Send him to the minors.
2. Trade him to another team, even if the trading deadline has passed, or do nothing at all.

Note: Any trades involving a 40-man roster player from July 31 to the end of the season may only involve players who have cleared major league waivers. If a player does not clear waivers—he is claimed by another team or teams—the club requesting waivers may withdraw the waiver request. If the club does not withdraw the waiver request, the player's contract is assigned as follows:

a. If only one claim is entered, the player's contract is assigned to the claiming club.
b. If more than one club in the same league makes claims, the club currently lower in the standings gets the player.
c. If clubs in both leagues claim the player, preference shall always go to the club in the same league as the club requesting waivers.

■ Designated for Assignment
This rule allows a club to open a roster spot for up to 10 days while waiting for a player to clear waivers.

Recalled vs. Contract Purchased
If a player is on the 40-man roster, he is "recalled." If not, then his contract is purchased from the minor league team. A player must be added to the 40-man roster when his contract is purchased.

■ Free agency
Six years of major league service are required to be eligible for free agency. A player has 15 days from the first day after the World Series to file for free agency.

By Dec. 7, a player's former club must offer to arbitrate or it becomes ineligible to sign the player. By Dec. 19, the player must accept the club's offer or on Jan. 9 the former club becomes ineligible to sign the player.

Six-year free agent (minor leagues). A player is eligible for free agency if he has played all or part of seven seasons in the major or minor leagues and is not placed on a major league team's 40-man roster as of Oct. 15.

■ Salary Arbitration
Three years of major league service are required for eligibility. A player with at least two years but less than three years of major league service will also be eligible if he ranks in the top 17 percent in total service in the class of players who have at least two but less than three years of major league service, however accumulated, but with at least 86 days of service accumulated during the immediately preceding season.

■ Rule 5 Draft
A player not on a major league 40-man roster as of Nov. 20 is eligible for the Rule 5 draft if:

1. The player was 18 or younger when he first signed a pro contract and this is the fourth Rule 5 draft since he signed.
2. The player was 19 or older when he first signed a pro contract and this is the third Rule 5 draft since he signed.

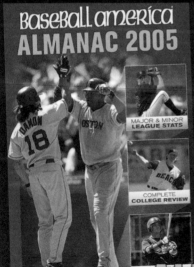

■ **Consecutive Game Hitting Streak**
A consecutive game hitting streak shall not be terminated if all the player's plate appearances (one or more) result in a base on balls, hit-by-pitch, defensive interference or a sacrifice bunt. The streak shall terminate if the player has a sacrifice fly and no hit.

■ **Consecutive Games Played Streak**
A consecutive games played streak shall be extended if the player plays one-half inning on defense, or if he completes a time at bat by reaching base or being put out.

■ **Major League Service**
A full year of service in the major leagues constitutes 172 days.

■ **Rookie Qualifications**
A player shall be considered a rookie if:
1. He does not have more than 130 at-bats or 50 innings pitched in the major leagues during a previous season or seasons and,
2. He has not accumulated more than 45 days on a major league roster during the 25-player limit, excluding time on the disabled list.

■ **Save Rule**
A pitcher shall be credited with a save when he meets the following three conditions:
1. He is the finishing pitcher in a game won by his club, and
2. He is not the winning pitcher, and
3. He qualifies under one of the following conditions:
   a. he enters the game with a lead of no more than three runs and pitches for at least one inning, or
   b. he enters the game with the potential tying run either on base, at bat or on deck, or
   c. he pitches effectively for at least three innings.
Blown save. When a relief pitcher enters a game in a save situation and departs with the save situation no longer in effect because he has given up the lead, he is charged with a blown save.

■ **Qualifying Marks**
Batting Championship. Major leagues—To qualify, a player must have a minimum of 502 plate appearances (3.1 plate appearances for each of the scheduled 162 games). Minor leagues—To qualify, a player must have accumulated 2.7 plate appearances for each scheduled game.
Earned Run Average. Major leagues—To qualify, a pitcher must have at least 162 innings pitched and have the lowest ERA. Minor leagues—To qualify, a pitcher must have pitched a number of innings at least .8 times the number of scheduled games.
Fielding Average. To qualify as a leader at the positions of first base, second base, third base, shortstop and outfield, a player must have appeared in a minimum of two-thirds of his team's games. For catcher, a player must have appeared in a minimum of one half of his team's games. For pitcher, the player with the highest average and the greatest number of total chances qualifies as the leader.

■ **Batting Average**
Divide the number of hits by the number of at-bats (H/AB).

■ **Earned Run Average**
Multiply the number of earned runs by nine; take that number and divide it by the number of innings pitched (ER x 9/IP).

■ **Slugging Percentage**
Divide the total bases of all safe hits by the total of times at bat. At-bats do not include walks, sacrifices, hit-by-pitches or times awarded first base because of interference or obstruction (TB/AB).

■ **On-Base Percentage**
Add the total number of hits, walks and number of times hit by pitches and divide by the total of at-bats, walks, hit-by-pitches and sacrifice flies (H+BB+HBP/AB+BB+HBP+SF).

■ **Fielding Percentage**
Divide the total number of putouts and assists by total chances—putouts, assists and errors (PO+A/PO+A+E).

■ **Winning Percentage**
Divide the number of games won by the total games won and lost (W/W+L).

■ **Magic Number**
Determine the number of games yet to be played, add one, and then subtract the number of games ahead in the loss column of the standings from the closest opponent.

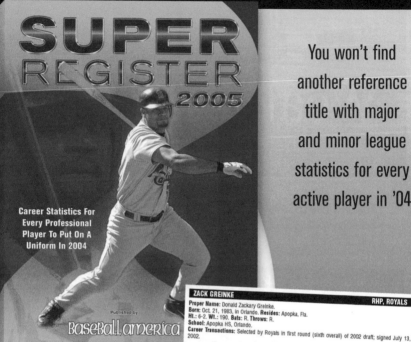

DRIVING DIRECTIONS

AMERICAN LEAGUE STADIUMS

ANGEL STADIUM, ANAHEIM
Highway 57 (Orange Freeway) to Orangewood exit, west on Orangewood, stadium on west side of Orange Freeway.

CAMDEN YARDS, BALTIMORE
From the north and east on I-95, take I-395 (exit 53), downtown to Russell Street; from the south or west on I-95, take exit 52 to Russell Street North.

FENWAY PARK, BOSTON
Massachusetts Turnpike (I-90) to Prudential exit (stay left), right at first set of lights, right on Dalton Street, left on Boylston Street, right on Ipswich Street.

U.S. CELLULAR FIELD, CHICAGO
Dan Ryan Expressway (I-90/94) to 35th Street exit.

JACOBS FIELD, CLEVELAND
From south, I-77 North to East Ninth Street exit, to Ontario Street; From east, I-90/Route 2 west to downtown, remain on Route 2 to East Ninth Street, left to stadium.

COMERICA PARK, DETROIT
I-75 to Grand River exit, follow service drive east to stadium, located off Woodward Avenue.

KAUFFMAN STADIUM, KANSAS CITY
From north or south, take I-435 to stadium exits. From east or west, take I-70 to stadium exits.

METRODOME, MINNESOTA
I-35W south to Washington Avenue exit or I-35W north to Third Street exit. I-94 East to I-35W north to Third Street exit or I-94 West to Fifth Street exit.

YANKEE STADIUM, NEW YORK
From I-95 North, George Washington Bridge to Cross Bronx Expressway to exit 1C; Major Deegan South (I-87) to exit G (161st Street); I-87 North to 149th or 155th Streets; I-87 South to 161st Street.

NETWORK ASSOCIATES COLISEUM, OAKLAND
From I-880, take either the 66th Avenue or Hegenberger Road exit.

SAFECO FIELD, SEATTLE
I-5 or I-90 to Fourth Avenue South exit.

TROPICANA FIELD, TAMPA BAY
I-275 South to St. Petersburg, exit 11, left onto Fifth Avenue, right onto 16th Street.

AMERIQUEST FIELD IN ARLINGTON, TEXAS
From I-30, take Ballpark Way exit, south on Ballpark Way; From Route 360, take Randol Mill exit, west on Randol Mill.

ROGERS CENTRE, TORONTO
From west, take QEW/Gardiner Expressway eastbound and exit at Spadina Avenue, north on Spadina one block, right on Bremner Boulevard. From east, take Gardiner Expressway westbound and exit at Spadina Avenue, north on Spadina one block, right on Bremner Boulevard.

NATIONAL LEAGUE STADIUMS

BANK ONE BALLPARK, ARIZONA
I-10 to Seventh Street exit, turn south; I-17 to Seventh Street, turn north.

TURNER FIELD, ATLANTA
I-75/85 northbound/southbound, take exit 246 (Fulton Street); I-20 westbound, take exit 58A (Capitol Avenue); I-20 eastbound, take exit 56B (Windsor Street), right on Windsor Street, left on Fulton Street.

WRIGLEY FIELD, CHICAGO
I-90/94 to Addison Street exit, follow Addison five miles to ballpark. One mile west of Lakeshore Drive, exit at Belmont going northbound, exit at Irving Park going southbound.

GREAT AMERICAN BALL PARK, CINCINNATI
I-75 southbound, take Second Street exit. Ballpark is located off Second Street at Main Street. I-71 southbound, take Third Street exit, right on Broadway. I-75/I-71 northbound, take Second Street exit—far right lane on Brent Spence Bridge. Ballpark is located off Second Street at Main Street.

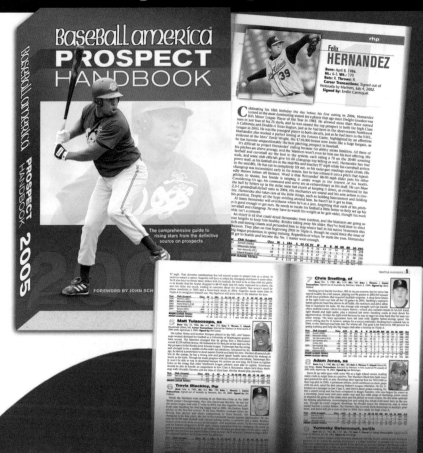

COORS FIELD, COLORADO
I-70 to I-25 South to exit 213 (Park Avenue) or 212C (20th Street); I-25 to 20th Street, east to park.

DOLPHINS STADIUM, FLORIDA
From south, Florida Turnpike extension to stadium exit; From north, I-95 to I-595 West to Florida Turnpike to stadium exit; From west, I-75 to I-595 to Florida Turnpike to stadium exit; From east, Highway 826 West to NW 27th Avenue, north to Dan Marino Blvd., right to stadium.

MINUTE MAID PARK, HOUSTON
From I-10 East, take Smith Street (exit 769A), left at Texas Ave., 0.6 miles to park at corner of Texas Ave. and Crawford St.; from I-10 West, take San Jacinto St. (exit 769B), right on Fannin St., left on Texas Ave., 0.3 miles to park; From Hwy. 59 North: take Gray Ave./Pierce Ave. exit, 0.3 miles on Gray St. to Crawford St., one mile to park.

DODGER STADIUM, LOS ANGELES
I-5 to Stadium Way exit, left on Stadium Way, right on Academy Road, left to Stadium Way to Elysian Park Avenue, left to stadium; I-110 to Dodger Stadium exit, left on Stadium Way, right on Elysian Park Avenue; US 101 to Alvarado exit, right on Sunset, left on Elysian Park Avenue.

MILLER PARK, MILWAUKEE
From airport/south, I-94 West to Madison exit, to stadium.

SHEA STADIUM, NEW YORK
From Bronx and Westchester, take Cross Bronx Expressway to Bronx-Whitestone Bridge, then take bridge to Whitestone Expressway to Northern Boulevard/Shea Stadium exit. From Brooklyn, take Eastbound BQE to Eastbound Grand Central Parkway. From Long Island, take either Northern State Parkway or LIE to Westbound Grand Central Parkway. From northern New Jersey, take George Washington Bridge to Cross Bronx Expressway. From Southern New Jersey, take any of bridge crossings to Verazzano Bridge, and then take either Belt Parkway or BQE to Grand Central Parkway.

CITIZENS BANK PARK, PHILADELPHIA
From I-95 or I-76, take the Broad Street exit. The ballpark is on on the north side of Pattison Avenue, between 11th and Darien Streets.

PNC PARK, PITTSBURGH
From south, I-279 through Fort Pitt Tunnel, make left off bridge to Fort Duquesne Bridge, cross Fort Duquesne Bridge, follow signs to PNC Park. From north, I-279 to PNC Park (exit 12, left lane), follow directions to parking.

BUSCH STADIUM, ST. LOUIS
From Illinois, take I-55 South, I-64 West, I-70 West or US 40 West across the Mississippi River (Poplar Street Bridge) to Busch Stadium exit. In Missouri, take I-55 North, I-64 East, I-70 East, I-44 East or US 40 East to downtown St. Louis and Busch Stadium exit.

PETCO PARK, SAN DIEGO
Four major thoroughfares feed into and out of downtown in all directions: Pacific Highway, I-5, State Route 163 and State Route 94/Martin Luther King Freeway. In addition, eight freeway on- and off-ramps service the area immediately around the ballpark.

SBC PARK, SAN FRANCISCO
From Peninsula/South Bay, I-280 north (or U.S. 101 north to I-280 north) to Mariposa Street exit, right on Mariposa, left on Third Street. From East Bay (Bay Bridge), I-80/Bay Bridge to Fifth Street exit, right on Fifth Street, right on Folsom Street, right on Fourth Street, continue on Fourth Street to parking lots (across bridge). From North Bay (Golden Gate Bridge), U.S. 101 south/Golden Gate Bridge to Downtown/Lombard Street exit, right on Van Ness Ave., left on Golden Gate Ave., right on Hyde Street and across Market Street to Eighth Street, left on Bryant Street, right on Fourth Street.

RFK STADIUM, WASHINGTON
Follow I-95 South (merge with I-495 toward Virginia). Exit onto the Baltimore-Washington Parkway south toward D.C. On the B-W parkway, follow signs toward I-295. Take East Capitol St. Exit.

Ripken Baseball

Ripken Baseball Summer Camps

Each year, more than 2,000 youth baseball campers between the ages of 7-18 will have an opportunity to learn baseball the Ripken Way at our Youth Baseball Academy in Aberdeen, MD. Ripken Baseball camps provide youth players with the once-in-a-lifetime opportunity to learn the game exactly the way Cal and Bill learned from their father; Cal Ripken, Sr.

Both overnight and day camp formats are offered. Campers will improve their skills and play games on professional-quality fields modeled after famous ballparks such as Oriole Park at Camden Yards, Wrigley Field, Fenway Park and Memorial Stadium. Our staff to camper ratio is 8:1 and all instructors are trained to teach and coach the Ripken Way. Bill Ripken is a frequent instructor at Ripken Baseball Camps and the Ripken Experience program features Cal, Bill and several of their former major league teammates.

Ripken Baseball Coaching Clinics

One of the primary goals of Ripken Baseball is to positively impact the lives of as many kids as possible. Cal & Bill believe that one of the ways to have the greatest impact is to share their knowledge with other baseball coaches. Ripken Baseball Coaching Clinics have been held in many parts of the country and feature a full day's worth of instruction from Cal & Bill in the areas of pitching, hitting, infield, outfield, and practice preparation. Positive and competent leadership is essential to providing young people with a productive baseball experience.

Ripken Baseball Tournament Series

In an effort to provide the unique opportunity for young ball players to experience the Ripken Youth Baseball Academy and to celebrate all that is great about the game, Ripken Baseball created a series of youth tournaments last year. Hundreds of youth teams with thousands of players will be able to play against other teams from around the country throughout the spring, summer and fall on the Academy's major league quality fields. Tournaments begin in March and run through October.

Ripken Baseball Fantasy Camps

Ripken Baseball will be hosting its first ever "Ripken Baseball Minor League Experience Fantasy Camp". This unique program will introduce adult participants to the minor-league lifestyle-from life on the road to post-game celebrations. Games will be played at the Orioles, Mets and Yankees minor league stadiums.

For more information please call
800-486-0850
www.ripkenbaseball.com

The Nation's Elite
HIGH SCHOOL
&
COLLEGE BASEBALL SCOUTING SERVICE

The Prospects Plus website database provides enhanced prospect profiles and coverage extending to the class of 2008

Choose the level that's right for you and call or log on today!

PROSPECTS PLUS
SCOUTING SERVICES

Level A . . . For industry insiders

Premium service. A complete scouting database including comprehensive biographical sketches and contact information as well as scouting reports on thousands of high school players, with a focus on the upcoming draft class. Lists and rankings of all the top college and high school players in the draft classes of 2005, 2006 and 2007, broken down nationally, by state, position, graduation year, ranking and more. Information will be updated constantly. This package is now available for a 12-month period beginning at the time of payment.

$395

PROSPECTS PLUS

Level B . . . For prospects, parents and fans

Regular service. Comprehensive lists and rankings of all the top college and high school players in the 2005, 2006 and 2007 draft classes, broken down nationally, by state and by position. This service now includes detailed scouting reports on prospects' performances at high school games, workouts, showcases and other tournaments throughout the calendar year. The subscription term is 12 months from the time of payment.

$120

WE IDENTIFY THE PLAYERS
+
WE SCOUT THEM
+
WE RANK THEM

800-845-2726 • BaseballAmerica.com/prospectsplus

The Leader in Baseball Information Management

by E Solutions Corporation

Bringing analysis and unrivaled access to your scouting and other player information, customized to meet your needs.

Discover what a third of MLB teams already know:

E Solutions' ScoutAdvisor™ system drastically improves the way baseball operations collect, organize and analyze critical data - downloaded securely and reliably to your PC, laptop or handheld (PDA) device.

Want to get the competitive edge other MLB teams already have?

Call 800-422-9892 or send an email to info@esnet.com.

Brought to you by

Key Features

> Daily automated MLB transaction and stats updates

> Custom daily player listings, scouting reports, and game schedules

> "Super Search" that returns only relevant results

> Comprehensive medical module for trainer input and incident tracking

> Encrypted front office communications

> Major & Minor League game day reports

> Player development tracking with built-in statistical analysis

> Wireless-ready from laptop or PDA

MAJOR
LEAGUES

MAJOR LEAGUE
BASEBALL

Mailing Address: 245 Park Ave., New York, NY 10167.
Telephone: (212) 931-7800.
Website: www.mlb.com.

Commissioner: Allan H. "Bud" Selig.
Senior Executive Assistant to Commissioner: Kathy Dubinski. **Executive Protection Supervisor:** Earnell Lucas. **Administrative Assistant to Commissioner:** Sandy Ronback. **Supervisor, Investigations:** Tom Christopher. **Assistant to Commissioner:** Lori Keck.
President/Chief Operating Officer: Bob DuPuy.
Executive Vice President, Baseball Operations: Sandy Alderson. **Executive VP, Administration:** John McHale. **Executive VP, Labor Relations/Human Resources:** Robert Manfred. **Executive VP, Business:** Tim Brosnan. **Executive VP, Finance:** Jonathan Mariner.

Bud Selig

Baseball Operations

Senior Vice President, Baseball Operations: Jimmie Lee Solomon. **VP, Baseball Operations/Administration:** Ed Burns. **Senior Director, Major League Operations:** Roy Krasik. **Manager, Baseball Operations:** Jeff Pfeifer.
Manager, Waivers/Major League Records: Brian Small. **Senior Manager, Minor League Operations:** Sylvia Lind. **VP, International Baseball Operations/Security:** Lou Melendez. **Senior Manager, Dominican Operations:** Rafael Perez.
VP, On-Field Operations: Bob Watson.
Director, Umpire Administration: Tom Lepperd. **Director, Umpire Medical Services:** Mark Letendre. **Umpiring Supervisors:** Rich Garcia, Jim McKean, Steve Palermo, Frank Pulli, Rich Rieker, Marty Springstead.
Director, Arizona Fall League: Steve Cobb.
Director, Major League Scouting Bureau: Frank Marcos. **Assistant Director, Scouting Bureau:** Rick Oliver.

Security, Facilities

Senior Vice President, Security/Facilities: Kevin Hallinan. **Senior Director, Security Operations:** Dan Mullin. **Director, Security Investigations:** George Hanna. **Senior Manager, Facilities Operations:** Linda Pantell. **Manager, Security Operations:** Paul Padilla. **Manager, Investigations:** Leroy Hendricks.

Bob DuPuy

General Administration

Vice President, Accounting/Treasurer: Bob Clark. **VP, Finance:** Kathleen Torres. **Director, Risk Management/Financial Reporting:** Anthony Avitable. **Manager, Payroll/Pension:** Rich Hunt.
Senior VP/General Counsel: Tom Ostertag. **Senior Manager, Records:** Mildred Delgado.
Senior VP/General Counsel: Ethan Orlinsky. **Deputy General Counsel:** Domna Candido, Jennifer Simms. **Director, Quality Control:** Peggy O'Neill-Janosik.
VP, Information Technologies: Julio Carbonell. **Director, Operations/Technical Support:** Peter Surhoff. **Manager, Software Development:** John Moran. **Senior Manager, Enterprise Systems:** Mike Morris.
Director, Baseball Assistance Team: Jim Martin.
Senior VP/General Counsel, Labor Relations: Frank Coonelly. **Deputy General Counsel, Labor:** Jennifer Gefsky. **Director, Salary/Contract Administration:** John Abbamondi.
VP, Strategic Planning for Recruitment/Diversity: Wendy Lewis. **Director, Recruitment:** Denise Males. **Senior Director, Office Services:** Donna Hoder.
VP, Human Resources: Ray Scott. **Manager, Benefits/Human Resources Information Systems:** Diane Cuddy.

Public Relations

Sandy Alderson

Telephone: (212) 931-7878. **FAX:** (212) 949-5654.
Senior Vice President, Public Relations: Richard Levin. **Vice President, PR Operations:** Patrick Courtney. **Director, Marketing Communications:** Kathleen Fineout. **Senior Manager, Baseball Information System:** Robert Doelger. **Manager, Media Relations:** Matthew Gould. **Manager, Marketing Communications:** Carmine Tiso. **Specialist, Baseball Information System:** John Blundell. **Specialist, Marketing Communications:** Matt Burton. **Coordinator, Media Relations:** Michael Teevan. **Coordinator, Marketing Communications:** Daniel Queen. **Senior Administrative Assistant:** Heather Flock. **Administrative Assistant:** Adriana Arcia. **Baseball Historian:** Jerome Holtzman.

Licensing

Senior Vice President, Licensing: Howard Smith.
VP, Adult Wearables/Authentics: Steve Armus. **VP, Collectibles/Cooperstown:** Colin Hagen. **Director, Licensing/Minor Leagues:** Eliot Runyon. **Senior Manager, Apparel Retail:** Adam Blinderman. **Director, Authentics:** Dennis Nolan. **Director, Novelties/Gifts:** Maureen Mason. **Director, New Technology/New Business:** Mike Napolitano. **Director, Business Affairs:** Geary Sellers. **Director, Non-Authentics:** Greg Sim. **Senior Manager, Presence Marketing:** Robin Jaffe.

Publishing and Photographs
Vice President, Publishing/Photographs: Don Hintze. Editor, Publishing/Photographs: Mike McCormick. Art Director, Publications: Faith Matorin. Director, MLB Photographs: Rich Pilling.

Special Events
Senior Vice President, Special Events: Marla Miller. Senior Director, Special Events: Brian O'Gara. Director, Special Events: Morgan Littlefield. Senior Manager, Special Events: Eileen Buser. Manager, Special Events: Joe Fitzgerald.

Broadcasting
Senior Vice President, Broadcasting: Chris Tully. VP, Broadcast Administration/Operations: Bernadette McDonald. Director, Distribution Development: Susanne Hilgefort. Manager, Broadcast Administration/Operations: Chuck Torres.

Community Affairs/Educational Programming
Vice President, Community Affairs/Educational Programming: Tom Brasuell. Manager, Community Affairs/Educational Programming: Jana Perry.

Corporate Sales
Senior VP, Corporate Sales: John Brody. Director, Local Sales: Joe Grippo. Director, Partner Services: Jeremy Cohen.

Advertising
Senior VP, Advertising/Marketing: Jacqueline Parkes. Director, Marketing: Mary Beck. Director, Research: Dan Derian. Manager, Advertising: Eric Cohen.
Vice President, Design Services: Anne Occi.

Club Relations
Senior VP, Club Relations/Scheduling: Katy Feeney. Coordinator, Club Relations/Scheduling: Chris Tropeano. Senior Administrative Assistant, Club Relations/Scheduling: Raxel Concepcion.
Senior VP, Club Relations: Phyllis Merhige. Coordinator, Club Relations: David Murphy. Senior Administrative Assistant, Club Relations: Angelica Cintron.

Major League Baseball Productions
Office Address: 75 Ninth Ave., New York, NY 10011. Telephone: (212) 931-7777. FAX: (212) 931-7788.
Vice President/Executive Producer: Dave Gavant.
Senior Coordinating Producer: David Check. Managing Producer: Adam Schlackman. Director, Productions/Operations: Shannon Valine. Vice President, Productions Programming/Business Affairs: Elizabeth Scott. Manager, Videotape Library: Frank Caputo.

International Business Operations
Mailing Address: 245 Park Ave., 34th Floor, New York, NY 10167. Telephone: (212) 931-7500. FAX: (212) 949-5795.
Senior VP, International Operations: Paul Archey. VP, International Licensing/Sponsorship: Shawn Lawson-Cummings. Director, International Broadcast Sales: Italo Zanzi. Managing Director, MLB Japan: Jim Small. Director, Australian Operations: Thomas Nicholson. Director, European Operations: Clive Russell. Director, Market Development/Events: James Pearce. Executive Producer, MLB International: Russell Gabay.

Umpires
Ted Barrett (Gilbert, AZ), Wally Bell (Boardman, OH), Joe Brinkman (Chiefland, FL), C.B. Bucknor (Brooklyn, NY), Mark Carlson (Shorewood, IL), Gary Cederstrom (Minot, ND), Eric Cooper (Johnston, IA), Derryl Cousins (El Segundo, CA), Terry Craft (Bradenton, FL), Jerry Crawford (Tiera Verde, FL), Fieldin Culbreth (Inman, SC), Phil Cuzzi (Nutley, NJ), Kerwin Danley (Los Angeles, CA), Gary Darling (Phoenix, AZ), Gerry Davis (Appleton, WI), Dana DeMuth (Gilbert, AZ), Laz Diaz (Orlando, FL), Mike DiMuro (Chandler, AZ), Bruce Dreckman (Marcus, IA), Doug Eddings (Las Cruces, NM), Paul Emmel (Bradenton, FL), Mike Everitt (Clive, IA), Andy Fletcher (Olive Branch, MS), Marty Foster (Beloit, WI), Bruce Froemming (Mequon, WI), Greg Gibson (Catlettsburg, KY), Brian Gorman (Camarillo, CA), Angel Hernandez (Loxahatchee, FL), John Hirschbeck (Youngstown, OH), Bill Hohn (Blue Bell, PA), Sam Holbrook (Lexington, KY), Marvin Hudson (Washington, GA), Dan Iassogna (Marietta, GA), Jim Joyce (Beaverton, OR), Jeff Kellogg (Mattawan, MI), Ron Kulpa (Maryland Heights, MO), Jerry Layne (Winter Haven, FL), Alfonso Marquez (Gilbert, AZ), Randy Marsh (Edgewood, KY), Tim McClelland (West Des Moines, IA), Jerry Meals (Salem, OH), Chuck Meriwether (Nashville, TN), Bill Miller (San Clemente, CA), Ed Montague (San Mateo, CA), Paul Nauert (Lawrenceville, GA), Jeff Nelson (Windermere, FL), Brian O'Nora (Canfield, OH), Larry Poncino (Tucson, AZ), Tony Randazzo (Las Cruces, NM), Ed Rapuano (Boca Raton, FL), Rick Reed (Rochester Hills, MI), Mike Reilly (Battle Creek, MI), Charlie Reliford (Bradenton, FL), Jim Reynolds (Scottsdale, AZ), Brian Runge (Oceanside, CA), Paul Schrieber (Scottsdale, AZ), Dale Scott (Portland, OR), Tim Timmons (New Albany, OH), Tim Tschida (Turtle Lake, WI), Larry Vanover (Owensboro, KY), Mark Wegner (Plant City, FL), Tim Welke (Kalamazoo, MI), Bill Welke (Marshall, MI), Hunter Wendelstedt (Madisonville, LA), Joe West (Fort Lauderdale, FL), Mike Winters (Carlsbad, CA), Jim Wolf (Phoenix, AZ), Larry Young (Roscoe, IL).

EVENTS
2005 Major League All-Star Game: July 12 at Comerica Park, Detroit.
2005 World Series: Begins Oct. 22 at winning league in All-Star Game.

AMERICAN LEAGUE

Years League Active: 1901-.
2005 Opening Date: April 3. **Closing Date:** Oct. 2.
Regular Season: 162 games.
Division Structure: East—Baltimore, Boston, New York, Tampa Bay, Toronto. **Central**—Chicago, Cleveland, Detroit, Kansas City, Minnesota. **West**—Anaheim, Oakland, Seattle, Texas.
Playoff Format: Three division champions and second-place team with best record meet in best-of-5 Division Series. Winners meet in best-of-7 League Championship Series.
All-Star Game: July 12, Comerica Park, Detroit (American League vs. National League).
Roster Limit: 25, through Aug. 31 when rosters expand to 40.
Brand of Baseball: Rawlings.
Statistician: Elias Sports Bureau, 500 Fifth Ave., New York, NY 10110.

STADIUM INFORMATION

City	Stadium	LF	Dimensions CF	RF	Capacity	2004 Att.
Anaheim	Angel Stadium	365	406	365	45,050	3,375,677
Baltimore	Camden Yards	333	410	318	48,876	2,744,013
Boston	Fenway Park	310	390	302	33,871	2,837,304
Chicago	U.S. Cellular Field	300	400	335	44,321	1,930,537
Cleveland	Jacobs Field	325	405	325	43,863	1,814,401
Detroit	Comerica Park	346	422	330	40,000	1,917,004
Kansas City	Kauffman Stadium	330	400	330	40,529	1,661,478
Minnesota	Hubert H. Humphrey Metrodome	343	408	327	48,678	1,879,222
New York	Yankee Stadium	318	408	314	57,545	3,775,292
Oakland	Network Associates Coliseum	330	400	367	43,662	2,201,516
Seattle	Safeco Field	331	405	326	45,600	2,940,731
Tampa Bay	Tropicana Field	315	407	322	45,200	1,275,011
Texas	Ameriquest Field in Arlington	334	400	325	49,166	2,513,685
Toronto	Rogers Centre	328	400	328	50,516	1,900,041

NATIONAL LEAGUE

Years League Active: 1876-.
2005 Opening Date: April 4. **Closing Date:** Oct. 2.
Regular Season: 162 games.
Division Structure: East—Atlanta, Florida, New York, Philadelphia, Washington. **Central**—Chicago, Cincinnati, Houston, Milwaukee, Pittsburgh, St. Louis. **West**—Arizona, Colorado, Los Angeles, San Diego, San Francisco.
Playoff Format: Three division champions and second-place team with best record meet in best-of-5 Division Series. Winners meet in best-of-7 League Championship Series.
All-Star Game: July 12 at Comerica Park, Detroit (American League vs. National League).
Roster Limit: 25, through Aug. 31 when rosters expand to 40.
Brand of Baseball: Rawlings.
Statistician: Elias Sports Bureau, 500 Fifth Ave., New York, NY 10110.

STADIUM INFORMATION

City	Stadium	LF	Dimensions CF	RF	Capacity	2004 Att.
Arizona	Bank One Ballpark	330	407	334	48,500	2,519,560
Atlanta	Turner Field	335	401	330	50,528	2,322,565
Chicago	Wrigley Field	355	400	353	38,884	3,170,184
Cincinnati	Great American Ball Park	328	404	325	42,263	2,287,250
Colorado	Coors Field	347	415	350	50,200	2,338,069
Florida	Dolphins Stadium	335	410	345	40,585	1,723,105
Houston	Minute Maid Park	315	435	326	42,000	3,087,872
Los Angeles	Dodger Stadium	330	395	330	56,000	3,488,283
Milwaukee	Miller Park	315	402	315	53,192	2,062,382
New York	Shea Stadium	338	410	338	55,777	2,318,321
Philadelphia	Citizens Bank Park	329	401	330	43,500	3,206,532
Pittsburgh	PNC Park	335	400	335	48,044	1,583,031
St. Louis	Busch Stadium	330	402	330	49,676	3,048,427
San Diego	Petco Park	334	398	322	42,000	3,040,046
San Francisco	SBC Park	335	404	307	40,800	3,258,864
*Washington	Robert F. Kennedy Stadium	335	410	335	56,000	748,550

*Franchise operated in Montreal in 2004.

ANAHEIM ANGELS

Office Address: Angel Stadium of Anaheim, 2000 Gene Autry Way, Anaheim, CA 92806.
Mailing Address: P.O. Box 2000, Anaheim, CA 92803.
Telephone: (714) 940-2000. **FAX:** (714) 940-2001.
Website: www.angelsbaseball.com.

Ownership
Operated by: Angels Baseball LP.
Chairman, Chief Executive Officer: Arturo Moreno.

BUSINESS OPERATIONS
President: Dennis Kuhl.

Arte Moreno

Finance, Administration
Chief Financial Officer: Bill Beverage. **Vice President, Finance/Administration:** Molly Taylor. **Senior Financial Analyst:** Amy Langdale. **Assistant Controller:** Cris Fisher. **Accountants:** Lorelei Largey, Jean Ouyang. **Assistant, Accounting:** Linda Chubak.
Director, Human Resources: Jenny Price. **Human Resources Generalist:** Nathan Andres. **Benefits Coordinator:** Tracie Key. **Assistant, Human Resources:** Lidia Argomaniz. **Insurance Risk Manager:** David Cohen.

Marketing, Corporate Sales
Senior Vice President, Sales/Marketing: John Carpino. **Director, Corporate Sales:** Richard McClemmy. **Corporate Sales Managers:** Bill Pedigo, Sabrina Warner.
Corporate Account Executives: Mike Gullo, Michael Means.
Sponsorship Services Manager: Carrie Basham. **Administrative Assistant:** Maria Dinh.
Director, Marketing/Promotions: Robert Alvarado. **Administrative Assistant, Marketing/Promotions:** Monica Campanis. **Director, Ticket/Suites Sales:** Steve Shiffman. **Administrative Assistant, Sales:** Pat Lissy. **Guest Relations Assistant:** Dave Paterson. **Senior Marketing Representative:** Jennifer Randall. **Marketing Coordinator/Designer:** Nancy Herrera. **Account Executives:** Dan Carnahan, Lisa Gaspar, Mike Kirby, Damon Roschke, Keith Rowe.
Group Sales Manager: Joe Furmanski. **Group Sales Account Executives:** Scott Booth, Carla Enriquez, Ernie Prukner, Ryan Redmond, Angel Rodriguez, Michael Sandoval. **Telemarketing Supervisor:** Tom DeTemple.
Manager, Entertainment: Peter Bull. **Producer, Video/Scoreboard Operations:** Robert Castillo.

Public/Media Relations, Communications
Telephone: (714) 940-2014. **FAX:** (714) 940-2205.
Vice President, Communications: Tim Mead. **Administrative Assistant:** Cathy Carey.
Manager, Baseball Information: Larry Babcock. **Manager, Media Services:** Nancy Mazmanian. **Media Relations Representatives:** Eric Kay, Marty Sewell.
Manager, Community Development: Matt Bennett. **Coordinator, Community Relations:** Anne Blasius
Publicity/Broadcasting Manager: Aaron Tom. **Publications Manager:** Doug Ward.
Speakers' Bureau: Jim Anderson, Dave Frost, Bobby Grich, Jay Johnstone, Darrell Miller, Clyde Wright.

Ballpark Operations
Director, Ballpark Operations: John Drum. **Manager, Facility Services:** Mike McKay. **Assistant Operations Manager:** Sam Maida.
Manager, Security: Keith Cleary. **Manager, Field/Ground Maintenance:** Barney Lopas. **Purchasing Specialist:** Ron Sparks. **Office Specialist:** Linda Fitzgerald. **Purchasing Assistant:** Suzanne Peters. **Office Support Assistant:** Calvin Ching.
Manager, Information Services: Al Castro. **Senior Network Engineer:** Neil Farris.
PA Announcer: David Courtney. **Organist:** Peggy Duquesnel.

Ticketing
Manager, Ticket Operations: Sheila Brazelton. **Assistant Ticket Manager:** Susan Weiss. **Supervisor, Ticketing:** Amer Nadler. **Ticketing Representatives:** Sandra Alonso, Clancy Holligan, Kim Weaver.

Travel, Clubhouse
Traveling Secretary: Tom Taylor.
Clubhouse Manager: Ken Higdon. **Assistant Clubhouse Manager:** Keith Tarter. **Visiting Clubhouse Manager:** Brian Harkins.
Senior Video Coordinator: Diego Lopez. **Video Coordinator:** Ruben Montano.

GENERAL INFORMATION
Stadium (year opened): Angel Stadium of Anaheim (1998).
Home Dugout: Third Base. **Playing Surface:** Grass.
Team Colors: Red, dark red, blue and silver.
Player Representative: Unavailable.

BASEBALL OPERATIONS

Vice President, General Manager: Bill Stoneman.
Assistant GM: Ken Forsch. **Special Assistants to GM:** Preston Gomez, Gary Sutherland.
Administrative Assistant, Scouting/General Manager: Laura Fazioli.

Major League Staff

Manager: Mike Scioscia.
Coaches: Bench—Joe Maddon; Pitching—Bud Black; Batting—Mickey Hatcher; First Base—Alfredo Griffin; Third Base—Ron Roenicke; Bullpen—Orlando Mercado; Bullpen Catcher—Steve Soliz.

Bill Stoneman

Medical, Training

Medical Director: Dr. Lewis Yocum. **Team Physician:** Dr. Craig Milhouse.
Head Athletic Trainer: Ned Bergert. **Athletic Trainer:** Rick Smith. **Assistant Athletic Trainer:** Adam Nevala. **Strength/Conditioning Coach:** Brian Grapes. **Administrative Assistant:** Chris Titchenal.

Player Development

Telephone: (714) 940-2031. **FAX:** (714) 940-2203.
Director, Player Development: Tony Reagins. **Manager, Baseball Operations:** Abe Flores. **Administrative Assistant, Player Development:** Juana Maria Arellano.
Director, Arizona Operations: Eric Blum.
Field Coordinator: Bruce Hines. **Roving Instructors:** Mike Butcher (pitching), Trent Clark (strength/conditioning), Geoff Hostetter (training coordinator), Bill Lachemann (catching/special assignment), Bobby Mitchell (outfield/baserunning/bunting), Bobby Ramos (catching), Ty Van Burkleo (hitting).

Mike Scioscia

Farm System

Class	Farm Team	League	Manager	Coach	Pitching Coach
AAA	Salt Lake	Pacific Coast	Dino Ebel	Jim Eppard	Bryn Smith
AA	Arkansas	Texas	Tom Gamboa	Todd Takayoshi	Keith Comstock
High A	Rancho Cucamonga	California	Ty Boykin	James Rowson	Eric Bennett
Low A	Cedar Rapids	Midwest	Bobby Magallanes	Justin Baughman	Kernan Ronan
Rookie	Orem	Pioneer	Tom Kotchman	Keith Johnson	Zeke Zimmerman
Rookie	Mesa	Arizona	Brian Harper	Unavailable	Felipe Suarez
Rookie	Angels	Dominican	Charlie Romero	Edgal Rodriguez	Santos Alcala

Scouting

Telephone: (714) 940-2038. **FAX:** (714) 940-2203.
Director, Amateur Scouting: Eddie Bane.
Director, Professional Scouting: Gary Sutherland.
Major League Scouts: Rich Schlenker (Walnut Creek, CA), Jeff Schugel (Denver, CO), Brad Sloan (Brimfield, IL), Moose Stubing (Villa Park, CA), Dale Sutherland (La Crescenta, CA).
National Crosscheckers: Jeff Malinoff (Lopez, WA), Ric Wilson (Chandler, AZ). **Regional Supervisors:** West—Bo Hughes (Sherman Oaks, CA); Midwest—Ron Marigny (New Orleans, LA); East—Marc Russo (Clearwater, FL).
Area Scouts: Arnold Braithwaite (Steger, IL), John Burden (Fairfield, OH), Arnold Cochrane (Ponce, PR), Tim Corcoran (La Verne, CA), Jeff Crane (Tuscaloosa, AL), Bobby DeJardin (San Clemente, CA), John Gracio (Mesa, AZ), Kevin Ham (El Paso, TX), Tom Kotchman (Seminole, FL), Dan Lynch (Marlboro, MA), Chris McAlphin (Huntersville, NC), Chad MacDonald (Arlington, TX), Dan Radcliffe (Green Belt, MD), Scott Richardson (Vacaville, CA), Jeff Scholzen (Hurricane, UT), Mike Silvestri (Davie, FL), Jack Uhey (Vancouver, WA).

Eddie Bane

International Supervisor: Clay Daniel (Jacksonville, FL).
International Scouts: Amador Arias (Venezuela), Felipe Gutierrez (Mexico), Tak Kawamoto (Japan), Charlie Kim (Seoul, Korea), Alex Messier (Canada), Leo Perez (Dominican Republic), Carlos Porte (Venezuela), Dennys Suarez (Venezuela), Ramon Valenzuela (Dominican Republic), Cesar Velasquez (Panama), Grant Weir (Australia).

ARIZONA DIAMONDBACKS

Office Address: Bank One Ballpark, 401 E. Jefferson St., Phoenix, AZ 85004.
Mailing Address: P.O. Box 2095, Phoenix, AZ 85001.
Telephone: (602) 462-6500. **FAX:** (602) 462-6599.
Website: www.diamondbacks.com.

Ownership

Operated by: AZPB Limited Partnership.
General Partners: Mike Chipman, Dale Jensen, Ken Kendrick, Jeff Moorad, Jeffrey Roger.

Ken Kendrick

BUSINESS OPERATIONS

President: Richard Dozer. **Assistant to President:** Michelle Libonati.
General Counsel: Tom O'Malley.
Vice President, Human Resources: Peter Wong.

Finance

Senior Vice President, Finance: Tom Harris. **VP, Information Systems:** Bill Bolt.
Controller: Craig Bradley. **Executive Assistant to Senior VP of Finance/Office Manager:** Sandy Cox.

Marketing, Sales

Vice President, Sales/Marketing: Mark Fernandez. **VP, Broadcasting:** Scott Geyer.
Director, Hispanic Marketing: Richard Saenz. **Tucson Operations Manager:** Jack Donovan. **Senior Director, Marketing:** Mike Malo.

Community Affairs

Director, Community Affairs: Karen Conway. **Senior Manager, Community Affairs:** Veronica Zapata Zendejas.

Public Relations, Communications

Telephone: (602) 462-6519. **FAX:** (602) 462-6527.
Director, Public Relations: Mike Swanson. **Senior Director, Publications:** Joel Horn. **Assistants to Director, Public Relations:** David Pape, Casey Wilcox. **Media Coordinator:** Susan Webner. **Staff Assistant:** Jeff Munn.

Stadium Operations

General Manager: Paige Peterson.
Vice President, Facilities Management: Alvan Adams. **VP, Event Services:** Russ Amaral. **VP, Security:** George Bevans. **Director, Suite Services:** Diney Ransford. **Director, Ballpark Attractions:** Charlene Vazquez-Inzunza. **Assistant Managers, Guest Relations:** Leslie Northcutt, Summer Terrell. **Director, Event Operations:** Jim Bochenek. **Head Groundskeeper:** Grant Trenbeath.
PA Announcer: Jeff Munn. **Official Scorer:** Rodney Johnson.

Ticketing

Telephone: (602) 514-8400. **FAX:** (602) 462-4141.
Senior Vice President, Ticket Operations/Special Services: Dianne Aguilar.
VP, Sales/Group and Season Tickets: Rob Kiese. **Director, Ticket Operations:** Darrin Mitch.

Travel, Clubhouse

Director, Team Travel: Roger Riley. **Visitors Clubhouse:** Bob Doty.

BASEBALL OPERATIONS

Telephone: (602) 462-6500. **FAX:** (602) 462-6599.

GENERAL INFORMATION

Stadium (year opened): Bank One Ballpark (1998).
Home Dugout: Third Base. **Playing Surface:** Grass.
Team Colors: Purple, copper and turquoise.
Player Representative: Mike Koplove.

Senior Vice President, General Manager: Joe Garagiola Jr.
Vice President, Special Assistant to GM: Bob Gebhard.
Assistant to GM: Valerie Dietrich.

Major League Staff
Manager: Bob Melvin.
Coaches: Bench—Jay Bell; Pitching—Mark Davis; Batting—Mike Aldrete; First Base—Brett Butler; Third Base—Carlos Tosca; Bullpen—Glenn Sherlock.

Medical, Training
Club Physicians: Dr. Michael Lee, Dr. Roger McCoy.
Head Trainer: Paul Lessard. Assistant Trainer: Dave Edwards.
Strength and Conditioning Coach: David Page.

Joe Garagiola Jr.

Minor Leagues
Telephone: (602) 462-4400. FAX: (602) 462-6421.
Assistant General Manager: Bob Miller. Business Manager, Baseball Operations: Jeff Jacobs. Administrative Assistant, Player Development/Scouting: Lisa Ventresca.
Coordinators: Dennis Lewallyn (pitching), David Nilsson (catching), Lee Tinsley (outfield), Rick Schu (hitting), Jack Howell (infield).
Head Trainer/Rehabilitation Coordinator: Greg Latta. Tucson Complex Coordinator: Bob Bensinger. Rehabilitation Coordinator: Ed Vosberg.

Bob Melvin

Farm System
Class	Farm Team	League	Manager	Coach	Pitching Coach
AAA	Tucson	Pacific Coast	Chip Hale	Lorenzo Bundy	Mike Parrott
AA	Tennessee	Southern	Tony Perezchica	Eric Fox	Dan Carlson
High A	Lancaster	California	Bill Plummer	Damon Mashore	Jeff Pico
Low A	South Bend	Midwest	Mark Haley	Tony Dello	Wellington Cepeda
Short season	Yakima	Northwest	Jay Gainer	Luis De los Santos	Erik Sabel
Rookie	Missoula	Pioneer	Hector De la Cruz	Jerry Stitt	Mel Stottlemyre Jr.
Rookie	Diamondbacks	Dominican	Audo Vicente	Juan Ballara	Jose Tapia

Scouting
Telephone: (602) 462-6518. FAX: (602) 462-6425.
Director, Scouting: Mike Rizzo. Scouting Assistant: Michele Copes.
Major League Scouts: Mack Babbit (Richmond, CA), Chris Bando (Gilbert, AZ), Bill Earnhart (Point Clear, AL), Mike Piatnik (Winter Haven, FL), Mike Sgobba (Scottsdale, AZ), Bill Singer (Decatur, AL), Paul Weaver (Phoenix, AZ).
National Supervisor: Kendall Carter (Scottsdale, AZ).
Regional Supervisors: East—Ed Durkin (Safety Harbor, FL), West—Kris Kline (Anthem, AZ), Central—Steve McAllister (Chillicothe, IL).
Scouts: Mark Baca (Temecula, CA), Ray Blanco (Miami, FL), Fred Costello (Livermore, CA), Trip Couch (Sugar Land, TX), Mike Daughtry (St. Charles, IL), Ed Gustafson (Spokane, WA), Scott Jaster (Midland, MI), Steve Kmetko (Phoenix, AZ), Hal Kurtzman (Van Nuys, CA), Greg Loniqro (Connellsville, PA), Howard McCullough (Greenville, NC), Matt Merullo (Madison, CT), Joe Robinson (St. Louis, MO), Mike Valarezo (Cantonment, FL), Luke Wrenn (Lakeland, FL).

Mike Rizzo

Director, Latin American Operations: Junior Noboa (Santo Domingo, DR). Coordinator, Mexico: Mike Sgobba (Scottsdale, AZ). Venezuela Supervisor: Miguel Nava (Tampa, FL).

ATLANTA BRAVES

Office Address: 755 Hank Aaron Dr., Atlanta, GA 30315.
Mailing Address: P.O. Box 4064, Atlanta, GA 30302.
Telephone: (404) 522-7630. **FAX:** (404) 614-1392.
Website: www.atlantabraves.com.

Ownership

Operated by: Atlanta National League Baseball Club, Inc.
Owner: Time Warner.
Chairman Emeritus: Bill Bartholomay.
Chairman/President: Terry McGuirk. **Senior Vice President/Assistant to President:** Henry Aaron.

BUSINESS OPERATIONS

Executive Vice President, Business Operations: Mike Plant. **Senior VP, Sales/Marketing:** Derek Schiller. **VP/Team Counsel:** John Cooper.

Finance

Vice President, Controller: Chip Moore.

Terry McGuirk

Marketing, Sales

Director, Ticket Sales: Paul Adams. **Director, Corporate Sales:** Jim Allen.

Public Relations, Communications

Telephone: (404) 614-1556. **FAX:** (404) 614-1391.
Senior Vice President, Public Relations/Communications: Greg Hughes.
Director, Communications: Walter Ward. **Manager, Media Relations:** Brad Hainje. **Administrative Assistant, Public Relations:** Anne McAlister. **Junior Publicists:** Adam Liberman, Meagan Swingle. **Publications Manager**: Andy Pressley.
Broadcasting Manager: Sue Vandiver.

Stadium Operations

Director, Stadium Operations/Security: Larry Bowman. **Field Director:** Ed Mangan.
PA Announcer: Bill Bowers. **Official Scorers:** Mark Frederickson, Mike Stamus.
Director, Audio-Video Operations: Jennifer Berger.

Ticketing

Telephone: (800) 326-4000. **FAX:** (404) 614 -2480.
Director, Ticket Operations: Ed Newman.

Travel, Clubhouse

Director, Team Travel/Equipment Manager: Bill Acree. **Visiting Clubhouse Manager:** John Holland.

GENERAL INFORMATION

Stadium (year opened): Turner Field (1997).
Home Dugout: First Base. **Playing Surface:** Grass.
Team Colors: Red, white and blue.
Player Representative: Johnny Estrada.

BASEBALL OPERATIONS

John Schuerholz

Telephone: (404) 522-7630. **FAX:** (404) 614-3308.
Executive Vice President, General Manager: John Schuerholz.
VP/Assistant GM: Frank Wren. **Special Assistant to GM/Player Development:** Jose Martinez. **Executive Assistant:** Melissa Stone.

Major League Staff
Manager: Bobby Cox.
Coaches: Dugout—Pat Corrales; Pitching—Leo Mazzone; Batting—Terry Pendleton; First Base—Glenn Hubbard; Third Base—Fredi Gonzalez; Bullpen—Bobby Dews.

Medical, Training
Director, Medical Services: Dr. Joe Chandler.
Trainer: Jeff Porter. **Assistant Trainer:** Jim Lovell. **Strength/ Conditioning Coach:** Frank Fultz.

Player Development
Telephone: (404) 522-7630. **FAX:** (404) 614-1350.
Director, Player Personnel: Dayton Moore. **Director, Baseball Operations:** Tyrone Brooks. **Director, Latin American Operations:** Marco Paddy. **Assistant Director, Player Development:** J.J. Picollo. **Administrative Assistants:** Lena Burney, Chris Rice. **Baseball Operations Assistant:** Matt Price.
Field Coordinator, Instruction: Chino Cadahia. **Pitching Coordinator:** Bill Fischer. **Field Supervisor:** Jim Beauchamp.
Roving Instructors: Rafael Belliard (infield), Jeff Blauser (general), Phil Falco (strength/conditioning), Ralph Henriquez (catching), Jack Maloof (hitting).

Bobby Cox

Farm System

Class	Farm Team	League	Manager	Coach	Pitching Coach
AAA	Richmond	International	Pat Kelly	Rick Albert	Mike Alvarez
AA	Mississippi	Southern	Brian Snitker	Philip Wellman	Kent Willis
High A	Myrtle Beach	Carolina	Randy Ingle	Franklin Stubbs	Bruce Dal Canton
Low A	Rome	South Atlantic	Rocket Wheeler	Bobby Moore	Jim Czajkowski
Rookie	Danville	Appalachian	Paul Runge	Mel Roberts	Derek Botelho
Rookie	Kissimmee	Gulf Coast	Luis Ortiz	Sixto Lezcano/Jim Saul	Derrick Lewis
Rookie	Braves I	Dominican	Jose Motta	Argenis Salazar/Jose Villar	Luis Alvarez
Rookie	Braves II	Dominican	Gabriel Luckert	Tommy Herrera	Juan Pablo Rojas

Scouting
Telephone: (404) 614-1354. **FAX:** (404) 614-1350.
Director, Scouting: Roy Clark. **Administrative Assistant:** Dixie Keller.
Advance Scout: Bobby Wine (Norristown, PA).
Special Assignment Scouts: Dick Balderson (Englewood, CO), Tim Conroy (Monroeville, PA), Jim Fregosi (Tarpon Springs, FL), Duane Larson (Knoxville, TN), Chuck McMichael (Grapevine, TX), Paul Snyder (Murphy, NC).
Professional Scouts: Rod Gilbreath (Lilburn, GA), Bobby Myrick (Colonial Heights, VA), Bob Wadsworth (Westminster, CA).
Crosscheckers: Hep Cronin (Cincinnati, OH), Paul Faulk (Little River, SC), John Flannery (Austin, TX), Kurt Kemp (Vancouver, WA).
Area Supervisors: Mike Baker (Santa Ana, CA), Daniel Bates (Phoenix, AZ), Tom Battista (Tustin, CA), Billy Best (Holly Springs, NC), Stu Cann (Bradley, IL), Sherard Clinkscales (Indianapolis, IN), Ralph Garr (Missouri City, TX), Al Goetz (Duluth, GA), Nick Hostetler (Sacramento, CA), Gregg Kilby (Jupiter, FL), Chris Knabenshue (Helton, TX), Robert Lucas (Atlanta, GA), Tim Moore (Kirkland, WA), John Stewart (Granville, NY), Don Thomas (Baton Rouge, LA), Terry Tripp (Shawnee, OK).
International Supervisors: Phil Dale (Victoria, Australia), Julian Perez (Levittown, PR).
International Scouts: Roberto Aquino (Dominican Republic), Neil Burke (Australia), Nehomar Caldera (Venezuela), Richard Castro (Venezuela), Jeremy Chou (Taiwan), Jose Pedro Flores (Venezuela), Carlos Garcia (Colombia), Ruben Garcia (Venezuela), Lonnie Goldberg (Canada), Courtland Hall (Germany), Daniel Latham (Japan), Jason Lee (Korea), Jose Leon (Venezuela), Hiroyuki Oya (Japan), Rolando Petit (Venezuela), Elvis Pineda (Dominican Republic), Manuel Samaniego (Mexico), Miguel Teran (Colombia), Marvin Throneberry (Nicaragua), Carlos Torres (Venezuela).

Dayton Moore

BALTIMORE ORIOLES

Office Address: 333 W. Camden St., Baltimore, MD 21201.
Telephone: (410) 685-9800. **FAX**: (410) 547-6272.
E-Mail Address: birdmail@orioles.com. **Website**: www.orioles.com.

Ownership
Operated by: The Baltimore Orioles Limited Partnership, Inc.
Chairman/Chief Executive Officer: Peter G. Angelos.

BUSINESS OPERATIONS
Vice Chairman, Community Projects/Public Affairs: Thomas Clancy.
Vice Chairman, Chief Operating Officer: Joe Foss.
Executive Vice President: John Angelos.
VP/Special Liaison to Chairman: Lou Kousouris.
General Legal Counsel: Russell Smouse.
Director, Human Resources: Lisa Tolson. **Director, Information Systems**: James Kline.

Finance
Vice President, Chief Financial Officer: Robert Ames.
Controller: Edward Kabernagel.

Peter Angelos

Marketing, Sales
Vice President/Corporate Sales and Sponsorships: T.J. Brightman.

Public Relations, Communications
Telephone: (410) 547-6150. **FAX**: (410) 547-6272.
Executive Director, Communications: Spiro Alafassos.
Director, Media Relations/Publications: Bill Stetka. **Manager, Baseball Information**: Kevin Behan. **Manager, Communications**: Monica Pence.
Senior Director, Advertising/Promotions: Matthew Dryer. **Director, Events/Programs**: Kristen Schultz.

Ballpark Operations
Director, Ballpark Operations: Roger Hayden. **Manager, Event Operations**: Doug Rosenberger.
Head Groundskeeper: Dave Nehila.
PA Announcer: Dave McGowan. **Official Scorers**: Jim Henneman, Marc Jacobsen.

Fan, Ticket Services
Telephone: (410) 685-9800. **FAX**: (410) 547-6270.
Senior Director, Fan/Ticket Services: Don Grove. **Assistant Director, Sales**: Mark Hromalik.
Ticket Manager: Audrey Brown. **Systems Inventory Manager**: Steve Kowalski.

Travel, Clubhouse
Traveling Secretary: Phil Itzoe. **Equipment Manager (Home)**: Jim Tyler. **Equipment Manager (Road)**: Fred Tyler.
Umpires, Field Attendant: Ernie Tyler.

GENERAL INFORMATION
Stadium (year opened): Oriole Park at Camden Yards (1992).
Home Dugout: First Base. **Playing Surface**. Grass.
Team Colors: Orange, black and white.
Player Representative: Jay Gibbons.

Jim Beattie

BASEBALL OPERATIONS

Telephone: (410) 547-6121. **FAX:** (410) 547-6271.
Executive Vice President, Baseball Operations: Jim Beattie. **VP, Baseball Operations:** Mike Flanagan.
Director, Baseball Administration: Ed Kenney Jr.
Executive Assistant to VP, Baseball Operations: Ann Lange.

Major League Staff

Manager: Lee Mazzilli.
Coaches: Bench—Sam Perlozzo; Pitching—Ray Miller; Batting—Terry Crowley; First Base—Rick Dempsey; Third Base—Tom Trebelhorn; Bullpen—Elrod Hendricks.

Medical, Training

Club Physician: Dr. William Goldiner. **Club Physician, Orthopedics:** Dr. Charles Silberstein.
Head Athletic Trainer: Richie Bancells. **Assistant Athletic Trainer**: Brian Ebel. **Strength/Conditioning Coach**: Tim Bishop.

Minor Leagues

Telephone: (410) 547-6120. **FAX**: (410) 547-6298.
Director, Minor League Operations: David Stockstill. **Assistant Director, Minor League Operations**: Tripp Norton. **Assistant, Minor League Operations**: Kevin Ibach. **Administrative Assistant**: Judy Grinblat.
Field/Hitting Coordinator: Julio Vinas. **Pitching Coordinator**: Doc Watson. **Medical Coordinator**: Dave Walker. **Strength/Conditioning Coach**: Jay Shiner. **Facilities Coordinator**: Jaime Rodriguez. **Camp Coordinator**: Len Johnston.
Roving Instructors: Moe Drabowsky (rehab pitching), Andy Etchebarren (catching), Cedric Landrum (outfield), Tom Lawless (infield/baserunnng), Denny Walling (hitting).

Lee Mazzilli

Farm System

Class	Farm Team	League	Manager	Coach	Pitching Coach
AAA	Ottawa	International	Dave Trembley	Dave Cash	Steve McCatty
AA	Bowie	Eastern	Don Werner	Butch Davis	Larry McCall
High A	Frederick	Carolina	Bien Figueroa	Moe Hill	Scott McGregor
Low A	Delmarva	South Atlantic	Gary Kendall	Orlando Gomez	Kennie Steenstra
Short season	Aberdeen	New York-Penn	Andy Etchebarren	Cesar Devarez	Dave Schmidt
Rookie	Bluefield	Appalachian	Jesus Alfaro	Cedric Landrum	Larry Jaster
Rookie	Orioles	Dominican	Miguel Jabalera	Benny Adames	Robert Perez
Rookie	Orioles	Venezuelan	Russell Vasquez	Luis Salazar	Carlos Leal

Scouting

Telephone: (410) 547-6187. **FAX:** (410) 547-6298.
Director, Scouting: Joe Jordan.
Administrative Assistant: Marcy Zerhusen.
Advance Scout: Deacon Jones (Sugar Land, TX).
Professional Scouts: Todd Frohwirth (Waukesha, WI), Bruce Kison (Bradenton, FL), Gus Quattlebaum (Hermosa Beach, CA), Gary Roenicke (Oceanside, CA), Tim Thompson (Lewiotown, PA), Fred Uhlman Sr. (Baltimore, MD).
National Crosschecker: Alan Marr (Sarasota, FL).
Regional Crosscheckers: East—Jeff Taylor (Newark, DE), Central—Deron Rombach (Arlington, TX), West—Dave Blume (Elk Grove, CA).
Full-Time Scouts: Dean Albany (Baltimore, MD), Bill Bliss (Gilbert, AZ), Ty Brown (Ruther Glen, VA), Ralph Garr Jr. (Grand Prairie, TX), John Gillette (Kirkland, WA), Troy Hoerner (Gurnee, IL), Jim Howard (Clifton Park, NY), Dave Jennings (Daphne, AL), James Keller (Sacramento, CA), Gil Kubski (Huntington Beach, CA), Lamar North (Rossville, GA), Nick Presto (West Palm Beach, FL), Mark Ralston (San Diego, CA), Jim Richardson (Marlow, OK), Harry Shelton (Ocoee, FL), Mike Tullier (River Ridge, LA), Dominic Viola (Cary, NC), Marc Ziegler (Columbus, OH).
Director, Latin American Scouting: Carlos Bernhardt (San Pedro de Macoris, D.R.). **Supervisor, Central/South America, Lesser Antilles:** Jesus Halabi (Aruba).
International Scouts: Ubaldo Heredia (Venezuela), Salvador Ramirez (Dominican Republic), Arturo Sanchez (Venezuela).

Joe Jordan

BOSTON RED SOX

Office Address: Fenway Park, 4 Yawkey Way, Boston, MA 02215.
Telephone: (617) 226-6000. FAX: (617) 226-6416.
Website: www.redsox.com.

Ownership
Principal Owner: John Henry. Chairman: Tom Werner. Vice Chairmen: David Ginsberg, Les Otten, Phillip Morse.
President/Chief Executive Officer: Larry Lucchino.
Director: George Mitchell. Chief Legal Officer, New England Sports Ventures: Lucinda Treat.

BUSINESS OPERATIONS
Chief Operating Officer: Mike Dee. Executive Vice President, Public Affairs: Dr. Charles Steinberg. Senior VP, Fenway Affairs: Larry Cancro. Senior VP, Corporate Relations: Meg Vaillancourt. Senior Advisor, Baseball Projects: Jeremy Kapstein.
Director, Human Resources/Office Administration: Michele Julian.
Director, Information Technology: Steve Conley. Senior Systems Analyst: Randy George.

Larry Lucchino

Finance, Legal
Vice President, Chief Financial Officer: Bob Furbush.
VP, Controller: Steve Fitch. Director, Finance: Ryan Oremus.
VP, Club Counsel: Elaine Steward. Staff Counsel: Jennifer Flynn. Law Clerk: Laura O'Neill.

Sales, Marketing
Senior Vice President, Sales/Marketing: Sam Kennedy. Director, Corporate Partnerships: Joe Januszewski. Director, Client Services: Troup Parkinson. Director, Sales: Sean Curtin. Senior Manager, Season/Group Sales: Corey Bowdre. Manager, .406 Club/VIP Services: Carole Alkins. Manager, Premium Seating Sales: Stephanie Nelson. Sponsor Services Coordinator: Martha Gibbings. Premium Seating Services Coordinator: Erin Burgoyne.
Senior Director, Fenway Enterprises: Chuck Steedman. Manager, Fenway Enterprises: Marcita Thompson.

Media, Community Relations
Vice President, Media Relations: Glenn Geffner. Manager, Media Relations: Kerri Moore. Media Relations Coordinator: Peter Chase. Media Relations Assistant/Credentials: Meghan Williams. Media Relations Assistants: Mark Rogoff, Andrew Merle.
Vice President, Club Historian: Dick Bresciani. Executive Consultant: Lou Gorman. Director, Publications: Debbie Matson. Manager, Publications/Archives: Rod Oreste. Coordinator, Alumni/Archives: Pam Ganley. Publications Assistant: Henry Mahegan. Staff Photographer: Julie Cordeiro.
Manager, Community Relations: Vanessa Leyvas. Director, Fan/Neighborhood Services: Sarah McKenna. Manager, Community Athletic Programs: Ron Burton Jr. Community Relations Coordinator: Sarah Stevenson.
Director, Advertising/Television/Video Production: Tom Catlin. Manager, Scoreboard/Video Production: Danny Kischel. Advertising Production Coordinators: John Carter, Megan Kaiser, Jon Mancini.

Stadium Operations
Senior Vice President, Planning/Development: Janet Marie Smith. Coordinator, Planning/Development: Paul Hanlon. Director, Security/Emergency Services: Charles Cellucci. Director, Facilities Management: Tom Queenan. Facilities Maintenance: Donnie Gardner, Glen McGlinchey, Tom Barnard.
Director, Event Operations: Jeff Goldenberg. Manager, Event Operations: Dan Lyons. Director Emeritus, Grounds: Joe Mooney. Director, Grounds: Dave Mellor. Assistant Director, Grounds: Charles Brunetti.
PA Announcer: Carl Beane. Official Scorers: Charles Scoggins, Joe Guiliotti.

Ticket Services, Operations
Telephone: (617) 482-4769, (877) REDSOX-9. FAX: (617) 226-6640.
Director, Ticket Operations: Richard Beaton. Director, Ticket Services/Information: Michael Schetzel. Senior Manager, Season Ticket Services: Joe Matthews. Manager, Ticket Services: Marcell Saporita. Manager, Ticket Accounting Administration: Sean Carragher. Senior Advisor, Ticketing: Ron Bumgarner. Ticket Services Coordinators: Naomi Calder, Sandi Quinn.

Travel, Clubhouse
Traveling Secretary: Jack McCormick. Administrative Assistant: Jean MacDougall. Equipment Manager/Clubhouse Operations: Joe Cochran. Assistant Equipment Manager: Edward "Pookie" Jackson. Visiting Clubhouse Manager: Tom McLaughlin. Video/Advance Scouting Coordinator: Billy Broadbent.

GENERAL INFORMATION
Stadium (year opened): Fenway Park (1912).
Home Dugout: First Base. Playing Surface: Grass.
Team Colors: Navy blue, red and white.
Player Representative: Johnny Damon.

Theo Epstein

BASEBALL OPERATIONS
Telephone: (617) 226-6000. **FAX:** (617) 226-6695.
Senior Vice President, General Manager: Theo Epstein.
VP, Baseball Operations: Mike Port. **Assistant GM:**
Josh Byrnes. **Special Assistant to GM, Player
Development/International Scouting:** Craig Shipley.
Senior Baseball Operations Advisor: Bill James. **Director, Baseball Operations/Assistant
Director, Player Development:** Peter Woodfork. **Assistant to GM:** Jed Hoyer. **Manager,
Major League Administration:** Brian O'Halloran. **Baseball Operations Assistant:** Zack Scott.

Major League Staff
Manager: Terry Francona.
Coaches: Bench—Brad Mills; Pitching—Dave Wallace; Batting—Ron Jackson; First
Base—Lynn Jones; Third Base—Dale Sveum; Bullpen—Bill Haselman.

Medical, Training
Medical Director: Dr. Thomas Gill.
Head Trainer: Jim Rowe. **Assistant Trainer/Rehab Coordinator:** Chris Correnti. **Assistant Trainer:** Chang-Ho Lee.

Player Development
Telephone: (617) 226-6000. **FAX:** (617) 226-6695.
Director, Player Development: Ben Cherington. **Director, Minor League Administration:**
Raquel Ferreira. **Administrative Assistant, Scouting/Player Development:** Victor Cruz.
Player Development Consultants: Dick Berardino, Tony Cloninger, Dwight Evans, Tommy
Harper, Felix Maldonado, Frank Malzone, Charlie Wagner, Carl Yastrzemski.
Coordinator, Florida Operations: Todd Stephenson. **Minor League Equipment Manager:**
Mike Stelmach. **Latin Education Coordinator:** Brian Whelan.
Field Coordinator: Rob Leary.
Roving Instructors/Coordinators: Orv Franchuk (hitting), Lou Frazier (outfield/baserun-
ning), Goose Gregson (Latin pitching), Al Nipper (pitching), Victor Rodriguez (Latin field),
U.L. Washington (infield).
Associate Medical Director: Dr. Brian Busconi, **Minor League Athletic Training
Coordinator:** Jim Young. **Assistant Minor League Athletic Training Coordinator:** Jon Jochim.
Sport Psychology Coach: Bob Tewksbury.

Terry Francona

Farm System

Class	Farm Team	League	Manager	Coach	Pitching Coach
AAA	Pawtucket	International	Ron Johnson	Mark Budaska	Mike Griffin
AA	Portland	Eastern	Todd Claus	Russ Morman	Fernando Arroyo
High A	Wilmington	Carolina	Dann Bilardello	Bruce Crabbe	Ace Adams
Low A	Greenville	South Atlantic	Chad Epperson	Randy Phillips	Bob Kipper
Short season	Lowell	New York-Penn	Luis Alicea	Alan Mauthe	Walter Miranda
Rookie	Fort Myers	Gulf Coast	Ralph Treuel	Cesar Hernandez	G. Gregson/D. Tomlin
Rookie	Red Sox	Dominican	Nelson Paulino	Jovel Jimenez	J. Gonzalez/D. Reyes
Rookie	Red Sox	Venezuelan	Josman Robles	Jesus Laya	Carlos Perez

Scouting
Director, Amateur Scouting: Jason McLeod. **Assistant Director, Professional/International
Scouting:** Tom Moore. **Assistant Scouting Director:** Amiel Sawdaye.
Coordinator, Advance Scouting: Galen Carr.
National Crosscheckers: Ray Crone (Cedar Hill, TX), Dave Finley (San Diego, CA).
Regional Crosscheckers: East—Mike Rikard (Durham, NC), West—Fred Peterson (Glendale,
CA), Central—Mark Wasinger (El Paso, TX).
Pro Scouts: Murray Cook (Miami, FL), David Howard (Kansas City, KS), Dave Jauss (Boston,
MA), Bill Latham (Birmingham, AL), Dana Levangie (Boston, MA), Joe McDonald (Lakeland,
FL), Rene Mons (Manchester, NH), Gary Rajsich (Temecula, CA), Alan Regier (Phoenix, AZ),
John Sanders (Atlanta, GA), Matt Sczesny (New York, NY), Jerry Stephenson (Fullerton, CA).
Area Scouts: John Booher (Vancouver, WA), Rob English (Duluth, GA), Ray Fagnant (East

Jason McLeod

Granby, CT), Danny Haas (Paducah, KY), Matt Haas (Cincinnati, OH), Nakia Hill (San Francisco,
CA), Ernie Jacobs (Wichita, KS), Wally Komatsubara (Aiea, HI), Jon Lukens (Orlando, FL), Dan
Madsen (Murrieta, CA), Darryl Milne (Denver, CO), Ed Roebuck (Lakewood, CA), Jim Robinson (Arlington, TX), Anthony
Turco (Tampa, FL), Danny Watkins (Tuscaloosa, AL), Jim Woodward (Claremont, CA), Jeff Zona (Mechanicsville, VA).
Consulting Scouts: Buzz Bowers (East Orleans, MA), Kelvin Bowles (Rocky Mount, VA), Alex Mesa (Miami, FL),
Cucho Rodriguez (San Juan, PR), Dick Sorkin (Potomac, MD), Terry Sullivan (La Grange, IL).
Coordinator, Latin American Scouting: Miguel Garcia. **Coordinator, Pacific Rim Scouting:** Jon Deeble. **Director,
Dominican Operations:** Jesus Alou. **Director, Baseball Operations, Dominican Republic:** Elvio Jimenez.

CHICAGO CUBS

Office Address: Wrigley Field, 1060 W. Addison St., Chicago, IL 60613. **Telephone:** (773) 404-2827. **FAX:** (773) 404-4129.

E-Mail Address: cubs@cubs.com.
Website: www.cubs.com.

Ownership

Operated by: Chicago National League Ball Club, Inc. **Owner:** Tribune Company.
Board of Directors: Dennis Fitzsimmons, Andy MacPhail.
President, Chief Executive Officer: Andy MacPhail. **Special Assistant to President:** Billy Williams.

BUSINESS OPERATIONS

Executive Vice President, Business Operations: Mark McGuire.
Director, Information Systems/Special Projects: Carl Rice. **PC Systems Analyst:** Sean True. **Senior Legal Counsel/Corporate Secretary:** Crane Kenney. **Executive Secretary, Business Operations:** Gayle Finney. **Director, Human Resources:** Jenifer Surma.

Andy MacPhail

Finance

Controller: Jodi Reischl. **Manager, Accounting:** Terri Lynn. **Payroll Administrator:** Mary Jane Iorio. **Senior Accountant:** Unavailable.

Marketing, Broadcasting

Senior Vice President, Marketing/Broadcasting: John McDonough.
Vice President, Community Relations/General Counsel: Michael Lufrano.
Director, Promotions/Advertising: Jay Blunk. **Manager, Cubs Care/Community Relations:** Rebecca Polihronis. **Coordinator, Marketing/Community Affairs:** Mary Dosek. **Manager, Mezzanine Suites:** Louis Artiaga. **Manager, Special Events/Entertainment:** Joe Rios.

Media Relations, Publications

Telephone: (773) 404-4191. **FAX:** (773) 404-4129.
Director, Media Relations: Sharon Pannozzo. **Manager, Media Relations:** Samantha Newby. **Assistant, Media Relations:** B.R. Koehnemann.
Director, Publications: Lena McDonagh. **Manager, Publications:** Jim McArdle. **Editorial Specialist, Publications:** Michael Huang. **Senior Graphic Designer:** Juan Alberto Castillo. **Graphic Design Specialist:** Joaquin Castillo. **Photographer:** Stephen Green.

Stadium Operations

Director, Stadium Operations: Paul Rathje.
Manager, Event Operations/Security: Mike Hill. **Coordinator, Event Operations/Security:** Julius Farrell. **Head Groundskeeper:** Roger Baird. **Facility Supervisor:** Bill Scott. **Coordinator, Office Services:** Randy Skocz. **Coordinator, Stadium Operations:** Danielle Alexa. **Switchboard Operator:** Brenda Morgan.
PA Announcers: Paul Friedman, Wayne Messmer. **Official Scorers:** Bob Rosenberg, Don Friske.

Ticketing

Telephone: (773) 404-2827. **FAX:** (773) 404-4014.
Director, Ticket Operations: Frank Maloney. **Assistant Director, Ticket Sales:** Brian Garza. **Assistant Director, Ticket Services:** Joe Kirchen. **Vault Room Supervisor:** Cherie Blake.

Travel, Clubhouse

Traveling Secretary: Jimmy Bank.
Home Clubhouse Manager: Tom Hellmann. **Visiting Clubhouse Manager:** Michael Berkhart.

GENERAL INFORMATION

Stadium (year opened): Wrigley Field (1916).
Home Dugout: Third Base. **Playing Surface:** Grass.
Team Colors: Royal blue, red and white.
Player Representative: Mark Prior.

Jim Hendry

BASEBALL OPERATIONS

Telephone: (773) 404-2827. **FAX:** (773) 404-4111.
Vice President/General Manager: Jim Hendry.
Executive Assistant to President/GM: Arlene Gill.
Director, Baseball Operations: Scott Nelson. **Manager, Baseball Information:** Chuck Wasserstrom
    Special Assistants to GM: Keith Champion (Ballwin, MO), Gary Hughes (Lantana, FL), Ken Kravec (Sarasota, FL), Ed Lynch (Scottsdale, AZ). **Scouting Consultant/Assistant to GM:** Randy Bush.

Major League Staff

Manager: Dusty Baker.
    Coaches: Dugout—Dick Pole; Pitching—Larry Rothschild; Batting—Gene Clines; First Base—Gary Matthews; Third Base—Chris Speier; Bullpen—Juan Lopez.

Medical, Training

Team Physicians: Dr. Stephen Adams, Dr. Michael Schafer, Dr. Stephen Gryzlo.
Head Trainer: Mark O'Neal. **Assistant Trainer:** Ed Halbur. **Strength/Conditioning Coordinator:** Tim Buss.

Player Development

Telephone: (773) 404-4035. **FAX:** (773) 404-4147.
Director, Player Development/Latin American Operations: Oneri Fleita. **Coordinator, Minor League Operations:** Patti Kargakis.
Field Coordinator: Dave Bialas. **Pitching Coordinator:** Lester Strode.
Minor League Medical/Rehab Coordinator: Greg Keuter.
Roving Instructors: Vince Coleman (outfield/baserunning), Jeff Huson (infield), Dave Keller (hitting), Grady Little (catching), Nao Masamoto (strength/conditioning).

Dusty Baker

Farm System

Class	Farm Team	League	Manager	Coach	Pitching Coach
AAA	Iowa	Pacific Coast	Mike Quade	Pat Listach	Rick Kranitz
AA	West Tenn	Southern	Bobby Dickerson	Von Joshua	Alan Dunn
High A	Daytona	Florida State	Richie Zisk	Mike Micucci	Mike Anderson
Low A	Peoria	Midwest	Julio Garcia	Ricardo Medina	Tom Pratt
Short season	Boise	Northwest	Trey Forkerway	Tom Beyers	David Rosario
Rookie	Mesa	Arizona	Steve McFarland	C. Martinez/A. Grissom	Rick Tronerud
Rookie	Cubs	Dominican	Franklin Font	Ramon Carabello	Leo Hernandez

Scouting

Telephone: (773) 404-2827. **FAX:** (773) 404-4147.
Director, Scouting: John Stockstill. **Administrative Assistant:** Patricia Honzik.
Advance Scout: Bob Didier (Federal Way, WA).
Major League Scout: Bill Harford (Chicago, IL). **Professional Scouts:** Tom Bourque (Cambridge, MA), Jim Crawford (Petal, MS), Demie Manieri (South Bend, IN), Joe Housey (Hollywood, FL), Mark Servais (LaCrosse, WI), Charlie Silvera (Millbrae, CA), Bob Lofrano (Woodland Hills, CA).
Special Assignment Scouts: Gene Handley (Huntington Beach, CA), Glen Van Proyen (Lisle, IL).
National Crosschecker: Brad Kelley (Glendale, AZ). **Crosscheckers:** Mark Adair (Florissant, MO), Sam Hughes (Smyrna, GA), Scott Pleis (Tampa, FL).
Full-Time Scouts: John Bartsch (Rocklin, CA), Billy Blitzer (Brooklyn, NY), Steve Fuller (Brea, CA), Antonio Grissom (Red Oak, GA), Denny Henderson (Orange, CA), Steve Hinton (Mather, CA), Steve McFarland (Scottsdale, AZ), Lukas McKnight (Gurnee, IL), Brian Milner (Fort Worth, TX), Rolando Pino (Pembroke Pines, FL), Steve Riha (Houston, TX), Bob Rossi (Baton Rouge, LA), Tom Shafer (Olathe, KS), Keith Stohr (Viera, FL), Billy Swoope (Norfolk, VA), Stan Zielinski (Winfield, IL).
International Scouts: Hector Ortega (Venezuela), Jose Serra (Dominican Republic).

John Stockstill

CHICAGO WHITE SOX

Office Address: 333 W. 35th St., Chicago, IL 60616.
Telephone: (312) 674-1000. **FAX:** (312) 674-5116.
Website: www.whitesox.com.

Ownership

Operated by: Chicago White Sox, Ltd.
Chairman: Jerry Reinsdorf. **Vice Chairman:** Eddie Einhorn.
Board of Directors: Fred Brzozowski, Robert Judelson, Judd Malkin, Robert Mazer, Allan Muchin, Jay Pinsky, Larry Pogofsky, Lee Stern, Sanford Takiff, Burton Ury, Charles Walsh.
General Counsel: Allan Muchin.
Special Assistant to Chairman: Dennis Gilbert. **Assistant to Chairman:** Anita Fasano.

Jerry Reinsdorf

BUSINESS OPERATIONS

Executive Vice President: Howard Pizer.
Senior Director, Information Services: Don Brown.
Senior Director, Human Resources: Moira Foy. **Administrator, Human Resources:** Leslie Gaggiano.

Finance

Senior Vice President, Administration/Finance: Tim Buzard. **Senior Director, Finance:** Bill Waters. **Accounting Manager:** Chris Taylor.

Marketing, Sales

Vice President, Marketing: Brooks Boyer. **Senior Director, Business Development/Broadcasting:** Bob Grim. **Manager, Promotions/Marketing Services:** Sharon Sreniawski. **Manager, Scoreboard Operations/Production:** Jeff Szynal. **Director, Game Operations:** Nichole Manning. **Coordinator, Promotions/Marketing Services:** Amy Sheridan. **Senior Director, Corporate Partnerships:** Jim Muno. **Manager, Corporate Partnerships:** Ryan Gribble, Gail Tucker. **Coordinators, Corporate Partnerships Services:** Stephanie Brewer, Jorie Sax. **Director, Ticket Sales:** Tom Sheridan. **Manager, Premium Seating Service:** Debbie Theobald. **Senior Directors, Community Relations:** Christine O'Reilly. **Director, Mass Communications:** Amy Kress. **Manager, Design Services:** Nicole Stack. **Senior Coordinator, Design Services:** Kyle White. **Senior Coordinators, Community Relations:** Nicole Arceneaux, Danielle Disch. **Coordinators, Community Relations:** Stephanie Carew, Dane Walkington.

Public Relations

Telephone: (312) 674-5300. **FAX:** (312) 674-5116.
Vice President, Communications: Scott Reifert. **Director, Media Relations:** Bob Beghtol. **Director, Public Relations:** Katie Kirby. **Manager, Media Relations:** Pat O'Connell. **Coordinator, Public Relations:** Ryan Barry. **Coordinator, Media Relations:** Vivian Stalling.

Stadium Operations

Senior Vice President, Stadium Operations: Terry Savarise. **Senior Director, Park Operations:** David Schaffer. **Senior Director, Guest Services/Diamond Suite Operations:** Julie Taylor.
Head Groundskeeper: Roger Bossard.
PA Announcer: Gene Honda. **Official Scorers:** Bob Rosenberg, Don Friske, Scott Reed.

Ticketing

Telephone: (312) 674-1000. **FAX:** (312) 674-5102.
Senior Director, Ticket Operations: Bob Devoy. **Manager, Ticket Operations:** Mike Mazza. **Manager, Ticket Accounting Administration:** Ken Wisz.

Travel, Clubhouse

Manager, Team Travel: Ed Cassin. **Equipment Manager, Clubhouse Operations:** Vince Fresso. **Visiting Clubhouse:** Gabe Morell. **Umpires Clubhouse:** Joey McNamara.

GENERAL INFORMATION

Stadium (year opened): U.S. Cellular Field (1991).
Home Dugout: Third Base. **Playing Surface:** Grass.
Team Colors: Black, white and silver.
Player Representative: Unavailable.

BASEBALL OPERATIONS

Senior Vice President/General Manager: Ken Williams. **Assistant GM:** Rick Hahn. **Executive Advisor to GM:** Roland Hemond. **Special Assistants to GM:** Bill Scherrer, Dave Yoakum. **Executive Assistant to GM:** Nancy Nesnidal.

Senior Director, Player Personnel: Duane Shaffer. **Director, Baseball Operations Systems:** Dan Fabian. **Assistant Director, Scouting/Baseball Operations Systems:** Andrew Pinter. **Assistant, Baseball Operations:** J.J. Lally.

Major League Staff

Manager: Ozzie Guillen.

Coaches: Bench—Harold Baines; Pitching—Don Cooper; Hitting—Greg Walker; First Base—Tim Raines; Third Base—Joey Cora; Bullpen—Art Kusnyer.

Ken Williams

Medical, Training

Senior Team Physician: Unavailable. **Head Trainer:** Herm Schneider. **Assistant Trainer:** Brian Ball. **Director, Conditioning:** Allen Thomas.

Player Development

Telephone: (312) 674-1000. **FAX:** (312) 674-5105.

Director, Player Development: David Wilder. **Assistant Director, Player Development:** Brian Porter.

Director, Minor League Administration: Grace Zwit. **Coordinator, Minor League Administration:** Kathy Potoski. **Manager, Clubhouse/Equipment:** Dan Flood.

Director, Instruction: Jim Snyder.

Roving Instructors/Coordinators: Kirk Champion (pitching), Mike Lum (hitting), Daryl Boston (outfield), Rafael Santana (infield), Tommy Thompson (catching), Nate Oliver (bunting), Dale Torborg (conditioning coordinator), Trung Cao (conditioning assistant). **Coordinator, Minor League Trainers/Rehabilitation:** Scott Takao.

Ozzie Guillen

Farm System

Class	Farm Team	League	Manager	Hitting Coach	Pitching Coach
AAA	Charlotte	International	Nick Leyva	Manny Trillo	Juan Nieves
AA	Birmingham	Southern	Razor Shines	Gregg Ritchie	Richard Dotson
High A	Winston-Salem	Carolina	Chris Cron	Andy Tomberlin	Sean Snedeker
Low A	Kannapolis	South Atlantic	Nick Capra	Ryan Long	J.R. Perdew
Rookie	Great Falls	Pioneer	John Orton	Joe Hall	Curt Hasler
Rookie	Bristol	Appalachian	Jerry Hairston	Bobby Tolan	Roberto Espinoza
Rookie	White Sox	Dominican	Denny Gonzalez	None	Gustavo Martinez

Scouting

Telephone: (312) 674-1000. **FAX:** (312) 451-5105.

Vice President, Free Agent/Major League Scouting: Larry Monroe.

Professional Scouts: Dan Durst (Rockford, IL), Doug Laumann (Florence, KY), Reggie Lewis (Elkton, MD), Gary Pellant (Chandler AZ), Paul Provas (Arlington, TX), Daraka Shaheed (Vallejo, CA), Derek Valenzuela (Temecula, CA), Bill Young (Long Beach, CA).

National Crosschecker: Ed Pebley (Brigham City, UT). **Regional Supervisors:** East Coast—John Tumminia (Newburgh, NY), West Coast—Joe Butler (Long Beach, CA), Midwest—Nathan Durst (Sycamore, IL).

Full-Time Area Scouts: Jayme Bane (Riverview, FL), Alex Cosmidis (Raleigh, NC), Chuck Fox (Summit, NJ), Larry Grefer (Park Hills, KY), Matt Hattabaugh (Westminster, CA), Warren Hughes (Mobile, AL), George Kachigian (Coronado, CA), John Kazanas (Phoenix, AZ), Larry Maxie (Upland, CA), Danny Ontiveras (Irvine, CA), Jose Ortega (Fort Lauderdale, FL), Clay Overcash (Oologan, OK), Mike Shirley (Anderson, IN), Alex Slattery (Maumelle, AR), Keith Staab (College Station, TX), Adam Virchis (Modesto, CA).

Duane Shaffer

Part-Time Scouts: Tom Butler (East Rancho Dominguez, CA), Javier Centeno (Guaynabo, PR), E.J. Chavez (El Paso, TX), John Doldoorian (Whitinsville, MA), Jason Morvant (Abbeville, LA), Phil Gulley (Morehead, KY), Blair Henry (Roberts, WI), Jack Jolly (Murfreesboro, TN), Dario Lodigiani (Napa, CA), Bill Moran (Portsmouth, VA), Glen Murdock (Livonia, MI), Howard Nakagama (Salt Lake City, UT), Al Otto (Schaumburg, IL), Mike Paris (Boone, IA), Scott Ramsey (Colbert, WA).

International Scouts: Derek Bryant (Mexico), Mariano DeLeon (Dominican Republic), Roberto Espinoza (Venezuela), Denny Gonzalez (Dominican Republic), Miguel Ibarra (Panama), Jorge Oquendo (Puerto Rico), Wuarnner Rincones (Venezuela), Ivan Robi (Panama), Tony Rodriguez (Dominican Republic), Oswaldo Salazar (Venezuela).

CINCINNATI REDS

Office Address: 100 Main St., Cincinnati, OH 45202.
Telephone: (513) 765-7000. **FAX:** (513) 765-7342.
Website: www.cincinnatireds.com.

Ownership

Operated by: The Cincinnati Reds, LLC.
Ownership Group: Carl Lindner, Mrs. Louis Nippert, William Reik Jr., George Strike, Gannett Co. Inc.
Chief Executive Officer: Carl Lindner. **Chief Operating Officer:** John Allen. **Executive Assistant to Chief Operating Officer:** Joyce Pfarr.

John Allen

BUSINESS OPERATIONS

General Counsel: James Evans. **Secretary Counsel:** Karl Grafe.

Finance, Administration

Senior Director, Finance and Administration/Controller: Anthony Ward. **Accounting Manager:** Jason Randolph. **Staff Accountant:** Jill Niemeyer. **Accounts Payable Clerk:** Sarah Lance. **Payroll Manager:** Leanna Weiss. **Payroll Accountant:** Ayanna Goddard. **Administrative Assistant:** Alice Wynn.
Human Resources Manager: Barbara Boles. **Administrator, Business/Broadcasting:** Ginny Kamp.

Marketing, Sales

Senior Director, Business Development: Brad Blettner. **Director, Marketing:** Cal Levy. **Manager, Scoreboard Operations:** Russ Jenisch. **Media Designer, Scoreboard Operations:** David Storm. **Coordinator, Marketing Operations/Events:** Zach Bonkowski. **Manager, Promotions:** Lori Watt. **Marketing Assistant, Corporate Services:** Michelle Weisman. **Marketing Assistant:** Brandon Bowman.
Director, Season/Group Sales: Pat McCaffrey. **Director, Premium Sales/Service**: Jenny Gardner. **Manager, Group Ticket Sales:** Brad Callahan. **Manager, Season Ticket Sales:** Cyndi Strzynski. **Manager, Special Events:** Jennifer Green. **Manager, Suite/Premium Services:** Maya Wadleigh. **Suite Sales Representative:** Dave Collins. **Sales Representatives:** Jodi Czanik, Chris Herrell, Patrick Korosec, Ryan Niemeyer, Ryan Rizzo. **Events Coordinator:** Abby Dawkins. **Assistant, Sales:** Kim Knapp. **Coordinator, Season Sales:** Amanda Phelps. **Coordinator, Group Sales:** Eric Keller. **Assistant, Season/Group Sales:** Laura Kellison. **Associate, Season/Group Sales:** Josh Rowley.
Manager, Merchandise: Amy Hafer. **Manager, Game Day Retail:** Alicia King. **Manager, Reds Team Shop:** Brian Stoehr. **Coordinator, Merchandise Operations:** Shelley Haas. **Merchandise Inventory Control Clerk:** Paul Kidwell.

Public Relations, Communications

Telephone: (513) 765-7800. **FAX:** (513) 765-7180.
Director, Media Relations: Rob Butcher. **Assistant Director, Media Relations:** Michael Vassallo. **Coordinator, Media Relations:** Larry Herms. **Assistant, Media Relations:** Jamie Ramsey.
Director, Creative Services: Ralph Mitchell. **Manager, Creative Services:** Dann Stupp. **Coordinator, Production/Design:** Julie Hammel. **Executive Director, Reds Community Fund:** Charlie Frank. **Manager, Community Relations:** Lorrie Platt. **Assistant, Community Relations:** Mary Goebel

Ballpark Operations

Senior Director, Ballpark Operations: Declan Mullin. **Assistant Director, Ballpark Operations:** Mike Maddox. **Chief Engineer:** Roger Smith. **Assistant to Chief Engineer:** Eric Dearing. **Superintendent, Ballpark Operations:** Bob Harrison. **Guest Relations Manager:** Jan Koshover.
Manager, Public Safety/Security: Kerry Rowland. **Switchboard Manager:** Lauren Gaghan.
Head Groundskeeper: Doug Gallant. **Assistant Groundskeeper:** Jon Phelps. **Grounds Supervisor:** Derrick Grubbs.

Ticketing

Telephone: (513) 765-7400. **FAX:** (513) 765-7119.
Director, Ticket Operations: John O'Brien. **Assistant Director, Ticket Operations:** Ken Ayer. **Ticket Operations Administration Manager:** Hallie Kinney. **Ticket Operations Accountant:** Jim Hall. **Ticket Operations Assistant:** Kevin Barnhill.

Travel, Clubhouse

Traveling Secretary: Gary Wahoff.
Senior Clubhouse/Equipment Manager: Bernie Stowe. **Reds Clubhouse/Equipment Manager:** Rick Stowe. **Visiting Clubhouse Manager:** Mark Stowe. **Reds Clubhouse Assistant:** Josh Stewart.

GENERAL INFORMATION

Stadium (year opened): Great American Ball Park (2003).
Home Dugout: First Base. **Playing Surface:** Grass.
Team Colors: Red, white and black.
Player Representative: Sean Casey.

Dan O'Brien

Dave Miley

BASEBALL OPERATIONS
Telephone: (513) 765-7700. **FAX:** (513) 765-7797.
General Manager: Dan O'Brien.
Director, Major League Operations: Brad Kullman.
Special Consultants to GM: Johnny Bench, Ken Griffey
Sr. **Executive Assistant to GM:** Debbie Bent. **Coordinator, Major League Scouting/Video Operations:** Nick Krall.

Major League Staff
Manager: Dave Miley.
Coaches: Bench—Jerry Narron; Pitching—Don Gullett; Batting—Chris Chambliss; First Base—Randy Whisler; Third Base—Mark Berry; Bullpen—Tom Hume; Bullpen Catcher—Mike Stefanski.

Medical, Training
Medical Director: Dr. Tim Kremchek.
Head Trainer: Mark Mann. **Assistant Trainer:** Tim Elser, Steve Baumann. **Strength/Conditioning Coach:** Matt Krause.

Player Development
Telephone: (513) 765-7700. **FAX:** (513) 765-7799.
Director, Player Development: Tim Naehring. **Assistant Director, Player Development:** Grant Griesser. **Senior Advisor:** Chief Bender. **Administrative Coordinator, Player Development:** Lois Hudson. **Manager, Florida Operations:** Jeff Maultsby. **Assistant Manager, Florida Operations:** Unavailable. **Minor League Equipment Manager:** Tim Williamson.
Minor League Field Coordinator: Bob Miscik. **Roving Coordinators:** Freddie Benavides (infield), Sammy Ellis (pitching), Jim Hickman (hitting), John Moses (outfield/baserunning), Leon Roberts (hitting), Vern Ruhle (pitching), Donnie Scott (catching). **Coordinator, Rehabilitation:** John Walker. **Coordinator, Medical:** Mark Farnsworth. **Coordinator, Strength/Conditioning:** Sean Marohn.

Farm System

Class	Farm Team	League	Manager	Coach(es)	Pitching Coach
AAA	Louisville	International	Rick Sweet	A. Garrett/Rod McCray	Mack Jenkins
AA	Chattanooga	Southern	Jayhawk Owens	Jamie Dismuke	Bill Moloney
High A	Sarasota	Florida State	Edgar Caceres	Billy White	Ed Hodge
Low A	Dayton	Midwest	Alonzo Powell	Chris Sabo	Larry Pierson
Rookie	Billings	Pioneer	Rick Burleson	Jeff Young	Butch Henry
Rookie	Sarasota	Gulf Coast	Luis Aguayo	Joe Ayrault	Jamie Garcia
Rookie	Reds	Dominican	Frank Laureano	Victor Franco/M.Gomez	Manuel Solano
Rookie	Reds	Venezuela	Jose Villa	JaimeTorres/Carlos Barrios	Jorge Lopez

Scouting
Telephone: (513) 765-7700. **FAX:** (513) 765-7799.
Assistant GM/Professional Scouting: Dean Taylor. **Assistant, Professional Scouting:** Matt Arnold.
Senior Special Assistant to GM/Advance Scout: Gene Bennett. **Special Assistants to GM/Professional Scouts:** Larry Barton Jr., Leland Maddox, Bill Wood.
Professional Scouts: Kelly Heath, Dan Huston, Greg McClain, Tom Mooney, Les Parker, Ross Sapp, Michael Williams.
Director, Amateur Scouting: Terry Reynolds. **Assistant Director, Amateur Scouting:** Paul Pierson. **Director, Scouting Administration:** Wilma Mann.
National Crosschecker: Butch Baccala (Weimar, CA). **Regional Crosscheckers:** East—Jim Thrift (Sarasota, FL); Midwest—Jim Gonzales (San Antonio, TX); West—Jeff Barton (Higley, AZ).
Scouting Supervisors: Jason Baker (Rome, NY), Howard Bowens (Tacoma, WA), Jeff Brookens (Chambersburg, PA), Jerry Flowers (Baton Rouge, LA), Mike Keenan (Manhattan, KS), Craig Kornfeld (Rancho Santa Margarita, CA), Steve Kring (Charlotte, NC), Mike Misuraca (Pomona, CA), Jeff Morris (Tucson, AZ), Rick Sellers (Remus, MI), Joe Siers (Wesley Chapel, FL), Perry Smith (Charlotte, NC), Tom Wheeler (Martinez, CA), Brian Wilson (Albany, TX), Tyler Wilt (Chicago, IL), Greg Zunino (Cape Coral, FL).

Terry Reynolds

International Scouting
Director, International Scouting/Player Development: Johnny Almaraz. **Coordinator, International Scouting:** Jhonathan Leyva. **Latin American Field Coordinator:** Marco Davalillo.
International Scouts: Oswaldo Alvarez (Mexico), Victor Aramas (Venezuela), Luis Baez (Dominican Republic), Luis Davalillo (Venezuela), Felix Delgado (Venezuela), Evereth Gomez (Venezuela), Carlos Moreno (Dominican Republic), Robert Morillo (Venezuela), Anibal Reluz (Panama), Maximo Rombley (Dominican Republic).

CLEVELAND INDIANS

Office Address: Jacobs Field, 2401 Ontario St., Cleveland, OH 44115.
Telephone: (216) 420-4200. **FAX:** (216) 420-4396.
Website: www.indians.com.

Ownership
Owner, Chief Executive Officer: Lawrence Dolan.
President: Paul Dolan.

BUSINESS OPERATIONS
Executive Vice President, Business: Dennis Lehman. **Senior Director, Human Resources:** Sara Lehrke.
Manager, Spring Training: Alex Slemc.

Larry Dolan

Finance
Senior Vice President, Finance/Chief Financial Officer: Ken Stefanov.
Controller: Sarah Taylor. **Senior Director, Information Systems:** Dave Powell. **Director, Planning, Analysis/Reporting:** Rich Dorffer. **Manager, Accounting:** Karen Menzing.

Marketing, Merchandising
Senior Vice President, Sales/Marketing: Vic Gregovits. **Director, Corporate Marketing:** Chris Previte. **Director, Marketing:** Sanaa Julien. **Manager, Publications/Graphic Design:** Bernadette Repko. **Manager, Brand Development/Special Events:** Dan Foust. **Manager, Scoreboard Operations:** Steve Warren. **Manager, Broadcasting:** Alex Slemc. **Coordinator, Production:** Justin White.
VP, Merchandising/Licensing: Jayne Churchmack. **Director, Merchandise:** Kurt Schloss. **Buyers, Retail:** Iris Delgado, Karen Fox. **Retail Controller:** Marjorie Ruhl. **District Manager:** Joanne Kahr.

Public Relations, Communications
Telephone: (216) 420-4350. **FAX:** (216) 420-4396.
Vice President, Public Relations: Bob DiBiasio. **Coordinators, Public Relations:** Angela Brdar, Stephanie Hierro. **Director, Media Relations:** Bart Swain. **Manager, Media Relations/Administration:** Susie Giuliano. **Manager, Media Relations:** Curtis Danburg. **Coordinator, Media Relations:** Jeff Sibel. **Press Box Supervisor:** John Krepop.
Director, Charitable Programs: Melissa Zapanta. **Manager, Community Relations:** John Carter.

Stadium Operations
Vice President, Ballpark Operations: Jim Folk. **Director, Ballpark Operations:** Jerry Crabb. **Director, Facility Maintenance:** Chris Donahoe. **Head Groundskeeper:** Brandon Koehnke.
PA Announcers: Duane Robinson, Bob Tayak. **Official Scorers:** Chuck Murr, Chad Broski, Bob Price, Hank Kozloski.

Ticketing
Telephone: (216) 420-4487. **FAX:** (216) 420-4481.
Director, Ticket Services: Marie Patten. **Manager, Public Sales:** Michael Blackert. **Manager, Vault/Processing:** Kelly Kelly. **Director, Ticket Sales:** Mike Mulhall. **Director, Luxury Seating:** Bill Lavelle. **Manager, Luxury Seating:** Cassy Baskin. **Manager, Customer Service/Sales:** Dave Murray.

Travel, Clubhouse
Director, Team Travel: Mike Seghi.
Home Clubhouse/Equipment Manager: Tony Amato. **Assistant Home Clubhouse/Equipment Manager:** Tommy Foster. **Visiting Clubhouse Manager:** Cy Buynak. **Manager, Equipment Acquisition/Distribution:** Jeff Sipos.

GENERAL INFORMATION
Stadium (year opened): Jacobs Field (1994).
Home Dugout: Third Base. **Playing Surface:** Grass.
Team Colors: Navy blue, red and silver.
Player Representative: Jody Gerut.

Mark Shapiro

BASEBALL OPERATIONS

Telephone: (216) 420-4200. **FAX:** (216) 420-4321.
Executive Vice President, General Manager: Mark Shapiro.
Assistant GM: Chris Antonetti. **Special Assistant to GM:** Neal Huntington.
Director, Player Personnel: Steve Lubratich. **Special Advisor, Baseball Operations:** Karl Kuehl. **Special Assistants, Baseball Operations:** Charles Nagy, Tim Belcher, Robby Thompson.
Director, Baseball Administration: Wendy Hoppel. **Assistant Director, Baseball Operations:** Mike Chernoff. **Executive Administrative Assistant, Baseball Operations:** Marlene Lehky. **Administrative Assistant, Baseball Operations:** Barbara Lessman. **Senior Coordinator, Baseball Systems:** Dan Mendlik. **Sport Psychologist/Director, Psychological Services:** Dr. Charles Maher.

Major League Staff

Manager: Eric Wedge.
Coaches: Bench—Buddy Bell; Pitching—Carl Willis; Batting—Eddie Murray; First Base—Jeff Datz; Third Base—Joel Skinner; Bullpen—Luis Isaac; Bullpen Catcher—Dan Williams.

Medical, Training

Director, Orthopaedic Services: Dr. Mark Schickendantz.
Head Trainer: Lonnie Soloff. **Assistant Trainers:** Rick Jameyson, Nick Kenney. **Senior Consultant, Athletic Training:** Paul Spicuzza. **Strength/Conditioning Coach:** Tim Maxey. **Director, Rehabilitation:** Jim Mehalik.

Player Development

Telephone: (216) 420-4308. **FAX:** (216) 420-4321.
Director, Player Development: John Farrell. **Director, Latin American Operations:** Ross Atkins. **Assistant Director, Player Development:** Mike Hazen. **Advisor, Player Development:** Johnny Goryl. **Assistant Director, Player Development/Latin American Operations:** Lino Diaz. **Mental Skills Coordinator:** John Couture. **Nutrition Consultant:** Jackie Berning.
Field Coordinator: Tim Tolman. **Coordinators:** Al Bumbry (outfield/baserunning), Ted Kubiak (defense), Lee Kuntz (rehab/medical), Jim Malone (strength/conditioning), Dave Miller (pitching), Derek Shelton (hitting).
Field Coordinator, Latin America: Minnie Mendoza.

Eric Wedge

Farm System

Class	Farm Team	League	Manager	Coach	Pitching Coach
AAA	Buffalo	International	Marty Brown	Felix Fermin	Ken Rowe
AA	Akron	Eastern	Torey Lovullo	Wayne Kirby	Greg Hibbard
High A	Kinston	Carolina	Luis Rivera	Lee May Jr.	Steve Lyons
Low A	Lake County	South Atlantic	Mike Sarbaugh	Jim Rickon	Scott Radinsky
Short season	Mahoning Valley	New York-Penn	Rouglas Odor	Jack Mull	Tony Arnold
Rookie	Burlington	Appalachian	Sean McNally	Unavailable	Ruben Niebla
Rookie	Indians I	Dominican	Junior Betances	Carlos Fermin	Kevin Carcamo
Rookie	Indians II	Dominican	Jose Stela	Luis Chavez	Juan Jimenez

Scouting

Telephone: (216) 420-4300. **FAX:** (216) 420-4321.
Assistant General Manager/Scouting Operations: John Mirabelli.
Assistant Director, Scouting: Brad Grant.
Major League Scouts: Don Poplin (Norwood, NC), Gary Tuck (Nashville, IN), DeJon Watson (Phoenix, AZ). **Professional Scouts:** Doug Carpenter (North Palm Beach, FL), Rodney Davis (Glendale, AZ), Dave Malpass (Huntington Beach, CA), Pat Murtaugh (Lafayette, IN), Chuck Tanner (New Castle, PA).
National Crosschecker: Jim Olander (Tucson, AZ). **Free-Agent Supervisors:** Southeast—Jerry Jordan (Kingsport, TN), Northeast—Chuck Ricci (Myersville, MD), Midwest—Ken Stauffer (Katy, TX), West Coast—Paul Cogan (Rocklin, CA).
Full-Time Area Scouts: Scott Barnsby (Old Hickory, TN), Henry Cruz (Fajardo, PR), Mike Daly (Kansas City, MO), Joe Graham (Phoenix, AZ), Chris Jefts (Sugar Hill, GA), Don Lyle (Sacramento, CA), Bob Mayer (Somerset, PA), Scott Meaney (Humble, TX), Les Pajari (Duluth, MN), Derrick Ross (Olmsted Township, OH), Phil Rossi (Jessup, PA), Matt Ruebel (Oklahoma City, OK), Vince Sagisi (Encino, CA), Bill Schudlich (Dearborn, MI), Jason Smith (Long Beach, CA), Mike Soper (Tampa, FL), Shawn Whalen (Vancouver, WA).

John Mirabelli

Director, Latin America Operations: Ross Atkins (Miami, FL). **Dominican Advisor:** Winston Llenas.
Latin America Supervisors: Henry Centeno (Venezuela), Felix Fermin (Dominican Republic), Johnny Martinez (Dominican Republic).

COLORADO ROCKIES

Office Address: 2001 Blake St., Denver, CO 80205.
Telephone: (303) 292-0200. **FAX:** (303) 312-2116.
Website: www.coloradorockies.com.

Ownership
Operated by: Colorado Rockies Baseball Club, Ltd.
Vice Chairman, Chief Executive Officer: Charles Monfort. **Vice Chairman:** Richard Monfort. **Executive Assistant to Vice Chairmen:** Patricia Penfold.

BUSINESS OPERATIONS
President: Keli McGregor. **Executive Assistant to President:** Terry Douglass.
Senior Vice President, Business Operations: Greg Feasel. **Assistant to Senior VP:** Donna Reed. **Senior Director, Personnel/Administration:** Elizabeth Stecklein. **Director, Information Systems:** Bill Stephani.

Finance

Senior Vice President/Chief Financial Officer: Hal Roth. **Assistant to Senior VP/Chief Financial Officer:** Tammy Vergara.

Charles Monfort

VP, Finance: Michael Kent. **Senior Director, Accounting:** Gary Lawrence. **Payroll Administrator:** Phil Emerson. **Accountants:** Phil Delany, Laine Campbell.

Marketing, Sales
Senior Director, Corporate Sales: Marcy English Glasser. **Account Executives:** Kari Anderson, Beth Beard. **Coordinators, Corporate Sales:** Kathy Wilson, Ted Tseng.
Senior Director, Promotions/Broadcasting: Alan Bossart. **Assistant to Senior Director, Promotions/Broadcasting:** Elizabeth Coates.
Manager, Promotions: Jason Fleming. **Coordinator, Broadcasting/Video Services:** Brian Ives. **Assistant, Broadcasting/Video Services:** Dan Storey.
Senior Director, Community/Retail Operations: Jim Kellogg. **Assistant to Senior Director, Community/Retail Operations:** Kelly Hall. **Manager, Community Affairs:** Stacy Schafer. **Coordinator, Community Affairs:** Antigone Vigil. **Manager, Coors Field Receiving/Distribution Center:** Steve Tomlinson.

Public Relations/Communications
Telephone: (303) 312-2325. **FAX:** (303) 312-2319.
Vice President, Communications/Public Relations: Jay Alves. **Assistant to VP, Communications/Public Relations:** Irma Thumim. **Coordinators, Communications/Public Relations:** Billy Witter, Brendan McNicholas.

Stadium Operations
Vice President, Ballpark Operations: Kevin Kahn.
Director, Coors Field Administration/Development: Dave Moore. **Manager, Ballpark Services:** Mary Beth Benner. **Director, Guest Services:** Steven Burke. **Scheduling/Payroll Assistant:** Beth Spiegel. **Managers, Guest Services:** Kathryn Coates, Brian Schneringer, Sandy Seta.
Director, Security: Don Lyon. **Senior Director, Engineering/Facilities:** James Wiener. **Assistant Director, Engineering:** Randy Carill. **Assistant Director, Facilities:** Dan Olsen.
Head Groundskeeper: Mark Razum. **Assistant Head Groundskeeper:** Jose Gonzalez. **Assistants, Groundskeeping:** Tim Holt, James Sowl.
PA Announcer: Kelly Burnham. **Official Scorers:** Dave Einspahr, Dave Plati.

Ticketing
Telephone: (303) 762-5437, (800) 388-7625. **FAX:** (303) 312-2115.
Vice President, Ticket Operations/Sales: Sue Ann McClaren. **Senior Director, Ticket Operations/Development:** Kevin Fenton. **Director, Ticket Operations/Finances:** Kent Hakes. **Assistant Director, Vault:** Scott Donaldson.
Senior Director, Advertising/Publications: Jill Roberts. **Manager, Advertising:** Angela Keenan. **Manager, Publications:** Mike Kennedy. **Director, Ticket Services/Spring Training Business Operations:** Chuck Javernick. **Director, Group Sales:** Jeff Spector. **Director, Season Tickets:** Jeff Benner. **Supervisor, Ticket Services:** Michael Bishop.

Travel, Clubhouse
Director, Major League Operations: Paul Egins.
Director, Clubhouse Operations: Keith Schulz. **Assistant to Director, Clubhouse Operations:** Eric Allen. **Visiting Clubhouse Manager:** Kurt Schlogl. **Video Coordinator:** Mike Hamilton.

GENERAL INFORMATION

Stadium (year opened): Coors Field (1995).
Home Dugout: First Base. **Playing Surface:** Grass.
Team Colors: Purple, black and silver.
Player Representative: Jason Jennings.

Dan O'Dowd

BASEBALL OPERATIONS

Telephone: (303) 292-0200. **FAX:** (303) 312-2320.
Executive Vice President/General Manager: Dan O'Dowd. **Assistant to Executive VP/GM:** Adele Armagost. **VP/Assistant GM:** Bill Geivett. **Senior Director, Baseball Operations:** Thad Levine.

Special Assistants to GM: Pat Daugherty (Aurora, CO), Marcel Lachemann (Penryn, CA), Kasey McKeon (Stoney Creek, NC).

Major League Staff

Manager: Clint Hurdle.
Coaches: Bench—Jamie Quirk; Pitching—Bob Apodaca; Batting—Duane Espy; First Base—Dave Collins; Third Base—Mike Gallego; Bullpen—Rick Mathews; Bullpen Catcher—Mark Strittmatter; Strength—Brad Andress; Video—Mike Hamilton.

Medical, Training

Director, Medical Operations: Tom Probst. **Medical Director:** Dr. Thomas Noonan. **Senior Associate Orthopedist:** Dr. Richard Hawkins. **Club Physicians:** Dr. Allen Schreiber, Dr. Douglas Wyland. **Rehabilitation Coordinator:** Scott Murayama.
Head Athletic Trainer: Keith Dugger. **Assistant Athletic Trainer:** Scott Gehret.

Player Development

Telephone: (303) 292-0200. **FAX:** (303) 312-2320.
Assistant Director, Player Development: Marc Gustafson. **Manager, Minor League Operations:** Jeff Bridich. **Roving Instructors:** Jim Johnson (hitting), Brian Jordan (strength/conditioning), Fred Kendall (catching), Bobby Meacham (infield), Jim Wright (pitching).
Video Coordinator: Brian Jones. **Mental Skills Coach:** Ronn Svetich. **Coordinator, Cultural Development:** Lori Brown. **Equipment Manager:** Joe Tamowski.

Clint Hurdle

Farm System

Class	Farm Team	League	Manager	Coach	Pitching Coach
AAA	Colorado Springs	Pacific Coast	Marv Foley	Alan Cockrell	Bob McClure
AA	Tulsa	Texas	Tom Runnells	Darron Cox	Bo McLaughlin
High A	Modesto	California	Stu Cole	Glenallen Hill	Butch Hughes
Low A	Asheville	South Atlantic	Joe Mikulik	Dave Hajek	Greg Booker
Short season	Tri-City (Wash.)	Northwest	Ron Gideon	Fred Ocasio	Russ Swan
Rookie	Casper	Pioneer	P.J. Carey	Tony Diaz	Richard Palacios
Rookie	Rockies	Dominican	Mauricio Gonzalez	Edison Lora	Pablo Paredes
Rookie	Rockies	Venezuela	Maurio Mendez	Unavailable	Unavailable

Scouting

Telephone: (303) 292-0200. **FAX:** (303) 312-2320.
Senior Director, Scouting: Bill Schmidt. **Director, Professional Scouting:** Jerry Dipoto. **Manager, Professional Scouting:** Matt Vinnola. **Administrator, Scouting:** Zach Wilson.
Major League Scout: Will George (Woolwich Township, NJ). **Professional Scouts:** Mike Berger (Oakmont, PA), Jack Gillis (Sarasota, FL), Art Pontarelli (Cranston, RI).
Special Assignment Scouts: Dave Holliday (Coalgate, OK), Terry Wetzel (Overland Park, KS).
National Crosscheckers: Ty Coslow (Louisville, KY), Danny Montgomery (Charlotte, NC).
Scouting Advisor: Dave Snow (Seal Beach, CA).
Full-Time Area Scouts: Todd Blyleven (Fountain Valley, CA), John Cedarburg (Fort Myers, FL), Scott Corman (Lexington, KY), Dar Cox (Frisco, TX), Jeff Edwards (Houston, TX), Mike Ericson (Glendale, AZ), Mike Garlatti (Edison, NJ), Mark Germann (Atkins, IA), Jeff Hipps (Long Beach, CA), Bert Holt (Visalia, CA), Damon Iannelli (Brandon, MS), Clarence Johns (Metairie, LA), Jay Matthews (Charlotte, NC), Jorge de Posada (Rio Piedras, PR), Ed Santa (Powell, OH), Gary Wilson (Sacramento, CA).

Bill Schmidt

Scouts: Steve Bernhardt (Perry Hall, MD), Norm DeBriyn (Fayetteville, AR), Casey Harvie (Lake Stevens, WA), Marc Johnson (Centennial, CO), Bobby Knopp, Don Lindeberg (Anaheim, CA), Dave McQueen (Bossier City, LA).
Director, Latin America Operations: Rolando Fernandez. **Coordinator, Pacific Rim Scouting:** Kent Blasingame (Fountain Hills, AZ).
International Scouts: Phil Allen (Australia), Francisco Cartaya (Venezuela), Felix Feliz (Dominican Republic), Carlos Gomez (Venezuela), Cristobal Giron (Panama), Orlando Medina (Venezuela), Frank Roa (Dominican Republic).

DETROIT TIGERS

Office Address: 2100 Woodward Ave., Detroit, MI, 48201.
Telephone: (313) 471-2000. FAX: (313) 471-2138.
Website: www.detroittigers.com.

Ownership

Operated by: Detroit Tigers, Inc.
Owner: Michael Ilitch.
President, Chief Executive Officer: Dave Dombrowski. Special Assistants to President: Al Kaline, Willie Horton. Executive Assistant to President/CEO: Patricia McConnell.
Senior Vice President: Jim Devellano.

BUSINESS OPERATIONS

Senior Vice President, Sales: Duane McLean. Executive Assistant to Senior VP, Sales: Tamara Mitin.

Finance

Vice President, Chief Financial Officer: Steve Quinn. Assistant to VP/CFO: Peggy Bacarella.

Mike Ilitch

Director, Finance: Kelli Kollman. Manager, Accounting/Finance: Karla Felton. Financial Analyst: Sheila Robine. Accounts Payable Coordinator: Debbie Sword. Purchasing Manager: DeAndre Berry.
Director, Human Resources: Karen Gruca.
Senior Manager, Payroll Administration: Maureen Kraatz. Payroll/Human Resources Coordinator: Stephanie Jenkins. Mail Services: Paul Kustra. Switchboard Operator: Janet Ware.

Marketing, Communications

Vice President, Public Affairs/Strategic Planning: Elaine Lewis. Administrative Assistant, Public Affairs/Strategic Planning: Tiffani Langford. Director, Community Affairs: Celia Bobrowsky. Coordinator, Community Affairs: Corey Bell.

Sales, Marketing

Vice President, Corporate Sales: Steve Harms. Managers, Corporate Sales: Tara Doyle, Greg Paddock, John Wolski. Corporate Sales Coordinator: Jill Chamberlain.
Director, Marketing: Ellen Hill Zeringue. Coordinator, Marketing: Ed Sanchez.
Director, Promotions/In-Game Entertainment: Joel Scott. Coordinator, Promotions/Special Events: Eli Bayless.
Vice President, Corporate Suite Sales and Services/Hospitality: Charles Jones. Manager, Suite Sales/Service: Scot Pett. Suite Services Coordinator: Amy Howard.
Director, Fantasy Camps: Jerry Lewis.

Media Relations, Communications

Telephone: (313) 471-2114. FAX: (313) 471-2138.
Senior Director, Communications: Cliff Russell. Media Relations Coordinator, Baseball Information: Brian Britten. Media Relations Coordinator: Rick Thompson. Media Relations/Broadcast Manager: Molly Light.

Park Operations

Vice President, Park Operations: Tim Padgett. Director, Park Operations: Mike Churchill.
Head Groundskeeper: Heather Nabozny. Senior Manager, Park Operations: Ed Goward. Managers, Ballpark Services: DuShawn Brandy, Allan Carrise. Park Operations Coordinators: Luke Hyvonen, Tessa Lawrence.
Scoreboard/Video Producer: Scott Fearncombe.

Ticketing

Telephone: (313) 471-2255.
Vice President, Ticket Sales/Service: Bob Raymond.
Director, Ticket Sales: Steve Fox. Director, Group Sales: Dwain Lewis.
Director, Ticket Services: Victor Gonzalez.

Travel, Clubhouse

Traveling Secretary: Bill Brown
Manager, Home Clubhouse: Jim Schmakel. Assistant Manager, Visiting Clubhouse: John Nelson. Clubhouse Assistant: Tyson Steele.
Ballpark Video Operations: Jeremy Kelch.

GENERAL INFORMATION

Stadium (year opened): Comerica Park (2000).
Home Dugout: Third Base. Playing Surface: Grass.
Team Colors: Navy blue, orange and white.
Player Representative: Mike Maroth.

BASEBALL OPERATIONS
Telephone: (313) 471-2059. **FAX:** (313) 471-2099.
General Manager: Dave Dombrowski.
Vice President/Assistant GM: Al Avila. **VP/Baseball Legal Counsel:** John Westhoff.
Administrative Assistant to VP/Assistant GM, Baseball Legal Counsel: Eileen Surma.
VP, Player Personnel: Scott Reid.
Director, Baseball Operations: Mike Smith. **Assistant, Baseball Operations/Foreign Affairs:** Ramon Pena. **International Liaison:** Joe Alvarez.

Major League Staff

Dave Dombrowski

Manager: Alan Trammell.
Coaches: Bench—Kirk Gibson; Pitching—Bob Cluck; Batting—Bruce Fields; First Base—Mick Kelleher; Third Base—Juan Samuel; Bullpen—Lance Parrish.

Medical, Training
Team Physicians: Dr. Kyle Anderson, Dr. David Collon, Dr. Michael Workings. **Director, Medical Services/Head Athletic Trainer:** Kevin Rand. **Assistant Athletic Trainer:** Steve Carter. **Strength/Conditioning Coach:** Dennie Taft.

Player Development
Telephone, Detroit: (313) 471-2096. **FAX:** (313) 471-2099. **Telephone, Florida Operations:** (863) 686-8075. **FAX:** (863) 688-9589.
Director, Minor League Operations: Dan Lunetta. **Administrative Assistant, Minor Leagues:** Audrey Zielinski.
Field Coordinator: Glenn Ezell. **Roving Instructors:** Bill Freehan (catching), Javiar Gillett (strength/conditioning), Toby Harrah (hitting), Rafael Landestoy (infield), Jon Matlack (pitching), Brian Peterson (performance enhancement), Gene Roof (outfield/baserunning), Doug Teter (medical coordinator).

Alan Trammell

Farm System

Class	Farm Team	League	Manager	Coach	Pitching Coach
AAA	Toledo	International	Larry Parrish	Leon Durham	Jeff Jones
AA	Erie	Eastern	Duffy Dyer	Pete Incaviglia	Mike Caldwell
High A	Lakeland	Florida State	Mike Rojas	Larry Herndon	Britt Burns
Low A	West Michigan	Midwest	Matt Walbeck	Tony Jaramillo	A.J. Sager
Short season	Oneonta	New York-Penn	Tom Brookens	Basilio Cabrera	Bill Monbouquette
Rookie	Lakeland	Gulf Coast	Kevin Bradshaw	Scott Makarewicz	Greg Sabat
Rookie	Tigers	Dominican	Unavailable	Unavailable	Unavailable

Scouting
Telephone: (313) 471-2098. **FAX:** (313) 471-2099.
Vice President, Amateur Scouting: David Chadd. **Assistant Director, Scouting:** James Orr. **Administrative Assistant, Scouting:** Gwen Keating.
Major League Scouts: Scott Bream (Phoenix, AZ), Dick Egan (Phoenix, AZ), Rob Guzik (Latrobe, PA), Al Hargesheimer (Arlington Heights, IL), Mike Russell (Troy, AL).
Special Assignment Scout: Greg Smith.
National Crosschooker: Curtis Dishman (Seabrook, TX). **Regional Supervisors:** Southeast—Steve Williams (Raleigh, NC), Northeast—Bob Cummings (Oak Lawn, IL), Midwest—Mike Hankins (Lee's Summit, MO), West—Joe Ferrone (Santa Clarita, CA).
Area Scouts: Rich Aude (Woodland Hills, CA), Bill Buck (Manassas, VA), Vaughn Calloway (Detroit, MI), Rolando Casanova (Miami, FL), Scott Cerny (Rocklin, CA), Jerome Cochran (Slidell, LA), Mike Gambino (West Roxbury, MA), Tim Grieve (Katy, TX), Mike Herbert (Chicago, IL), Joe Hodges (Rockwood, TN), Tim McWilliam (San Diego, CA), Marty Miller (Chicago, IL), Mark Monahan (Saline, MI), Steve Nichols (Mount Dora, FL), Tom Osowski (Dublin, OH), Brian Reid (Phoenix, AZ), Dennis Sheehan (Glasco, NY), Steve Taylor (Shawnee, OK), Clyde Weir (Portland, MI), Harold Zonder (Louisville, KY).
Assistant, Baseball Operations/Foreign Affairs: Ramon Pena (Dominican Republic).

David Chadd

FLORIDA MARLINS

Office Address: Dolphins Stadium, 2267 Dan Marino Blvd. Miami, FL 33056.
Telephone: (305) 626-7400. **FAX:** (305) 626-7428.
Website: www.floridamarlins.com.

Ownership

Owner: Jeffrey Loria. **Vice Chairman:** Joel Mael.
President: David Samson. **Special Assistants to President:** Andre Dawson, Tony Perez.

BUSINESS OPERATIONS

Senior Vice President, Chief Financial Officer: Michel Bussiere.
Director, Human Resources: Ana Hernandez. **Supervisor, Office Services:** Karl Heard.
Assistant, Office Services: Donna Kirton. **Senior Receptionist:** Kathy Lanza. **Receptionist:** Christina Fredericks.

Finance

Vice President, Finance: Susan Jaison. **Manager, Accounting:** Julio Garrido.
Director, Information Technology: Roger Sosa. **Manager, Business Information Systems:** Ken Strand. **Manager, Telecommunications:** Sam Mora.

Jeffrey Loria

Marketing, Sales

Vice President, Marketing: Sean Flynn. **Manager, Promotions:** Matt Britten. **Manager, Merchandise:** Robyn Fogel. **Manager, Hispanic Sales/Marketing:** Juan Martinez.
Vice President, New Business Development: Dale Hendricks.
Director, Corporate Sales: Brendan Cunningham. **Director, Season/Group Sales:** Joe Hovancak. **Director, Customer Service:** Spencer Linden. **Manager, Season/Group Sales:** Marty Mulford.
Manager, Community Affairs: Angela Smith. **Assistant, Player Relations:** Manny Colon. **Assistants, Community Affairs:** Paul Resnick, Ron Sklar.
Executive Director, Florida Marlins Community Foundation: Nancy Olson. **Assistant Directors:** Doug Harris, Jeremy Stern.

Media Relations, Communications

Telephone: (305) 626-7429. **FAX:** (305) 626-7302.
Vice President, Communications/Broadcasting: P.J. Loyello.
Director, Media Relations: Unavailable. **Manager, Media Relations:** Mike Gazda. **Coordinator, Media Relations:** Alex Horowitz. **Administrative Assistant, Media Relations:** Maria Armella.
Director, Broadcast Services: Suzanne Rayson.

Stadium Operations

Director, In-Game Entertainment: Gary Levy. **Associate Producer:** Eric Ramirez. **Video Archivist:** Chris Myers. **Organist:** Lowery Ballew.
PA Announcer: Dick Sanford. **Official Scorer:** Ron Jernick.

Ticketing

Telephone: (305) 930-4487. **FAX:** (305) 626-7432.
Customer Service Manager: Spencer Linden.

Travel, Clubhouse

Director, Team Travel: Bill Beck.
Equipment Manager: John Silverman. **Assistant Equipment Manager:** Mark Brown. **Visiting Clubhouse Manager:** Bryan Greenberg. **Assistant, Clubhouse and Umpire's Room:** Michael Hughes.

GENERAL INFORMATION

Stadium (year opened): Dolphins Stadium (1993).
Home Dugout: First Base. **Playing Surface:** Grass.
Team Colors: Teal, black and white.
Player Representative: Josh Beckett.

BASEBALL OPERATIONS
Telephone: (305) 626-7400. **FAX:** (305) 626-7433.
Senior Vice President/General Manager: Larry Beinfest.
Vice President, Player Personnel: Dan Jennings. **Assistant GM:**
Michael Hill. **Special Assistant to GM/Pro Scout:** Orrin Freeman.
Manager, Baseball Information Systems: David Kuan.
Video Coordinator: Cullen McRae.

Major League Staff
Manager: Jack McKeon.
Coaches: Bench—Harry Dunlop; Pitching—Mark Wiley;
Batting—Bill Robinson; First Base—Perry Hill; Third Base—Jeff
Cox; Bullpen—Luis Dorante; Bullpen Coordinator—Pierre
Arsenault.

Larry Beinfest

Medical, Training
Team Physician: Dr. Daniel Kanell.
Head Trainer: Sean Cunningham. **Assistant Trainer:** Mike Kozak. **Director,
Strength/Conditioning:** Paul Fournier.

Player Development
Vice President, Player Development/Scouting: Jim Fleming.
Director, Player Development: Brian Chattin.
Field Coordinator: John Pierson. **Coordinators:** Gene Basham (training/rehabilitation),
Doug Davis (catching/baserunning), John Mallee (hitting), Ed Romero (infield), Wayne
Rosenthal (pitching), Mike West (strength/conditioning).

Jack McKeon

Farm System
Class	Farm Team	League	Manager	Coach	Pitching Coach
AAA	Albuquerque	Pacific Coast	Dean Treanor	Reggie Jefferson	Jeff Schwarz
AA	Carolina	Southern	Gary Allenson	Steve Phillips	Scott Mitchell
High A	Jupiter	Florida State	Tim Cossins	Paul Sanagorski	Reid Cornelius
Low A	Greensboro	South Atlantic	Brandon Hyde	Bo Porter	Steve Foster
Short-season	Jamestown	New York-Penn	Mike Mordecai	Matt Raleigh	John Duffy
Rookie	Jupiter	Gulf Coast	Edwin Rodriguez	Johnny Rodriguez	Gary Buckels
Rookie	Marlins	Dominican	Jose Zapata	Basilio Alvarado	Edison Santana
Rookie	Marlins	Venezuelan	Romulo Oliveros	None	Rene Garcia

Scouting
Telephone: (305) 626-7400. **FAX:** (305) 626-7294.
Director, Scouting: Stan Meek. **Assistant Director, Scouting:** Gregg Leonard.
Advance Scout: Joe Moeller (Manhattan Beach, CA). **Pro Scouts:** Guy Mader (Greenville,
NC), Tommy Thompson (La Mesa, CA), Gene Watson.
National Crosschecker: David Crowson (College Station, TX). **Regional Supervisors:**
East—Mike Cadahia (Miami Springs, FL); Central—Ray Hayward (Norman, OK); West—
Scott Goldby (Yuba City, CA); Canada—Steve Payne (Barrington, RI).
Area Scouts: Alex Agostino (St. Bruno, Quebec), Matt Anderson (Williamsport, PA), Carlos
Berroa (San Juan, PR), Brian Bridges (Kennesaw, GA), Dennis Cardoza (College Station, TX),
John Cole (Lake Forest, CA), Robby Corsaro (Adelanto, CA), Dave Dangler (Birmingham, AL),
Scot Engler (Montgomery, IL), Ryan Fox (Broken Arrow, OK), John Hughes (Walnut Creek,
CA), John Martin (Tampa, FL), Joel Matthews (Concord, NC), Bob Oldis (Iowa City, IA), Steve
Payne (Barrington, RI), David Post (Hillsboro, OR), Scott Stanley (Phoenix, AZ).

Stan Meek

Senior Vice President/Director, International Operations: Fred Ferreria.
Director, International Scouting: Marc Delpiano. **International Supervisors:** Venezuela—Carlos Acosta (Caracas,
Venez.); Dominican Republic—Jesus Campos (San Pedro de Macoris, D.R.); Europe—A.B. Jesurun (Waddinxveen,
Netherlands).
International Scouts: Wilmer Adrian (Venezuela), Evelio Areas (Nicaragua), Greg Burrows (Bahamas), Aristides
Bustamonte (Panama/Costa Rica), Nelson Castro (Venezuela), Enrique Constante (Dominican Republic), Nathan
Davison (Australia), Scott Dawes (Australia), Luis Fermin (Venezuela), Rene Garcia (Venezuela), Carlos Guzman
(Guatemala), Jason Hewitt (Australia), Ton Hofstede (Netherlands), Go Ikeda (Japan), Brian Lombard (South Africa),
Roberto Marquez (Venezuela), Pedro Martinez (Venezuela), Willie Marrugo (Colombia), Ellerton Maynard (Virgin
Islands), Spencer Mills (Netherlands Antilles), Romulo Oliveros (Venezuela), Rene Picota (Panama), Carlos Rivero
(Venezuela), Craig Stoves (Australia), Orlando Tejera (Venezuela), Francis Wanga (Bonaire).

HOUSTON ASTROS

Office Address: Minute Maid Park, Union Station, 501 Crawford, Suite 400, Houston, TX 77002.
Mailing Address: P.O. Box 288, Houston, TX 77001.
Telephone: (713) 259-8000. **FAX:** (713) 259-8981.
E-Mail Address: fanfeedback@astros.mlb.com. **Website:** www.astros.com.

Ownership
Operated by: McLane Group, LP.
Chairman, Chief Executive Officer: Drayton McLane.
Board of Directors: Drayton McLane, Bob McClaren, G.W. Sanford, Webb Stickney.

BUSINESS OPERATIONS
President, Business Operations: Pam Gardner. **Executive Assistant:** Eileen Colgin.

Finance/Administration
Senior Vice President, Finance/Administration: Jackie Traywick.
Director, Treasury/Office Services: Damian Babin. **Controller:** Jonathan Germer. **Accounting Coordinator:** Evelyn Tremaine. **Ticket System Account Manager:** Brooke Ellenberger.
Director, Human Resources: Larry Stokes. **Human Resources Coordinator:** Jordon Kalina.

Drayton McLane

Marketing, Sales
Vice President, Broadcasting/Advertising Sales: Jamie Hildreth. **Director, Advertising Sales:** Alicia Nevins.
Manager, Advertising Sales/Promotions: Yvette Casares-Willis.
VP, Market Development: Rosi Hernandez. **VP, Marketing:** Andrew Huang. **Market Development Coordinator:** Caroline Montano.

Public Relations, Communications
Telephone: (713) 259-8900. **FAX:** (713) 259-8981.
Senior Vice President, Communications: Jay Lucas.
Director, Media Relations: Jimmy Stanton. **Assistant Director, Media Relations:** Lisa Ramsperger.
VP, Community Development: Marian Harper. **Director, Business Communications:** Todd Fedewa. **Communications Assistant:** Leah Tobin.
Manager, Community Development: Rita Suchma.
Director, Information Technology/Procurement: Brad Bourland. **Information Technology Coordinator:** Arlene Hebert. **Network Administrator:** Rob Weaver.

Stadium Operations
Senior Vice President, Ballpark Operations/Customer Service: Rob Matwick.
Vice President, Special Events: Kala Sorenson. **Senior Director, Engineering/Maintenance:** Bobby Forrest. **Manager, Engineering:** David McKenzie. **Audio-Visual Coordinator:** Lowell Matheny. **Security Manager:** Kirk Benoit.
Director, Ballpark Entertainment: Kirby Kander. **Production Coordinator:** Brock Jessel. **Marketing Coordinator:** Clint Pasche. **Director, Telecommunications/Broadcast Technology:** Mike Cannon.
Director, Customer Service: Michael Kenny. **Manager, Customer Service:** Rebecca Bond. **Coordinator, Ballpark Operations/Customer Service:** April Matthews.
Manager, Special Events: Leigh Ann Dawson. **Conference Center/Special Events Sales:** Christine O'Beirne.
Director, Field Operations: Dan Bergstrom. **Groundskeeper:** Willie Berry. **Assistant Groundskeepers:** Colin Castille, Michael Ranc.
PA Announcer: Bob Ford. **Official Scorers:** Rick Blount, Ivy McLemore, David Matheson, Trey Wilkinson.

Ticketing
Telephone: (713) 259-8500. **FAX:** (713) 259-8326.
Vice President, Ticket Sales/Services: John Sorrentino.
Director, Ticket Operations: Marcia Coronado. **Director, Box Office Operations:** Bill Cannon. **Manager, Sales Support:** Matt Rogers. **Manager, Premium Sales:** Andrea Levine-Spier. **Administrative Assistant, Ticket Services:** Joannie Cobb. **Senior Account Executive:** Brent Broussard. **Ticket Production Coordinator:** Sandy Luna.

Travel, Clubhouse
Director, Team Travel: Barry Waters. **Equipment Director, Payroll/Employee Benefits:** Ruth Kelly. **Manager, Payroll/Benefits:** Jessica Horton. **Manager:** Dennis Liborio. **Assistant Equipment Managers:** Carl Schneider, Butch New. **Visiting Clubhouse Manager:** Steve Perry. **Umpires/Clubhouse Assistant:** Chuck New.

GENERAL INFORMATION
Stadium (year opened): Minute Maid Park (2000).
Home Dugout: First Base. **Playing Surface:** Grass.
Team Colors: Brick red, sand beige and black.
Player Representative: Morgan Ensberg.

Tim Purpura

BASEBALL OPERATIONS
Telephone: (713) 259-8000. **FAX:** (713) 259-8600.
President, Baseball Operations: Tal Smith.
General Manager: Tim Purpura. **Senior Director, Baseball Operations:** David Gottfried. **Special Assistants to General Manager:** Enos Cabell, Al Pedrique, Nolan Ryan. **Consultant, Baseball Operations:** Matt Galante. **Executive Assistant, Major League Operations:** Traci Dearing. **Video Coordinator:** Jim Summers.

Major League Staff
Manager: Phil Garner.
Coaches: Bench—Cecil Cooper; Pitching—Jim Hickey; Batting—Gary Gaetti; First Base—Jose Cruz Sr.; Third Base—Doug Mansolino; Bullpen—Mark Bailey.

Medical, Training
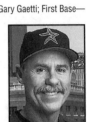

Medical Director: Dr. David Lintner. **Team Physicians:** Dr. Tom Mehlhoff, Dr. Jim Muntz. **Head Trainer:** Dave Labossiere. **Assistant Trainer:** Rex Jones. **Strength/Conditioning Coach:** Dr. Gene Coleman.

Player Development
Telephone: (713) 259-8922. **FAX:** (713) 259-8600.
Assistant General Manager/Director, Player Development: Ricky Bennett. **Assistant Directors, Baseball Operations:** Jay Edmiston, Bryan Frazier, Carlos Perez.
Field Coordinator: Tom Wiedenbauer. **Minor League Coordinators:** Sean Berry (hitting), Jim Pankovits (defense), Dewey Robinson (pitching).
Coordinator, Training/Rehabilitation: Pete Fagan. **Coordinator, Strength/Conditioning:** Nate Lucero.

Phil Garner

Farm System

Class	Farm Team	League	Manager	Coach	Pitching Coach
AAA	Round Rock	Pacific Coast	Jackie Moore	Spike Owen/Harry Spilman	Burt Hooton
AA	Corpus Christi	Texas	Dave Clark	John Tamargo Jr.	Joe Slusarski
High A	Salem	Carolina	Ivan DeJesus	Chuck Carr	Stan Boroski
Low A	Lexington	South Atlantic	Tim Bogar	Rodney Linares	Charley Taylor
Short season	Tri-City (N.Y.)	New York-Penn	Gregg Langbehn	Jorge Orta	Don Alexander
Rookie	Greeneville	Appalachian	Russ Nixon	Pete Rancont	Bill Ballou
Rookie	Astros	Dominican	Rafael Ramirez	A. DeFreitas/M. De laC ruz	Rick Aponte
Rookie	Astros	Venezuela	Mario Gonzalez	Omar Lopez	Oscar Padron

Scouting

Telephone: (713) 259-8921. **FAX:** (713) 259-8600.
Senior Director, Player Personnel: Paul Ricciarini. **Assistant Director, Baseball Operations:** Charlie Norton.
Coordinator, Major League Scouting: Fred Nelson. **Major League Scouts:** Gordy MacKenzie (Fruitland Park, FL), Walt Matthews (Texarkana, TX), Tom Romenesko (Santee, CA), Bob Skinner (San Diego, CA).
Coordinator, Professional Scouting: J.D. Elliby (Orlando, FL). **Professional Scouts:** Glen Barker (Albany, NY), Ken Califano (Stafford, VA), Gene DeBoor (Brandon, WI), Scipio Spinks (Missouri City, TX).
National Supervisor: Tad Slowik (Arlington Heights, IL).
Regional Supervisors: East—Gerry Craft (St. Clairsville, OH); Central—Ralph Bratton (Dripping Springs, TX); West—Dough Deutsch (Costa Mesa, CA).

Paul Ricciarini

Area Scouts: Ted Brzenk (Waukesha, WI), Chuck Carlson (Treasure Island, FL), Tom DeLong (Ocala, FL), Ellis Dungan (Pensacola, FL), Ed Edwards (Landisburg, PA), James Farrar (Shreveport, LA), Paul Gale (Keizer, OR), Tim Harrington (Boston, MA), David Henderson (Edmond, OK), Brian Keegan (Matthews, NC), Bob King (La Mesa, CA), Mike Maggart (Penn Yan, NY), Tom McCormack (University City, MO), Jerry Merz (Henderson, NV), Pat Murphy (The Woodlands, TX), Mel Nelson (Highland, CA), Rusty Pendergrass (Houston, TX), Bob Poole (Redwood City, CA), Mike Rosamond (Madison, MS), Mark Ross (Tucson, AZ), Joey Sola (Caguas, PR), Kevin Stein (Columbus, OH), Dennis Twombley (Redondo Beach, CA), Nick Venuto (Massillon, OH), Gene Wellman (Danville, CA).
Special Assistant to GM, Dominican Scouting/Development: Julio Linares. **Special Assistant to GM, Venezuelan Scouting/Development:** Andres Reiner. **Coordinator, Venezuela:** Pablo Torrealba.

KANSAS CITY ROYALS

Office Address: One Royal Way, Kansas City, MO 64129.
Mailing Address: P.O. Box 419969, Kansas City, MO 64141.
Telephone: (816) 921-8000. FAX: (816) 921-1366.
Website: www.kcroyals.com.

Ownership
Operated by: Kansas City Royals Baseball Club, Inc.
Chairman/Chief Executive Officer: David Glass. President: Dan Glass. Board of Directors:
Ruth Glass, Don Glass, Dayna Martz, Julia Irene Kauffman, Herk Robinson.
Executive Administrative Assistant: Ginger Salem.
General Counsel: Dick Nixon.

BUSINESS OPERATIONS
Senior Vice President, Business Operations: Mark Gorris. Executive Administrative
Assistant: Cindy Hamilton.

Finance
Vice President, Finance/Administration: Dale Rohr. Senior Administrative Assistant:
Janet Milone.

David Glass

Senior Director/Controller: John Luther. Manager, Accounting: Sean Ritchie. Manager, Ticket
Operations/Concessions Accounting: Lisa Kresha. Accounts Payable Coordinator: Sarah Kosfeld. Senior Director,
Payroll/Benefits/Human Resources: Tom Pfannenstiel. Manager, Human Resources: Lynne Elder.
Senior Director, Information Systems: Jim Edwards. Manager, Programming/Systems Analyst: Becky Randall.

Communications, Marketing
Telephone: (816) 921-8000. FAX: (816) 921-5775.
Vice President, Communications/Marketing: David Witty. Director, Royals Charities: Betty Kaegel.
Director, Media Relations: Aaron Babcock. Manager, Broadcast/Media Services: Chris Stathos. Coordinator,
Media Relations: David Holtzman. Director, Public Relations: Lora Grosshans. Manager, Public Relations: Ben
Aken. Administrative Assistant: Precious Washington. Mascot Coordinator: Byron Shores.
Director, Broadcast Services/Royals Alumni: Fred White. Manager, Radio Network Operations: Don Free.
Director, Marketing: Kim Hillix. Manager, Marketing: Curt Nelson. Manager, Game Entertainment: Chris DeRuyscher.

Business Development
Vice President, Business Development: Neil Harwell. Vice President, Corporate/Group Sales: Mike Phillips.
Director, Corporate Sponsorships: Michele Kammerer. Account Executive: Brian Legenza.
Director, Season Ticket Sales/Royals Lancers: Rick Amos. Manager, Group Sales: Scott Wadsworth.

Ballpark Operations
Vice President, Ballpark Operations/Development: Bob Rice.
Director, Event Operations/Guest Services: Chris Richardson. Managers, Event Operations/Guest Services:
Courtney Files, Renee VanLaningham. Manager, Stadium Tours/Operations: Morrie Carlson.
Director, Groundskeeping/Landscaping: Trevor Vance. Manager, Groundskeeping: Jerad Minnick. Landscape
Assistant: Anthony Bruce.
Director, Stadium Operations: Rodney Lewallen. Coordinators, Stadium Operations: Jermaine Goodwin, Matthew
Pellant. Coordinator, Telephone Services: Kathy Butler. Coordinator, Mail Services: Larry Garrett. Manager, Stadium
Services: Johnny Williams. Manager, Stadium Engineering: Jim Lang.
PA Announcer: Mike McCartney. Official Scorers: Del Black, Alan Eskew, Will Rudd.

Ticketing
Telephone: (816) 921-8000. FAX: (816) 504-4144.
Senior Director, Ticket Operations: Lance Buckley. Director, Ticket Services: Chris Darr. Director, Season Ticket
Services: Joe Grigoli. Coordinator, Season Tickets: Mary Lee Martino. Manager, Call Center: Jim Evans.
Coordinators, Ticket Operations: Betty Bax, Jacque Tschirhart.

Travel, Clubhouse
Senior Director, Team Travel: Jeff Davenport.
Equipment Manager: Mike Burkhalter. Assistant Equipment Manager: Patrick Gorman. Visiting Clubhouse
Manager: Chuck Hawke.
Video Coordinator: Mark Topping.

GENERAL INFORMATION
Stadium (year opened): Ewing M. Kauffman Stadium (1973).
Home Dugout: First Base. Playing Surface: Grass.
Team Colors: Royal blue and white.
Player Representative: Jeremy Affeldt.

Allard Baird

BASEBALL OPERATIONS

Telephone: (816) 921-8000. **FAX:** (816) 924-0347.
Senior Vice President/General Manager: Allard Baird. **Vice President/Assistant GM:** Muzzy Jackson. **Senior Advisor to GM:** Art Stewart. **Assistant to GM:** Brian Murphy. **Special Assistants to GM:** Pat Jones, Luis Medina. **Manager, Major League Operations:** Karol Kyte.
Vice President, Baseball Operations: George Brett. **Director, Baseball Operations:** Jin Wong.
Senior Director, Player Personnel: Donny Rowland.

Major League Staff

Manager: Tony Pena.
Coaches: Bench—Bob Schaefer; Pitching—Guy Hansen; Batting—Jeff Pentland; First Base—Joe Jones; Third Base—Luis Silverio; Bullpen—Brian Poldberg.

Medical, Training

Team Physician: Dr. Steven Joyce. **Associate Physicians:** Dr. Tim Badwey, Dr. Mark Bernhardt, Dr. Dan Gurba, Dr. Thomas Phillips, Dr. Charles Rhoades.
Athletic Trainer: Nick Swartz. **Assistant Athletic Trainer:** Frank Kyte. **Strength/Conditioning Coordinator:** Andy Kettler.

Player Development

Telephone: (816) 921-8000. **FAX:** (816) 924-0347.
Senior Director, Player Development: Shaun McGinn. **Manager, Minor League Operations:** Amy Buckler.
Special Assignment, Player Development/Scouting: John Wathan.
Coordinator, Instruction: Jeff Garber. **Roving Instructors:** Ron Clark (infield), Andre David (hitting), Ty Hill (strength/conditioning), Dale Gilbert (rehabilitation), Mike Mason (pitching), John Mizerock (catching). **Minor League Equipment Coordinator:** Johnny O'Donnell.
Latin American Strength/Conditioning Coordinator: Ryan Stoneberg.

Tony Pena

Farm System

Class	Farm Team	League	Manager	Coach	Pitching Coach
AAA	Omaha	Pacific Coast	Mike Jirschele	Terry Bradshaw	Mark Brewer
AA	Wichita	Texas	Frank White	Nelson Liriano	Larry Carter
High A	High Desert	California	Billy Gardner Jr.	Boots Day	Andy Hawkins
Low A	Burlington	Midwest	Jim Gabella	Patrick Anderson	Tom Burgmeier
Rookie	Idaho Falls	Pioneer	Brian Rupp	Pookie Wilson	Jose Bautista
Rookie	Surprise	Arizona	Lloyd Simmons	Tom Poquette	Royal Clayton
Rookie	Royals	Dominican	Julio Bruno	M. Garcia/B. Liriano	Carlos Martinez

Scouting

Telephone: (816) 921-8000. **FAX:** (816) 924-0347.
Senior Director, Scouting: Deric Ladnier. **Manager, Scouting Operations:** Linda Smith.
Professional Scouts: Brannon Bonifay (Stuart, FL), Orlando Estevez (Pembroke Pines, FL), Earl Winn (Bowling Green, KY).
Advance Scout: Mike Paczik (Bethesda, MD).
Special Assignment Scout: Carlos Pascual (Miami, FL).
Regional Supervisors: Jeff McKay (Walterville, OR), Junior Vizcaino (Durham, NC), Dennis Woody (Danville, AR).
Area Supervisors: Bob Bishop (San Dimas, CA), Mike Brown (Chandler, AZ), Jason Bryans (Detroit, MI), Steve Connelly (Glasco, NY), Albert Gonzalez (Coral Springs, FL), Spencer Graham (Raleigh, NC), Phil Huttmann (Kansas City, MO), Gary Johnson (Costa Mesa, CA), Cliff Pastornicky (Bradenton, FL), John Ramey (Wildomar, CA), Johnny Ramos (Carolina, PR), Sean Rooney (Tinton Falls, NJ), Max Semler (Lake City, FL), Chet Sergo (Houston, TX), Greg Smith (Davenport, WA), Keith Snider (Stockton, CA), Gerald Turner (Euless, TX), Jon Weil (Atlanta, GA), Mark Willoughby (Hammond, LA).

Deric Ladnier

Coordinator, Latin America Operations: Albert Gonzalez (Coral Springs, FL). **Dominican Republic Academy Administrator/Scouting:** Pedro Silverio. **Venezuelan Scouting Supervisor:** Juan Carlos Indriago.
International Scouts: Wilmer Castillo (Venezuela), Luis Cordoba (Panama), Juan Lopez (Nicaragua), Ramon Martinez (Dominican Republic), Daurys Nin (Dominican Republic), Mike Randall (South Africa), Rafael Vasquez (Dominican Republic).

LOS ANGELES DODGERS

Office Address: 1000 Elysian Park Ave., Los Angeles, CA 90012.
Telephone: (323) 224-1500. **FAX:** (323) 224-1269.
Website: www.dodgers.com.

Ownership

Operated by: Los Angeles Dodgers, LLC.
Principal Owner/Chairman of the Board: Frank McCourt. **Vice Chairman:** Jamie McCourt.

BUSINESS OPERATIONS

Executive Vice President, Chief Operating Officer: Marty Greenspun. **Executive Vice President, Chief Marketing Officer:** Lon Rosen. **Executive Vice President, Public Affairs:** Howard Sunkin.
Senior Vice President: Tommy Lasorda.
Senior VP, General Counsel: Sam Fernandez. **Associate Counsel:** Christine Chrisman. **Secretary, Legal:** Irma Duenas.

Finance

Vice President, Chief Financial Officer: Cris Hurley.
Director, Finance/Accounting: Amanda Shearer. **Manager, Payroll:** Rebecca Aguilar.

Frank McCourt

Sales, Advertising, Client Services

Chief Sales Officer: Greg McElroy. **Vice President, Sales:** Sergio del Prado. **Directors, Sponsorship Sales:** Jason Klein, Karen Marumoto. **Manager, Advertising/Special Events:** Dan Brewster.

Public Relations, Communications

Vice President, Communications: Gary Miereanu. **Director, Public Relations:** John Olguin. **Assistant Director, Public Relations:** Josh Rawitch. **Supervisor, Broadcast/Publications:** Paul Gomez.
Director, Community Affairs: Erikk Aldridge. **Director, Community Relations:** Don Newcombe.

Stadium Operations

Vice President, Stadium Operations: Doug Duennes.
Director, Stadium Operations: Lon Rosenberg. **Assistant Director, Stadium Operations:** Charles Taylor. **Assistant Director, Stadium Operations/Turf and Grounds:** Eric Hansen.
PA Announcer: Eric Smith. **Official Scorers:** Don Hartack, Ed Munson.-**Organist:** Nancy Bea Hefley.

Ticketing

Telephone: (323) 224-1471. **FAX:** (323) 224-2609.
Director, Ticket Operations: Billy Hunter. **Assistant Director, Ticket Operations:** Chris Frumento.

Travel, Clubhouse

Manager, Team Travel: Unavailable. **Home Clubhouse Managers:** Dave Dickinson, Mitch Poole. **Visiting Clubhouse Manager:** Jerry Turner.

GENERAL INFORMATION

Stadium (year opened): Dodger Stadium (1962).
Home Dugout: Third Base. **Playing Surface:** Grass.
Team Colors: Dodger blue and white.
Player Representative: David Ross.

BASEBALL OPERATIONS
Telephone: (323) 224-1500. **FAX:** (323) 224-1463.
Executive Vice President, General Manager: Paul DePodesta. **VP, Assistant GM:** Kim Ng.
Special Assistant to GM/Advance Scout: Mark Weidemaier (Tierre Verde, FL). **Senior Advisor, Baseball Operations:** Joe Amalfitano.
    Coordinator, Baseball Operations: Dan Feinstein. **Analyst, Baseball Operations:** Jason Amoroso. **Administrator, Baseball Operations:** Ellen Harrigan. **Executive Assistant, Baseball Operations:** Adriana Urzua.
    Vice President, Spring Training/Minor League Facilities: Craig Callan.
    Director, Asian Operations: Acey Kohrogi. **Manager, Japanese Affairs:** Scott Akasaki. **Manager, Korean Affairs:** Curtis Jung. **Manager, Chinese/Taiwanese Affairs:** Vincent Liao.

Paul DePodesta

Major League Staff
Manager: Jim Tracy.
Coaches: Bench—Jim Lett, Manny Mota; Pitching—Jim Colborn; Batting— Tim Wallach; First Base—John Shelby; Third Base—Glenn Hoffman; Bullpen—Jon Debus.

Medical, Training
Team Physicians: Dr. Frank Jobe, Dr. Michael Mellman, Dr. Ralph Gambardella, Dr. Herndon Harding.
Head Trainer: Stan Johnston. **Assistant Trainer:** Matt Wilson. **Physical Therapist:** Pat Screnar. **Strength/Conditioning Coach:** Todd Clausen.

Player Development
Telephone: (323) 224-1431. **FAX:** (323) 224-1359.
Vice President, Scouting/Player Development: Roy Smith.
Director, Player Development: Terry Collins. **Assistant Director, Player Development:** Luchy Guerra. **Coordinator, Minor League Operations:** Chris Haydock.
    Roving Coordinators: Dave Anderson (infield), George Hendrick (hitting), Rick Honeycutt (pitching), Doug Jarrow (strength/conditioning), David Rivera (physical therapy).
    Director, Campo Las Palmas/Dominican Republic: Eleodoro Arias. **Coordinators, Dominican Republic Operations:** Victor Baez (field), Antonio Bautista (hitting), Martin Berroa (training), Pedro Mega (infield), Jose Rosario (strength/conditioning).
    Supervisor, Venezuelan Operations: Camilo Pascual.

Jim Tracy

Farm System

Class	Farm Team	League	Manager	Coach	Pitching Coach
AAA	Las Vegas	Pacific Coast	Jerry Royster	Mariano Duncan	Roger McDowell
AA	Jacksonville	Southern	John Shoemaker	Steve Yeager	Ken Howell
High A	Vero Beach	Florida State	Scott Little	Dan Radison	Marty Reed
Low A	Columbus	South Atlantic	Travis Barbary	Garey Ingram	Glenn Dishman
Rookie	Ogden	Pioneer	Juan Bustabad	Unavailable	Bob Welch
Rookie	Vero Beach	Gulf Coast	Luis Salazar	M. Singleton/R. Ortiz	George Culver
Rookie	Dodgers I	Dominican	Antonio Bautista	Juan Davalillo	Hector Eduardo
Rookie	Dodgers II	Dominican	Jose Mija	Rafael Rijo	K. Martinez/Carlos Gil

Scouting
Director, Amateur Scouting: Logan White. **Special Advisor to Amateur Scouting Director/National Crosschecker:** Gib Bodet (San Clemente, CA). **Administrator, Scouting:** Jane Capobianco. **Coordinator, Scouting Operations:** Bill McLaughlin.
    Major League Scout: Carl Loewenstine (Hamilton, OH). **Professional Scouts:** Dan Freed (Lexington, IL), Vance Lovelace (Tampa, FL), Ron Rizzi (Joppa, MD).
    Special Assignment Scout: Tim Kelly (New Lenox, IL).
    National Crosschecker: Tim Hallgren (Roanoke, TX). **Regional Supervisors:** East—John Barr (Palm City, FL); Midwest—Gary Nickels (Naperville, IL); West Coast—Tom Thomas (Phoenix, AZ).
    Area Scouts: Doug Carpenter (Jupiter, FL), Jim Chapman (Delta, BC), Bobby Darwin (Cerritos, CA), Scott Groot (Mission Viejo, CA), Clarence Johns (New Orleans, LA), Calvin Jones (Henderson, NV), Hank Jones (Vancouver, WA), Lon Joyce (Spartanburg, SC), John Kosciak (Milford, MA), Marty Lamb (Lexington, KY), Mike Leuzinger (Mansfield, TX), James Merriweather (Los Angeles, CA), Bill Pleis (Parrish, FL), Clair Rierson (Frederick, MD), Mark Sheehy (Sacramento, CA), Chris Smith (Montgomery, TX), Brian Stephenson (Phoenix, AZ), Mitch Webster (Great Bend, KS).
    Director, International Scouting: Rene Francisco.**International Scouts:** Mike Brito (Mexico), Tony Harris (Australia), Pat Kelly (Pacific Rim), Camilo Pascual (Venezuela).

Logan White

MILWAUKEE BREWERS

Office Address: Miller Park, One Brewers Way, Milwaukee, WI 53214.
Telephone: (414) 902-4400. **FAX:** (414) 902-4053.
Website: www.milwaukeebrewers.com.

Ownership
Owner: Mark L. Attanasio.
Operated by: Milwaukee Brewers Baseball Club.

BUSINESS OPERATIONS
Executive Vice President: Rick Schlesinger. **General Counsel:** Marti Wronski.
Director, Human Resources/Office Management: Sally Andrist. **Manager, Human Resources:** Mariela Garcia-Danet. **Executive Assistant, Business Operations:** Adela Reeve. **Senior Director, Broadcasting/Entertainment:** Aleta Mercer. **Manager, Audio/Video Productions:** Deron Anderson.

Finance
Senior Vice President, Chief Financial Officer: Robert Quinn Jr.

Mark Attanasio

Controller: Joe Zidanic. **Director, Management Information Systems:** Dan Krautkramer. **Systems Administrator:** Tristan Benson. **Payroll Coordinator/Accountant:** Brian Krueger. **Financial Analysts:** Wes Seidel, Vicki Wise.

Corporate Affairs, Sales/Marketing
Senior Director, Marketing: Kathy Schwab.
Directors, Corporate Partnerships: Amy Deering, Dave Tamburrino. **Manager, Corporate Sales/Promotions:** David Barnes. **Administrative Assistant, Marketing:** Lisa Brzeski.

Public Relations, Community Relations
Telephone: (414) 902-4500. **FAX:** (414) 902-4053.
Director, Media Relations: Jon Greenberg. **Manager, Media Relations:** Nicole Saunches. **Publications Assistant:** Robbin Barnes. **Team Photographer:** Scott Paulus. **Director, Community Relations:** Leonard Peace. **Coordinator, Community Relations:** Patricia Ramirez. **Manager, Youth Baseball Programs:** Larry Hisle.

Stadium Operations
Vice President, Stadium Operations: Steve Ethier.
Director, Grounds: Gary Vanden Berg. **Manager, Grounds:** Raechal Volkening. **Coordinator, Guest Relations:** Kristy Suworoff. **Supervisor, Warehouse:** Patrick Rogo. **Manager, Event Sales:** Amy Barnes.
President, Brewers Charities: Lynn Sprangers.
PA Announcer: Robb Edwards. **Official Scorers:** Tim O'Driscoll, Wayne Franke.

Ticketing
Telephone: (414) 902-4000. **FAX:** (414) 902-4100.
Assistant Vice President, Ticket Sales: Jim Bathey. **Assistant VP, Ticket Services:** John Barnes.
Manager, Corporate Partner Services: Patty Harsch. **Manager, Group Sales:** Chris Barlow. **Manager, Season Ticket Sales:** Billy Friess. **Administrative Assistant:** Irene Bolton. **Assistant Director, Ticket Services:** Nancy Jorgensen. **Manager, Ticket Services/Phone Center:** Glenn Kurylo. **Representative, Ticket Office Support Services:** Diane Schoenfeld. **Senior Account Executives:** Beau Bradle, Bill Junker, Kara Kabitzke, Chris Kimball.

Travel, Clubhouse
Director, Team Travel: Dan Larrea.
Director, Clubhouse Operations/Equipment Manager: Tony Migliaccio. **Visiting Clubhouse Manager:** Phil Rozewicz. **Assistant, Home Clubhouse:** Mike Moulder. **Coordinator, Umpires Room:** Duane Lewis.

GENERAL INFORMATION
Stadium (year opened): Miller Park (2001).
Home Dugout: First Base. **Playing Surface:** Grass.
Team Colors: Navy blue, gold and white.
Player Representative: Wes Helms.

BASEBALL OPERATIONS

Executive Vice President, General Manager: Doug Melvin. **Assistant GM:** Gord Ash. **Senior Special Assistant to GM:** Larry Haney (Barboursville, VA). **Special Assistant to GM/Scouting:** Dick Groch (Marysville, MI). **Senior Administrator, Baseball Operations:** Barb Stark.

Major League Staff

Manager: Ned Yost.
Coaches: Bench—Rich Dauer; Pitching—Mike Maddux; Batting—Butch Wynegar; First Base—Dave Nelson; Third Base—Rich Donnelly; Bullpen—Bill Castro.

Doug Melvin

Medical, Training

Head Team Physician: Dr. William Raasch. **Head Athletic Trainer:** Roger Caplinger. **Assistant Athletic Trainer/Coordinator, Strength and Conditioning:** Dan Wright. **Assistant Athletic Trainer:** Paul Anderson.

Player Development

Telephone: (414) 902-4400. **FAX:** (414) 902-4059.
Special Assistant to General Manager/Player Development: Reid Nichols. **Assistant Director, Player Development:** Scott Martens. **Assistant to Player Development:** Mark Mueller.

Field Coordinator: Ed Sedar. **Coordinators:** Frank Neville (trainers), Jim Rooney (pitching), Jim Skaalen (hitting). **Roving Instructors:** Charlie Greene (catching), Norberto Martin (infield). **Equipment Manager:** J.R. Rinaldi. **Clubhouse Manager, Arizona:** Matt Bass. **Employee Assistance Coordinator** Tim Hewes.

Ned Yost

Farm System

Class	Farm Team	League	Manager	Coach	Pitching Coach
AAA	Nashville	Pacific Coast	Frank Kremblas	Gary Pettis	Stan Kyles
AA	Huntsville	Southern	Don Money	Sandy Guerrero	Rich Sauveur
High A	Brevard County	Florida State	John Tamargo	Johnny Narron	Fred Dabney
Low A	West Virginia	South Atlantic	Ramon Aviles	Tony Diggs	Mark Littell
Rookie	Helena	Pioneer	Ed Sedar	Bobby Randall	John Curtis
Rookie	Phoenix	Arizona	Mike Guerrero	Joel Youngblood	Steve Cline

Scouting

Telephone: (414) 902-4400. **FAX:** (414) 902-4059.
Director, Scouting: Jack Zduriencik. **Assistant Director, Scouting:** Tom Flanagan. **Administrative Assistant:** Amanda Klecker.

Special Assignment Scout: Lee Thomas (Chesterfield, MO).

Professional Scouts: Lary Aaron (Atlanta, GA), Hank Allen (Upper Marlboro, MD), Chris Bourjos (Scottsdale, AZ), Brad Del Barba (Fort Mitchell, KY), Larry Haney (Barboursville, VA), J Harrison (Antelope, CA), Tom Hinkle (Atascadero, CA), Toney Howell (Gurnee, IL), Leon Wurth (Nashville, TN).

National Crosscheckers: Larry Doughty (Leawood, KS), John Poloni (Tarpon Springs, FL). **Regional Supervisors:** West Coast—Tom Allison (Austin, TX); Midwest—Jeff Cornell (Lee's Summit, MO); East Coast—Bobby Heck (Apopka, FL).

Jack Zduriencik

Area Supervisors: Charles Allano (Land O' Lakes, FL), Tony Blengino (Magnolia, NJ), Grant Brittain (Hickory, NC), Mike Farrell (Indianapolis, IN), Manolo Hernandez (Moca, PR), Brian Johnson (Avondale, AZ), Harvey Kuenn Jr. (New Berlin, WI), Joe Mason (Millbrook, AL), Justin McCray (Davis, CA), Ray Montgomery (Pearland, TX), Brandon Newell (Bellingham, WA), Larry Pardo (Miami, FL), Doug Reynolds (Tallahassee, FL), Corey Rodriguez (Hermosa Beach, CA), Bruce Seid (Aliso Viejo, CA), Jim Stevenson (Tulsa, OK).

Scouts: Edward Fastaia (Brooklyn, NY), Roger Janeaway (Englewood, OH), John Logan (Milwaukee, WI), Mike Rasdall (Colorado Springs, CO), Brad Stoll (Lawrence, KS).

Latin America Supervisor—Fernando Arango (Dania, FL). **International Scouts:** Richard Clemons (Canada), John Haar (Canada), Mike LaBossiere (Canada), James Lapp (Canada), Fausto Sosa Pena (Dominican Republic), Jean Roy (Canada), Dale Tilleman (coordinator, Canada), Freddy Torres (Venezuela).

MINNESOTA TWINS

Office Address: 34 Kirby Puckett Place, Minneapolis, MN 55415.
Telephone: (612) 375-1366. **FAX:** (612) 375-7480.
Website: www.twinsbaseball.com.

Ownership
Operated by: The Minnesota Twins.
Owner: Carl Pohlad. **Chairman, Executive Committee:** Howard Fox.
Executive Board: Jerry Bell, Carl Pohlad, James Pohlad, Robert Pohlad, William Pohlad, Dave St. Peter.
President, Minnesota Twins: Dave St. Peter. **President, Twins Sports Inc.:** Jerry Bell.
Administrative Assistant to President/Office Manager: Joan Boeser.

Carl Pohlad

BUSINESS OPERATIONS

Human Resources
Vice President, Human Resources/Diversity: Raenell Dorn. **Payroll Manager:** Lori Beasley. **Human Resources Generalist:** Leticia Fuentes.

Finance
Chief Financial Officer: Kip Elliott. **Director, Financial Planning:** Andy Weinstein. **Director, Financial Reporting:** Michelle Stukel. **Accountant:** Jerry McLaughlin. **Accounts Payable:** Amy Fong.
Director, Information Systems: Wade Navratil. **Director, Network/Baseball Information Systems:** John Avenson.

Marketing
Vice President, Marketing: Patrick Klinger. **Director, Advertising:** Nancy O'Brien. **Director, Corporate Communications:** Brad Ruiter. **Promotions Coordinator:** Chris Hodapp. **Director, Game Presentation:** Andy Price. **Executive Director, Twins Community Fund:** Peter Martin. **Manager, Community Relations:** Bryan Donaldson. **Coordinators, Community Relations:** Andrea Knutson, Gloria Westerdahl.

Corporate Sales
Vice President, Corporate Partnerships: Eric Curry. **Managers, Corporate Sales:** Kernal Buhler, Dick Schultz, Mark Zobel. **Account Executive:** Willie Wong. **Manager, Client Services:** Bodie Rykken. **Coordinators, Client Services:** Jordan Gross, Katie Hartman.

Ticket Sales
Vice President, Ticket Sales/Service: Steve Smith. **Director, Ticket Sales/Service:** Scott O'Connell.
Customer Sales/Service Account Executives: Mike Leonard, Chris Malek, Lisa Rasmussen, Jason Stern. **Sales Development Representatives:** Chris Carson, Craig Gumz, Eric Hudson, Rob Malec. **Group Sales Development Representatives:** Dan Craighead, Jeff Hibicke. **Manager, Ticket Sales/Service Support:** Beth Vail.

Communications
Telephone: (612) 375-7471. **FAX:** (612) 375-7473.
Director, Team Travel/Baseball Communications: Remzi Kiratli. **Manager, Baseball Communications:** Sean Harlin. **Manager, Media/Player Relations:** Mike Herman. **Coordinator, Baseball Communications/Media Relations:** Molly Gallatin. **Official Scorer:** Tom Mee.

Stadium Operations
Vice President, Operations: Matt Hoy. **Director, Stadium Operations:** Dave Horsman. **Director, Special Events:** Heidi Sammon. **Manager, Stadium Operations:** Jeff Flom. **Manager, Security:** Dick Dugan. **Manager, Merchandise:** Matt Noll. **Manager, Roseville Pro Shop:** Joel Davis. **Manager, Minnetonka Pro Shop:** Courtney Pahlke. **Manager, Apple Valley Pro Shop:** Maris McEachran.
Coordinator, Office Services: John McEvoy. **Office Services Assistant:** Mike Sather. **Receptionist:** TaMica Tody. **PA Announcer:** Bob Casey.

Ticket Operations
Telephone: (612) 338-9467, (800) 338-9467. **FAX:** (612) 375-7464.
Director, Ticket Operations: Paul Froehle. **Manager, Box Office:** Mike Stiles. **Supervisor, Ticket Office:** Karl Dedenbach. **Coordinator, Ticket Office:** Mike Johnson. **Manager, Telemarketing:** Patrick Forsland.

Clubhouse
Equipment Manager: Jim Dunn. **Visitors Clubhouse:** Troy Matchan. **Internal Video Specialist:** Nyal Peterson.

GENERAL INFORMATION
Stadium (year opened): Hubert H. Humphrey Metrodome (1982).
Home Dugout: Third Base. **Playing Surface:** Field turf.
Team Colors: Burgundy, navy blue and white.
Player Representative: Kyle Lohse.

Terry Ryan

BASEBALL OPERATIONS
Telephone: (612) 375-7484. **FAX:** (612) 375-7417.
Vice President, General Manager: Terry Ryan.
VP, Assistant GM: Bill Smith. **Assistant GM:** Wayne Krivsky. **Special Assistants to GM:** Larry Corrigan, Joe McIlvaine, Tom Kelly.
Director, Baseball Operations: Rob Antony. **Assistant, Baseball Operations:** Brad Steil. **Administrative Assistant, Major League Operations:** Juanita Lagos-Benson.

Major League Staff
Manager: Ron Gardenhire.
Coaches: Bench—Steve Liddle; Pitching—Rick Anderson; Batting—Scott Ullger; First Base—Jerry White; Third Base—Al Newman; Bullpen—Rick Stelmaszek.

Medical, Training
Club Physicians: Dr. Dan Buss, Dr. Vijay Eyunni, Dr. Tom Jetzer, Dr. John Steubs, Dr. Jon Hallberg, Dr. Alvaro Sanchez.
Head Trainer: Rick McWane. **Assistant Trainer:** Dave Pruemer. **Strength/Conditioning Coach:** Randy Popple.

Player Development
Telephone: (612) 375-7488. **FAX:** (612) 375-7417.
Director, Minor Leagues: Jim Rantz. **Administrative Assistant, Minor Leagues:** Julie Rohloff.
Minor League Field Coordinator: Joe Vavra. **Roving Instructors:** Jim Dwyer (hitting), Rick Knapp (pitching).

Ron Gardenhire

Farm System

Class	Farm Team	League	Manager	Coach	Pitching Coach
AAA	Rochester	International	Phil Roof	Rich Miller	Bobby Cuellar
AA	New Britain	Eastern	Stan Cliburn	Floyd Rayford	Stu Cliburn
High A	Fort Myers	Florida State	Riccardo Ingram	Jeff Carter	Eric Rasmussen
Low A	Beloit	Midwest	Kevin Boles	Rudy Hernandez	Gary Lucas
Rookie	Elizabethton	Appalachian	Ray Smith	Jeff Reed	Jim Shellenback
Rookie	Fort Myers	Gulf Coast	Nelson Prada	Milt Cuyler	Steve Mintz
Rookie	Twins	Dominican	Nelson Norman	J. Valdez/C. Almonte	Pablo Frias
Rookie	Twins	Venezuela	Asdrubal Estrada	Ramon Borrego	Pablo Torres

Scouting
Telephone: (612) 375-7525. **FAX:** (612) 375-7417.
Director, Scouting: Mike Radcliff (Overland Park, KS).
Administrative Assistant, Scouting: Jack Goin.
Special Assignment Scouts: Larry Corrigan (Fort Myers, FL), Cal Ermer (Chattanooga, TN), Joe McIlvaine (Newtown Square, PA).
Major League Scout: Bill Harford (Chicago, IL). **Coordinator, Professional Scouting:** Vern Followell (Buena Park, CA). **Advance Scout:** Bob Hegman (Lee's Summit, MO).
Scouting Supervisors: East—Earl Frishman (Tampa, FL), West—Deron Johnson (Sacramento, CA), Midwest—Joel Lopci (Plato, MN), Mike Ruth (Lee's Summit, MO).

Mike Radcliff

Area Scouts: Kevin Bootay (Sacramento, CA), Dan Cox (Santa Ana, CA), Marty Esposito (Robinson, TX), Sean Johnson (Chandler, AZ), John Leavitt (Garden Grove, CA), Bill Lohr (Centralia, WA), Gregg Miller (Chandler, OK), Billy Milos (Crown Point, IN), Tim O'Neil (Lexington, KY), Hector Otero (Trujillo Alto, PR), Mark Quimuyog (Lynn Haven, FL), Ricky Taylor (Hickory, NC), Brad Weitzel (Haines City, FL), Jay Weitzel (Salamanca, NY), John Wilson (Blairstown, NJ), Mark Wilson (Lindstrom, MN).
Coordinator, International Scouting: Howard Norsetter (Australia)
International Scouts: John Cortese (Italy), Gene Grimaldi (Europe), David Kim (South Korea), Jose Leon (Venezuela), Yoshi Okamoto (Japan), Jim Ridley (Canada), Ken-Su (Taiwan), Koji Takahashi (Japan).

NEW YORK METS

Office Address: 123-01 Roosevelt Ave., Flushing, NY 11368.
Telephone: (718) 507-6387. FAX: (718) 507-6395.
Website: www.mets.com.

Ownership
Operated by: Sterling Mets, LP.
Board of Directors: Arthur Friedman, Steve Greenberg, David Katz, Michael Katz, Saul Katz, Tom Osterman, Stuart Sucherman, Marvin Tepper, Fred Wilpon, Jeff Wilpon, Richard Wilpon.
Chairman, Chief Executive Officer: Fred Wilpon. President: Saul Katz. Senior Executive Vice President, Chief Operating Officer: Jeff Wilpon.

BUSINESS OPERATIONS
Executive Vice President, Business Operations: David Howard. Senior Vice President, General Counsel: David Cohen.

Finance
Fred Wilpon

Chief Financial Officer: Mark Peskin. Vice President/Controller: Lenny Labita. Director, Information Systems: Dot Pope. Chief Accountant: Rebecca Mahadeva.

Marketing, Sales
Vice President, Corporate Sales/Services: Paul Danforth.
Director, Marketing: Tina Bucciarelli. Director, Marketing Productions: Tim Gunkel.
Director, Corporate Services: Jim Plummer. Director, Corporate Sales/Services: Paul Asencio. Manager, Marketing Communications: Jill Grabill. Director, Community Outreach: Jill Knee. Coordinator, Community Outreach: Chris Brown.

Media Relations
Telephone: (718) 565-4330. FAX: (718) 639-3619.
Vice President, Media Relations: Jay Horwitz. Manager, Media Relations: Shannon Dalton. Manager, Corporate/Media Services: Stella Fiore. Media Relations Specialist: Ethan Wilson. Media Relations Coordinator: Owen Bochner.

Stadium Operations
Vice President, Facilities: Karl Smolarz. Director, Stadium Operations: Kevin McCarthy. Manager, Stadium Operations: Sue Lucchi. Manager, Field Operations: Mike Williams.
PA Announcer: Alex Anthony. Official Scorers: Joe Donnelly, Howie Karpin, Bill Shannon, Jordan Sprechman.

Ticketing
Telephone: (718) 507-7499. FAX: (718) 507-6396.
Vice President, Ticket Sales/Services: Bill Ianniciello.
Director, Ticket Operations: Dan DeMato. Director, Ticket Sales Development: Jamie Ozure. Manager, Ticket Sales Development: Jeff Schindle. Director, Group/Ticket Sales Services: Thomas Fersch. Manager, Group/Ticket Sales Services: Mark Phillips.

Travel, Clubhouse
Equipment Manager, Associate Travel Director: Charlie Samuels. Assistant Equipment Manager: Vinny Greco. Visiting Clubhouse Manager: Tony Carullo. Video Editor: Joe Scarola.

GENERAL INFORMATION
Stadium (year opened): Shea Stadium (1964).
Home Dugout: First Base. Playing Surface: Grass.
Team Colors: Blue and orange.
Player Representative: Eric Valent.

BASEBALL OPERATIONS
Telephone: (718) 565-4315. **FAX:** (718) 507-6391.
Executive Vice President/General Manager: Omar Minaya. **Senior Vice President, Baseball Operations:** Jim Duquette. **Special Assistants to GM:** Tony Bernazard, Al Goldis, Sandy Johnson, Bill Livesey. **Executive Assistant to GM:** Leonor Colon.

Major League Staff
Manager: Willie Randolph
Coaches: Bench—Sandy Alomar Sr.; Pitching—Rick Peterson; Batting—Rick Down; First Base—Jerry Manuel; Third Base—Manny Acta; Bullpen—Guy Conti; Catching—Tom Nieto.

Omar Minaya

Medical, Training
Medical Director: Dr. David Altchek. **Team Physician:** Dr. Ainsworth Allen.
Head Trainer: Ray Ramirez. **Assistant Trainer:** Mike Herbst. **Coordinator, Strength/Conditioning:** Rick Slate. **Assistant Coordinator, Fitness/Conditioning:** Jose Vazquez.

Player Development
Telephone: (718) 565-4302. **FAX:** (718) 205-7920.
Vice President, Scouting/Player Development: Gary LaRocque.
Director, Minor League Operations: Kevin Morgan. **Assistant Director, Minor League Operations:** John Fantauzzi. **Assistant, Player Development:** Amy Neal.
Advisor to Minor League Director: Ray Rippelmeyer. **Infield Consultant:** Chico Fernandez.
Field Coordinator: Tony Tijerina. **Coordinator, Instruction:** Bobby Floyd. **Coordinators:** Edgar Alfonzo (infield), Lamar Johnson (hitting), Rick Patterson (baserunning/bunting), John Stearns (catching), Rick Waits (pitching).
Director, Athletic Development: Vern Gambetta. **Coordinator, Athletic Development:** Jason Craig. **Training Coordinator:** Bill Wagner. **Assistant Coordinator, Athletic Development:** Ken Coward. **Coordinator, Rehabilitation Pitching:** Randy Niemann. **Coordinator, Rehabilitation:** Jason Wulf. **Equipment Manager:** Kevin Kierst. **Assistant Equipment Manager:** Jack Brenner.

Willie Randolph

Farm System
Class	Farm Team	League	Manager	Coach	Pitching Coach
AAA	Norfolk	International	Ken Oberkfell	Howard Johnson	Dan Warthen
AA	Binghamton	Eastern	Jack Lind	Dave Hollins	Blaine Beatty
High A	St. Lucie	Florida State	Tim Teufel	Al LeBoeuf	Rick Mahler
Low A	Hagerstown	South Atlantic	Unavailable	Luis Natera	Shawn Barton
Short season	Brooklyn	New York-Penn	Mookie Wilson	Donovan Mitchell	Steve Merriman
Rookie	Kingsport	Appalachian	Jesse Levis	Juan Lopez	Dan Murray
Rookie	Mets	Gulf Coast	Gary Carter	Nelson Silverio	Hector Berrios
Rookie	Mets	Dominican	Lupe Jabalera	Liliano Castro	J. Hernaiz/B. Marte
Rookie	Mets	Venezuelan	Jesus Tiamo	Leo Hernandez	J. Hernaiz/R. Lazo

Scouting
Telephone: Amateur—(718) 565-4311; Professional—(718) 803-4013. **FAX:** (718) 205-7920.
Director, Amateur Scouting: Russ Bove. **Assistant Director, Amateur Scouting:** Rudy Torraono. **Assistant, Amateur Scouting:** Elizabeth Gadsden.
Coordinator, Professional Scouting: Bryan Lambe. **Assistant Professional/International Scouting:** Anne Fairbanks.
Special Assignment Scout: Bruce Benedict.
Professional Scouts: Dave Engle (San Diego, CA), Howie Freiling (Apex, NC), Roland Johnson (Newington, CT), Harry Minor (Long Beach, CA), Joe Nigro (Staten Island, NY).
National Crosscheckers: Paul Fryer (Calabasas, CA), Terry Tripp (Harrisburg, IL).
Regional Supervisors: West—Bob Minor (Garden Grove, CA); North—Gene Kerns (Hagerstown, MD); South—Joe DelliCarri (Longwood, FL).

Gary LaRocque

Area Supervisors: Dave Birecki (Flagstaff, AZ), Quincy Boyd (Plainfield, IL), Erwin Bryant (Lexington, KY), Jon Bunnell (Tampa, FL), Larry Chase (Pearcy, AR), Doug Gassaway (Blum, TX), Rodney Henderson (Lexington, KY), Chuck Hensley Jr. (Sacramento, CA), Scott Hunter (Mount Laurel, NJ), Steve Leavitt (Huntington Beach, CA), Fred Mazuca (Tustin, CA), Marlin McPhail (Irmo, SC), Greg Morhardt (South Windsor, CT), Claude Pelletier (St. Lazare, Quebec), Jim Reeves (Camas, WA), Junior Roman (San Sebastian, PR), Joe Salermo (Hallandale Beach, FL), Matt Wondolowski (Oakton, VA).
Director, International Scouting: Rafael Bournigal. **Director, Pacific Rim Scouting:** Isao O'Jimi (Japan).
International Scouts (full time): Eddy Toledo (Dominican Republic), Gregorio Machado (Venezuela), Tony Harris (Australia).

NEW YORK YANKEES

Office Address: Yankee Stadium, East 161st Street and River Avenue, Bronx, NY 10451.
Telephone: (718) 293-4300. **FAX:** (718) 293-8431.
Website: www.yankees.com.

Ownership
Principal Owner: George Steinbrenner. **General Partners:** Harold Steinbrenner, Henry Steinbrenner, Stephen Swindal.
Vice President: Felix Lopez.

BUSINESS OPERATIONS
President: Randy Levine.
Chief Operating Officer: Lonn Trost.
Vice President, Administration: Sonny Hight.

Finance
Vice President, Chief Financial Officer: Steve Dauria.
VP, Finance: Robert Brown.

George Steinbrenner

Business Development
Senior Vice President, Marketing: Deborah Tymon.
VP, Corporate/Community Relations: Brian Smith.
VP, Sponsorship Sales/Services: Michael Tusiani.

Media Relations, Publications
Telephone: (718) 579-4460. **FAX:** (718) 293-8414.
Senior Advisor: Arthur Richman. **Senior Director, Media Relations/Publicity:** Rick Cerrone. **Assistant Director, Media Relations/Publicity:** Jason Zillo. **Coordinator, Media Relations:** Ben Tuliebitz. **Director, Publications/Multimedia:** Mark Mandrake.

Stadium Operations
Director, Stadium Operations: Doug Behar. **Assistant Director, Stadium Operations:** Cliff Rowley. **Stadium Superintendent:** Pete Pullara.
Head Groundskeeper: Dan Cunningham. **Scoreboard/Broadcasting Manager:** Mike Bonner.
Director, Concessions: Joel White. **Director, Hospitality:** David Bernstein.
PA Announcer: Bob Sheppard. **Official Scorers:** Bill Shannon, Howie Karpin.

Ticketing
Telephone: (718) 293-6000. **FAX:** (718) 293-4841.
Vice President, Ticket Operations: Frank Swaine.
Senior Director, Ticket Operations: Irfan Kirimca.

Travel, Clubhouse
Traveling Secretary: David Szen.
Equipment Manager: Rob Cucuzza. **Visiting Clubhouse Manager:** Lou Cucuzza Jr.

GENERAL INFORMATION
Stadium (year opened): Yankee Stadium (1923).
Home Dugout: First Base. **Playing Surface:** Grass.
Team colors: Navy blue and white.
Player representative: Mike Mussina.

BASEBALL OPERATIONS
Telephone: (718) 293-4300. **FAX:** (718) 293-0015.
Senior Vice President/General Manager: Brian Cashman.
VP, Assistant GM: Jean Afterman. **Senior VP, Player Personnel:** Gordon Blakeley. **Coordinator, Major League Operations:** Anthony Flynn. **VP/Senior Advisor:** Gene Michael.
Special Assistants, Baseball Operations: Frank Howard, Jerry Krause.
Special Advisory Group: Yogi Berra, Reggie Jackson, Clyde King.

Major League Staff
Manager: Joe Torre.
Coaches: Bench/Catchers—Joe Girardi; Pitching—Mel Stottlemyre; Batting—Don

Brian Cashman   Mattingly; First Base—Roy White; Third Base—Luis Sojo; Bullpen—Neil Allen.

Medical, Training
Team Physician, New York: Dr. Stuart Hershon. **Team Physician, Tampa:** Dr. Andrew Boyer.
Head Trainer: Gene Monahan. **Assistant Trainer:** Steve Donohue.
Strength/Conditioning Coach: Jeff Mangold.

Player Development
Florida Complex: 3102 N. Himes Ave., Tampa, FL 33607. **Telephone:** (813) 875-7569.
FAX: (813) 873-2302.
Senior Vice President, Baseball Operations: Mark Newman.
VP, Player Personnel: Billy Connors. **Director, Player Development:** Pat Roessler.
Assistant Director, Player Development: Billy Eppler.
Minor League Coordinators: Nardi Contreras (pitching), Andy Stankiewicz (infield).
Head Trainer: Mark Littlefield. **Coordinator, Strength/Conditioning:** E.J. Amo. **Equipment**
Manager: David Hays. **Clubhouse Manager:** Jack Terry.

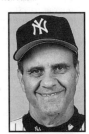

Joe Torre

Farm System

Class	Farm Club	League	Manager	Coach	Pitching Coach
AAA	Columbus	International	Bucky Dent	Kevin Long	Gil Patterson
AA	Trenton	Eastern	Bill Masse	Ty Hawkins	Dave Eiland
High A	Tampa	Florida State	Joe Breeden	Bill Doran	Greg Pavlick
Low A	Charleston	South Atlantic	Bill Mosiello	Torre Tyson	Steve Renko
Short season	Staten Island	New York-Penn	Andy Stankiewicz	Rob Ducey	Mike Thurman
Rookie	Tampa	Gulf Coast	Oscar Acosta	Matt Martin	Carlos Reyes
Rookie	Yankees I	Dominican	Carlos Mota	Julio Valdez	Wilfrido Cordova
Rookie	Yankees II	Dominican	Freddie Tiburcio	Sonder Encarnacion	Jose Duran

Scouting
Telephone: (813) 875-7569. **FAX:** (813) 348-2302.
Vice President, Scouting: Damon Oppenheimer.
Assistant Director, Professional Scouting: John Coppolella. **Assistant Director, Amateur Scouting:** John Kremer.
Advance Scouts: Chuck Cottier (Tampa, FL), Wade Taylor (Orlando, FL).
Professional Scouts: Jim Benedict (Bradenton, FL), Ron Brand (Mesa, AZ), Joe Caro (Tampa, FL), Bill Emslie (Safety Harbor, FL), Greg Orr (Sacramento, CA), Jeff Wetherby (Wesley Chapel, FL).
National Crosschecker: Wayne Britton (Waynesboro, VA). **Regional Crosscheckers:** East—Joe Arnold (Lakeland, FL); Midwest—Tim Kelly (New Lenox, IL); West—Jeff Patterson (Anaheim, CA).

Mark Newman

Area Scouts: Mike Baker (Cave Creek, AZ), Brian Barber (Winter Garden, FL), Mark Batchko (Arlington, TX), Steve Boros (Kingwood, TX), Mike Gibbons (Liberty Township, OH), Steve Lemke (Lincolnshire, IL), Bill Mele (El Segundo, CA), Cesar Presbott (Bronx, NY), Trevor Schaffer (Tampa, FL), D.J. Svihlik (Birmingham, AL), Steve Swail (Charlotte, NC), Fay Thompson (Callejo, CA), Mike Thurman (Corvallis, OR).
Vice President, International Scouting: Lin Garrett. **Vice President, International Operations:** Abel Guerra.
Assistant Director, International Operations: Stephanie Carapazza.
Coordinator, Latin American Scouting: Carlos Rios (Santo Domingo, DR). **Coordinator, Pacific Rim Scouting:** John Cox (Redlands, CA).
International Scouts: Darwin Bracho (Venezuela), Ricardo Finol (Venezuela), Ricardo Heron (Panama), Jose Luna (Dominican Republic), Victor Mata (Dominican Republic), Tito Quintero (Colombia), Hector Rincones (Venezuela), Edgar Rodriguez (Nicaragua), Cesar Suarez (Venezuela), Jesus Valdiva (Dominican Republic).

OAKLAND ATHLETICS

Office Address: 7000 Coliseum Way, Oakland, CA 94621.
Telephone: (510) 638-4900. FAX: (510) 562-1633.
Website: www.oaklandathletics.com.

Ownership

Operated by: Athletics Investment Group LLC (1996).
Co-Owner/Managing Partner: Steve Schott. Co-Owner/Partner: Ken Hofmann.
President: Michael Crowley. Executive Assistant to President: Carolyn Jones.
General Counsel: Nick Rossi. Assistant General Counsels: Caleb Jay, Rob Schantz.

BUSINESS OPERATIONS

Finance, Administration

Vice President, Finance: Paul Wong.
Director, Finance: Linda Rease. Payroll Manager: Kathy Leviege. Senior Accountant:
Isabelle Mahaffey. Assistant Ticket Accountant: David Fucillo.

Steve Schott

Manager, Human Resources: Kim Chen. Human Resources/Finance Coordinator: Janet
Aquino. Information Systems Manager: Debbie Dean.

Sales, Marketing

Vice President, Sales/Marketing: David Alioto.
Director, Corporate Sales: Franklin Lowe. Corporate Account Managers: Jill Golden, Kelle Venezia, Susan
Weiglein. Manager, Sales/Marketing: Lisa Wood. Manager, Interactive Marketing: Cameron Stewart. Coordinator,
Sales/Marketing: Katie Kelly. Manager, Creative Services: Mike Ono.
Director, Merchandising/Purchasing: Drew Bruno. Coordinator, Merchandising: Josh Vargo.

Public Relations, Communications

Telephone: (510) 563-2207. FAX: (510) 562-1633.
Vice President, Broadcasting/Communications: Ken Pries.
Director, Public Relations: Jim Young. Manager, Media Relations: Kristy Fick. Manager, Baseball Information:
Mike Selleck. Coordinator, Media Services: Debbie Gallas. Team Photographer: Michael Zagaris.
Manager, Community Relations: Detra Paige. Coordinator, Community Relations/Broadcasting: Warren Chu.

Stadium Operations

Vice President, Stadium Operations: David Rinetti.
Director, Stadium Operations: David Avila. Manager, Stadium Operations: Paul La Veau. Manager, Stadium
Operations Systems: Eric Nelson. Manager, Stadium Services: Randy Duran. Manager, Stadium Operations Events:
Kristy Ledbetter. Coordinator, Stadium Services: David Cochran. Coordinator, Stadium Operations: Shannon Bruener.
Director, In-Stadium Entertainment: Troy Smith. Director, Multimedia Services: David Don. Coordinator,
Multimedia Services: Jon Martin. Coordinator, In-Stadium Entertainment: Jeff Gass.
Head Groundskeeper: Clay Wood. Arizona Groundskeeper: Chad Huss.
PA Announcer: Roy Steele. Official Scorers: Chuck Dybdal, Art Santo Domingo, Al Talboy.

Ticketing

Director, Ticket Operations: Steve Fanelli.
Senior Manager, Ticket Operations: Doug Vanderheyden. Manager, Ticket Services: Josh Ziegenbusch. Manager,
Box Office: Anthony Silva. Coordinator, Group Tickets: David Adame. Coordinator, Ticket Operations: Katherine
Greenberg. Manager, Spring Training Marketing/Operations: Mike Saverino.
Director, Premium Seating Services: Dayn Floyd. Manager, Premium Seating Services: Susie Campion.
Manager, Special Events: Adrienne Carew. Coordinator, Special Events: Heather Rajeski.
Senior Manager, Ticket Sales: Grant Christensen.
Senior Account Managers, Outside Sales: Phil Chapman, Craig Kadden, Parker Newton. Account Managers,
Outside Sales: Adam Clar, Chris Corda, Brian DiTucci, Ryan Jones, Kimberlee Kelso, Sean O'Keefe, Chris Van Dyne.
Inside Sales Representatives: Aaron Dragomir, Christina Espinoza, Luke Pushee.

Travel, Clubhouse

Director, Team Travel: Mickey Morabito. Travel Specialist: Colleen Osterberg.
Equipment Manager: Steve Vucinich. Visitors Clubhouse: Mike Thalblum. Assistant Equipment Manager: Brian
Davis. Clubhouse Assistant: William Angel. Manager, Arizona Clubhouse: Jesse Sotomayor.

GENERAL INFORMATION

Stadium (year opened): Network Associates Coliseum (1968).
Home Dugout: Third Base. Playing Surface: Grass.
Team Colors: Kelly green and gold.
Player Representative: Bobby Crosby.

Billy Beane

BASEBALL OPERATIONS

Vice President, General Manager: Billy Beane.
Assistant GM: David Forst. **Special Assistants to GM:**
Randy Johnson, Matt Keough. **Executive Assistant:** Betty
Shinoda.
Director, Baseball Administration: Pamela Pitts.
Baseball Analyst: Farhan Zahidi.

Major League Staff

Manager: Ken Macha.
Coaches: Dugout—Rene Lachemann; Pitching—Curt Young; Batting—Dave Hudgens;
First Base—Brad Fischer; Third Base—Ron Washington; Bullpen—Bob Geren.
Medical, Training
Team Physician: Dr. Allan Pont. **Team Orthopedist:** Dr. Jerrald
Goldman. **Consulting Orthopedists:** Dr. John Frazier, Dr. Lewis Yocum. **Arizona Team**
Physician: Dr. Fred Dicke.
Head Trainer: Larry Davis. **Assistant Trainer:** Steve Sayles. **Strength and Conditioning:**
Clarence Cockrell.

Player Development

Telephone, Oakland: (510) 638-4900. **FAX:** (510) 563-2376.
Arizona Complex: Papago Park Baseball Complex, 1802 N. 64th St., Phoenix, AZ 85008.
Telephone: (602) 949-5951. **FAX:** (602) 945-0557.
Director, Player Development: Keith Lieppman. **Director, Minor League Operations:** Ted
Polakowski.
Roving Instructors: Juan Navarrete (infield), Ron Plaza, Ron Romanick (pitching), Greg
Sparks (hitting).
Medical Coordinator: Jeff Collins. **Strength and Conditioning:** Chris Lantz.

Ken Macha

Farm System

Class	Farm Team	League	Manager	Coach	Pitching Coach
AAA	Sacramento	Pacific Coast	Tony DeFrancesco	Brian McArn	Rick Rodriguez
AA	Midland	Texas	Von Hayes	Eddie Williams	Jim Coffman
High A	Stockton	California	Todd Steverson	Darren Bush	Scott Emerson
Low A	Kane County	Midwest	Dave Joppie	Aaron Nieckula	Garvin Alston
Short season	Vancouver	Northwest	Webster Graham	Jeremy Scheid	Craig Lefferts
Rookie	Phoenix	Arizona	Ruben Escalera	Juan Dilone	Mike Holmes
Rookie	Athletics I	Dominican	Unavailable	Unavailable	Unavailable
Rookie	Athletics II	Dominican	Unavailable	Unavailable	Unavailable

Scouting

Telephone: (510) 638-4900. **FAX:** (510) 563-2376.
Director, Scouting: Eric Kubota. **Coordinator, Scouting:** Bryn Alderson.
Assistant General Manager/Coordinator, Professional Scouting: David Forst.
Advance/Major League Scout: Joe Sparks.
National Field Coordinator: Chris Pittaro (Robbinsville, NJ). **National Crosschecker:** Ron
Vaughn (Corona, CA).
Scouting Supervisors: East Coast—Billy Owens (Tampa, FL); Midwest—Steve Bowden
(Cypress, TX); West Coast—Will Schock (Oakland, CA).
Area Scouts: Steve Barningham (Dunedin, FL), Jeff Bittiger (Saylorsburg, NJ), Blake Davis
(Dallas, TX), Ruben Escalera (San Juan, PR), Mike Holmes (Winston-Salem, NC), Scott Kidd
(Rocklin, CA), Rick Magnante (Van Nuys, CA), Kelcey Mucker (Metairie, LA), Jim Pransky
(Bettendorf, IA), Jeremy Schied (Phoenix, AZ), Rich Sparks (Sterling Heights, MI).
Coordinator, Dominican Republic: Raymond Abreu (Santo Domingo, DR).
International Scouts: Ruben Barradas (Venezuela), Juan Carlos De la Cruz (Dominican Republic), Angel Eusebio
(Dominican Republic), Julio Franco (Venezuela), Juan Martinez (Dominican Republic), Fausto Pena (Dominican
Republic), Bernardino Rosario (Dominican Republic), Oswaldo Troconis (Venezuela).

Eric Kubota

PHILADELPHIA PHILLIES

Office Address: Citizens Bank Park, One Citizens Bank Way, Philadelphia, PA 19148.
Telephone: (215) 463-6000.
Website: www.phillies.com.

Ownership
Operated by: The Phillies.
President, Chief Executive Officer: David Montgomery. **Chairman:** Bill Giles.

BUSINESS OPERATIONS
Vice President, General Counsel: Bill Webb.
Director, Business Development: Joe Giles. **Director, Human Resources:** Terry DeRugeriis.

Finance
Senior Vice President, Chief Financial Officer: Jerry Clothier.
Director, Finance/Accounting: John Nickolas. **Manager, Payroll Services:** Karen Wright.
Director, Information Systems: Brian Lamoreaux.

David Montgomery

Marketing, Promotions
Vice President, Advertising Sales: David Buck.
Manager, Client Services/Alumni Relations: Debbie Nocito. **Manager, National Sales:** Rob MacPherson. **Manager, Advertising Sales:** Scott Nickle. **Manager, Corporate Sales:** Brian Mahoney. **Director, Events:** Kurt Funk. **Director, Entertainment:** Chris Long. **Director, Broadcasting/Video Services:** Rory McNeil. **Manager, Advertising/Internet Services:** Jo-Anne Levy-Lamoreaux.

Public Relations, Communications
Telephone: (215) 463-6000. **FAX:** (215) 389-3050.
Vice President, Public Relations: Larry Shenk.
Director, Media Relations: Leigh Tobin. **Director, Print/Creative Services:** Tina Urban. **Coordinator, Publications:** Christine Negley. **Media Relations Representative:** Greg Casterioto. **Media Relations Administrator:** Mary Ann Gettis. **Director, Community Relations:** Gene Dias. **Speakers' Bureau Representative:** Maje McDonnell. **Community/Fan Development Representative:** Dick Allen.

Ballpark Operations
Vice President, Operations/Administration: Michael Stiles.
Director, Facility Management: Mike DiMuzio. **Director, Event Operations:** Eric Tobin. **Manager, Event Contract Services:** Bruce Leith.
PA Announcer: Dan Baker. **Official Scorers:** Jay Dunn, Bob Kenney, John McAdams.

Ticketing
Telephone: (215) 463-1000. **FAX:** (215) 463-9878.
Vice President, Ticket Operations: Richard Deats.
Director, Ticket Department: Dan Goroff. **Director, Sales:** John Weber. **Director, Group Sales:** Kathy Killian. **Manager, Ticket Technology/Development:** Chris Pohl. **Manager, Suite Sales/Services:** Tom Mashek.
Manager, Phone Center: Phil Feather. **Manager, Club Sales/Services:** Derek Schuster. **Manager, Season Ticket Services:** Mike Holdren.

Travel, Clubhouse
Manager, Equipment/Team Travel: Frank Coppenbarger. **Assistant Equipment Manager:** Dan O'Rourke. **Manager, Visiting Clubhouse:** Kevin Steinhour. **Assistant, Home Clubhouse:** Phil Sheridan.

GENERAL INFORMATION
Stadium (year opened): Citizens Bank Park (2004).
Home Dugout: First Base. **Playing Surface:** Natural grass.
Team Colors: Red, blue and white.
Player Representative: Randy Wolf.

BASEBALL OPERATIONS

Vice President, General Manager: Ed Wade.
Assistant GM: Ruben Amaro Jr. **Director, Baseball Administration:** Susan Ingersoll. **Computer Analysis:** Jay McLaughlin. **Senior Advisor to GM:** Dallas Green. **Special Assistant to GM:** John Vukovich.

Major League Staff

Manager: Charlie Manuel.
Coaches: Dugout—Gary Varsho; Pitching—Rich Dubee; Batting—Milt Thompson; First Base—Marc Bombard; Third Base—Bill Dancy; Bullpen—Ramon Henderson; Catching—Mick Billmeyer.

Ed Wade

Medical, Training

Director, Medical Services: Dr. Michael Ciccotti.
Head Trainer: Jeff Cooper. **Assistant Trainer:** Mark Andersen. **Conditioning Coordinator:** Scott Hoffman.

Player Development

Telephone: (215) 463-6000. **FAX:** (215) 755-9324.
Assistant General Manager, Scouting/Player Development: Mike Arbuckle.
Director, Minor League Operations: Steve Noworyta. **Administrative Assistant, Minor Leagues/Scouting:** Mike Ondo.
Director, Latin American Operations: Sal Artiaga. **Director, Florida Operations:** John Timberlake. **Assistant Director, Florida Operations:** Lee McDaniel.
Field Coordinator: Mike Compton. **Coordinators:** Roly deArmas (catching), Dale Ellicott (conditioning), Gorman Heimueller (pitching), Don Long (hitting), Jerry Martin (outfield/baserunning), Dave Owen (infield), Scott Sheridan (trainers).

Charlie Manuel

Farm System

Class	Farm Team	League	Manager	Coach	Pitching Coach
AAA	Scranton/W-B	International	Gene Lamont	Sal Rende	Rod Nichols
AA	Reading	Eastern	Steve Swisher	John Morris	Tom Filer
High A	Clearwater	Florida State	Greg Legg	Ken Dominguez	Scott Lovekamp
Low A	Lakewood	South Atlantic	P.J. Forbes	J.P. Roberge	Steve Schrenk
Short season	Batavia	New York-Penn	Manny Amador	Greg Gross	Ken Patterson
Rookie	Clearwater	Gulf Coast	Jim Morrison	Luis Melendez	Carlos Arroyo
Rookie	Phillies	Dominican	Sammy Mejia	Domingo Brito	Cesar Mejia
Rookie	Phillies	Venezuelan	Rafael DeLima	Silverio Navas	Lester Straker

Scouting

Telephone: (215) 218-5204. **FAX:** (215) 755-9324.
Director, Scouting: Marti Wolever (Papillion, NE). **Assistant Director, Scouting:** Rob Holiday.
Coordinators, Scouting: Jim Fregosi Jr. (Murrieta, CA), Mike Ledna (Arlington Heights, IL).
Director, Major League Scouts: Gordon Lakey (Barker, TX). **Major League Scout:** Jimmy Stewart (Odessa, FL). **Advance Scout:** Hank King (Limerick, PA).
Professional Scouts: Sonny Bowers (Hewitt, TX), Ron Hansen (Baldwin, MD), Dean Jongewaard (Fountain Valley, CA), Larry Rojas (Clearwater, FL), Del Unser (Scottsdale, AZ).
Scout/Instructor: Ruben Amaro Sr. (Weston, FL).
Regional Supervisors: East—John Castleberry (High Point, NC); Central—Brian Kohlscheen (Norman, OK); West—Billy Moore (Alta Loma, CA).
Area Scouts: Sal Agostinelli (Kings Park, NY), Therron Brockish (Anthem, AZ), Steve Cohen (Cary, NC), Darrell Conner (Riverside, CA), Joey Davis (Rancho Murrieta, CA), Tim Kissner (Long Beach, CA), Jerry Lafferty (Kansas City, MO), Chip Lawrence (Somerfield, FL), Miguel Machado (Miami Lakes, FL), Paul Murphy (Wilmington, DE), Gene Schall (Harleysville, PA), Paul Scott (Frisco, TX), Stewart Smothers (Los Angeles, CA), Mike Stauffer (Ridgeland, MS), Bob Szymkowski (Chicago, IL), Roy Tanner (Charleston, SC).

Mike Arbuckle

International Supervisor: Sal Agostinelli (Kings Park, NY).
International Scouts: Tomas Herrera (Mexico), Allan Lewis (Panama, Central America), Jesus Mendez (Venezuela), Wil Tejada (Dominican Republic).

PITTSBURGH PIRATES

Office Address: PNC Park at North Shore, 115 Federal St., Pittsburgh, PA 15212.
Mailing Address: P.O. Box 7000, Pittsburgh, PA 15212.
Telephone: (412) 323-5000. **FAX:** (412) 325-4412.
Website: www.pittsburghpirates.com.

Ownership

Operated by: Pittsburgh Pirates Acquisition, Inc.
Chief Executive Officer, Managing General Partner: Kevin McClatchy.
Board of Directors: Don Beaver, Frank Brenner, Kevin McClatchy, Thomas Murphy Jr., Ogden Nutting, Robert Nutting (chairman).

BUSINESS OPERATIONS

Finance

Vice President, Finance: Jim Plake.
Controller: David Bowman. **Director, Office Services:** Patti Mistick. **Director, Information Technology:** Terry Zeigler.

Kevin McClatchy

Marketing, Sales

Vice President, Sales/Marketing: Tim Schuldt.
Senior Director, Ticket Sales/Fan Development: Jim Alexander. **Senior Director, Corporate Development:** Bob Derda. **Director, Licensing/Promotions:** Joe Billetdeaux. **Director, Corporate Partnerships:** Mike Egan.

Communications

Telephone: (412) 325-4976. **FAX:** (412) 325-4413.
Vice President, Communications: Patty Paytas. **Director, Media Relations:** Jim Trdinich. **Manager, Media Services:** Dan Hart. **Manager, Broadcasting:** Marc Garda. **Director, Community Development:** Wende Torbert. **Manager, Communications/Special Events:** Christine Serkoch. **In-Game Entertainment:** Eric Wolff, Alex Moser.
VP, Corporate Projects: Nelson Briles.
Alumni Liaison: Sally O'Leary.

Stadium Operations

Vice President, PNC Park Operations/Facilities Management: Dennis DaPra.
Director, Operations: Chris Hunter. **Director, Security/Contract Services:** Jeff Podobnik. **Field Maintenance Manager:** Steve Peeler.
PA Announcer: Tim DeBacco. **Official Scorers:** Bob Hertzel, Tony Krizmanich, Evan Pattak, Bob Webb.

Ticketing

Telephone: (800) 289-2827. **FAX:** (412) 325-4404.
Manager, Ticket Services: Dave Wysocki.

Travel, Clubhouse

Traveling Secretary: Greg Johnson.
Equipment Manager/Home Clubhouse Operations: Roger Wilson. **Visitors Clubhouse Operations:** Kevin Conrad.

GENERAL INFORMATION

Stadium (year opened): PNC Park (2004).
Home Dugout: Third Base. **Playing Surface:** Grass.
Team Colors: Black, gold, red and white
Player Representative: Josh Fogg.

David Littlefield

BASEBALL OPERATIONS

Telephone: (412) 325-4743. **FAX:** (412) 325-4414.
Senior Vice President, General Manager: David Littlefield.
Assistant GM: Doug Strange. **Special Assistants to GM:** Jack Bowen, Louie Eljaua, Jesse Flores, Jax Robertson, Pete Vuckovich.
Director, Baseball Operations: Jon Mercurio. **Baseball Operations Assistant:** Bryan Minniti. **Administrative Assistant, Baseball Operations:** Jeannie Donatelli.

Major League Staff

Manager: Lloyd McClendon.
Coaches: Bench—Pete Mackanin; Pitching—Spin Williams; Batting—Gerald Perry; First Base—Rusty Kuntz; Third Base—John Russell; Bullpen—Bruce Tanner.

Medical, Training

Medical Director: Dr. Patrick DeMeo. **Team Physician:** Dr. Edward Snell.
Head Trainer: Brad Henderson. **Assistant Trainers:** Mark Rogow, Mike Sandoval. **Strength/Conditioning Coordinator:** Frank Velasquez.

Minor Leagues

Telephone: (412) 325-4737. **FAX:** (412) 325-4414.
Director, Player Development: Brian Graham. **Administrator, Minor Leagues:** Diane DePasquale.
Coordinator, Instruction: Jeff Banister. **Roving Instructors:** Jeff Manto (hitting), Gary Redus (outfield/baserunning), Gary Ruby (pitching).
Latin American Field Coordinator: Euclides Rojas. **Director, Dominican Republic Academy:** Esteban Beltre.

Lloyd McClendon

Farm System

Class	Farm Team	League	Manager	Coach	Pitching Coach
AAA	Indianapolis	International	Trent Jewett	Hensley Meulens	Darold Knowles
AA	Altoona	Eastern	Tony Beasley	John Wehner	Jeff Andrews
High A	Lynchburg	Carolina	Tim Leiper	Matt Winters	Bob Milacki
Low A	Hickory	South Atlantic	Jeff Branson	Greg Briley	Ray Searage
Short season	Williamsport	New York-Penn	Tom Prince	B. Moore/R. Sambo	Dave Lundquist
Rookie	Bradenton	Gulf Coast	Jeff Livesey	Woody Huyke	R. Newman/M. Bonilla
Rookie	Pirates	Dominican	Ramon Zapata	Ceciliio Beltre	Miguel Valdez
Rookie	Pirates	Venezuelan	Osmin Melendez	Ivan Colmenares	J. Prieto/D. Urbina

Scouting

Telephone: (412) 325-4738. **FAX:** (412) 325-4414.
Director, Scouting: Ed Creech. **Coordinator, Scouting Systems:** Sandy Deutsch.
National Supervisors: Tony DeMacio (Virginia Beach, VA), Jimmy Lester (Columbus, GA).
Regional Supervisors: John Green (West Grove, PA), Mark McKnight (Acworth, GA), Bump Merriweather (Los Angeles, CA).
Area Scouts: Kevin Clouser (Santa Monica, CA), Steve Fleming (Louisa, VA), Duane Gustavson (Columbus, OH), Greg Hopkins (Beaverton, OR), Mike Leuzinger (Mansfield, TX), Jaron Madison (Fairfield, CA), Jon Mecurio (Pittsburgh, PA), Buddy Paine (Hartsdale, NY), Jack Powell (Sweetwater, TN), Jim Rough (Wichita, KS), Everett Russell (Thibodaux, LA), Rob Sidwell (Windermere, FL), Charlie Sullivan (Miami Beach, FL), Ted Williams (Peoria, AZ).

Part-Time Scouts: Tom Barnard (Arlington Heights, IL), Elmer Gray (Pittsburgh, PA), Homer Newlin (Tallahassee, FL), William Price (Austin, TX), Tom Rogers (Clearwater, FL), Jose Rosario (Bayamon, PR), Troy Williams (Winder, GA).
Director, Latin American Scouting: Rene Gayo. **Supervisor, Dominican Republic:** Josue Herrera. **Supervisor, Venezuela:** Rodolfo Petit. **Scouts, Dominican Republic:** Marciano Alvarez, Ramon Perez, Frank Tavares. **International Scouts:** Daniel Garcia (Colombia), Jose Pineda (Panama), Jesus Valdez (Mexico), Marc Van Zanten (Netherlands Antilles), Alex Zapata (Panama).

Ed Creech

ST. LOUIS CARDINALS

Office Address: 250 Stadium Plaza, St. Louis, MO 63102.
Telephone: (314) 421-3060. FAX: (314) 425-0640.
Website: www.stlcardinals.com.

Ownership
Operated by: St. Louis Cardinals, LLC.
General Partner: Bill DeWitt Jr. Vice Chairman: Fred Hanser. Secretary/Treasurer: Andrew Baur.
President: Mark Lamping.
Senior Administrative Assistant to Chairman: Grace Hale. Senior Administrative Assistant to President: Julie Laningham.

BUSINESS OPERATIONS
Senior Vice President, Business Development: Bill DeWitt III.
VP, Event Services: Vicki Bryant. Coordinator, Event Services: Missy Tobey. Director, Government Affairs/Special Projects: Ron Watermon.
VP, Public Affairs/Employee Relations: Marian Rhodes. Manager, Office Administration/Human Resources Specialist: Karen Brown.

Mark Lamping

Finance
Senior Vice President, Controller: Brad Wood.
Director, Accounting: Deborah Pfaff. Director, Finance: Rex Carter. Supervisor, Ticket Accounting/Reporting: Michelle Flach. Senior Accountant: Tracey Sessions.

Marketing, Sales
Senior Vice President, Sales/Marketing: Dan Farrell. Administrative Assistant, Corporate Sales: Gail Ruhling.
Senior Director, Corporate Sales/Marketing: Thane van Breusegen. Director, Target Marketing: Ted Savage. Corporate Sales Account Executives: Jeff Floerke, Valerie Kotys, Theron Morgan, Tony Simokaitis.

Public Relations, Community Relations
Telephone: (314) 421-3060. FAX: (314) 982-7399.
Director, Media Relations: Brian Bartow. Assistants to Director, Media Relations: Jim Anderson, Melody Yount.
Director, Publications: Steve Zesch. Publications Assistant: Tom Raber.
VP, Community Relations: Marty Hendin. Community Relations Communications Specialist: Gabrielle Martin.
VP/Group Director, Community Outreach/Cardinals Care: Tim Hanser. Coordinator, Cardinals Care: Lucretia Payne. Youth Baseball Commissioner, Cardinals Care: Keith Brooks.

Stadium Operations
Vice President, Stadium Operations: Joe Abernathy. Administrative Assistant: Nan Bommarito.
Director, Stadium Operations: Mike Bertani. Director, Security/Special Services: Joe Walsh. Administrative Assistant, Security: Hope Baker.
Director, Quality Assurance/Guest Services: Mike Ball. Manager, Stadium Operations: Cindy Richards.
Head Groundskeeper: Bill Findley. Assistant Head Groundskeeper: Chad Casella.
PA Announcer: John Ulett. Official Scorers: Gary Mueller, Jeff Durbin, Mike Smith.

Ticketing
Telephone: (314) 421-2400. FAX: (314) 425-0649.
Vice President, Ticket Operations: Josie Arnold.
Senior Director, Ticket Sales: Joe Strohm.
Manager, Ticket Operations: Kim Kleeschulte. Manager, Box Office: Julie Baker. Director, Season/Premium Ticket Sales: Mark Murray. Coordinator, Premium Seats: Julia Kelley. Coordinator, Prime Seat Club: Jennifer Needham.
Director, Group Sales: Michael Hall. Manager, Group Sales: Mary Clare Bena. Supervisor, Customer Service: Marilyn Mathews.

Travel, Clubhouse
Traveling Secretary: C.J. Cherre.
Equipment Manager: Rip Rowan. Assistant Equipment Manager: Ernie Moore. Visiting Clubhouse Manager: Jerry Risch. Video Coordinator: Chad Blair.

GENERAL INFORMATION
Stadium (year opened): Busch Stadium (1966).
Home Dugout: First Base. Playing Surface: Grass.
Team Colors: Red and white.
Player Representative: Ray King.

Walt Jocketty

BASEBALL OPERATIONS
Telephone: (314) 425-0687. **FAX:** (314) 425-0648.
Senior Vice President, General Manager: Walt Jocketty. **Assistant GM:** John Mozeliak. **Special Assistants to GM:** Mike Jorgensen, Red Schoendienst.
VP, Player Personnel: Jerry Walker. **Director, Major League Administration/Senior Executive Assistant to GM:** Judy Carpenter-Barada.

Major League Staff
Manager: Tony La Russa.
Coaches: Bench—Joe Pettini; Pitching—Dave Duncan; Batting—Hal McRae; First Base—Dave McKay; Third Base—Jose Oquendo; Bullpen—Marty Mason.

Medical, Training
Senior Medical Advisor: Dr. Stan London. **Club Physician:** Dr. George Paletta.
Head Trainer: Barry Weinberg. **Assistant Trainer:** Greg Hauck.

Player Development
Telephone: (314) 425-0628. **FAX:** (314) 425-0638.
Director, Player Development: Bruce Manno. **Assistant Director, Player Development/Manager, Baseball Information:** John Vuch. **Administrative Assistant:** Judy Francis.
Player Development Advisor/Infield Instructor: George Kissell.
Field Coordinator: Jim Riggleman. **Coordinators:** Mark Riggins (pitching), Gene Tenace (hitting), Tom Spencer (baserunning/outfield).
Minor League Equipment Manager: Buddy Bates.

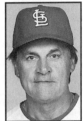

Tony La Russa

Farm System

Class	Farm Team	League	Manager	Coach	Pitching Coach
AAA	Memphis	Pacific Coast	Danny Sheaffer	Tommy Gregg	Dyar Miller
AA	Springfield	Texas	Chris Maloney	Dallas Williams	Blaise Ilsley
High A	Palm Beach	Florida State	Ron Warner	Derrick May	Derek Lilliquist
Low A	Quad Cities	Midwest	Joe Cunningham	Keith Mitchell	Bryan Eversgerd
Short season	New Jersey	New York-Penn	Mark DeJohn	Unavailable	Sid Monge
Rookie	Johnson City	Appalachian	Tom Kidwell	Unavailable	Al Holland

Scouting
Telephone: (314) 516-0435. **FAX:** (314) 425-0638.
Vice President, Player Procurement: Jeff Luhnow. **Assistant Scouting Director:** Dan Kantrovitz. **Administrative Assistant:** Linda Brauer.
Director, Professional Scouting: Marteese Robinson.
Major League/Special Assignment Scouts: Bing Devine (St. Louis, MO), Mike Jorgensen (St. Louis, MO), Jim Leyland (Pittsburgh, PA), Fred McAlister (Katy, TX).
Professional Scouts: Bill Harford (Chicago, IL), Marty Keough (Scottsdale, AZ), Mike Squires (Kalamazoo, MI).
National/Regional Supervisors: Chuck Fick (Newbury Park, CA), Marty Maier (St. Louis, MO), Joe Rigoli (Parsippany, NJ), Mike Roberts (Hot Springs, AR).
Area Supervisors: Joe Almaraz (San Antonio, TX), Clark Crist (Tucson, AZ), Steve Gossett (Broken Arrow, OK), Brian Hopkins (Cleveland, OH), Scott Melvin (Quincy, IL), Scott Nichols (Richland, MS), Jay North (Vacaville, CA), Joel Ronda (Puerto Rico), Tommy Shields (Lititz, PA), Mike Shildt (Charlotte, NC), Anup Sinha (Rancho Cucamonga, CA), Roger Smith (Eastman, GA), Steve Turco (Clearwater, FL), Dane Walker (Canby, OR).
International Group Coordinator: Maria Valentin. **Administrative Latin American Scouting Coordinator:** Enrique Brito (Venezuela). **International Scouts:** Wilmer Becerra (Venezuela), Neder Horta (Colombia), Rene Rojas (Dominican Republic).

Jeff Luhnow

SAN DIEGO PADRES

Office Address: Petco Park, 100 Park Blvd., San Diego, CA 92101.
Mailing Address: P.O. Box 122000, San Diego, CA 92112.
Telephone: (619) 795-5000.
E-Mail Address: comments@padres.com. **Website:** www.padres.com

Ownership

Operated by: Padres, LP.
Principal Owner, Chairman: John Moores. **Co-Vice Chairman:** Charlie Noell.
President/Chief Executive Officer: Dick Freeman

BUSINESS OPERATIONS

Finance

Vice President/Chief Financial Officer: Fred Gerson. **VP/Controller:** Dan Fumai. **Director, Information Systems:** Joe Lewis.

Marketing, Sales

Executive Vice President/Business Affairs: Steve Violetta.
Executive Director, Corporate Partnerships: Jim Ballweg. **Assistant Director, Corporate Partnerships:** Marty Gorsich.

John Moores

Public Relations, Community Relations

Telephone: (619) 795-5265. **FAX:** (619) 795-5266.
Executive Vice President/Communications: Jeff Overton.
Director, Media Relations: Luis Garcia. **Assistant Director, Media Relations:** Michael Uhlenkamp. **Coordinator, Baseball Information:** Dustin Morse.
Vice President, Community Relations: Michele Anderson.
Director, Padres Foundation: Sue Botos.
Manager, Community Relations: Nhu Tran. **Coordinator, Community Relations:** Sarah Rodriguez.

Stadium Operations

Executive Vice President/Managing Director, Ballpark Management: Richard Andersen.
VP, Ballpark Operations: Mark Guglielmo.
Director, Security/Transportation: Ken Kawachi. **Director, Landscape/Field Maintenance:** Luke Yoder.
PA Announcer: Frank Anthony. **Official Scorers:** Dennis Smythe, Bill Zavestoski.

Ticketing

Telephone: (619) 795-8025. **FAX:** (619) 795-5034.
Executive Director, Ticket Sales: Mark Tilson.

Travel, Clubhouse

Director, Team Travel/Equipment Manager: Brian Prilaman. **Home Clubhouse Operations:** Tony Petricca. **Visitors Clubhouse Operations:** David Bacharach.

GENERAL INFORMATION

Stadium (year opened): Petco Park (2004).
Home Dugout: First Base. **Playing Surface:** Grass.
Team Colors: Padres sand, navy blue, sky blue.
Player Representative: Adam Eaton.

Kevin Towers

BASEBALL OPERATIONS

Telephone: (619) 795-5076. **FAX:** (619) 795-5036.
Executive Vice President, General Manager: Kevin Towers.
Assistant GM: Fred Uhlman Jr. **Special Assistants to GM:** Ken Bracey, Grady Fuson.
Assistant, Major League Operations: Jeff Kingston. **Administrative Assistant:** Herta Bingham.

Major League Staff
Manager: Bruce Bochy.
Coaches: Bench—Tony Muser; Pitching—Darren Balsley; Batting—Dave Magadan; First Base—Davey Lopes; Third Base—Rob Picciolo; Bullpen—Darrel Akerfelds.

Medical, Training
Club Physician: Scripps Clinic medical staff.
Head Trainer: Todd Hutcheson. **Assistant Trainer:** Jim Daniel. **Strength/Conditioning Coach:** Joe Hughes.

Player Development
Telephone: (619) 795-5335. **FAX:** (619) 795-5036.
Director, Player Development: Tye Waller. **Director, Minor League Operations:** Priscilla Oppenheimer. **Assistant to Director, Player Development:** Juan Lara.
Special Assistant to GM/Field Coordinator: Bill Bryk.
Roving Instructors: Mike Couchee (pitching), Doug Dascenzo (outfield/baserunning), Rob Deer (hitting), Joe Ferguson (catching), Tony Franklin (infield). **Coordinator, Trainers:** Lance Cacanindin. **Strength/Conditioning Coordinator:** Danny Stinnett.

Bruce Bochy

Farm System

Class	Farm Team	League	Manager	Coach	Pitching Coach
AAA	Portland	Pacific Coast	Craig Colbert	Jose Castro	Gary Lance
AA	Mobile	Southern	Gary Jones	Mike Davis	Mike Harkey
High A	Lake Elsinore	California	Rick Renteria	Tom Tornincasa	Dave Rajsich
Low A	Fort Wayne	Midwest	Randy Ready	Max Venable	Steve Webber
Short season	Eugene	Northwest	Roy Howell	Ben Oglivie	Wally Whitehurst
Rookie	Peoria	Arizona	Carlos Lezcano	Luis Quinones	Jim Bennett
Rookie	Padres	Dominican	Pablo Martinez	Jose Mateo	Rafael Valdez

Scouting
Telephone: (619) 795-5343. **FAX:** (619) 795-5036.
Director, Scouting: Bill Gayton. **Assistant Director, Scouting:** Mike Wickham.
Major League Scouts: Ken Bracey (Morton, IL), Ray Crone (Waxahachie, TX), Moose Johnson (Arvada, CO), Ted Simmons (Wildwood, MO), Gene Thompson (Scottsdale, AZ).
Advance Scout: Jeff Gardner (Newport Beach, CA).
Professional Scouts: Charley Kerfeld (Gig Harbor, WA), Ben McLure (Hummelstown, PA), Tom McNamara (Lakewood Ranch, FL), Van Smith (Belleville, IL), Elanis Westbrooks (Houston, TX).
National Crosschecker: Jay Darnell (Plano, TX). **Regional Crosscheckers:** West Coast—Chris Gwynn (Alta Loma, CA); East Coast—Scott Littlefield (Long Beach, CA); Midwest—Tim Holt (Allen, TX).
Scouting Supervisor, Independent Leagues: Mal Fichman.
Full-Time Scouts: Joe Bochy (Plant City, FL), Rich Bordi (Rohnert Park, CA), Josh Boyd (Gig Harbor, WA), Jim Bretz (South Windsor, CT), Lane Decker (Piedmont, OK), Bob Filotei (Wilmer, AL), Brendan Hause (San Diego, CA), Hank King (Monroe, GA), Bob Laurie (Plano, TX), Ashley Lawson (Cary, NC), Dave Lottsfeldt (Greenwood Village, CO), Billy Merkel (Columbia, TN), Jeff Stewart (Normal, IL), Jake Wilson (El Segundo, CA).
Part-Time Scouts: Robert Beattie (Sioux Falls, SD), Dan Bleiwas (Thornhill, Ontario), Leroy Dreyer (Brenham, TX), Robert Gutierrez (Carol City, FL), William Killian (Stanwood, MA), Hank Krause (Akron, IA), Willie Ronda (Rio Piedras, PR), Cam Walker (Centerville, IA).
Director, Professional/International Scouting: Randy Smith (Scottsdale, AZ).
International Scouts: Rafael Beleo (Dominican Republic), Jorge Carolus (Netherlands Antilles), Milton Croes (Caribbean), Marcial Del Valle (Colombia), Akira Ejiri (Japan), Felix Francisco (Dominican Republic), Elvin Jarquin (Nicaragua), Victor Magdaleno (Venezuela), Daniel Mavares (Colombia), Ricardo Montenegro (Panama), Francis Mojica (Dominican Republic), Ricardo Petit (Venezuela), Ronald Petit (Venezuela), Robert Rowley (Panama), Jose Salado (Dominican Republic), Trevor Schumm (Australia), Illich Salazar (Venezuela).

Bill Gayton

SAN FRANCISCO GIANTS

Office Address: SBC Park, 24 Willie Mays Plaza, San Francisco, CA 94107.
Telephone: (415) 972-2000. **FAX:** (415) 947-2800.
Website: www.sfgiants.com.

Ownership
Operated by: San Francisco Baseball Associates, LP.
President, Managing General Partner: Peter Magowan.
Senior General Partner: Harmon Burns. **General Partner:** William Neukom. **Special Assistant:** Willie Mays. **Senior Advisor:** Willie McCovey.

BUSINESS OPERATIONS
Executive Vice President, Chief Operating Officer: Larry Baer.
Senior VP, General Counsel: Jack Bair. **Vice President, Human Resources:** Joyce Thomas.

Peter Magowan

Finance
Senior Vice President, Chief Financial Officer: John Yee. **VP, Chief Information Officer:** Bill Schlough. **Director, Management Information Systems:** John Winborn.
VP, Administration: Alfonso Felder.
VP, Finance: Lisa Pantages.

Marketing, Sales
Senior Vice President, Corporate Marketing: Mario Alioto. **VP, Corporate Sponsorship:** Jason Pearl. **Director, Special Events:** Valerie McGuire.
Senior VP, Consumer Marketing: Tom McDonald. **Director, Marketing/Entertainment:** Bryan Srabian. **Director, Client Relations:** Annemarie Hastings. **Director, Sales/Ticket Marketing:** Rob Sullivan. **Manager, Season Ticket Sales:** Craig Solomon. **VP/General Manager, Retail:** Connie Kullberg. **Director, Retail:** Derik Landry.

Media Relations, Community Relations
Telephone: (415) 972-2448. **FAX:** (415) 947-2800.
Manager, Media Relations: Jim Moorehead. **Director, Broadcasting/Media Services:** Maria Jacinto. **Director, Media Relations:** Blake Rhodes. **Coordinator, Media Relations:** Matt Hodson.
VP, Print Publications/Creative Services: Nancy Donati. **VP, Communications:** Staci Slaughter. **Director, Public Affairs:** Shana Daum. **Manager, Photography/Archives:** Missy Mikulecky.

Ballpark Operations
Senior Vice President, Ballpark Operations: Jorge Costa.
VP, Guest Services: Rick Mears. **Senior Director, Ballpark Operations:** Gene Telucci. **Manager, Maintenance:** Frank Peinado. **Security Manager:** Tinie Roberson. **Head Groundskeeper:** Scott MacVicar.
PA Announcer: Renel Brooks-Moon. **Official Scorers:** Chuck Dybdal, Art Santo Domingo, Al Talboy.

Ticketing
Telephone: (415) 972-2000. **FAX:** (415) 947-2500.
Vice President, Ticket Services/Client Relations: Russ Stanley. **Director, Ticket Services:** Devin Lutes. **Director, Luxury Suites:** Amy Luskotoff. **Manager, Ticket Services:** Bob Bisio. **Manager, Ticket Accounting:** Kem Easley. **Manager, Ticket Operations:** Anita Sprinkles. **Special Events Ticket Manager:** Todd Pierce.

Travel, Clubhouse
Director, Travel: Reggie Younger. **Equipment Manager:** Miguel Murphy. **Visitors Clubhouse:** Harvey Hodgerney. **Umpires Attendant:** Richard Cacace.

GENERAL INFORMATION
Stadium (year opened): SBC Park (2000).
Home Dugout: Third Base. **Playing Surface:** Grass.
Team Colors: Black, orange and cream.
Player Representative: Michael Tucker.

BASEBALL OPERATIONS

Telephone: (415) 972-1922. **FAX:** (415) 947-2737.
Senior Vice President, General Manager: Brian Sabean.
VP, Assistant GM: Ned Colletti. **Special Assistant to GM:** Ron Perranoski. **Executive Assistant, Baseball Operations:** Karen Sweeney. **Coordinator, Baseball Operations:** Jeremy Shelley.

Major League Staff

Manager: Felipe Alou.
Coaches: Bench—Ron Wotus; Pitching—Dave Righetti; Batting—Joe Lefebvre; First Base—Luis Pujols; Third Base—Gene Glynn; Bullpen—Mark Gardner; Bullpen Catcher—Bill Hayes.

Brian Sabean

Medical, Training

Team Physicians: Dr. Robert Murray, Dr. Gary Fanton, Dr. Ken Akizuki.
Medical Director/Head Trainer: Stan Conte. **Assistant Trainers:** Dave Groeschner, Ben Potenziano.

Player Development

Telephone: (415) 972-1922. **FAX:** (415) 947-2929.
Vice President, Player Personnel: Dick Tidrow.
Director, Player Development: Jack Hiatt. **Director, Minor League Operations:** Bobby Evans. **Assistant, Minor League Operations:** Yeshayah Goldfarb. **Special Assistant, Player Personnel:** Jim Davenport.
Coordinator, Instruction: Fred Stanley. **Coordinator, Minor League Pitching:** Bert Bradley. **Coordinator, Minor League Hitting:** Willie Upshaw. **Coordinator, Minor League Hitting Instruction:** Bob Mariano.
Roving Instructors: Joe Amalfitano (infield), Darren Lewis (baserunning/outfield), Kirt Manwaring (catching), Lee Smith (pitching).

Felipe Alou

Farm System

Class	Farm Team	League	Manager	Coach	Pitching Coach
AAA	Fresno	Pacific Coast	Shane Turner	Jim Bowie	Tom Brown
AA	Norwich	Eastern	Dave Machemer	Roger LaFrancois	Bob Stanley
High A	San Jose	California	Lenn Sakata	Gary Davenport	Trevor Wilson
Low A	Augusta	South Atlantic	Roberto Kelly	Jerry Browne	Ross Grimsley
Short season	Salem-Keizer	Northwest	Steve Decker	Ricky Ward	Jerry Cram
Rookie	Scottsdale	Arizona	Bert Hunter	Leo Garcia	Will Malerich
Rookie	Giants	Dominican	Manuel Jimenez	Hector Ortiz	Luis Prieto

Scouting

Telephone: (415) 972-1922. **FAX:** (415) 947-2737.
Coordinator, Scouting: Matt Nerland.
Major League Scouts: Joe DiCarlo (Ringwood, NJ), Stan Saleski (Dayton, OH), Paul Turco Sr. (Sarasota, FL), Ted Uhlaender (Parshall, CO), Tom Zimmer (St. Petersburg, FL).
Advance Scout: Pat Dobson (El Cajon, CA).
Special Assignment Scouts: Dick Cole (Costa Mesa, CA), Larry Osborne (Woodstock, GA).
National Crosschecker: Doug Mapson (Chandler, AZ). **Regional Crosscheckers:** Canada—Steve Arnieri (Barrington, IL); Southwest—Lee Carballo (Westchester, CA); East Coast—Paul Turco Jr. (Tampa, FL); West Coast—Darren Wittcke (Gresham, OR).
Area Scouts: Dean Decillis (Weston, FL), Rex Delanuez (Burbank, CA), John DiCarlo (Glenwood, NJ), Lee Elder (Martinez, GA), Tom Korenek (Houston, TX), Ray Krawczyk (Corona, CA), Felix Negron (Bayamon, PR), Sean O'Connor (Westerville, OH), Pat Portugal (Raleigh, NC), John Shafer (Portland, OR), Joe Strain (Englewood, CO), Todd Thomas (Dallas, TX), Glenn Tufts (Bridgewater, MA), Harry Stavrenos (Soquel, CA), Matt Woodward (Vancouver, WA).

Dick Tidrow

Coordinator, International Operations: Rick Ragazzo (Leona Valley, CA).
Director, Dominican Republic Operations: Pablo Peguero (Santo Domingo, DR). **Special Assignment Scout:** Matty Alou (Santo Domingo, DR). **Venezuela Supervisor:** Ciro Villalobos (Zulia, VZ).
International Scouts: Enrique Burgos (Panama), Jorge Diaz (Colombia), Philip Elhage (Curacao), Martin Hernandez (Venezuela), Juan Marquez (Venezuela), Sebastian Martinez (Venezuela), Fausto Pena (Dominican Republic), Luis Pena (Mexico), Jesus Stephens (Dominican Republic), Alex Torres (Nicaragua), Aguedo Vasquez (Dominican Republic), Carlos Zerpa (Venezuela).

SEATTLE MARINERS

Office Address: 1250 First Ave. S., Seattle, WA 98134.
Mailing Address: P.O. Box 4100, Seattle, WA 98194.
Telephone: (206) 346-4000. **FAX:** (206) 346-4400.
Website: www.seattlemariners.com.

Ownership

Operated by: Baseball Club of Seattle, LP.
Board of Directors: Minoru Arakawa, John Ellis, Chris Larson, Howard Lincoln, Wayne Perry, Frank Shrontz, Craig Watjen.
Chairman, Chief Executive Officer: Howard Lincoln. **President, Chief Operating Officer:** Chuck Armstrong.

BUSINESS OPERATIONS

Finance

Executive Vice President, Finance/Ballpark Operations: Kevin Mather.
VP, Finance: Tim Kornegay. **Assistant Controller:** Greg Massey.
VP, Human Resources: Marianne Short. **VP, Technology Services:** Larry Witherspoon.

Chuck Armstrong

Marketing, Sales

Executive Vice President, Business/Operations: Bob Aylward.
VP, Marketing: Kevin Martinez. **Director, Marketing:** Jon Schuller. **Director, Promotions:** Gregg Greene. **Director, Retail Operations:** Jim La Shell. **Suite Sales:** Moose Clausen.
Baseball Information, Communications
Telephone: (206) 346-4000. **FAX:** (206) 346-4400.
Vice President, Communications: Randy Adamack.
Director, Baseball Information: Tim Hevly. **Assistants, Baseball Information:** Gillian Hagamen, Kelly Munro.
Director, Public Information: Rebecca Hale. **Director, Graphic Design:** Carl Morton.
Director, Community Relations: Gina Hasson. **Manager, Community Programs:** Sean Grindley.

Ticketing

Telephone: (206) 346-4001. **FAX:** (206) 346-4100.
Director, Ticket Services: Kristin Fortier. **Manager, Ticket Operations:** Connie McKay. **Manager, Group/Suite Tickets Services:** Steve Belling. **Manager, Box Office:** Malcolm Rogel. **Director, Season Tickets/Group Sales:** Bob Hellinger. **Senior Director, Sales:** Frances Traisman.

Stadium Operations

Vice President, Ballpark Operations: Neil Campbell. **Director, Safeco Field Operations:** Tony Pereira.
Head Groundskeeper: Bob Christofferson.
PA Announcer: Tom Hutyler. **Official Scorer:** Unavailable.

Travel, Clubhouse

Director, Team Travel: Ron Spellecy.
Clubhouse Manager: Ted Walsh. **Visiting Clubhouse Manager:** Henry Genzale.
Video Coordinator: Carl Hamilton.

GENERAL INFORMATION

Stadium (year opened): Safeco Field (1999).
Home Dugout: First Base. **Playing Surface:** Grass.
Team Colors: Northwest green, silver and navy blue.
Player Representative: Joel Pineiro.

Bill Bavasi

BASEBALL OPERATIONS
Executive Vice President, General Manager: Bill Bavasi.
VP, Baseball Administration: Lee Pelekoudas. **Special Assistants to Executive VP, Player Personnel:** John Boles, Dan Evans. **Special Consultant to GM:** Pat Gillick.
Administrator, Baseball Operations: Debbie Larsen.
Baseball Operations Assistant/Systems Coordinator: Jim Na.

Major League Staff
Manager: Mike Hargrove.
Coaches: Dugout—Ron Hassey; Pitching—Bryan Price; Batting—Don Baylor; First Base—Carlos Garcia; Third Base—Jeff Newman; Bullpen—Jim Slaton.

Medical, Training
Medical Director: Dr. Larry Pedegana. **Club Physician:** Dr. Mitchel Storey.
Head Trainer: Rick Griffin. **Assistant Trainer:** Tom Newberg. **Strength/Conditioning Coach:** Allen Wirtala.

Player Development
Telephone: (206) 346-4313. **FAX:** (206) 346-4300.
Vice President, Player Development/Scouting: Benny Looper.
Director, Minor League Operations: Greg Hunter. **Director, Player Development:** Frank Mattox. **Administrator, Player Development:** Jan Plein.
Coordinator, Minor League Instruction: Mike Goff. **Trainer Coordinator:** Mickey Clarizio.
Roving Instructors: Glenn Adams (hitting), James Clifford (strength/conditioning), Darrin Garner (infield), Roger Hansen (catching), Pat Rice (pitching). **Special Assignment Coaches:** Norm Charlton, Buzzy Keller, Cal McLish, Dave Myers.

Mike Hargrove

Farm System

Class	Farm Team	League	Manager	Coach	Pitching Coach
AAA	Tacoma	Pacific Coast	Dan Rohn	Terry Pollreisz	Rafael Chaves
AA	San Antonio	Texas	Dave Brundage	Gary Thurman	Dwight Bernard
High A	Inland Empire	California	Daren Brown	Henry Cotto	Scott Budner
Low A	Wisconsin	Midwest	Scott Steinmann	Tommy Cruz	Brad Holman
Short season	Everett	Northwest	Pedro Grifol	James Horner	Marcos Garcia
Rookie	Peoria	Arizona	Dana Williams	Andy Bottin	Gary Wheelock
Rookie	Mariners	Dominican	Juan Castillo	R. Mejia/A. Morillo	Manuel Marrero
Rookie	Mariners	Venezuela	Jose Moreno	Angel Escobar	Jesus Hernandez

Scouting
Telephone: (206) 346-4000. **FAX:** (206) 346-4300.
Vice President, Scouting: Bob Fontaine. **Scouting Assistant:** Jim Fitzgerald. **Administrator, Scouting:** Hallie Larson.
Special Assignments/Amateur Scouting: Tom Davis.
Advance Scout: Steve Peck (Phoenix, AZ).
Director, Professional Scouting: Ken Compton (Cypress, CA).
Major League Scouts: John Boles (Melbourne, FL), Dan Evans (La Canada, CA), David Garcia (El Cajon, CA), Bob Harrison (Long Beach, CA), Bill Kearns (Milton, MA), Bob Miske (Amherst, NY), Wayne Morgan (Pebble Beach, CA), Chris Pelekoudas (Goodyear, AZ), Steve Pope (Asheville, NC), Tim Schmidt (San Bernardino, CA).
National Coordinators: Rick Ingalls (Long Beach, CA), Steve Jongewaard (Fountain Valley, CA).

Bob Fontaine

Territorial Supervisors: West—Ron Tostenson (El Dorado Hills, CA); East—John McMichen (Treasure Island, FL); Midwest—Carroll Sembera (Shiner, TX), Ken Madeja (Novi, MI).
Full-Time Scouts: Craig Bell (Asheboro, NC), Joe Bohringer (DeKalb, IL), Phil Geisler (Bellevue, WA), Pedro Grifol (Miami, FL), Mark Leavitt (Maitland, FL), Mark Lummus (Cleburne, TX), David May (Bear, DE), Rob Mummau (Stephens City, VA), Stacey Pettis (Antioch, CA), Tim Reynolds (Irvine, CA), Alvin Rittman (Memphis, TN), Rafael Santo Domingo (San Juan, PR), Kyle Van Hook (Brenham, TX), Greg Whitworth (Canyon Country, CA).
Director, International Operations: Bob Engle (Tampa, FL). **Assistant Director, International Operations:** Hide Sueyoshi (Bellevue, WA). **Director, Pacific Rim Operations:** Ted Heid (Glendale, AZ). **Coordinator, Canada/Europe:** Wayne Norton (Port Moody, BC).
Supervisors, International Scouting: Pedro Avila (Venezuela), Emilio Carrasquel (Venezuela), Patrick Guerrero (Dominican Republic), Matt Stark (Mexico), Jamey Storvick (Taiwan), Curtis Wallace (Colombia), Yasushi Yamamoto (Japan).

TAMPA BAY DEVIL RAYS

Office Address: Tropicana Field, One Tropicana Dr., St. Petersburg, FL 33705.
Telephone: (727) 825-3137. FAX: (727)-825-3111.
Website: www.devilrays.com.

Ownership

Owned by: P.J. Benton, Joseph Chlapaty, Mel Danker, Franklin Eck, Florida Progress Corporation, Claude Focardi, Jim Goodmon, Robert Kleinert, Gary Markel, Arthur Nagle, Vincent Naimoli, Daniel O'Connell, Frank Richardson, Lance Ringhaver, Thomas Sansone, Gus Stavros, Stuart Sternberg, Stephen Waters.

Operated by: Tampa Bay Devil Rays, Ltd.

Managing General Partner, Chief Executive Officer: Vincent Naimoli. Executive Assistant: Diane Villanova. Administrative Assistant: Jennifer Lyn Tran

Vince Naimoli

BUSINESS OPERATIONS

Senior Vice President, Administration/Chief Financial Officer: John Higgins. Senior VP, Business Operations: David J. Auker. Administrative Assistant: Silvia Bynes.

VP, Employee/Guest Relations: Jose Tavarez.

Finance

Vice President, Planning/Development: Matt Silverman. Director, Business Administration: Bill Wiener. Controller: Patrick Smith. Supervisor, Accounting: Sandra Faulkner. Payroll Supervisor: Jill Baetz. Benefits Coordinator: Debra Perry. Accounts Payable Coordinator: Sam Reams. Purchasing Coordinator: Mike Yodis.

Sales, Ticketing

Vice President, Sales: Unavailable. Administrative Assistant: Kristi Capone.

Director, Event Productions/Entertainment: John Franzone. Assistant Event Producer: Stephanie Renica. Manager, Print/Graphic Production: Charles Parker. Manager, Video/Graphic Production: Jason Rundle. Graphic Designer/Photo Manager: Erik Ruiz. Video Producer: Doug Elsberry. Matrix Producer: Laura Cuozzo.

Director, Ticket Operations: Robert Bennett. Assistant Director, Ticket Operations: Ken Mallory. Ticket Operations Representative: Karen Richardson. Customer Service Director: John Heffernan. Customer Service Representative: Craig Champagne. Director, Sales: Clark Beacom. Senior Account Executives: Jake Dunlap, Brian Ross, Jeremy White.

Marketing

Vice President, Marketing: John Browne.

Senior Director, Corporate Partnerships/Broadcasting: Larry McCabe. Directors, Corporate Partnerships: Aaron Cohn, Kevin Gallagher, P.J. Laferla, George Manias, Dana Metz. Managers, Corporate Partnership Coordination: Erin Buscemi, Jason Wilmoth. Account Executives, Corporate Partnerships: Wes Engram, Kraig Obarski. Manager, Sponsorship Coordination: Beth Bohnsack. Manager, Corporate Partnership Coordination/Television Operations: Joe Ciaravino.

Public Relations

Telephone: (727) 825-3242. FAX: (727) 825-3111.

Vice President, Public Relations: Rick Vaughn.

Coordinator, Public Relations: Carmen Molina. Director, Media Relations: Chris Costello. Coordinator, Media Relations: Jason Latimer. Website Manager: Eric Helmer.

Vice President, Community Relations/Business Affairs: Veronica Costello. Executive Director, Community Development/Rays of Hope Foundation: Dick Crippen. Director, Community Relations: Liz-Beth Lauck. Manager, Promotions/Advertising: Brian Killingsworth. Merchandise Manager: Debbie Brooks.

Stadium Operations

Vice President, Operations/Facilities: Rick Nafe. Administrative Assistant: Lorra Gillespie.

Building Manager: Scott Kelyman. Event Manager: Tom Karac. Event Coordinator: Todd Hardy. Manager, Suites/Customer Liaison Services: Cass Halpin. Booking Coordinator: Caren Gramley.

Head Groundskeeper: Dan Moeller. Director, Audio/Visual Services: Ron Golick.

PA Announcer: Bill Couch.

Travel, Clubhouse

Director, Team Travel: Jeff Ziegler.

Equipment Manager, Home Clubhouse: Chris Westmoreland. Visitors Clubhouse: Guy Gallagher.

GENERAL INFORMATION

Stadium (year opened): Tropicana Field (1998).
Home Dugout: First Base. Playing Surface: FieldTurf.
Team Colors: Black, blue and green.
Player Representative: Rocco Baldelli.

BASEBALL OPERATIONS

Senior Vice President, Baseball Operations/ General Manager: Chuck LaMar.

Assistant GMs: Bart Braun, Scott Proefrock. **Director, Major League Administration:** Sandy Dengler. **Special Assistant to GM:** Rick Williams. **Senior Baseball Advisor:** Don Zimmer. **Video Coordinator:** Chris Fernandez.

Major League Staff

Manager: Lou Piniella. **Coaches:** Bench—John McLaren; Pitching—Chuck Hernandez; Batting—Lee Elia; First Base—Billy Hatcher; Third Base—Tom Foley; Bullpen—Matt Sinatro.

Medical, Training

Chuck LaMar

Medical Director: Dr. James Andrews. **Medical Team Physician:** Dr. Michael Reilly. **Orthopedic Team Physician:** Dr. Koco Eaton. **Head Athletic Trainer:** Ken Crenshaw. **Assistant Athletic Trainer:** Ron Porterfield. **Strength/Conditioning Coach:** Kevin Barr.

Minor Leagues

Telephone: (727) 825-3267. **FAX:** (727) 825-3493.

Director, Player Personnel/Scouting: Cam Bonifay. **Assistant, Player Development/Scouting:** Mitch Lukevics. **Assistant, Player Development:** Andrew Friedman. **Administrative Assistant, Player Development:** Giovanna Rodriguez.

Field Coordinator: Jim Hoff. **Minor League Coordinators:** Paul Harker (medical/rehabilitation), Steve Henderson (hitting), Jerry Nyman (pitching), Nate Shaw (strength/conditioning). **Equipment Manager:** Tim McKechney.

Lou Piniella

Farm System

Class	Farm Team	League	Manager	Coach	Pitching Coach
AAA	Durham	International	Bill Evers	Richie Hebner	Joe Coleman
AA	Montgomery	Southern	Mako Oliveras	Skeeter Barnes	Xavier Hernandez
High A	Visalia	California	Steve Livesey	Omer Munoz	Marty DeMerritt
Low A	SW Michigan	Midwest	Joe Szekely	Skeeter Barnes	R.C. Lichtenstein
Short season	Hudson Valley	New York-Penn	Dave Howard	Matt Quatraro	Dick Bosman
Rookie	Princeton	Appalachian	Jamie Nelson	Manny Castillo	Rafael Montalvo

Scouting

Telephone: (727) 825-3241. **FAX:** (727) 825-3493.

Special Assistant to General Manager/Scouting: Tim Wilken. **Assistant to Scouting Director:** Nancy Berry.

Major League Scouts: Bart Johnson (Bridgeview, IL), Roger Jongewaard (Fallbrook, CA), Don Williams (Paragould, AR), Stan Williams (Lakewood, CA). **Major League Consultants:** Jerry Gardner (Los Alamitos, CA), George Zuraw (Englewood, FL).

Assistant Scouting Director/National Coordinator: R.J. Harrison (Phoenix, AZ). **Regional Scouting Coordinators:** Dave Roberts (Portland, OR), Mac Siebert (Molino, FL). **Special Assignment Scout:** Benny Latino (Hammond, LA).

Scouting Supervisors: Jonathan Bonifay (Austin, TX), Jim Bonnici (Ortonville, MI), Skip Bundy (Birmingham, AL), Tom Couston (Chicago, IL), Rickey Drexler (Jeanerette, LA), Kevin Elfering (Wesley Chapel, FL), Milt Hill (Cumming, GA), Paul Kirsch (Sherwood, OR), Brad Matthews (Concord, NC), Fred Repke (Rancho Cucamonga, CA), Craig Weissmann (LaCosta, CA), Doug Witt (Brooklyn MD).

Cam Bonifay

Area Scouts: Joe Murphy (Rock Island, IL), Lee Seras (Flanders, NJ).

Director, International Scouting: Rudy Santin (Miami, FL). **Scout:** Junior Ramirez (Dominican Republic).

TEXAS RANGERS

Office Address: 1000 Ballpark Way, Arlington, TX 76011.
Mailing Address: P.O. Box 90111, Arlington, TX 76004.
Telephone: (817) 273-5222. **FAX:** (817) 273-5110.
Website: www.texasrangers.com.

Ownership

Owner: Southwest Sports Group, Inc.
Chairman, Chief Executive Officer: Tom Hicks.
President: Jeff Cogen.
Executive Vice President, Southwest Sports Group: Casey Shilts. **Executive Director to President:** Jim Sundberg. **Executive Assistant to President:** Carla Rosenberg.

Tom Hicks

BUSINESS OPERATIONS

Executive Vice President, Business Operations: Rick McLaughlin. **Executive Assistant, Business Operations/Security:** Judy Southworth.
Assistant VP, Human Resources: Terry Turner. **Manager, Benefits/Compensation:** Carla Clack. **Supervisor, Staffing/Development:** Shannon Cain. **Staff Attorney:** Lucy Meyers.
Director, Information Technology: Mike Bullock. **Director, Application Systems:** Russell Smutzer. **Manager, Systems Administration:** Karl Clark.

Finance

Vice President, Finance: Kellie Fischer. **Executive Assistant, Legal/Finance:** Kay Turner.
Controller: Starr Pritchard **Director, Treasury/Reporting:** Christie Steblein. **Manager, Payroll:** Donna Blaylock. **Manager, Accounting:** Donna Kee. **Senior Staff Accountant:** Paula Murphy.

Marketing, Sales

Vice President, Sponsorship: Brad Alberts. **Directors, Sponsorship Sales:** Jim Cochrane, Grady Raskin, Lillian Richey. **Director, Broadcasting Sales Services:** Angie Swint. **Director, Corporate/Suite Sales:** Thomas Hicks Jr.
Vice President, Marketing/In-Park Entertainment: Chuck Morgan. **Assistant VP, Marketing:** Kelly Calvert. **Senior Director, Graphic Design:** Rainer Uhlir. **Director, Publications:** Kurt Daniels. **Director, Promotions/Special Events:** Sherry Flow. **Director, Graphic Design:** Michelle Hays. **Director, Media:** Heidi Leonards. **Creative Director, Media:** Rush Olson. **Director, New Market Development:** Karin Morris. **Producer/Videographer:** Hugo Carbajal.
Assistant Vice President, Merchandising: Todd Grizzle. **Director, Merchandising:** Diane Atkinson. **Manager, Warehouse Operations:** Gabriel Naggar. **Manager, Ballpark Retail Operations:** Stephen Moore.

Public Relations, Communications

Telephone: (817) 273-5203. **FAX:** (817) 273-5110.
Senior Director, Baseball Media Relations: Gregg Elkin. **Assistant Director, Baseball Media Relations:** Rich Rice. **Manager, Business Communications:** Jessica Beard. **VP, Player/Community Relations:** Norm Lyons. **Director, Community Relations:** Taunee Paur Taylor. **Assistant Director, Community Relations:** Tyler Beckstrom.

Stadium Operations

Vice President, Event Operations/Security: John Hardin. **Senior Director, Customer Service:** Donnie Pordash.
Assistant VP, Facilities Operations: Gib Searight. **Director, Grounds:** Tom Burns. **Director, Maintenance:** Mike Call. **Coordinator, Facility Services:** Duane Arber. **Coordinator, General Maintenance:** John Deardorff.
PA Announcer: Chuck Morgan. **Official Scorers:** John Mocek, Steve Weller.

Ticketing

Telephone: (817) 273-5100. **FAX:** (817) 273-5190.
Director, Ticket Services: Mike Lentz. **Manager, Ticket Operations:** David Larson. **Coordinator, Ticket Accounting Administration:** Ranae Lewis. **Coordinator, Season Tickets:** Ben Rogers. **Coordinator, Group Tickets:** Ryan Spaeny. **Coordinator, Box Office:** Jesus Morillo.
Vice President, Ticket Sales: Andy Silverman. **Assistant VP, Luxury Suite Sales:** Paige Jackson Farragut. **Director, Ticket Sales:** Ken Troupe. **Director, Baseball Programs/Youth Ballpark:** Breon Dennis.

Travel, Clubhouse

Director, Travel: Chris Lyngos.
Equipment/Home Clubhouse Manager: Zack Minasian. **Assistant Clubhouse Manager:** Dave Bales. **Visiting Clubhouse Manager:** Kelly Terrell. **Video Coordinator:** Josh Frasier.

GENERAL INFORMATION

Stadium (year opened): Ameriquest Field in Arlington (1994).
Home Dugout: First Base. **Playing Surface:** Grass.
Team Colors: Royal blue and red.
Player Representative: Mark Teixeira.

John Hart

BASEBALL OPERATIONS
Telephone: (817) 273-5222. **FAX:** (817) 273-5285.
Executive Vice President, General Manager: John Hart.
Assistant GM: Jon Daniels. **Special Assistant to GM:** Jay Robertson. **Senior Advisor to GM:** Tom Giordano.
Director, Major League Administration: Judy Johns.
Assistant, Baseball Operations: Jake Krug.

Major League Staff
Manager: Buck Showalter.
Coaches: Bench—Don Wakamatsu; Pitching—Orel Hershiser; Batting—Rudy Jaramillo; First Base/Outfield—DeMarlo Hale; Third Base—Steve Smith; Bullpen—Mark Connor.

Medical, Training
Team Physician: Dr. Keith Meister. **Team Internist:** Dr. David Hunter.
Head Trainer/Medical Director: Jamie Reed. **Assistant Trainer:** Kevin Harmon. **Director, Strength/Conditioning:** Fernando Montes.

Player Development
Telephone: (817) 273-5224. **FAX:** (817) 273-5285.
Director, Player Personnel: Dom Chiti. **Director, Minor League Operations:** John Lombardo. **Administrative Assistant, Player Development/Scouting:** Margaret Bales.
Roving Instructors: Rick Adair (pitching), Damon Berryhill (catching), Tim Ireland (baserunning/bunting), Brook Jacoby (hitting), Don Kalksteoin (performance enhancement), Napoleon Pichardo (strength), Kyle Turner (medical).
Manager, Minor League Complex Operations: Chris Guth. **Assistant Equipment Manager:** Russ Oliver. **Arizona Clubhouse Manager:** Troy Timney.

Buck Showalter

Farm System

Class	Farm Team	League	Manager	Coach	Pitching Coach
AAA	Oklahoma	Pacific Coast	Bobby Jones	Paul Carey	Lee Tunnell
AA	Frisco	Texas	Darryl Kennedy	Ronnie Ortegon	Steve Luebber
High A	Bakersfield	California	Arnie Beyeler	Mike Boulanger	David Chavarria
Low A	Clinton	Midwest	Carlos Subero	Brian Dayett	Stan Hilton
Short season	Spokane	Northwest	Greg Riddoch	Mark Whiten	Glenn Abbott
Rookie	Surprise	Arizona	Pedro Lopez	Unavailable	Aris Tirado
Rookie	Rangers	Dominican	Guillermo Mercedes	Fermin Infante	Francisco Saneaux

Scouting
Telephone: (817) 273-5277. **FAX:** (817) 273-5285.
Director, Scouting: Ron Hopkins (Seattle, WA). **Manager, Pro/International Scouting:** A.J. Preller.
Professional Scouts: Keith Boeck (Chandler, AZ), Mel Didier (Phoenix, AZ), Bob Johnson (University Park, FL), Woody Woodward (Palm Coast, FL).
Regional Crosscheckers: Kip Fagg (Gilbert, AZ), Dave Klipstein (Roanoke, TX), Doug Harris (Carlisle, PA).
Area Scouts: Russ Ardolina (Baltimore, MD), Guy DeMutis (Windermere, FL), Jay Eddings (Sperry, OK), Steve Flores (Temecula, CA), Tim Fortugno (Elk Grove, CA), Mark Ciogler (Fenton, MI), Mike Grouse (Olathe, KS), Todd Guggiana (Long Beach, CA), Derek Lee (Homewood, IL), Gary McGraw (Gaston, OR), Rick Schroeder (Phoenix, AZ), Scott Sharp (Charlotte, NC), Doug Simons (Decatur, AL), Randy Taylor (Katy, TX), Frankie Thon (Guaynabo, PR), Jeff Wood (New York, NY).
Part-time Scouts: Seth Brizek (Hartwell, GA), Ron Toenjes (Georgetown, TX).
Latin Coordinator: Manny Batista (Vega Alta, PR). **Dominican Program Coordinator:** Danilo Troncoso (La Romana, DR) **Dominican Program/English Instructor:** Dennys Sanchez. **International Crosschecker:** Don Welke (Louisville, KY). **International Scouts:** Andres Espinoso (Venezuela), Jesus Ovalle (Dominican Republic), Rodolfo Rosario (Dominican Republic), Edgar Suarez (Venezuela), Eduardo Thomas (Panama).

Dom Chiti

TORONTO BLUE JAYS

Office/Mailing Address: 1 Blue Jays Way, Suite 3200, Toronto, Ontario M5V 3M7.
Telephone: (416) 341-1000. **FAX:** (416) 341-1250.
E-Mail Address: bluejay@bluejays.ca **Website:** www.bluejays.com.

Ownership
Operated by: Toronto Blue Jays Baseball Club.
Principal Owner: Rogers Communications, Inc.
President, Chief Executive Officer: Paul Godfrey. **Executive Assistant to President/CEO:** Julie Stoddart.

BUSINESS OPERATIONS
Senior Vice President, Operations/Corporate Development: Lisa Novak. **Director, Business Affairs:** Matthew Shuber. **Executive Assistant, Operations/Corporate Development:** Alina Szwed.
VP, Special Projects: Howard Starkman.

Finance
Vice President, Finance/Administration: Susan Brioux. **Controller:** Tony Loffreda.
Manager, Human Resources: Michelle Carter.
Director, Information Technology: Jacques Farand. **IT Project Manager:** Anthony Miranda. **IT Support Analyst:** Vidal Abad. **Network Administrator:** Donny Catinari. **Ticket System Administrator:** Darlene Samakese.

Paul Godfrey

Marketing, Sales
Director, Consumer Marketing: Laurel Lindsay. **Manager, Promotions:** Jillian Stoltz. **Executive Producer, Game Entertainment:** Deb Belinsky. **Manager, Game Entertainment/Productions:** Tim Sullivan. **Manager Brand Development:** Greg Arbour. **Coordinator, Promotions:** Rob Jack. **Executive Assistant:** Maria Cresswell.
Managing Director, Merchandising: Anthony Partipilo. **Director, Stadium Merchandising:** Michael Andrejek. **Manager, Purchasing/Mail Order Operations:** Helen Maunder. **Manager, Stadium Events:** Linda Mykytyshyn.
VP, Corporate Partnerships/Business Development: Mark Lemmon. **Director, Corporate Partnerships:** Robert Mackay. **Managers, Corporate Partnerships:** Bryan Reinblatt, Honsing Leung. **Director, Corporate Marketing:** Wilna Behr.

Media Relations, Communications
Telephone: (416) 341-1301/1303. **FAX:** (416) 341-1250.
Senior Vice President, Communications/External Relations: Rob Godfrey. **Executive Assistant to Senior VP of Communications/External Relations:** Jacey Chae.
Director, Communications: Jay Stenhouse. **Director, Public Relations:** Will Hill. **Manager, Baseball Information:** Ryan Mittleman. **Coordinator, Communications:** Sue Mallabon. **Communications Assistant:** Erik Grosman.

Stadium Operations
Director, Stadium Operations: Mario Coutinho. **Manager, Guest Relations:** Paul So. **Office Manager:** Anne Fulford. **Supervisor, Maintenance/Housekeeping Services:** Mick Bazinet. **Administrative Assistant, Operations:** June Sym. **PA Announcer:** Murray Eldon. **Official Scorers:** Louis Cauz, Doug Hobbs, Joe Sawchuk. **Head Groundskeeper:** Tom Farrell.

Ticketing
Telephone: (416) 341-1234. **FAX:** (416) 341-1177. .
Vice President, Ticket Sales/Service: Patrick Elster.
Senior Advisor/Director, Special Projects: Sheila Stella. **Director, Ticket Sales/Service:** Jason Diplock. **Manager, Ticket System/Box Office:** Doug Barr.
Manager, Direct Marketing: Tanya Rynyk. **Coordinator, Direct Marketing:** Sherry Thurston. **Manager, Sales Channel Development:** Franc Rota. **Manager, Sales Channel Integration:** Craig Johnson.
Manager, Retail Development: Scott Clark. **Manager, Premier Client Services:** Chris Gill. **Manager, Consumer Sales:** Paul Fruitman. **Supervisors, Consumer Sales:** Michael Hook, John Santana.
Manager, Group Development: Shelby Nelson. **Coordinator, Group Development:** Cindy Hewitt.

Travel, Clubhouse
Manager, Team Travel: Mike Shaw.
Equipment Manager: Jeff Ross. **Clubhouse Manager:** Kevin Malloy. **Visiting Clubhouse Manager:** Len Frejlich. **Video Operations:** Robert Baumander.

GENERAL INFORMATION
Stadium (year opened): Rogers Centre (1989).
Home Dugout: Third Base. **Playing Surface:** Artificial turf.
Team Colors: Blue, metallic silver, metallic graphite, black and white.
Player Representative: Vernon Wells.

BASEBALL OPERATIONS
Senior Vice President, Baseball Operations/General Manager: J.P. Ricciardi. **VP, Baseball Operations/Assistant GM:** Tim McCleary. **Special Assistants to GM:** Keith Law, Chris Buckley. **Executive Assistant to GM:** Fran Brown. **Executive Assistant, Major League Operations:** Heather Connolly. **Assistant, Baseball Operations:** Bart Given.
Director, Player Personnel: Tony LaCava.
Director, Florida Operations: Ken Carson.
Ambassador, Amateur Baseball/Canada: Jim Fanning. **Baseball Camp Coordinator:** John Milton.

Major League Staff
Manager: John Gibbons.
Coaches: Bench—Ernie Whitt; Pitching—Brad Arnsberg; Batting—Mike Barnett; First Base—Mickey Brantley; Third Base—Brian Butterfield; Bullpen—Bruce Walton.

J.P. Ricciardi

Medical, Training
Medical Advisor: Dr. Bernie Gosevitz. **Team Physician:** Dr. Ron Taylor.
Head Trainer: George Poulis. **Assistant Trainer:** Dave Abraham. **Strength/Conditioning Coordinator:** Donovan Santas.
Director, Team Safety: Ron Sandelli.

Player Development
Telephone: (727) 734-1807. **FAX:** (727) 734-8162.
Director, Player Development: Dick Scott. **Manager, Minor League Operations:** Charlie Wilson. **Assistant, Player Development:** Joanna Nelson. **Administrative Assistant:** Kim Marsh.
Roving Instructors: Dane Johnson (pitching), Merv Rettenmund (hitting).
Minor League Coordinators: Jay Inouye (training), Chris Joyner (strength/conditioning), Billy Wardlow (equipment).

John Gibbons

Farm System

Class	Farm Team	League	Manager	Coach	Pitching Coach
AAA	Syracuse	International	Marty Pevey	Dwayne Murphy	Chuck Kniffin
AA	New Hampshire	Eastern	Mike Basso	John Valentin	Dave LaRoche
High A	Dunedin	Florida State	Omar Malave	Paul Elliott	Rick Langford
Low A	Lansing	Midwest	Ken Joyce	Charles Poe	Tom Bradley
Short season	Auburn	New York-Penn	Dennis Holmberg	Dave Pano	Tom Signore
Rookie	Pulaski	Appalachian	Gary Cathcart	Justin Mashore	Antonio Caceres
Rookie	Blue Jays	Dominican	Unavailable	None	Oswald Peraza
Rookie	Blue Jays	Venezuelan	Domingo Carrasquel	Hedbertt Hurtado	Unavailable

Scouting
Telephone: (416) 341-1115. **FAX:** (416) 341-1245.
Director, Scouting: Jon Lalonde.
Professional Scouts: Sal Butera (Lake Mary, FL), Kimball Crossley (Providence, RI), Ted Lekas (Worcester, MA), Kevin O'Brien (Brockton, MA).
National Crosscheckers: Tom Clark (Shrewsbury, MA), Tim Huff (Cave Creek, AZ), Mike Mangan (Clermont, FL).
Scouting Coordinators: Andrew Tinnish (Tallahassee, FL), Alex Anthopoulos (Montreal, Quebec).
Area Scouts: Tony Arias (Miami Lakes, FL), Andy Beene (Center Point, TX), Matt Briggs (Ridgeland, MS), Tom Burns (Harrisburg, PA), Billy Gasparino (Los Angeles, CA), Joel Grampietro (Tampa, FL), Aaron Jersild (Chicago, IL), Alvin Morrow (Phoenix, AZ), Brandon Mozley (Sacramento, CA), Ty Nichols (Broken Arrow, OK), Demerius Pittman (Corona, CA), Jorge Rivera (Puerto Nuevo, PR), Tom Tanous (Barrington, RI), Marc Tramuta (Charlotte, NC).

Jon Lalonde

Director, Canadian Scouting: Kevin Briand (Etobicoke, Ontario). **Canadian Scouts:** Greg Brons (Saskatoon, Saskatchewan), Jean Marc Mercier (Montreal, Quebec). **Associate Scout, Canada:** Sean McCann (Toronto, Ontario).
Director, Latin America Operations: Tony Arias (Miami Lakes, FL).
International Scouts: Robinson Garces (Venezuela), Takashi Ishikawa (Japan), Boris Miranda (Panama), Rafael Moncada (Venezuela), Juan Salavarria (Venezuela), Hilario Soriano (Dominican Republic), Greg Wade (Australia).

WASHINGTON NATIONALS

Office Address: 2400 East Capitol St., SE Washington, DC 20003.
Telephone: (202) 675-5100. **FAX:** (202) 547-0025.
Website: www.nationals.com.

Ownership
Operated by: Baseball Expos, LP.
President: Tony Tavares. **Executive Assistant:** Tanya Archie.

BUSINESS OPERATIONS
Executive Vice President, Business Affairs: Claude Delorme. **VP/General Manager, Space Coast Stadium:** Andy Dunn.

Tony Tavares

Sales, Marketing
Vice President, Sales/Marketing: David Cope. **Director, Ticket Sales:** Joe Deoudes. **Director, Marketing/Promotions:** Carleen Martin. **Director, Corporate Sales:** Joe Hickey.

Media Relations, Communications
Vice President, Communications: Chartese Berry.
Director, Baseball Information: John Dever. **Coordinator, Media Relations:** Lars Thorn.
Director, Community Relations: Barbra Silva. **Coordinator, Community Relations:** Jennifer Skolochenko. **Assistant, Communications:** Lisa Pagano.

Stadium Operations
Director, Game Operations: Unavailable. **Manager, Entertainment/Events:** Josh Golden. **Director, Management Information Systems:** Jim Bernhardt.
PA Announcer: Unavailable. **Official Scorers:** Unavailable.

Ticketing
Director, Ticket Operations: Derek Younger. **Assistant Director, Ticketing:** Tracey Kirkbride.

TRAVEL, CLUBHOUSE
Director, Team Travel: Rob McDonald.
Equipment Manager: Mike Wallace. **Visiting Clubhouse:** Matt Rosenthal.

GENERAL INFORMATION
Stadium (year opened): Robert F. Kennedy Stadium (1966).
Home Dugout: Third Base. **Playing Surface:** Grass.
Team Colors: Red, white and blue.
Player Representative: Brian Schneider.

BASEBALL OPERATIONS

General Manager: Jim Bowden. **Assistant GM:** Tony Siegle. **Special Assistants to GM:** Bob Boone, Barry Larkin, Jose Rijo. **Special Advisor to GM**: Jose Cardenal. **Director, Major League Administration:** Lee MacPhail.

Major League Staff

Manager: Frank Robinson.

Coaches: Bench—Eddie Rodriguez; Pitching—Randy St. Claire; Hitting—Tom McCraw; First Base—Don Buford; Third Base—Dave Huppert; Bullpen/Catchers—Bob Natal; Roving—Jack Voigt.

Jim Bowden

Medical, Training

Medical Director: Dr. Tom Graham. **Orthopedic Physicians:** Dr. Wiemi Douoghui, Dr. Dave Johnson. **Consultant:** Dr. Tim Kremchek. **Consultants:** Dr. James Andrews, Dr. Lewis Yocum.

Head Trainer: Tim Abraham. **Assistant Trainer:** Scott Lawrenson. **Strength/Conditioning Coach:** Kazuhiko Tomooka.

Player Development

Director, Player Development: Adam Wogan. **Assistant Director, Player Development:** Nick Manno.

Field Coordinator: Doug Sisson. **Roving Coordinators:** Jose Alguacil (infield), Michael Arndt (strength/conditioning), Mike McGowan (athletic training/rehab), Mitchell Page (hitting), Brent Strom (pitching).

Manager, Florida Operations: Tyler Holmes. **Minor League Equipment Coordinator:** Ryan Strefelder.

Frank Robinson

Farm System

Class	Farm Team	League	Manager	Coach	Pitching Coach
AAA	New Orleans	Pacific Coast	Tim Foli	Mike Hart	Charlie Corbell
AA	Harrisburg	Eastern	Keith Bodie	Frank Cacciatore	Rick Tomlin
High A	Potomac	Carolina	Bob Henley	Troy Gingrich	Ricky Bones
Low A	Savannah	South Atlantic	Randy Knorr	Joel Chimelis	Mark Grater
Short season	Vermont	New York-Penn	Bobby Williams	Rick Eckstein	Craig Bjornson
Rookie	Melbourne	Gulf Coast	Wendell Kim	Jason Camilli	Franklin Bravo
Rookie	Nationals	Dominican	Sergio Mendez	Angel Abreu	

Manuel Santana

Scouting

Director, Scouting: Dana Brown. **Assistant Director, Scouting:** Brian Parker.

Advance Scout: Mike Paul (Tucson, AZ).

Professional Scouts: Mike Toomey (Gaithersburg, MD), Fred Wright (Harrisburg, NC).

Regional Crosscheckers: East—Paul Tinnell (Bradenton, FL); Midwest—Ray Jackson (Ocala, FL); West—Charles Scott (Novato, CA).

Area Scouts: Anthony Arango (Davie, FL), Ray Corbett (College Station, TX), Eric Robinson (Hiram, GA), Larry Izzo (Deer Park, NY), Bon Jones (Fort Wayne, IN), Doug McMillan (Shingle Springs, CA), Lance Nichols (Dodge City, KS), Delvy Santiago (Vega Alta, PR), Alex Smith (Abingdon, MD), Bob Hamelin (Concord, NC), Brian Hunter (Lake Elsinore, CA), Mitch Sokol (Phoenix, AZ), Denis Boucher (Montreal, Quebec).

Dana Brown

Director, Latin American Operations: Ismael Cruz. **Coordinator, Latin American Operations:** Pablo Cruz. **Scouts, Dominican Republic:** Sandi Rosaro, Jose Baez.

MAJOR LEAGUE
SCHEDULES

2004 STANDINGS
SPRING TRAINING

AMERICAN LEAGUE

2004 STANDINGS

EAST	W	L	Pct.	GB	Manager(s)	General Manager(s)
New York Yankees	101	61	.623	—	Joe Torre	Brian Cashman
*Boston Red Sox	98	64	.605	3	Terry Francona	Theo Epstein
Baltimore Orioles	78	84	.481	23	Lee Mazzilli	Jim Beattie/Mike Flanagan
Tampa Bay Devil Rays	70	91	.435	301/2	Lou Piniella	Chuck LaMar
Toronto Blue Jays	67	94	.416	331/2	Carlos Tosca/John Gibbons	J.P. Ricciardi

CENTRAL	W	L	Pct.	GB	Manager	General Manager
Minnesota Twins	92	70	.568	—	Ron Gardenhire	Terry Ryan
Chicago White Sox	83	79	.512	9	Ozzie Guillen	Ken Williams
Cleveland Indians	80	82	.494	12	Eric Wedge	Mark Shapiro
Detroit Tigers	72	90	.444	20	Alan Trammell	Dave Dombrowski
Kansas City Royals	58	104	.358	34	Tony Pena	Allard Baird

WEST	W	L	Pct.	GB	Manager	General Manager
Anaheim Angels	92	70	.568	—	Mike Scioscia	Bill Stoneman
Oakland Athletics	91	71	.562	1	Ken Macha	Billy Beane
Texas Rangers	89	73	.549	3	Buck Showalter	John Hart
Seattle Mariners	63	99	.389	29	Bob Melvin	Bill Bavasi

*Won wild-card playoff berth

PLAYOFFS: Division Series (best-of-5)—New York defeated Minnesota 3-1; Boston defeated Anaheim 3-0. **League Championship Series** (best-of-7)—Boston defeated New York 4-3.

NATIONAL LEAGUE

2004 STANDINGS

EAST	W	L	Pct.	GB	Manager	General Manager
Atlanta Braves	96	66	.593	—	Bobby Cox	John Schuerholz
Philadelphia Phillies	86	76	.531	10	Larry Bowa	Ed Wade
Florida Marlins	83	79	.512	13	Jack McKeon	Larry Beinfest
New York Mets	71	91	.438	25	Art Howe	Jim Duquette
Montreal Expos	67	95	.414	29	Frank Robinson	Omar Minaya

CENTRAL	W	L	Pct.	GB	Manager(s)	General Manager
St. Louis Cardinals	105	57	.648	—	Tony La Russa	Walt Jocketty
*Houston Astros	92	70	.568	13	Jimy Williams/Phil Garner	Gerry Hunsicker
Chicago Cubs	89	73	.549	16	Dusty Baker	Jim Hendry
Cincinnati Reds	76	86	.469	29	Dave Miley	Dan O'Brien
Pittsburgh Pirates	72	89	.447	321/2	Lloyd McClendon	Dave Littlefield
Milwaukee Brewers	67	94	.416	371/2	Ned Yost	Doug Melvin

WEST	W	L	Pct.	GB	Manager(s)	General Manager
Los Angeles Dodgers	93	69	.574	—	Jim Tracy	Paul DePodesta
San Francisco Giants	91	71	.562	2	Felipe Alou	Brian Sabean
San Diego Padres	87	75	.537	6	Bruce Bochy	Kevin Towers
Colorado Rockies	68	94	.420	25	Clint Hurdle	Dan O'Dowd
Arizona Diamondbacks	51	111	.315	42	Bob Brenly/Al Pedrique	Joe Garagiola Jr.

*Won wild-card playoff berth

PLAYOFFS: Division Series (best-of-5)—Houston defeated Atlanta 3-2; St. Louis defeated Los Angeles 3-1. **League Championship Series** (best-of-7)—St. Louis defeated Houston 4-3.

2004 WORLD SERIES

(Best-of-7)
Boston (American) defeated St. Louis (National) 4-0.

AMERICAN
LEAGUE

ANAHEIM ANGELS
Angel Stadium of Anaheim

■ Standard Game Times: 7:05 p.m.; Sun. 1:05.

APRIL
5-6-7 .... Texas
8-9-10 .... Kansas City
11-12-13 .... at Texas
15-16-17 .... at Oakland
18-19 .... Seattle
20-21 .... Cleveland
22-23-24 .... Oakland
26-27-28 .... at Yankees
29-30 .... at Minnesota

MAY
1 .... at Minnesota
2-3-4 .... at Seattle
6-7-8 .... Detroit
9-10-11 .... Cleveland
13-14-15 .... at Detroit
16-17-18 .... at Oakland
20-21-22 .. *at Los Angeles
23-24-25-26 ..... White Sox
27-28-29 .... Kansas City
30-31 .... at White Sox

JUNE
1 .... at White Sox
3-4-5 .... at Boston
6-7-8 .... *at Atlanta
10-11-12 .... *at Mets
13-14-15 ...... *Washington
17-18-19 .... *Florida
20-21-22 .... Texas
24-25-26 ...... *Los Angeles
27-28-29-30 .... at Texas

JULY
1-2-3 .... at Kansas City
4-5-6 .... Minnesota
7-8-9-10 .... Seattle
14-15-16-17 . at Minnesota
18-19-20 .... Oakland
21-22-23-24 .... Yankees
26-27-28 .... at Toronto
29-30-31 .... at Yankees

AUGUST
2-3-4 .... Baltimore
5-6-7 .... Tampa Bay
9-10-11 .... at Oakland
12-13-14 .... at Seattle
15-16-17 .... Toronto
18-19-20-21 .... Boston
23-24-25 .... at Baltimore
26-27-28 ...... at Tampa Bay
30-31 .... Oakland

SEPTEMBER
1 .... Oakland
2-3-4 .... Seattle
6-7-8 .... at Boston
9-10-11 .... at White Sox
12-13-14 .... at Seattle
15-16-17-18 .... Detroit
20-21-22 .... Texas
23-24-25 .... Tampa Bay
26-27-28-29 ..... at Oakland
30 .... at Texas

OCTOBER
1-2 .... at Texas

2-3-4 .... at Anaheim
5-6-7 .... at Texas
9-10-11 .... Tampa Bay
12-13-14 .... Toronto
15-16-17 .... at Oakland
19-20-21 ...... at Cleveland
23-24-25 .... Anaheim
26-27-28-29 .... Oakland
30-31 .... at Toronto

SEPTEMBER
1 .... at Toronto

2-3-4 .... at Boston
5-6-7 .... Toronto
9-10-11 .... at Seattle
12-13-14 .... at Texas
16-17-18 .... Tampa Bay
19-20-21-22 ..... at Yankees
23-24-25 .... Boston
27-28-29 .... Yankees
30 .... at Tampa Bay

OCTOBER
1-2 .... at Tampa Bay

BOSTON RED SOX
Fenway Park

■ Standard Game Times: 7:05 p.m.; Sat. 1:20, 7:05; Sun. 2:05.

APRIL
3 .... at Yankees
5-6 .... at Yankees
8-9-10 .... at Toronto
11 .... Yankees
13-14 .... Yankees
15-16-17 .... Tampa Bay
18-19 .... Toronto
20-21 .... at Baltimore
22-23-24 .... at Tampa Bay
25-26-27 .... Baltimore
29-30 .... at Texas

MAY
1 .... at Texas
2-3-4-5 .... at Detroit
6-7-8 .... Seattle
9-10-11 .... Oakland
13-14-15 .... at Seattle
16-17-18 .... at Oakland
20-21-22 .... *Atlanta
24-25-26 .... at Toronto
27-28-29 .... at Yankees
30-31 .... Baltimore

JUNE
1 .... Baltimore
3-4-5 .... Anaheim
6-7-8 .... *at St. Louis
10-11-12 .... *at Cubs
13-14-15 .... *Cincinnati
17-18-19 .... *Pittsburgh
20-21-22 .... at Cleveland
24-25-26 .. *at Philadelphia
27-28-29 .... Cleveland

JULY
1-2-3 .... Toronto
4-5-6 .... at Texas
7-8-9-10 .... at Baltimore
14-15-16-17 .... Yankees
18-19-20 .... Tampa Bay
21-22-23-24 . at White Sox
25-26-27 .... at Tampa Bay
29-30-31 .... Minnesota

AUGUST
2-3-4 .... Kansas City
5-6-7 .... at Minnesota
8-9-10 .... Texas
12-13-14 .... White Sox
15-16-17 .... at Detroit
18-19-20-21 .... at Anaheim
23-24-25 ..... at Kansas City
26-27-28 .... Detroit
29-30-31 .... Tampa Bay

SEPTEMBER
1 .... Tampa Bay
2-3-4 .... Baltimore
6-7-8 .... Anaheim
9-10-11 .... at Yankees
12-13-14 .... at Toronto
15-16-17-18 .... Oakland
19-20-21 ...... at Tampa Bay
23-24-25 .... at Baltimore
26-27-28-29 .... Toronto
30 .... Yankees

OCTOBER
1-2 .... Yankees

BALTIMORE ORIOLES
Oriole Park at Camden Yards

■ Standard Game Times: 7:05 p.m.; Sat. 4:35; Sun. 1:35.

APRIL
4 .... Oakland
6-7 .... Oakland
8-9-10 .... at Yankees
12-13-14 ...... at Tampa Bay
15-16-17 .... Yankees
18-19 .... Detroit
20-21 .... Boston
22-23-24 .... at Toronto
25-26-27 .... at Boston
29-30 .... Tampa Bay

MAY
1 .... Tampa Bay
2-3-4 .... Toronto
6-7-8 .... Kansas City
9-10-11 .... Minnesota
12-13-14-15 . at White Sox
17-18-19 .... at Kansas City
20-21-22 ...... *Philadelphia
24-25-26 .... Seattle
27-28-29 .... Detroit
30-31 .... at Boston

JUNE
1 .... at Boston
3-4-5 .... at Detroit
6-7-8 .... *at Pittsburgh
10-11-12 ...... *at Cincinnati
13-14-15 .... *Houston
17-18-19 .... *Colorado
20-21-22-23 .... at Toronto
24-25-26 .... *at Atlanta
27-28-29 .... Yankees
30 .... Cleveland

JULY
1-2-3 .... Cleveland
4-5 .... at Yankees
7-8-9-10 .... Boston
9-10-11 .... Kansas City
14-15-16-17 ...... at Seattle
18-19-20 .... at Minnesota
22-23-24 ...... at Tampa Bay
25-26-27-28 .... Texas
29-30-31 .... White Sox

AUGUST
1 .... White Sox

CHICAGO WHITE SOX
U.S. Cellular Field

■ Standard Game Times: 7:05 p.m.; Sat. 6:05; Sun. 2:05.

APRIL
4 .... Cleveland
6-7 .... Cleveland
8-9-10 .... at Minnesota
11 .... at Cleveland
13-14 .... at Cleveland
15-16-17 .... Seattle
18-19 .... Minnesota
20-21 .... at Detroit
22-23-24 ..... at Kansas City
25-26-27 .... at Oakland

29-30 .... Detroit

MAY
1 .... Detroit
3-4-5 .... Kansas City
6-7-8 .... at Toronto
9-10-11 .... at Tampa Bay
12-13-14-15 .... Baltimore
16-17-18 .... Texas
20-21-22 .... *at Cubs
23-24-25-26 .... at Anaheim
27-28-29 .... at Texas

30-31 ... Anaheim

JUNE

1 ... Anaheim
3-**4-5** ... Cleveland
6-7-8 ... *at Colorado
10-11-**12** ... *at San Diego
13-14-15 ... *Arizona
17-18-19 ... *Los Angeles
20-21-**22** ... Kansas City
24-25-**26** ... *Cubs
28-29-**30** ... at Detroit

JULY

1-2-**3** ... at Oakland
4-5-6 ... Tampa Bay
8-9-10 ... Oakland
14-15-**16-17** ... at Cleveland
18-19-**20** ... Detroit
21-22-23-**24** ... Boston
25-26-**27** ... at Kansas City
29-**30-31** ... at Baltimore

AUGUST

1 ... at Baltimore
2-3-**4** ... Toronto
5-6-**7** ... Seattle
8-9-**10** ... at Yankees
12-13-**14** ... at Boston
15-16-17 ... Minnesota
19-**20-21** ... Yankees
23-24-**25** ... at Minnesota
26-27-**28** ... at Seattle
29-30-**31** ... at Texas

SEPTEMBER

1-2-3-**4** ... Detroit
6-7-8 ... Kansas City
9-10-**11** ... Anaheim
13-14-**15** ... at Kansas City
16-**17-18** ... at Minnesota
19-20-21 ... Cleveland
22-23-24-**25** ... Minnesota
26-27-28-**29** ... at Detroit
30 ... at Cleveland

OCTOBER

1-**2** ... at Cleveland

CLEVELAND INDIANS
Jacobs Field

■ **Standard Game Times:** 7:05 p.m.; Sat-Sun. 1:05.

APRIL

4 ... at White Sox
6-7 ... at White Sox
8-**9-10** ... at Detroit
11 ... White Sox
13-14 ... White Sox
15-**16-17** ... Minnesota
18-**19** ... at Kansas City
20-21 ... at Anaheim
22-23-**24** ... at Seattle
26-27-28 ... Detroit
29-**30** ... Kansas City

MAY

1 ... Kansas City
3-4-**5** ... at Minnesota
6-7-**8** ... at Texas
9-10-**11** ... at Anaheim
13-**14-15** ... Toronto
16-17-**18** ... Anaheim
20-21-**22** ... *at Cincinnati
23-24-25-26 ... Minnesota
27-28-**29** ... Oakland
31 ... at Minnesota

JUNE

1-**2** ... at Minnesota
3-**4-5** ... at White Sox
7-8-**9** ... *at San Diego
10-11-**12** ... *at San Francisco
14-15-16 ... *Colorado
17-18-**19** ... *Arizona
20-21-22 ... Boston
24-25-**26** ... *Cincinnati
27-28-**29** ... at Boston
30 ... at Baltimore

JULY

1-**2**-3 ... at Baltimore
4-5-6 ... Detroit
7-8-**9-10** ... at Yankees
14-15-**16-17** ... White Sox
18-19-20-**21** ... Kansas City
22-**23-24** ... Seattle
25-26-**27** ... at Oakland
28-29-**30-31** ... at Seattle

AUGUST

2-3-4 ... Yankees
5-6-**7** ... at Detroit
9-10-11 ... at Kansas City
12-13-**14** ... Tampa Bay
16-17-**18** ... Texas
19-20-**21** ... Baltimore
22-23-24-25 ... at Tampa Bay
26-**27-28** ... at Toronto
29-30-31 ... Detroit

SEPTEMBER

2-3-**4** ... at Minnesota
5-6-7 ... at Detroit
9-10-**11** ... Minnesota
12-13-14 ... Oakland
16-17-**18** ... Kansas City
19-20-21 ... at White Sox
22-23-24-**25** ... at Kansas City
27-28-29 ... Tampa Bay
30 ... White Sox

OCTOBER

1-**2** ... White Sox

DETROIT TIGERS
Comerica Park

■ **Standard Game Times:** 7:05 p.m.; Thur./Sat.–Sun. 1:05.

APRIL

4 ... Kansas City
6-7 ... Kansas City
8-**9-10** ... Cleveland
12-13-14 ... at Minnesota
15-**16-17** ... at Kansas City
18-19 ... at Baltimore
20-**21** ... White Sox
22-**23-24** ... Minnesota
26-27-28 ... at Cleveland
29-30 ... at White Sox

MAY

1 ... at White Sox
2-3-4-**5** ... Boston
6-7-**8** ... at Anaheim
9-10-**11** ... at Texas
13-**14-15** ... Anaheim
17-18-**19** ... Tampa Bay
20-21-**22** ... *Arizona
24-25-26 ... at Yankees
27-**28-29** ... at Baltimore
31 ... Texas

JUNE

1-**2** ... Texas
3-4-**5** ... Baltimore
6-7-8 ... *at Los Angeles
10-11-**12** ... *at Colorado
14-15-**16** ... *San Diego
17-18-**19** ... *San Francisco
21-22-**23** ... at Minnesota
24-25-**26** ... *at Arizona
28-29-**30** ... White Sox

JULY

1-2-**3** ... Yankees
4-5-6 ... at Cleveland
7-8-9-**10** ... at Tampa Bay
14-15-16-**17** ... Kansas City
18-19-**20** ... at White Sox
21-22-23-**24** ... Minnesota
25-26-27 ... at Seattle
29-**30-31** ... at Oakland

AUGUST

2-3-**4** ... Seattle
5-6-**7** ... Cleveland
8-9-10-11 ... at Toronto
12-13-**14** ... at Kansas City
15-16-17 ... Boston
19-20-**21** ... Toronto
23-24-**25** ... Oakland
26-27-**28** ... at Boston
29-30-31 ... at Cleveland

SEPTEMBER

1-2-3-**4** ... at White Sox
5-6-7 ... Cleveland
9-10-**11** ... Kansas City
12-13-14 ... Minnesota
15-16-17-**18** ... at Anaheim
19-20-**21** ... at Kansas City
23-24-**25** ... Seattle
26-27-28-**29** ... White Sox
30 ... at Minnesota

OCTOBER

1-**2** ... at Minnesota

KANSAS CITY ROYALS
Kauffman Stadium

■ **Standard Game Times:** 7:10 p.m.; Sat. 6:10; Sun. 1:10.

APRIL

4 ... at Detroit
6-7 ... at Detroit
8-9-**10** ... at Anaheim
11 ... Seattle
13-14 ... Seattle
15-**16-17** ... Detroit
18-**19** ... Cleveland
20-**21** ... at Minnesota
22-23-**24** ... White Sox
26-27-**28** ... Minnesota
29-**30** ... at Cleveland

MAY

1 ... at Cleveland
3-4-**5** ... at White Sox
6-7-**8** ... at Baltimore
9-10-**11** ... at Toronto
12-13-14-**15** ... Tampa Bay
17-18-**19** ... Baltimore
20-21-**22** ... *St. Louis
24-25-26 ... at Texas
27-28-**29** ... at Anaheim
31 ... Yankees

JUNE

1-2 ... Yankees
3-**4-5** ... Texas
7-8-**9** ... *at San Francisco
10-11-**12** ... *at Arizona
14-15-16 ... *Los Angeles
17-18-**19** ... *Houston
20-21-**22** ... at White Sox
24-25-**26** ... *at Colorado
27-28-**29** ... at Minnesota

JULY

1-2-3 ... Anaheim
4-5-6 ... Seattle
7-8-9-**10** ... Minnesota
14-15-16-**17** ... at Detroit
18-19-20-**21** ... at Cleveland
22-23-**24** ... Toronto
25-26-**27** ... White Sox
28-29-30-**31** at Tampa Bay

AUGUST

2-3-**4** ... at Boston
5-6-**7** ... Oakland
9-10-11 ... Cleveland
12-13-**14** ... Detroit
15-16-**17** ... at Seattle
19-20-**21** ... at Oakland
23-24-25 ... Boston
26-**27-28** ... at Yankees
29-**30-31** ... Minnesota

SEPTEMBER

1-2-3-**4** ... Texas
6-7-8 ... at White Sox
9-10-**11** ... at Detroit
13-14-**15** ... White Sox
16-17-**18** ... at Cleveland
19-20-**21** ... Detroit
22-23-24-**25** ... Cleveland
26-27-28-29 . at Minnesota
30 ... at Toronto

OCTOBER

1-2 ... at Toronto

MINNESOTA TWINS
Hubert H. Humphrey Metrodome

■ **Standard Game Times:** 7:10 p.m.; Sat 6:10, Sun. 1:10.

APRIL

4-5-**6** ... at Seattle
8-9-10 ... White Sox
12-13-14 ... Detroit

15-**16**-**17** .... at Cleveland
18-19 .... at White Sox
20-**21** .... Kansas City
22-**23**-**24** .... at Detroit
26-27-**28** .... at Kansas City
29-**30** .... Anaheim

MAY
1 .... Anaheim
3-4-**5** .... Cleveland
6-**7**-**8** .... at Tampa Bay
9-10-**11** ...... at Baltimore
13-14-**15** .... Texas
17-18-**19** .... Toronto
20-21-**22** ..... *Milwaukee
23-24-25-26 ... at Cleveland
27-**28**-**29** .... at Toronto
31 .... Cleveland

JUNE
1-**2** .... Cleveland
3-4-**5** .... Yankees
7-8-9 .... *at Arizona
10-11-**12** .. *at Los Angeles
14-15-16 ... *San Francisco
17-18-**19** .... *San Diego
21-22-**23** .... Detroit
24-25-**26** ... *at Milwaukee
27-28-**29** .... Kansas City

JULY
1-2-**3** .... Tampa Bay

4-5-**6** .... at Anaheim
7-8-**9**-**10** ..... at Kansas City
14-15-**16**-**17** .... Anaheim
18-19-**20** .... Baltimore
21-22-23-**24** .... at Detroit
26-**27**-**28** .... at Yankees
29-30-**31** .... at Boston

AUGUST
1-2-3-**4** .... Oakland
5-**6**-**7** .... Boston
8-9-10 .... at Seattle
12-**13**-**14** .... at Oakland
15-16-17 ...... at White Sox
18-19-20-**21** .... Seattle
23-24-**25** .... White Sox
26-**27**-**28** .... at Texas
29-30-**31** .... at Kansas City

SEPTEMBER
2-3-**4** .... Cleveland
5-6-**7** .... Texas
9-10-**11** .... at Cleveland
12-13-14 .... at Detroit
16-**17**-**18** .... White Sox
19-20-**21** .... at Oakland
22-23-24-**25** . at White Sox
26-27-28-29 ... Kansas City
30 .... Detroit

OCTOBER
1-**2** .... Detroit

NEW YORK YANKEES
Yankee Stadium

■ **Standard Game Times:** 7:05 p.m.; Sat.–Sun. 1:05.

APRIL
3 .... Boston
5-**6** .... Boston
8-**9**-**10** .... Baltimore
11 .... at Boston
13-14 .... at Boston
18-19 .... Tampa Bay
20-21 .... at Toronto
22-**23**-**24** .... Texas
26-27-28 .... Anaheim
29-**30** .... Toronto

MAY
1 .... Toronto
2-3-4-5 ...... at Tampa Bay
6-**7**-**8** .... Oakland
9-10-**11** .... Seattle
13-14-15 .... at Oakland
16-17-18 .... at Seattle
20-**21**-**22** .... at Mets
24-25-26 .... Detroit
27-**28**-29 .... Boston
31 .... at Kansas City

JUNE
1-2 .... at Kansas City
3-4-**5** .... at Minnesota
6-7-8 .... *at Milwaukee
10-**11**-**12** ... *at St. Louis
14-15-16 ...... *Pittsburgh
17-**18**-**19** .... *Cubs
20-21-**22**-23 .... Tampa Bay
24-**25**-26 .... *Mets
27-28-29 .... at Baltimore

JULY
1-2-**3** .... at Detroit
4-**5** .... Baltimore
7-8-**9**-**10** .... Cleveland
14-15-**16**-17 ...... at Boston
18-19-20 .... at Texas
21-22-23-**24** .... at Anaheim
26-27-**28** .... Minnesota
29-**30**-**31** .... Anaheim

AUGUST
2-3-4 .... at Cleveland
5-**6**-**7** .... at Toronto
8-9-10 .... White Sox
11-12-**13**-**14** .... Texas
15-16-17 ...... at Tampa Bay
19-**20**-**21** ...... at White Sox
22-23-24-**25** .... Toronto
26-**27**-**28** .... Kansas City
29-30-31 .... at Seattle

SEPTEMBER
1 .... Seattle
2-**3**-**4** .... at Oakland
6-7-8 .... Tampa Bay
9-**10**-**11** .... Boston
13-14-15 .... at Tampa Bay
16-**17**-**18** .... at Toronto
19-20-21-22 ...... Baltimore
23-**24**-**25** .... Toronto
27-28-29 .... at Baltimore
30 .... at Boston

OCTOBER
1-**2** .... at Boston

OAKLAND ATHLETICS
Network Associates Coliseum

■ **Standard Game Times:** 7:05 p.m.; Sat.–Sun. 1:05.

APRIL
4 .... at Baltimore
6-7 .... at Baltimore
8-9-**10** .... at Tampa Bay
11-12-13 .... Toronto
15-**16**-**17** .... Anaheim
18-**19** .... at Texas
20-21 .... at Seattle
22-23-24 .... Anaheim
25-26-**27** .... White Sox
29-**30** .... Seattle

MAY
1 .... Seattle
2-3-**4** .... Texas
6-**7**-**8** .... at Yankees
9-10-**11** .... at Boston
13-14-**15** ....Yankees
16-17-**18** .... Boston
20-21-22 . *at San Francisco
24-25-**26** ...... at Tampa Bay
27-28-**29** .... at Cleveland
30-31 .... Tampa Bay

JUNE
1 .... Tampa Bay
2-3-4-**5** .... Toronto
7-8-9 .... *at Washington
10-**11**-**12** ... *at Atlanta
14-15-**16** .... *Mets
17-**18**-**19** ..... *Philadelphia
20-21-22-**23** .... at Seattle
24-**25**-**26** .. *San Francisco
28-29-**30** .... Seattle

JULY
1-2-**3** .... White Sox
5-**6**-**7** .... at Toronto
8-9-10 .... at White Sox
14-15-**16**-**17** .... Texas
18-19-20 .... at Anaheim
21-22-23-**24** .... at Texas
25-26-27 .... Cleveland
29-**30**-**31** .... Detroit

AUGUST
1-2-3-**4** .... at Minnesota
5-6-**7** .... at Kansas City
9-10-**11** .... Anaheim
12-**13**-**14** .... Minnesota
15-16-**17** .... Baltimore
19-20-21 .... Kansas City
23-24-**25** .... at Detroit
26-**27**-**28**-**29** .. at Baltimore
30-31 .... at Anaheim

SEPTEMBER
1 .... at Anaheim
2-**3**-**4** .... Yankees
5-6-**7** .... Seattle
9-10-**11** .... at Texas
12-13-14 .... at Cleveland
15-16-17-**18** .... at Boston
19-20-21 .... Minnesota
23-**24**-**25** .... Texas
26-27-28-29 .... Anaheim
30 .... at Seattle

OCTOBER
1-**2** .... at Seattle

SEATTLE MARINERS
Safeco Field

■ **Standard Game Times:** 7:05 p.m.; Sat. 1:05, 7:05; Sun. 1:05.

APRIL
4-5-**6** .... Minnesota
8-**9**-**10** .... Texas
11 .... at Kansas City
13-**14** .... at Kansas City
15-**16**-**17** ...... at White Sox
18-**19** .... at Anaheim
20-21 .... Oakland
22-23-**24** .... Cleveland
26-27-28 .... at Texas
29-**30** .... at Oakland

MAY
1 .... at Oakland
2-3-**4** .... Anaheim
6-**7**-**8** .... at Boston
9-10-**11** .... at Yankees
13-14-**15** .... Boston
16-17-18 .... Yankees
20-21-**22** .... *San Diego
24-25-26 ...... at Baltimore
27-28-**29**....... at Tampa Bay
30-31 .... Toronto

JUNE
1 .... Toronto
3-4-**5** .... Tampa Bay
7-8-9 .... *at Florida
10-11-**12** .. *at Washington
14-15-16 ...... *Philadelphia
17-18-**19** .... *Mets

20-21-22-**23** .... Oakland
24-25-**26** ..... *at San Diego
28-29-**30** .... at Oakland

JULY
1-**2**-**3** .... Texas
4-5-6 .... at Kansas City
7-8-9-**10**........... at Anaheim
14-15-**16**-**17** ...... Baltimore
19-20-**21** .... at Toronto
22-**23**-**24** .... at Cleveland
25-26-27 .... Detroit
28-29-30-**31** .... Cleveland

AUGUST
2-**3**-**4** .... at Detroit
5-6-**7** .... at White Sox
8-9-10 .... Minnesota
12-**13**-**14** .... Anaheim
15-16-**17** .... Kansas City
18-19-20-**21** ... at Minnesota
23-24-**25** .... at Texas
26-**27**-**28** .... White Sox
29-30-31 .... Yankees

SEPTEMBER
1 .... Yankees
2-**3**-**4** .... at Anaheim
5-6-**7** .... at Oakland
9-10-**11**............... Baltimore
12-13-**14** .... Anaheim
15-16-17-**18** .... at Texas

19-20-21-22...... at Toronto	30 .... Oakland
23-24-**25** .... at Detroit	**OCTOBER**
27-28-**29** .... Texas	1-**2** .... Oakland

TAMPA BAY DEVIL RAYS
Tropicana Field

■ **Standard Game Times:** 7:15 p.m.; Sat. 6:15; Sun. 2:15.

APRIL		JULY	
4-5-**6** .... Toronto		1-2-**3** .... at Minnesota	
8-9-**10** .... Oakland		4-5-6 .... at White Sox	
12-13-14 .... Baltimore		7-8-9-**10** .... Detroit	
15-16-**17** .... at Boston		14-15-16-**17** ..... at Toronto	
18-19 .... at Yankees		18-19-**20** .... at Boston	
20-21 .... Texas		22-23-**24** .... Baltimore	
22-23-**24** .... Boston		25-26-**27** .... Boston	
26-27-**28** .... at Toronto		28-29-30-**31** ... Kansas City	
29-**30** .... at Baltimore		**AUGUST**	
MAY		2-3-4 .... at Texas	
1..................... at Baltimore		5-6-7 .... at Anaheim	
2-3-4-5 .... Yankees		9-10-11 .... at Baltimore	
6-7-8 .... Minnesota		12-13-**14**........ at Cleveland	
9-10-**11** .... White Sox		15-16-17 .... Yankees	
12-13-14-**15** ...... at Kansas		19-20-**21** .... Texas	
City		22-23-24-25 .... Cleveland	
17-18-**19** .... at Detroit		26-27-**28** .... Anaheim	
20-21-**22** .... *at Florida		29-30-31 .... at Boston	
24-25-**26** .... Oakland		**SEPTEMBER**	
27-28-**29** .... Seattle		1......................at Boston	
30-31 .... at Oakland		2-3-**4** .... at Toronto	
JUNE		6-7-8 .... at Yankees	
1 .... at Oakland		9-10-**11** .... Toronto	
3-4-**5** .... at Seattle		13-14-15 .... Yankees	
7-8-9 .... *at Cincinnati		16-**17-18** .... at Baltimore	
10-11-**12** .. *at Pittsburgh		19-20-21 .... Boston	
13-14-15 ...... *Milwaukee		23-24-**25** .... at Anaheim	
17-18-19 .... *St. Louis		27-28-29 .... at Cleveland	
20-21-**22**-23 ... at Yankees		30 .... Baltimore	
24-25-**26** .... *Florida		**OCTOBER**	
27-28-**29** .... Toronto		1-2 .... Baltimore	

TEXAS RANGERS
Ameriquest Field in Arlington

■ **Standard Game Times:** 7:05 p.m.; Sun. 1:05.

APRIL			
5-6-7 .... at Anaheim		20-**21-22** .... *Houston	
8-**9-10** .... at Seattle		24-25-26 .... Kansas City	
11-12-13 .... Anaheim		27-**28-29** .... White Sox	
14-15-16-**17** .... Toronto		31 .... at Detroit	
18-**19** .... Oakland		**JUNE**	
20-21 .... at Tampa Bay		1-2 .... at Detroit	
22-**23-24** .... at Yankees		3-**4-5** .... at Kansas City	
26-27-28 .... Seattle		7-8-9 ...... *at Philadelphia	
29-30 .... Boston		10-**11-12** .... *at Florida	
MAY		13-14-15 .... *Atlanta	
1............................ Boston		17-18-**19** ...... *Washington	
2-3-**4** .... at Oakland		20-21-22 .... at Anaheim	
6-7-**8** .... Cleveland		24-**25-26** .... *at Houston	
9-10-**11** .... Detroit		27-28-29-**30** .... Anaheim	
13-14-**15** ...... at Minnesota		**JULY**	
16-17-**18** .... at White Sox		1-**2-3** .... at Seattle	
		4-5-6 .... Boston	

8-9-**10** .... Toronto	26-**27-28** .... Minnesota
14-15-**16-17** ...... at Oakland	29-30-**31** .... White Sox
18-19-20 .... Yankees	**SEPTEMBER**
21-22-23-**24** .... Oakland	1-2-3-**4** .... at Kansas City
25-26-27-28 .. at Baltimore	5-6-**7** .... at Minnesota
29-**30-31** .... at Toronto	9-10-**11** .... Oakland
AUGUST	12-13-**14** .... Baltimore
2-3-4 .... Tampa Bay	15-16-17-**18** .... Seattle
5-6-**7** .... Baltimore	20-21-22 .... at Anaheim
8-9-**10** .... at Boston	23-**24-25** .... at Oakland
11-12-**13-14** .... at Yankees	27-28-**29** .... at Seattle
16-17-**18** .... at Cleveland	30 .... Anaheim
19-20-**21** ...... at Tampa Bay	**OCTOBER**
23-24-**25** .... Seattle	1-**2** .... Anaheim

TORONTO BLUE JAYS
Rogers Centre

■ **Standard Game Times:** 7:07 p.m.; Sat. 4:07; Sun. 1:07.

APRIL			
4-5-**6** .... at Tampa Bay		5-6-7 .... Oakland	
8-9-10 .... Boston		8-9-**10** .... at Texas	
11-12-13 .... at Oakland		14-15-**16-17** .... Tampa Bay	
14-15-**16-17** .... at Texas		19-20-**21** .... Seattle	
18-19 .... at Boston		22-23-**24** ..... at Kansas City	
20-21 .... Yankees		26-27-28 .... Anaheim	
22-**23-24** .... at Boston		29-**30-31** .... Texas	
26-27-**28** .... Tampa Bay		**AUGUST**	
29-**30** .... at Yankees		2-3-**4** .... at White Sox	
MAY		5-**6-7** .... Yankees	
1 .... at Yankees		8-9-10-**11** .... Detroit	
2-3-**4** .... at Baltimore		12-**13-14** .... at Baltimore	
6-**7-8** .... White Sox		13-**14-15** .... Baltimore	
9-10-11 .... Kansas City		15-16-17 .... at Anaheim	
13-**14-15** .... at Cleveland		19-20-21 .... at Detroit	
17-18-**19** .... at Minnesota		22-23-24-**25** ..... at Yankees	
20-**21-22** .... *Washington		26-**27-28** .... Cleveland	
24-25-26 .... Boston		30-31 .... Baltimore	
27-**28-29** .... Minnesota		**SEPTEMBER**	
30-31 .... at Seattle		1 .... Baltimore	
JUNE		2-3-**4** .... Tampa Bay	
1 .... at Seattle		5-6-**7** .... at Tampa Bay	
2-3-4-**5** .... at Oakland		9-10-**11** ...... at Tampa Bay	
6-**7-8** .... *at Cubs		12-13-14 .... Boston	
10-11-**12** .... *at Houston		16-**17-18** .... Yankees	
13-14-15 .... *St. Louis		19-20-21-22 .... Seattle	
17-**18-19** .... *Milwaukee		23-**24-25** .... at Yankees	
20-21-22-23 ...... Baltimore		26-27-28-29 ...... at Boston	
24-25-**26** .. *at Washington		30 .... Kansas City	
27-28-**29** ...... at Tampa Bay		**OCTOBER**	
JULY		1-2 .... Kansas City	
1-2-**3** .... at Boston			

NOTE: Dates in **bold** indicate afternoon games. All game times are subject to change. Gaps in dates indicate scheduled off-days but may be affected by rainouts.

* Interleague Series.

NATIONAL LEAGUE

ARIZONA DIAMONDBACKS
Bank One Ballpark

■ **Standard Game Times:** 6:40 p.m.; Sun. 1:40.

APRIL	
4-5-6	Cubs
8-9-**10**	Los Angeles
11-12-**13**	Colorado
14	at Washington
16-**17**	at Washington
18-**19**	at Colorado
20-21	at San Francisco
22-23-**24**	San Diego
25-26-27	at Los Angeles
29-30	at San Diego

MAY	
1	at San Diego
2-3-**4**	San Francisco
5-6-7-**8**	Pittsburgh
9-10-**11**	Washington
12-13-14-**15**	at Colorado
17-18-19	at Houston
20-21-**22**	*at Detroit
24-25-26	San Diego
27-28-**29**	Los Angeles
31	at Mets

JUNE	
1-2	at Mets
3-4-**5-6**	at Philadelphia
7-8-9	*Minnesota
10-11-**12**	*Kansas City
13-14-15	*at White Sox
17-18-19	*at Cleveland
20-21-22-**23**	at San Francisco
24-25-**26**	*Detroit
28-29-30	San Francisco

JULY	
1-**2**-3	at Los Angeles
4-5-6-**7**	St. Louis
8-9-**10**	Cincinnati
14-15-16-**17**	at San Diego
18-19-20	Florida
22-23-24	Atlanta
25-26-**27**	at Milwaukee
28-29-30-**31**	at Cubs

AUGUST	
2-3-4	Houston
5-6-**7**	Colorado
9-10-11	at Florida
12-**13-14**	at Atlanta
16-17-18	at St. Louis
19-20-**21**	at Cincinnati
22-23-24-25	Mets
26-**27**-28	Philadelphia
29-30-**31**	at San Diego

SEPTEMBER	
2-3-**4**	San Francisco
6-**7**-**8**	at Pittsburgh
9-10-**11**	at Colorado
13-14-15	Milwaukee
16-**17-18**	Colorado
20-21-22	Los Angeles
23-24-**25**	San Diego
27-28-29	Los Angeles
30	San Francisco

OCTOBER	
1-2	at San Francisco

ATLANTA BRAVES
Turner Field

■ **Standard Game Times:** 7:35 p.m.; Wed./Sat. 7:05; Sun. 1:05

APRIL	
5-6-7	at Florida
8-9-**10**	Mets
11-12-**13**	Washington
15-**16-17**	at Philadelphia
18-19	at Houston
20-21	at Washington
22-23-**24**	Philadelphia
25-26-**27**	at Mets
29-30	St. Louis

MAY	
1	St. Louis
3-**4**	Florida
5-6-7-**8**	Houston
9-10-**11**	at Colorado
13-14-**15**	at Los Angeles
16-17-**18**	at San Diego
20-21-**22**	*at Boston
23-24-25	Mets
27-**28-29**	Philadelphia
30-31	at Washington

JUNE	
1-2	at Washington

3-4-**5**	at Pittsburgh
6-7-8	*Anaheim
10-**11-12**	*Oakland
13-14-15	*at Texas
16-17-18-**19**	at Cincinnati
21-22-23	Florida
24-**25-26**	*Baltimore
27-28-29-30	at Florida

JULY	
1-2-3	at Philadelphia
4-5-6-7	Cubs
8-9-**10**	Milwaukee
14-15-16-**17**	at Mets
18-19-**20**	at San Francisco
22-23-24	at Arizona
26-27-**28**	Washington
29-30-**31**	Pittsburgh

AUGUST	
1	Pittsburgh
2-3-4	at Cincinnati
5-6-**7**	at St. Louis
9-10-11	San Francisco
12-**13-14**	Arizona
16-17-18	Los Angeles

CHICAGO CUBS
Wrigley Field

■ **Standard Game Times:** 1:20 p.m., 7:05 p.m.; Fri. 2:20; Sat.–Sun. 1:20.

APRIL	
4-5-6	at Arizona
8-9-**10**	Milwaukee
11-12-**13**	San Diego
15-16-**17**	at Pittsburgh
18-19	at Cincinnati
20-21	at St. Louis
22-23-24	Pittsburgh
25-26-**27**	Cincinnati
29-30	at Houston

MAY	
1	at Houston
3-4-**5**	at Milwaukee
6-7-8	Philadelphia
9-10-**11**	Mets
13-14-**15**	at Washington
17-**18**	at Pittsburgh
20-21-22	*White Sox
23-24-25	Houston
26-27-28-29	Colorado
30-31	at Los Angeles

JUNE	
1	at Los Angeles
2-3-4-**5**	at San Diego
6-7-**8**	*Toronto
10-11-12	*Boston
13-14-15	Florida
17-**18**-19	*at Yankees
20-21-22-**23**	at Milwaukee
24-25-26	*at White Sox
28-**29**-**30**	Milwaukee

JULY	
1-**2**-3	Washington
4-5-6-**7**	at Atlanta
8-9-**10**	at Florida
15-16-17	Pittsburgh
18-19-20-**21**	at Cincinnati
22-**23-24**	at St. Louis
25-26-**27**	San Francisco
28-29-30-31	Arizona

AUGUST	
2-3-**4**	at Philadelphia
5-**6-7**	at Mets
8-9-**10**	Cincinnati
11-12-13-14	St. Louis
15-16-17	at Houston
19-20-21	at Colorado
22-23-24	Atlanta
26-27-28	Florida
29-30-**31**	Los Angeles

SEPTEMBER	
2-3-**4**	at Pittsburgh
5-6-**7**	at St. Louis
8-9-**10-11**	at San Francisco
12-13-14	Cincinnati
15-**16-17-18**	St. Louis
20-21-**22**	at Milwaukee
23-24-25	Houston
27-**28**	Pittsburgh
29-30	at Houston

OCTOBER	
1-2	at Houston

CINCINNATI REDS
Great American Ball Park

■ **Standard Game Times:** 7:10 p.m.; Sat. 7:10, 1:15; Sun. 1:15.

APRIL	
4	Mets
6-7	Mets
8-9-**10**	at Houston
12-**13**	at St. Louis
15-**16-17**	Houston
18-19	Cubs
20-21	Pittsburgh
22-**23-24**	at Florida
25-26-**27**	at Cubs
29-30	at Milwaukee

MAY	
1	at Milwaukee
2-3-4	St. Louis

6-7-8	Los Angeles
9-10-11	San Diego
12-13-14-**15**	at Philadelphia
16-**17-18**	at Mets
20-21-22	*Cleveland
23-24-**25**	Washington
26-27-28-**29**	Pittsburgh
30-31	at Houston

JUNE	
1	at Houston
3-4-**5**	at Colorado
7-8-9	*Tampa Bay
10-11-**12**	*Baltimore
13-14-15	*at Boston

Also in second column of Arizona September part:

19-**20-21**	San Diego
22-23-**24**	at Cubs
26-27-**28**	at Milwaukee
29-30-31	Washington

SEPTEMBER	
1	Washington
2-3-**4**	Cincinnati
5-6-**7**	Mets
9-**10-11**	at Washington

16-17-18-**19** .... Atlanta
20-21-**22** .... St. Louis
24-25-**26** ..... at Cleveland
28-29 .... at St. Louis
30 .... Houston
JULY
1-2-**3** .... Houston
4-5-6-7 ... at San Francisco
8-9-**10** .... at Arizona
15-16-**17** .... Colorado
18-19-20-**21** .... Cubs
22-23-**24** .... Milwaukee
25-26-27-**28** .... at L.A.
29-**30-31** ..... at San Diego
AUGUST
2-3-4 .... Atlanta
5-6-**7** .... Florida
8-9-**10** .... at Cubs
12-13-**14** ...... at Milwaukee

COLORADO ROCKIES
Coors Field

■ **Standard Game Times:** 7:05 p.m.; Thurs. 1:05; Sat. 6:05; Sun. 1:05.

APRIL
4 .... San Diego
6 .... San Diego
8-**9-10** ..... at San Francisco
11-12-**13** .... at Arizona
15-16-**17** ..... San Francisco
18-**19** .... Arizona
20-**21** ...... at Philadelphia
22-23-**24** .... Los Angeles
26-27-**28** .... Florida
29-30 .... at Los Angeles
MAY
1 .... at Los Angeles
2-3-**4** .... at San Diego
6-7-**8** .... at Florida
9-10-**11** .... Atlanta
12-13-14-**15** .... Arizona
17-18-**19** ..... San Francisco
20-21-**22** ..... at Pittsburgh
23-24-**25** .... at Milwaukee
26-27-28-29 ..... at Cubs
30-31 .... St. Louis
JUNE
1-2 .... St. Louis
3-4-**5** .... Cincinnati
6 7 8 .... *White Sox
10-11-12 .... *Detroit
14-15-16 ... *at Cleveland
17-**18-19** ... *at Baltimore
20-21-**22** .... at Houston
24-25-**26** .... *Kansas City
27-28-**29** .... Houston

30 .... at St. Louis
JULY
1-2-**3** .... at St. Louis
4-5-6-**7** .... Los Angeles
8-9-**10** .... San Diego
15-16-**17** .... at Cincinnati
18-19-20 ..... at Washington
21-22-23-**24** . at Pittsburgh
25-26-27 .... Mets
28-29-30-**31** ... Philadelphia
AUGUST
2-3-**4** .... at San Francisco
5-6-**7** .... at Arizona
9-10-**11** .... Pittsburgh
12-13-**14** .... Washington
15-16-17 .... Milwaukee
19-20-21 .... Cubs
23-24-25 .... at Los Angeles
26-27-**28** ...... at San Diego
29-30-**31** . at San Francisco
SEPTEMBER
2-3-**4** .... Los Angeles
6-7-8 .... at San Diego
9-10-11 .... Arizona
12-13-14 ... at Los Angeles
16-**17-18** .... at Arizona
19-20-21-**22** ..... San Diego
23-24-**25** ..... San Francisco
26-27-28 .... at Atlanta
29-30 .... at Mets
OCTOBER
1-2 .... at Mets

FLORIDA MARLINS
Pro Player Stadium

■ **Standard Game Times:** 7:05 p.m.; Fri. 7:35; Sat. 6:05; Sun. 1:05.

APRIL
5-6-**7** .... Atlanta
8-9-**10** .... Washington
11-12-**13** .... Philadelphia
15-16-17 .... at Mets
18-19 .... at Washington
20-21 .... Mets
22-**23-24** .... Cincinnati
26-27-**28** ...... at Colorado

29-30 .... at Philadelphia
MAY
1 .... at Philadelphia
3-4 .... at Atlanta
6-7-**8** .... Colorado
9-10-11 .... Houston
13-14-**15** .... at San Diego
16-17-**18** .... at Los Angeles
20-21-**22** .... *Tampa Bay

23-24-25 .... Philadelphia
26-27-28-**29** .... Mets
30-31 .... at Pittsburgh
JUNE
1-2 .... at Pittsburgh
3-4-**5** .... at Washington
7-8-9 .... *Seattle
10-11-**12** .... *Texas
13-14-**15** .... at Cubs
17-**18-19** ... *at Anaheim
21-22-23 .... at Atlanta
24-25-**26** ... *at Tampa Bay
27-28-29-30 .... Atlanta
JULY
1-**2-3** .... at Mets
4-5-6-**7** .... Milwaukee
8-9-**10** .... Cubs
14-15-16-**17** .. at Philadelphia
18-19-20 .... at Arizona
22-23-**24** . at San Francisco
26-27-28 .... Pittsburgh
29-**30-31** .... at Washington

HOUSTON ASTROS
Minute Maid Park

■ **Standard Game Times:** 7:05 p.m.; Sat. 6:05; Sun. 1:05.

APRIL
5-6 .... St. Louis
8-9-**10** .... Cincinnati
11 .... at Mets
13-14 .... at Mets
15-**16-17** .... at Cincinnati
18-19 .... Atlanta
20-21 .... Milwaukee
22-23-24 .... at St. Louis
25-26-**27** ...... at Pittsburgh
29-30 .... Cubs
MAY
1 .... Cubs
2-3-4 .... Pittsburgh
5-6-7-**8** .... at Atlanta
9-10-11 .... at Florida
12-13-14-15 .. San Francisco
17-18-19 .... Arizona
20-**21-22** .... *at Texas
23-24-25 .... at Cubs
27-28-**29** ...... at Milwaukee
30-**31** .... Cincinnati
JUNE
1 .... Cincinnati
3-**4-5** .... St. Louis
7-8-9 .... at Mets
10-11-**12** .... *Toronto
13-14-15 ...*at Baltimore
17-18-**19** .. *at Kansas City
20-21-**22** .... Colorado
24-25-**26** .... *Texas
27-28-**29** ...... at Colorado
30 .... at Cincinnati

JULY
1-2-**3** .... at Cincinnati
4-5-6-**7** .... San Diego
8-9-**10** .... Los Angeles
15-**16-17** .... at St. Louis
18-19-**20** ...... at Pittsburgh
21-22-23-**24** .. at Washington
25-26-27 .... Philadelphia
28-29-30-**31** .... Mets
AUGUST
2-3-4 .... at Arizona
5-**6-7** .... at San Francisco
9-10-11 .... Washington
12-13-**14** .... Pittsburgh
15-16-17 .... Cubs
18-19-20-**21** ..... Milwaukee
22-23-24 ..... at Los Angeles
26-27-**28** ... at Los Angeles
30-31 .... Cincinnati
SEPTEMBER
1 .... Cincinnati
2-3-**4** .... St. Louis
5-6-7 .... at Philadelphia
9-10-**11** ...... at Milwaukee
12-13-14-15 ...... Florida
16-17-18 .... Milwaukee
19-20-21-**22** . at Pittsburgh
23-24-25 .... at Cubs
27-28 .... at St. Louis
29-30 .... Cubs
OCTOBER
1-2 .... Cubs

LOS ANGELES DODGERS
Dodger Stadium

■ **Standard Game Times:** 7:10 p.m.; Sun. 1:10.

APRIL
5-6-**7** .... at San Francisco
8-9-**10** .... at Arizona
12-13 .... San Francisco
15-16-**17** .... San Diego
18-**19** .... at Milwaukee

20-21 .... at San Diego
22-23-**24** .... at Colorado
25-26-27 .... Arizona
29-30 .... Colorado
MAY
1 .... Colorado

2-3-4 .... Washington
6-7-8 .... at Cincinnati
9-10-11-**12** ..... at St. Louis
13-14-**15** .... Atlanta
16-17-**18** .... Florida
20-**21-22** .... *Anaheim
24-25-26 . at San Francisco
27-28-**29** .... at Arizona
30-31 .... Cubs

JUNE

1 .... Cubs
2-3-4-**5** .... Milwaukee
6-7-8 .... *Detroit
10-11-**12** .... *Minnesota
14-15-16 ... *at Kansas City
17-18-19 ..... *at White Sox
20-21-22-**23** . at San Diego
24-25-**26** ..... *at Anaheim
27-28-29 .... San Diego

JULY

1-2-**3** .... Arizona
4-5-6-**7** .... at Colorado
8-**9-10** .... at Houston
14-15-**16-17** .. San Francisco
19-20-**21** .... at Philadelphia

MILWAUKEE BREWERS
Miller Park

■ **Standard Game Times:** 7:05 p.m.; Thur. 1:05; Sat. 6:05; Sun. 1:05.

APRIL

4 .... at Pittsburgh
6 .... at Pittsburgh
8-9-10 .... at Cubs
11-12-13 .... Pittsburgh
15-**16-17** .... St. Louis
18-**19** .... Los Angeles
20-21 .... at Houston
22-**23-24** . at San Francisco
25-26-**27** .... at St. Louis
29-**30** .... Cincinnati

MAY

1 .... Cincinnati
3-4-**5** .... Cubs
6-7-**8** .... Mets
9-10-**11** .... Philadelphia
13-14-**15** .... at Pittsburgh
16-17-18-**19** .. at Washington
20-**21-22** ...... *at Minnesota
23-24-25 .... Colorado
27-28-**29** .... Houston
30-31 . at San Diego

JUNE

1 .... at San Diego
2-3-4-**5** ...... at Los Angeles
6-7-**8** .... *Yankees
10-11-**12** ...... at Philadelphia
13-14-15 .... *at Tampa Bay
17-**18-19** .... *at Toronto
20-21-22-**23** .... Cubs
24-25-**26** .... *Minnesota
28-**29-30** .... at Cubs

JULY

1-2-**3** .... Pittsburgh
4-5-6-**7** .... at Florida
8-9-**10** .... at Atlanta
14-15-16-**17** ...... Washington
18-19-20-**21** .... at St. Louis
22-23-**24** ...... at Cincinnati
25-26-**27** .... Arizona
28-29-30-**31** .. San Francisco

AUGUST

2-3-**4** .... at Mets
5-6-**7** .... at Philadelphia
8-9-**10** .... St. Louis
12-13-**14** .... Cincinnati
15-16-17 .... at Colorado
18-19-20-**21** .... at Houston
23-24-**25** .... Florida
26-27-**28** .... Atlanta
30-31 .... Pittsburgh

SEPTEMBER

1-2-3-**4** .... San Diego
5-6-**7** .... at Cincinnati
9-10-**11** .... Houston
13-14-15 .... at Arizona
16-17-**18** .... at Houston
20-21-**22** .... Cubs
23-24-**25** .... St. Louis
26-27-28-**29** ...... Cincinnati
30 .... at Pittsburgh

OCTOBER

1-2 .... at Pittsburgh

NEW YORK METS
Shea Stadium

■ **Standard Game Times:** 7:10 p.m.; Sat. 1:10, 1:20, 7:10; Sun. 1:10.

APRIL

4 .... at Cincinnati
6-7 .... at Cincinnati

8-9-**10** .... at Atlanta
11 .... Houston
13-14 .... Houston

22-**23-24** .... at Mets
25-26-27-**28** ...... Cincinnati
29-**30-31** .... St. Louis

AUGUST

2-3-4 .... at Washington
5-6-**7** .... at Pittsburgh
9-10-11 .... Philadelphia
12-**13-14** .... Mets
16-17-18 .... at Atlanta
19-20-**21-22** .... at Florida
23-24-25 .... Colorado
26-27-**28** .... Houston
29-30-**31** .... at Cubs

SEPTEMBER

2-3-4 .... at Colorado
5-6-7 .... San Francisco
9-**10-11** .... San Diego
12-13-14 .... Colorado
15-16-**17-18** .... at S.F.
20-21-22 .... at Arizona
23-24-25-**26** ...... Pittsburgh
27-28-29 .... Arizona
30 .... at San Diego

OCTOBER

1-2 .... at San Diego

15-**16-17** .... Florida
18-19 .... at Philadelphia
20-21 .... at Florida
22-**23-24** .... Washington
25-26-27 .... Atlanta
29-30 .... at Washington

MAY

1 .... at Washington
2-3-4-**5** .... Philadelphia
6-7-**8** .... at Milwaukee
9-10-**11** .... at Cubs
13-14-15 .... St. Louis
16-17-**18** .... Cincinnati
20-**21-22** .... *Yankees
23-24-25 .... at Atlanta
26-27-28-**29** ...... at Florida
31 .... Arizona

JUNE

1-2 .... Arizona
3-4-5 .... San Francisco
7-8-9 .... Houston
10-11-**12** .... *Anaheim
14-15-16 ...... *at Oakland
17-18-**19** ..... *at Seattle
21-22-23 .. at Philadelphia
24-**25-26** .... *at Yankees
28-29-**30** .... Philadelphia

JULY

1-2-3 .... Florida
4-5-6-**7** ...... at Washington

PHILADELPHIA PHILLIES
Citizens Bank Park

■ **Standard Game Times:** 7:05, 1:05 p.m.; Sun. 1:35.

APRIL

4 .... Washington
6-7 .... Washington
8-9-10 .... at St. Louis
11-12-13 .... at Florida
15-**16-17** .... Atlanta
18-19 .... Mets
20-21 .... Colorado
22-23-**24** .... at Atlanta
25-26-**27** .... at Washington
29-30 .... Florida

MAY

1 .... Florida
2-3-4-**5** .... at Mets
6-7-8 .... at Cubs
9-10-**11** .... at Milwaukee
12-13-14-**15** ...... Cincinnati
17-18-**19** .... St. Louis
20-**21-22** .... *at Baltimore
23-24-25 .... at Cubs
27-**28-29** .... at Atlanta
31 .... San Francisco

JUNE

1-2 .... San Francisco
3-4-**5-6** .... Arizona
7-8-9 .... *Texas
10-11-**12** .... Milwaukee
14-15-16 .... *at Seattle
17-**18-19** .... *at Oakland
21-22-23 .... Mets
24-**25-26** .... *Boston
28-29-**30** .... at Mets

8-9-**10** .... at Pittsburgh
14-15-16-**17** .... Atlanta
19-20-21 .... San Diego
22-**23-24** .... Los Angeles
25-26-27 .... at Colorado
28-29-30-**31** .... at Houston

AUGUST

2-3-**4** .... Milwaukee
5-**6-7** .... Cubs
9-10-**11** ...... at San Diego
12-**13-14** ..... at Los Angeles
16-17-18 .... Pittsburgh
19-20-**21** .... Washington
22-23-24-25 ...... at Arizona
26-**27-28** . at San Francisco
30-31 .... Philadelphia

SEPTEMBER

1 .... Philadelphia
2-3-**4** .... at Florida
5-6-7 .... at Atlanta
8-9-10-**11** ...... at St. Louis
13-14-**15** .... Washington
16-**17-18** .... Atlanta
20-21-22 .... Florida
23-24-**25** .... at Mets
26-27-28 .. at Philadelphia
29-30 .... Colorado

OCTOBER

1-2 .... Colorado

JULY

1-2-**3** .... Atlanta
4-5-6-**7** .... at Pittsburgh
8-**9-10** .... Washington
14-15-**16-17** .... Florida
19-20-**21** .... Los Angeles
22-**23-24** .... San Diego
25-26-27 .... at Houston
28-29-30-**31** .... at Colorado

AUGUST

2-3-**4** .... Cubs
5-6-**7** .... Milwaukee
9-10-11 ...... at Los Angeles
12-13-**14** ...... at San Diego
15-16-17-18 ... Washington
19-20-**21** .... Pittsburgh
22-23-24 . at San Francisco
26-**27-28** .... at Arizona
30-31 .... at Mets

SEPTEMBER

1 .... at Mets
2-3-**4** .... at Washington
5-6-7 .... Houston
9-10-**11** .... Florida
12-13-14-15 .... Atlanta
16-**17-18** .... at Florida
20-21-**22** .... at Atlanta
23-24-**25** ..... at Cincinnati
26-27-28 .... Mets
30 .... at Washington

OCTOBER

1-2 .... at Washington

PITTSBURGH PIRATES
PNC Park

■ **Standard Game Times:** 7:05 p.m.; Sun. 1:35.

APRIL		JULY	
4	Milwaukee	1-2-3	at Milwaukee
6	Milwaukee	4-5-6-7	Philadelphia
7-8-9-**10**	at San Diego	8-9-**10**	Mets
11-12-**13**	at Milwaukee	**15**-**16**-**17**	at Cubs
15-16-**17**	Cubs	18-19-**20**	Houston
18-19	St. Louis	21-22-23-**24**	Colorado
20-**21**	at Cincinnati	26-27-28	at Florida
22-23-24	at Cubs	29-30-**31**	at Atlanta
25-26-**27**	Houston	**AUGUST**	
29-30	San Francisco	1	at Atlanta
MAY		2-3-**4**	San Diego
1	San Francisco	5-6-**7**	Los Angeles
2-3-4	at Houston	9-10-**11**	at Colorado
5-6-7-**8**	at Arizona	12-13-**14**	at Houston
9-10-**11**	at San Diego	16-17-18	at Mets
13-14-**15**	Milwaukee	19-20-**21**	at Phillies
17-**18**	Cubs	22-23-24-25	St. Louis
20-21-**22**	Colorado	26-27-28-29	Cincinnati
23-24-25	at St. Louis	30-**31**	at Milwaukee
26-27-28-**29**	at Cincinnati	**SEPTEMBER**	
30-31	Florida	2-3-**4**	Cubs
JUNE		6-7-8	Arizona
1-2	Florida	9-10-**11**	at Cincinnati
3-4-**5**	Atlanta	12-13-**14**	at St. Louis
6-7-8	*Baltimore	16-17-**18**	Cincinnati
10-11-**12**	*Tampa Bay	19-20-21-**22**	Houston
14-15-16	*at Yankees	23-24-**25**-26	at L.A.
17-18-**19**	*at Boston	27-28	at Cubs
20-21-**22**	Washington	30	Milwaukee
23-24-25-**26**	at St. Louis	**OCTOBER**	
28-29-**30**	at Washington	1-2	Milwaukee

ST. LOUIS CARDINALS
Busch Stadium

■ **Standard Game Times:** 7:10 p.m.; Thurs. (April-May) 12:10; Sat. 1:15, 6:15; Sun. 1:15.

APRIL		23-24-25-**26**	Pittsburgh
5-**6**	at Houston	28-29	Cincinnati
8-9-**10**	Philadelphia	30	Colorado
12-**13**	Cincinnati	**JULY**	
15-**16**-**17**	at Milwaukee	1-2-**3**	Colorado
18-19	at Pittsburgh	4-5-6-**7**	at Arizona
20-**21**	Cubs	8-9-**10**	at San Francisco
22-**23** 24	Houston	15-**16**-**17**	Houston
25-26-**27**	Milwaukee	18-19-20-**21**	Milwaukee
29-30	at Atlanta	**22**-23-24	Cubs
MAY		26-27-**28**	at San Diego
1	at Atlanta	29-**30**-**31**	at Los Angeles
2-3-4	at Cincinnati	**AUGUST**	
5-6-7-**8**	San Diego	1-2-3-4	Florida
9-10-11-**12**	Los Angeles	5-**6**-**7**	Atlanta
13-**14**-**15**	at Mets	8-9-**10**	at Milwaukee
17-18-**19**	at Philadelphia	**11**-**12**-**13**-**14**	at Cubs
20-21-**22**	at Kansas City	16-17-18	Arizona
23-24-25	Pittsburgh	19-**20**-**21**	San Francisco
27-28-**29**	Washington	22-23-24-25	at Pittsburgh
30-31	at Colorado	26-**27**-**28**	at Washington
JUNE		29-30-31	at Florida
1-**2**	at Colorado	**SEPTEMBER**	
3-**4**-**5**	at Houston	2-3-**4**	at Houston
6-7-8	*Boston	5-**6**-**7**	Cubs
10-**11**-**12**	*Yankees	8-9-10-**11**	Mets
13-14-15	*at Toronto	12-13-**14**	Pittsburgh
17-18-**19**	*at Tampa Bay	15-**16**-**17**-**18**	at Cubs
20-21-**22**	at Cincinnati	20-21-22	at Cincinnati

23-24-**25**	at Milwaukee
27-28	Houston
30	Cincinnati

OCTOBER

1-**2**	Cincinnati

SAN DIEGO PADRES
PETCO Park

■ **Standard Game Times:** 7:05 p.m.; Sun. 1:05.

APRIL		JULY	
4	at Colorado	1-2-**3**	San Francisco
6	at Colorado	4-5-6-**7**	at Houston
7-8-9-**10**	Pittsburgh	8-9-**10**	at Colorado
11-**12**-**13**	at Cubs	14-15-16-**17**	Arizona
15-16-**17**	at Los Angeles	19-20-**21**	at Mets
18-19	San Francisco	22-23-24	at Philadelphia
20-21	Los Angeles	26-27-**28**	St. Louis
22-23-**24**	at Arizona	29-30-**31**	Cincinnati
25-26-**27**	at San Francisco	**AUGUST**	
29-30	Arizona	2-3-**4**	at Pittsburgh
MAY		5-6-**7**	at Washington
1	Arizona	9-10-**11**	Mets
2-3-**4**	Colorado	12-13-**14**	Philadelphia
5-6-**7**-**8**	at St. Louis	16-17-18	at Florida
9-10-**11**	at Cincinnati	19-**20**-**21**	at Atlanta
13-14-**15**	Florida	22-23-24	Houston
16-17-**18**	Atlanta	26-27-**28**	Colorado
20-21-**22**	at Seattle	29-30-**31**	Arizona
24-25-26	at Arizona	**SEPTEMBER**	
27-**28**-**29**	at San Francisco	1-2-3-**4**	at Milwaukee
30-31	Milwaukee	6-7-8	Colorado
JUNE		9-**10**-**11**	at Los Angeles
1	Milwaukee	12-13-**14**	at San Francisco
2-3-4-**5**	Cubs	16-17-**18**	Washington
7-8-**9**	*Cleveland	19-20-21-**22**	at Colorado
10-11-**12**	*White Sox	23-24-25	at Arizona
14-15-16	*at Detroit	26-27-28-29	San Francisco
17-18-**19**	*at Minnesota	30	Los Angeles
20-21-22-**23**	Los Angeles	**OCTOBER**	
24-25-**26**	*Seattle	1-**2**	Los Angeles
27-28-**29**	at Los Angeles		

SAN FRANCISCO GIANTS
SBC Park

■ **Standard Game Times:** 7:15 p.m.; Thurs. 12:35, 7:15; Sat. 1:05, 7:15; Sun. 1:05.

APRIL		14-15-16	*at Minnesota
5-6-7	Los Angeles	17-18-**19**	*at Detroit
8-**9**-**10**	Colorado	20-21-22-**23**	*at Oakland
12-**13**	at Los Angeles	24-**25**-**26**	*at Oakland
15-16-**17**	at Colorado	28-29-30	at Arizona
18-19	at San Diego	**JULY**	
20-21	Arizona	1-2-**3**	at San Diego
22-**23**-**24**	Milwaukee	4-5-6-**7**	Cincinnati
25-26-**27**	San Diego	8-**9**-**10**	St. Louis
29-30	at Pittsburgh	14-15-**16**-**17**	at Los Angeles
MAY		18-19-**20**	Atlanta
1	at Pittsburgh	22-23-**24**	Florida
2-3-**4**	at Arizona	25-26-**27**	at Cubs
6-**7**-**8**	Washington	28-29-30-**31**	at Milwaukee
9-10-**11**	Pittsburgh	**AUGUST**	
12-13-14-15	at Houston	2-3-**4**	Colorado
17-18-**19**	at Colorado	5-**6**-**7**	Houston
20-21-**22**	*Oakland	9-10-11	at Atlanta
24-25-26	Los Angeles	12-13-**14**	at Florida
27-**28**-**29**	San Diego	15-16-17-**18**	at Cincinnati
31	at Philadelphia	19-**20**-**21**	at St. Louis
JUNE		22-23-24	Philadelphia
1-2	at Philadelphia	26-**27**-**28**	Mets
3-4-5	at Mets	29-30-**31**	Colorado
7-8-**9**	*Kansas City	**SEPTEMBER**	
10-11-**12**	*Cleveland	2-3-**4**	at Arizona

5-6-7 .... at Los Angeles	23-24-**25** .... at Colorado
8-9-**10-11** .... Cubs	26-27-28-29 .. at San Diego
12-13-**14** .... San Diego	30 .... Arizona
15-16-**17-18** .. Los Angeles	
20-21-**22** .... at Washington	

| OCTOBER |
| **1-2** .... Arizona |

WASHINGTON NATIONALS
RFK Stadium

■ **Standard Game Times:** 7:05 p.m.; Thur. 1:05p.m., 7:05p.m.; Sun. 1:05.

APRIL		MAY	
4 .... at Philadelphia		1 .... Mets	
6-7 .... at Philadelphia		2-3-4 .... at Los Angeles	
8-9-**10** .... at Florida		6-**7-8** ...... at San Francisco	
11-12-**13** .... at Atlanta		9-10-**11** .... at Arizona	
14 .... Arizona		13-14-**15** .... Cubs	
16-**17** .... Arizona		16-17-18-**19** ..... Milwaukee	
18-19 .... Florida		20-**21-22** .... *at Toronto	
20-**21** .... Atlanta		23-24-**25** .... at Cincinnati	
22-**23-24** .... at Mets		27-28-**29** .... at St. Louis	
25-26-**27** .... Philadelphia		30-31 .... Atlanta	
29-30 .... Mets			

| JUNE |
| 1-2 .... Atlanta |
| 3-4-**5** .... Florida |
| 7-8-9 .... *Oakland |
| 10-11-**12** .... *Seattle |
| 13-14-15 .... *at Anaheim |
| 17-18-**19** .... *at Texas |
| 20-21-**22** ...... at Pittsburgh |
| 24-25-**26** .... *Toronto |
| 28-29-**30** .... Pittsburgh |

| JULY |
| **1-2-3** .... at Cubs |
| 4-5-6-**7** .... Mets |
| 8-**9-10** .... at Philadelphia |
| **14**-15-16-**17** . at Milwaukee |
| 18-19-20 .... Colorado |
| 21-22-23-**24** .... Houston |
| 26-27-**28** .... at Atlanta |
| 29-**30-31** .... at Florida |

| AUGUST |
| 2-3-4 .... Los Angeles |

| 5-6-**7** .... San Diego |
| 9-10-11 .... at Houston |
| 12-13-**14** .... at Colorado |
| 15-16-17-18 .... at Phil. |
| 19-20-**21** .... at Mets |
| 23-24-**25** .... Cincinnati |
| 26-**27-28** .... St. Louis |
| 29-30-31 .... at Atlanta |

| SEPTEMBER |
| 1 .... at Atlanta |
| 2-3-**4** .... Philadelphia |
| **5**-6-**7-8** .... Florida |
| 9-**10-11** .... Atlanta |
| 13-14-**15** .... at Mets |
| 16-17-**18** ...... at San Diego |
| 20-21-**22** ..... San Francisco |
| 23-24-**25** .... Mets |
| 26-27-28 .... at Florida |
| 30 .... Philadelphia |

| OCTOBER |
| **1-2** .... Philadelphia |

NOTE: Dates in **bold** indicate afternoon games. All game times are subject to change. Gaps in dates indicate scheduled off-days but may be affected by rainouts.

* Interleague Series

INTERLEAGUE
SCHEDULE

May 20
Anaheim at Los Angeles
Arizona at Detroit
Atlanta at Boston
Cleveland at Cincinnati
Houston at Texas
Milwaukee at Minnesota
Oakland at San Francisco
Philadelphia at Baltimore
San Diego at Seattle
St. Louis at Kansas City
Tampa Bay at Florida
Washington at Toronto
White Sox at Cubs
Yankees at Mets

May 21
Anaheim at Los Angeles
Arizona at Detroit
Atlanta at Boston
Cleveland at Cincinnati
Houston at Texas
Milwaukee at Minnesota
Oakland at San Francisco
Philadelphia at Baltimore
San Diego at Seattle
St. Louis at Kansas City
Tampa Bay at Florida
Washington at Toronto
White Sox at Cubs
Yankees at Mets

May 22
Anaheim at Los Angeles
Arizona at Detroit
Atlanta at Boston
Cleveland at Cincinnati
Houston at Texas
Milwaukee at Minnesota
Oakland at San Francisco
Philadelphia at Baltimore
San Diego at Seattle
St. Louis at Kansas City
Tampa Bay at Florida
Washington at Toronto
White Sox at Cubs
Yankees at Mets

June 6
Anaheim at Atlanta
Baltimore at Pittsburgh
Boston at St. Louis
Detroit at Los Angeles
Toronto at Cubs
White Sox at Colorado
Yankees at Milwaukee

June 7
Anaheim at Atlanta
Baltimore at Pittsburgh
Boston at St. Louis
Cleveland at San Diego
Detroit at Los Angeles

Kansas City at San Francisco
Minnesota at Arizona
Oakland at Washington
Seattle at Florida
Tampa Bay at Cincinnati
Texas at Philadelphia
Toronto at Cubs
White Sox at Colorado
Yankees at Milwaukee

June 8
Anaheim at Atlanta
Baltimore at Pittsburgh
Boston at St. Louis
Cleveland at San Diego
Detroit at Los Angeles
Kansas City at San Francisco
Minnesota at Arizona
Oakland at Washington
Seattle at Florida
Tampa Bay at Cincinnati
Texas at Philadelphia
Toronto at Cubs
White Sox at Colorado
Yankees at Milwaukee

June 9
Cleveland at San Diego
Kansas City at San Francisco
Minnesota at Arizona
Oakland at Washington
Seattle at Florida
Tampa Bay at Cincinnati
Texas at Philadelphia

June 10
Anaheim at Mets
Baltimore at Cincinnati
Boston at Cubs
Cleveland at San Francisco
Detroit at Colorado
Kansas City at Arizona
Minnesota at Los Angeles
Oakland at Atlanta
Seattle at Washington
Tampa Bay at Pittsburgh
Texas at Florida
Toronto at Houston
White Sox at San Diego
Yankees at St. Louis

June 11
Anaheim at Mets
Baltimore at Cincinnati
Boston at Cubs
Cleveland at San Francisco
Detroit at Colorado
Kansas City at Arizona
Minnesota at Los Angeles
Oakland at Atlanta
Seattle at Washington
Tampa Bay at Pittsburgh
Texas at Florida

Toronto at Houston
White Sox at San Diego
Yankees at St. Louis

June 12
Anaheim at Mets
Baltimore at Cincinnati
Boston at Cubs
Cleveland at San Francisco
Detroit at Colorado
Kansas City at Arizona
Minnesota at Los Angeles
Oakland at Atlanta
Seattle at Washington
Tampa Bay at Pittsburgh
Texas at Florida
Toronto at Houston
White Sox at San Diego
Yankees at St. Louis

June 13
Arizona at White Sox
Atlanta at Texas
Cincinnati at Boston
Houston at Baltimore
Milwaukee at Tampa Bay
St. Louis at Toronto
Washington at Anaheim

June 14
Arizona at White Sox
Atlanta at Texas
Cincinnati at Boston
Colorado at Cleveland
Houston at Baltimore
Los Angeles at Kansas City
Mets at Oakland
Milwaukee at Tampa Bay
Philadelphia at Seattle
Pittsburgh at Yankees
San Diego at Detroit
San Francisco at Minnesota
St. Louis at Toronto
Washington at Anaheim

June 15
Arizona at White Sox
Atlanta at Texas
Cincinnati at Boston
Colorado at Cleveland
Houston at Baltimore
Los Angeles at Kansas City
Mets at Oakland
Milwaukee at Tampa Bay
Philadelphia at Seattle
Pittsburgh at Yankees
San Diego at Detroit
San Francisco at Minnesota
St. Louis at Toronto
Washington at Anaheim

June 16
Colorado at Cleveland

Los Angeles at Kansas City
Mets at Oakland
Philadelphia at Seattle
Pittsburgh at Yankees
San Diego at Detroit
San Francisco at Minnesota

June 17
Arizona at Cleveland
Colorado at Baltimore
Cubs at Yankees
Florida at Anaheim
Houston at Kansas City
Los Angeles at White Sox
Mets at Seattle
Milwaukee at Toronto
Philadelphia at Oakland
Pittsburgh at Boston
San Diego at Minnesota
San Francsico at Detroit
St. Louis at Tampa Bay
Washington at Texas

June 18
Arizona at Cleveland
Colorado at Baltimore
Cubs at Yankees
Florida at Anaheim
Houston at Kansas City
Los Angeles at White Sox
Mets at Seattle
Milwaukee at Toronto
Philadelphia at Oakland
Pittsburgh at Boston

San Diego at Minnesota
San Francsico at Detroit
St. Louis at Tampa Bay
Washington at Texas

June 19
Arizona at Cleveland
Colorado at Baltimore
Cubs at Yankees
Florida at Anaheim
Houston at Kansas City
Los Angeles at White Sox
Mets at Seattle
Milwaukee at Toronto
Philadelphia at Oakland
Pittsburgh at Boston
San Diego at Minnesota
San Francsico at Detroit
St. Louis at Tampa Bay
Washington at Texas

June 24
Baltimore at Atlanta
Boston at Philadelphia
Cincinnati at Cleveland
Cubs at White Sox
Detroit at Arizona
Florida at Tampa Bay
Kansas City at Colorado
Los Angeles at Anaheim
Mets at Yankees
Minnesota at Milwaukee
San Francisco at Oakland
Seattle at San Diego

Texas at Houston
Toronto at Washington

June 25
Baltimore at Atlanta
Boston at Philadelphia
Cincinnati at Cleveland
Cubs at White Sox
Detroit at Arizona
Florida at Tampa Bay
Kansas City at Colorado
Los Angeles at Anaheim
Mets at Yankees
Minnesota at Milwaukee
San Francisco at Oakland
Seattle at San Diego
Texas at Houston
Toronto at Washington

June 26
Baltimore at Atlanta
Boston at Philadelphia
Cincinnati at Cleveland
Cubs at White Sox
Detroit at Arizona
Florida at Tampa Bay
Kansas City at Colorado
Los Angeles at Anaheim
Mets at Yankees
Minnesota at Milwaukee
San Francisco at Oakland
Seattle at San Diego
Texas at Houston
Toronto at Washington

SPRING TRAINING
ARIZONA CACTUS LEAGUE

ANAHEIM ANGELS
Major League Club
Complex Address (first year): Diablo Stadium (1993), 2200 W. Alameda, Tempe, AZ 85282. Telephone: (602) 438-4300. FAX: (602) 438-7950. **Seating Capacity:** 9,785. **Location:** I-10 to exit 153B (48th Street), south one mile on 48th Street to Alameda Drive, left on Alameda.
Minor League Clubs
Complex Address: Gene Autry Park, 4125 E. McKellips, Mesa, AZ 85205. Telephone: (480) 830-4137. FAX: (480) 438-7950. **Hotel Address:** Homestead Suites, 1920 W. Isabella, Mesa, AZ 85202.

ARIZONA DIAMONDBACKS
Major League Club
Complex Address (first year): Tucson Electric Park (1998), 2500 Ajo Way, Tucson, AZ 85713. Telephone: (520) 434-1400. FAX: (520) 434-1443. **Seating Capacity:** 11,000. **Location:** I-10 to exit 262 (Park Street) or 263 (Kino Street), south to Ajo Way, left (east) on Ajo Way to park.
Hotel Address: JW Marriott Starr Pass Resort, 3800 W. Starr Pass Blvd., Tucson, AZ 85745. Telephone: (520) 792-3500.
Minor League Clubs
Complex Address: Kino Veterans Memorial Sportspark, 3600 S. Country Club, Tucson, AZ 85713. Telephone: (520) 434-1400. FAX: (520) 434-1443. **Hotel Address:** Radisson City Center, 181 W. Broadway, Tucson, AZ 85701. Telephone: (520) 624-8711.

CHICAGO CUBS
Major League Club
Complex Address (first year): HoHoKam Park (1979), 1235 N. Center St., Mesa, AZ 85201. Telephone: (480) 668-0500. FAX: (480) 668-4541. **Seating Capacity:** 8,963. **Location:** Main Street (U.S. Highway 60) to Center Street, north 1½ miles on Center Street.
Hotel Address: Best Western Dobson Ranch Inn, 1666 S. Dobson Rd., Mesa, AZ 85202. Telephone: (480) 831-7000.
Minor League Clubs
Complex Address: Fitch Park, 160 E. Sixth Place, Mesa, AZ 85201. Telephone: (480) 668-0500. FAX: (480) 668-4501. **Hotel Address:** Best Western Mezona, 250 W. Main St., Mesa, AZ 85201. Telephone: (480) 834-9233.

CHICAGO WHITE SOX
Major League Club
Complex Address (first year): Tucson Electric Park (1998), 2500 E. Ajo Way, Tucson, AZ 85713. Telephone: (520) 434-1300. FAX: (520) 434-1151. **Seating Capacity:** 11,000. **Location:** I-10 to exit 262 (Park Street) or 263 (Kino Street), south to Ajo Way, left (east) on Ajo Way to park.
Hotel Address: Doubletree Guest Suites, 6555 E. Speedway Blvd., Tucson, AZ 85710. Telephone: (520) 721-7100.
Minor League Clubs
Complex Address: Same as major league club. **Hotel Address:** Ramada Palo Verde, 5251 S. Julian Dr., Tucson,

AZ 85706. Telephone: (520) 294-5250.

COLORADO ROCKIES
Major League Club
Complex Address (first year): Hi Corbett Field (1993), 3400 E. Camino Campestre, Tucson, AZ 85716. Telephone: (520) 322-4500. **Seating Capacity:** 8,655. **Location:** I-10 to Broadway exit, east on Broadway to Randolph Park.
Hotel Address: Hilton Tucson East, 7600 Broadway, Tucson, AZ 85710.
Minor League Clubs
Complex Address: Same as major league club. **Hotel Address:** Clarion Hotel, 102 N. Alvernon, Tucson, AZ 85711. Telephone: (520) 795-0330.

KANSAS CITY ROYALS
Major League Club
Complex Address (first year): Surprise Stadium (2003), 15946 N. Bullard Ave., Surprise, AZ 85374. **Telephone:** (623) 266-4400. **FAX:** (623) 266-4584. **Seating Capacity:** 10,700. **Location:** I-10 West to Route 101 North, 101 North to Bell Road, left on Bell for five miles, stadium on left.
Hotel Address: Wingate Inn & Suites, 1188 N. Dysart Rd., Avondale, AZ 85323. Telephone: (623) 547-1313.
Minor League Clubs
Complex/Hotel Address: Same as major league club.

MILWAUKEE BREWERS
Major League Club
Complex Address (first year): Maryvale Baseball Park (1998), 3600 N. 51st Ave., Phoenix, AZ 85031. Telephone: (623) 245-5555. FAX: (623) 245-5580. **Seating Capacity:** 9,000. **Location:** I-10 to exit 139 (51st Ave.), north on 51st Ave.; I-17 to exit 202 (Indian School Road), west on Indian School Road.
Hotel Address: Holiday Inn Express-Tempe, 5300 S. Priest Dr., Tempe, AZ 85283. Telephone: (480) 820-7500.
Minor League Clubs
Complex Address: Maryvale Baseball Complex, 3805 N. 53rd Ave., Phoenix, AZ 85031. Telephone: (623) 245-5600. FAX: (623) 245-5607. **Hotel Address:** Same as major league club.

OAKLAND ATHLETICS

Major League Club
Complex Address (first year): Phoenix Municipal Stadium (1982), 5999 E. Van Buren, Phoenix, AZ 85008. Telephone: (602) 225-9400. FAX: (602) 225-9473. **Seating Capacity:** 8,500. **Location:** I-10 to exit 153 (48th Street), HoHoKam Expressway to Van Buren Street (U.S. Highway 60), right on Van Buren; park two miles on right.
Hotel Address: Doubletree Suites Hotel, 320 N. 44th St., Phoenix, AZ 85008. Telephone: (602) 225-0500.

Minor League Clubs
Complex Address: Papago Park Baseball Complex, 1802 N. 64th St., Phoenix, AZ 85008. Telephone: (480) 949-5951. FAX: (480) 945-0557. **Hotel Address:** Fairfield Inn, 5101 N. Scottsdale Rd., Scottsdale, AZ 85251. Telephone: (480) 945-4392.

SAN DIEGO PADRES

Major League Club
Complex Address (first year): Peoria Sports Complex (1994), 8131 W. Paradise Lane, Peoria, AZ 85382. Telephone: (623) 486-7000. FAX: (623) 412-9382. **Seating Capacity:** 10,000. **Location:** I-17 to Bell Road exit, west on Bell to 83rd Ave.
Hotel Address: Comfort Suites, 8473 W. Paradise Lane, Peoria, AZ 85382. Telephone: (623) 334-3993.

Minor League Clubs
Complex Address: Same as major league club. **Hotel Address:** Sheraton Crescent, 2620 W. Dunlap Ave., Phoenix, AZ 85021. Telephone: (623) 943-8200.

SAN FRANCISCO GIANTS

Major League Club
Complex Address (first year): Scottsdale Stadium (1981), 7408 E. Osborn Rd., Scottsdale, AZ 85251. Telephone: (480) 990-7972. FAX: (480) 990-2643. **Seating Capacity:** 10,500. **Location:** Scottsdale Road to Osborne Road, east on Osborne ½ mile.
Hotel Address: Courtyard Marriott, 3311 N. Scottsdale Rd., Scottsdale, AZ 85251. Telephone: (480)

429-7785.

Minor League Clubs
Complex Address: Indian School Park, 4415 N. Hayden Road at Camelback Road, Scottsdale, AZ 85251. Telephone: (480) 990-0052. FAX: (480) 990-2349. **Hotel Address:** Days Inn, 4710 N. Scottsdale Rd., Scottsdale, AZ 85351. Telephone: (480) 947-5411.

SEATTLE MARINERS

Major League Club
Complex Address (first year): Peoria Sports Complex (1993), 15707 N. 83rd Ave., Peoria, AZ 85382. Telephone: (623) 776-4800. FAX: (480) 776-4829. **Seating Capacity:** 10,000. **Location:** I-17 to Bell Road exit, west on Bell to 83rd Ave.
Hotel Address: LaQuinta Inn & Suites, 16321 N. 83rd Ave., Peoria, AZ 85382 Telephone: (623) 487-1900.

Minor League Clubs
Complex Address: Peoria Sports Complex (1993), 15707 N. 83rd Ave., Peoria, AZ 85382. Telephone: (602) 412-9000. FAX: (602) 412-9382. **Hotel Address:** Hampton Inn, 8408 W. Paradise Lane, Peoria, AZ 85382. Telephone: (623) 486-9918.

TEXAS RANGERS

Major League Club
Complex Address (first year): Surprise Stadium (2003), 15754 N. Bullard Ave., Surprise, AZ 85374. **Telephone:** (623) 266-8100. **FAX:** (623) 266-8120. **Seating Capacity:** 10,714. **Location:** I-10 West to Route 101 North, 101 North to Bell Road, left at Bell for seven miles, stadium on left.
Hotel Address: Windmill Suites at Sun City West, 12545 W. Bell Rd., Surprise, AZ 85374. Telephone: (623) 583-0133.

Minor League Clubs
Complex Address: Same as major league club. **Hotel Address:** Hampton Inn, 2000 N. Litchfield Rd., Goodyear, AZ 85338. Telephone: (623) 536-1313; Holiday Inn Express, 1313 N. Litchfield Rd., Goodyear, AZ 85338.

FLORIDA GRAPEFRUIT LEAGUE

ATLANTA BRAVES

Major League Club
Stadium Address (first year): Disney's Wide World of Sports Complex (1998), Cracker Jack Stadium, 700 S. Victory Way, Kissimmee, FL 34747. Telephone: (407) 939-2200. **Seating Capacity:** 9,500. **Location:** I-4 to exit 25B (Highway 192 West), follow signs to Magic Kingdom/Wide World of Sports Complex, right on Victory Way.
Hotel Address: World Center Marriott, World Center Drive, Orlando, FL 32821. Telephone: (407) 239-4200.

Minor League Clubs
Complex Address: Same as major league club. Telephone: (407) 939-2232. FAX: (407) 939-2225. **Hotel Address:** Days Suites, 5820 W. Hwy. 92, Kissimmee, FL 34746. Telephone: (407) 396-7900.

BALTIMORE ORIOLES

Major League Club
Complex Address (first year): Fort Lauderdale Stadium (1996), 1301 NW 55th St., Fort Lauderdale, FL 33309. Telephone: (954) 776-1921. FAX: (954) 776-

9116. **Seating Capacity:** 8,340. **Location:** I-95 to exit 32 (Commercial Blvd.), West on Commercial, right on Orioles Blvd. (NW 55th Street), stadium on left.
Hotel Address: Sheraton Suites, 555 NW 62nd St., Fort Lauderdale, FL 33309. Telephone: (954) 772-5400.

Minor League Clubs
Complex Address: Twin Lakes Park, 6700 Clark Rd., Sarasota, FL 34241. Telephone: (941) 923-1996. FAX: (941) 922-3751. **Hotel Address:** Ramada Inn Limited, 5774 Clark Road, Sarasota, FL 34233. Telephone: (941) 921-7812; Americinn, 5931 Fruitville Rd., Sarasota, FL 34232. Telephone: (941) 342-8778.

BOSTON RED SOX
Major League Club
Complex Address (first year): City of Palms Park (1993), 2201 Edison Ave., Fort Myers, FL 33901. Telephone: (239) 334-4799. FAX: (239) 334-6060. **Seating Capacity:** 8,200. **Location:** I-75 to exit 39, three miles west on Tuttle Ave., right on Tuttle to 12th Street, stadium on left.
Hotel Address: Homewood Suites Hotel, 5255 Big Pine Way, Fort Myers, FL 33907. Telephone: (239) 275-6000.
Minor League Clubs
Complex Address: Red Sox Minor League Complex, 4301 Edison Ave., Fort Myers, FL 33916. Telephone: (239) 461-4500. FAX: (239) 332-8107. **Hotel Address:** Ramada Inn, 2500 Edwards Dr., Fort Myers, FL 33901. Telephone: (239) 337-0300.

CINCINNATI REDS
Major League Club
Complex Address (first year): Ed Smith Stadium (1998), 1090 N. Euclid Avenue, Sarasota, FL 34237. Telephone: (941) 955-6501. FAX: (941) 955-6365. **Seating Capacity:** 7,500. **Location:** I-75 to exit 39, west on Fruitville Road (Route 780) for four miles, right on Tuttle.
Hotel Address—Staff: Marriott Residence Inn, 1040 University Pkwy., Sarasota, FL 34234. Telephone: (941) 358-1468. FAX: (941) 358-0850.
Players: Wellesley Inn, 1803 N. Tamiami Trail, Sarasota, FL 34234. Telephone: (941) 366-5128. FAX: (941) 953-4322.
Minor League Clubs
Complex Address: Same as major league club. **Hotel Address:** Holiday Inn, 7150 N. Tamiami Trail, Sarasota, FL 34243. Telephone: (941) 355-2781.

CLEVELAND INDIANS
Major League Club
Complex Address (first year): Chain O' Lakes Park (1993), Cypress Gardens Blvd. at U.S. 17, Winter Haven, FL 33880. Telephone: (863) 293-5405. FAX: (863) 291-5772. **Seating Capacity:** 7,000. **Location:** U.S. 17 (Third Street) south through Winter Haven to Cypress Gardens Boulevard.
Hotel Address: Holiday Inn, 1150 Third St. SW, Winter Haven, FL 33880. Telephone: (863) 294-4451.
Minor League Clubs
Complex Address/Hotel: Same as major league club.

DETROIT TIGERS
Major League Club
Complex Address (first year): Joker Marchant Stadium (1946), 2301 Lakeland Hills Blvd., Lakeland, FL 33805. Telephone: (863) 686-8075. FAX: (863) 688-9589. **Seating Capacity:** 9,000. **Location:** I-4 to exit 19 (Lakeland Hills Boulevard), left 1½ miles.
Hotel Address: Wellesley Inn, 3520 Hwy. 98 N., Lakeland, FL 33805. Telephone: (863) 859-3399.

Minor League Clubs
Complex/Hotel Address: Tigertown, 2125 N. Lake Ave., Lakeland, FL 33805. Telephone: (863) 686-8075. FAX: (863) 688-9589.

FLORIDA MARLINS
Major League Club
Complex Address (first year): Roger Dean Stadium (1998), 4751 Main St., Jupiter, FL 33458. Telephone: (561) 775-1818. **Seating Capacity:** 7,000. **Location:** I-95 to exit 58, east on Donald Ross Road for ¼ mile.
Hotel Address: Hampton Inn, 401 RCA Blvd., Palm Beach Gardens, FL 33410. Telephone: 561-625-8880. FAX: (561) 625-6766.
Minor League Clubs
Complex Address: Same as major league club.
Hotel Address: Fairfield Inn, 6748 W. Indiantown Rd., Jupiter, FL 33458. Telephone: (561) 748-5252.

HOUSTON ASTROS
Major League Club
Complex Address (first year): Osceola County Stadium (1985), 631 Heritage Park Way, Kissimmee, FL 34744. Telephone: (321) 697-3150. FAX: (321) 697-3199. **Seating Capacity:** 5,300. **Location:** From Florida Turnpike South, take exit 244, west on U.S. 192, right on Bill Beck Boulevard; From Florida Turnpike North, take exit 242, west on U.S. 192, right on Bill Beck Blvd.; From I-4, take exit onto 192 East for 12 miles, stadium on left; From 17-92 South, take U.S. 192, left for three miles.
Hotel Address: Renaissance Orlando Resort at Seaworld, 6677 Sea Harbor Dr., Orlando, FL 32821. Telephone: (407) 351-3555.
Minor League Clubs
Complex Address: 1000 Bill Beck Blvd., Kissimmee, FL 34744. Telephone: (321) 697-3100. FAX: (321) 697-3195. **Hotel Address:** Same as major league club.

LOS ANGELES DODGERS
Major League Club
Complex Address (first year): Holman Stadium (1948). **Seating Capacity:** 6,500. **Location:** Exit I-95 to Route 60 East, left on 43rd Avenue, right on 26th Street.
Hotel Address: Dodgertown, 4001 26th St., Vero Beach, FL 32960. Telephone: (772) 569-4900. FAX: (772) 567-0819.
Minor League Clubs
Complex/Hotel Address: Same as major league club.

MINNESOTA TWINS
Major League Club
Complex Address (first year): Lee County Sports Complex/Hammond Stadium (1991), 14100 Six Mile Cypress Pkwy., Fort Myers, FL 33912. Telephone: (239) 768-4282. FAX: (239) 768-4211. **Seating Capacity:** 7,500. **Location:** Exit 21 off I-75, west on Daniels Parkway, left on Six Mile Cypress Parkway.
Hotel Address: Radisson Inn, 12635 Cleveland Ave., Fort Myers, FL 33907. Telephone: (239) 936-4300.
Minor League Clubs
Complex Address/Hotel: Same as major league club.

NEW YORK METS
Major League Club
Complex Address (first year): St. Lucie Sports Complex/Tradition Field (1987), 525 NW Peacock Blvd., Port St. Lucie, FL 34986. Telephone: (772) 871-2100. FAX: (772) 878-9802. **Seating Capacity:** 7,000.

Location: Exit 121C (St. Lucie West Boulevard) off I-95, east ¼ mile, left onto NW Peacock Boulevard.
Hotel Address: Spring Hill Suites, 2000 NW Courtyard Circle, Port St. Lucie, FL 34986. Telephone: (772) 871-2929.
Minor League Clubs
Complex Address: Same as major league club. **Hotel Address:** Holiday Inn, 10120 South Federal Hwy, Port St. Lucie, FL 34952. Telephone: (772) 337-2200.

NEW YORK YANKEES
Major League Club
Complex Address (first year): Legends Field (1996), One Steinbrenner Dr., Tampa, FL 33614. Telephone: (813) 875-7753. FAX: (813) 673-3199. **Seating Capacity:** 10,000. **Location:** I-275 to Martin Luther King, west on Martin Luther King to Dale Mabry.
Hotel Address: Radisson Bay Harbor Inn, 770 Courtney Campbell Causeway, Tampa, FL 33607. Telephone: (813) 281-8900.
Minor League Clubs
Complex Address: Yankees Player Development/ Scouting Complex, 3102 N. Himes Ave., Tampa, FL 33607. Telephone: (813) 875-7569. FAX: (813) 873-2302. **Hotel Address:** Holiday Inn Express, 4732 N. Dale Mabry, Tampa, FL 33614.

PHILADELPHIA PHILLIES
Major League Club
Complex Address (first year): Bright House Networks Field (2004), 601 N. Old Coachman Rd., Clearwater, FL 33765. Telephone: (727) 467-4457. FAX: (727) 712-4498. **Seating Capacity:** 7,300. **Location:** U.S. Highway 19 North, left on Drew Street, right on Old Coachman Road, ballpark on right.
Hotel: None.
Minor League Clubs
Complex Address: Carpenter Complex, 651 N. Old Coachman Rd., Clearwater, FL 33765. Telephone: (727) 799-0503. FAX: (727) 726-1793. **Hotel Addresses:** Hampton Inn, 21030 U.S. Highway 19 North, Clearwater, FL 34625. Telephone: (727) 797-8173; Econolodge, 21252 U.S. Highway 19, Clearwater, FL 34625. Telephone: (727) 799-1569.

PITTSBURGH PIRATES
Major League Club
Stadium Address (first year): McKechnie Field (1969), 17th Ave. West and Ninth Street West, Bradenton, FL 34205. **Seating Capacity:** 6,562. **Location:** U.S. 41 to 17th Ave, west to Ninth Street.
Complex/Hotel Address: Pirate City, 1701 27th St. E., Bradenton, FL 34208. Telephone: (941) 747-3031. FAX: (941) 747-9549.
Minor League Clubs
Complex/Hotel Address: Same as major league club.

ST. LOUIS CARDINALS
Major League Club
Complex Address (first year): Roger Dean Stadium

(1998), 4795 University Dr., Jupiter, FL 33458. Telephone: (561) 775-1818. FAX: (561) 799-1380. **Seating Capacity:** 6,864. **Location:** I-95 to exit 58, east on Donald Ross Road for ¼ mile.
Hotel Address: Embassy Suites Hotel, 4350 PGA Blvd., Palm Beach, FL 33410. Telephone: (561)622-1000.
Minor League Clubs
Complex: Same as major league club. **Hotel:** Doubletree Hotel, 4431 PGA Blvd., Palm Beach Gardens, FL 33410. Telephone: (561) 622-2260.

TAMPA BAY DEVIL RAYS
Major League Club
Stadium Address (first year): Progress Energy Park/Home of Al Lang Field (1998), 180 Second Ave. SE, St. Petersburg, FL 33701. Telephone: (727) 825-3137. FAX: (727) 825-3167. **Seating Capacity:** 6,438. **Location:** I-275 to exit 23C, left on First Street South to Second Avenue South, stadium on right.
Complex/Hotel Address: Raymond A. Naimoli Complex, 7901 30th Ave. N., St. Petersburg, FL 33710. Telephone: (727) 384-5517.
Minor League Clubs
Complex/Hotel Address: Same as major league club.

TORONTO BLUE JAYS
Major League Club
Stadium Address (first year): Knology Park (1977), 373 Douglas Ave. #A, Dunedin, FL 34698. Telephone: (727) 733-9302. **Seating Capacity:** 5,509. **Location:** From I-275, north on Highway 19, left on Sunset Point Road for four miles, right on Douglas Avenue, stadium one mile on right.
Hotel Address: Red Roof Inn, 3200 U.S. 19 N., Palm Harbor, FL 34684. Telephone: (727) 786-2529.
Minor League Clubs
Complex Address: Bobby Mattick Training Facility at Englebert Complex, 1700 Solon Ave., Dunedin, FL 34698. Telephone: (727) 734-8007. **Hotel Address:** Same as major league club.

WASHINGTON NATIONALS
Major League Club
Complex Address (first year): Space Coast Stadium (2003), 5800 Stadium Pkwy., Viera, FL 32940. Telephone: (321) 633-9200. **Seating Capacity:** 7,200. **Location:** I-95 southbound to Fiske Blvd. (exit 74), south on Fiske/Stadium Parkway to stadium; I-95 northbound to State Road #509/Wickham Road (exit 73), left off exit, right on Lake Andrew Drive to complex.
Hotel Address: Melbourne Airport Hilton, 200 Rialto Place, Melbourne, FL 32901. Telephone: (321) 768-0200.
Minor League Clubs
Complex Address: Carl Barger Complex, 5600 Stadium Pkwy., Viera, FL 32940. Telephone: (321) 633-8119. **Hotel Address:** Imperial Hotel & Conference Center, 8298 N. Wickman Rd., Viera, FL 32940. Telephone: (321) 255-0077.

MEDIA
INFO

LOCAL MEDIA
INFORMATION

ANAHEIM ANGELS

Radio Announcers: Rory Markas, Terry Smith. Spanish—Ivan Lara, Jose Mota. **Flagship Station:** KSPN 710-AM, KTWQ 1090-AM (Spanish).

TV Announcers: Rex Hudler, Steve Physioc, Jose Mota. **Flagship Stations:** KCAL Channel 9, Fox Sports Net (regional cable).

NEWSPAPERS, Daily Coverage (*national/beat writers): Long Beach Press Telegram, Los Angeles Times (Mike DiGiovanna, *Ross Newhan), Orange County Register (Mark Saxon), Riverside Press Enterprise (Matt Tresaugue), San Gabriel Valley Tribune (*Joe Haakenson, Gabe Lacques), Inland Valley Daily Bulletin. **MLB.com:** Doug Miller.

BALTIMORE ORIOLES

Radio Announcers: Jim Hunter, Fred Manfra, Chuck Thompson. **Flagship Station:** WBAL 1090-AM.

TV Announcers: Jim Palmer, Michael Reghi. **Flagship Station:** Comcast SportsNet.

NEWSPAPERS, Daily Coverage (*national/beat writers): Baltimore Sun (Roch Kubatko, *Peter Schmuck), Washington Post (Jorge Arangure), Washington Times, York, Pa., Daily Record. **MLB.com:** Gary Washburn.

BOSTON RED SOX

Radio Announcers: Joe Castiglione, Jerry Trupiano. **Flagship Station:** WEEI 850-AM.

TV Announcers: Don Orsillo, Jerry Remy. **Flagship Stations:** WSBK 38, New England Sports Network (regional cable).

NEWSPAPERS, Daily Coverage (*national/beat writers): Boston Globe (Gordon Edes, Chris Snow, *Larry Whiteside), Boston Herald (Jeff Horrigan, Tony Massarotti, Michael Silverman), Providence Journal (Steve Krasner, Sean McAdam), Worcester Telegram & Gazette (Bill Ballou, Phil O'Neill), Hartford Courant (Paul Doyle, Dave Heuschkel). **MLB.com:** Ian Browne.

CHICAGO WHITE SOX

Radio Announcers: John Rooney, Ed Farmer. **Flagship Station:** WMVP/ESPN Radio 1000-AM.

TV Announcers: Ken Harrelson, Darrin Jackson. **Flagship Stations:** WGN Channel 9 (national cable), Comcast SportsNet (regional cable), WCIU-TV Channel 26.

NEWSPAPERS, Daily Coverage (*national/beat writers): Chicago Sun-Times (Doug Padilla), Chicago Tribune (Bob Foltman, *Phil Rogers), Arlington Heights Daily Herald (Scot Gregor), Daily Southtown (Joe Cowley). **MLB.com:** Scott Merkin, Damon Young.

CLEVELAND INDIANS

Radio Announcers: Tom Hamilton, Mike Hegan, Matt Underwood. **Flagship Station:** WTAM 1100-AM.

TV Announcers: Rick Manning, John Sanders, Mike Hegan. **Flagship Station:** Fox Sports Net.

NEWSPAPERS, Daily Coverage (beat writers): Canton Repository, Cleveland Plain Dealer (Paul Hoynes), Lake County News-Herald (Jim Ingraham), Akron Beacon-Journal (Sheldon Ocker), Canton Repository (Andy Call). **MLB.com:** Justice Hill.

DETROIT TIGERS

Radio Announcers: Dan Dickerson, Jim Price. **Flagship Station:** WXYT 1270-AM.

TV Announcers: Rod Allen, Mario Impemba. **Flagship Station:** Fox Sports Net Detroit.

NEWSPAPERS, Daily Coverage (beat writers): Detroit Free Press (John Lowe, Gene Guidi), Detroit News (Tom Gage), Oakland Press (Crystal Evola, Pat Caputo), Booth Newspapers (Danny Knobler), Windsor Star (Jim Parker). **MLB.com:** Jason Beck.

KANSAS CITY ROYALS

Radio Announcers: Ryan Lefebvre, Denny Matthews. **Flagship Station:** WHB 810-AM.

TV Announcers: Bob Davis, Paul Splittorff. **Flagship Stations:** Royals Television Network.

NEWSPAPERS, Daily Coverage (beat writers): Kansas City Star (Bob Dutton). **MLB.com:** Dick Kaegel, Chris Shaeffer.

MINNESOTA TWINS

Radio Announcers: Herb Carneal, John Gordon, Dan Gladden. **Flagship Station:** WCCO 830-AM.

TV Announcers: Bert Blyleven, Dick Bremer. **Flagship Station:** Fox Sports Net.

NEWSPAPERS, Daily Coverage (beat writers): St. Paul Pioneer Press (Gordon Wittenmyer), Minneapolis Star Tribune (LaVelle Neal). **MLB.com:** Mark Sheldon.

NEW YORK YANKEES

Radio Announcers: John Sterling, Suzyn Waldman. **Flagship Station:** WCBS 880-AM.

TV Announcers: Michael Kay, Jim Kaat, Ken Singleton, Paul O'Neill. **Flagship Stations:** YES (Yankees Entertainment & Sports) Network.

NEWSPAPERS, Daily Coverage (*national/beat writers): New York Daily News (*John Harper, *Bill Madden, Anthony McCarron), New York Post (George King, *Joel Sherman), New York Times (*Murray Chass, *Jack Curry, Tyler Kepner), Newark Star-Ledger (Dan Graziano, *Larry Rocca), The Bergen Record (Pete Caldera, *Bob Klapisch), Newsday (Jim Baumbach, *Jon Heyman), Hartford Courant (Dom Amore, *Jack O'Connell), The Journal News (John Delcos). **MLB.com:** Mark Feinsand, Tom Singer.

OAKLAND ATHLETICS

Radio Announcers: Bill King, Ray Fosse, Ken Korach. **Flagship Station:** KFRC 610-AM. **TV Announcers:** Ray Fosse,

Hank Greenwald, Tim Roye, Glen Kuiper. **Flagship Stations:** KICU, Fox Sports Net (regional cable).
   NEWSPAPERS, Daily Coverage (*national/beat writers): San Francisco Chronicle (*John Shea, Susan Slusser), Oakland Tribune (Josh Suchon), Contra Costa Times/San Jose Mercury News (Joe Roderick), Sacramento Bee (Tim Casey), Santa Rosa Press Democrat (Jeff Fletcher). **MLB.com:** John Schlegel.

SEATTLE MARINERS
   TV/Radio Announcers: Ron Fairly, Dave Henderson, Dave Niehaus, Rick Rizzs, Dave Valle.
   Flagship Stations: KOMO 1000-AM (radio), Fox Sports Net (TV).
   NEWSPAPERS, Daily Coverage (*national/beat writers): Seattle Times (Bob Finnigan, *Larry Stone), Seattle Post-Intelligencer (*Dave Andriesen, John Hickey), Tacoma News Tribune (Larry LaRue), The Everett Herald (Kirby Arnold), Kyodo News (Keizo Konishi), Nikkan Sports (Mamoru Shikama). **MLB.com:** Jim Street.

TAMPA BAY DEVIL RAYS
   Radio Announcers: Andy Freed, Dave Wills. **Flagship Station:** WHNZ 1250-AM.
   TV Announcers: Dewayne Staats, Joe Magrane. **Flagship Stations:** WXPX-TV PAX 66, Fox Sports Net (regional cable).
   NEWSPAPERS, Daily Coverage (beat writers): St. Petersburg Times (Marc Topkin), Tampa Tribune (Carter Gaddis), Bradenton Herald (Roger Mooney), Port Charlotte Sun-Herald (John Fineran), Lakeland Ledger (Dick Scanlan), Sarasota Herald-Tribune (Dennis Maffazoli). **MLB.com:** Paul Smith.

TEXAS RANGERS
   Radio Announcers: Eric Nadel, Victor Rojas; Spanish—Eleno Ornelas, Jose Guzman. **Flagship Station:** KRLD 1080-AM, KESS 1270-AM (Spanish).
   TV Announcers: Josh Lewin, Tom Grieve. **Flagship Stations:** KDFI, KDFW, Fox Sports Net (regional cable).
   NEWSPAPERS, Daily Coverage (beat writers): Dallas Morning News (Evan Grant, Ben Shpigel), Fort Worth Star-Telegram (T.R. Sullivan, Kathleen O'Brien). **MLB.com:** Jesse Sanchez.

TORONTO BLUE JAYS
   Radio Announcers: Tom Cheek, Jerry Howarth. **Flagship Station:** The Fan 590-AM.
   TV Announcers: Rogers SportsNet—Unavailable. TSN—Rod Black, Pat Tabler. **Flagship Stations:** Rogers SportsNet (regional cable), The Sports Network.
   NEWSPAPERS, Daily Coverage (*national/beat writers): Toronto Sun (Mike Rutsey, *Bob Elliott, Mike Ganter), Toronto Star (Geoff Baker, *Richard Griffin, Alan Ryan, Mark Zwolinski), Globe and Mail (Larry Millson, *Jeff Blair). **MLB.com:** Spencer Fordin.

NATIONAL LEAGUE

ARIZONA DIAMONDBACKS
   Radio Announcers: Thom Brennaman, Jeff Munn, Ken Phelps, Greg Schulte; Spanish—Miguel Quintana, Oscar Soria, Richard Saenz. **Flagship Stations:** KTAR 620-AM, KSUN 1400-AM (Spanish).
   TV Announcers: Thom Brennaman, Mark Grace, Joe Garagiola, Greg Schulte. **Flagship Stations:** KTVK-TV 3, Fox Sports Net (regional cable).
   Newspapers, Daily Coverage (beat writers): Arizona Republic (Bob McManaman), East Valley Tribune (Jack Magruder), Arizona Daily Star, Tucson Citizen (Ken Brazzle). **MLB.com:** Steve Gilbert.

ATLANTA BRAVES
   Radio Announcers: Skip Caray, Chip Caray, Joe Simpson, Don Sutton, Pete Van Wieren. **Flagship Station:** WGST 640-AM.
   TV Announcers: TBS—Skip Caray, Chip Caray, Joe Simpson, Don Sutton, Pete Van Wieren; Fox Sports Net—Bob Rathbun, Tom Paciorek. **Flagship Stations:** TBS (national cable); Fox Sports Net, Turner South (regional cable).
   NEWSPAPERS, Daily Coverage (*national/beat writers): Atlanta Journal-Constitution (*Guy Curtwright, Dave O'Brien). **MLB.com:** Mark Bowman.

CHICAGO CUBS
   Radio Announcers: Pat Hughes, Ron Santo. **Flagship Station:** WGN 720-AM.
   TV Announcers: Len Kasper, Bob Brenly. **Flagship Stations:** WGN Channel 9 (national cable), Comcast SportsNet (regional cable), WCIU-TV Channel 26.
   NEWSPAPERS, Daily Coverage (*national/beat writers): Chicago Tribune (*Phil Rogers, Paul Sullivan), Chicago Sun-Times (Mike Kiley), Arlington Heights Daily Herald (Bruce Miles), Daily Southtown (Jeff Vorva). **MLB.com:** Carrie Muskat.

CINCINNATI REDS
   Radio Announcers: Marty Brennaman, Steve Stewart, Joe Nuxhall. **Flagship Station:** WLW 700-AM.
   TV Announcers: George Grande, Chris Welsh. **Flagship Station:** Fox Sports Net.
   NEWSPAPERS, Daily Coverage (beat writers): Cincinnati Enquirer (John Fay), Cincinnati Post (Marc Lancaster), Dayton Daily News (Hal McCoy), Columbus Dispatch (Jim Massie). **MLB.com:** Todd Lorenz.

COLORADO ROCKIES
   Radio Announcers: Jack Corrigan, Jeff Kingery. **Flagship Station:** KOA 850-AM.
   TV Announcers: Drew Goodman, George Frazier. **Flagship Stations:** KTVD Channel 20, Fox Sports Net (regional cable).
   NEWSPAPERS, Daily Coverage (*national/beat writers): Rocky Mountain News (*Tracy Ringolsby, Jack Etkin), Denver Post (Troy Renck, *Mike Klis). **MLB.com:** Thomas Harding.

FLORIDA MARLINS
   Radio Announcers: Jon Sciambi, Dave Van Horne. Spanish—Felo Ramirez, Luis Quintana. **Flagship Stations:** WQAM 560-AM, WQBA 1140-AM (Spanish).
   TV Announcer: Tommy Hutton. **Flagship Stations:** PAX 35 and 67, Fox Sports Net (regional cable).
   NEWSPAPERS, Daily Coverage (*national/beat writers): Miami Herald (Kevin Baxter, Clark Spencer), Fort

Lauderdale Sun-Sentinel (*Mike Berardino, Juan Rodriguez), Palm Beach Post (Joe Capozzi). Spanish—El Nuevo Herald (Jorge Ebro). **MLB.com:** Joe Frisaro.

HOUSTON ASTROS

Radio Announcers: Alan Ashby, Milo Hamilton; Spanish—Francisco Ernesto Ruiz, Alex Trevino. **Flagship Stations:** KTRH 740-AM, KLAT 1010-AM (Spanish).

TV Announcers: Bill Brown, Jim Deshaies, Larry Dierker. **Flagship Station:** Fox Sports Net.

NEWSPAPERS, Daily Coverage (beat writers): Houston Chronicle (Jesus Ortiz, Richard Justice, Brian McTaggert), Beaumont Enterprise (Paula Hunt), Port Arthur News (Tom Halliburton), The Herald Coaster (Bill Hartman). **MLB.com:** Alyson Footer, Jim Molony.

LOS ANGELES DODGERS

Radio Announcers: Vin Scully, Rick Monday, Charley Steiner; Spanish—Jaime Jarrin, Fernando Valenzuela, Pepe Yniguez. **Flagship Stations:** KFWB 980-AM, KWKW 1330-AM (Spanish).

TV Announcers: Vin Scully, Rick Monday. **Flagship Stations:** KCOP Channel 13, Fox Sports Net (regional cable).

NEWSPAPERS, Daily Coverage (*national/beat writers): Los Angeles Times (Tim Brown, Steve Henson, *Ross Newhan), South Bay Daily Breeze (Bill Cizek), Los Angeles Daily News (Tony Jackson), Orange County Register (Bill Plunkett), Riverside Press-Enterprise (Allison Otto). Spanish—La Opinion (Carlos Alvarado). **MLB.com:** Ken Gurnick.

MILWAUKEE BREWERS

Radio Announcers: Bob Uecker, Jim Powell. **Flagship Station:** WTMJ 620-AM.

TV Announcers: Bill Schroeder, Daron Sutton. **Flagship Station:** Fox Sports Net.

NEWSPAPERS, Daily Coverage (beat writers): Milwaukee Journal Sentinel (Tom Haudricourt, Drew Olson), Wisconsin State Journal (Vic Feuerherd). **MLB.com:** Adam McCalvy.

NEW YORK METS

Radio Announcers: Gary Cohen, Ed Coleman, Howie Rose. **Flagship Station:** WFAN 660-AM.

TV Announcers: Fran Healy, Keith Hernandez, Ralph Kiner, Matt Loughlin, Tim O'Brien, Ted Robinson, Tom Seaver. **Flagship Stations:** WPIX-TV, Fox Sports Net (regional cable), Madison Square Garden (regional cable).

NEWSPAPERS, Daily Coverage (*national/beat writers): New York Times (*Murray Chass, *Jack Curry, Lee Jenkins), New York Daily News (*Bill Madden, Adam Rubin), New York Post (Mark Hale, *Joel Sherman), Newsday (*Jon Heyman, Dave Lennon), Newark Star-Ledger (Don Burke, *Larry Rocca), The Bergen Record (*Bob Klapisch, Steve Popper), The News Journal (Pete Abraham). **MLB.com:** Kevin Czerwinski.

PHILADELPHIA PHILLIES

Radio Announcers: Larry Andersen, Scott Graham, Harry Kalas, Tom McCarthy, Chris Wheeler. **Flagship Stations:** WPHT 1210-AM, WIP 610-AM.

TV Announcers: Larry Andersen, Harry Kalas, Chris Wheeler. **Flagship Stations:** WPSG UPN-57, Comcast SportsNet (regional cable).

NEWSPAPERS, Daily Coverage (*national/beat writers): Philadelphia Inquirer (Todd Zolecki, *Jim Salisbury), Philadelphia Daily News (*Paul Hagen, Marcus Hayes), Bucks County Courier Times (Randy Miller), Delaware County Times (Dennis Deitch), Wilmington News-Journal (Edward de la Fuente). **MLB.com:** Ken Mandel.

PITTSBURGH PIRATES

Radio Announcers: Steve Blass, Greg Brown, Lanny Frattare, Bob Walk. **Flagship Station:** KDKA 1020-AM.

TV Announcers: Steve Blass, Greg Brown, Lanny Frattare, Bob Walk. **Flagship Station:** Fox Sports Net.

NEWSPAPERS, Daily Coverage (beat writers): Pittsburgh Post-Gazette (Dejan Kovacevic), Pittsburgh Tribune-Review (Joe Rutter), Beaver County Times (John Perrotto). **MLB.com:** Ed Eagle.

ST. LOUIS CARDINALS

Radio Announcers: Mike Shannon, Wayne Hagin. **Flagship Station:** KMOX 1120-AM.

TV Announcers: Joe Buck , Al Hrabosky, Dan McLaughlin, Rick Horton, Bob Carpenter. **Flagship Stations:** KPLR Channel 11, Fox Sports Net (regional cable).

NEWSPAPER, Daily Coverage (beat writers): St. Louis Post-Dispatch (Joe Strauss, Rick Hummel), Belleville, Ill., News-Democrat (Joe Ostermeier, David Wilhelm). **MLB.com:** Matthew Leach.

SAN DIEGO PADRES

Radio Announcers: Jerry Coleman, Ted Leitner. **Flagship Station:** XPRS 1090-AM.

TV Announcers: Matt Vasgersian, Mark Grant, Tony Gwynn. **Flagship Station:** Channel 4 Padres (cable).

NEWSPAPERS, Daily Coverage (beat writers): San Diego Union-Tribune (Tom Krasovic, Bill Center), North County Times (Brian Hiro, John Maffei). **MLB.com:** Mike Scarr.

SAN FRANCISCO GIANTS

Radio Announcers: Mike Krukow, Duane Kuiper, Jon Miller, Greg Papa, Dave Flemming. **Flagship Station:** KNBR 680-AM. **TV Announcers:** FOX—Mike Krukow, Duane Kuiper; KTVU—Jon Miller, Duane Kuiper, Mike Krukow, Greg Papa. **Flagship Stations:** KTVU-TV 2, Fox Sports Net (regional cable).

NEWSPAPERS, Daily Coverage (*national/beat writers): San Francisco Chronicle (Henry Schulman, *John Shea), San Jose Mercury News (Chris Haft), Sacramento Bee (Nick Peters), Oakland Tribune (Andrew Baggarly), Santa Rosa Press Democrat (Jeff Fletcher). **MLB.com:** Rich Draper.

WASHINGTON NATIONALS

Radio Announcers: Unavailable. **Flagship Station:** Unavailable.

TV Announcers: Unavailable. **Flagship Station:** Unavailable.

NEWSPAPERS, Daily Coverage (beat writers): Baltimore Sun, Washington Post, Washington Times. **MLB.com:** Bill Ladson.

NATIONAL MEDIA
INFORMATION

ELIAS SPORTS BUREAU INC.
Official Major League Statistician

Mailing Address: 500 Fifth Ave., Suite 2140, New York, NY 10110. **Telephone:** (212) 869-1530. **FAX:** (212) 354-0980. **Website:** www.esb.com.
President: Seymour Siwoff.
Executive Vice President: Steve Hirdt. **Vice President:** Peter Hirdt. **Data Processing Manager:** Chris Thorn.

MAJOR LEAGUE BASEBALL ADVANCED MEDIA
Official Minor League Statistician

Mailing Address: 75 Ninth Ave., New York, NY 10011. **Telephone:** (212) 485-3444. **FAX:** (212) 485-3456.
Director, Minor League Baseball Advanced Media: Misann Ellmaker. **Deputy Project Manager, Minor League Baseball Advanced Media:** Nathan Blackmon. **Manager, Data Syndication:** Chris Lentine. **Senior Reporter:** Jonathan Mayo. **Editorial Producer:** Andrew Tarica.

STATS, Inc.
Mailing Address: 8130 Lehigh Ave., Morton Grove, IL 60053. **Telephone:** (847) 583-2100. **FAX:** (847) 470-9140. **Website:** biz.stats.com.
Chief Executive Officers: Gary Walrath. **Senior Vice Presidents:** Steve Byrd, Robert Schur. **Director, Sales:** Jim Capuano, Greg Kirkorsky. **Director, Marketing:** Walter Lis. **Director, Sports Operations:** Allan Spear. **Manager, Baseball Operations:** Jeff Chernow.

ESPN/ESPN2

- Baseball Tonight
- Sunday Night Baseball
- Monday Night Baseball
- Wednesday Night Doubleheaders
- Wednesday Afternoon Baseball
- ESPN DayGame
- Opening Day, Holidays
- Home Run Derby, All-Star programming
- Spring Training Games

Mailing Address, ESPN Connecticut: ESPN Plaza, 935 Middle St., Bristol, CT 06010. **Telephone:** (860) 766-2000. **FAX:** (860) 766-2213.
Mailing Address, ESPN New York Executive Offices: 77 W. 66th St., New York, NY, 10023. **Telephone:** (212) 456-7777. **FAX:** (212) 456-2930.
President: George Bodenheimer.
Executive Vice President, Administration: Ed Durso. **Executive VP, Production/Technical Operations:** Steve Anderson. **Executive VP, Programming/Production:** Mark Shapiro.
Executive Vice President/Executive Editor: John Walsh. **Senior VP, Programming Strategy:** Len Deluca. **Vice President, Programming:** Mike Ryan. **Senior VP, Remote Production:** Jed Drake. **Senior Coordinating Producer, Remote Production:** Tim Scanlan. **Coordinating Producer, Remote Production:** Patrick Cavanagh. **Senior VPs/Managing Editors, Studio Production:** Bob Eaton, Norby Williamson. **Senior Coordinating Producer, Baseball Tonight:** Jay Levy.

ESPN.com
Executive Editor: Leonardo Lampugnale.

ESPN Classic
Vice President, Programming/Acquisitions: Crowley Sullivan.

ESPN International, ESPN Deportes
Senior Vice President/Managing Director, ESPN International: Russell Wolff. **Senior VP, International Productions, ESPN Classic and ESPNEWS:** Jodi Markley. **VP, International Production and Operations:** Chris Calcinari

Communications
Senior Vice Presidents: Rosa Gatti, Chris LaPlaca. **Senior Director:** Diane Lamb. **Senior Publicist:** Nate Smeltz.
Commentators, Sunday Night Baseball: Play-by-play—Jon Miller. Analyst—Joe Morgan.
Commentators, ESPN Deportes: Play-by-play—Ernesto Jerez. Analysts—Candy Maldonado Jr.
Other Commentators: Dave Barnett, Chris Berman, Larry Bowa, Jeff Brantley, Dave Campbell, Tom Candiotti, Bob Carpenter, Peter Gammons, Tony Gwynn, David Justice, John Kruk, Tim Kurkjian, Buck Martinez, Gary Miller, Dave O'Brien, Kyle Peterson, Karl Ravech, Harold Reynolds, Dave Ryan, Samantha Ryan, Dan Shulman, Jayson Stark, Rick Sutcliffe.

FOX SPORTS

- Saturday Game of the Week
- All-Star Game, 2005-2006
- Division Series, 2005-2006
- American League Championship Series, 2005-2006
- National League Championship Series, 2005-2006
- World Series, 2005-2006

Mailing Address, Los Angeles: Fox Network Center, Building 101, Fifth floor, 10201 West Pico Blvd., Los Angeles, CA 90035. **Telephone:** (310) 369-6000. **FAX:** (310) 969-9467.

Mailing Address, New York: 1211 Avenue of the Americas, 28th Floor, New York, NY 10036. **Telephone:** (212) 556-2500. **FAX:** (212) 354-6902. **Website:** www.foxsports.com.

Chairman/Chief Executive Officer, Fox Sports Television Group: David Hill. **President, Executive Producer:** Ed Goren. **Executive Vice President, Production/Coordinating Studio Producer:** Scott Ackerson. **Executive VP, Production/Senior Producer:** Bill Brown. **Senior VP, Production:** Jack Simmons. **VP, Operations/MLB on Fox:** Jerry Steinberg. **Studio Producer, MLB on Fox:** Gary Lang. **Studio Director, MLB on Fox:** Bob Levy.

Senior VP, Communcations: Lou D'Ermilio. **VP, Communications:** Dan Bell. **Manager, Communications:** Tim Buckman. **Publicist:** Ileana Pena.

Broadcasters: Thom Brennaman, Joe Buck, Josh Lewin, Kevin Kennedy, Steve Lyons, Tim McCarver, Jeanne Zelasko.

FOX SPORTS NET

- Regional Coverage

Mailing Address: 10201 W. Pico Blvd., Building 101, Los Angeles, CA 90035. **Telephone:** (310) 369-1000. **FAX:** (310) 969-6049.

President, Chief Executive Officer/Fox Sports Television Group: David Hill. **President, Fox Sports Net/Fox Sports Cable Networks:** Bob Thompson. **Chief Operating Officer, Fox Sports Net:** Randy Freer. **President, Advertising Sales, Fox Cable Networks:** Lou LaTorre. **Executive VP, Programming/Production:** George Greenberg. **Manager, Communications:** Justin Simon. **FSN News Manager:** Geoffrey Birchfield. **Publicist:** Emily Corliss.

Other Television Networks

ABC SPORTS

Mailing Address: 47 West 66th St., New York, NY 10023. **Telephone:** (212) 456-4878. **FAX:** (212) 456-2877. **Website:** www.abcsports.com.

President, ABC Sports: George Bodenheimer. **Senior Vice President, Programming:** Loren Matthews. **VP, Media Relations:** Mark Mandel. **Publicist, Media Relations:** Adam Freifeld.

CBS SPORTS

Mailing Address: 51 W. 52nd St., New York, NY 10019. **Telephone:** (212) 975-5230. **FAX:** (212) 975-4063.

President, CBS Sports: Sean McManus. **Executive Producer:** Tony Petitti. **Senior Vice Presidents, Programming:** Mike Aresco, Rob Correa. **Vice President, Communications:** Leslie Anne Wade.

NBC SPORTS

Mailing Address: 30 Rockefeller Plaza, Suite 1558, New York, NY 10112. **Telephone:** (212) 664-2014. **FAX:** (212) 664-6365.

Chairman, NBC Sports: Dick Ebersol. **President, NBC Sports:** Ken Schanzer.

Vice President, Sports Communications: Kevin Sullivan.

Superstations

ROGERS SPORTSNET (Canada)

Mailing Address: 333 Bloor St. East, Toronto, Ontario M4W 1G9. **Telephone:** (416) 332-5600. **FAX:** (416) 332-5767. **Website:** www.sportsnet.ca.

President, Rogers Media: Tony Viner. **President, Rogers Sportsnet:** Doug Beeforth. **Vice President, Communications:** Jan Innes. **Director, Communications/Promotions:** Dave Rashford.

THE SPORTS NETWORK (Canada)

Mailing Address: Bell Globemedia Inc., 9 Channel Nine Court, Scarborough, Ontario M1S 4B5. **Telephone:** (416) 332-5000. **FAX:** (416) 332-4337. **Website:** www.tsn.ca

Executive Producer, News: Marc Milliere. **Senior Vice President, Programming:** Phil King. **Executive Producer:** Paul McLean. **VP, Production:** Rick Chisholm. **Communications Manager:** Andrea Goldstein. **Executive Producer, tsn.ca:** Mike Day.

TBS

(Atlanta Braves)

Mailing Address: One CNN Center, P.O. Box 105366, Atlanta, GA 30348. **Telephone:** (404) 827-1700. **FAX:** (404) 827-1593. **Website:** www.superstation.com.

Executive Producer: Glenn Diamond.

WGN

(Chicago Cubs, Chicago White Sox)

Mailing Address: 2501 W Bradley Pl., Chicago, IL 60618. **Telephone:** (773) 528-2311. **FAX:** (773) 528-6050.

Website: www.wgntv.com.
Director, Programming: Bob Vorwald.

RADIO NETWORKS

ESPN RADIO
- Game of the Week
- Sunday Night Baseball
- All-Star Game
- Division Series
- League Championship Series
- World Series

Mailing Address: ESPN Plaza, 935 Middle St., Bristol, CT 06010. **Telephone:** (860) 766-2000. **FAX:** (860) 589-5523.

General Manager: Bruce Gilbert. **Executive Producer, Remote Broadcasts:** John Martin. **Chief Engineer:** Tom Evans. **Director, Operations:** Keith Goralski. **Program Director:** Pete Gianesini. **Marketing/Promotions Coordinator:** Janet Alden. **Vice President, Sports/ABC Radio Network:** T. J. Lambert.

Commentators: Joe D'Ambrosio, Dave Barnett, Dave Campbell, Jim Durham, Jon Miller, Chris Moore, Joe Morgan, Harold Reynolds, Dan Shulman.

MLB.COM RADIO

Mailing Address: 75 Ninth Ave., New York, NY 10011. **Telephone:** (212) 485-3444. **FAX:** (212) 485-3456. **E-Mail Address:** radio@mlb.com. **Website:** www.mlb.com.

Hosts: Seth Everett, Billy Sample. **Contributor:** Brian McRae. **Coordinator:** Craig Chambers. **Producers:** Mike Dillon, Dan Gentile, Vinny Micucci, Mike Siano.

XM SATELLITE RADIO
- 24-hour MLB Home Plate channel
- MLB live play-by-play for spring training, regular season, playoffs, World Series
- MLB En Espanol channel

Mailing Address: 1500 Eckington Place NE, Washington, DC 20002. **Telephone:** (202) 380-4000. **FAX:** 202-380-4500. **E-Mail Address:** mlb@xmradio.com. **Website:** www.xmradio.com.

Executive Vice President, Programming: Eric Logan. **Vice President, Talk Programming:** Kevin Straley. **Vice President, Corporate Affairs:** Chance Patterson. **Program Director, MLB Home Plate channel:** Chuck Dickemann. **Director, Sports Marketing:** George Perry. **Commentators:** Cal Ripken, Jr., Billy Ripken, Rob Dibble, Larry Bowa, Kevin Kennedy, Buck Martinez, Mark Patrick, Charley Steiner, Phil Wood, Ronnie Lane, Joe Castellano.

ABC SPORTS RADIO

Mailing Address: 125 West End Ave., Sixth Floor, New York, NY 10023. **Telephone:** (212) 456-5185. **Studio:** (800) 221-4559. **E-Mail Address:** abcsportsradio@abc.com.

Vice President, Radio: Steve Jones. **General Manager, News/Sports:** Michael Rizzo. **Operations Manager:** Cliff Bond. **Producers:** Andrew Bogusch, Eric Duetsch, Howie Karpin, Mike Kirk, Tim McDermott, Yvette Michael, Tushar Saxena. Steve White. **Anchors:** Todd Ant, John Cloghessy, Johnny Holliday.

SPORTING NEWS RADIO NETWORK

Mailing Address: P.O. Box 509, Techny, IL 60082. **Telephone:** (847) 509-1661. **Producers Line:** (800) 224-2004. **FAX:** (847) 509-1677. **Website:** www.sportingnewsradio.com.

President: Clancy Woods. **Executive Vice President, Sales:** Bill Peterson. **Acting Director, Affiliate Relations:** Ryan Williams. **Program Director:** Matt Nahigian. **Sports Director:** Randy Merkin. **Executive Producer:** Jen Williams.

SPORTS BYLINE USA

Mailing Address: 300 Broadway, Suite 8, San Francisco, CA 94133. **Telephone:** (415) 434-8300. **Guest Line:** (800) 358-4457. **Studio Line:** (800) 878-7529. **FAX:** (415) 391-2569. **E-Mail Address:** byline@pacbell.net. **Website:** www.sportsbyline.com.

President: Darren Peck. **Executive Producer:** Alex Murillo.

NEWS ORGANIZATIONS

ASSOCIATED PRESS

Mailing Address: 450 W. 33rd St., New York, NY 10010. **Telephone:** (212) 621-1630. **FAX:** (212) 621-1639. **Website:** www.ap.org.

Sports Editor: Terry Taylor. **Deputy Sports Editor:** Aaron Watson. **Sports Photo Editor:** Mike Feldman. **Baseball Writers:** Ron Blum, Mike Fitzpatrick, Jim Litke, Ben Walker, Steve Wilstein.

BLOOMBERG SPORTS NEWS

Address: 400 College Road East, P.O. Box 888, Princeton, NJ 08540. **Telephone:** (609) 750-4691. **FAX:** (609) 897-8397.

Sports Editor: Jay Beberman. **Deputy Sports Editor:** Mike Sillup.

CANADIAN PRESS

Mailing Address, Toronto: 36 King St. East, Toronto, Ontario M5C 2L9. **Mailing Address, Montreal:** 215 Saint-Jacques St., Suite 100, Montreal, Quebec H2Y 1M6. **Telephone:** (416) 507-2154 (Toronto), (514) 849-3212 (Montreal). **FAX:** (416) 507-2074 (Toronto), (514) 282-6915 (Montreal). **E-Mail Address:** sports@cp.org.

Sports Editor: Neil Davidson. **Baseball Writer:** Shi Davidi. **Baseball Writer, Montreal:** Bill Beacon.

MLB ADVANCED MEDIA (MLB.COM)

Office Address: 75 Ninth Ave., 5th Floor, New York, NY 10011. **Telephone:** (212) 485-3444. **FAX:** (212) 485-3456. **Chief Executive Officer:** Bob Bowman.

Senior Vice President, Chief Marketing Officer: Holly Arnowitz. **Director, Ticketing:** Heather Benz. **VP, Multi-Media:** Jane Buford. **VP, Human Resources:** Leslie Knickerbocker.

Senior VP/Chief Technical Officer: Joe Choti. **VP, Chief Financial Officer:** Jeff D'Onofrio. **Senior VP, Corporate Communications:** Jim Gallagher. **Senior VP, E-Commerce:** Noah Garden. **Senior VP/Editor-In-Chief, mlb.com:** Dinn Mann. **VP, Design:** Deck Rees.

Senior VP/General Counsel: Michael Mellis, **Senior VP, Business Development:** George Kliavkoff. **VP, Sponsorship:** Mark Sage.

SPORTSTICKER

Mailing Address: ESPN Plaza, Building B, Fourth Floor, Bristol, CT 06010. **Telephone:** (860) 766-1899. **FAX:** (800) 336-0383. **E-Mail Address:** newsroom@sportsticker.com.

News Director: Chris Bernucca. **Baseball Editor:** Anthony Mormile. **Manager, Customer Marketing/Communications:** Lou Monaco.

Senior Bureau Manager: Michael Walczak. **Bureau Managers:** Tom Diorio, Brian Rabufetti. **Programmer Analysts:** John Foley, Walter Kent.

Historical Consultant: Bill Weiss.

PRESS ASSOCIATIONS

BASEBALL WRITERS ASSOCIATION OF AMERICA

Mailing Address: P.O. Box 610611, Bayside, NY 11361. **Telephone:** (718) 767-2582. **FAX:** (718) 767-2583. **E-Mail Address:** bbwaa@aol.com.

President: T.R. Sullivan (Fort Worth Star Telegram). **Vice President:** Peter Schmuck (Baltimore Sun). **Secretary-Treasurer:** Jack O'Connell (BBWAA).

Board of Directors: Paul Hagen (Philadelphia Daily News), Danny Knobler (Booth Newspapers), Drew Olson (Milwaukee Journal Sentinel), Susan Slusser (San Francisco Chronicle).

NATIONAL COLLEGIATE BASEBALL WRITERS ASSOCIATION

Mailing Address: 2201 Stemmons Fwy., 28th Floor, Dallas, TX 75207. **Telephone:** (214) 753-0102. **FAX:** (214) 753-0145. **E-Mail Address:** bo@big12sports.com.

Executive Director, Newsletter Editor: Bo Carter (Big 12 Conference).

President: Mike Montore (Southern Mississippi). **First Vice President:** Todd Lamb (Ohio State). **Second VP:** Dave Fanucchi (USA Baseball). **Third VP:** Michael Carey (St. John's). **Secretary/Treasurer:** Russ Anderson (Conference USA)

NEWSPAPERS/PERIODICALS

USA TODAY

Mailing Address: 7950 Jones Branch Dr., McLean, VA 22108. **Telephones/Baseball Desk:** (703) 854-5286, 854-5954, 854-3706, 854-3744, 854-3746. **FAX:** (703) 854-2072. **Website:** www.usatoday.com.

Publishing Frequency: Daily (Monday-Friday).

Baseball Editors: Cesar Brioso, Peter Barzilai, Matt Cimento, John Tkach. **Baseball Columnist:** Hal Bodley. **Baseball Writers:** Mel Antonen, Rod Beaton, Mike Dodd, Gary Graves, Chuck Johnson.

THE SPORTING NEWS

Mailing Address: 10176 Corporate Square Dr., Suite 200, St. Louis, MO 63132. **Telephone:** (314) 997-7111. **FAX:** (314) 997-0765. **Website:** www.sportingnews.com.

Publishing Frequency: Weekly.

Senior Vice President/Editorial Director: John Rawlings. **Executive Editor:** Bob Hille. **Managing Editor:** Stan McNeal. **Senior Writer:** Ken Rosenthal. **Senior Editor:** Tom Gatto. **Senior Photo Editor:** Paul Nisely.

SPORTS ILLUSTRATED

Mailing Address: 135 W. 50th St., New York, NY 10020. **Telephone:** (212) 522-1212. **FAX, Editorial:** (212) 522-4543. **FAX, Public Relations:** (212) 522-4832. **Website:** www.si.com.

Publishing Frequency: Weekly.

Managing Editor: Terry McDonnell. **Senior Editor:** Larry Burke. **Associate Editor:** B.J. Schecter. **Senior Writers:** Jeff Pearlman, Tom Verducci. **Staff Writer:** Danny Habib. **Writers/Reporters:** Albert Chen, Gene Menez. **Vice President, Communications:** Art Berke.

USA TODAY SPORTS WEEKLY

Mailing Address: 7950 Jones Branch Dr., McLean, VA 22108. **Telephone:** (800) 872-1415, (703) 854-6319. **FAX:** (703) 854-2034. **Website:** www.usatoday.com.

Publishing Frequency: Weekly.

Publisher/Executive Editor: Lee Ivory. **Managing Editor:** Tim McQuay. **Deputy Managing Editor:** Scott Zucker. **Senior Editor:** Frank Cooney. **Operations Editor:** Amanda Tinkham Boltax. **Senior Writers:** Bob Nightengale, Paul White, Lisa Winston. **Writers:** Chris Colston, Steve DiMeglio, Seth Livingstone.

STREET AND SMITH'S SPORTS BUSINESS JOURNAL

Mailing Address: 120 W. Morehead St., Suite 310, Charlotte, NC 28202. **Telephone:** (704) 973-1400. **FAX:** (704)

973-1401. **Website:** www.sportsbusinessjournal.com.
Publishing Frequency: Weekly.
Publisher: Richard Weiss. **Editor-in-chief:** Abraham Madkour. **Managing Editor:** Ross Nethery.

ESPN THE MAGAZINE

Mailing Address: 19 E. 34th St., Seventh Floor, New York, NY 10016. **Telephone:** (212) 515-1000. **FAX:** (212) 515-1290. **Website:** www.espn.com.
Publishing Frequency: Bi-weekly.
Executive Editor: Steve Wulf. **Senior Editor:** Jon Scher. **General Editor:** Ed McGregor. **Senior Writers:** Jeff Bradley, Peter Gammons, Tim Keown, Tim Kurkjian, Buster Olney. **Photo Editor:** Catriona Ni Aolain. **Photo Operations Coordinator:** Tricia Reed. **Manager, Communications:** Ashley Swadel.

BASEBALL AMERICA

Address: 201 West Main St., Suite 201, Durham, NC 27702. **Mailing Address:** P.O. Box 2089, Durham, NC 27702. **Telephone:** (919) 682-9635. **FAX:** (919) 682-2880.
Publishing Frequency: Bi-weekly.
President: Catherine Silver. **Publisher:** Lee Folger. **Editor:** Allan Simpson. **Managing Editor:** Will Lingo. **Executive Editor:** Jim Callis. **Senior Writer:** Alan Schwarz.

BASEBALL DIGEST

Mailing Address: 990 Grove St., Evanston, IL 60201. **Telephone:** (847) 491-6440. **FAX:** (847) 491-6203. **E-Mail Address:** bkuenster@centurysports.net. **Website:** www.centurysports.net/baseball.
Publishing Frequency: Monthly, April through January.
Publisher: Norman Jacobs. **Editor:** John Kuenster. **Managing Editor:** Bob Kuenster.

COLLEGIATE BASEBALL

Mailing Address: P.O. Box 50566, Tucson, AZ 85703. **Telephone:** (520) 623-4530. **FAX:** (520) 624-5501. **E-Mail Address:** editor@baseballnews.com. **Website:** www.baseballnews.com.
Publishing Frequency: Bi-weekly, January-June; September, October.
Publisher: Lou Pavlovich. **Editor:** Lou Pavlovich Jr.

JUNIOR BASEBALL MAGAZINE

Mailing Address: P.O. Box 9099, Canoga Park, CA 91309. **Telephone:** (818) 710-1234. **Customer Service:** (888) 487-2448. **FAX:** (818) 710-1877. **E-Mail Address:** editor@juniorbaseball.com. **Website:** www.juniorbaseball.com.
Publishing Frequency: Bi-monthly.
Publisher/Editor: Dave Destler. **Publishing Director:** Dayna Destler.

SPORTS ILLUSTRATED FOR KIDS

Mailing Address: 135 W. 50th St., Fourth Floor, New York, NY 10020. **Telephone:** (212) 522-1212. **FAX:** (212) 522-0120. **Website:** www.sikids.com.
Publishing Frequency: Monthly.
Publisher: Peter Krieger. **Managing Editor:** Neil Cohen. **Assistant Managing Editor:** Peter Kay. **Senior Editor:** John Rolfe.

BASEBALL ANNUALS

ATHLON SPORTS BASEBALL

Mailing Address: 220 25th Ave. N., Suite 200, Nashville, TN 37203. **Telephone:** (615) 327-0747. **FAX:** (615) 327-1149. **E-Mail Address:** info@athlonsports.com. **Website:** www.athlonsports.com.
Chief Executive Officer: Roger Di Silvestro. **President:** Charles Allen. **Managing Editor:** Charlie Miller. **Senior Editor:** Rob Doster. **Editor:** Mitch Light.

SPORTING NEWS BASEBALL YEARBOOK

Mailing Address: 10176 Corporate Square Dr., Suite 200, St. Louis, MO 63132. **Telephone:** (314) 997-7111. **FAX:** (314) 997-0765. **Website:** www.sportingnews.com.
Senior Vice President/Editorial Director: John Rawlings. **Executive Editor:** Bob Hille. **Managing Editor:** Stan McNeal. **Senior Writer:** Ken Rosenthal. **Senior Editor:** Tom Gatto. **Senior Photo Editor:** Paul Nisely.

SPRING TRAINING BASEBALL YEARBOOK

Mailing Address: Vanguard Publications, P.O. Box 667, Chapel Hill, NC 27514. **Telephone:** (919) 967-2420. **FAX:** (919) 967-6294. **E-Mail Address:** vanguard3@mindspring.com. **Website:** www.springtrainingmagazine.com.
Publisher: Merle Thorpe. **Editor:** Myles Friedman.

STREET AND SMITH'S BASEBALL YEARBOOK

Mailing Address: 120 West Morehead St., Suite 230, Charlotte, NC 28202. **Telephone:** (704) 973-1575. **FAX:** (704) 973-1576. **E-Mail Address:** annuals@streetandsmiths.com. **Website:** www.streetandsmiths.com.
Publisher: Mike Kallay. **Managing Editor:** Scott Smith.

Baseball Encyclopedias

THE BASEBALL ENCYCLOPEDIA

Mailing Address: Barnes & Noble Publishing Inc., 122 Fifth Ave., 5th Floor, New York, NY 10011. **Telephone:** (212) 633-3516. **FAX:** (212) 633-3327. **E-Mail Address:** jboudinot@bn.com. **Website:** www.247baseball.com.
Editors: Pete Palmer, Gary Gillette.

THE SPORTS ENCYCLOPEDIA: BASEBALL
Mailing Address: St. Martin's Press, 175 Fifth Ave., New York, NY 10010. **Telephone:** (212) 764-5151. **E-Mail Address:** joseph.rinaldi@stmartins.com. **Website:** www.stmartins.com.
Authors: David Neft, Richard Cohen, Michael Neft. **Editor:** Marc Resnick.

TOTAL BASEBALL
Mailing Address: SportClassic Books, Sport Media Publishing, 21 Carlaw Ave., Toronto, ON M4M 2R6. **Telephone:** (416) 466-0418. **FAX:** (416) 466-9530. **E-Mail Address:** info@sportclassicbooks.com. **Website:** www.sportclassic-books.com.
Editors: John Thorn, Phil Birnbaum, Bill Deane.

HOBBY PUBLICATIONS

BECKETT INC.
Beckett Baseball Collector
Mailing Address: 15850 Dallas Pkwy., Dallas, TX 75248. **Telephone:** (972) 991-6657, (800) 840-3137. **FAX:** (972) 991-8930. **Website:** www.beckett.com.
Chief Executive Officer, Publisher: James Beckett. **President, beckett.com:** Mark Harwell. **Editor:** Mike Payne.

KRAUSE PUBLICATIONS
Mailing Address: 700 E. State St., Iola, WI 54990. **Telephone:** (715) 445-4612. **FAX:** (715) 445-4087. **Website:** www.krause.com, www.collect.com, www.fantasysportsmag.com.
Publisher: Dean Listle.
Editor, Fantasy Sports: Greg Ambrosius. **Editor, Sports Collectors Digest:** T.S. O'Connell. **Editor, Tuff Stuff:** Rocky Landsverk.

TEAM PUBLICATIONS

CITADEL MEDIA
Diehard (Boston Red Sox), Mets Inside Pitch (New York Mets)
Mailing Address: 1916 Pike Place, Suite 12-250, Seattle, WA 98101. **Telephone:** (888) 979-0979. **FAX:** (206) 728-7744.
Publisher, Diehard: J.C. Heckman. **Managing Editor:** Jerry Beach.
Publisher, Inside Pitch: Glen Nelson. **Managing Editor:** Bryan Hoch.

VINE LINE
(Chicago Cubs)
Mailing Address: Chicago Cubs Publications, 1060 W. Addison St., Chicago, IL 60613. **Telephone:** (773) 404-2827. **FAX:** (773) 404-4129. **E-Mail Address:** vineline@cubs.com. **Managing Editor:** Lena McDonagh. **Editor:** Jim McArdle.

YANKEES MAGAZINE
(New York Yankees)
Mailing Address: Yankee Stadium, Bronx, NY 10451. **Telephone:** (800) 469-2657. **Publisher/Director, Publications and Media:** Mark Mandrake. **Managing Editor:** Glenn Slavin.

INDIANS INK
(Cleveland Indians)
Mailing Address: P.O. Box 539, Mentor, OH 44061. **Telephone:** (440) 953-2200. **FAX:** (440) 953-2202. **Editor:** Frank Derry.

OUTSIDE PITCH
(Baltimore Orioles)
Mailing Address: P.O. Box 27143, Baltimore, MD 21230. **Telephone:** (410) 234-8888, (800) 342-4737. FAX: (410) 234-1029. **Website:** www.outsidepitch.com. **Publisher:** David Simone. **Editor:** David Hill.

REDS REPORT
(Cincinnati Reds)
Mailing Address: Columbus Sports Publications, P.O. Box 12453, Columbus, OH 43212. **Telephone:** (614) 486-2202. **FAX:** (614) 486-3650. **Publisher:** Frank Moskowitz. **Editor:** Mark Schmetzer. **Managing Editor:** Mark Rae.

OTHER
INFO

GENERAL
INFORMATION

MAJOR LEAGUE BASEBALL PLAYERS ASSOCIATION

Mailing Address: 12 E. 49th St., 24th Floor, New York, NY 10017. **Telephone:** (212) 826-0808. **FAX:** (212) 752-4378. **E-Mail Address:** feedback@mlbpa.org. **Website:** www.mlbplayers.com.

Year Founded: 1966.

Executive Director, General Counsel: Donald Fehr.

Chief Operating Officer: Gene Orza. **General Counsel:** Michael Weiner. **Assistant General Counsel:** Doyle Pryor, Robert Lenaghan, Jeff Fannell.

Special Assistants to Executive Director: Bobby Bonilla, Phil Bradley, Steve Rogers, Allyne Price.

Managing Officer: Martha Child. **Manager, Financial Operations:** Marietta DiCamillo. **Contract Administrator:** Cindy Abercrombie. **Accounting Assistants:** Terri Hinkley, Yolanda Largo. **Administrative Assistants:** Virginia Carballo, Aisha Hope, Melba Markowitz, Sharon O'Donnell, Lisa Pepin. **Receptionist:** Rebecca Rivera.

Director, Business Affairs/Licensing: Judy Heeter. **General Manager, Licensing:** Richard White. **Director, Communications:** Greg Bouris. **Assistant General Counsel, Licensing:** Evie Goldstein. **Category Director, Interactive Games:** John Olshan. **Communications Manager:** Chris Dahl. **Category Director, Trading Cards/Collectibles:** Evan Kaplan. **Category Manager, Apparel/Novelties:** Nancy Willis. **Manager, Player Trust:** Melissa Persaud. **Administrative Manager:** Heather Gould. **Program Coordinator:** Hillary Falk. **Licensing Assistant:** Eric Rivera. **Manager, Office Services:** Victor Lugo. **Executive Secretary/Licensing:** Sheila Peters.

Executive Board: Player representatives of the 30 major league clubs.

League Representatives: American League—Tony Clark; **National League**—Mark Loretta.

SCOUTING

MAJOR LEAGUE SCOUTING BUREAU

Mailing Address: 3500 Porsche Way, Suite 100, Ontario, CA 91764. **Telephone:** (909) 980-1881. **FAX:** (909) 980-7794.

Year Founded: 1974.

Director: Frank Marcos. **Assistant Director:** Rick Oliver. **Office Coordinator:** Joanne Costanzo. **Administrative Assistant:** Debbie Keedy.

Board of Directors: Sandy Alderson (Major League Baseball), Dave Dombrowski (Tigers), Bob Gebhard (Diamondbacks), Roland Hemond (White Sox), Frank Marcos (MLSB), Omar Minaya (Mets), Randy Smith (Padres), Jimmie Lee Solomon (Major League Baseball), Art Stewart (Royals), Kevin Towers (Padres).

Scouts: Rick Arnold (Spring Mills, PA), Matt Barnicle (Huntington Beach, CA), Andy Campbell (Chandler, AZ), Mike Childers (Lexington, KY), Dick Colpaert (Utica, MI), Craig Conklin (Cayucos, CA), Dan Dixon (Temecula, CA), Jim Elliott (Winston-Salem, NC), Art Gardner (Walnut Grove, MS), Rusty Gerhardt (New London, TX), Dennis Haren (San Diego, CA), Chris Heidt (Austin, TX), Doug Horning (Schererville, IN), Don Jacoby (Winter Haven, FL), Brad Kohler (Bethlehem, PA), Don Kohler (Asbury, NJ), Mike Larson (Waseca, MN), Wayne Mathis (Kansas City, MO), Jethro McIntyre (Pittsburg, CA), Paul Mirocke (Wesley Chapel, FL), Carl Moesche (Gresham, OR), Alex Morales (Wellington, FL), Tim Osborne (Woodstock, GA), Gary Randall (Rock Hill, SC), Willie Romay (Miami Springs, FL), Kevin Saucier (Pensacola, FL), Pat Shortt (South Hempstead, NY), Craig Smajstrla (Pearland, TX), Christie Stancil (Raleigh, NC), Ed Sukla (Irvine, CA), Marv Thompson (Corona, CA), Jim Walton (Shattuck, OK).

Supervisor, Canada: Walt Burrows (Brentwood Bay, BC). **Canadian Scouts:** Curtis Bailey (Red Deer, AB), Jason Chee-Aloy (Toronto, ON), Bill Green (Vancouver, BC), Andrew Halpenny (Winnipeg, MB), Sean Gulliver (St. John's, NF), Ian Jordan (Kirkland, QC), Ken Lenihan (Bedford, NS), Dave McConnell (Kelowna, BC), Dan Mendham (Dorchester, ON), Todd Plaxton (Saskatoon, SK), Jasmin Roy (Longueuil, QC), Tony Wylie (Anchorage, AK).

Supervisor, Puerto Rico: Pepito Centeno (Bayamon, PR).

PROFESSIONAL BASEBALL SCOUTS FOUNDATION

Mailing Address: 9665 Wilshire Blvd., Suite 801, Beverly Hills, CA 90212. **Telephone:** (310) 858 1935. **FAX:** (310) 246-4862. **E-Mail Address:** hitter19@aol.com. **Website:** www.professionalbaseballscoutsfoundation.com.

Chairman: Dennis Gilbert. **Chief Financial Officer:** Joey Behrstock.

Directors: Dan Evans, Bill Gayton, Pat Gillick, Derrick Hall, Roland Hemond, Gary Hughes, Lisa Jackson, Tommy Lasorda, Roberta Mazur, Harry Minor, Bob Nightengale, Tracy Ringolsby, Dale Sutherland, Dave Yoakum, John Young.

SCOUT OF THE YEAR FOUNDATION

Mailing Address: P.O. Box 211585, West Palm Beach, FL 33421. **Telephone:** (561) 798-5897, (561) 818-4329. **FAX:** (561) 798-4644. **E-Mail Address:** bertmazur@aol.com.

President: Roberta Mazur. **Vice President:** Tracy Ringolsby. **Treasurer:** Ron Mazur II.

Board of Advisers: Joe L. Brown, Bob Fontaine, Pat Gillick, Roland Hemond, Gary Hughes, Tommy Lasorda, Allan Simpson, Ron Shapiro, Ted Spencer, Bob Watson.

SCOUTING SERVICES

INSIDE EDGE, INC.

Mailing Address: 5049 Emerson Ave. S., Minneapolis, MN 55419. **Telephone:** (800) 858-3343. **FAX:** (508) 526-6145. **E-Mail Address:** insideedge@aol.com. **Website:** www.inside-edge.com.

Partners: Jay Donchetz, Randy Istre.

PROSPECTS PLUS
(A Joint Venture of Baseball America and Perfect Game USA)
Mailing Address: Baseball America, P.O. Box 2089, Durham, NC 27702. **Telephone:** (800) 845-2726. **FAX:** (919) 682-2880. **E-Mail Addresses:** alanmatthews@baseballamerica.com; jerry@perfectgame.org. **Website:** www.baseballamerica.com/prospectsplus; www.perfectgame.org.
Editors, Baseball America: Alan Matthews, Allan Simpson. **Director, Perfect Game USA:** Jerry Ford.

SKILLSHOW, INC.
Mailing Address: 290 King of Prussia Rd., Suite 322, Radnor, PA 19087. **Telephone:** (610) 687-9072. **FAX:** (610) 687-9629. **E-Mail Address:** info@skillshow.com. **Website:** www.skillshow.com.
Chief Executive Officer: Tom Koerick Jr. **President/Director, Sales:** Tom Koerick Sr.

UMPIRES

WORLD UMPIRES ASSOCIATION
Major Leagues
Mailing Address: P.O. Box 394, Neenah, WI 54957. **Telephone:** (920) 969-1580. **FAX:** (920) 969-1892. **E-Mail Address:** worldumpiresassn@aol.com.
Year Founded: 2000.
President: John Hirschbeck. **Vice President:** Joe Brinkman. **Secretary/Treasurer:** Jeff Nelson. **Labor Counsel:** Joel Smith. **Administrator:** Phil Janssen.

PROFESSIONAL BASEBALL UMPIRE CORPORATION
Minor Leagues
Office Address: 201 Bayshore Dr. SE, St. Petersburg, FL 33701. **Mailing Address:** P.O. Box A, St. Petersburg, FL 33731. **Telephone:** (727) 822-6937. **FAX:** (727) 821-5819.
President: Mike Moore. **Treasurer/Vice President, Administration:** Pat O'Conner. **Secretary/General Counsel:** Scott Poley. **Administrator:** Eric Krupa. **Assistant to Administrator:** Lillian Dixon.
Executive Director, PBUC: Mike Fitzpatrick (Kalamazoo, MI).
Field Evaluators/Instructors: Jorge Bauza, (San Juan, PR), Dennis Cregg (Webster, MA), Mike Felt (Lansing, MI), Justin Klemm (North Bethesda, MD), Larry Reveal (Chesapeake, VA).

UMPIRE DEVELOPMENT SCHOOLS
Harry Wendelstedt Umpire School
Mailing Address: 88 S. St. Andrews Dr., Ormond Beach, FL 32174. **Telephone:** (386) 672-4879. **FAX:** (386) 672-3212. **E-Mail:** admin@umpireschool.com. **Website:** www.umpireschool.com.
Operators: Harry Wendelstedt, Hunter Wendelstedt.

Jim Evans Academy of Professional Umpiring
Mailing Address: 12741 Research Blvd., Suite 401, Austin, TX 78759. **Telephone:** (512) 335-5959. **FAX:** (512) 335-5411. **E-Mail:** jimsacademy@earthlink.net. **Website:** www.umpireacademy.com.
Operator: Jim Evans.

TRAINERS

PROFESSIONAL BASEBALL ATHLETIC TRAINERS SOCIETY
Mailing Address: 400 Colony Square, Suite 1750, 1201 Peachtree St., Atlanta, GA 30361. **Telephone:** (404) 875-4000. **FAX:** (404) 892-8560. **E-Mail Address:** rmallernee@mallernee-branch.com. **Website:** www.pbats.org.
Year Founded: 1983.
President: Jamie Reed (Texas Rangers). **Secretary:** Jim Rowe (Boston Red Sox). **Treasurer:** Jeff Porter (Atlanta Braves). **American League Head Athletic Trainer Representative:** Kevin Rand (Detroit Tigers). **American League Assistant Athletic Trainer Representative:** Brian Ebel (Baltimore Orioles). **National League Head Athletic Trainer Representative:** Jeff Porter (Atlanta Braves). **National League Assistant Athletic Trainer Representative:** Rex Jones (Houston Astros).
General Counsel: Rollin Mallernee.

MUSEUMS

BABE RUTH BIRTHPLACE and OFFICIAL ORIOLES MUSEUM
Office Address: 216 Emory St., Baltimore, MD 21230. **Telephone:** (410) 727-1539. **FAX:** (410) 727-1652. **E-Mail Address:** info@baberuthmuseum.com. **Website:** www.baberuthmuseum.com.
Year Founded: 1973.
Executive Director: Mike Gibbons. **Curator:** Greg Schwalenberg.
Museum Hours: April-October, 10 a.m.-6 p.m. (10 a.m.-7:30 p.m. for Baltimore Orioles home games); November-March: Tuesday-Sunday, 10 a.m.-5 p.m. (10 a.m.-8 p.m. for Baltimore Ravens home games).

CANADIAN BASEBALL HALL OF FAME AND MUSEUM
Museum Address: 386 Church St., St. Marys, Ontario N4X 1C2. **Mailing Address:** P.O. Box 1838, St. Marys, Ontario N4X 1C2. **Telephone:** (519) 284-1838. **FAX:** (519) 284-1234. **E-Mail Address:** baseball@baseballhalloffame.ca. **Website:** www.baseballhalloffame.ca.

Year Founded: 1983.

President/Chief Executive Officer: Tom Valcke. **Director, Operations:** Scott Crawford. **Curator:** Carl McCoomb.

Museum Hours: May—weekends only, Sat. 10:30 a.m.-4 p.m.; Sun. noon-4 p.m.; June 1-Oct. 9—Mon.-Sat. 10:30 a.m.-4:30 p.m.; Sun. noon-4 p.m.

2005 Induction Ceremonies: June 25.

Boys/Girls Weeklong Camps: July.

FIELD OF DREAMS MOVIE SITE

Address: 28963 Lansing Rd., Dyersville, IA 52040. **Telephone:** (888) 875-8404. **FAX:** (319) 875-7253. **E-Mail Address:** shoelessjoe@fieldofdreamsmoviesite.com. **Website:** www.fieldofdreamsmoviesite.com.

Year Founded: 1989.

Manager, Business/Marketing: Betty Boeckenstedt.

Hours: April-November, 9 a.m.-6 p.m.

LEGENDS OF THE GAME BASEBALL MUSEUM

Address: 1000 Ballpark Way Suite 400, Arlington, TX 76011. **Telephone:** (817) 273-5600. **FAX:** (817) **E-Mail Address:** museum@texasrangers.com. **Website:** www.texasrangers.com. **Director:** Amy Polley.

Hours: April-September, game days, 9 a.m.-7:30 p.m.; non game days, Mon.-Sat. 9 a.m.-4 p.m., Sunday 11 a.m.-4 p.m.; October-March, Tues.-Sat. 10 a.m.-4 p.m.

LITTLE LEAGUE BASEBALL MUSEUM

Office Address: 525 Route 15 S., Williamsport, PA 17701. **Mailing Address:** P.O. Box 3485, Williamsport, PA 17701. **Telephone:** (570) 326-3607. **FAX:** (570) 326-2267. **E-Mail Address:** museum@littleleague.org. **Website:** www.littleleague.org/museum.

Year Founded: 1982.

Director: Janice Ogurcak. **Administrative Assistant:** Adam Thompson.

Museum Hours: Memorial Day-Labor Day, 10 a.m.-7 p.m. (Sun. noon-7 p.m.); October-May, Mon., Thurs. and Fri. 10 a.m.-5 p.m., Sat. noon-5 p.m., Sun. noon-4 p.m.

LOUISVILLE SLUGGER MUSEUM

Office Address: 800 W. Main St., Louisville, KY 40202. **Telephone:** (502) 588-7228. **FAX:** (502) 585-1179. **Website:** www.sluggermuseum.org.

Year Founded: 1996.

Executive Director: Anne Jewell.

Museum Hours: Monday through Saturday, Jan. 2-Dec. 23, 9 a.m.-5 p.m,; Sunday (April-Nov.), noon-5p.m.

THE NATIONAL PASTIME: MUSEUM OF MINOR LEAGUE BASEBALL
(Under Development)

Museum Address: 175 Toyota Plaza, Suite 300, Memphis, TN 38103. **Telephone:** (901) 722-0207. **FAX:** (901) 527-1642. **E-Mail Address:** dchase@memphisredbirds.com. **Website:** www.memphisredbirds.com/autozone_park/museum.html.

Founders: Dean Jernigan, Kristi Jernigan.

Executive Director: Dave Chase.

NATIONAL BASEBALL HALL OF FAME AND MUSEUM

Office Address: 25 Main St., Cooperstown, NY 13326. **Mailing Address:** P.O. Box 590, Cooperstown, NY 13326. **Telephone:** (888) 425-5633, (607) 547-7200. **FAX:** (607) 547-2044. **E-Mail Address:** info@baseballhalloffame.org. **Website:** www.baseballhalloffame.org.

Year Founded: 1939.

Chairman: Jane Forbes Clark. **Vice Chairman:** Joe Morgan. **President:** Dale Petroskey. **Senior Vice President:** Bill Haase. **VP, Communications/Education:** Jeff Idelson. **VP/Chief Curator:** Ted Spencer. **Curator, Collections:** Peter Clark. **Librarian:** Jim Gates. **Controller:** Fran Althiser. **Director, Public Relations:** Brad Horn.

Museum Hours: Memorial Day Weekend-Labor Day—9 a.m.-9 p.m.; remainder of year—9 a.m.-5 p.m. Open daily except Thanksgiving, Christmas, New Year's Day.

2005 Hall of Fame Induction Ceremonies: July 31, 1:30 p.m. **2005 Hall of Fame Game:** May 23, 2 p.m., Boston Red Sox vs. Detroit Tigers.

NEGRO LEAGUES BASEBALL MUSEUM

Mailing Address: 1616 E. 18th St., Kansas City, MO 64108. **Telephone:** (816) 221-1920. **FAX:** (816) 221-8424. **E-Mail Address:** Unavailable. **Website:** www.nlbm.com.

Year Founded: 1990.

Chairman: Buck O'Neil. **President:** Mark Bryant.

Executive Director: Don Motley. **Marketing Director:** Bob Kendrick. **Curator:** Raymond Doswell.

Museum Hours: Tues.-Sat. 9 a.m.-6 p.m., Sun. noon-6 p.m. Closed Monday.

NOLAN RYAN FOUNDATION AND EXHIBIT CENTER

Address: 2925 S. Bypass 35, Alvin, TX 77511. **Telephone:** (281) 388-1134. **FAX:** (281) 388-1135. **Website:** www.nolanryanfoundation.org/museum.htm.

Hours: Mon.-Sat. 9 a.m.-4 p.m.

TED WILLIAMS MUSEUM and HITTERS HALL OF FAME

Mailing Address: 2455 N. Citrus Hills Blvd., Hernando, FL 34442. **Telephone:** (352) 527-6566. **FAX:** (352) 527-4163. **E-Mail Address:** twmuseum@hitter.net. **Website:** twmuseum.com.

Executive Director: Dave McCarthy. **Museum Director:** Mike Colabelli.

Museum Hours: Tues.-Sun., 10 a.m.-4 p.m.

RESEARCH

SOCIETY FOR AMERICAN BASEBALL RESEARCH
Mailing Address: 812 Huron Rd. E., Suite 719, Cleveland, OH 44115. **Telephone:** (216) 575-0500. **FAX:** (216) 575-0502. **Website:** www.sabr.org.
Year Founded: 1971.
President: Dick Beverage. **Vice President:** Bill Nowlin. **Secretary:** Neil Traven. **Treasurer:** F.X. Flinn. **Directors:** Daniel Ginsburg, Tom Hufford, Norman Macht, Andy McCue.
Executive Director: John Zajc. **Membership Services Associate:** Ryan Chamberlain. **Director, Publications:** Jim Charlton.

ALUMNI ASSOCIATIONS

MAJOR LEAGUE BASEBALL PLAYERS ALUMNI ASSOCIATION
Mailing Address: 1631 Mesa Ave., Suite B, Colorado Springs, CO 80906. **Telephone:** (719) 477-1870. **FAX:** (719) 477-1875. **E-Mail Address:** postoffice@mlbpaa.com. **Website:** www.baseball-legends.com.
President: Brooks Robinson. **Chief Executive Officer:** Dan Foster.
Board of Directors: Sandy Alderson, Nelson Briles, John Doherty, Denny Doyle, Brian Fisher, Jim "Mudcat" Grant, Rich Hand, Jim Hannan (chairman), Jim Poole, Steve Rogers, Will Royster, Jose Valdivielso, Fred Valentine (vice chairman).
Legal Counsel: Sam Moore. **Vice President, Player Appearances:** Chris Torgusen. **VP, Special Events:** Geoffrey Hixson. **VP, Special Events—Youth Programming:** Lance James. **Director, Administration:** Blaze Bautista. **Special Events Coordinator:** Mike Groll.

ASSOCIATION OF PROFESSIONAL BALL PLAYERS OF AMERICA
Mailing Address: 1820 W. Orangewood Ave., Suite 206, Orange, CA 92868. **Telephone:** (714) 935-9993. **FAX:** (714) 935-0431. **E-Mail Address:** ballplayersassn@aol.com. **Website:** www.apbpa.org.
Year Founded: 1924.
President: Roland Hemond. **First Vice President:** Tal Smith. **Second VP:** Dick Wagner. **Third VP:** Bob Kennedy. **Secretary/Treasurer:** Dick Beverage. **Administrative Assistant:** Patty Helmsworth.
Directors: Sparky Anderson, Mark Grace, Tony Gwynn, Orel Hershiser, Whitey Herzog, Tony La Russa, Tom Lasorda, Brooks Robinson, Nolan Ryan, Tom Seaver.

BASEBALL ASSISTANCE TEAM (BAT)
Mailing Address: 245 Park Ave., 31st Floor, New York, NY 10167. **Telephone:** (212) 931-7822, (866) 605-4594. **FAX:** (212) 949-5433.
Year Founded: 1986.
President, Chief Executive Officer: Ted Sizemore. **Vice Presidents:** Frank Torre, Greg Wilcox, Earl Wilson. **Chairman:** Bobby Murcer.
Executive Director: James Martin. **Secretary:** Thomas Ostertag. **Treasurer:** Jonathan Mariner. **Consultant:** Sam McDowell.

MINOR LEAGUE BASEBALL ALUMNI ASSOCIATION
Mailing Address: P.O. Box A, St. Petersburg, FL 33731. **Telephone:** (727) 822-6937. **FAX:** (727) 821-5819. **E-Mail Address:** alumni@minorleaguebaseball.com. **Website:** www.minorleaguebaseball.com. **President:** Mike Moore.

MINISTRY

BASEBALL CHAPEL
Mailing Address: P.O. Box 302, Springfield, PA 19064.**Telephone:** (610) 690-2474. **E-Mail Address:** office@baseballchapel.org. **Website:** www.baseballchapel.org.
Year Founded: 1973.
President: Vince Nauss.
Director, Latin America: Rich Sparling. **Assistant Director:** Cali Magallanes. **Director, Ministry Materials:** Kyle Abbot. **Director, Ministry Operations:** Rob Crose. **Coordinator, Baseball Family:** Colleen Endres.
Board of Directors: Don Christenson, Dave Dravecky, Greg Groh, Dave Howard, Jim Lane, Mike Matheny, Chuck Murphy, Vince Nauss, Bill Sampen, Tye Waller, Walt Wiley (chairman).

TRADE, EMPLOYMENT

THE BASEBALL TRADE SHOW
Mailing Address: P.O. Box A, St. Petersburg, FL 33731. **Telephone:** (727) 822-6937, (727) 456-1718. **FAX:** (727) 825-3785.
Manager, Exhibition Services/Alumni Association: Noreen Brantner.
2005 Convention: Dec. 5-7 at Dallas, TX (Trinity Hall, Wyndham Anatole).

PROFESSIONAL BASEBALL EMPLOYMENT OPPORTUNITIES
Mailing Address: P.O. Box A, St. Petersburg, FL 33731. **Telephone:** (866) 937-7236. **FAX:** (727) 821-5819. **E-Mail:** info@pbeo.com. **Website:** www.pbeo.com.
Contact: Scott Kravchuk.

BASEBALL CARD MANUFACTURERS

DONRUSS/PLAYOFF
Mailing Address: 2300 E. Randol Mill, Arlington, TX 76011. **Telephone:** (817) 983-0300. **FAX:** (817) 983-0400. **E-Mail Address:** lshelton@donruss.com. **Website:** www.donruss.com.

FLEER/SKYBOX INTERNATIONAL
Mailing Address: 1120 Route 73 S., Suite 300, Mount Laurel, NJ 08054. **Telephone:** (800) 343-6816. **FAX:** (856) 231-0383. **E-Mail Address:** info@fleer.com. **Website:** www.fleer.com.

GRANDSTAND CARDS
Mailing Address: 22647 Ventura Blvd., #192, Woodland Hills, CA 91364. **Telephone:** (818) 992-5642. **FAX:** (818) 348-9122. **E-Mail Address:** gscards1@pacbell.net. **Website:** www.grandstandcards.com.

MULTI-AD SPORTS
Mailing Address: 1720 W. Detweiller Dr., Peoria, IL 61615. **Telephone:** (800) 348-6485, ext. 5111. **FAX:** (309) 692-8378. **E-Mail Address:** bjeske@multi-ad.com. **Website:** www.multi-ad.com/sports.

TOPPS
Mailing Address: One Whitehall St., New York, NY 10004. **Telephone:** (212) 376-0300. **FAX:** (212) 376-0573. **Website:** www.topps.com.

UPPER DECK
Mailing Address: 5909 Sea Otter Place, Carlsbad, CA 92008. **Telephone:** (800) 873-7332. **FAX:** (760) 929-6548. **E-Mail Address:** customer_service@upperdeck.com. **Website:** www.upperdeck.com.

MINOR
LEAGUES

MINOR LEAGUE
BASEBALL

NATIONAL ASSOCIATION
OF PROFESSIONAL BASEBALL LEAGUES

Office Address: 201 Bayshore Dr. SE, St. Petersburg, FL 33701. **Mailing Address:** P.O. Box A, St. Petersburg, FL 33731. **Telephone:** (727) 822-6937. **FAX:** (727) 821-5819. **Website:** www.milb.com.

Year Founded: 1901.
President, Chief Executive Officer: Mike Moore.
Vice President: Stan Brand (Washington, D.C.).
Treasurer, Chief Operating Officer/VP, Administration: Pat O'Conner. **Assistant to VP, Administration:** Mary Wooters.
Secretary/General Counsel: Scott Poley. **Administrator, Legal Affairs:** Sandie Olmsted.
Special Counsel: George Yund (Cincinnati, OH)

MINOR LEAGUE BASEBALL

Mike Moore

Executive Director, Business Operations: John Cook.
Director, Baseball Operations: Tim Brunswick.
Director, Media Relations: Jim Ferguson. **Assistant Director, Media Relations:** Steve Densa.
Director, Business/Finance: Eric Krupa. **Manager, Accounting:** Jeff Carrier.
Director, Information Technology: Rob Colamarino.
Official Statistician: Major League Baseball Advanced Media, 75 Ninth Ave., New York, NY 10011. **Telephone:** (212) 485-3444.
2005 Winter Meetings: Dec. 5-8 at Dallas, TX.

Affiliated Members/Council of League Presidents

Class AAA

League	President	Telephone	FAX Number
International	Randy Mobley	(614) 791-9300	(614) 791-9009
Mexican	Alejandro Hutt	011-555-557-1007	011-555-395-2454
Pacific Coast	Branch Rickey	(719) 636-3399	(719) 636-1199

Class AA

League	President	Telephone	FAX Number
Eastern	Joe McEacharn	(207) 761-2700	(207) 761-7064
Southern	Don Mincher	(770) 321-0400	(770) 321-0037
Texas	Tom Kayser	(210) 545-5297	(210) 545-5298

High Class A

League	President	Telephone	FAX Number
California	Joe Gagliardi	(408) 369-8038	(408) 369-1409
Carolina	John Hopkins	(336) 691-9030	(336) 691-9070
Florida State	Chuck Murphy	(386) 252-7479	(386) 252-7495

Low Class A

League	President	Telephone	FAX Number
Midwest	George Spelius	(608) 364-1188	(608) 364-1913
South Atlantic	John Moss	(704) 739-3466	(704) 739-1974

Short-Season Class A

League	President	Telephone	FAX Number
New York-Penn	Ben Hayes	(727) 576-6300	(727) 576-6307
Northwest	Bob Richmond	(208) 429-1511	(208) 429-1525

Rookie Advanced

League	President	Telephone	FAX Number
Appalachian	Lee Landers	(704) 873-5300	(704) 873-4333
Pioneer	Jim McCurdy	(509) 456-7615	(509) 456-0136

Rookie

League	President	Telephone	FAX Number
Arizona	Bob Richmond	(208) 429-1511	(208) 429-1525
Dominican Summer	Freddy Jana	(809) 532-3619	(809) 532-3619
Gulf Coast	Tom Saffell	(941) 966-6407	(941) 966-6872
Venezuela Summer	Saul Gonzalez	011-58-41-24-0321	011-58-41-24-0705

PROFESSIONAL BASEBALL
PROMOTION CORPORATION

Office Address: 201 Bayshore Dr. SE, St. Petersburg, FL 33701. **Mailing Address:** P.O. Box A, St. Petersburg, FL 33731. **Telephone:** (727) 822-6937. **FAX/Marketing:** (727) 894-4227. **FAX/Licensing:** (727) 825-3785.
President, Chief Executive Officer: Mike Moore.
Treasurer, Chief Operating Officer/VP, Administration: Pat O'Conner.
Executive Director, Business Operations: John Cook. **Senior Assistant Director, Special Operations:** Kelly Ryan. **Assistant Director, Special Operations:** Scott Kravchuk.
Director, Licensing: Brian Earle. **Assistant Director, Licensing:** Tina Gust.
Director, Marketing: Rod Meadows. **Senior Manager, Marketing:** Derek Johnson. **Account Manager, Marketing:** Jen Reinhardt. **Club Coordinator, Marketing:** Melissa Keilen
Professional Baseball Employment Opportunities Contact: Scott Kravchuk. **Manager, Exhibition Services/Alumni Association:** Noreen Brantner. **Manager, Trademarks/Contracts:** Susan Pinckney. **Assistant, Special Operations:** Jill Rusinko. **Administrative Assistant, Special Operations:** Jeannette Machicote.

PROFESSIONAL BASEBALL
UMPIRE CORPORATION

Office Address: 201 Bayshore Dr. SE, St. Petersburg, FL 33701. **Mailing Address:** P.O. Box A, St. Petersburg, FL 33731. **Telephone:** (727) 822-6937. **FAX:** (727) 821-5819.
President: Mike Moore.
Treasurer/Vice President, Administration: Pat O'Conner. **Secretary/General Counsel:** Scott Poley.
Administrator: Eric Krupa. **Assistant to Administrator:** Lillian Patterson
Executive Director, PBUC: Mike Fitzpatrick (Kalamazoo, MI).
Field Evaluators/Instructors: Dennis Cregg (Webster, MA), Mike Felt (Lansing, MI), Justin Klemm (Washington, DC), Jorge Bauza (San Juan, PR), Larry Reveal (Chesapeake, VA).

GENERAL
INFORMATION

	Teams	Games	Regular Season Opening Day	Closing Day	All-Star Games Date	Site
International	14	144	April 7	Sept. 5	*July 13	Sacramento
Pacific Coast	16	144	April 7	Sept. 5	*July 13	Sacramento
Eastern	12	142	April 7	Sept. 5	July 13	Portland
Southern	10	140	April 7	Sept. 5	July 13	Mobile
Texas	8	140	April 7	Sept. 4	June 21	Frisco
California	10	140	April 7	Sept. 5	#June 28	Frederick
Carolina	8	140	April 7	Sept. 5	#June 28	Frederick
Florida State	12	140	April 7	Sept. 4	June 18	Clearwater
Midwest	14	140	April 7	Sept. 5	June 21	Peoria
South Atlantic	16	140	April 7	Sept. 5	June 28	Augusta
New York-Penn	14	76	June 21	Sept. 8	Aug. 23	Brooklyn
Northwest	8	76	June 21	Sept. 7	None	
Appalachian	10	68	June 21	Aug. 30	None	
Pioneer	8	76	June 21	Sept. 8	None	
Arizona	9	56	June 22	Aug. 30	None	
Gulf Coast	12	54	June 24	Aug. 25	None	

*Triple-A All-Star Game
#California League vs. Carolina League

MINOR LEAGUES

Parent club in parentheses. **2004 STANDINGS** *Split-season champion. #Wild card.

INTERNATIONAL LEAGUE   AAA

NORTH	W	L	Pct.	GB	Manager
Buffalo Bisons (Indians)	83	61	.576	—	Marty Brown
Pawtucket Red Sox (Red Sox)	73	71	.507	10	Buddy Bailey
Rochester Red Wings (Twins)	73	71	.507	10	Phil Roof
Scranton/Wilkes-Barre Red Barons (Phillies)	69	73	.486	13	Marc Bombard
Ottawa Lynx (Orioles)	66	78	.458	17	Tim Leiper
Syracuse SkyChiefs (Blue Jays)	66	78	.458	17	Marty Pevey
SOUTH	**W**	**L**	**Pct.**	**GB**	**Manager**
Richmond Braves (Braves)	79	62	.560	—	Pat Kelly
#Durham Bulls (Devil Rays)	77	67	.535	3½	Bill Evers
Norfolk Tides (Mets)	72	72	.500	8½	John Stearns
Charlotte Knights (White Sox)	68	74	.479	11½	Nick Capra
WEST	**W**	**L**	**Pct.**	**GB**	**Manager**
Columbus Clippers (Yankees)	80	64	.556	—	Bucky Dent
Louisville RiverBats (Reds)	67	77	.465	13	Rick Burleson
Indianapolis Indians (Brewers)	66	78	.458	14	Cecil Cooper
Toledo Mud Hens (Tigers)	65	78	.455	14½	Larry Parrish

GOVERNORS' CUP PLAYOFFS—Semifinals: Buffalo defeated Durham 3-2 and Richmond defeated Columbus 3-2 in best-of-5 series. **Finals:** Buffalo defeated Richmond 3-1 in best-of-5 series.

PACIFIC COAST LEAGUE   AAA

CENTRAL	W	L	Pct.	GB	Manager
Iowa Cubs (Cubs)	79	64	.552	—	Mike Quade
Colorado Springs Sky Sox (Rockies)	78	65	.545	1	Marv Foley
Omaha Royals (Royals)	71	73	.493	8½	Mike Jirschele
Albuquerque Isotopes (Marlins)	67	77	.465	12½	Tracy Woodson
EAST	**W**	**L**	**Pct.**	**GB**	**Manager**
Oklahoma RedHawks (Rangers)	81	63	.563	—	Bobby Jones
Memphis Redbirds (Cardinals)	73	71	.507	8	Danny Sheaffer
New Orleans Zephyrs (Astros)	66	78	.458	15	Chris Maloney
Nashville Sounds (Pirates)	63	79	.444	17	Trent Jewett
NORTH	**W**	**L**	**Pct.**	**GB**	**Manager**
Portland Beavers (Padres)	84	60	.583	—	Craig Colbert
Tacoma Rainiers (Mariners)	79	63	.556	4	Dan Rohn
Edmonton Trappers (Expos)	69	74	.483	14½	Dave Huppert
Salt Lake Stingers (Angels)	56	88	.389	28	Mike Brumley
SOUTH	**W**	**L**	**Pct.**	**GB**	**Manager**
Sacramento River Cats (Athletics)	79	65	.549	—	Tony DeFrancesco
Tucson Sidewinders (Diamondbacks)	74	70	.514	5	Chip Hale
Las Vegas 51s (Dodgers)	67	76	.469	11½	Terry Kennedy
Fresno Grizzlies (Giants)	62	82	.431	17	Fred Stanley

PLAYOFFS—Semifinals: Sacramento defeated Portland 3-1 and Iowa defeated Oklahoma 3-2 in best-of-5 series. **Finals:** Sacramento defeated Iowa 3-0 in best-of-5 series.

EASTERN LEAGUE   AA

NORTH	W	L	Pct.	GB	Manager
New Hampshire Fisher Cats (Blue Jays)	84	57	.596	—	Mike Basso
#Binghamton Mets (Mets)	76	66	.535	8½	Ken Oberkfell
New Britain Rock Cats (Twins)	70	70	.500	13½	Stan Cliburn
Norwich Navigators (Giants)	69	73	.486	15½	Shane Turner
Portland Sea Dogs (Red Sox)	69	73	.486	15½	Ron Johnson
Trenton Thunder (Yankees)	64	78	.451	20½	Stump Merrill
SOUTH	**W**	**L**	**Pct.**	**GB**	**Manager**
Altoona Curve (Pirates)	85	56	.603	—	Tony Beasley
#Erie Seawolves (Tigers)	80	62	.563	5½	Rick Sweet
Bowie Baysox (Orioles)	73	69	.514	12½	Dave Trembley
Reading Phillies (Phillies)	64	77	.454	21	Greg Legg
Akron Aeros (Indians)	63	78	.447	22	Brad Komminsk
Harrisburg Senators (Expos)	52	90	.366	33½	Dave Machemer

PLAYOFFS—Semifinals: New Hampshire defeated Binghamton 3-1 and Altoona defeated Erie 3-0 in best-of-5 series. **Finals:** New Hampshire defeated Altoona 3-0 in best-of-5 series.

SOUTHERN LEAGUE

AA

EAST	W	L	Pct.	GB	Manager
*Chattanooga Lookouts (Reds)	87	53	.621	—	Jayhawk Owens
Carolina Mudcats (Marlins)	73	66	.525	13½	Ron Hassey
*Tennessee Smokies (Cardinals)	69	71	.493	18	Mark DeJohn
Jacksonville Suns (Dodgers)	66	71	.482	19½	Dino Ebel
Greenville Braves (Braves)	63	76	.453	23½	Brian Snitker
WEST	W	L	Pct.	GB	Manager
*Birmingham Barons (White Sox)	73	66	.525	—	Razor Shines
*Mobile BayBears (Padres)	73	67	.521	½	Gary Jones
West Tenn Diamond Jaxx (Cubs)	70	68	.507	2½	Bobby Dickerson
Huntsville Stars (Brewers)	65	75	.464	8½	Frank Kremblas
Montgomery Biscuits (Devil Rays)	57	83	.407	16½	Charlie Montoyo

PLAYOFFS—Semifinals: Tennessee defeated Chattanooga 3-1 and Mobile defeated Birmingham 3-1 in best-of-five series. **Finals:** Cancelled—Mobile and Tennessee declared co-champions.

TEXAS LEAGUE

AA

EAST	W	L	Pct.	GB	Manager
*Frisco RoughRiders (Rangers)	81	59	.579	—	Tim Ireland
Wichita Wranglers (Royals)	73	66	.525	7½	Frank White
*Tulsa Drillers (Rockies)	71	68	.511	9½	Tom Runnells
Arkansas Travelers (Angels)	59	80	.424	21½	Tyrone Boykin
WEST	W	L	Pct.	GB	Manager
**Round Rock Express (Astros)	86	54	.614	—	Jackie Moore
Midland RockHounds (Athletics)	72	68	.514	14	Webster Garrison
San Antonio Missions (Mariners)	66	72	.478	19	Dave Brundage
El Paso Diablos (Diamondbacks)	48	89	.350	36½	Scott Coolbaugh

PLAYOFFS—Semifinals: Frisco defeated Tulsa 3-0 in best-of-5 series; Round Rock received first-round bye. **Finals:** Frisco defeated Round Rock 4-1 in best-of-7 series.

CALIFORNIA LEAGUE

HIGH A

NORTH	W	L	Pct.	GB	Manager
**Modesto A's (Athletics)	90	50	.643	—	Von Hayes
#San Jose Giants (Giants)	74	66	.529	16	Lenn Sakata
#Stockton Ports (Rangers)	72	68	.514	18	Arnie Beyeler
Bakersfield Blaze (Devil Rays)	59	81	.421	31	Mako Oliveras
Visalia Oaks (Rockies)	56	84	.400	34	Stu Cole
SOUTH	W	L	Pct.	GB	Manager
**Lancaster JetHawks (Diamondbacks)	86	54	.614	—	Wally Backman
#Inland Empire 66ers (Mariners)	77	63	.550	9	Steve Roadcap
#Rancho Cucamonga Quakes (Angels)	69	71	.493	17	Bobby Meacham
Lake Elsinore Storm (Padres)	68	72	.486	18	Rick Renteria
High Desert Mavericks (Brewers)	49	91	.350	37	Mel Queen

PLAYOFFS—Quarterfinals: San Jose defeated Stockton 2-1 and Inland Empire defeated Rancho Cucamonga 2-0 in best-of-3 series. **Semifinals:** Modesto defeated San Jose 3-2 and Lancaster defeated Inland Empire 3-1 in best-of-5 series. **Finals:** Modesto defeated Lancaster 3-2 in best-of-5 series.

CAROLINA LEAGUE

HIGH A

NORTH	W	L	Pct.	GB	Manager(s)
*Wilmington Blue Rocks (Royals)	77	62	.554	—	Billy Gardner
*Potomac Cannons (Reds)	67	72	.482	10	Edgar Caceres
Lynchburg Hillcats (Pirates)	57	81	.413	19½	Jay Loviglio/Tom Prince
Frederick Keys (Orioles)	52	87	.374	25	Tom Lawless
SOUTH	W	L	Pct.	GB	Manager(s)
*Kinston Indians (Indians)	88	50	.638	—	Torey Lovullo
Myrtle Beach Pelicans (Braves)	75	63	.543	13	Randy Ingle
*Winston-Salem Warthogs (White Sox)	74	66	.529	15	Ken Dominguez/Nick Leyva
Salem Avalanche (Astros)	65	74	.468	23½	Russ Nixon

PLAYOFFS—Semifinals: Wilmington defeated Potomac 2-1 and Kinston defeated Winston-Salem 2-1 in best-of-3 series. **Finals:** Kinston defeated Wilmington 3-2 in best-of-5 series.

FLORIDA STATE LEAGUE

HIGH A

EAST	W	L	Pct.	GB	Manager
*Vero Beach Dodgers (Dodgers)	77	57	.575	—	Scott Little
*Daytona Cubs (Cubs)	70	56	.556	3	Steve McFarland
Palm Beach Cardinals (Cardinals)	73	61	.545	4	Tom Nieto
St. Lucie Mets (Mets)	64	65	.496	10½	Tim Teufel
Jupiter Hammerheads (Marlins)	64	71	.474	13½	Luis Dorante
Brevard County Manatees (Expos)	53	72	.424	19½	Tim Raines
WEST	W	L	Pct.	GB	Manager
*Dunedin Blue Jays (Blue Jays)	76	57	.571	—	Omar Malave

	W	L	Pct.	GB	Manager(s)
*Tampa Yankees (Yankees)	75	58	.564	1	Bill Masse
Sarasota Red Sox (Red Sox)	76	61	.555	2	Todd Claus
Fort Myers Miracle (Twins)	61	74	.452	16	Jose Marzan
Clearwater Phillies (Phillies)	55	82	.401	23	Mike Schmidt
Lakeland Tigers (Tigers)	51	81	.386	24½	Gary Green

PLAYOFFS—Semifinals: Daytona defeated Vero Beach 2-0 and Tampa defeated Dunedin 2-0 in best-of-3 series. **Finals:** Cancelled—Daytona and Tampa declared co-champions.

MIDWEST LEAGUE — LOW A

EAST	W	L	Pct.	GB	Manager(s)
#Lansing Lugnuts (Cubs)	77	63	.550	—	Julio Garcia
*South Bend Silver Hawks (Diamondbacks)	77	63	.550	—	Tony Perezchica
#Fort Wayne Wizards (Padres)	72	68	.514	5	Randy Ready
Battle Creek Yankees (Yankees)	71	68	.511	5½	Mitch Seoane/Bill Mosiello
*West Michigan Whitecaps (Tigers)	69	70	.496	7½	Matt Walbeck
Dayton Dragons (Reds)	48	92	.343	29	Alonzo Powell

WEST	W	L	Pct.	GB	Manager
**Kane County Cougars (Athletics)	83	56	.597	—	Dave Joppie
#Cedar Rapids Kernels (Angels)	75	64	.540	8	Bobby Magallanes
#Peoria Chiefs (Cardinals)	75	64	.540	8	Joe Cunningham
#Clinton LumberKings (Rangers)	74	64	.536	8½	Carlos Subero
Beloit Snappers (Brewers)	72	68	.514	9½	Don Money
Swing of the Quad Cities (Twins)	68	68	.500	13½	Kevin Boles
Wisconsin Timber Rattlers (Mariners)	57	82	.410	26	Daren Brown
Burlington Bees (Royals)	56	84	.400	27½	Jim Gabella

PLAYOFFS—Quarterfinals: Clinton defeated Cedar Rapids 2-0, South Bend defeated Fort Wayne 2-0, Kane County defeated Peoria 2-1 and West Michigan defeated Lansing 2-1 in best-of-3 series. **Semifinals:** Kane County defeated Clinton 2-0 and West Michigan defeated South Bend 2-0 in best-of-3 series. **Finals:** West Michigan defeated Kane County 3-2 in best-of-5 series.

SOUTH ATLANTIC LEAGUE — LOW A

NORTH	W	L	Pct.	GB	Manager
*Hickory Crawdads (Pirates)	85	55	.607	—	Dave Clark
*Charleston, W.Va., Alley Cats (Blue Jays)	84	56	.600	1	Ken Joyce
Lake County Captains (Indians)	73	66	.525	11½	Luis Rivera
Lakewood BlueClaws (Phillies)	70	66	.515	13	P.J. Forbes
Delmarva Shorebirds (Orioles)	69	69	.500	15	Bien Figueroa
Kannapolis Intimidators (White Sox)	69	70	.496	15½	Chris Cron
Lexington Legends (Astros)	67	72	.482	17½	Ivan DeJesus
Hagerstown Suns (Giants)	49	88	.358	34½	Mike Ramsey

SOUTH	W	L	Pct.	GB	Manager
**Capital City Bombers (Mets)	89	47	.654	—	Jack Lind
#Charleston, S.C., RiverDogs (Devil Rays)	76	63	.547	14½	Steve Livesey
Rome Braves (Braves)	70	70	.500	21	Rocket Wheeler
Columbus Catfish (Dodgers)	69	69	.500	21	Dann Bilardello
Augusta GreenJackets (Red Sox)	66	73	.475	24½	Chad Epperson
Asheville Tourists (Rockies)	64	75	.460	26½	Joe Mikulik
Savannah Sand Gnats (Expos)	58	80	.420	32	Bob Henley
Greensboro Bats (Marlins)	50	89	.360	40½	Steve Phillips

PLAYOFFS—Semifinals: Hickory defeated Charleston, W.Va., 2-0 and Capital City defeated Charleston, S.C., 2-0 in best-of-3 series. **Finals:** Hickory defeated Capital City 3-0 in best-of-5 series.

NEW YORK-PENN LEAGUE — SHORT-SEASON A

McNAMARA	W	L	Pct.	GB	Manager
Brooklyn Cyclones (Mets)	43	31	.581	—	Tony Tijerina
New Jersey Cardinals (Cardinals)	41	34	.547	2½	Tommy Shields
Hudson Valley Renegades (Devil Rays)	39	33	.542	3	Dave Howard
Aberdeen Ironbirds (Orioles)	35	40	.467	8½	Don Buford
Williamsport Crosscutters (Pirates)	34	40	.459	9	Jeff Branson
Staten Island Yankees (Yankees)	28	44	.389	14	Tommy John

PINCKNEY	W	L	Pct.	GB	Manager
Auburn Doubledays (Blue Jays)	50	24	.676	—	Dennis Holmberg
#Mahoning Valley Scrappers (Indians)	42	34	.553	9	Mike Sarbaugh
Jamestown Jammers (Marlins)	30	45	.400	20½	Benny Castillo
Batavia Muckdogs (Phillies)	28	46	.378	22	Luis Melendez

STEDLER	W	L	Pct.	GB	Manager
Tri-City ValleyCats (Astros)	50	25	.667	—	Gregg Langbehn
Vermont Expos (Expos)	34	38	.472	14½	Jose Alguacil
Oneonta Tigers (Tigers)	33	41	.446	16½	Mike Rojas
Lowell Spinners (Red Sox)	32	44	.421	18½	Luis Alicea

PLAYOFFS—Semifinals: Mahoning Valley defeated Auburn 2-0 and Tri-City defeated Brooklyn 2-1 in best-of-3 series. **Finals:** Mahoning Valley defeated Tri-City 2-0 in best-of-3 series.

NORTHWEST LEAGUE

SHORT-SEASON A

EAST	W	L	Pct.	GB	Manager
Boise Hawks (Cubs)	42	34	.553	—	Tom Beyers
Spokane Indians (Rangers)	41	35	.539	1	Darryl Kennedy
Tri-City Dust Devils (Rockies)	40	36	.526	2	Ron Gideon
Yakima Bears (Diamondbacks)	35	41	.461	7	Bill Plummer
WEST	**W**	**L**	**Pct.**	**GB**	**Manager**
Vancouver Canadians (Athletics)	42	34	.553	—	Dennis Rogers
Everett AquaSox (Mariners)	41	35	.539	1	Pedro Grifol
Salem-Keizer Volcanoes (Giants)	37	39	.487	5	Joe Strain
Eugene Emeralds (Padres)	26	50	.342	16	Roy Howell

PLAYOFFS—Boise defeated Vancouver 3-0 in best-of-5 series for league championship.

APPALACHIAN LEAGUE

ROOKIE ADVANCED

EAST	W	L	Pct.	GB	Manager
Danville Braves (Braves)	41	25	.621	—	Jim Saul
Pulaski Blue Jays (Blue Jays)	40	27	.597	1½	Gary Cathcart
Burlington Indians (Indians)	31	35	.470	10	Rouglas Odor
Bluefield Orioles (Orioles)	28	39	.418	13½	Gary Kendall
Princeton Devil Rays (Devil Rays)	23	44	.343	18½	Jamie Nelson
WEST	**W**	**L**	**Pct.**	**GB**	**Manager**
Greeneville Astros (Astros)	41	26	.612	—	Tim Bogar
Elizabethton Twins (Twins)	38	29	.567	3	Ray Smith
Johnson City Cardinals (Cardinals)	33	35	.485	8½	Tom Kidwell
Kingsport Mets (Mets)	32	36	.471	9½	Mookie Wilson
Bristol White Sox (White Sox)	27	38	.415	13	Jerry Hairston

PLAYOFFS—Greeneville defeated Danville 2-1 in best-of-3 series for league championship.

PIONEER LEAGUE

ROOKIE ADVANCED

NORTH	W	L	Pct.	GB	Manager
*Great Falls White Sox (White Sox)	42	33	.560	1½	John Orton
Helena Brewers (Brewers)	40	37	.519	4½	Johnny Narron
*Billings Mustangs (Reds)	37	37	.500	6	Donnie Scott
Missoula Osprey (Diamondbacks)	27	46	.370	15½	Jim Presley
SOUTH	**W**	**L**	**Pct.**	**GB**	**Manager**
**Provo Angels (Angels)	44	32	.579	—	Tom Kotchman
#Idaho Falls Chukars (Royals)	42	35	.545	2½	Brian Rupp
Ogden Raptors (Dodgers)	35	40	.467	8½	Travis Barbary
Casper Rockies (Rockies)	33	40	.452	9½	P.J. Carey

PLAYOFFS—Semifinals: Billings defeated Great Falls 2-0 and Provo defeated Idaho Falls 2-1 in best-of-3 series. **Finals:** Provo defeated Billings 2-0 in best-of-3 series.

ARIZONA LEAGUE

ROOKIE

	W	L	Pct.	GB	Manager
*Giants	36	19	.655	—	Bert Hunter
*Athletics	34	22	.607	2½	Ruben Escalera
Rangers	32	24	.571	4½	Pedro Lopez
Mariners	31	25	.554	5½	Scott Steinmann
Royals	29	27	.518	7½	Lloyd Simmons
Cubs	27	29	.482	9½	Trey Forkerway
Padres	26	30	.464	10½	Carlos Lezcano
Brewers	24	32	.429	12½	Mike Guerrero
Angels	12	43	.218	24	Brian Harper

PLAYOFF—Giants defeated Athletics in one-game playoff.

GULF COAST LEAGUE

ROOKIE

EAST	W	L	Pct.	GB	Manager
Mets	36	24	.600	—	Brett Butler
Marlins	31	29	.517	5	Tim Cossins
Dodgers	31	29	.517	5	Luis Salazar
Expos	22	38	.367	14	Arturo DeFreites
SOUTH	**W**	**L**	**Pct.**	**GB**	**Manager**
Red Sox	34	24	.586	—	Ralph Treuel
Twins	31	26	.544	2½	Riccardo Ingram
Pirates	30	28	.517	4	Woody Huyke
Reds	20	37	.351	13½	Freddie Benavides
NORTH	**W**	**L**	**Pct.**	**GB**	**Manager**
Yankees	36	23	.610	—	Oscar Acosta
Phillies	36	24	.600	½	Roly deArmas
Tigers	24	36	.400	12½	Kevin Bradshaw
Braves	23	36	.390	13	Ralph Henriquez

PLAYOFFS—Semifinal: Red Sox defeated Mets in one-game playoff; Yankees received first-round bye. **Finals:** Yankees defeated Red Sox 2-0 in best-of-3 series.

INTERNATIONAL
LEAGUE

CLASS AAA

Office Address: 55 S. High St., Suite 202, Dublin, OH 43017.
Telephone: (614) 791-9300. **FAX:** (614) 791-9009.
E-Mail Address: office@ilbaseball.com. **Website:** www.ilbaseball.com.
Years League Active: 1884-.

President/Treasurer: Randy Mobley.
Vice Presidents: Harold Cooper, Dave Rosenfield (Norfolk), Tex Simone (Syracuse), George Sisler Jr. **Corporate Secretary:** Max Schumacher (Indianapolis).
Directors: Bruce Baldwin (Richmond), Don Beaver (Charlotte), George Habel (Durham), Rick Muntean (Scranton/Wilkes-Barre), Joe Napoli (Toledo), Ray Pecor Jr. (Ottawa), Bob Rich Jr. (Buffalo), Dave Rosenfield (Norfolk), Ken Schnacke (Columbus), Max Schumacher (Indianapolis), Naomi Silver (Rochester), John Simone (Syracuse), Mike Tamburro (Pawtucket), Gary Ulmer (Louisville).
Administrative Assistant: Chris Sprague. **Office Manager:** Loretta Holland.
Division Structure: North—Buffalo, Ottawa, Pawtucket, Rochester, Scranton/Wilkes-Barre, Syracuse. **West**—Columbus, Indianapolis, Louisville, Toledo. **South**—Charlotte, Durham, Norfolk, Richmond.

Randy Mobley

Regular Season: 144 games. **2005 Opening Date:** April 7. **Closing Date:** Sept. 5.
All-Star Game: July 13 at Sacramento, CA (IL vs. Pacific Coast League).
Playoff Format: West champion meets South champion in best-of-5 series; wild-card club (non-division winner with best record) meets North champion in best-of-5 series. Winners meet in best-of-5 series for Governors' Cup championship.
Roster Limit: 24. **Player Eligibility Rule:** No restrictions.
Brand of Baseball: Rawlings ROM-INT.
Statistician: Major League Baseball Advanced Media, 75 Ninth Ave., New York, NY 10011.
Umpires: Scott Barry (Quincy, MI), Damien Beal (Fultondale, AL), Michael Belin (Niagara Falls, NY), Tyler Bolick (Woodstock, GA), Kevin Causey (Maple Grove, MN), Paul Chandler (Silverdale, WA), Brad Cole (Jacksonville, FL), Dan Cricks (Birmingham, AL), Dusty Dellinger (China Grove, NC), Michael Estabrook (Tampa, FL), Chad Fairchild (Sarasota, FL), Mike Fichter (Munster, IN), Troy Fullwood (Hampton, VA), Chris Griffith (Fort Worth, TX), Brian Hale (Trussville, AL), James Hoye (Brookpark, OH), Chris Hubler (Durant, IA), Adrian Johnson (Houston, TX), Joe Judkowitz (Coral Springs, FL), Trey Nelson (Lincoln, NE), Brent Persinger (Lexington, KY), David Riley (Fridley, MN), Andy Roberts (Birmingham, AL), R.J. Thompson (Mt. Carmel, TN), A.J. Wendel (Arlington, TX), John Woods (Phoenix, AZ).

STADIUM INFORMATION

Club	Stadium	Opened	Dimensions LF	CF	RF	Capacity	2004 Att.
Buffalo	Dunn Tire Park	1988	325	404	325	18,150	574,088
Charlotte	Knights Stadium	1990	325	400	325	10,002	265,271
Columbus	Cooper Stadium	1977	355	400	330	15,000	489,177
Durham	Durham Bulls Athletic Park	1995	305	400	327	10,000	490,615
Indianapolis	Victory Field	1996	320	402	320	15,500	576,067
Louisville	Louisville Slugger Field	2000	325	400	340	13,200	648,092
Norfolk	Harbor Park	1993	333	410	338	12,067	485,260
Ottawa	Lynx Stadium	1993	325	404	325	10,332	159,619
Pawtucket	McCoy Stadium	1946	325	400	325	10,031	657,067
Richmond	The Diamond	1985	330	402	330	12,134	368,436
Rochester	Frontier Field	1997	335	402	325	10,840	437,088
Scranton/WB	Lackawanna County Stadium	1989	330	408	330	10,982	402,676
Syracuse	Alliance Bank Stadium	1997	330	400	330	11,671	364,648
Toledo	Fifth Third Field	2002	320	412	315	8,943	544,778

BUFFALO
BISONS

Office Address: 275 Washington St., Buffalo, NY 14203.
Telephone: (716) 846-2000. **FAX:** (716) 852-6530.
E-Mail Address: info@bisons.com. **Website:** www.bisons.com.
Affiliation (first year): Cleveland Indians (1995). **Years in League:** 1886-90, 1912-70, 1998-.

OWNERSHIP, MANAGEMENT
Operated by: Rich Products Corp.
Chairman: Robert Rich Sr. **Principal Owner, President:** Robert Rich Jr.
President, Rich Entertainment Group: Melinda Rich. **President, Rich Baseball Operations:** Jon Dandes. **Vice President/Treasurer:** David Rich. **VP/Secretary:** William Gisel.
VP/General Manager: Mike Buczkowski. **VP, Finance:** Joseph Segarra. **Corporate Counsel:** Jill Bond, William Grieshober. **Director, Sales:** Christopher Hill. **Director, Stadium Operations:** Tom Sciarrino. **Controller:** John Rupp. **Manager, Ticket Office/Accounting:** Rita Clark. **Accounting Assistant:** Amy Delaney. **Accountants:** Kevin Parkinson, Nicole Winiarski. **Manager, Ticket Operations:** Mike Poreda. **Public Relations Coordinator:** Brad Bisbing. **Marketing/Game Day Coordinator:** Mike Sciortino. **Sales Account Representatives:** Kristen Burwell, Ryan Bennett, Mark Gordon, Jim Harrington, Brendan Kelly, Geoff Lundquist, Burt Mirti, Frank Mooney, Anthony Sprague. **Coordinator, Sales:** Susan Kirk. **Manager, Merchandise:** Kathleen Wind. **Manager, Office Services:** Margaret Russo. **Executive Assistant:** Tina Sarcinelli. **Director, Food/Beverages:** John Corey. **Assistant Concessions Manager:** Roger Buczek. **Assistant Manager, Pettibones Grill:** Robert Free. **Head Groundskeeper:** Kari Allen. **Chief Engineer:** Pat Chella. **Home Clubhouse/Equipment Manager:** Scott Lesher. **Visiting Clubhouse Manager:** Mike Crouse.

FIELD STAFF
Manager: Marty Brown. **Coach:** Felix Fermin. **Pitching Coach:** Ken Rowe. **Trainer:** Todd Tomczyk.

GAME INFORMATION
Radio Announcers: Jim Rosenhaus, Duke McGuire. **No. of Games Broadcast:** Home-72, Away-72. **Flagship Station:** WECK 1230-AM.
PA Announcer: John Summers. **Official Scorers:** Mike Kelly, Kevin Lester.
Stadium Name: Dunn Tire Park. **Location:** From north, take I-190 to Elm Street exit, left onto Swan Street. From east, take I-90 West to exit 51 (Route 33) to end, exit at Oak Street, right onto Swan Street. From west, take I-90 East, exit 53 to I-190 North, exit at Elm Street, left onto Swan Street. **Standard Game Times:** 7:05 p.m.; Thur. 1:05; Sat. 2:05, 7:05; Sun 2:05. **Ticket Price Range:** $5-18.
Visiting Club Hotel: Downtown Holiday Inn, 620 Delaware Ave., Buffalo, NY 14202. Telephone: (716) 886-2121.

CHARLOTTE
KNIGHTS

Office Address: 2280 Deerfield Dr., Fort Mill, SC 29715.
Telephone: (704) 357-8071. **FAX:** (704) 329-2155.
E-Mail Address: knights@charlotteknights.com. **Website:** www.charlotteknights.com.
Affiliation (first year): Chicago White Sox (1999). **Years in League:** 1993-.

OWNERSHIP, MANAGEMENT
Operated by: Knights Baseball, LLC.
Principal Owners: Bill Allen, Don Beaver. **President:** Don Beaver.
Vice President/General Manager: Bill Blackwell. **Assistant GM:** Jon Percival. **Director, Group Sales/Ticket Operations:** Sean Owens. **Director, Media/Community Relations:** Ryan Gerds. **Director, Creative Services:** Mike Riviello. **Director, Broadcasting/Team Travel:** Matt Swierad. **Director, Corporate Accounts:** Chris Semmens. **Business Manager:** Jay McAllister. **Corporate Account Manager:** Brooke Varner. **Group Event Coordinators:** Thomas Lee, Sean O'Connor, Natalie Pope. **Box Office Coordinator:** Kelly Crawford. **Operations Manager:** Tom Humrickhouse. **Office Manager/Merchandise:** Anne Kelley. **Head Groundskeeper:** Eddie Busque. **Assistant Groundskeeper:** Mike Headd. **Facility Maintenance Manager:** Joe Sistare. **Clubhouse Manager:** John Bare.

FIELD STAFF
Manager: Nick Leyva. **Coach:** Manny Trillo. **Pitching Coach:** Juan Nieves. **Trainer:** Scott Johnson.

GAME INFORMATION
Radio Announcer: Matt Swierad. **No. of Games Broadcast:** Home-72, Away-72. **Flagship Station:** WFNA 1660-AM.
PA Announcer: Ken Conrad. **Official Scorers:** Brent Stastny, Ed Walton, Sam Copeland.
Stadium Name: Knights Stadium. **Location:** Exit 88 off I-77, east on Gold Hill Road. **Standard Game Times:** 7:15 p.m.; Sun. 2:15. **Ticket Price Range:** $6-10.
Visiting Club Hotel: Hampton Inn and Suites, 401 Towne Centre Blvd., Pineville NC 28134. Telephone: (704) 889-2700.

COLUMBUS
CLIPPERS

Office Address: 1155 W. Mound St., Columbus, OH 43223.
Telephone: (614) 462-5250. FAX: (614) 462-3271.
E-Mail Address: info@clippersbaseball.com. Website: www.clippersbaseball.com.
Affiliation (first year): New York Yankees (1979). Years in League: 1955-70, 1977-.

OWNERSHIP, MANAGEMENT

Operated by: Columbus Baseball Team, Inc.
Principal Owner: Franklin County, Ohio.
Board of Directors: Ralph Anderson, Donald Borror, Stephen Cheek, Wayne Harer, Richard Smith, Cathy Lyttle, John Wolfe.
President, General Manager: Ken Schnacke. Assistant GM: Mark Warren. Director, Stadium Operations: Steve Dalin. Director, Ticket Operations: Scott Ziegler. Director, Group Sales: Ty Debevoise. Director, Marketing: Mark Galuska. Director, Promotions: Jason Kidik. Director, Broadcasting: Todd Bell. Director, Advertising: Keif Fetch. Director, Communications: Joe Santry. Director, Community/Media Relations: Unavailable. Director, Merchandising: Krista Oberlander. Director, Finance: Bonnie Badgley. Assistant Director, Group Sales: Travis Hall. Assistant Director, Promotions: Tommy Hampton. Assistant to GM: Judi Timmons. Administrative Assistants: Kelly Ryther, Brittney Heimann.

FIELD STAFF

Manager: Bucky Dent. Coaches: Frank Howard, Kevin Long. Pitching Coach: Gil Patterson. Trainer: Darren London.

GAME INFORMATION

Radio Announcers: Todd Bell, Gary Richards. No. of Games Broadcast: Home-72, Away-72. Flagship Station: WSMZ 103.1-FM.
PA Announcer: Rich Hanchette. Official Scorer: Wil Christensen.
Stadium Name: Cooper Stadium. Location: From north/south, I-71 to I-70 West, exit at Mound Street. From west, I-70 East, exit at Broad Street, east to Glenwood, south to Mound Street. From east, I-70 West, exit at Mound Street. Standard Game Times: 7:05 p.m.; Fri. 7:05/7:25; Sat. 6:05/7:05; Sun. 1:05. Ticket Price Range: $5-9.
Visiting Club Hotels: Radisson Hotel, 7007 N. High St., Columbus, OH 43085. Telephone: (614) 436-0700; Sheraton Suites-Columbus, 201 Hutchinson Ave., Columbus, OH 43235. Telephone: (614) 781-7316; Holiday Inn, 175 Hutchinson Ave., Columbus, OH 43235. Telephone: (614) 431-4457.

DURHAM
BULLS

Office Address: 409 Blackwell St., Durham, NC 27701.
Mailing Address: P.O. Box 507, Durham, NC 27702.
Telephone: (919) 687-6500. FAX: (919) 687-6560.
Website: www.durhambulls.com.
Affiliation (first year): Tampa Bay Devil Rays (1998). Years in League: 1998-.

OWNERSHIP, MANAGEMENT

Operated by. Capitol Broadcasting Co., Inc.
President, Chief Executive Officer: Jim Goodmon.
Vice President: George Habel. VP, Legal Counsel: Mike Hill.
General Manager: Mike Birling. Manager, Sales: Chip Hutchinson. Account Executives, Sponsorship: Heath Brown, Chris Overby, Neil Solondz. Coordinator, Sponsorship Services: Nicola Mattis. Director, Media Relations/Promotions: Matt DeMargel. Director, Multimedia Operations: Aaron Bare. Assistant, Media Relations: Lee Aldridge. Assistant, Community Relations/Promotions: Stacy Sheppard. Director, Ticket Services: Brad Lanphear. Director, Group Sales: Tim Seaton. Business Development Coordinators: Kevin Crittendon, Dustin Hickman, Mary Beth Warfford. Group Sales Assistants: Vince Logan, Jamie Patterson, Jerry Wilson, Doug Yopp. Director, Stadium Operations: Shawn Kisson. Supervisor, Operations: Derek Walsh. Manager, Merchandise: Allan Long. General Manager, Concessions: Jamie Jenkins. Assistant GM, Concessions: Tammy Scott. Head Groundskeeper: Scott Strickland. Manager, Business: Rhonda Carlisle. Accountants: Theresa Stocking, Delesia Rogers. Director, Security: Ed Sarvis. Receptionist/Secretary: Barbara Goss. Box Office Sales: Jerry Mach.

FIELD STAFF

Manager: Bill Evers. Coach: Richie Hebner. Pitching Coach: Joe Coleman. Trainer: Tom Tisdale.

GAME INFORMATION

Radio Announcers: Steve Barnes, Neil Solondz. No. of Games Broadcast: Home-72, Away-72. Flagship Station: WDNC 620-AM.

PA Announcer: Bill Law. **Official Scorer:** Brent Belvin.

Stadium Name: Durham Bulls Athletic Park. **Location:** From Raleigh, I-40 West to Highway 147 North, exit 12B to Willard, two blocks on Willard to stadium. From I-85, Gregson Street exit to downtown, left on Chapel Hill Street, right on Mangum Street. **Standard Game Times:** 7 p.m.; Sun. 5. **Ticket Price Range:** $5-8.

Visiting Club Hotel: Durham Marriott at the Civic Center, 201 Foster St., Durham, NC 27701. Telephone: (919) 768-6000.

INDIANAPOLIS
INDIANS

Office Address: 501 W. Maryland St., Indianapolis, IN 46225.
Telephone: (317) 269-3542. **FAX:** (317) 269-3541.
E-Mail Address: indians@indyindians.com **Website:** www.indyindians.com.
Affiliation (first year): Pittsburgh Pirates (2005). **Years in League:** 1963, 1998-.

OWNERSHIP, MANAGEMENT

Operated by: Indians, Inc.
Chairman, President: Max Schumacher.
General Manager: Cal Burleson. **Assistant GM, Operations:** Randy Lewandowski. **Director, Corporate Development:** Bruce Schumacher. **Director, Marketing:** Chris Herndon. **Director, Ticket Operations:** Matt Guay. **Director, Ticket Sales:** Byron Stevens. **Manager, Box Office:** Courtney Parker. **Manager, Premium Services:** Kerry Vick. **Manager, Media Relations:** Matt Segal. **Director, Community Relations:** Traci Vernon. **Director, Merchandising:** Mark Schumacher. **Marketing Coordinator:** Beth Miller. **Ticket Sales Executives:** Jake Oakman, Chad Bohm, David Tingley, Kathryn Thompson. **Director, Broadcasting:** Howard Kellman. **Director, Business Operations:** Brad Morris. **Director, Stadium/Baseball Operations:** Scott Rubin. **Control Room Coordinator:** Adam Lane. **Facility Director:** Bill Sampson. **Director, Stadium Maintenance:** Tim Hughes. **Maintenance Assistant:** Allan Danehy. **Head Groundskeeper:** Jamie Mehringer. **Assistant Groundskeeper:** Jeff Hermesch. **Administrative Assistant:** Stu Tobias. **Equipment/Clubhouse Manager:** Unavailable. **Director, Food Services:** Carey Landis.

FIELD STAFF

Manager: Trent Jewett. **Coach:** Hensley Meulens. **Pitching Coach:** Darold Knowles. **Trainer:** Jose Ministral.

GAME INFORMATION

Radio Announcer: Howard Kellman. **No. of Games Broadcast:** Home-72, Away-72. **Flagship Station:** ESPN 950-AM.

PA Announcer: Bruce Schumacher. **Official Scorers:** Kim Rogers, Tom Akins, Mark Walpole.

Stadium Name: Victory Field. **Location:** I-70 to West Street exit, north on West Street to ballpark; I-65 to Martin Luther King and West Street exit, south on West Street to ballpark. **Standard Game Times:** 7 p.m.; Sun. 2/6. **Ticket Price Range:** $7-12.

Visiting Club Hotel: The Comfort Inn, 530 S. Capitol, Indianapolis, IN 46225. Telephone: (317) 631-9000.

LOUISVILLE
BATS

Office Address: 401 E. Main St., Louisville, KY 40202.
Telephone: (502) 212-2287. **FAX:** (502) 515-2255.
E-Mail Address: info@batsbaseball.com. **Website:** www.batsbaseball.com.
Affiliation (first year): Cincinnati Reds (2000). **Years in League:** 1998-.

OWNERSHIP, MANAGEMENT

Operated by: Louisville Baseball Club, Inc.
Board of Directors: Ed Glasscock, Jack Hillerich, Kenny Huber, Bob Stallings, Dan Ulmer, Gary Ulmer, Steve Trager, Mike Brown.
Chairman: Dan Ulmer. **President:** Gary Ulmer.
Vice President/General Manager: Dale Owens. **Assistant GM/Director, Marketing:** Greg Galiette. **Director, Baseball Operations:** Mary Barney. **Director, Stadium Operations:** Scott Shoemaker. **Director, Ticket Sales:** James Breeding. **Director, Broadcasting:** Jim Kelch. **Controller:** Michele Anderson. **Manager, Tickets:** George Veith. **Director, Public/Media Relations:** Svend Jansen. **Director, Suite Level Services:** Kyle Reh. **Manager, Ticket Accounting:** Earl Stubblefield. **Coordinator, Group Sales:** Bryan McBride. **Senior Account Executives:** Jason Abraham, Courtney Myers, Jason Hartings, Hal Norwood. **Assistant Director, Public/Media Relations:** Megan Dimond. **Manager, Community Relations:** Karrie Harper. **Operations Assistant:** Doug Randol. **Senior Account Executive:** Matt Andrews. **Account Executives:** Matt Wilmes, Nick Evans. **Assistant Ticket Manager:** Josh Hargreaves. **Administrative Assistant:** Jodi Tischendorf. **Head Groundskeeper:** Tom Nielsen. **Assistant Groundskeeper:** Brad Smith.

FIELD STAFF

Manager: Rick Sweet. **Coaches:** Adrian Garrett, Rodney McCray. **Pitching Coach:** Mack Jenkins. **Trainer:** Chris

Lapole.

GAME INFORMATION

Radio Announcers: Jim Kelch, Matt Andrews. **No. of Games Broadcast:** Home-72, Away-72. **Flagship Station:** WGTK 970-AM.

PA Announcer: Charles Gazaway. **Official Scorer:** Ken Horn.

Stadium Name: Louisville Slugger Field. **Location:** I-64 and I-71 to I-65 South/North to Brook Street exit, right on Market Street, left on Jackson Street, stadium on Main Street between Jackson and Preston. **Standard Game Times:** 7:15 p.m.; Sat. 6:15, Sun. 1:15/6:15. **Ticket Price Range:** $4-9.

Visiting Club Hotel: Marriott Louisville Downtown, 280 West Jefferson St., Louisville, KY 40202. Telephone: (502) 627-5044.

NORFOLK
TIDES

Office Address: 150 Park Ave., Norfolk, VA 23510.
Telephone: (757) 622-2222. **FAX:** (757) 624-9090.
E-Mail Address: receptionist@norfolktides.com. **Website:** www.norfolktides.com.
Affiliation (first year): New York Mets (1969). **Years in League:** 1969-.

OWNERSHIP, MANAGEMENT

Operated by: Tides Baseball Club, LP.
President: Ken Young.
General Manager: Dave Rosenfield. **Coordinator, Sales/Promotions:** Ben Giancola. **Director, Media Relations:** Ian Locke. **Director, Community Relations:** Heather Harkins. **Director, Ticket Operations:** Glenn Riggs. **Director, Group Sales:** Dave Harrah. **Business Manager:** Mike Giedlin. **Director, Stadium Operations:** John Slagle. **Assistant, Stadium Operations:** Matt Newbold. **Local Sales Manager:** Jack Kotarides. **Sales Representative:** Anne Valihura. **Coordinator, Group Sales:** Stephanie Brammer. **Coordinator, Group Sales:** Brooke Briggs. **Manager, Merchandising:** Mandy Cormier. **Ticket Manager:** Linda Waisanen. **Administrative Assistant:** Jenn Moore. **Assistant Box Office Manager:** Jonathan Slagle. **Director, Video Operations:** Jody Cox. **Equipment/Clubhouse Manager:** Stan Hunter. **Head Groundskeeper:** Ken Magner. **Assistant Groundskeeper:** Keith Collins.

FIELD STAFF

Manager: Ken Oberkfell. **Coach:** Howard Johnson. **Pitching Coach:** Dan Warthen. **Trainer:** Brian Chicklo.

GAME INFORMATION

Radio Announcers: Jeff McCarragher, John Castleberry. **No. of Games Broadcast:** Home-72, Away-72. **Flagship Station:** ESPN 1310-AM.

PA Announcer: Unavailable. **Official Scorer:** Unavailable.

Stadium Name: Harbor Park. **Location:** Exit 9, 11A or 11B off I-264, adjacent to the Elizabeth River in downtown Norfolk. **Standard Game Times:** 7:15 p.m.; Sun. (April-June) 1:15, (July-Sept.) 6:15. **Ticket Price Range:** $8.50-10.

Visiting Club Hotels: Sheraton Waterside, 777 Waterside Dr., Norfolk, VA 23510. Telephone: (757) 622-6664; Doubletree Club Hotel, 880 N. Military Hwy., Norfolk, VA 23502. Telephone: (757) 461-9192.

OTTAWA
LYNX

Office Address: Lynx Stadium, 300 Coventry Rd., Ottawa, Ontario K1K 4P5.
Telephone: (613) 747-5969. **FAX:** (613) 747-0003.
E-Mail Address: lynx@ottawalynx.com. **Website:** www.ottawalynx.com.
Affiliation (first year): Baltimore Orioles (2003). **Years in League:** 1951-54, 1993-.

OWNERSHIP, MANAGEMENT

Operated By: Ottawa Lynx Company.
Principal Owner: Ray Pecor Jr.
General Manager: Kyle Bostwick. **Assistant GM:** Mark Sluban. **Office Administrator:** Lorraine Charrette. **Director, Media/Public Relations:** Brian Morris. **Director, Ticket Operations:** Melissa Rumble. **Promotions:** Angie Lynch. **Equipment Manager:** John Bryk. **Visiting Clubhouse Manager:** Jason Ross. **Head Groundskeeper:** Steve Bennett.

FIELD STAFF

Manager: Dave Trembley. **Coach:** Dave Cash. **Pitching Coach:** Steve McCatty. **Trainer:** P.J. Mainville. **Strength/Conditioning Coach:** Joe Hogarty.

GAME INFORMATION

Radio: Unavailable.
PA Announcer: Jeff Lefebvre. **Official Scorer:** Frank Calamatas.
Stadium Name: Lynx Stadium. **Location:** Highway 417 to Vanier Parkway exit, Vanier Parkway north to Coventry

Road to stadium. **Standard Game Times:** 7:05 p.m.; Sat. 6:05, Sun./holidays 1:05. **Ticket Price Range:** $6.50-11. **Visiting Club Hotel:** Chimo Hotel, 1199 Joseph Cyr Rd., Ottawa, Ontario K1K 3P5. Telephone: (613) 744-1060.

PAWTUCKET
RED SOX

Office Address: One Ben Mondor Way, Pawtucket, RI 02860.
Mailing Address: P.O. Box 2365, Pawtucket, RI 02861.
Telephone: (401) 724-7300. **FAX:** (401) 724-2140.
E-Mail Address: info@pawsox.com. **Website:** www.pawsox.com.
Affiliation (first year): Boston Red Sox (1973). **Years in League:** 1973-.

OWNERSHIP, MANAGEMENT

Operated by: Pawtucket Red Sox Baseball Club, Inc.
Chairman: Ben Mondor. **President:** Mike Tamburro.
Vice President/General Manager: Lou Schwechheimer. **VP, Chief Financial Officer:** Matt White. **VP, Sales/Marketing:** Michael Gwynn. **VP, Stadium Operations:** Mick Tedesco. **VP, Public Relations:** Bill Wanless. **Assistant to GM:** Daryl Jasper. **Director, Broadcasting/Community Affairs:** Andy Freed. **Director, Ticket Operations:** Mike McAtee. **Manager, Finance:** Kristy Batchelder. **Director, Community Relations:** Jeff Bradley. **Director, Merchandising:** Eric Petterson. **Director, Media Services:** Jeff Ouimette. **Director, Warehouse Operations:** Dave Johnson. **Director, Concession Services:** Jim Hogan. **Director, Corporate Services:** Sarah Keane. **Account Executive:** Bill Crawford. **Secretary:** Kim Garcia. **Clubhouse Manager:** Unavailable. **Head Groundskeeper:** Casey Erven. **Assistant Groundskeeper:** Matt McKinnon. **Facility Operations:** Kevin Galligan. **Executive Chef:** Dom Rendine.

FIELD STAFF

Manager: Ron Johnson. **Coach:** Mark Budaska. **Pitching Coach:** Mike Griffin. **Trainer:** Greg Barajas.

GAME INFORMATION

Radio Announcer: Steve Hyder. **No. of Games Broadcast:** Home-72, Away-72. **Flagship Station:** WSKO 790-AM. **PA Announcer:** Jim Martin. **Official Scorer:** Bruce Guindon.
Stadium Name: McCoy Stadium. **Location:** From north, Route 95 South to exit 2A in Massachusetts (Newport Ave./Pawtucket), follow Newport Ave. for 2 miles, right on Columbus Ave., follow Columbus Ave. for one mile, stadium on right. From south, Route 95 North to exit 28 (School Street), right at bottom of exit ramp, through two sets of lights, left onto Pond Street, right on Columbus Ave., stadium entrance on left. From west (Worcester), Route 146 South to Route 295 North to Route 95 South and follow directions from north. From east (Fall River), Route 195 West to Route 95 North and follow directions from south. **Standard Game Times:** 7 p.m.; Sat. 6, Sun. 1. **Ticket Price Range:** $6-9.
Visiting Club Hotel: Comfort Inn, 2 George St., Pawtucket, RI 02860. Telephone: (401) 723-6700.

RICHMOND
BRAVES

Office Address: 3001 North Blvd., Richmond, VA 23230.
Mailing Address: P.O. Box 6667, Richmond, VA 23230.
Telephone: (804) 359-4444. **FAX:** (804) 359-0731.
E-Mail Address: info@rbraves.com. **Website:** www.rbraves.com.
Affiliation (first year): Atlanta Braves (1966). **Years in League:** 1884, 1915-17, 1954-64, 1966-.

OWNERSHIP, MANAGEMENT

Operated by: Atlanta National League Baseball, Inc.
General Manager: Bruce Baldwin. **Assistant GM:** Toby Wyman. **Office Manager:** Joanne Curnutt. **Receptionist:** Janet Zimmerman. **Manager, Stadium Operations:** Jonathan Griffith. **Manager, Field Maintenance:** Chad Mulholland. **Manager, Public Relations:** Unavailable. **Assistant Manager, Community Relations:** Elizabeth Snavely. **Assistant Manager, Promotions/Entertainment:** Noir Fowler. **Manager, Corporate Sales:** Ben Terry. **Manager, Ticket Operations:** Meghan Lynch. **Assistant Manager, Ticket Operations:** Mike Castle. **Corporate Sales Representative:** Chris Kelley. **Clubhouse Manager:** Jodie Cahoon.

FIELD STAFF

Manager: Pat Kelly. **Coach:** Rick Albert. **Pitching Coach:** Mike Alvarez. **Trainer:** Jay Williams.

GAME INFORMATION

Radio Announcers: Robert Fish, John Emmett. **No. of Games Broadcast:** Home-72, Away-72. **Flagship Station:** WXGI 950-AM.
PA Announcer: Mike Blacker. **Official Scorers:** Leonard Alley, Roscoe Puckett.
Stadium Name: The Diamond. **Location:** Exit 78 (Boulevard) at junction of I-64 and I-95, follow signs to park. **Standard Game Times:** 7 p.m., 4; Sun. 2. **Ticket Price Range:** $6-9.
Visiting Club Hotel: Quality Inn, 8008 W. Broad St., Richmond, VA 23230. Telephone: (804) 346-0000.

ROCHESTER
RED WINGS

Office Address: One Morrie Silver Way, Rochester, NY 14608.
Telephone: (585) 454-1001. **FAX**: (585) 454-1056, (585) 454-1057.
E-Mail Address: info@redwingsbaseball.com **Website**: www.redwingsbaseball.com.
Affiliation (first year): Minnesota Twins (2003). **Years in League**: 1885-89, 1891-92, 1895-.

OWNERSHIP, MANAGEMENT
Operated by: Rochester Community Baseball.
Chairman, Chief Operating Officer: Naomi Silver. **President, Chief Executive Officer**: Gary Larder.
General Manager: Dan Mason. **Assistant GM**: Will Rumbold. **Controller**: Darlene Giardina. **Operations Coordinator**: Mary Goldman. **Head Groundskeeper**: Gene Buonomo. **Director, Media/Public Relations**: Chuck Hinkel. **Director, Corporate Development**: Nick Sciarratta. **Group/Picnic Director**: Parker Allen. **Director, Promotions**: Matt Cipro. **Director, Game Day Production**: Brian Golding. **Director, Ticket Operations**: Joe Ferrigno. **Director, Merchandising**: Rosemarie Bianco. **Director, Human Resources**: Paula LoVerde. **Assistant Director, Groups/Picnics**: Zach Holmes. **Account Executive**: Andy DiLaura. **APAR Manager**: Liz Ammons. **Executive Secretary**: Ginny Colbert. **Director, Food Services**: Jeff Dodge. **Manager, Suites/Catering**: Jennifer Pierce. **Catering Sales Manager**: Sarah Bradley. **Manager, Concessions**: Jeff DeSantis. **Business Manager, Concessions**: Dave Bills. **Clubhouse Operations**: Terry Costello. **Night Secretary**: Cathie Costello.

FIELD STAFF
Manager: Phil Roof. **Coach**: Rich Miller. **Pitching Coach**: Bobby Cueller. **Trainer**: Tony Leo.

GAME INFORMATION
Radio Announcers: Josh Whetzel, Joe Altobelli. **No. of Games Broadcast**: Home-72, Away-72. **Flagship Stations**: WHTK 1280-AM, WYSL 1040-AM.
PA Announcer: Mike Pazdyk. **Official Scorer**: Lary Bump.
Stadium Name: Frontier Field. **Location**: I-490 East to exit 12 (Brown/Broad Street) and follow signs. I-490 West to exit 14 (Plymouth Ave.) and follow signs. **Standard Game Times**: 7:05 p.m., Sun 1:35. **Ticket Price Range**: $5.50-9.50
Visiting Club Hotel: Crown Plaza, 70 State St., Rochester, NY 14608. Telephone: (585) 546-3450.

SCRANTON/WILKES-BARRE
RED BARONS

Office Address: 235 Montage Mountain Rd., Moosic, PA 18507.
Mailing Address: P.O. Box 3449, Scranton, PA 18505.
Telephone: (570) 969-2255. **FAX**: (570) 963-6564.
E-Mail Address: barons@epix.net. **Website**: www.redbarons.com.
Affiliation (first year): Philadelphia Phillies (1989). **Years in League**: 1989-.

OWNERSHIP, MANAGEMENT
Operated by: Lackawanna County Stadium Authority.
Chairman: John Grow.
General Manager: Jeremy Ruby. **Director, Media/Public Relations**: Mike Cummings. **Director, Promotions**: Unavailable. **Executive Assistant**: Kelly Byron. **Director, Sales/Marketing**: Unavailable. **Senior Account Representatives**: Joe Shaughnessy, Mike Trudnak, Jennette LePori. **Director, Ticket Sales**: Ann Marie Nocera. **Director, Merchandising**: Ray Midura. **Director, Food Services**: Rich Sweeney. **Clubhouse Operations**: Red Brower, Rich Revta. **Director, Accounts Payable**: Karen Healey. **Office Manager**: Donna Kunda. **Controller**: Unavailable. **Head Groundskeeper**: Bill Casterline.

FIELD STAFF
Manager: Gene Lamont. **Coach**: Sal Rende. **Pitching Coach**: Rod Nichols. **Trainer**: Brian Cammarota.

GAME INFORMATION
Radio Announcer: Kent Westling. **No. of Games Broadcast**: Home-72, Away-72. **Flagship Station**: WWDL 104.9-FM.
PA Announcer: Johnny Davies. **Official Scorers**: Bob McGoff, Jeep Fanucci.
Stadium Name: Lackawanna County Stadium. **Location**: I-81 to exit 182 (Davis Street/Montage Mountain Road), take Montage Mountain Road one mile to stadium. **Standard Game Times**: 7 p.m.; Sun. 2, 6. **Ticket Price Range**: $5-8.
Visiting Club Hotel: Radisson at Lackawanna Station, 700 Lackawanna Ave., Scranton, PA 18503. Telephone: (570) 342-8300.

SYRACUSE
SKYCHIEFS

Office Address: One Tex Simone Dr., Syracuse, NY 13208.
Telephone: (315) 474-7833. **FAX:** (315) 474-2658.
E-Mail Address: baseball@skychiefs.com. **Website:** www.skychiefs.com.
Affiliation (first year): Toronto Blue Jays (1978). **Years in League:** 1885-89, 1891-92, 1894-1901, 1918, 1920-27, 1934-55, 1961-.

OWNERSHIP, MANAGEMENT

Operated by: Community Owned Baseball Club of Central New York, Inc.
Chairman: Charles Rich. **President:** Donald Waful. **Vice President/Treasurer:** Anton Kreuzer. **Vice President/Chief Operating Officer:** Anthony "Tex" Simone.
General Manager: John Simone. **Assistant GM, Business:** Don Lehtonen. **Director, Group Sales:** Victor Gallucci. **Director, Operations:** H.J. Refici. **Director, Corporate Sales/Community Relations:** Andy Gee. **Associate Director, Group/Corporate Sales:** Mike Voutsinas. **Director, Merchandising:** Wendy Shoen. **Director, Ticket Office:** Jon Blumenthal. **Team Historian:** Ron Gersbacher. **Receptionist:** Priscilla Venditti. **Field Maintenance:** Jim Jacobson.

FIELD STAFF

Manager: Marty Pevey. **Coach:** Dwayne Murphy. **Pitching Coach:** Chuck Kniffin. **Trainer:** Jon Woodworth.

GAME INFORMATION

Radio Announcer: Bob McElligott. **No. of Games Broadcast:** Home-72, Away-72. **Flagship Station:** WFBL 1390-AM.
PA Announcer: Jim Donovan. **Official Scorer:** Tom Leo, Johnny Stats.
Stadium Name: Alliance Bank Stadium. **Location:** New York State Thruway to exit 36 (I-81 South), to 7th North Street exit, left on 7th North, right on Hiawatha Boulevard. **Standard Game Times:** 7 p.m., Sun. 6. **Ticket Price Range:** $4-7.
Visiting Club Hotel: Ramada Inn, 1305 Buckley Rd., Syracuse, NY 13212. Telephone: (315) 457-8670.

TOLEDO
MUD HENS

Office Address: 406 Washington St., Toledo, OH 43604.
Telephone: (419) 725-4367. **FAX:** (419) 725-4368.
E-Mail Address: mudhens@mudhens.com. **Website:** www.mudhens.com.
Affiliation (first year): Detroit Tigers (1987). **Years in League:** 1889, 1965-.

OWNERSHIP, MANAGEMENT

Operated by: Toledo Mud Hens Baseball Club, Inc.
Chairman, President: Michael Miller. **Vice President:** David Huey. **Secretary/Treasurer:** Charles Bracken.
General Manager: Joseph Napoli. **Assistant GM/Director, Marketing:** Scott Jeffer. **Assistant GM/Director, Corporate Partnerships:** Neil Neukam. **Assistant GM, Ticket Sales/Operations:** Erik Ibsen. **Chief Financial Officer:** Bob Eldridge. **Manager, Promotions:** Jamay Edwards. **Director, Public/Media Relations:** Jason Griffin. **Director, Ticket Sales/Services:** Thom Townley. **Manager of Group Sales & Services:** Brian Perkins. **Manager, Box Office Sales/Services:** Greg Setola. **Manager, Community Relations:** Cheri Bohnsack. **Corporate Sales Associate:** Neil Stein. **Season Ticket/Group Sales Associates:** Chris Hole, John Mulka, Eric Tomaszewski, Nathan Steinmetz. **Manager, Video Board Operations:** Mike Ramirez. **Manager, Merchandising:** Craig Katz. **Assistant Manager, Merchandising:** Ed Sintic. **Manager, Stadium Operations:** Kirk Sausser. **Assistant Manager, Operations:** Melissa Ball. **Business Manager:** Dorothy Welniak. **Office Manager:** Carol Hamilton. **Maintenance Supervisor:** L.C. Bates. **Maintenance Assistant:** Erick Coleman. **Head Groundskeeper:** Jake Tyler. **Assistant Groundskeeper:** Kris Fawcett. **Clubhouse Manager:** Joe Sarkisian. **Team Historian:** John Husman.

FIELD STAFF

Manager: Larry Parrish. **Coach:** Leon Durham. **Pitching Coach:** Jeff Jones. **Trainer:** Matt Rankin.

GAME INFORMATION

Radio/Television Announcers: Jim Weber, Frank Gilhooley, Jason Griffin. **No. of Games Broadcast:** Home-72, Away-72. **Flagship Station:** WLQR 1470-AM.
PA Announcer: Kevin Mullan. **Official Scorers:** Jeff Businger, Ron Kleinfelter, Guy Lammers.
Stadium Name: Fifth Third Field. **Location:** From Ohio Turnpike 80/90, exit 54 (4A) to I-75 North, follow I-75 North to exit 201-B, left onto Erie Street, right onto Washington Street. From Detroit, I-75 South to exit 202-A, right onto Washington Street. From Dayton, I-75 North to exit 201-B, left onto Erie Street, right onto Washington Street. From Ann Arbor, Route 23 South to I-475 East, I-475 East to I-75 South, I-75 South to exit 202-A, right onto Washington Street. **Standard Game Times:** 7 p.m.; Sun. 2. **Ticket Prices:** $8.
Visiting Club Hotel: Radisson, 101 North Summit, Toledo, OH 43604. Telephone: (419) 241-3000.

PACIFIC COAST
LEAGUE

CLASS AAA

Mailing Address: 1631 Mesa Ave., Suite A, Colorado Springs, CO 80906.
Telephone: (719) 636-3399. **FAX:** (719) 636-1199.
E-Mail Address: office@pclbaseball.com. **Website:** www.pclbaseball.com.
President: Branch B. Rickey.
Vice President: Don Logan (Las Vegas).

PACIFIC COAST LEAGUE

Directors: Don Beaver (New Orleans), Sam Bernabe (Iowa), Hilary Buzas-Drammis (Salt Lake), Tony Ensor (Colorado Springs), Pat Filippone (Fresno), George Foster (Tacoma), Al Gordon (Nashville), Dean Jernigan (Memphis), Don Logan (Las Vegas), Jay Miller (Round Rock), Matt Minker (Omaha), Scott Pruitt (Oklahoma), Branch Rickey (Portland), Art Savage (Sacramento), Ken Young (Albuquerque), Jay Zucker (Tucson).

Director, Operations: George King. **Office Manager:** Melanie Fiore. **Operations Assistant:** Steve Hurlbert.

Division Structure. American Conference—Northern: Iowa, Memphis, Nashville, Omaha. **Southern:** Albuquerque, New Orleans, Oklahoma, Round Rock. **Pacific Conference—Northern:** Colorado Springs, Portland, Salt Lake, Tacoma. **Southern:** Fresno, Las Vegas, Sacramento, Tucson.

Branch Rickey

Regular Season: 144 games. **2005 Opening Date:** April 7. **Closing Date:** Sept. 5.

All-Star Game: July 13 at Sacramento (PCL vs. International League).

Playoff Format: Pacific Conference/Northern champion meets Southern champion, and American Conference/Northern champion meets Southern champion in best-of-5 semifinal series. Winners meet in best-of-5 series for league championship.

Roster Limit: 24. **Player Eligibility Rule:** No restrictions.

Brand of Baseball: Rawlings ROM.

Statistician: Major League Baseball Advanced Media, 75 Ninth Ave., New York, NY 10011.

Umpires: Ramon Armendariz (Vista, CA), David Aschwege (Lincoln, NE), Lance Barksdale (Jackson, MS), Angel Campos (Ontario, CA), Ben Clanton (Nesbit, MS), Frank Coffland (San Antonio, TX), Adam Dowdy (Pontiac, IL), Robert Drake (Mesa, AZ), Chris Guccione (Brighton, CO), Cameron Keller (Westminster, CO), Kevin Kelley (St. Louis, MO), Scott Kennedy (Louisville, KY), Brian Knight (Helena, MT), Scott Letendre (Shasta, CA), Mark Mauro (San Mateo, CA), John McMasters (Tacoma, WA), Casey Moser (Iowa Park, TX), Michael Muchlinski (Ephrata, WA), Shawn Rakos (Orting, WA), Travis Reininger (Brighton, CO), Jack Samuels (Orange, CA), Kevin Sweeney (Rio Rancho, NM), Todd Tichenor (Holcomb, KS), Ryan West (Littleton, CO).

STADIUM INFORMATION

Club	Stadium	Opened	LF	CF	RF	Capacity	2004 Att.
Albuquerque	Isotopes Park	2003	360	410	340	12,700	575,607
Colorado Springs	Sky Sox Stadium	1988	350	400	350	9,000	236,022
Fresno	Grizzlies Stadium	2002	324	402	335	12,500	531,040
Iowa	Principal Park	1992	335	400	335	10,800	540,055
Las Vegas	Cashman Field	1983	328	433	323	9,334	306,628
Memphis	AutoZone Park	2000	319	400	322	14,200	730,565
Nashville	Herschel Greer Stadium	1978	327	400	327	10,700	405,536
New Orleans	Zephyr Field	1997	333	405	332	11,000	324,324
Oklahoma	SBC Bricktown Ballpark	1998	325	400	325	13,066	474,206
Omaha	Johnny Rosenblatt Stadium	1948	332	408	332	24,000	318,537
Portland	PGE Park	1926	319	405	321	19,810	312,678
*Round Rock	The Dell Diamond	2000	330	400	325	10,000	*252,557
Sacramento	Raley Field	2000	330	405	325	14,111	751,156
Salt Lake	Franklin Covey Field	1994	345	420	315	15,500	448,153
Tacoma	Cheney Stadium	1960	325	425	325	9,600	310,680
Tucson	Tucson Electric Park	1998	340	405	340	11,000	285,378

*Franchise operated in Edmonton in 2004

ALBUQUERQUE
ISOTOPES

Office Address: 1601 Avenida Cesar Chavez SE, Albuquerque, NM 87106.
Telephone: (505) 924-2255. **FAX:** (505) 242-8899.
E-Mail Address: info@albuquerquebaseball.com. **Website:** www.albuquerque-baseball.com.
Affiliation (first year): Florida Marlins (2003). **Years in League:** 1972-2000, 2003-.

OWNERSHIP, MANAGEMENT

Operated by: Albuquerque Baseball Club, LLC.
President: Ken Young. **Secretary/Treasurer:** Emmett Hammond.
General Manager: John Traub. **Assistant GM, Sales/Marketing:** Nick LoBue. **Director, Accounting:** Barbara Campbell. **Director, Stadium Operations:** Drew Stuart. **Director, Community Relations:** Melissa Gomez. **Director, Group Sales/Season Tickets:** Jennifer Steger. **Director, Retail Operations:** Chrissy Baines. **Box Office Manager:** Jake Smith. **Manager, Media Relations:** David Bearman. **Manager, Corporate Sales/Promotions:** Chris Holland. **Manager, Suite Relations:** Paul Hartenberger. **Stadium Operations Assistant:** Eddie Enriquez. **Community Relations Assistant:** Rosie Matlock. **Executive, Corporate Sales:** Renee Hoyden. **Executives, Group/Ticket Sales:** Adam Beggs, Cheryl Hull. **Office Manager:** Cristien Camp. **General Manager, Ovations Food Services:** Jay Satenspiel. **Head Groundskeeper:** Jarad Alley. **Home Clubhouse Manager:** Gerald Bass. **Visiting Clubhouse Manager:** Rick Pollack.

FIELD STAFF

Manager: Dean Treanor. **Coach:** Reggie Jefferson. **Pitching Coach:** Jeff Schwarz. **Trainer:** Unavailable.

GAME INFORMATION

Radio Announcer: Bob Socci. **No. of Games Broadcast:** Home-72, Away-72. **Flagship Station:** KNML 610-AM.
PA Announcer: Stu Walker. **Official Scorers:** Gary Herron, John Miller.
Stadium Name: Isotopes Park. **Location:** From 1-25, exit east on Avenida Cesar Chavez SE to University Boulevard; from I-40, exit south on University Boulevard SE to Avenida Cesar Chavez. **Standard Game Times:** 7:05 p.m.; Sun. (April-May) 1:35, (June-Sept.) 6:05. **Ticket Price Range:** $5-20.
Visiting Club Hotel: MCM Elegante, 2020 Menaul NE, Albuquerque, NM 87107. Telephone: (505) 884-2511.

COLORADO SPRINGS
SKY SOX

Office Address: 4385 Tutt Blvd., Colorado Springs, CO 80922.
Telephone: (719) 597-1449. **FAX:** (719) 597-2491.
E-Mail Address: info@skysox.com. **Website:** www.skysox.com.
Affiliation (first year): Colorado Rockies (1993). **Years in League:** 1988-.

OWNERSHIP, MANAGEMENT

Operated by: Colorado Springs Sky Sox, Inc.
Principal Owner: David Elmore.
President/General Manager: Tony Ensor. **Senior Vice President, Administration:** Sam Polizzi. **Senior VP, Operations:** Dwight Hall. **Senior VP, Marketing:** Rai Henniger. **Senior VP, Stadium Operations:** Mark Leasure. **Coordinator, Special Events:** Brien Smith. **Assistant GM, Public Relations:** Gabe Ross. **Accountant:** Kelly Hanlon. **Director, Broadcast Operations:** Dan Karcher. **Assistant GM, Community Relations:** Corey Wynn. **Director, Corporate Events:** Lara Wroblewski. **Group Sales/Ticket Operations:** Chip Dreamer. **Promotions/Public Relations Coordinator:** Kazuhito Oki. **Director, Season Ticket Sales:** Whitney Shellem. **Corporate Event Planner:** Gina D'Ambrosio. **Home Clubhouse Manager:** Ricky Grima. **Visiting Clubhouse Manager:** Greg Grimaldo. **Marketing Representatives:** Jimmy Donnellon, Greg Gilbertson, Andrew Painter, Tasuhiro Yamamoto.

FIELD STAFF

Manager: Marv Foley. **Coach:** Alan Cockrell. **Pitching Coach:** Bob McClure. **Trainer:** Jeremy Moeller.

GAME INFORMATION

Radio Announcers: Dan Karcher, Dick Chase. **No. of Games Broadcast:** Home-72, Away-72. **Flagship Station:** KRDO 1240-AM.
PA Announcer: Chip Dreamer. **Official Scorer:** Marty Grantz.
Stadium Name: Sky Sox Stadium. **Location:** I-25 South to Woodmen Road exit, east on Woodmen to Powers Boulevard, right on Powers to Barnes Road. **Standard Game Times:** 7:05 p.m.; Sun. 1:05. **Ticket Price Range:** $5-9.
Visiting Club Hotel: LeBaron Hotel Downtown Colorado Springs, 314 W. Bijou St., Colorado Springs, CO 80905. Telephone: (800) 477-8610.

FRESNO
GRIZZLIES

Office Address: 1800 Tulare St., Fresno, CA 93721.
Telephone: (559) 320-4487. **FAX:** (559) 264-0795.
E-Mail Address: info@fresnogrizzlies.com. **Website:** www.fresnogrizzlies.com.
Affiliation (first year): San Francisco Giants (1998). **Years in League:** 1998-.

OWNERSHIP, MANAGEMENT

Operated by: Fresno Diamond Group, LLC.
President: Pat Filippone. **Vice President:** Gerry McKearney.
VP, Tickets: Andrew Stuebner. **VP, Corporate Sales:** Mike Maiorana. **Executive/Administrative Assistant:** Janet Anderson. **Director, Community Relations:** Heather Raburn. **Manager, Community Relations:** Sarah Marten. **Marketing Manager:** Megan Curdy. **Director, Media Relations:** Matt Blankenheim. **Director, Entertainment:** Kelly Reed. **Director, Ticketing:** Tom Backemeyer. **Ticket Manager:** Luke Reiff. **Director, Business Development:** Stacie Johnson. **Director, Group Sales:** Brian Merrell. **Manager, Group Sales:** Andrew Bragman. **Account Executives:** Joe Toler, Brett Marshall. **Account Executive/Merchandise Manager:** Brian Sheets. **Inside Sales Manager:** Ash Anunsen. **Accounts Receivable/Ticket Office:** Karen Thomas. **Corporate Sales:** Evan Cole. **Manager, Corporate Sponsorships:** Michelle Sanchez. **Director, Events Operations:** Garrett Fahrmann. **Manager, Operations:** Chris Althoff. **Assistant Operations Manager:** Harvey Kawasaki. **Head Groundskeeper:** Monty Sowell. **Projects Manager:** Mike Palazzolo. **Finance Manager:** Bryan Humphreys. **Booking Manager:** Maria Ortiz. **Director, Accounting:** Murray Shamp. **Receptionist:** Ashley Thomas.

FIELD STAFF

Manager: Shane Turner. **Coach:** Jim Bowie. **Pitching Coach:** Tom Brown. **Trainer:** Richard Stark.

GAME INFORMATION

Radio Announcers: Doug Greenwald (English), Jess Gonzalez (Spanish). **No. of Games Broadcast:** Home-72, Away-72. **Flagship Stations:** KAAT 103.1-FM (English), KGST 1600-AM (Spanish).
PA Announcer: Brian Anthony. **Official Scorer:** Unavailable.
Stadium Name: Grizzlies Stadium. **Location:** From 99 North, take Fresno Street exit, left on Fresno Street, left on Inyo or Tulare to stadium; from 99 South, take Fresno Street exit, left on Fresno Street, right on Broadway to H Street; from 41 North, take Van Ness exit towards downtown Fresno, left on Van Ness, left on Inyo or Tulare, stadium is straight ahead; from 41 South, take Tulare exit, stadium is located at Tulare and H Streets, or take Van Ness exit, right on Van Ness, left on Inyo or Tulare, stadium is straight ahead. **Standard Game Times:** 7:05 p.m., Sun. (April-June 15) 2:05. **Ticket Price Range:** $5-15.
Visiting Club Hotel: Unavailable.

IOWA
CUBS

Office Address: One Line Drive, Des Moines, IA 50309.
Telephone: (515) 243-6111. **FAX:** (515) 243-5152.
E-Mail Address: info@iowacubs.com. **Website:** www.iowacubs.com.
Affiliation (first year): Chicago Cubs (1981). **Years in League:** 1969-.

OWNERSHIP, MANAGEMENT

Operated by: Raccoon Baseball Inc.
Chairman, Principal Owner: Michael Gartner. **Executive Vice President:** Michael Giudicessi.
President, General Manager: Sam Bernabe. **VP, Assistant GM:** Jim Nahas. **VP, Chief Financial Officer:** Sue Tollefson. **VP/Director, Stadium Operations:** Tom Greene. **VP/Director, Broadcast Operations:** Deene Ehlis. **Director, Media Relations:** Jeff Lantz. **Coordinator, Public Relations:** Matt Nordby. **Director, Logistics:** Scott Sailor. **Director, Community Relations:** Matt Johnson. **Coordinators, Group Sales:** Kenny Houser, Ryan Ulrich. **Director, Sales:** Rich Gilman. **Director, Luxury Suites:** Brent Conkel. **Manager, Stadium Operations:** Jeff Tilley. **Corporate Sales Executives:** Greg Ellis, Michael Broadhurst, Nate Teut. **Corporate Relations:** Red Hollis. **Manager, Broadcast Operations:** David Raymond. **Head Groundskeeper:** Chris Schlosser. **Director, Merchandise:** Chad Mescher. **Coordinator, Merchandise:** Rick Giudicessi. **Accountant:** Lori Auten. **Manager, Cub Club:** Rick Cooper. **Office Manager:** Lindsey Cox. **Director, Information Systems:** Larry Schunk.

FIELD STAFF

Manager: Mike Quade. **Coach:** Pat Listach. **Pitching Coach:** Rick Kranitz. **Trainer:** Bob Grimes.

GAME INFORMATION

Radio Announcers: Deene Ehlis, David Raymond. **No. of Games Broadcast:** Home-72, Away-72. **Flagship Station:** KXNO 1460-AM.
PA Announcers: Mark Pierce, Geoff Conn. **Official Scorers:** Dirk Brinkmeyer, Brian Gibson, Mike Mahon.

Stadium Name: Principal Park. **Location:** I-80 or I-35 to I-235, to Third Street exit, south on Third Street, left on Line Drive. **Standard Game Times:** 7:05 p.m.; Sun. 1:05. **Ticket Price Range:** $6-10.

Visiting Club Hotel: Valley West Inn, 3535 Westown Pkwy., West Des Moines, IA 50266 . Telephone: (515) 225-2524.

LAS VEGAS
51s

Office Address: 850 Las Vegas Blvd. N., Las Vegas, NV 89101.
Telephone: (702) 386-7200. **FAX:** (702) 386-7214.
E-Mail Address: info@lv51.com. **Website:** www.lv51.com.
Affiliation (first year): Los Angeles Dodgers (2001). **Years in League:** 1983-.

OWNERSHIP, MANAGEMENT

Operated by: Mandalay Baseball Properties.

President, General Manager: Don Logan. **Vice President, Finance:** Allen Taylor. **VP, Operations/Security:** Nick Fitzenreider. **Director, Business Development:** Derek Eige. **Director, Ticket Operations:** Mike Rodriguez. **Director, Corporate Sponsorships:** Mike Hollister. **Director, Marketing:** Chuck Johnson. **Director, Merchandise:** Laurie Wanser. **Director, Broadcasting:** Russ Langer. **Managers, Corporate Marketing:** Anthony Albert, David Byrne, Melissa Harkavy, John Spoley. **Manager, Community Relations:** Larry Brown. **Manager, Baseball Administration:** Denise Korach. **Media Relations Director:** Jim Gemma. **Special Assistant to GM:** Bob Blum. **Administrative Assistants:** Michelle Taggart, Pat Dressel. **Operations Manager:** Chip Vespe.

FIELD STAFF

Manager: Jerry Royster. **Coach:** Mariano Duncan. **Pitching Coach:** Roger McDowell. **Trainer:** Jason Mahnke.

GAME INFORMATION

Radio Announcer: Russ Langer. **No. of Games Broadcast:** Home-72, Away-72. **Flagship Station:** KENO 1460-AM. **PA Announcer:** Dan Bickmore. **Official Scorer:** Unavailable.

Stadium Name: Cashman Field. **Location:** I-15 to US 95 exit (Downtown), east to Las Vegas Boulevard North exit, one-half mile north to Cashman Field. **Standard Game Times:** 7:05 p.m.; Sun. 12:05. **Ticket Price Range:** $7-12.

Visiting Club Hotel: Golden Nugget Hotel & Casino, 129 Fremont St., Las Vegas, NV 89101. Telephone: (702) 385-7111.

MEMPHIS
REDBIRDS

Office Address: 175 Toyota Plaza, Suite 300, Memphis, TN 38103.
Telephone: (901) 721-6000. **FAX:** 901-842-1222.
Website: www.memphisredbirds.com.
Affiliation (first year): St. Louis Cardinals (1998). **Years in League:** 1998-.

OWNERSHIP, MANAGEMENT

Operated by: Memphis Redbirds Baseball Foundation, Inc. **Founders:** Dean Jernigan, Kristi Jernigan.

President/General Manager: Dave Chase. **Manager, Operations:** Tony Martin. **Controller:** Garry Condrey. **Accounting Specialist:** Leslie Wilkes. **Human Resources Specialist:** Pam Abney. **VP, Marketing:** Kerry Sewell. **Director, Game Entertainment:** Kim Jackson. **Multimedia Coordinator:** Nick Benyo. **Media Relations Coordinator:** Molly Darnofall. **Marketing Coordinator:** Tim Whang. **Graphic Designer:** Iris Horne. **Retail Supervisor:** Starr Taiani. **Mascot Coordinator:** Chris Pegg. **Director, Broadcasting:** Tom Stocker. **Senior VP, Sales:** Pete Rizzo. **Executive Assistant:** Cindy Compton. **Senior Account Executive:** Rob Edgerton. **Account Executives:** Lisa Shurden, Steve Berneman. **Sales Coordinator:** Sommer Collins. **VP, Community Relations:** Reggie Williams. **Community Relations Coordinator:** Emma Glover. **Programs Coordinator:** Jamison Morris. **Director, Field Operations:** Steve Horne. **Groundskeepers:** Ed Collins, Jeff Vincent. **Manager, Ticket Sales:** Brady Bruhn. **Manager, Season Tickets:** Cathy Allen. **Group Sales Coordinator:** Kristi Smith. **Group Sales Executive:** Dan Schaefer. **Ticket Sales Executives:** Ryan Thompson, Ivery Yarbrough, Tom Tilney. **Chief Engineer:** Danny Abbott. **Maintenance:** Spencer Shields. **Manager, Stadium Operations:** Asim Thomas. **Office Coordinator:** Linda Smith.

FIELD STAFF

Manager: Danny Sheaffer. **Coach:** Tommy Gregg. **Pitching Coach:** Dyar Miller. **Trainer:** Chris Conroy.

GAME INFORMATION

Radio Announcers: Tom Stocker, Steve Selby. **No. of Games Broadcast:** Home-72, Away-72. **Flagship Station:** WHBQ 560-AM.

PA Announcer: Tim Van Horn. **Official Scorer:** J.J. Guinozzo.

Stadium Name: AutoZone Park. **Location:** North on I-240, exit at Union Avenue West, approx. 1½ miles to park. **Standard Game Times:** 7:05 p.m.; Sat. 6:05; Sun. 2:05. **Ticket Price Range:** $5-17.

Visiting Club Hotel: Sleep Inn at Court Square, 40 N. Front, Memphis, TN 38103. Telephone: (901) 522-9700.

NASHVILLE
SOUNDS

Office Address: 534 Chestnut St., Nashville, TN 37203.
Telephone: (615) 242-4371. FAX: (615) 256-5684.
E-Mail Address: info@nashvillesounds.com. Website: www.nashvillesounds.com.
Affiliation (first year): Milwaukee Brewers (2005). Years in League: 1998-.

OWNERSHIP, MANAGEMENT

Operated by: AmeriSports LLC.
President/Owner: Al Gordon.
General Manager: Glenn Yaeger. Assistant GM: Chris Snyder. Vice President, Sales: Brent High. Director, Accounting: Barb Walker. Director, Sales: Joe Hart. Director, Ticketing: Ricki Schlabach. Director, Media Relations/Baseball Operations: Doug Scopel. Director, Marketing/Promotions: Brandon Vonderharr. Director, Food/Beverage: Mark Lawrence. Director, Corporate Sales: Jason Bennett. Director, Community Relations: Sarah Barthol. Director, Merchandising/Sales Associate: Cody Berry. Manager, Sponsorships/Marketing: Julie Hager. Manager, Stadium Operations: P.J. Harrison. Manager, Community Relations: Amy Alder. Manager, Mascot/Entertainment: Buddy Yelton. Office Manager: Sharon Ridley. Broadcaster: Chuck Valenches. Clubhouse Manager: J.R. Rinaldi. Head Groundskeeper: Chris Pearl.

FIELD STAFF

Manager: Frank Kremblas. Coach: Gary Pettis. Pitching Coach: Stan Kyles. Trainer: Jeff Paxson.

GAME INFORMATION

Radio Announcer: Chuck Valenches. No. of Games Broadcast: Home-72, Away-72. Flagship Station: Unavailable. PA Announcer: Dale Conquest. Official Scorers: Eric Jones, Matt Wilson.
Stadium Name: Herschel Greer Stadium. Location: I-65 to Wedgewood exit, west to Eighth Avenue, right on Eighth to Chestnut Street, right on Chestnut. Standard Game Times: 7 p.m.; Wed. 12; Sat. 6; Sun. (April-May) 2, (June-Aug.) 6. Ticket Price Range: $6-10.
Visiting Club Hotel: Select Hotel by Holiday Inn, 2613 West End Ave., Nashville, TN 37203. Telephone: (615) 327-4707.

NEW ORLEANS
ZEPHYRS

Office Address: 6000 Airline Dr., Metairie, LA 70003.
Telephone: (504) 734-5155. FAX: (504) 734-5118.
E-Mail Address: zephyrs@zephyrsbaseball.com. Website: www.zephyrsbaseball.com.
Affiliation (first year): Washington Nationals (2005). Years in League: 1998-.

OWNERSHIP, MANAGEMENT

Operated by: New Orleans Zephyrs Baseball Club, LLC.
Managing Partner/President: Don Beaver.
General Manager: Mike Schline. Director, Community Relations: Marc Allen. Director, Broadcasting: Tim Grubbs. Director, Operations: Jon Peterson. Director, Corporate Sales: Alex Sheffield. Director, Marketing/Special Events: Jaime Burchfield. Director, Corporate Events/Merchandising: Pattie Feder. Director, Ticket Operations: Preston Gautrau. Director, Finance: Kim Topp. Personal Assistant, GM: Jessica DeOro. Corporate Sales Executive: Jason Adzigian. Group Sales Representatives: Leah Rigby, Ben Sonnier, Adam Wasch. Director, Media Relations: Kevin Maney. Media Manager: Ron Swoboda. Head Groundskeeper: Thomas Marks. Assistant Groundskeeper: Craig Shaffer. Maintenance Coordinator: Bill Rowell. Assistant Director, Operations: Todd Wilson. GM, Food Services: George Messina. Administrative Assistant, Food Services: Priscilla Arbello.

FIELD STAFF

Manager: Tim Foli. Coach: Mike Hart. Pitching Coach: Charlie Corbell. Trainer: Jeff Paxson.

GAME INFORMATION

Radio Announcers: Tim Grubbs, Ron Swoboda (English), Herman Rodriguez (Spanish). No. of Games Broadcast: English—Home-72, Away-72; Spanish—Home-38. Flagship Stations: WTIX 690-AM, WSLA 1560 -AM, WFNO 830-AM (Spanish).
PA Announcer: Doug Moreau. Official Scorer: J.L. Vangilder.
Stadium Name: Zephyr Field. Location: I-10 West toward Baton Rouge, exit at Clearview Parkway (exit 226) and continue south, right on Airline Drive (U.S. 61 North) for 1 mile, stadium on left; From airport, take Airline Drive (U.S. 61) east for 4 miles, stadium on right. Standard Game Times: 7:05 p.m.; Sat. 6:05; Sun. (April-May) 2:05, (June-

Sept.) 5:05. **Ticket Price Range:** $5-9.50.
  Visiting Club Hotel: Airport Hilton, 901 Airline Dr., Kenner LA 70062. Telephone: (504) 469-5000.

OKLAHOMA
REDHAWKS

  Mailing Address: 2 S. Mickey Mantle Dr., Oklahoma City, OK 73104.
  Telephone: (405) 218-1000. **FAX:** (405) 218-1001.
  E-Mail Address: info@oklahomaredhawks.com. **Website:** www.oklahomared-
hawks.com.
  Affiliation (first year): Texas Rangers (1983). **Years in League:** 1963-1968, 1998-.

OWNERSHIP, MANAGEMENT

  Operated by: Oklahoma Baseball Club, LLC
  Principal Owner: Robert Funk. **Managing General Partner:** Scott Pruitt.
  Executive Director: John Allgood. **Chief Financial Officer:** Steve McEwen. **Director, Corporate/Public Relations:** Laurie Gore. **Director, Facility Operations:** Harlan Budde. **Director, Guest Services:** Nancy Simmons. **Director, Operations:** Mike Prange. **Director, Sponsorships:** David Patterson. **Director, Ticket Sales:** Mary Ramsey. **Senior Accountant:** Nicole Lamb. **Accountant:** Patty Hoecker. **Promotions Manager:** Brandon Baker. **Ticket Sales Manager:** Johnny Walker. **Fan Scouts:** Barry Harvey, Kristin Packnett, Kendra Sauer. **Receptionist:** Trina Gross. **Clubhouse Manager:** Russ Oliver. **Head Groundskeeper:** Monte McCoy.

FIELD STAFF

  Manager: Bobby Jones. **Coach:** Paul Carey. **Pitching Coach:** Lee Tunnell. **Trainer:** Chris DeLucia.

GAME INFORMATION

  Radio Announcer: Jim Byers. **No. of Games Broadcast:** Home-72, Away-72. **Flagship Station:** WKY 930-AM.
  PA Announcer: Randy Kemp. **Official Scorers:** Bob Colon, Mike Treps.
  Stadium Name: SBC Bricktown Ballpark. **Location:** At interchange of I-235 and I-40, take Reno exit, east on Reno. **Standard Game Times:** 7:05 p.m.; Sun. 2:05. **Ticket Price Range:** $6-14.
  Visiting Club Hotel: Sheraton, One N. Broadway, Oklahoma City, OK 73102. Telephone: (405) 235-2780.

OMAHA
ROYALS

  Office Address: Rosenblatt Stadium, 1202 Bert Murphy Ave., Omaha, NE 68107.
  Telephone: (402) 734-2550. **FAX:** (402) 734-7166.
  E-Mail Address: info@oroyals.com. **Website:** www.oroyals.com.
  Affiliation (first year): Kansas City Royals (1969). **Years in League:** 1998-.

OWNERSHIP, MANAGEMENT

  Operated by: Omaha Royals Limited Partnership.
  Principal Owners: Matt Minker, Warren Buffett, Walter Scott. **Managing General Partner/President:** Matt Minker.
  Senior Vice President, General Manager: Doug Stewart. **VP, Sales/Assistant GM:** Matt Brown. **VP, Business/Baseball Operations:** Kyle Fisher. **Director, Broadcasting:** Mark Nasser. **Director, Media Relations:** Kevin McNabb. **Director, Ticket Operations/Group Sales:** Don Wilson. **Director, Merchandise/Promotions:** Cassie Duncan. **Director, Administrative Services:** Rose Swenson. **Sponsorship Sales Representative:** Angela Mullen. **Manager, Marketing:** Karen Cohick. **Manager, Community Relations:** Melissa Harder. **Manager, Ticket Office:** Jeff Gogerty. **Manager, Ticket Sales:** Gregg Jones. **Group Sales Representatives:** Brock Shaw, Jason Camp. **Ticket Office Assistant:** Natalie Duncan. **Administrative Assistants:** Kay Besta, Lois Biggs. **Head Groundskeeper:** Jesse Cuevas. **General Manager, Concessions:** Ryan Slane.

FIELD STAFF

  Manager: Mike Jirschele. **Coach:** Terry Bradshaw. **Pitching Coach:** Mark Brewer. **Trainer:** Jeff Stevenson.

GAME INFORMATION

  Radio Announcers: Mark Nasser, Kevin McNabb. **No. of Games Broadcast:** Home-72, Away-72. **Flagship Station:** KOSR 1490-AM.
  PA Announcer: Bill Jensen. **Official Scorer:** Rob White.
  Stadium Name: Johnny Rosenblatt Stadium. **Location:** I-80 to 13th Street exit, one block south. **Standard Game Times:** 7:05 p.m.; Sat. 6:05; Sun. 1:35. **Ticket Price Range:** $6-10.
  Visiting Club Hotel: Hilton Omaha, 1001 Cass St., Omaha, NE 68102. Telephone: (402) 342-4313.

PORTLAND
BEAVERS

Office Address: 1844 SW Morrison, Portland, OR 97205.
Telephone: (503) 553-5400. FAX: (503) 553-5405.
E-Mail Address: info@pgepark.com. Website: www.portlandbeavers.com.
Affiliation (first year): San Diego Padres (2001). Years in League: 1903-1917, 1919-1972, 1978-1993, 2001-.

OWNERSHIP, MANAGEMENT

Operated by: Beavers PCL Baseball, LLC.
General Manager: Jack Cain. Vice President, Corporate Partnerships/Suite Sales: Ryan Brach. Vice President, Ticket Sales/Marketing: Ripper Hatch. Director, Communications: Chris Metz. Director, Operations: Ken Puckett. Director, Client Services: Jennifer Gartz. Manager, Tickets/Merchandise: Bob Cain. Manager, Community Outreach: Keri Stoller. Manager, Group Sales: Ben Hoel. Manager, Accounting: Diane Rogers. Manager, Corporate Partnership Sales: Brian Rogers. Manager, Suite Sales: Rick Barr. Manager, Facility Maintenance: Dave Tankersley. Coordinator, Promotions: Jadira Ruiz. Coordinator, Ticket Sales/Marketing: Danna Bubalo. Coordinator, Ticket Renewals: Dan Zusman. Account Executives, Group Tickets: Kim Berger, Ashley Bedford. Account Executives, Ticket Sales: Chad Doing, Greg Herbst. Account Executives, Corporate Ticket Sales: Jo Bullock, Greg Stone. Assistant, Media Relations: Collin Romer. Senior Accounting Clerk: Penny Bishop. Office Manager/Receptionist: Jeanne Nichols. Head Groundskeeper: Jesse Smith. Home Clubhouse Manager: James Cameron.

FIELD STAFF

Manager: Craig Colbert. Coach: Jose Castro. Pitching Coach: Gary Lance. Trainer: John Maxwell.

GAME INFORMATION

Radio Announcers: Rich Burk. No. of Games Broadcast: Home-72, Away-72. Flagship Station: Unavailable.
PA Announcer: Mike Stone. Official Scorer: Blair Cash.
Stadium Name: PGE Park. Location: I-405 to West Burnside exit, SW 20th Street to park. Standard Game Times: 7:05 p.m.; Sun. 2:05. Ticket Price Range: $7-12.
Visiting Club Hotel: Portland Marriott-Downtown, 1401 SW Naito Pkwy., Portland, OR 97201. Telephone: (503) 226-7600.

ROUND ROCK
EXPRESS

(Franchise Operated in Edmonton in 2005)
Office Address: 3400 East Palm Valley Blvd., Round Rock, TX 78664.
Telephone: (512) 255-2255. FAX: (512) 255-1558.
E-Mail Address: info@rrexpress.com. Website: www.roundrockexpress.com.
Affiliation (first year): Houston Astros (2005). Years in League: 2005-.

OWNERSHIP, MANAGEMENT

Operated by: Ryan-Sanders Baseball, LP.
Principal Owners: Eddie Maloney, Jay Miller, Nolan Ryan, Reese Ryan, Reid Ryan, Don Sanders, Brad Sanders, Bret Sanders.
Chief Executive Officer: Reid Ryan. President: Jay Miller. Chief Financial Officer: Reese Ryan.
Vice President, General Manager: Dave Fendrick. Controller: Debbie Coughlin. Assistant GM, Promotions/Stadium Entertainment: Derrick Grubbs. Director, Media/Public Relations: Kirk Dressendorfer. Director, Merchandising: Sue Denny. Director, Ticket Operations: Ross Scott. Director, United Heritage Center: Scott Allen. Director, Special Events: Laura Whatley. Director, Group Sales: Henry Green. Director, Sales: Gary Franke. Director, Customer Relations: George Smith. Account Executives: Gregg Miller, Brent Green, Richard Tapia. Receptionist: Wendy Gordon. Field Superintendent: Dennis Klein. Director, Broadcasting: Mike Capps. Clubhouse Manager: Kenny Bufton. Marketing/Retail Coordinator: Jamie Schroeder.

FIELD STAFF

Manager: Jackie Moore. Coaches: Spike Owen, Harry Spilman. Pitching Coach: Burt Hooton. Trainer: Mike Freer.

GAME INFORMATION

Radio Announcer: Mike Capps. No. of Games Broadcast: Home-72, Away-72. Flagship Station: KWNX 1260-AM.
PA Announcer: Derrick Grubbs. Official Scorer: Tommy Tate.
Stadium Name: The Dell Diamond. Location: I-35 North to exit 253 (Highway 79 East/Taylor), stadium on left 3½ miles. Standard Game Times: 7:05 p.m.; Sun. (April-May) 2:05. Ticket Price Range: $5-10.
Visiting Club Hotel: Hilton Garden Inn, 2310 N. IH-35, Round Rock, TX 78681. Telephone: (512) 341-8200.

SACRAMENTO
RIVER CATS

Office Address: 400 Ballpark Dr., West Sacramento, CA 95691.
Telephone: (916) 376-4700. **FAX:** (916) 376-4710.
E-Mail Address: info@rivercats.com. **Website:** www.rivercats.com
Affiliation (first year): Oakland Athletics (2000). **Years in League:** 1903, 1909-11, 1918-60, 1974-76, 2000-

OWNERSHIP, MANAGEMENT

Owned by: Sacramento River Cats Baseball Club, LLC.
Principal Owner/Chief Executive Officer: Art Savage. **President, General Manager:** Alan Ledford. **Executive Vice Presidents:** Bob Hemond, Warren Smith.
Senior VP, Chief Financial Officer: Dan Vistica. **General Counsel:** Matt Re. **VP, Corporate Partnerships/Broadcasting:** Darrin Gross. **VP, Stadium Operations/Special Events:** Matt LaRose. **VP, Ticket Sales/Marketing:** Andy Fiske. **Senior Director, Community Relations:** Tony Asaro. **Senior Director, Guest Services, Parking/Security:** Mike Reichert. **Assistant GM/Director, Media Relations:** Gabe Ross. **Director, Ticket Operations:** Steve Hill. **Director, Marketing:** Joe Wagoner. **Director, Ticket Sales:** Justin Piper. **Director, Ticket Services:** Cory Dolich. **Director, Corporate Service/Broadcasting:** Scott Druskin. **Manager, Merchandise:** Trish Dolan. **Manager, Marketing:** Alexis Lee. **Manager, Promotions:** Jamie Von Sossan. **Manager, Grounds:** Chris Fahrner. **Manager, Baseball/Stadium Operations:** Matt Thomas. **Manager, Personnel:** Larisa Collins. **Manager, Luxury Suite Sales/Service:** Josh Morin. **Manager, Season Tickets:** Bob Dunham. **Manager, Ticket Operations:** Larry Martinez. **Manager, Accounting:** Stan Kelly.

FIELD STAFF

Manager: Tony DeFrancesco. **Coach:** Brian McArn. **Pitching Coach:** Rick Rodriguez. **Trainer:** Walt Horn.

GAME INFORMATION

Radio Announcers: Johnny Doskow (English), Jose Reynoso (Spanish). **No. of Games Broadcast:** Home-72, Away-72 (English); Home-72, Away-28 (Spanish). **Flagship Stations:** KTKZ 1380-AM (English), KCFA 106.1-FM (Spanish).
PA Announcer: Unavailable. **Official Scorers:** Mark Honbo, Brian Berger.
Stadium Name: Raley Field. **Location:** I-5 to Business-80 West, exit at Jefferson Boulevard. **Standard Game Times:** 7:05 p.m. **Ticket Price Range:** $5-18.
Visiting Club Hotel: Holiday Inn, Capitol Plaza, 300 J St., Sacramento, CA 95814. Telephone: (916) 446-0100.

SALT LAKE
STINGERS

Office Address: 77 W. 1300 South, Salt Lake City, UT 84115.
Mailing Address: P.O. Box 4108, Salt Lake City, UT 84110.
Telephone: (801) 325-2273. **FAX:** (801) 485-6818.
Website: www.stingersbaseball.com. **E-Mail Address:** info@stingersbaseball.com.
Affiliation: Anaheim Angels (2001). **Years in League:** 1915-25, 1958-65, 1970-84, 1994-.

OWNERSHIP, MANAGEMENT

Operated by: Larry H. Miller Baseball, Inc.
Principal Owner: Larry Miller.
Chief Operating Officer: Dennis Haslam. **Senior VP/Chief Marketing Officer:** Jay Francis. **Senior VP/Chief Financial Officer:** Robert Hyde. **Senior VP/Broadcasting:** Randy Rigby. **Senior VP/Facilities:** Scott Williams. **VP/General Manager:** Marc Amicone. **VP/Finance:** John Larson. **VP/Ticket Sales:** Jim Olson. **VP/Communications:** Caroline Shaw. **VP/Sponsorship Sales:** Mike Snarr. **VP/Special Events:** Brent Allenbach. **VP/Security:** Jim Bell. **VP/Food Services:** Mark Stedman. **Concession Manager:** Dave Dalton. **Assistant GM/Operations:** Dorsena Picknell. **Assistant GM/Corporate Sales:** Brad Tammen. **Controller:** Travis Court. **Director, Ticket Sales:** Bobbie Walker. **Director, Broadcasting/Public Relations:** Steve Klauke. **Box Office Manager:** Richard Lahr. **Corporate Account Managers:** Mike Daniels, Darren Feller. **Ticket Sales Executives:** John Kruse, Brian Prutch, Gary Tomlinson. **Office Manager:** Julie Empey. **Team Photographer:** Brent Asay.

FIELD STAFF

Manager: Dino Ebel. **Coach:** Jim Eppard. **Pitching Coach:** Bryn Smith. **Trainer:** Jaime Welch.

GAME INFORMATION

Radio Broadcaster: Steve Klauke. **No. of Games Broadcast:** Home-72, Away-72. **Flagship Station:** KJQS 1230-AM.
PA Announcer: Jeff Reeves. **Official Scorers:** Bruce Hilton, Howard Nakagama.
Stadium name: Franklin Covey Field. **Location:** I-15 to 1300 South exit, east to ballpark at West Temple. **Standard Game Times:** 7 p.m., 6:30 (April-May); Sun. 2. **Ticket Price Range:** $7-10.
Visiting Club Hotel: Sheraton City Centre, 150 W. 500 South, Salt Lake City, UT 84101. Telephone: (801) 401-2000.

TACOMA
RAINIERS

Office Address: 2502 S. Tyler St., Tacoma, WA 98405.
Telephone: (253) 752-7707. FAX: (253) 752-7135.
E-Mail Address: rainiers@tacomarainiers.com. Website: www.tacomarainiers.com.
Affiliation: Seattle Mariners (1995). Years in League: 1904-1905, 1960-.

OWNERSHIP, MANAGEMENT

Operated by: George's Pastime, Inc.
President: George Foster.
Board of Directors: George Foster, Jeff Foster, Jonathan Foster, Sue Foster, Mark Kanai, Jack Pless.
General Manager: Dave Lewis. Assistant GM, Baseball Operations: Kevin Kalal. Assistant GM, Stadium Operations: Philip Cowan. Director, Marketing: Rachel Marecle. Director, Sales: Tim Sexton. Director, Promotions: Jocelyn Hill. Account Executives: Shane Santman, Ryan Barabe, Stephanie Carlson, Chris Anderson. Director, Food/Beverage: Corey Brandt. Director, Merchandise: Kathy Baxter. Director, Tickets: Kurt Swanson. Staff Accountant: Joyce Hardin. Office Manager: Patti Stacy. Community Fund President: Margaret McCormick. Head Groundskeeper: Ryan Schutt. Maintenance Supervisor: Jim Smith. Clubhouse Manager: Jeff Bopp. Assistant Clubhouse Manager: Rich Arneson.

FIELD STAFF

Manager: Dan Rohn. Coach: Terry Pollreisz. Pitching Coach: Rafael Chaves. Trainer: Rob Nodine.

GAME INFORMATION

Radio Broadcaster: Mike Curto. No. of Games Broadcast: Home-72, Away-72. Flagship Station: KHHO 850-AM. PA Announcer: Unavailable. Official Scorers: Darin Padur, Mark Kalal.
Stadium name: Cheney Stadium. Location: From I-5, take exit 132 (Highway 16 West) for 1.2 miles to 19th Street East exit, right on Tyler Street for ⅓ mile. Standard Game Times: 7:05 p.m., 6:05 (April-May); Sundays/holidays 1:35. Ticket Price Range: $5-12.
Visiting Club Hotel: La Quinta Inn, 1425 E. 27th St., Tacoma, WA 98421. Telephone: (253) 383-0146.

TUCSON
SIDEWINDERS

Office Address: 2500 E. Ajo Way, Tucson, AZ 85713.
Mailing Address: P.O. Box 27045, Tucson, AZ 85726.
Telephone: (520) 434-1021. FAX: (520) 889-9477.
E-Mail Address: mail@tucsonsidewinders.com. Website: www.tucsonsidewinders.com.
Affiliation (first year): Arizona Diamondbacks (1998). Years in League: 1969-.

OWNERSHIP, MANAGEMENT

Operated by: Tucson Baseball LLC.
Principal Owner/President: Jay Zucker.
Vice President/General Manager: Rick Parr. Assistant GM/Director, Sales: Sean Smock. Director, Broadcasting: Brett Dolan. Director, Stadium Operations: Matthew Burke. Director, Group Sales: Brian Moss. Director, Community Relations: Sergio Pedroza. Director, Media Relations: Landon Vincent. Director, Promotions/Account Executive: Jessica Withers. Director, Ticket Operations: Brad Hudecek. Director, Inside Sales: Sandy Davis. Account Executive/Promotions Coordinator: Nick Wesoky. Group Sales Representatives: Kimberly Levin, Whitney Evenchik. Office Manager: Stacy Griffitts. Home Clubhouse Manager: Unavailable. Visiting Clubhouse Manager: Brian Sprague. Groundskeeper: Chris Bartos.

FIELD STAFF

Manager: Chip Hale. Coach: Lorenzo Bundy. Pitching Coach: Mike Parrott. Trainer: Greg Barber.

GAME INFORMATION

Radio Announcer: Brett Dolan. No. of Games Broadcast: Home-72, Away-72. Flagship Station: KTZR 1450-AM. PA Announcer: Dale Lopez. Official Scorer: Unavailable.
Stadium Name: Tucson Electric Park. Location: From northwest, I-10 to Ajo exit, east on Ajo to stadium; from southeast, I-10 to Palo Verde exit, north to Ajo, west to stadium. Standard Game Times: 7 p.m., (April-May) 6:30; Sun. 6:30. Ticket Price Range: $5-8.
Visiting Club Hotel: Viscount Suite Hotel, 4855 E. Broadway, Tucson, AZ 85711. Telephone: (520) 745-6500.

EASTERN
LEAGUE

Office Address: 30 Danforth St., Suite 208, Portland, ME 04101.
Telephone: (207) 761-2700. **FAX:** (207) 761-7064.
E-Mail Address: elpb@easternleague.com. **Website:** www.easternleague.com.
Years League Active: 1923-.
President, Treasurer: Joe McEacharn.

          Vice President, Secretary: Rick Brenner.
Assistant to President: Bill Rosario.
          Directors: Greg Agganis (Akron), Bill Dowling (New Britain), Charles Eshbach (Portland), Joe Finley (Trenton), Barry Gordon (Norwich), Chuck Greenberg (Altoona), Greg Martini (Harrisburg), Frank Miceli (Bowie), Shawn Smith (New Hampshire), Craig Stein (Reading), Hank Stickney (Erie), Mike Urda (Binghamton).
          Division Structure: North—Binghamton, New Britain, New Hampshire, Norwich, Portland, Trenton. **South**—Akron, Altoona, Bowie, Erie, Harrisburg, Reading.
          Regular Season: 142 games. **2005 Opening Date:** April 7. **Closing Date:** Sept. 5.
          All-Star Game: July 13 at Portland.
          Playoff Format: Top two teams in each division meet in best-of-5 series. Winners meet in best-of-5 series for league championship.
          Roster Limit: 23; 24 until 30th day of season and after Aug. 9. **Player Eligibility Rule:**

Joe McEacharn   No restrictions.
          Brand of Baseball: Rawlings ROM-EL.
  Statistician: Major League Baseball Advanced Media, 75 Ninth Ave., New York, NY 10011.
  Umpires: Chris Conroy (Williamstown, MA), John Coons (Streator, IL), Brandon Cooper (Louisville, KY), Mike Edwards (Chesapeake, VA), Rob Healey (Cranston, RI), Jason Klein (Orange, CT), Keith McConkey (St. Catharines, Ontario), Stephen McMullen (Willingboro, NJ), Jonathan Merry (Dahlonega, GA), Josh Miller (Coconut Creek, FL), Brian Reilly (Lansing, MI), Daniel Reyburn (Nashville, TN), Brent Rice (Jackson, MI), Jeff Spisak (Indianapolis, IN), Art Stewart (Frankfort, IL), Jacob Uhlenhopp (Nevada, IA), David Uyl (Caledonia, IL), Andrew Vincent (Simsburg, CT).

STADIUM INFORMATION

Club	Stadium	Opened	Dimensions			Capacity	2004 Att.
			LF	CF	RF		
Akron	Canal Park	1997	331	400	337	9,297	478,611
Altoona	Blair County Ballpark	1999	315	400	325	7,200	394,062
Binghamton	NYSEG Stadium	1992	330	400	330	6,012	216,493
Bowie	Prince George's Stadium	1994	309	405	309	10,000	312,354
Erie	Jerry Uht Park	1995	312	400	328	6,000	245,117
Harrisburg	Commerce Bank Park	1987	335	400	335	6,300	255,978
New Britain	New Britain Stadium	1996	330	400	330	6,146	311,671
New Hampshire	Unavailable	2005	326	400	306	6,500	215,961
Norwich	Thomas J. Dodd Memorial Stadium	1995	309	401	309	6,275	168,559
Portland	Hadlock Field	1994	315	400	330	6,975	434,684
Reading	First Energy Stadium	1950	330	400	330	9,000	478,257
Trenton	Mercer County Waterfront Park	1994	330	407	330	6,341	402,280

AKRON
AEROS

Office Address: 300 S. Main St., Akron, OH 44308.
Telephone: (330) 253-5151. **FAX:** (330) 253-3300.
E-Mail Address: info@akronaeros.com. **Website:** www.akronaeros.com.
Affiliation (first year): Cleveland Indians (1989). **Years in League:** 1989-.

OWNERSHIP, MANAGEMENT

Operated by: Akron Professional Baseball, Inc.
Principal Owners: Mike Agganis, Greg Agganis.
Chief Executive Officer: Greg Agganis. **Executive Vice President/General Manager:** Jeff Auman. **Vice President:** Drew Cooke. **Chief Financial Officer:** Bob Larkins. **Director, Public Relations:** James Carpenter. **Director, Corporate Sales:** Dan Burr. **Director, Ticket Sales:** Kim Usselman-Fogel. **Manager, Package Sales:** Kevin Snyder. **Senior Account Representative, Group Sales:** Thomas Craven. **Account Representatives, Group Sales:** Keith Solar, Matt Kurilec. **Director, Merchandising:** Kris Roukey. **Director, Field/Stadium Maintenance:** Matt Duncan. **Director, Player Facilities:** Fletcher Wilkes. **Office Manager:** Arlene Vidumanksy. **AeroFare General Manager:** John Weletyk. **AeroFare Office Manager:** Stephanie Ulery.

FIELD STAFF

Manager: Torey Lovullo. **Coach:** Wayne Kirby. **Pitching Coach:** Greg Hibbard. **Trainer:** Jeff Desjardins.

GAME INFORMATION

Radio Announcer: Jim Clark. **No. of Games Broadcast:** Home-71, Away-71. **Flagship Station:** FOX Sports 1350-AM.
PA Announcer: Joe Jastrzemski/Joe Dunn. **Official Scorers:** Roger Grecni, Adam Widman.
Stadium Name: Canal Park. **Location:** From I-76 East or I-77 South, exit onto Route 59 East, exit at Exchange/Cedar, right onto Cedar, left at Main Street. From I-76 West or I-77 North, exit at Main Street/Downtown, follow exit onto Broadway Street, left onto Exchange Street, right at Main Street. **Standard Game Times:** 7:05 p.m.; Sat. (April) 2:05; Sun. 2:05. **Ticket Price Range:** $7-10.
Visiting Club Hotel: Radisson Hotel Akron City Centre, 20 W. Mill St., Akron, OH 44308. Telephone: (330) 384-1500.

ALTOONA
CURVE

Office Address: 1000 Park Ave., Altoona, PA 16602.
Mailing Address: P.O. Box 1029, Altoona, PA 16603.
Telephone: (814) 943-5400. **FAX:** (814) 942-9132, (814) 943-9050.
E-Mail Address: frontoffice@altoonacurve.com. **Website:** www.altoonacurve.com.
Affiliation (first year): Pittsburgh Pirates (1999). **Years in League:** 1999-.

OWNERSHIP, MANAGEMENT

Operated by: Curve Baseball LP.
President, Managing Partner: Chuck Greenberg. **General Manager:** Todd Parnell. **Assistant GM:** Rick Janac. **Senior Director, Ticketing/New Business Development:** Brent Boznanski. **Director, Broadcasting:** Rob Egan. **Director, Media Relations:** Jason Dambach. **Director, Community Relations:** Elsie Zengel. **Director, Ballpark Operations:** Kirk Stiffler. **Director, Finance:** Machelle Noel. **Director, Ticket Sales:** Jeff Garner. **Assistant Director, Ticket Sales:** Chris Mundhenk. **Ticketing Associates:** Jeff Adams, Corey Homan, Derek Martin, Randy Pfarr, Chris Phillips. **Box Office Manager:** Tammie Duran. **Information Services Specialist/Graphic Designer:** Bill Edevane. **Executive Producer, In-Game Entertainment:** Matt Zidik. **Assistant Director, Ballpark Operations/Merchandising:** Ben Rothrock. **Head Groundskeeper:** Patrick Coakley. **Assistant Groundskeeper:** Matt Neri. **Director, Food Services:** Eric Shoup. **Assistant Manager, Concessions:** Yvonne Hunter. **Director, Clubhouse Operations:** Ken Thomas.

FIELD STAFF

Manager: Tony Beasley. **Coach:** John Wehner. **Pitching Coach:** Jeff Andrews. **Trainer:** Jason Palmer.

GAME INFORMATION

Radio Announcers: Rob Egan, Jason Dambach. **No. of Games Broadcast:** Home-71, Away-71. **Flagship Station:** WFBG 1290-AM.
PA Announcer: Rich DeLeo. **Official Scorer:** Ted Beam.
Stadium Name: Blair County Ballpark. **Location:** Frankstown Road exit off I-99. **Standard Game Times:** 7:05 p.m. (June-Sept.), 6:35 (April-May); Sun. 6:05 (June-Sept.), 3:05 (April-May). **Ticket Price Range:** $4-12.
Visiting Club Hotel: Ramada Inn of Altoona, Route 220 and Plank Road, Altoona, PA 16602. Telephone: (814) 946-1631.

BINGHAMTON
METS

Office Address: 211 Henry St., Binghamton, NY 13901.
Mailing Address: P.O. Box 598, Binghamton, NY 13902.
Telephone: (607) 723-6387. **FAX:** (607) 723-7779.
E-Mail Address: bmets@bmets.com. **Website:** www.bmets.com.
Affiliation (first year): New York Mets (1992). **Years in League:** 1923-37, 1940-63, 1966-68, 1992-.

OWNERSHIP, MANAGEMENT

Operated by: Binghamton Mets Baseball Club, Inc.
Principal Owners: Bill Maines, David Maines, George Scherer, Michael Urda.
President: Michael Urda. **Special Advisor to President:** Bill Terlecky.
General Manager: Scott Brown. **Assistant GM:** Jim Weed. **Director, Stadium Operations:** Richard Tylicki. **Director of Food/Beverage:** Matt Bednar. **Director, Sales:** Scott Gruver. **Ticket Office Manager:** Mike Catalano. **Coordinator, Special Events:** Dan Abashian. **Director, Group Sales:** Jason Hall. **Merchandising Manager:** Lisa Shattuck. **Director, Broadcasting:** Robert Ford. **Office Manager:** Rebecca Brown. **Community Relations Coordinator:** Nancy Wiseman.

FIELD STAFF

Manager: Jack Lind. **Coach:** Dave Hollins. **Pitching Coach:** Blaine Beatty. **Trainer:** Victor Trassof-Jilg.

GAME INFORMATION

Radio Announcer: Matt Park. **No. of Games Broadcast:** Home-71, Away-71. **Flagship Station:** WNBF 1290-AM.
PA Announcer: Roger Neel. **Official Scorer:** Steve Kraly.
Stadium Name: NYSEG Stadium. **Location:** I-81 to exit 4S (Binghamton), Route 11 exit to Henry Street. **Standard Game Times:** 7 p.m., (April-May) 6; Sat. 6; Sun. 1:30. **Ticket Price Range:** $7-8.
Visiting Club Hotel: Holiday Inn Arena, 8 Hawley St., Binghamton, NY 13901. Telephone: (607) 722-1212.

BOWIE
BAYSOX

Office Address: 4101 NE Crain Hwy., Bowie, MD 20716.
Telephone: (301) 805-6000. **FAX:** (301) 464-4911.
E-Mail Address: info@baysox.com. **Website:** www.baysox.com.
Affiliation (first year): Baltimore Orioles (1993). **Years In League:** 1993-.

OWNERSHIP, MANAGEMENT

Operated by: Comcast-Spectacor.
Directors: Peter Luukko, Frank Miceli.
General Manager: Brian Shallcross. **Director, Ticket Operations:** Addie Staebler. **Director, Marketing:** Phil Wrye. **Manager, Communications:** Unavailable. **Assistant Director, Marketing:** Marlene Engberg. **Manager, Ticket Office:** Charlene Fewer. **Sponsorship Sales Manager:** Bill Snitcher. **Director, Stadium Operations:** Matt Parrott. **Manager, Stadium Operations:** Craig Burden. **Managers, Group Events:** Clark Baker, Pete Sekulow, Matt Murphy, Mike Zatchey, Marsha Darbouze, Matt McLaughlin. **Corporate Partnerships:** Kyle Droppers, Brian Bauer. **Bookkeeper:** Carol Terwillger. **Assistant, Communications:** Jon Shoup-Mendizabal. **Assistant, Marketing:** Brandan Kaiser. **Coordinators, Group Events:** Karida Jordan, Chris Keefer. **Coordinator, Box Office:** Rob Finn.

FIELD STAFF

Manager: Don Werner. **Coach:** Butch Davis. **Pitching Coach:** Larry McCall. **Trainer:** Mark Shires.

GAME INFORMATION

Radio: None.
PA Announcers: Thom Jones, Byron Hudtloff. **Official Scorer:** Unavailable.
Stadium Name: Prince George's Stadium. **Location:** ¼ mile south of U.S. 50-U.S. 301 interchange at Bowie.
Standard Game Times: 7:05 p.m.; Sun. (April-June) 1:05, (July-Aug.) 6:05. **Ticket Price Range:** $6-14.
Visiting Club Hotel: Ramada Inn-Laurel, 3400 Fort Meade Rd., Laurel, MD 20724. Telephone: (301) 498-0900.

ERIE
SEAWOLVES

Office Address: 110 E. 10th St., Erie, PA 16501.
Telephone: (814) 456-1300. **FAX:** (814) 456-7520.
E-Mail Address: seawolves@seawolves.com **Website:** www.seawolves.com.
Affiliation (first year): Detroit Tigers (2001). **Years in League:** 1999-.

OWNERSHIP, MANAGEMENT

Operated by: Mandalay Baseball Properties.

General Manager: John Frey. **Head Groundskeeper:** Brandon Shanz. **Assistant GM/Business Development:** Matt Bresee. **Director, Marketing/Promotions:** Rob Magee. **Director, Ticket Operations:** Mark Pirrello. **Director, Group Sales:** Joe Etling. **Director, Concessions/Stadium Operations:** Ragen Walker. **Ticket Sales Representatives:** Becky Obradovic, Ross Swaldo, Brent Curry. **Accountant:** Bernie Mulvihill. **Administrative Assistant:** Christine Gates.

FIELD STAFF

Manager: Duffy Dyer. **Coach:** Pete Incaviglia. **Pitching Coach:** Mike Caldwell. **Trainer:** Rob Sonnenberg.

GAME INFORMATION

Radio Announcer: Mike Antonellis. **No. of Games Broadcast:** Home-71, Away-71. **Flagship Station:** WFNN 1330-AM.

PA Announcer: Dean Pepicello. **Official Scorer:** Les Caldwell.

Stadium Name: Jerry Uht Park. **Location:** U.S. 79 North to East 12th Street exit, left on State Street, right on 10th Street. **Standard Game Times:** 7:05 p.m., 6:35 (April-May); Sun. 1:05. **Ticket Price Range:** $5-8.

Visiting Club Hotel: Avalon Hotel, 16 W. 10th St., Erie, PA 16501. Telephone: (814) 459-2220.

HARRISBURG
SENATORS

Office Address: Commerce Bank Park, City Island, Harrisburg, PA 17101.
Mailing Address: P.O. Box 15757, Harrisburg, PA 17105.
Telephone: (717) 231-4444. **FAX:** (717) 231-4445.
E-Mail Address: hbgsenator@aol.com. **Website:** www.senatorsbaseball.com.
Affiliation (first year): Washington Nationals (2005). **Years in League:** 1924-35, 1987-.

OWNERSHIP, MANAGEMENT

Operated by: Harrisburg Civic Baseball Club, Inc.

Chairman: Greg Martini.

General Manager: Todd Vander Woude. **Assistant GM, Baseball Operations:** Mark Mattern. **Assistant GM, Business Operations:** Mark Clarke. **Director, Facilities Operations:** Tim Foreman. **Director, Concessions Operations:** Steve Leininger. **Manager, Concessions:** Traci Kirkhoff. **Director, Ticket Sales:** Tom Wess. **Director, Group Sales:** Brian Egli. **Picnic Operations:** Carol Baker. **Associate, Ticket Sales:** Mark Brindle. **Turf Manager:** Ryan Schmidt. **Interns:** Melissa Altemose, Wes Bonadio, Amber Wiest, Michael Franken, Lynn Fuller, Patrick McMaster, Rick Nehf.

FIELD STAFF

Manager: Keith Bodie. **Coach:** Frank Cacciatore. **Pitching Coach:** Rick Tomlin. **Trainer:** Beth Jarrett.

GAME INFORMATION

Radio Announcer: Terry Byrom, Mark Mattern. **No. of Games Broadcast:** Home-71, Away-71. **Flagship Station:** WKBO 1230-AM.

PA Announcer: Chris Andree. **Official Scorer:** Dave Wright.

Stadium Name: Commerce Bank Park. **Location:** I-83, exit 23 (Second Street) to Market Street, bridge to City Island. **Standard Game Times:** 6:35 p.m.; Sat. 6:05; Sun. 1:05. **Ticket Price Range:** $3-9.

Visiting Club Hotel: Hilton Hotel, One N. Second St., Harrisburg, PA 17101. Telephone: (717) 233-6000.

NEW BRITAIN
ROCK CATS

Office Address: 230 John Karbonic Way, New Britain, CT 06051.
Mailing Address: P.O. Box 1718, New Britain, CT 06050.
Telephone: (860) 224-8383. **FAX:** (860) 225-6267.
E-Mail Address: rockcats@rockcats.com. **Website:** www.rockcats.com.
Affiliation (first year): Minnesota Twins (1995). **Years in League:** 1983-.

OWNERSHIP, MANAGEMENT

Operated by: New Britain Baseball Club, Inc.

Principal Owners: Bill Dowling, Coleman Levy. **Chairman of Board:** Coleman Levy.

President, General Manager: Bill Dowling. **Assistant GMs:** Evan Levy, John Willi. **Controller:** Paula Perdelwitz. **Director, Broadcasting:** Jeff Dooley. **Director, Ticket Operations:** Peter Colon. **Director, Media Relations:** Bob Dowling. **Account Executives:** Frank Novak, Ricky Ferrell, Dennis Meehan, Jenny Haag. **Coordinator, Stadium Operations:** Mike Hyland. **Coordinator, Community Relations:** Lauren Griswold. **Assistant, Corporate Sales:** Logan Smith. **Assistant, Media Relations:** Courtney Nogas. **Home Clubhouse Manager:** Tyler Greco. **Visiting Clubhouse Manager:** Anthony Desanto.

FIELD STAFF
Manager: Stan Cliburn. **Coach:** Floyd Rayford. **Pitching Coach:** Stu Cliburn. **Trainer:** Chad Jackson.

GAME INFORMATION
Radio Announcers: Jeff Dooley, Dan Lovallo. **No. of Games Broadcast:** Home-71, Away-71. **Flagship Station:** WDRC 1360-AM.
PA Announcer: Don Shamber. **Official Scorer:** Unavailable.
Stadium Name: New Britain Stadium. **Location:** From I-84, take Route 72 East (exit 35) or Route 9 South (exit 39A), left at Ellis Street (exit 25), left at South Main Street, stadium one mile on right. From Route 91 or Route 5, take Route 9 North to Route 71 (exit 24), first exit.
Standard Game Times: 7:05 p.m., 6:35 (April-June); Sun. 1:35. **Ticket Price Range:** $5-10.
Visiting Club Hotel: Holiday Inn Express, 120 Laning St., Southington, CT 06489. Telephone: 860-276-0736.

NEW HAMPSHIRE
FISHER CATS

Office Address: One Line Dr., Manchester, NH 03101.
Telephone: (603) 641-2005. **FAX:** (603) 641-2055.
E-Mail Address: baseballinfo@nhfishercats.com. **Website:** www.nhfishercats.com.
Affiliation (first year): Toronto Blue Jays (2004). **Years in League:** 2004-

OWNERSHIP, MANAGEMENT
Operated By: 6 to 4 to 3, LLC.
Principal Owner, Chief Executive Officer: Drew Weber.
President, General Manager: Shawn Smith. **Corporate Controller:** Sheri-Lynn Fournier. **Assistant GM:** Jeff Tagliaferro. **Director, Corporate Events:** John Egan. **Director, Baseball/Event Operations:** Mike Biagini. **Director, Media Relations:** John Zahr. **Director, Food/Beverage:** Tim Restall. **Director, Group Sales:** Erik Lesniak. **Director, Ticket Operations:** Kendra Krauss. **Group Sales:** Brent Weigler, Brian Weigler, Randy Menken. **Corporate Partnership Specialist:** Danielle Matteau. **Director, Corporate Sales:** Tim Dalton.

FIELD STAFF
Manager: Mike Basso. **Coach:** John Valentin. **Pitching Coach:** Dave LaRoche. **Trainer:** Voon Chong.

GAME INFORMATION
Radio Announcers: Mike Murphy, Bob Lipman. **No. of Games Broadcast:** Unavailable. **Flagship Station:** Unavailable.
PA Announcer: John Zahr. **Official Scorer:** Unavailable.
Stadium Name: Unavailable. **Location:** From I-93, take I-293 to exit 5 (Granite Street), go right on Granite Street, right on South Commercial Street. **Standard Game Times:** 6:35 p.m.; Sat. 5:05, (April-May) 1:05; Sun. 1:05. **Ticket Price Range:** $4-12.
Visiting Club Hotel: Comfort Inn, 298 Queen City Ave., Manchester, NH 03102. Telephone: (603) 668-2600.

NORWICH
NAVIGATORS

Office Address: 14 Stott Ave., Norwich, CT 06360.
Mailing Address: P.O. Box 6003, Yantic, CT 06389.
Telephone: (860) 887-7962. **FAX:** (860) 886-5996.
E-Mail Address: tater@gators.com. **Website:** www.gators.com.
Affiliation (first year): San Francisco Giants (2003). **Years in League:** 1995-.

OWNERSHIP, MANAGEMENT
Operated by: Navigators Baseball, LP.
President/Managing Partner: Lou DiBella.
General Manager: Keith Hallal. **Assistant GM/Director, Marketing:** Tom Hinsch. **Director, Finance:** Richard Darling. **Senior Director, Stadium Operations:** John Gilbert. **Group Sales Managers:** Johnny Gill, John Muszkewycz, David Uden. **Director, Merchandise/Internet:** John Fleming. **Ticket Manager:** Neil Frisch. **Director, Media/Broadcasting:** Shawn Holliday. **Community Relations:** Meaghan Davis. **Office Manager:** Michelle Sadowski. **Head Groundskeeper:** Chris Berube.

FIELD STAFF
Manager: Dave Machemer. **Coach:** Roger La Francois. **Pitching Coach:** Bob Stanley. **Trainer:** Patrick Serbus.

GAME INFORMATION
Radio Announcers: Shawn Holliday, Jeremy Lechan. **No. of Games Broadcast:** Home-71, Away-71. **Flagship Station:** WICH 1310-AM.
PA Announcer: Ed Weyant. **Official Scorer:** Gene Gumbs.

Stadium Name: Sen. Thomas J. Dodd Memorial Stadium. Location: I-395 to exit 82, follow signs to Norwich Industrial Park, stadium is in back of industrial park. Standard Game Times: 7:05 p.m.; Mon., Tue., Thur. (April-May) 6:35; Wed. (April-May) 12:35; Sat. (April-May) 1:05; Sun. 1:05. Ticket Price Range: $7-10.
    Visiting Club Hotel: Days Inn-Niantic, 265 Flanders Rd., Niantic, CT 06357. Telephone: (860) 739-6921.

PORTLAND
SEA DOGS

Office Address: 271 Park Ave., Portland, ME 04102.
Mailing Address: P.O. Box 636, Portland, ME 04104.
Telephone: (207) 874-9300. FAX: (207) 780-0317.
E-Mail Address: seadogs@portlandseadogs.com. Website: www.seadogs.com.
Affiliation (first year): Boston Red Sox (2003). Years in League: 1994-.

OWNERSHIP, MANAGEMENT
Operated By: Portland, Maine Baseball, Inc.
Principal Owner, Chairman: Daniel Burke.
President, General Manager: Charles Eshbach. Vice President/Assistant GM: John Kameisha. Assistant GM, Business Operations: Jim Heffley. Director, Public Relations: Chris Cameron. Director, Sales and Marketing/Promotions Coordinator: Geoff Iacuessa. Director, Group Sales: Corey Thompson. Director, Ticketing: Dave Strong. Assistant Director, Ticketing: Tony Cameron. Director, Broadcasting: Todd Jamison. Director, Food Services: Mike Scorza. Director, Video Operations: A.J. Gosselin. Special Projects: Peter Drivas. Office Manager: Judy Bray. Administrative Assistants: Adam Brunno, Kim Buchmann, Nick Cliche, Brice Greenleaf, Liz Knox, Jonathan Mercier, Drew Palmer, Jeremy Porter, Brian White.
Clubhouse Managers: Craig Candage Jr., Craig Candage Sr., Rick Goslin. Head Groundskeeper: Rick Anderson.

FIELD STAFF
Manager: Todd Claus. Coach: Russ Morman. Pitching Coach: Fernando Arroyo. Trainer: Masai Takahashi.

GAME INFORMATION
Radio Announcers: Todd Jamison. No. of Games Broadcast: Home-71, Away-71. Flagship Station: WBAE-1490 AM.
PA Announcer: Dean Rogers. Official Scorer: Mike Beveridge, Thom Hinton.
Stadium Name: Hadlock Field. Location: From South, I-295 to exit 5, merge onto Congress Street, left at St. John Street, merge right onto Park Ave. From North, I-295 to exit 6A, right onto Park Ave. Standard Game Times: 7 p.m., (April-May) 6; Sat. 6, (April-May) 1; Sun. 1. Ticket Price Range: $3-8.
Visiting Club Hotel: DoubleTree Hotel, 1230 Congress St., Portland, ME 04102. Telephone: (207) 774-5611.

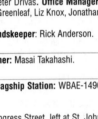

READING
PHILLIES

Office Address: Route 61 South/1900 Centre Ave., Reading, PA 19601.
Mailing Address: P.O. Box 15050, Reading, PA 19612.
Telephone: (610) 375-8469. FAX: (610) 373-5868.
E-Mail Address: info@readingphillies.com. Website: www.readingphillies.com.
Affiliation (first year): Philadelphia Phillies (1967). Years in League: 1933-35, 1952-61, 1963-65, 1967-.

OWNERSHIP, MANAGEMENT
Operated By: E&J Baseball Club, Inc.
Principal Owner, President: Craig Stein.
General Manager: Chuck Domino. Assistant GM: Scott Hunsicker. Director, Stadium Operations/Concessions: Andy Bortz. Director, Maintenance/Game Staff Operations: Troy Potthoff. Director, Stadium Grounds: Dan Douglas. Office Manager: Deneen Giesen. Controller: Kristyne Haver. Director, Merchandise: Kevin Sklenarik. Director, Ticket Operations: Mike Becker. Manager, Group Sales/Deck Buffets: Ryan Bardi. Manager, Group Sales/Pool and Picnic Buffets: Christie Chrisanthon. Manager, Group Sales/Customer Service: Mike Robinson. Director, Group Sales/Game Presentation: Ashley Forlini. Director, Communications: Rob Hackash. Communications Assistant: Andy Kauffman. Director, Sales: Joe Bialek. Corporate Sales/Game Entertainment/Graphic Artist: Matt Jackson. Ticket Assistant/Fundraising: Ben Rupp. Special Events Coordinator: Josh Holly.

FIELD STAFF
Manager: Steve Swisher. Coach: John Morris. Pitching Coach: Tom Filer. Trainer: Joel Kennedy.

GAME INFORMATION
Radio Announcer: Steve Degler. No. of Games Broadcast: Home-71, Away-71. Flagship Station: ESPN 1240-AM.
PA Announcer: Dave Bauman. Official Scorer: John Lemcke.
Stadium Name: FirstEnergy Stadium. Location: From east, take Pennsylvania Turnpike West to Morgantown exit, to 176 North, to 422 West, to Route 12 East, to Route 61 South exit. From west, take 422 East to Route 12 East, to

Route 61 South exit. From north, take 222 South to Route 12 exit, to Route 61 South exit. From south, take 222 North to 422 West, to Route 12 East exit at Route 61 South.

Standard Game Times: 7:05 p.m., Mon.-Thurs. (April-May) 6:35; Sun. 1:05. **Ticket Price Range:** $4-9.

Visiting Club Hotel: Wellesley Inn, 910 Woodland Ave., Wyomissing, PA 19610. Telephone: (610) 374-1500.

TRENTON
THUNDER

Office Address: One Thunder Rd., Trenton, NJ 08611.
Telephone: (609) 394-3300. **FAX:** (609) 394-9666.
E-Mail Address: office@trentonthunder.com. **Website:** www.trentonthunder.com.
Affiliation (first year): New York Yankees (2003). **Years in League:** 1994-.

OWNERSHIP, MANAGEMENT

Operated by: Garden State Baseball, LLP.

General Manager/Chief Operating Officer: Rick Brenner. **Assistant GM:** Brad Taylor. **Executive Director, Marketing:** Eric Lipsman. **Chief Financial Officer:** Steve Ripa. **Director, Stadium Operations:** Josh Watson. **Director, Merchandising:** Joe Pappalardo. **Director, Media Relations/Broadcasting:** Dan Loney. **Director, Ticket Operations:** Matt Pentima. **Director, Group Sales:** Brian Cassidy. **Director, Public Relations:** Bill Cook. **Office Manager:** Kathy Gallagher. **Assistant Directors, Group Sales:** Jason Schubert, Brian Fox. **Assistant Director, Ticket Sales:** Patience Purdy. **Assistant Controller:** Jeff Kluge. **Manager, Community Relations:** Ellen Donahue. **Manager, Stadium Operations:** Ryan Crammer. **Manager, Group Sales:** Frank Chimera. **Conference Center Specialist/Group Sales Manager:** Vicki Siesta. **Specialist, Ticket Office:** Jeff Hurley. **Assistant, Merchandise:** Amy Noble. **Assistant, Ticket Office:** Adam Smedberg. **Assistant, Group Sales:** Ross Mehalko. **Interns:** Melanie Astore, John Brilla, Bobby Capaldo, Joseph Compitello, Desiree DiAngelo, Josh DiCamillo, Jack Dooley, Steven Dilemme, Chris Deubert, Robert Fox, Megan Higgenbotham, Matt Karpel, Leora Kleist, Kyle Krug, Michael Lenard, C.J. Nami, Evan Olesh, Ross Rodriguez, Kenneth Ruch, Matt Schwartz, Nadia Silk, Evan Steinberg, Greg Welikson. **Head Groundskeeper:** Nicole Sherry. **Clubhouse Manager:** Daniel Rose.

FIELD STAFF

Manager: Bill Masse. **Coach:** Ty Hawkins. **Pitching Coach:** Dave Eiland. **Trainer:** Zac Womack.

GAME INFORMATION

Radio Announcers: Dan Loney, Jim Jackson. **Flagship Station:** WBUD 1260-AM. **No. of Games Broadcast:** Home-71, Away-71.

PA Announcer: Bill Bromberg. **Official Scorers:** Jay Dunn, Mike Maconi.

Stadium Name: Samuel J. Plumeri Sr. Field at Mercer County Waterfront Park. **Location:** From I-95, take Route 1 North to Route 29 South, stadium entrance just before tunnel. **Standard Game Times:** 7:05 p.m.; Sun. 1:35. **Ticket Price Range:** $6-9.

Visiting Club Hotel: McIntosh Hotel, 3270 Brunswick Pike, Lawrenceville, NJ 08648. Telephone: (609) 896-3700.

SOUTHERN
LEAGUE

President: Don Mincher.
Vice President: Steve DeSalvo.
Directors: Peter Bragan Jr. (Jacksonville), Steve Bryant (Carolina), Frank Burke (Chattanooga), Steve DeSalvo (Mississippi), Tom Dickson (Montgomery), Doug Kirchhofer (Tennessee), Robert Lozinak (West Tenn), Jonathan Nelson (Birmingham), Miles Prentice (Huntsville), Bill Shanahan (Mobile).
Vice President, Operations: Lori Webb. **Coordinator, Media Relations:** Jason Risley.
Division Structure: North—Carolina, Chattanooga, Huntsville, Tennessee, West Tenn.
South—Birmingham, Jacksonville, Mississippi, Mobile, Montgomery.
Regular Season: 140 games (split schedule). **2005 Opening Date:** April 7. **Closing Date:** Sept. 5.
All-Star Game: July 13 at Mobile.
Playoff Format: First-half division champions meet second-half division champions in best-of-5 series. Winners meet in best-of-5 series for league championship.
Don Mincher
Roster Limit: 23; 24 until 30th day of season and after Aug. 9. **Player Eligibility Rule:** No restrictions.
Brand of Baseball: Rawlings.
Statistician: Major League Baseball Advanced Media, 75 Ninth Ave., New York, NY 10011.
Umpires: Brandon Bushee (Tocsin, IL), Joshua Carlisle (New Philadelphia, OH), Scot Chamberlain (Strawberry Plains, TN), Maria Cortesio (Rock Island, IL), Robert Hansen (Corona, CA), Edwin Hickox (Daytona Beach, FL), Brian Kennedy (Charlotte, NC), Jeffrey Latter (Gresham, OR), Brian Martin (Mooresville, NC), Todd Paskiet (Venice, FL), Pete Pedersen (Orlando, FL), Will Robinson (Marion, AR), Jamie Roebuck (Connelly Springs, NC), R.J. Thompson (Mt. Carmel, TN), Garrett Watson (Las Vegas, NV).

STADIUM INFORMATION

Club	Stadium	Opened	Dimensions			Capacity	2004 Att.
			LF	CF	RF		
Birmingham	Hoover Metropolitan Stadium	1988	340	405	340	10,800	280,879
Carolina	Five County Stadium	1991	330	400	330	6,500	245,810
Chattanooga	BellSouth Park	2000	325	400	330	6,160	244,961
Huntsville	Joe W. Davis Municipal Stadium	1985	345	405	330	10,200	180,506
Jacksonville	Baseball Grounds of Jacksonville	2003	321	420	317	11,000	420,495
*Mississippi	Mississippi Braves Stadium	2005	337	332	400	6,000	143,443
Mobile	Hank Aaron Stadium	1997	325	400	310	6,000	193,885
Montgomery	Montgomery Riverwalk Stadium	2004	314	401	332	6,000	322,946
Tennessee	Smokies Park	2000	330	400	330	6,000	253,756
West Tenn	Pringles Park	1998	310	395	320	6,000	159,308

* Franchise operated in Greenville, S.C., in 2004

BIRMINGHAM
BARONS

Office Address: 100 Ben Chapman Dr., Hoover, AL 35244.
Mailing Address: P.O. Box 360007, Birmingham, AL 35236.
Telephone: (205) 988-3200. **FAX:** (205) 988-9698.
E-Mail Address: barons@barons.com. **Website:** www.barons.com.
Affiliation (first year): Chicago White Sox (1986). **Years in League:** 1964-65, 1967-75, 1981-.

OWNERSHIP, MANAGEMENT
Operated by: Elmore Sports Group, Ltd.
Principal Owner: Dave Elmore.
General Manager: Jonathan Nelson. **Director, Stadium Operations:** James Young. **Head Groundskeeper:** Luke Davis. **Director, Broadcasting:** Curt Bloom. **Director, Media Relations:** Mike Hobson. **Director, Sales:** Kevin Anderson. **Director, Marketing:** Jason Lehr. **Director, Promotions:** Jeremy Neisser. **Director, Season Tickets:** Jim Stennett. **Director, Group Sales:** Michael Pepper. **Director, Food Services:** Eric Crook. **Director, Catering:** Theresa Fiebrich. **Corporate Events Planners:** John Wilson, Blair Holden, Clark McDuff. **Office Manager:** Kecia Arnold.

FIELD STAFF
Manager: Razor Shines. **Coach:** Gregg Ritchie. **Pitching Coach:** Richard Dotson. **Trainer:** Joe Geck.

GAME INFORMATION
Radio Announcer: Curt Bloom. **No. of Games Broadcast:** Home-70, Away-70. **Flagship Station:** WYDE 101.1-FM.
PA Announcer: Chris Champion. **Official Scorer:** Mike Sullivan.
Stadium Name: Hoover Metropolitan Stadium. **Location:** I-459 to Highway 150 (exit 10) in Hoover. **Standard Game Times:** 7 p.m., Wed (April-June) 11 a.m.; Sun. (April-June) 2, (July-Aug.) 6. **Ticket Price Range:** $5-10.
Visiting Club Hotel: Best Western Riverchase Inn, 1800 Riverchase Dr., Birmingham, AL 35244. Telephone: (205) 985-7500.

CAROLINA
MUDCATS

Office Address: 1501 N.C. Hwy. 39, Zebulon, NC 27597.
Mailing Address: P.O. Drawer 1218, Zebulon, NC 27597.
Telephone: (919) 269-2287. **FAX:** (919) 269-4910.
E-Mail Address: muddy@gomudcats.com. **Website:** www.gomudcats.com.
Affiliation (first year): Florida Marlins (2003). **Years in League:** 1991-.

OWNERSHIP, MANAGEMENT
Operated by: Carolina Mudcats Professional Baseball Club, Inc.
Principal Owner: Steve Bryant.
General Manager: Joe Kremer. **Assistant GM:** Eric Gardner. **Director, Broadcasting:** Patrick Kinas. **Directors, Stadium Operations:** Alex Paul, Jeff Dowd **Corporate Sales Representatives:** Adam Dyer, Paul Windley. **Director, Group Sales:** Elizabeth Henderson. **Director, Tickets:** Erin Wallace. **Director, Special Events:** Nathan Priddy. **Head Groundskeeper:** John Packer. **Office Manager:** Jackie DiPrimo. **Community Relations/Marketing:** Brian DeWine. **Director, Food/Beverage:** David Turska. **Group Sales Associates:** Holden Royall, Hampton Terry. **Coordinator, Video Production:** Scott Timmreck.

FIELD STAFF
Manager: Gary Allenson. **Coach:** Steve Phillips. **Pitching Coach:** Scott Mitchell. **Trainer:** Steve Miller.

GAME INFORMATION
Radio Announcer: Patrick Kinas. **No. of Games Broadcast:** Home-70, Away-70. **Flagship Station:** Unavailable.
PA Announcer: Duke Sanders. **Official Scorer:** John Hobgood.
Stadium Name: Five County Stadium. **Location:** From Raleigh, U.S. 64 East to 264 East, exit at Highway 39 in Zebulon. **Standard Game Times:** 7:15 p.m.; Sun. 4, (April, May, Sept) 2. **Ticket Price Range:** $4.50-8.50.
Visiting Club Hotel: Best Western Raleigh North, 2715 Capital Blvd., Raleigh, NC 27604. Telephone: (919) 872-5000.

CHATTANOOGA
LOOKOUTS

Office Address: 201 Power Alley, Chattanooga, TN 37402.
Mailing Address: P.O. Box 11002, Chattanooga, TN 37401.

SOUTHERN LEAGUE

Telephone: (423) 267-2208. **FAX**: (423) 267-4258.
E-Mail Address: lookouts@lookouts.com. **Website**: www.lookouts.com.
Affiliation (first year): Cincinnati Reds (1988). **Years in League**: 1964-65, 1976-.

OWNERSHIP, MANAGEMENT

Operated by: Scenic City Baseball, LLC.
Principal Owners: Daniel Burke, Frank Burke, Charles Eshbach.
President/General Manager: Frank Burke. **Assistant GM/Director, Media Relations**: John Maedel. **Assistant GM**: Debbie Triplett **Director, Business Administration**: Trevor Reeves. **Director, Group Sales**: Bill Wheeler. **Director, Merchandising**: Kristin Dillard. **Director, Ticketing Operations**: Beth Elliott. **Director, Concessions**: Steve Sullivan. **Director, Broadcasting**: Larry Ward. **Head Groundskeeper**: Bo Henley.

FIELD STAFF

Manager: Jayhawk Owens. **Coach**: Jamie Dismuke. **Pitching Coach**: Bill Moloney. **Trainer**: Unavailable.

GAME INFORMATION

Radio Announcer: Larry Ward. **No. of Games Broadcast**: Home-70, Away-70. **Flagship Station**: WDOD 1310-AM. **PA Announcer**: John Maedel. **Official Scorers**: Wirt Gammon, Andy Paul.
Stadium Name: BellSouth Park. **Location**: From I-24, take U.S. 27 North to exit 1C (Fourth Street), first left onto Chestnut Street, left onto Third Street. **Standard Game Times**: 7:15 p.m.; Wed. 12:15; Sun. 2:15. **Ticket Price Range**: $4-8.
Visiting Club Hotel: Holiday Inn, 2345 Shallowford Rd., Chattanooga, TN 37412. Telephone: (423) 855-2898.

HUNTSVILLE
STARS

Office Address: 3125 Leeman Ferry Rd., Huntsville, AL 35801.
Mailing Address: P.O. Box 2769, Huntsville, AL 35804.
Telephone: (256) 882-2562. **FAX**: (256) 880-0801.
E-Mail Address: info@huntsvillestars.com. **Website**: www.huntsvillestars.com.
Affiliation (first year): Milwaukee Brewers (1999). **Years In League**: 1985-.

OWNERSHIP, MANAGEMENT

Operated by: Huntsville Stars, LLC.
President: Miles Prentice.
General Manager: Tom Van Schaack. **Director, Broadcasting/Sales**: Unavailable. **Director, Media Relations**: Bryan Neece. **Marketing/Community Relations**: Erin Moroney. **Director, Ticketing**: Gary Ward. **Director, Field Maintenance**: Kyle Lewis. **Director, Stadium Operations**: Cason Warren. **Group Sales Executives**: Matt Price, Erin Moroney, Gary Ward. **Office Manager/Assistant, Community Relations**: Earl Grilliot.

FIELD STAFF

Manager: Don Money. **Coach**: Sandy Guerrero. **Pitching Coach**: Rich Sauveur. **Trainer**: David Yeager.

GAME INFORMATION

Radio Announcer: Unavailable. **No. of Games Broadcast**: Home-70, Away-70. **Flagship Station**: WTKI 1450-AM. **PA Announcer**: Todd Blass. **Official Scorer**: Don Rizzardi.
Stadium Name: Joe W. Davis Municipal Stadium. **Location**: I-65 to I-565 East, south on Memorial Parkway to Drake Avenue exit, right on Don Mincher Drive. **Standard Game Times**: 7:05 p.m., Tues.-Wed. (April-June 20) 12:05; Sun. (April-June 20) 2:05. (June 22-Sept.) 6:05. **Ticket Price Range**: $5-8.
Visiting Club Hotel: La Quinta Inn, 3141 University Dr., Huntsville, AL 35805. Telephone: (256) 533-0756.

JACKSONVILLE
SUNS

Office Address: 301 A. Philip Randolph Blvd, Jacksonville, FL 32202.
Mailing Address: P.O. Box 4756, Jacksonville, FL 32201.
Telephone: (904) 358-2846. **FAX**: (904) 358-2845.
E-Mail Address: jaxsuns@bellsouth.net. **Website**: www.jaxsuns.com.
Affiliation (second year): Los Angeles Dodgers (2001). **Years In League**: 1970-.

OWNERSHIP, MANAGEMENT

Operated by: Baseball Jax, Inc.
Principal Owner, President: Peter Bragan Sr. **President**: Mary Frances Bragan.
Vice President/General Manager: Peter Bragan Jr. **Assistant GM**: Kirk Goodman. **Director, Ticket Operations**: Karlie Evatt. **Director, Broadcasting**: Joe Block. **Director, Community Relations**: Tana Stavinoha. **Director, Field Operations**: Ed Attalla. **Director, Group Sales**: Robyn Wassman. **Director, Food/Beverage**: Bill Schumpp. **Director, Merchandise**: Traci Barbour. **Director, Sponsorships/Promotions**: Brady Ballard. **Director, Stadium Operations**:

Shannon Leach. **Assistant Director, Food/Beverage:** Don Gardner. **Manager, Box Office:** Lana Lundell. **Office Manager:** Barbara O'Berry. **Business Manager:** Craig Barnett. **Executive Assistant:** Darlene Short. **Groundskeeper:** Joe Soenksen. **Administrative Assistants:** Betsy Pellicer, Bradley Rodriguez, Brendan Bledsoe, Mark Hannah.

FIELD STAFF
Manager: John Shoemaker. **Coach:** Steve Yeager. **Pitching Coach:** Ken Howell. **Trainer:** Tony Cordova. **Strength/Conditioning:** Ron Quintana

GAME INFORMATION
Radio Announcer: Joe Block. **No. of Games Broadcast:** Home-70, Away-70. **Flagship Station:** The Fox 930-AM. **PA Announcer:** John Leard. **Official Scorer:** Jason Eliopulos.
Stadium Name: The Baseball Grounds of Jacksonville. **Location:** I-95 South to Martin Luther King Parkway exit, follow Gator Bowl Boulevard around Alltel Stadium; I-95 North to Exit 347 (Emerson Street), go right to Hart Bridge Expressway, take Sports Complex exit, left at light to stop sign, take left and follow around Alltel Stadium; From Mathews Bridge, take A. Philip Randolph exit, right on A. Philip Randolph, straight to stadium. **Standard Game Times:** 7:05 p.m, Wed. 1:05; Sun. 3:05, 5:05. **Ticket Price Range:** $5.50-17.50.
Visiting Club Hotel: Adam's Mark Jacksonville, 225 Coastline Dr., Jacksonville, FL 32202. Telephone: (904) 633-9095.

MISSISSIPPI
BRAVES

Office Address: 226 St. Paul St., Pearl, MS 39208.
Mailing Address: P.O. Box 97389, Pearl, MS 39288.
Telephone: (601) 932-8788. **FAX:** (601) 936-3567.
Website: www.mississippibraves.com.
Affiliation (first year): Atlanta Braves (2005). **Years in League:** 2005.

OWNERSHIP, MANAGEMENT
Operated by: Atlanta National League Baseball Club, Inc. **Principal Owner:** Time Warner.
General Manager: Steve DeSalvo. **Assistant GM:** Jim Bishop. **Promotions Director:** Brian Prochilo. **Ticket Manager:** Bob Askin. **Head Groundskeeper:** Matt Taylor. **Director, Food Services:** Jim Rawson. **Office Manager:** Kate Loftin. **Sales Associates:** Sean Guillotte, Tracy Echols.

FIELD STAFF
Manager: Brian Snitker. **Coach:** Phillip Wellman. **Pitching Coach:** Kent Willis. **Trainer:** Mike Graus.

GAME INFORMATION
Radio Announcer: Unavailable. **No. of Games Broadcast:** Home-70, Away-70. **Flagship Station:** Unavailable.
PA Announcer: Unavailable. **Official Scorer:** Unavailable.
Stadium Name: Mississippi Braves Stadium. **Location:** I-20 to exit 48/Pearl (Pearson Road). **Standard Game Times:** Unavailable. **Ticket Price Range:** $8-12.
Visiting Club Hotel: Best Western Jackson North, 593 E. Beasley Rd., Jackson, MS 39206. Telephone: (601) 956-8686.

MOBILE
BAYBEARS

Office Address: Hank Aaron Stadium, 755 Bolling Bros. Blvd., Mobile, AL 36606.
Telephone: (251) 479-2327. **FAX:** (251) 476-1147.
E-Mail Address: baybears@mobilebaybears.com. **Website:** www.mobilebay-bears.com.
Affiliation (first year): San Diego Padres (1997). **Years in League:** 1966, 1970, 1997-.

OWNERSHIP, MANAGEMENT
Operated by: HWS Group.
Principal Owner: Mike Savit.
President/General Manager: Bill Shanahan. **Vice President/General Sales Manager:** Travis Toth. **Assistant GM, Finance:** Betty Adams. **Assistant GM, Ticket Operations:** Doug Stephens. **Assistant GM, Facility Operations/Head Groundskeeper:** Pat White. **Director, Group Sales:** Jeff Long. **Director, Baseball Operations:** Jason Kirksey. **Director, Banquet Facilities:** Mike Callahan. **Office Manager:** LaLoni Taylor. **Director, Stadium Operations:** Nick Krause. **Sales Representatives:** John Hilliard, Ira Yates. **Broadcaster/Media Relations:** Tim Hagerty. **Merchandising:** Matt Taylor. **Clubhouse Manager:** A.J. Niland. **Stadium Operations Assistant:** Wade Vadakin. **Internet Liaison/Team Chaplain:** Lorin Burr. **Interns:** Jeremy Howard, Ryan Perdue.

FIELD STAFF
Manager: Gary Jones. **Coach:** Mike Davis. **Pitching Coach:** Mike Harkey. **Trainer:** Will Sinon.

GAME INFORMATION
Radio Announcer: Tim Hagerty. **No. Of Games Broadcast:** Home-70, Away-70. **Flagship Station:** WABB 1480-AM. **PA Announcers:** Jay Hasting, Matt McCoy. **Official Scorer:** Unavailable.
Stadium Name: Hank Aaron Stadium. **Location:** I-65 to exit 1 (Government Blvd. East), right at Satchel Paige Drive, right at Bolling Bros. Boulevard. **Standard Game Times:** 7:05 p.m.; Sun. (April-May) 2:05, (June-Aug.) 6:05. **Ticket Price Range:** $4-8.
Visiting Club Hotel: Ashbury Suites, 600 West I-65 Service Rd., Mobile, AL 36608. Telephone: (251) 344-8030.

MONTGOMERY
BISCUITS

Office Address: 200 Coosa St., Montgomery, AL 36104.
Telephone: (334) 323-2255. **FAX:** (334) 323-2225.
E-Mail Address: info@biscuitsbaseball.com. **Website:** www.biscuitsbaseball.com.
Affiliation (first year): Tampa Bay Devil Rays (2004). **Years in League:** 1965-1980, 2004-.

OWNERSHIP, MANAGEMENT
Operated by: Montgomery Professional Baseball, LLC.
Principal Owners: Tom Dickson, Sherrie Myers.
General Manager, Operations: Greg Rauch. **Assistant GM:** Patrick Day. **GM, Sales/Marketing:** Megan Frazer. **Marketing Assistants:** Marla Terranova, Jim Tocco, DeAndrae Watson. **Sponsorship Manager:** Gretchen Pickle. **Corporate Account Executives:** Travis Burkett, Brian Toy. **Box Office Manager:** Kerry Cranford. **Season Ticket Coordinator/Head Concierge:** Kent Rose. **Director, Operations:** Steve Blackwell. **Group Sales Representatives:** Ben Charlton, Eric Clements, Alton Gorum. **Director, Food Service:** Nick Kavalauskas. **Concession Supervisor:** Ben Blankenship. **Director, Catering:** Jason Wilson. **Kitchen Supervisor:** Andy Day. **Business Manager:** Linda Fast. **Retail Manager:** Monte Meyers. **Client Service Executive:** Hope Fussell. **Bookkeeper:** Tranitra Avery. **Office Assistant:** Bill Sisk. **Warehouse Supervisor:** Edward Sole. **Head Groundskeeper:** Lane Oglesvy.

FIELD STAFF
Manager: Mako Oliveras. **Coach:** Skeeter Barnes. **Pitching Coach:** Xavier Hernandez. **Trainer:** Matt Lucero.

GAME INFORMATION
Radio Announcer: Jim Tocco. **No. of Games Broadcast:** Home-70, Away-70. **Flagship Station:** WLWI 1440-AM. **PA Announcer:** Rick Hendrick. **Official Scorers:** Travis Jarome, A.A. Moore.
Stadium Name: Montgomery Riverwalk Stadium. **Location:** I-65 to exit 172, east on Herron Street, left on Coosa Street. **Standard Game Times:** 7:05 p.m.; Sun. (April-June) 2:05, (July-Sept.) 6:05. **Ticket Price Range:** $6-10.
Visiting Club Hotel: Unavailable.

TENNESSEE
SMOKIES

Office Address: 3540 Line Dr., Kodak, TN 37764.
Telephone: (865) 286-2300. **FAX:** (865) 523-9913.
E-Mail Address: info@smokiesbaseball.com. **Website:** www.smokiesbaseball.com.
Affiliation (first year): Arizona Diamondbacks (2005) **Years in League:** 1964-67, 1972-.

OWNERSHIP, MANAGEMENT
Operated by: SPBC, LLC.
President: Doug Kirchhofer.
General Manager: Brian Cox. **Assistant GM:** Jeff Shoaf. **Director, Broadcasting/Media Relations:** Tom Hart. **Director, Sales:** Jon Kuka. **Corporate Sales Executive:** Tom Luebbe. **Director, Stadium Operations:** Brian Webster. **Director, Ticket Operations:** Kamryn Hollar. **Director, Community Relations:** Lauren Chesney. **Director, Field Operations:** Ross D'Lugos. **Assistant Director, Field Operations:** Bob Shoemaker. **Director, Food/Beverage:** Tony DaSilveira. **Director, Group Sales:** Bryce Patton. **Group Sales Representatives:** Gabe Bowman, Amanda Turner, Ryan Koehler. **Business Manager:** Suzanne French. **Assistant, Broadcast/Media Relations:** Chip Kain. **Merchandise Assistant:** Mark French. **Operations Assistants:** Cory Barker, Matt Blue, Ryan Cox, Matt Zahler. **Administrative Assistants:** Kay Campbell, Tolena Trout.

FIELD STAFF
Manager: Tony Perezchica. **Coach:** Eric Fox. **Pitching Coach:** Dan Carlson. **Trainer:** Rodger Fleming. **Strength Coach:** Ed Yong.

GAME INFORMATION
Radio Announcers: Tom Hart, Chip Kain. **No. of Games Broadcast:** Home-70, Away-70. **Flagship Stations:** WNOX 990-AM, WSEV 930-AM.
PA Announcer: George Yardley. **Official Scorers:** Randy Corrado, Paul Barger.
Stadium Name: Smokies Park. **Location:** I-40 to exit 407, Highway 66 North. **Standard Game Times:** 7:15 p.m.,

Sun. 5. **Ticket Price Range:** $5-9.
   Visiting Club Hotel: Days Inn-Exit 407, 3402 Winfield Dunn Pkwy., Kodak TN 37764. Telephone: (865) 933-4500.

WEST TENN
DIAMOND JAXX

   Office Address: 4 Fun Place, Jackson, TN 38305.
   Telephone: (731) 988-5299. **FAX:** (731) 988-5246.
   E-Mail Address: fun@diamondjaxx.com. **Website:** www.diamondjaxx.com.
   Affiliation (first year): Chicago Cubs (1998). **Years in League:** 1998-.

OWNERSHIP, MANAGEMENT
   Operated by: Lozinak Baseball Properties, LLC.
   General Manager: Jeff Parker. **Director, Operations:** Robert Jones. **Director, Broadcasting/Media Relations:** Ron Potesta. **Director, Advertising/Group Sales:** Dave Jojola. **Director, Ticketing/Merchandise Sales:** Jason Compton. **Manager, Community Relations/Group Sales:** Stephanie Pierce. **Manager, Advertising Sales/Promotions:** Mark Vanderhaar. **Manager, Ticketing/Merchandising and Publications:** Liz Malone. **Account Executive/Group Sales:** John-Michael Tolar. **Administrative Assistant:** Jackie Nelson. **Head Groundskeeper:** Justin Spillman. **Concessions Manager:** Barbara Newsom. **Clubhouse Manager:** Bradley Arnold.

FIELD STAFF
   Manager: Bobby Dickerson. **Coach:** Von Joshua. **Pitching Coach:** Alan Dunn. **Trainer:** Chuck Baughman. **Strength/Conditioning:** Brad Krieg.

GAME INFORMATION
   Radio Announcer: Ron Potesta. **No. of Games Broadcast:** Home-70, Away-70. **Flagship Station:** Unavailable. **PA Announcer:** Unavailable. **Official Scorer:** Tracy Brewer.
   Stadium Name: Pringles Park. **Location:** From I-40, take exit 85 South on F.E. Wright Drive, left onto Ridgecrest Road. **Standard Game Times:** 7:05 p.m., 6:35 (April-May); Wed. 12:05, Sun. 1:05. **Ticket Prices:** $4-8.50.
   Visiting Club Hotel: Doubletree Hotel, 1770 Hwy. 45 Bypass, Jackson, TN 38305. Telephone: (731) 664-6900.

TEXAS
LEAGUE

Mailing Address: 2442 Facet Oak, San Antonio, TX 78232.
Telephone: (210) 545-5297. **FAX:** (210) 545-5298.
E-Mail Address: texasleague@sbcglobal.net. **Website:** www.texas-league.com.
Years League Active: 1888-1890, 1892, 1895-1899, 1902-1942, 1946-.

President, Treasurer: Tom Kayser.
Vice President: Mike McCall. **Corporate Secretary:** Burl Yarbrough. **Administrative Assistant:** Tim Watts.
Directors: Jon Dandes (Wichita), J.J. Gottsch (Corpus Christi), Mike Lamping (Springfield), Chuck Lamson (Tulsa), Mike McCall (Frisco), Miles Prentice (Midland), Bill Valentine (Arkansas), Burl Yarbrough (San Antonio).
Division Structure: East—Arkansas, Springfield, Tulsa, Wichita. **West**—Corpus Christi, Frisco, Midland, San Antonio.
Regular Season: 140 games (split schedule). **2005 Opening Date:** April 7. **Closing Date:** Sept. 4.
All-Star Game: June 21 at Frisco.
Playoff Format: First-half division champions play second-half division champions in best-of-5 series. Winners meet in best-of-7 series for league championship.
Roster Limit: 23; 24 for first 30 days of season and after Aug. 9. **Player Eligibility Rule:** No restrictions.

Tom Kayser

Brand of Baseball: Rawlings.
Statistician: Major League Baseball Advanced Media, 75 Ninth Ave., New York, NY 10011.
Umpires: Delfin Colon (Houston, TX), Stephen Fritzoni (Hesperio, CA), Matt Kaylor (Grain Valley, MO), Jason Kiser (Columbia, MO), Barry Larson (Lewiston, ID), Joseph Maiden (West Hills, CA), David Rackley (Seabrook, TX), Jeremy Sparling (Hughson, CA), Joe Stegner (Boise, ID), Jason Stein (Forth Worth, TX), Chris Tiller (Tyler, TX), Todd Waters (Coppell, TX).

STADIUM INFORMATION

Club	Stadium	Opened	LF	CF	RF	Capacity	2004 Att.
Arkansas	Ray Winder Field	1932	330	390	345	6,083	178,655
*Corpus Christi	Whataburger Field	2005	325	400	315	7,500	689,286
Frisco	Dr. Pepper/Seven-Up Ballpark	2003	330	410	322	10,000	553,312
Midland	First America Bank Ballpark	2002	330	410	322	6,669	256,110
San Antonio	Nelson Wolff Municipal Stadiumj	1994	310	402	340	6,200	278,080
#Springfield	John Q. Hammonds Field	2003	315	400	330	8,458	229,315
Tulsa	Drillers Stadium	1981	335	390	340	11,003	320,733
Wichita	Lawrence-Dumont Stadium	1934	344	401	312	6,055	161,638

*Franchise operated in Round Rock in 2004.
#Franchise operated in El Paso in 2004.

ARKANSAS TRAVELERS

Office Address: Ray Winder Field at War Memorial Park, Little Rock, AR 72205.
Mailing Address: P.O. Box 55066, Little Rock, AR 72215.
Telephone: (501) 664-1555. **FAX:** (501) 664-1834.
E-Mail Address: travs@travs.com. **Website:** www.travs.com.
Affiliation (first year): Anaheim Angels (2001). **Years In League:** 1966-.

OWNERSHIP, MANAGEMENT
Operated by: Arkansas Travelers Baseball Club, Inc.
President: Bert Parke.
Executive Vice President, General Manager: Bill Valentine. **Assistant GM:** Pete Laven. **Director, Community Relations:** Lauren Rew. **Director, Media Relations/Broadcasting:** Phil Elson. **Director, Concessions:** John Evans. **Director, Stadium Operations:** Fifty Greene. **Office Manager:** John Paige. **Park Superintendent:** Greg Johnston. **Assistant Park Superintendent:** Reggie Temple. **Bookkeeper:** Nena Valentine.

FIELD STAFF
Manager: Tom Gamboa. **Coach:** Todd Takayoshi. **Pitching Coach:** Keith Comstock. **Trainer:** Armando Rivas.

GAME INFORMATION
Radio Announcer: Phil Elson. **No. of Games Broadcast:** Home-70, Away-70. **Flagship Station:** KDXE 1380-AM. **PA Announcer:** Kevin Cruise. **Official Scorers:** Tim Cooper, Dan Floyd.
Stadium Name: Ray Winder Field. **Location:** I-630 to Fair Park Boulevard exit, north off exit, right after zoo. **Standard Game Times:** 7:10 p.m., 6:30 DH; Sun. 2. **Ticket Price Range:** $5-9.
Visiting Club Hotel: La Quinta Inn, 4100 East McCain Blvd., North Little Rock, AR 72117. Telephone: (501) 945-0808.

CORPUS CHRISTI HOOKS

(Club operated in Round Rock in 2004)
Office Address: 734 East Port Ave., Corpus Christi, TX 78401.
Mailing Address: P.O. Box H, Corpus Christi, TX 78469.
Telephone: (361) 561-4665. **FAX:** (361) 561-4666 .
E-Mail Address: info@cchooks.com. **Website:** www.cchooks.com.
Affiliation (first year): Houston Astros (2005). **Years in League:** 1958-59, 2005.

OWNERSHIP, MANAGEMENT
Operated by: Ryan Sanders Baseball
Principal Owners: Reese Ryan, Reid Ryan, Nolan Ryan, Brad Sanders, Bret Sanders, Don Sanders. **Chairman, President:** Reid Ryan. **Chief Financial Officer:** Reese Ryan. **President:** J.J. Gottsch.
General Manager: Ken Schrom. **Assistant GM, Ticket Operations:** Michael Wood. **Director, Community Relations:** Elisa Macias. **Controller:** Christy Lockard. **Director, Ballpark Entertainment:** Clint Musslewhite. **Director, Media/Public Relations:** Matt Hicks. **Director, Merchandising:** Brooke Sims. **Director, Group Sales:** Joe McMahon. **Director, Customer Relations:** Tina Athans. **Account Executive:** Adam Nuse. **Head Groundskeeper:** Brad Detmore. **Stadium Operations:** Leslie Hitt. **Clubhouse Manager:** Sven Offerson.

FIELD STAFF
Manager: Dave Clark. **Coach:** John Tamargo. **Pitching Coach:** Joe Slusarski. **Trainer:** Jamey Snodgrass.

GAME INFORMATION
Radio Announcer: Matt Hicks. **No. of Games Broadcast:** Home-70, Away-70. **Flagship Station:** KOUL 103.7-FM. **PA Announcer:** Clint Musslewhite. **Official Scorer:** Unavailable.
Stadium Name: Whataburger Field. **Location:** I-37 to end of interstate, left at Chaparral, left at Port Ave. **Standard Game Times:** 7:05 p.m.; Sun. (April-May) 2:05, (June-Sept.) 6:05. **Ticket Price Range:** $5-9.
Visiting Club Hotel: Omni Marina Hotel, 707 N. Shoreline, Corpus Christi, TX 78401. Telephone: 361-886-3553.

FRISCO ROUGHRIDERS

Office Address: 7300 RoughRiders Trail, Frisco, TX 75034.
Telephone: (972) 731-9200. **FAX:** (972) 731-7455.
E-Mail Address: info@ridersbaseball.com. **Website:** www.ridersbaseball.com.

Affiliation (first year): Texas Rangers (2003). **Years in League:** 2003-.

OWNERSHIP, MANAGEMENT

Operated by: Mandalay Sports Entertainment.
Principal Owners: Mandalay Sports Entertainment.
President, General Manager: Mike McCall. **Assistant General Manager:** Mike deMaine. **Senior Vice Presidents, Sponsorships:** Scott Sanju. **VP, Ticket Sales:** Brent Stehlik. **VP, Finance/Human Resources:** Sally Morris. **VP, Corporate Partnerships:** Mark Clayton. **Senior Director, Corporate Partnerships:** Rebecca King. **Director, Group Sales:** Marcia Steinberg. **Director, Customer Service:** Dick Harmon. **Director, Special Projects:** Jennifer Knaup. **Director, Sponsor Promotions:** Todd McVeigh. **Director, Ticket Operations:** Michael Byrnes. **Creative Director:** Aaron Artman. **Special Events/Suite Services Coordinator:** Jennifer Jimenez. **Senior Corporate Marketing Manager:** Brandon Raphael. **Corporate Marketing Managers:** Jason Cohen, Michael Drake, Matt Goodman, Andrew Kahn, Ryan Limburg, Justin McCord, Brett Salsbury, Dallas Shults, Aaron Windham. **Customer Account Managers:** Gretchen Kiker, Josh Loinette, Jason Weaver. **Group Sales Coordinators:** Ryan Byrne, Carrie Caldwell, Matt Centofonti, Jenna Snider, Kai Murray, Michael Davidow. **Corporate Partners Service Coordinator:** Keri Butler, Scott Burchett. **Stadium/Team Operations Manager:** Mike Poole. **Maintenance Manager:** Alfonso Bailon. **Head Groundskeeper:** Unavailable. **Director, Game Entertainment:** Unavailable. **Administrative Assistant:** Collette Robbins.

FIELD STAFF

Manager: Darryl Kennedy **Coach:** Ronnie Ortegon. **Pitching Coach:** Steve Luebber. **Trainer:** Mark Ryan.

GAME INFORMATION

Radio Announcer: Scott Garner. **No. of Games Broadcast:** Home-70, Away-70. **Radio Station:** KBTK 1700-AM.
PA Announcer: Ken Buckner. **Official Scorer:** Unavailable.
Stadium Name: Dr Pepper/Seven Up Ballpark. **Location:** Dallas North Tollway to State Highway 121. **Standard Game Times:** 7 p.m.; Fri.-Sat. 7:30; Sun. (April-May) 2, (June-Aug.) 6. **Ticket Price Range:** $7-15.
Visiting Club Hotel: Embassy Suites, 7600 John Q. Hammons Dr., Frisco, TX 75034. Telephone: (972) 712-8200.

MIDLAND
ROCKHOUNDS

Office Address: 5514 Champions Dr., Midland, TX 79706.
Telephone: (432) 520-2255. **FAX:** (432) 520-8326.
Website: www.midlandrockhounds.org.
Affiliation (first year): Oakland Athletics (1999). **Years in League:** 1972-.

OWNERSHIP, MANAGEMENT

Operated By: Midland Sports, Inc.
Principal Owners: Miles Prentice, Bob Richmond.
President: Miles Prentice. **Executive Vice President:** Bob Richmond.
General Manager: Monty Hoppel. **Assistant GM:** Jeff VonHolle. **Assistant GM, Marketing/Tickets:** Jamie Richardson. **Assistant GM, Corporate Sales:** Harold Fuller. **Director, Broadcasting/Publications:** Bob Hards. **Executive Director, Midland Concessions:** Dave Baur. **Concessions Assistant:** Edwin White. **Director, Merchandising/Manager, Stadium Facilities:** Ray Fieldhouse. **Director, Business Operations:** Eloisa Galvan. **Manager, Season Ticket Sales:** Kevin Smith. **Director, Group Sales:** Bob Flannery. **Office/Customer Service Manager:** Stacy Fielding. **Head Groundskeeper:** Erick Ferland. **Assistant Groundskeeper:** Ben Browning. **Director, Community Relations:** Sarah Wallace. **Administrative Assistant:** Greg Bergman. **Assistant Facilities Manager:** Tony De Grande. **Sales Representative:** Chuck Dunton

FIELD STAFF

Manager: Von Hayes. **Coach:** Eddie Williams. **Pitching Coach:** Jim Coffman. **Trainer:** Javier Alvidrez.

GAME INFORMATION

Radio Announcer: Bob Hards. **No. of Games Broadcast:** Home-70, Away-70. **Flagship Station:** KCRS 550-AM.
PA Announcer: Ace O'Connell. **Official Scorer:** Paul Burnette.
Stadium Name: First American Bank Ballpark. **Location:** From I-20, exit Loop 250 North to Highway 191 intersection. **Standard Game Times:** 7 p.m., 6:30 (April-May); Sun. (April-May) 2, (June-Aug.) 6. **Ticket Price Range:** $5-9.
Visiting Club Hotel: Holiday Inn Hotel and Suites, 4300 W. Hwy. 80, Midland, TX 79703. Telephone: (432) 697-3181.

SAN ANTONIO
MISSIONS

Office Address: 5757 Hwy. 90 W., San Antonio, TX 78227.
Telephone: (210) 675-7275. **FAX:** (210) 670-0001.
E-Mail Address: sainfo@samissions.com. **Website:** www.samissions.com.

Affiliation (first year): Seattle Mariners (2001). **Years In League:** 1888, 1892, 1895-99, 1907-42, 1946-64, 1968-.

OWNERSHIP, MANAGEMENT

Operated by: Elmore Sports Group.

Principal Owner: Dave Elmore. **President:** Burl Yarbrough.

General Manager: David Gasaway. **Assistant GMs:** Doug Campbell, Jeff Long, Jeff Windle. **Comptroller:** Dennis Mancias. **Controller:** Marc Frey. **Stadium Manager:** Tom McAfee. **Director, Media Relations:** Mickey Holt. **Director, Group Sales:** Emmy Roberts. **Manager, Group Sales:** Bill Gerlt. **Director, Marketing:** Jose Melendez. **Director, Box Office:** Tiffany Johnson. **Director, Broadcasting:** Roy Acuff. **Account Executives:** Christina Fanuzzi, Stu Paul, Mac Simmons, Michael Zamora. **Office Manager:** Delia Rodriguez. **Merchandising:** Karen Sada. **Clubhouse Operations:** Matt Martinez (home), Jim Vasaldua (visitors).

FIELD STAFF

Manager: Dave Brundage. **Coach:** Gary Thurman. **Pitching Coach:** Dwight Bernard. **Trainer:** Chris Gorosics.

GAME INFORMATION

Radio Announcers: Roy Acuff, Stu Paul. **No. of Games Broadcast:** Home-70, Away-70. **Flagship Station:** KKYX 680-AM, KZDC 1250-AM (Spanish—Sunday home games only).

PA Announcer: Stan Kelly. **Official Scorer:** David Humphrey.

Stadium Name: Nelson W. Wolff Municipal Stadium. **Location:** From I-10, I-35 or I-37, take U.S. 90 West to Callaghan Road exit, stadium on right. **Standard Game Times:** 7:05 p.m.; Sun. 6:05. **Ticket Price Range:** $4-9.

Visiting Club Hotel: Red Roof Inn, 1011 E. Houston St., San Antonio, TX 78205. Telephone: (210) 229-9973.

SPRINGFIELD
CARDINALS

(Club operated in El Paso, Texas, in 2004)

Office Address: 955 East Trafficway, Springfield, MO 65802.

Telephone: (417) 863-2143. **FAX:** (417) 863-0388.

E-Mail Address: springfield@stlcardinals.com. **Website:** www.springfieldcardinals.com.

Affiliation (first year): St. Louis Cardinals (2005). **Years in League:** 2005-.

OWNERSHIP, MANAGEMENT

Operated by: St. Louis Cardinals.

Principal Owner: St. Louis Cardinals.

Vice President/General Manager: Matt Gifford. **VP, Sales/Marketing:** Kirk Elmquist. **VP, Baseball/Business Operations:** Scott Smulczenski. **VP, Facility Operations:** Bill Fischer. **Operations Manager:** Ron Henderson. **Box Office Manager:** Angela Deke. **Customer Relations Coordinator:** Nikki Love. **Head Groundskeeper:** Brock Phipps. **Assistant Groundskeeper:** Aaron Lowrey. **Manager, Public Relations:** Mike Lindskog. **Media Relations Assistant:** Brittany Bremer. **Account Executives:** Shannon Handwerker, Heather Luetkemeyer, Kate Mata, Duane Miller, Dan Reiter, Eric Tomb.

FIELD STAFF

Manager: Chris Maloney. **Coach:** Dallas Williams. **Pitching Coach:** Blake Ilsley. **Trainer:** Brad LaRosa.

GAME INFORMATION

Radio Announcers: Mike Lindskog, Rob Evans. **No. of Games Broadcast:** Home-70, Away-70. **Flagship Station:** JOCK 98.7-FM.

PA Announcer: Unavailable. **Official Scorer:** Unavailable.

Stadium Name: John Q. Hammons Field. **Location:** Highway 65 to Chestnut Expressway exit, west to National, south on National, west on Trafficway. **Standard Game Time:** 7:10 p.m. **Ticket Price Range:** $5-22.50.

Visiting Club Hotel: Unavailable.

TULSA
DRILLERS

Office Address: 4802 E. 15th St., Tulsa, OK 74112.

Telephone: (918) 744-5998. **FAX:** (918) 747-3267.

E-Mail Address: mail@tulsadrillers.com. **Website:** www.tulsadrillers.com.

Affiliation (first year): Colorado Rockies (2003). **Years in League:** 1933-42, 1946-65, 1977-.

OWNERSHIP, MANAGEMENT

Operated by: Tulsa Baseball, Inc.

Principal Owner, President: Went Hubbard.

Executive Vice President, General Manager: Chuck Lamson. **Assistant GM:** Mike Melega. **Bookkeeper:** Cheryll Couey. **Office Manager:** D.D. Bristol. **Director, Promotions/Merchandise:** Jason George. **Manager, Ticket Sales:** Jeremy Lawson. **Director, Public/Media Relations:** Brian Carroll. **Director, Stadium Operations/Group Sales:** Mark

Hilliard. **Operations Manager:** Cary Stidham. **Head Groundskeeper:** Gary Shepherd. **Corporate Sales Associate:** Kristine Garner. **Group Ticket Sales Assistant:** Brian Carr. **Promotions/Merchandise Assistant:** David McCarthy. **Ticket Sales Assistant:** Matt Adams. **Assistant Groundskeeper:** Brian Hilliard.

FIELD STAFF
Manager: Tom Runnells. **Coach:** Darron Cox. **Pitching Coach:** Bo McLaughlin. **Trainer:** Heath Townsend.

GAME INFORMATION
Radio Announcer: Mark Neely. **No. of Games Broadcast:** Home-70, Away-70. **Flagship Station:** KTBZ AM 1430. **PA Announcer:** Kirk McAnany. **Official Scorers:** Unavailable.
Stadium Name: Drillers Stadium. **Location:** Three miles north of I-44 and 1½ miles south of I-244 at 15th Street and Yale Avenue. **Standard Game Times:** 7:05 p.m.; Sun. (April-June, Sept.) 2:05, (July-Aug.) 6:05. **Ticket Price Range:** $5-9.
Visiting Club Hotel: Hampton Inn, 3209 S. 79th E. Ave., Tulsa, OK 74145. Telephone: (918) 663-1000.

WICHITA
WRANGLERS

Office Address: 300 S. Sycamore, Wichita, KS 67213.
Mailing Address: P.O. Box 1420, Wichita, KS 67201.
Telephone: (316)-267-3372. **FAX:** (316)-267-3382.
E-Mail Address: wranglers@wichitawranglers.com. **Website:** www.wichitawranglers.com.
Affiliation (first year): Kansas City Royals (1995). **Years in League:** 1987 -

OWNERSHIP, MANAGEMENT
Operated By: Wichita Baseball, Inc.
Principal Owner: Rich Products Corp.
Chairman: Robert Rich Sr. **President:** Robert Rich Jr. **Executive Vice President:** Melinda Rich.
General Manager: Eric Edelstein. **Assistant GM, Director of Stadium/Baseball Operations:** Josh Robertson. **Assistant GM, Director of Sales/Marketing:** Kyle Ebers. **Director, Business Operations:** Sindy Dick. **Manager, Marketing/Media Relations:** Matt Rogers. **Assistant, Marketing Coordinator:** Staci Flinchbaugh. **Assistant, Stadium/Baseball Operations:** Jeff Kline. **Senior Account Executive:** Robert Slaughter. **Account Executive:** Justin Cole. **Ticket Manager:** Stephanie White. **Game Day/Merchandise Manager:** Unavailable.

FIELD STAFF
Manager: Frank White. **Coach:** Nelson Liriano. **Pitching Coach:** Larry Carter. **Trainer:** Charles Leddon.

GAME INFORMATION
Radio Announcers: Rick Page. **No. of Games Broadcast:** Home-70, Away-70. **Flagship Station:** WKME 93.5-FM. **PA Announcer:** Unavailable. **Official Scorers:** Ted Woodward, Edd Cream.
Stadium Name: Lawrence-Dumont Stadium. **Location:** I-35 to Kellogg Avenue West, North on Broadway, West on Lewis. **Standard Game Times:** 7 p.m.; Sun. 6, (April-May) 2. **Ticket Price Range:** $5-10.
Visiting Club Hotel: La Quinta-Towne East, 7700 E. Kellogg, Wichita, KS 67207. Telephone: (316)-681-2881.

CALIFORNIA LEAGUE

CLASS A ADVANCED

Office Address: 2380 S. Bascom Ave., Suite 200, Campbell, CA 95008.
Telephone: (408) 369-8038. **FAX:** (408) 369-1409.
E-Mail Address: cabaseball@aol.com. **Website:** www.californialeague.com.
Years League Active: 1941-1942, 1946-.

Joe Gagliardi

President/Treasurer: Joe Gagliardi.

Vice President: Mike Ellis (Lancaster). **Corporate Secretary:** John Oldham.

Directors: Bobby Brett (High Desert), Chris Chen (Modesto), Mike Ellis (Lancaster), Joe Gagliardi (Bakersfield), Gary Jacobs (Lake Elsinore), Chris Lampe (San Jose), Dave Oldham (Inland Empire), Tom Seidler (Visalia), Hank Stickney (Rancho Cucamonga), Tom Volpe (Stockton).

Director, Marketing: Steve Fields. **League Administrator:** Kathleen Kelly. **Director, Umpire Development:** John Oldham.

Division Structure: North—Bakersfield, Modesto, San Jose, Stockton, Visalia. **South**—High Desert, Inland Empire, Lake Elsinore, Lancaster, Rancho Cucamonga.

Regular Season: 140 games (split schedule). **2005 Opening Date:** April 7. **Closing Date:** Sept. 5.

Playoff Format: Six teams. First-half champions in each division earn first-round bye; second-half champions meet wild card with next best overall record in best-of-3 quarterfinals. Winners meet first-half champions in best-of-5 semifinals. Winners meet in best-of-5 series for league championship.

All-Star Game: June 28 at Frederick, MD (California League vs. Carolina League).

Roster Limit: 25 active. **Player Eligibility Rule:** No more than two players and one player-coach on active list may have more than six years experience.

Brand of Baseball: Rawlings.

Statistician: Major League Baseball Advanced Media, 75 Ninth Ave., New York, NY 10011.

Umpires: Shane Alexander (Smyrna, TN), Chris Bakke (Alexandria, MN), Aaron Banks (Olathe, KS), Jeremy Barbe (White Barrel Lake, MN), Lance Barrett (Las Vegas, NV), Brandon Coony (Andrews, TX), Scott Jarrad (Berthoud, CO), Jeffrey Macias (Glendale, AZ), Mark Ripperger (Carlsbad, CA), Gregory Tucker (Pearland, TX).

STADIUM INFORMATION

			Dimensions				
Club	**Stadium**	**Opened**	**LF**	**CF**	**RF**	**Capacity**	**2004 Att.**
Bakersfield	Sam Lynn Ballpark	1941	328	354	328	4,200	69,922
High Desert	Mavericks Stadium	1991	340	401	340	3,808	122,265
Inland Empire	Arrowhead Credit Union Park	1996	330	410	330	5,000	201,633
Lake Elsinore	The Diamond	1994	330	400	310	7,866	236,746
Lancaster	Lancaster Municipal Stadium	1996	350	410	350	4,500	129,442
Modesto	John Thurman Field	1952	312	400	319	4,000	145,019
Rancho Cucamonga	The Epicenter	1993	335	400	335	6,615	286,198
San Jose	Municipal Stadium	1942	340	390	340	4,000	151,414
Stockton	Banner Island Ballpark	2005	300	399	326	5,200	98,035
Visalia	Recreation Park	1946	320	405	320	1,647	66,254

BAKERSFIELD
BLAZE

Office Address: 4009 Chester Ave., Bakersfield, CA 93301.
Mailing Address: P.O. Box 10031, Bakersfield, CA 93389.
Telephone: (661) 716-4487. FAX: (661) 322-6199.
E-Mail Address: blaze@bakersfieldblaze.com. Website: www.bakersfieldblaze.com.
Affiliation: Texas Rangers (2005). Years In League: 1941-42, 1946-75, 1978-79, 1982-.

OWNERSHIP, MANAGEMENT
Principal Owner: Bakersfield Baseball, LLC.
Vice President, General Manager: Chris Freshour. Assistant GM: Brian Thomas. Ticket Sales Manager: Shawn Schoolcraft. Community Relations Manager: Erika Bakeman. Corporate Sales/Operations Manager: Russell Blatt. Food Service Coordinator: Kelsey Scritchfield. Ticket/Merchandise Coordinator: Tracy Baca.

FIELD STAFF
Manager: Arnie Beyeler. Coach: Mike Boulanger. Pitching Coach: David Chavarria. Trainer: Brian Bobier.

GAME INFORMATION
Radio Announcers: Brian Thomas. No. of Games Broadcast: Home-70, Away-70. Flagship Station: KGEO 1230-AM.
PA Announcer: Unavailable. Official Scorer: Tim Wheeler.
Stadium Name: Sam Lynn Ballpark. Location: Highway 99 to California Avenue, east three miles to Chester Avenue, north two miles to stadium. Standard Game Times: 7:05 p.m. Ticket Price Range: $4-8.
Visiting Club Hotel: Holiday Inn Select, 801 Truxtun Ave., Bakersfield, CA 93301. Telephone: (661) 323-1900.

HIGH DESERT
MAVERICKS

Office Address: 12000 Stadium Way, Adelanto, CA 92301.
Telephone: (760) 246-6287. FAX: (760) 246-3197.
E-Mail Address: mavsinfo@hdmavs.com. Website: www.hdmavs.com.
Affiliation (first year): Kansas City Royals (2005). Years in League: 1991-.

OWNERSHIP, MANAGEMENT
Operated by: High Desert Mavericks, Inc.
Principal Owner: Bobby Brett. President: Andy Billig. Vice President: Brent Miles
General Manager: Bruce Mann. Director, Group Sales: Monica Ortega. Account Executive: Shaun Northrup. Director, Marketing: Nate Liberman. Director, Promotions: Autumn Rose Saenz. Office Manager: Robin Buckles. Head Groundskeeper: Tino Gonzales. Clubhouse Manager: Brandon Weil.

FIELD STAFF
Manager: Billy Gardner Jr. Coach: Boots Day. Pitching Coach: Andy Hawkins. Trainer: Steve Guadalupe.

GAME INFORMATION
Radio Announcer: Roxy Bernstein. No. of Games Broadcast: Home-70, Away-70. Flagship Station: KRAK 910-AM.
PA Announcer: Ernie Escajeda. Official Scorer: Jack Tucker.
Stadium Name: Mavericks Stadium. Location: I-15 North to Highway 395 to Adelanto Road. Standard Game Times: 7:05 p.m.; Sun. (April-May) 3:05, (June-Aug.) 5:05. Ticket Price Range: $6-8.
Visiting Club Hotel: Ramada Inn, I-15 and Palmdale Road, Victorville, CA 92392. Telephone: (760) 245-6565.

INLAND EMPIRE
66ERS

Office Address: 280 South E St., San Bernardino, CA 92401.
Telephone: (909) 888-9922. FAX: (909) 888-5251.
Website: www.ie66ers.
Affiliation (first year): Seattle Mariners (2001). Years in League: 1941, 1987-.

OWNERSHIP, MANAGEMENT
Operated by: Inland Empire 66ers Baseball Club of San Bernardino.
Principal Owners: David Elmore, Donna Tuttle.
President/General Manager: Dave Oldham. Vice President/Assistant GM: Paul Stiritz. Senior VP, Sales: Pete Thuresson. Chief Financial Officer: Carol Spivey. Director, Food and Beverage/Stadium Manager: Joe Henderson.

Director, Corporate Communications: Laura Tolbirt. Director, Broadcasting: Mike Saeger. Director, Merchandise: Laurie Oldham. Director, Tickets: Brett Tyndale. Manager, Stadium Operations: Ryan English. Director, Group Sales: Steve James. Assistant Director, Food/Beverage: Joe Hudson. Assistant Director, Broadcasting: Mike Wagenheim. Account Executives: Bobby Gearing, Brad Graham. Administrative Assistant: Ashley Rojas. Head Groundskeeper: Jesse Sandoval.

FIELD STAFF
Manager: Daren Brown. Coach: Henry Cotto. Pitching Coach: Scott Budner. Trainer: Andrew Nelson.

GAME INFORMATION
Radio Announcer: Mike Saeger. No. of Games Broadcast: Mon.-Sat. games only. Flagship Station: KVCR 91.9-FM. PA Announcer: J.J. Gould. Official Scorer: Unavailable.

Stadium Name: Arrowhead Credit Union Park. Location: From south, I-215 to 2nd Street exit, east on 2nd, right on G Street. From north, I-215 to 3rd Street exit, left on Rialto, right on G Street. Standard Game Times: 7:11 p.m.; Sun. (April-May) 2:11, (June-Sept.) 6:11. Ticket Price Range: $5-8.

Visiting Club Hotel: Radisson Hotel, 295 North E St., San Bernardino, CA 92401. Telephone: (909) 381-6181.

LAKE ELSINORE
STORM

Office Address: 500 Diamond Dr., Lake Elsinore, CA 92530.
Mailing Address: P.O. Box 535, Lake Elsinore, CA 92531.
Telephone: (951) 245-4487. FAX: (951) 245-0305.
E-Mail Address: info@stormbaseball.com. Website: www.stormbaseball.com.
Affiliation (first year): San Diego Padres (2001). Years in League: 1994-.

OWNERSHIP, MANAGEMENT
Operated by: Storm, LLC.
Principal Owner: Gary Jacobs.
President/General Manager: Dave Oster. Assistant GM/Vice President, Marketing: Chris Jones. Assistant GM/Vice President, Stadium Operations: Bruce Kessman. Assistant GM, Community Development: Tracy Kessman. Director, Corporate Sales: Paul Engl. Assistant Director, Corporate Sales: Kerstin Becker. Director, Broadcasting: Sean McCall. Director, Media/Public Relations: Casey Hauan. Director, Graphic Communications: Mark Beskid. Director, Merchandising: Donna Grunow. Director, Concessions/Operations: Frank White. Assistant Director, Concessions/Operations: Tom Anderson. Director, Group Sales: Dave Endress. Account Executive: Allen Benavides. Director, Ticket Operations: Corrine Roberge. Director, Stadium Operations: Matt Thompson. Assistant Director, Marketing: Amanda Heglin. Director, Business Administration: Yvonne Hunneman. Office Manager: Jo Equila. Director, Field Maintenance: Francisco Castaneda. Clubhouse Manager: Unavailable.

FIELD STAFF
Manager: Rick Renteria. Coach: Tom Tornincasa. Pitching Coach: Dave Rajsich. Trainer: Jason Haeussinger.

GAME INFORMATION
Radio Announcer: Sean McCall. No. of Games Broadcast: Home-70, Away-70. Flagship Station: KTMQ 103.3 FM. PA Announcer: Joe Martinez. Official Scorer: Unavailable.

Stadium Name: The Diamond. Location: From I-15, exit at Diamond Drive, west one mile to stadium. Standard Game Times: 7:05 p.m.; Wed. 6:05; Sun. (first half) 2:05, (second half) 6:05. Ticket Price Range: $5-9.

Visiting Club Hotel: Lake Elsinore Hotel and Casino, 20930 Malaga St., Lake Elsinore, CA 92530. Telephone: (951) 674-3101.

LANCASTER
JETHAWKS

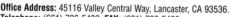

Office Address: 45116 Valley Central Way, Lancaster, CA 93536.
Telephone: (661) 726-5400. FAX: (661) 726-5406.
E-Mail Address: info@jethawks.com. Website: www.jethawks.com.
Affiliation (first year): Arizona Diamondbacks (2001). Years in League: 1996-.

OWNERSHIP, MANAGEMENT
Operated By: Clutch Play Baseball, LLC.
Chairman: Horn Chen. President: Mike Ellis.
General Manager: Brad Seymour. Assistant General Manager: Joe Reinsch. Director, Stadium Operations: John Laferney. Director, Sponsorships: Matt Allen. Director, Community Relations: Dan Hubbard. Director, Promotions/Marketing: Thom Carter. Director, Food/Beverage: Brady Alanis. Account Executives: Craig Czubik, Gary Hunt. Director, Merchandising: Amy Schrecengost. Head Groundskeeper: Dave Phatenhaur.

CALIFORNIA LEAGUE

FIELD STAFF

Manager: Bill Plummer. **Coach:** Damon Mashore. **Pitching Coach:** Jeff Pico. **Trainer:** Adam Weyer.

GAME INFORMATION

Radio Announcer: Dan Hubbard. **No. of Games Broadcast:** Home-70, Away-70. **Flagship Station:** KTPI 1340-AM.
PA Announcers: Mitchell Chase, Dave Kelli. **Official Scorer:** David Guenther.
Stadium Name: Lancaster Municipal Stadium. **Location:** Highway 14 in Lancaster to Avenue I exit, west one block to stadium. **Standard Game Times:** 7 p.m., (April-May) 6:30; Sat. (April-May) 5; Sun (April–May) 2, (June–Sept) 6.
Ticket Price Range: $5-8.
Visiting Club Hotel: Best Western Antelope Valley Inn, 44055 North Sierra Hwy., Lancaster, CA 93534 . Telephone: (661) 948-4651.

MODESTO
NUTS

Office Address: 601 Neece Dr., Modesto, CA 95351.
Mailing Address: P.O. Box 883, Modesto, CA 95353.
Telephone: (209) 572-4487. **FAX:** (209) 572-4490.
E-Mail Address: fun@modestonuts.com. **Website:** www.modestonuts.com.
Affiliation (first year): Colorado Rockies (2005). **Years in League:** 1946-64, 1966-.

OWNERSHIP, MANAGEMENT

Operated by: Modesto Nuts Baseball Club, Inc.
Principal Owner, President: Chris Chen.
Vice President, Business Development: Tim Marting. **General Manager:** Michael Gorrasi. **Assistant GM/Director, Operations:** Alex Schwerin. **Director, Sales/Marketing:** Matt Person. **Director, Broadcasting:** Paul Chiofar. **Director, Tickets:** Bob Angus. **Office/Accounting Manager:** Debra Baucom. **Director, Public Relations:** Brian LaFountain.

FIELD STAFF

Manager: Stu Cole. **Coach:** Glenallen Hill. **Pitching Coach:** Butch Hughes. **Trainer:** Jason Skolnik.

GAME INFORMATION

Radio Announcer: Paul Chiofar. **No. of Games Broadcast:** Home-50, Away-50. **Flagship Station:** KESP 970-AM.
PA Announcer: Unavailable. **Official Scorer:** Unavailable.
Stadium Name: John Thurman Field. **Location:** Highway 99 in southwest Modesto to Tuolomne Boulevard exit, west on Tuolomne for one block to Neece Drive, left for ¼ mile to stadium. **Standard Game Times:** 7:05 p.m.; Sun. (April-June) 1:05, (July-Aug.) 6:05. **Ticket Price Range:** $5-9.
Visiting Club Hotel: Ramada Inn, 2001 W. Orangeburg Ave., Modesto, CA 95350. Telephone: (209) 521-9000.

RANCHO CUCAMONGA
QUAKES

Office Address: 8408 Rochester Ave., Rancho Cucamonga, CA 91730.
Mailing Address: P.O. Box 4139, Rancho Cucamonga, CA 91729.
Telephone: (909)481-5000. **FAX:** (909) 481-5005.
E-Mail Address: rcquakes@aol.com. **Website:** www.rcquakes.com.
Affiliation (first year): Anaheim Angels (2001). **Years in League:** 1993-.

OWNERSHIP, MANAGEMENT

Operated by: Valley Baseball Inc.
Principal Owners: Hank Stickney, Jack Cooley, Scott Ostlund.
Chairman: Hank Stickney.
General Manager: North Johnson. **Assistant GM:** Chris Bitters. **Head Groundskeeper:** Rex Whitney. **Director, Entertainment:** Kristin Beernink. **Director, Group Sales:** Scott Carter. **Director, Guest Relations:** Linda Rathfon. **Director, Finance:** Heidi Acedo. **Director, Concessions:** Anita Johnson. **Director, Broadcasting/Media Relations:** Jason Anaforian. **Manager, Stadium Operations:** Ryan Ross. **Manager, Sponsorship Services:** Brandon Tanner. **Manager, Group Sales:** Dan Wesolowski. **Corporate Sales Executive:** Tim Renyi. **Manager, Ticket Office:** James Annos. **Ticket Sales Representatives:** Jim Fleming, Matt Payne, Jan Selasky. **Office Manager:** Stacie Lord.

FIELD STAFF

Manager: Ty Boykin. **Coach:** James Rowson. **Pitching Coach:** Eric Bennett. **Trainer:** Unavailable.

GAME INFORMATION

Radio Announcer: Jason Anaforian. **No. of Games Broadcast:** Home-70, Away-70. **Flagship Station:** KWRM 1370-AM.
PA Announcer: David Jeremiah.
Stadium Name: The Epicenter. **Location:** I-10 to I-15 North, exit at Foothill Boulevard, left on Foothill, left on

Rochester to stadium. **Standard Game Times:** 7:15 p.m.; Sun. (first half) 2:15, (second half) 5:15. **Ticket Price Range:** $7-10.

 Visiting Club Hotel: Best Western Heritage Inn, 8179 Spruce Ave., Rancho Cucamonga, CA 91730. Telephone: (909) 466-1111.

SAN JOSE
GIANTS

Office Address: 588 E. Alma Ave., San Jose, CA 95112.
Mailing Address: P.O. Box 21727, San Jose, CA 95151.
Telephone: (408) 297-1435. **FAX:** (408) 297-1453.
E-Mail Address: sanjosegiants@sjgiants.com **Website:** www.sjgiants.com.
Affiliation (first year): San Francisco Giants (1988). **Years in League:** 1942, 1947-58, 1962-76, 1979-.

OWNERSHIP, MANAGEMENT

 Operated by: Progress Sports Management.
 Principal Owners: Heidi Cox, Richard Beahrs. **Chief Operating Officer:** Chris Lampe.
 General Manager: Mark Wilson. **Assistant GM, Operations:** Zach Walter. **Assistant GM, Marketing/Media:** Erik Holland. **Director, Sales:** Linda Pereira. **Ticket Director/Group Sales:** Chris DiGiorgio. **Director, Public Relations:** Joe Ritzo. **Manager, Stadium Operations/Head Groundskeeper:** Leyton Lampe. **Account Executives:** Darin Dodd, Elizabeth Dyson, John Nagai, Lindsay Thrasher.

FIELD STAFF

 Manager: Lenn Sakata. **Coach:** Gary Davenport. **Pitching Coach:** Trevor Wilson. **Trainer:** Rob Knepper.

GAME INFORMATION

 Radio Announcers: Rocky Koplik, Joe Ritzo. **No. of Games Broadcast:** Saturdays and Sundays only. **Flagship Station:** KNTS 1220-AM.
 PA Announcer: Brian Burkett. **Official Scorer:** John Pletsch.
 Stadium Name: Municipal Stadium. **Location:** From I-280, 10th Street exit to Alma, left on Alma, stadium on right. From U.S. 101, Tully Road exit to Senter, right on Senter, left on Alma, stadium on left. **Standard Game Times:** 7 p.m.; Sat. 5; Sun. 1. **Ticket Price Range:** $5-10.
 Visiting Club Hotel: Pruneyard Inn, 1995 S. Bascom Ave., Campbell, CA 95008. Telephone: (408) 559-4300.

STOCKTON
PORTS

Mailing Address: P.O. Box 8365, Stockton, CA 95208.
Telephone: (209) 644-1900. **FAX:** (209) 644-1931.
E-Mail Address: info@stocktonports.com. **Website:** www.stocktonports.com.
Affiliation (first year): Oakland Athletics (2005). **Years in League:** 1941, 1946-72, 1978-.

OWNERSHIP, MANAGEMENT

 Operated by: 7th Inning Stretch, LLC.
 Chairman, Chief Executive Officer: Tom Volpe.
 Executive Vice President: John Katz. **General Manager:** Mike McCarroll. **Assistant GM/Operations:** Trevor Fawcett. **Director, Media Relations:** Michael Swope. **Director, Group Sales:** Nikki Pruett. **Group Account Executive:** David Nielsen. **Ticket Account Executive:** David Espinoza.

FIELD STAFF

 Manager: Todd Steverson. **Coach:** Darren Bush. **Pitching Coach:** Scott Emerson. **Trainer:** Brian Thorson.

GAME INFORMATION

 Radio Announcer: Toby Hyde. **No. of Games Broadcast:** Home-70, Away-70. **Flagship Station:** KSTN 1420-AM.
 PA Announcer: Unavailable. **Official Scorer:** Unavailable.
 Stadium Name: Banner Island Ballpark. **Location:** From I-5/99, take Crosstown Freeway (Highway 4) exit to El Dorado Street, north on El Dorado to Freemont Street, left on Freemont. **Standard Game Times:** 7:05 p.m.; Sun. 1:05. **Ticket Price Range:** $4-9.
 Visiting Club Hotel: Hampton Inn-Stockton, 5045 S. State Rt. 99, Stockton, CA 95215. Telephone: (209) 946-1234.

VISALIA
OAKS

Office Address: 440 N. Giddings St., Visalia, CA 93291.
Telephone: (559) 625-0480. **FAX:** (559) 739-7732.
E-Mail Address: oaksbaseball@hotmail.com. **Website:** www.oaksbaseball.com.
Affiliation (first year): Tampa Bay Devil Rays (2005). **Years in League:** 1946-62, 1968-75, 1977-.

OWNERSHIP, MANAGEMENT
Operated by: Top of the Third, Inc.
Principal Owners: Tom Seidler, Kevin O'Malley.
General Manager: Jennifer Whiteley. **Director, Sales/Marketing:** Kevin Huffine. **Director, Broadcasting/Media Relations:** Ira Liebman. **Group Sales Executive:** John Drigotas. **Head Groundskeeper:** Ken Peterson.

FIELD STAFF
Manager: Steve Livesey. **Coach:** Omer Muñoz. **Pitching Coach:** Marty DeMerritt. **Trainer:** Jimmy Southard.

GAME INFORMATION
Radio Announcer: Ira Liebman. **No. of Games Broadcast:** Home-70, Away-70. **Flagship Station:** KJUG 1270-AM.
PA Announcer: Matt White. **Official Scorer:** Harry Kargenian.
Stadium Name: Recreation Park. **Location:** From Highway 99, take 198 East to Mooney Boulevard exit, left on Giddings Avenue. **Standard Game Times:** 6:35 p.m.; Fri.-Sat. 7:05; Sun. 1:35. **Ticket Price Range:** $5-7.
Visiting Club Hotel: Radisson Hotel, 300 S. Court St., Visalia, CA 93291. Telephone: (559) 636-1111.

CAROLINA
LEAGUE

Office Address: 1806 Pembroke Rd., Greensboro, NC 27408.
Mailing Address: P.O. Box 9503, Greensboro, NC 27429.
Telephone: (336) 691-9030. **FAX:** (336) 691-9070.
E-Mail Address: office@carolinaleague.com. **Website:** www.carolinaleague.com.
Years League Active: 1945-.

John Hopkins

President/Treasurer: John Hopkins.
Vice Presidents: Kelvin Bowles (Salem), Calvin Falwell (Lynchburg). **Corporate Secretary:** Matt Minker (Wilmington).
Directors: Kelvin Bowles (Salem), Calvin Falwell (Lynchburg), George Habel (Myrtle Beach), Peter Luukko (Frederick), Cam McRae (Kinston), Matt Minker (Wilmington), Billy Prim (Winston-Salem), Art Silber (Potomac).
Administrative Assistants: Michael Albrecht, Marnee Larkins.
Division Structure: North—Frederick, Lynchburg, Potomac, Wilmington. **South**—Kinston, Myrtle Beach, Salem, Winston-Salem.
Regular Season: 140 games (split schedule). **2005 Opening Date:** April 7. **Closing Date:** Sept. 5.
All-Star Game: June 28 at Frederick (Carolina League vs. California League).
Playoff Format: First-half division champions play second-half division champions in best-of-3 series (team that wins both halves plays wild-card). Division champions meet in best-of-5 series for Mills Cup.

Roster Limit: 25 active. **Player Eligibility Rule:** No age limit. No more than two players and one player-coach on active list may have six or more years of prior minor league service.
Brand of Baseball: Rawlings.
Statistician: Major League Baseball Advanced Media, 75 Ninth Ave., New York, NY 10011.
Umpires: Cory Blaser (Westminister, CO), John Brammer (Marlow, OK), Fran Burke (Apex, NC), Tim Donald (Mount Forest, Ontario), Tom Hallion (Louisville, KY), Mark Lollo (New Lexington, OH), Karreem Mebane (Hamden, CT), Alan Porter (Warminster, PA).

STADIUM INFORMATION

Club	Stadium	Opened	LF	CF	RF	Capacity	2004 Att.
Frederick	Harry Grove Stadium	1990	325	400	325	5,400	266,257
Kinston	Grainger Stadium	1949	335	390	335	4,100	103,015
Lynchburg	City Stadium	1940	325	390	325	4,000	148,067
Myrtle Beach	Coastal Federal Field	1999	325	405	328	4,324	209,095
Potomac	Pfitzner Stadium	1984	315	400	315	6,000	170,278
Salem	Salem Memorial Stadium	1995	325	401	325	6,300	224,991
Wilmington	Frawley Stadium	1993	325	400	325	6,532	320,788
Winston-Salem	Ernie Shore Field	1956	325	400	325	6,000	134,144

FREDERICK
KEYS

Office Address: 21 Stadium Dr., Frederick, MD 21703.
Mailing Address: P.O. Box 3169, Frederick, MD 21705.
Telephone: (301) 662-0013. **FAX:** (301) 662-0018.
E-Mail Address: info@frederickkeys.com. **Website:** www.frederickkeys.com.
Affiliation (first year): Baltimore Orioles (1989). **Years in League:** 1989-.

OWNERSHIP, MANAGEMENT

Operated by: Comcast-Spectacor.
Directors: Peter Luukko, Frank Miceli.
General Manager: Dave Ziedelis. **Director, Marketing:** Keri Scrivani. **Assistant Director, Marketing:** Jennifer Smoral. **Director, Public Relations:** Ryan Sakamoto. **Public Relations Assistant:** Eric Jarinko. **Director, Stadium Operations:** Dave Wisner. **Sponsorship Sales Manager:** Shaun O'Neal. **Senior Account Manager:** Mark Ziegler. **Account Manager:** Joe Izzo. **Ticket Sales Manager:** Deanna Contorchick. **Box Office Manager:** Unavailable. **Box Office Assistant:** Unavailable. **Events Coordinators:** Jason Grose, Darcie Hartwick, Paul Weinberg, Doug Winter. **Administrative Assistant:** Barb Freund. **Bookkeeper:** Tami Hetrick. **Clubhouse Manager:** George Bell. **GM, Food Services:** Chris Inouye. **Assistant GM, Food Services:** Kelly Downes. **Head Groundskeeper:** Unavailable.

FIELD STAFF

Manager: Bien Figueroa. **Coach:** Moe Hill. **Pitching Coach:** Scott McGregor. **Trainer:** Trek Schuler.

GAME INFORMATION

Radio: None.
PA Announcer: Victoria Gordon. **Official Scorers:** George Richardson, Dennis Hetrick.
Stadium Name: Harry Grove Stadium. **Location:** From I-70, take exit 54 (Market Street), left at light. From I-270, take exit 32 (I-70 Baltimore/Hagerstown) towards Baltimore (I-70 East), to exit 54, left at Market Street. **Standard Game Times:** 7:05 p.m., Sun. 2:05. **Ticket Price Range:** $8-11.
Visiting Club Hotel: Quality Inn, 420 Prospect Blvd., Frederick, MD 21701. Telephone: (301) 695-6200.

KINSTON
INDIANS

Office Address: 400 E. Grainger Ave., Kinston, NC 28501.
Mailing Address: P.O. Box 3542, Kinston, NC 28502.
Telephone: (252) 527-9111. **FAX:** (252) 527-0498.
E-Mail Address: info@kinstonindians.com. **Website:** www.kinstonindians.com.
Affiliation (first year): Cleveland Indians (1987). **Years in League:** 1956-57, 1962-74, 1978-.

OWNERSHIP, MANAGEMENT

Operated by: Slugger Partners, LP.
Principal Owners: Cam McRae, North Johnson.
Chairman: Cam McRae. **President:** North Johnson.
General Manager: Marty Wheeler. **Assistant GM:** Shari Massengill. **Director, Broadcasting/Public Relations:** Rob Sinclair. **Director, Sales:** Ryan Eason. **Director, Food/Beverage:** Unavailable. **Head Groundskeeper:** Tommy Walston. **Clubhouse Operations:** Robert Smeraldo. **Team Photographer:** Carl Kline.

FIELD STAFF

Manager: Luis Rivera. **Coach:** Lee May Jr. **Pitching Coach:** Steve Lyons. **Trainer:** Jeff Desjardins.

GAME INFORMATION

Radio Announcer: Rob Sinclair. **No. of Games Broadcast:** Home-70, Away-70. **Flagship Station:** WRNS 960-AM.
PA Announcer: Jeff Diamond. **Official Scorer:** Taplie Coile.
Stadium Name: Grainger Stadium. **Location:** From west, take U.S. 70 Business (Vernon Avenue), left on East Street; from east, take U.S. 70 West, right on Highway 58, right on Vernon Avenue, right on East Street. **Standard Game Times:** 7 p.m.; Sun. (April-June) 2, (July-Aug.) 5. **Ticket Price Range:** $2-6.
Visiting Club Hotel: Hampton Inn, Highway 70 Bypass, Kinston NC 28504. Telephone: (252) 523-1400.

LYNCHBURG
HILLCATS

Office Address: Lynchburg City Stadium, 3180 Fort Ave., Lynchburg, VA 24501.
Mailing Address: P.O. Box 10213, Lynchburg, VA 24506.

Telephone: (434) 528-1144. **FAX:** (434) 846-0768.
E-Mail Address: info@lynchburg-hillcats.com. **Website:** www.lynchburg-hillcats.com.
Affiliation (first year): Pittsburgh Pirates (1995). **Years in League:** 1966-.

OWNERSHIP, MANAGEMENT
Operated by: Lynchburg Baseball Corp.
President: Calvin Falwell.
General Manager: Paul Sunwall. **Assistant GM:** Ronnie Roberts. **Director, Group Sales/Promotions:** Kevin Donahue. **Head Groundskeeper/Sales:** Darren Johnson. **Director, Broadcasting/Publications:** Jon Schaeffer. **Stadium Operations/Concessions Director:** Chris Johnson. **Ticket Manager:** Brent Monticue. **Director, Game Day Operations:** Robert Finley. **Office Manager:** Diane Tucker.

FIELD STAFF
Manager: Tim Leiper. **Coach:** Matt Winters. **Pitching Coach:** Bob Milacki. **Trainer:** Thomas Pribyl.

GAME INFORMATION
Radio Announcer: Jon Schaeffer. **No. of Games Broadcast:** Home-70, Away-70. **Flagship Station:** WKDE 105.5-FM.
PA Announcer: Chuck Young. **Official Scorers:** Malcolm Haley, Chuck Young.
Stadium Name: Calvin Falwell Field at Lynchburg City Stadium. **Location:** U.S. 29 South to Lynchburg City Stadium (exit 6); U.S. 29 North to Lynchburg City Stadium (exit 4). **Standard Game Times:** 7:05 p.m.; Sun. (first half) 2:05, (second half) 6:05. **Ticket Price Range:** $4-7.
Visiting Club Hotel: Best Western, 2815 Candlers Mountain Rd., Lynchburg, VA 24502. Telephone: (434) 237-2986.

MYRTLE BEACH
PELICANS

Office Address: 1251 21st Ave. N., Myrtle Beach, SC 29577.
Telephone: (843) 918-6002. **FAX:** (843) 918-6001.
E-Mail Address: info@myrtlebeachpelicans.com. **Website:** www.myrtlebeachpeli-cans.com.
Affiliation (first year): Atlanta Braves (1999). **Years in League:** 1999-.

OWNERSHIP, MANAGEMENT
Operated by: Capitol Broadcasting Company.
Principal Owner: Jim Goodmon. **Vice President:** George Habel.
VP, General Manager: Matt O'Brien. **Manager, Corporate Sales:** Neil Fortier. **Manager, Sales:** Mike Junga. **Manager, Community Relations:** Angela Barwick. **Director, Broadcasting:** Garry Griffith. **Ticket Sales Manager:** Vince Nicoletti. **Accounting Manager:** Anne Frishmuth. **Director, Ticket Operations:** Richard Graves. **Director, Retail Operations:** Richard Graves. **Director, Field Operations:** Chris Ball. **Manager, Marketing/Media:** Ryan Ibbotson. **Ticket Sales/Account Executive:** Bradley Bell. **Account Executive:** Gwen Pobanz. **Assistant Groundskeeper:** Greg Jones. **Clubhouse Manager:** Unavailable.

FIELD STAFF
Manager: Randy Ingle. **Coach:** Franklin Stubbs. **Pitching Coach:** Bruce Dal Canton. **Trainer:** Drew Van Dam.

GAME INFORMATION
Radio Announcers: Garry Griffith, Ryan Ibbotson. **No. of Games Broadcast:** Home-70, Away-70. **Flagship Station:** The TEAM 93.9-FM, 93.7-FM, 1050-AM.
PA Announcer: Unavailable. **Official Scorer:** Bill Walsh.
Stadium Name: Coastal Federal Field. **Location:** U.S. Highway 17 Bypass to 21st Avenue North, ½ mile to stadium. **Standard Game Time:** 7:05 p.m. **Ticket Price Range:** $5.50-8.50.
Visiting Club Hotel: Holiday Inn Express-Broadway at the Beach, U.S. Highway 17 Bypass & 29th Avenue North, Myrtle Beach, SC 29578. Telephone: (843) 916-4993.

POTOMAC
NATIONALS

Office Address: 7 County Complex Ct., Woodbridge, VA 22192.
Mailing Address: P.O. Box 2148, Woodbridge, VA 22195.
Telephone: (703) 590-2311. **FAX:** (703) 590-5716.
E-Mail Address: info@potomacnationals.com. **Website:** www.potomacnationals.com.
Affiliation (first year): Washington Nationals (2005). **Years in League:** 1978-.

OWNERSHIP, MANAGEMENT
Operated by: Prince William Professional Baseball Club, Inc.
Principal Owner: Art Silber. **President:** Lani Silber Weiss.

General Manager: Jay Richardson. **Director, Operations:** Eric Enders. **Director, Ticket Operations:** Brian Keller. **Director, Group Sales:** Brian Beck. **Assistant Director, Operations:** Colin Smith. **Director, Community Relations:** Maureen Connolly. **Director, Food Services:** Unavailable. **Marketing Coordinator:** Patrick Delaney. **Public Relations/Media Manager:** Amy Plourd. **Business Manager:** Jason Choi. **Group Sales Representative:** Heather Moody. **Director, Broadcasting:** Dan Laing. **Head Groundskeeper:** Mike Lundy.

FIELD STAFF
Manager: Bobby Henley. **Coach:** Troy Gingrich. **Pitching Coach:** Ricky Bones. **Trainer:** Steve Gober.

GAME INFORMATION
Radio: None.
PA Announcer: Jarrod Wronski. **Official Scorer:** David Vincent.
Stadium Name: G. Richard Pfitzner Stadium. **Location:** From I-95, take exit 158B and continue on Prince William Parkway for 5 miles, right into County Complex Court. **Standard Game Times:** 7:05 p.m.; Sun. 1:35. **Ticket Price Range:** $7-11.
Visiting Club Hotel: Best Western Potomac Mills, 14619 Potomac Mills Rd., Woodbridge, VA 22192. Telephone: (703) 494-4433.

SALEM
AVALANCHE

Office Address: 1004 Texas St., Salem, VA 24153.
Mailing Address: P.O. Box 842, Salem, VA 24153.
Telephone: (540) 389-3333. **FAX:** (540) 389-9710.
E-Mail Address: info@salemavalanche.com. **Website:** www.salemavalanche.com.
Affiliation (first year): Houston Astros (2003). **Years in League:** 1968-.

OWNERSHIP, MANAGEMENT
Operated by: Salem Professional Baseball Club, Inc.
Principal Owner/President: Kelvin Bowles.
General Manager: Jamie Toole. **Assistant GM:** Chris Allen. **Director, Finance:** Brian Bowles. **Senior Director, Stadium Operations:** Allen Lawrence. **Director, Multimedia Operations:** Chris Deines. **Director, Broadcasting, Media/Public Relations:** Unavailable. **Director, Tickets Sales/Service:** Clint Thebeau. **Director, Group Sales:** Matt Krantz. **Sales Executive:** Nick Basso. **Director, Operations/Merchandising:** Chuck Roberts. **Office Manager:** Jennifer Brown. **Head Groundskeeper:** Tracy Schneweis. **Sales Associates:** Sharon Cupp, Christy Dennis, Meghan Fuller, Graham Hall, Christina Kjolhede, John LeGacy, Andrew Rosh, Alison Sander, Mike Tesoro.

FIELD STAFF
Manager: Ivan DeJesus. **Coach:** Chuck Carr. **Pitching Coach:** Stan Boroski. **Trainer:** Eric Montague.

GAME INFORMATION
Radio Announcer: Unavailable. **No. of Games Broadcast:** Home-69, Away-71. **Flagship Stations:** WGMN 1240-AM, WVGM 1320-AM.
PA Announcer: Adam Ranzer. **Official Scorer:** Bob Teitelbaum.
Stadium Name: Salem Memorial Baseball Stadium. **Location:** I-81 to exit 141 (Route 419), follow signs to Salem Civic Center Complex. **Standard Game Times:** 7:05 p.m.; Sun. (April-June) 2:05, (July-Aug) 6:05. **Ticket Price Range:** $5-7.
Visiting Club Hotel: Comfort Inn Airport, 5070 Valley View Blvd., Roanoke VA 24012. Telephone: (540) 527-2020.

WILMINGTON
BLUE ROCKS

Office Address: 801 S. Madison St., Wilmington, DE 19801.
Telephone: (302) 888-2015. **FAX:** (302) 888-2032.
E-Mail Address: info@bluerocks.com. **Website:** www.bluerocks.com.
Affiliation (first year): Boston Red Sox (2005). **Years in League:** 1993-.

OWNERSHIP, MANAGEMENT
Operated by: Wilmington Blue Rocks, LP.
President: Matt Minker.
General Manager: Chris Kemple. **Assistant GM:** Andrew Layman. **Director, Marketing:** Tripp Baum. **Assistants, Marketing:** Jamie Wilson, Spencer Malcom. **Director, Merchandise:** Jim Beck. **Merchandise Assistant:** Mark Makowski. **Director, Broadcasting/Media Relations:** Steve Lenox. **Assistant, Media Relations:** Kyle Berger. **Director, Community Relations:** Dave Brown. **Assistant, Community Relations:** Brandon Harrison. **Director, Group Sales:** Melissa Golden. **Assistant Director, Group Sales:** Shawn Vascellaro. **Executive, Sales/Group Sales:** Kevin Linton. **Director, Tickets/Advertising:** Jared Forma. **Assistant, Ticket Sales:** Steve Datz. **Ticket Office Assistants:** Steve Lovergine, Matt Walker. **Director, Field Operations:** Steve Gold. **Office Manager:** Terra Crump. **Centerplate General**

Manager: Bobby Dichiaro. **Centerplate Office Manager:** Nicole Houtman.

FIELD STAFF
Manager: Dann Bilardello. **Coach:** Bruce Crabbe. **Pitching Coach:** Ace Adams. **Trainer:** Lee Slagle.

GAME INFORMATION
Radio Announcers: Steve Lenox, Kyle Berger. **No. of Games Broadcast:** Home-70, Away-70. **Flagship Station:** WWTX 1290-AM.

PA Announcer: John McAdams. **Official Scorers:** E.J. Casey, Jay Dunn, Dick Shute.

Stadium Name: Judy Johnson Field at Daniel S. Frawley Stadium. **Location:** I-95 North to Maryland Ave. (exit 6), right onto Maryland Ave., right on Read Street, right on South Madison Street to ballpark; I-95 South to Maryland Ave. (exit 6), left at Martin Luther King Blvd., right on South Madison Street. **Standard Game Times:** 7:05 p.m., (April-May) 6:35; Sat. 6:05; Sun. 1:35. **Ticket Price Range:** $2-9.

Visiting Club Hotel: Quality Inn-Skyways, 147 N. DuPont Hwy., New Castle, DE 19720. Telephone: (302) 328-6666.

WINSTON-SALEM
WARTHOGS

Office Address: 401 Deacon Blvd., Winston-Salem, NC 27105.
Mailing Address: P.O. Box 4488, Winston-Salem, NC 27115.
Telephone: (336) 759-2233. **FAX:** (336) 759-2042.
E-Mail Address: warthogs@warthogs.com. **Website:** www.warthogs.com.
Affiliation (first year): Chicago White Sox (1997). **Years in League:** 1945-.

OWNERSHIP, MANAGEMENT
Operated by: Sports Menagerie, Corp.

Co-Owners: Billy Prim, Andrew Filipowski. **President:** Guy Schuman.

General Manager, Baseball Operations: Ryan Manuel. **Special Assistant to GM:** David Beal. **Chief Financial Operator:** Kurt Gehsmann. **Office Manager:** Amanda Elbert. **Director, Broadcasting/Media Relations:** Alan York. **Director, Community Relations:** Mel Klunder. **Director, Merchandise/Tickets:** Jim Gleitman. **Account Executives:** Sarcanda Bellissimo, Shaun McElhinny, Vinny Pannutti. **Interns:** Logan Collins, Cass Ferguson, Jacqueline Jones, Nicole Miller.

FIELD STAFF
Manager: Chris Cron. **Coach:** Andy Tomberlin. **Pitching Coach:** Sean Snedeker. **Trainer:** Josh Fallin.

GAME INFORMATION
Radio Announcer: Alan York. **No. of Games Broadcast:** Home-70, Away-70. **Flagship Station:** Unavailable.

PA Announcer: Larry Berry. **Official Scorer:** Unavailable.

Stadium Name: Ernie Shore Field. **Location:** I-40 Business to Cherry Street exit, north through downtown, right on Deacon Boulevard, park on left. **Standard Game Times:** 7 p.m.; Wed. 12; Sun. 2. **Ticket Price Range:** $5-7.

Visiting Club Hotel: Holiday Inn, Hanes Mall, 2008 S. Hawthorne Rd., Winston-Salem, NC 27103. Telephone: (336) 765-6670.

FLORIDA STATE
LEAGUE

CLASS A ADVANCED

Street Address: 115 E. Orange Ave., Daytona Beach, FL 32114.
Mailing Address: P.O. Box 349, Daytona Beach, FL 32115.
Telephone: (386) 252-7479. **FAX:** (386) 252-7495.
E-Mail Address: fslbaseball@cfl.rr.com. **Website:** www.floridastateleague.com.
Years League Active: 1919-1927, 1936-1941, 1946-.

President, Treasurer: Chuck Murphy.
Vice Presidents: Ken Carson (Dunedin), Rob Rabenecker (Jupiter).
Corporate Secretary: David Hood.
Directors: Sammy Arena (Tampa), Brian Barnes (Jupiter), Ken Carson (Dunedin), Emily Christy (Vero Beach), Andy Dunn (Brevard County), Chris Easom (Palm Beach), Marvin Goldklang (Fort Myers), Jeff Maultsby (Sarasota), Ron Myers (Lakeland), Andrew Rayburn (Daytona), Paul Taglieri (St. Lucie), John Timberlake (Clearwater).
Office Secretary: Peggy Catigano.
Division Structure: East—Brevard County, Daytona, Jupiter, Palm Beach, St. Lucie, Vero Beach. **West**—Clearwater, Dunedin, Fort Myers, Lakeland, Sarasota, Tampa.
Regular Season: 140 games (split schedule). **2005 Opening Date:** April 7. **Closing Date:** Sept. 4.

Chuck Murphy

All-Star Game: June 18 at Clearwater.
Playoff Format: First-half division champions meet second-half champions in best-of-3 series. Winners meet in best-of-5 series for league championship.
Roster Limit: 25. **Player Eligibility Rule:** No age limit. No more than two players and one player-coach on active list may have six or more years of prior minor league service.
Brand of Baseball: Rawlings.
Statistician: Major League Baseball Advanced Media, 75 Ninth Ave., New York, NY 10011.
Umpires: Jason Bradley (Blackshear, GA), Scott Childers (Martinez, GA), Steven Cummings (Satsuma, FL), Robert Davidson (Littleton, CO), Russell Dunn (Savannah, TN), Tyler Funneman (Moweaqua, IL), Richard Laird (Norfolk, VA), Eric Loveless (Layton, UT), Clinton Mahan (Taylorville, IL), Jason Nakaishi (Syracuse, UT), Robert Price (Grand Rapids, MI), James Robertson (Hampton, GA), John Tumpane (Oak Lawn, IL).

STADIUM INFORMATION

Club	Stadium	Opened	Dimensions			Capacity	2004 Att.
			LF	CF	RF		
Brevard County	Space Coast Stadium	1994	340	404	340	7,500	98,430
Clearwater	Bright House Networks Field	2004	330	400	330	8,500	135,082
Daytona	Jackie Robinson Ballpark	1930	317	400	325	4,000	110,223
Dunedin	Knology Park	1977	335	400	315	6,106	36,844
Fort Myers	William H. Hammond Stadium	1991	330	405	330	7,500	96,150
Jupiter	Roger Dean Stadium	1998	330	400	325	6,871	06,003
Lakeland	Joker Marchant Stadium	1966	340	420	340	7,100	32,301
Palm Beach	Roger Dean Stadium	1998	330	400	325	6,871	92,806
St. Lucie	Tradition Field	1988	338	410	338	7,500	85,991
Sarasota	Ed Smith Stadium	1989	340	400	340	7,500	40,715
Tampa	Legends Field	1996	318	408	314	10,386	71,648
Vero Beach	Holman Stadium	1953	340	400	340	6,500	66,945

BREVARD COUNTY
MANATEES

Office Address: 5800 Stadium Pkwy., Melbourne, FL 32940.
Telephone: (321) 633-9200. **FAX:** (321) 633-9210.
E-Mail Address: info@spacecoaststadium.com. **Website:** www.manateesbaseball.com.
Affiliation (first year): Milwaukee Brewers (2005). **Years in League:** 1994-.

OWNERSHIP, MANAGEMENT
Operated by: Washington Nationals.
Director, Florida Operations: Buck Rogers. **Assistant General Manager:** Trey Fraser. **Manager, Group Sales:** Babs Rogers. **Manager, Sales/Promotions:** Calvin Funkhouser. **Manager, Accounting:** Chris Roberson. **Manager, Sales/Marketing:** Mark Hughes. **Manager, Ticket Sales/Public Relations:** Jeff Weinhold. **Account Executives:** Tyler Hubbard, Joe McGrail. **Administrative Assistant:** Kelley Wheeler. **Facilities Engineer:** Charles Bunch. **Office Manager, Concessions:** Siv Donovan.

FIELD STAFF
Manager: John Tamargo. **Coach:** Johnny Narron. **Pitching Coach:** Fred Dabney. **Trainer:** Masa Koyanagi.

GAME INFORMATION
Radio: None.
PA Announcer: Unavailable. **Official Scorer:** Ron Jernick.
Stadium Name: Space Coast Stadium. **Location:** I-95 North to Wickham Road (exit 191), left on Wickham, right on Lake Andrew Drive, left onto Judge Fran Jameson Way, right on Stadium Parkway; I-95 South to Fiske Boulevard (exit 195), left on Fiske, follow Fiske/Stadium Parkway to ballpark. **Standard Game Times:** 7:05 p.m., Sun. 1:35. **Ticket Price Range:** $4-7.
Visiting Club Hotel: Baymont Inn & Suites, 7200 George T. Edwards Dr., Melbourne, FL 32940. Telephone: (321) 242-9400.

CLEARWATER
THRESHERS

Office Address: 601 N. Old Coachman Rd, Clearwater, FL 33765.
Telephone: (727) 712-4300. **FAX:** (727) 712-4498.
Website: www.threshersbaseball.com.
Affiliation (first year): Philadelphia Phillies (1985). **Years in League:** 1985-.

OWNERSHIP, MANAGEMENT
Operated by: The Philadelphia Phillies.
Chairman: Bill Giles. **President:** David Montgomery. **Director, Florida Operations:** John Timberlake. **Assistant Director, Florida Operations:** Lee McDaniel. **Business Manager:** Dianne Gonzalez.
General Manager: Unavailable. **Assistant GM/Director, Sales:** Dan McDonough. **Assistant GM/Ticketing:** Jason Adams. **Coordinator, Merchandising/Special Events:** Carrie Jenkins. **Manager, Food/Beverage:** Dan Madden. **Group Sales:** Jennifer Mastry, Bobby Mitchell. **Ballpark Operations:** Jay Warren. **Ticket Manager:** Kevin Brahm. **Maintenance Coordinator:** Cory Sipe. **Special Projects Coordinator:** Tony Lenning. **Office Manager:** De De Angelillis. **Head Groundskeeper:** Opie Cheek. **Clubhouse Operations:** Cliff Armbruster.

FIELD STAFF
Manager: Greg Legg. **Coaches:** Dan Roberts, Ken Dominguez. **Pitching Coach:** Scott Lovekamp. **Trainer:** Shawn Fcasni.

GAME INFORMATION
Radio: None.
PA Announcer: Don Guckian. **Official Scorer:** Larry Wiederecht.
Stadium Name: Bright House Networks Field. **Location:** U.S. 19 North and Drew Street in Clearwater. **Standard Game Times:** 7:05 p.m., Sun. 2:05. **Ticket Price Range:** $2-8.
Visiting Club Hotel: Econo Lodge, 21252 U.S. 19 N., Clearwater, FL 33765. Telephone: (727) 796-3165.

DAYTONA
CUBS

Office Address: 105 E. Orange Ave., Daytona Beach, FL 32114.
Telephone: (386) 257-3172. **FAX:** (386) 257-3382.
E-Mail Address: info@daytonacubs.com. **Website:** www.daytonacubs.com.

Affiliation (first year): Chicago Cubs (1993). **Years in league:** 1920-24, 1928, 1936-41, 1946-73, 1977-87, 1993-.

OWNERSHIP/MANAGEMENT

Operated by: Big Game Florida, LLC.
Principal Owner/President: Andrew Rayburn.
General Manager: Bill Papierniak. **Assistant GM:** Matthew Provence. **Director, Sales:** Jeremiah Johnson. **Director, Stadium Operations:** Erik Malvik. **Director, Media:** Bo Fulginiti. **Director, Tickets:** Betsy Gladish. **Director, Merchandise:** Nobutaka Egashira. **Director, Facilities:** J.R. Laub. **Stadium Operations Assistants:** Jeff De Caito, Josh Lawther, Rick Polster, Robbie Zombeck. **Office Manager:** Tammy Devine. **Clubhouse Manager:** J.R. Laub.

FIELD STAFF

Manager: Richie Zisk. **Coach:** Mike Micucci. **Pitching Coach:** Mike Anderson. **Trainer:** Steve Melendez.

GAME INFORMATION

Radio Announcers: Bo Fulginiti, Shawn Flickinger. **No. of Games Broadcast:** Home-70, Away-70. **Flagship Station:** WELE 1380-AM.
PA Announcer: Tim Lecras. **Official Scorer:** Lyle Fox.
Stadium Name: Jackie Robinson Ballpark. **Location:** I-95 to International Speedway Blvd. exit (Route 92), east to Beach Street, south to Magnolia Ave., east to ballpark; A1A North/South to Orange Ave., west to ballpark. **Standard Game Times:** 7:05 p.m.; Sun. 6:05. **Ticket Price Range:** $6-9.
Visiting Club Hotel: Treasure Island Resort, 2025 S. Atlantic Ave., Daytona Beach Shores, FL 32118. Telephone: (386) 255-8371.

DUNEDIN
BLUE JAYS

Office Address: 373-A Douglas Ave., Dunedin, FL 34698.
Telephone: (727) 733-9302. **FAX:** (727) 734-7661.
E-Mail Address: feedback@dunedinbluejays.com. **Website:** www.dunedinblue-jays.com.
Affiliation (first year): Toronto Blue Jays (1987). **Years in League:** 1978-79, 1987-.

OWNERSHIP, MANAGEMENT

Operated by: Toronto Blue Jays.
Director, Florida Operations/General Manager: Ken Carson. **Assistant GM:** Carrie Johnson. **Manager, Ticket Sales:** Russ Williams. **Manager, Group Sales:** James O'Brien. **Office Manager:** Pat Smith. **Sales Representatives:** Jared Gates, Janette Talbot. **Head Groundskeeper:** Budgie Clark. **Clubhouse Operations:** Unavailable.

FIELD STAFF

Manager: Omar Malave. **Coach:** Paul Elliott. **Pitching Coach:** Rick Langford. **Trainer:** Mike Frostad.

GAME INFORMATION

Radio: None.
PA Announcers: Ed Groth, Dave Bell. **Official Scorer:** Bobby Porter.
Stadium Name: Dunedin Stadium. **Location:** From I-275, north on Highway 19, left on Sunset Point Road for 4½ miles, right on Douglas Avenue, stadium is ½ mile on right. **Standard Game Times:** 7 p.m.; Sun 1. **Ticket Price Range:** $3-5.
Visiting Club Hotel: Econo Lodge, 21252 U.S. 19 N., Clearwater, FL 34625. Telephone: (727) 799-1569.

FORT MYERS
MIRACLE

Office Address: 14400 Six Mile Cypress Pkwy., Fort Myers, FL 33912.
Telephone: (239) 768-4210. **FAX:** (239) 768-4211.
E-Mail Address: miracle@miraclebaseball.com. **Website:** www.miraclebaseball.com.
Affiliation: Minnesota Twins (1993). **Years in League:** 1926, 1978-87, 1991-.

OWNERSHIP, MANAGEMENT

Operated by: Greater Miami Baseball Club, LP.
Principal Owner/Chairman: Marvin Goldklang. **Chief Executive Officer:** Mike Veeck. **President:** Linda McNabb.
General Manager: Steve Gliner. **Assistant GM:** Andrew Seymour. **Director, Business Operations:** Suzanne Reaves. **Manager, Sales/Marketing:** Terry Simon. **Head Groundskeeper:** Keith Blasingim. **Manager, Media Relations/Broadcasting:** Sean Aronson. **Sales Representatives:** Stephen Kaufman, Justin Stecz. **Manager, Food/Beverage:** John Acquavella. **Assistant Manager, Food/Beverage:** Kris Koch.

FIELD STAFF

Manager: Riccardo Ingram. **Coach:** Jeff Carter. **Pitching Coach:** Eric Rasmussen. **Trainer:** Larry Bennese.

GAME INFORMATION

Radio Announcer: Sean Aronson. **No of Games Broadcast:** Home-70, Away-70. **Flagship Station:** ESPN 770-AM. **PA Announcer:** Sean Fox. **Official Scorer:** Benn Norton.

Stadium Name: William H. Hammond Stadium. **Location:** Exit 131 off I-75, west on Daniels Parkway, left on Six Mile Cypress Parkway. **Standard Game Times:** 7:05 p.m.; Sun. 1:05. **Ticket Price Range:** $4-6.

Visiting Club Hotel: Wellesley Inn and Suites, 4400 Ford St. Extension, Fort Myers, FL 33909. Telephone: (239) 278-3949.

JUPITER
HAMMERHEADS

Office Address: 4751 Main St., Jupiter, FL 33458.
Telephone: (561) 775-1818. **FAX:** (561) 691-6886.
E-Mail Address: info@rogerdeanstadium.com. **Website:** www.jupiterhammer-heads.com.
Affiliation (first year): Florida Marlins (2002). **Years in League:** 1998-.

OWNERSHIP, MANAGEMENT

Owned by: Florida Marlins.
Operated by: Jupiter Stadium, LTD.
General Manager, JSL: Rob Rabenecker. **Executive Assistant to GM, JSL:** Carol McAteer.

GM, Jupiter Hammerheads: Brian Barnes. **Associate GM:** Chris Easom. **Director, Sales/Marketing:** Jennifer Brown. **Manager, Merchandising:** Jordan Schneider. **Manager, Stadium Building:** Jorge Toro. **Manager, Facility Operations:** Marshall Jennings. **Assistant Manager, Facility Operations:** Karsten Blackwelder, Johnny Simmons. **Office Manager:** Tom Vanatta. **Manager, Tickets:** Chris LaRoy. **Marketing Sales Representatives:** Sandi O'Malley, Amanda Sinclair. **Senior Sales Representative:** Scott Hodge. **Sales Representatives:** Bryan Knapp, Lainey Ruskay. **Interns:** Caitlin Bakum, Zack Bayrouty, Krista Boyd, Miriam Hyder, Ryan Morgan, Joe Schuler, Adam Shelton, Brett Stang, Shawn Sterling, Tony Suarez, Jordan Treadway, Andrew Waterson, Amanda Welcomer, Kelvin Woodson.

FIELD STAFF

Manager: Tim Cossins. **Coach:** Paul Sanagorski. **Pitching Coach:** Reid Cornelius. **Trainer:** Josh Seligman.

GAME INFORMATION

Radio: None.
PA Announcers: John Frost, Lou Palmer, Dick Sanford. **Official Scorer:** Zack Bayrouty.

Stadium Name: Roger Dean Stadium. **Location:** I-95 to exit 83, east on Donald Ross Road for ¼ mile. **Standard Game Times:** 7:05 p.m.; (Tues.) 6:35, (Sat.) 6:05, (Sun.) 2:05. **Ticket Price Range:** $6-7.

Visiting Club Hotel: Comfort Inn & Suites Jupiter, 6752 West Indiantown Road, Jupiter, FL 33458-3978. Telephone: (561) 745-7997.

LAKELAND
TIGERS

Office Address: 2125 N. Lake Ave., Lakeland, FL 33805.
Mailing Address: P.O. Box 90187, Lakeland, FL 33804.
Telephone: (863) 686-8075. **FAX:** (863) 688-9589.
E-Mail Address: info@lakelandtigers.net.
Affiliation (first year): Detroit Tigers (1967). **Years in League:** 1919-26, 1953-55, 1960, 1962-64, 1967-.

OWNERSHIP, MANAGEMENT

Operated by: Detroit Tigers.
Principal Owner: Mike Ilitch. **President:** Dave Dombrowski. **Director, Florida Operations:** Ron Myers.

General Manager: Todd Pund. **Assistant GM:** Shannon Follett. **Ticket Operations:** Erik Veenhuis. **Director, Merchandising/Concessions:** Kay LaLonde. **Clubhouse Operations:** Unavailable. **Head Groundskeeper:** Bryan French.

FIELD STAFF

Manager: Mike Rojas. **Coach:** Larry Herndon. **Pitching Coach:** Britt Burns. **Trainer:** Chris McDonald.

GAME INFORMATION

Radio: None.
PA Announcer: Shari Szabo. **Official Scorer:** Sandy Shaw.

Stadium Name: Joker Marchant Stadium. **Location:** I-4 to Exit 33, left 1½ miles. **Standard Game Times:** 7 p.m.; Sun. 1. **Ticket Price Range:** $4-5.

Visiting Club Hotel: Baymont Inns and Suites, 4315 Lakeland Park Dr., Lakeland, FL 33809. Telephone: (863) 815-0606.

PALM BEACH
CARDINALS

Office Address: 4751 Main St., Jupiter, FL 33458.
Telephone: (561) 775-1818. **FAX:** (561) 691-6886.
E-Mail Address: info@rogerdeanstadium.com. **Website:** www.palmbeach cardinals.com.
Affiliation (first year): St. Louis Cardinals (2003). **Years in League:** 2003-.

OWNERSHIP, MANAGEMENT
Owned by: St. Louis Cardinals.
Operated by: Jupiter Stadium, LTD.
General Manager, JSL: Rob Rabenecker. **Executive Assistant to GM, JSL:** Carol McAteer.
GM, Palm Beach Cardinals: Chris Easom. **Associate GM:** Brian Barnes. **Director, Sales/Marketing:** Jennifer Brown. **Manager, Merchandising:** Jordan Schneider. **Manager, Stadium Building:** Jorge Toro. **Manager, Facility Operations:** Marshall Jennings. **Assistant Managers, Facility Operations:** Karsten Blackwelder, Johnny Simmons. **Office Manager:** Tom Vanatta. **Manager, Tickets:** Chris LaRoy. **Marketing Sales Representatives:** Sandi O'Malley, Amanda Sinclair. **Senior Sales Representative:** Scott Hodge. **Sales Representatives:** Bryan Knapp, Lainey Ruskay. **Interns:** Caitlin Bakum, Zack Bayrouty, Krista Boyd, Miriam Hyder, Ryan Morgan, Joe Schuler, Adam Shelton, Brett Stang, Shawn Sterling, Tony Suarez, Jordan Treadway, Andrew Waterson, Amanda Welcomer, Kelvin Woodson.

FIELD STAFF
Manager: Ron "Pop" Warner. **Coach:** Derrick May. **Pitching Coach:** Derek Lilliquist. **Trainer:** Allen Thompson.

GAME INFORMATION
Radio: None.
PA Announcers: John Frost, Lou Palmer, Dick Sanford. **Official Scorer:** Tony Suarez.
Stadium Name: Roger Dean Stadium. **Location:** I-95 to exit 83, east on Donald Ross Road for ¼ mile. **Standard Game Times:** 7:05 p.m.; (Tues.) 6:35, (Sat.) 6:05, (Sun.) 2:05. **Ticket Price Range:** $6-7.
Visiting Club Hotel: Comfort Inn & Suites Jupiter, 6752 West Indiantown Road, Jupiter, FL 33458-3978. Telephone: (561) 745-7997.

SARASOTA
REDS

Office Address: 2700 12th St., Sarasota, FL 34237.
Mailing Address: 1090 N. Euclid Ave., Sarasota, FL 34237.
Telephone: (941) 365-4460. **FAX:** (941) 365-4217.
Affiliation (first year): Cincinnati Reds (2005). **Years in League:** 1927, 1961-65, 1989-.

OWNERSHIP, MANAGEMENT
Operated by: Cincinnati Reds, LLP.
General Manager: Dan Wolfert. **Assistant GM:** Blaine Smith. **Director, Operations/Marketing:** Dan Wolfert. **Manager, Ticketing:** Barbara Robinson. **Clubhouse Manager:** Tim Williamson.

FIELD STAFF
Manager: Edgar Caceres. **Coach:** Billy White. **Pitching Coach:** Ed Hodge. **Trainer:** Trevor Carter.

GAME INFORMATION
Radio: None.
PA Announcer: Unavailable. **Official Scorer:** Howard Spungen.
Stadium Name: Ed Smith Stadium. **Location:** I-75 to exit 210, three miles west to Tuttle Avenue, right on Tuttle 1/2 mile to 12th Street, stadium on left. **Standard Game Times:** 7:00 p.m., Sun. 1:00. **Ticket Price Range:** Unavailable.
Visiting Club Hotel: AmericInn and Suites, 5931 Fruitville Rd., Sarasota, FL 34232. Telephone: (941) 342-8778.

ST. LUCIE
METS

Office Address: 525 NW Peacock Blvd., Port St. Lucie, FL 34986.
Telephone: (772) 871-2100. **FAX:** (772) 878-9802.
Website: www.stluciemets.com.
Affiliation (first year): New York Mets (1988). **Years in League:** 1988-.

OWNERSHIP, MANAGEMENT
Operated by: Sterling Mets, LP.

Chairman: Fred Wilpon. President: Saul Katz. Executive Vice President/Chief Operating Officer: Jeff Wilpon. Director, Florida Operations/General Manager: Paul Taglieri. Manager, Stadium Operations: Traer Van Allen. Manager, St. Lucie Mets Operations: Ari Skalet. Manager, Concessions: Brian Paupeck. Catering/Special Events Manager: Sally Gibson. Ticketing/Merchandise Coordinator: Erin Rescigno. Office Assistant: Cynthia Malaspino. Administrative Assistant: Matt Ross. Head Groundskeeper: Tommy Bowes. Clubhouse Manager: Jack Brenner.

FIELD STAFF

Manager: Tim Teufel. Coach: Al LeBoeuf. Pitching Coach: Rick Mahler. Trainer: Ruben Barrera.

GAME INFORMATION

Radio: None.
PA Announcer: Unavailable. Official Scorer: Bob Adams.
Stadium Name: Tradition Field. Location: Exit 121 (St. Lucie West Blvd.) off I-95, east ½ mile, left on NW Peacock Blvd. Standard Game Times: 7 p.m.; Sun 5. Ticket Price Range: $3-4.
Visiting Club Hotel: Holiday Inn, 10120 S. Federal Hwy., Port St. Lucie, FL 34952. Telephone: (772) 337-2200.

TAMPA
YANKEES

Office Address: One Steinbrenner Dr., Tampa, FL 33614.
Telephone: (813) 875-7753. FAX: (813) 673-3174.
E-Mail Address: sarena@yankees.com.
Affiliation (first year): New York Yankees (1994). Years in League: 1919-27, 1957-1988, 1994-.

OWNERSHIP, MANAGEMENT

Operated by: New York Yankees, LP.
Principal Owner: George Steinbrenner.
General Manager: Sammy Arena. Assistant GM: Julie Kremer. Director, Stadium Operations: Dean Holbert. Director, Sales/Marketing: Howard Grosswirth. Account Representative: Heath Hardin. Director, Ticket Sales: Vance Smith. Head Groundskeeper: Ritchie Anderson.

FIELD STAFF

Manager: Joe Breeden. Coach: Bill Doran. Pitching Coach: Greg Pavlick. Trainer: Mike Wickland.

GAME INFORMATION

Radio: None.
PA Announcer: Steve Hague. Official Scorer: Unavailable.
Stadium Name: Legends Field. Location: I-275 to Martin Luther King, west on Martin Luther King to Dale Mabry. Standard Game Times: 7 p.m.; Sun. 1. Ticket Price Range: $5-7.
Visiting Club Hotel: Holiday Inn Express, 4732 N. Dale Mabry Hwy., Tampa, FL 33614. Telephone: (813) 877-6061.

VERO BEACH
DODGERS

Office Address: 4101 26th St., Vero Beach, FL 32960.
Mailing Address: P.O. Box 2887, Vero Beach, FL 32961.
Telephone: (772) 569-4900. FAX: (772) 567-0819.
E-Mail Address: info@vbdodgers.com. Website: www.vbdodgers.com.
Affiliation (first year): Los Angeles Dodgers (1980). Years in League: 1980-.

OWNERSHIP, MANAGEMENT

Operated by: Los Angeles Dodgers.
President: Martin Greenspun.
General Manager: Emily Christy. Assistant GM: Unavailable. Head Groundskeeper: Steve Carlsward. Director, Ticket Sales: Louise Boissy. Manager, Concessions/Souvenirs: Kathy Bond. Secretary: Edith Marcelle. Advertising Secretary: Betty Rollins. Administrative Assistants: Matt Blaney, Brent Gambill, Shawn Marette.

FIELD STAFF

Manager: Scott Little. Coach: Dan Radison. Pitching Coach: Marty Reed. Trainer: Carlos Olivas.

GAME INFORMATION

Radio Announcer: Brian Petrotta. No. of Games Broadcast: Home-70, Away-70. Flagship Station: WTTB 1490-AM.
PA Announcers: Joe Sanchez, Steve Stone. Official Scorer: Randy Phillips.
Stadium Name: Holman Stadium. Location: I-95 to Route 60 East, left on 43rd Avenue, right on Aviation Boulevard. Standard Game Times: 7 p.m.; Sun. (April-June) 1. Ticket Price Range: $4-6.
Visiting Club Hotel: Unavailable.

MIDWEST LEAGUE

Office Address: 1118 Cranston Rd., Beloit, WI 53511.
Mailing Address: P.O. Box 936, Beloit, WI 53512.
Telephone: (608) 364-1188. **FAX:** (608) 364-1913.
E-Mail Address: mwl@midwestleague.com. **Website:** www.midwestleague.com.
Years League Active: 1947-.

President, Treasurer: George Spelius.
Vice President: Ed Larson. **Legal Counsel/Secretary:** Richard Nussbaum.
Directors: Andrew Appleby (Fort Wayne), Tom Barbee (Cedar Rapids), Lew Chamberlin (West Michigan), Dennis Conerton (Beloit), Tom Dickson (Lansing), Kevin Krause (Quad Cities), Alan Levin (South Bend), Robert Murphy (Dayton), Paul Schnack (Clinton), William Shea (Southwest Michigan), Rocky Vonachen (Peoria), Dave Walker (Burlington), Mike Woleben (Kane County), Rob Zerjav (Wisconsin).
League Administrator: Holly Voss.
Division Structure: East—Dayton, Fort Wayne, Lansing, South Bend, Southwest Michigan West Michigan. **West**—Beloit, Burlington, Cedar Rapids, Clinton, Kane County, Peoria, Quad City, Wisconsin.
Regular Season: 140 games (split-schedule). **2005 Opening Date:** April 7. **Closing Date:** Sept. 5.
All-Star Game: June 21 at Peoria.

George Spelius

Playoff Format: Eight teams qualify. First-half and second-half division champions, and wild-card teams, meet in best-of-3 quarterfinal series. Winners meet in best-of-3 series for division championship. Division champions meet in best-of-5 final for league championship.
Roster Limit: 25 active. **Player Eligibility Rule:** No age limit. No more than two players and one player-coach on active list may have more than five years experience.
Brand of Baseball: Rawlings ROM-MID.
Statistician: Major League Baseball Advanced Media, 75 Ninth Ave., New York, NY 10011.
Umpires: Unavailable.

STADIUM INFORMATION

Club	Stadium	Opened	LF	CF	RF	Capacity	2004 Att.
Beloit	Pohlman Field	1982	325	380	325	3,500	96,677
Burlington	Community Field	1947	338	403	318	3,200	63,376
Cedar Rapids	Veterans Memorial Stadium	2002	315	400	325	5,300	177,888
Clinton	Alliant Energy Field	1937	335	390	325	2,500	91,804
Dayton	Fifth Third Field	2000	338	402	338	7,230	593,663
Fort Wayne	Memorial Stadium	1993	330	400	330	6,516	278,351
Kane County	Philip B. Elfstrom Stadium	1991	335	400	335	7,400	522,042
Lansing	Oldsmobile Park	1996	305	412	305	11,000	392,256
Peoria	O'Brien Field	2002	310	400	310	7,200	211,598
Quad City	John O'Donnell Stadium	1931	343	400	318	4,024	173,364
South Bend	Coveleski Regional Stadium	1988	336	405	336	5,000	213,617
Southwest Michigan	C.O. Brown Stadium	1990	322	402	333	4,500	95,845
West Michigan	Fifth Third Ballpark	1994	317	402	327	10,900	390,033
Wisconsin	Fox Cities Stadium	1995	325	400	325	5,500	206,487

BELOIT
SNAPPERS

Office Address: 2301 Skyline Dr., Beloit, WI 53511.
Telephone: (608) 362-2272. **FAX:** (608) 362-0418.
E-Mail Address: snappy@snappersbaseball.com. **Website:** www.snappersbaseball.com.
Affiliation (first year): Minnesota Twins (2005). **Years in League:** 1982-.

OWNERSHIP, MANAGEMENT
Operated by: Beloit Professional Baseball Association, Inc.
Chairman: Dennis Conerton. **President:** Marcy Olsen.
General Manager: Jeff Vohs. **Director, Community/Media Relations:** Jeremy Neuman. **Director, Gameday Operations:** Jason Collins. **Director, Ticket Operations/Merchandise:** Brandon Smith. **Director, Corporate Sales:** Riley Gostisha.

FIELD STAFF
Manager: Kevin Boles. **Coach:** Rudy Hernandez. **Pitching Coach:** Gary Lucas. **Trainer:** Alan Rail.

GAME INFORMATION
Radio Announcer: Unavailable. **No. of Games Broadcast:** Unavailable. **Flagship Station:** WTJK 1380-AM.
PA Announcer: Unavailable. **Official Scorer:** Jeremy Neuman.
Stadium Name: Pohlman Field. **Location:** I-90 to exit 185-A, right at Cranston Road for 1½ miles; I-43 to Wisconsin 81 to Cranston Road, right at Cranston for 1½ miles. **Standard Game Times:** 7 p.m., (April-May) 6:30; Sun. 2. **Ticket Price Range:** $5-7.
Visiting Club Hotel: Econo Lodge, 2956 Milwaukee Rd., Beloit, WI 53511. Telephone: (608) 364-4000.

BURLINGTON
BEES

Office Address: 2712 Mt. Pleasant St., Burlington, IA 52601.
Telephone: (319) 754-5705. **FAX:** (319) 754-5882.
E-Mail Address: staff@gobees.com. **Website:** www.gobees.com.
Affiliation (first year): Kansas City Royals (2001). **Years in League:** 1962-.

OWNERSHIP, MANAGEMENT
Operated by: Burlington Baseball Association, Inc.
President: Dave Walker.
General Manager: Chuck Brockett. **Assistant GM, Baseball Operations:** Randy Wehofer. **Assistant GM, Sales/Marketing:** Adam Small. **Director, Group Outings:** Trish Renken. **Head Groundskeeper:** Dave Vander Heyden.

FIELD STAFF
Manager: Jim Gabella. **Coach:** Patrick Anderson. **Pitching Coach:** Tom Burgmeier. **Trainer:** Mark Stubblefield.

GAME INFORMATION
Radio Announcer: Randy Wehofer. **No. of Games Broadcast:** Home-70, Away-70. **Flagship Stations:** KBUR 1490-AM, KBKB 1360-AM.
PA Announcer: Bob Engberg. **Official Scorer:** Scott Logas.
Stadium Name: Community Field. **Location:** From U.S. 34, take U.S. 61 North to Mt. Pleasant Street, east ⅛ mile. **Standard Game Times:** 7 p.m.; Sat. (April-May) 6; Sun. 2. **Ticket Price Range:** $4-7.
Visiting Club Hotel: Pzazz Best Western, 3001 Winegard Dr., Burlington, IA 52601. Telephone: (319) 753-2223.

CEDAR RAPIDS
KERNELS

Office Address: 950 Rockford Rd. SW, Cedar Rapids, IA 52404.
Telephone: (319) 363-3887. **FAX:** (319) 363-5631.
E-Mail Address: kernels@kernels.com. **Website:** www.kernels.com.
Affiliation (first year): Anaheim Angels (1993). **Years in League:** 1962-.

OWNERSHIP, MANAGEMENT
Operated by: Cedar Rapids Baseball Club, Inc.
President: Tom Barbee.
General Manager: Jack Roeder. **Chief Operating Officer:** Doug Nelson. **Sports Turf Manager:** Jesse Roeder.

Director, Tickets/Group Sales: Andrea Murphy. Director, Broadcasting: John Rodgers. Director, Finance: Charlie Patrick. Director, Graphics/Technology: Andrew Pantini. Entertainment Manager: Josh Boots. Stadium Operations Manager: Seth Dohrn. Customer Services/Suite Manager: Jessica Fergesen. Concessions Manager: Dave Soper.

FIELD STAFF

Manager: Bobby Magallanes. Coach: Justin Baughman. Pitching Coach: Kernan Ronan. Trainer: Unavailable.

GAME INFORMATION

Radio Announcer: John Rodgers. No. of Games Broadcast: Home-70, Away-70. Flagship Station: KCRG 1600-AM. PA Announcer: Dale Brodt. Official Scorer: Al Gruwell.
Stadium Name: Veterans Memorial Stadium. Location: I-380 to Wilson Ave. exit, west to Rockford Road, right one mile to corner of 8th Ave. and 15th Street SW. Standard Game Times: 7 p.m., (April-May, Sept.) 6:30; Sat. (April-May) 5, (June-Aug.) 7; Sun. 2. Ticket Price Range: $5-8.
Visiting Club Hotel: Best Western Village Inn, 100 F Ave. NW, Cedar Rapids, IA 52405. Telephone: (319) 366-5323.

CLINTON
LUMBERKINGS

Mailing Address: P.O. Box 1295, Clinton, IA 52733.
Telephone: (563) 242-0727. FAX: (563) 242-1433.
E-Mail Address: lumberkings@lumberkings.com. Website: www.lumberkings.com.
Affiliation (first year): Texas Rangers (2003). Years in League: 1956-.

OWNERSHIP, MANAGEMENT

Operated by: Clinton Baseball Club, Inc.
Chairman: Don Roode. President: Paul Schnack.
General Manager: Ted Tornow. Director, Operations: Nate Kreinbrink. Director, Promotions: Derick Stoulil. Groundskeeper: Unavailable.

FIELD STAFF

Manager: Carlos Subero. Coach: Brian Dayett. Pitching Coach: Stan Hilton. Trainer: Brian Bodenhamer.

GAME INFORMATION

Radio Announcer: Chris Lake. No. of Games Broadcast: Home-70, Away-70. Flagship Station: KCLN 1390-AM. PA Announcer: Brad Seward. Official Scorer: Tom Whaley.
Stadium Name: Alliant Energy Field. Location: Highway 67 North to Sixth Avenue North, right on Sixth, cross railroad tracks, stadium on right. Standard Game Times: 7 p.m.; (April-May) 6; Sun. 2. Ticket Price Range: $4-6.
Visiting Club Hotel: Super 8 Motel, 1711 Lincoln Way, Clinton, IA 52732. Telephone: (563) 242-8870.

DAYTON
DRAGONS

Office Address: Fifth Third Field, 220 N. Patterson Blvd., Dayton, OH 45402.
Mailing Address: P.O. Box 2107, Dayton, OH 45401.
Telephone: (937) 228-2287. FAX: (937) 228-2284.
E-Mail Address: dragons@daytondragons.com. Website: www.daytondragons.com.
Affiliate (first year): Cincinnati Reds (2000). Years in League: 2000-.

OWNERSHIP, MANAGEMENT

Operated by: Dayton Professional Baseball, LLC.
Owners: Hank Stickney, Ken Stickney, Peter Guber, Paul Schaeffer, Magic Johnson, Archie Griffin.
President: Robert Murphy. Executive Vice President: Eric Deutsch.
Vice President, Baseball/Stadium Operations: Gary Mayse. VP, Sponsorships: Jeff Webb. Director, Ticket Sales: John Davis. Director, Marketing: Jim Francis. Director, Entertainment: Shari Sharkins. Director, Media Relations/Broadcasting: Mike Vander Wood. VP, Finance: Jim Goodrich. Box Office Manager: Sally Ledford. Corporate Marketing Managers: Michael Blanton, Jermaine Cage, Clint Taylor, Mark Wilhjelm. Marketing Managers: Brandy Abney, Brad Eaton, Kevin Johnson, Laura Rose, Emily Tincher. Operations Manager: Joe Eaglowski. Facilities Operations Manager: Joe Elking. Team Operations Manager: John Wallace. Head Groundskeeper: Ryan Kaspiztke. Staff Accountant: Dorothy Day. Office Manager: Leslie Stuck. Administrative Assistant: Lisa Rike.

FIELD STAFF

Manager: Alonzo Powell. Coach: Chris Sabo. Pitching Coach: Larry Pierson. Trainer: Randy Brackney.

GAME INFORMATION

Radio Announcer: Mike Vander Wood. No. of Games Broadcast: Home-70, Away-70. Flagship Station: WING 1410-AM.
PA Announcer: Unavailable. Official Scorers: Unavailable.
Stadium Name: Fifth Third Field. Location: I-75 South to downtown Dayton, left at First Street; I-75 North, right at

First Street exit. **Standard Game Times:** 7 p.m.; Sun. 2. **Ticket Price Range:** $7-12.75.
  Visiting Club Hotel: Fairfield Inn, Dayton North, 6960 Miller Lane, Dayton, OH 45414. Telephone: (937) 898-1120.

FORT WAYNE
WIZARDS

  Office Address: 1616 E. Coliseum Blvd., Fort Wayne, IN 46805.
  Telephone: (260) 482-6400. **FAX:** (260) 471-4678.
  E-Mail Address: info@fortwaynewizards.com. **Website:** www.fortwaynewizards.com
  Affiliation (first year): San Diego Padres (1999). **Years in League:** 1993-.

OWNERSHIP, MANAGEMENT
  Operated by: General Sports and Entertainment, LLC.
  Owner: Andrew Appleby.
  General Manager: Mike Nutter. **Assistant GM, Business Operations:** Brian Schackow. **Senior Assistant GM:** David Lorenz. **Director, Marketing/Graphic Design:** Michael Limmer. **Director, Community/Media Relations:** Jared Parcell. **Director, Ticket Operations:** Patrick Ventura. **Director, Broadcasting:** Terry Byrom. **Group Sales Representatives:** Tony Desplaines, Kevin Duplaga, Brad Shank. **Group Sales Representative:** Jeff Bierly. **Office Manager:** Cathy Tinney.

FIELD STAFF
  Manager: Randy Ready. **Coach:** Max Venable. **Pitching Coach:** Steve Webber. **Trainer:** Paul Navarro.

GAME INFORMATION
  Radio Announcers: Terry Byrom, Kent Hormann. **No. of Games Broadcast:** Home-70, Away-70. **Flagship Station:** WKJG 1380-AM.
  PA Announcers: Jared Parcell, Jim Shovlin. **Official Scorers:** Mike Maahs; Mike Jewell.
  Stadium Name: Memorial Stadium. **Location:** Exit 112A (Coldwater Road South) off I-69 to Coliseum Blvd., left to stadium. **Standard Game Times:** 6 p.m., (June-July) 7; Wed. 11, (June-July) 12; Sat. 4, (June-July) 6:15; Sun. 2. **Ticket Price Range:** $6.50-9.
  Visiting Club Hotel: Best Western Luxbury, 5501 Coventry Lane, Fort Wayne, IN 46804. Telephone: (260) 436-0242.

KANE COUNTY
COUGARS

  Office Address: 34W002 Cherry Lane, Geneva, IL 60134.
  Telephone: (630) 232-8811. **FAX:** (630) 232-8815.
  E-Mail Address: info@kccougars.com. **Website:** www.kccougars.com.
  Affiliation (first year): Oakland Athletics (2003). **Years in League:** 1991-.

OWNERSHIP, MANAGEMENT
  Operated by: Cougars Baseball Partnership/American Sports Enterprises, Inc.
  President: Mike Woleben. **Vice President:** Mike Murtaugh.
  VP/General Manager: Jeff Sedivy. **Assistant GMs:** Curtis Haug, Jeff Ney. **Business Manager:** Mary Almlie. **Comptroller:** Doug Czurylo. **Concessions Accountant:** Chris McGorry. **Director, Ticket Operations:** Amy Mason. **Assistant Director, Ticket Operations:** Mike Gilreath. **Season Ticket Coordinator:** Lindsey Bast. **Ticket Operations:** Erin Wiencek, Shawn Touney. **Director, Ticket Sales:** Michael Patterson. **Account Executives:** David Edison, Steve McNelley, Patti Savage. **Director, Food/Beverage:** Rich Essegian. **Director, Catering:** Mike Klafehn. **Concessions Supervisor:** Tim Howe. **Director, Public Relations:** Kari Kuefler. **Design, Graphics:** Emmet Broderick, Todd Koenitz. **Manager, Advertising:** Bill Baker. **Manager, Merchandise:** Chris McGorry. **Head Groundskeeper:** Ryan Nieuwsma. **Office Manager:** Carol Huppert. **Facilities Management:** Jeff Snyder. **Clubhouse Manager:** Sean Gallick.

FIELD STAFF
  Manager: Dave Joppie. **Coach:** Aaron Nieckula. **Pitching Coach:** Garvin Alston. **Trainer:** Justin Whitehouse.

GAME INFORMATION
  Radio Announcer: Chris Rushin. **No. of Games Broadcast:** Home-70, Away-70. **Flagship Station:** WBIG 1280-AM.
  PA Announcer: Kevin Sullivan. **Official Scorer:** Bill Baker.
  Stadium Name: Philip B. Elfstrom Stadium. **Location:** From east or west, I-88 (East-West Tollway) to Farnsworth Avenue North exit, north five miles to Cherry Lane, left into stadium complex; from north, Route 59 south to Route 64 (North Ave.), west to Kirk Road, south past Route 38 to Cherry Lane, right into stadium complex; from northwest, I-90 to Randall Road South exit, south to Fabyan Parkway, east to Kirk Road, north to Cherry Lane, left into stadium complex. **Standard Game Times:** 6:30 p.m., (April-May 26) 6:00; Sat. (April-May 6) 4, (May 14-Sept.) 6; Sun. 2. **Ticket Price Range:** $8-9.
  Visiting Club Hotel: Best Western Naperville Inn, 1617 Naperville Rd., Naperville, IL 60563. Telephone: (630) 505-0200.

LANSING
LUGNUTS

Office Address: 505 E. Michigan Ave., Lansing, MI 48912.
Telephone: (517) 485-4500. **FAX:** (517) 485-4518.
E-Mail Address: info@lansinglugnuts.com. **Website:** www.lansinglugnuts.com.
Affiliation (first year): Toronto Blue Jays (2005). **Years In League:** 1996-.

OWNERSHIP, MANAGEMENT
Operated by: Take Me Out to the Ballgame, LLC.
Principal Owners: Tom Dickson, Sherrie Myers.
General Manager: Jeff Calhoun. **Vice President, Marketing:** Darla Bowen. **Director, Food Service:** Dave Parker. **Director, Sponsorship/Marketing:** Valerie Claus. **Manager, Tickets:** Chris Troub. **Director, Retail:** Cherie Hargitt. **Director, Sales:** Nick Grueser. **Marketing Manager:** Seth VanHoven. **Marketing Assistant:** Justin Furr. **Head Groundskeeper:** Matt Anderson. **Group Sales Representatives:** Mike MacKenzie, Nick Brzenzinski. **Corporate Account Executives:** Jim LaPorte, Nathan Greene. **Sponsorship Service Representative:** Kelly Love. **Business Manager:** Suzanne Green. **Front Desk Administrator:** Sharon Jackson. **Sponsorship Intern:** Erin Pierce.

FIELD STAFF
Manager: Ken Joyce. **Coach:** Charles Poe. **Pitching Coach:** Tom Bradley. **Trainer:** Andrew Muccino.

GAME INFORMATION
Radio Announcer: Seth VanHoven. **No. of Games Broadcast:** Home-65, Away-65. **Flagship Station:** The Ticket 92.1/92.7-FM.
PA Announcer: J.J. Wright. **Official Scorer:** Mike Clark.
Stadium Name: Oldsmobile Park. **Location:** I-96 East/West to U.S. 496, exit at Larch Street, go north, stadium on left. **Standard Game Times:** 7:05 p.m., (April-May) 6:05; Sun. 2:05. **Ticket Price Range:** $6.50-8.
Visiting Club Hotel: Holiday Inn South, 6820 South Cedar, Lansing, MI 48911. Telephone: (517) 694-8123.

PEORIA
CHIEFS

Office Address: 730 SW Jefferson, Peoria, IL 61602.
Telephone: (309) 680-4000. **FAX:** (309) 680-4080.
Website: www.peoriachiefs.com.
Affiliation (first year): Chicago Cubs (2005). **Years in League:** 1983-.

OWNERSHIP, MANAGEMENT
Operated by: Peoria Chiefs Community Baseball Club, LLC.
President: Rocky Vonachen.
General Manager: Ralph Converse. **Director, Guest Services/Account Executive:** Howard Yates. **Manager, Box Office:** Ryan Sivori. **Manager, Broadcast/Media:** Nathan Baliva. **Manager, Marketing/Promotions:** Geoff Brigham. **Account Executives:** George Moore, Jeremy Wieburg, Holly Fisher, Shari Phipps. **Head Groundskeeper:** T.J. Shine.

FIELD STAFF
Manager: Julio Garcia. **Coach:** Ricardo Medina. **Pitching Coach:** Tom Pratt. **Trainer:** Chuck Baughman.

GAME INFORMATION
Radio Announcer: Nathan Baliva. **No. of Games Broadcast:** Home-70, Away-70. **Flagship Station:** WOAM 1350-AM.
PA Announcer: Unavailable. **Official Scorer:** Unavailable.
Stadium Name: O'Brien Field. **Location:** From South/East, I-74 to exit 93 (Jefferson Street), west one mile, stadium is one block west of Kumpf Boulevard on left. From North/West, I-74 to exit 91 (Glendale Avenue), straight through stoplight and follow Kumpf Boulevard left for five blocks, right on Jefferson Street, stadium on left. **Standard Game Times:** 7 p.m.; (April-May) 6:30; Sat. 6:30; Sun. 2. **Ticket Price Range:** $6-10.
Visiting Club Hotel: Holiday Inn City Centre, 500 Hamilton Blvd., Peoria, IL 61602. Telephone: (309) 674-2500.

SWING OF THE
QUAD CITIES

Office Address: 209 S. Gaines St., Davenport, IA 52802.
Telephone: (563) 324-3000. **FAX:** (563) 324-3109.
E-Mail Address: jazzed@swingbaseball.com. **Website:** www.swingbaseball.com.
Affiliation (first year): St. Louis Cardinals (2005). **Years in League:** 1960-.

OWNERSHIP, MANAGEMENT

Operated by: Seventh Inning Stretch, LC.
President/General Manager: Kevin Krause.
Vice President, Sales/Marketing: Michael Weindruch. **Assistant GM:** Josh Eagan. **Director, Baseball Operations/Groundskeeper:** Andy Duyvejonck. **Director, Sales:** Michael Corrigan. **Ticket Manager:** Greg Sprott. **Director, Food/Beverage:** James Johnson. **Premium Services/Banquets Manager:** Melissa Muehler. **Director, Broadcasting/Media Relations:** Andrew Rudnik. **Account Executive:** Bill Bubon. **Office Manager:** Carrie Brus.

FIELD STAFF

Manager: Joe Cunningham. **Coach:** Keith Mitchell. **Pitching Coach:** Bryan Eversgerd. **Trainer:** Brian Puchalski.

GAME INFORMATION

Radio Announcer: Andrew Rudnik. **No. of Games Broadcast:** Home-70, Away-70. **Flagship Station:** Unavailable. **PA Announcer:** Unavailable. **Official Scorer:** Unavailable.
Stadium Name: John O'Donnell Stadium. **Location:** From I-74, take State Street exit, west onto River Drive, south on Gaines Street. From I-80, take Brady/Harrison Street exit south, west onto River Drive, south on Gaines Street. **Standard Game Times:** 7 p.m., April 6:30; Sun. 2. **Ticket Price Range:** $6-12.
Visiting Club Hotel: Holiday Inn, 5202 Brady St., Davenport, IA 52806. Telephone: (563) 391-1230

SOUTH BEND
SILVER HAWKS

Office Address: 501 W. South St., South Bend, IN 46601.
Telephone: (574) 235-9988. **FAX:** (574) 235-9950.
E-Mail Address: hawks@silverhawks.com. **Website:** www.silverhawks.com.
Affiliation (first year): Arizona Diamondbacks (1997). **Years in League:** 1988-.

OWNERSHIP, MANAGEMENT

Operated by: Palisades Baseball, Ltd.
Principal Owner: Alan Levin. **Executive Vice President:** Erik Haag. **Director, Finance:** Cheryl Case.
Assistant General Manager: Tim Arseneau. **Director, Sales/Marketing:** Tony Wittrock. **Manager, Box Office:** Stephen Hinkel. **Director, Stadium Operations:** Mike Cook. **Director, Concessions:** Dennis Watson. **Account Executives:** Billy Richards, Ian Zelenski. **Office Manager:** Kelly Devon. **Director, Media Relations:** Mike Lockert. **Head Groundskeeper:** Joel Reinebold.

FIELD STAFF

Manager: Mark Haley. **Coach:** Tony Dello. **Pitching Coach:** Wellington Cepeda. **Trainer:** Scott Jones.

GAME INFORMATION

Radio Announcer: Mike Lockert. **No. of Games Broadcast:** Unavailable. **Flagship Station:** Unavailable. **PA Announcer:** Unavailable. **Official Scorer:** Unavailable.
Stadium Name: Stanley Coveleski Regional Stadium. **Location:** I-80/90 toll road to exit 77, take US 31/33 south to South Bend, to downtown (Main Street), to Western Avenue, right on Western, left on Taylor. **Standard Game Times:** 7 p.m., (April-May) 6:30; Sun. 1:30. **Ticket Price Range:** $5-7.
Visiting Club Hotel: Quality Inn-University Area, 515 Dixie Way North, South Bend, IN 46637. Telephone: (574) 272-6600.

SOUTHWEST MICHIGAN
DEVIL RAYS

Office Address: 189 Bridge St., Battle Creek, MI 49017.
Telephone: (269) 660-2287. **FAX:** (269) 660-2288.
E-Mail Address: info@southwestmichigandevilrays.com. **Website:** www.southwestmichigandevilrays.com.
Affiliation: Tampa Bay Devil Rays (2005). **Years in League:** 1995-

OWNERSHIP, MANAGEMENT

Operated by: Fun Entertainment, LLC
President: William Shea. **Chief Operating Officer:** Alan Stein. **General Manager:** Martie Cordaro. **Business Manager:** Brian Cheever. **Media Relations Director:** Brett Carow. **Director, Group Sales/Operations:** Luke Kuboushek. **Corporate Sales Executive:** Steve Glasgow. **Regional Sales Managers:** Mike Knipper, Greg Kruger, Rob Crain. **Director, Concessions:** Pete Cummins. **Field Turf Manager:** Len Matthews. **Executive Assistant:** Robin Santiago. **Merchandise/Box Office Manager:** Shauna Fiegel. **Stadium Manager:** Steve Kaylor.

FIELD STAFF

Manager: Joe Szekely. **Coach:** Skeeter Barnes. **Pitching Coach:** R.C. Lichtenstein. **Trainer:** Chris Tomashoff.

GAME INFORMATION

Radio: Unavailable.

PA Announcer: Unavailable. **Official Scorer:** Unavailable.
Stadium Name: C.O. Brown Stadium. **Location:** I-94 to exit 98B (downtown), to Capital Avenue and continue five miles to stadium. **Standard Game Times:** 7:05 p.m., (April-May) 6:35; Sunday 2:05. **Ticket Price Range:** $6-8.
Visiting Club Hotel: Comfort Inn, 2590 Capital Ave. SW, Battle Creek, MI 49017. Telephone: (269) 965-3201

WEST MICHIGAN
WHITECAPS

Office Address: 4500 W. River Dr., Comstock Park, MI 49321.
Mailing Address: P.O. Box 428, Comstock Park, MI 49321.
Telephone: (616) 784-4131. **FAX:** (616) 784-4911.
E-Mail Address: playball@whitecaps-baseball.com. **Website:** www.whitecaps-baseball.com.
Affiliation (first year): Detroit Tigers (1997). **Years in League:** 1994-.

OWNERSHIP, MANAGEMENT
Operated by: Whitecaps Professional Baseball Corp.
Principal Owners: Denny Baxter, Lew Chamberlin.
Chief Executive Officer, Managing Partner: Lew Chamberlin. **Chief Financial Officer:** Denny Baxter. **President:** Scott Lane.
Vice President, Operations: Jim Jarecki. **Director, Ticket Sales:** Steve McCarthy. **Director, Operations/Outside Events:** Matt Costello. **Managers, Human Resources:** Ellen Chamberlin, Tina Porcelli. **Manager, Food/Beverage:** Matt Timon. **Director, Corporate Sales:** Dan McCrath. **Marketing Manager:** Mickey Graham. **Ticket Sales Manager:** Kerri Troyer. **Manager, Website/Merchandise:** Lori Ashcroft. **Manager, Public Relations:** Jamie Farber. **Manager, Ticket Operations:** Steve Klein. **Head Groundskeeper:** Ryan Baumbach. **Manager, Facility Maintenance:** Dutch VanSingel. **Promotions Manager:** Jason Lewandowski. **Corporate Sales:** Dave Skoczen, Trevor Tkach. **Ticket Sales Consultants:** Alanna Kuhn, Brian Hamilton, Jay Lockett, Scott Lutz, Chad Sayen, Craig Yust. **Assistant, Accounts Receivable:** Barb Renteria. **Assistant, Food/Beverage:** Bill Moore. **Receptionists:** Kim Castle, Susie Former.

FIELD STAFF
Manager: Matt Walbeck. **Coach:** Tony Jaramillo. **Pitching Coach:** A.J. Sager. **Trainer:** Dustin Campbell.

GAME INFORMATION
Radio Announcer: Dave Skoczen. **No. of Games Broadcast:** Home-70, Away-70. **Flagship Station:** WBBL 1340-AM
PA Announcers: Bob Wells, Mike Newell. **Official Scorers:** Mike Dean, Don Thomas.
Stadium Name: Fifth Third Ballpark. **Location:** U.S. 131 North from Grand Rapids to exit 91 (West River Drive). **Standard Game Times:** 7 p.m., (April-May) 6:35; Sat. (April-May) 2; Sun. 2. **Ticket Price Range:** $5-9.
Visiting Club Hotel: Days Inn-Downtown, 310 Pearl St. NW, Grand Rapids, MI 49504. Telephone: (616) 235-7611.

WISCONSIN
TIMBER RATTLERS

Office Address: 2400 N. Casaloma Dr., Appleton, WI 54913.
Mailing Address: P.O. Box 7464, Appleton, WI 54912.
Telephone: (920) 733-4152. **FAX:** (920) 733-8032.
E-Mail Address: info@timberrattlers.com. **Website:** www.timberrattlers.com.
Affiliation (first year): Seattle Mariners (1993). **Years in League:** 1962 .

OWNERSHIP, MANAGEMENT
Operated by: Appleton Baseball Club, Inc.
Chairman: Dave Anderson.
President, General Manager: Rob Zerjav. **Director, Operations:** Tom Kulczewski. **Controller:** Cathy Spanbauer. **Director, Community/Media Relations:** Nikki Becker. **Director, Promotions/Graphic Design:** Angie Ceranski. **Manager, Merchandise/Internet Specialist:** Logan Waetje. **Director, Ticket Sales:** Scott Moudry. **Managers, Group Sales:** Lisa Nortman, Lindsay Kray, Tiffany Timmerman. **Director, Sales:** Laurie Schill. **Managers, Corporate Sales:** Nicole DeBoth, Chris Mehring. **Office Manager:** Mary Robinson. **Head Groundskeeper:** Jesse Mallmann.

FIELD STAFF
Manager: Scott Steinmann. **Coach:** Tommy Cruz. **Pitching Coach:** Brad Holman. **Trainer:** Jeremy Clipperton.

GAME INFORMATION
Radio Announcer: Chris Mehring. **No. of Games Broadcast:** Home-70, Away-70. **Flagship Station:** WJMQ 92.3-FM.
PA Announcer: Matt Wittlin. **Official Scorer:** Jay Grusznski.
Stadium Name: Fox Cities Stadium. **Location:** Highway 41 to Highway 15 (OO) exit, west to Casaloma Drive, left to stadium. **Standard Game Times:** 7:05 p.m., (April-May) 6:35; Sun. 1:05. **Ticket Price Range:** $4-7.50.
Visiting Club Hotel: Microtel Inn & Suites, 321 Metro Dr., Appleton, WI 54913. Telephone: (920) 997-3121.

SOUTH ATLANTIC
LEAGUE

Office Address: 504 Crescent Hill, Kings Mountain, NC 28086.
Mailing Address: P.O. Box 38, Kings Mountain, NC 28086.
Telephone: (704) 739-3466. **FAX:** (704) 739-1974.
E-Mail Address: saleague@bellsouth.net. **Website:** www.southatlanticleague.com.
Years League Active: 1904-1964, 1979 -.

President/Secretary-Treasurer: John Moss.
Vice President: Ron McKee (Asheville).
Directors: Don Beaver (Hickory), Cooper Brantley (Greensboro), Peter Carfagna (Lake County), Joseph Finley (Lakewood), Marvin Goldklang (Charleston), Larry Hedrick (Kannapolis), David Heller (Columbus), Alan Levin (West Virginia), Ron McKee (Asheville), Frank Miceli (Delmarva), Chip Moore (Rome), Rich Mozingo (Capital City), Rich Neumann (Hagerstown), Michael Savit (Augusta), Ken Silver (Savannah), Alan Stein (Lexington).
Administrative Assistant: Patrick Heavner.
Division Structure: North—Delmarva, Greensboro, Hagerstown, Hickory, Lake County, Lakewood, Lexington, West Virginia. **South**—Asheville, Augusta, Capital City, Charleston, Columbus, Kannapolis, Rome, Savannah.
Regular Season: 140 games (split-schedule). **2005 Opening Date:** April 7. **Closing Date:** Sept. 5.

John Moss

All-Star Game: June 28 at Augusta.
Playoff Format: First-half and second-half division champions meet in best-of-3 semifinal series. Winners meet in best-of-5 series for league championship.
Roster Limit: 25 active. **Player Eligibility Rule:** No age limit. No more than two players and one player-coach on active list may have more than five years of experience.
Brand of Baseball: Rawlings.
Statistician: Major League Baseball Advanced Media, 75 Ninth Ave., New York, NY 10011.
Umpires: Shea Abbott (Clearwater, FL), Russell Barrett (Las Vegas, NV), Brett Cavins (Versailles, KY), Vernon Chamberlain (Lake City, FL), Thomas Clarke (Andover, MA), Tim Daub (Ellicott, MD), Adam Ficken (Huntsville, AL), John Gelatt (East Greenbush, NY), Clay Gillentine (Greenville, TX), Manuel Gonzalez (Valencia, Venez.), Eugene McDonald (Waycross, GA), Jason Millsap (Bryan, TX), Jesse Redwine (Del City, OK), Justin Vogel (Jacksonville, FL), Richard Young (Cayce, SC).

STADIUM INFORMATION

Club	Stadium	Opened	Dimensions LF	CF	RF	Capacity	2004 Att.
Asheville	McCormick Field	1992	328	402	300	4,000	140,634
Augusta	Lake Olmstead Stadium	1995	330	400	330	4,322	160,378
Capital City	Capital City Stadium	1991	330	395	320	6,000	100,798
Charleston	Joseph P. Riley Ballpark	1997	306	386	336	5,800	255,793
Columbus	Golden Park	1951	330	415	330	5,000	51,352
Delmarva	Arthur W. Perdue Stadium	1996	309	402	309	5,200	230,536
Greensboro	First Horizon Park	2005	322	400	320	8,000	200,477
Hagerstown	Municipal Stadium	1931	335	400	330	4,600	128,508
Hickory	L.P. Frans Stadium	1993	330	401	330	5,062	178,439
Kannapolis	Fieldcrest Cannon Stadium	1995	330	400	310	4,700	105,214
Lake County	Eastlake Ballpark	2003	320	400	320	7,273	406,096
Lakewood	FirstEnergy Park	2001	325	400	325	6,588	440,521
Lexington	Applebee's Park	2001	320	401	318	6,033	401,191
Rome	State Mutual Stadium	2003	335	400	330	5,100	246,674
Savannah	Grayson Stadium	1941	290	410	310	8,000	113,359
West Virginia	Unavailable	2005	330	400	320	4,300	125,979

ASHEVILLE
TOURISTS

Office Address: McCormick Field, 30 Buchanan Pl., Asheville, NC 28801.
Mailing Address: P.O. Box 1556, Asheville, NC 28802.
Telephone: (828) 258-0428. **FAX:** (828) 258-0320.
E-Mail Address: touristsbb@mindspring.com. **Website:** www.theashevilletourists.com.
Affiliation (first year): Colorado Rockies (1994). **Years in League:** 1976-.

OWNERSHIP, MANAGEMENT
Operated by: Asheville Tourists Baseball, Inc.
Principal Owners: Peter Kern, Ron McKee.
President: Ron McKee.
General Manager: Larry Hawkins. **Assistant GM:** Chris Smith. **Director, Business Operations:** Carolyn McKee.
Director, Media Relations: Bill Ballew. **Director, Group Sales:** David King. **Concessions Manager:** Carter Buschman.
Head Groundskeeper: Patrick Schrimplin.

FIELD STAFF
Manager: Joe Mikulik. **Coach:** Dave Hajek. **Pitching Coach:** Greg Booker. **Trainer:** Chris Strickland.

GAME INFORMATION
Radio: None.
PA Announcer: Rick Diggler. **Official Scorer:** Mike Gore.
Stadium Name: McCormick Field. **Location:** I-240 to Charlotte Street South exit, south one mile on Charlotte, left on McCormick Place. **Standard Game Times:** 7 p.m.; Sun. 2. **Ticket Price Range:** $6-8.
Visiting Club Hotel: Holiday Inn East, 1450 Tunnel Rd., Asheville, NC 28805. Telephone: (828) 298-5611.

AUGUSTA
GREENJACKETS

Office Address: 78 Milledge Rd., Augusta, GA 30904.
Telephone: (706) 736-7889. **FAX:** (706) 736-1122.
E-Mail Address: grnsox@aol.com. **Website:** www.greenjacketsbaseball.com.
Affiliation (first year): San Francisco Giants (2005). **Years in League:** 1988-.

OWNERSHIP, MANAGEMENT
Operated by: H.W.S. Baseball, LLC.
Chief Executive Officer: Michael Savit. **Chief Operating Officer:** Jeffrey Savit. **Executive Vice President:** Chris Scheuer. **General Manager:** Nick Brown. **Director, Stadium Operations:** David Ryther Jr. **Director, Ticket Sales:** Frank Coppola. **Groundskeeper:** Andrew Wright.

FIELD STAFF
Manager: Roberto Kelly. **Coach:** Jerry Browne. **Pitching Coach:** Ross Grimsley. **Trainer:** Jeffrey Shanlee.

GAME INFORMATION
Radio: None.
PA Announcer: Scott Skadan. **Official Scorer:** Steve Cain.
Stadium Name: Lake Olmstead Stadium. **Location:** I-20 to exit 199 (Washington Road), east to Broad Street, left onto Milledge Road, stadium on right. **Standard Game Times:** 7:15 p.m., Sun. 2:15. **Ticket Price Range:** $6-10.
Visiting Club Hotel: Fairfield Inn by Marriott, 201 Boy Scout Rd., Augusta, GA 30909. Telephone: (706) 733-8200.

CHARLESTON
RIVERDOGS

RIVERDOGS

Office Address: 360 Fishburne St., Charleston, SC 29403.
Mailing Address: P.O. Box 20849, Charleston, SC 29413.
Telephone: (843) 723-7241. **FAX:** (843) 723-2641.
E-Mail Address: dogsrus@riverdogs.com. **Website:** www.riverdogs.com.
Affiliation (first year): New York Yankees (2005). **Years in League:** 1973-78, 1980-.

OWNERSHIP, MANAGEMENT
Operated by: The Goldklang Group/South Carolina Baseball Club, LP.
Principal Owners: Marv Goldklang, Mike Veeck, Bill Murray.
General Manager: Dave Echols. **Assistant GM:** Andy Lange. **Director, Stadium Operations:** Ben Danosky. **Director,**

Promotions: Jim Pfander. **Coordinator, Media Relations:** Unavailable. **Business Manager:** Aubra Carlton. **Director, Special Events:** Dale Stickney. **Director, Food/Beverage:** Jason Kerton. **Director, Technology Services:** Chris Ginnett. **Office Manager:** Kristal Lessington. **Director, Community Relations:** Danielle Swigart. **Coordinator, Sales:** Harold Craw. **Director, Merchandise:** Kristi Tolley. **Manager, Food/Beverage:** Jason Fuller. **Manager, Ticket:** Jake Terrell. **Manager, Sales:** Unavailable. **Head Groundskeeper:** Mike Geiger.

FIELD STAFF

Manager: Bill Mosiello. **Coach:** Torre Tyson. **Pitching Coach:** Steve Renko. **Trainer:** Tim Lentych.

GAME INFORMATION

Radio Announcer: Josh Mauer. **No. of Games Broadcast:** Home-70, Away-70. **Flagship Station:** WTMZ 910-AM. **PA Announcer:** Ken Carrington. **Official Scorer:** Chuck Manka.
Stadium Name: Joseph P. Riley Jr. Ballpark. **Location:** From U.S. 17, take Lockwood Drive North, right on Fishburne Street. **Standard Game Times:** 7:05 p.m.; Sun. 2:05. **Ticket Price Range:** $4-8.
Visiting Club Hotel: Howard Johnson Riverfront, 250 Spring St., Charleston, SC 29403. Telephone: (843) 722-4000.

COLUMBUS
CATFISH

Office Address: Golden Park, 100 Fourth St., Columbus, GA 31901.
Telephone: (706) 571-8866. **FAX:** (706) 571-9984.
E-Mail Address: info@columbuscatfish.com. **Website:** www.columbuscatfish.com.
Affiliation (first year): Los Angeles Dodgers (2002). **Years in League:** 2001-.

OWNERSHIP, MANAGEMENT

Operated by: Main Street Baseball, LLC.
Owner: David Heller.
General Manager: Jim Beaudoin. **Director, Sales/Marketing:** Jim Asher. **Director, Ticket Operations:** Coulson Barbiche. **Director, Media/Community Relations:** John Youngblood. **Director, Stadium Operations:** J.J. Reali. **Director, Broadcasting:** Chad Goldberg. **Head Groundskeeper:** Brock Van Faussien. **Office Manager:** Brandi Kohl. **Administrative Assistants:** Mike Daggett, Chelsea Dalton, Samantha Dunn, Brad Hudson, Takeshi Sakurayama, Peter Trent.

FIELD STAFF

Manager: Travis Barbary. **Coach:** Garey Ingram. **Pitching Coach:** Glenn Dishman. **Trainer:** Jason Roberts. **Strength/Conditioning Coach:** Ed Kohl.

GAME INFORMATION

Radio Announcer: Chad Goldberg. **No. of Games Broadcast:** Home-70, Away-70. **Flagship Station:** WDAK 540- AM.
Stadium Name: Golden Park. **Location:** I-85 South to exit 7 (Manchester Expressway), right on Manchester Expressway for one mile, left on Veterans Parkway into South Commons complex. **Standard Game Times:** 6/7 p.m.; Sat. 1/7; Sun. 2. **Ticket Price Range:** $4-7.
Visiting Club Hotel: Holiday Inn North, 2800 Manchester Expwy., Columbus, GA 31904. Telephone: (706) 324-0231.

DELMARVA
SHOREBIRDS

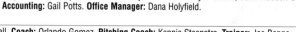

Office Address: 6400 Hobbs Rd., Salisbury, MD 21804.
Mailing Address: P.O. Box 1557, Salisbury, MD 21802.
Telephone: (410) 219-3112. **FAX:** (410) 219-9164.
E-Mail Address: information@theshorebirds.com. **Website:** www.theshorebirds.com.
Affiliation (first year): Baltimore Orioles (1997). **Years in League:** 1996-.

OWNERSHIP, MANAGEMENT

Operated by: Comcast-Spectacor.
Directors: Peter Luukko, Frank Miceli.
General Manager: Steve Yaros. **Director, Sales:** Greg Beckman. **Director, Stadium Operations:** Deandre Ewell. **Head Groundskeeper:** Kelly Burns. **Senior Corporate Sales Manager:** Jimmy Sweet. **Group Event Manager/Ticket Sales Representative:** Kris Rutledge. **Director, Community Relations/Customer Service:** Norb Sadilek. **Marketing Communications Manager/Public Relations:** Nick Mirabello. **Marketing Manager/Media Relations:** Brian Patey. **Marketing Manager/Mascot Coordinator:** Brad Collins. **Group Event Managers/Ticket Sales Representatives:** Erin Dunn, Tom Denlinger, Randy Atkinson. **Corporate Account Representatives:** Ryan Sachs, John Houser. **Box Office Manager:** Tiana Humes. **Accounting:** Gail Potts. **Office Manager:** Dana Holyfield.

FIELD STAFF

Manager: Gary Kendall. **Coach:** Orlando Gomez. **Pitching Coach:** Kennie Steenstra. **Trainer:** Joe Benge.

GAME INFORMATION

Radio Announcer: Ryan Sachs. **No. of Games Broadcast:** Home-70, Away-70. **Flagship Station:** WTGM 960-AM.

PA Announcer: Jim Whittemore. **Official Scorer:** Unavailable.
   Stadium Name: Arthur W. Perdue Stadium. **Location:** From U.S. 50 East, right on Hobbs Road; From U.S. 50 West, left on Hobbs Road. **Standard Game Times:** 6:35 p.m. (first half), 7:05 (second half); Sun. 1:35. **Ticket Price Range:** $4-12.
   Visiting Club Hotel: Best Value Inn 2625 N. Salisbury Blvd., Salisbury, MD 21801. Telephone: (410) 742-7194.

GREENSBORO
GRASSHOPPERS

   Office Address: 408 Bellemeade St., Greensboro, NC 27401.
   Telephone: (336) 268-2255. **FAX:** (336) 273-7350.
   E-Mail Address: info@gsohoppers.com. **Website:** www.gsohoppers.com.
   Affiliation (first year): Florida Marlins (2003). **Years in League:** 1979-.

OWNERSHIP, MANAGEMENT
   Operated by: Greensboro Baseball, LLC.
   Principal Owners: Cooper Brantley, Wes Elingburg, Len White.
   President, Chief Operating Officer: Donald Moore. **General Manager:** Tom Howe. **Assistant GM/Head Groundskeeper:** Jake Holloway. **Director, Marketing/Community Relations:** Cari Powell. **Director, Media Relations:** Megan Thomas. **Director, Creative Services:** Amanda Williams. **Director, Finance/Merchandise:** Sue DeRocco. **Director, Stadium Operations:** Tim Vangel. **Director, Front Office/Game Day Operations:** Ashley Stephens. **Executive Assistant:** Rosalee Brewer. **Director, Ticketing:** Kim Gordon.

FIELD STAFF
   Manager: Brandon Hyde. **Coach:** Bo Porter. **Pitching Coach:** Steve Foster. **Trainer:** Frank Briceland.

GAME INFORMATION
   Radio Announcer: Andy Durham. **No. of Games Broadcast:** Home-70. **Flagship Station:** WPET 950-AM.
   PA Announcer: Jim Scott. **Official Scorer:** Paul Wirth.
   Stadium Name: First Horizon Park. **Location:** From I-85, take Higway 220 South (exit 36) to Coliseum Boulevard, continue on Edgeworth Street, ballpark at corner of Edgeworth and Bellemeade Streets. **Standard Game Times:** 7 p.m.; Sun. 5. **Ticket Price Range:** $6-9.
   Visiting Club Hotel: Ramada Inn Airport, 7067 Albert Pick Rd., Greensboro, NC 27409. Telephone: (336) 668-3900.

GREENVILLE
BOMBERS

   Office Address: One Braves Avenue, Greenville, SC 29607.
   Mailing Address: Unavailable.
   Telephone: (864) 422-1510. **FAX:** Unavailable.
   E-Mail Address: info@bomberball.com. **Website:** www.bomberball.com.
   Affiliation (first year): Boston Red Sox (2005). **Years in League:** 2005-.

OWNERSHIP, MANAGEMENT
   Operated by: RB3, LLC.
   President/General Manager: Rich Mozingo. **Director, Tickets/Merchandise:** Luis Gonzalez. **Director, Media Relations/Group Sales:** Pete Ehmke. **Director, Concessions:** Skip Anderson.

FIELD STAFF
   Manager: Chad Epperson. **Coach:** Randy Phillips. **Pitching Coach:** Bob Kipper. **Trainer:** Brad Pearson.

GAME INFORMATION
   Radio: None.
   PA Announcer: Unavailable. **Official Scorer:** Unavailable.
   Stadium Name: Greenville Municipal Stadium. **Location:** I-85 to exit 46 (Mauldin Road), east two miles. **Standard Game Times:** 7:05 p.m., Sun., 2:05. **Ticket Price Range:** Unavailable.
   Visiting Club Hotel: Unavailable.

HAGERSTOWN
SUNS

   Office Address: 274 E. Memorial Blvd., Hagerstown, MD 21740.
   Telephone: (301) 791-6266. **FAX:** (301) 791-6066.

**HAGERSTOWN
SUNS**

E-Mail Address: info@hagerstownsuns.com. **Website:** www.hagerstownsuns.com.
Affiliation (first year): New York Mets (2005). **Years in League:** 1993-.

OWNERSHIP, MANAGEMENT

Operated by: Mandalay Baseball Properties.
Principal Owners: Peter Guber, Paul Schaeffer, Hank Stickney, Ken Stickney.
General Manager: Kurt Landes. **Assistant GM:** Will Smith. **Director, Business Operations:** Carol Gehr. **Director, Stadium Operations:** Mike Showe. **Director, Marketing:** C.J. Johnson. **Director, Group Sales:** Drew Himsworth. **Director, Food/Beverage:** Alan Aust. **Manager, Ticket Sales**: Jason Bucur. **Manager, Media Relations:** Jason Gordon. **Interns:** Dave Fera, Kuni Miyajima, Joe Moore, Joel Pagliaro, Keith Pellicane, Jason Rhea, Chris Worstell. **Clubhouse Manager:** Todd Terpstra.

FIELD STAFF

Manager: Unavailable. **Coach:** Luis Natera. **Pitching Coach:** Shawn Barton. **Trainer:** Unavailable.

GAME INFORMATION

Radio Announcers: Jason Gordon, Joe Moore. **No. of Games Broadcast:** Home-70, Away-70. **Flagship Station:** WHAG 1410-AM.
PA Announcer: Rick Reeder. **Official Scorer:** Chris Spaid.
Stadium Name: Municipal Stadium. **Location:** Exit 32B (U.S. 40 West) on I-70 West, left at Eastern Boulevard; Exit 6A (U.S. 40 East) on I-81, right at Eastern Boulevard. **Standard Game Times:** 7:05 p.m., (April-May) 6:35; Sun. (April–June) 1:35, (July-Sept) 5:35. **Ticket Price Range:** $5-8.
Visiting Club Hotel: Clarion Hotel & Conference Center, 901 Dual Hwy., Hagerstown, MD 21740. Telephone: (301) 733-5100.

HICKORY
CRAWDADS

Office Address: 2500 Clement Blvd. NW, Hickory, NC 28601.
Mailing Address: P.O. Box 1268, Hickory, NC 28603.
Telephone: (828) 322-3000. **FAX:** (828) 322-6137.
E-Mail Address: crawdad@hickorycrawdads.com. **Website:** www.hickorycrawdads.com.
Affiliation (first year): Pittsburgh Pirates (1999). **Years in League:** 1952, 1960, 1993-.

OWNERSHIP, MANAGEMENT

Operated by: Hickory Baseball, Inc.
Principal Owners: Don Beaver, Luther Beaver, Charles Young.
President: Don Beaver.
General Manager: David Haas. **Assistant GM:** Brad Dail. **Ticket Manager:** Harry Schroeder. **Director, Operations:** Dan Brokos. **Director, Merchandise**: Barbara Beatty. **Office Manager/Special Events:** Jeanna Homesley. **Director, Broadcasting/Media Relations:** Dave Friedman. **Director, Public Relations:** Amanda Starnes. **Account Executives:** Luke Heim, Kevin Huisman, Mark Parker, Charlie Patton.

FIELD STAFF

Manager: Jeff Branson. **Coach:** Greg Briley. **Pitching Coach:** Ray Searage. **Trainer:** Bryan Housand.

GAME INFORMATION

Radio Announcer: David Friedman. **No. of Games Broadcast:** Home-70, Away-70. **Flagship Station:** WMNC 92.1-FM.
PA Announcers: JuJu Phillips, Steve Fisher. **Official Scorer:** Gary Olinger.
Stadium Name: L.P. Frans Stadium (1993). **Location:** I-40 to exit 123 (Lenoir North), 321 North to Clement Blvd., left for 1/2 mile. **Standard Game Times:** 7 p.m., 6:30 (school nights); Sun. (April-May) 2, (June-Aug.) 6. **Ticket Price Range:** $5-8.
Visiting Club Hotel: Red Roof Inn, 1184 Lenoir Rhyne Blvd., Hickory, NC 28602. Telephone: (828) 323-1500.

KANNAPOLIS
INTIMIDATORS

Office Address: 2888 Moose Rd., Kannapolis, NC 28083.
Mailing Address: P.O. Box 64, Kannapolis, NC 28082.
Telephone: (704) 932-3267. **FAX:** (704) 938-7040.
E-Mail Address: info@intimidatorsbaseball.com. **Website:** www.intimidatorsbaseball.com.
Affiliation (first year): Chicago White Sox (2001). **Years in League:** 1995-.

OWNERSHIP, MANAGEMENT

Operated by: Smith Family Baseball, Inc.
President: Brad Smith.
General Manager: Tim Mueller. **Associate GM:** Randy Long. **Assistant GM/Director, Stadium Operations:** Jaime

Pruitt. **Director, Tickets/Merchandise**: Tracy Snelbaker. **Director, Corporate/Group Sales**: Chad Thomas. **Interns**: Shannon Dente, Dave Williams.

FIELD STAFF
Manager: Nick Capra. **Coach**: Ryan Long. **Pitching Coach**: J.R. Perdew. **Trainer**: Thomas Vera.

GAME INFORMATION
Radio: None.
PA Announcer: John Homa. **Official Scorer**: Tom Reilly.
Stadium Name: Fieldcrest Cannon Stadium. **Location**: Exit 63 on I-85, west on Lane Street to Stadium Drive.
Standard Game Times: 7:05 p.m.; Sun. 5:05. **Ticket Price Range**: $4-7.
Visiting Club Hotel: Hampton Inn, 612 Dickens Place NE, Concord, NC 28025. Telephone: (704) 793-9700.

LAKE COUNTY
CAPTAINS

Office Address: 35300 Vine St., Eastlake, OH 44095.
Mailing Address: P.O. Box 7129, Eastlake, OH 44095.
Telephone: (440) 975-8085. **FAX**: (440) 975-8958.
E-Mail Address: info@captainsbaseball.com. **Website**: www.captainsbaseball.com.
Affiliation (first year): Cleveland Indians (2003). **Years in League**: 2003-.

OWNERSHIP, MANAGEMENT
Operated by: Cascia, LLC.
Chairman: Peter Carfagna. **Vice Chairman**: Rita Murphy Carfagna. **Vice President**: Ray Murphy.
General Manager: Casey Stump. **Senior Consultant, Sales/Marketing**: Graham Hearns. **Assistant GM, Sales/Marketing**: Gary Thomas. **Assistant GM, Operations**: Paul Siegwarth. **Assistant GM, Public Relations**: Katie Dannemiller. **Director, Merchandise**: Scott Beaman. **Director, Ticket Sales**: Kevin Brodzinski. **Sports Turf Manager**: Greg Elliott. **Director, Community Relations**: Kate Furman. **Controller**: Ken Fogel. **Director, Group Sales**: Jeff Hull. **Assistant Sports Turf Manager**: Josh Klute. **Director, Promotions**: Arica Kress. **Ticket Account Manager**: Julia LaManna. **Director, Special Projects/Account Executive**: Bill Levy. **Box Office Manager**: Morris Seiden. **Manager, Food Service**: Linda Stringham. **Assistant GM, Food/Beverage**: Ashley Teichart. **Director, Broadcasting/Media Relations**: Dave Wilson. **Receptionist**: Tabitha Walters. **Account Executives**: Matt Phillips, Brock Richards, Beth West. **Interns**: Jennifer Berkshire, Eric Nelson, Ryan Petrus.

FIELD STAFF
Manager: Mike Sarbaugh. **Coach**: Jim Rickon. **Pitching Coach**: Scott Radinsky. **Trainer**: Unavailable.

GAME INFORMATION
Radio Announcers: Dave Wilson, Craig Deas. **No. of Games Broadcast**: Home-70, Away-70. **Flagship Station**: WELW 1330-AM.
PA Announcer: Ray Milavec. **Official Scorer**: Fred Heyer.
Stadium Name: Eastlake Ballpark. **Location**: From Route 2 East, exit at Ohio 91, stadium 1/4 mile north. **Standard Game Times**: 7:05 p.m.; Sat. (April-May) 2:05; Sun. 2:05. **Ticket Price Range**: $5-8.
Visiting Club Hotel: Radisson Hotel-Eastlake, 35000 Curtis Blvd., Eastlake, OH 44095. Telephone: (440) 953-8000.

LAKEWOOD
BLUECLAWS

Office Address: 2 Stadium Way, Lakewood, NJ 08701.
Telephone: (732) 901-7000. **FAX**: (732) 901-3967.
E-Mail Address: info@lakewoodblueclaws.com. **Website**: www.lakewoodblue-claws.com.
Affiliation: Philadelphia Phillies (2001). **Years In League**: 2001-.

OWNERSHIP, MANAGEMENT
Operated by: American Baseball Company, LLC.
President: Joseph Finley. **Partners**: Joseph Caruso, Joseph Plumeri, Craig Stein.
General Manager: Geoff Brown. **Assistant GM**: John Clark. **Director, Operations**: Brandon Marano. **Operations Manager**: Joe Scalise. **Director, Marketing**: Mike Ryan. **Director, Promotions**: Hal Hansen. **Manager, Media/Public Relations**: Ben Wagner. **Director, Community Relations**: Jim DeAngelis. **Special Events Manager**: Michelle Casserly. **Director, Ticket Sales**: Jeremy Fishman. **Ticket Sales Managers**: Jim Doughty, Dan Kurland. **Director, Group Sales**: Nelson Constantino. **Group Sales Managers**: Dan Higgins, Jim McNamara, Johanna Reilly. **Manager, Merchandise**: Alicia Pishnick. **Chief Financial Officer**: Steve Ripa. **Controller**: Denise Casazza. **Front Office Manager**: Robin Hill. **Head Groundskeeper**: Ryan Radcliffe. **Assistant Groundskeeper/Clubhouse Manager**: Russ Schaefer. **Director, Food/Beverage Service**: Steve Tracy. **Assistant Director, Food/Beverage Service**: Chris Tafrow. **Catering Manager**: Mike Donahue. **Office Manager, Food Service**: Joanna DiBella. **Assistants**: Nick Barrale, Kathleen Carosi, Erin Coyne,

Brett Handelman, Dan Kish, Matthew Pribbemow, Morgan Prosser, Andrew Smith, Michael Van Hise.

FIELD STAFF

Manager: P.J. Forbes. **Coach:** J.P. Roberge. **Pitching Coach:** Steve Schrenk. **Trainer:** Jason Kirkman.

GAME INFORMATION

Radio Announcers: Nick Barrale, Ben Wagner. **No. of Games Broadcast:** Home-70, Away-70. **Flagship Station:** WADR 1310-AM.

PA Announcer: Kevin Clark. **Official Scorer:** Lisa Clark.

Stadium Name: FirstEnergy Park. **Location:** Route 70 to New Hampshire Ave., north on New Hampshire for 2½ miles to ballpark. **Standard Game Times:** 7:05 p.m.; Mon.-Thur. (April-May) 6:35, Sat. (April) 1:05; Sun 1:05, (July-Aug.) 5:05. **Ticket Prices:** $9.

Visiting Team Hotel: Super 8, 2016 Hwy. 37 W., West Manchester, NJ. 08759. Telephone: (732) 657-7100.

LEXINGTON
LEGENDS

Office Address: 207 Legends Lane, Lexington, KY 40505.
Mailing Address: P.O. Box 11458, Lexington, KY 40575. **Telephone:** (859) 252-4487. **FAX:** (859) 252-0747.
E-Mail Address: webmaster@lexingtonlegends.com. **Website:** www.lexingtonlegends.com.
Affiliation (first year): Houston Astros (2001). **Years in League:** 2001-.

OWNERSHIP, MANAGEMENT

Operated by: Lexington Professional Baseball Company.
President/Chief Operating Officer: Alan Stein. **Chief Financial Officer:** Sandy Canon. **Executive Assistant:** Monica Johnson.
General Manager: Kevin Kulp. **VP, Operations:** Gary Durbin. **Director, Stadium Operations/Human Resources:** Shannon Kidd. **Director, Marketing:** Catherine Hayden. **Director, Broadcasting/ Media Relations:** Larry Glover. **Director, Community Relations:** Tiffany King. **Director, Special Events:** Rick Bryant. **Director, Field Maintenance:** Ben Heiple. **Assistant Groundskeeper:** Erin Sherrell. **Box Office Manager:** Missy Carl. **Group Sales Representatives:** Justin Ball, David Barry, Brad Link, Lenore Sparks. **Birthday Party Representative:** Monica Johnson. **Business Manager:** Jeff Black. **Senior Sales Executive:** Ron Borkowski. **Advertising Sales Executives:** Seth Poteat, Sarah Frazier. **Director, Ticket Operations:** Beth Goldenberg. **Receptionist:** Beverly Howard.

FIELD STAFF

Manager: Tim Bogar. **Coach:** Rodney Linares. **Pitching Coach:** Charley Taylor. **Trainer:** Unavailable.

GAME INFORMATION

Radio Announcer: Larry Glover. **No. of Games Broadcast:** Home-70, Away-70. **Flagship Station:** WLXG 1300-AM. **PA Announcer:** Brad Link. **Official Scorer:** Unavailable.

Stadium Name: Applebee's Park. **Location:** From I-64/75, take exit 113, right onto North Broadway toward downtown Lexington for 1.2 miles, past New Circle Road (Highway 4), right into stadium, located adjacent to Northland Shopping Center. **Standard Game Times:** 7:05 p.m.; Mon.-Thur. (April-May) 6:35; Sun. (April-May) 2:05, (June-Aug.) 6:05. **Ticket Price Range:** $4-7.

Visiting Club Hotel: Ramada Inn and Conference Center, 2143 N. Broadway, Lexington, KY 40505. Telephone: (859) 299-1261.

ROME
BRAVES

Office Address: State Mutual Stadium, 755 Braves Blvd, Rome, GA 30161.
Mailing Address: P.O. Box 5515, Rome, GA 30162.
Telephone: (706) 368-9388. **FAX:** (706) 368-6525.
E-Mail Address: rome.braves@turner.com. **Website:** www.romebraves.com.
Affiliation (first year): Atlanta Braves (2003). **Years in League:** 2003-.

OWNERSHIP, MANAGEMENT

Operated by: Time Warner/Atlanta National League Baseball Club, Inc.
General Manager: Michael Dunn. **Assistant GM:** Jim Jones. **Director, Stadium Operations:** Eric Allman. **Director, Ticket Sales:** Erin White. **Director, Food/Beverage:** Dave Atwood. **Manager, Community Relations:** Unavailable. **Administrative Manager:** Kristie Hancock. **Account Representatives:** Dave Butler, Jennifer Collins. **Head Groundskeeper:** Mike Hurd. **Receptionist:** Starla Roden. **Retail Manager:** Seline McCoy. **Warehouse Manager:** Terry Morgan.

FIELD STAFF

Manager: Rocket Wheeler. **Coach:** Bobby Moore. **Pitching Coach:** Jim Czajkowski. **Trainer:** Mike Dart.

SOUTH ATLANTIC LEAGUE

GAME INFORMATION

Radio Announcer: Randy Davis. **No. of Games Broadcast:** Home-70, Away-70. **Flagship Stations:** WLAQ 1410-AM, WATG 95.7-FM.

PA Announcer: Eddie Brock. **Official Scorer:** Ron Taylor.

Stadium Name: State Mutual Stadium. **Location:** I-75 North to exit 290 (Rome/Canton), left off exit and follow Highway 411/Highway 20 to Rome, right at intersection of Highway 411 and Highway 1 (Veterans Memorial Highway), stadium is at intersection of Veterans Memorial Highway and Riverside Parkway. **Standard Game Times:** 7 p.m.; Sun. 2. **Ticket Price Range:** $4-10.

Visiting Club Hotel: Days Inn, 840 Turner McCall Blvd., Rome, GA 30161. Telephone: (706) 295-0400.

SAVANNAH
SAND GNATS

Office Address: 1401 E. Victory Dr., Savannah, GA 31404.
Mailing Address: P.O. Box 3783, Savannah, GA 31414.
Telephone: (912) 351-9150. **Fax:** (912) 352-9722.
Website: www.sandgnats.com.
Affiliation (first year): Washington Nationals (2005). **Years in League:** 1962, 1984 -.

OWNERSHIP, MANAGEMENT

Operated by: Rickshew Baseball.

Co-General Managers: Bradley Dodson, Brian Sheaffer. **Director, Merchandise/Sales:** Matt Barry. **Director, Community Relations:** Chris Turner. **Director, Marketing/Public Relations:** Kevin Gray. **Public Relations/Marketing Manager:** Scott Gierman. **Director, Ticket Operations:** Greg Vojtanek. **Group Sales Manager:** Jonathan Kaplan. **Ticket Manager:** John Crimmins. **Director, Client Services:** Katie Stocz. **Ticket Assistant/Clubhouse Manager:** Joe Mann. **Groundskeeper:** Chuck Cannon.

FIELD STAFF

Manager: Randy Knorr. **Coach:** Joel Chimelis. **Pitching Coach:** Mark Grater. **Trainer:** Sean Wayne.

GAME INFORMATION

Radio: None.

PA Announcer: Jeffery McDermott. **Official Scorer:** Marcus Holland.

Stadium Name: Grayson Stadium. **Location:** I-16 to 37th Street exit, left on 37th, right on Abercorn Street, left on Victory Drive; From I-95 to exit 16 (Savannah/Pembroke), east on 204, right on Victory Drive, stadium is on right in Daffin Park. **Standard Game Times:** 7 p.m.; Mon.-Thurs. (April-May) 6:35; Sun. (April-May) 2. **Ticket Price Range:** $5-8.

Visiting Club Hotel: Days Inn–Oglethorpe Mall, 114 Mall Blvd., Savannah, GA 31406. Telephone: (912) 352-4455.

WEST VIRGINIA
POWER

Office Address: 601 Morris St., Charleston, WV 25301.
Telephone: (304) 344-2287. **FAX:** (304) 344-0083.
E-Mail Address: team@wvpower.com. **Website:** www.wvpower.com.
Affiliation (first year): Milwaukee Brewers (2005). **Years in League:** 1987-.

OWNERSHIP, MANAGEMENT

Operated by: Palisades Baseball.
Principal Owner: Alan Levin.

General Manager: Andy Milovich. **Director, Business Development:** Ryan Gates. **Director, Marketing:** Chad Hodson. **Accountant:** Jeremy Young. **Client Services:** Brian Harrigan. **Director, Concessions:** Ryan Montgomery. **Director, Broadcast/Media Relations:** Andy Barch. **Director, Stadium Operations:** John Phillips. **Senior Sales Executive:** Marty Nash. **Groundskeeper:** Eric Bailey. **Ticket Sales Executives:** Jeremy Taylor, Matt Thompson, Josh Brown.

FIELD STAFF

Manager: Ramon Aviles. **Coach:** Tony Diggs. **Pitching Coach:** Mark Littell. **Trainer:** Alan Diamond.

GAME INFORMATION

Radio Announcer: Andy Barch. **No. of Games Broadcast:** Unavailable. **Flagship Station:** WSWW 1490-AM.

PA Announcer: Donald Cook. **Official Scorer:** Lee France.

Stadium Name: Unavailable. **Location:** I-77 South to Capitol Street exit, left on Lee Street, left on Brooks Street. **Standard Game Times:** 7:05 p.m., Sun. 2:05. **Ticket Price Range:** $5-8.

Visiting Club Hotel: Ramada Plaza Hotel, 2nd Avenue and B Street, South Charleston, WV 25303. Telephone: (304) 744-4641.

NEW YORK-PENN
LEAGUE

Mailing Address: One Progress Plaza, 200 Central Ave., Suite 2300, St. Petersburg, FL 33701.
Telephone: (727) 576-6300. **FAX:** (727) 822-3768.
Website: www.nypennleague.com.

Years League Active: 1939-.
President: Ben Hayes.
Presidents Emeritus: Leo Pinckney, Bob Julian.
Vice President: Sam Nader (Oneonta). **Treasurer:** Jon Dandes (Jamestown). **Corporate Secretary:** Tony Torre (New Jersey).
Directors: Tim Bawmann (Lowell), David Burke (Hudson Valley), Steve Cohen (Brooklyn), Jon Dandes (Jamestown), Jeff Eiseman (Aberdeen), Josh Getzler (Staten Island), Bill Gladstone (Tri-City), Barry Gordon (New Jersey), Alan Levin (Mahoning Valley), Paul Marriott (Batavia), Sam Nader (Oneonta), Ray Pecor (Vermont), Leo Pinckney (Auburn), Paul Velte (Williamsport).
League Administrator: Debbie Carlisle. **League Historian:** Charles Wride.
Division Structure: McNamara—Aberdeen, Brooklyn, Hudson Valley, New Jersey, Staten Island, Williamsport. **Pinckney**—Auburn, Batavia, Jamestown, Mahoning Valley. **Stedler**—Lowell, Oneonta, Tri-City, Vermont.

Ben Hayes

Regular Season: 76 games. **2005 Opening Date:** June 21. **Closing Date:** Sept. 8.
All-Star Game: Aug. 23 at Brooklyn. **Hall of Fame Game:** Tri-City vs. Oneonta, July 24 at Cooperstown, NY.
Playoff Format: Division champions and wild-card team meet in best-of-3 semi-finals. Winners meet in best-of-3 series for league championship.
Roster Limit: 30 active, but only 25 may be in uniform and eligible to play in any given game. **Player Eligibility Rule:** No more than four players 23 or older; no more than three players on active list may have four or more years of prior service.
Brand of Baseball: Rawlings.
Statistician: Major League Baseball Advanced Media, 75 Ninth Ave., New York, NY 10011.
Umpires: Unavailable.

STADIUM INFORMATION

Club	Stadium	Opened	LF	CF	RF	Capacity	2004 Att.
Aberdeen	Ripken Stadium	2002	310	400	310	6,000	228,925
Auburn	Falcon Park	1995	330	400	330	2,800	63,679
Batavia	Dwyer Stadium	1996	325	400	325	2,600	37,086
Brooklyn	KeySpan Park	2001	315	412	325	7,500	294,261
Hudson Valley	Dutchess Stadium	1994	325	400	325	4,494	155,606
Jamestown	Russell E. Diethrick Jr. Park	1941	335	410	353	3,324	57,523
Lowell	Edward LeLacheur Park	1998	337	400	302	5,000	185,000
Mahoning Valley	Eastwood Field	1999	335	405	335	6,000	160,832
New Jersey	Skylands Park	1994	330	392	330	4,356	115,324
Oneonta	Damaschke Field	1906	350	406	350	4,200	42,100
Staten Island	Richmond County Bank Ballpark	2001	325	400	325	6,500	156,895
Tri-City	Joseph L. Bruno Stadium	2002	325	400	325	5,000	110,497
Vermont	Centennial Field	1922	330	405	323	4,400	93,796
Williamsport	Bowman Field	1923	345	405	350	4,200	75,785

Dimensions

ABERDEEN
IRONBIRDS

Office Address: 873 Long Dr., Aberdeen, MD 21001.
Telephone: (410) 297-9292. **FAX:** (410) 297-6653.
E-Mail Address: info@ironbirdsbaseball.com. **Website:** www.ironbirdsbaseball.com.
Affiliation (first year): Baltimore Orioles (2002). **Years in League:** 2002-.

OWNERSHIP, MANAGEMENT
Operated by: Ripken Professional Baseball, LLC.
Principal Owner: Cal Ripken Jr.
General Manager: Jeff Eiseman. **Assistant GM:** Aaron Moszer. **Director, Sales:** Amy Venuto. **Manager, Public Relations/Broadcasting:** Jay Moskowitz.

FIELD STAFF
Manager: Andy Etchebarren. **Coach:** Cesar Devarez. **Pitching Coach:** Dave Schmidt. **Trainer:** Spencer Elliott.

GAME INFORMATION
Radio Announcer: Steve Melewski. **No. of Games Broadcast:** Home-38, Away-38. **Flagship Station:** WAMD 970-AM.
PA Announcer: Andrew Holly. **Official Scorer:** Joe Stetka.
Stadium Name: Ripken Stadium. **Location:** I-95 to exit 85 (Route 22), west on 22 West, right onto Long Drive.
Standard Game Times: 7:05 p.m. **Ticket Price Range:** $5-14.
Visiting Club Hotel: Wingate Inn, Riverside Parkway, Aberdeen, MD 21001. Telephone: (410) 272-2929.

AUBURN
DOUBLEDAYS

Office Address: 130 N. Division St., Auburn, NY 13021.
Telephone: (315) 255-2489. **FAX:** (315) 255-2675.
E-Mail Address: ddays@auburndoubledays.com. **Website:** www.auburndouble-days.com.
Affiliation (first year): Toronto Blue Jays (2001). **Years in League:** 1958-80, 1982-.

OWNERSHIP, MANAGEMENT
Operated by: Auburn Community Non-Profit Baseball Association, Inc.
Chairman: Tom Ganey. **President:** Leo Pinckney.
General Manager: Carl Gutelius. **Assistant GM:** Kevin Breen. **Head Groundskeeper:** Rich Wild. **Director, Media/Public Relations:** Unavailable.

FIELD STAFF
Manager: Dennis Holmberg. **Coach:** Dave Pano. **Pitching Coach:** Tom Signore. **Trainer:** Chris Vernon.

GAME INFORMATION
Radio Announcer: Unavailable. **No of Games Broadcast:** Away-38. **Flagship Station:** WDWN 89.1-FM.
PA Announcer: Unavailable. **Official Scorer:** Unavailable.
Stadium Name: Falcon Park. **Location:** I-90 to exit 40, right on Route 34 for 8 miles to York Street, right on York, left on North Division Street. **Standard Game Times:** 7 p.m., Sun. 6. **Ticket Price Range:** $4-5.50.
Visiting Club Hotel: Microtel, 12 Seminary Ave., Auburn, NY 13021. Telephone: (315) 253-5000.

BATAVIA
MUCKDOGS

Office Address: Dwyer Stadium, 299 Bank St., Batavia, NY 14020.
Telephone: (585) 343-5454. **FAX:** (585) 343-5620.
E-Mail Address: info@muckdogs.com. **Website:** www.muckdogs.com.
Affiliation (first year): Philadelphia Phillies (1988). **Years in League:** 1939-53, 1957-59, 1961-.

OWNERSHIP, MANAGEMENT
Operated by: Genesee County Baseball Club.
President: Brian Paris.
General Manager: Paul Marriott. **Assistant GM:** Jennifer Pacino. **Director, Media/Public Relations:** Unavailable. **Director, Community Relations:** Linda Crook. **Clubhouse Operations:** Tony Pecora. **Director, Stadium Operations:** Don Rock.

FIELD STAFF

Manager: Manny Amador. **Coach:** Greg Gross. **Pitching Coach:** Ken Patterson. **Trainer:** Chris Mudd.

GAME INFORMATION

Radio Announcer: Unavailable. **No. of Games Broadcast:** Away-38. **Flagship Station:** WBSU 89.1-FM. **PA Announcer/Official Scorer:** Wayne Fuller.
Stadium Name: Dwyer Stadium. **Location:** I-90 to exit 48, left on Route 98 South, left on Richmond Avenue, left on Bank Street. **Standard Game Times:** 7:05 p.m. **Ticket Price Range:** $4-5.
Visiting Club Hotel: Days Inn of Batavia, 200 Oak St., Batavia, NY 14020. Telephone: (585) 343-1440.

BROOKLYN
CYCLONES

Office Address: 1904 Surf Ave., Brooklyn, NY 11224.
Telephone: (718) 449-8497. **FAX:** (718) 449-6368.
E-Mail Address: info@brooklyncyclones.com. **Website:** www.brooklyncyclones.com.
Affiliation (first year): New York Mets (2001). **Years in League:** 2001-.

OWNERSHIP, MANAGEMENT

Operated by: Brooklyn Baseball Co., LLC.
Managing Member: Fred Wilpon. **Senior Executive Vice President/Chief Operating Officer:** Jeff Wilpon.
General Manager: Steve Cohen. **Assistant GM:** Kevin Mahoney. **Manager, Media Relations:** Dave Campanaro.
Account Executive/Community Relations: Robert Field. **Account Executives:** Elizabeth Lombardi, Kimberly Patterson, Greg Radin, Ricky Viola. **Manager, Brooklyn Baseball Gallery/Community Relations:** Anna Isaacson. **Manager, Merchandise:** Kevin Jimenez. **Bookkeeper:** Tatiana Kanevsky. **Manager, Operations:** Vladimir Lipsman. **Receptionist/Community Relations:** Sharon Lundy-Ross. **Manager, Tickets:** Chris Parsons. **Head Groundskeeper:** Kevin Ponte. **Maintenance/Grounds Crew:** George Reeder. **Manager, Promotions/Entertainment:** Howie Wolpoff.

FIELD STAFF

Manager: Mookie Wilson. **Coach:** Donovan Mitchell. **Pitching Coach:** Steve Merriman. **Trainer:** Unavailable.

GAME INFORMATION

Radio Announcer: Warner Fusselle. **No. of Games Broadcast:** Home-38, Away-38. **Flagship Station:** Unavailable. **PA Announcer:** Dominick Alagia. **Official Scorer:** David Freeman.
Stadium Name: KeySpan Park. **Location:** Belt Parkway to Cropsey Avenue South, continue on Cropsey until it becomes West 17th Street, continue to Surf Avenue, stadium on south side of Surf Avenue. By subway, west to Stillwell Avenue/Coney Island Station. **Standard Game Times:** 7 p.m., Sat. 6, Sun. 5. **Ticket Price Range:** $7-12.
Visiting Club Hotel: Comfort Inn, 8315 Fourth Ave., Brooklyn, NY 11209. Telephone: (718) 238-3737.

HUDSON VALLEY
RENEGADES

Office Address: Dutchess Stadium, Route 9D, Wappingers Falls, NY 12590.
Mailing Address: P.O. Box 661, Fishkill, NY 12524.
Telephone: (845) 838-0094. **FAX:** (845) 838-0014.
E-Mail Address: info@hvrenegades.com. **Website:** www.hvrenegades.com.
Affiliation (first year): Tampa Bay Devil Rays (1996). **Years in League:** 1994-.

OWNERSHIP, MANAGEMENT

Operated by: Keystone Professional Baseball Club, Inc.
Principal Owner: Marv Goldklang. **President:** Mike Veeck.
General Manager: David Burke. **Vice President/Assistant GM:** Kathy Butsko. **Assistant GM:** Derek Sharp. **Director, Ticket Operations:** Bonnie Johnson. **Director, Food Services:** Joe Ausanio. **Director, Business Operations:** Jennifer Vitale. **Director, Entertainment:** Corey Whitted. **Director, Special Events/Renegades Charitable Foundation:** Rick Zolzer. **Director, Foundation Operations:** Rich McClane. **Director, Client Services/Foundation:** John Church. **Head Groundskeeper/Director, Stadium Maintenance:** Tom Hubmaster. **Director, Client Services/Media Relations:** Tyler Tumminia. **Director, Ticket Sales:** Michael Branda. **Director, Operations:** Jay Martyn.

FIELD STAFF

Manager: Dave Howard. **Coach:** Matt Quatraro. **Pitching Coach:** Dick Bosman. **Trainer:** Unavailable.

GAME INFORMATION

Radio Announcer: Sean Ford. **No. of Games Broadcast:** Home-38, Away-38. **Flagship Stations:** WBNR 1260-AM, WLNA 1420-AM.
PA Announcer: Rick Zolzer. **Official Scorer:** James Bouffard.
Stadium Name: Dutchess Stadium. **Location:** I-84 to exit 11 (Route 9D North), north one mile to stadium. **Standard Game Times:** 7:11 p.m., Sun. 5:11. **Ticket Price Range:** $4-9.

Visiting Club Hotel: The Wellesley Inn, Route 9, Fishkill, NY 12524. Telephone (845) 896-4995.

JAMESTOWN
JAMMERS

Office Address: 485 Falconer St., Jamestown, NY 14701.
Mailing Address: P.O. Box 638, Jamestown, NY 14702.
Telephone: (716) 664-0915. **FAX:** (716) 664-4175.
E-Mail Address: email@jamestownjammers.com. **Website:** www.jamestownjammers.com.
Affiliation (first year): Florida Marlins (2002). **Years in League:** 1939-57, 1961-73, 1977-.

OWNERSHIP, MANAGEMENT
Operated by: Rich Baseball Operations.
Principal Owner, President: Robert Rich Jr. **Chairman:** Robert Rich Sr. **President, Rich Baseball Operations:** Jonathon Dandes.
General Manager: Matthew Drayer. **Director, Sales/Marketing:** George Sisson. **Director, Baseball Operations:** Benjamin Burnett. **Head Groundskeeper:** Jamie Bloomquist. **Director, Food Services:** Unavailable.

FIELD STAFF
Manager: Mike Mordecai. **Coach:** Matt Raleigh. **Pitching Coach:** John Duffy. **Trainer:** Will Morin.

GAME INFORMATION
Radio Announcer: Unavailable. **No. of Games Broadcast:** Away-38. **Flagship Station:** Unavailable.
PA Announcer: Unavailable. **Official Scorer:** Jim Riggs.
Stadium Name: Russell E. Diethrick Jr. Park. **Location:** From I-90, south on Route 60, left on Buffalo Street, left on Falconer Street. **Standard Game Times:** 7:05 p.m., Sun. 4:05. **Ticket Price Range:** $4-6.
Visiting Club Hotel: Red Roof Inn, 1980 E. Main St., Falconer, NY 14733. Telephone: (716) 665-3670.

LOWELL
SPINNERS

Office Address: 450 Aiken St., Lowell, MA 01854.
Telephone: (978) 459-2255. **FAX:** (978) 459-1674.
E-Mail Address: generalinfo@lowellspinners.com. **Website:** www.lowellspinners.com.
Affiliation (first year): Boston Red Sox (1996). **Years in League:** 1996-.

OWNERSHIP, MANAGEMENT
Operated by: Diamond Action, Inc.
Owners: Drew Weber, Joann Weber. **Chief Executive Officer:** Drew Weber. **President:** Shawn Smith.
General Manager: Tim Bawmann. **Vice President, Business Operations:** Brian Lindsay. **Controller:** Priscilla Harbour. **Director, Stadium Operations:** Dan Beaulieu. **Assistant Director, Stadium Operations:** Gareth Markey. **Director, Corporate Communications:** Jon Goode. **Director, Merchandising:** Joann Weber. **Merchandising Manager:** Justin Panarese. **Director, Ticket Sales:** Shannon Feehan. **Director, Ticket Group Sales:** Jon Healy. **Head Groundskeeper:** Rick Walker. **Clubhouse Manager:** Del Christman.

FIELD STAFF
Manager: Luis Alicea. **Coach:** Alan Mauthe. **Pitching Coach:** Walter Miranda. **Trainer:** Jon Jochim.

GAME INFORMATION
Radio: Unavailable.
PA Announcers: John Rafferty, Peter Mundy. **Official Scorers:** Dave Rourke, Rusty Eggen, Bob Ellis.
Stadium Name: Edward LeLacheur Park. **Location:** From Routes 495 and 3, take exit 35C (Lowell Connector), follow connector to exit 5B (Thorndike Street) onto Dutton Street, past city hall, left onto Father Morrissette Boulevard, right on Aiken Street. **Standard Game Times:** 7:05 p.m.; Sat.-Sun. 5:05. **Ticket Price Range:** $3.50-7.50.
Visiting Club Hotel: Doubletree Inn, 50 Warren St., Lowell, MA 01852. Telephone: (978) 452-1200.

MAHONING VALLEY
SCRAPPERS

Office Address: 111 Eastwood Mall Blvd., Niles, OH 44446.
Mailing Address: P.O. Box 1357, Niles, OH 44446.
Telephone: (330) 505-0000. **FAX:** (330) 505-9696.
E-Mail Address: mvscrappers@onecom.com. **Website:** www.mvscrappers.com.

Affiliation (first year): Cleveland Indians (1999). **Years in League:** 1999-.

OWNERSHIP, MANAGEMENT
Operated by: Palisades Baseball, Ltd.
Managing General Partner: Alan Levin. **Executive Vice President:** Erik Haag. **Director, Finance:** Cheryl Carlson. **General Manager:** Dave Smith. **Director, Business Development:** Joe Gregory. **Director, Stadium Operations:** Chris Walsh. **Director, Ticket Operations:** Jordan Taylor. **Director, Box Office:** Heather Safarek. **Accountant:** Debbie Primmer. **Director, Client Services:** Mike Brent. **Director, Promotions/Marketing:** Jim Riley. **Senior Account Representative:** Scott MacDonald. **Ticket Sales Representatives:** Mike Link, Brad Hooser. **Director, Concessions:** Unavailable. **Administrative Assistant:** Andrea Zagger.

FIELD STAFF
Manager: Rouglas Odor. **Coach:** Jack Mulli. **Pitching Coach:** Tony Arnold. **Trainer:** Chad Wolfe.

GAME INFORMATION
Radio Announcer: Greg Gania. **No. of Games Broadcasts:** Home-38, Away-38. **Flagship Station:** WNIO 1390-AM. **PA Announcer:** Ryan Pritt. **Official Scorer:** Al Thorne.
Stadium Name: Eastwood Field. **Location:** I-80 to 11 North to 82 West to 46 South, stadium located behind Eastwood Mall. **Standard Game Times:** 7 p.m.; Sun. 2. **Ticket Price Range:** $6-8.
Visiting Club Hotel: Unavailable.

NEW JERSEY
CARDINALS

Office Address: 94 Championship Place, Suite 2, Augusta, NJ 07822.
Telephone: (973) 579-7500. **FAX:** (973) 579-7502.
E-Mail Address: office@njcards.com. **Website:** www.njcards.com.
Affiliation (first year): St. Louis Cardinals (1994). **Years in League:** 1994-.

OWNERSHIP, MANAGEMENT
Operated by: Minor League Heroes, LP.
Chairman: Barry Gordon. **President:** Marc Klee.
Vice President, General Manager: Tony Torre. **Assistant GM:** Herm Sorcher. **Head Groundskeeper:** Ralph Naifeh. **Director, Marketing/Merchandising:** Bob Commentucci. **Director, Ticket Operations/Corporate, Group Sales:** Matt Millet. **Director, Sponsorships/Group Sales:** Gregg Kubala. **Director, Community Relations/Group Sales:** Lisa Howell. **Director, Finance:** Tullia Mowery.

FIELD STAFF
Manager: Mark DeJohn. **Coach:** Unavailable. **Pitching Coach:** Sid Monge. **Trainer:** Manabu Kawazuru.

GAME INFORMATION
Radio Announcers: Phil Pepe, Joel Konya. **No. of Games Broadcast:** Home-38. **Flagship Station:** SportsNetAmerica.com.
PA Announcer: Mike Griffone. **Official Scorer:** Ken Hand.
Stadium Name: Skylands Park. **Location:** In New Jersey, I-80 to exit 34B (Route 15 North) to Route 565 East; From Pennsylvania, I-84 to Route 6 (Matamoras) to Route 206 North to Route 565 East. **Standard Game Times:** 7:15 p.m., Sat.-Sun. 5. **Ticket Price Range:** $7-12.
Visiting Club Hotel: Wellesley Inn, 1255 Route 10, Whippany, NJ 07981. Telephone: (973) 539-8350.

ONEONTA
TIGERS

Office Address: 95 River St., Oneonta, NY 13820.
Telephone: (607) 432-6326. **FAX:** (607) 432-1965.
E-Mail Address: naderas@telenet.net. **Website:** www.oneontatigers.com.
Affiliation (first year): Detroit Tigers (1999). **Years in League:** 1966-.

OWNERSHIP, MANAGEMENT
Operated by: Oneonta Athletic Corp.
President, General Manager: Sam Nader. **Director, Business/Stadium Operations:** John Nader. **Controller:** Sidney Levine. **Head Groundskeeper:** Mike Dunn. **Director, Media/Public Relations:** Alice O'Conner. **Director, Marketing/Merchandising:** Suzanne Longo. **Director, Special Projects:** Mark Nader. **Director, Operations/Ticket Sales:** Bob Zeh. **Director, Food Services:** Brad Zeh.

FIELD STAFF
Manager: Tom Brookens. **Coach:** Basilio Cabrera. **Pitching Coach:** Bill Monbouquette. **Trainer:** Unavailable.

GAME INFORMATION

Radio: None.
PA Announcer: John Horne. **Official Scorer:** Tom Heitz.
Stadium Name: Damaschke Field. **Location:** Exit 15 off I-88. **Standard Game Times:** 7 p.m., Sun. 6. **Ticket Price Range:** $4-6.
Visiting Club Hotel: Oasis Motor Inn, 366 Chestnut St., Oneonta, NY 13820. Telephone: (607) 432-6041.

STATEN ISLAND
YANKEES

Stadium Address: 75 Richmond Terrace, Staten Island, NY 10301.
Telephone: (718) 720-9265. **FAX:** (718) 273-5763.
E-Mail Address: siyanks@siyanks.com. **Website:** www.siyanks.com.
Affiliation (first year): New York Yankees (1999). **Years in League:** 1999-.

OWNERSHIP, MANAGEMENT

Operated by: Staten Island Minor League Holdings, LLC.
Principal Owners: Josh Getzler, Phyllis Getzler, Stan Getzler.
Chairman: Stan Getzler. **President:** Henry Steinbrenner. **Chief Operating Officer:** Josh Getzler. **Vice President, Operations:** Jeff Dumas.
General Manager: Jane Rogers. **Assistant GMs:** John Davison, Gary Perone. **Director, Media Relations:** Jim Mauceri. **Director, Community Relations:** Polo Burgos. **Director, Ticket Operations/Group Sales:** Dominic Costantino. **Technical Director:** Mike D'Amboise. **Director, Stadium Operations:** Ryan Bellmier. **Bookkeeper:** Ruth Rizzo. **Head Groundskeeper:** Unavailable.

FIELD STAFF

Manager: Andy Stankiewicz. **Coach:** Rob Ducey. **Pitching Coach:** Mike Thurman. **Trainer:** Jeff Zabba.

GAME INFORMATION

Radio Announcer: Unavailable. **No. of Games Broadcast:** Home-38, Away-38. **Flagship Station:** Unavailable.
PA Announcer: Unavailable. **Official Scorer:** Unavailable.
Stadium Name: Richmond County Bank Ballpark at St. George. **Location:** St. George located in Staten Island, next to Staten Island Ferry Terminal. **Standard Game Times:** 7:05 p.m., Sun 5:05. **Ticket Price Range:** $9-11.
Visiting Club Hotel: The Navy Lodge, 408 North Path Rd., Staten Island, NY 10305. Telephone: (718) 442-0413.

TRI-CITY
VALLEYCATS

Stadium Address: 80 Vandenburgh Ave., Troy, NY 12180.
Mailing Address: P.O. Box 694, Troy, NY 12181.
Telephone: (518) 629-2287. **FAX:** (518) 629-2299.
E-Mail Address: info@tcvalleycats.com. **Website:** www.tcvalleycats.com.
Affiliation: Houston Astros (2002). **Years in League:** 2002-.

OWNERSHIP, MANAGEMENT

Operated by: National Pastime Corporation.
Principal Owners: Martin Barr, John Burton, William Gladstone, Richard Murphy, Alfred Roberts, Stephen Siegel.
President: William Gladstone.
Vice President, General Manager: R.C. Reuteman. **Assistant GM:** Vic Christopher. **Director, Sales:** Peter Rosenberg. **Account Executives:** Brett Gilmore, Scott Obergefell, Kristan Pelletier. **Director, Corporate Communications:** Eileen McCarthy. **Administrative Assistant:** Liz Litsch.

FIELD STAFF

Manager: Gregg Langbehn. **Coach:** Jorge Orta. **Pitching Coach:** Donny Alexander. **Trainer:** John Patton.

GAME INFORMATION

Radio Announcer: Unavailable. **No. of Games Broadcast:** Home-38, Away-38. **Flagship Station:** WABY 1160 AM.
PA Announcer: Tony Pettograsso. **Official Scorer:** Unavailable.
Stadium Name: Joseph L. Bruno Stadium. **Location:** From north, I-87 to exit 7 (Route 7), go east approximately 1 ½ miles to I-787 South, to Route 378 East, go over bridge to Route 4, right to Route 4 South, one mile to Hudson Valley Community College campus on left. From south, I-87 to exit 23 (I-787), I-787 north six miles to exit for Route 378 east, Route 378 over bridge to Route 4, go right to Route 4 South, one mile to Hudson Valley Community College campus on left. From east, Massachusetts Turnpike to exit B-1 (I-90), go nine miles to Exit 8 (Defreestville), left off ramp to Route 4 North, Route 4 North for five miles, Hudson Valley Community College on right. From West, I-90 to exit 24 (I-90 East), I-90 east for six miles to I-787 North (Troy), take I-787 North for 2.2 miles to exit for Route 378 East, take Route 378 over bridge to Route 4,, right to Route 4 south for one mile to Hudson Valley Community College campus on left. **Standard Game Times:** 7 p.m.; Sun. 6. **Ticket Price Range:** $4.50-7.50.

Visiting Club Hotel: Days Inn, 14 Wolf Rd., Albany, NY 12205. Telephone: (518) 459-3600.

VERMONT
EXPOS

Office Address: 1 Main St., Suite 4, Winooski, VT 05404.
Telephone: (802) 655-4200. FAX: (802) 655-5660.
E-Mail Address: mail@vermontexpos.com. Website: www.vermontexpos.com.
Affiliation (first year): Washington Nationals (2005). Years in League: 1994-.

OWNERSHIP, MANAGEMENT
Operated by: Vermont Expos, Inc.
Principal Owner, President: Ray Pecor. Vice President: Kyle Bostwick.
General Manager: C.J. Knudsen. Director, Stadium Operations: Jim O'Brien. Head Groundskeeper: Unavailable. Executive Operations Manager/Director, Promotions: Adrienne Wilson. Director, Media/Stadium Administration: Paul Stanfield. Director, Sales: Shawn Quinn. Director, Marketing/Ticket Operations: Nate Cloutier. Director, Food Services: Steve Bernard. Director, Special Projects: Onnie Matthews. Clubhouse Operations: Phil Schelzo.

FIELD STAFF
Manager: Bobby Williams. Coach: Rick Eckstein. Pitching Coach: Craig Bjornson. Trainer: Unavailable.

GAME INFORMATION
Radio Announcer: George Commo. No. of Games Broadcast: Home-25, Away-25. Flagship Station: Unavailable.
PA Announcer: Rich Haskell. Official Scorer: Ev Smith.
Stadium Name: Centennial Field. Location: I-89 to exit 14W, right on East Avenue for one mile, right at Colchester Avenue. Standard Game Times: 7:05 p.m., Sun. 5:05. Ticket Price Range: $3-7.
Visiting Club Hotel: University Inn & Suites, 5 Dorset St., South Burlington, VT 05403. Telephone: (802) 863-5541.

WILLIAMSPORT
CROSSCUTTERS

Office Address: Bowman Field, 1700 W. Fourth St., Williamsport, PA 17701.
Mailing Address: P.O. Box 3173, Williamsport, PA 17701.
Telephone: (570) 326-3389. FAX: (570) 326-3494.
E-Mail Address: mail@crosscutters.com. Website: www.crosscutters.com.
Affiliation (first year): Pittsburgh Pirates (1999). Years in League: 1968-72, 1994-.

OWNERSHIP, MANAGEMENT
Operated by: Geneva Cubs Baseball, Inc.
Principal Owners: Paul Velte, John Schreyer. President: Paul Velte. Vice President: John Schreyer.
General Manager: Doug Estes. Director, Marketing/Public Relations: Gabe Sinicropi. Director, Food/Beverage: Bill Gehron. Director, Ticket Operations/Community Relations: Kelle Renninger. Assistant, Ticket Operations: Pete Frikker. Head Groundskeeper: Unavailable. Clubhouse Manager: Unavailable.

FIELD STAFF
Manager: Tom Prince. Coaches: Brandon Moore, Ramon Sambo. Pitching Coach: Dave Lundquist. Trainer: Bob Westwood.

GAME INFORMATION
Radio: Unavailable.
PA Announcer: Rob Thomas. Official Scorer: John Green.
Stadium Name: Bowman Field. Location: From south, Route 15 to Maynard Street, right on Maynard, left on Fourth Street for one mile; From north, Route 15 to Fourth Street, left on Fourth. Standard Game Time: 7:05 p.m. Ticket Price Range: $3.75-6.
Visiting Club Hotel: Holiday Inn, 1840 E. Third St., Williamsport, PA 17701. Telephone: (570) 326-1981.

NORTHWEST
LEAGUE

SHORT-SEASON CLASS A

Office Address: 910 Main St., Suite 351, Boise, ID 83702.
Mailing Address: P.O. Box 1645, Boise, ID 83701.
Telephone: (208) 429-1511. **FAX:** (208) 429-1525.
E-Mail Address: bobrichmond@worldnet.att.net.
Years League Active: 1954-.

President, Treasurer: Bob Richmond.
Vice President: Mike McMurray (Yakima). **Corporate Secretary:** Jerry Walker (Salem-Keizer).
Directors: Bob Beban (Eugene), Bobby Brett (Spokane), Peter Carfagna (Everett), Fred Herrmann (Vancouver), Mike McMurray (Yakima), Brent Miles (Tri-City), Jerry Walker (Salem-Keizer), Thomas Wick (Boise).
Administrative Assistant: Rob Richmond.
Division Structure: East—Boise, Spokane, Tri-City, Yakima. **West**—Eugene, Everett, Salem-Keizer, Vancouver.
Regular Season: 76 games. **2005 Opening Date:** June 21. **Closing Date:** Sept. 7.
Playoff Format: Division winners meet in best-of-5 series for league championship.
All-Star Game: None.
Roster Limit: 30 active, 35 under control. **Player Eligibility Rule:** No more than four players 23 or older. No more than three players on active list may have four or more years of prior service.

Bob Richmond

Brand of Baseball: Rawlings.
Statistician: Major League Baseball Advanced Media, 75 Ninth Ave., New York, NY 10011.
Umpires: Unavailable.

STADIUM INFORMATION

Club	Stadium	Opened	Dimensions LF	CF	RF	Capacity	2004 Att.
Boise	Memorial Stadium	1989	335	405	335	4,500	107,936
Eugene	Civic Stadium	1938	335	400	328	6,800	117,547
Everett	Everett Memorial Stadium	1984	330	395	330	3,682	104,010
Salem-Keizer	Volcanoes Stadium	1997	325	400	325	4,100	118,929
Spokane	Avista Stadium	1958	335	398	335	7,162	169,075
Tri-City	Dust Devils Stadium	1995	335	400	335	3,730	54,087
Vancouver	Nat Bailey Stadium	1951	335	395	335	6,500	140,037
Yakima	Yakima County Stadium	1993	295	406	295	3,000	51,544

BOISE HAWKS

Office Address: 5600 N. Glenwood St., Boise, ID 83714.
Telephone: (208) 322-5000. **FAX:** (208) 322-6846.
Website: www.boisehawks.com.
Affiliation (first year): Chicago Cubs (2001). **Years in League:** 1975-76, 1978, 1987-.

OWNERSHIP, MANAGEMENT
Operated by: Boise Hawks Baseball Club LCC.
President/General Manager: Todd Rahr. **Assistant GM:** Dina Duncan. **Controller:** Pam Linebarger. **Stadium Operations/Head Groundskeeper:** Boyd Mauer. **Marketing Manager:** Ken Hyde. **Director, Ticket Sales:** Nat Reynolds. **Group Sales Manager:** Dorothy Gutierrez. **Ticket Operations Manager:** Amanda Compson. **Sales Representatives:** Andrew Logsdon, Andy Simon.

FIELD STAFF
Manager: Trey Forkerway. **Coach:** Tom Beyers. **Pitching Coach:** David Rosario. **Trainer:** Nick Frangella.

GAME INFORMATION
Radio Announcer: Mike Safford. **No. of Games Broadcast:** Home-38, Away-38. **Flagship Station:** KTIK 1350-AM. **PA Announcer:** Chris Walton. **Official Scorer:** Unavailable.
Stadium Name: Memorial Stadium. **Location:** I-84 to Cole Road, north to Western Idaho Fairgrounds at 5600 North Glenwood Street. **Standard Game Times:** 7:15 p.m., Sun. 6:15. **Ticket Price Range:** $2-8.
Visiting Club Hotel: Holiday Inn Airport, 3300 Vista Ave., Boise, ID 83705. Telephone: (208) 344-8365.

EUGENE EMERALDS

Office Address: 2077 Willamette St., Eugene, OR 97405.
Mailing Address: P.O. Box 5566, Eugene, OR 97405.
Telephone: (541) 342-5367. **FAX:** (541) 342-6089.
E-Mail Address: ems@go-ems.com. **Website:** www.go-ems.com.
Affiliation (first year): San Diego Padres (2001). **Years in League:** 1955-68, 1974-.

OWNERSHIP, MANAGEMENT
Operated by: Elmore Sports Group, Ltd.
Principal Owner: David Elmore.
President, General Manager: Bob Beban. **Assistant GMs:** Sergio Apodaca, Bryan Beban. **Director, Business Operations:** Eileen Beban. **Director, Food Services/Stadium Operations:** Jim Brelsford. **Director, Tickets/Special Events:** Brandy Evenson. **Grounds Superintendent:** Peter Lockwood.

FIELD STAFF
Manager: Roy Howell. **Coach:** Ben Oglivie. **Pitching Coach:** Wally Whitehurst. **Trainer:** Jo Jo Tarantino.

GAME INFORMATION
Radio Announcer: Ben Ingram. **No. of Games Broadcast:** Home-38, Away-38. **Flagship Station:** KPNW 1120-AM. **PA Announcer:** Unavailable. **Official Scorer:** George McPherson.
Stadium Name: Civic Stadium. **Location:** From I-5, take I-105 to Exit 2, stay left and follow to downtown, cross over Ferry Street Bridge to Eighth Avenue, left on Pearl Street, south to 20th Avenue. **Standard Game Times:** 7:05 p.m., Sun. 5:05. **Ticket Price Range:** $5.50-9.
Visiting Club Hotel: Valley River Inn, 1000 Valley River Way, Eugene, OR 97401. Telephone: (541) 687-0123.

EVERETT AQUASOX

Mailing Address: 3802 Broadway, Everett, WA 98201.
Telephone: (425) 258-3673. **FAX:** (425) 258-3675.
E-Mail Address: aquasox@aquasox.com. **Website:** www.aquasox.com.
Affiliation (first year): Seattle Mariners (1995). **Years in League:** 1984-.

OWNERSHIP, MANAGEMENT
Operated by: Famiglia II.
President: Peter Carfagna. **Vice President, Baseball Operations:** Pete Carfagna.
General Manager: Dan Lewis. **Director, Corporate Sales:** Brian Sloan. **Director, Broadcasting/Corporate Sales:**

Pat Dillon. **Director, Ballpark Operations:** Jason Jarett. **Director, Ticket Services:** Dave Roberts. **Director, Food/Beverage:** Cathy Bierman. **Director, Merchandising:** Victoria Dearborn. **Director, Special Projects:** Todd Holterhoff. **Director, Media Relations:** Erin Johns.

FIELD STAFF
Manager: Pedro Grifol. **Coach:** James Horner. **Pitching Coach:** Marcos Garcia. **Trainer:** Spyder Webb.

GAME INFORMATION
Radio Announcer: Pat Dillon. **No. of Games Broadcast:** Home-38, Away-38. **Flagship Station:** KRKO 1380-AM. **PA Announcer:** Tom Lafferty. **Official Scorer:** Pat Castro.
Stadium Name: Everett Memorial Stadium. **Location:** I-5, exit 192. **Standard Game Times:** 7:05 p.m., Sun. 4:05. **Ticket Price Range:** $8-13.
Visiting Club Hotel: Best Western Cascadia Inn, 2800 Pacific Ave., Everett, WA 98201. Telephone: (425) 258-4141.

SALEM-KEIZER
VOLCANOES

Street Address: 6700 Field of Dreams Way NE, Keizer, OR 97307.
Mailing Address: P.O. Box 20936, Keizer, OR 97307.
Telephone: (503) 390-2225. **FAX:** (503) 390-2227.
E-Mail Address: probasebal@aol.com. **Website:** www.volcanoesbaseball.com.
Affiliation (first year): San Francisco Giants (1997). **Years in League:** 1997-.

OWNERSHIP, MANAGEMENT
Operated By: Sports Enterprises, Inc.
Principal Owners: Jerry Walker, Bill Tucker.
President, General Manager: Jerry Walker. **Vice President, Operations:** Rick Nelson. **Manager, Corporate Sales/Director, Promotions:** Lisa Walker. **Corporate Sponsorships:** Steve Wertz, Sheryl Kelsh. **Director, Sales/Media Relations:** Pat Lafferty. **Director, Community Relations:** Unavailable. **Corporate Ticket Sales:** John Banks, Christine Campbell, Matt Palumbo. **Director, Merchandising/Ticket Office Operations:** Kate Hamm.

FIELD STAFF
Manager: Steve Decker. **Coach:** Ricky Ward. **Pitching Coach:** Jerry Cram. **Trainer:** Larry Duensing.

GAME INFORMATION
Radio Announcer: Pat Lafferty. **No. of Games Broadcast:** Home-38, Away-38. **Flagship Station:** KYKN 1430-AM. **PA Announcer:** Unavailable. **Official Scorer:** Dawn Hills.
Stadium Name: Volcanoes Stadium. **Location:** I-5 to exit 260 (Chemawa Road), west one block to Radiant Drive, north six blocks to stadium. **Standard Game Times:** 6:35 p.m.; Fri-Sat. 7:05, Sun. 5:05. **Ticket Price Range:** $6-10.
Visiting Club Hotel: Comfort Suites, 630 Hawthorne Ave. SE, Salem, OR 97301. Telephone: (503) 585-9705.

SPOKANE
INDIANS

Office Address: 602 N. Havana, Spokane, WA 99202.
Mailing Address: P.O. Box 4758, Spokane, WA 99220.
Telephone: (509) 535-2922. **FAX:** (509) 534-5368.
E-Mail Address: mail@spokaneindiansbaseball.com. **Website:** www.spokaneindiansbaseball.com.
Affiliation (first year): Texas Rangers (2003). **Years in League:** 1972, 1983-.

OWNERSHIP, MANAGEMENT
Operated by: Longball, Inc.
Principal Owners: Bobby Brett, George Brett, J.B. Brett.
President: Andrew Billig.
Vice President, General Manager: Paul Barbeau. **VP, Sponsorships:** Otto Klein. **Assistant GM, Ticket Sales:** Paul Zilm. **Assistant GM, Operations:** Chris Duff. **Assistant GM, Concessions:** Lesley DeHart. **Director, Sponsorships/Public Relations:** Jared Rose. **Director, Ticket Sales:** Brian Burton. **Director, Promotions:** Brad Poe. **Director, Accounting:** Greg Sloan. **Account Executives:** Sarah Travis, Evan Wagner. **Coordinator, Group Sales:** Randi Aud. **Head Groundskeeper:** Bret Whiteman. **Assistant Director, Stadium Operations:** Larry Blumer.

FIELD STAFF
Manager: Greg Riddoch. **Coach:** Mark Whiten. **Pitching Coach:** Glenn Abbott. **Trainer:** Cesar Roman.

GAME INFORMATION
Radio Announcer: Bob Robertson. **No. of Games Broadcast:** Home-38, Away-38. **Flagship Station:** KFAN 790-AM. **PA Announcer:** Brad Moon. **Official Scorer:** Unavailable.
Stadium Name: Avista Stadium at Spokane County Fair and Expo Center. **Location:** From west, I-90 to exit 283B (Thor/Freya), east on 3rd Avenue, left onto Havana; from east, I-90 to Broadway exit, right onto Broadway, left onto

Havana. **Standard Game Time:** 6:30 p.m. **Ticket Price Range:** $4-8.
Visiting Club Hotel: Mirabeau Park Hotel & Convention Center, N. 1100 Sullivan Road, Spokane, WA 99037. Telephone: (509) 924-9000.

TRI-CITY
DUST DEVILS

Office Address: 6200 Burden Rd., Pasco, WA 99301.
Telephone: (509) 544-8789. **FAX:** (509) 547-9570.
E-Mail Address: info@dustdevilsbaseball.com. **Website:** www.dustdevilsbaseball.com.
Affiliation (first year): Colorado Rockies (2001). **Years in League:** 1955-1974, 1983-1986, 2001-.

OWNERSHIP, MANAGEMENT

Operated by: Northwest Baseball Ventures.
Principal Owner: George Brett. **President:** Brent Miles.
General Manager: Derrel Ebert. **Assistant GM:** Scott Litle. **Group Sales Coordinator:** C.J. Loper. **Account Executive:** Matt Nash. **Promotions Coordinator:** Ashley Lee. **Director, Accounting:** Tim Gittel. **Head Groundskeeper:** Michael Angel.

FIELD STAFF

Manager: Ron Gideon. **Coach:** Freddie Ocasio. **Pitching Coach:** Russ Swan. **Trainer:** Chris Dovey.

GAME INFORMATION

Radio Announcer: Tom Barket. **No. of Games Broadcast:** Home-38, Away-38. **Flagship Station:** KJOX 970-AM.
PA Announcer: Shane Edinger. **Official Scorer:** Tony Wise.
Stadium Name: Dust Devils Stadium. **Location:** I-182 to exit 9 (Road 68), north to Burden Road, right to stadium.
Standard Game Times: 7:15 p.m. **Ticket Price Range:** $4-7.
Visiting Club Hotel: Red Lion Hotel-Columbia Center, 1101 N. Columbia Center Blvd., Kennewick, WA 99336. Telephone: (509) 783-0611.

VANCOUVER
CANADIANS

Office Address: 4601 Ontario St., Vancouver, British Columbia V5V 3H4.
Telephone: (604) 872-5232. **FAX:** (604) 872-1714.
E-Mail Address: staff@canadiansbaseball.com. **Website:** www.canadiansbaseball.com.
Affiliation (first year): Oakland Athletics (2000). **Years in League:** 2000-.

OWNERSHIP, MANAGEMENT

Operated by: National Sports Organization, Inc.
Principal Owners: Dwain Cross, Fred Herrmann, Bud Kaufman. **President:** Dan Kilgras.
General Manager: Delany Dunn. **Assistant GM:** Ben Ekren. **Special Assistant to Owner:** Bill Posthumus. **Assistant Marketing Manager:** Jeff Dye. **Ticket Manager:** Lori Bonang. **Director, Finance:** Carol Miner. **Director, Media Relations:** Leanne Cass. **Clubhouse Manager:** Jordan Wilson.

FIELD STAFF

Manager: Webster Garrison. **Coach:** Jeremy Schied. **Pitching Coach:** Craig Lefferts. **Trainer:** Chris Lessner.

GAME INFORMATION

Radio: The Team 1040-AM.
PA Announcer: Delany Dunn. **Official Scorer:** Pat Karl.
Stadium Name: Nat Bailey Stadium. **Location:** From downtown, take Cambie Street Bridge, left on East 29th Avenue, left on Clancy Loringer Way, right to stadium; from south, take Highway 99 to Oak Street, right on 41st Avenue, left on Ontario to 30th Avenue. **Standard Game Times:** 7:05 p.m., Sun. 1:05. **Ticket Price Range:** $8-20.
Visiting Club Hotel: Accent Inns, 10551 Edwards Dr., Richmond, B.C. V6X 3L8. Telephone: (604) 273-3311.

YAKIMA
BEARS

Office Address: 8 N. 2nd St., Yakima, WA 98901.
Mailing Address: P.O. Box 483, Yakima, WA 98907.
Telephone: (509) 457-5151. **FAX:** (509) 457-9909.
E-Mail Address: info@yakimabears.com. **Website:** www.yakimabears.com.

Affiliation (first year): Arizona Diamondbacks (2001). **Years in League:** 1955-66, 1990-.

OWNERSHIP, MANAGEMENT
Operated by: Short Season, LLC.
Managing Partners: Mike McMurray, Mike Ellis, Josh Weinman, Myron Levin. **President:** Mike McMurray.
General Manager: K.L. Wombacher. **Director, Sales/Promotions:** Teddi Fowler. **Account Executives:** Amanda Baker, Nathan Wagner. **Head Groundskeeper:** Unavailable. **Clubhouse Operations:** Aaron Arndt. **Director, Concessions:** Broc Arndt. **Administrative Assistants:** Tyler Edison, Justin Glaser.

FIELD STAFF
Manager: Jay Gainer. **Coach:** Luis De los Santos. **Pitching Coach:** Erik Sabel. **Trainer:** Jason Lieuw.

GAME INFORMATION
Radio Announcer: Unavailable. **No. of Games Broadcast:** Home-38, Away-38. **Flagship Station:** KUTI 1460-AM.
PA Announcer: Todd Lyons. **Official Scorer:** Mike McMurray.
Stadium Name: Yakima County Stadium. **Location:** I-82 to exit 34 (Nob Hill Boulevard), west to Fair Avenue, right on Fair, right on Pacific Avenue. **Standard Game Times:** 7:05 p.m., Sun. 6:05. **Ticket Price Range:** $3.50-7.50.
Visiting Club Hotel: Best Western Ahtanum Inn, 2408 Rudkin Rd., Union Gap, WA 98903. Telephone: (509) 248-9700.

APPALACHIAN
LEAGUE

ROOKIE ADVANCED

Mailing Address: 283 Deerchase Circle, Statesville, NC 28625.
Telephone: (704) 873-5300. **FAX:** (704) 873-4333.
E-Mail Address: appylg@direcway.com.
Years League Active: 1921-25, 1937-55, 1957-.

President, Treasurer: Lee Landers. **Corporate Secretary:** Jim Holland (Princeton).

Directors: Ricky Bennett (Greeneville), Cam Bonifay (Princeton), John Farrell (Burlington), Dave Wilder (Bristol), Len Johnston (Bluefield), Bruce Manno (Johnson City), Dayton Moore (Danville), Kevin Morgan (Kingsport), Jim Rantz (Elizabethton), Dick Scott (Pulaski).

League Administrator: Bobbi Landers.

Division Structure: East—Bluefield, Burlington, Danville, Princeton, Pulaski. **West**—Bristol, Elizabethton, Greeneville, Johnson City, Kingsport.

Regular Season: 68 games. **2005 Opening Date:** June 21. **Closing Date:** Aug. 30.

All-Star Game: None.

Playoff Format: Division winners meet in best-of-3 series for league championship.

Roster Limit: 35 active. **Player Eligibility Rule:** No more than two years of prior minor league service. No more than 15 players 21 years of age or older, provided no more than two of the 15 are 23 years of age or older. No more than 12 of the 21-year-olds may be listed on line-up card for any game.

Lee Landers

Brand of Baseball: Rawlings.
Statistician: Major League Baseball Advanced Media, 75 Ninth Ave., New York, NY 10011.
Umpires: Unavailable.

STADIUM INFORMATION

Club	Stadium	Opened	Dimensions LF	CF	RF	Capacity	2004 Att.
Bluefield	Bowen Field	1939	335	365	335	2,250	24,910
Bristol	DeVault Memorial Stadium	1969	325	400	310	2,000	21,120
Burlington	Burlington Athletic Stadium	1960	335	410	335	3,000	34,219
Danville	Dan Daniel Memorial Park	1993	330	400	330	2,588	32,194
Elizabethton	Joe O'Brien Field	1974	335	414	326	1,500	27,017
Greeneville	Pioneer Park	2004	331	400	331	2,400	51,183
Johnson City	Howard Johnson Field	1956	320	410	320	2,500	19,940
Kingsport	Hunter Wright Stadium	1995	330	410	330	2,500	30,765
Princeton	Hunnicutt Field	1988	330	396	330	1,950	25,374
Pulaski	Calfee Park	1935	335	405	310	2,500	25,659

BLUEFIELD
ORIOLES

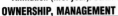

Office Address: 2003 Stadium Dr., Bluefield, WV 24701.
Mailing Address: P.O. Box 356, Bluefield, WV 24701.
Telephone: (276) 326-1326. **FAX:** (276) 326-1318.
Affiliation (first year): Baltimore Orioles (1958). **Years in League:** 1946-55, 1957-.

OWNERSHIP, MANAGEMENT
Operated by: Bluefield Baseball Club, Inc.
Director: Len Johnston (Baltimore Orioles).
Vice President: Cecil Smith. **Secretary:** M.K. Burton. **Counsel:** David Kersey.
President, General Manager: George McGonagle. **Controller:** Charles Peters. **Director, Special Projects:** Tuillio Ramella.

FIELD STAFF
Manager: Jesus Alfaro. **Coach:** Cedric Landrum. **Pitching Coach:** Larry Jaster. **Trainer:** Patrick Wesley.

GAME INFORMATION
Radio Announcer: Buford Early. **No. of Games Broadcast:** Unavailable. **Flagship Station:** Unavailable.
PA Announcer: Buford Early. **Official Scorers:** Will Prewitt, Tim Richardson.
Stadium Name: Bowen Field. **Location:** I-77 to Bluefield exit, Route 290 to Route 460 West, right onto Leatherwood Lane, left at first light, past Chevron station and turn right, stadium 1/4 mile on left. **Standard Game Times:** 7 p.m., DH 6; Sun. 6, DH 5. **Ticket Prices:** $3.50.
Visiting Club Hotel: Unavailable.

BRISTOL
WHITE SOX

Office Address: 1501 Euclid Ave., Bristol, VA 24201.
Mailing Address: P.O. Box 1434, Bristol, VA 24203.
Telephone: (540) 645-7275. **FAX:** (540) 669-7686.
E-Mail Address: bwsox@3wave.com. **Website:** www.bristolsox.com.
Affiliation (first year): Chicago White Sox (1995). **Years in League:** 1921-25, 1940-55, 1969-.

OWNERSHIP, MANAGEMENT
Operated by: Chicago White Sox.
Director: Dave Wilder (Chicago White Sox).
President: Boyce Cox. **General Manager:** Robert Childress.

FIELD STAFF
Manager: Jerry Hairston. **Coach:** Bobby Tolan. **Pitching Coach:** Roberto Espinoza. **Trainer:** Unavailable.

GAME INFORMATION
Radio: None.
PA Announcer: Boyce Cox. **Official Scorer:** Allen Shepherd.
Stadium Name: DeVault Memorial Stadium. **Location:** I-81 to exit 3 onto Commonwealth Ave., right on Euclid Ave. for 1/2 mile. **Standard Game Time:** 7 p.m. **Ticket Price Range:** $3-5.
Visiting Club Hotel: Ramada Inn, 2122 Euclid Ave., Bristol, VA 24201. Telephone: (540) 669-7171.

BURLINGTON
INDIANS

Office Address: 1450 Graham St., Burlington, NC 27217.
Mailing Address: P.O. Box 1143, Burlington, NC 27217.
Telephone: (336) 222-0223. **FAX:** (336) 226-2498.
E-Mail Address: info@burlingtonindians.net. **Website:** www.burlingtonindians.net.
Affiliation (first year): Cleveland Indians (1986). **Years in League:** 1986-.

OWNERSHIP, MANAGEMENT
Operated by: Burlington Baseball Club, Inc.
Director: John Farrell (Cleveland Indians).
President: Miles Wolff. **Vice President:** Dan Moushon.
General Manager: Mark Cryan. **Assistant GM:** Jeremy Auker. **Director, Media Relations:** Adam Pohl. **Director,**

Stadium Operations: Josh Hall.

FIELD STAFF

Manager: Sean McNally. **Coach:** Unavailable. **Pitching Coach:** Ruben Niebla. **Trainer:** Teddy Blackwell.

GAME INFORMATION

Radio Announcer: Adam Pohl. **No. of Games Broadcast:** Home-34, Away-34. **Flagship Station:** WBAG 1150-AM. **PA Announcer:** Brad Hines. **Official Scorer:** Unavailable.

Stadium Name: Burlington Athletic Stadium. **Location:** I-40/85 to exit 145, north on Route 100 (Maple Avenue) for 1½ miles, right on Mebane Street for 1½ miles, right on Beaumont, left on Graham. **Standard Game Time:** 7 p.m. **Ticket Price Range:** $4-6.

Visiting Club Hotel: Holiday Inn-Outlet Center, 2444 Maple Ave., Burlington, NC 27215. Telephone: (336) 229-5203.

DANVILLE
BRAVES

Office Address: Dan Daniel Memorial Park, 302 River Park Dr., Danville, VA 24540. **Mailing Address:** P.O. Box 378, Danville, VA 24543.
Telephone: (434) 797-3792. **FAX:** (434) 797-3799.
E-Mail Address: info@dbraves.com. **Website:** www.dbraves.com.
Affiliation (first year): Atlanta Braves (1993). **Years in League:** 1993-.

OWNERSHIP, MANAGEMENT

Operated by: Atlanta National League Baseball Club, Inc.
Director: Dayton Moore (Atlanta Braves).
General Manager: David Cross. **Assistant GM:** Bob Kitzmiller. **Sales/Marketing Manager:** Unavailable. **Office Manager:** Shelby Tate. **Head Groundskeeper:** Richard Gieselman.

FIELD STAFF

Manager: Paul Runge. **Coach:** Mel Roberts. **Pitching Coach:** Derek Botelho. **Trainer:** Tyson Burton.

GAME INFORMATION

Radio: None.
PA Announcer: Nick Pierce. **Official Scorer:** Sam Ferguson.
Stadium Name: American Legion Post 325 Field at Dan Daniel Memorial Park. **Location:** U.S. 29 Bypass to River Park Drive/Dan Daniel Memorial Park exit; follow signs to park. **Standard Game Times:** 7 p.m.; Sun. 4. **Ticket Price Range:** $3.50-6.50.
Visiting Club Hotel: Innkeeper-West, 3020 Riverside Dr., Danville, VA 24541. Telephone: (434) 799-1202.

ELIZABETHTON
TWINS

Office Address: 208 N. Holly Lane, Elizabethton, TN 37643. **Mailing Address:** 136 S. Sycamore St., Elizabethton, TN 37643.
Telephone: (423) 547-6441. **FAX:** (423) 547-6442.
E-Mail Address: etwins@preferred.com. **Website:** www.elizabethtontwins.com.
Affiliation (first year): Minnesota Twins (1974). **Years in League:** 1937-42, 1945-51, 1974-.

OWNERSHIP, MANAGEMENT

Operated by: City of Elizabethton.
Director: Jim Rantz (Minnesota Twins).
President: Harold Mains.
General Manager: Mike Mains. **Clubhouse Operations:** David McQueen. **Head Groundskeeper:** David Nanney. **Director, Ticket/Group Sales:** Kim Hodge. **Director, Merchandising:** Linda Church. **Director, Food Services:** Cindy Walker.

FIELD STAFF

Manager: Ray Smith. **Coach:** Jeff Reed. **Pitching Coach:** Jim Shellenback. **Trainer:** Masauki Nakatsukasa.

GAME INFORMATION

Radio Announcer: Frank Santore. **No. of Games Broadcast:** Home-34, Away-6. **Flagship Station:** WBEJ 1240-AM. **PA Announcer:** Tom Banks. **Official Scorer:** Bill Crow.
Stadium Name: Joe O'Brien Field. **Location:** I-81 to Highway I-26, exit at Highway 321/67, left on Holly Lane. **Standard Game Times:** 7 p.m., DH 6. **Ticket Price Range:** $3-5.
Visiting Club Hotel: Holiday Inn, 101 W. Springbrook Dr., Johnson City, TN 37601. Telephone: (423) 282-4611.

GREENEVILLE
ASTROS

Office Address: 135 Shiloh Rd., Greeneville, TN 37743.
Mailing Address: P.O. Box 5192, Greeneville, TN 37743.
Telephone: (423) 638-0411. **FAX:** (423) 638-9450.
E-Mail Address: info@greenevilleastros.com. **Website:** www.greenevilleastros.com.
Affiliation (first year): Houston Astros (2004). **Years in League:** 2004-.

OWNERSHIP, MANAGEMENT
Operated by: Houston Astros Baseball Club.
Director: Ricky Bennett (Houston Astros).
General Manager: Lynsi House. **Assistant GM:** Omar Roque. **Director, Group Sales/Media Relations:** John Doyle.
Head Groundskeeper: Blair Waller **Clubhouse Operations:** Unavailable.

FIELD STAFF
Manager: Russ Nixon. **Coach:** Pete Rancont. **Pitching Coach:** Bill Ballou. **Trainer:** J.D. Shields.

GAME INFORMATION
Radio Announcers: Bobby Rader, Brian Stayton. **No. of Games Broadcast:** Home-34. **Flagship Station:** WSMG 1450-AM.
PA Announcer: Unavailable. **Official Scorer:** Johnny Painter.
Stadium Name: Pioneer Park. **Location:** From the north, take South US 11E, turn left at red light at Hardee's onto Erwin Highway (TN 107). From the south, take North US 11E, turn right at red light at Hardee's onto Erwin Highway. Once on Erwin Highway, Stadium is one mile on the right on the Tusculum College Campus. **Standard Game Times:** 7 p.m., Sun. 6. **Ticket Price Range:** $4-6.
Visiting Club Hotel: The Jameson Inn, 3160 E. Andrew Johnson Hwy., Greeneville, TN 37743. Telephone: (423) 638-7511.

JOHNSON CITY
CARDINALS

Office Address: 111 Legion St., Johnson City, TN 37601.
Mailing Address: P.O. Box 179, Johnson City, TN 37605.
Telephone: (423) 461-4866. **FAX:** (423) 461-4864.
E-Mail Address: info@jccardinals.com. **Website:** www.jccardinals.com.
Affiliation (first year): St. Louis Cardinals (1975). **Years in League:** 1911-13, 1921-24, 1937-55, 1957-61, 1964-.

OWNERSHIP, MANAGEMENT
Operated by: Johnson City Sports Foundation, Inc.
President: Dr. Jeff Banyas.
Director: Bruce Manno (St. Louis Cardinals).
General Manager: Brandon Cross. **Clubhouse Operations:** Pat Kramer. **Groundskeeper:** Mike Whitson.

FIELD STAFF
Manager: Tommy Kidwell. **Coach:** Joe Almaraz. **Pitching Coach:** Al Holland. **Trainer:** Eric Bauer.

GAME INFORMATION
Radio: Unavailable. **No. of Games Broadcast:** Home-34. **Flagship Station:** WKPT 1590-AM.
PA Announcer: Unavailable. **Official Scorer:** Unavailable.
Stadium Name: Howard Johnson Field. **Location:** I-181 to exit 32, left on East Main, through light onto Legion Street. **Standard Game Times:** 7 p.m. **Ticket Price Range:** $3-5.
Visiting Club Hotel: Holiday Inn, 101 W. Springbrook Dr., Johnson City, TN 37601. Telephone: (423) 282-4611.

KINGSPORT
METS

Office Address: 800 Granby Rd., Kingsport, TN 37660.
Mailing Address: P.O. Box 1128, Kingsport, TN 37662.
Telephone: (423) 378-3744. **FAX:** (423) 392-8538.
E-Mail Address: info@kmets.com. **Website:** www.kmets.com.
Affiliation (first year): New York Mets (1980). **Years in League:** 1921-25, 1938-52, 1957, 1960-63, 1969-82, 1984-.

OWNERSHIP, MANAGEMENT
Operated by: S&H Baseball, LLC.
Director: Kevin Morgan (New York Mets).
President: Rick Spivey. **Vice President:** Steve Harville.
General Manager: Roman Stout. **Director, Housing:** Peggy Lozier. **Head Groundskeeper:** Josh Warner.

FIELD STAFF
Manager: Jesse Levis. **Coach:** Juan Lopez. **Pitching Coach:** Dan Murray. **Trainer:** Unavailable.

GAME INFORMATION
Radio: None.
PA Announcer: Don Spivey. **Official Scorer:** Eddie Durham.
Stadium Name: Hunter Wright Stadium. **Location:** I-81 to I-181 North, exit 11E (Stone Drive), left on West Stone Drive (U.S. 11W), right on Granby Road. **Standard Game Times:** 7 p.m., DH 6. **Ticket Price Range:** $3-5.
Visiting Club Hotel: Jameson Inn, 304 Bays Mountain Plaza, Kingsport, TN 37660. Telephone: (423) 230-0534.

PRINCETON
DEVIL RAYS

Office Address: Hunnicutt Field, Old Bluefield Road, Princeton, WV 24740.
Mailing Address: P.O. Box 5646, Princeton, WV 24740.
Telephone: (304) 487-2000. **FAX:** (304) 487-8762.
E-Mail Address: raysball@sunlitsurf.com. **Website:** www.princetondevilrays.com.
Affiliation (first year): Tampa Bay Devil Rays (1997). **Years in League:** 1988-.

OWNERSHIP, MANAGEMENT
Operated by: Princeton Baseball Association, Inc.
Director: Cam Bonifay (Tampa Bay Devil Rays).
President: Dewey Russell.
General Manager: Jim Holland. **Director, Stadium Operations:** Mick Bayle. **Head Groundskeeper:** Frankie Bailey.
Account Representative: Paul Lambert. **Clubhouse Manager:** Shane Rossetti.

FIELD STAFF
Manager: Jamie Nelson. **Coach:** Manny Castillo. **Pitching Coach:** Rafael Montalvo. **Trainer:** Kris Russell.

GAME INFORMATION
Radio Announcer: Jarrod Talbott. **No. of Games Broadcast:** Away-34. **Flagship Station:** WAEY 1490-AM.
PA Announcer: Unavailable. **Official Scorer:** Dick Daisey.
Stadium Name: Hunnicutt Field. **Location:** Exit 9 off I-77, U.S. 460 West to downtown exit, left on Stafford Drive, stadium located behind Mercer County Technical Education Center. **Standard Game Times:** 7 p.m., DH 5:30; Sun. 4. **Ticket Price Range:** $3-5.
Visiting Club Hotel: Days Inn, I-77 and Ambrose Lane, Princeton, WV 24740. Telephone: (304) 425-8100.

PULASKI
BLUE JAYS

Mailing Address: P.O. Box 676, Pulaski, VA 24301.
Telephone: (540) 980-1070. **FAX:** (540) 980-1850.
E-Mail Address: mail@pulaskibluejays.com. **Website:** www.pulaskibluejays.com.
Affiliation (first year): Toronto Blue Jays (2003). **Years in League:** 1946-50, 1952-55, 1957-58, 1969-77, 1982-92, 1997-.

OWNERSHIP, MANAGEMENT
Operated by: Pulaski Baseball, Inc.
General Manager: Shawn Hite.

FIELD STAFF
Manager: Gary Cathcart. **Coach:** Justin Mashore. **Pitching Coach:** Antonio Caceres. **Trainer:** Unavailable.

GAME INFORMATION
Radio: None.
PA Announcer: Andy French. **Official Scorer:** Edgar Williams.
Stadium Name: Calfee Park. **Location:** I-81 to exit 89B (Route 11), north to Pulaski, right on Pierce Avenue.
Standard Game Time: 7 p.m. **Ticket Price Range:** $4-6.
Visiting Club Hotel: Comfort Inn, 4424 Cleburne Blvd., Dublin, VA 24084. Telephone: (540) 674-1100.

PIONEER
LEAGUE

Office Address: 157 S. Lincoln Ave., Spokane, WA 99201.
Mailing Address: P.O. Box 2564, Spokane, WA 99220.
Telephone: (509) 456-7615. **FAX:** (509) 456-0136.
E-Mail Address: fanmail@pioneerleague.com. **Website:** www.pioneerleague.com.
Years League Active: 1939-42, 1946-.

President/Secretary-Treasurer: Jim McCurdy.
Vice President: Mike Ellis (Missoula).
Directors: Dave Baggott (Ogden), Mike Ellis (Missoula), D.G. Elmore (Helena), Kevin Greene (Idaho Falls), Kevin Haughian (Casper), Jeff Katofsky (Orem), Vinny Purpura (Great Falls), Bob Wilson (Billings).
Administrative Assistant: Teryl MacDonald.
Division Structure: North—Billings, Great Falls, Helena, Missoula. **South**—Casper, Idaho Falls, Ogden, Orem.
Regular Season: 76 games (split schedule). **2005 Opening Date:** June 21. **Closing Date:** Sept. 8.
Playoff Format: First-half division winners meet second-half division winners in best-of-3 series. Winners meet in best-of-3 series for league championship.
All-Star Game: None.

Jim McCurdy

Roster Limit: 35 active, 30 dressed for each game. **Player Eligibility Rule:** No more than 17 players 21 and older, provided that no more than two are 23 or older. No player on active list may have three or more years of prior minor league service.
Brand of Baseball: Rawlings.
Statistician: Major League Baseball Advanced Media, 75 Ninth Ave., New York, NY 10011.
Umpires: Unavailable.

STADIUM INFORMATION

Club	Stadium	Opened	Dimensions LF	CF	RF	Capacity	2004 Att.
Billings	Cobb Field	1948	335	405	325	4,200	106,837
Casper	Mike Lansing Field	2002	355	400	345	2,500	42,938
Great Falls	Legion Park	1956	335	414	335	3,800	109,779
Helena	Kindrick Field	1939	335	400	325	1,700	37,568
Idaho Falls	McDermott Field	1976	340	400	350	2,928	61,237
Missoula	Missoula Civic Stadium	2004	309	398	287	2,600	64,942
Ogden	Lindquist Field	1997	335	396	334	5,000	133,886
*Orem	Parkway Crossing Stadium	2005	305	408	312	4,000	43,920

*Franchise operated in Provo in 2004.

BILLINGS
MUSTANGS

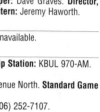

Office Address: Cobb Field, 901 N. 27th St., Billings, MT 59101.
Mailing Address: P.O. Box 1553, Billings, MT 59103.
Telephone: (406) 252-1241. **FAX:** (406) 252-2968.
E-Mail Address: mustangs@billingsmustangs.com. **Website:** www.billingsmustangs.com.
Affiliation (first year): Cincinnati Reds (1974). **Years in League:** 1948-63, 1969-.

OWNERSHIP, MANAGEMENT
Operated by: Billings Pioneer Baseball Club, Inc.
President: Bob Wilson.
General Manager: Gary Roller. **Director, Sales:** Allen Reynolds. **Head Groundskeeper:** Dave Graves. **Director, Broadcasting:** Unavailable. **Director, Clubhouse Operations:** Alex Kimmet. **Operations Intern:** Jeremy Haworth.

FIELD STAFF
Manager: Rick Burleson. **Coach:** Jeff Young. **Pitching Coach:** Butch Henry. **Trainer:** Unavailable.

GAME INFORMATION
Radio Announcer: Unavailable. **No. of Games Broadcast:** Home-38, Away-38. **Flagship Station:** KBUL 970-AM.
PA Announcer: Kyle Riley. **Official Scorer:** Matt Bender.
Stadium Name: Cobb Field. **Location:** I-90 to 27th Street North exit, north to Ninth Avenue North. **Standard Game Times:** 7:05 p.m., Sun. 4:05. **Ticket Price Range:** $4-6.50.
Visiting Club Hotel: Rimrock Inn, 1203 N. 27th St., Billings, MT 59101. Telephone: (406) 252-7107.

CASPER
ROCKIES

Office Address: 330 Kati Lane, Casper, WY 82602.
Mailing Address: P.O. Box 1293, Casper, WY 82602.
Telephone: (307) 232-1111. **FAX:** (307) 265-7867.
E-Mail Address: homerun@casperrockies.com. **Website:** www.casperrockies.com.
Affiliation (first year): Colorado Rockies (2001). **Years in League:** 2001-.

OWNERSHIP, MANAGEMENT
Operated by: Casper Professional Baseball Club, LLC.
Principal Owner, Chief Executive Officer: Kevin Haughian.
President, General Manager: Danny Tetzlaff. **Assistant GM:** Aaron McCrieght.

FIELD STAFF
Manager: P.J. Carey. **Coach:** Tony Diaz. **Pitching Coach:** Richard Palacios. **Trainer:** Austin O'Shea.

GAME INFORMATION
Radio Announcer: Unavailable. **No. of Games Broadcast:** Unavailable. **Flagship Station:** KVOC 1230-AM.
PA Announcer: Unavailable. **Official Scorer:** Unavailable.
Stadium Name: Mike Lansing Field. **Location:** I-25 to Poplar Street exit, north on Poplar Street, right into Crossroads Park. **Standard Game Times:** 7:05 p.m., Sun. 5:05. **Ticket Price Range:** $7.50-9.
Visiting Club Hotel: Parkway Plaza, 123 W. "E" St., Casper, WY 82601. Telephone (307) 235-1777.

GREAT FALLS
WHITE SOX

Office/Stadium Address: 1015 25th St. N., Great Falls, MT 59401.
Mailing Address: P.O. Box 1621, Great Falls, MT 59403.
Telephone: (406) 452-5311. **FAX:** (406) 454-0811.
E-Mail Address: whitesox@greatfallswhitesox.com. **Website:** www.greatfallswhitesox.com.
Affiliation: Chicago White Sox (2003). **Years in League:** 1948-1963, 1969-.

OWNERSHIP, MANAGEMENT
Operated by: Great Falls Baseball Club, Inc.
President: Vinny Purpura.
General Manager: Jim Keough. **Assistant GM:** Ginger Burcham. **Head Groundskeeper:** Carl Christofferson.

FIELD STAFF
Manager: John Orton. **Coach:** Joe Hall. **Pitching Coach:** Curt Hasler. **Trainer:** Kevin Pillifant.

GAME INFORMATION

Radio Announcer: Ray Alexander. **No. of Games Broadcast:** Home-38, Away-38. **Flagship Station:** KMON 560-AM. **PA Announcer:** Tim Paul. **Official Scorer:** Mike Lewis.

Stadium Name: Legion Park. **Location:** From I-15, take 10th Ave. South (exit 281) for four miles to 26th Street, left to 8th Ave. North, left to 25th Street North, right to ballpark. **Standard Game Times:** 7 p.m., Sun. 4. **Ticket Price Range:** $5-8.

Visiting Club Hotel: Midtown Hotel, 526 Second Ave. N., Great Falls, MT 59401. Telephone: (406) 453-2411.

HELENA
BREWERS

Office Address: 1300 N. Ewing, Helena, MT 59601.
Mailing Address: P.O. Box 6756, Helena, MT 59604.
Telephone: (406) 495-0500. **FAX:** (406) 495-0900.
E-Mail Address: info@helenabrewers.net. **Website:** www.helenabrewers.net.
Affiliation (first year): Milwaukee Brewers (2003). **Years in League:** 1978-2000, 2003-.

OWNERSHIP, MANAGEMENT

Operated by: Helena Baseball Club LLC.
Principal Owner: D.G. Elmore.
General Manager: Paul Fetz. **Assistant GM:** Travis Brower. **Director, Tickets:** Chad Moore. **Director, Broadcasting/Media Relations:** Steve Wendt.

FIELD STAFF

Manager: Eddie Sedar. **Coach:** Bobby Randall. **Pitching Coach:** John Curtis. **Trainer:** Tim Steinhaus.

GAME INFORMATION

Radio Announcer: Steve Wendt. **No. of Games Broadcast:** Home-38, Away-38. **Flagship Station:** KCAP 1340-AM. **PA Announcer:** Unavailable. **Official Scorer:** Unavailable.

Stadium Name: Kindrick Field. **Location:** Cedar Street exit off I-15, west to Main Street, left at Memorial Park. **Standard Game Time:** 7:05 p.m. **Ticket Price Range:** $5-7.

Visiting Club Hotel: Red Lion Colonial Hotel, 2301 Colonial Dr., Helena, MT 59601. Telephone: (406) 443-2100.

IDAHO FALLS
CHUKARS

Office Address: 568 W. Elva, Idaho Falls, ID 83402.
Mailing Address: P.O. Box 2183, Idaho Falls, ID 83403.
Telephone: (208) 522-8363. **FAX:** (208) 522-9858.
E-Mail Address: chukars@ifchukars.com. **Website:** www.ifchukars.com.
Affiliation (first year): Kansas City Royals (2004). **Years in League:** 1940-42, 1946-.

OWNERSHIP, MANAGEMENT

Operated by: The Elmore Group.
Principal Owner: David Elmore.
President, General Manager: Kevin Greene. **Assistant GM, Merchandise:** Marcus Loyola. **Director, Public Relations/Concessions:** Nathan Peck. **Director, Corporate Sales:** Andrea Villalpando. **Head Groundskeeper:** Christopher Michaels.

FIELD STAFF

Manager: Brian Rupp. **Coach:** Pookie Wilson. **Pitching Coach:** Jose Bautista. **Trainer:** Yoshi Kitaura.

GAME INFORMATION

Radio Announcers: John Balginy, Jim Garshow. **No. of Games Broadcast:** Home-38, Away-38. **Flagship Station:** KUPI 980-AM.

PA Announcer: Steve Davis. **Official Scorer:** John Balginy.

Stadium Name: McDermott Field. **Location:** I-15 to West Broadway exit, left onto Memorial Drive, right on Mound Avenue, ¼ mile to stadium. **Standard Game Times:** 7:15 p.m., Sun. 5. **Ticket Price Range:** $5-8.

Visiting Club Hotel: Guesthouse Inn & Suites, 850 Lindsay Blvd., Idaho Falls, ID 83402. Telephone: (208) 522-6260.

MISSOULA
OSPREY

Office Address: 137 E. Main St., Missoula, MT 59802.
Telephone: (406) 543-3300. **FAX:** (406) 543-9463.
E-Mail Address: generalmgr@missoulaosprey.com. **Website:** www.missoula
osprey.com.
Affiliation (first year): Arizona Diamondbacks (1999). **Years in League:** 1956-60, 1999-.

OWNERSHIP, MANAGEMENT
Operated by: Mountain Baseball, LLC.
President: Mike Ellis. **Executive Vice President:** Judy Ellis.
Vice President/General Manager: Matt Ellis. **Assistant GMs:** Chris Hale, Jared Amoss. **Director, Finance/Human Resources:** Shelly Ellis. **Manager, Group Sales:** Mark Cline. **Director, Merchandise:** Lori Hale. **Office Administrator:** Barb Holmes-Smith. **Clubhouse Manager:** Unavailable.

FIELD STAFF
Manager: Hector De la Cruz. **Coach:** Jerry Stitt. **Pitching Coach:** Mel Stottlemyre Jr. **Trainer:** Tim Higgins.

GAME INFORMATION
Radio Announcer: Tim Boulware. **No. of Games Broadcast:** Home-38, Away-38. **Flagship Station:** 1340-AM.
PA Announcer: Patrick Nikolay. **Official Scorer:** Unavailable.
Stadium Name: Missoula Civic Stadium. **Location:** Orange Street to Cregg Lane, west on Cregg Lane, stadium west of McCormick Park. **Standard Game Times:** 7:05 p.m., Sun. 5:05. **Ticket Price Range:** $4-10.
Visiting Club Hotel: Campus Inn, 744 E. Broadway, Missoula, MT 59802. Telephone: (406) 549-5134.

OGDEN
RAPTORS

Office Address: 2330 Lincoln Ave., Ogden, UT 84401.
Telephone: (801) 393-2400. **FAX:** (801) 393-2473.
E-Mail Address: homerun@ogden-raptors.com. **Website:** www.ogden-
raptors.com.
Affiliation (first year): Los Angeles Dodgers (2003). **Years in League:** 1939-42, 1946-55, 1966-74, 1994-.

OWNERSHIP, MANAGEMENT
Operated by: Ogden Professional Baseball, Inc.
Principal Owners: Dave Baggott, John Lindquist. **Chairman, President:** Dave Baggott.
General Manager: Joe Stein. **Director, Marketing:** John Stein. **Controller:** Carol Spickler. **Head Groundskeeper:** Ken Kopinski. **Director, Merchandising:** Geri Kopinski.

FIELD STAFF
Manager: Juan Bustabad. **Coach:** Unavailable. **Pitching Coach:** Bob Welch. **Trainer:** Unavailable.

GAME INFORMATION
Radio Announcer: Unavailable. **No. of Games Broadcast:** Home-38, Away-38. **Flagship Station:** KXOL 1660-AM.
PA Announcer: Pete Diamond. **Official Scorer:** Dennis Kunimura.
Stadium Name: Lindquist Field. **Location:** I-15 North to 21st Street exit, east to Lincoln Avenue, south three blocks to park. **Standard Game Times:** 7 p.m., Sun. 1. **Ticket Price Range:** $6-8.
Visiting Club Hotel: Marriott, 247 24th St., Odgen, UT 84401. Telephone: (801) 627-1190.

OREM
OWLZ

(Franchise operated in Provo in 2004)
Office Address: Parkway Crossing Stadium, 970 West University Pkwy., Orem, UT 84058.
Telephone: (801) 377-2255. **FAX:** (801) 377-2345.
E-Mail Address: fan@oremowlz.com. **Website:** www.oremowlz.com.
Affiliation: Anaheim Angels (2001). **Years in League:** 2001-.

OWNERSHIP, MANAGEMENT
Operated by: Bery Bery Gud To Me, LLC.
Principal Owners: Jeff Katofsky, Harvey Katofsky.

General Manager: Dave Jacobsen. **Assistant GM:** Ryan Pace. **Director, Communications/Marketing:** Zachary Fraser. **Director, Public Relations:** Karrie Broderick. **Senior Sales Manager:** Jim Daniels.

FIELD STAFF

Manager: Tom Kotchman. **Coach:** Kevin Johnson. **Pitching Coach:** Zeke Zimmerman. **Trainer:** Aaron Wells.

GAME INFORMATION

Radio Announcers: Trevor Kelly, Joey Hurley. **No. of Games Broadcast:** Home-38, Away-38. **Flagship Station:** KSRR 1400-AM.

PA Announcer: Lincoln Fillmore. **Official Scorer:** Sara Harris.

Stadium Name: Parkway Crossing Stadium. **Location:** Exit 272 (University Parkway) off 1-15 at Utah Valley State College campus. **Standard Game Times:** 7:05 p.m., Sun. 4:05. **Ticket Price Range:** $3-8.

Visiting Club Hotel: Provo Days Inn, 1675 N. 200 West, Provo, UT 84604. Telephone: (801) 375-8600.

ARIZONA LEAGUE

Office Address: 910 Main St., Suite 351, Boise, ID 83702.
Mailing Address: P.O. Box 1645, Boise, ID 83701.
Telephone: (208) 429-1511. **FAX:** (208) 429-1525. **E-Mail Address:** bobrichmond@worldnet.att.net.
Years League Active: 1988-.
President/Treasurer: Bob Richmond.
Vice President: Bobby Evans (Giants). **Corporate Secretary:** Ted Polakowski (Athletics).
Administrative Assistant: Rob Richmond.
Division Structure: None.
Regular Season: 56 games (split schedule). **2005 Opening Date:** June 22. **Closing Date:** Aug. 30. **Standard Game Times:** 10:30 a.m.; night games—7 p.m.
Playoff Format: First-half winner meets second-half winner in one-game championship.
All-Star Game: None.
Roster Limit: 35 active. **Player Eligibility Rule:** No more than 12 players 20 or older, no more than eight players 21 or older, and no more than four players of any age not selected in 2005 first-year draft. A maximum of four foreign players not subject to the draft playing in the United States for the first time are exempt from the age limits.
Brand of Baseball: Rawlings.
Statistician: Major League Baseball Advanced Media, 75 Ninth Ave., New York, NY 10011.

Clubs	Playing Site	Manager	Coach	Pitching Coach
Angels	Gene Autry Park, Mesa	Brian Harper	Unavailable	Felipe Suarez
Athletics	Papago Park Sports Complex, Phoenix	Ruben Escalera	Juan Dilone	Mike Holmes
Brewers	Maryvale Baseball Complex, Phoenix	Mike Guerrero	Joel Youngblood	Steve Cline
Cubs	Fitch Park, Mesa	Steve McFarland	C.Martinez/A. Grissom	Rick Tronerud
Giants	Giants minor league complex, Scottsdale	Bert Hunter	Leo Garcia	Will Malerich
Mariners	Peoria Sports Complex, Peoria	Dana Williams	Andy Bottin	Gary Wheelock
Padres	Peoria Sports Complex, Peoria	Carlos Lezcano	Luis Quinones	Jim Bennett
Rangers	Surprise Recreation Campus	Pedro Lopez		Aris Tirado
Royals	Surprise Recreation Campus	Lloyd Simmons	Tom Poquette	Royal Clayton

GULF COAST LEAGUE

Rookie Classification
Office Address: 1503 Clower Creek Dr., Suite H-262, Sarasota, FL 34231.
Telephone: (941) 966-6407. **FAX:** (941) 966-6872.
Years League Active: 1964-.
President/Secretary-Treasurer: Tom Saffell.
First Vice President: Steve Noworyta (Phillies). **Second Vice President:** Jim Rantz (Twins).
Administrative Assistant: Bill Ventolo.
Division Structure: East—Dodgers, Marlins, Mets, Nationals. **North**—Braves, Phillies, Tigers, Yankees. **South**—Pirates, Reds, Red Sox, Twins.
Regular Season: 54 games. **2005 Opening Date:** June 24. **Closing Date:** Aug. 25.
Playoff Format: Division winner with best regular season record meets winner of one-game playoff between other two division winners in best-of-3 series for championship.
Roster Limit: 35 active, but only 30 eligible for each game. **Player Eligibility Rule:** No age restrictions. No more than two years of prior service, excluding Rookie leagues outside the United States and Canada; a third year is allowed for players under 20.
Brand of Baseball: Rawlings.
Statistician: Major League Baseball Advanced Media, 75 Ninth Ave., New York, NY 10011.

Clubs	Playing Site	Manager	Coach(es)	Pitching Coach
Braves	Disney's Wide World of Sports, Orlando	Luis Ortiz	S. Lezcano/J. Saul	Derrick Lewis
Dodgers	Dodgertown, Vero Beach	Luis Salazar	M. Singleton/R. Ortiz	George Culver
Marlins	Roger Dean Stadium, Jupiter	Edwin Rodriguez	Johnny Rodriguez	Gary Buckels
Mets	St. Lucie Sports Complex, St. Lucie	Gary Carter	Nelson Silverio	Hector Berrios
Nationals	Carl Barger Baseball Complex, Melbourne	Wendell Kim	Jason Camilli	Franklin Bravo
Phillies	Carpenter Complex, Clearwater	Jim Morrison	Luis Melendez	Carlos Arroyo
Pirates	Pirate City Complex, Bradenton	Jeff Livesey	Woody Huyke	M. Bonilla/R. Newman
Reds	Ed Smith Stadium, Sarasota	Luis Aguayo	Joe Ayrault	Jamie Garcia
Red Sox	City of Palms Park, Fort Myers	Ralph Treuel	Cesar Hernandez	G. Gregson/D. Tomlin
Tigers	Tigertown, Lakeland	Kevin Bradshaw	Scott Makarewicz	Greg Sabat
Twins	Lee County Stadium, Fort Myers	Nelson Prada	Milt Cuyler	Steve Mintz
Yankees	Yankee Complex, Tampa	Oscar Acosta	Matt Martin	Carlos Reyes

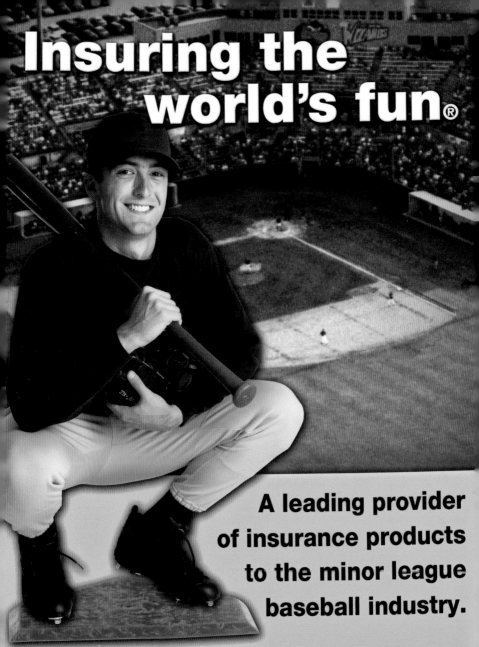

MINOR LEAGUE
SCHEDULES

CLASS AAA
INTERNATIONAL LEAGUE

BUFFALO

APRIL
7-8-9-10	Richmond
11-12	Syracuse
13-14	at Syracuse
15-16-17-18	at Paw.
19-20-21	Rochester
22-23-24-25	Pawtucket
26-27	at Syracuse
28-29-30	at Ottawa

MAY
1	at Ottawa
3-4-5-6	Scranton
7-8	Ottawa
9-10-11-12	at Durham
13-14-15-16	at Charlotte
17-18-19-20	Louisville
21-22-23-24	Charlotte
26-27-28-29	at Roch.
30-31	Toledo

JUNE
1-2	Toledo
3-4-5-6	Columbus
7-8	at Syracuse
9-10	Syracuse
11-12-13-14	at Louisville
16-17-18-19	at Indy
20-21-22-23	Norfolk
24-25-26-27	Durham
28-29	at Scranton
30	Scranton

JULY
1	Scranton
2-3	Ottawa
4-5	at Rochester
6-7	at Scranton
8-9-10	Rochester
14-15-16-17	at Toledo
18-19-20-21	at Col.
22-23	at Scranton
24-25	Scranton
26-27-28-29	Pawtucket
30-31	Indianapolis

AUGUST
1-2	Indianapolis
4-5	at Rochester
6-7-8-9	at Pawtucket
11-12-13-14	Ottawa
15-16-17-18	at Rich.
19-20-21-22	at Norfolk
23-24-25-26	Syracuse
27-28	at Scranton
29-30	Rochester
31	at Ottawa

SEPTEMBER
1-2-3	at Ottawa
4-5	at Syracuse

CHARLOTTE

APRIL
7-8-9-10	Columbus
11-12-13-14	Toledo
15-16-17-18	at Col.
19-20-21-22	at Toledo
23-24-25-26	Richmond
27-28	Norfolk
29	Durham
30	at Durham

MAY
1	at Durham
3-4	at Richmond
5-6-7-8	at Norfolk
9-10-11-12	Ottawa
13-14-15-16	Buffalo
17-18-19-20	at Ottawa
21-22-23-24	at Buffalo
25-26-27-28	Ind.
30-31	Scranton

JUNE
1-2	Scranton
3-4-5-6	at Indianapolis
7-8-9-10	at Louisville
11-12	Norfolk
14-15	at Norfolk
16-17-18-19	Syracuse
20-21-22-23	Louisville
24-25-26-27	at Scranton
28-29-30	Pawtucket

JULY
1	Pawtucket
2-3-4-5	at Pawtucket
7-8	at Indianapolis
9-10	at Louisville
14-15	Indianapolis
16-17	Louisville
18-19-20-21	Rochester
22-23-24-25	at Syracuse
26-27-28-29	at Roch.
30-31	Richmond

AUGUST
1	at Durham
2-3	Columbus
4-5-6-7	Durham
9-10	at Norfolk
11-12	at Richmond
13-14	Richmond
15-16	at Toledo
17-18	at Columbus
19-20-21	at Durham
22-23	Toledo
24-25	at Durham
26-27-28-29	Norfolk
30-31	at Richmond

SEPTEMBER
1-2	at Richmond
3-4-5	Durham

COLUMBUS

APRIL
7-8-9-10	at Charlotte
11-12-13-14	at Durham
15-16-17-18	Charlotte
19-20-21-22	Durham
23-24-25	at Louisville
26-27-28-29	at Ind.
30	at Toledo

MAY
1	at Toledo
3-4	Louisville
5-6-7-8	Indianapolis
9-10-11-12	at Rochester
13-14-15-16	at Syracuse
17-18-19-20	Rochester
21-22-23-24	Syracuse
26-27	Toledo
28-29	at Toledo
30-31	at Ottawa

JUNE
1-2	at Ottawa
3-4-5-6	at Buffalo
7-8-9-10	Ottawa
11-12-13-14	Pawtucket
16-17-18-19	at Paw.
20-21-22-23	at Scranton
24-25-26-27	Norfolk
28-29-30	Richmond

JULY
1	Richmond
2-3	at Durham
4-5	at Richmond
6-7-8	at Norfolk
9-10	Toledo
14-15-16-17	Scranton
18-19-20-21	Buffalo
22-23-24-25	at Ind.
26-27-28-29	at Rich.
30-31	at Norfolk

AUGUST
1	at Norfolk
2-3	at Charlotte
4-5	Louisville
6-7	Richmond
8-9	Toledo
11-12-13-14	at Toledo
15-16	Norfolk
17-18	Charlotte
19-20-21	at Louisville
22-23	Durham
24-25	Louisville
26-27-28-29	Ind.
31	at Louisville

SEPTEMBER
1	at Louisville
2-3	Toledo
4-5	Louisville

DURHAM

APRIL
7-8-9-10	Toledo
11-12-13-14	Columbus
15-16-17-18	at Toledo
19-20-21-22	at Col.
23-24-25-26	Norfolk
27-28	Richmond
29	at Charlotte
30	Charlotte

MAY
1	Charlotte
3-4	at Norfolk
5-6-7-8	at Richmond
9-10-11-12	Buffalo
13-14-15-16	at Scranton
17-18-19-20	at Scranton
21-22-23-24	Ind.
26-27-28-29	Pawtucket
30-31	at Syracuse

JUNE
1-2	at Syracuse
3-4-5-6	at Ottawa
7-8	at Norfolk
9-10	Norfolk
11-12-13-14	Scranton
16-17-18-19	Louisville
20-21-22-23	at Paw.
24-25-26-27	at Buffalo
28-29-30	Syracuse

JULY
1	Syracuse
2-3	Columbus
4-5	Toledo
7-8	at Louisville
9-10	at Indianapolis
14-15-16-17	Rochester
18-19	at Richmond
20-21	Richmond
22-23-24-25	at Roch.
26-27-28-29	at Louisville
30-31	at Toledo

AUGUST
1	Charlotte
2-3	Norfolk
4-5-6-7	at Charlotte
9-10	at Richmond
11-12	Indianapolis
13-14	Louisville
15-16-17-18	at Ind.
19-20-21	Charlotte
22-23	at Columbus
24-25	Charlotte
26-27-28-29	Richmond
30-31	at Norfolk

SEPTEMBER
1-2	at Norfolk
3-4-5	at Charlotte

INDIANAPOLIS

APRIL
7-8-9-10	Pawtucket
11-12-13-14	Ottawa
15-16-17-18	at Norfolk
19-20-21-22	at Rich.
23-24-25	Toledo
26-27-28-29	Columbus
30	Louisville

MAY
1	Louisville
3-4	at Toledo
5-6-7-8	at Columbus
9-10-11-12	Richmond
13-14-15-16	Norfolk
17-18-19-20	at Paw.
21-22-23-24	at Durham
25-26-27-28	at Charlotte
30-31	Louisville

JUNE
1-2	at Louisville
3-4-5-6	Charlotte
7-8-9-10	at Scranton
11-12-13-14	at Roch.
16-17-18-19	Buffalo
20-21-22-23	Rochester
24-25-26-27	at Toledo
28-29-30	at Ottawa

JULY
1	at Ottawa
2-3	at Louisville
4-5	Louisville
6	at Louisville
7-8	Charlotte
9-10	Durham
14-15	at Charlotte
16-17	at Richmond
18-19-20-21	Syracuse
22-23-24-25	Columbus
26-27-28-29	at Syracuse
30-31	at Buffalo

AUGUST
1-2	at Buffalo
4-5	Norfolk
6-7	Toledo
8-9-10	at Louisville
11-12	at Durham
13-14	at Norfolk
15-16-17-18	Durham
19-20-21-22	Scranton
24-25	Richmond
26-27-28-29	at Col.
30-31	Toledo

SEPTEMBER
1	Toledo
2-3	Louisville
4-5	at Toledo

LOUISVILLE

APRIL
7-8-9-10	Ottawa
11-12-13-14	Pawtucket
15-16-17-18	at Rich.
19-20-21-22	at Norfolk
23-24-25	Columbus
26-27-28-29	Toledo
30	at Indianapolis

MAY
1	at Indianapolis
3-4	at Columbus
5-6-7-8	at Toledo
9-10-11-12	Norfolk
13-14-15-16	Richmond
17-18-19-20	at Buffalo
21-22-23-24	at Scranton
26-27-28-29	Syracuse
30-31	at Indianapolis

JUNE
1-2	Indianapolis
3-4-5-6	at Syracuse
7-8-9-10	Charlotte
11-12-13-14	Buffalo
16-17-18-19	at Durham
20-21-22-23	at Charlotte
24-25-26-27	Rochester
28-29-30	at Rochester

JULY
1	at Rochester
2-3	Indianapolis
4-5	at Indianapolis
6	Indianapolis
7-8	Durham
9-10	Charlotte
14-15	at Richmond
16-17	at Charlotte
18-19-20-21	at Paw.
22-23-24-25	Toledo
26-27-28-29	Durham
30-31	at Ottawa

AUGUST
1-2	at Ottawa
4-5	at Columbus
6-7	Norfolk
8-9-10	Indianapolis
11-12	at Norfolk
13-14	at Durham
15-16-17-18	Scranton
19-20-21	Columbus
22-23	Richmond
24-25	at Columbus
26-27-28-29	at Toledo
31	Columbus

SEPTEMBER
1	Columbus
2-3	at Indianapolis
4-5	at Columbus

NORFOLK

APRIL
7-8-9-10	at Scranton
11-12-13-14	at Roch.
15-16-17-18	Ind.
19-20-21-22	Louisville
23-24-25-26	at Durham
27-28	at Charlotte
29-30	Richmond

MAY
1	at Richmond
3-4	Durham
5-6-7-8	Charlotte
9-10-11-12	at Louisville
13-14-15-16	at Ind.
17-18	Richmond
19-20	at Richmond
21-22-23-24	Pawtucket
26-27-28-29	Ottawa
30-31	at Pawtucket

JUNE
1-2	at Pawtucket
3-4-5-6	Rochester
7-8	Durham
9-10	at Durham
11-12	at Charlotte
14-15	Charlotte
16-17-18-19	Scranton
20-21-22-23	at Buffalo
24-25-26-27	at Col.
28-29-30	at Toledo

JULY
1	at Toledo
2-3-4-5	Syracuse
6-7-8	Columbus
9-10	at Richmond
14-15-16-17	at Syracuse
18-19-20-21	at Ottawa
22-23-24	Richmond
25	at Richmond
26-27-28-29	Toledo
30-31	Columbus

AUGUST
1	Columbus
2-3	at Durham
4-5	at Indianapolis
6-7	at Louisville
9-10	Charlotte
11-12	Louisville
13-14	Indianapolis
15-16	at Columbus
17-18	at Toledo
19-20-21-22	Buffalo
24-25	Toledo
26-27-28-29	at Charlotte
30-31	Durham

SEPTEMBER
1-2	Durham
3	at Richmond
4	Richmond
5	at Richmond

OTTAWA

APRIL
7-8-9-10	at Louisville
11-12-13-14	at Ind.
16-17-18	Rochester
19-20	Scranton
22-23-24-25	at Roch.
26-27	at Scranton
28-29-30	Buffalo

MAY
1	Buffalo
3-4-5-6	Syracuse
7-8	at Buffalo
9-10-11-12	at Charlotte
13-14-15-16	at Durham
17-18-19-20	Charlotte
21-22-23-24	at Rich.
26-27-28-29	at Norfolk
30-31	Columbus

JUNE
1-2	Columbus
3-4-5-6	Durham
7-8-9-10	at Columbus
11-12-13-14	at Toledo
16-17-18-19	Richmond
20-21-22-23	Toledo
24-25-26-27	at Syracuse
28-29-30	Indianapolis

JULY
1	Indianapolis
2-3	at Buffalo
4-5	at Scranton
6-7	at Pawtucket
8-9-10	Scranton
14-15-16-17	Pawtucket
18-19-20-21	Norfolk
22-23-24-25	at Paw.
26-27-28-29	at Scranton
30-31	Louisville

AUGUST
1-2	Louisville
3-4-5	Scranton
6-7	Rochester
9-10	at Rochester
11-12-13-14	at Buffalo
15-16	at Syracuse
17-18	Pawtucket
19-20-21-22	Syracuse
23-24	at Pawtucket
25-26	at Rochester
27-28	at Syracuse
29-30	Pawtucket
31	Buffalo

SEPTEMBER
1-2-3	Buffalo
4-5	Rochester

PAWTUCKET

APRIL
7-8-9-10	at Indianapolis
11-12-13-14	at Louisville
15-16-17-18	Buffalo
20-21	Syracuse
22-23-24-25	at Buffalo
26-27	at Rochester
28-29-30	Scranton

MAY
1	Scranton
3-4-5-6	Rochester
7-8	at Syracuse
9-10-11-12	at Scranton
13-14-15-16	Toledo
17-18-19-20	Ind.
21-22-23-24	at Norfolk
26-27-28-29	at Durham
30-31	Norfolk

JUNE
1-2	Norfolk
3-4-5-6	Richmond
7-8-9-10	at Toledo
11-12-13-14	at Col.
16-17-18-19	Columbus
20-21-22-23	Durham
24-25-26-27	at Rich.
28-29-30	at Charlotte

JULY
1	at Charlotte
2-3-4-5	Charlotte
6-7	Ottawa
8-9-10	at Syracuse
14-15-16-17	at Ottawa
18-19-20-21	Louisville
22-23-24-25	Ottawa
26-27-28-29	at Buffalo
30-31	Syracuse

AUGUST
1-2	Syracuse
3-4-5	at Syracuse
6-7-8-9	Buffalo
11-12	at Scranton
13-14-15-16	at Roch.
17-18	at Ottawa
19-20-21-22	Rochester
23-24	Ottawa
25-26	at Scranton
27-28	at Rochester
29-30	at Ottawa
31	Syracuse

SEPTEMBER
1	Syracuse
2-3-4-5	Scranton

RICHMOND

APRIL
7-8-9-10	at Buffalo
11-12-13-14	at Scranton

LOUISVILLE (continued)

Date	Opponent
15-16-17-18	Louisville
19-20-21-22	Ind.
23-24-25-26	at Charlotte
27-28	at Durham
29-30	at Norfolk

MAY
Date	Opponent
1	Norfolk
3-4	Charlotte
5-6-7-8	Durham
9-10-11-12	at Ind.
13-14-15-16	at Louisville
17-18	at Norfolk
19-20	Norfolk
21-22-23-24	Ottawa
26-27-28-29	Scranton
30-31	at Rochester

JUNE
Date	Opponent
1-2	at Rochester
3-4-5-6	at Pawtucket
7-8-9-10	Rochester
11-12-13-14	Syracuse
16-17-18-19	at Ottawa
20-21-22-23	at Syracuse
24-25-26-27	Pawtucket
28-29-30	at Columbus

JULY
Date	Opponent
1	at Columbus
2-3	at Toledo
4-5	Columbus
6-7-8	Toledo
9-10	Norfolk
14-15	Louisville
16-17	Indianapolis
18-19	Durham
20-21	at Durham
22-23-24	at Norfolk
25	Norfolk
26-27-28-29	Columbus
30-31	at Charlotte

AUGUST
Date	Opponent
2-3-4-5	at Toledo
6-7	at Columbus
9-10	Durham
11-12	Charlotte
13-14	at Charlotte
15-16-17-18	Buffalo
19-20-21	Toledo
22-23	at Louisville
24-25	at Indianapolis
26-27-28-29	at Durham
30-31	Charlotte

SEPTEMBER
Date	Opponent
1-2	Charlotte
3	Norfolk
4	at Norfolk
5	Norfolk

ROCHESTER
APRIL
Date	Opponent
7-8	at Syracuse
9-10	Syracuse
11-12-13-14	Norfolk
16-17-18	at Ottawa
19-20-21	at Buffalo
22-23-24-25	Ottawa
26-27	Pawtucket
28-29	at Syracuse
30	Syracuse

MAY
Date	Opponent
1	Syracuse
3-4-5-6	at Pawtucket
7-8	at Scranton
9-10-11-12	Columbus
13-14-15-16	Scranton
17-18-19-20	at Col.
21-22-23-24	at Toledo
26-27-28-29	Buffalo
30-31	Richmond

JUNE
Date	Opponent
1-2	Richmond
3-4-5-6	at Norfolk
7-8-9-10	at Richmond
11-12-13-14	Ind.
16-17-18-19	Toledo
20-21-22-23	at Ind.
24-25-26-27	at Louisville
28-29-30	Louisville

JULY
Date	Opponent
1	Louisville
2-3	Scranton
4-5	Buffalo
6-7	Syracuse
8-9-10	at Buffalo
14-15-16-17	at Durham
18-19-20-21	at Charlotte
22-23-24-25	Durham
26-27-28-29	Charlotte
30-31	at Scranton

AUGUST
Date	Opponent
1-2	at Scranton
4-5	Buffalo
6-7	at Ottawa
9-10	Ottawa
11-12	at Syracuse
13-14-15-16	Pawtucket
17-18	at Syracuse
19-20-21-22	at Paw.
23-24	at Scranton
25-26	Ottawa
27-28	Pawtucket
29-30	at Buffalo
31	Scranton

SEPTEMBER
Date	Opponent
1	Scranton
2-3	Syracuse
4-5	at Ottawa

SCRANTON
APRIL
Date	Opponent
7-8-9-10	Norfolk
11-12-13-14	Richmond
15-16-17-18	at Syracuse
19-20	at Ottawa
22-23-24-25	Syracuse
26-27	Ottawa
28-29-30	at Pawtucket

MAY
Date	Opponent
1	at Pawtucket
3-4-5-6	at Buffalo
7-8	Rochester
9-10-11-12	Pawtucket
13-14-15-16	at Roch.
17-18-19-20	Durham
21-22-23-24	Louisville
26-27-28-29	at Rich.
30-31	at Charlotte

JUNE
Date	Opponent
1-2	at Charlotte
3-4-5-6	Toledo
7-8-9-10	Indianapolis
11-12-13-14	at Durham
16-17-18-19	at Norfolk
20-21-22-23	Columbus
24-25-26-27	Charlotte
28-29	Buffalo
30	at Buffalo

JULY
Date	Opponent
1	at Buffalo
2-3	at Rochester
4-5	Ottawa
6-7	Buffalo
8-9-10	at Ottawa
14-15-16-17	at Col.
18-19-20-21	at Toledo
22-23	Buffalo
24-25	at Buffalo
26-27-28-29	Ottawa
30-31	Rochester

AUGUST
Date	Opponent
1-2	Rochester
3-4-5	at Ottawa
6-7	Syracuse
9-10	at Syracuse
11-12	Pawtucket
13-14	Syracuse
15-16-17-18	at Louisville
19-20-21-22	at Ind.
23-24	Rochester
25-26	Pawtucket
27-28	Buffalo
29-30	at Syracuse
31	at Rochester

SEPTEMBER
Date	Opponent
1	at Rochester
2-3-4-5	at Pawtucket

SYRACUSE
APRIL
Date	Opponent
7-8	Rochester
9-10	at Rochester
11-12	at Buffalo
13-14	Buffalo
15-16-17-18	Scranton
20-21	at Pawtucket
22-23-24-25	at Scranton
26-27	Buffalo
28-29	Rochester
30	at Rochester

MAY
Date	Opponent
1	at Rochester
3-4-5-6	at Ottawa
7-8	Pawtucket
9-10-11-12	Toledo
13-14-15-16	Columbus
17-18-19-20	at Toledo
21-22-23-24	at Col.
26-27-28-29	at Louisville
30-31	Durham

JUNE
Date	Opponent
1-2	Durham
3-4-5-6	Louisville
7-8	Buffalo
9-10	at Buffalo
11-12-13-14	at Rich.
16-17-18-19	at Charlotte
20-21-22-23	Richmond
24-25-26-27	Ottawa
28-29-30	at Durham

JULY
Date	Opponent
1	at Durham
2-3-4-5	at Norfolk
6-7	at Rochester
8-9-10	Pawtucket
14-15-16-17	Norfolk
18-19-20-21	at Ind.
22-23-24-25	Charlotte
26-27-28-29	Ind.
30-31	at Pawtucket

AUGUST
Date	Opponent
1-2	at Pawtucket
3-4-5	Pawtucket
6-7	at Scranton
9-10	Scranton
11-12	Rochester
13-14	at Scranton
15-16	Ottawa
17-18	Rochester
19-20-21-22	at Ottawa
23-24-25-26	at Buffalo
27-28	Ottawa
29-30	Scranton
31	at Pawtucket

SEPTEMBER
Date	Opponent
1	at Pawtucket
2-3	at Rochester
4-5	Buffalo

TOLEDO
APRIL
Date	Opponent
7-8-9-10	at Durham
11-12-13-14	at Charlotte
15-16-17-18	Durham
19-20-21-22	Charlotte
23-24-25	at Indianapolis
26-27-28-29	at Louisville
30	Columbus

MAY
Date	Opponent
1	Columbus
3-4	Indianapolis
5-6-7-8	Louisville
9-10-11-12	at Syracuse
13-14-15-16	at Paw.
17-18-19-20	Syracuse
21-22-23-24	Rochester
26-27	at Columbus
28-29	Columbus
30-31	at Buffalo

JUNE
Date	Opponent
1-2	at Buffalo
3-4-5-6	at Scranton
7-8-9-10	Pawtucket
11-12-13-14	Ottawa
16-17-18-19	at Roch.
20-21-22-23	at Ottawa
24-25-26-27	Ind.
28-29-30	Norfolk

JULY
Date	Opponent
1	Norfolk
2-3	Richmond
4-5	at Durham
6-7-8	at Richmond
9-10	at Columbus
14-15-16-17	Buffalo
18-19-20-21	Scranton

22-23-24-25	at Louisville	6-7	at Indianapolis	19-20-21	at Richmond
26-27-28-29	at Norfolk	8-9	at Columbus	22-23	at Charlotte
30-31	**Durham**	**11-12-13-14**	**Columbus**	24-25	at Norfolk
	AUGUST	**15-16**	**Charlotte**	**26-27-28-29**	**Louisville**
2-3-4-5	**Richmond**	**17-18**	**Norfolk**	30-31	at Indianapolis

SEPTEMBER
1 at Indianapolis
2-3 at Columbus
4-5 Indianapolis

PACIFIC COAST LEAGUE

ALBUQUERQUE

APRIL
7-8-9-10 **Iowa**
11-12-13-14 **Omaha**
15-16-17-18 at Iowa
19-20-21-22 at Omaha
23-24-25-26 **Oklahoma**
28-29-30 at New Orleans

MAY
1 at New Orleans
2-3-4-5 at Oklahoma
6-7-8-9 **New Orleans**
10-11-12-13 **Portland**
14-15-16-17 **Tacoma**
19-20-21-22 at L.V.
23-24-25-26 at Tucson
27-28-29-30 **Omaha**
31 **Nashville**

JUNE
1-2-3 **Nashville**
4-5-6-7 at Oklahoma
9-10-11-12 **Round Rock**
13-14-15-16 at Nashville
17-18-19-20 at Memphis
21-22-23-24 **Nashville**
25-26-27-28 at R.R.
30 at Omaha

JULY
1-2-3 at Omaha
4-5-6-7 **Oklahoma**
8-9-10 **Memphis**
14-15-16-17 at Nashville
18-19-20-21 at Iowa
22-23-24-25 at N.O.
26-27-28-29 **Salt Lake**
30-31 **Colo. Springs**

AUGUST
1-2 **Colo. Springs**
4-5-6-7 at Sacramento
8-9-10-11 at Fresno
12-13-14-15 **N.O.**
16-17-18-19 **Iowa**
20-21-22-23 at R.R.
24-25-26-27-28 **Mem.**
29-30-31 **Round Rock**

SEPTEMBER
1 **Round Rock**
2-3-4-5 at Memphis

COLORADO SPRINGS

APRIL
7-8-9-10 **Las Vegas**
11-12-13-14 **Tucson**
15-16-17-18 at L.V.
19-20-21-22 at Tucson
23-24-25-26 **Tacoma**
28-29-30 Portland

MAY
1 **Portland**

2-3-4-5 at Tacoma
6-7-8-9 at Portland
10-11-12-13 **Iowa**
14-15-16-17 **Omaha**
19-20-21-22 at N.O.
23-24-25-25 at Okla.
27-28-29-30 **Portland**
31 at Las Vegas

JUNE
1-2-3 at Las Vegas
4-5-6-7 at Tucson
9-10-11-12 **Sacramento**
13-14-15-16 at Fresno
17-18-19-20 at Sac.
21-22-23-24 at Salt Lake
25-26-27-28 **Fresno**
30 at Tacoma

JULY
1-2-3 at Tacoma
4-5-6-7 **Sacramento**
8-9-10 **Salt Lake**
14-15-16-17 at Sac.
18-19-20-21 **Las Vegas**
22-23-24-25 **Tacoma**
26-27-28-29 at R.R.
30-31 at Albuquerque

AUGUST
1-2 at Albuquerque
4-5-6-7 **Nashville**
8-9-10-11 **Memphis**
12-13-14-15 at Portland
16-17-18-19 at Fresno
20-21-22-23 **Tucson**
24-25-26-27-28 **S.L.**
29-30-31 at Salt Lake

SEPTEMBER
1 at Salt Lake
2-3-4-5 **Fresno**

FRESNO

APRIL
7-8-9-10 **Tacoma**
11-12-13-14 **Portland**
15-16-17-18 at Tacoma
19-20-21-22 at Portland
23-24-25-26 **Tucson**
28-29-30 Las Vegas

MAY
1 **Las Vegas**
2-3-4-5 at Las Vegas
6-7-8-9 at Tucson
10-11-12-13 **N.O.**
14-15-16-17 **Oklahoma**
19-20-21-22 at Iowa
23-24-25-26 at Omaha
27-28-29-30 **Tacoma**
31 **Tucson**

JUNE
1-2-3 **Tucson**
4-5-6-7 at Las Vegas

9-10-11-12 at Salt Lake
13-14-15-16 **C.S.**
17-18-19-20 **Salt Lake**
21-22-23-24 at Portland
25-26-27-28 at C.S.
30 at Tucson

JULY
1-2-3 at Tucson
4-5-6-7 **Las Vegas**
8-9-10 **Sacramento**
14-15-16-17 at Salt Lake
18-19-20-21 **Salt Lake**
22-23-24-25 **Portland**
26-27-28-29 at Nashville
30-31 at Memphis

AUGUST
1-2 at Memphis
4-5-6-7 **Round Rock**
8-9-10-11 **Albuquerque**
12-13-14-15 at Sac.
16-17-18-19 **C.S.**
20-21-22-23 at Tacoma
24-25-26-27-28 **Sac.**
29-30-31 at Sacramento

SEPTEMBER
1 at Sacramento
2-3-4-5 at C.S.

IOWA

APRIL
7-8-9-10 at Albuquerque
11-12-13-14 at R.R.
15-16-17-18 **Albu.**
19-20-21-22 **R.R.**
23-24-25-26 at Nashville
28-29-30 at Memphis

MAY
1 at Memphis
2-3-4-5 **Nashville**
6-7-8-9 **Memphis**
10-11-12-13 at C.S.
14-15-16-17 at Salt Lake
19-20-21-22 **Fresno**
23-24-25-26 **Sac.**
27-28-29-30 at R.R.
31 **Oklahoma**

JUNE
1-2-3 **Oklahoma**
4-5-6-7 at Memphis
9-10-11-12 **Nashville**
13-14-15-16 **N.O.**
17-18-19-20 at Nashville
21-22-23-24 **Oklahoma**
25-26-27-28 **Omaha**
30 at Oklahoma

JULY
1-2-3 at Oklahoma
4-5-6-7 **Round Rock**
8-9-10 at New Orleans
14-15-16-17 **Omaha**

18-19-20-21 Albu.
22-23-24-25 at Okla.
26-27-28-29 at Tacoma
30-31 at Portland

AUGUST
1-2 at Portland
4-5-6-7 **Tucson**
8-9-10-11 **Las Vegas**
12-13-14-15 at Omaha
16-17-18-19 at Albu.
20-21-22-23 **Memphis**
24-25-26-27-28 at N.O.
29-30-31 at Omaha

SEPTEMBER
1 at Omaha
2-3-4-5 **New Orleans**

LAS VEGAS

APRIL
7-8-9-10 at C.S.
11-12-13-14 at Salt Lake
15-16-17-18 **C.S.**
19-20-21-22 **Salt Lake**
23-24-25-26 at Sac.
28-29-30 at Fresno

MAY
1 at Fresno
2-3-4-5 **Fresno**
6-7-8-9 **Sacramento**
10-11-12-13 at Nashville
14-15-16-17 at Nashville
19-20-21-22 **Albu.**
23-24-25-26 **R.R.**
27-28-29-30 at Tucson
31 **Colo. Springs**

JUNE
1-2-3 **Colo. Springs**
4-5-6-7 **Fresno**
9-10-11-12 at Tacoma
13-14-15-16 at Sac.
17-18-19-20 **Tacoma**
21-22-23-24 **Sac.**
25-26-27-28 at Tucson
30 **Portland**

JULY
1-2-3 **Portland**
4-5-6-7 at Fresno
8-9-10 at Portland
14-15-16-17 **Tucson**
18-19-20-21 at C.S.
22-23-24-25 at Salt Lake
26-27-28-29 **N.O.**
30-31 **Oklahoma**

AUGUST
1-2 **Oklahoma**
4-5-6-7 at Omaha
8-9-10-11 at Iowa
12-13-14-15 **Tucson**
16-17-18-19 at Tacoma
20-21-22-23 **Portland**

24-25-26-27-28	at Port.
29-30-31	**Tacoma**

SEPTEMBER

1	**Tacoma**
2-3-4-5	**Salt Lake**

MEMPHIS

APRIL

7-8-9-10	**Oklahoma**
11-12-13-14	**N.O.**
15-16-17-18	at Okla.
20-21-21-22	at N.O.
23-24-25-26	**Omaha**
28-29-30	**Iowa**

MAY

1	**Iowa**
2-3-4-5	at Omaha
6-7-8-9	at Iowa
10-11-12-13	**Las Vegas**
14-15-16-17	**Tucson**
19-20-21-22	at Portland
23-24-25-26	at Tacoma
27-28-29-30	**Oklahoma**
31	at Round Rock

JUNE

1-2-3	at Round Rock
4-5-6-7	**Iowa**
9-10-11-12	at Omaha
13-14-15-16	at R.R.
17-18-19-20	**Albu.**
21-22-23-24	**R.R.**
25-26-27-28	at N.O.
30	at Nashville

JULY

1-2-3	at Nashville
4-5-6-7	**Omaha**
8-9-10	at Albuquerque
14-15-16-17	**N.O.**
18-19-20-21	at Nashville
22-23-24-25	**R.R.**
26-27-28-29	**Sac.**
30-31	**Fresno**

AUGUST

1-2	**Fresno**
4-5-6-7	at Salt Lake
8-9-10-11	at C.S.
12-13-14-15	**Nashville**
16-17-18-19	at Okla.
20-21-22-23	at Iowa
24-25-26-27-28	at Albu.
29-30-31	**Nashville**

SEPTEMBER

1	**Nashville**
2-3-4-5	**Albuquerque**

NASHVILLE

APRIL

7-8-9-10	**New Orleans**
11-12-13-14	**Oklahoma**
15-16-17-18	at N.O.
19-20-21-22	at Okla.
23-24-25-26	**Iowa**
28-29-30	**Omaha**

MAY

1	**Omaha**
2-3-4-5	at Iowa
6-7-8-9	at Omaha
10-11-12-13	**Tucson**
14-15-16-17	**Las Vegas**

19-20-21-22	at Tacoma
23-24-25-26	at Portland
27-28-29-30	**N.O.**
31	at Albuquerque

JUNE

1-2-3	at Albuquerque
4-5-6-7	**Omaha**
9-10-11-12	at Iowa
13-14-15-16	**Albu.**
17-18-19-20	**Iowa**
21-22-23-24	at Albu.
25-26-27-28	at Okla.
30	**Memphis**

JULY

1-2-3	**Memphis**
4-5-6-7	at New Orleans
8-9-10	at Round Rock
14-15-16-17	**Albu.**
18-19-20-21	**Memphis**
22-23-24-25	at Omaha
26-27-28-29	**Fresno**
30-31	**Sacramento**

AUGUST

1-2	**Sacramento**
4-5-6-7	at Colo. Springs
8-9-10-11	at Salt Lake
12-13-14-15	at Memphis
16-17-18-19	**R.R.**
20-21-22-23	**Oklahoma**
24-25-26-27-28	at R.R.
29-30-31	at Memphis

SEPTEMBER

1	at Memphis
2-3-4-5	**Round Rock**

NEW ORLEANS

APRIL

7-8-9-10	at Nashville
11-12-13-14	at Memphis
15-16-17-18	**Nashville**
20-21-21-22	**Memphis**
23-24-25-26	at R.R.
28-29-30	**Albuquerque**

MAY

1	**Albuquerque**
2-3-4-5	**Round Rock**
6-7-8-9	at Albuquerque
10-11-12-13	at Fresno
14-15-16-17	at Sac.
19-20-21-22	**C.S.**
23-24-25-26	**Salt Lake**
27-28-29-30	at Nashville
31	at Omaha

JUNE

1-2-3	at Omaha
4-5-6-7	**Round Rock**
9-10-11-12	**Oklahoma**
13-14-15-16	at Iowa
17-18-19-20	at Okla.
21-22-23-24	**Omaha**
25-26-27-28	**Memphis**
30	at Round Rock

JULY

1-2-3	at Round Rock
4-5-6-7	**Nashville**
8-9-10	**Iowa**
14-15-16-17	at Memphis
18-19-20-21	**Oklahoma**

22-23-24-25	**Albu.**
26-27-28-29	at L.V.
30-31	at Tucson

AUGUST

1-2	at Tucson
4-5-6-7	**Tacoma**
8-9-10-11	**Portland**
12-13-14-15	at Albu.
16-17-18-19	**Omaha**
20-21-22-23	at Omaha
24-25-26-27-28	**Iowa**
29-30-31	at Oklahoma

SEPTEMBER

1	at Oklahoma
2-3-4-5	at Iowa

OKLAHOMA

APRIL

7-8-9-10	at Memphis
11-12-13-14	at Nashville
15-16-17-18	**Memphis**
19-20-21-22	**Nashville**
23-24-25-26	at Albu.
28-29-30	at Round Rock

MAY

1	at Round Rock
2-3-4-5	**Albuquerque**
6-7-8-9	**Round Rock**
10-11-12-13	at Sac.
14-15-16-17	at Fresno
19-20-21-22	**Salt Lake**
23-24-25	**C.S.**
27-28-29-30	at Memphis
31	at Iowa

JUNE

1-2-3	at Iowa
4-5-6-7	**Albuquerque**
9-10-11-12	at N.O.
13-14-15-16	**Omaha**
17-18-19-20	**N.O.**
21-22-23-24	at Iowa
25-26-27-28	**Nashville**
30	**Iowa**

JULY

1-2-3	**Iowa**
4-5-6-7	at Albuquerque
8-9-10	at Omaha
14-15-16-17	**R.R.**
18-19-20-21	at N.O.
22-23-24-25	**Iowa**
26-27-28-29	at Tucson
30-31	at Las Vegas

AUGUST

1-2	at Las Vegas
4-5-6-7	**Portland**
8-9-10-11	**Tacoma**
12-13-14-15	at R.R.
16-17-18-19	**Memphis**
20-21-22-23	at Nashville
24-25-26-27-28	at Oma.
29-30-31	**New Orleans**

SEPTEMBER

1	**New Orleans**
2-3-4-5	**Omaha**

OMAHA

APRIL

7-8-9-10	at Round Rock
11-12-13-14	at Albu.

15-16-17-18	**R.R.**
19-20-21-22	**Albu.**
23-24-25-26	at Memphis
28-29-30	at Nashville

MAY

1	at Nashville
2-3-4-5	**Memphis**
6-7-8-9	**Nashville**
10-11-12-13	at Salt Lake
14-15-16-17	at C.S.
19-20-21-22	**Sac.**
23-24-25-26	**Fresno**
27-28-29-30	at Albu.
31	**New Orleans**

JUNE

1-2-3	**New Orleans**
4-5-6-7	at Nashville
9-10-11-12	**Memphis**
13-14-15-16	at Okla.
17-18-19-20	at R.R.
21-22-23-24	at N.O.
25-26-27-28	at Iowa
30	**Albuquerque**

JULY

1-2-3	**Albuquerque**
4-5-6-7	at Memphis
8-9-10	**Oklahoma**
14-15-16-17	at Iowa
18-19-20-21	**R.R.**
22-23-24-25	**Nashville**
26-27-28-29	at Portland
30-31	at Tacoma

AUGUST

1-2	at Tacoma
4-5-6-7	**Las Vegas**
8-9-10-11	**Tucson**
12-13-14-15	**Iowa**
16-17-18-19	at N.O.
20-21-22-23	**N.O.**
24-25-26-27-28	**Okla.**
29-30-31	**Iowa**

SEPTEMBER

1	**Iowa**
2-3-4-5	at Oklahoma

PORTLAND

APRIL

7-8-9-10	at Sacramento
11-12-13-14	at Fresno
15-16-17-18	**Sac.**
19-20-21-22	**Fresno**
23-24-25-26	at Salt Lake
28-29-30	at C.S.

MAY

1	at C.S.
2-3-4-5	**Salt Lake**
6-7-8-9	**C.S.**
10-11-12-13	at Albu.
14-15-16-17	at R.R.
19-20-21-22	**Memphis**
23-24-25-26	**Nashville**
27-28-29-30	at C.S.
31	at Salt Lake

JUNE

1-2-3	at Salt Lake
4-5-6-7	**Tacoma**
9-10-11-12	**Tucson**
13-14-15-16	at Tacoma

17-18-19-20 at Tucson
21-22-23-24 **Fresno**
25-26-27-28 at Sac.
30 at Las Vegas
JULY
1-2-3 at Las Vegas
4-5-6-7 Tacoma
8-9-10 Las Vegas
14-15-16-17 at Tacoma
18-19-20-21 Sac.
22-23-24-25 at Fresno
26-27-28-29 Omaha
30-31 Iowa
AUGUST
1-2 Iowa
4-5-6-7 at Oklahoma
8-9-10-11 at N.O.
12-13-14-15 C.S.
16-17-18-19 Salt Lake
20-21-22-23 at L.V.
24-25-26-27-28 L.V.
29-30-31 at Tucson
SEPTEMBER
1 at Tucson
2-3-4-5 Tucson

ROUND ROCK
APRIL
7-8-9-10 Omaha
11-12-13-14 Iowa
15-16-17-18 at Omaha
19-20-21-22 at Iowa
23-24-25-26 N.O.
28-29-30 Oklahoma
MAY
1 Oklahoma
2-3-4-5 at New Orleans
6-7-8-9 at Oklahoma
10-11-12-13 Tacoma
14-15-16-17 Portland
19-20-21-22 at Tucson
23-24-25-26 at L.V.
27-28-29-30 Iowa
31 Memphis
JUNE
1-2-3 Memphis
4-5-6-7 at New Orleans
9-10-11-12 at Albu.
13-14-15-16 Memphis
17-18-19-20 Omaha
21-22-23-24 at Memphis
25-26-27-28 Albu.
30 New Orleans
JULY
1-2-3 New Orleans
4-5-6-7 at Iowa
8-9-10 Nashville
14-15-16-17 at Okla.
18-19-20-21 at Omaha
22-23-24-25 at Memphis
26-27-28-29 C.S.
30-31 Salt Lake
AUGUST
1-2 Salt Lake
4-5-6-7 at Fresno
8-9-10-11 at Sacramento
12-13-14-15 Oklahoma
16-17-18-19 at Nashville

20-21-22-23 **Albu.**
24-25-26-27-28 **Nash.**
29-30-31 at Albuquerque
SEPTEMBER
1 at Albuquerue
2-3-4-5 at Nashville

SACRAMENTO
APRIL
7-8-9-10 Portland
11-12-13-14 Tacoma
15-16-17-18 at Portland
19-20-21-22 at Tacoma
23-24-25-26 Las Vegas
28-29-30 Tucson
MAY
1 Tucson
2-3-4-5 at Tucson
6-7-8-9 at Las Vegas
10-11-12-13 Oklahoma
14-15-16-17 N.O.
19-20-21-22 at Omaha
23-24-25-26 at Iowa
27-28-29-30 Salt Lake
31 Tacoma
JUNE
1-2-3 Tacoma
4-5-6-7 at Salt Lake
9-10-11-12 at C.S.
13-14-15-16 Las Vegas
17-18-19-20 C.S.
21-22-23-24 at L.V.
25-26-27-28 Portland
30 Salt Lake
JULY
1-2-3 Salt Lake
4-5-6-7 at Colo. Springs
8-9-10 at Fresno
14-15-16-17 C.S.
18-19-20-21 at Portland
22-23-24-25 Tucson
26-27-28-29 at Memphis
30-31 at Nashville
AUGUST
1-2 at Nashville
4-5-6-7 Albuquerque
8-9-10-11 Round Rock
12-13-14-15 Fresno
16-17-18-19 at Tucson
20-21-22-23 at Salt Lake
24-25-26-27-28 at Fres.
29-30-31 Fresno
SEPTEMBER
1 Fresno
2-3-4-5 at Tacoma

SALT LAKE
APRIL
7-8-9-10 Tucson
11-12-13-14 Las Vegas
15-16-17-18 at Tucson
19-20-21-22 at L.V.
23-24-25-26 Portland
28-29-30 Tacoma
MAY
1 Tacoma
2-3-4-5 at Portland
6-7-8-9 at Tacoma
10-11-12-13 Omaha

14-15-16-17 **Iowa**
19-20-21-22 at Okla.
23-24-25-26 at N.O.
27-28-29-30 at Sac.
31 Portland
JUNE
1-2-3 Portland
4-5-6-7 Sacramento
9-10-11-12 Fresno
13-14-15-16 at Tucson
17-18-19-20 at Fresno
21-22-23-24 C.S.
25-26-27-28 Tacoma
30 at Sacramento
JULY
1-2-3 at Sacramento
4-5-6-7 Tucson
8-9-10 at C.S.
14-15-16-17 Fresno
18-19-20-21 at Fresno
22-23-24-25 Las Vegas
26-27-28-29 at Albu.
30-31 at Round Rock
AUGUST
1-2 at Round Rock
4-5-6-7 Memphis
8-9-10-11 Nashville
12-13-14-15 at Tacoma
16-17-18-19 at Portland
20-21-22-23 Sac.
24-25-26-27-28 at C.S.
29-30-31 C.S.
SEPTEMBER
1 Colo. Springs
2-3-4-5 at Las Vegas

TACOMA
APRIL
7-8-9-10 at Fresno
11-12-13-14 at Sac.
15-16-17-18 Fresno
19-20-21-22 Sac.
23-24-25-26 at C.S.
28-29-30 at Salt Lake
MAY
1 at Salt Lake
2-3-4-5 C.S.
6-7-8-9 Salt Lake
10-11-12-13 at R.R.
14-15-16-17 at Albu.
19-20-21-22 Nashville
23-24-25-26 Memphis
27-28-29-30 at Fresno
31 at Sacramento
JUNE
1-2-3 at Sacramento
4-5-6-7 at Portland
9-10-11-12 Las Vegas
13-14-15-16 Portland
17-18-19-20 at L.V.
21-22-23-24 Tucson
25-26-27-28 at Salt Lake
30 C.S.
JULY
1-2-3 C.S.
4-5-6-7 at Portland
8-9-10 at Tucson
14-15-16-17 Portland

18-19-20-21 **Tucson**
22-23-24-25 at C.S.
26-27-28-29 **Iowa**
30-31 **Omaha**
AUGUST
1-2 Omaha
4-5-6-7 at New Orleans
8-9-10-11 at Oklahoma
12-13-14-15 Salt Lake
16-17-18-19 Las Vegas
20-21-22-23 Fresno
24-25-26-27-28 at Tuc.
29-30-31 at Las Vegas
SEPTEMBER
1 at Las Vegas
2-3-4-5 Sacramento

TUCSON
APRIL
7-8-9-10 at Salt Lake
11-12-13-14 at C.S.
15-16-17-18 Salt Lake
19-20-21-22 C.S.
23-24-25-26 at Fresno
28-29-30 at Sacramento
MAY
1 at Sacramento
2-3-4-5 Sacramento
6-7-8-9 Fresno
10-11-12-13 at Nashville
14-15-16-17 at Memphis
19-20-21-22 R.R.
23-24-25-26 Albu.
27-28-29-30 Las Vegas
31 at Fresno
JUNE
1-2-3 at Fresno
4-5-6-7 C.S.
9-10-11-12 at Portland
13-14-15-16 Salt Lake
17-18-19-20 Portland
21-22-23-24 at Tacoma
25-26-27-28 Las Vegas
30 Fresno
JULY
1-2-3 Fresno
4-5-6-7 at Salt Lake
8-9-10 Tacoma
14-15-16-17 at L.V.
18-19-20-21 at Tacoma
22-23-24-25 at Sac.
26-27-28-29 Oklahoma
30-31 New Orleans
AUGUST
1-2 New Orleans
4-5-6-7 at Iowa
8-9-10-11 at Omaha
12-13-14-15 at L.V.
16-17-18-19 Sac.
20-21-22-23 at C.S.
24-25-26-27-28 Tacoma
29-30-31 Portland
SEPTEMBER
1 Portland
2-3-4-5 at Portland

CLASS AA
EASTERN LEAGUE

AKRON

APRIL

7-8-9-10	**Binghamton**
11-12-13	**Bowie**
14-15-16-17	at Bowie
18-19-20	at Altoona
21-22-23-24	**Altoona**
25-26-27	**Bowie**
29-30	at Harrisburg

MAY

1	at Harrisburg
2-3-4-5	at Binghamton
6-7-8	**Harrisburg**
9-10-11-12	at Erie
13-14-15	at New Britain
16-17-18	at Norwich
20-21-22	**Norwich**
23-24-25-26	**Erie**
27-28-29-30	at Bowie
31	at Binghamton

JUNE

1-2	at Binghamton
3-4-5	**Bowie**
7-8-9	**N.H.**
10-11-12	at Altoona
13-14-15	at Erie
17-18-19	**Bowie**
20-21-22-23	**Reading**
24-25-26	at Harrisburg
28-29-30	at Reading

JULY

1-2-3	**Binghamton**
4-5-6-7	at Reading
8-9-10-11	**Erie**
14-15-16-17	at Portland
18-19-20	at N.H.
22-23-24	**Trenton**
25-26-27-28	**Harrisburg**
29-30-31	at Binghamton

AUGUST

1-2-3-4	**Reading**
5-6-7	at Altoona
8 0 10	**Erie**
11-12-13-14	at Trenton
16-17-18	**Altoona**
19-20-21	**Harrisburg**
22-23-24-25	at Erie
26-27-28	at Altoona
30-31	**New Britain**

SEPTEMBER

1	**New Britain**
2-3-4-5	**Portland**

ALTOONA

APRIL

7-8-9-10	at Reading
11-12-13	at Trenton
14-15-16-17	**Erie**
18-19-20	**Akron**
21-22-23-24	at Akron

25-26-27	at Erie
29-30	**Trenton**

MAY

1	**Trenton**
2-3-4-5	**Reading**
6-7-8	at Trenton
9-10-11	**Harrisburg**
13-14-15	**N.H.**
16-17-18	at Bowie
20-21-22	at Binghamton
23-24-25-26	**Norwich**
27-28-29-30	**Reading**
31	at Harrisburg

JUNE

1-2	at Harrisburg
3-4-5	at Reading
7-8-9	**Binghamton**
10-11-12	**Akron**
13-14-15-16	at Norwich
17-18-19	at New Britain
20-21-22-23	**Bowie**
24-25-26	**New Britain**
28-29-30	at Portland

JULY

1-2-3	at N.H.
4-5-6-7	**Erie**
8-9-10-11	**Harrisburg**
14-15-16-17	at Harris.
18-19-20	at Erie
22-23-24	**Harrisburg**
25-26-27-28	**Bing.**
29-30-31	at Trenton

AUGUST

1-2-3-4	at Erie
5-6-7	**Akron**
8-9-10	**Bowie**
11-12-13-14	at Reading
16-17-18	at Akron
19-20-21	**Reading**
22-23-24-25	at Bowie
26-27-28	**Akron**
30-31	**Portland**

SEPTEMBER

1	**Portland**
2-3-4-5	at Bowie

BINGHAMTON

APRIL

7-8-9-10	at Akron
11-12-13	at Erie
14-15-16-17	**N.H.**
18-19-20	at Portland
21-22-23-24	at N.H.
26-27-28	**Portland**
29-30	**Erie**

MAY

1	**Erie**
2-3-4-5	**Akron**
6-7-8	at Erie
9-10-11	**Bowie**
13-14-15	at Norwich

17-18-19	at Reading
20-21-22	**Altoona**
23-24-25-26	at Portland
27-28-29-30	**Trenton**
31	**Akron**

JUNE

1-2	**Akron**
3-4-5	at Trenton
7-8-9	at Altoona
10-11-12	**Norwich**
13-14-15-16	**N.H.**
17-18-19	at Norwich
20-21-22-23	at N.B.
24-25-26	**Erie**
28-29-30	**New Britain**

JULY

1-2-3	at Akron
4-5-6-7	**N.H.**
8-9-10-11	at Norwich
14-15-16-17	**Reading**
18-19-20	**New Britain**
22-23-24	at Bowie
25-26-27-28	at Altoona
29-30-31	**Akron**

AUGUST

1-2-3-4	at Harrisburg
5-6-7	**Portland**
8-9-10	**Norwich**
11-12-13-14	at N.H.
15-16-17	at Portland
19-20-21	**Trenton**
22-23-24-25	**Harrisburg**
26-27-28	at Trenton
30-31	at N.H.

SEPTEMBER

1	at N.H.
2-3-4-5	**New Britain**

BOWIE

APRIL

7-8-9-10	at Harrisburg
11-12-13	at Akron
14-15-16-17	**Akron**
18-19-20	**Erie**
21-22-23-24	at Erie
25-26-27	at Akron
29-30	**Reading**

MAY

1	**Reading**
2-3-4-5	**Trenton**
6-7-8	at Reading
9-10-11	at Binghamton
13-14-15	**Portland**
16-17-18	**Altoona**
20-21-22	at Portland
23-24-25-26	at N.H.
27-28-29-30	**Akron**
31	**Reading**

JUNE

1-2	**Reading**
3-4-5	at Akron

ERIE

APRIL

7-8-9-10	**Trenton**
11-12-13	**Binghamton**
14-15-16-17	at Altoona
18-19-20	at Bowie
21-22-23-24	**Bowie**
25-26-27	**Altoona**
29-30	at Binghamton

MAY

1	at Binghamton
2-3-4-5	at Harrisburg
6-7-8	**Binghamton**
9-10-11-12	**Akron**
13-14-15	at Reading
16-17-18	**Portland**
20-21-22	**New Britain**
23-24-25-26	at Akron
27-28-29-30	at Harris.
31	**Trenton**

JUNE

1-2	**Trenton**
3-4-5	**Harrisburg**
7-8-9	at Trenton
10-11-12	**N.H.**
13-14-15	**Akron**
17-18-19	at Portland
20-21-22-23	at N.H.
24-25-26	at Binghamton
27-28-29	**Harrisburg**

JULY

Date	Opponent
1-2-3	Reading
4-5-6-7	at Altoona
8-9-10-11	at Akron
14-15-16-17	Norwich
18-19-20	Altoona
22-23-24	at Reading
25-26-27-28	at Reading
29-30-31	Reading

AUGUST

Date	Opponent
1-2-3-4	Altoona
5-6-7	at Bowie
8-9-10	at Akron
11-12-13-14	Bowie
16-17-18	at New Britain
19-20-21	at Norwich
22-23-24-25	Akron
26-27-28	at Harrisburg
30-31	at Bowie

SEPTEMBER

Date	Opponent
1	at Bowie
2-3-4-5	Reading

HARRISBURG

APRIL

Date	Opponent
7-8-9-10	Bowie
11-12-13	at Reading
14-15-16-17	at N.B.
18-19-20	N.H.
21-22-23-24	at Portland
25-26-27	at N.H.
29-30	Akron

MAY

Date	Opponent
1	Akron
2-3-4-5	Erie
6-7-8	at Akron
9-10-11	at Altoona
13-14-15	Trenton
16-17-18	New Britain
20-21-22	at Trenton
23-24-25-26	at Reading
27-28-29-30	Erie
31	Altoona

JUNE

Date	Opponent
1-2	Altoona
3-4-5	at Erie
7-8-9	at Bowie
10-11-12	Reading
13-14-15-16	Portland
17-18-19	at Reading
20-21-22-23	Norfolk
24-25-26	Akron
27-28-29	at Erie

JULY

Date	Opponent
1-2-3	Trenton
4-5-6-7	at Bowie
8-9-10-11	at Altoona
14-15-16-17	Altoona
18-19-20	Trenton
22-23-24	at Altoona
25-26-27-28	at Akron
29-30-31	Bowie

AUGUST

Date	Opponent
1-2-3-4	Binghamton
5-6-7	at Norwich
8-9-10	at N.H.
11-12-13-14	N.B.
16-17-18	Bowie
19-20-21	at Akron
22-23-24-25	at Bing.
26-27-28	Erie
30-31	Reading

SEPTEMBER

Date	Opponent
1	Reading
2-3-4-5	at Trenton

NEW BRITAIN

APRIL

Date	Opponent
7-8-9-10	at N.H.
11-12-13	at Portland
14-15-16-17	Harrisburg
18-19-20	Reading
21-22-23-24	at Trenton
25-26-27	at Reading
29-30	N.H.

MAY

Date	Opponent
1	N.H.
2-3-4-5	Portland
6-7-8	at N.H
9-10-11	Norwich
13-14-15	Akron
16-17-18	at Harrisburg
20-21-22	at Erie
23-24-25-26	Trenton
27-28-29-30	N.H.
31	at Norwich

JUNE

Date	Opponent
1-2	at Norwich
3-4-5	at Portland
7-8-9	Norwich
10-11-12	Trenton
13-14-15-16	at Reading
17-18-19	Altoona
20-21-22-23	Bing.
24-25-26	at Altoona
28-29-30	at Binghamton

JULY

Date	Opponent
1-2-3	Bowie
4-5-6-7	at Norwich
8-9-10-11	at Bowie
14-15-16-17	N.H.
18-19-20	at Binghamton
22-23-24	at Norwich
25-26-27-28	Portland
29-30-31	Norwich

AUGUST

Date	Opponent
1-2-3-4	at Portland
5-6-7	Trenton
8-9-10	Portland
11-12-13-14	at Harris.
16-17-18	Erie
19-20-21	at Bowie
22-23-24-25	Reading
26-27-28	Norwich
30-31	at Akron

SEPTEMBER

Date	Opponent
1	at Akron
2-3-4-5	at Binghamton

NEW HAMPSHIRE

APRIL

Date	Opponent
7-8-9-10	New Britain
11-12-13	Norwich
14-15-16-17	at Bing.
18-19-20	at Harrisburg
21-22-23-24	Bing.
25-26-27	Harrisburg
29-30	at New Britain

MAY

Date	Opponent
1	at New Britain
2-3-4-5	at Norwich
6-7-8	New Britain
9-10-11	at Portland
13-14-15	at Altoona
17-18-19	at Trenton
20-21-22	Reading
23-24-25-26	Bowie
27-28-29-30	at N.B.
31	Portland

JUNE

Date	Opponent
1-2	Portland
3-4-5	Norwich
7-8-9	at Akron
10-11-12	at Erie
13-14-15-16	at Bing.
17-18-19	Trenton
20-21-22-23	Erie
24-25-26	at Bowie
28-29-30	at Trenton

JULY

Date	Opponent
1-2-3	Altoona
4-5-6-7	at Binghamton
8-9-10-11	Portland
14-15-16-17	at N.B.
18-19-20	Akron
22-23-24	Portland
25-26-27-28	at Norwich
29-30-31	at Portland

AUGUST

Date	Opponent
1-2-3-4	Trenton
5-6-7	at Reading
8-9-10	Harrisburg
11-12-13-14	Bing.
16-17-18	at Norwich
19-20-21	Portland
22-23-24-25	Norwich
26-27-28	at Portland
30-31	Binghamton

SEPTEMBER

Date	Opponent
1	Binghamton
2-3-4-5	at Norwich

NORWICH

APRIL

Date	Opponent
7-8-9-10	at Portland
11-12-13	at N.H.
14-15-16-17	Reading
18-19-20	Trenton
21-22-23-24	at Reading
26-27-28	at Trenton
29-30	Portland

MAY

Date	Opponent
1	Portland
2-3-4-5	N.H.
6-7-8	at Portland
9-10-11	at New Britain
13-14-15	Binghamton
16-17-18	Akron
20-21-22	at Akron
23-24-25-26	at Altoona
27-28-29-30	Portland
31	New Britain

JUNE

Date	Opponent
1-2	New Britain
3-4-5	at N.H.
7-8-9	at New Britain
10-11-12	at Binghamton
13-14-15-16	Altoona
17-18-19	Binghamton
20-21-22-23	at Harris.
24-25-26	Portland
28-29-30	Bowie

JULY

Date	Opponent
1-2-3	at Portland
4-5-6-7	New Britain
8-9-10-11	Binghamton
14-15-16-17	at Erie
18-19-20	at Bowie
22-23-24	New Britain
25-26-27-28	N.H.
29-30-31	at New Britain

AUGUST

Date	Opponent
1-2-3-4	at Bowie
5-6-7	Harrisburg
8-9-10	at Binghamton
11-12-13-14	at Portland
16-17-18	N.H.
19-20-21	Erie
22-23-24-25	at N.H.
26-27-28	at New Britain
30-31	Trenton

SEPTEMBER

Date	Opponent
1	Trenton
2-3-4-5	N.H.

PORTLAND

APRIL

Date	Opponent
7-8-9-10	Norwich
11-12-13	New Britain
14-15-16-17	at Trenton
18-19-20	Binghamton
21-22-23-24	Harrisburg
26-27-28	at Binghamton
29-30	at Norwich

MAY

Date	Opponent
1	at Norwich
2-3-4-5	at New Britain
6-7-8	Norwich
9-10-11	N.H.
13-14-15	at Akron
16-17-18	at Erie
20-21-22	Bowie
23-24-25-26	Bing.
27-28-29-30	at Norwich
31	at N.H.

JUNE

Date	Opponent
1-2	at N.H.
3-4-5	New Britain
7-8-9	at Reading
10-11-12	at Bowie
13-14-15-16	at Harris.
17-18-19	Erie
20-21-22-23	Trenton
24-25-26	at Norwich

28-29-30	Altoona		

JULY
1-2-3 — Norwich
4-5-6-7 — at Trenton
8-9-10-11 — at N.H.
14-15-16-17 — Akron
18-19-20 — Reading
22-23-24 — at N.H.
25-26-27-28 — at N.B.
29-30-31 — N.H.

AUGUST
1-2-3-4 — New Britain
5-6-7 — at Binghamton
8-9-10 — at New Britain
11-12-13-14 — Norwich
15-16-17 — Binghamton
19-20-21 — at N.H.
22-23-24-25 — Trenton
26-27-28 — N.H.
30-31 — at Altoona

SEPTEMBER
1 — at Altoona
2-3-4-5 — at Akron

READING

APRIL
7-8-9-10 — Altoona
11-12-13 — Harrisburg
14-15-16-17 — at Norwich
18-19-20 — at New Britain
21-22-23-24 — Norwich
25-26-27 — New Britain
29-30 — at Bowie

MAY
1 — at Bowie
2-3-4-5 — at Altoona
6-7-8 — Bowie
9* — Trenton
10-11-12 — at Trenton
13-14-15 — Erie
17-18-19 — Binghamton
20-21-22 — at N.H.
23-24-25-26 — Harrisburg
27-28-29-30 — at Altoona
31 — at Bowie

JUNE
1-2 — at Bowie
3-4-5 — Altoona
7-8-9 — Portland
10-11-12 — at Harrisburg
13-14-15-16 — N.B.
17-18-19 — Harrisburg
20-21-22-23 — at Akron
24-25-26 — at Trenton
28-29-30 — Akron

JULY
1-2-3 — at Erie
4-5-6-7 — Akron
8-9-10 — Trenton
14-15-16-17 — at Bing.
18-19-20 — at Portland
22-23-24 — Erie
25-26-27-28 — Bowie
29-30-31 — at Erie

AUGUST
1-2-3-4 — at Akron

5-6-7 — N.H.
8-9-10 — at Trenton
11-12-13-14 — Altoona
16-17-18 — Trenton
19-20-21 — at Altoona
22-23-24-25 — at N.B.
26-27-28 — Bowie
30-31 — at Harrisburg

SEPTEMBER
1 — at Harrisburg
2-3-4-5 — at Erie
*at Citizen's Bank Park, Philadelphia

TRENTON

APRIL
7-8-9-10 — at Erie
11-12-13 — Altoona
14-15-16-17 — Portland
18-19-20 — at Norwich
21-22-23-24 — N.B.
26-27-28 — Norwich
29-30 — at Altoona

MAY
1 — at Altoona
2-3-4-5 — at Bowie
6-7-8 — Altoona
10-11-12 — Reading
13-14-15 — at Harrisburg
17-18-19 — N.H.
20-21-22 — Harrisburg
23-24-25-26 — at N.B.
27-28-29-30 — at Bing.

31 — at Erie

JUNE
1-2 — at Erie
3-4-5 — Binghamton
7-8-9 — Erie
10-11-12 — at New Britain
13-14-15-16 — Bowie
17-18-19 — at N.H.
20-21-22-23 — at Portland
24-25-26 — Reading
28-29-30 — N.H.

JULY
1-2-3 — at Harrisburg
4-5-6-7 — Portland
8-9-10 — at Reading
14-15-16-17 — Bowie
18-19-20 — at Harrisburg
22-23-24 — at Akron
25-26-27-28 — Erie
29-30-31 — Altoona

AUGUST
1-2-3-4 — at N.H.
5-6-7 — at New Britain
8-9-10 — Reading
11-12-13-14 — Akron
16-17-18 — at Reading
19-20-21 — at Binghamton
22-23-24-25 — at Portland
26-27-28 — Binghamton
30-31 — at Norwich

SEPTEMBER
1 — at Norwich
2-3-4-5 — Harrisburg

SOUTHERN LEAGUE

BIRMINGHAM

APRIL
7-8-9-10 — at Jacksonville
11-12-13 — at Carolina
15-16-17 — Montgomery
18-19-20-21 — Jack.
22-23-24 — at Montgomery
25-26-27 — at Tennessee
28-29-30 — Chattanooga

MAY
1 — Chattanooga
2-3-4 — West Tenn
6-7-8 — at Chattanooga
9-10-11-12 — Mississippi
13-14-15 — Jacksonville
16-17-18 — at Mississippi
20-21-22 — West Tenn
23-24-25-26 — at Tenn.
27-28-29-30 — at W. Tenn
31 — Montgomery

JUNE
1-2-3 — Montgomery
4-5-6-7 — at Tennessee
9-10-11-12 — at Mobile
13-14-15 — Tennessee
16-17-18-19 — Mobile
21-22-23-24 — at Chat.
25-26-27-28 — at Carolina
30 — Montgomery

JULY
1-2-3 — Montgomery
4-5-6-7 — at Huntsville
8-9-10-11 — Mobile
15-16-17 — at Chattanooga
18-19-20-21 — at Jack.
22-23-24 — Huntsville
26-27-28 — Montgomery
29-30-31 — at Chattanooga

AUGUST
2-3-4 — Mississippi
5-6-7 — al Montgomery
8-9-10 — at Mississippi
11-12-13-14 — Huntsville
15-16-17 — Carolina
19-20-21 — at Mobile
22-23-24-25 — Tennessee
26-27-28-29 — at Jack.
30-31 — West Tenn

SEPTEMBER
1 — West Tenn
2-3-4-5 — Jacksonville

CAROLINA

APRIL
7-8-9-10 — Huntsville
11-12-13 — Birmingham
15-16-17 — at Hunstville
18-19-20-21 — at Chat.
22-23-24 — Tennessee

25-26-27 — at Jacksonville
28-29-30 — at Mont.

MAY
1 — at Montgomery
2-3-4 — at Mobile
6-7-8 — Montgomery
9-10-11-12 — Chattanooga
13-14-15 — at Tennessee
16-17-18 — at West Tenn
20-21-22 — Tennessee
23-24-25-26 — Huntsville
27-28-29-30 — at Chat.
31 — Chattanooga

JUNE
1-2-3 — Chattanooga
4-5-6-7 — West Tenn
9-10-11-12 — at Jack.
13-14-15 — Jacksonville
16-17-18-19 — at Tenn.
21-22-23-24 — Miss.
25-26-27-28 — Birm.
30 — at Jacksonville

JULY
1-2-3 — at Jacksonville
4-5-6-7 — Chattanooga
8-9-10-11 — West Tenn
15-16-17 — at Huntsville
18-19-20-21 — at Chat.
22-23-24 — Jacksonville

25-26-27 — Chattanooga
29-30-31 — at West Tenn

AUGUST
2-3-4 — at Chattanooga
5-6-7 — Tennessee
8-9-10 — West Tenn
11-12-13-14 — at Tenn.
15-16-17 — at Birmingham
19-20-21 — Chattanooga
22-23-24-25 — at Chat.
26-27-28-29 — Mobile
30-31 — at Jacksonville

SEPTEMBER
1 — at Jacksonville
2-3-4-5 — at Mississippi

CHATTANOOGA

APRIL
7-8-9-10 — at West Tenn
11-12-13 — at Mobile
15-16-17 — West Tenn
18-19-20-21 — Carolina
22-23-24 — at Jacksonville
25-26-27 — Mobile
28-29-30 — at Birmingham

MAY
1 — at Birmingham
2-3-4 — Tennessee
6-7-8 — Birmingham
9-10-11-12 — at Carolina

West Tenn (continued)

Date	Opponent
13-14-15	West Tenn
16-17-18	at Tennessee
19-20-21	at Huntsville
23-24-25-26	Mississippi
27-28-29-30	Carolina
31	at Carolina

JUNE
Date	Opponent
1-2-3	at Carolina
4-5-6-7	Jacksonville
8-9	Huntsville
10-11	at Huntsville
13-14-15	at Mississippi
17-18-19-20	at Hunt.
21-22-23-24	Birm.
25-26-27-28	at Mont.
30	Tennessee

JULY
Date	Opponent
1-2-3	Tennessee
4-5-6-7	at Carolina
8-9-10-11	at Tennessee
15-16-17	Birmingham
18-19-20-21	Carolina
22-23-24	at Tennessee
25-26-27	at Carolina
29-30-31	Birmingham

AUGUST
Date	Opponent
2-3-4	Carolina
5-6-7	West Tenn
8-9-10	at Jacksonville
11-12-13-14	Mississippi
16-17-18	Huntsville
19-20-21	at Carolina
22-23-24-25	Carolina
26-27-28-29	at W. Tenn
30-31	at Mississippi

SEPTEMBER
Date	Opponent
1	at Mississippi
2-3	at Huntsville
4-5	Huntsville

HUNTSVILLE
APRIL
Date	Opponent
7-8-9-10	at Carolina
11-12-13	at Jacksonville
15-16-17	Carolina
18-19-20-21	Mobile
22-23-24	at West Tenn
25-26-27	at Mississippi
28-29-30	Tennessee

MAY
Date	Opponent
1	Tennessee
2-3-4	Mississippi
6-7-8	at Tennessee
9-10-11-12	at Mobile
13-14-15	at Mont.
16-17-18	Jacksonville
19-20-21	Chattanooga
23-24-25-26	at Carolina
27-28-29-30	Tennessee
31	at Mississippi

JUNE
Date	Opponent
1-2-3	at Mississippi
4-5-6-7	Mississippi
8-9	at Chattanooga
10-11	Chattanooga
13-14-15	West Tenn
17-18-19-20	Chat.
21-22-23-24	at Mobile
25-26-27-28	Jack.
30	at West Tenn

JULY
Date	Opponent
1-2-3	at West Tenn
4-5-6-7	Birmingham
8-9-10-11	at Mississippi
15-16-17	Carolina
18-19-20-21	at Mobile
22-23-24	at Birmingham
26-27-28	West Tenn
29-30-31	Montgomery

AUGUST
Date	Opponent
2-3-4	at West Tenn
5-6-7	Mississippi
8-9-10	Mobile
11-12-13-14	at Birm.
16-17-18	at Chattanooga
19-20-21	at Tennessee
22-23-24-25	Mobile
26-27-28-29	Tennessee
30-31	at Tennessee

SEPTEMBER
Date	Opponent
1	at Tennessee
2-3	Chattanooga
4-5	at Chattanooga

JACKSONVILLE
APRIL
Date	Opponent
7-8-9-10	Birmingham
11-12-13	Huntsville
15-16-17	Mississippi
18-19-20-21	at Birm.
22-23-24	Chattanooga
25-26-27	Carolina
28-29-30	at Mobile

MAY
Date	Opponent
1	at Mobile
2-3-4	at Montgomery
6-7-8	Mississippi
9-10-11-12	Mont.
13-14-15	at Birm.
16-17-18	at Huntsville
20-21-22	Mississippi
23-24-25-26	at Mont.
27-28-29-30	at Mobile
31	Mobile

JUNE
Date	Opponent
1-2-3	Mobile
4-5-6-7	at Chattanooga
9-10-11-12	Carolina
13-14-15	at Carolina
16-17-18-19	Mont.
21-22-23-24	at W. Tenn
25-26-27-28	at Hunt.
30	Carolina

JULY
Date	Opponent
1-2-3	Carolina
4-5-6-7	at Mobile
8-9-10-11	Montgomery
15-16-17	at Mont.
18-19-20-21	Birm.
22-23-24	at Carolina
25-26-27	Tennessee
29-30-31	Mobile

AUGUST
Date	Opponent
2-3-4	at Tennessee
5-6-7	at Mobile
8-9-10	Chattanooga
11-12-13-14	West Tenn
16-17-18-19-20-21	at Miss.
22-23-24-25	at Mont.
26-27-28-29	Birm.
30-31	Carolina

SEPTEMBER
Date	Opponent
1	Carolina
2-3-4-5	at Birmingham

MISSISSIPPI
APRIL
Date	Opponent
7-8-9-10	at Montgomery
11-12-13	at West Tenn
15-16-17	at Jacksonville
18-19-20-21	Mont.
22-23-24	at Mobile
25-26-27	Huntsville
28-29-30	West Tenn

MAY
Date	Opponent
1	West Tenn
2-3-4	at Huntsville
6-7-8	at Jacksonville
9-10-11-12	at Birm.
13-14-15	Mobile
16-17-18	Birmingham
20-21-22	at Jacksonville
23-24-25-26	at Chat.
27-28-29-30	Mont.
31	Huntsville

JUNE
Date	Opponent
1-2-3	Huntsville
4-5-6-7	at Huntsville
9-10-11-12	at West Tenn
13-14-15	Chattanooga
16-17-18-19	West Tenn
21-22-23-24	at Carolina
25-26-27-28	at Tenn.
30	Mobile

JULY
Date	Opponent
1-2-3	Mobile
4-5-6-7	at Montgomery
8-9-10-11	Huntsville
15-16-17	at West Tenn
18-19-20-21	Mont.
22-23-24	Mobile
26-27-28	at Mobile
29-30-31	Tennessee

AUGUST
Date	Opponent
2-3-4	at Birmingham
5-6-7	at Huntsville
8-9-10	Birmingham
11-12-13-14	at Chat.
16-17-18-19-20-21	Jack.
22-23-24-25	West Tenn
26-27-28-29	at Carolina
30-31	Chattanooga

SEPTEMBER
Date	Opponent
1	Chattanooga
2-3-4-5	Carolina

MOBILE
APRIL
Date	Opponent
7-8-9-10	Tennessee
11-12-13	Chattanooga
15-16-17	at Tennessee
18-19-20-21	at Hunt.
22-23-24	Mississippi
25-26-27	at Chattanooga
28-29-30	Jacksonville

MAY
Date	Opponent
1	Jacksonville
2-3-4	Carolina
6-7	at West Tenn
9-10-11-12	Huntsville
13-14-15	at Mississippi
16-17-18	at Mont.
20-21-22	Montgomery
23-24-25-26	at W. Tenn
27-28-29-30	Jack.
31	at Jacksonville

JUNE
Date	Opponent
1-2-3	at Jacksonville
4-5-6-7	at Montgomery
9-10-11-12	Birmingham
13-14-15	Montgomery
16-17-18-19	at Birm.
21-22-23-24	Huntsville
25-26-27-28	West Tenn
30	at Mississippi

JULY
Date	Opponent
1-2-3	at Mississippi
4-5-6-7	Jacksonville
8-9-10-11	at Birm.
15-16-17	Tennessee
18-19-20-21	Huntsville
22-23-24	at Mississippi
26-27-28	Mississippi
29-30-31	at Jacksonville

AUGUST
Date	Opponent
2-3-4	at Montgomery
5-6-7	Jacksonville
8-9-10	at Huntsville
12-13-14-15	Mont.
16-17-18	at West Tenn
19-20-21	Birmingham
22-23-24-25	at Hunt.
26-27-28-29	at Carolina
31	West Tenn

SEPTEMBER
Date	Opponent
1	West Tenn
2-3-4-5	Jacksonville

MONTGOMERY
APRIL
Date	Opponent
7-8-9-10	Mississippi
11-12-13	Tennessee
15-16-17	at Birmingham
18-19-20-21	at Miss.
22-23-24	Birmingham
25-26-27	at West Tenn
28-29-30	Carolina

MAY
Date	Opponent
1	Carolina
2-3-4	Jacksonville
6-7-8	at Carolina
9-10-11-12	at Jack.
13-14-15	Huntsville
16-17-18	Mobile
20-21-22	at Mobile

Texas League / Southern League Schedules

23-24-25-26	Jack.
27-28-29-30	at Miss.
31	at Birmingham

JUNE

1-2-3	at Birmingham
4-5-6-7	Mobile
9-10-11-12	Tennessee
13-14-15	at Mobile
16-17-18-19	at Jack.
21-22-23-24	Tennessee
25-26-27-28	Chat.
30	at Birmingham

JULY

1-2-3	at Birmingham
4-5-6-7	Mississippi
8-9-10-11	at Jacksonville
15-16-17	Jacksonville
18-19-20-21	at Miss.
22-23-24	West Tenn
26-27-28	at Mobile
29-30-31	at Huntsville

AUGUST

2-3-4	Mobile
5-6-7	Birmingham
8-9-10	at Tennessee
12-13-14-15	at Mobile
16-17-18	Tennessee
19-20	at West Tenn
22-23-24-25	Jack.
26-27-28-29	Miss.
31	at Mobile

SEPTEMBER

1	at Mobile
2-3-4-5	at Tennessee

TENNESSEE

APRIL

7-8-9-10	at Mobile
11-12-13	at Mont.
15-16-17	Mobile
18-19-20-21	West Tenn
22-23-24	at Carolina
25-26-27	Birmingham
28-29-30	at Huntsville

MAY

1	at Huntsville
2-3-4	at Chattanooga
6-7-8	Huntsville
9-10-11-12	at West Tenn
13-14-15	Carolina
16-17-18	Chattanooga
20-21-22	at Carolina
23-24-25-26	Birm.
27-28-29-30	at Huntsville
31	West Tenn

JUNE

1-2-3	West Tenn
4-5-6-7	Birmingham
9-10-11-12	at Mont.
13-14-15	at Birmingham
16-17-18-19	Carolina
21-22-23-24	at Mont.
25-26-27-28	Mississippi
30	at Chattanooga

JULY

1-2-3	at Chattanooga
4-5-6-7	West Tenn
8-9-10-11	Chattanooga
15-16-17	at Mobile

18-19-20-21	at W. Tenn
22-23-24	Chattanooga
25-26-27	at Jacksonville
29-30-31	at Mississippi

AUGUST

2-3-4	Jacksonville
5-6-7	at Carolina
8-9-10	Mont.
11-12-13-14	Carolina
16-17-18	at Montgomery
19-20-21	Huntsville
22-23-24-25	at Birm.
26-27-28-29	at Hunt.
30-31	Huntsville

SEPTEMBER

1	Huntsville
2-3-4-5	Montgomery

WEST TENNESSEE

APRIL

7-8-9-10	Chattanooga
11-12-13	Mississippi
15-16-17	at Chat.
18-19-20-21	at Tenn.
22-23-24	Huntsville
25-26-27	Montgomery
28-29-30	at Mississippi

MAY

1	at Mississippi
2-3-4	at Birmingham
6-7	Mobile
9-10-11-12	Tennessee
13-14-15	at Chat.
16-17-18	Carolina
20-21-22	at Birm.

23-24-25-26	Mobile
27-28-29-30	Birm.
31	at Tennessee

JUNE

1-2-3	at Tennessee
4-5-6-7	at Carolina
9-10-11-12	Mississippi
13-14-15	at Huntsville
16-17-18-19	at Miss.
21-22-23-24	Jacksonville
25-26-27-28	at Mobile
30	Huntsville

JULY

1-2-3	Huntsville
4-5-6-7	at Tennessee
8-9-10-11	at Carolina
15-16-17	Mississippi
18-19-20-21	Tennessee
22-23-24	at Mont.
26-27-28	at Huntsville
29-30-31	Carolina

AUGUST

2-3-4	Huntsville
5-6-7	at Chattanooga
8-9-10	at Carolina
11-12-13-14	at Jack.
16-17-18	Mobile
19-20	Montgomery
22-23-24-25	at Miss.
26-27-28-29	Chattanooga
30-31	at Birmingham

SEPTEMBER

1	at Birmingham
2-3-4-5	Mobile

TEXAS LEAGUE

ARKANSAS

APRIL

7-8-9-10	Springfield
12-13-14-15-16	Wichita
17-18-19-20-21	at Tulsa
22-23-24-25-26	at Wich.
28-29-30	San Antonio

MAY

1	San Antonio
2-3-4	Corpus Christi
5-6-7	at San Antonio
8-9-10-11	at C.C.
13-14-15-16-17	Tulsa
18-19-20-21-22	at Spring.
23-24-25	Frisco
26-27-28-29	at Midland
30-31	at Frisco

JUNE

1-2	at Frisco
3-4-5	Midland
7-8-9-10	Tulsa
11-12-13-14-15	Spring.
16-17-18-19	at Wichita
23-24-25-26	C.C.
27-28-29	San Antonio

JULY

1-2-3-4-5	at Tulsa

6-7-8-9-9	Wichita
11-12-13-14	at S.A.
15-16-17	at C.C.
19-20-21-22-23	Tulsa
24-25-26-27	at Spring.
28-29-29-30-31	at Wich.

AUGUST

2-3-4-5-6	Springfield
8-9-10	at Midland
11-12-13	at Frisco
15-16-16-17	Midland
18-19-20-21	Frisco
23-24-25-26	Wichita
27-28-29-30	at Tulsa
31	at Springfield

SEPTEMBER

1-2-3-4	at Springfield

CORPUS CHRISTI

APRIL

7-8-9-10	at San Antonio
12-13-14-15-16	at Frisco
17-18-19-20-21	Midland
22-23-24-25-26	Frisco
28-29-30	at Springfield

MAY

1	at Springfield
2-3-4	at Arkansas

5-6-7	Springfield
8-9-10-11	Arkansas
13-14-15-16-17	at Mid.
18-19-20-21-22	S.A.
23-24-25	at Wichita
26-27-28-29	at Tulsa
30-31	Wichita

JUNE

1-2	Wichita
3-4-5	Tulsa
7-8-9-10	at Midland
11-12-13-14-15	at S.A.
16-17-18-19	Frisco
23-24-25-26	at Arkansas
27-28-29	at Spring.

JULY

1-2-3-4-5	Midland
6-7-8-9-10	at Frisco
11-12-13-14	Spring.
15-16-17	Arkansas
19-20-21-22-23	at Mid.
24-25-26-27	S.A.
28-29-30-31	Frisco

AUGUST

1	Frisco
2-3-4-5-6	at San Antonio
7-8-9-10	Tulsa
11-12-13	Wichita

15-16-17	at Tulsa
18-19-20-21	at Wichita
23-24-25-26	at Frisco
27-28-29-30	Midland
31	San Antonio

SEPTEMBER

1-2-3-4	San Antonio

FRISCO

APRIL

7-8-9-10	at Midland
12-13-14-15-16	C.C.
17-18-19-20-21	at S.A.
22-23-24-25-26	at C.C.
28-29-30	Tulsa

MAY

1	Tulsa
2-3-4	Wichita
5-6-7	at Tulsa
8-9-10-11	at Wichita
13-14-15-16-17	S.A.
18-19-20-21-22	Midland
23-24-25	at Arkansas
26-27-28-29	Spring.
30-31	Arkansas

JUNE

1-2	Arkansas
3-4-5	at Springfield

7-8-9-10	San Antonio
11-12-13-14-15	at Mid.
16-17-18-19	at C.C.
23-24-25-26	Wichita
27-28-29	Tulsa
30	at San Antonio

JULY
1-2-3-4	at San Antonio
6-7-8-9-10	C.C.
11-12-13-14	at Tulsa
15-16-17	at Wichita
19-20-21-22-23	S.A.
24-25-26-27	Midland
28-29-30-31	at C.C.

AUGUST
1	at Corpus Christi
3-4-5-6-7	at Midland
8-9-10	Springfield
11-12-13	Arkansas
15-16-17	at Springfield
18-19-20-21	at Arkansas
23-24-25-26	C.C.
27-28-29-30	at S.A.
31	Midland

SEPTEMBER
| 1-2-3-4 | Midland |

MIDLAND

APRIL
7-8-9-10	Frisco
12-13-14-15-16	S.A.
17-18-19-20-21	at C.C.
22-23-24-25-26	at S.A.
28-29-30	Wichita

MAY
1	Wichita
2-3-4	Tulsa
5-6-7	at Wichita
8-9-10-11	at Tulsa
13-14-15-16-17	C.C.
18-19-20-21-22	at Frisco
23-24-25	Springfield
26-27-28-29	Arkansas
30-31	at Springfield

JUNE
1-2	at Springfield
3-4-5	at Arkansas
7-8-9-10	Corpus Christi
11-12-13-14-15	Frisco
16-17-18-19	at S.A.
23-24-25	at Tulsa
27-28-29	Wichita

JULY
1-2-3-4-5	at C.C.
6-7-8-9-10	San Antonio
11-12-13-14	at Wichita
15-16-17-18	Tulsa
19-20-21-22-23	C.C.
24-25-26-27	at Frisco
28-29-30-31	at S.A.

AUGUST
1	at San Antonio
3-4-5-6-7	Frisco
8-9-10	Arkansas
11-12-13	at Springfield

15-16-16-17	at Arkansas
18-19-20-21	Springfield
23-24-25-26	S.A.
27-28-29-30	at C.C.
31	at Frisco

SEPTEMBER
| 1-2-3-4 | at Frisco |

SAN ANTONIO

APRIL
7-8-9-10	Corpus Christi
12-13-14-15-16	at Mid.
17-18-19-20-21	Frisco
22-23-24-25-26	Midland
28-29-30	at Arkansas

MAY
1	at Arkansas
2-3-4	at Springfield
5-6-7	Arkansas
8-9-10-11	Springfield
13-14-15-16-17	at Frisco
18-19-20-21-22	at C.C.
23-24-25	Tulsa
26-27-28-29	Wichita
30-31	at Tulsa

JUNE
1-2	at Tulsa
3-4-5	at Wichita
7-8-9-10	at Frisco
11-12-13-14-15	C.C.
16-17-18-19	Midland
23-24-25-26	at Spring.
27-28-29	at Arkansas
30	Frisco

JULY
1-2-3-4	Frisco
6-7-8-9-10	at Midland
11-12-13-14	Arkansas
15-16-17	Springfield
19-20-21-22-23	at Frisco
24-25-26-27	at C.C.
28-29-30-31	Midland

AUGUST
1	Midland
2-3-4-5-6	Corpus Christi
8-9-10	Wichita
12-13-14	at Tulsa
15-16-16-17	at Wichita
18-19-20-21	Tulsa
23-24-25-26	at Midland
27-28-29-30	at Wichita
31	at Corpus Christi

SEPTEMBER
| 1-2-3-4 | at Corpus Christi |

SPRINGFIELD

APRIL
7-8-9-10	at Arkansas
12-13-14-15-16	Tulsa
17-18-19-20-21	at Wich.
22-23-24-25-26	at Tulsa
28-29-30	Corpus Christi

MAY
| 1 | Corpus Christi |
| 2-3-4 | San Antonio |

5-6-7	at Corpus Christi
8-9-10-11	at S.A.
13-14-15-16-17	Wichita
18-19-20-21-22	Ark.
23-24-25	at Midland
26-27-28-29	at Frisco
30-31	Midland

JUNE
1-2	Midland
3-4-5	Frisco
7-8-9-10	Wichita
11-12-13-14-15	at Ark.
16-17-18-19	at Tulsa
23-24-25	S.A.
27-28-29	Corpus Christi

JULY
1-2-3-4-5	at Wichita
6-7-8-9-10	Tulsa
11-12-13-14	at C.C.
15-16-17	at San Antonio
19-20-21-22-23	Wichita
24-25-26-27	Arkansas
28-29-30-31	at Tulsa

AUGUST
1	at Tulsa
2-3-4-5-6	at Arkansas
8-9-10	at Frisco
11-12-13	Midland
14-15-16-17	Frisco
18-19-20-21	at Midland
23-24-25-26	Tulsa
27-28-29-30	at Wichita
31	Arkansas

SEPTEMBER
| 1-2-3-4 | Arkansas |

TULSA

APRIL
7-8-9-10	at Wichita
12-13-14-15-16	at Spring.
17-18-19-20-21	Ark.
22-23-24-25-26	Spring.
28-29-30	at Frisco

MAY
1	at Frisco
2-3-4	at Midland
5-6-7	Frisco
8-9-10-11	Midland
13-14-15-16-17	at Ark.
18-19-20-21-22	Wichita
23-24-25	at San Antonio
26-27-28-29	C.C.
30-31	San Antonio

JUNE
1-2	San Antonio
3-4-5	at Corpus Christi
7-8-9-10	at Arkansas
11-12-13-14-15	at Wich.
16-17-18-19	Springfield
23-24-25	Midland
27-28-29	at Frisco

JULY
1-2-3-4-5	Arkansas
6-7-8-9-10	at Spring.
11-12-13-14	Frisco

15-16-17-18	at Midland
19-20-21-22-23	at Ark.
24-24-25-26-27	at Wich.
28-29-30-31	Spring.

AUGUST
1	Springfield
3-4-5-6	Wichita
7-8-9-10	at C.C.
12-13-14	San Antonio
15-16-17	Corpus Christi
18-19-20-21	at S.A.
23-24-25-26	at Spring.
27-28-29-30	Arkansas
31	Wichita

SEPTEMBER
| 1-2-3-4 | Wichita |

WICHITA

APRIL
7-8-9-10	Tulsa
12-13-14-15-16	at Ark.
17-18-19-20-21	Spring.
22-23-24-25-26	Ark.
28-29-30	at Midland

MAY
1	at Midland
2-3-4	at Frisco
5-6-7	Midland
8-9-10-11	Frisco
13-14-15-16-17	at Spring.
18-19-20-21-22	at Tulsa
23-24-25	Corpus Christi
26-27-28-29	at S.A.
30-31	at Corpus Christi

JUNE
1-2	at Corpus Christi
3-4-5	San Antonio
7-8-9-10	at Spring.
11-12-13-14-15	Tulsa
16-17-18-19	Arkansas
23-24-25-26	at Frisco
27-28-29	at Midland

JULY
1-2-3-4-5	Spring.
6-7-8-9-9	at Arkansas
11-12-13-14	Midland
15-16-17	Frisco
19-20-21-22-23	at Spring.
24-24-25-26-27	Tulsa
28-29-29-30-31	Ark.

AUGUST
3-4-5-6	at Tulsa
8-9-10	at San Antonio
11-12-13	at C.C.
15-16-16-17	S.A.
18-19-20-21	C.C.
23-24-25-26	at Arkansas
27-28-29-30	Springfield
31	at Tulsa

SEPTEMBER
| 1-2-3-4 | at Tulsa |

HIGH CLASS A
CALIFORNIA LEAGUE

BAKERSFIELD

APRIL
7-8-9	at Inland Empire
11-12-13	at Visalia
15-16-17-17	**Visalia**
18-19-20	at Modesto
22-23-24	**Inland Empire**
25	**Modesto**
26-27-28	**High Desert**
29-30	**San Jose**

MAY
1	**San Jose**
2-3-4	at R.C.
5-6-7-8	at San Jose
10-11-12	**Modesto**
13-14-15	**Visalia**
16-17-18	at Modesto
19-20-21-22	at Stockton
23-24-25-26	**San Jose**
27-28-29	**Lake Elsinore**
30-31	at San Jose

JUNE
1	at San Jose
2-3-4-5	at Stockton
7-8-9	**Lancaster**
10-11-12-13	**Stockton**
14-15-16	at Lancaster
17-18-19	at High Desert
20-21-22	at Visalia
23-24-25	at High Desert

JULY
1-2-3	**Inland Empire**
4	at Lancaster
5-6	at R.C.
8-9-10	**Stockton**
11-12-13	**Lake Elsinore**
14	at Modesto
15-16-17	at Stockton
18-19-20	**R.C.**
21-22-23-24	**Visalia**
26-27-28	at Modesto
29-30-31	at San Jose

AUGUST
1	at San Jose
2-3-4	**Modesto**
5-6-7	at Visalia
8-9-10-11	at San Jose
12-13-14	**San Jose**
15-16-17-18	**Modesto**
19-20-21	at Lancaster
23-24-25	**Lancaster**
26-27-28	**Stockton**
29-30-31	**Visalia**

SEPTEMBER
1	**Visalia**
2-3-4	at Lake Elsinore

HIGH DESERT

APRIL
7-8-9-10	**Lancaster**
11-12-13-14	**I.E.**
15-16-17	at R.C.
18-19	**San Jose**
21-22-23-24	at L.E.
26-27-28	at Bakersfield
29-30	at Modesto

MAY
1	at Modesto
2-3-4	at Lake Elsinore
5-6-7-8	**R.C.**
9-10-11-12	**L.E.**
13-14-15-16	at Lan.
17-18-19	at I.E.
20-21-22	**Inland Empire**
24-25-26	at Stockton
27-28-29	at I.E.
30-31	at Lancaster

JUNE
1-2	at Lancaster
3-4-5	**Modesto**
7-8-9	**R.C.**
10-11-12-13	at R.C.
14-15-16	**Visalia**
17-18-19	**Bakersfield**
20-21-22	at Modesto
23-24-25	**Bakersfield**
30	at Lancaster

JULY
1-2-3	**Lake Elsinore**
4-5-6-7	at I.E.
8-9-10	at Lancaster
11-12-13	**R.C.**
14-15-16-17	**San Jose**
18-19-20	at Visalia
22-23-24	at San Jose
26-27-28	**Visalia**
29-30-31	at L.E.

AUGUST
1-2-3-4	at R.C.
5-6-7	**Lancaster**
8-9-10-11	**Inland Empire**
12-13-14	at L.E.
16-17-18	**Stockton**
19-20-21-22	**R.C.**
23-24-25	at R.C.
26-27-28	at Lancaster
29-30-31	**Lake Elsinore**

SEPTEMBER
1	**Lake Elsinore**
2-3-4	**Lancaster**

INLAND EMPIRE

APRIL
7-8-9	**Bakersfield**
11-12-13-14	at H.D.
15-16-17	**Modesto**
18-19-20-21	**Lancaster**
22-23-24	at Bakersfield
25-26-27	at Visalia
29-30	at R.C.

MAY
1	at R.C.
2-3-4-5	**Lancaster**
6-7-8	**Stockton**
10-11-12	at Lancaster
13-14-15	at L.E.
16	**Lake Elsinore**
17-18-19	**High Desert**
20-21-22	at High Desert
23	**R.C.**
24-25	at R.C.
27-28-29	**High Desert**
30-31	**R.C.**

JUNE
1-2	**R.C.**
3-4-5-6	at Lake Elsinore
7-8-9	at Stockton
10-11-12	at San Jose
13-14-15	at L.E.
16-17-18-19	**L.E.**
20-21-22	**Stockton**
23	at Lake Elsinore
24-25	**Lake Elsinore**

JULY
1-2-3	at Bakersfield
4-5-6-7	**High Desert**
8-9-10	**Modesto**
11-12-13	at San Jose
15-16-17	at Modesto
18-19-20	**Lake Elsinore**
21	**R.C.**
22-23	at R.C.
25-26-27-28	**Lancaster**
29	at R.C.
30-31	**R.C.**

AUGUST
1-2-3-4	**Lancaster**
5	**R.C.**
6-7	at Rancho Cuca
8-9-10-11	at High Desert
12-13-14	**Lancaster**
15-16-17	**San Jose**
19-20-21	at Visalia
22-23-24-25	at L.E.
26-27-28	**Visalia**
29	**R.C.**
30-31	at Lancaster

SEPTEMBER
1	at Lancaster
2-3-4-5	**R.C.**

LAKE ELSINORE

APRIL
7	**R.C.**
8-9-10	at R.C.
12-13-14	**Stockton**
15-16-17	**San Jose**
18-19-20	at R.C.
21-22-23-24	**H.D.**
25-26-27	**R.C.**
28	at R.C.
29-30	at Visalia

MAY
1	at Visalia
2-3-4	**High Desert**
6-7-8	**Lancaster**
9-10-11-12	at H.D.
13-14-15	**Inland Empire**
16	at Inland Empire
17-18-19	**Visalia**
20-21-22	at Lancaster
23-24-25	**Lancaster**
27-28-29	at Bakersfield
31	**Modesto**

JUNE
1-2	**Modesto**
3-4-5-6	**Inland Empire**
7-8-9	at San Jose
10-11-12	at Modesto
13-14-15	**Inland Empire**
16-17-18-19	at I.E.
20-21-22	**R.C.**
23	**Inland Empire**
24-25	at Inland Empire
30	**R.C.**

JULY
1-2-3	at High Desert
4	**R.C.**
5-6-7	**Lancaster**
8-9-10	**R.C.**
11-12-13	at Bakersfield
15-16-17	at Visalia
18-19-20	at I.E.
22-23-24	**Modesto**
25-26-27-28	at R.C.
29-30-31	**High Desert**

AUGUST
2-3-4	at San Jose
5-6-7	at Stockton
8-9-10-11	at Lancaster
12-13-14	**High Desert**
16-17-18	at Lancaster
19-20-21	**Stockton**
22-23-24-25	**I.E.**
26-27-28	at R.C.
29-30-31	at High Desert

SEPTEMBER
1	at High Desert
2-3-4	**Bakersfield**
5	at Lancaster

LANCASTER

APRIL
7-8-9-10	at High Desert
11	at R.C.
12-13-14	**San Jose**
15-16-17	**Stockton**
18-19-20-21	at I.E.
21-22-23	**R.C.**
26-27-28	at Modesto
29-30	at Stockton

MAY
1	at Stockton
2-3-4-5	at Inland Empire
6-7-8	at Lake Elsinore
10-11-12	Inland Empire
13-14-15-16	H.D.
17-18-19	at R.C.
20-21-22	Lake Elsinore
23-24-25	at L.E.
26-27-28-29	R.C.
30-31	High Desert

JUNE
1-2	High Desert
3-4-5	at R.C.
7-8-9	at Bakersfield
10-11-12	at Visalia
14-15-16	Bakersfield
17-18-19	Visalia
20-21-22	at San Jose
23-24-25	at Modesto
30	High Desert

JULY
1-2	R.C.
3	at R.C.
4	Bakersfield
5-6-7	at Lake Elsinore
8-9-10	High Desert
11-12-13	Modesto
14-15-16-17	at R.C.
18-19-20	San Jose
22-23-24	at Stockton
25-26-27-28	at I.E.
29-30-31	Visalia

AUGUST
1-2-3-4	Inland Empire
5-6-7	at High Desert
8-9-10-11	Lake Elsinore
12-13-14	at I.E.
16-17-18	Lake Elsinore
19-20-21	Bakersfield
23-24-25	at Bakersfield
26-27-28	High Desert
30-31	Inland Empire

SEPTEMBER
1	Inland Empire
2-3-4	at High Desert
5	Lake Elsinore

MODESTO

APRIL
7-8-9-10	Stockton
12-13-14	R.C.
15-16-17	at I.E.
18-19-20	Bakersfield
21-22-23-24	at San Jose
25	at Bakersfield
26-27-28	Lancaster
29-30	High Desert

MAY
1	High Desert
2-3-4	at Stockton
5-6-7-8	at Visalia
10-11-12	at Bakersfield
13-14-15	at Stockton
16-17-18	Bakersfield
20-21-22	San Jose
23-24-25-26	at Visalia
27-28-29	Stockton
31	at Lake Elsinore

JUNE
1-2	at Lake Elsinore
3-4-5	at High Desert
6-7-8-9	Visalia
10-11-12	Lake Elsinore
14-15-16	at R.C.
17-18-19	at San Jose
20-21-22	High Desert
23-24-25	Lancaster

JULY
1-2-3	at San Jose
4-5-6-7	Visalia
8-9-10	at Inland Empire
11-12-13	at Lancaster
14	Bakersfield
15-16-17	Inland Empire
19-20-21	Stockton
22-23-24	at L.E.
26-27-28	Bakersfield
29-30-31	Stockton

AUGUST
2-3-4	at Bakersfield
5-6-7	San Jose
9-10-11	at Visalia
12-13-14	R.C.
15-16-17-18	at Bak.
19-20-21	at San Jose
22-23-24	Visalia
25-26-27-28	San Jose
29-30-31	at Stockton

SEPTEMBER
1	at Stockton
2-3-4-5	at Visalia

RANCHO CUCAMONGA

APRIL
7	at Lake Elsinore
8-9-10	Lake Elsinore
11	Lancaster
12-13-14	at Modesto
15-16-17	High Desert
18-19-20	Lake Elsinore
22-23-24	at Lancaster
25-26-27	at L.E.
28	Lake Elsinore
29-30	Inland Empire

MAY
1	Inland Empire
2-3-4	Bakersfield
5-6-7-8	at High Desert
10-11-12	at Visalia
13-14-15	at San Jose
17-18-19	Lancaster
20-21-22	Visalia
23	at Inland Empire
24-25	Inland Empire
26-27-28-29	at Lan.
30-31	at Inland Empire

JUNE
1-2	at Inland Empire
3-4-5	Lancaster
7-8-9	at High Desert
10-11-12-13	H.D.
14-15-16	Modesto
17-18-19	at Stockton
20-21-22	at L.E.
23-24-25	Stockton
30	at Lake Elsinore

JULY
1-2	at Lancaster
3	Lancaster
4	at Lake Elsinore
5-6	Bakersfield
8-9-10	at Lake Elsinore
11-12-13	at High Desert
14-15-16-17	Lancaster
18-19-20	at Bakersfield
21	at Inland Empire
22-23	Inland Empire
25-26-27-28	L.E.
29	Inland Empire
30-31	at Inland Empire

AUGUST
1-2-3-4	High Desert
5	at Inland Empire
6-7	Inland Empire
9-10-11	at Stockton
12-13-14	at Modesto
16-17-18	Visalia
19-20-21-22	at H.D.
23-24-25	High Desert
26-27-28	Lake Elsinore
29	at Inland Empire
30-31	San Jose

SEPTEMBER
1	San Jose
2-3-4-5	at Inland Empire

SAN JOSE

APRIL
7-8-9-10	at Visalia
12-13-14	at Lancaster
15-16-17	at L.E.
18-19	at High Desert
21-22-23-24	Modesto
25-26-27	Stockton
28	at Stockton
29-30	at Bakersfield

MAY
1	at Bakersfield
2-3-4	Visalia
5-6-7-8	Bakersfield
9	Stockton
10-11-12	at Stockton
13-14-15	R.C.
16-17-18	Stockton
20-21-21-22	at Modesto
23-24-25-26	at Bak.
27-28-29	at Visalia
30-31	Bakersfield

JUNE
1	Bakersfield
2-3-4-5	at Visalia
7-8-9	Lake Elsinore
10-11-12	Inland Empire
14-15-16	at Stockton
17-18-19	Modesto
20-21-22	Lancaster
23-24-25	Visalia

JULY
30	Stockton
1-2-3	Modesto
4-5-6-7	at Stockton
8-9-10	Visalia
11-12-13	Inland Empire
14-15-16-17	at H.D.
18-19-20	at Lancaster
22-23-24	High Desert
26-27-28	at Stockton
29-30-31	Bakersfield

AUGUST
1	Bakersfield
2-3-4	Lake Elsinore
5-6-7	at Modesto
8-9-10-11	Bakersfield
12-13-14	at Bakersfield
15-16-17	at I.E.
19-20-21	Modesto
22-23-24	Stockton
25-26-27-28	at Modesto
30-31	at R.C.

SEPTEMBER
1	at R.C.
2-3-4	at Stockton
5	Stockton

STOCKTON

APRIL
7-8-9-10	at Modesto
12-13-14	at L.E.
15-16-17	at Lancaster
18-19-20	at Visalia
21-22-23-24	Visalia
25-26-27	at San Jose
28	San Jose
29-30	Lancaster

MAY
1	Lancaster
2-3-4	Modesto
6-7-8	at Inland Empire
9	at San Jose
10-11-12	San Jose
13-14-15	Modesto
16-17-18	at San Jose
19-20-21-22	High Desert
24-25-26	High Desert
27-28-29	at Modesto
30-31	at Visalia

JUNE
1	at Visalia
2-3-4-5	Bakersfield
7-8-9	Inland Empire
10-11-12-13	at Bak.
14-15-16	San Jose
17-18-19	R.C.
20-21-22	at I.E.
23-24-25	at R.C.
30	at San Jose

JULY
1-2-3	at Visalia
4-5-6-7	San Jose
8-9-10	at Visalia
12-13-14	Visalia
15-16-17	Bakersfield
19-20-21	at Modesto

<table>
<tr><td>22-23-24</td><td>Lancaster</td></tr>
<tr><td>26-27-28</td><td>San Jose</td></tr>
<tr><td>29-30-30-31</td><td>at Modesto</td></tr>
</table>

AUGUST
1-2-3-4	at Visalia
5-6-7	Lake Elsinore
9-10-11	R.C.
12-13-13-14	Visalia
16-17-18	at High Desert
19-20-21	at L.E.
22-23-24	at San Jose
26-27-28	at Bakersfield
29-30-31	Modesto

SEPTEMBER
1	Modesto
2-3-4	San Jose
5	at San Jose

VISALIA

APRIL
7-8-9-10	San Jose
11-12-13	Bakersfield
15-16-17-17	at Bak.
18-19-20-21-22-23-24	Stock.
25-26-27	Inland Empire
29-30	Lake Elsinore

MAY
1	Lake Elsinore
2-3-4	at San Jose
5-6-7-8	Modesto
10-11-12	R.C.
13-14-15	at Bakersfield
17-18-19	at L.E.
20-21-22	at R.C.
23-24-25-26	Modesto

27-28-29	San Jose
30-31	at Stockton

JUNE
1	at Stockton
2-3-4-5	San Jose
6-7-8-9	at Modesto
10-11-12	Lancaster
14-15-16	at High Desert
17-18-19	at Lancaster
20-21-22	Bakersfield
23-24-25	at San Jose
30	Bakersfield

JULY
1-2-3	Stockton
4-5-6-7	at Modesto
8-9-10	at San Jose
12-13-14	at Stockton
15-16-17	Lake Elsinore

18-19-20	High Desert
21-22-23-24	at Bak.
26-27-28	at High Desert
29-30-31	at Lancaster

AUGUST
1-2-3-4	Stockton
5-6-7	Bakersfield
9-10-11	Modesto
12-13-13-14	at Stockton
16-17-18	at R.C.
19-20-21	Inland Empire
22-23-24	at Modesto
26-27-28	at I.E.
29-30-31	at Bakersfield

SEPTEMBER
1	at Bakersfield
2-3-4-5	Modesto

CAROLINA LEAGUE

FREDERICK

APRIL
8-9-10	at Lynchburg
11-12-13-14	Salem
15-16-17	Kinston
18-19-20	at Salem
21-22-23-24	Wilmington
26-27-28	at W.-S.
29-30	at Potomac

MAY
1	at Potomac
2-3-4-5	Winston-Salem
6-7-8	Wilmington
9-10-11-12	at M.B.
13-14-15	at Kinston
16-17-18	Myrtle Beach
20-21-22	Lynchburg
23-24-25	at Wilmington
26-27-28-29	at Lynch.
30-31	Salem

JUNE
1	Salem
2-3-4-5	Kinston
6-7-8	at Salem
10-11-12	Potomac
13-14-15-16	at W.-S.
17-18-19	Potomac
20-21-22	W.-S.
24-25-26	at Potomac
30	at Myrtle Beach

JULY
1-2	at Myrtle Beach
3-4-5	at Lynchburg
6-7-8	Myrtle Beach
9-10-11	Lynchburg
13-14-15-16	at Wilm.
18-19-20-21	at Kinston
22-23-24	Salem
25-26-27	Kinston
28-29-30-31	at Salem

AUGUST
1-2-3	Wilmington
4-5-6	at W.-S.
7-8-9-10	at Potomac

12-13-14	Winton-Salem
15-16-17-18	Potomac
19-20-21	at M.B.
22-23-24	at Kinston
26-27-28-29	M.B.
30-31	Lynchburg

SEPTEMBER
1-2	Lynchburg
3-4-5	at Wilmington

KINSTON

APRIL
8-9-10	W.-S.
11-12-13-14	Wilmington
15-16-17	at Frederick
18-19-20	at Wilm.
21-22-23-24	M.B.
26-27-28	Lynchburg
29-30	at Salem

MAY
1	at Salem
2-3-4-5	at Lynchburg
6-7-8	Salem
9-10-11-12	at Potomac
13-14-15	Frederick
16-17-18	Potomac
20-21-22	at W.-S.
23-24-25	at Salem
26-27-28-29	W.-S.
30-31	Wilmington

JUNE
1	Wilmington
2-3-4-5	at Frederick
6-7-8	at Wilmington
10-11-12	Myrtle Beach
13-14-15-16	Lynchburg
17-18-19	at M.B.
21-22-23	at Lynchburg
24-25-26	Salem
30	at Potomac

JULY
1-2	at Potomac
3-4-5	at W.-S.
6-7-8	Wilmington
9-10-11	Winston-Salem

13-14-15-16	at Salem
18-19-20-21	Frederick
22-23-24	Potomac
25-26-27	at Frederick
28-29-30-31	at Wilm.

AUGUST
1-2-3	Myrtle Beach
4-5-6	Lynchburg
8-9-10-11	at M.B.
12-13-14	at Lynchburg
15-16-17-18	Salem
19-20-21	at Potomac
22-23-24	Frederick
26-27-28-29	Potomac
30-31	at W.-S.

SEPTEMBER
1-2	at W.-S.
3-4-5	at Myrtle Beach

LYNCHBURG

APRIL
8-9-10	Frederick
11-12-13-14	Potomac
15-16-17	at W.-S.
18-19-20	at Potomac
21-22-23-24	Salem
26-27-28	at Kinston
29-30	at Myrtle Beach

MAY
1	at Myrtle Beach
2-3-4-5	Kinston
6-7-8	Myrtle Beach
9-10-11-12	at Wilm.
13-14-15	W.-S.
16-17-18	Wilmington
20-21-22	at Frederick
23-24-25	at Potomac
26-27-28-29	Frederick
30-31	Potomac

JUNE
1	Potomac
2-3-4-5	at W.-S.
6-7-8	at M.B.
10	Salem
11	at Salem

11	Salem
13-14-15-16	at Kinston
17-18	at Salem
19	Salem
21-22-23	Kinston
24-25-26	Myrtle Beach
30	at Wilmington

JULY
1-2	at Wilmington
3-4-5	Frederick
6-7-8	Salem
9-10-11	at Frederick
14-15-16-17	at Potomac
18-19-20-21	W.-S.
22-23-24	Wilmington
25-26-27	at W.-S.
28-29-30-31	at M.B.

AUGUST
1-2-3	Potomac
4-5-6	at Kinston
8-9-10-11	at Salem
12-13-14	Kinston
15-16-17-18	M.B.
19-20-21	at Wilmington
22-23-24	W.-S.
26-27-28-29	Wilmington
30-31	at Frederick

SEPTEMBER
1-2	at Frederick
3-4-5	at Salem

MYRTLE BEACH

APRIL
7-8-9-10	Wilmington
11-12-13-14	at W.-S.
15-16-17	Potomac
18-19-20	W.-S.
21-22-23-24	at Kinston
26-27-28	Salem
29-30	Lynchburg

MAY
1	Lynchburg
2-3-4-5	at Salem
6-7-8	at Lynchburg
9-10-11-12	Frederick

13-14-15	at Potomac
16-17-18	at Frederick
19-20-21	at Wilmington
23-24-25	**W.-S.**
27-28-29	**Wilmington**
30-31	at W.-S.

JUNE
1	at Winston-Salem
2-3-4-5	at Potomac
6-7-8	**Lynchburg**
10-11-12	at Kinston
13-14-15-16	**Salem**
17-18-19	**Kinston**
21-22-23	**Salem**
24-25-26	at Lynchburg
30	**Frederick**

JULY
1-2	**Frederick**
3-4-5	at Potomac
6-7-8	at Frederick
9-10-11	**Wilmington**
13-14-15-16	**W.-S.**
18-19-20-21	at Wilm.
22-23-24	at W.-S.
25-26-27	**Potomac**
28-29-30-31	**Lynchburg**

AUGUST
1-2-3	at Kinston
4-5-6	at Salem
8-9-10-11	**Kinston**
12-13-14	at Salem
15-16-17-18	at Lynch.
19-20-21	**Frederick**
23-24-25	at Wilmington
26-27-28-29	at Frederick
30-31	**Potomac**

SEPTEMBER
1-2	**Potomac**
3-4-5	**Kinston**

POTOMAC

APRIL
8-9-10	at Salem
11-12-13-14	at Lynch.
15-16-27	at M.B.
18-19-20	**Lynchburg**
21-22-23-24	at W-S
26-27-28	**Wilmington**
29-30	**Frederick**

MAY
1	**Frederick**
2-3-4-5	at Wilmington
6-7-8	at W.-S.
9-10-11-12	**Kinston**
13-14-15	**Myrtle Beach**
16-17-18	at Kinston
20-21-22	**Salem**
23-24-25	**Lynchburg**
26-27-28-29	at Salem
30-31	at Lynchburg

JUNE
1	at Lynchburg
2-3-4-5	**Myrtle Beach**
6-7-8	**W.-S.**
10-11-12	at Frederick

13-14-15-16	**Wilmington**
17-18-19	at Frederick
21-22-23	at Wilmington
24-25-26	**Frederick**
30	**Kinston**

JULY
1-2	**Kinston**
3-4-5	**Myrtle Beach**
6-7-8	at W.-S.
9-10-11	at Salem
14-15-16-17	**Lynchburg**
18-19-20-21	**Salem**
22-23-24	at Kinston
25-26-27	at M.B.
28-29-30-31	**W.-S.**

AUGUST
1-2-3	at Lynchburg
4-5-6	**Wilmington**
7-8-9-10	**Frederick**
12-13-14	at Wilmington
15-16-17-18	at Frederick
19-20-21	**Kinston**
23-24-25	**Salem**
26-27-28-29	at Kinston
30-31	at Myrtle Beach

SEPTEMBER
1-2	at Myrtle Beach
3-4-5	**Winston-Salem**

SALEM

APRIL
8-9-10	**Potomac**
11-12-13-14	at Frederick
15-16-17	at Wilmington
18-19-20	**Frederick**
21-22-23-24	at Lynch.
26-27-28	at M.B.
29-30	**Kinston**

MAY
1	**Kinston**
2-3-4-5	**Myrtle Beach**
6-7-8	at Kinston
9-10-11-12	**W.-S.**
13-14-15	**Wilmington**
17-18-19	at W.-S.
20-21-22	at Potomac
23-24-25	**Kinston**
26-27-28-29	**Potomac**
30-31	at Frederick

JUNE
1	at Frederick
2-3-4-5	at Wilmington
6-7-8	**Frederick**
10	at Lynchburg
11	**Lynchburg**
11	at Lynchburg
13-14-15-16	at M.B.
17-18	**Lynchburg**
19	at Lynchburg
21-22-23	at M.B.
24-25-26	at Kinston
30	at Winston-Salem

JULY
1-2	at Winston-Salem
3-4-5	at Wilmington

6-7-8	at Lynchburg
9-10-11	**Potomac**
13-14-15-16	**Kinston**
18-19-20-21	at Potomac
22-23-24	at Frederick
25-26-27	**Wilmington**
28-29-30-31	**Frederick**

AUGUST
1-2-3	**Winston-Salem**
4-5-6	**Myrtle Beach**
8-9-10-11	**Lynchburg**
12-13-14	**Myrtle Beach**
15-16-17-18	at Kinston
19-20-21	**W.-S.**
23-24-25	at Potomac
26-27-28-29	at W.-S.
30-31	**Wilmington**

SEPTEMBER
1-2	**Wilmington**
3-4-5	**Lynchburg**

WILMINGTON

APRIL
7-8-9-10	at M.B.
11-12-13-14	at Kinston
15-16-17	**Salem**
18-19-20	**Kinston**
21-22-23-24	at Frederick
26-27-28	at Potomac
29-30	**Winston-Salem**

MAY
1	**Winston-Salem**
2-3-4-5	**Potomac**
6-7-8	at Frederick
9-10-11-12	**Lynchburg**
13-14-15	at Salem
16-17-18	at Lynchburg
19-20-21	**Myrtle Beach**
23-24-25	**Frederick**
27-28-29	at M.B.
30-31	at Kinston

JUNE
1	at Kinston
2-3-4-5	**Salem**
6-7-8	**Kinston**
10-11-12	at W.-S.
13-14-15-16	at Potomac
17-18-19	**W.-S.**
21-22-23	**Potomac**
24-25-26	at W.-S.
30	**Lynchburg**

JULY
1-2	**Lynchburg**
3-4-5	**Salem**
6-7-8	at Kinston
9-10-11	at M.B.
13-14-15-16	**Frederick**
18-19-20-21	**M.B.**
22-23-24	at Lynchburg
25-26-27	at Salem
28-29-30-31	**Kinston**

AUGUST
1-2-3	at Frederick
4-5-6	at Potomac
8-9-10-11	**W.-S.**

12-13-14	**Potomac**
15-16-17-18	at W-S
19-20-21	**Lynchburg**
23-24-25	**Myrtle Beach**
26-27-28-29	at Lynch.
30-31	at Salem

SEPTEMBER
1-2	at Salem
3-4-5	**Frederick**

WINSTON-SALEM

APRIL
8-9-10	at Kinston
11-12-13-14	**M.B.**
15-16-17	**Lynchburg**
18-19-20	at M.B.
21-22-23-24	**Potomac**
26-27-28	**Frederick**
29-30	at Wilmington

MAY
1	at Wilmington
2-3-4-5	at Frederick
6-7-8	**Potomac**
9-10-11-12	at Salem
13-14-15	at Lynchburg
17-18-19	**Salem**
20-21-22	**Kinston**
23-24-25	at M.B.
26-27-28-29	at Kinston
30-31	**Myrtle Beach**

JUNE
1	**Myrtle Beach**
2-3-4-5	**Lynchburg**
6-7-8	at Potomac
10-11-12	**Wilmington**
13-14-15-16	**Frederick**
17-18-19	at Wilmington
20-21-22	at Frederick
24-25-26	**Wilmington**
30	**Salem**

JULY
1-2	**Salem**
3-4-5	**Kinston**
6-7-8	**Potomac**
9-10-11	at Kinston
13-14-15-16	at M.B.
18-19-20-21	at Lynch.
22-23-24	**Myrtle Beach**
25-26-27	**Lynchburg**
28-29-30-31	at Potomac

AUGUST
1-2-3	at Salem
4-5-6	**Frederick**
8-9-10-11	at Wilmington
12-13-14	at Frederick
15-16-17-18	**Wilmington**
19-20-21	at Salem
22-23-24	at Lynchburg
26-27-28-29	**Salem**
30-31	**Kinston**

SEPTEMBER
1-2	**Kinston**
3-4-5	at Potomac

FLORIDA STATE LEAGUE

BREVARD

APRIL
7-8	Daytona
9-10	at Daytona
11-12-13	at St. Lucie
14-15-16	Jupiter
18-19-20	St. Lucie
21-22-23	at Jupiter
24-25-26	at Palm Beach
27-28-29	Vero Beach
30	Palm Beach

MAY
1-2	Palm Beach
3-4-5	at Vero Beach
6-7-8	Dunedin
11-12-13-14	Clearwater
15-16-17-18	at Tampa
19-20-21-22	Sarasota
23-24-25-26	at Lakeland
27-28-29-30	at F.M.

JUNE
1-2	Daytona
3-4	at Daytona
5-6-7	Jupiter
8-9-10	at St. Lucie
11-12-13	at Vero Beach
14-15-16	Palm Beach
20-21-22	Vero Beach
23-24-25	at Palm Beach
26-27-28	at Jupiter
29-30	St. Lucie

JULY
1	St. Lucie
2	Daytona
3-4-5	at Daytona
6-7-8-9	at Clearwater
11-12-13-14	at Dunedin
15-16-17-18	Fort Myers
20-21-22	Daytona
23	at Daytona
24-25-26-27	Lakeland
28-29-30-31	Tampa

AUGUST
2-3-4-5	at Sarasota
6-7-8	at St. Lucie
9-10-11	Jupiter
12-13-14	St. Lucie
16-17-18	at Jupiter
19-20-21	at Palm Beach
22-23-24	Vero Beach
26-27-28	Palm Beach
29-30-31	at Vero Beach

SEPTEMBER
1-2	Daytona
3-4	at Daytona

CLEARWATER

APRIL
7-8	at Dunedin
9-10	Dunedin
11-12-13	Lakeland
14-15-16	Tampa
18-19-20	at Fort Myers
21-22-23	at Sarasota
24-25-26	Fort Myers
27-28-29	at Tampa
30	Sarasota

MAY
1-2	Sarasota
3-4-5	at Lakeland
6-7-8-9	Vero Beach
11-12-13-14	at Brevard
15-16-17-18	P.B.
19-20-21-22	Daytona
23-24-25-26	at Jupiter
27-28-29-30	at St. Lucie

JUNE
1-2	Dunedin
3-4	at Dunedin
5-6-7	Tampa
8-9-10	Lakeland
11-12-13	at Sarasota
14-15-16	at Fort Myers
20-21-22	Sarasota
23-24-25	Fort Myers
26-27-28	at Tampa
29-30	at Lakeland

JULY
1	at Lakeland
2-3	Dunedin
4-5	at Dunedin
6-7-8-9	Brevard
11-12-13-14	at V.B.
15-16-17-18	St. Lucie
20-21	at Dunedin
22-23	Dunedin
24-25-26-27	Jupiter
28-29-30-31	at P.B.

AUGUST
2-3-4-5	at Daytona
6	at Tampa
7-8	Tampa
9-10-11	Lakeland
12-13-14	at Sarasota
16-17-18	at Fort Myers
19-20-21	Sarasota
22-23-24-25	Fort Myers
26-27	at Tampa
29-30-31	at Lakeland

SEPTEMBER
1-2	Dunedin
3-4	at Dunedin

DAYTONA

APRIL
7-8	at Brevard
9-10	Brevard
11-12-13	Jupiter
14-15-16	at Vero Beach
17-18-19	at Jupiter
21-22-23	Vero Beach
24-25-26	St. Lucie
27-28-29	at Palm Beach
30	at St. Lucie

MAY
1-2	at St. Lucie
3-4-5	Palm Beach
6-7-8-9	at Tampa
11-12-13-14	Lakeland
15-16-17-18	Fort Myers
19-20-21-22	at Clear.
23-24-25-26	at Dunedin
27-28-29-30	Sarasota

JUNE
1-2	at Brevard
3-4	Brevard
5-6-7	at Vero Beach
8-9-10	Jupiter
11-12-13	Palm Beach
14-15-16	at St. Lucie
20-21-22	at Palm Beach
23-24-25	St Lucie
26-27-28	Vero Beach
29-30	at Jupiter

JULY
1	at Jupiter
2	at Brevard
3-4-5	Brevard
6-7-8-9	at Lakeland
11-12-13-14	Tampa
15-16-17-18	at Sarasota
20-21-22	at Brevard
23	Brevard
24-25-26-27	Dunedin
28-29-30-31	at F.M.

AUGUST
2-3-4-5	Clearwater
6-7-8	Jupiter
9-10-11	at Vero Beach
12-13-14	at Jupiter
16-17-18	Vero Beach
19-20-21	St. Lucie
22-23-24	at Palm Beach
25-26-27	at St. Lucie
29-30-31	Palm Beach

SEPTEMBER
1-2	at Brevard
3-4	Brevard

DUNEDIN

APRIL
7-8	Clearwater
9-10	at Clearwater
11-12	at Sarasota
13	Sarasota
14-15-16	at Fort Myers
18	Lakeland
19	at Lakeland
20	Lakeland
21-22	Tampa
23	at Tampa
24-25	at Lakeland
26	Lakeland
27-28-29	Fort Myers
30	Tampa

MAY
1-2	at Tampa
3	at Sarasota
4-5	Sarasota
6-7-8-9	at Brevard
11-12-13-14	P.B.
15-16-17-18	at Jupiter
19-20-21-22	at St. Lucie
23-24-25-26	Daytona
27-28-29-30	Vero Beach

JUNE
1-2	at Clearwater
3-4	Clearwater
5-6-7	at Fort Myers
8-9-10	at Sarasota
11-12-13	Tampa
14-15-16	Lakeland
20-21-22	at Tampa
24-25-26	at Lakeland
26-27-28	Fort Myers
29	at Sarasota
30	Sarasota

JULY
1	Sarasota
2-3	at Clearwater
4-5	Clearwater
6-7-8-9	at Palm Beach
11-12-13-14	Brevard
15-16-17-18	at V.B.
20-21	Clearwater
22-23	at Clearwater
24-25-26-27	at Daytona
28-29-30-31	Jupiter

AUGUST
2-3-4-5	St. Lucie
6-7-8	at Fort Myers
9	at Sarasota
10	Sarasota
11	at Sarasota
12-13-15	Tampa
16	Lakeland
17	at Lakeland
18	Lakeland
19-20-21	at Tampa
22	at Lakeland
23	Lakeland
24	at Lakeland
25-26-27	Fort Myers
29-30-31	Sarasota

SEPTEMBER
1-2	at Clearwater
3-4	Clearwater

FORT MYERS

APRIL
7-8	at Sarasota
9-10	Sarasota
11-12-13	at Tampa
14-15-16	Dunedin
18-19-20	Clearwater
21-22-23	at Lakeland
24-25-26	at Clearwater
27-28-29	at Dunedin
30	Lakeland

MAY
1-2	Lakeland
3-4-5	Tampa
6-7-8-9	at Palm Beach
11-12-13-14	St. Lucie

Date	Opponent
15-16-17-18	at Daytona
19-20-21-22	**Jupiter**
23-24-25-26	at V.B.
27-28-29-30	**Brevard**

JUNE
Date	Opponent
1-2	at Sarasota
3-4	**Sarasota**
5-6-7	**Dunedin**
8-9-10	at Tampa
11-12-13	at Lakeland
14-15-16	**Clearwater**
20-21-22	**Lakeland**
23-24-25	at Clearwater
26-27-28	at Dunedin
29-30	**Tampa**

JULY
Date	Opponent
1	**Tampa**
2-3	**Sarasota**
4-5	at Sarasota
6-7-8-9	at St. Lucie
11-12-13-14	**P.B.**
15-16-17-18	at Brevard
20	at Sarasota
21	**Sarasota**
22	at Sarasota
23	**Sarasota**
24-25-26-27	**Vero Beach**
28-29-30-31	**Daytona**

AUGUST
Date	Opponent
2-3-4-5	at Jupiter
6-7-8	**Dunedin**
9-10-11	at Tampa
12-13-14	at Lakeland
16-17-18	**Clearwater**
19-20-21	**Lakeland**
22-23-24	at Clearwater
25-26-27	at Dunedin
29-30-31	**Tampa**

SEPTEMBER
Date	Opponent
1-2	at Sarasota
3-4	**Sarasota**

JUPITER
APRIL
Date	Opponent
7-8	at Palm Beach
9-10-	**Palm Beach**
11-12-13	at Daytona
14-15-16	at Brevard
17-18-19	**Daytona**
21-22-23	**Brevard**
24-25-26	at Vero Beach
27-28-29	at St. Lucie
30	**Vero Beach**

MAY
Date	Opponent
1-2	**Vero Beach**
3-4-5	**St. Lucie**
6-7-8-9	at Sarasota
11-12-13-14	**Tampa**
15-16-17-18	**Dunedin**
19-20-21-22	at F.M.
23-24-25-26	**Clearwater**
27-28-29-30	at L'wood

JUNE
Date	Opponent
1-2	at Palm Beach
3-4	**Palm Beach**
5-6-7	at Brevard

Date	Opponent
8-9-10	at Daytona
11-12-13	**St. Lucie**
14-15-16	**Vero Beach**
20-21-22	at St. Lucie
23-24-25	at Vero Beach
26-27-28	**Brevard**
29-30	**Daytona**

JULY
Date	Opponent
1	**Daytona**
2-3	at Palm Beach
4	**Palm Beach**
5	at Palm Beach
6-7-8-9	at Tampa
11-12-13-14	**Sarasota**
15-16-17-18	**Lakeland**
20	at Palm Beach
21-22-23	**Palm Beach**
24-25-26-27	at Clear.
28-29-30-31	at Dunedin

AUGUST
Date	Opponent
2-3-4-5	**Fort Myers**
6-7-8	at Daytona
9-10-11	at Brevard
12-13-14	**Daytona**
16-17-18	**Brevard**
19-20-21	at Vero Beach
22-23-24	at St. Lucie
25-26-27	**Vero Beach**
29-30-31	**St. Lucie**

SEPTEMBER
Date	Opponent
1-2	**Palm Beach**
3-4	at Palm Beach

LAKELAND
APRIL
Date	Opponent
7-8	at Tampa
9-10	**Tampa**
11-12-13	at Clearwater
14-15-16	at Sarasota
18	at Dunedin
19	**Dunedin**
20	at Dunedin
21-22-23	**Fort Myers**
24-25	**Dunedin**
26	at Dunedin
27-28-29	**Sarasota**
30	at Fort Myers

MAY
Date	Opponent
1-2	at Fort Myers
3-4-5	**Clearwater**
6-7-8-9	at St. Lucie
11-12-13-14	at Daytona
15-16-17-18	**Vero Beach**
19-20-21-22	at P.B.
23-24-25-26	**Brevard**
27-28-29-30	**Jupiter**

JUNE
Date	Opponent
1-2	at Tampa
3-4	**Tampa**
5-6-7	**Sarasota**
8-9-10	at Clearwater
11-12-13	**Fort Myers**
14-15-16	at Dunedin
20-21-22	at Fort Myers
23-24-25	**Dunedin**
26-27-28	at Sarasota

Date	Opponent
29-30	**Clearwater**

JULY
Date	Opponent
1	**Clearwater**
2-3	at Tampa
4-5	**Tampa**
6-7-8-9	**Daytona**
11-12-13-14	**St. Lucie**
15-16-17-18	at Jupiter
20-21	**Tampa**
22-23	at Tampa
24-25-26-27	at Brevard
28-29-30-31	at V.B.

AUGUST
Date	Opponent
2-3-4-5	**Palm Beach**
6-7	**Sarasota**
8	at Sarasota
9-10-11	at Clearwater
12-13-14	**Fort Myers**
16	at Dunedin
17	**Dunedin**
18	at Dunedin
19-20-21	at Fort Myers
22	**Dunedin**
23	at Dunedin
24	**Dunedin**
25-26	at Sarasota
27	**Sarasota**
29-30-31	**Clearwater**

SEPTEMBER
Date	Opponent
1-2	**Tampa**
3-4	at Tampa

PALM BEACH
APRIL
Date	Opponent
7-8	**Jupiter**
9-10	at Jupiter
11-12-13	**Vero Beach**
14-15-16	**St. Lucie**
18-19-20	at Vero Beach
21-22-23	at St. Lucie
24-25-26	**Brevard**
27-28-29	**Daytona**
30	at Brevard

MAY
Date	Opponent
1-2	at Brevard
3-4-5	at Daytona
6-7-8-9	**Fort Myers**
11-12-13-14	at Dunedin
15-16-17-18	at Clear.
19-20-21-22	**Lakeland**
23-24-25-26	at Sarasota
27-28-29-30	**Tampa**

JUNE
Date	Opponent
1-2	**Jupiter**
3-4	at Jupiter
5-6-7	**St. Lucie**
8-9-10	**Vero Beach**
11-12-13	at Daytona
14-15-16	at Brevard
20-21-22	**Daytona**
23-24-25	**Brevard**
26-27-28	at St. Lucie
29-30	at Vero Beach

JULY
Date	Opponent
1	at Vero Beach
2-3	**Jupiter**

Date	Opponent
4	at Jupiter
5	**Jupiter**
6-7-8-9	**Dunedin**
11-12-13-14	at F.M.
15-16-17-18	at Tampa
20	**Jupiter**
21-22-23	at Jupiter
24-25-26-27	**Sarasota**
28-29-30-31	**Clearwater**

AUGUST
Date	Opponent
2-3-4-5	at Lakeland
6-7-8	**Vero Beach**
9-10	**St. Lucie**
11	at St. Lucie
12-13-14	at Vero Beach
15	**St. Lucie**
17-18	at St. Lucie
19-20-21	**Brevard**
22-23-24	**Daytona**
26-27-28	at Brevard
29-30-31	at Daytona

SEPTEMBER
Date	Opponent
1-2	at Jupiter
3-4	**Jupiter**

SARASOTA
APRIL
Date	Opponent
7-8	**Fort Myers**
9-10	at Fort Myers
11-12	**Dunedin**
13	at Dunedin
14-15-16	**Lakeland**
18-19	at Tampa
20	**Tampa**
21-22-23	**Clearwater**
24	at Tampa
25-26	**Tampa**
27-28-29	at Lakeland
30	at Clearwater

MAY
Date	Opponent
1-2	at Clearwater
3	**Dunedin**
4-5	at Dunedin
6-7-8-9	**Jupiter**
11-12-13-14	at V.B.
15-16-17-18	**St. Lucie**
19-20-21-22	at Brevard
23-24-25-26	**P.B.**
27-28-29-30	at Daytona

JUNE
Date	Opponent
1-2	**Fort Myers**
3-4	at Fort Myers
5-6-7	at Lakeland
8-9-10	**Dunedin**
11-12-13	**Clearwater**
14-15-16	at Tampa
20-21-22	at Clearwater
23-24-25	**Tampa**
26-27-28	**Lakeland**
29	**Dunedin**
30	at Dunedin

JULY
Date	Opponent
1	at Dunedin
2-3	at Fort Myers
4-5	**Fort Myers**
6-7-8-9	**Vero Beach**

11-12-13-14	at Jupiter
15-16-17-18	Daytona
20	Fort Myers
21	at Fort Myers
22	Fort Myers
23	at Fort Myers
24-25-26-27	at P.B.
28-29-30-31	at St. Lucie

AUGUST

2-3-4-5	Brevard
6-7	at Lakeland
8	Lakeland
9	Dunedin
10	at Dunedin
11	Dunedin
12-13-14	Clearwater
16-17-18	at Tampa
19-20-21	at Clearwater
22-23-24	Tampa
25-26	Lakeland
27	at Lakeland
29-30-31	at Dunedin

SEPTEMBER

1-2	Fort Myers
3-4	at Fort Myers

ST. LUCIE

APRIL

7	Vero Beach
8	at Vero Beach
9	Vero Beach
10	at Vero Beach
11-12-13	Brevard
14-15-16	at Palm Beach
18-19-20	at Brevard
21-22-23	Palm Beach
24-25-26	at Daytona
27-28-29	Jupiter
30	Daytona

MAY

1-2	Daytona
3-4-5	at Jupiter
6-7-8-9	Lakeland
11-12-13-14	at F.M.
15-16-17-18	at Sara.
19-20-21-22	Dunedin
23-24-25-26	at Tampa
27-28-29-30	Clearwater

JUNE

1	at Vero Beach
2-3	Vero Beach
4	at Vero Beach
5-6-7	at Palm Beach

8-9-10	Brevard
11-12-13	at Jupiter
14-15-16	Daytona
20-21-22	Jupiter
23-24-25	at Daytona
26-27-28	Palm Beach
29-30	at Brevard

JULY

1	at Brevard
2	Vero Beach
3	at Vero Beach
4	Vero Beach
5	at Vero Beach
6-7-8-9	Fort Myers
11-12-13-14	at L'wood
15-16-17-18	at Clear.
20-21	Vero Beach
22-23	at Vero Beach
24-25-26-27	Tampa
28-29-30-31	Sarasota

AUGUST

2-3-4-5	at Dunedin
6-7-8	Brevard
9-10	at Palm Beach
11	Palm Beach
12-13-14	at Vero Beach
15	at Palm Beach
17-18	Palm Beach
19-20-21	at Daytona
22-23-24	Jupiter
25-26-27	Daytona
29-30-31	at Jupiter

SEPTEMBER

1-2	Vero Beach
3-4	at Vero Beach

TAMPA

APRIL

7-8	Lakeland
9-10	at Lakeland
11-12-13	Fort Myers
14-15-16	at Clearwater
18-19	Sarasota
20	at Sarasota
21-22	at Dunedin
23	Dunedin
24	Sarasota
25-26	at Sarasota
27-28-29	Clearwater
30	at Dunedin

MAY

1-2	Dunedin
3-4-5	at Fort Myers

6-7-8-9	Daytona
11-12-13-14	at Jupiter
15-16-17-18	Brevard
19-20-21-22	at V.B.
23-24-25-26	St. Lucie
27-28-29-30	at P.B.

JUNE

1-2	Lakeland
3-4	at Lakeland
5-6-7	at Clearwater
8-9-10	Fort Myers
11-12-13	at Dunedin
14-15-16	Sarasota
20-21-22	Dunedin
23-24-25	at Sarasota
26-27-28	Clearwater
29-30	at Fort Myers

JULY

1	at Fort Myers
2-3	Lakeland
4-5	at Lakeland
6-7-8-9	Jupiter
11-12-13-14	Daytona
15-16-17-18	P.B.
20-21	at Lakeland
22-23	Lakeland
24-25-26-27	at St. Lucie
28-29-30-31	at Brevard

AUGUST

2-3-4-5	Vero Beach
6	Clearwater
7-8	at Clearwater
9-10-11	Fort Myers
12-13-15	at Dunedin
16-17-18	Sarasota
19-20-21	Dunedin
22-23-24	at Clearwater
25	at Clearwater
26-27	Clearwater
29-30-31	at Fort Myers

SEPTEMBER

1-2	at Lakeland
3-4	Lakeland

VERO BEACH

APRIL

7	at St. Lucie
8	St. Lucie
9	at St. Lucie
10	St. Lucie
11-12-13	at Palm Beach
14-15-16	Daytona
18-19-20	Palm Beach

21-22-23	at Daytona
24-25-26	Jupiter
27-28-29	at Brevard
30	at Jupiter

MAY

1-2	at Jupiter
3-4-5	Brevard
6-7-8-9	at Clear.
11-12-13-14	Sarasota
15-16-17-18	at L'wood
19-20-21-22	Tampa
23-24-25-26	Fort Myers
27-28-29-30	at Dunedin

JUNE

1	St. Lucie
2-3	at St. Lucie
4	St. Lucie
5-6-7	Daytona
8-9-10	at Palm Beach
11-12-13	Brevard
14-15-16	at Jupiter
20-21-22	at Brevard
23-24-25	Jupiter
26-27-28	at Daytona
29-30	Palm Beach

JULY

1	Palm Beach
2	at St. Lucie
3	St. Lucie
4	at St. Lucie
5	St. Lucie
6-7-8-9	at Sarasota
11-12-13-14	Clearwater
15-16-17-18	Dunedin
20-21	at St. Lucie
22-23	St. Lucie
24-25-26-27	at F.M.
28-29-30-31	Lakeland

AUGUST

2-3-4-5	at Tampa
6-7-8	at Palm Beach
9-10-11	Daytona
12-13-14	Palm Beach
16-17-18	at Daytona
19-20-21	Jupiter
22-23-24	Brevard
25-26-27	at Jupiter
29-30-31	Brevard

SEPTEMBER

1-2	at St. Lucie
3-4	St. Lucie

LOW CLASS A
MIDWEST LEAGUE

BELOIT

APRIL

7-8-9-10	Quad Cities
12-13-14	at K.C.
15-16-17-18	Lansing
19-20-21-22	at Clinton
23-24-25-26	at Wis.
28-29-30	Fort Wayne

MAY

1	Fort Wayne
2-3-4-5	at C.R.
6-7-8-9	at F.W.
10-11-12-13	Peoria
14-15-16-17	at Q.C.
19-20-21-22	S.B.
23-24-25-26	C.R.
31	at Burlington

JUNE

1-2-3	at Burlington
4-5-6-7	Clinton
9-10-11-12	at Peoria
13-14-15	Kane County
16-17-18-19	Wisconsin
23-24-25-26	at Burl.
27-28-29	Kane County
30	Dayton

JULY

1-2-3	Dayton
4-5-6-7	at Wisconsin
8-9-10-11	Burlington
13-14-15	at K.C.
16-17-18-19	SW Mich.
21-22-23-24	at C.R.
25-26-27-28	at S.B.
29-30-31	Clinton

AUGUST

1	Clinton
2-3-4-5	W. Mich.
6-7-8-9	at W. Mich.
11-12-13-14	at Lansing
15-16-17-18	Quad Cities
19-20-21-22	at K.C.
25-26-27-28	at Dayton
29-30-31	Peoria

SEPTEMBER

1	Peoria
2-3-4-5	Wisconsin

BURLINGTON

APRIL

7-8-9-10	at Clinton
12-13-14	Cedar Rapids
15-16-17-18	K.C.
19-20-21-22	at Wis.
23-24-25-26	at F.W.
28-29-30	Clinton

MAY

1	Clinton
2-3-4-5	W. Mich.
6-7-8-9	at C.R.

10-11-12-13	Lansing
14-15-16-17	at Peoria
19-20-21-22	Quad Cities
23-24-25-26	at S.B.
27-28-29-30	Dayton
31	Beloit

JUNE

1-2-3	Beloit
4-5-6-7	at Dayton
9-10-11-12	Fort Wayne
13-14-15	at C.R.
16-17-18-19	at K.C.
23-24-25-26	Beloit
27-28-29	at Clinton
30	at Peoria

JULY

1-2-3	at Peoria
4-5-6-7	South Bend
8-9-10-11	at Beloit
13-14-15	Peoria
16-17-18-19	at Clinton
21-22-23-24	K.C.
25-26-27-28	at W.M.
29-30-31	Wisconsin

AUGUST

1	Wisconsin
2-3-4	at Lansing
5-6-7	at Quad Cities
9-10	at Quad Cities
11-12-13-14	SW Mich.
15-16-17-18	Wisconsin
19-20-21-22	at SW Mich.
25-26-27-28	C.R.
29-30-31	Clinton

SEPTEMBER

1	Clinton
2-3-4-5	at Clinton

CEDAR RAPIDS

APRIL

7-8-9-10	Kane County
12-13-14	at Burlington
15-16-17-18	at W.M.
19-20-21-22	Peoria
23-24-25-26	at Lansing
28-29-30	at Quad Cities

MAY

1	at Quad Cities
2-3-4-5	Beloit
6-7-8-9	Burlington
11-12-13	at Quad Cities
14-15-16-17	at Dayton
18	at Quad Cities
19-20-21-22	W. Mich.
23-24-25-26	at Beloit
27-28-29-30	South Bend
31	Wisconsin

JUNE

1-2-3	Wisconsin
4-5-6-7	at South Bend
9-10-11-12	at Wis.

13-14-15	Burlington
16-17-18-19	Clinton
23-24-25-26	Peoria
27-28-29	at Peoria
30	Lansing

JULY

1-2-3	Lansing
4-5-6-7	Fort Wayne
8-9-10-11	at Q.C.
13-14-15	Clinton
16-17-18-19	at Peoria
21-22-23-24	Beloit
25-26-27-28	at F.W.
29-30-31	Dayton

AUGUST

1	Dayton
2-3-4-5	at SW Mich.
6-7-8-9	at Wisconsin
11-12-13-14	K.C.
15-16-17-18	SW Mich.
19-20-21-22	at Clinton
25-26-27-28	at Burl.
29-30-31	Quad Cities

SEPTEMBER

1	Quad Cities
2-3-4-5	at Kane County

CLINTON

APRIL

7-8-9-10	Burlington
12-13-14	at Peoria
15-16-17	at Quad Cities
19-20-21-22	Beloit
23-24-25-26	SW Mich.
27	at Quad Cities
28-29-30	at Burlington

MAY

1	at Burlington
2-3-4-5	at South Bend
6-7-8-9	Quad Cities
10-11-12-13	Dayton
14-15-16-17	at K.C.
19-20-21-22	at Wis.
23-24-25-26	Fort Wayne
27-28-29-30	Peoria
31	at Lansing

JUNE

1-2-3	at Lansing
4-5-6-7	at Beloit
9-10-11-12	Kane County
13-14-15	Wisconsin
16-17-18-19	at C.R.
23-24-25-26	K.C.
27-28-29	Burlington
30	at West Michigan

JULY

1-2-3	at West Michigan
4-5-6-7	at SW Michigan
8-9-10-11	W. Mich.
13-14-15	at C.R.
16-17-18-19	Burlington

13-14-15	Burlington
16-17-18-19	Clinton
23-24-25-26	Peoria
27-28-29	at Peoria
30	Lansing

JULY

1-2-3	Lansing
4-5-6-7	Fort Wayne
8-9-10-11	at Q.C.
13-14-15	Clinton
16-17-18-19	at Peoria
21-22-23-24	Beloit
25-26-27-28	at F.W.
29-30-31	Dayton

AUGUST

1	Dayton
2-3-4-5	at SW Mich.
6-7-8-9	at Wisconsin
11-12-13-14	K.C.
15-16-17-18	SW Mich.
19-20-21-22	at Clinton
25-26-27-28	at Burl.
29-30-31	Quad Cities

SEPTEMBER

1	Quad Cities
2-3-4-5	at Kane County

21-22-23-24	at Wis.
25-26-27-28	Lansing
29-30-31	at Beloit

AUGUST

1	at Beloit
2-3-4-5	at Quad Cities
6-7-8-9	Peoria
11-12-13-14	at Dayton
15-16-17-18	at F.W.
19-20-21-22	C.R.
25-26-27-28	South Bend
29-30-31	at Burlington

SEPTEMBER

1	at Burlington
2-3-4-5	Burlington

DAYTON

APRIL

7-8-9-10	at South Bend
12-13-14	W.M.
15-16-17-18	Fort Wayne
19-20-21-22	at SW Michigan
23-24-25-26	at Q.C.
28-29-30	Lansing

MAY

1	Lansing
2-3-4-5	Kane County
6-7-8-9	at Wisconsin
10-11-12-13	at Clinton
14-15-16-17	C.R.
19-20-21-22	Peoria
23-24-25-26	at W.M.
27-28-29-30	at Burl.
31	South Bend

JUNE

1-2-3	South Bend
4-5-6-7	Burlington
9-10-11-12	at Lansing
13-14-15	at South Bend
16-17-18-19	SW Mich.
23-24-25-26	at F.W.
27-28-29	W.M.
30	at Beloit

JULY

1-2-3	at Beloit
4-5-6-7	Lansing
8-9-10-11	SW Michigan
13-14-15	at W. Mich.
16-17-18-19	Quad Cities
21-22-23-24	South Bend
25-26-27-28	at Peoria
29-30-31	at C.R.

AUGUST

1	at Cedar Rapids
2-3-4-5	Fort Wayne
6-7-8-9	at Kane County
11-12-13-14	Clinton
15-16-17-18	at Lansing
19-20-21-22	at S.B.
25-26-27-28	Beloit
29-30-31	Wisconsin

CLASS A SCHEDULES

1	**Wisconsin**
2-3-4-5	at Fort Wayne

FORT WAYNE

APRIL
7-8	at Lansing
9-10	**Lansing**
12-13-14	at SW Mich.
15-16-17-18	at Dayton
19-20-21-22	**South Bend**
23-24-25-26	**Burlington**
28-29-30	at Beloit

MAY
1	at Beloit
2-3-4-5	at Peoria
6-7-8-9	**Beloit**
10-11-12-13	**SW Mich.**
14-15-16-17	at W.M.
19-20-21-22	**K.C.**
23-24-25-26	at Clinton
27-28-29-30	**W. Mich.**
31	**Quad Cities**

JUNE
1-2-3	**Quad Cities**
4-5-6-7	at Kane County
9-10-11-12	at Burlington
13-14-15	**SW Michigan**
16-17	**Lansing**
18-19	at Lansing
23-24-25-26	**Dayton**
27-28-29	at South Bend
30	**Wisconsin**

JULY
1-2-3	**Wisconsin**
4-5-6-7	at Cedar Rapids
8-9-10-11	at South Bend
13-14-15	**South Bend**
16-17	**Lansing**
18-19	at Lansing
21-22-23-24	at Q.C.
25-26-27-28	**C.R.**
29-30-31	**Peoria**

AUGUST
1	**Peoria**
2-3-4-5	at Dayton
6-7-8-9	at SW Michigan
11-12-13-14	**South Bend**
15-16-17-18	**Clinton**
19-20-21-22	at W.M.
25-26-27-28	at Wis.
29-30	**Lansing**
31	at Lansing

SEPTEMBER
1	at Lansing
2-3-4-5	**Dayton**

KANE COUNTY

APRIL
7-8-9-10	at C.R.
12-13-14	**Beloit**
15-16-17-18	at Burl.
19-20-21-22	**Quad Cities**
23-24-25-26	**South Bend**
28-29-30	at Peoria

MAY
1	at Peoria
2-3-4-5	at Dayton
6-7-8-9	**Peoria**
10-11-12-13	at S.B.
14-15-16-17	**Clinton**
19-20-21-22	at F.W.
23-24-25-26	**Wisconsin**
23-28-29-30	**Lansing**
31	at West Michigan

JUNE
1-2-3	at West Michigan
4-5-6-7	**Fort Wayne**
9-10-11-12	at Clinton
13-14-15	at Beloit
16-17-18-19	**Burlington**
23-24-25-26	at Clinton
27-28-29	at Beloit
30	**SW Michigan**

JULY
1-2-3	**SW Michigan**
4-5	**Peoria**
6-7	at Peoria
8-9-10-11	at Lansing
13-14-15	**Beloit**
16-17-18-19	**Wisconsin**
21-22-23-24	at Burl.
25-26-27-28	at Wis.
29-30-31	**Quad Cities**

AUGUST
1	**Quad Cities**
2-3	at Peoria
4-5	**Peoria**
6-7-8-9	**Dayton**
11-12-13-14	at C.R.
15-16-17-18	**W. Mich.**
19-20-21-22	**Beloit**
25-26-27-28	at Q.C.
29-30-31	at SW Mich.

SEPTEMBER
1	at SW Michigan
2-3-4-5	**Cedar Rapids**

LANSING

APRIL
7-8	**Fort Wayne**
9-10	at Fort Wayne
12-13-14	**South Bend**
15 16 17 18	at Beloit
19-20-21-22	**W. Mich.**
23-24-25-26	**C.R.**
28-29-30	at Dayton

MAY
1	at Dayton
2-3-4-5	**Quad Cities**
6-7-8-9	**SWMichigan**
10-11-12-13	at Burl.
14-15-16-17	**Wisconsin**
19-20-21-22	at SW Mich.
23-24-25-26	at Q.C.
27-28-29-30	at K.C.
31	**Clinton**

JUNE
1-2-3	**Clinton**
4-5-6-7	at Peoria
9-10-11-12	**Dayton**

13-14-15	at W. Mich.
16-17	at Fort Wayne
18-19	**Fort Wayne**
23-24-25-26	at W.M.
27-28-29	**SW Michigan**
30	at Cedar Rapids

JULY
1-2-3	at Cedar Rapids
4-5-6-7	at Dayton
8-9-10-11	**Kane County**
13-14-15	at SW Mich.
16-17	at Fort Wayne
18-19	**Fort Wayne**
21-22-23-24	**Peoria**
25-26-27-28	at Clinton
29-30-31	at South Bend

AUGUST
1	at South Bend
2-3-4-5	**Burlington**
6-7-8-9	at South Bend
11-12-13-14	**Beloit**
15-16-17-18	**Dayton**
19-20-21-22	at Wis.
25-26-27-28	**SW Mich.**
29-30	at Fort Wayne
31	**Fort Wayne**

SEPTEMBER
1	**Fort Wayne**
2-3-4-5	**West Michigan**

PEORIA

APRIL
7-8-9-10	at Wisconsin
12-13-14	**Clinton**
15-16-17-18	**Wisconsin**
19-20-21-22	at C.R.
23-24-25-26	at W.M.
28-29-30	**Kane County**

MAY
1	**Kane County**
2-3-4-5	**Fort Wayne**
6-7-8-9	at Kane County
10-11-12	at Beloit
13	**SW Michigan**
14-15-16-17	**Burlington**
19-20-21-22	at Dayton
23-24-25-26	**SW Mich.**
27-28-29-30	at Clinton
31	at SW Michigan

JUNE
1-2-3	at SW Michigan
4-5-6-7	**Lansing**
8	at Quad Cities
9-10-11-12	**Beloit**
14-15	at Quad Cities
16-17-18-19	**Quad Cities**
23-24-25-26	at C.R.
27-28-29	**Cedar Rapids**
30	**Burlington**

JULY
1-2-3	**Burlington**
4-5	at Kane County
6-7	**Kane County**
8-9-10-11	**Wisconsin**
13-14-15	at Burlington
16-17-18-19	**C.R.**

21-22-23-24	at Lansing
25-26-27-28	**Dayton**
29-30-31	at Fort Wayne

AUGUST
1	at Fort Wayne
2-3	**Kane County**
4-5	at Kane County
6-7-8-9	at Clinton
11-12-13-14	**Quad Cities**
15-16-17-18	at S.B.
19-20-21	at Quad Cities
24	at Quad Cities
25-26-27-28	**W. Mich.**
29-30-31	at Beloit

SEPTEMBER
1	at Beloit
2-3-4-5	**South Bend**

QUAD CITIES

APRIL
7-8-9-10	at Beloit
12-13-14	at Wisconsin
15-16-17	**Clinton**
19-20-21-22	at K.C.
23-24-25-26	**Dayton**
27	**Clinton**
28-29-30	**Cedar Rapids**

MAY
1	**Cedar Rapids**
2-3-4-5	at Lansing
6-7-8-9	at Clinton
11-12-13	**Cedar Rapids**
14-15-16-17	**Beloit**
18	**Cedar Rapids**
19-20-21-22	at Burl.
23-24-25-26	**Lansing**
27-28-29-30	**Wisconsin**
31	at Fort Wayne

JUNE
1-2-3	at Fort Wayne
4-5-6-7	at W. Mich.
8	**Peoria**
9-10-11-12	**South Bend**
14-15	**Peoria**
16-17-18-19	at Peoria
23-24-25-26	at Wis.
27-28-29	**Wisconsin**
31	at South Bend

JULY
1-2-3	at South Bend
4-5-6-7	**West Michigan**
8-9-10-11	**Cedar Rapids**
13-14-15	at Wisconsin
16-17-18-19	at Dayton
21-22-23-24	**Fort Wayne**
25-26-27-28	**SW Mich.**
29-30-31	at K.C.

AUGUST
1	at Kane County
2-3-4-5	**Clinton**
6-7	**Burlington**
9-10	**Burlington**
11-12-13-14	at Peoria
15-16-17-18	at Beloit
19-20-21	**Peoria**
24	**Peoria**

25-26-27-28	K.C.
29-30-31	at C.R.

SEPTEMBER

1	at Cedar Rapids
2-3-4-5	at SW Mich.

SOUTH BEND

APRIL

7-8-9-10	Dayton
12-13-14	at Lansing
15-16-17-18	SW Mich.
19-20-21-22	at F.W.
23-24-25-26	at K.C.
28-29-30	Wisconsin

MAY

1	Wisconsin
2-3-4-5	Clinton
6-7-8-9	at W. Mich.
10-11-12-13	K.C.
14-15-16-17	at SW Mich.
19-20-21-22	at Beloit
23-24-25-26	Burlington
27-28-29-30	at C.R.
31	at Dayton

JUNE

1-2-3	at Dayton
4-5-6-7	Cedar Rapids
9-10-11-12	at Q.C.
13-14-15	Dayton
16-17-18-19	W. Mich.
23-24-25-26	at SW Mich.
27-28-29	Fort Wayne
30	Quad Cities

JULY

1-2-3	Quad Cities
4-5-6-7	at Burlington
8-9-10-11	Fort Wayne
13-14-15	at Fort Wayne
16-17-18-19	W. Mich.
21-22-23-24	at Dayton
25-26-27-28	Beloit
29-30-31	Lansing

AUGUST

1	Lansing
2-3-4-5	at Wisconsin
6-7-8-9	Lansing
15-16-17-18	Peoria
19-20-21-22	Dayton
25-26-27-28	at Clinton
29-30-31	at W. Mich.

SEPTEMBER

1	at West Michigan

2-3-4-5	at Peoria

SW MICHIGAN

APRIL

7-8	West Michigan
9-10	at West Michigan
12-13-14	Fort Wayne
15-16-17-18	at S.B.
19-20-21-22	Dayton
23-24-25-26	at Clinton
28-29	at West Michigan
30	West Michigan

MAY

1	West Michigan
2-3-4-5	Wisconsin
6-7-8-9	at Lansing
10-11-12-13	at F.W.
14-15-16-17	South Bend
19-20-21-22	Lansing
23-24-25-26	at Peoria
27-28-29-30	Beloit
31	Peoria

JUNE

1-2-3	Peoria
4	at Wisconsin
6-7	at Wisconsin
9-10-11-12	W. Mich.
13-14-15	at Fort Wayne
16-17-18-19	at Dayton
23-24-25-26	South Bend
27-28-29	at Lansing
30	at Kane County

JULY

1-2-3	at Kane County
4-5-6-7	Clinton
8-9-10-11	at Dayton
13-14-15	Lansing
16-17-18-19	at Beloit
21-22-23-24	W. Mich.
25-26-27-28	at Q.C.
29-30-31	at W. Mich.

AUGUST

1	at West Michigan
2-3-4-5	Cedar Rapids
6-7-8-9	Fort Wayne
11-12-13-14	at Burl.
15-16-17-18	at C.R.
19-20-21-22	Burlington
25-26-27-28	at Lansing
29-30-31	Kane County

SEPTEMBER

1	Kane County

2-3-4-5	Quad Cities

WEST MICHIGAN

APRIL

7-8	at SW Michigan
9-10	SW Michigan
12-13-14	at Dayton
15-16-17-18	C.R.
19-20-21-22	at Lansing
23-24-25-26	Peoria
28-29	SW Michigan
30	at SW Michigan

MAY

1	at SW Michigan
2-3-4-5	at Burlington
6-7-8-9	South Bend
10-11-12-13	at Wis.
14-15-16-17	F.W.
19-20-21-22	at C.R.
23-24-25-26	Dayton
27-28-29-30	at F.W.
31	Kane County

JUNE

1-2-3	Kane County
4-5-6-7	Quad Cities
9-10-11-12	at SW Mich.
13-14-15	Lansing
16-17-18-19	at S.B.
23-24-25-26	Lansing
27-28-29	at Dayton
30	Clinton

JULY

1-2-3	Clinton
4-5-6-7	at Quad Cities
8-9-10-11	at Clinton
13-14-15	Dayton
16-17-18-19	at S.B.
21-22-23-24	at SW Mich.
25-26-27-28	Burlington
29-30-31	SW Michigan

AUGUST

1	SW Michigan
2-3-4-5	at Beloit
6-7-8-9	Beloit
11-12-13-14	Wisconsin
15-16-17-18	at K.C.
19-20-21-22	Fort Wayne
25-26-27-28	at Peoria
29-30-31	South Bend

SEPTEMBER

1	South Bend
2-3-4-5	at Lansing

WISCONSIN

APRIL

7-8-9-10	Peoria
12-13-14	Quad Cities
15-16-17-18	at Peoria
19-20-21-22	Burlington
23	Beloit
24	SW Michigan
25-26	Beloit
28-29-30	at South Bend

MAY

1	at South Bend
2-3-4-5	at SW Michigan
6-7-8-9	Dayton
10-11-12-13	W. Mich.
14-15-16-17	at Lansing
19-20-21-22	Clinton
23-24-25-26	at K.C.
27-28-29-30	at Q.C.
31	at Cedar Rapids

JUNE

1-2-3	at Cedar Rapids
4	SW Michigan
6-6	SW Michigan
7	SW Michigan
9-10-11-12	C.R.
13-14-15	at Clinton
16-17-18-19	at Beloit
23-24-25-26	Quad Cities
27-28-29	at Quad Cities
30	at Fort Wayne

JULY

1-2-3	at Fort Wayne
4-5-6-7	Beloit
8-9-10-11	at Peoria
13-14-15	Quad Cities
16-17-18-19	at K.C.
21-22-23-24	Clinton
25-26-27-28	K.C.
29-30-31	at Burlington

AUGUST

1	at Burlington
2-3-4-5	South Bend
6-7-8-9	Cedar Rapids
11-12-13-14	at W.M.
15-16-17-18	at Burl.
19-20-21-22	Lansing
25-26-27-28	Fort Wayne
29-30-31	at Dayton

SEPTEMBER

1	at Dayton
2-3-4-5	at Beloit

SOUTH ATLANTIC LEAGUE

ASHEVILLE

APRIL

7-8-9-10	at Kannapolis
11-12-13	Hickory
14-15-16-17	Kannapolis
18-19-20	at Hickory
21-22-23-24	G'boro
26-27-28	at Delmarva
30	at Lakewood

MAY

1-2-3	at Lakewood
5-6-7-8	Hagerstown
9-10-11-12	Lake County
13-14-15-16	at Lex.
17-18-19-20	W. Va.
21-22-23-24	at Rome
25-26-27-28	Lexington
30-31	Savannah

JUNE

1-2	Savannah
3-4-5-6	at Columbus
7-8-9-10	at Augusta
11-12-13-14	Greenville
16-17-18-19	at G'boro
21-22-23	Kannapolis
24-25-26	Hickory
30	at Greenville

JULY

1-2-3	at Greenville
4-5-6-7	Augusta
8-9-10-11	Columbus
13-14-15-16	at Sav.
17-18-19-20	at Char.
21-22-23-24	Rome
25-26-27	at Greensboro
28-29-30-31	Lexington

AUGUST
2-3-4-5 at West Virginia
6-7-8-9 Lakewood
10-11-12-13 Delmarva
15-16-17-18 at L.C.
19-20-21-22 at Hag.
23-24-25 Greensboro
26-27 at Rome
29-30 Hickory
31 at Kannapolis

SEPTEMBER
1-2 at Kannapolis
3-4-5 at Hickory

AUGUSTA

APRIL
7-8-9-10 at Charleston
11-12-13 at Rome
14-15-16-17 Savannah
18-19-20 Rome
21-22-23-24 at Sav.
30 at Greenville

MAY
1-2-3 at Greenville
4-5-6-7 at Columbus
9-10-11-12 Rome
13-14-15-16 Columbus
17-18-19-20 at Rome
21-22-23-24 at G'boro
26-27-28-29 Greenville
30-31 Hickory

JUNE
1-2 Hickory
3-4-5-6 at Kannapolis
7-8-9-10 Asheville
11-12-13-14 at Char.
16-17-18-19 Savannah
21-22-23 Rome
24-25-26 Charleston
22-23-24 Greensboro
30 Kannapolis

JULY
1-2-3 Kannapolis
4-5-6-7 at Asheville
8-9-10-11 Charleston
13-14-15-16 G'boro
17-18-19-20 at Sav.
21-22-23-24 at Hickory
26-27-28-20 Groonvillo
30-31 at Charleston

AUGUST
1 at Columbus
3-4-5-6 Rome
8-9-10-11 Columbus
12-13-14-15 at Sav.
16-17-18-19 at G'ville
20-21-22-23 Charleston
25-26-27-28 at Rome
29-30-31 at Columbus

SEPTEMBER
1-2 at Charleston
2-3-4-5 Savannah

CHARLESTON

APRIL
7-8-9-10 Augusta
11-12-13 Columbus
14-15-16-17 at G'ville
18-19-20 at Columbus
22-23-24-25 Greenville
26-27-28-29 at Augusta
30 Rome

MAY
1-2-3 Rome
5-6-7-8 at Savannah
9-10-11-12 at Col.
13-14-15-16 Savannah
17-18-19-20 Columbus
21-22-23-24 at Hickory
25-26-27-28 at L'wood
30-31 Greensboro

JUNE
1-2 Greensboro
3-4-5-6 at Rome
7-8-9-10 Kannapolis
11-12-13-14 Augusta
16-17-18-19 at G'ville
21-22-23 at Savannah
24-25-26 Augusta
30 Rome

JULY
1-2-3 Rome
4-5-6-7 at Greensboro
8-9-10-11 at Augusta
13-14-15-16 Hickory
18-19-20 Asheville
21-22-23-24 at Kann.
26-27-28-29 at Sav.
30-31 Augusta

AUGUST
1-2 Augusta
3-4-5-6 Greenville
8-9-10-11 at Rome
12-13-14-15 Columbus
16-17-18-19 Asheville
20-21-22-23 at Augusta
24-25-26-27 at G'ville
29-30-31 Rome

SEPTEMBER
1 Rome
2-3-4-5 at Columbus

COLUMBUS

APRIL
7-8-9-10 at Savannah
11-12-13 at Charleston
14-15-16-17 Rome
18-19-20 Charleston
21-22-23-24 at Rome
26-27-28-29 Greenville
30 at Savannah

MAY
1-2-3 at Savannah
4-5-6-7 Augusta
9-10-11-12 Charleston
13-14-15-16 at Augusta
17-18-19-20 at Char.
21-22-23-24 Savannah
26-27-28-29 Hickory
30-31 at Greenville

JUNE
1-2 at Greenville
3-4-5-6 Asheville
7-8-9-10 at Greensboro
11-12-13-14 at Kann.
16-17-18-19 Rome
21-22-23 Greenville
24-25-26 at Rome
22-23-24 Charleston
30 Greensboro

JULY
1-2-3 Greensboro
4-5-6-7 at Hickory
8-9-10-11 at Asheville
13-14-15-16 at G'ville
17-18-19-20 Kannapolis
21-22-23-24 Savannah
26-27-28-29 at Rome
30-31 at Greenville

AUGUST
1-2 at Greenville
4-5-6-7 Savannah
8-9-10-11 at Augusta
12-13-14-15 at Char.
16-17-18-19 Rome
20-21-22-23 Greenville
25-26-27-28 at Sav.
29-30-31 Augusta

SEPTEMBER
1 Augusta
2-3-4-5 Charleston

DELMARVA

APRIL
7-8-9-10 at Lexington
11-12-13 at Lake County
15-16-17-18 Lexington
19-20-21 Lake County
22-23-24-25 at Hag.
26-27-28-29 Asheville
30 Hickory

MAY
1-2-3 Hickory
5-6-7-8 at Greensboro
9-10-11-12 W. Va.
13-14-15-16 Lakewood
17-18-19-20 at Kann.
21-22-23-24 at W.Va.
26-27 Hagerstown
28-29 at Hagerstown
30-31 West Virginia

JUNE
1-2 West Virginia
3-4-5-6 at Lake County
7-8 at Lakewood
9-10 Lakewood
11-12-13-14 L.C.
16-17-18-19 Lakewood
21-22-23-24 at L.C.
25-26 at Lakewood
30 West Virginia

JULY
1-2-3-4 West Virginia
4-5-6 Lakewood
7-8-9-10 at Lake County
12-13-14-15 Lexington
16-17-18-19 L.C.
21-22-23-24 at Lex.

---

25 at Hagerstown
26-27 Hagerstown
28-29-30-31 at Kann.

AUGUST
1-2-3-4 Greensboro
6-7-8-9 at Hickory
10-11-12-13 at Asheville
15-16-17-18 Kannapolis
19-20 Lakewood
21-22-23-24 at L'wood
25-26-27-28 Hag.
29-30-31 at W. Va.

SEPTEMBER
1 at West Virginia
2-3-4-5 at Lakewood

GREENSBORO

APRIL
7-8 at Hickory
9-10 Hickory
11-12-13 at Kannapolis
14-15 Hickory
16-17 at Hickory
18-19-20 Kannapolis
21-22-23-24 at Ashe.
26-27-28-29 Lakewood
30 at West Virginia

MAY
2-3-4 at West Virginia
5-6-7-8 Delmarva
9-10-11-12 Lexington
13-14-15-16 at Hag.
17-18-19-20 at L.C.
21-22-23-24 Augusta
26-27-28-29 Rome
30 at Charleston

JUNE
1-2 at Charleston
3-4-5-6 at Greenville
7-8-9-10 Columbus
11-12-13-14 at Sav.
16-17-18-19 Asheville
21-22-23 at Hickory
24-25-26 at Kannapolis

JULY
1-2-3 at Columbus
4-5-6-7 Charleston
8-9-10-11 Savannah
13-14-15-16 at Augusta
17-18-19-20 at Rome
21-22-23-24 Greenville
25-26-27 Asheville
28-29-30 at Lakewood

AUGUST
2-3-4-5 at Delmarva
6-7-8-9 West Virginia
10-11-12-13 Hag.
15-16-17-18 at Lex.
19-20-21-22 L.C.
23-24-25 at Asheville
26-27 at Kannapolis
29-30 Kannapolis

SEPTEMBER
1-2 Hickory
3-4-5 Kannapolis

GREENVILLE

APRIL
7-8-9-10	at Rome
11-12-13	at Savannah
14-15-16-17	**Charleston**
18-19-20	**Savannah**
22-23-24-25	at Char.
28-29-30	at Columbus

MAY
1-2-3	**Augusta**
4-5-6-7	at Rome
9-10-11-12	**Savannah**
13-14-15-16	**Rome**
17-18-19-20	at Sav.
21-22-23-24	**Kannapolis**
26-27-28-29	at Augusta
30-31	**Columbus**

JUNE
1-2	**Columbus**
3-4-5-6	**Greensboro**
7-8-9-10	at Hickory
11-12-13-14	at Asheville
16-17-18-19	**Charleston**
21-22-23	at Columbus
24-25-26	**Savannah**
30	**Asheville**

JULY
1-2-3	**Asheville**
4-5-6-7	at Rome
8-9-10-11	at Kannapolis
13-14-15-16	**Columbus**
17-18-19-20	**Hickory**
21-22-23-24	at G'boro
26-27-28-29	at Augusta
30-31	**Columbus**

AUGUST
1-2	**Columbus**
3-4-5-6	at Charleston
8-9-10-11	**Savannah**
12-13-14-15	at Rome
16-17-18-19	**Augusta**
20-21-22-23	at Col.
24-25-26-27	**Charleston**
29-30-31	at Savannah

SEPTEMBER
1	at Savannah
2-3-4-5	**Rome**

HAGERSTOWN

APRIL
7-8-9-10	**West Virginia**
11-12-13	**Lakewood**
14-15-16-17	at W. Va.
18-19-20	at Lakewood
22-23-24-25	**Delmarva**
26-27-28-29	at L.C.
30	**Kannapolis**

MAY
1-2-3	**Kannapolis**
5-6-7-8	at Asheville
9-10-11-12	at Hickory
13-14-15-16	**G'boro**
17-18-19-20	at L'wood
21-22-23-24	**Lexington**
26-27	at Delmarva

28-29	**Delmarva**
30-31	**Lakewood**

JUNE
1-2	**Lakewood**
3-4-5-6	at Lexington
7-8-9-10	at Lake County
11-12-13-14	at Lex.
16-17-18-19	**W. Va.**
21-22-23-24	at L'wood
25-26	**Lexington**
30	at Lakewood

JULY
1	at Lakewood
2-3	**Lakewood**
4-5-6	at Delmarva
7-8	**West Virginia**
9-10	at West Virginia
11-12	at Lake County
14-15	**Lake County**
16-17	**West Virginia**
18-19	at West Virginia
21-22	at Lake County
23-24	**Lake County**
25	**Delmarva**
26-27	at Delmarva
28-29-30-31	at Kann.

AUGUST
2-3-4-5	**Lake County**
6-7-8-9	at Lexington
10-11-12-13	at G'boro
15-16-17-18	**Hickory**
19-20-21-22	**Asheville**
23-24	**Lexington**
25-26-27-28	at Delmarva
29-30	at Lakewood
31	**Lakewood**

SEPTEMBER
1	**Lakewood**
2-3-4-5	**Lexington**

HICKORY

APRIL
7-8	**Greensboro**
9-10	at Greensboro
11-12-13	at Asheville
14-15	at Greensboro
16-17	**Greensboro**
18-19-20	**Asheville**
21-22-23-24	at Kann.
26-27-28-29	**W. Va.**
30	at Delmarva

MAY
1-2-3	at Delmarva
4-5-6-7	at Lakewood
9-10-11-12	**Hagerstown**
13-14-15-16	**L.C.**
17-18-19-20	at Lex.
21-22-23-24	**Charleston**
26-27-28-29	at Col.
30-31	at Augusta

JUNE
1-2	at Augusta
3-4-5-6	**Savannah**
7-8-9-10	**Greenville**
11-12-13-14	at Rome
16-17-18-19	**Kannapolis**

21-22-23	**Greensboro**
24-25-26	at Asheville
30	at Savannah

JULY
1-2-3	at Savannah
4-5-6-7	**Columbus**
8-9-10-11	**Rome**
13-14-15-16	at Char.
17-18-19-20	at G'ville
21-22-23-24	**Augusta**
25-26-27-28	**Kannapolis**
29-30-31	at W. Va.

AUGUST
2-3-4-5	**Lakewood**
6-7-8-9	**Delmarva**
11-12-13-14	at L.C.
15-16-17-18	at Hag.
19-20-21-22	**Lexington**
23-24-25	at Kannapolis
26-27	**Asheville**
29-30	**Asheville**
31	at Greensboro

SEPTEMBER
1-2	at Greensboro
3-4-5	**Asheville**

KANNAPOLIS

APRIL
7-8-9-10	**Asheville**
11-12-13	**Greensboro**
14-15-16-17	at Asheville
18-19-20	at Greensboro
21-22-23-24	**Hickory**
26-27-28-29	**Lexington**
30	at Hagerstown

MAY
1-2-3	at Hagerstown
4-5-6-7	at Lake County
9-10-11-12	**Lakewood**
13-14-15-16	at W. Va.
17-18-19-20	**Delmarva**
21-22-23-24	at G'ville
25-26-27-28	at Sav.
30-31	**Rome**

JUNE
1-2	**Rome**
3-4-5-6	**Augusta**
7-8-9-10	at Charleston
11-12-13-14	**Columbus**
16-17-18-19	at Hickory
21-22-23	at Asheville
24-25-26	**Greensboro**
30	at Augusta

JULY
1-2-3	at Augusta
4-5-6-7	**Savannah**
8-9-10-11	**Greenville**
13-14-15-16	at Rome
17-18-19-20	at Col.
21-22-23-24	**Charleston**
25-26-27	at Hickory
28-29-30-31	**Hag.**

AUGUST
2-3-4-5	at Lexington
6-7-8-9	**Lake County**
11-12-13-14	at L'wood

15-16-17-18	at Del.
19-20-21-22	**W. Va.**
23-24-25	**Hickory**
26-27	**Greensboro**
29-30	at Greensboro
31	**Asheville**

SEPTEMBER
1-2	**Asheville**
3-4-5	at Greensboro

LAKE COUNTY

APRIL
7-8-9-10	at Lakewood
11-12-13	**Delmarva**
14-15-16-17	**Lakewood**
19-20-21	at Delmarva
22-23-24-25	**W. Va.**
26-27-28-29	**Hag.**
30	at Lexington

MAY
1-2-3	at Lexington
4-5-6-7	**Kannapolis**
9-10-11-12	at Asheville
13-14-15-16	at Hickory
17-18-19-20	**G'boro**
21-22-23-24	**Lakewood**
26-27-28-29	**W. Va.**
30-31	at Lexington

JUNE
1-2	at Lexington
3-4-5-6	**Delmarva**
7-8-9-10	at Hagerstown
11-12-13-14	at Delmarva
16-17-18-19	**Lexington**
21-22-23-24	**Delmarva**
25-26	at West Virginia
30	at Lexington

JULY
1-2-3	at Lexington
4-5-6	**Lakewood**
7-8-9-10	**Delmarva**
11-12	**Hagerstown**
14-15	at Hagerstown
16-17-18-19	at Delmarva
21-22	**Hagerstown**
23-24	at Hagerstown
25-26-27	at Lakewood
28-29-30-31	**Delmarva**

AUGUST
2-3-4-5	at Hagerstown
6-7-8-9	at Kannapolis
11-12-13-14	**Hickory**
15-16-17-18	**Asheville**
19-20-21-22	at G'boro
23-24	at West Virginia
25-26-27-28	at L'wood
29-30-31	**Lexington**

SEPTEMBER
1	**Lexington**
2-3-4-5	**West Virginia**

LAKEWOOD

APRIL
7-8-9-10	**Lake County**
11-12-13	at Hagerstown
14-15-16-17	at L.C.

18-19-20 **Hagerstown**
22-23-24-25 at Lex.
26-27-28-29 at G'boro
30 Asheville

MAY
1-2-3 Asheville
4-5-6-7 Hickory
9-10-11-12 Kannapolis
13-14-15-16 at Delmarva
17-18-19-20 Hag.
21-22-23-24 at L.C.
25-26-27-28 Charleston
30-31 at Hagerstown

JUNE
1-2 at Hagerstown
3-4-5-6 West Virginia
7-8 Delmarva
9-10 at Delmarva
11-12-13-14 at W. Va.
16-17-18-19 at Del.
21-22-23-24 Hag.
25-26 Delmarva
30 Hagerstown

JULY
1 Hagerstown
2-3 at Hagerstown
4-5-6 at Lake County
7-8-9-10 at Lexington
12-13-14-15 W. Va.
16-17-18-19 Lexington
20-21-22-23-24 at W.Va.
25-26-27 Lake County
28-29-30-31 Greensboro

AUGUST
2-3-4-5 at Hickory
6-7-8-9 at Asheville
11-12-13-14 Kannapolis
16-17-18 at W. Va.
19-20 at Delmarva
21-22-23-24 Delmarva
25-26-27-28 L.C.
29-30 Hagerstown
31 at Hagerstown

SEPTEMBER
1 at Hagerstown
2-3-4-5 Delmarva

LEXINGTON

APRIL
7-8-9-10 Delmarva
11-12-13 West Virginia
15-16-17-18 at Delmarva
19-20-21 at W. Va.
22-23-24-25 Lakewood
26-27-28-29 at Kann.
30 Lake County

MAY
1-2-3 Lake County
5-6-7-8 at W. Va.
9-10-11-12 at G'boro
13-14-15-16 Asheville

17-18-19-20 Hickory
21-22-23-24 at Hag.
25-26-27-28 at Asheville
30-31 **Lake County**

JUNE
1-2 Lake County
3-4-5-6 Hagerstown
7-8-9-10 at W. Va.
11-12-13-14 Hag.
16-17-18-19 at L.C.
21-22-23-24 W. Va.
25-26 at Hagerstown
30 Lake County

JULY
1-2-3 at Lake County
4-5-6 at West Virginia
7-8-9-10 Lakewood
12-13-14-15 at Delmarva
16-17-18-19 at L'wood
21-22-23-24 Delmarva
25-26-27 West Virginia
28-29-30-31 at Asheville

AUGUST
2-3-4-5 Kannapolis
6-7-8-9 Hagerstown
11-12-13-14 at W.Va.
15-16-17-18 G'boro
19-20-21-22 at Hickory
23-24 at Hagerstown
25-26-27-28 W. Va.
29-30-31 at Lake County

SEPTEMBER
1 at Lake County
2-3-4-5 at Hagerstown

ROME

APRIL
7-8-9-10 Greenville
11-12-13 Augusta
14-15-16-17 at Col.
18-19-20 at Augusta
21-22-23-24 Columbus
26-27-28-29 Savannah
30 at Charleston

MAY
1-2-3 at Charleston
4-5-6-7 Greenville
9-10-11-12 at Augusta
13 14 15 16 at G'ville
17-18-19-20 Augusta
21-22-23-24 Asheville
26-27-28-29 at G'boro
30-31 at Kannapolis

JUNE
1-2 at Kannapolis
3-4-5-6 Charleston
7-8-9-10 at Savannah
11-12-13-14 Hickory
16-17-18-19 at Col.
21-22-23 at Augusta
24-25-26 Columbus

---

30 at Charleston

JULY
1-2-3 at Charleston
4-5-6-7 Greenville
8-9-10-11 at Hickory
13-14-15-16 Kannapolis
17-18-19-20 G'boro
21-22-23-24 at Ashe.
26-27-28-29 Columbus
30-31 at Savannah

AUGUST
1-2 at Savannah
3-4-5-6 at Augusta
8-9-10-11 Charleston
12-13-14-15 Greenville
16-17-18-19 at Col.
20-21-22-23 Savannah
25-26-27-28 Augusta
29-30-31 at Charleston

SEPTEMBER
1 at Charleston
2-3-4-5 at Greenville

SAVANNAH

APRIL
7-8-9-10 Columbus
11-12-13 Greenville
14-15-16-17 at Augusta
18-19-20 at Greenville
21-22-23-24 Augusta
26-27-28-29 at Rome
30 Columbus

MAY
1-2-3 Columbus
5-6-7-8 Charleston
9-10-11-12 at G'ville
13-14-15-16 at Char.
17-18-19-20 Greenville
21-22-23-24 at Col.
25-26-27-28 Kannapolis
30-31 at Asheville

JUNE
1-2 at Asheville
3-4-5-6 at Hickory
7-8-9-10 Rome
11-12-13-14 G'boro
16-17-18-19 at Augusta
21-22-23 Charleston
24-25-26 at Greenville
30 Hickory

JULY
1-2-3 Hickory
4-5-6-7 at Kannapolis
8-9-10-11 at G'boro
13-14-15-16 at Ashe.
17-18-19-20 Augusta
21-22-23-24 at Col.
26-27-28-29 Charleston
30-31 **Rome**

AUGUST
1-2 Rome

4-5-6-7 at Columbus
8-9-10-11 at Greenville
12-13-14-15 Augusta
16-17-18-19 at Char.
20-21-22-23 at Rome
25-26-27-28 Columbus
29-30-31 Greenville

SEPTEMBER
1 **Greenville**
2-3-4-5 at Augusta

WEST VIRGINIA

APRIL
7-8-9-10 at Hagerstown
11-12-13 at Lexington
14-15-16-17 Hag.
19-20-21 Lexington
22-23-24-25 at L.C.
26-27-28-29 at Hickory
30 Greensboro

MAY
1-2-3 Greensboro
5-6-7-8 Lexington
9-10-11-12 at Delmarva
13-14-15-16 Kannapolis
17-18-19-20 at Ashe.
21-22-23-24 Delmarva
26-27-28-29 L.C.
30-31 at Delmarva

JUNE
1-2 at Delmarva
3-4-5-6 at Lakewood
7-8-9-10 Lexington
11-12-13-14 Lakewood
16-17-18-19 at Hag.
21-22-23-24 at Lex.
25-26 Lake County
30 at Delmarva

JULY
1-2-3 at Delmarva
4-5-6 Lexington
7-8-9-10 Hagerstown
12-13-14-15 at L'wood
16-17-18-19 at Hag.
20-21-22-23-24 L'wood
25-26-27 at Lexington
28-29-30-31 Hickory

AUGUST
2-3-4-5 Asheville
6-7-8-9 at Greensboro
11-12-13-14 Lexington
16-17-18 Lakewood
19-20-21-22 at Kann.
23-24 at Lake County
25-26-27-28 at Lex.
29-30-31 Delmarva

SEPTEMBER
1 **Delmarva**
2-3-4-5 at Lake County

SHORT-SEASON CLASS A
NEW YORK-PENN LEAGUE

ABERDEEN
JUNE
21-22-23	Hudson Valley
24-25-26	at Brooklyn
27-28-29	at Williamsport
30	Brooklyn

JULY
1-2	Brooklyn
3-4-5	Williamsport
6-7-8	at Hudson Valley
9-10-11	New Jersey
13-14-15	Staten Island
16-17-18	at Tri-City
19-20-21	at Vermont
22-23-24	M.V.
25-26-27	Oneonta
28-29-30	at New Jersey
31	at Jamestown

AUGUST
1-2	at Jamestown
4-5-6	Batavia
7-8-9	Lowell
10-11-12	at Auburn
13-14-15	at S.I.
16-17	Hudson Valley
18-19	at New Jersey
20-21	at Brooklyn
24-25	New Jersey
26-27-28	Williamsport
29-30	Staten Island
31	at Williamsport

SEPTEMBER
1-2	at Williamsport
3-4	at Staten Island
5-6	Brooklyn
7-8	at Hudson Valley

AUBURN
JUNE
21	Batavia
22-23	at Batavia
24-25-26	M.V.
27-28-29	Jamestown
30	at Mahoning Valley

JULY
1-2	at Mahoning Valley
3-4-5	at Jamestown
6-7	Batavia
8	at Batavia
9-10-11	at Lowell
13-14-15	Vermont
16-17-18	at Brooklyn
19-20-21	New Jersey
22-23-24	at Tri-City
25-26-27	Hudson Valley
28-29-30	at M.V.
31	at Staten Island

AUGUST
1-2	at Staten Island
4-5-6	Oneonta
7-8-9	at Williamsport
10-11-12	Aberdeen
13	at Batavia
14	Batavia
15	at Batavia
16	Batavia
17	at Batavia
18-19-20-21	Jamestown
24	Batavia
25	at Batavia
26	Batavia
27-28	at M.V.
29-30-31	at Jamestown

SEPTEMBER
1	at Jamestown
2-3-4-5-6	M.V.
7	at Batavia
8	Batavia

BATAVIA
JUNE
21	at Auburn
22-23	Auburn
24	at Jamestown
25	Jamestown
26	at Jamestown
27-28-29	at M.V.
30	Jamestown

JULY
1	at Jamesotwn
2	Jamestown
3-4-5	Mahoning Valley
6-7	at Auburn
8	Auburn
9-10-11	Tri-City
13-14-15	at Oneonta
16-17-18	Staten Island
19-20-21	at Lowell
22-23-24	at H.V.
25-26-27	Brooklyn
28	Jamestown
29	at Jamestown
30	Jamestown
31	Williamsport

AUGUST
1-2	Williamsport
4-5-6	at Aberdeen
7-8-9	at New Jersey
10-11-12	Vermont
13	Auburn
14	at Auburn
15	Auburn
16	at Auburn
17	Auburn
18-19-20-21	at M.V.
24	at Auburn
25	Auburn
26	at Auburn
27	Jamestown
29-30-31	M.V.

SEPTEMBER
1	Mahoning Valley
2	at Jamestown
3	Jamestown
4	at Jamestown
5	Jamestown
6	at Jamestown
7	Auburn
8	at Auburn

BROOKLYN
JUNE
21	Staten Island
22	at Staten Island
23	at Staten Island
24-25-26	Aberdeen
27	New Jersey
28	at New Jersey
29	New Jersey
30	at Aberdeen

JULY
1-2	at Aberdeen
3-4	at New Jersey
5	New Jersey
6-7	Staten Island
8	at Staten Island
10-11-12	at H.V.
13-14-15	Williamsport
16-17-18	Auburn
19-20-21	at Oneonta
22-23-24	Jamestown
25-26-27	at Batavia
28-29-30	Hudson Valley
31	at Lowell

AUGUST
1-2	at Lowell
4-5-6	Vermont
7-8-9	at Mahoning Valley
10-11-12	Tri-City
13-14-15	at Williamsport
16-17	New Jersey
18-19	Williamsport
20-21	Aberdeen
24-25	at Williamsport
26-27	at Staten Island
28	Staten Island
29-30	Hudson Valley
31	Staten Island

SEPTEMBER
1	Staten Island
2	at Staten Island
3-4	at Hudson Valley
5-6	at Aberdeen
7-8	at New Jersey

HUDSON VALLEY
JUNE
21-22-23	at Aberdeen
24-25-26	Williamsport
27	at Staten Island
28-29	Staten Island
30	at Williamsport

JULY
1-2	at Williamsport
3	at Staten Island
4	Staten Island
5	at Staten Island
6-7-8	Aberdeen
9-10-11	Brooklyn
13-14-15	at New Jersey
16-17-18	at Jamestown
19-20-21	M.V.
22-23-24	Batavia
25-26-27	at Auburn
28-29-30	at Brooklyn

AUGUST
1-2-3	Oneonta
4-5-6	at Tri-City
7-8-9	at Vermont
10-11-12	Lowell
13-14-15	New Jersey
16-17	at Aberdeen
18	Staten Island
19	at Staten Island
20-21	Williamsport
24	Staten Island
25	at Staten Island
26-27-28	New Jersey
29-30	at Brooklyn
31	at New Jersey

SEPTEMBER
1-2	at New Jersey
3-4	Brooklyn
5-6	at Williamsport
7-8	Aberdeen

JAMESTOWN
JUNE
21-22-23	at M.V.
24	Batavia
25	at Batavia
26	Batavia
27-28-29	at Auburn
30	at Batavia

JULY
1	Batavia
2	at Batavia
3-4-5	Auburn
6-7-8	Mahoning Valley
9-10-11	at Vermont
13-14-15	Lowell
16-17-18	Hudson Valley
19-20-21	at S.I.
22-23-24	at Brooklyn
25-26-27	Tri-City
28	at Batavia
29	Batavia
30	at Batavia
31	Aberdeen

AUGUST
1-2	Aberdeen
4-5-6	New Jersey
7-8-9	at Oneonta
10-11-12	at Williamsport
13-14-15-16-17	M.V.
18-19-20-21	at Auburn
24-25-26	at M.V.
27	at Batavia
29-30-31	Auburn

SEPTEMBER
1	Auburn
2	Batavia
3	at Batavia
4	Batavia
5	at Batavia
6	Batavia
7-8	at Mahoning Valley

LOWELL

JUNE
21-22-23	**Vermont**
24-25-26	at Oneonta
27-28-29	**Tri City**
30	**Oneonta**

JULY
1-2	**Oneonta**
3-4-5	at Tri-City
6-7-8	at Vermont
9-10-11	**Auburn**
13-14-15	at Jamestown
16-17-18	at M.V.
19-20-21	**Batavia**
22-23-24	**Staten Island**
25-26-27	at New Jersey
28-29-30	at Vermont
31	**Brooklyn**

AUGUST
1-2	**Brooklyn**
4-5-6	**Williamsport**
7-8-9	at Aberdeen
10-11-12	at H.V.
13-14-15-16-17	**Oneonta**
18-19-20-21	at Tri-City
24-25	at Vermont
26-27-28-29	**Tri-City**
30-31	**Vermont**

SEPTEMBER
1-2-3	**Vermont**
4-5-6-7-8	at Oneonta

MAHONING VALLEY

JUNE
21-22-23	**Jamestown**
24-25-26	at Auburn
27-28-29	**Batavia**
30	**Auburn**

JULY
1-2	**Auburn**
3-4-5	at Batavia
6-7-8	at Jamestown
9-10-11	**Oneonta**
13-14-15	at Tri City
16-17-18	**Lowell**
19-20-21	at H.V.
22-23-24	at Aberdeen
25-26-27	**Williamsport**
28-29-30	**Auburn**
31	at Vermont

AUGUST
1-2	at Vermont
4-5-6	**Staten Island**
7-8-9	**Brooklyn**
10-11-12	at New Jersey
13-14-15-16-17	at Jam.
18-19-20-21	**Batavia**
24-25-26	**Jamestown**
27-28	**Auburn**
29-30-31	at Batavia

SEPTEMBER
1	at Batavia
2-3-4-5-6	at Auburn
7-8	**Jamestown**

NEW JERSEY

JUNE
21-22-23	**Williamsport**
24-25	at Staten Island

26	**Staten Island**
27	at Brooklyn
28	**Brooklyn**
29	at Brooklyn
30	at Staten Island

JULY
1-2	**Staten Island**
3-4	**Brooklyn**
5	at Brooklyn
6-7-8	at Williamsport
9-10-11	at Aberdeen
13-14-15	**Hudson Valley**
16-17-18	**Oneonta**
19-20-21	at Auburn
22-23-24	at Vermont
25-26-27	**Lowell**
28-29-30	**Aberdeen**

AUGUST
1-2-3	at Tri City
4-5-6	at Jamestown
7-8-9	**Batavia**
10-11-12	**M.V.**
13-14-15	at H.V.
16-17	at Brooklyn
18-19	**Aberdeen**
20-21	**Staten Island**
24-25	at Aberdeen
26-27-28	at H.V.
29-30	**Williamsport**
31	**Hudson Valley**

SEPTEMBER
1-2	**Hudson Valley**
3-4	at Williamsport
5-6	at Staten Island
7-8	**Brooklyn**

ONEONTA

JUNE
21	at Tri-City
22	**Tri-City**
23	at Tri-City
24-25-26	**Lowell**
27-28-29	at Vermont
30	at Lowell

JULY
1-2	at Lowell
3-4-5	**Vermont**
6	**Tri-City**
7	at Tri-City
8	**Tri-City**
9-10-11	at M.V.
13-14-15	**Batavia**
16-17-18	at New Jersey
19-20-21	**Brooklyn**
22-23-24	**Williamsport**
25-26-27	at Aberdeen
29-30-31	**Tri-City**

AUGUST
1-2-3	at Hudson Valley
4-5-6	at Auburn
7-8-9	**Jamestown**
10-11-12	**Staten Island**
13-14-15-16-17	at Low.
18-19-20-21	at Vermont
24-25	**Tri City**
26-27-28-29	**Vermont**
30-31	at Tri-City

SEPTEMBER
1-2-3	at Tri-City
4-5-6-7-8	**Lowell**

STATEN ISLAND

JUNE
21	at Brooklyn
22-23	**Brooklyn**
24-25	**New Jersey**
26	at New Jersey
27	**Hudson Valley**
28-29	at Hudson Valley
30	**New Jersey**

JULY
1-2	at New Jersey
3	**Hudson Valley**
4	at Hudson Valley
5	**Hudson Valley**
6-7	at Brooklyn
8	at Staten Island
9-10-11	**Williamsport**
13-14-15	at Aberdeen
16-17-18	at Batavia
19-20-21	**Jamestown**
22-23-24	at Lowell
25-26-27	**Vermont**
28-29-30	at Williamsport
31	**Auburn**

AUGUST
1-2	**Auburn**
4-5-6	at Mahoning Valley
7-8-9	**Tri-City**
10-11-12	at Oneonta
13-14-15	**Aberdeen**
16-17	**Williamsport**
18	at Hudson Valley
19	**Hudson Valley**
20-21	at New Jersey
24	at Hudson Valley
25	**Hudson Valley**
26-27	**Brooklyn**
28	at Brooklyn
29-30	at Aberdeen
31	at Brooklyn

SEPTEMBER
1	at Brooklyn
2	**Brooklyn**
3-4	**Aberdeen**
5-6	**New Jersey**
7-8	at Williamsport

TRI-CITY

JUNE
21	**Oneonta**
22	at Oneonta
23	**Oneonta**
24-25-26	at Vermont
27-28-29	at Lowell
30	**Vermont**

JULY
1-2	**Vermont**
3-4-5	**Lowell**
6	at Oneonta
7	**Oneonta**
8	at Oneonta
9-10-11	at Batavia
13-14-15	**M.V.**
16-17-18	**Aberdeen**
19-20-21	at Williamsport
22-23-24	**Auburn**
25-26-27	at Jamestown
29-30-31	at Oneonta

AUGUST
1-2-3	**New Jersey**
4-5-6	**Hudson Valley**
7-8-9	at Staten Island
10-11-12	at Brooklyn
13-14-15	**Vermont**
16-17	at Vermont
18-19-20-21	**Lowell**
24-25	at Oneonta
26-27-28-29	at Lowell
30-31	**Oneonta**

SEPTEMBER
1-2-3	**Oneonta**
4-5-6	at Vermont
7-8	**Vermont**

VERMONT

JUNE
21-22-23	at Lowell
24-25-26	**Tri-City**
27-28-29	**Oneonta**
30	at Tri-City

JULY
1-2	at Tri-City
3-4-5	at Oneonta
6-7-8	**Lowell**
9-10-11	**Jamestown**
13-14-15	at Auburn
16-17-18	at Williamsport
19-20-21	**Aberdeen**
22-23-24	**New Jersey**
25-26-27	at S.I.
28-29-30	**Lowell**
31	**Mahoning Valley**

AUGUST
1-2	**Mahoning Valley**
4-5-6	at Brooklyn
7-8-9	**Hudson Valley**
10-11-12	at Batavia
13-14-15	at Tri-City
16-17	**Tri-City**
18-19-20-21	**Oneonta**
24-25	**Lowell**
26-27-28-29	at Oneonta
30-31	at Lowell

SEPTEMBER
1-2-3	at Lowell
4-5-6	**Tri-City**
7-8	at Tri-City

WILLIAMSPORT

JUNE
21-22-23	at New Jersey
24-25-26	at H.V.
27-28-29	**Aberdeen**
30	**Hudson Valley**

JULY
1-2	**Hudson Valley**
3-4-5	at Aberdeen
6-7-8	**New Jersey**
9-10-11	at Staten Island
13-14-15	at Brooklyn
16-17-18	**Vermont**
19-20-21	**Tri-City**
22-23-24	at Oneonta
25-26-27	at M.V.
28-29-30	**Staten Island**
31	at Batavia

AUGUST		
1-2	at Batavia	
4-5-6	at Lowell	
7-8-9	Auburn	
10-11-12	Jamestown	

13-14-15	Brooklyn
16-17	at Staten Island
18-19	at Brooklyn
20-21	at Hudson Valley
24-25	Brooklyn

26-27-28	at Aberdeen
29-30	at New Jersey
31	Aberdeen

SEPTEMBER	
1-2	Aberdeen
3-4	New Jersey
5-6	Hudson Valley
7-8	Staten Island

NORTHWEST LEAGUE

BOISE

JUNE
21-22-23-24-25	at Ever.
26-27-28-29-30	Eugene

JULY
1-2-3	at Tri-City
4-5-6-7-8	Everett
9-10-11	at Yakima
13-14-15	Tri-City
16-17-18-19-20	at Eug.
21-22-23	Yakima
24-25-26	at Yakima
27-28-29-30-31	Van.

AUGUST
2-3-4-5-6	at S.-K.
7-8-9	at Spokane
10-11-12	Spokane
13-14-15-16-17	S.-K.
19-20-21-22-23	at Van.
24-25-26	at Spokane
27-28-29	at Tri-City
30-31	Tri-City

SEPTEMBER
1	Tri City
2-3-4	Yakima
5-6-7	Spokane

EVERETT

JUNE
21-22-23-24-25	Boise
26-27-28-29-30	at Spok.

JULY
1-2-3	Vancouver
4-5-6-7-8	at Boise
9-10-11	Salem-Keizer
13-14-15	at Vancouver
16-17-18-19-20	Spok.
21-22-23	at S.-K.
24-25-26	Eugene
27-28-29-30-31	Tri-City

AUGUST
2-3-4-5-6	Yakima
7-8-9	Eugene
10-11-12	at Eugene
13-14-15-16-17	Yakima
19-20-21-22-23	at T.-C.
24-25-26	Salem-Keizer
27-28-29	at Vancouver
30-31	Vancouver

SEPTEMBER
1	Vancouver
2-3-4	at Salem-Keizer
5-6-7	at Eugene

SPOKANE

JUNE
21-22-23-24-25	at Eug.
26-27-28-29-30	Everett

JULY
1-2-3	at Yakima
4-5-6-7-8	Eugene
9-10-11	at Tri-City
13-14-15	Yakima
16-17-18-19-20	at Ever.
21-22-23	Tri-City
24-25-26	at Tri-City
27-28-29-30-31	S.-K.

AUGUST
2-3-4-5-6	at Vancouver
7-8-9	Boise
10-11-12	at Boise
13-14-15-16-17	Van.
19-20-21-22-23	at S.-K.
24-25-26	Boise
27-28-29	Yakima
30-31	at Yakima

SEPTEMBER
1	at Yakima
2-3-4	Tri-City
5-6-7	at Boise

VANCOUVER

JUNE
21-22-23-24-25	at Yak.
26-27-28-29-30	Tri-City

JULY
1-2-3	at Everett
4-5-6-7-8	Yakima
9-10-11	at Eugene
13-14-15	Everett
16-17-18-19-20	at T.-C.
21-22-23	Eugene
24-25-26	at S.-K.
27-28-29-30-31	at Boise

AUGUST
2-3-4-5-6	Spokane
7-8-9	Salem-Keizer
10-11-12	at S.-K.
13-14-15-16-17	at Spok.
19-20-21-22-23	Boise
24-25-26	at Eugene
27-28-29	Everett
30-31	at Everett

SEPTEMBER
1	at Everettt
2-3-4	Eugene
5-6-7	Salem Keizer

EUGENE

JUNE
21-22-23-24-25	Spok.
26-27-28-29-30	at Boise

JULY
1-2-3	Salem-Keizer
4-5-6-7-8	at Spokane
9-10-11	Vancouver
13-14-15	at S.-K.
16-17-18-19-20	Boise
21-22-23	at Vancouver
24-25-26	at Everett
27-28-29-30-31	Yakima

AUGUST
2-3-4-5-6	at Tri-City
7-8-9	at Everett
10-11-12	Everett
13-14-15-16-17	Tri-City
19-20-21-22-23	at Yak.
24-25-26	Vancouver
27-28-29	at S.-K.
30-31	Salem-Keizer

SEPTEMBER
1	Salem-Keizer
2-3-4	at Vancouver
5-6-7	Everett

SALEM-KEIZER

JUNE
21-22-23-24-25	at T.-C.
26-27-28-29-30	Yakima

JULY
1-2-3	at Eugene
4-5-6-7-8	Tri-City
9-10-11	at Everett
13-14-15	Eugene
16-17-18-19-20	at Yak.
21-22-23	Everett
24-25-26	Vancouver
27-28-29-30-31	at Spok.

AUGUST
2-3-4-5-6	Boise
7-8-9	at Vancouver
10-11-12	Vancouver
13-14-15-16-17	at Boise
19-20-21-22-23	Spok.
24-25-26	at Everett
27-28-29	Eugene
30-31	at Eugene

SEPTEMBER
1	at Eugene
2-3-4	Everett
5-6-7	at Vancouver

TRI-CITY

JUNE
21-22-23-24-25	S.-K.
26-27-28-29-30	at Van.

JULY
1-2-3	Boise
4-5-6-7-8	at S.-K.
9-10-11	Spokane
13-14-15	at Yakima
16-17-18-19-20	Van.
21-22-23	at Spokane
24-25-26	Spokane
27-28-29-30-31	at Ever.

AUGUST
2-3-4-5-6	Eugene
7-8-9	Yakima
10-11-12	at Yakima
13-14-15-16-17	at Eug.
19-20-21-22-23	Everett
24-25-26	at Yakima
27-28-29	Boise
30-31	at Boise

SEPTEMBER
1	at Boise
2-3-4	at Spokane
5-6-7	Yakima

YAKIMA

JUNE
21-22-23-24-25	Van.
26-2-28-29-30	at S.-K.

JULY
1-2-3	Spokane
4-5-6-7-8	at Vancouver
9-10-11	Boise
13-14-15	at Spokane
16-17-18-19-20	S.-K.
21-22-23	at Boise
24-25-26	Boise
27-28-29-30-31	at Eug.

AUGUST
2-3-4-5-6	Everett
7-8-9	at Tri-City
10-11-12	Tri-City
13-14-15-16-17	at Ever.
19-20-21-22-23	Eugene
24-25-26	Tri-City
27-28-29	at Spokane
30-31	Spokane

SEPTEMBER
1	Spokane
2-3-4	at Boise
5-6-7	at Tri-City

ROOKIE LEAGUES
APPALACHIAN LEAGUE

BLUFIELD

JUNE

21-22-23	at Elizabethton
24-25-26	Danville
27-28-29	Bristol
30	at Princeton

JULY

1-2-3	at Princeton
4	Princeton
5-6-7	Johnson City
8-9-10	at Danville
12-13-14	at Bristol
15-16-17	Kingsport
18-19-20	Burlington
21-22-23	at Pulaski
24-25-26	Princeton
27-28-29	at Burlington
30-31	at Kingsport

AUGUST

1	at Kingsport
3-4-5	Greeneville
6-7-8	at Johnson City
9-10-11	Princeton
12-13-14	at Pulaski
16-17-18	Burlington
19-20-21	Pulaski
22-23-24	at Greeneville
25-26-27	Elizabethton
28-29-30	at Danville

BRISTOL

JUNE

21-22-23	Greeneville
24-25-26	at Kingsport
27-28-29	at Bluefield
30	Burlington

JULY

1-2	Burlington
3	Pulaski
4-5-6-7	at Pulaski
8-9-10	at Burlington
12-13-14	Bluefield
15-16-17	Pulaski
18-19-20	at Elizabethton
21-22-23	at Greeneville
24-25-26	Kingsport
28-29-30	at J.C.
31	Danville

AUGUST

1-2	Danville
3-4-5	Johnson City
6-7-8	at Danville
9-10-11	at Johnson City
12-13-14	Greeneville
16-17-18	at Elizabethton
19-20-21	Princeton
22-23-24	Elizabethton
25-26-27	at Princeton
28-29-30	Kingsport

BURLINGTON

JUNE

21-22-23	at Princeton
24-25-26	at Elizabethton
27-28-29	Pulaski
30	at Bristol

JULY

1-2	at Bristol
3	at Danville
4	Danville
5-6-7	Princeton
8-9-10	Bristol
12-13-14	at Princeton
15-16-17	Danville
18-19-20	at Bluefield
21-22-23	at Danville
24-25-26	Elizabethton
27-28-29	Bluefield
30-31	at Pulaski

AUGUST

1	at Pulaski
3-4-5	Pulaski
6-7-8	Kingsport
9-10-11	at Greeneville
12-13-14	Danville
16-17-18	at Bluefield
19-20-21	at Kingsport
22-23-24	Johnson City
25-26-27	Greeneville
28-29-30	at J.C.

DANVILLE

JUNE

21-22-23	at Pulaski
24-25-26	at Bluefield
27-28-29	Princeton
30	Greeneville

JULY

1-2	Greeneville
3	at Burlington
5-6-7	at Greeneville
8-9-10	Bluefield
12-13-14	Kingsport
15-16-17	at Burlington
18-19-20	at Pulaski
21-22-23	Burlington
24-25-26	Pulaski
28-29-30	at Elizabethton
31	at Bristol

AUGUST

1-2	at Bristol
3-4-5	at Princeton
6-7-8	Bristol
9-10-11	Elizabethton
12-13-14	at Burlington
16-17-18	Princeton
19-20-21	at J.C.
22-23-24	at Kingsport
25-26-27	at J.C.
28-29-30	Bluefield

ELIZABETHTON

JUNE

21-22-23	Bluefield
24-25-26	Burlington
27-28-29	at J.C.
30	Kingsport

JULY

1-2	Kingsport
3	Greeneville
4	at Greeneville
5-6-7	at Kingsport
8-9-10	Greeneville
12-13-14	Pulaski
15-16-17	at Greeneville
18-19-20	Bristol
21-22-23	at Princeton
24-25-26	at Burlington
28-29-30	Danville
31	Johnson City

AUGUST

1-2	Johnson City
3-4-5	at Kingsport
6-7-8	at Pulaski
9-10-11	at Danville
12-13-14	Johnson City
16-17-18	Bristol
19-20-21	at Greeneville
22-23-24	at Bristol
25-26-27	at Bluefield
28-29-30	Princeton

GREENEVILLE

JUNE

21-22-23	at Bristol
24-25-26	Johnson City
27-28-29	Kingsport
30	at Danville

JULY

1-2	at Danville
3	at Elizabethton
4	Elizabethton
5-6-7	Danville
8-9-10	at Elizabethton
12-13-14	at J.C.
15-16-17	Elizabethton
18-19-20	at Kingsport
21-22-23	Bristol
24-25-26	at J.C.
27-28-29	Kingsport
30-31	Princeton

AUGUST

1	Princeton
3-4-5	at Bluefield
6-7-8	at Princeton
9-10-11	Burlington
12-13-14	at Bristol
16-17-18	at Pulaski
19-20-21	Elizabethton
22-23-24	Bluefield
25-26-27	at Burlington
28-29-30	Pulaski

JOHNSON CITY

JUNE

21-22	at Kingsport
23	Kingsport
24-25-26	at Greeneville
27-28-29	Elizabethton
30	Pulaski

JULY

1-2	Johnson City
3	at Kingsport
4	Kingsport
5-6-7	at Bluefield
8-9-10	at Pulaski
12-13-14	Greeneville
15-16-17	Princeton
18-19-20	at Princeton
21-22-23	at Kingsport
24-25-26	Greeneville
28-29-30	Bristol
31	at Elizabethton

AUGUST

1-2	at Elizabethton
3-4-5	at Bristol
6-7-8	Bluefield
9-10-11	Bristol
12-13-14	at Elizabethton
16	at Kingsport
17-18	Kingsport
19-20-21	Danville
22-23-24	at Burlington
25-26-27	at Danville
28-29-30	Burlington

KINGSPORT

JUNE

21-22	Johnson City
23	at Johnson City
24-25-26	Bristol
27-28-29	at Greeneville
30	at Elizabethton

JULY

1-2	at Elizabethton
3	at Johnson City
4	at Johnson City
5-6-7	Elizabethton
8-9-10	Princeton
12-13-14	at Danville
15-16-17	at Bluefield
18-19-20	Greeneville
21-22-23	Johnson City
24-25-26	at Bristol
27-28-29	at Greeneville
30-31	Bluefield

AUGUST

1	Bluefield
3-4-5	Elizabethton
6-7-8	at Burlington
9-10-11	Pulaski
12-13-14	at Princeton
16	at Johnson City
17-18	Johnson City
19-20-21	Burlington
22-23-24	Danville
25-26-27	at Pulaski
28-29-30	at Bristol

PRINCETON

JUNE

21-22-23	Burlington
24-25-26	at Pulaski
27-28-29	at Danville
30	Bluefield

JULY

1-2-3	Bluefield
4	at Bluefield
5-6-7	at Burlington

8-9-10	at Kingsport	9-10-11	at Bluefield	30	at Johnson City	30-31	Burlington
12-13-14	**Burlington**	**12-13-14**	**Kingsport**	**JULY**		**AUGUST**	
15-16-17	at J.C.	16-17-18	at Danville	1-2	at Johnson City	1	Burlington
18-19-20	**Johnson City**	19-20-21	at Bristol	3	at Bristol	3-4-5	at Burlington
21-22-23	**Elizabethton**	**22-23-24**	**Pulaski**	**4-5-6-7**	**Bristol**	**6-7-8**	**Elizabethton**
24-25-26	at Bluefield	**25-26-27**	**Bristol**	**8-9-10**	**Johnson City**	9-10-11	at Kingsport
27-28-29	**Pulaski**	28-29-30	at Elizabethton	12-13-14	at Elizabethton	**12-13-14**	**Bluefield**
30-31	at Greeneville	**PULASKI**		15-16-17	at Bristol	**16-17-18**	**Greeneville**
AUGUST		**JUNE**		**18-19-20**	**Danville**	19-20-21	at Bluefield
1	at Greeneville	**21-22-23**	**Danville**	**21-22-23**	**Bluefield**	22-23-24	at Princeton
3-4-5	**Danville**	**24-25-26**	**Princeton**	24-25-26	at Danville	**25-26-27**	**Kingsport**
6-7-8	**Greeneville**	27-28-29	at Burlington	27-28-29	at Princeton	28-29-30	at Greeneville

PIONEER LEAGUE

BILLINGS

JUNE
21-22-23-24	at G.F.
25-26	at Missoula
27-28	**Great Falls**
29-30	**Helena**

JULY
1	Helena
2-3-4	at Missoula
5-6-7	**Missoula**
8-9	**Helena**
11-12-13-14	at I.F.
15-16-17	**Casper**
18-19-20-21	**Idaho Falls**
22-23-24	at Casper
25-26-27	at Helena
28-29-30	**Great Falls**

AUGUST
1-2-3	at Missoula
4-5	at Helena
6-7-8	**Helena**
10-11-12	at Ogden
13-13-15-16	at Orem
18-19-20-21	**Ogden**
22-23-24	**Orem**
25-26-27	at Helena
28-29-30	**Great Falls**
31	**Missoula**

SEPTEMBER
1	Missoula
2-3-4-5	at Great Falls
6-7-8	**Missoula**

CASPER

JUNE
21-22-23-24	Idaho Falls
25-26	at Idaho Falls
27-28-29	at Ogden
30	**Orem**

JULY
1	Orem
2-3-4	**Ogden**
5-6-7	at Orem
8-9	at Ogden
11-12-13-14	**Great Falls**
15-16-17	at Billings
18-19-20-21	at G.F.
22-23-34	**Billings**
25-26-27	**Orem**
28-29-30	at Idaho Falls

AUGUST
1-2-3	at Orem
4-5-6	**Ogden**
7-8-9	**Orem**
10-11-12	at Helena
13-14-15-16	at Missoula
18-29-20	**Missoula**
21-22-23-24	**Helena**
26-27-28	at Ogden
29-30	at Orem
31	at Idaho Falls

SEPTEMBER
1-2	at Idaho Falls
3-4-5-6	**Idaho Falls**
7-8	**Ogden**

GREAT FALLS

JUNE
21-22-23-24	Billings
25-26	at Helena
27-28	at Billings
29-30	**Missoula**

JULY
1	Missoula
2-3-4	**Helena**
5-6-7	at Helena
8-9	**Missoula**
11-12-13-14	at Casper
15-16-17	at Idaho Falls
18-19-20-21	**Casper**
22-23-24	**Idaho Fall**
25-26-27	at Missoula
28-29-30	at Billings

AUGUST
1-2-3	Helena
4-5	at Missoula
6-7-8	**Missoula**
10-11-12	at Orem
13-14-15-16	at Ogden
18-19-20-21	**Orem**
22-23-24	**Ogden**
25-26-27	at Missoula
28-29-30	at Billing
31	**Helena**

SEPTEMBER
1	Helena
2-3-4-5	**Billings**
6-7-8	at Helena

HELENA

JUNE
21-22-23-24	at Missoula
25-26	**Great Falls**
27-28	**Missoula**
29-30	at Billings

JULY
1	at Billings
2-3-4	at Great Falls
5-6-7	**Great Falls**
8-9	at Billings
11-12-13-14	**Ogden**
15-16-17	**Orem**
18-19-20	at Ogden
21-22-23-24	at Orem
25-26-27	**Billings**
28-29-30	**Missoula**

AUGUST
1-2-3	at Great Falls
4-5	**Billings**
6-7-8	at Billings
10-11-12	**Casper**
13-14-15-16	**Idaho Falls**
18-29-20	at Idaho Falls
21-22-23-24	at Casper
25-26-27	**Billings**
28-29-30	**Missoula**
31	at Great Falls

SEPTEMBER
1	at Great Falls
2-3-4-5	at Missoula
6-7-8	**Great Falls**

IDAHO FALLS

JUNE
21-22-23-24	at Casper
25-26	**Casper**
27-28-29	at Orem
30	**Ogden**

JULY
1	Ogden
2-3-4	**Orem**
5-6-7	at Ogden
8-9	at Orem
11-12-13-14	**Billings**
15-16-17	**Great Falls**
18-19-20-21	at Billings
22-23-24	at Great Falls
25-26-27	**Ogden**
28-29-30	**Casper**

AUGUST
1-2-3	at Ogden
4-5-6	**Orem**
7-8-9	**Ogden**
10-11-12	at Missoula
13-14-15-16	at Helena
18-19-20	**Helena**
21-22-23-24	**Missoula**
26-27-28	at Orem
29-30	at Ogden
31	**Casper**

MISSOULA

JUNE
21-22-23-24	Helena
25-26	**Billings**
27-28	at Helena
29-30	at Great Falls

JULY
1	at Great Falls
2-3-4	**Billings**
5-6-7	at Billings
8-9	at Great Falls
11-12-13-14	**Orem**
15-16-17	**Ogden**
18-19-20	at Orem
21-22-23-24	at Orem
25-26-27	**Great Falls**
28-29-30	at Helena

AUGUST
1-2-3	Billings
4-5	**Great Falls**
6-7-8	at Great Falls
10-11-12	**Idaho Falls**
13-14-15-16	**Casper**
18-19-20	at Casper
21-22-23-24	at I.F.
25-26-27	**Great Falls**
28-29-30	at Helena
31	at Billings

SEPTEMBER
1	at Billings
2-3-4-5	**Helena**
6-7-8	at Billings

OGDEN

JUNE
21-22-23-24	at Orem
25-26	**Orem**
27-28-29	**Casper**
30	at Idaho Falls

JULY
1	at Idaho Falls
2-3-4	at Casper
5-6-7	**Idaho Falls**
8-9	**Casper**
11-12-13-14	at Helena
15-16-17	at Missoula
18-19-20	**Helena**
21-22-23-24	**Missoula**
25-26-27	at Idaho Falls

Pioneer League (continued)

Date	Opponent
28-29-30	Orem
AUGUST	
1-2-3	Idaho Falls
4-5-6	at Casper
7-8-9	at Idaho Falls
10-11-12	Billings
13-14-15-16	Great Falls
18-19-20-21	at Billings
22-23-24	at Great Falls
26-27-28	Casper
29-30	Idaho Falls
31	Orem

Date	Opponent
SEPTEMBER	
1-2	Orem
3-4-5-6	at Orem
7-8	at Casper
OREM	
JUNE	
21-22-23-24	Ogden
25-26	at Ogden
27-28-29	Idaho Falls
30	at Casper
JULY	
1	at Casper

Date	Opponent
2-3-4	at Idaho Falls
5-6-7	Casper
8-9	Idaho Falls
11-12-13-14	at Missoula
15-16-17	at Helena
18-19-20	Missoula
21-22-23-24	Helena
25-26-27	at Casper
28-29-30	at Ogden
AUGUST	
1-2-3	Casper
4-5-6	at Idaho Falls
7-8-9	at Casper

Date	Opponent
10-11-12	Great Falls
13-13-15-16	Billings
18-19-20-21	at G.F.
22-23-24	at Billings
26-27-28	Idaho Falls
29-30	Casper
31	at Ogden
SEPTEMBER	
1-2	at Ogden
3-4-5-6	Ogden
7-8	at Idaho Falls

ARIZONA LEAGUE

ANGELS

Date	Opponent
JUNE	
22	at Cubs
23	Mariners
25	at Giants
26	Rangers
27	Athletics
28	Cubs
30	at Mariners
JULY	
1-21	Athletics
2-11-22	Padres
3-23	at Brewers
5-25	Giants
6-16	Rangers
7-10	Royals
8-28	Brewers
12-18	Cubs
13	Mariners
15	at Giants
17	at Athletics
20	at Mariners
26	at Rangers
27-30	at Royals
31	at Padres
AUGUST	
1-7-21	at Cubs
2-22	Mariners
4-24	at Giants
5-15	at Rangers
6-10-26	at Athletics
9	at Mariners
11-20	at Padres
12	at Brewers
14	Giants
16-27	at Royals
17-29	Brewers
19	Royals
25	Rangers
30	Padres

ATHLETICS

Date	Opponent
JUNE	
22	Giants
23	at Brewers
24	Royals
26	at Padres
27	at Angels
28	at Giants
29	Mariners
JULY	
1-21	at Angels
2-22	Rangers
3-23	at Royals
4-24	at Cubs
6-26	Padres
7-27	at Mariners
8-28	at Rangers
9-29	Cubs
11-31	Brewers
12	Giants
13	at Brewers
14	Royals
16	at Padres
17	Angels
18	at Giants
19	Mariners
AUGUST	
1-21	Giants
2-22	at Brewers
3-23	Royals
5-25	at Padres
6-10-26	Angels
7	at Giants
8	Mariners
11	Rangers
12	at Royals
13	at Cubs
15	Padres
16-27	at Mariners
17-28	at Rangers
18-30	Cubs
20	Brewers

BREWERS

Date	Opponent
JUNE	
23	Athletics
24	at Padres
25	at Mariners
26	Cubs
28	Mariners
29	at Rangers
30	at Royals
JULY	
1-21	Rangers
3-23	Angels
4-24	at Giants
5-25	Royals
6-26	at Cubs
8-28	at Angels
9-29	Giants
10-30	Padres
11-31	at Athletics
13	Athletics
14	at Padres
15	at Mariners
16	Cubs
18	Mariners
19	at Rangers
20	at Royals
AUGUST	
2-22	Athletics
3-23	at Padres
4-24	at Mariners
5-25	Cubs
7	Mariners
8	at Rangers
9-28	at Royals
10-30	Rangers
12	Angels
13	at Giants
14	Royals
15	at Cubs
17-29	at Angels
18-27	Giants
19	Padres
20	at Athletics

CUBS

Date	Opponent
JUNE	
22	Angels
23	at Royals
24	Giants
26	at Brewers
27	Padres
28	at Angels
29	Royals
JULY	
1-21	at Padres
2-22	Mariners
3-23	at Rangers
4-24	Athletics
6-26	Brewers
7-27	at Giants
8-28	at Mariners
9-29	at Athletics
11-31	Rangers
12-18	at Angels
13	at Royals
14	Giants
16	at Brewers
17	Padres
19	Royals
AUGUST	
1-7-21	Angels
2-22	at Royals
3-23	Giants
5-25	at Brewers
6-28	Padres
8	Royals
10	at Padres
11-26	Mariners
12-27	at Rangers
13	Athletics
15	Brewers
16	at Giants
17	at Mariners
18-30	at Athletics
20	Rangers

GIANTS

Date	Opponent
JUNE	
22	at Athletics
23	Rangers
24	at Cubs
25	Angels
27	at Rangers
28	Athletics
29	at Padres
30	Padres
JULY	
2-22	at Royals
3-23	Mariners
4-24	Brewers
5-25	at Angels
7-27	Cubs
8-28	Royals
9-29	at Brewers
10-30	at Mariners
12	at Athletics
13	Rangers
14	at Cubs
15	Angels
17	at Rangers
18	Athletics
19	at Padres
20	Padres
AUGUST	
1-21	at Athletics
2-22	Rangers
3-23	at Cubs
4-24	Angels
6	at Rangers
7	Athletics
8-29	at Padres
9	Padres
11	at Royals
12-28	Mariners
13	Brewers
14	at Angels
16	Cubs
17-26	Royals
18-27	at Brewers
19	at Mariners

MARINERS

JUNE
22	Padres
23	at Angels
24	at Rangers
25	Brewers
27	Royals
28	at Brewers
29	at Athletics
30	Angels

JULY
2-22	at Cubs
3-23	at Giants
4-24	Rangers
5-25	at Padres
7-27	Athletics
8-28	Cubs
9-29	at Royals
10-30	Giants
12	Padres
13	at Angels
14	at Rangers
15	Brewers
17	Royals
18	at Brewers
19	at Athletics
20	Angels

AUGUST
1-21	Padres
2-22	at Angels
3-23	at Rangers
4-24	Brewers
6-29	Royals
7	at Brewers
8	at Athletics
9	Angels
11-26	at Cubs
12-28	at Giants
13	Rangers
14	at Padres
16-27	Athletics
17	Cubs
18	at Royals
19	Giants

PADRES

JUNE
22	at Mariners
24	Brewers
25	at Royals
26	Athletics
27	at Cubs
29	Giants
30	at Giants

JULY
1-21	Cubs
2-22	at Angels
4-24	Royals
5-25	Mariners
6-26	at Athletics
7-27	Rangers
9-29	at Rangers
10-30	at Brewers
11	at Angels
12	at Mariners
14	Brewers
15	at Royals
16	Athletics
17	at Cubs
19	Giants
20	at Giants
31	Angels

AUGUST
1-21	at Mariners
3-23	Brewers
4-24	at Royals
5-25	Athletics
6-28	at Cubs
8-29	Giants
9	at Giants
10	Cubs
11-20	Angels
13	Royals
14	Mariners
15	at Athletics
16-26	Rangers
18	at Rangers
19	at Brewers
30	at Angels

RANGERS

JUNE
22	Royals
23	at Giants
24	Mariners
26	at Angels
27	Giants
28	at Royals
29	Brewers

JULY
1-21	at Brewers
2-22	at Athletics
3-23	Cubs
4-24	at Mariners
6-16	at Angels
7-27	at Padres
8-28	Athletics
9-29	Padres
11-31	at Cubs
12	Royals
13	at Giants
14	Mariners
17	Giants
18	at Royals
19	Brewers
26	Angels

AUGUST
1-21	Royals
2-22	at Giants
3-23	Mariners
5-15	Angels
6	Giants
7	at Royals
8	Brewers
10-30	at Brewers
11	at Athletics
12-27	Cubs
13	at Mariners
16-26	at Padres
17-28	Athletics
18	Padres
20	at Cubs
25	at Angels

ROYALS

JUNE
22	at Rangers
23	Cubs
24	at Athletics
25	Padres
27	at Mariners
28	Rangers
29	at Cubs
30	Brewers

JULY
2-22	Giants
3-23	Athletics
4-24	at Padres
5-25	at Brewers
7-27	at Angels
8-28	at Giants
9-29	Mariners
10	at Angels
12	at Rangers
13	Cubs
14	at Athletics
15	Padres
17	at Mariners
18	Rangers
19	at Cubs
20	Brewers
30	Angels

AUGUST
1-21	at Rangers
2-22	Cubs
3-23	at Athletics
4-24	Padres
6-29	at Mariners
7	Rangers
8	at Cubs
9-28	Brewers
11	Giants
12	Athletics
13	at Padres
14	at Brewers
16-27	Angels
17-26	at Giants
18	Mariners
19	at Angels

GULF COAST LEAGUE

BRAVES

JUNE
24	at Yankees
25	Yankees
27	at Tigers
28	Tigers
29	Phillies
30	at Phillies

JULY
1-9-15-23-30	at Yankees
2-8-16-22-29	Yankees
4-12-18-26	Tigers
5-11-19-25	at Tigers
6-14-20-28	at Phillies
7-13-21-27	Phillies

AUGUST
1-9-16-22	Tigers
2-8-15-23	at Tigers
3-11-17-25	at Phillies
4-10-18-24	Phillies
5-12-20	at Yankees
6-13-19	Yankees

DODGERS

JUNE
24	Mets
25	at Mets
27	Nationals
28	at Nationals
29	at Marlins
30	Marlins

JULY
1-9-15-23-30	Mets
2-8-16-22-29	at Mets
4-12-18-26	at Nationals
5-11-19-25	Nationals
6-14-20-28	Marlins
7-13-21-27	at Marlins

AUGUST
1-9-16-22	at Nationals
2-8-15-23	Nationals
3-11-17-25	Marlins
4-10-18-24	at Marlins
5-12-20	Mets
6-13-19	at Mets

MARLINS

JUNE
24	Nationals
25	at Nationals
27	Mets
28	at Mets
29	Dodgers
30	at Dodgers

JULY
1-9-15-23-29	Nationals
2-8-16-22-30	at Nationals
4-12-18-26	at Mets
5-11-19-25	Mets
6-14-20-28	at Dodgers
7-13-21-27	Dodgers

AUGUST
1-9-16-22	at Mets
2-8-15-23	Mets
3-11-17-25	at Dodgers
4-10-18-24	Dodgers
5-13-19	at Nationals
6-12-20	Nationals

METS

JUNE
24	at Dodgers
25	Dodgers
27	at Marlins
28	Marlins
29	Nationals
30	at Nationals

JULY
1-9-15-23-30	at Dodgers
2-8-16-22-29	Dodgers
4-12-18-26	Marlins
5-11-19-25	at Marlins

6-14-20-28 at Nationals
7-13-21-27 **Nationals**

AUGUST
1-9-16-22 **Marlins**
2-8-15-23 at Marlins
3-11-17-25 at Nationals
4-10-18-24 **Nationals**
5-12-20 at Dodgers
6-13-19 **Dodgers**

NATIONALS

JUNE
24 at Marlins
25 **Marlins**
27 at Dodgers
28 **Dodgers**
29 at Mets
30 **Mets**

JULY
1-9-15-23-29 at Marlins
2-8-16-22-30 **Marlins**
4-12-18-26 **Dodgers**
5-11-19-25 at Dodgers
6-14-20-28 **Mets**
7-13-21-27 at Mets

AUGUST
1-9-16-22 **Dodgers**
2-8-15-23 at Dodgers
3-11-17-25 **Mets**
4-10-18-24 at Mets
5-13-19 **Marlins**
6-12-20 at Marlins

PHILLIES

JUNE
24 at Tigers
25 **Tigers**
27 at Yankees
28 **Yankees**
29 at Braves
30 **Braves**

JULY
1-9-15-23-29 at Tigers
2-8-16-22-30 **Tigers**
4-12-18-26 **Yankees**
5-11-19-25 at Yankees
6-14-20-28 **Braves**
7-13-21-27 at Braves

AUGUST
1-9-16-22 **Yankees**
2-8-15-23 at Yankees
3-11-17-25 **Braves**
4-10-18-24 at Braves
5-13-19 **Tigers**
6-12-20 at Tigers

PIRATES

JUNE
24 **Red Sox**
25 at Red Sox
27 **Reds**
28 at Reds
29 **Twins**
30 at Twins

JULY
1-9-15-23-29 **Red Sox**
2-8-16-22-30 at Red Sox
4-12-18-19 at Reds
5-11-25-26 **Reds**
6-14-20-28 at Twins
7-13-21-27 **Twins**

AUGUST
1-9-16-24 at Reds
2-8-15-25 **Reds**
3-11-17-22 at Twins
4-10-18-23 **Twins**
5-13-19 at Red Sox
6-12-20 **Red Sox**

REDS

JUNE
24 at Twins
25 **Twins**
27 at Pirates
28 **Pirates**
29 **Red Sox**
30 at Red Sox

JULY
1-9-22-23-29 at Twins
2-8-15-16-30 **Twins**
4-12-18-19 **Pirates**
5-11-25-26 at Pirates
6-14-27-28 at Red Sox
7-13-20-21 **Red Sox**

AUGUST
1-9-16-24 **Pirates**
2-8-15-25 at Pirates
3-11-17-22 at Red Sox
4-10-18-23 **Red Sox**
5-12-20 at Twins
6-13-19 **Twins**

RED SOX

JUNE
24 at Pirates
25 **Pirates**
27 at Twins
28 **Twins**
29 at Reds
30 **Reds**

JULY
1-9-15-23-29 at Pirates
2-8-16-22-30 **Pirates**
4-12-18-26 at Twins
5-11-19-25 at Twins
6-14-27-28 **Reds**
7-13-20-21 at Reds

AUGUST
1-9-16-25 **Twins**
2-8-15-24 at Twins
3-11-17-22 **Reds**
4-10-18-23 at Reds
5-13-19 **Pirates**
6-12-20 at Pirates

TIGERS

JUNE
24 **Phillies**
25 at Phillies
27 **Braves**
28 at Braves
29 **Yankees**
30 at Yankees

JULY
1-9-15-23-29 **Phillies**
2-8-16-22-30 at Phillies
4-12-18-26 at Braves
5-11-19-25 **Braves**
6-14-20-28 at Yankees
7-13-21-27 **Yankees**

AUGUST
1-9-16-22 at Braves
2-8-15-23 **Braves**
3-11-17-25 at Yankees
4-10-18-24 **Yankees**
5-13-19 at Phillies
6-12-20 **Phillies**

TWINS

JUNE
24 **Reds**
25 at Reds
27 **Red Sox**
28 at Red Sox
29 at Pirates
30 **Pirates**

JULY
1-9-22-23-29 **Reds**
2-8-15-16-30 at Reds
4-12-18-26 at Red Sox
5-11-19-25 **Red Sox**
6-14-20-28 **Pirates**
7-13-21-27 at Pirates

AUGUST
1-9-16-25 at Red Sox
2-8-15-24 **Red Sox**
3-11-17-22 **Pirates**
4-10-18-23 at Pirates
5-12-20 **Reds**
6-13-19 at Reds

YANKEES

JUNE
24 **Braves**
25 at Braves
27 **Phillies**
28 at Phillies
29 at Tigers
30 **Tigers**

JULY
1-9-15-23-30 **Braves**
2-8-16-22-29 at Braves
4-12-18-26 at Phillies
5-11-19-25 **Phillies**
6-14-20-28 **Tigers**
7-13-21-27 at Tigers

AUGUST
1-9-16-22 at Phillies
2-8-15-23 **Phillies**
3-11-17-25 **Tigers**
4-10-18-24 at Tigers
5-12-20 **Braves**
6-13-19 at Braves

INDEPENDENT
LEAGUES

INDEPENDENT
LEAGUES

ATLANTIC LEAGUE

NORTH	W	L	PCT	GB
Bridgeport Bluefish	72	53	.576	—
*Nashua Pride	65	61	.515	7½
*Long Island Ducks	64	61	.512	8
Pennsylvania Road Warriors	23	103	.182	49½

SOUTH	W	L	PCT	GB
*Camden Riversharks	75	49	.604	—
*Atlantic City Surf	71	53	.572	4
Somerset Patriots	68	57	.544	7½
Newark Bears	62	63	.496	13½

PLAYOFFS: Semifinals— Long Island defeated Atlantic City 2-1 and Camden defeated Nashua 2-0 in best-of-5 series. **Finals—**Long Island defeated Camden 3-0 in best-of-5 series.

CENTRAL LEAGUE

EAST	W	L	PCT	GB
*Pensacola Pelicans	55	40	.578	—
Fort Worth Cats	50	43	.537	4½
*Shreveport Sports	50	45	.526	5
Jackson Senators	40	55	.421	15

WEST	W	L	PCT	GB
**Edinburg Roadrunners	68	27	.715	—
Coastal Bend Aviators	43	53	.447	26½
San Angelo Colts	36	57	.387	31
#Amarillo Dillas	36	58	.382	31½

PLAYOFFS: Semifinals—Edinburg defeated Amarillo 3-0 and Shreveport defeated Pensacola 3-2 in best-of-5 series. **Finals—**Edinburg defeated Shreveport 3-0 in best-of-5 series.

FRONTIER LEAGUE

EAST	W	L	PCT	GB
Washington Wild Things	62	34	.646	—
Evansville Otters	54	42	.563	8
Kalamazoo Kings	51	45	.531	11
Chillicothe Paints	48	48	.500	14
Richmond Roosters	43	53	.448	19
Florence Freedom	31	65	.323	31

WEST	W	L	PCT	GB
Rockford Riverhawks	59	37	.615	—

	56	38	.596	2
Gateway Grizzlies	56	38	.596	2
River City Rascals	51	43	.543	7
Springfield-Ozark Ducks	52	44	.542	7
Windy City Thunderbolts	37	57	.394	21
Mid-Missouri Mavericks	28	66	.298	30

PLAYOFFS: Semifinals—Rockford defeated Gateway 3-2 and Evansville defeated Washington 3-0 in best-of-5 series. **Finals—**Rockford defeated Evansville 3-0 in best-of-5 series.

NORTHEAST LEAGUE

NORTH	W	L	PCT	GB
*Quebec Les Capitales	58	34	.630	—
*North Shore Spirit	57	35	.619	1
#Bangor Lumberjacks	56	36	.608	2
Brockton Rox	45	47	.489	13

SOUTH	W	L	PCT	GB
*New Jersey Jackals	54	39	.580	—
New Haven County Cutters	39	54	.419	15
Elmira Pioneers	32	60	.347	21½
Aces	28	64	.304	25½

PLAYOFFS: Semifinals—New Jersey defeated Bangor 3-1 and North Shore defeated Quebec 3-2 in best-of-5 series. **Finals—**New Jersey defeated North Shore 3-2 in best-of-5 series.

NORTHERN LEAGUE

NORTH	W	L	PCT	GB
*St. Paul Saints	61	34	.642	—
Winnipeg Goldeyes	56	39	.589	5
*Fargo-Moorhead RedHawks	55	41	.572	5½
Sioux City Explorers	39	57	.406	23
Sioux Falls Canaries	33	63	.343	29

SOUTH	W	L	PCT	GB
*Schaumburg Flyers	58	38	.604	—
Lincoln Saltdogs	49	47	.510	9
Joliet Jackhammers	49	47	.510	9
*Kansas City T-Bones	48	48	.500	10
Gary Southshore Railcats	31	65	.322	27

PLAYOFFS: Semifinals—St. Paul defeated Fargo-Moorhead 3-1 and Schaumburg defeated Kansas City 3-2 in best-of-5 series. **Finals—**St. Paul defeated Schaumburg 3-2 in best-of-5 series

ATLANTIC
LEAGUE

Mailing Address: 401 N. Delaware Ave., Camden, NJ 08102.
Telephone: (856) 541-9400. **FAX:** (856) 541-9410.
E-Mail Address: atllge@aol.com. **Website:** www.atlanticleague.com.
Year Founded: 1998.

Chief Executive Officer: Frank Boulton. **Executive Director:** Joe Klein. **Vice President:** Mickey Herbert (Bridgeport).
Directors: Mark Berson (Newark), Frank Boulton (Long Island), Chris English (Nashua), Mickey Herbert (Bridgeport), Steve Kalafer (Somerset), Peter Kirk (Lancaster), Tony Rosenthal (Atlantic City).
League Operations Coordinator: Terence Archer
Division Structure: North—Bridgeport, Lancaster, Long Island, Nashua. **South**—Atlantic City, Camden, Newark, Somerset.
Regular Season: 140 games (split schedule). **2005 Opening Date:** April 27. **Closing Date:** Sept. 25.
All-Star Game: July 13 at Atlantic City.
Playoff Format: First-half division winners meet second-half winners in best-of-3 series. Winners meet in best-of-5 final for league championship.
Roster Limit: 25. **Eligibility Rule:** No restrictions.
Brand of Baseball: Rawlings.
Statistician: SportsTicker, ESPN Plaza—Building B, Bristol, CT 06010.

STADIUM INFORMATION

Club	Stadium	Opened	Dimensions LF	CF	RF	Capacity	2004 Att.
Atlantic City	The Sandcastle	1998	307	408	307	5,900	133,521
Bridgeport	The Ballpark at Harbor Yard	1998	325	405	325	5,300	242,608
Camden	Campbell's Field	2001	325	405	325	6,425	293,018
*Lancaster	Clipper Magazine Stadium	2005	372	400	300	6,000	—
Long Island	Citibank Park	2000	325	400	325	6,002	440,540
Nashua	Historic Holman Stadium	1937	307	401	315	4,375	117,768
Newark	Bears & Eagles Riverfront Stadium	1999	302	394	323	6,200	189,468
Somerset	Commerce Bank Ballpark	1999	317	402	315	6,100	376,315

*Franchise operated as Pennsylvania Road Warriors (travel team) in 2004

ATLANTIC CITY
SURF

Office Address: 545 N. Albany Ave., Atlantic City, NJ 08401.
Telephone: (609) 344-8873. **FAX:** (609) 344-7010.
E-Mail Address: surf@acsurf.com. **Website:** www.acsurf.com.

Operated by: Atlantic City Surf Professional Baseball LLC.
General Manager: Mario Perrucci. **Assistant GM/Director, Group Sales:** John Kiphorn. **Assistant Director, Group Sales:** Frank Dougherty. **Director, Media Relations/Marketing:** Chuck Betson. **Director, Ticket Sales:** Dennis Watson. **Director, Merchandising/Stadium Operations:** Danny Petrazzolo. **Director, Promotions/Community Relations:** Carl Grider. **Director, Finance:** Tom Clark. **Director, Baseball Operations:** Jeff Ball. **Clubhouse Operations:** Bob Schaffer.
Manager: Mitch Williams. **Coaches:** Tim Lindecamp, Greg Luzinski.

GAME INFORMATION

Radio Announcer: Jacob Issac. **No. of Games Broadcast:** Home-70, Away-70. **Flagship Station:** WUSS 1490-AM.
PA Announcer: Greg Maiuro. **Official Scorer:** Jeff Bohrer.
Stadium Name: The Sandcastle. **Location:** Atlantic City Expressway to exit 2, east on Routes 40/322. **Standard Game Times:** 6:35 p.m.; Sun. 1:35, (May-June, Sept.) 5:05.
Visiting Club Hotel: Fairfield Inn, 405 White Horse Pike, Absecon, NJ. **Telephone:** (609) 646-5000.

BRIDGEPORT
BLUEFISH

Office Address: 500 Main St., Bridgeport, CT 06604.
Telephone: (203) 345-4800. **FAX:** (203) 345-4830.
E-Mail Address jcunningham@bridgeportbluefish.com. **Website:** www.bridge-

portbluefish.com.

Operated by: Bridgeport Bluefish Professional Baseball Club, LLC.
Owners: Charlie Dowd, Mickey Herbert, Ken Paul.
President, Chief Executive Officer: Mickey Herbert. **Senior Vice President:** Ken Paul.
General Manager: Charlie Dowd. **Assistant GM:** John Cunningham. **Controller:** Tammy Nolin. **Senior Account Executive:** John Harris. **Account Executives:** Mary Cappello, Andy Paul, Joe Skarupa. **Administrator, Sales:** Shannon Walsh. **Manager, Box Office:** Rebecca Ramos. **Manager, Group Sales:** Jennifer Davis. **Group Sales Representatives:** Kim Pizighelli, Courtney Smith, Bryan Wideman. **Manager, Accounts Receivable:** Alison Mester. **Assistant, Finance:** Barbara Prato. **Receptionist:** Melissa Perkins. **Head Groundskeeper:** Craig Veeder.
Manager: Jose Lind. **Coaches:** Unavailable. **Trainer:** Unavailable.

GAME INFORMATION

Radio Announcer: Jeff Holtz. **No. of Games Broadcast:** Unavailable. **Flagship Station:** WVOF 88.5-FM.
PA Announcer: Bill Jensen. **Official Scorer:** Joel Pleban.
Stadium Name: The Ballpark at Harbor Yard. **Location:** I-95 to exit 27, Route 8/25 to exit 1. **Standard Game Times:** 6:35 p.m., Sun. 1:35.
Visiting Club Hotel: Holiday Inn Bridgeport, 1070 Main St., Bridgeport, CT 06604. Telephone: (203) 334-1234.

CAMDEN RIVERSHARKS

Office Address: 401 N. Delaware Ave., Camden, NJ 08102.
Telephone: (856) 963-2600. **FAX:** (856) 963-8534.
E-Mail Address: riversharks@riversharks.com. **Website:** www.riversharks.com.

Operated by: BKK Sports, LLC.
Principal Owners: Frank Boulton, Steve Kalafer, Peter Kirk, BKK Sports LLC. **President:** Jon Danos.
General Manager: John Brandt. **Director, Marketing:** Kristen Daffin. **Director, Corporate Partnerships:** Adam Lorber.
Director, Ticket Sales: Gina Stepoulos. **Director, Operations:** Matthew Tirrell. **Corporate Partnerships Managers:** Brad Strauss, Natalie Filomeno. **Corporate Sales:** Joel Seiden. **Ticket Operations Manager:** Randy Newsome. **Group Account Managers:** Robert Nehring, Ryan Arnold, Marissa Perri, Beverly Monk. **Bookkeeper:** Dawn Norton. **Director, Baseball Operations:** Patty MacLuckie. **Receptionist:** Dolores Rozier. **Groundskeeper:** Michael Nicotra.
Manager: Wayne Krenchicki. **Coach:** Victor Torres. **Pitching Coach:** Steve Foucault. **Trainer:** Unavailable.

GAME INFORMATION

Radio: Unavailable.
PA Announcer: Kevin Casey. **Official Scorer:** Dick Shute.
Stadium Name: Campbell's Field. **Location:** From Philadelphia, right on Sixth Street, right after Ben Franklin Bridge toll booth, right on Cooper Street until it ends at Delaware Ave. From Camden, I-676 to exit 5B, follow signs to field. **Standard Game Times:** 6:35 p.m., Sun. 1:35.
Visiting Club Hotel: Holiday Inn, Route 70 and Sayer Avenue, Cherry Hill, NJ 08002. Telephone: (856) 663-5300.

LANCASTER BARNSTORMERS

Office Address: 3708 Hempland Rd., Mountville, PA 17554.
Telephone: (717) 509-4487 **FAX:** (717) 509-4456
E-Mail Address: info@lancasterbarnstormers.com. **Website:** www.lancasterbarn-stormers.com.

Operated by: Keystone Baseball, LLC.
Principal Owners: Peter Kirk, Keystone Baseball, LLC. **President:** Jon Danos.
General Manager: Joe Pinto. **Assistant GM:** Gina Stepoulos. **Director, Public Affairs:** Andy Frankel. **Director, Corporate Partnerships:** Vince Bulik. **Corporate Partnerships Managers:** Jeff Bertoni, Andy Shultz, Pete Tsirigotis. **Group Events Managers:** Shawn Gelnett, Meagan Hample, Cory Harpin. **Ticket Operations Manager:** Joan Dubord. **Marketing Manager:** Jason Jesberger. **Marketing Assistants:** Amanda Elia, Bryan Hubbard, Ted Serro. **Executive Assistant:** Kim Draude. **Bookkeeper:** Jackie Zanghi. **Receptionist:** Amanda Kowalski. **Director, Stadium Operations:** Don Pryer. **Food Service Manager:** Josh Leatherman.
Manager: Tom Herr. **Coach:** Bert Pena. **Pitching Coach:** Rick Wise. **Trainer:** Unavailable.

GAME INFORMATION

Radio Announcer: Unavailable. **No. of Games Broadcast:** Home-70, Away-70. **Flagship Station:** The Ticket 1390-AM.
PA Announcer: Unavailable. **Official Scorer:** Unavailable.
Stadium Name: Clipper Magazine Stadium. **Location:** From Route 30, take Fruitville Pike or Harrisburg Pike towards downtown Lancaster, stadium at intersection of Prince Street and Harrisburg Pike. **Standard Game Times:**

7:05 p.m., Sun. 1:35.
Visiting Club Hotel: Days Inn-Lancaster, 30 Keller Ave., Lancaster, PA 17601. Telephone: (717) 299-5700.

LONG ISLAND
DUCKS

Mailing Address: 3 Court House Dr., Central Islip, NY 11722.
Telephone: (631) 940-3825. **FAX:** (631) 940-3800.
E-Mail Address: info@liducks.com. **Website:** www.liducks.com.

Operated by: Long Island Ducks Professional Baseball, LLC.
Principal Owner, Chief Executive Officer: Frank Boulton. **Owner/Senior Vice President, Baseball Operations:** Bud Harrelson.
General Manager: Michael Hirsch. **Assistant GM:** Doug Cohen. **Director, Communications:** Michael Pfaff. **Director, Group Sales:** Mike Pacella. **Director, Promotions:** Jami Dock. **Business Manager:** Gerry Anderson. **Controller:** Alex Scannella. **Manager, Ticket Sales:** Ben Harper. **Manager, Operations:** Andrew Washington. **Manager, Community Relations:** Michele Connizzo. **Manager, Merchandise:** Jessica Fleming. **Manager, Clubhouse Operations:** Jimmy Russell. **Assistant Manager, Facilities:** Jon Archer. **Assistant Manager, Tickets:** Bill Harney. **Coordinator, Administration:** Erica Cuddy.
Manager: Don McCormack. **Coach:** Bud Harrelson. **Pitching Coach:** Dave LaPoint. **Trainers:** Tony Amin, Adam Lewis.

GAME INFORMATION
Radio Announcers: Chris King, David Weiss. **No. of Games Broadcast:** 66. **Flagship Station:** WLIE 540-AM.
PA Announcer: Unavailable. **Official Scorers:** Joe Donnelly, Red Foley.
Stadium Name: Citibank Park. **Location:** Southern State Parkway east to Carleton Avenue North (exit 43 A), right onto Courthouse Drive, stadium behind Federal Courthouse Complex. **Standard Game Times:** 7:05 p.m.; Sun. 1:35.
Visiting Club Hotels: Holiday Inn Express-Stony Brook, 3131 Nesconset Hwy., Stony Brook, NY 11720. Telephone: (631) 471-8000. Holiday Inn Express-Hauppauge, 2050 Express Dr. South, Hauppauge, NY 11788. Telephone: (631) 348-1400.

NASHUA
PRIDE

Office Address: 67 Amherst St., Nashua, NH 03064.
Telephone: (603) 883-2255. **FAX:** (603) 883-0880.
E-Mail Address: info@nashuapride.com. **Website:** www.nashuapride.com.

Operated by: BKK Nashua LLC.
Principal Owner: Unavailable
General Manager: Todd Marlin. **Director of Tickets:** Jason Marshall. **Account Executives:** Anna Turbe, Greg Cross, Nick Majocha. **Office Manager:** Beverly Taylor.
Manager: Butch Hobson. **Pitching Coach:** Andre Rabouin.

GAME INFORMATION
Radio: Unavailable.
PA Announcer: Ken Cail. **Official Scorer:** Roger Pepin.
Stadium Name: Historic Holman Stadium. **Location:** Route 3 to exit 7E (Amherst Street), stadium one mile on left.
Standard Game Time: 6:35 p.m., (Fri.-Sat.) 7, (Sun.) 1:30.
Visiting Club Hotel: Unavailable.

NEWARK
BEARS

Office Address: 450 Broad St., Newark, NJ 07102.
Telephone: (973) 848-1000. **FAX:** (973) 621-0095.
Website: www.newarkbears.com.

Operated by: Newark Bears Professional Baseball Club, Inc.
Owners: Steven Kalafer, Marc Berson.
Senior Vice President, General Manager: Dean Rivera. **VP, Sales and Marketing/Assistant GM:** Melissa Manfre. **Director, Media Relations/Broadcasting:** Jim Cerny. **Controller:** Scott Janner. **Manager, Stadium Operations:** Joe Sobeski. **Director, Tickets:** Keith Butler. **Manager, Group Sales:** Rocco Scannielo. **Director, Fan Development:** Mark Gallego. **Head Groundskeeper:** Carlos Aroacho.

Manager: Chris Jones. Director, Player Personnel, Coach: Henry Cruz. Pitching Coach: Pete Filson.

Radio Announcer: Jim Cerny. No. of Games Broadcast: Unavailable. Flagship Station: Unavailable. PA Announcer: Steve Boland. Official Scorer: Unavailable.

Stadium Name: Bears & Eagles Riverfront Stadium. Location: New Jersey Parkway North/South to exit 145 (280 East), to exit 15; New Jersey Turnpike North/South to 280 West, to exit 15A. Standard Game Times: 7:05 p.m., Sat. 6:05, Sun. 1:35.

Visiting Club Hotel: Wellesley Inn & Suites, 265 Route 3 East, Clifton, NJ 07014. Telephone: (973) 778-6500.

SOMERSET PATRIOTS

Office Address: One Patriots Park, Bridgewater, NJ 08807.
Telephone: (908) 252-0700. FAX: (908) 252-0776.
Website: www.somersetpatriots.com.

Operated by: Somerset Patriots Baseball Club, LLC.
Principal Owners: Steven Kalafer, Jack Cust, Byron Brisby, Don Miller. Chairman: Steven Kalafer.
President, General Manager: Patrick McVerry. Vice President, Ticketing: Brendan Fairfield. VP, Marketing: Dave Marek. VP, New Business Development: Chris Bryan. Controller: Wayne Seguin. Head Groundskeeper: Ray Cipperly. Director, Public Relations: Marc Russinoff. Assistant GM: Rob Lukachyk. Account Representatives: John Gibson, Dan Neville. Manager, Community Relations: Matt Rothenberg. Director, Ticket Sales: Bryan Iwicki. Group Sales: Chris Aubertin, Matthew Kopas. Manager, Ticket Sales: Tim Ur. Executive Assistant to GM: Michele DaCosta. Accountants: Stephanie Diez, Wendy Miervaldis. Receptionist: Lorraine Ott. GM, Centerplate: Mike McDermott. Grounds Crew: Joe Zavodnick.
Director, Player Procurement: Adam Gladstone. Manager: Sparky Lyle. Pitching Coach: John Montefusco. Trainer: Paul Kolody.

Radio Announcer: Brian Bender. No. of Games Broadcast: Home-70, Away-70. Flagship Station: WCTC 1450-AM. PA Announcer: Paul Spychala. Official Scorer: John Nolan.
Stadium Name: Commerce Bank Ballpark. Location: Route 287 North to exit 13B/Route 287 South to exit 13 (Somerville Route 28 West); follow signs to ballpark. Standard Game Times: 7:05 p.m., Sun. 1:35.
Visiting Club Hotel: Somerset Ramada, 60 Cottontail Lane, Somerset, NJ 08873. Telephone: (732) 560-9880.

CAN-AM
LEAGUE

(Previously called Northeast League)

Office Address: 1415 Hwy. 54 West, Suite 210, Durham, NC 27707.
Telephone: (919) 401-8150. FAX: (919) 401-8152.
E-Mail Address: info@canamleague.com. Website: www.canamleague.com.
Year Founded: 2005.

Commissioner: Miles Wolff. President: Dan Moushon. Supervisor, Umpires: Kevin Winn.
Division Structure: North—Bangor, Brockton, North Shore, Quebec. South—Elmira, New Haven County, New Jersey, Worcester.
Regular Season: 92 games (split schedule). 2005 Opening Date: May 26. Closing Date: Sept. 5.
All-Star Game: July 19 at Brockton, MA (Can-Am League vs. Central League).
Playoff Format: First-half division winners meet second-half division winners in best-of-5 series. Winners meet in best-of-5 series for league championship.
Roster Limit: 22. Eligibility Rule: Minimum of five first-year players; maximum of four veterans with at least four years of professional experience.
Brand of Baseball: Rawlings.
Statistician: SportsTicker, ESPN Plaza-Building B, Bristol, CT 06010.

STADIUM INFORMATION

Club	Stadium	Opened	Dimensions			Capacity	2004 Att.
			LF	CF	RF		
Bangor	John Winkin Baseball Complex	2003	330	400	330	3,000	62,987
Brockton	Campanelli Stadium	2002	340	404	320	4,750	203,094
Elmira	Dunn Field	1939	325	386	325	4,020	55,710
New Haven County	Yale Field	1927	330	405	315	5,000	56,982
New Jersey	Yogi Berra Stadium	1998	308	398	308	3,784	106,110

North Shore	Fraser Field	1940	320	400	320	3,804	115,118
Quebec	Stade Municipal de Quebec	1938	315	385	315	4,800	156,899
*Worcester	Unavailable	—	—	—	—	—	—

*Franchise operated as Aces (travel team) in 2004

BANGOR
LUMBERJACKS

Office Address: 663 Stillwater Ave., Bangor, Maine 04401.
Telephone: (207) 947-1900. **FAX:** (207) 947-9900.
E-Mail address: info@bangorlumberjacks.com. **Website:** www.bangorlumber-jacks.com.

Operated by: Lumberjack Baseball LLC.
Principal Owner: Chip Hutchins.
General Manager: Curt Jacey. **Assistant GM:** Ryan Conley.
Manager: Chris Carminucci. **Coaches:** Unavailable.

GAME INFORMATION
Radio Announcer: Unavailable. **No. of Games Broadcast:** Home-36. **Flagship Station:** WHCF 88.5-FM.
PA Announcer: Unavailable. **Official Scorer:** Unavailable.
Stadium Name: John Winkin Baseball Complex. **Location:** I-95 to exit 48, right on Broadway, left on Husson Ave. to Husson College, straight ahead one mile. **Standard Game Times:** Unavailable.
Visiting Team Hotel: Unavailable.

BROCKTON
ROX

Office Address: 1 Lexington Ave, Brockton, MA 02301.
Telephone: (508) 559-7000. **FAX:** (508) 587-2802.
Website: www.brocktonrox.com.

Principal Owner: Van Schley. **President:** Jim Lucas.
General Manager: Dave Sacchetti. **Assistant GM:** Andy Crossley. **Director, Corporate Sales:** Gary MacKinnon. **Director, Ticket Sales:** Brian Voelkel. **Director, Business Operations:** Mary Scarlett. **Director, Promotions:** Andrea Thrubis. **Director, Community Relations/Merchandise:** Kari Gast. **Director, Special Events:** Danni Barrall. **Director, Media Relations:** Dave Raymond. **Food/Beverage:** Michael Canina, Kevin Long. **Box Office Manager:** Drew Cunningham. **Ticket Sales Representatives:** Greg Berry, Matt Meola. **Receptionist:** Me'Shay Hurt.
Director, Player Procurement: Barry Moss. **Manager:** Ed Nottle. **Coaches:** Chris Miyake, Shad Williams. **Trainer:** Lauren Eck.

GAME INFORMATION
Radio Announcer: Dave Raymond. **No. of Games Broadcast:** Home-46, Away-46. **Flagship Station:** WBET 1460-AM.
PA Announcer: Unavailable. **Official Scorer:** Unavailable.
Stadium name: Campanelli Stadium. **Directions:** Route 24 North/South to Route 123 East, stadium is two miles on right. **Standard Game Times:** 7:11 p.m.; Sun. (May-June) 2:05, (July-Sept.) 5:05.
Visiting Club Hotel: Residence Inn, 124 Liberty St., Brockton, MA 02301. Telephone: (508) 583-3600.

ELMIRA
PIONEERS

Office Address: 546 Luce St., Elmira, NY 14904.
Telephone: (607) 734-1270. **FAX:** (607) 734-0891.
E-Mail Address: pioneers@elmirapioneers.com. **Website:** www.elmirapioneers.com.

Operated by: Elmira Baseball, LLC.
President: Phil Kramer.
General Manager: Tom Sullivan. **Assistant GM:** Ryan Ehrhart. **Director, Operations:** Shawn Van Etten. **Head Groundskeeper:** Tony Spallone.
Manager: Greg Keagle. **Coach:** Trey Beamon. **Pitching Coach:** Allen Levrault.

GAME INFORMATION
Radio: Unavailable.
PA Announcer: Unavailable. **Official Scorer:** James Wilson.

Stadium Name: Dunn Field. Location: I-86 (Route 17) to exit 56 (Church Street), left on Madison Ave., left on Maple Ave., left on Luce Street. Standard Game Times: 7:05 p.m., Sun. 2:05.
Visiting Club Hotel: Holiday Inn Elmira-Riverview, 760 E. Water, Elmira, NY 14901. Telephone: (607) 734-4211.

NEW HAVEN COUNTY
CUTTERS

Office Address: 252 Derby Ave., West Haven, CT 06516.
Telephone: (203) 777-5636. FAX: (203) 777-4369.
Website: www.cuttersbaseball.com.

Operated by: Flying Bats and Balls, LLC.
Principal Owner: Jonathan Fleisig. President: Rick Handelman.
General Manager: Marie Heikkinen Webb. Assistant GM: Jason Horn. Director, Food/Beverage: Rob Keener. Director, Promotions/Special Events: Stephen Colvin. Corporate Sales Representative: Jim Ingram. Ticket Sales Representatives: Shannon Geerlings, Ted Shepard. Coordinator, Community Relations/Entertainment: Matt D'Amato. Director, Player Personnel: Bob Wirz. Manager: Mike Church. Coach: Andy Walker. Trainer: Unavailable.

GAME INFORMATION
Radio: None.
PA Announcer: Stephen Colvin. Official Scorer: Unavailable.
Stadium Name: Yale Field. Directions: From I-95, take eastbound exit 44 or westbound exit 45 to Route 10 and follow the Yale Bowl signs. From Merritt Parkway, take exit 57, follow to 34 East. Standard Game Times: 7:05 p.m., Sun. 2:05.
Visiting Club Hotel: Unavailable.

NEW JERSEY
JACKALS

Office Address: One Hall Dr., Little Falls, NJ 07424.
Telephone: (973) 746-7434. FAX: (973) 655-8021.
E-Mail Address: info@jackals.com. Website: www.jackals.com.

Operated by: Floyd Hall Enterprises, LLC.
Principal Owner, Chairman: Floyd Hall. President: Greg Lockard.
General Manager: Ben Wittkowski. Business Manager: Jennifer Fertig. Director, Ticket Operations: Matt Abel. Director, Corporate Sales: Ken Yudman. Corporate Sales Representative: Jim Rodriguez. Group Sales Representatives: Brooke Kenna, Trish Vignola. Media Relations: Joe Ameruoso. Facilities Manager: Aldo Licitra. Concessions Manager: Michele Guarino. Clubhouse Manager: Wally Brackett.
Manager: Joe Calfapietra. Coaches: Kevin Dattola, Ani Ramos. Pitching Coach: Brian Drahman. Trainer: Mitch Rosenthal.

GAME INFORMATION
Radio Announcer: Unavailable. No. of Games Broadcast: Home-46, Away-46. Flagship Station: WPSC 88.7-FM.
PA Announcer: Unavailable. Official Scorer: Kim DeRitter.
Stadium Name: Yogi Berra Stadium. Location: Route 80 or Garden State Parkway to Route 46, take Valley Road exit to Montclair State University. Standard Game Times: 7:05 p.m.; Sun. 2:05.
Visiting Club Hotel: Wellesley Inn, 265 Route 3 East, Clifton, NJ 07014. Telephone: (973) 778-6500.

NORTH SHORE
SPIRIT

Office Address: 365 Western Ave, Lynn, MA 01904.
Mailing Address: P.O. Box 8120, Lynn, MA 01904.
Telephone: (781) 592-0007. FAX: (781) 592-0004.
E-Mail Address: info@northshorespirit.com. Website: www.northshorespirit.com.

Operated by: Spirit of New England Baseball Club, LLC.
Principal Owner: Nicholas Lopardo.
General Manager: Brent Connolly. Director, Ticket Sales/Entertainment: Andy Seguin. Director, Entertainment: Chris Ames. Director Sales/Marketing: Kevin Kelly. Senior Account Executive: Kurt Cochran. Account Executive, Groups: Marty Giniven. Account Executive: Bryce Scottron. Media Relations: Julie Wetherbee. Group Sales: Luis Breazeale. Administrative/Advertising Assistant: Courtney Deveau. Ticket Sales Manager: Seth Bettan.
Manager: John Kennedy. Coaches: Rich Gedman, Frank Carey, Jim Tgettis. Pitching Coach: Dick Radatz.

Strength/Conditioning Coach: Paul Melanson.

GAME INFORMATION

Radio Announcer: Unavailable. **No. of Games Broadcast:** Home-46, Away-46. **Flagship Station:** WESX 1230-AM.
PA Announcer: Unavailable. **Official Scorer:** Unavailable.
Stadium Name: Fraser Field. **Location:** Route 129 (Lynn exit) into Lynn on Lynnfield Street, left at Chestnut Street; right at Western Ave. (Route 107), stadium on right. **Standard Game Times:** 7:05 p.m., Sun. 2:05.
Visiting Club Hotel: Sheraton Ferncroft, 50 Ferncroft Rd., Danvers, MA 01923. Telephone: (978) 777-2500.

QUEBEC

LES CAPITALES

Office Address: 100 Rue du Cardinal Maurice-Roy, Quebec City, Quebec G1K 8Z1.
Telephone: (418) 521-2255. **FAX:** (418) 521-2266.
E-Mail Address: baseball@capitalesdequebec.com. **Website:** www.capitalesde-quebec.com.

President: Richard Cloutier.
General Manager: Nicolas Labbé. **Director, Business Operations:** Rémi Bolduc. **Director, Media/Public Relations:** Alexandre Harvey. **Sales/Marketing:** Ed Sweeney. **Director, Ticket Sales:** Nathalie Gauthier.
Manager: Michel Laplante. **Coaches:** Unavailable.

GAME INFORMATION

Radio Announcer: Unavailable. **No. of Games Broadcast:** Unavailable. **Flagship Station:** CHRC 800-AM.
PA Announcer: Damien Miville-Deschênes. **Official Scorer:** Stéphan Lévesque.
Stadium Name: Stade Municipal de Québec. **Location:** Highway 40 to Highway 173 (Centre-Ville) exit 2 to Parc Victoria. **Standard Game Times:** 7:05 p.m., Sun. 1:05.
Visiting Club Hotel: Hotel du Nord, 640 St. Vallier W., Quebec City, Quebec G1N 1C5. Telephone: (418) 522-1554.

WORCESTER

Office Address: P.O. Box 2221, Worcester, MA 01613.
Telephone: (508) 792-2288. **FAX:** (508) 926-3662.
E-Mail Address: info@worcesterprobaseball.com. **Website:** www.worcester-probaseball.com.

President/Chief Executive Officer: Alan Stone.
General Manager: Mike Lieberman. **Ticket Sales Representative:** Christina Tashjian.
Manager: Rich Gedman. **Coaches:** Unavailable.

GAME INFORMATION

Radio: Unavailable.
PA Announcer: Unavailable. **Official Scorer:** Unavailable.
Stadium Name: Unavailable. **Location:** Unavailable. **Standard Game Times:** Unavailable.
Visiting Club Hotel: Unavailable.

CENTRAL
LEAGUE

Mailing Address/Baseball Operations: 1415 Hwy. 54 West, Suite 210, Durham, NC 27707.
Telephone: (919) 401-8150. **FAX:** (919) 401-8152.
Mailing Address/Business Operations: P.O. Box 2712, Colorado Springs, CO 87901.
Telephone: (719) 520-0060. **FAX:** (719) 520-0221.
E-Mail Address: info@centralleaguebaseball.com. **Website:** www.centralleaguebaseball.com.
Year Founded: 1994.

Commissioner: Miles Wolff. **Vice President, Baseball Operations:** Dan Moushon. **Supervisor, Umpires:** Kevin Winn. **Division Structure:** None.
Regular Season: 94 games (split schedule). **2005 Opening Date:** May 5. **Closing Date:** Aug. 20.
All-Star Game: July 19 at Brockton, MA (Central League vs. Can-Am League).
Playoff Format: First-half winner and second-half winner meet wild card teams in best-of-5 series. Winners meet

in best-of-5 series for league championship.

Roster Limit: 22. **Player Eligibility Rule:** Minimum of five first-year players, maximum of four veterans with at least four years of professional experience.

Brand of Baseball: Rawlings.

Statistician: SportsTicker, ESPN Plaza-Building B, Bristol, CT 06010 .

STADIUM INFORMATION

Club	Stadium	Opened	Dimensions LF	CF	RF	Capacity	2004 Att.
Coastal Bend	Aviators Stadium	2003	330	400	330	4,000	103,049
Edinburg	Edinburg Stadium	2001	325	400	325	4,000	145,370
Fort Worth	LaGrave Field	2002	325	400	335	5,100	151,374
Jackson	Smith-Wills Stadium	1975	330	400	330	5,200	71,349
Pensacola	Pelican Park	1991	320	390	320	2,500	44,584
San Angelo	Foster Field	2000	330	395	330	4,044	82,758
Shreveport	Fair Grounds Field	1986	330	400	330	4,500	55,207
*El Paso	Cohen Stadium	1990	340	410	340	9,725	58,627

*Franchise operated in Amarillo in 2004

COASTAL BEND
AVIATORS

Mailing Address: 1151 E. Main Ave., Robstown, TX 78380.
Telephone: (361) 387-8585. **FAX:** (361) 387-3535.
Website: www.aviatorsbaseball.com.

General Manager: Shane Tritz. **Office Manager:** Brandi Ramon. **Director, Sales/Marketing:** Ray Hunt. **Sales Executive:** Javier Limon. **Bookkeeper:** Lalita Hughes.
Manager: Murray Wilson. **Coach:** Unavailable.

GAME INFORMATION

Radio Announcer: Unavailable. **No. of Games Broadcast:** Home-47, Away-47. **Flagship Stations:** KSIX 1230-AM, KCCT 1150-AM.

PA Announcer: Unavailable. **Official Scorer:** Unavailable.

Stadium Name: Aviators Stadium. **Location:** 12 miles west of downtown Corpus Christi at junction of Highway 77 and Highway 44. **Standard Game Times:** 7:05 p.m., Sun. 6:05.

Visiting Club Hotel: U.S. Travel Center, 2217 N. U.S. Hwy. 77, Robstown, TX 78380. Telephone: (361) 767-2656.

EDINBURG
ROADRUNNERS

Office Address: 920 N. Sugar Rd., Edinburg, TX 78541.
Mailing Address: P.O. Box 4119, Edinburg, TX 78540.
Telephone: (956) 289-8800. **FAX:** (956) 289-8833.
E-Mail Address: winstonayala@yahoo.com. **Website:** www.roadrunnersbaseball.com.

General Manager: Winston Ayala. **Director, Sales/Marketing:** Bob Flanagan. **Director, Business Operations:** Rudy Rodriguez, **Manager, Sales:** Mike Patrick. **Office Manager:** Imelda Palacios.
Manager: Chad Tredaway. **Assistant Coaches:** Reggie Tredaway, John Harris.

GAME INFORMATION

Radio: Unavailable.

PA Announcer: Tony Forina. **Official Scorer:** Unavailable.

Stadium Name: Edinburg Stadium. **Location:** Highway 281, left at Schuinor Street to Sugar Road, stadium on right. **Standard Game Time:** 7:05 p.m.

Visiting Club Hotel: Unavailable.

EL PASO
DIABLOS

Mailing Address: 9700 Gateway North Blvd., El Paso, Texas, 79924.
Telephone: (915) 755-2000. **FAX:** (915) 757-0671.
Website: www.diablos.com.

Owners: Mark Schuster, Tom Whaley, David Pearlman.

General Manager: Unavailable. **Assistant GM/Operations:** Jimmy Hicks. **Corporate Marketing Manager:** Bernie Ricono. **Corporate Sales:** Jeff Stewart. **Director, Ticket Sales:** Angela Martinez. **Group Sales:** Miguel Flores. **Manager, Marketing/Promotions:** Kelly Rogers. **Manager, Communications:** Valerie Venegas. **Group/Ticket Sales:** Delbert Arnold. **Maintenance Manager:** Richard Bellah.

Manager: Mike Marshall. **Pitching Coach:** Jack Kucek.

GAME INFORMATION

Radio Announcers: Unavailable (English), Miguel Flores (Spanish). **No. of Games Broadcast:** Home-47, Away-47. Home-47 (Spanish). **Flagship Stations:** KHEY 1380-AM, XEP 1300-AM (Spanish).

PA Announcer: Unavailable. **Official Scorer:** Unavailable.

Stadium Name: Cohen Stadium. **Location:** I-10 to U.S. 54 (Patriot Freeway), east to Diana exit to Gateway North Boulevard. **Standard Game Time:** 7:05 p.m.

Visiting Club Hotel: Best Western Airport Inn, 7144 Gateway Blvd. E., El Paso, TX 79915. Telephone: (915) 779-7700.

FORT WORTH
CATS

Mailing Address: P.O Box 4411, Fort Worth, TX 76106.
Telephone: (817) 226-2287. **FAX:** (817) 534-4620.
E-Mail Address: info@fwcats.com. **Website:** www.fwcats.com.

Operated By: Texas Independent Baseball.
Principal Owner: Carl Bell.

President, Chief Operating Officer: John Dittrich. **Senior Vice President, General Manager:** Monty Clegg. **Senior VP, Business Development:** Mark Presswood. **VP, Marketing/Administration:** Kevin Forrester. **VP, Corporate Sales/Sponsorships:** John Bilbow. **VP, Special Projects:** Maury Wills. **Director, Communications:** David Hatchett. **Assistant Communications Director/Website:** Emil Moffatt. **Director, Community Relations:** Erika Wrage. **Director, Promotions:** Stacy Navarro. **Business Manager:** Lois Dittrich. **Group Sales:** Joby Raymond. **Corporate Sales:** Mike Forrester. **Director, Stadium Operations:** Dick Smith.

Director, Player Development: Barry Moss. **Manager:** Wayne Terwilliger. **Coach:** Stan Hough. **Pitching Coach:** Dan Smith. **Trainer:** Alan Reid.

GAME INFORMATION

Radio Announcers: John Nelson, David Hatchett, Emil Moffatt. **No. of Games Broadcast:** Home-47, Away-47. **Flagship Station:** KTFW 1460-AM.

PA Announcer: Frankie Gasca. **Official Scorer:** Mike McAbee.

Stadium Name: LaGrave Field. **Location:** From I-30, take I-35 North to North Side Drive exit, left (west) off exit to Main Street, left (south) on Main, left (east) onto NE Sixth Street. **Standard Game Times:** 7:05 p.m.; Sun. 1:05.

Visiting Club Hotel: Clarion Hotel, 600 Commerce St., Fort Worth, TX 76102. Telephone: (871) 332-6900.

JACKSON
SENATORS

Office Address: 1200 Lakeland Dr., Jackson, MS 39216.
Mailing Address: P.O. Box 4934, Jackson, MS 39296.
Telephone: (601) 362-2294. **FAX:** (601) 362-9577.
E-Mail Address: info@jacksonsenators.com. **Website:** www.jacksonsenators.com.

Operated By: Mississippi Baseball Club, LLC.
Managing Partner: Calvin Wells.

Vice President, General Manager: Craig Brasfield. **Assistant GM/Director, Sales and Marketing:** Chet Carey. **Controller/Director, Merchandising:** Carrie Brasfield. **Director, Group Sales/Ticket Operations:** Scott Jacobs. **Director, Media Relations/Broadcasting:** Unavailable. **Director, Food/Beverage:** Unavailable. **Head Groundskeeper:** Ken Estes. **Administrative Assistant:** Lane Smith.

Manager: Hill Denson. **Coaches:** Unavailable. **Trainer:** John Dussouy.

GAME INFORMATION

Radio Announcer: Unavailable. **No. of Games Broadcast:** Home-46, Away-48. **Flagship Station:** ESPN 1240-AM.

PA Announcer: Glen Waddle. **Official Scorer:** Denny Hales.

Stadium Name: Smith-Wills Stadium. **Location:** I-55 to Lakeland Drive, left at Cool Papa Bell Drive. **Standard Game Times:** 7:05 p.m.; Sun. 2:05, 6:05.

Visiting Club Hotel: Unavailable.

PENSACOLA
PELICANS

Mailing Address: 913 Gulf Breeze Pkwy., Suite 36, Gulf Breeze, FL 32561.
Telephone: (850) 934-8444. **FAX**: (850)934-8744.
E-Mail Address: info@pensacolapelicans.com. **Website**: www.pensacolapelicans.com.

Owners: Quint Studer, Rishy Studer. **President**: Rishy Studer. **Chief Executive Officer**: Quint Studer.
General Manager: George Stavrenos. **Senior Sales Executive**: Talmadge Nunnari. **Sales Executive**: Mike Coziahr.
Director, Media Relations: Jason Libbert. **Manager, Front Office/Ticket Operations**: Casey Flanagan. **Coordinator, Community Relations**: Jessica Morris. **Coordinator, Promotions/Merchandise**: Michael Ann Riley. **Coordinator, Stadium Operations**: Gregg Buckles.
Director, Player Procurement: James Gamble. **Manager**: Bernie Carbo.

GAME INFORMATION

Radio Announcer: Unavailable. **No. of Games Broadcast**: Home-47, Away-47. **Flagship Station**: 1620-AM.
PA Announcer: Unavailable. **Official Scorer**: Jake Fish.
Stadium Name: Pelican Park. **Location**: Highway 65 to CC&J exit, right on 17th Street, follow signs to stadium.
Standard Game Times: 6:35 p.m., weekend 6:05.

SHREVEPORT
SPORTS

Mailing Address: 2901 Pershing Blvd, Shreveport, LA 71109.
Telephone: (318) 636-5555. **FAX**: (318) 636-5670.
Website: www.shreveportsports.com.

Owners: Gary Elliston, Carl Bell.
General Manager: Brian Viselli. **Corporate Sales**: Joe Bernis. **Account Executives**: George Reynolds, Mitchell Person. **Merchandising**: Terri Sipes. **Concessions Manager**: John Riffon.
Manager: Unavailable. **Coaches**: Unavailable.

GAME INFORMATION

Radio Announcer: Dave Nitz. **No. of Games Broadcast**: Home-47. Away-47. **Flagship Station**: KRMD-AM.
PA Announcer: Dennis Buddie. **Official Scorer**: Unavailable.
Stadium Name: Fair Grounds Field (1986). **Location**: Hearne Ave. (Highway 171), exit off of I-20 at Louisiana State Fairgrounds. **Standard Game Times**: 7:05 p.m., Sun. 2:05 (May-June), 6:05 (July-Aug.).
Visiting Club Hotel: Unavailable.

SAN ANGELO
COLTS

Office Address: 1600 University Ave., San Angelo, TX 76904.
Telephone: (325) 042 6687. **FAX**: (325) 947-9480.
E-Mail Address: colts@zipnet.us. **Website**: www.sanangelocolts.com.

Operated by: San Angelo Colts Baseball Club, LLC.
President, Executive General Manager: Harlan Bruha. **Assistant GM**: Paige Jackson. **Director, Marketing**: Bruce McLaren. **Marketing Executives**: Courtney Neal, Katrina Buckner. **Intern**: Karenrose Honea. **Stadium Superintendent**: Joe Stapp.
Manager: John Harris. **Coach**: Unavailable. **Trainer**: Jeff Mann.

GAME INFORMATION

Radio Announcer: Mark Moesner. **No. of Games Broadcast**: Home-47, Away-47. **Flagship Station**: KKSA 1260-AM.
PA Announcer: Unavailable. **Official Scorer**: Unavailable.
Stadium Name: Colts Stadium. **Location**: From north/south, take U.S. 87 to Knickerbocker Road, west to stadium; From east/west, take U.S. 67 to U.S. 87 South, to Knickerbocker Road, west to stadium. **Standard Game Time**: 7:05 p.m.
Visiting Club Hotel: Howard Johnson, 415 W. Beauregard Blvd., San Angelo, TX 76903. Telephone: (915) 653-2995.

FRONTIER
LEAGUE

Office Address: 408 W. U.S. Hwy 40, Suite 100, Troy, IL 62294.
Mailing Address: P.O. Box 62, Troy, IL 62294.
E-Mail Address: office@frontierleague.com. **Website:** www.frontierleague.com.
Year Founded: 1993.

Commissioner: Bill Lee. **Chairman:** Chris Hanners (Chillicothe).
President: Rich Sauget. **Vice Presidents:** John Swiatek (Washington), Duke Ward (Richmond). **Corporate Secretary/Treasurer:** Bob Wolfe. **Legal Council/Deputy Commissioner:** Kevin Rouch. **Director, Development:** Leo Trich.
Directors: Dan Brennan (Windy City), Clint Brown (Florence), Harold Burkemper (River City), Bill Bussing (Evansville), Dave Ciarrachi (Rockford), Mike Hayes (Ohio Valley), Chris Hanners (Chillicothe), Rich Sauget (Gateway), John Swiatek (Washington), Duke Ward (Richmond), Gary Wendt (Mid-Missouri), Bill Wright (Kalamazoo).
Division Structure: East—Chillicothe, Evansville, Florence, Ohio Valley, Richmond, Washington. **West**—Gateway, Kalamazoo, Mid-Missouri, River City, Rockford, Windy City.
Regular Season: 96 games. **2005 Opening Date:** May 25. **Closing Date:** Sept. 5.
All-Star Game: July 13 at Washington.
Playoff Format: Top two teams in each division meet in best-of-5 semifinal series. Winners meet in best-of-5 series for league championship.
Roster Limit: 24. **Eligibility Rule:** Minimum of 10 first-year players; maximum of seven players with one year of professional experience; maximum of two players with two years of experience and maximum of three players with three or more years of experience. No player may be 27 prior to Jan. 1 of current season.
Brand of Baseball: Wilson
Statistician: SportsTicker, ESPN Plaza—Building B, Bristol, CT 06010 .

STADIUM INFORMATION

Club	Stadium	Opened	Dimensions LF	CF	RF	Capacity	2004 Att.
Chillicothe	V.A. Memorial Stadium	1954	328	400	325	4,000	82,183
Evansville	Bosse Field	1915	315	415	315	5,181	121,733
Florence	Champion Window Field	2004	325	395	325	4,200	68,250
Gateway	GMC Stadium	2002	318	385	301	6,500	217,500
Kalamazoo	Homer Stryker Field	1995	306	400	330	4,806	135,654
Mid-Missouri	Taylor Stadium	2000	340	400	340	3,084	45,511
*Ohio Valley							67,028
Richmond	McBride Stadium	1936	324	402	322	1,800	46,019
River City	T.R. Hughes Ballpark	1999	320	382	299	4,989	185,333
Rockford	RiverHawks Stadium	2005	315	380	312	4,056	103,140
Washington	Falconi Field	2002	325	400	325	3,200	154,963
Windy City	Hawkinson Ford Field	1999	335	390	335	4,000	67,397

*Franchise operated in Springfield-Ozark in 2004, will operate as traveling team in 2005.

CHILLICOTHE
PAINTS

Office Address: 59 N. Paint St., Chillicothe, OH 45601.
Telephone: (740) 773-8326. **FAX:** (740) 773-8338.
E-Mail Address: paints@bright.net. **Website:** www.chillicothepaints.com.

Operated by: Chillicothe Paints Professional Baseball Association, Inc.
Principal Owner: Chris Hanners. **President:** Shirley Bandy.
Vice President, General Manager: Bryan Wickline. **Stadium Superintendent:** Jim Miner. **Director, Finance:** Maleine Davis. **Director, Sales/Marketing:** John Wend. **Director of Game Day Operations/Group Sales:** Unavailable. **Director, Merchandise:** Unavailable. **Director, Concessions:** Unavailable. **Head Groundskeeper:** Jim Miner.
Manager: Glenn Wilson. **Coach:** Marty Dunn. **Trainer:** Scott Street.

GAME INFORMATION

Radio Announcer: Ryan Mitchell. **No. of Games Broadcast:** Home-51, Away-45. **Flagship Station:** WXIZ 100.9-FM.
PA Announcer: John Wend. **Official Scorer:** Aaron Lemaster.
Stadium Name: V.A. Memorial Stadium. **Location:** Route 23 to Bridge Street, west on Route 35, north on Route 104. **Standard Game Times:** 7:05 p.m., Sun. 6:05.
Visiting Club Hotel: Unavailable.

EVANSVILLE
OTTERS

Office Address: 1701 N. Main St., Evansville, IN 47711.
Mailing Address: P.O. Box 3565, Evansville, IN 47734.
Telephone: (812) 435-8686. **FAX:** (812) 435-8688.
E-Mail Address: ottersbb@evansville.net. **Website:** www.evansvilleotters.com.

Operated by: Evansville Baseball, LLC.
President: Bill Bussing. **Senior Vice President:** Pat Rayburn.
Vice President, General Manager: Steve Tahsler. **Director, Ticketing:** Andrew Aldenderfer. **Director, Baseball Operations:** Jeff Pohl. **Facilities Manager:** Mike Duckworth. **Account Executives:** Chad Cooper, Deana Johnson, Dan McGinn, Liam Miller, Joel Padfield. **Promotions Coordinator:** Scot Trible. **Assistant, Operations:** Tammy Berg. **Head Groundskeeper:** Joe Parker. **Flag Chairman:** Marvin Gray.
Manager: Greg Jelks. **Coaches:** George Fisher, J.R. Seymour. **Pitching Coach:** Jeff Pohl. **Trainer:** Unavailable.

GAME INFORMATION
Radio Announcers: Chad Cooper, Dan McGinn. **No. of Games Broadcast:** Home-51, Away-45. **Flagship Station:** WUEV 91.5-FM.
PA Announcer: Unavailable. **Official Scorer:** Steve Rhoads.
Stadium Name: Bosse Field. **Location:** U.S. 41 to Diamond Ave. West, left at Heidelbach Ave. **Standard Game Times:** 7:05 p.m., Sun. 6:05.
Visiting Club Hotel: Home Life Studios & Suites, 100 South Green River Rd., Evansville, IN 47715. Telephone: 812-475-1700.

FLORENCE
FREEDOM

Office Address: 7950 Freedom Way, Florence, KY 41042.
Telephone: (859) 594-4487. **FAX:** (859) 647-4639.
Website: florencefreedom.com.

Operated by: Canterbury Baseball, LLC.
President, Managing Partner: Clint Brown.
General Manager: Pat Daly. **Assistant GM:** Morgan West. **Director, Ticket Operations:** Yumi Blackburn. **Director, Media/Public Relations:** Kili Hood. **Groundskeeper:** Lyle Travis.
Director, Baseball Operations/Manager: Jamie Keefe. **Coach:** Unavailable. **Pitching Coach:** Unavailable. **Trainer:** Unavailable.

GAME INFORMATION
Radio: Unavailable.
PA Announcer: Unavailable. **Official Scorer:** Unavailable.
Stadium: Champion Window Field. **Location:** I-71/75 South to exit 180, left onto U.S. 42, right on Freedom Way; I-71/75 North to exit 180. **Standard Game Times:** 7:05 p.m.; Tues. 12:35, Sun. 6:05.
Visiting Club Hotel: Microtel Inns and Suites, 7490 Woodspoint Dr., Florence, KY 41042. Telephone: (859) 746-8100.

GATEWAY
GRIZZLIES

Mailing Address: 2301 Grizzlie Bear Blvd., Sauget, IL 62206.
Telephone: (618) 337-3000. **FAX:** (618) 332-3625.
E-Mail Address: grizzlies@accessus.net. **Website:** www.gatewaygrizzlies.com.

Operated by: Gateway Baseball, LLC.
Managing Officer: Richard Sauget.
General Manager: Tony Funderburg. **Assistant GM:** Steven Gomric. **Administrative Assistant to GM:** Gina Perschbacher. **Director, Group Sales:** Jason Roeslein. **Office Operations:** Brent Pownall. **Corporate Sales Associate:** Joe Pott. **Director, Promotions:** Corey Stephens. **Director, Corporate Sales:** C.J. Hendrickson. **Director, Stadium Operations/Corporate Sales Associate:** Heath Kassing. **Director, Mechandise/Ticket Sales Associate:** Kelly Kicielinski. **Head Groundskeeper/Corporate Sales Associate:** Craig Kuhl. **Interns:** Ethan Barrett, Ryan Bundy, Katy Gerard, Jevon Heany, Christine Hopper, Lindsey Meyer, Lindsey Rabe, Michael Smelik.
Manager: Danny Cox. **Coaches:** Tim Mueth, Neil Fiala. **Trainer:** Geof Manzo.

Radio Announcer: Joe Pott. No of Games Broadcast: Home-48, Away-48. Flagship Station: ESPN 1380-AM. PA Announcer: Tom Calhoun. Official Scorer: Amanda Haas.
Stadium Name: GMC Stadium. Location: I-255 at exit 15 (Mousette Lane). Standard Game Times: 7:05 p.m., Sun. 6:05.
Visiting Club Hotel: Econo Lodge, 1409 W. Highway 50, O'Fallon, IL. Telephone: (618) 628-8895.

KALAMAZOO
KINGS

Mailing Address: 251 Mills St., Kalamazoo, MI 49048.
Telephone: (269) 388-8326. FAX: (269) 388-8333.
E-Mail Address: kalamazookings@kalamazookings.com. Website: www.kalamazookings.com.

Operated by: Team Kalamazoo, LLC.
Owners: Bill Wright, Mike Seelye, Pat Seelye, Joe Rosenhagen, Ed Bernard, Scott Hocevar.
General Manager/Managing Partner: Joe Rosenhagen. Fundraising Coordinator/Community Relations: Chris Peake. Sales Manager: Becky Smith. Marketing: Lee Naplin.
Director, Baseball Operations/Field Manager: Fran Riordan. Pitching Coach: Wes Crawford.

GAME INFORMATION
Radio Announcers: Mike Levine, Ryan Maguire. No. of Games Broadcast: Home-51, Away-45. Flagship Station: WQSN 1660-AM.
PA Announcers: Jim Lefler, Tom Dukesherer. Official Scorer: Jason Zerban.
Stadium Name: Homer Stryker Field. Location: I-94 to Sprinkle Road (exit 80), north on Sprinkle Road, left on Business Loop I-94, left on Kings Highway, right on Mills Street. Standard Game Times: 6:35 p.m., Sun. 5:35.
Visiting Club Hotel: Days Inn Airport Hotel, 3522 Sprinkle Rd., Kalamazoo, MI 49002. Telephone: (269) 381-7070.

MID-MISSOURI
MAVERICKS

Mailing Address: 810 E. Walnut, Columbia, MO 65201.
Telephone: (573) 256-4004. FAX: (573) 256-4003.
E-Mail Address: info@midmomavs.com. Website: www.midmomavs.com.

Operated by: Columbia Professional Baseball LLC.
President: Gary Wendt.
Director, Community Relations: Ann Wilhelm. Director, Sales/Marketing: Rich Stoneking. Coordinator, Community Relations/Marketing Coordinator: Amanda Heenan. Director, Business Affairs: Melissa Wheeler.

GAME INFORMATION
Radio Announcer: Unavailable. No. of Games Broadcast: Home-47, Away-49. Flagship Station: KFRU 1400-AM.
PA Announcer: Unavailable. Official Scorer: Unavailable.
Stadium Name: Taylor Stadium. Location: I-70 to Providence Road exit, south to Research Park Drive, right to stadium. Standard Game Times: 7:05 p.m., Sun. 6:05.
Visiting Club Hotel: Regency Downtown Hotel, 1111 E. Broadway, Columbia, MO 65201.

OHIO VALLEY
REDCOATS

The franchise will operate as a traveling team in 2005, although it will play 15 games in Lafayette, Ind., and six games in Marietta, Ohio.
General manager: Unavailable.
Manager: Unavailable. Coaches: Unavailable.

RICHMOND
ROOSTERS

Mailing Address: 201 NW 13th St., Richmond, IN 47374.
Telephone: (765) 935-7529. FAX: (765) 962-7047.
E-Mail Address: staff@richmondroosters.com. Website: www.richmondroosters.com.

Operated by: Richmond Roosters Baseball, LLC.
Owner/President: Allen Brady.
Vice President/General Manager: Deanna Beaman. Director, Group Sales/Community Relations: Tom Linehan.
Director, Food Services/Office Manager: LaDonna White.
Manager: Chris Mongiardo. Coach: Unavailable. Trainer: Theresa Wright-Reed.

GAME INFORMATION

Radio Announcer: Scott Leo. No. of Games Broadcast: Home-48, Away-48. Flagship Stations: WKBV 1490-AM, WCNB 1580-AM, Star 98.3-FM.
PA Announcer: Scott Beaman. Official Scorer: Unavailable.
Stadium Name: McBride Stadium. Location: I-70 to exit 149A (Williamsburg Pike), right on West Main Street, right on NW 13th Street. Standard Game Times: 6:35 p.m.; Sun. 4:35.
Visiting Club Hotel: Unavailable.

RIVER CITY
RASCALS

Office Address: 900 Ozzie Smith Dr., O'Fallon, MO 63366.
Mailing Address: P.O. Box 662, O'Fallon, MO 63366.
Telephone: (636) 240-2287. FAX: (636) 240-7313.
E-Mail Address: info@rivercityrascals.com. Website: www.rivercityrascals.com.

Operated by: Missouri River Baseball, LLC.
Managing Partner: Harold Burkemper. Executive Director: Bob Wente. Assistant General Manager: Allen Gossett.
Director, Merchandising: Bobby Rhoden. Director, Ticket Sales/Operations: Bryan Schubert. Director, Community/Media Relations: Alan Jackson. Group Sales Associates: John Aebischer, David Biesenthal. Head Groundskeeper: Chris Young.
Manager: Randy Martz. Coaches: Brian Lewis, Mike Barger. Trainer: Missouri Bone & Joint.

GAME INFORMATION

Radio Announcer: Mike Morgan. No. of Games Broadcast: Home-48, Away-48. Flagship Station: Unavailable.
PA Announcer: Joe Sutton. Official Scorer: Keith Deshurley.
Stadium Name: T.R. Hughes Ballpark. Location: I-70 to exit 219, north on T.R. Hughes Road, follow signs to ballpark. Standard Game Times: 7:05 p.m., Sun. 6:05.
Visiting Club Hotel: Hilton Garden Inn, 2310 Technology Dr., O'Fallon, MO 63366. Telephone: (636) 625-2700.

ROCKFORD
RIVERHAWKS

Office Address: 4503 Interstate Blvd., Loves Park, IL 61111.
Telephone: (815) 964-2255. FAX: (815) 964-2462.
E-Mail Address: playball@rockfordriverhawks.com. Website: www.rockfordriverhawks.com.

Operated by: Rockford Baseball, LLC.
Managing Partner: Dave Ciarrachi.
General Manager: Mike Babcock. Assistant GM: Todd Fulk. Director, Broadcasting: Bill Czaja. Director, Sales: Josh Olerud. Account Executives: Scotty Haulter, Sam Knaack. Director, Group Sales: Tim Wilson. Head Groundskeeper: Unavailable.
Manager: Mike Young. Coach: Sam Knaack. Trainer: Unavailable.

GAME INFORMATION

Radio Announcer: Bill Czaja. No. of Games Broadcast: Home-51, Away-45. Flagship Station: WRHL 102.3-FM.
PA Announcer: Scott Bentley. Official Scorer: Aaron Nester.
Stadium Name: RiverHawks Stadium. Location: I-90 to Riverside Boulevard exit, east to Interstate Drive, left on Interstate Drive. Standard Game Times: 7:05 p.m., Sun 6:05.
Visiting Club Hotel: Sleep Inn, 725 Clark Rd., Rockford, IL 61107. Telephone: (815) 398-8900.

WASHINGTON
WILD THINGS

Office Address: Falconi Field, One Washington Federal Way, Washington, PA 15301.
Telephone: (724) 250-9555. FAX: (724) 250-2333.

E-Mail Address: info@washingtonwildthings.com. **Website:** www.washingtonwildthings.com.

Owned by: Sports Facility, LLC. **Operated by:** Washington Frontier League Baseball, LLC. **Managing Partner:** John Swiatek.

President/Chief Executive Officer: John Swiatek. **General Manager:** Ross Vecchio. **Director, Marketing:** Christine Blaine. **Director, Merchandise:** Scott Eafrati. **Director, Sales/Service:** Jeff Ptak. **Director, Stadium Operations:** Steve Zavacky. **Group/Season Ticket Manager:** Ricci Rich.

Manager: John Massarelli. **Coach:** Ryan Ellis. **Pitching Coach:** Mark Mason. **Trainer:** Craig Castor.

GAME INFORMATION

Radio Announcer: Bob Gregg. **No. of Games Broadcast:** Home-48, Away-48. **Flagship Station:** WJPA 95.3-FM. **PA Announcer:** Bill DiFabio. **Official Scorer:** Skip Hood.

Stadium Name: Falconi Field. **Location:** I-70 to exit 15 (Chesnut Street), right on Chesnut Street to Washington Crown Center Mall, right at mall entrance, right on to Mall Drive to stadium. **Standard Game Times:** 7:05 p.m., Sun. 6:35.

Visiting Club Hotel: Unavailable.

WINDY CITY
THUNDERBOLTS

Office Address: 14011 South Kenton Ave., Crestwood, IL 60445.

Telephone: (708) 489-2255. **FAX:** (708) 489-2999.

E-Mail Address: info@wcthunderbolts.com. **Website:** www.wcthunderbolts.com.

Owned by: Crestwood Professional Baseball, LLC.

General Manager: Cory Dirksen. **Assistant GM:** Terry Fenton. **Director, Sales:** Mike McAdams. **Director, Group Sales:** Pete Kelly. **Account Executive/Promotions Director:** Rosario Cappello. **Account Executive/Stadium Operations:** Mike Lucas. **Merchandise Director/Office Manager:** Joanna Bauer.

Director, Business Operations/Player Personnel: Brian Hooper. **Manager:** Brent Bowers. **Coaches:** Steve Trout, Mike Kashirsky. **Trainer:** Unavailable.

GAME INFORMATION

Radio: Unavailable.

PA Announcer: Unavailable. **Official Scorer:** Unavailable.

Stadium Name: Hawkinson Ford Field. **Location:** I-294 to Cicero Ave. exit (Route 50), south for 1½ miles, left at Midlothian Turnpike, right on Kenton Ave.; I-57 to 147th Street, west on 147th to Cicero, north on Cicero, right on Midlothian Turnpike, right on Kenton. **Standard Game Times:** 7:05 p.m., Sun. 5:05.

Visiting Club Hotel: Georgio's Comfort Inn, 8800 W. 159th St., Orland Park, IL 60462. **Telephone:** (708) 403-1100.

NORTHERN
LEAGUE

Office Address: 309 West Seventh St., Suite 901, Fort Worth, TX 76102.

Telephone: (817) 378-9898. **FAX:** 817-378-9805.

E-Mail Address: info@northernleague.com. **Website:** www.northernleague.com.

Founded: 1993.

Commissioner: Mike Stone. **Chief Operating Officer:** John Blake. **Supervisor, Umpires:** Randy Hoback.

Directors: Jim Abel (Lincoln), John Ehlert (Kansas City), Rich Ehrenreich (Schaumburg), Jeff Gidney (Calgary), Marv Goldklang (St. Paul), Mike Hansen (Joliet), Sam Katz (Winnipeg), Dan Orlich (Edmonton), John Roost (Sioux Falls), Mike Tatoian (Gary), Bruce Thom (Fargo-Moorhead), Ben Zuraw (Sioux Falls).

Division Structure: North—Calgary, Edmonton, Fargo-Moorhead, Sioux City, Sioux Falls, Winnipeg. **South**—Gary, Joliet, Kansas City, Lincoln, St. Paul, Schaumburg.

Regular Season: 96 games (split schedule). **2005 Opening Date:** May 20. **Closing Date:** Sept. 4.

All-Star Game: July 19 at Gary.

Playoff Format: First-half division winner meets second half division winner in best-of-5 semifinal series. Winners meet in best-of-5 series for league championship.

Roster Limit: 22. **Eligibility Rule:** Minimum of five first-year players; maximum of four players with at least five years of professional experience.

Brand of Baseball: Rawlings.

Statistician: SportsTicker, ESPN Plaza-Building B, Bristol, CT 06010.

STADIUM INFORMATION

Club	Stadium	Opened	LF	CF	RF	Capacity	2004 Att.
*Calgary	Foothills Stadium	1966	345	400	345	8,000	—
*Edmonton	TELUS Field	1995	340	420	320	9,200	—

Fargo-Moorhead	Newman Outdoor Field	1996	318	400	314	4,513	179,665
Gary	U.S. Steel Yard	2003	320	400	335	6,139	147,801
Joliet	Silver Cross Field	2002	330	400	327	4,616	198,250
Kansas City	Community America Ballpark	2003	300	396	328	4,365	238,745
Lincoln	Haymarket Park	2001	335	395	325	4,500	204,354
St. Paul	Midway Stadium	1982	320	400	320	6,069	280,375
Schaumburg	Alexian Field	1999	355	400	353	7,048	200,060
Sioux City	Lewis and Clark Park	1993	330	400	330	3,630	120,681
Sioux Falls	Sioux Falls Stadium	1964	312	410	312	4,029	108,096
Winnipeg	CanWest Global Park	1999	325	400	325	7,481	323,241

*Expansion franchises

CALGARY
VIPERS

Office Address: 2255 Crowchild Trail NW, Calgary, Alberta T2N 3R5. **Telephone:** (403) 277-2255.
E-Mail Address: info@calgaryvipers.com. **Website:** www.calgaryvipers.com.

Owner: Jeff Gidney. **President, Chief Operating Officer:** Peter Young. **Merchandise Manager:** Branden Young. **Manager:** Unavailable. **Coaches:** Unavailable.

GAME INFORMATION
Radio: Unavailable.
PA Announcer: Unavailable. **Official Scorer:** Unavailable.
Stadium Name: Foothills Stadium. **Location:** Crowchild Trail NW to 24th Avenue. **Standard Game Times:** 7:05 p.m., Sun. 1:35.
Visiting Club Hotel: Unavailable.

EDMONTON
CRACKER-CATS

Office Address: 10233 96th Ave., Edmonton, Alberta T5K 0A5.
Telephone: (780) 423-2255. **FAX:** (780) 423-3112.
E-Mail address: info@crackercats.ca. **Website:** www.crackercats.ca.

Operated by: Northern League in Edmonton Inc.
General Manager: Mel Kowalchuk. **Assistant GM:** Fraser Murray. **Office Manager:** Nancy Yeo. **Accountant:** Heather Pick. **Senior Account Executive:** Ken Charuk. **Director, Broadcasting:** Al Coates. **Account Executive:** Dale Roy. **Ticket Manager/Community Relations:** Kendra Morten. **Stadium Manager:** Don Benson. **Head Groundskeeper:** Tom Archibald. **Clubhouse Operations:** Dan Rosnau.
Manager/Director, Player Procurement: Terry Bevington. **Assistant Director, Player Procurement:** Mark Randall. **Coaches:** John Barlow, Brad Hall. **Trainer:** Unavailable.

GAME INFORMATION
Radio Announcer: Al Coates. **No. of Games Broadcast:** Unavailable. **Flagship Station:** Unavailable.
PA Announcer: Ron Rimer/Bill Cowen. **Official Scorer:** Al Coates.
Stadium Name: TELUS Field. **Location:** From north, 101st Street to 96th Avenue, left on 96th, one block east; from south, Calgary Trail North to Queen Elizabeth Hill, right across Walterdale Bridge, right 96th Avenue. **Standard Game Times:** 7:05 p.m.; Sun. 1:35.
Visiting Club Hotel: Unavailable.

FARGO-MOORHEAD
REDHAWKS

Office Address: 1515 15th Ave. N., Fargo, ND 58102.
Telephone: (701) 235-6161. **FAX:** (701) 297-9247.
E-Mail Address: redhawks@fmredhawks.com. **Website:** www.fmredhawks.com.

Operated by: Fargo Baseball, LLC.
President: Bruce Thom. **Vice President:** Brad Thom.
General Manager: Lee Schwartz. **Director, Baseball Operations/Communications:** Josh Buchholz. **Senior Accountant:** Sue Wild. **Accounting Assistant:** Tina Lesmeister. **Stadium Superintendent/Head Groundskeeper:** Blair

Tweet. **Director, Promotions:** Kristie Schwan. **Director, Merchandise/Special Events, Advertising:** Sara Garaas. **Director, Ticket Sales:** Nicole Ellis. **Assistant, Media Relations:** Justin Stottlemyre. **Clubhouse Operations:** Brent Tehven.

Manager/Director, Player Procurement: Doug Simunic. **Assistant Director, Player Procurement/Consultant:** Jeff Bittiger. **Pitching Coach:** Steve Montgomery. **Coach:** Bucky Burgau, Robbie Lopez. **Trainer:** Don Bruenjes.

GAME INFORMATION

Radio Announcers: Jack Michaels, Maury Wills. **No. of Games Broadcast:** Home-48, Away-48. **Flagship Station:** WDAY 970-AM.

PA Announcer: Merrill Piepkorn. **Official Scorer:** Rob Olson.

Stadium Name: Newman Outdoor Field. **Location:** I-29 North to exit 67, right on 19th Ave. North, right on Albrecht Boulevard. **Standard Game Times:** 7:05 p.m., Sun. 2:05.

Visiting Club Hotel: Comfort Inn West, 3825 9th Ave. SW, Fargo, ND 58103. Telephone: (701) 282-9596.

GARY SOUTHSHORE
RAILCATS

Office Address: One Stadium Plaza, Gary, IN 46402.
Telephone: (219) 882-2255. **FAX:** (219) 882-2259.
E-Mail Address: info@railcatsbaseball.com Website: www.railcatsbaseball.com.

Operated by: SouthShore Baseball, LLC. **Principal Owners:** Victory Sports Group, LLC.
Chairman: George Huber. **President, Chief Executive Officer:** Mike Tatoian.
Vice President, General Manager: Roger Wexelberg. **Assistant GM:** Kevin Spudic. **Director, Broadcasting:** Tom Nichols. **Director, Facility:** Mike Figg. **Group Sales Manager:** Mike Smith. **Corporate Sales Managers:** Renee Connelly, Milton Thaxton. **Merchandise Manager/Community Relations:** Jamie Kurpiel. **Manager, Field Maintenance:** Tom Preslar. **Director, Ticket Operations:** Cayla Pearson. **Marketing/Promotions Assistant:** Jahi Garrett. **Group Sales/Community Relations Assistant:** Becky Kremer. **Executive Assistant:** Tomika Hicks.
Manager: Greg Tagert. **Coaches:** Unavailable.

GAME INFORMATION

Radio Announcer: Tom Nichols. **No. of Games Broadcast:** Home-48, Away-48. **Flagship Station:** WEFM 95.5-FM.

Stadium Name: U.S. Steel Yard. **Location:** I-65 to I-90 West (toll), one mile to Broadway South, left on Fifth Street. **Standard Game Times:** 7 p.m., Sat. 6, Sun. 2.

Visiting Club Hotel: Trump Hotel, 21 Buffington Harbor Dr., Gary, IN 46406. Telephone: (219) 977-9999.

JOLIET
JACKHAMMERS

Office Address: 1 Mayor Art Schultz Dr., Joliet, IL 60432.
Telephone: (815) 726-2255. **FAX:** (815) 726-9223.
E-Mail Address: info@jackhammerbaseball.com. **Website:** www.jackhammer-baseball.com.

Operated by: Joliet Professional Baseball Club, LLC.
Chairman: Peter Ferro. **Vice Chairman:** Charles Hammersmith. **Chief Executive Officer/General Counsel:** Michael Hansen. **Chief Financial Officer/President:** John Costello.
Executive Vice President/General Manager: Steve Malliet. **Assistant GM:** Kelly Sufka. **Director, Ticket Sales:** Rich Kuchar. **Ticket Operations Manager:** Chad Therrien. **Ticket Sales Manager:** Kyle Kreger. **Ticket Sales Representatives:** Ryan Harris, Damon Shoultz. **Director, Broadcasting/Media Relations:** Bryan Dolgin. **Director, Community Relations/Promotions:** Sarah Heth. **Director, Corporate Sales:** Keri Rumfield. **Director, Field/Stadium Operations:** Jeff Eckert. **Director, Accounting/Human Resources:** Tammy Harvey. **Administrative Assistant:** Sonia Little.
Manager: Jeff Isom. **Coach:** Bobby Bell. **Pitching Coach:** Rich Hyde. **Trainer:** Scott Wilson.

GAME INFORMATION

Radio Announcers: Bryan Dolgin, Mark Vasko. **No. of Games Broadcast:** Home-48, Away-48. **Flagship Stations:** WJOL 1340-AM.

PA Announcer: Elwood Blues. **Official Scorer:** Dave Laketa.

Stadium Name: Silver Cross Field. **Location:** I-80 to Chicago Street/Route 53 North exit, go ½ mile on Chicago Street, right on Washington Street to Jefferson Street/U.S. 52, right on Jefferson, ballpark on left. **Standard Game Times:** 7:05 p.m., Tues. 6:05 p.m., Sun. 2:05/5:05.

Visiting Club Hotel: Hampton Inn, 3555 Mall Loop Dr., Joliet, IL 60431. Telephone: (815) 439-9500.

KANSAS CITY
T-BONES

Office Address: 1800 Village West Pkwy., Kansas City, KS 66111.
Telephone: (913) 328-2255. **FAX:** (913) 328-5652.
E-Mail Address: batterup@tbonesbaseball.com. **Website:** www.tbonesbaseball.com.

Operated By: T-Bones Baseball Club, LLC; Ehlert Development.
Owner, President: John Ehlert. **Vice President:** Adam Ehlert.
Vice President/General Manager: Rick Muntean. **VP, Marketing/Corporate Partnerships:** Kevin Battle. **Assistant General Manager:** Chris Browne. **Director, Merchandising:** Tracy Lewis. **Director, Media Relations:** Loren Foxx. **Director, Promotions:** Justin Stancil. **Director, Group Sales:** Brandon Smith. **Head Groundskeeper:** Don Frantz. **Stadium Operations:** Jason Hoss. **Bookkeeper:** Nikki White. **Director, Corporate Sponsorships:** Mike Meyers.
Manager: Al Gallagher. **Coach:** Darryl Motley. **Pitching Coach:** Unavailable. **Trainer:** Unavailable.

GAME INFORMATION
Radio Announcer: Unavailable. **No. of Games Broadcast:** Home-48, Away-48. **Flagship Station:** Unavailable.
PA Announcer: Unavailable. **Official Scorer:** Unavailable.
Stadium Name: Community America Ballpark. **Location:** State Avenue West off I-435, corner of 110th and State Avenue. **Standard Game Times:** 7:05 p.m., Sun. 5:05.
Visiting Club Hotel: Unavailable.

LINCOLN
SALTDOGS

Office Address: 403 Line Dr., Suite A, Lincoln, NE 68508.
Telephone: (402) 474-2255. **FAX:** (402) 474-2254.
E-Mail Address: info@saltdogs.com. **Website:** www.saltdogs.com.

Owner: Jim Abel. **President:** Charlie Meyer.
Vice President, General Manager: Tim Utrup. **Assistant GM/Director, Marketing:** Bret Beer. **Director, Broadcasting/Communications:** Len Clark. **Director, Merchandising/Promotions:** Anne Duchek. **Director, Ticketing:** Tim Petersen. **Director, Stadium Operations:** Ryan Lockhart. **Assistant Director, Stadium Operations:** Shane Godel. **Ticket Account Executive:** Kendall Christensen. **Marketing Consultant:** Sherrie Hannerman. **Office Manager:** Jeanette Eagleton.
Manager: Tim Johnson. **Coach:** Mike Workman. **Trainers:** Corey Courtney, Joel Jasa.

GAME INFORMATION
Radio Announcers: Len Clark, John Baylor. **No. of Games Broadcast:** Home-48, Away-48. **Flagship Station:** KFOR 1240-AM.
PA Announcer: Unavailable. **Official Scorer:** Unavailable.
Stadium Name: Haymarket Park. **Location:** I-80 to Cornhusker Highway West, left on First Street, right on Sun Valley Blvd., left on Line Drive. **Standard Game Times:** 7:05 p.m., Sun. 5:05.
Visiting Club Hotel: Embassy Suites, 1040 P St., Lincoln, NE 68508. Telephone: (402) 474-1111.

ST. PAUL
SAINTS

Saints
St. Paul

Office Address: 1771 Energy Park Dr., St. Paul, MN 55108.
Telephone: (651) 644-3517. **FAX:** (651) 644-1627.
E-Mail Address: funsgood@saintsbaseball.com. **Website:** www.saintsbaseball.com.

Operated By: St. Paul Saints Baseball Club, Inc.
Principal Owners: Marv Goldklang, Mike Veeck, Bill Murray.
Chairman: Marv Goldklang. **President:** Mike Veeck.
Executive Vice President, General Manager: Derek Sharrer. **VP, Business Development:** Tom Whaley. **Assistant GM:** Eben Yager. **Community Relations/Customer Service Director:** Annie Huidekoper. **Marketing Director:** Dan Lehv. **Promotions Director:** Stephanie Harris. **Corporate Sales Director:** Matt Hansen. **Corporate Sales Manager:** Jack Weatherman. **Group Sales Director:** Matt Bomberg. **Group Sales Manager:** Ron Wade. **Special Events Manager:** Heather Westrom. **Media Relations Director:** Dave Wright. **Merchandise Director:** Amy Alt. **Concessions Director:** Tom Farrell. **International Development Director:** Seigo Masubuchi. **Controller:** Wayne Engel. **Business Manager:** Leesa Anderson. **Office Manager:** Jennifer Jensen. **Stadium Operations Director:** Bib Klepperich. **Groundskeeper:** Connie Rudolph.

Manager: George Tsamis. **Coaches:** Ben Fleetham, Jackie Hernandez, Lamarr Rogers, T.J. Wiesner. **Trainer:** Unavailable.

GAME INFORMATION

Radio Announcer: Kris Atteberry. **No. of Games Broadcast:** Home-48, Away-48. **Flagship Station:** KSNB 950-AM. **PA Announcer:** Rusty Kath. **Official Scorers:** Jeff Lehtinen, Rick Kubitschek.
Stadium Name: Midway Stadium. **Location:** From I-94, take Snelling Avenue North exit, west onto Energy Park Drive. **Standard Game Times:** 7:05 p.m., Sun. 1:05.
Visiting Club Hotel: AmericInn of Mounds View, 1100 Highway 10, Mounds View, MN 55112. Telephone: (763) 786-2000.

SCHAUMBURG
FLYERS

Office Address: 1999 S. Springinsguth Rd., Schaumburg, IL 60193.
Telephone: (847) 891-2255. **FAX:** (847) 891-6441.
E-Mail Address: info@flyersbaseball.com. **Website:** www.flyersbaseball.com.

Principal Owners: Richard Ehrenreich, John Hughes, Gregory Smith. **Managing Partner/President:** Richard Ehrenreich.
General Manager: Rick Rungaitis. **Director, Media Relations:** Matt McLaughlin. **Manager, Group Sales:** Robin Lemke. **Ticket Manager:** Scott Boor. **Director, Graphics/Publications:** Shannan Kelly. **Group Sales Assistant/Merchandise:** Shannon Allen. **Director, Stadium Operations/Head Groundskeeper:** Ryan Pfeiffer. **Human Resources/Corporate Sales:** Ben Burke. **Clubhouse Manager:** Greg Garofalo. **Director, Security:** Dean Norman.
Manager: Andy McCauley. **Coach:** Gregg Neuman. **Pitching Coach:** Jim Boynewicz. **Trainer:** Mike Hickey.

GAME INFORMATION

Radio Announcer: Matt McLaughlin. **No. of Games Broadcast:** Home-48, Away-48. **Flagship Station:** www.flyers-baseball.com.
PA Announcer: Steve Brandy. **Official Scorers:** Tim Calderwood, Greg Swiderski.
Stadium Name: Alexian Field. **Location:** From north, I-290 to Elgin-O'Hare Expressway (Thorndale), west on expressway to Irving Park Road exit, left on Springinsguth under expressway, stadium on left; From south, U.S. 20 West (Lake Street) to Elgin-O'Hare Expressway (Thorndale), east on expressway, south on Springinsguth Road. **Standard Game Times:** 7:05 p.m.; Sat. 6:20; Sun. 1:20.
Visiting Club Hotel: Unavailable.

SIOUX CITY
EXPLORERS

Office Address: 3400 Line Dr., Sioux City, IA 51106.
Telephone: (712) 277-9467. **FAX:** (712) 277-9406.
E-Mail Address: siouxcityxs@yahoo.com. **Website:** www.xsbaseball.com.

Operated by: Sioux City Explorers Baseball Club, LLC.
General Manager: Chuck Robbins. **Assistant GM:** Luke Nielsen. **Assistant GM, Game Day Operations:** Mike Gorsett. **Director, Broadcasting:** Chris Varney. **Director, Stadium Operations:** Jim LeMoine. **Office Manager:** Karla Hertz.
Manager: Steve Shirley. **Coaches:** Jay Kirkpatrick, Jim Scholten.

GAME INFORMATION

Radio Announcer: Chris Varney. **No. of Games Broadcast:** Home-48, Away-48. **Flagship Station:** KSCJ 1360-AM. **PA Announcer:** Unavailable. **Official Scorer:** Unavailable.
Stadium Name: Lewis and Clark Park. **Location:** I-29 to Singing Hills Blvd. North, right on Line Drive. **Standard Game Times:** 7:05 p.m., Sun. 5:05.
Visiting Club Hotel: Unavailable.

SIOUX FALLS
CANARIES

Office Address: 1001 N. West Ave., Sioux Falls, SD 57104.
Telephone: (605) 333-0179. **FAX:** (605) 333-0139.
E-Mail Address: canaries@canariesbaseball.com. **Website:** www.canariesbase-ball.com.

Operated by: Sioux Falls Canaries Professional Baseball Club, LLC.
Principal Owner, Chairman: Ben Zuraw. **President:** Jeff Loebl.
General Manager: John Kuhn. **Assistant GM:** Larry McKenney. **Assistant GM/Director, Corporate Sales:** Ned Gavlick. **Group Sales Manager:** Kevin Heibut. **Tickets Sales Specialist:** Chris Schwab. **Marketing Manager:** Andy Henning. **Community Relations Coordinator:** Misten Schelhaas. **Client Relations, Sales/Marketing:** Tamara Nelson. **Director of Fun:** Dan Christopherson.
Manager: Mike Pinto. **Director, Player Personnel:** Doc Edwards. **Coaches:** Unavailable. **Trainer:** Brian Pickering.

GAME INFORMATION
Radio Announcer: Jarrod Shadrick. **No. of Games Broadcast:** Home-48, Away-48. **Flagship Station:** KWSN 1230-AM.
PA Announcer: Dan Christopherson. **Official Scorer:** Bob Beattie.
Stadium Name: Sioux Falls Stadium. **Location:** I-29 to Russell Street, south one mile, right on West Avenue. **Standard Game Times:** 7:05 p.m., Sun. 5:05.
Visiting Club Hotel: Baymont Inn, 3200 Meadow Ave., Sioux Falls, SD 57106. Telephone: (605) 362-0835.

WINNIPEG
GOLDEYES

Office Address: One Portage Ave. E., Winnipeg, Manitoba R3B 3N3.
Telephone: (204) 982-2273. **FAX:** (204) 982-2274.
E-Mail Address: goldeyes@goldeyes.com. **Website:** www.goldeyes.com.

Operated by: Winnipeg Goldeyes Baseball Club, Inc.
Principal Owner, President: Sam Katz.
General Manager: Andrew Collier. **Director, Marketing:** Dan Chase. **Director, Communications:** Jonathan Green. **Director, Promotions:** Barb McTavish. **Director, Sales:** Lorraine Maciboric. **Director, Group Sales:** Regan Katz. **Account Representatives:** Paul Edmonds, Dave Loat, Darren McCabe, Dennis McLean. **Director, Merchandising:** Carol Orchard. **Comptroller:** Judy Jones. **Facility Manager:** Scott Horn. **Administrative Assistants:** Heather Mann-O'Hara, Angela Sanche. **Head Groundskeeper:** Don Ferguson.
Manager/Director, Player Procurement: Hal Lanier. **Coach:** Tom Vaeth. **Pitching Coach:** Rick Forney. **Trainer:** Dong Lien.

GAME INFORMATION
Radio Announcer: Paul Edmonds. **No. of Games Broadcast:** Home-48, Road-48. **Flagship Station:** 1290 CFRW AM.
PA Announcer: Ron Arnst. **Official Scorer:** Steve Eitzen.
Stadium Name: CanWest Global Park. **Location:** Pembina Highway (Route 75), east on River Ave., north on Main Street, east on Water Ave. **Standard Game Times:** 7:05 p.m., Sun. 1:35.
Visiting Club Hotel: Ramada Marlborough, 331 Smith St., Winnipeg, Manitoba R3B 2G9. Telephone: (204) 942-6411.

GOLDEN
LEAGUE

Office Address: 6140 Stoneridge Mall Rd., Suite 550, Pleasanton, CA 94588.
Telephone: (925) 226-2889. **FAX:** (925)226-2891.
E-Mail Address: info@goldenbaseball.com. **Website:** www.goldenbaseball.com.
Year Founded: 2005.

Chief Executive Officer: David Kaval. **President:** Amit Patel. **Commissioner:** Kevin Outcalt. **Chief Operating Officer:** Greg Coleman. **Chief Marketing Officer:** Jim Weyermann. **League Historian and Secretary:** Bill Weiss. **Supervisor of Officials:** Dan Perugini. **Director of Player Development/Scouting:** Kash Beauchamp. **Controller:** Mike Munson. **Executive Assistant:** Joyce Prescott.
Member Clubs, Division Structure: California—Chico, Fullerton, Long Beach, San Diego. **Arizona**—Mesa, Surprise, Tijuana, Yuma.
Regular Season: 90 games. **2005 Opening Date:** May 26. **Closing Date:** Aug. 28.
All-Star Game: Unavailable.
Playoff Format: Four team championship tournament.
Roster Limit: 22. **Eligibility Rules:** Six first-year players minimum, four veterans (27 or older) maximum.
Brand of Baseball: Rawlings ROM-GBL.
Statistician: Sportsticker, ESPN Plaza-Building B, Bristol, CT 06010.

INDEPENDENT SCHEDULES

HOME GAMES ONLY

ATLANTIC LEAGUE

ATLANTIC CITY
APRIL	
28-29-30	Newark

MAY	
1	Newark
2-3	Long Island
13-14-15	Somerset
23-24-25-26	Camden
27-28-29	Bridgeport

JUNE	
3-4-5	Nashua
7-8-9	Lancaster
17-18-19	Newark
20-21-22	Long Island
30	Somerset

JULY	
1-2-3	Somerset
18-19-20-21	Nashua
22-23-24	Long Island

AUGUST	
2-3-4	Lancaster
12-13-14	Camden
15-16-17-18	Bridgeport
22-23-24	Nashua
25-26-27-28	Lancaster

SEPTEMBER	
2-3-4	Somerset
5-6-7	Newark
20-21-22	Camden
23-24-25	Bridgeport

BRIDGEPORT
APRIL	
28-29-30	Long Island

MAY	
1	Long Island
6-7-8	Lancaster
10-11-12	Nashua
20-21-22	Atlantic City
23-24-25-26	Somerset
30-31	Newark

JUNE	
1-2	Newark
14-15-16	Atlantic City
17-18-19	Long Island
27-28-29	Nashua

JULY	
1-2-3	Camden
15-16-17	Newark
25-26-27	Lancaster
28-29-30-31	Nashua

AUGUST	
5-6-7	Somerset
8-9-10-11	Camden

19-20-21	Newark
29-30-31	Lancaster

SEPTEMBER	
1	Lancaster
2-3-4	Camden
12-13-14	Long Island
15-16-17-18	Atl. City
20-21-22	Somerset

CAMDEN
APRIL	
28-29-30	Nashua

MAY	
1	Nashua
2-3-4-5	Lancaster
13-14-15	Bridgeport
16-17-18-19	Atl. City
27-28-29	Somerset

JUNE	
3-4-5	Newark
7-8-9	Long Island
17-18-19	Nashua
20-21-22	Lancaster

JULY	
4-5-6	Atlantic City
7-8-9-10	Bridgeport
18-19-20-21	Newark
22-23-24	Lancaster

AUGUST	
2-3-4	Bridgeport
5-6-7	Atlantic City
15-16-17-18	Somerset
22-23-24	Newark
25-26-27-28	L.I.

SEPTEMBER	
9-10-11	Long Island
12-13-14	Nashua
23-24-25	Somerset

LANCASTER
MAY	
11-12	Atlantic City
17-18-19	Long Island
20-21-22	Newark
30-31	Camden

JUNE	
1-2	Camden
3-4-5	Bridgeport
10-11-12	Somerset
13	Atlantic City
14-15-16	Nashua
23-24-25-26	Bridgeport
27-28-29	Atlantic City

JULY	
4-5-6-7	Long Island
15-16-17	Camden

18-19-20-21	Somerset
28-29-30-31	Newark

AUGUST	
5-6-7	Long Island
8-9-10-11	Atlantic City
19-20-21	Camden

SEPTEMBER	
2-3-4	Nashua
5-6-7	Bridgeport
12-13-14	Somerset
15-16-17-18	Nashua
23-24-25	Newark

LONG ISLAND
MAY	
4-5	Atlantic City
6-7-8	Somerset
10-11-12	Camden
20-21-22	Nashua
23-24-25-26	Lancaster
30-31	Atlantic City

JUNE	
1-2	Atlantic City
10-11-12	Bridgeport
14-15-16	Newark
23-24-25-26	Somerset
27-28-29	Camden

JULY	
8-9-10	Nashua
15-16-17	Atlantic City
18-19-20-21	Bridgeport
28-29-30-31	Camden

AUGUST	
	Nashua
12-13-14	Lancaster
19-20-21	Atlantic City
22-23-24	Bridgeport

SEPTEMBER	
2-3-4	Newark
5-6-7	Somerset
15-16-17-18	Newark
20-21-22	Lancaster

NASHUA
MAY	
2-3-4-5	Bridgeport
6-7-8	Atlantic City
13-14-15	Lancaster
16-17-18-19	Newark
27-28-29	Long Island
31	Somerset

JUNE	
1-2	Somerset
10-11-12	Camden
20-21-22	Bridgeport
23-24-25-26	Atl. City

18-19-20-21	Somerset
28-29-30-31	Newark

AUGUST	
5-6-7	Long Island
8-9-10-11	Atlantic City
19-20-21	Camden

SEPTEMBER	
2-3-4	Nashua
5-6-7	Bridgeport
12-13-14	Somerset
15-16-17-18	Nashua
23-24-25	Newark

NEWARK
APRIL	
27	Somerset

MAY	
3-4-5	Somerset
6-7-8	Camden
13-14-15	Long Island
23-24-25-26	Nashua
27-28-29	Lancaster

JUNE	
7-8-9	Bridgeport
10-11-12	Atlantic City
20-21-22	Somerset
23-24-25-26	Camden
30	Long Island

JULY	
1-2-3	Long Island
8-9-10	Lancaster
22-23-24	Somerset
25-26-27	Camden

AUGUST	
2-3-4	Long Island
12-13-14	Nashua
15-16-17-18	Lancaster
25-26-27-28	Bridgeport
29-30-31	Atlantic City

SEPTEMBER	
1	Atlantic City
9-10-11	Bridgeport
12-13-14	Atlantic City
20-21-22	Nashua

SOMERSET
APRIL	
28-29-30	Lancaster

MAY	
1	Lancaster

10-11-12	Newark	17-18-19	Lancaster	28-29-30-31	Atl. City
16-17-18-19	Bridgeport	27-28-29	Newark		

JUNE (col 1) / **JULY** (col 2) / **AUGUST** (col 3) / **SEPTEMBER** (col 4)

20-21-22	Camden				
		JULY		**AUGUST**	
JUNE		4-5-6	Bridgeport	8-9-10-11	Newark
3-4-5	Long Island	8-9-10	Atlantic City	12-13-14	Bridgeport
6-7-8-9	Nashua	15-16-17	Nashua	19-20-21	Nashua
14-15-16	Camden	25-26-27	Long Island	22-23-24	Lancaster
				29-30-31	Long Island

SEPTEMBER

1	Long Island
9-10-11	Atlantic City
15-16-17-18	Camden

CANADIAN-AMERICAN LEAGUE

BANGOR
MAY
26-27-28-29	N.J.
JUNE
7-8-9	Elmira
10-11-12	North Shore
20-21-22	Quebec
JULY
1-2-3-4	Brockton
5-6-7	Worcester
11-12-13	New Haven
14-15-16	Quebec
25-26-27	New Haven
28-29-30-31	N.J.
AUGUST
8-9-10	Worcester
12-13-14	Brockton
23-24-25	Elmira
SEPTEMBER
2-3-4-5	North Shore

BROCKTON
MAY
26-27-28-29	Elmira
30-31	Worcester
JUNE
1	Worcester
10-11-12	New Haven
13-14-15-16	Bangor
24-25-26	New Jersey
28-29-30	Quebec
JULY
8-9-10	North Shore
21-22-23-24	Worcester
AUGUST
1-2-3	Elmira
4-5-6-7	New Haven
15-16-17	Quebec
19	North Shore
21	North Shore
29-30-31	Bangor

ELMIRA
SEPTEMBER
2-3-4-5	New Jersey
MAY
30-31	North Shore
JUNE
1	North Shore
2-3-4-5	Brockton
13-14-15-16	N.J.
17-18-19	Quebec
24-25-26	Bangor
28-29-30	New Haven
JULY
	Worcester
21-22-23-24	Bangor
25-26-27	Brockton
AUGUST
4-5-6-7	North Shore
8-9-10	New Jersey
19-20-21	Worcester
26-27-28	Quebec
29-30-31	New Haven

NEW HAVEN
MAY
30-31	Bangor
JUNE
1	Bangor
2-3-4-5	Quebec
13-14-15-16	Worcester
17-18-19	Brockton
24-25-26	North Shore
JULY
5-6-7	Elmira
8-9-10	New Jersey
15-16-17	New Jersey
28-29-30-31	Quebec
AUGUST
1-2-3	Bangor
12-13-14	Elmira
16-17-18	North Shore
23-24-25	North Shore

NEW JERSEY
SEPTEMBER
2-3-4-5	Worcester
JUNE
2-3-4-5	Bangor
6-7-8	Quebec
17-18-19	New Haven
21-22-23	New Haven
27-28-29	North Shore
JULY
1-2-3-4	Elmira
11-12-13	Brockton
21-22-23-24	N.S.
AUGUST
1-2-3	Quebec
4-5-6-7	Bangor
15-16-17	Elmira
19-20-21	New Haven
26-27-28	Brockton
30-31	Worcester
SEPTEMBER
1	Worcetser

NORTH SHORE
JUNE
2-3-4-5	Worcester
7-8-9	New Haven
17-18-19	Bangor
21-22-23	Brockton
JULY
1-2-3-4	Quebec
5-6-7	New Jersey
11-12-13	Elmira
15-16-17	Brockton
25-26-27	Worcester
28-29-30-31	Elmira
AUGUST
8-9-10	New Haven
12-13-14	Quebec
20	Brockton
23-24-25	New Jersey
26-27-28	Bangor

QUEBEC
MAY
26-27-28-29	N.H.
30-31	New Jersey
JUNE
1	New Jersey
10-11-12	Elmira
13-14-15-16	N.S.
24-25-26	Worcester
JULY
5-6-7	Brockton
8-9-10	Bangor
21-22-23-24	N.H.
25-26-27	New Jersey
AUGUST
4-5-6	Worcester
9-10-11	Brockton
19-20-21	Bangor
30-31	North Shore
SEPTEMBER
1	North Shore
2-3-4-5	Elmira

WORCESTER
MAY
28-29-29	North Shore
JUNE
6-7-8	Brockton
10-11-12	New Jersey
20	North Shore
21-22-23	Elmira
27-28-29	Bangor
JULY
1-2-3-4	New Haven
11-12-13	Quebec
14-15-16	Elmira
28-29-30-31	Brockton
AUGUST
1-2-3	North Shore
11-12-13	New Jersey
16-17-18	Bangor
22-23-24-25	Quebec
26-27-28	New Haven

CENTRAL LEAGUE

COASTAL BEND
MAY
5-6-7-8	Edinburg
10-11-12	San Angelo
20-21-22	Shreveport
31	Pensacola
JUNE
1-2	Pensacola
3-4-5-6	El Paso
10-11-12	Fort Worth
14-15-16	Jackson
27	Edinburg
29-30	Edinburg
JULY
5-6-7-8-9	El Paso
10-11-12	San Angelo
28-29-30-31	Pensacola
AUGUST
1-2-3	Shreveport
8-9-10	Fort Worth
18-19-20	Jackson

EDINBURG
MAY
10-11-12	El Paso
17-18-19	Shreveport
20-21-22	San Angelo
23	Coastal Bend

27-28-29-30	Pensacola

JUNE
8-9	Edinburg
13-14-15	Fort Worth
17-18-19-20	Jackson
28	Coastal Bend

JULY
1-2-3-4	El Paso
6-7-8-9	San Angelo
21-22-23	Shreveport
25-26-27	Pensacola

AUGUST
5-6-7	Coastal Bend
15-16-17	Jackson
18-19-20	Fort Worth

EL PASO

MAY
5-6-7-8	San Angelo
13-14-15	Jackson
16-17-18	Pensacola
27-28-29-30	C.B.
31	Fort Worth

JUNE
1-2	Fort Worth
10-11-12	Edinburg
22-23-24-25	Shreveport
27-28-29-30	San Angelo

JULY
11-12-13	Edinburg
14-15-16	Coastal Bend
24-25-26	Jackson
28-29-30-31	Fort Worth

AUGUST
8-9-10	Pensacola

11-12-13	Shreveport

FORT WORTH

MAY
13-14-15	Edinburg
16-17-18	Coastal Bend
24-25-26	Jackson

JUNE
4-5-6	San Angelo
7-8-9	El Paso
17-18-19-20	Shreveport
22-23-24-25	Pensacola

JULY
1-2-3-4-5	Jackson
6-7-8-9	Pensacola
21-22-23	El Paso
25-26-27	San Angelo

AUGUST
4-5-6	Shreveport
11-12-13	Edinburg
14-15-16	Coastal Bend

JACKSON

MAY
5-6-7-8	Pensacola
9-10-11	Jackson
20-21-22	El Paso
28-29-30	Shreveport
31	Edinburg

JUNE
1-2	Edinburg
10-11-12	San Angelo
22-23-24-25	C.B.
26-27-28	Pensacola

JULY
12-13	Fort Worth
14-15-16-17	Shreveport
28-29-30-31	Edinburg

AUGUST
1-2-3	El Paso
8-9-10	San Angelo
11-12-13	Coastal Bend

PENSACOLA

MAY
9-10-11	Shreveport
20-21-22	Fort Worth
23-24-25	El Paso

JUNE
3-4-5-6	Edinburg
7-8-9	Pensacola
13-14-15	San Angelo
18-19-20-21	C.B.

JULY
1-2-3-4	Shreveport
14-15-16-17	Fort Worth
21-22-23	Coastal Bend

AUGUST
1-2-3	Edinburg
4-5-6-7	Jackson
15-16-17	El Paso
18-19-20	San Angelo

SAN ANGELO

MAY
13-14-15	Penascola
16-17-18	Jackson
24-25-26	Coastal Bend
27-28-29-30	Fort Worth

JUNE
7-8-9	Shreveport
17-18-19-20	El Paso
22-23-24-25	Edinburg

JULY
1-2-3-4	Coastal Bend
14-15-16-17	Edinburg
21-22-23	Jackson

AUGUST
1-2-3	Fort Worth
4-5-6	El Paso
11-12-13	Pensacola
14-15-16	Shreveport

SHREVEPORT

MAY
5-6-7-8	Fort Worth
13-14-15	Coastal Bend
24-25-26	Edinburg
31	San Angelo

JUNE
1-2	San Angelo
3-4-5-6	Jackson
10-11-12	Pensacola
14-15-16	El Paso
27-28-29-30	Fort Worth

JULY
6-7-8-9	Shreveport
10-11-12	Pensacola
24-25-26	Coastal Bend
28-29-30-31	San Angelo

AUGUST
8-9-10	Edinburg
18-19-20	El Paso

FRONTIER LEAGUE

CHILLICOTHE

MAY
25-26-27	Evansville

JUNE
1-2-3	Washington
4-5-6	Richmond
11-12-13	Evansville
21-22-23	River City
24-25-26	Mid-Missouri
30	Ohio Valley

JULY
1-2	Ohio Valley
9-10-11	Kalamazoo
15-16-17	Ohio Valley
18-19-20	Richmond
24-25-26	Florence
30-31	Windy City

AUGUST
1	Windy City
3-4-5	Rockford
9-10-11	Washington
16-17-18	Gateway
25-26-27	Florence
31	Ohio Valley

SEPTEMBER
1-2	Ohio Valley

EVANSVILLE

MAY
28-29-30	Ohio Valley

JUNE
4-5-6	Washington
8-9-10	Richmond
14-15-16	Windy City
17-18-19	Gateway
27-28-29	Florence
30	Richmond

JULY
1-2	Richmond
9-10-11	River City
18-19-20	Washington
21-22-23	Chillicothe
27-28-29	Rockford
30-31	Kalamazoo

AUGUST
1	Kalamazoo
9-10-11	Florence
12-13-14	Ohio Valley
16-17-18	Mid-Missouri
25-26-27	Ohio Valley

SEPTEMBER
3-4-5	Chillicothe

FLORENCE

MAY
28-29-30	Chillicothe

JUNE
1-2-3	Evansville
4-5-6	Ohio Valley
11-12-13	Richmond
21-22-23	Mid-Missouri
24-25-26	River City
30	Washington

JULY
1-2	Washington
3-4-5	Ohio Valley
6-7-8	Kalamazoo
18-19-20	Ohio Valley
27-28-29	Windy City
30-31	Gateway

AUGUST
1	Gateway
6-7-8	Rockford
12-13-14	Chillicothe
22-23-24	Richmond
31	Washington

SEPTEMBER
1-2	Washington
3-4-5	Richmond

GATEWAY

MAY
25-26-27	Rockford
28-29-30	Kalamazoo

JUNE
4	Mid-Missouri
8-9-10	Windy City
14-15-16	Ohio Valley
21-22-23	Washington
24-25-26	Richmond

JULY
3-4-5	River City
15-16-17	Mid-Missouri
21-22-23	River City
27-28-29	Chillicothe

AUGUST
3-4-5	Ohio Valley
6-7-8	Evansville
12-13-14	Rockford
19-20-21	Florence
22-23-24	Mid-Missouri
28-29-30	Windy City

INDEPENDENT LEAGUE SCHEDULES

SEPTEMBER
1-2 Kalamazoo

KALAMAZOO
JUNE
1-2-3 Rockford
8-9-10 Mid-Missouri
11-12-13 Gateway
17-18-19 Richmond
21-22-23 Ohio Valley
24-25-26 Evansville
JULY
3-4-5 Rockford
15-16-17 River City
18-19-20 Gateway
24-25-26 River City
27-28-29 Ohio Valley
AUGUST
3-4-5 Florence
6-7-8 Chillicothe
12-13-14 Windy City
16-17-18 Washington
25-26-27 Windy City
SEPTEMBER
3-4-5 Mid-Missouri

MID-MISSOURI
MAY
25-26-27 River City
28-29-30 Rockford
JUNE
5-6 Gateway
14-15-16 Florence
17-18-19 Chillicothe
27-28-29 Kalamazoo
JULY
3-4-5 Windy City
6-7-8 Evansville
18-19-20 Windy City
21-22-23 Kalamazoo
27-28-29 Richmond
30-31 Washington
AUGUST
1 Washington
9-10-11 Gateway
19-20-21 Ohio Valley

25-26-27 River City
28-29-30 Rockford

OHIO VALLEY
JUNE
1-2-3 Richmond
8-9-10 Chillicothe
11-12-13 Washington
JULY
9-10-11 Mid-Missouri
24-25-26 Evansville
AUGUST
16-17-18 River City
22-23-24 Richmond
28-29-30 Florence

RICHMOND
MAY
25-26-27 Florence
JUNE
14-15-16 Rockford
21-22-23 Windy City
27-28-29 Ohio Valley
JULY
3-4-5 Chillicothe
9-10-11 Gateway
15-16-17 Evansville
21-22-23 Florence
24-25-26 Washington
30-31 River City
AUGUST
1 River City
3-4-5 Mid-Missouri
9-10-11 Ohio Valley
19-20-21 Kalamazoo
25-26-27 Washington
28-29-30 Chillicothe
31 Evansville
SEPTEMBER
1-2 Evansville

RIVER CITY
MAY
28-29-30 Windy City
JUNE
1-2-3 Gateway
4-5-6 Kalamazoo

14-15-16 Chillicothe
17-18-19 Florence
27-28-29 Rockford
30 Mid-Missouri
JULY
1-2 Mid-Missoui
6-7-8 Ohio Valley
18-19-20 Rockford
27-28-29 Washington
AUGUST
6-7-8 Richmond
12-13-14 Mid-Missouri
19-20-21 Evansville
22-23-24 Windy City
28-29-30 Kalamazoo
SEPTEMBER
3-4-5 Gateway

ROCKFORD
JUNE
8-9-10 River City
11-12-13 Mid-Missouri
17-18-19 Washington
21-22-23 Evansville
24-25-26 Ohio Valley
30 Gateway
JULY
1-2 Gateway
6-7-8 Chillicothe
9-10-11 Florence
21-22-23 Windy City
24-25-26 Mid-Missouri
30-31 Ohio Valley
AUGUST
1 Ohio Valley
9-10-11 Kalamazoo
16-17-18 Richmond
22-23-24 Kalamazoo
25-26-27 Gateway
31 River City
SEPTEMBER
1-2 River City
3-4-5 Windy City

WASHINGTON
MAY
25-26-27 Ohio Valley

28-29-30 Richmond
JUNE
8-9-10 Florence
14-15-16 Kalamazoo
24-25-26 Windy City
27-28-29 Chillicothe
JULY
3-4-5 Evansville
6-7-8 Gateway
15-16-17 Florence
21-22-23 Ohio Valley
AUGUST
3-4-5 River City
6-7-8 Mid-Missouri
12-13-14 Richmond
19-20-21 Rockford
22-23-24 Chillicothe
28-29-30 Evansville
SEPTEMBER
3-4-5 Ohio Valley

WINDY CITY
MAY
25-26-27 Kalamazoo
JUNE
1-2-3 Mid-Missouri
4-5-6 Rockford
11-12-13 River City
17-18-19 Ohio Valley
27-28-29 Gateway
30 Kalamazoo
JULY
1-2 Kalamazoo
6-7-8 Richmond
9-10-11 Washington
15-16-17 Rockford
24-25-26 Gateway
AUGUST
3-4-5 Evansville
6-7-8 Ohio Valley
9-10-11 River City
16-17-18 Florence
19-20-21 Chillicothe
31 Mid-Missouri
SEPTEMBER
1-2 Mid-Missouri

NORTHERN LEAGUE

CALGARY
MAY
27-28-29 Joliet
30-31 Sioux Falls
JUNE
1 Sioux Falls
10-11-12 Sioux City
13-14-15 Winnipeg
24-25-26-27 Edmonton
28-29-30 Schaumburg
JULY
1-2-3 Fargo-Moorhead
12-13-14 Sioux City
15-16-17 Gary

29-30-31 Edmonton
AUGUST
1-2-3-4 Lincoln
16-17-18 Sioux Falls
19-20-21-22 F-M
30-31 Winnipeg
SEPTEMBER
1 Winnipeg
2-3-4 Kansas City

EDMONTON
MAY
23 Gary
27-28-29 Sioux Falls

30-31 Joliet
JUNE
1 Joliet
10-11-12 Winnipeg
13-14-15 Sioux City
16-17-18-19 Calgary
28-29-30 F-M
JULY
Schaumburg
12-13-14 Gary
15-16-17 Sioux City
AUGUST
2-3-4 St. Paul
5-6-7-8 Calgary

16-17-18 F-M
19-20-21-22 S.F.
30-31 Kansas City
SEPTEMBER
1 Kansas City
2-3-4 Winnipeg

FARGO-MOORHEAD
MAY
20-21-22 Winnipeg
31 Sioux City
JUNE
1-2 Sioux City
6-7-8 Edmonton

| 21-22-23 | Joliet |
| 24-25-26 | Sioux Falls |

JULY

4-5-6	Gary
7-8-9-10	Calgary
15-16-17	Winnipeg
22-22-23-24	St. Paul
25-26-27	Edmonton

AUGUST

1-2-3-4	Sioux Falls
5-6-7-8	Sioux City
12-13-14	Schaumburg
26-27-28	Calgary
30-31	Lincoln

SEPTEMBER

| 1 | Lincoln |

GARY

MAY

| 24-25-26 | Edmonton |
| 31 | St. Paul |

JUNE

1-2	St. Paul
3-4-5	Calgary
13-14-15	Sioux Falls
17-18-19-20	Schaum.
27-28-29-30	Lincoln

JULY

8-9-10	Kansas City
22-23-24	Lincoln
29-30-31	Schaumburg

AUGUST

2-3-4	Kansas City
9-10-11	F-M
12-13-14	Winnipeg
26-27-28	Joliet
30-31	St. Paul

SEPTEMBER

| 1 | St. Paul |
| 2-3-4 | Joliet |

JOLIET

MAY

| 20-21-22 | Gary |
| 23-24-25-26 | K.C. |

JUNE

3-4-5-6	St. Paul
7-8-9	Gary
16-17-18-19	Sioux Falls
24-25-26	Lincoln
27-28-29	Sioux City

JULY

8-9	Schaumburg
10	Kansas City
13-14	St. Paul

| 22-23-24 | Calgary |

AUGUST

5-6-7	Kansas City
12-13-14	Lincoln
16-17-18	Winnipeg
23-24-25	Edmonton
30-31	Schaumburg

SEPTEMBER

| 1 | Schaumburg |

KANSAS CITY

MAY

| 20-21-22 | Edmonton |
| 31 | Lincoln |

JUNE

1-2	Lincoln
3-4-5	Schaumburg
6-7-8	Calgary
13-14-15	Joliet
24-25-26	Gary
27-28-29-30	St. Paul

JULY

12-13-14	F-M
15-16-17	Schaumburg
25-26-27	Lincoln
28-29-30-31	Joliet

AUGUST

12-13-14	St. Paul
16-17-18	Sioux City
19-20-21-22	Gary
26-27-28	Sioux Falls

LINCOLN

MAY

| 23-24-25-26 | Winnipeg |
| 27-28-29 | F-M |

JUNE

6-7-8-9	Schaumburg
10-11-12	Kansas City
17-18-19	St. Paul
21-22-23	Gary

JULY

1-2-3	Joliet
4-5-6	Edmonton
15-16-17	Joliet
28-29-30	Sioux Falls

AUGUST

9-10-11	Kansas City
16-17-18	Gary
19-20-21-22	St. Paul
23-24-25	Schaumburg

SEPTEMBER

| 2-3-4 | Sioux City |

ST. PAUL

MAY

20-21-22-23	Schaum.
24-25-26	Calgary
27-28-29	Kansas City

JUNE

10-11-12	Gary
13-14-15	F-M
24-25-26	Winnipeg

JULY

4-5-6	Joliet
8-9-10	Lincoln
15-16-17	Sioux Falls
25-26-27-28	Gary

AUGUST

5-6-7	Lincoln
9-10-11	Joliet
16-17-18	Schaumburg
23-24-25	Kansas City
26-27-28-29	Sioux City

SCHAUMBURG

MAY

| 24-25-26 | F-M |
| 27-28-29-29 | Schaum. |

JUNE

10-11-12	Kansas City
13-14-15	Lincoln
21-22-23	St. Paul
24-25-26	Sioux City

JULY

4-5-6	Kansas City
12-13-14	Lincoln
21-22-23-24	K.C.
25-26-27	Calgary

AUGUST

1-2-3	Joliet
5-6-7-8	Gary
19-20-21	Winnipeg
26-27-28	Edmonton

SEMPTEMBER

| 2-3-4 | St. Paul |

SIOUX CITY

MAY

| 20-21-22 | Calgary |

JUNE

3-4-5	Lincoln
7-8-9	St. Paul
17-18-19-20	F-M
21-22-23	Edmonton

JULY

| 1-2-3 | Kansas City |
| 4-5-6-7 | Winnipeg |

8-9-10	Sioux Falls
26-27-28	Winnipeg
29-30-31	F-M

AUGUST

9-10-11	Edmonton
12-13-14	Calgary
19-20-21-22	Joliet
23-24-25	Gary
30-31	Sioux Falls

SEPTEMBER

| 1 | Sioux Falls |

SIOUX FALLS

MAY

| 20-21-22 | Lincoln |
| 23-24-25-26 | Sioux City |

JUNE

3-4-5	Edmonton
6-7-8	Winnipeg
9-10-11-12	F-M
21-22-23	Kansas City

JULY

1-2-3	St. Paul
4-5-6	Calgary
22-23-24	Sioux City
25-26-27	Joliet

AUGUST

5-6-7-8	Winnipeg
9-10-11	Schaumburg
12-13-14	Edmonton
23-24-25	Calgary

SEPTEMBER

| 2-3-4 | Fargo-Moorhead |

WINNIPEG

MAY

| 27-28-29 | Sioux City |
| 31 | Schaumburg |

JUNE

1-2	Schaumburg
3-4-5	Fargo-Moorhead
17-18-19	Kansas City
21-22-23	Calgary
27-28-29	Sioux Falls

JULY

1-2-3	Gary
8-9-10	Edmonton
12-13-14	Sioux Falls
21-22-23-24	Edmonton
29-30-31	St. Paul

AUGUST

2-3-4	Sioux City
9-10-11	Calgary
23-24-25	F-M
26-27-28-29	Lincoln

INTERNATIONAL
LEAGUES

FOREIGN
LEAGUES

2004 STANDINGS

AMERICAS

MEXICAN LEAGUE
TRIPLE-A CLASSIFICATION

NORTH	W	L	PCT	GB
*Puebla Parrots	63	34	.649	—
+Saltillo Sarape Makers	63	34	.649	—
Monterrey Sultans	56	41	.577	7
Tijuana Bulls	49	48	.505	14
Laguna Cowboys	45	54	.454	19
Aguascalientes Rieleros	45	55	.450	19½
Monclova Steelers	39	60	.393	25
San Luis Potosi Tuneros	32	66	.326	31½

SOUTH	W	L	PCT	GB
*Mexico City Red Devils	60	40	.600	—
+Campeche Pirates	55	42	.567	3½
Angelopolis Tigers	54	45	.545	5½
Oaxaca Warriors	50	48	.510	9
Tabasco Cattlemen	48	48	.500	10
Veracruz Reds	44	56	.440	16
Yucatan Lions	43	55	.438	16
Cancun Lobstermen	40	60	.400	20

*first half champion+second half champion

PLAYOFFS—First Round: Puebla defeated Aguascalientes 4-0; Campeche defeated Tabasco 4-1; Monterrey defeated Tijuana 4-3; Mexico City defeated Yucatan 4-1; Angelopolis defeated Oaxaca 4-1 in best-of-7 series. **Second Round:** Puebla defeated Tijuana 4-1; Campeche defeated Angelopolis 4-1; Saltillo defeated Monterrey 4-2; Mexico City defeated Oaxaca 4-0. **Semifinals:** Campeche defeated Mexico City 4-3; Saltillo defeated Puebla 4-2 in best-of-7 series. **Final:** Campeche defeated Saltillo 4-1 in best-of-7 series.

MEXICAN ACADEMY
ROOKIE CLASSIFICATION

	W	L	PCT	GB
Celaya	32	15	.681	—
Guanajuato	28	20	.583	4½
Queretaro	19	28	.404	13
Salamanca	17	33	.340	16½

DOMINICAN SUMMER LEAGUE
ROOKIE CLASSIFICATION

SANTO DOMINGO EAST/American	W	L	PCT	GB
Indians I	53	16	.768	—
Tigers	44	25	.638	9
Indians II	36	31	.537	16
Twins	36	33	.522	17
Red Sox	33	35	.485	19½

SANTO DOMINGO EAST/National	W	L	PCT	GB
Giants	36	32	.529	—
Diamondbacks	33	36	.478	3½
Rockies	33	37	.471	4
Cubs	27	42	.391	9 1/2
Reds	24	46	.343	13
Dodgers I	22	44	.333	13

SANTO DOMINGO NORTH	W	L	PCT	GB
Mariners	50	21	.704	—
Dodgers II	47	23	.671	2½

	W	L	PCT	GB
Athletics I	34	36	.486	15½
Phillies	31	39	.443	18½
Expos	30	38	.441	18½
Athletics II	18	53	.254	32

SANTO DOMINGO WEST	W	L	PCT	GB
Yankees I	50	21	.704	—
Padres	40	31	.563	10
Mets	34	37	.479	16
Yankees II	18	53	.254	32

SAN PEDRO de MACORIS	W	L	PCT	GB
Blue Jays	51	19	.729	—
Angels	45	26	.634	6½
Orioles	33	38	.465	18½
Astros	31	39	.443	20
Pirates	26	44	.371	25
Rangers	26	46	.361	26

CIBAO	W	L	PCT	GB
Royals	49	14	.778	—
White Sox	36	26	.581	12½
Marlins	29	36	.446	21
Braves II	27	36	.429	22
Braves I	17	46	.270	32

PLAYOFFS: Quarterfinals—Yankees I defeated Mariners 2-1 and Blue Jays defeated Giants 2-0 in best-of-3 series. **Semifinals—**Indians defeated Blue Jays 2-0 and Yankees I defeated Royals 2-1 in best-of-3 series. **Finals—**Indians defeated Yankees I 3-2 in best-of-5 series.

VENEZUELAN SUMMER LEAGUE
ROOKIE CLASSIFICATION

	W	L	PCT	GB
Venoco I (Astros)	37	25	.594	—
Tronconero II (Mets)	37	25	.594	—
Universidad (Marlins/Padres)	34	29	.539	3½
Aguirre (Mariners)	32	28	.532	4
Tronconero I (Phillies)	29	31	.484	7
Ciudad Alianza (Red Sox)	29	33	.469	8
Cagua (Reds)	28	32	.468	8
San Joaquin (Pirates)	28	35	.445	9½
Venoco II (Orioles)	22	38	.373	14

PLAYOFFS: Tronconero II defeated Venoco I 2-1 in best-of-3 series.

CUBA
WEST

GROUP A	W	L	PCT	GB
Pinar del Rio	57	33	.633	—
Isla de la Juventud	46	43	.517	10½
Metropolitans	43	47	.478	14
Matanzas	27	63	.300	30

GROUP B	W	L	PCT	GB
Sancti Spiritus	54	35	.607	—
Industriales	52	38	.578	2½
Havana	38	51	.422	16
Cienfuegos	27	62	.303	27

EAST

GROUP C	W	L	PCT	GB
Villa Clara	57	33	.633	—

	W	L		PCT	GB
Ciego de Avila	55	34		.611	1½
Las Tunas	44	46		.489	13
Camaguey	38	52		.422	19
GROUP D	**W**	**L**		**PCT**	**GB**
Santiago de Cuba	53	37		.589	—
Granma	49	41		.544	4
Holguin	43	48		.467	11
Guantanamo	35	54		.393	17½

PLAYOFFS—Quarterfinals: Santiago defeated Ciego de Avila 3-0; Villa Clara defeated Granma 3-0; Industriales defeated Sancti Spiritus 3-2; and Pinar del Rio defeated Isla de la Juventud 3-0 in best-of-5 series. **Semifinals:** Villa Clara defeated Santiago 4-3; and Industriales defeated Pinar del Rio 4-2 in best-of-7 series. **Finals:** Industriales defeated Villa Clara 4-0 in best-of-7 series.

ASIA

JAPANESE LEAGUES

CENTRAL	W	L	T	PCT	GB
Chunichi Dragons	79	56	3	.585	—
Yakult Swallows	72	64	2	.529	7½
Yomiuri Giants	71	64	3	.526	8
Hanshin Tigers	66	70	2	.485	13½
Hiroshima Carp	60	77	1	.438	20
Yokohama BayStars	59	76	3	.437	20

PACIFIC LEAGUE	W	L	T	PCT	GB
Fukuoka Daiei Hawks	77	52	4	.597	—
Seibu Lions	74	58	1	.561	4½
Hokkaido Nippon Ham Fighters	66	65	2	.504	12
Chiba Lotte Marines	65	65	3	.500	12½
Osaka Kintetsu Buffaloes	61	70	2	.466	17
Orix BlueWave	49	82	2	.374	29

PLAYOFFS—Seibu defeated Hokkaido 2-1 in best-of-3 series; Seibu defeated Fukuoka 3-2 in best-of-5 series for league championship.

KOREA BASEBALL ORGANIZATION

	W	L	T	PCT	GB
Hyundai Unicorns	75	53	5	.586	—
Samsung Lions	73	52	8	.584	1½
Doosan Bears	70	62	1	.530	7
Kia Tigers	67	61	5	.523	8
SK Wyverns	61	64	8	.488	12½
LG Twins	59	70	4	.457	16½
Hanwha Eagles	53	74	6	.417	21½
Lotte Giants	50	72	11	.410	22

PLAYOFFS: First Round—Doosan defeated Kia 2-0 in best-of-3 series. **Second Round**—Samsung defeated Doosan 3-1 in best-of-5 series. **Finals**—Hyundai defeated Samsung 4-2-3 in best-of-7 series.

TAIWAN

	W	L	T	PCT	GB
*President Lions	54	40	4	.551	—

	W	L		PCT	GB
Brother Elephants	54	45	1	.540	3½
+Sinon Bulls	52	43	3	.530	4½
China Trust Whales	45	50	2	.463	9½
Macoto Cobras	43	54	0	.438	13½
La New Bears	40	56	2	.408	15½

*first half champion +second half champion

PLAYOFFS: Sinon Bulls defeated President Lions 4-3 in best-of-7 series.

CHINA

	W	L	PCT	GB
Tianjin Lions	21	15	.583	—
Beijing Tigers	21	15	.583	—
Guandong Leopards	20	16	.556	1
Shanghai Golden Eagles	10	26	.278	11

PLAYOFFS: Beijing defeated Tianjin 3-2 in best-of-5 series.

EUROPE

ITALY

	W	L	PCT	GB
Grosseto	47	7	.870	—
Bologna	43	11	.796	4
Parma	32	22	.593	15
Nettuno	30	24	.556	17
Rimini	29	25	.537	18
Paterno	24	30	.444	23
San Marino	23	31	.426	24
Modena	23	31	.426	24
Anzio	13	41	.241	34
Rho	6	48	.111	41

PLAYOFFS—Semifinals: Grosseto defeated Nettuno 4-1 and Bologna defeated Parma 4-0 in best-of-7 series. **Final:** Grosseto defeated Bologna 4-2 in best-of-7 series.

NETHERLANDS

	W	L	T	PCT	GB
HCAW	34	6	0	.850	—
Neptunus	32	7	1	.813	1½
Hoofddorp Pioniers	27	12	1	.688	6½
Kinheim	24	15	1	.613	9½
Amsterdam Pirates	17	23	0	.425	17
Hague Tornado's	16	24	0	.400	20
Almere	12	26	2	.325	21
Sparta/Feyenoord	9	30	1	.238	24½
Oosterhout Twins	6	34	0	.150	28

PLAYOFFS—Semifinals: Neptunus defeated Hoofddorp Pioniers 3-1 and HCAW defeated Kinheim 3-0 in best-of-5 series. **Final:** Neptunus defeated HCAW 3-1 in best-of-5 series.

AMERICAS

MEXICO

MEXICAN LEAGUE
Member, National Association
Class AAA

NOTE: *The Mexican League is a member of the National Association of Professional Baseball Leagues and has a Triple-A classification. However, its member clubs operate largely independent of the 30 major league teams, and for that reason the league is listed in the international and winter league section.*

Mailing Address: Angel Pola No. 16, Col. Periodista, CP 11220, Mexico, D.F. **Telephone:** (011-52) 555-557-1007. **FAX:** (011-52) 555-395-2454. **E-Mail Address:** mbl@prodigy.net.mx. **Website:** www.lmb.com.mx.

Years League Active: 1955-.

President: Alejandro Hutt. **Operations Manager:** Nestor Alba Brito.

Division Structure: North—Aquascalientes, Laguna, Monclova, Monterrey, Puebla, San Luis Potosi, Saltillo, Tijuana. **South**—Angelopolis, Campeche, Cancún, Mexico City, Oaxaca, Tabasco, Veracruz, Yucatan.

Regular Season: 110 games (split-schedule). **2005 Opening Date:** March 19. **Closing Date:** July 24.

All-Star Game: May 29 at Puebla (Angelopolis).

Playoff Format: Top six teams in each division qualify; first- and second-place teams in each division receive first-round byes. First, second and semifinal rounds are best-of-7 series; division champions meet in best-of-7 series for league championship.

Roster Limit: 28. **Roster Limit, Imports:** 6.

AGUASCALIENTES RAILROADMEN
Office Address: Calle Manuel Madrigal y Juan de la Barrera, Colonia Heroes, Aguascalientes, Aguascalientes, CP 20250. **Telephone:** (011-52) 449-970-4585. **E-Mail Address:** rieleros@lmb.com.mx. **Website:** www.rielerosdeaguascalientes.com.mx.

President: Jean Paul Mansur Beltran. **General Manager:** Antelmo Hernandez.

Manager: Alex Taveras.

ANGELOPOLIS TIGERS
Office Address: Calle Paseo de las Fuentes, #13 Col. Arbodedas de Guadalupe, CP 72210, Puebla, Puebla. **Telephone:** (011-52) 222-236-4909. **FAX:** (011-52) 222-234-0192. **E-Mail Address:** tigres@tigresdemexico.com.mx. **Website:** www.tigresdemexico.com.mx.

President: Cuauhtémoc Rodriguez. **General Manager:** Iram Campos Lara.

Manager: Enrique Reyes.

CAMPECHE PIRATES
Office Address: Unidad Deportiva 20 de Noviembre, Local 4, CP 24000, Campeche, Campeche. **Telephone:** (011-52) 981-816-2116. **FAX:** (011-52) 981-816-3807. **E-Mail Address:** piratasc@prodigy.net.mx.

President: Gabriel Escalante Castillo. **General Manager:** Maria del Socorro Morales.

Manager: Francisco Estrada Soto.

CANCUN LOBSTERMEN
Office Address: Av. Nader Super Mz 5 Lote 4 Edif Nader Col Centro, Col. Centro, CP 77500, Cancún, Quintana Roo. **Telephone/FAX:** (011-52) 998-898-2442.

E-Mail Address: cancun@lmb.com.mx. **Website:** www.langosterosdecancun.com.

President: Chara Mansur Beltran. **General Manager:** Ruben de la Cruz Herrera.

Manager: Juan Pacho.

LAGUNA COWBOYS
Office Address: Juan Gutenberg s/n, Col. Centro, CP 27000, Torreon, Coahuila. **Telephone:** (011-52) 871-718-5515. **FAX:** (011-52) 871-717-4335. **E-Mail Address:** unionlag@prodigy.net.mx. **Website:** www.vaqueroslaguna.com.

President: Jose Antonio Mansur Beltran. **General Manager:** Felipe Rodriguez.

Manager: Geraldo Sanchez.

MEXICO CITY RED DEVILS
Office Address: Av. Cuauhtemoc #451-101, Col. Narvarte, CP 03020, Mexico DF **Telephone:** (011-52) 555-639-8722. **FAX:** (011-52) 555-639-9722. **E-Mail Address:** diablos@diablos-rojos.com.mx. **Website:** www.diablos.com.mx.

President: Roberto Mansur Galán. **General Manager:** Eduardo de la Cerda.

Manager: Houston Jimenez.

MONCLOVA STEELERS
Office Address: Cuauhtemoc #299, Col. Ciudad Deportiva, CP 25750, Monclova, Coahuila. **Telephone:** (011-52) 866-636-2334. **FAX:** (011-52) 866-636-2688. **E-Mail Address:** acererosdelnorte@prodigy.net.mx. **Website:** www.acereros.com.mx.

President: Donaciano Garza Gutierrez. **General Manager:** Victor Favela Lopez.

Manager: Lino Rivera.

MONTERREY SULTANS
Office Address: Av. Manuel Barragan s/n, Estadio Monterrey, Apartado Postal 870, Monterrey, Nuevo Leon, CP 66460. **Telephone:** (011-52) 818-351-8022. **FAX:** (011-52) 818-351-8634. **E-Mail Address:** rmagdaleno@sultanes.com.mx. **Website:** www.sultanes.com.mx.

President: José Maiz García. **General Manager:** Roberto Magdaleno Ramírez.

Manager: Hector Torres.

OAXACA WARRIORS
Office Address: Privada del Chopo #105, Fraccionamiento El Chopo, CP 68050, Oaxaca, Oaxaca. **Telephone:** (011-52) 951-515-5522. **FAX:** (011-52) 951-515-4966. **E-Mail Address:** guerreros@guerrerosdeoaxaca.com. **Website:** www.guerrerosdeoaxaca.com.

President: Vicente Pérez Avellá Villa. **General Manager:** Guillermo Rodriguez Velazquez.

Manager: Homer Rojas.

PUEBLA PARROTS
Office Address: Calle Paseo de las Fuentes, #13 Col Arboledas de Guadalupe, CP 72210, Puebla, Puebla. **Telephone:** (011-52) 222-236-3313. **FAX:** (011-52) 222-236-2906. **E-Mail Address:** oficina@pericosdepuebla.com.mx. **Website:** www.pericosdepuebla.com.mx.

President: Samuel Lozano Molina. **General Manager:** Francisco Minjarez Garcia.

Manager: Armando Cabrera.

SALTILLO SARAPE MAKERS

Office Address: Blvd. Nazario Ortiz Esquina con Blvd. Jesus Sanchez, CP 25280, Saltillo, Coahuila. **Telephone:** (011-52) 844-416-9455. **FAX:** (011-52) 844-439-1330. **E-Mail Address:** aley@grupoley.com. **Website:** www.saraperos.com.mx.
President: Juan Manuel Ley. **General Manager:** Eduardo Valenzuela.
Manager: Derek Bryant.

SAN LUIS POTOSI TUNEROS

Office Address: Av. Himno Nacional #400, Col. Himno Nacional, San Luis Postosi, CP 78280. **Telephone:** (011-52) 444-812-4940. **FAX:** (011-52) 444-812-4939.
President: Marcello De los Santos. **General Manager:** Leo Clayton.
Manager: Dan Firova.

TABASCO CATTLEMEN

Office Address: Explanada de la Ciudad Deportiva, Parque de Beisbol Centenario del 27 de Febrero, Col. Atasta de Serra, CP 86100, Villahermosa, Tabasco. **Telephone:** (011-52) 993-352-2787. **FAX:** (011-52) 993-352-2788. **E-Mail Address:** olmecastab@prodigy.net.mx.
President: Maximo Evia Ramirez. **General Manager:** Raul Gonzalez Rodriguez.
Manager: Juan Francisco Rodriguez.

TIJUANA COLTS

Office Address: Av Netzahualcoyotl #1204-101 Zona Rio, Tijuana, Baja California. **Telephone:** (011-52) 664-683-5899. **FAX:** (011-52) 664-683-5899. **E-Mail Address:** Unavailable. **Website:** www.potrosdetijuana.com.
President: Belisario Cabrera. **General Manager:** David Gonzalez.
Manager: Unavailable.

VERACRUZ REDS

Office Address: Av. Jacarandas s/n, Esquina España, Fraccionamiento Virginia, CP 94294, Boca del Rio, Veracruz. **Telephone:** (011-52) 229-935-5004. **FAX:** (229) 935-5008. **Website:** www.rojosdelaguila.com.mx.
President/General Manager: Unavailable.
Manager: Marco Antonio Vazquez.

YUCATAN LIONS

Office Address: Calle 50 #406-B, Entre 35 y 37, Col. Jesus Carranza, CP 97109, Merida, Yucatán. **Telephone:** (011-52) 999-926-3022. **FAX:** (011-52) 999-926-3631. **E-Mail Addresses:** leonesy@prodigy.net.mx. **Website:** www.leonesdeyucatan.com.mx.
President: Gustavo Ricalde Durán. **General Manager:** Wilbert Valle Acevedo.
Manager: Bernie Tatis

MEXICAN ACADEMY

Rookie Classification
Mailing Address: Angel Pola No. 16, Col. Periodista, CP 11220, Mexico, D.F. **Telephone:** (011-52) 555-557-1007. **FAX:** (011-52) 555-395-2454. **E-Mail Address:** mbl@prodigy.net.mx. **Website:** www.lmb.com.mx.
Member Clubs: Celaya, Guanajuato, Queretaro, Salamanca.
Regular Season: 50 games. **2005 Opening Date:**

October. **Closing Date:** December.

DOMINICAN REPUBLIC

DOMINICAN SUMMER

Member, National Association
Rookie Classification
Mailing Address: Calle Segunda No. 64, Reparto Antilla, Santo Domingo, Dominican Republic. **Telephone/FAX:** (809) 532-3619.
Years League Active: 1985-.
President: Freddy Jana. **Administrative Assistant:** Orlando Diaz.
2005 Member Clubs/Participating Organizations: Angels, Astros, Athletics I, Athletics II, Blue Jays, Braves I, Braves II, Cardinals, Cubs, Diamondbacks, Dodgers I, Dodgers II, Giants, Indians I, Indians II, Mariners, Marlins, Mets, Nationals, Orioles, Padres, Phillies, Pirates, Rangers, Reds, Red Sox, Rockies, Royals, Tigers, Twins, White Sox, Yankees I, Yankees II.
Regular Season: 70-72 games, depending on divisions. **2005 Opening Date:** June 4. **Closing Date:** Aug. 26.
Playoff Format: Six divisions; two division champions with best winning percentages receive first-round byes. Four teams meet in best-of-3 quarterfinals; winners and division champions with first-round byes meet in best-of-3 semifinals; winners meet in best-of-5 series for league championship.
Roster Limit: 35; 30 active. **Player Eligibility Rule:** No more than eight players 20 or older and no more than two players 21 or older. At least 10 players must be pitchers. No more than four years of prior service, excluding Rookie leagues outside the U.S. and Canada.

VENEZUELA

VENEZUELAN SUMMER

Member, National Association
Rookie Classification
Mailing Address: C.C. Caribbean Plaza Modulo 8, P.A. Local 173-174, Valencia, Carabobo, Venezuela. **Telephone:** (011-58) 241-824-0321, (011) 58-241-824-0980. **FAX:** (011-58) 241-824-0705. **Website:** www.venezuelansummerleague.com.
Years League Active: 1997-.
Administrator: Saul Gonzalez Acevedo.
2005 Member Clubs: Aguirre, Cagua, Ciudad Alienza, San joaquin, Troconero 1, Tronconero 2, Universidad, Venoco 1, Venoco 2. **Participating Organizations:** Astros, Blue Jays, Mariners, Marlins, Mets, Orioles, Phillies, Pirates, Reds, Red Sox, Rockies, Twins.
Regular Season: 60 games. **2005 Opening Date:** May 16. **Closing Date:** Aug. 5.
Playoffs: Best-of-3 series between top two teams in regular season.
Roster Limit: 35; 30 active. **Player Eligibility Rule:** No player on active list may have more than three years of minor league service. Open to players from all Latin American Spanish-speaking countries except Dominican Republic and Puerto Rico.

ASIA

CHINA

CHINA BASEBALL ASSOCIATION

Mailing Address: 5, Tiyuguan Road, Beijing 100763, Peoples Republic of China. **Telephone:** (011-86) 10-85826002. **FAX:** (011-86) 10-85825994. **E-Mail Address:** chinabaseball2008@yahoo.com.cn.

Years League Active: 2002-.

Chairman: Hu Jian Guo. **Vice Chairmen:** Tom McCarthy, Shen Wei. **Executive Director:** Yang Jie. **General Manager, Marketing/Promotion:** Lin Xiao Wu.

Member Clubs: Beijing Tigers, China Hopestars, Guangdong Leopards, Shanghai Golden Eagles, Sichuan Dragons, Tianjin Lions.

Regular Season: 30 games. **2005 Opening Date:** April 1. **Closing Date:** June 26.

Playoff Format: Top two teams meet in best-of-5 series for league championship (July 2-10).

Import Rule: Three players on active roster.

JAPAN

Mailing Address: Imperial Tower, 14F, 1-1-1 Uchisaiwai-cho, Chiyoda-ku, Tokyo 100-0011. **Telephone:** 03-3502-0022. **FAX:** 03-3502-0140.

Commissioner: Yasuchika Negoro.

Executive Secretary: Kazuo Hasegawa. **Executive Director:** Kunio Shimoda. **Director, Baseball Operations:** Nobby Ito. **Assistant Directors, International Affairs:** Tack Nakajima, Tex Nakamura.

Japan Series: Best-of-7 series between Central and Pacific League champions, begins Oct. 22 at home of Pacific League club.

All-Star Series: July 22 at Seibu Dome; July 23 at Koshien Stadium.

Roster Limit: 70 per organization (one major league club, one minor league club). Major league club is permitted to register 28 players at a time, though just 25 may be available for each game.

Roster Limit, Imports: 4 (2 position players and 2 pitchers; 3 position players and 1 pitcher or 3 pitchers and 1 position player) in majors; unlimited in minors.

CENTRAL LEAGUE

Mailing Address: Asahi Bldg. 3F, 6-6-7 Ginza, Chuo-ku, Tokyo 104-0061. **Telephone:** 03-3572-1673. **FAX:** 03-3571-4545.

President: Hajime Toyokura.

Secretary General: Hideo Okoshi. **Planning Department:** Masaaki Nagino. **Public Relations:** Kazu Ogaki.

Regular Season: 146 games. **2005 Opening Date:** April 1. **Closing Date:** Oct. 6.

Playoff Format: None.

CHUNICHI DRAGONS

Mailing Address: Chunichi Bldg. 6F, 4-1-1 Sakae, Naka-ku, Nagoya 460-0008. **Telephone:** 052-252-5226. **FAX:** 052-263-7696.

Chairman: Bungo Shirai. **President:** Junnosuke Nishikawa. **General Manager:** Kazumasa Ito. **Field Manager:** Hiromitsu Ochiai.

2005 Foreign Players: Domingo Guzman, Luis Martinez, Alex Ochoa, Tyrone Woods, Chen Wei Yin (Taiwan).

HANSHIN TIGERS

Mailing Address: 1-47 Koshien-cho, Nishinomiya-shi, Hyogo-ken 663-8152. **Telephone:** 0798-46-1515. **FAX:** 0798-46-3555.

Chairman: Masatoshi Tezuka. **President:** Yoshihiro Makita. **Field Manager:** Akinobu Okada.

2005 Foreign Players: Jamie Brown, Darwin Cubillan, Andy Sheets, Shane Spencer, Jeff Williams.

HIROSHIMA TOYO CARP

Mailing Address: 5-25 Motomachi, Naka-ku, Hiroshima 730-8508. **Telephone:** 082-221-2040. **FAX:** 082-228-5013.

President: Hajime Matsuda. **General Manager:** Junro Anan. **Field Manager:** Koji Yamamoto.

2005 Foreign Players: John Bale, Juan Feliciano, Greg LaRocca, Mike Romano.

YAKULT SWALLOWS

Mailing Address: Shimbashi MCV Bldg. 5F, 5-13-5 Shimbashi, Minato-ku, Tokyo 105-0004. **Telephone:** 03-5470-8915. **FAX:** 03-5470-8916.

Chairman: Sumiya Hori. **President:** Yoshikazu Tagiku. **General Manager:** Kesanori Kurashima. **Field Manager:** Tsutomu Wakamatsu.

2005 Foreign Players: Dicky Gonzalez, Alex Ramirez, Alex Ramirez Jr., Adam Riggs.

YOKOHAMA BAYSTARS

Mailing Address: Kannai Arai Bldg, 7F, 1-8 Onoe-cho, Naka-ku, Yokohama 231-0015. **Telephone:** 045-681-0811. **FAX:** 045-661-2500.

Chairman: Kiyoshi Wakabayashi. **President:** Susumu Minegishi. **Field Manager:** Kazuhiko Ushijima.

2005 Foreign Players: Cedrick Bowers, Mike Holtz, Marc Kroon, Kevin Witt. **Coach:** John Turney.

YOMIURI GIANTS

Mailing Address: Takebashi 3-3 Bldg., 3-3 Kanda Nishiki-cho, Chiyoda-ku, Tokyo 101-8462. **Telephone:** 03-3295-7711. **FAX:** 03-3295-7734.

Chairman: Takuo Takihana. **President:** Tsunekazu Momoi. **General Manager:** Hidetoshi Kiyotake. **Field Manager:** Tsuneo Horiuchi.

2005 Foreign Players: Gabe Kapler, Dan Miceli, Tuffy Rhodes, Brian Sikorski.

PACIFIC LEAGUE

Mailing Address: Asahi Bldg. 9F, 6-6-7 Ginza, Chuo-ku, Tokyo 104-0061. **Telephone:** 03-3573-1551. **FAX:** 03-3572-5843.

President: Tadao Koike. **Secretary General:** Shigeru Murata. **Administration Department:** Katsuhisa Matsuzaki.

Regular Season: 136 games. **2005 Opening Date:** March 26. **Closing Date:** Sept. 28.

Playoff Format—Stage 1: second-place team meets third-place team in best-of-3 series. Stage 2: Winner of Stage 1 meets first-place team in best-of-5 series for league championship.

CHIBA LOTTE MARINES

Mailing Address: WBG Marive West 26F, 2-6 Nakase, Mihama-ku, Chiba-shi, Chiba-ken 261-8587. **Telephone:** 043-297-2101. **FAX:** 043-297-2181.

Chairman: Takeo Shigemitsu. **President:** Eisuke Hamamoto. **Field Manager:** Bobby Valentine.

2005 Foreign Players: Benny Agbayani, Matt Franco,

Val Pascucci, Dan Serafini, Lee Seung Yeop (Korea). **Coaches:** Frank Ramppen, Tom Robson.

FUKUOKA SOFTBANK HAWKS
Mailing Address: Fukuoka Dome, Hawks Town, Fukuoka 810-0065. **Telephone:** 092-844-1189. **FAX:** 092-844-4600.
Chairman: Masayoshi Son. **General Manager:** Masashi Tsunoda. **Field Manager:** Sadaharu Oh.
2005 Foreign Players: Tony Batista, Jolbert Cabrera, Pedro Feliciano, Anderson Gomes, Lindsay Gulin, Julio Zuleta.

HOKKAIDO NIPPON HAM FIGHTERS
Mailing Address: 1 Hitsujigaoka, Toyohira-ku, Sapporo 062-0045. **Telephone:** 011-857-3939. **FAX:** 011-857-3900.
Chairman: Hiroji Okoso. **Acting Owner:** Takeshi Kojima. **President:** Junji Iwamura. **General Manager:** Shigeru Takada. **Field Manager:** Trey Hillman.
2005 Foreign Players: Erick Almonte, Brandon Knight, Carlos Mirabal, Sherman Obando, Fernando Seguignol. **Coaches:** Mike Brown, Gary Denbo.

ORIX BUFFALOES
Mailing Address: 3251-10 Midoridai, Suma-ku, Kobe 654-0163. **Telephone:** 078-795-1203. **FAX:** 078-795-1205.
Chairman: Yoshihiko Miyauchi. **President:** Takashi Koizumi. **General Manager:** Katsuhiro Nakamura. **Field Manager:** Akira Ogi.
2005 Foreign Players: Kevin Beirne, Cliff Brumbaugh, Karim Garcia, Jose Parra, Jeremy Powell. **Coach:** Ralph Bryant.

SEIBU LIONS
Mailing Address: 2135 Kami-Yamaguchi, Tokorozawa-shi, Saitama-ken 359-1189. **Telephone:** 04-2924-1155. **FAX:** 04-2928-1919.
Team President: Yoshio Hoshino. **General Manager:** Akira Kuroiwa. **Field Manager:** Tsutomu Ito.
2005 Foreign Players: Alex Cabrera, Chang Chi-Chie (Taiwan), Jose Fernandez, Hsu Ming-chieh (Taiwan).

TOHOKU RAKUTEN GOLDEN EAGLES
Mailing Address: Midosuji Grand Bldg., 2-2-3 Namba, Chuo-ku, Osaka 542-0076. **Telephone:** 06-6212-9744. **FAX:** 06-6212-6834.
Chairman: Hiroshi Mikitani. **President:** Toru Shimada. **General Manager:** Marty Kuehnert. **Field Manager:** Yasushi Tao.
2005 Foreign Players: Kevin Hodges, Luis Lopez, Damon Minor, Aaron Myette, Gary Rath.

KOREA

KOREA BASEBALL ORGANIZATION
Mailing Address: 946-16 Dokokdong, Kangnam-gu, Seoul, Korea. **Telephone:** (02) 3460-4643. **FAX:** (02) 3460-4649.
Years League Active: 1982-.
Commissioner: Park Yong-oh. **Secretary General:** Lee Sang-kook. **Deputy Secretary General:** Lee Sang-il.
Division Structure: None.
Regular Season: 132. **2005 Opening Date:** March 12. **Closing Date:** Aug. 30.
Korean Series: Regular-season champion automatically qualifies for Korean Series. Third- and fourth-place teams meet in best-of-3 series; winner advances to meet second-place team in best-of-5 series; winner meets first-place team in best-of-7 series for league championship.
Roster Limit: 27 active through Sept. 1, when rosters

expand to 32. **Imports:** 2 active.

DOOSAN BEARS
Mailing Address: Chamsil Baseball Stadium, 10 Chamsil-1 dong, Songpa-ku, Seoul, Korea 138-221. **Telephone:** (02) 2240-1777. **FAX:** (02) 2240-1788. **Website:** www.doosanbears.com.
President: Kyung Chang-Ho. **Manager:** Kim Kyung-Moon.

HANHWA EAGLES
Mailing Address: 22-1 Youngjeon-dong, Dong-ku, Daejeon, Korea 300-200. **Telephone:** (042) 637-6001. **FAX:** (042) 632-2929. **Website:** www.hanwhaeagles.co.kr.
General Manager: Song Kyu-Soo. **Manager:** Yoo Seung-an.

HYUNDAI UNICORNS
Mailing Address: Hyundai Haesang Bldg., 9th Floor, 1014 Kwonseon-dong, Kwonseon-ku, Suwon, Kyungki-do, Korea 441-390. **Telephone:** (031) 226-9000. **FAX:** (031) 224-9107. **Website:** www.hd-unicorns.co.kr.
General Manager: Jeong Jae-ho. **Manager:** Kim Jae-park.

KIA TIGERS
Mailing Address: 266 Naebang-dong, Seo-ku, Gwangju, Korea 502-807. **Telephone:** (062) 370-1895. **FAX:** (062) 525-5350. **Website:** www.kiatigers.co.kr.
General Manager: Jeong Jae-kong. **Manager:** Kim Sung-han.

LG TWINS
Mailing Address: Chamshil Baseball Stadium, 10 Chamshil 1-dong, Songpa-ku, Seoul, Korea 138-221. **Telephone:** (02) 2005-5760-5. **FAX:** (02) 2005-5801. **Website:** www.lgtwins.com.
General Manager: You Sung-min. **Manager:** Lee Soon-Chul.

LOTTE GIANTS
Mailing Address: 930 Sajik-dong Dongrae-Ku, Pusan, Korea, 607-120. **Telephone:** (051) 505-7422. **FAX:** 51-506-0090. **Website:** www.lotte-giants.co.kr.
General Manager: Lee Sang-koo. **Manager:** Yang Sang-Moon.

SAMSUNG LIONS
Mailing Address: 184-3, Sunhwari-jinrliangyun, Kyungsan, Kyungsan, Kyungsangbuk-do, Korea 712-830. **Telephone:** (053) 859-3114. **FAX:** (053) 859-3117. **Website:** www.samsunglions.com.
General Manager: Kim Jae-ha. **Manager:** Kim Eung-yong.

SK WYVERNS
Mailing Address: 8 San, Moonhak-dong, Nam-ku, Inchon, Korea 402-070. **Telephone:** (032) 422-7949. **FAX:** (032) 429-4565. **Website:** www.skwyvers.com.
General Manager: Choi Jong-joon. **Manager:** Cho Bum-hyun.

TAIWAN

CHINESE PROFESSIONAL BASEBALL LEAGUE
Mailing Address: 2F, No. 32, Pateh Road, Sec. 3, Taipei, Taiwan. **Telephone:** 886-2-2577-6992. **FAX:** 886-2-2577-2606. **Website:** www.cpbl.com.tw.
Years League Active: 1990-.
Commissioner: Harvey Chen. **Secretary General:** Wayne Lee.
Member Clubs: Brother Elephants (Taipei), China Trust Whales (Chiayi City), President Lions (Tainan), Sinon Bulls (Taichung), La New Bears (Kaohsiung), Makoto Cobras (Taipei).

Regular Season: 100 games (split schedule). **2005 Opening Date:** Feb. 28. **Closing Date:** Oct. 31.

Championship Series: Split-season champions meet in best-of-7 series for league championship.

Import Rule: Only three import players may be active, and only two may be on the field at the same time.

EUROPE

HOLLAND

Mailing Address: Royal Dutch Baseball and Softball Association, "Twinstate II", Perkinsbaan 15, 3439 ND Nieuwegein, Holland. **Telephone:** 31-(0) 30-607-6070. **FAX:** 31-30- 294-3043. **Website:** www.knbsb.nl.
President: Hans Meijer.

ALMERE '90

Mailing Address: B.S.C. Almere '90, Estafettelaan 2, 1318 EG Almere. **Telephone:** 31 (0) 36-549 95 40. **Website:** www.almere90.nl .

AMSTERDAM PIRATES

Mailing Address: Postbus 8862, 1006 JB Amsterdam. **Telephone:** 31 (0) 20-6199591. **Website:** www.amsterdam-pirates.nl.

DEN HAAG TORNADOS

Mailing Address: Postbus 47994, 2504 CG Den Haag. **Telephone:** 31 (0) 70-366 97 22. **Website:** www.svado.nl.

HCAW

Mailing Address: Mr. Cocker HCAW, Postbus 1321, 1400 BH Bussum. **Telephone:** +31 (0) 35-693- 14 30. **Website:** www.hcaw.nl.

HOOFDDORP PIONIERS

Mailing Address: Postbus 475, 2130 AL Hoofddorp. **Telephone:** 31 (0) 23-561 35 57. **Website:** www.hoofddorp-pioniers.nl.

KINHEIM

Mailing Address: Gemeentelijk Sportpark, Badmintonpad, 2023 BT Haarlem. **Telephone:** 31 (0) 23-525 13 39. **Website:** www.kinheim.net.

NEPTUNUS

Mailing Address: Sportclub Neptunus, Postbus 35064, 3005 DB Rotterdam. **Telephone:** 31 (0) 10-437 53 69. **Website:** www.neptunussport.com.

SPARTA/FEYENOORD

Mailing Address: Postbus 9211, 3007 AE Rotterdam. **Telephone:** +31 (0) 10-479-04 83. **Website:** www.spartafeyenoord.com.

ITALY

Mailing Address: Federazione Italiana Baseball/Softball, Viale Tiziano 74, 00196 Roma, Italy. **Telephone:** 39-06-36858376. **FAX:** 39-06-36858201. **Website:** www.baseball-softball.it
President: Riccardo Fraccari. **General Secretary:** Marcello Standoli.

BOLOGNA

Mailing Address: Piazzale Atleti Azzurri d'Italia, 40122 Bologna. **Telephone:** 39-051-479618. **FAX:** 39-051-554000. **E-Mail Address:** fortitudobaseball@tin.it. **Website:** www.fortitudobaseball.com.
President: Alfredo Pacini. **Manager:** Mauro Mazzotti.

GROSSETO

Mailing Address: Via della Repubblica 2, 58100

Grosseto. **Telephone:** 39-0564-494149. **FAX:** 39-0564-476750 **Website:** www.bbcgrosseto.it
President: Claudio Banchi. **Manager:** Pedro Medina.

MODENA

Mailing Address: Casella Postale 69, 41010 Saliceto Panaro, Modena. **Telephone:** 39-059-371655. **FAX:** 39-059-365300. **E-Mail Address:** info@modenabaseball.com .
Website: www.modenabaseball.com
President: Giovanni Tinti. **Manager:** Mauro Paglioli.

NETTUNO

Mailing Address: Stadio Steno Borghese, Via Scipione Borghese, 00048 Nettuno (Roma). **Telephone/FAX:** 39-06-9854966. **E-Mail Address:** info@nettunobaseball.net **Website:** www.nettunobaseball.net
President: Cesare Augusto Spigoni. **Manager:** Ruggero Bagialemani.

PARMA

Mailing Address: Via Donatore 4, Collecchio, 43044 Parma. **Telephone:** 39-335-604-8969. **FAX:** 39-0521-802601. **E-Mail Address:** baseballcity@hotmail.com. **Website:** www.eteamz.com/cusparma.
President: Rossano Rinaldi. **Manager:** Chris Catanoso.

PATERNO

Mailing Address: Viale dei Platani 15 , 95047 Paterno **Telephone:** 39-095 843152. **E-Mail Address:** team@warriorspaterno.com. **Website:** www.warriorspaterno.com.
President: Mario Raciti. **Manager:** Alejandro Duret.

REGGIO EMILIA

Mailing Address: Via Petit Bon 1, 42100 Reggio Emilia. **Telephone/FAX:** 39-0522 558156. **E-Mail Address:** info@reggiobaseball.it **Website:** www.reggiobaseball.it.
President: Graziella Casali. **Manager:** Gilberto Gerali.

RIMINI

Mailing Address: Via Monaco 2, 47900 Rimini. **Telephone/FAX:** 39-0541-741761. **E-Mail Address:** pirati@baseballrimini.com **Website:** www.baseballrimini.com.
President: Cesare Zangheri. **Manager:** Michele Romano.

SAN MARINO

Mailing Address: Via Piana 37, 47031 Republic of San Marino **Telephone:** 39-0549-991170. **FAX:** 39-0549-991247.
President: Giorgio Pancotti. **Manager:** Doriano Bindi.

TRIESTE

Mailing Address: Via degli Alpini 15, 34100 Trieste. **Telephone:** 39-040-213826. **FAX:** 39-040-3773232. **E-Mail Address:** segreteria@alpinabaseball.it **Website:** www.alpinabaseball.it.
President: Igor Dolenc. **Manager:** Frank Pantoja.

WINTER
LEAGUES

2004-2005
STANDINGS

CARIBBEAN SERIES

	W	L	PCT	GB
Mexico	5	1	.833	—
Venezuela	3	3	.500	2
Dominican Republic	3	3	.500	2
Puerto Rico	1	5	.167	4

DOMINICAN LEAGUE

REGULAR SEASON	W	L	PCT	GB
Aguilas	30	19	.612	—
Gigantes	27	22	.551	3
Estrellas	26	23	.531	4
Licey	26	24	.520	4½
Escogido	22	28	.440	8½
Azucareros	17	32	.347	13
ROUND-ROBIN	W	L	PCT	GB
Aguilas	11	7	.611	—
Licey	10	8	.556	1
Estrellas	9	9	.500	2
Gigantes	6	12	.333	5

CHAMPIONSHIP SERIES: Aguilas defeated Licey 4-3 in best-of-7 series.

MEXICAN PACIFIC LEAGUE

	W	L	PCT	GB
*Culiacan	42	23	.646	—
*Obregon	37	29	.560	5½
Mazatlan	35	30	.538	7
Los Mochis	34	32	.515	8½
Guasave	33	31	.515	8½
Mexicali	30	33	.476	11
Hermosillo	28	38	.424	14½
Navojoa	21	44	.323	21

*Split season champion

PLAYOFFS: Quarterfinals—Culiacan defeated Guasave 4-1; Mexicali defeated Obregon 4-3 and Los Mochis defeated Mazatlan 4-3 in best-of-7 series. Semifinals—Mexicali defeated Mochis 4-2 and Mazatlan defeated Culican 4-3 in best-of-7 series. Final—Mazatlan defeated Mexicali 4-1 in best-of-7 series.

PUERTO RICAN LEAGUE

	W	L	PCT	GB
Caguas	24	16	.600	—
Mayaguez	22	18	.550	2
Ponce	21	19	.525	3
Carolina	20	20	.500	4
Santurce	19	21	.475	5
Manati	14	26	.350	10

PLAYOFFS: Final—Mayaguez defeated Carolina 5-3 in best-of-9 series for league championship.

VENEZUELAN LEAGUE

WEST	W	L	PCT	GB
Lara 33	29		.532	—
Occidente	31	30	.508	1½
Aragua	31	31	.500	2
Zulia	28	33	.459	4½
EAST	W	L	PCT	GB
Caracas	39	22	.639	—
Oriente	36	25	.590	3
Magallanes	27	35	.435	12½
La Guaira	21	41	.339	18½
ROUND-ROBIN	W	L	PCT	GB
Aragua	11	5	.688	—
Caracas	9	7	.563	2
Oriente	8	8	.500	3
Lara 6	10		.375	5
Occidente	6	10	.375	5

CHAMPIONSHIP SERIES: Aragua defeated Caracas 4-3 in best-of-7 series.

ARIZONA FALL LEAGUE

AMERICAN	W	L	PCT	GB
Scottsdale Scorpions	21	15	.583	—
Peoria Saguaros	17	17	.500	3
Mesa Solar Sox	14	22	.389	7
NATIONAL	W	L	PCT	GB
Phoenix Desert Dogs	21	15	.583	—
Grand Canyon Rafters	18	17	.514	2½
Peoria Javelinas	16	21	.432	5½

PLAYOFF: Mesa Solar Sox defeated Phoenix Desert Dogs 1-0.

WINTER
BASEBALL

CARIBBEAN BASEBALL CONFEDERATION

(Confederacion de Beisbol Profesional del Caribe)

Mailing Address: Frank Feliz Miranda No. 1 Naco, Santo Domingo, Dominican Republic. **Telephone:** (809) 562-4737, 562-4715. **FAX:** (809) 565-4654.

Commissioner: Juan Fco. Puello Herrera. **Secretary:** Benny Agosto.

Member Countries: Dominican Republic, Mexico, Puerto Rico, Venezuela.

2006 Caribbean Series: Dates/site unavailable.

DOMINICAN LEAGUE

Office Address: Estadio Quisqueya, 2da. Planta, Ens. La Fe, Santo Domingo, D.N., Dominican Republic. **Mailing Address:** Apartado Postal 1246, Santo Domingo, D.N., Dominican Republic. **Telephone:** (809) 567-6371, (809) 563-5085. **FAX:** (809) 567-5720. **E-Mail Address:** info@beisboldominicano.com. **Website:** www.beisboldominicano.com.

Years League Active: 1951-.

President: Dr. Leonardo Matos Berrido. **Administrator:** Marcos Rodriguez. **Public Relations Director:** Jorge Torres.

Regular Season: 50 games. **2005 Opening Date:** Oct. 22. **Closing Date:** Dec 29.

Playoff Format: Top four teams meet in 18-game round-robin. Top two teams advance to best-of-7 series for league championship. Winner advances to Caribbean Series.

Roster Limit: 30. **Roster Limit, Imports:** 7.

AGUILAS CIBAENAS

Office Address: Estadio Cibao, Apartado 111, Santiago, Dom. Rep. **Mailing Address:** Calle 3, No. 16, Reparto Oquet, Santiago, Dom. Rep.. **Telephone:** (809) 575-8250. **FAX:** (809) 575-0865. **E-Mail Address:** a.cibaenas@codetel.net.do. **Website:** www.lasaguilas.com.

President: Winston Llenas. **General Manager:** Reynaldo Bisono.

2004-2005 Manager: Felix Fermin.

AZUCAREROS DEL ESTE

Mailing Address: Estadio Francisco Micheli, La Romana, Dom. Rep. **Telephone:** (809) 556-6189. **FAX:** (809) 550-1550. **E-Mail Address:** torosdeleste@codetel.net.do. **Website:** www.azucarerosdeleste.com

President: Francisco Micheli. **General Manager:** Pablo Peguero.

2004-2005 Manager: Luis Silverio.

LEONES DEL ESCOGIDO

Office Address: Estadio Quisqueya, Ens. la Fe, Apartado Postal 1287, Santo Domingo, Dom. Rep. **Telephone:** (809) 565-1910. **FAX:** (809) 567-7643. **E-Mail Address:** info@escogido.com. **Website:** www.escogido.com.do.

President: Julio Hazim Risk. **General Manager:** Freddy Jana.

2004-2005 Manager: Juan Samuel.

ESTRELLAS ORIENTALES

Office Address: Estadio Tetelo Vargas, San Pedro de Macoris, Dom. Rep. **Telephone:** (809) 529-3618. **FAX:** (809) 526-7658. **E-Mail Address:** estrellasdeoriente@hotmail.com. **Website:** www.estrellasdeoriente.com

President: Manuel Antim Battle. **General Manager:** Manuel Antun.

2004-2005 Manager: Luis Natera.

TIGRES DE LICEY

Office Address: Estadio Quisqueya, Apartado Postal 1321, Santo Domingo, Dom. Rep. **Telephone:** (809) 567-3090. **FAX:** (809) 542-7714. **E-Mail Address:** fernando.ravelo@codetel.net.do. **Website:** www.licey.com.

President: Emigolo Garrido. **General Manager:** Fernando Ravelo Jana.

2004-2005 Manager: Manny Acta.

GIGANTES DEL CIBAO

Office Address: Estadio Julian Javier, San Francisco de Macoris, Dom. Rep. **Telephone:** (809) 482-0741. **FAX:** (809) 588-8733. **Website:** www.gigantesdelcibao.com.

President: Alberto Genao. **General Manager:** Martin Almanzar.

2004-2005 Manager: Arturo de Freites.

MEXICAN PACIFIC LEAGUE

Mailing Address: Av. Insurgentes No. 847 Sur, Interior 402, Edificio San Carlos, Col. Centro, CP 80120, Culiacan, Sinaloa. **Telephone/FAX:** (011-52) 667-761-25-70, (011-52) 667-761-25-71. **E-Mail Address:** ligadelpacifico@ligadelpacifico.com.mx. **Website:** www.ligadelpacifico.com.mx.

Years League Active: 1958-.

President: Renato Vega Alvarado. **General Manager:** Oviel Dennis Gonzalez.

Regular Season: 68 games. **2004-2005 Opening Date:** Oct. 11. **Closing Date:** Dec. 30.

Playoff Format: Six teams advance to best-of-7 quarterfinals. Three winners and losing team with best record advance to best-of-7 semifinals. Winners meet in best-of-7 series for league championship. Winner advances to Caribbean World Series.

Roster Limit: 30. **Roster Limit, Imports:** 5.

TOMATEROS DE CULIACAN

Street Address: Av Alvaro Obregon 340 Sur, CP 8000, Culiacan, Sinaloa, Mexico. **Telephone:** (011-52) 667-712-2446. **FAX:** (011-52) 667-715-6828. **E-Mail Address:** tomateros@infosel.com.mx.

President: Juan Manuel Ley Lopez. **General Managers:** Eduardo Valenzuela.

2004-2005 Manager: Jose Luis Ibarra.

ALGODONEROS DE GUASAVE

Mailing Address: Obregon No. 43, CP 81000, Guasave, Sinaloa, Mexico. **Telephone:** (011-52) 687-872-29-98. **FAX:** (011-52) 687-872-14-31. **E-Mail Address:** algodon@prodigy.net.mx.

President: Fausto Perez. **General Manager:** Jaime Blancarte.

2004-2005 Manager: Alfonso Jimenez.

NARANJEROS DE HERMOSILLO

Mailing Address: Blvd. Solidaridad s/n, Estadio

Hector Espino, E/Jose S. Healey Y Blvd., Luis Encinas, CP 83188, Hermosillo, Sonora, Mexico. **Telephone:** (011-52) 662-260-69-32. **FAX:** (011-52) 662-260-69-31. **E-Mail Address:** webmaster@naranjeros.com.mx.
President: Enrique Mazon Rubio. **General Manager:** Marco Antonio Manzo.
2004-2005 Manager: Tom Gamboa.

CANEROS DE LOS MOCHIS
Mailing Address: Francisco I. Madero No. 116 Oriente, CP 81200, Los Mochis, Sinaloa, Mexico. **Telephone:** (011-52) 668-812-86-02. **FAX:** (011-52) 668-812-67-40. **E-Mail Address:** verdes@infosel.net.mx.
President: Mario Lopez Valdez. **General Manager:** Antonio Castro Chavez.
2004-2005 Manager: Lorenzo Bundy.

VENADOS DE MAZATLAN
Mailing Address: Gutierrez Najera No. 821, CP 82000, Mazatlan, Sinaloa, Mexico. **Telephone:** (011-52) 669-981-17-10. **FAX:** (011-52) 669-981-17-11. **E-Mail Address:** club@venados.com.mx.
President: Jesus Ismael Barros Cebreros. **General Manager:** Alejandro Lizarraga Osuna.
2004-2005 Manager: Dan Firova.

AGUILAS DE MEXICALI
Mailing Address: Estadio De Beisbol De La Cd. Deportiva, Calz. Cuautemoc s/n, Las Fuentes Mexicali, Baja, CA, Mexico. **Telephone:** (011-52) 686-567-0040. **FAX:** (011-52) 686-567-0095. **E-Mail Address:** aguilas2@telnor.net
President: Dio Alberto Murillo. **General Manager:** Jesus Sommers.
2004-2005 Manager: Raul Cano.

MAYOS DE NAVOJOA
Mailing Address: Rosales No. 102, E/Pesqueira Y no Reeleccion, CP 85830, Navojoa, Sonora, Mexico. **Telephone:** (011-52) 642-422-14-33. **FAX:** (011-52) 642-422-89-97. **E-Mail Address:** clubmayos@hotmail.com.
President: Victor Cuevas Garibay. **General Manager:** Lauro Villalobos.
2004-2005 Manager: Bernie Tatis.

YAQUIS DE OBREGON
Mailing Address: Guerrero y Michoacan, Estadio de Beisbol Tomas Oroz Gaytan, CP 85130, Ciudad Obregon, Sonora, Mexico. **Telephone:** (011-52) 644-413-77-66. **FAX:** (011-52) 644-414-11-56. **E-Mail Address:** clubyaquisdeobregon@yaquisdeobregon.com.mx.
President: Luis Alfonso Lugo Platt. **General Manager:** Roberto Diaz Gonzalez.
2004-2005 Manager: Tim Johnson.

PUERTO RICAN LEAGUE
Office Address: Avenida Munoz Rivera 1056, Edificio First Federal, Suite 501, Rio Piedras, PR 00925. **Mailing Address:** P.O. Box 191852, San Juan, PR 00019. **Telephone:** (787) 765-6285, 765-7285. **FAX:** (787) 767-3028. **Website:** hitboricua.com.
Years League Active: 1938-.
President: Joaquin Monserrate Matienzo. **Executive Director:** Benny Agosto.
Regular Season: 40 games. **2004-2005 Opening Date:** Nov. 16. **Closing Date:** Jan. 6.
Playoff Format: Top four teams meet in best-of-7 semifinal series. Winners meet in best-of-9 series for league championship. Winner advances to Caribbean World Series.
Roster Limit: 30. **Roster Limit, Imports:** 5.

CRIOLLOS DE CAGUAS
Mailing Address: P.O. Box 1415, Caguas, PR 00726. **Telephone:** (787) 258-2222. **FAX:** (787) 743-0545.
President, General Manager: Filiberto Berrios. **2004-2005 Manager:** Jose Munoz.

CAROLINA GIANTS
Mailing Address: Roberto Clemente Stadium, P.O. Box 366246, San Juan, PR 00936. **Telephone:** (787) 643-4351. **FAX:** (787) 834-7480.
President: Benjamin Rivera. **General Manager/Manager:** Ramon Aviles.

MANATI ATHENIANS
Mailing Address: Direccion Postal Box 1155, Manati, PR 00674. **Telephone:** (787) 854-5757. **FAX:** (787) 854-6767.
President: Tony Valentin. **2004-2005 Manager:** Juan Lopez.

MAYAGUEZ INDIANS
Mailing Address: 3089 Marina Station, Mayaguez, PR 00681. **Telephone:** (787) 834-6111, 834-5211. **FAX:** (787) 834-7480.
President, General Manager: Daniel Aquino. **2004-2005 Manager:** Mako Oliveras.

LEONES DE PONCE
Mailing Address: P.O. Box 363148, San Juan, PR 00936. **Telephone:** (787) 848-8884. **FAX:** (787) 848-0050.
President: Antonio Munoz Jr. **2004-2005 Manager:** Jose Cruz Sr.

SANTURCE CRABBERS
Mailing Address: Unavailable. **Telephone:** (787) 773-0759, 773-0758. **FAX:** (787) 703-0756.
President: Carlos Baerga. **2004-2005 Manager:** Carmelo Martinez.

VENEZUELAN LEAGUE
Mailing Address: Avenida Casanova, Centro Comercial "El Recreo," Torre Sur, Piso 3, Oficinas 6 y 7, Sabana Grande, Caracas, Venezuela. **Telephone:** (011-58) 212-761-4932. **FAX:** (011-58) 212-761-7661. **Website:** www.lvbp.com.
Years League Active: 1946-.
President: Ramon Guillermo Aveledo. **General Manager:** Jose Domingo Alvarez.
Division Structure: East—Caracas, La Guaira, Magallanes, Oriente. **West**—Aragua, Lara, Pastora, Zulia.
Regular Season: 62 games. **2003-2004 Opening Date:** Oct. 14. **Closing Date:** Dec. 27.
Playoff Format: Top two teams in each division, plus a wild-card team, meet in 16-game round-robin series. Top two finishers meet in best-of-7 series for league championship. Winner advances to Caribbean Series.
Roster Limit: 26. **Roster Limit, Imports:** 7.

ARAGUA TIGERS
Mailing Address: Estadio Jose Perez Colmenares, Calle Campo Elias, Barrio Democratico, Maracay, Aragua, Venezuela. **Telephone:** (011-58) 243-554-4134. **FAX:** (011-58) 243-553-8655. **E-Mail Address:** tigres@tel-cel.net.ve. **Website:** www.tigresdearagua.com.ve.
President, General Manager: Rafael Rodriguez.
2004-2005 Manager: Buddy Bailey.

CARACAS LIONS
Mailing Address: Av. Francisco de Miranda, Centro Seguros la Paz, Piso 4, ofc. 42-C, La California Norte. **Telephone:** (011-58) 212-238-7733. **FAX:** (011-58) 212-238-0691. **E-Mail Address:** contacto@leones.com.

Website: www.leones.com.
President: Ariel Prat. **General Manager:** Oscar Prieto.
2004-2005 Manager: Omar Malave.

LA GUAIRA SHARKS
Mailing Address: Primera Transversal, Urbanizacion Miramar Pariata, Maiquetia, Vargas, Venezuela. **Telephone:** (011-58) 212-332-5579. **FAX:** (011-58) 212-332-3116. **E-Mail Addres:** tiburones@cantv.net. **Website:** www.tiburones.com.
President: Percy Chacin Armando Arratia. **General Manager:** Carlos Moreno.
2004-2005 Manager: Luis Salazar.

LARA CARDINALS
Mailing Address: Av. Rotaria, Estadio Antonio Herrera Gutiérrez, Barquisimeto, Lara, Venezuela. **Telephone:** (011-58) 251-442- 4543. **FAX:** (011-58) 251-442-1921. **E-Mail Address:** contacto@cardenalesdelara.com. **Website:** www.cardenalesdelara.com.
President, General Manager: Humberto Oropeza.
2004-2005 Manager: Dan Rohn.

MAGALLANES NAVIGATORS
Mailing Address: Centro Comercial Caribbean Plaza, Modulo 8, Local 173, Valencia, Carabobo, Venezuela. **Telephone:** (011-58) 241-824-0980. **FAX:** (011-58) 241-824-0705. **E-Mail address:** Magallanes@telcel.net.ve. **Website:** www.magallanes.com
President: Dr. Jorge Latoche. **General Manager:**

Roberto Ferrari.
2004-2005 Manager: Phil Regan.

ORIENTE CARIBBEANS
Mailing Address: Avenida Estadio Alfonso Carrasquel, Oficina Caribes de Oriente, Centro Comercial Novocentro, Piso 2, Local 2-4, Puerto la Cruz, Anzoategui, Venezuela. **Telephone:** (011-58) 281-266-2536. **FAX:** (011-58) 281-266-7054. **Website:** caribesbbc.com
President: Aurelio Fernandez-Concheso. **Vice President:** Pablo Ruggeri.
2004-2005 Manager: Dave Machemer.

PASTORA DE LOS LLANOS
Mailing Address: Estadio Bachiller Julio Hernandez Molina, Avenida Romulo Gallegos, Aruare, Portuguesa, Venezuela. **Telephone:** (011-58) 255-622-2945. **Fax:** (011-58) 255-621-8595.
President, General Manager: Enrique Finol.
2004-2005 Manager: Luis Dorante.

ZULIA EAGLES
Mailing Address: Avenida 8 con Calle 81, Urb. Santa Rita, Edificio Las Carolinas, Mezzanine Local M-3, Maracaibo, Zulia, Venezuela. **Telephone:** (011-58) 261-797-9834, (011-58) 261-798-0541. **FAX:** (011-58) 261-798-0579. **Website:** www.aguilas.com.
President: Lucas Rincon Colmenares. **General Manager:** Luis Rodolfo Machado Silva.
2004-2005 Manager: Pete Mackanin.

OTHER WINTER LEAGUES

ARIZONA FALL LEAGUE
Mailing Address: 10201 S. 51st St., Suite 230, Phoenix, AZ 85044. **Telephone:** (480) 496-6700. **FAX:** (480) 496-6384. **E-Mail Address:** afl@mlb.com **Website:** www.mlb.com.
Years League Active: 1992-.
Operated by: Major League Baseball.
Executive Vice President: Steve Cobb. **Executive Assistant:** Joan McGrath.
Division Structure: American—Mesa, Peoria Saguaros, Scottsdale; **West**—Grand Canyon, Peoria Javelinas, Phoenix.
Regular Season: 39 games. **2005 Opening Date:** Oct. 5. **Closing Date:** Nov. 20.
Playoff Format: Division champions meet in one-game championship.
Roster Limit: 30. Players with less than one year of major league service are eligible.

GRAND CANYON RAFTERS
Mailing Address: Scottsdale Stadium, 7408 East Osborn Rd., Scottsdale, AZ 85251.
Working Agreements: Atlanta Braves, Detroit Tigers, Minnesota Twins, New York Yannkees, San Francisco Giants.
2004 Manager: Bruce Fields (Tigers). **Coach:** Jose Marzan (Twins). **Pitching Coach:** Dave Eiland (Yankees).

MESA SOLAR SOX
Mailing Address: Mesa HoHoKam Park, 1235 N. Center, Mesa, AZ 85201.
Working Agreements: Chicago Cubs, Chicago White Sox, Colorado Rockies, St. Louis Cardinals, Tampa Bay Devil Rays.
2004 Manager: Charlie Montoya (Devil Rays). **Coach:** Glenallen Hill (Rockies). **Pitching Coach:** Sean Snedeker (White Sox).

PEORIA JAVELINAS
Mailing Address: Peoria Sports Complex, 16101 N. 83rd Ave., Peoria, AZ 85382.
Working Agreements: Baltimore Orioles, Cleveland Indians, Montreal Expos, San Diego Padres, Seattle Mariners.
2004 Manager: Mike Goff (Mariners). **Coach:** Torey Lovullo (Indians). **Pitching Coach:** Gary Lance (Padres).

PEORIA SAGUAROS
Mailing Address: Peoria Sports Complex, 16101 N. 83rd Ave., Peoria, AZ 85382.
Working Agreements: Boston Red Sox, New York Mets, Pittsburgh Pirates, Texas Rangers, Toronto Blue Jays.
2004 Manager: Marty Pevey (Blue Jays). **Coach:** John Russell (Pirates). **Pitching Coach:** Randy Niemann (Mets).

PHOENIX DESERT DOGS
Mailing Address: Phoenix Municipal Stadium, 5999 E. Van Buren St., Phoenix, AZ 85007.
Working Agreements: Anaheim Angels, Florida Marlins, Kansas City Royals, Oakland Athletics, Philadelphia Phillies.
2004 Manager: Dean Treanor (Marlins). **Coach:** Eric Richardson (Phillies). **Pitching Coiach:** Erik Bennett (Angels).

SCOTTSDALE SCORPIONS
Mailing Address: Scottsdale Stadium, 7408 East Osborn Rd., Scottsdale, AZ 85251.
Working Agreements: Arizona Diamondbacks, Cincinnati Reds, Houston Astros, Los Angeles Dodgers, Milwaukee Brewers.
2004 Manager: Ivan DeJesus (Astros). **Coach:** Lee Tinsley (Diamondbacks). **Pitching Coach:** Stan Kyles (Brewers).

COLLEGES

COLLEGE BASEBALL

NATIONAL COLLEGIATE ATHLETIC ASSOCIATION

Mailing Address: P.O. Box 6222, Indianapolis, IN 46206. **Telephone:** (317) 917-6222. **FAX:** (317) 917-6826 (championships), (317) 917-6857 (baseball). **E-Mail Addresses:** dpoppe@ncaa.org (Dennis Poppe), rbuhr@ncaa.org (Randy Buhr), dleech@ncaa.org (Damani Leech), dworlock@ncaa.org (David Worlock), jhamilton@ncaa.org (J.D. Hamilton), wburrow@ncaa.org (Wayne Burrow). **Websites:** www.ncaa.org, www.ncaasports.com.

President: Myles Brand. **Managing Director, Baseball:** Dennis Poppe. **Associate Director, Baseball:** Damani Leech. **Director, Championships:** Wayne Burrow. **Assistant Director, Championships:** Randy Buhr. **Media Contact, College World Series:** David Worlock. **Contact, Statistics:** Sean Straziscar.

Chairman, Division I Baseball Committee: Charlie Carr (senior associate athletic director, Florida State). **Division I Baseball Committee:** Michael Cross (senior associate athletic director, Princeton), John D'Argenio (athletic director, Siena), Rick Dickson (athletic director, Tulane), Mike Gaski (baseball coach, UNC Greensboro), Mike Hamrick (athletic director, Nevada-Las Vegas), Paul Krebs (athletic director, Bowling Green State), Bill Rowe (athletic director, Southwest Missouri State), Bob Steitz (senior associate athletic director, Villanova).

Chairman, Division II Baseball Committee: Britt Bonneau (baseball coach, Abilene Christian). **Chairman, Division III Baseball Committee:** Eric Etchison (baseball coach, Maryville, Tenn.).

2006 National Convention: Jan. 6-10 at Indianapolis.

2005 Championship Tournaments
NCAA Division I

59th College World Series	Omaha, NE, June 17-26/27
Super Regionals (8)	June 10-13
Regionals (16)	June 3-6

NCAA Division II

38th World Series	Montgomery, AL, May 28-June4
Regionals (8)	Campus sites, May 19-21

NCAA Division III

30th World Series	Appleton, WI, May 27-31
Regionals (8)	Campus sites, May 19-22

NATIONAL ASSOCIATION OF INTERCOLLEGIATE ATHLETICS

Mailing Address: 23500 W. 105th St., P.O. Box 1325, Olathe, KS 66051. **Telephone:** (913) 791-0044. **FAX:** (913) 791-9555. **Website:** www.naia.org.

President, Chief Executive Officer: Steve Baker. **Director, Championships:** Lori Thomas. **Administrators, Championship Events:** Ruth Feldblum, Scott McClure. **Sports Information Director:** Dawn Harmon.

2005 Championship Tournament

NAIA World Series	Lewiston, ID, May 27-June 3

NATIONAL JUNIOR COLLEGE ATHLETIC ASSOCIATION

Mailing Address: 1755 Telstar Dr., Suite 103, Colorado Springs, CO 80920. **Telephone:** (719) 590-9788. **FAX:** (719) 590-7324. **Website:** www.njcaa.org.

Executive Director: Wayne Baker. **Director, Division I Baseball Tournament:** Jamie Hamilton. **Director, Division II Baseball Tournament:** John Daigle. **Director, Division III Baseball Tournament:** Charles Adams.

2005 Championship Tournaments
Division I

World Series	Grand Junction, CO, May 28-June 4

Division II

World Series	Millington, TN, May 28-June 3

Division III

World Series	Glens Falls, NY, May 21-27

CALIFORNIA COMMUNITY COLLEGE COMMISSION ON ATHLETICS

Mailing Address: 2017 O St., Sacramento, CA 95814. **Telephone:** (916) 444-1600. **FAX:** (916) 444-2616. **E-Mail Address:** info@coasports.org. **Website:** www.coasports.org.

Commissioner of Athletics: Joanne Fortunato. **Associate Commissioner, Athletics:** Stuart Van Horn. **Director, Sports Information:** David Eadie.

2005 Championship Tournament

State Championship	Fresno City College, May 28-30

NORTHWEST ATHLETIC ASSOCIATION OF COMMUNITY COLLEGES

Mailing Address: 1800 E. McLoughlin Blvd., Vancouver, WA 98663. **Telephone:** (360) 992-2833. **FAX:** ((360) 696-6210. **Website:** www.nwaacc.org.

Executive Director: Dick McClain.

2005 Championship Tournament

NWCCAA Championship .... Longview, WA, May 26-30

AMERICAN BASEBALL COACHES ASSOCIATION

Office Address: 108 S. University Ave., Suite 3, Mount Pleasant, MI 48858. **Telephone:** (989) 775-3300. **FAX:** (989) 775-3600. **E-Mail Address:** abca@abca.org. **Website:** www.abca.org.

Executive Director: Dave Keilitz. **Assistant to Executive Director:** Betty Rulong. **Membership/Convention Coordinator:** Nick Phillips. **Assistant Coordinator:** Juahn Clark.

Chairman: Glen Tuckett (Brigham Young University). **President:** Irish O'Reilly (Lewis).

2006 National Convention: Jan. 5-8 at Chicago (Hyatt Regency Hotel).

NCAA DIVISION I CONFERENCES

AMERICA EAST CONFERENCE

Mailing Address: 10 High St., Suite 860, Boston, MA 02110. **Telephone:** (617) 695-6369. **FAX:** (617) 695-6385. **E-Mail Address:** bourque@americaeast.com. **Website:** www.americaeast.com.

Baseball Members (First Year): Albany (2002), Binghamton (2002), Hartford (1990), Maine (1990), Maryland-Baltimore County (2004), Northeastern (1990), Stony Brook (2002), Vermont (1990).

Assistant Commissioner/Communications: Matt Bourque.

2005 Tournament: Four teams, double-elimination. May 26-28 at Burlington, VT (University of Vermont).

ATLANTIC COAST CONFERENCE

Office Address: 4512 Weybridge Lane, Greensboro, NC 27407. **Mailing Address:** P.O. Drawer ACC, Greensboro, NC 27417. **Telephone:** (336) 851-6062. **FAX:** (336) 854-8797. **E-Mail Address:** ayakola@theacc.org. **Website:** www.theacc.com.

Baseball Members (First Year): Clemson (1953), Duke (1953), Florida State (1992), Georgia Tech (1980), Maryland (1953), Miami (2005), North Carolina (1953), North Carolina State (1953), Virginia (1953), Virginia Tech (2005), Wake Forest (1953).

Director of Public Relations: Amy Yakola.

2005 Tournament: Eleven teams, double-elimination. May 23-29 at Jacksonville, FL (The Baseball Grounds of Jacksonville).

ATLANTIC SUN CONFERENCE

Mailing Address: 3370 Vineville Ave., Suite 108-B, Macon, GA 31204.

Telephone: (478) 474-3394. **FAX:** (478) 474-4272. **E-Mail Address:** dpierce@atlanticsun.org. **Website:** www.atlanticsun.org.

Baseball Members (First Year): Belmont (2002), Campbell (1994), Central Florida (1992), Florida Atlantic (1993), Gardner-Webb (2003), Georgia State (1983), Jacksonville (1999), Lipscomb (1994), Mercer (1978), Stetson (1985), Troy (1998).

Assistant Commissioner, Media/Championships: Devlin Pierce. **Assistant Director, Communications:** Mike Holmes.

2005 Tournament: Six teams, double-elimination. May 25-28 at DeLand, FL (Stetson University).

ATLANTIC 10 CONFERENCE

Mailing Address: 230 S. Broad St., Suite 1700, Philadelphia, PA 19102. **Telephone:** (215) 545-6678. **FAX:** (215) 545-3342. **E-Mail Address:** shaug@atlantic10.org. **Website:** www.atlantic10.org.

Baseball Members (First Year): East—Fordham (1996), Massachusetts (1977), Rhode Island (1981), Saint Joseph's (1983), St. Bonaventure (1980), Temple (1983). **West**—Dayton (1996), Duquesne (1977), George Washington (1977), LaSalle (1996), Richmond (2002), Xavier (1996).

Director, Baseball Communications: Stephen Haug.

2005 Tournament: Six teams, double-elimination. May 25-28 at Dayton, OH (Fifth Third Field).

BIG EAST CONFERENCE

Mailing Address: 222 Richmond St., Suite 110, Providence, RI 02903. **Telephone:** (401) 453-0660. **FAX:** (401) 751-8540. **E-Mail Address:** jgust@bigeast.org. **Website:** www.bigeast.org.

Baseball Members (First Year): Boston College (1985), Connecticut (1985), Georgetown (1985), Notre Dame (1996), Pittsburgh (1985), Rutgers (1996), St. John's (1985), Seton Hall (1985), Villanova (1985), West Virginia (1996).

Director, Communications: John Gust.

2005 Championship: Four teams, double-elimination. May 26-28 at Bridgewater, NJ (Commerce Bank Ballpark).

BIG SOUTH CONFERENCE

Mailing Address: 6428 Bannington Dr., Suite A, Charlotte, NC 28226. **Telephone:** (704) 341-7990. **FAX:** (704) 341-7991. **E-Mail Address:** marks@bigsouth.org. **Website:** www.bigsouthsports.com.

Baseball Members (First Year): Birmingham-Southern (2002), Charleston Southern (1983), Coastal Carolina (1983), High Point (1999), Liberty (1991), UNC Asheville (1985), Radford (1983), Virginia Military Institute (2004), Winthrop (1983).

Director, Public Relations: Mark Simpson.

2005 Tournament: Six teams, double-elimination. May 25-28 at Conway, SC (Coastal Carolina University).

BIG TEN CONFERENCE

Mailing Address: 1500 W. Higgins Rd., Park Ridge, IL 60068. **Telephone:** (847) 696-1010. **FAX:** (847) 696-1110. **E-Mail Address:** schipman@bigten.org. **Website:** www.bigten.org.

Baseball Members (First Year): Illinois (1896), Indiana (1906), Iowa (1906), Michigan (1896), Michigan State (1950), Minnesota (1906), Northwestern (1898), Ohio State (1913), Penn State (1992), Purdue (1906).
Director, Communications: Scott Chipman.
2005 Tournament: Six teams, double-elimination. May 25-28 at regular-season champion.

BIG 12 CONFERENCE
Mailing Address: 2201 Stemmons Freeway, 28th Floor, Dallas, TX 75207. **Telephone:** (214) 753-0102. **FAX:** (214) 753-0145. **E-Mail Address:** bo@big12sports.com. **Website:** www.big12sports.com.
Baseball Members (First Year): Baylor (1997), Kansas (1997), Kansas State (1997), Missouri (1997), Nebraska (1997), Oklahoma (1997), Oklahoma State (1997), Texas (1997), Texas A&M (1997), Texas Tech (1997).
Sports Information Director: Bo Carter.
2005 Tournament: Eight teams, double-elimination. May 25-29 at Oklahoma City, OK (SBC Bricktown Park).

BIG WEST CONFERENCE
Mailing Address: 2 Corporate Park, Suite 206, Irvine, CA 92606. **Telephone:** (949) 261-2525. **FAX:** (949) 261-2528. **E-Mail Address:** dcouch@bigwest.org. **Website:** www.bigwest.org.
Baseball Members (First Year): Cal Poly (1997), UC Irvine (2002), UC Riverside (2002), UC Santa Barbara (1970), Cal State Fullerton (1975), Cal State Northridge (2001), Long Beach State (1970), Pacific (1972).
Assistant Director, Information: Darcy Couch.
2005 Tournament: None.

COLONIAL ATHLETIC ASSOCIATION
Mailing Address: 8625 Patterson Ave., Richmond, VA 23229. **Telephone:** (804) 754-1616. **FAX:** (804) 754-1830. **E-Mail Address:** rwashburn@caasports.com. **Website:** www.caasports.com.
Baseball Members (First Year): Delaware (2002), George Mason (1986), Hofstra (2002), James Madison (1986), UNC Wilmington (1986), Old Dominion (1992), Towson (2002), Virginia Commonwealth (1996), William & Mary (1986).
Sports Information Director: Rob Washburn.
2005 Tournament: Six teams, double-elimination. May 25-28 at Wilmington, NC (UNC Wilmington).

CONFERENCE USA
Mailing Address: 5201 N. O'Connor Blvd., Suite 300, Irving, TX 75039. **Telephone:** (214) 774-1300. **FAX:** (214) 496-0055. **E-Mail Address:** rdanderson@c-usa.org. **Website:** www.c-usasports.com.
Baseball Members (First Year): Alabama-Birmingham (1996), Charlotte (1996), Cincinnati (1996), East Carolina (2002), Houston (1997), Louisville (1996), Memphis (1996), Saint Louis (1996), South Florida (1996), Southern Mississippi (1996), Texas Christian (2002), Tulane (1996).
Assistant Commissioner, Media Relations: Russell Anderson.
2005 Tournament: Eight teams, double-elimination. May 25-29 at Hattiesburg, MS (Southern Mississippi).

HORIZON LEAGUE
Mailing Address: 201 S. Capitol Ave., Suite 500, Indianapolis, IN 46225.
Telephone: (317) 237-5622. **FAX:** (317) 237-5620. **E-Mail Address:** wroleson@horizonleague.org. **Website:** www.horizonleague.org.
Baseball Members (First Year): Butler (1979), Cleveland State (1994), Illinois-Chicago (1994), Wisconsin-Milwaukee (1994), Wright State (1994), Youngstown State (2002).
Director, Communications: Will Roleson.
2005 Tournament: Six teams, double-elimination. May 25-29 at Indianapolis, IN (Victory Field).

IVY LEAGUE
Mailing Address: 228 Alexander Rd., Second Floor, Princeton, NJ 08544.
Telephone: (609) 258-6426. **FAX:** (609) 258-1690. **E-Mail Address:** info@ivyleaguesports.com. **Website:** www.ivyleaguesports.com.
Baseball Members (First Year): Rolfe—Brown (1948), Dartmouth (1930), Harvard (1948), Yale (1930). **Gehrig**—Columbia (1930), Cornell (1930), Pennsylvania (1930), Princeton (1930).
Assistants, Public Information: Tyson Hubbard, Eddy Lentz.
2005 Tournament: Best-of-3 series between division champions. May 7-8 at team with best overall record.

METRO ATLANTIC ATHLETIC CONFERENCE
Mailing Address: 712 Amboy Ave., Edison, NJ 08837. **Telephone:** (732) 738-5455. **FAX:** (732) 738-8366. **E-Mail Address:** jill.skotarczak@maac.org. **Website:** www.maacsports.com.
Baseball Members (First Year): Canisius (1990), Fairfield (1982), Iona (1982), LeMoyne (1990), Manhattan (1982), Marist (1998), Niagara (1990), Rider (1998), St. Peter's (1982), Siena (1990).
Director, Media Relations: Jill Skotarczak
2005 Tournament: Four teams, double-elimination. May 26-28 at Fishkill, NY (Dutchess Stadium).

MID-AMERICAN CONFERENCE
Mailing Address: 24 Public Square, 15th Floor, Cleveland, OH 44113. **Telephone:** (216) 566-4622. **FAX:** (216) 858-9622. **E-Mail Address:** bmcgowan@mac-sports.com. **Website:** www.mac-sports.com.
Baseball Members (First Year): East—Akron (1992), Buffalo (2001), Kent State (1951), Marshall (1997), Miami (1947), Ohio (1946). **West**—Ball State (1973), Bowling Green State (1952), Central Michigan (1971), Eastern Michigan (1971), Northern Illinois (1997), Toledo (1950), Western Michigan (1947).
Associate Director, Media Relations: Bryan McGowan.
2005 Tournament: Six teams (top two in each division, two wild-card teams with next best conference winning per-

centage), double-elimination. May 25-28 at team with best conference winning percentage.

MID-CONTINENT CONFERENCE
Mailing Address: 340 W. Butterfield Rd., Suite 3-D, Elmhurst, IL 60126. **Telephone:** (630) 516-0661. **FAX:** (630) 516-0673. **E-Mail Address:** petersen@mid-con.com. **Website:** www.mid-con.com.
Baseball Members (First Year): Centenary (2004), Chicago State (1994), Oakland (2000), Oral Roberts (1998), Southern Utah (2000), Valparaiso (1984), Western Illinois (1984).
Director, Media Relations: Kristina Petersen.
2005 Tournament: Four teams, double-elimination. May 26-28 at Tulsa, OK (Oral Roberts University).

MID-EASTERN ATHLETIC CONFERENCE
Mailing Address: 102 N. Elm St., Suite 401, P.O. Box 21205, Greensboro, NC 27420. **Telephone:** (336) 275-9961. **FAX:** (336) 275-9964. **E-Mail Address:** jinksm@themeac.com. **Website:** www.meacsports.com.
Baseball Members (First Year): Bethune-Cookman (1979), Coppin State (1985), Delaware State (1970), Florida A&M (1979), Maryland-Eastern Shore (1970), Norfolk State (1998), North Carolina A&T (1970).
Director, Media Relations: Michelle Jinks.
2005 Tournament: Seven teams, double-elimination. April 29-May 1 at Orlando, FL (Disney Wide World of Sports Complex).

MISSOURI VALLEY CONFERENCE
Mailing Address: 1818 Chouteau Ave., St. Louis, MO 63103. **Telephone:** (314) 421-0339. **FAX:** (314) 421-3505. **E-Mail Address:** fricke@mvc.org. **Website:** www.mvc.org.
Baseball Members (First Year): Bradley (1955), Creighton (1976), Evansville (1994), Illinois State (1980), Indiana State (1976), Northern Iowa (1991), Southern Illinois (1974), Southwest Missouri State (1990), Wichita State (1945).
Assistant Director, Communications: Erica Fricke.
2005 Tournament: Six teams, double-elimination. May 25-28 at Wichita, KS (Wichita State University).

MOUNTAIN WEST CONFERENCE
Mailing Address: 15455 Gleneagle Dr., Suite 200B, Colorado Springs, CO 80921. **Telephone:** (719) 488-4040. **FAX:** (719) 487-7241. **E-Mail Address:** medge@TheMWC.com. **Website:** www.TheMWC.com.
Baseball Members (First Year): Air Force (2000), Brigham Young (2000), Nevada-Las Vegas (2000), New Mexico (2000), San Diego State (2000), Utah (2000).
Assistant Director, Communications: Marlon Edge.
2005 Tournament: Six teams, double-elimination. May 25-28 at Salt Lake City, UT (Franklin Covey Field).

NORTHEAST CONFERENCE
Mailing Address: 200 Cottontail Lane, Vantage Court North, Somerset, NJ 08873. **Telephone:** (732) 469-0440. **FAX:** (732) 469-0744. **E-Mail Address:** rratner@northeastconference.org. **Website:** www.northeastconference.org.
Baseball Members (First Year): Central Connecticut State (1999), Fairleigh Dickinson (1981), Long Island (1981), Monmouth (1985), Mount St. Mary's (1989), Quinnipiac (1999), Sacred Heart (2000), St. Francis, N.Y. (1981), Wagner (1981).
Associate Commissioner: Ron Ratner.
2005 Tournament: Four teams, double-elimination. May 20-22 at Lakewood, NJ (First Energy Park).

OHIO VALLEY CONFERENCE
Mailing Address: 215 Centerview Dr., Suite 115, Brentwood, TN 37027. **Telephone:** (615) 371-1698. **FAX:** (615) 371-1788. **E-Mail Address:** kmelcher@ovc.org. **Website:** www.ovcsports.com.
Baseball Members (First Year): Austin Peay (1962), Eastern Illinois (1996), Eastern Kentucky (1948), Jacksonville State (2003), Morehead State (1948), Murray State (1948), Samford (2003), Southeast Missouri State (1991), Tennessee-Martin (1992), Tennessee Tech (1949).
Assistant Commissioner: Kim Melcher.
2005 Tournament: Six teams, double-elimination. May 25-28 at Paducah, KY (Brooks Stadium).

PACIFIC-10 CONFERENCE
Mailing Address: 800 S. Broadway, Suite 400, Walnut Creek, CA 94596. **Telephone:** (925) 932-4411. **FAX:** (925) 932-4601. **E-Mail Address:** ncohan@pac-10.org. **Website:** www.pac-10.org.
Baseball Members (First Year): Arizona (1979), Arizona State (1979), California (1916), UCLA (1928), Oregon State (1916), Southern California (1922), Stanford (1917), Washington (1916), Washington State (1917).
Public Relations Intern: Noah Cohan.
2005 Tournament: None.

PATRIOT LEAGUE
Mailing Address: 3773 Corporate Pkwy., Suite 190, Center Valley, PA 18034. **Telephone:** (610) 289-1950. **FAX:** (610) 289-1952. **E-Mail Address:** jsiegel@patriotleague.com. **Website:** www.patriotleague.com.
Baseball Members (First Year): Army (1993), Bucknell (1991), Holy Cross (1991), Lafayette (1991), Lehigh (1991), Navy (1993).
Assistant Director, Media Relations: Jessica Siegel.
2005 Tournament: Top three teams; No. 2 plays No. 3 in one-game playoff. Winner faces No. 1 team in best-of-3 series at No. 1 seed, May 14-15.

SOUTHEASTERN CONFERENCE
Mailing Address: 2201 Richard Arrington Blvd. N., Birmingham, AL 35203. **Telephone:** (205) 458-3000. **FAX:** (205) 458-3030. **E-Mail Address:** cdunlap@sec.org. **Website:** www.secsports.com.

Baseball Members (First Year): East—Florida (1933), Georgia (1933), Kentucky (1933), South Carolina (1992), Tennessee (1933), Vanderbilt (1933). West—Alabama (1933), Arkansas (1992), Auburn (1933), Louisiana State (1933), Mississippi (1933), Mississippi State (1933).
Assistant Director, Media Relations: Chuck Dunlap.
2005 Tournament: Eight teams, modified double-elimination. May 25-29 at Birmingham, AL (Hoover Metropolitan Stadium).

SOUTHERN CONFERENCE
Mailing Address: 702 N. Pine St., Spartanburg, SC 29303. Telephone: (864) 591-5100. FAX: (864) 591-3448. E-Mail Address: sshutt@socon.org. Website: www.soconsports.com.
Baseball Members (First Year): Appalachian State (1971), Charleston (1998), The Citadel (1936), Davidson (1991), East Tennessee State (1978), Elon (2004), Furman (1936), Georgia Southern (1991), UNC Greensboro (1997), Western Carolina (1976), Wofford (1997).
Associate Commissioner, Public Affairs: Steve Shutt.
2005 Tournament: Eight teams, double-elimination. May 25-28 at Charleston, SC (The Citadel).

SOUTHLAND CONFERENCE
Mailing Address: 1700 Alma Dr., Suite 550, Plano, TX 75075. Telephone: (972) 422-9500. FAX: (972) 422-9225. E-Mail Address: bludlow@southland.org. Website: www.southland.org.
Baseball Members (First Year): Lamar (1999), Louisiana-Monroe (1983), McNeese State (1973), Nicholls State (1992), Northwestern State (1988), Sam Houston State (1988), Southeastern Louisiana (1998), Texas State (1988), Texas-Arlington (1964), Texas-San Antonio (1992).
Baseball Contact/Assistant Commissioner: Bruce Ludlow.
2005 Tournament: Six teams, double-elimination. May 25-28 at Natchitoches, LA (Northwestern State University).

SOUTHWESTERN ATHLETIC CONFERENCE
Mailing Address: A.G. Gaston Building, 1527 Fifth Ave. N., Birmingham, AL 35203. Telephone: (205) 252-7573, ext. 111. FAX: (205) 252-9997. E-Mail Address: w.dooley@swac.org. Website: www.swac.org.
Baseball Members (First Year): East—Alabama A&M (2000), Alabama State (1982), Alcorn State (1962), Jackson State (1958), Mississippi Valley State (1968). West—Arkansas-Pine Bluff (1999), Grambling State (1958), Prairie View A&M (1920), Southern (1934), Texas Southern (1954).
Assistant Commissioner, Media Relations: Wallace Dooley.
2005 Tournament: Six teams, double-elimination. May 6-9 at Houston, TX (Baseball USA—The Yard).

SUN BELT CONFERENCE
Mailing Address: 601 Poydras St., Suite 2355, New Orleans, LA 70130.
Telephone: (504) 299-9066. FAX: (504) 299-9068. E-Mail Address: broussard@sunbeltsports.org. Website: www.sunbeltsports.org.
Baseball Members (First Year): Arkansas-Little Rock (1991), Arkansas State (1991), Florida International (1999), Louisiana-Lafayette (1991), Middle Tennessee (2001), New Mexico State (2001), New Orleans (1976, 1991), South Alabama (1976), Western Kentucky (1982).
Director, Media Relations: Rob Broussard.
2005 Tournament: Eight teams, double-elimination. May 25-28 at Miami, FL (Florida International University).

WEST COAST CONFERENCE
Mailing Address: 1250 Bayhill Dr., Suite 101, San Bruno, CA 94066. Telephone: (650) 873-8622. FAX: (650) 873-7846. E-Mail Addresses: jwilson@westcoast.org; estyer@westcoast.org. Website: www.wccsports.com.
Baseball Members (First Year): Gonzaga (1996), Loyola Marymount (1968), Pepperdine (1968), Portland (1996), Saint Mary's (1968), San Diego (1979), San Francisco (1968), Santa Clara (1968).
Director, Communications: Joe Wilson. Assistant Director, Communications: Ellen Styer.
2005 Tournament: Division champions meet in best-of-3 series, May 27-29.

WESTERN ATHLETIC CONFERENCE
Mailing Address: 9250 East Costilla Ave., Suite 300, Englewood, CO 80112. Telephone: (303) 799-9221. FAX: (303) 799-3888. E-Mail Address: wac@wac.org. Website: www.wacsports.com.
Baseball Members (First Year): Fresno State (1993), Hawaii (1980), Louisiana Tech (2002), Nevada (2001), Rice (1997), San Jose State (1997).
Commissioner: Karl Benson. Senior Associate Commissioner: Jeff Hurd. Director, Sports Information: Dave Chaffin.
2005 Tournament: None.

NCAA DIVISION II CONFERENCES

CALIFORNIA COLLEGIATE ATHLETIC ASSOCIATION
Mailing Address: 800 S. Broadway, Suite 309, Walnut Creek, CA 94596. Telephone: (925) 472-8299. FAX: (925) 472-8887. Website: www.goccaa.org.
Baseball Members: UC San Diego, Cal State Dominguez Hills, Cal State Los Angeles, Cal Poly Pomona, Cal State San Bernardino, Cal State Stanislaus, Chico State, San Francisco State, Sonoma State.

CAROLINAS-VIRGINIA ATHLETIC CONFERENCE
Mailing Address: 26 Cub Dr., Thomasville, NC 27360. Telephone: (336) 884-0482. FAX: (336) 499-6031. E-Mail

Address: CVAC@triad.rr.com. **Website:** www.cvac.net.
   Baseball Members: Anderson (S.C.), Barton, Belmont Abbey, Coker, Erskine, Limestone, Mount Olive, Pfeiffer, St. Andrews Presbyterian.

CENTRAL ATLANTIC COLLEGIATE CONFERENCE
Mailing Address: NJIT Sports Information, University Heights, Newark, NJ 07102. **Telephone:** (973) 596-8324. **FAX:** (973) 596-8440. **E-Mail Address:** mentone@adm.njit.edu. **Website:** www.caccathletics.org.
   Baseball Members: Bloomfield, Caldwell, Dominican (N.Y.), Felician, New Jersey Institute of Technology, Nyack, University of the Sciences/Philadelphia, Teikyo Post, Wilmington (Del.).

CENTRAL INTERCOLLEGIATE ATHLETIC ASSOCIATION
Mailing Address: 303 Butler Farm Rd., Suite 102, Hampton, VA 23666. **Telephone:** (757) 865-0071. **FAX:** (757) 865-8436. **E-Mail Address:** TheCiaa@aol.com. **Website:** www.theciaa.com.
   Baseball Members: Elizabeth City State, Saint Augustine's, Saint Paul's, Shaw, Virginia State.

GREAT LAKES INTERCOLLEGIATE ATHLETIC CONFERENCE
Mailing Address: 1110 Washington Ave., Bay City, MI 48708. **Telephone:** (989) 894-2529. **FAX:** (989) 894-2825. **E-Mail Address:** tomjb@gliac.org. **Website:** www.gliac.org.
   Baseball Members: Ashland, Findlay, Gannon, Grand Valley State, Hillsdale, Mercyhurst, Northwood (Mich.), Saginaw Valley State, Wayne State (Mich.).

GREAT LAKES VALLEY CONFERENCE
Mailing Address: Pan Am Plaza, Suite 560, 201 S. Capitol Ave., Indianapolis, IN 46225. **Telephone:** (317) 237-5636. **FAX:** (317) 237-5632. **E-Mail Address:** jim@glvc-sports.org. **Website:** www.glvcsports.com.
   Baseball Members: Bellarmine, Indianapolis, Kentucky Wesleyan, Lewis, Missouri-Saint Louis, Northern Kentucky, Quincy, Saint Joseph's (Ind.), Southern Illinois-Edwardsville, Southern Indiana, Wisconsin-Parkside.

GULF SOUTH CONFERENCE
Mailing Address: 2101 Providence Park, Suite 200, Birmingham, AL 35242. **Telephone:** (205) 991-9880. **FAX:** (205) 437-0505. **E-Mail Address:** gcsid@mindspring.com. **Website:** www.gulfsouthconference.org.
   Baseball Members: Alabama-Huntsville, Arkansas-Monticello, Arkansas Tech, Central Arkansas, Christian Brothers, Delta State, Harding, Henderson State, Lincoln Memorial, Montevallo, North Alabama, Ouachita Baptist, Southern Arkansas, Valdosta State, West Alabama, West Florida, West Georgia.

HEARTLAND CONFERENCE
Mailing Address: P.O. Box 131569, Tyler, TX 75713. **Telephone:** (877) 505-6509. **FAX:** (877) 505-9542. **E-Mail Address:** peyton@heartlandsports.org. **Website:** www.heartlandsports.org.
   Baseball Members: Incarnate Word, Lincoln (Mo.), Rockhurst, St. Edward's, St. Mary's (Texas).

LONE STAR CONFERENCE
Mailing Address: 1221 W. Campbell Rd., No. 245, Richardson, TX 75080. **Telephone:** (972) 234-0033. **FAX:** (972) 234-4110. **E-Mail Address:** wagnons@lonestarconference.org. **Website:** www.lonestarconference.org.
   Baseball Members: Abilene Christian, Angelo State, Cameron, Central Oklahoma, East Central, Eastern New Mexico, Northeastern State, Southeastern Oklahoma State, Southwestern Oklahoma State, Tarleton State, Texas A&M-Kingsville, West Texas A&M.

MID-AMERICA INTERCOLLEGIATE ATHLETICS ASSOCIATION
Mailing Address: 10551 Barkley, Suite 501, Overland Park, KS 66212. **Telephone:** (913) 341-3839/3080. **FAX:** (913) 341-5887/2995. **E-Mail Address:** rmcfillen@themiaa.com. **Website:** www.themiaa.com.
   Baseball Members: Central Missouri State, Emporia State, Missouri-Rolla, Missouri Southern State, Missouri Western State, Northwest Missouri State, Pittsburg State, Southwest Baptist, Truman State, Washburn.

NEW YORK COLLEGIATE ATHLETIC CONFERENCE
Mailing Address: 24A Village Square, Glen Cove, NY 11542. **Telephone:** (516) 609-2714. **FAX:** (516) 609-0881. **E-Mail Address:** gonycac@hotmail.com. **Website:** www.nycac.net.
   Baseball Members: Adelphi, Bridgeport, Concordia (N.Y.), C.W. Post-Long Island, Dowling, Mercy, Molloy, New Haven, Philadelphia, Queens, St. Thomas Aquinas.

NORTH CENTRAL INTERCOLLEGIATE ATHLETIC CONFERENCE
Mailing Address: Ramkota Hotel, 3200 W. Maple St., Sioux Falls, SD 57107. **Telephone:** (605) 338-0907. **FAX:** (605) 338-1889. **E-Mail Address:** info@northcentralconference.org. **Website:** www.northcentralconference.org.
   Baseball Members: Augustana (S.D.), Minnesota-Duluth, Minnesota State-Mankato, Nebraska-Omaha, North Dakota, St. Cloud State.

NORTHEAST-10 CONFERENCE
Mailing Address: 16 Belmont St., South Easton, MA 02375. **Telephone:** (508) 230-9844. **FAX:** (508) 230-9845. **E-Mail:** kbelbin@northeast10.org. **Website:** www.northeast10.org.
   Baseball Members: American International, Assumption, Bentley, Bryant, Franklin Pierce, Massachusetts-Lowell, Merrimack, Pace, Saint Anselm, Saint Rose, Southern Connecticut State, Southern New Hampshire, Stonehill.

NORTHERN SUN INTERCOLLEGIATE CONFERENCE
Mailing Address: 161 Anthony Ave., Suite 920, St. Paul, MN 55103. **Telephone:** (651) 288-4016. **FAX:** (651) 224-8583. **E-Mail:** lind@northernsun.org. **Website:** www.northernsun.org.
   Baseball Members: Bemidji State, Concordia-St. Paul, Minnesota-Crookston, Minnesota State-Moorhead, Northern

State, Southwest Minnesota State, Wayne State (Neb.), Winona State.

PEACH BELT CONFERENCE

Mailing Address: P.O. Box 204290, Augusta, GA 30917. **Telephone:** (706) 860-8499. **FAX:** (706) 650-8113. **E-Mail Address:** sports@peachbelt.com. **Website:** www.peachbelt.com.

Baseball Members: Armstrong Atlantic State, Augusta State, Columbus State, Francis Marion, Georgia College & State, Kennesaw State, Lander, UNC Pembroke, North Florida, South Carolina-Aiken, South Carolina-Upstate.

PENNSYLVANIA STATE ATHLETIC CONFERENCE

Mailing Address: 204 Annex Building, Susquehanna Ave., Lock Haven, PA 17745. **Telephone:** (570) 893-2780. **FAX:** (570) 893-2206. **E-Mail Address:** wadair@lhup.edu. **Website:** www.psacsports.org.

Baseball Members: Bloomsburg, California (Pa.), Clarion, East Stroudsburg, Indiana (Pa.), Kutztown, Lock Haven, Mansfield, Millersville, Shippensburg, Slippery Rock, West Chester.

ROCKY MOUNTAIN ATHLETIC CONFERENCE

Mailing Address: 219 West Colorado Ave., Suite 212, Colorado Springs, CO 80903. **Telephone:** (719) 471-0066. **FAX:** (719) 471-0088. **E-Mail Address:** fitz@rmacsports.org. **Website:** www.rmacsports.org.

Baseball Members: Colorado School of Mines, Colorado State-Pueblo, Fort Hays State, Mesa State, Metro State, Nebraska-Kearney, New Mexico Highlands, Regis.

SOUTH ATLANTIC CONFERENCE

Mailing Address: Gateway Plaza, Suite 130, 226 N. Park Dr., Rock Hill, SC 29730. **Telephone:** (803) 981-5240. **FAX:** (803) 981-9444. **E-Mail Address:** thesac@comporium.net. **Website:** www.thesac.com.

Baseball Members: Carson-Newman, Catawba, Lenoir-Rhyne, Mars Hill, Newberry, Presbyterian, Tusculum, Wingate.

SOUTHERN INTERCOLLEGIATE ATHLETIC CONFERENCE

Mailing Address: 3469 Lawrenceville Hwy., Suite 207, Tucker, GA 30084. **Telephone:** (770) 908-0482. **FAX:** (770) 908-2772. **Website:** www.thesiac.com.

Baseball Members: Albany State (Ga.), Benedict (S.C.), Clark Atlanta, Kentucky State, Lane, LeMoyne-Owen, Miles, Morehouse, Paine, Tuskegee.

SUNSHINE STATE CONFERENCE

Mailing Address: 7061 Grand National Dr., Suite 140, Orlando, FL 32819. **Telephone:** (407) 248-8460. **FAX:** (407) 248-8325. **E-Mail Address:** info@ssconference.org. **Website:** www.ssconference.org.

Baseball Members: Barry, Eckerd, Florida Southern, Florida Tech, Lynn, Nova Southeastern, Rollins, Saint Leo, Tampa.

WEST VIRGINIA INTERCOLLEGIATE ATHLETIC CONFERENCE

Mailing Address: 1422 Main St., Princeton, WV 24740. **Telephone:** (304) 487-6298. **FAX:** (304) 487-6299. **E-Mail Address:** will@wviac.org. **Website:** www.wviac.org.

Baseball Members: Alderson-Broaddus, Bluefield State, Charleston (W.Va.), Concord, Davis & Elkins, Fairmont State, Ohio Valley, Salem International, Shepherd, West Liberty State, West Virginia State, West Virginia University Tech, West Virginia Wesleyan.

*Recruiting coordinator
Provisional Division I status in 2005

AIR FORCE ACADEMY Falcons
Conference: Mountain West.
Mailing Address: 2168 Field House Dr., USAF Academy, CO 80840. **Website:** www.airforcesports.com. **Head Coach:** Mike Hutcheon. **Assistant Coaches:** Marty Nelson, *Ryan Thompson. **Telephone:** (719) 333-7898. ◆ **Baseball SID:** Nick Arseniak. **Telephone:** (719) 333-9251. **FAX:** (719) 333-3798.

AKRON Zips
Conference: Mid-American (East).
Mailing Address: Rhodes Arena, 373 Carroll St., Akron, OH 44325. **Website:** www.gozips.com.
Head Coach: Tim Berenyi. **Assistant Coaches:** Lucas Fry, Trent McIlvain. **Telephone:** (330) 972-7290. ◆ **Baseball SID:** Shawn Nestor. **Telephone:** (330) 972-6292. **FAX:** (330) 374-8844.

ALABAMA Crimson Tide
Conference: Southeastern (West).
Mailing Address: P.O. Box 870391, Tuscaloosa, AL 35487. **Website:** www.rolltide.com.
Head Coach: Jim Wells. **Assistant Coaches:** *Todd Butler, Jim Gatewood, B.J. Green. **Telephone:** (205) 348-6171. ◆ **Baseball SID:** Barry Allen. **Telephone:** (205) 348-6084. **FAX:** (205) 348-8841.
Home Field: Sewell-Thomas Stadium. **Seating Capacity:** 6,118. **Outfield Dimensions:** LF—325, CF—400, RF—325. **Press Box Telephone:** (205) 348-4927.

ALABAMA-BIRMINGHAM Blazers
Conference: Conference USA.
Mailing Address: Bartow Arena, 617 13th St. S., Birmingham, AL 35294. **Website:** www.uabsports.com.
Head Coach: Larry Giangrosso. **Assistant Coach:** Nick Dumas, *Frank Walton. **Telephone:** (205) 934-5181. ◆ **Baseball SID:** Jeremy Hoffman. **Telephone:** (205) 976-2576. **FAX:** (205) 934-7505.
Home Field: Jerry D. Young Memorial Field. **Seating Capacity:** 1,000. **Outfield Dimensions:** LF—330, CF—400, RF—330. **Press Box Telephone:** (205) 934-0200.

ALABAMA A&M Bulldogs
Conference: Southwestern Athletic.
Mailing Address: P.O. Box 1597, Normal, AL 35762. **Website:** www.aamu.edu/PR/sports/athletics.
Head Coach: Thomas Wesley. **Telephone:** (256) 372-4004. ◆ **Baseball SID:** William Bright Jr. **Telephone:** (256) 372-4005. **FAX:** (256) 372-5951.

ALABAMA STATE Hornets
Conference: Southwestern Athletic.
Mailing Address: 915 S. Jackson St., Montgomery, AL 36101. **Website:** www.alasu.edu/asusports.
Head Coach: Larry Watkins. **Telephone:** (334) 229-4228. ◆ **Baseball SID:** Albert Moore. **Telephone:** (334) 229-4511. **FAX:** (334) 229-2971.

ALBANY Great Danes
Conference: America East.
Mailing Address: 1400 Washington Ave., Albany, NY 12222. **Website:** www.albany.edu/sports.
Head Coach: Jon Mueller. **Assistant Coaches:** Garrett Baron, *Mark Lavenia, Matt Quatraro. **Telephone:** (518) 442-3014. ◆ **Baseball SID:** Brianna LaBrecque. **Telephone:** (518) 442-5733. **FAX:** (518) 442-3139.

ALCORN STATE Braves
Conference: Southwestern Athletic.
Mailing Address: 1000 ASU Drive, Alcorn State, MS 39096. **Website:** www.alcorn.edu/athletics.
Head Coach: Willie McGowan. **Assistant Coaches:** *Marqus Johnson, Luis Marquez. **Telephone:** (601) 877-6279. ◆ **Baseball SID:** Tyrone Broxton. **Telephone:** (601) 877-6466. **FAX:** (601) 877-3821.

APPALACHIAN STATE Mountaineers
Conference: Southern.
Mailing Address: Owens Fieldhouse, Boone, NC 28608. **Website:** www.goasu.com.
Head Coach: Chris Pollard. **Assistant Coach:** Andrew See. **Telephone:** (828) 262-6097. ◆ **Baseball SID:** Mike Flynn. **Telephone:** (828) 262-2268. **FAX:** (828) 262-6106.

ARIZONA Wildcats
Conference: Pacific-10.
Mailing Address: Room 106, McKale Center, Tucson, AZ 85716. **Website:** www.arizonaathletics.com.
Head Coach: Andy Lopez. **Assistant Coaches:** Andy Diver, Steve Kling, *Mark Wasikowski. **Telephone:** (520) 621-4102. ◆ **Baseball SID:** Matt Rector. **Telephone:** (520) 621-0914. **FAX:** (520) 621-2681.
Home Field: Jerry Kindall Field at Frank Sancet Stadium. **Seating Capacity:** 6,500. **Outfield Dimensions:** LF—360, CF—400, RF—360. **Press Box Telephone:** (520) 621-4440.

ARIZONA STATE Sun Devils
Conference: Pacific-10.
Mailing Address: Carson Student-Athlete Center, 500 E. Veterans Way, Tempe, AZ 85287. **Website:** www.the-sundevils.com.
Head Coach: Pat Murphy. **Assistant Coaches:** Tim Esmay, Jack Krawczyk, *Jay Sferra. **Telephone:** (480) 965-5717. ◆ **Baseball SID:** Jeff Evans. **Telephone:** (480) 965-6594. **FAX:** (480) 965-5408.
Home Field: Packard Stadium. **Seating Capacity:** 3,879. **Outfield Dimensions:** LF—340, CF—395, RF—340. **Press Box Telephone:** (480) 727-7253.

ARKANSAS Razorbacks
Conference: Southeastern (West).
Mailing Address: P.O. Box 7777, Fayetteville, AR 72702. **Website:** www.hogwired.com.
Head Coach: Dave Van Horn. **Assistant Coaches:** *Matt Deggs, Dave Jorn. **Telephone:** (479) 575-3655. ◆ **Baseball SID:** Josh Maxson. **Telephone:** (479) 575-2751. **FAX:** (479) 575-7481.
Home Field: Baum Stadium. **Seating Capacity:** 10,000. **Outfield Dimensions:** LF—320, CF—400, RF—320. **Press Box Telephone:** (479) 575-4141.

ARKANSAS-LITTLE ROCK Trojans
Conference: Sun Belt.
Mailing Address: 2801 S. University Ave., Little Rock, AR 72204. **Website:** www.ualrtrojans.com.
Head Coach: Brian Rhees. **Assistant Coaches:** *Clint Culbertson, Bobby Pierce. **Telephone:** (501) 663-8095. ◆ **Baseball SID:** John Eckart. **Telephone:** (501) 569-7104. **FAX:** (501) 683-7002.

ARKANSAS-PINE BLUFF Golden Lions
Conference: Southwestern Athletic.
Mailing Address: 1200 N. University Dr., Mail Slot 4805, Pine Bluff, AR 71601. **Website:** www.uapb.edu/athletics.
Head Coach: Elbert Bennett. **Assistant Coach:** *Michael Bumpers. **Telephone:** (870) 575-8938. ◆

Baseball SID: Tamara Williams. **Telephone:** (870) 575-7174. **FAX:** (870) 543-7881.

ARKANSAS STATE Indians
Conference: Sun Belt.
Mailing Address: P.O. Box 1000, State University, AR 72467. **Website:** www.asuindians.com.
Head Coach: Keith Kessinger. **Assistant Coaches:** Brad Henderson, *Christian Ostrander. **Telephone:** (870) 972-2700. ◆ **Baseball SID:** Matt McCollester. **Telephone:** (870) 972-2541. **FAX:** (870) 972-2756.

ARMY Cadets
Conference: Patriot.
Mailing Address: 639 Howard Rd., West Point, NY 10996. **Website:** www.goarmysports.com.
Head Coach: Joe Sottolano. **Assistant Coaches:** Brendan Dougherty, Fritz Hamburg. **Telephone:** (845) 938-3712. ◆ **Baseball SID:** Bob Beretta. **Telephone:** (845) 938-6416. **FAX:** (845) 446-2556.

AUBURN Tigers
Conference: Southeastern (West).
Mailing Address: Auburn Athletic Department, Corner of Samford & Donahue, Auburn, AL 36830. **Website:** www.auburntigers.com.
Head Coach: Tom Slater. **Assistant Coaches:** *Chris Finwood, Matt Myers, Karl Nonemaker. **Telephone:** (334) 844-4975. ◆ **Baseball SID:** Kirk Sampson. **Telephone:** (334) 844-9803. **FAX:** (334) 844-9807.
Home Field: Plainsman Park. **Seating Capacity:** 4,096. **Outfield Dimensions:** LF—315, CF—385, RF—331. **Press Box Telephone:** (334) 844-4138.

AUSTIN PEAY STATE Governors
Conference: Ohio Valley.
Mailing Address: P.O. Box 4515, Clarksville, TN 37044. **Website:** www.apsu.edu/letsgopeay.
Head Coach: Gary McClure. **Assistant Coaches:** Casey Callaway, *Brian Hetland. **Telephone:** (931) 221-6266. ◆ **Baseball SID:** Cody Bush. **Telephone:** (931) 221-7561. **FAX:** (931) 221-7562.

BALL STATE Cardinals
Conference: Mid-American (West).
Mailing Address: HP 253, Ball State University, Muncie, IN 47306. **Website:** www.ballstatesports.com.
Head Coach: Greg Beals. **Assistant Coaches:** *Clint Albert, Mike Stafford. **Telephone:** (765) 285-8226. ◆ **Baseball SID:** Brad Caudill. **Telephone:** (765) 285-8242. **FAX:** (765) 285-8929.
Home Field: Ball Diamond. **Seating Capacity:** 1,700. **Outfield Dimensions:** LF—330, CF—400, RF—330. **Press Box Telephone:** (765) 285-8932.

BAYLOR Bears
Conference: Big 12.
Mailing Address: 150 Bear Run, Waco, TX 76711. **Website:** www.BaylorBears.com.
Head Coach: Steve Smith. **Assistant Coaches:** Chris Berry, Steve Johnigan, *Mitch Thompson. **Telephone:** (254) 710-3029. ◆ **Baseball SID:** Larry Little. **Telephone:** (254) 710-4389. **FAX:** (254) 710-1369.
Home Field: Baylor Ballpark at Ferrell Field. **Seating Capacity:** 5,000. **Outfield Dimensions:** LF—330, CF—400, RF—330. **Press Box Telephone:** (254) 754-5546.

BELMONT Bruins
Conference: Atlantic Sun.
Mailing Address: 1900 Belmont Blvd., Nashville, TN 37221. **Website:** www.belmont.edu/athletics.
Head Coach: Dave Jarvis. **Assistant Coaches:** Matt Barnett, *Jason Stein. **Telephone:** (615) 460-6166. ◆

Baseball SID: Ryan Herzberg. **Telephone:** (615) 460-8023. **FAX:** (615) 460-5584.

BETHUNE-COOKMAN Wildcats
Conference: Mid-Eastern Athletic.
Mailing Address: 640 Dr. Mary McLeod Bethune Blvd., Daytona Beach, FL 32114. **Website:** www.cookman.edu/athletics.
Head Coach: Mervyl Melendez. **Assistant Coaches:** Willie Brown, *Joel Sanchez, Jose Vazquez. **Telephone:** (386) 481-2224. ◆ **Baseball SID:** Opio Mashariki. **Telephone:** (386) 481-2206. **FAX:** (386) 481-2238.

BINGHAMTON Bearcats
Conference: America East.
Mailing Address: West Gym Office #25, Binghamton, NY 13902. **Website:** athletics.binghamton.edu.
Head Coach: Tim Sinicki. **Assistant Coaches:** *Mike Collins, Tim Harkness. **Telephone:** (607) 777-5808. **Baseball SID:** John Hartrick. **Telephone:** (607) 777-6800. **FAX:** (607) 777-4597.

BIRMINGHAM-SOUTHERN Panthers
Conference: Big South.
Mailing Address: P.O. Box 549041, Birmingham, AL 35254. **Website:** www.bscsports.net.
Head Coach: Brian Shoop. **Assistant Coaches:** *Doug Kovash, Perry Roth, Jared Walker. **Telephone:** (205) 226-4797. **Baseball SID:** Fred Sington. **Telephone:** (205) 226-7736. **FAX:** (205) 226-3049.

BOSTON COLLEGE Eagles
Conference: Big East.
Mailing Address: 140 Commonwealth Ave., Chestnut Hill, MA 02467. **Website:** www.bceagles.com.
Head Coach: Pete Hughes. **Assistant Coaches:** *Mikio Aoki, Steve Englert. **Telephone:** (617) 552-1131. ◆ **Baseball SID:** Josh Centor. **Telephone:** (617) 552-4508. **FAX:** (617) 552-4903.
Home Field: Commander Shea Field. **Seating Capacity:** 1,000. **Outfield Dimensions:** LF—330, CF—400, RF—320. **Press Box Telephone:** (617) 552-0119.

BOWLING GREEN STATE Falcons
Conference: Mid-American (West).
Mailing Address: 201 Perry Stadium East, Bowling Green, OH 43403. **Website:** www.bgsufalcons.com.
Head Coach: Danny Schmitz. **Assistant Coaches:** *Tod Brown, Dave Whitmire. **Telephone:** (419) 372-7065. ◆ **Baseball SID:** Kris Kamann. **Telephone:** (419) 372-7077. **FAX:** (419) 372-6015.
Home Field: Warren Steller Field. **Seating Capacity:** 1,100. **Outfield Dimensions:** LF—340, CF—400, RF—340. **Press Box Telephone:** (419) 372-1234.

BRADLEY Braves
Conference: Missouri Valley.
Mailing Address: 1501 W. Bradley Ave., Peoria, IL 61625. **Website:** www.bubraves.com.
Head Coach: Dewey Kalmer. **Assistant Coaches:** Mike Dunne, John Dyke, *Marc Wagner. **Telephone:** (309) 677-2644. ◆ **Baseball SID:** Bobby Parker. **Telephone:** (309) 677-2624. **FAX:** (309) 677-3626.
Home Field: O'Brien Field. **Seating Capacity:** 8,000. **Outfield Dimensions:** LF—310, CF—400, RF—310. **Press Box Telephone:** (309) 680-4045.

BRIGHAM YOUNG Cougars
Conference: Mountain West.
Mailing Address: 30 SFH, Brigham Young University, Provo, UT 84602. **Website:** www.byucougars.com.
Head Coach: Vance Law. **Assistant Coaches:** Bobby Applegate, *Ryan Roberts. **Telephone:** (801) 378-5049.

◆ **Baseball SID:** Ralph Zobell. **Telephone:** (801) 422-9769. **FAX:** (801) 422-0633.
Home Field: Larry Miller Field. **Seating Capacity:** 2,204. **Outfield Dimensions:** LF—345, CF—400, RF—345. **Press Box Telephone:** (801) 378-4041.

BROWN Bears
Conference: Ivy League (Rolfe).
Mailing Address: Brown University, Box 1932, Providence, RI 02912. **Website:** www.BrownBears.com.
Head Coach: Marek Drabinski. **Assistant Coaches:** Raphael Cerrato, Jim Foster, Jamie Grillo. **Telephone:** (401) 863-3090. ◆ **Baseball SID:** Kristen DiChiaro. **Telephone:** (401) 863-7014. **FAX:** (401) 863-1436.

BUCKNELL Bison
Conference: Patriot.
Mailing Address: Department of Athletics, Bucknell University, Lewisburg, PA 17837. **Website:** www.bucknellbison.com.
Head Coach: Gene Depew. **Assistant Coaches:** Scott Heather, Brian Hoyt. **Telephone:** (570) 577-3593. ◆ **Baseball SID:** Jess Riden. **Telephone:** (570) 577-3121. **FAX:** (570) 577-1660.

BUFFALO Bulls
Conference: Mid-American (East).
Mailing Address: 175 Alumni Arena, Buffalo, NY 14260. **Website:** www.buffalobulls.com.
Head Coach: Bill Breene. **Assistant Coaches:** Dave Borsuk, *Ron Torgalski. **Telephone:** (716) 645-6808. ◆ **Baseball SID:** Joe Guistina. **Telephone:** (716) 645-5523. **FAX:** (716) 645-6840.

BUTLER Bulldogs
Conference: Horizon.
Mailing Address: 510 W. 49th St., Indianapolis, IN 46208. **Website:** www.butlersports.com.
Head Coach: Steve Farley. **Assistant Coaches:** Dennis Kas, Bob Keeney, Joe Kornokovich. **Telephone:** (317) 940-9721. ◆ **Baseball SID:** Jim McGrath. **Telephone:** (317) 940-9414. **FAX:** (317) 940-9808.

CALIFORNIA Golden Bears
Conference: Pacific-10.
Mailing Address: 210 Memorial Stadium, Berkeley, CA 94720. **Website:** www.calbears.com.
Head Coach: David Esquer. **Assistant Coaches:** Jason Dennis, *Dan Hubbs, Jon Zuber. **Telephone:** (510) 642-9026. ◆ **Baseball SID:** Scott Ball. **Telephone:** (510) 643-1741. **FAX:** (510) 643-7778.
Home Field: Evans Diamond. **Seating Capacity:** 2,500. **Outfield Dimensions:** LF—320, CF—395, RF—320. **Press Box Telephone:** (510) 642-3098.

#UC DAVIS Aggies
Conference: Big West.
Mailing Address: One Shields Ave., Davis, CA 95616. **Website:** www.ucdavisaggies.com.
Head Coach: Rex Peters. **Assistant Coaches:** Lloyd Acosta, Bobby Calderon, *Matt Vaughn. **Telephone:** (530) 752-7513. ◆ **Baseball SID:** Bill Stevens. **Telephone:** (530) 754-5674. **FAX:** (530) 754-5674.
Home Field: Dobbins Stadium. **Seating Capacity:** 2,500. **Outfield Dimensions:** LF—310, CF—400, RF—310. **Press Box Telephone:** Unavailable.

UCLA Bruins
Conference: Pacific-10.
Mailing Address: P.O. Box 24044, Los Angeles, CA 90024. **Website:** www.uclabruins.com.
Head Coach: John Savage. **Assistant Coaches:** Brian Green, Matt Jones, Pat Shine, *Michael Sondheimer.

Telephone: (310) 794-8210. ◆ **Baseball SID:** Bryan DeSena. **Telephone:** (310) 206-4008. **FAX:** (310) 825-8664.
Home Field: Jackie Robinson Stadium. **Seating Capacity:** 1,250. **Outfield Dimensions:** LF—330, CF—390, RF—330. **Press Box Telephone:** (310) 794-8213.

UC IRVINE Anteaters
Conference: Big West.
Mailing Address: 1394 Crawford Hall, Irvine, CA 92697. **Website:** www.athletics.uci.edu.
Head Coach: Dave Serrano. **Assistant Coaches:** Chad Baum, Greg Bergeron, *Sergio Brown. **Telephone:** (949) 824-4292. ◆ **Baseball SID:** Fumi Kimura. **Telephone:** (949) 824-9474. **FAX:** (949) 824-5260.
Home Field: Anteater Stadium. **Seating Capacity:** 3,200. **Outfield Dimensions:** LF—335, CF—405, RF—335. **Press Box Telephone:** (949) 824-9905.

UC RIVERSIDE Highlanders
Conference: Big West.
Mailing Address: 900 University Ave., Riverside, CA 92521. **Website:** www.athletics.ucr.edu.
Head Coach: Doug Smith. **Assistant Coaches:** Randy Betten, *Andrew Checketts, Estevan Valencia. **Telephone:** (909) 787-5441. ◆ **Baseball SID:** Mark Dodson. **Telephone:** (909) 787-5438. **FAX:** (909) 787-5889.
Home Field: Riverside Sports Complex. **Seating Capacity:** 2,500. **Outfield Dimensions:** LF—330, CF—400, RF—330. **Press Box Telephone:** (909) 787-6415.

UC SANTA BARBARA Gauchos
Conference: Big West.
Mailing Address: Robertson Gym, Santa Barbara, CA 93106. **Website:** www.ucsbgauchos.com.
Head Coach: Bob Brontsema. **Assistant Coaches:** John Kirkgard, *Tom Myers, Bob Townsend. **Telephone:** (805) 893-3690. ◆ **Baseball SID:** Bill Mahoney. **Telephone:** (805) 893-3428. **FAX:** (805) 893-4537.
Home Field: Caesar Uyesaka Stadium. **Seating Capacity:** 1,000. **Outfield Dimensions:** LF—335, CF—400, RF—335. **Press Box Telephone:** (805) 893-4671.

CAL POLY Mustangs
Conference: Big West.
Mailing Address: One Grand Ave., San Luis Obispo, CA 93407. **Website:** www.gopoly.com.
Head Coach: Larry Lee. **Assistant Coaches:** Jerry Weinstein, *Jesse Zepeda. **Telephone:** (805) 756-6367. ◆ **Baseball SID:** Eric Burdick. **Telephone:** (805) 756-6550. **FAX:** (805) 756-2650.
Home Field: Robin Baggett Stadium. **Seating Capacity:** 1,734. **Outfield Dimensions:** LF—335, CF—405, RF—335. **Press Box Telephone:** (805) 756-7456.

CAL STATE FULLERTON Titans
Conference: Big West.
Mailing Address: P.O. Box 6810, Fullerton, CA 92834. **Website:** www.titansports.org.
Head Coach: George Horton. **Assistant Coaches:** *Jason Gill, Ted Silva, Rick Vanderhook. **Telephone:** (714) 278-3780. ◆ **Baseball SID:** Michael Greenlee. **Telephone:** (714) 278-3081. **FAX:** (714) 278-3141.
Home Field: Goodwin Field. **Seating Capacity:** 3,500. **Outfield Dimensions:** LF—330, CF—400, RF—330. **Press Box Telephone:** (714) 278-5327.

CAL STATE NORTHRIDGE Matadors
Conference: Big West.
Mailing Address: 18111 Nordhoff St., Northridge, CA 91330. **Website:** www.gomatadors.com.
Head Coach: Steve Rousey. **Assistant Coaches:** Grant

Hohman, Mark Kertenian, *Rob McKinley. **Telephone:** (818) 677-7055. ◆ **Baseball SID:** Tony La Torra. **Telephone:** (818) 677-3243. **FAX:** (818) 677-4950.
Home Field: Matador Field. **Seating Capacity:** 1,400. **Outfield Dimensions:** LF—325, CF—400, RF—330. **Press Box Telephone:** (818) 677-4293.

CAMPBELL Fighting Camels
Conference: Atlantic Sun.
Mailing Address: P.O. Box 10, Buies Creek, NC 27506. **Website:** www.gocamels.com.
Head Coach: Chip Smith. **Assistant Coaches:** *Kent Cox, Sean Fleming. **Telephone:** (910) 893-1338. ◆ **Baseball SID:** Jonathan Albert. **Telephone:** (910) 814-4367. **FAX:** (910) 893-1330.

CANISIUS Golden Griffins
Conference: Metro Atlantic.
Mailing Address: 2001 Main St., Buffalo, NY 14208. **Website:** www.gogriffs.com.
Head Coach: Mike McRae. **Assistant Coaches:** Don Bell, Marc Kunigonis. **Telephone:** (716) 888-3207. ◆ **Baseball SID:** Marc Gignac. **Telephone:** (716) 888-2978. **FAX:** (716) 888-3178.

CENTENARY Gents
Conference: Mid-Continent.
Mailing Address: 2911 Centenary Blvd., Shreveport, LA 71134. **Website:** www.centenary.edu/athletics.
Head Coach: Ed McCann. **Assistant Coaches:** Cory Burton, Mike Diaz, Jeff Poulin. **Telephone:** (318) 869-5298. ◆ **Baseball SID:** David Pratt. **Telephone:** (318) 869-5092. **FAX:** (318) 869-5128.

CENTRAL CONNECTICUT STATE Blue Devils
Conference: Northeast.
Mailing Address: 1615 Stanley St., New Britain, CT 06050. **Website:** www.ccsubluedevils.com.
Head Coach: Charlie Hickey. **Assistant Coaches:** *Paul LaBella, Jim Ziogas. **Telephone:** (860) 832-3074. ◆ **Baseball SID:** Tom Pincince. **Telephone:** (860) 832-3089. **FAX:** (860) 832-3084.

CENTRAL FLORIDA Golden Knights
Conference: Atlantic Sun.
Mailing Address: 4000 Central Florida Blvd., Orlando, FL 32816. **Website:** www.ucfathletics.com.
Head Coach: Jay Bergman. **Assistant Coaches:** Tim Boeth, *Craig Cozart, Derek Wolfe. **Telephone:** (407) 823-0140. ◆ **Baseball SID:** Jason Baum. **Telephone:** (407) 823-0994. **FAX:** (407) 823-5266.
Home Field: Jay Bergman Field. **Seating Capacity:** 1,980. **Outfield Dimensions:** LF—325, CF—400, RF—325. **Press Box Telephone:** (407) 823-4487.

CENTRAL MICHIGAN Chippewas
Conference: Mid-American (West).
Mailing Address: 100 Rose Arena, Mount Pleasant, MI 48859. **Website:** www.cmuchippewas.com.
Head Coach: Steve Jaksa. **Assistant Coaches:** Brad Stromdahl, *Mike Villano. **Telephone:** (989) 774-4392. ◆ **Baseball SID:** Fred Stabley Jr. **Telephone:** (989) 774-3277. **FAX:** (989) 774-7324.

CHARLESTON Cougars
Conference: Southern.
Mailing Address: 30 George St., Charleston, SC 29424. **Website:** www.cofcsports.com.
Head Coach: John Pawlowski. **Assistant Coaches:** *Scott Foxhall, Rob Reinstetle, Seth Von Behren. **Telephone:** (843) 953-5916. ◆ **Baseball SID:** Tony Ciuffo. **Telephone:** (843) 953-953-6720. **FAX:** (843) 953-8296.
Home Field: Patriots Point Stadium. **Seating**

Capacity: 2,000. **Outfield Dimensions:** LF—300, CF—400, RF—330. **Press Box Telephone:** (843) 953-9141.

CHARLESTON SOUTHERN Buccaneers
Conference: Big South.
Mailing Address: P.O. Box 118087, Charleston, SC 29423. **Website:** www.csusports.com.
Head Coach: Jason Murray. **Assistant Coaches:** Brian Hoop, *Mike Scolinos. **Telephone:** (843) 863-7591. ◆ **Baseball SID:** David Shelton. **Telephone:** (843) 863-7688. **FAX:** (843) 863-7676.

CHARLOTTE 49ers
Conference: Conference USA.
Mailing Address: 9201 University City Blvd., Charlotte, NC 28223. **Website:** www.charlotte49ers.com.
Head Coach: *Loren Hibbs. **Assistant Coaches:** Bo Durkac, Brandon Hall. **Telephone:** (704) 687-3935. ◆ **Baseball SID:** Matt McCullough. **Telephone:** (704) 687-6312. **FAX:** (704) 687-4918.
Home Field: Tom and Lib Phillips Field. **Seating Capacity:** 2,000. **Outfield Dimensions:** LF—335, CF—390, RF—335. **Press Box Telephone:** (704) 687-3148.

CHICAGO STATE Cougars
Conference: Mid-Continent.
Mailing Address: 9501 S. King Dr. JDC 100E, Chicago, IL 60628. **Website:** www.csu.edu/athletics.
Head Coach: Terrence Jackson. **Assistant Coaches:** *Dennis Bonebreak, Joe Ramirez, Adam Sanchez. **Telephone:** (773) 995-3659. ◆ **Baseball SID:** Ben Greenberg. **Telephone:** (773) 995-2217. **FAX:** (773) 995-3656.

CINCINNATI Bearcats
Conference: Conference USA.
Mailing Address: One Edwards Center, Suite 4150 ML 0021, Cincinnati, OH 45221. **Website:** www.ucbearcats.com.
Head Coach: Brian Cleary. **Assistant Coaches:** *Brad Meador, Joe Regruth. **Telephone:** (513) 556-1577. ◆ **Baseball SID:** Shawn Sell. **Telephone:** (513) 556-0618. **FAX:** (513) 556-0619.
Home Field: UC Baseball Stadium. **Seating Capacity:** 3,200. **Outfield Dimensions:** LF—325, CF—400, RF—325. **Press Box Telephone:** (513) 556-9645.

THE CITADEL Bulldogs
Conference: Southern.
Mailing Address: 171 Moultrie St., Charleston, SC 29409. **Website:** www.citadelsports.com.
Head Coach: Fred Jordan. **Assistant Coaches:** David Beckley, David Griffin, *Chris Lemonis. **Telephone:** (843) 953-5285. ◆ **Baseball SID:** Kevin Rhodes. **Telephone:** (843) 953 5120. **FAX:** (843) 953-5058.
Home Field: Joseph P. Riley Park. **Seating Capacity:** 6,000. **Outfield Dimensions:** LF—305, CF—398, RF—337. **Press Box Telephone:** (843) 965-4151.

CLEMSON Tigers
Conference: Atlantic Coast.
Mailing Address: P.O. Box 31, Clemson, SC 29633. **Website:** www.clemsontigers.com.
Head Coach: Jack Leggett. **Assistant Coaches:** Bradley LeCroy, *Kevin O'Sullivan, Tom Riginos. **Telephone:** (864) 656-1947. ◆ **Baseball SID:** Brian Hennessy. **Telephone:** (864) 656-1921. **FAX:** (864) 656-0299.
Home Field: Doug Kingsmore Stadium. **Seating Capacity:** 6,000. **Outfield Dimensions:** LF—320, CF—400, RF—330. **Press Box Telephone:** (864) 656-7731.

CLEVELAND STATE Vikings
Conference: Horizon.

Mailing Address: 2121 Euclid Ave., Cleveland, OH 44115. Website: www.csuvikings.com.

Head Coach: Jay Murphy. Assistant Coaches: Doug Besozzi, Brian Donohew, Dave Sprochi. Telephone: (216) 687-4822. ◆ Baseball SID: Chris Urban. Telephone: (216) 687-4818. FAX: (216) 523-7257.

COASTAL CAROLINA Chanticleers

Conference: Big South.

Mailing Address: P.O. Box 261954, Conway, SC 29528. Website: www.goccusports.com.

Head Coach: Gary Gilmore. Assistant Coaches: Clint Ayers, *Bill Jarman, Kevin Schnall. Telephone: (843) 349-2816. ◆ Baseball SID: Kent Reichert. Telephone: (843) 349-2840. FAX: (843) 349-2819.

Home Field: Watson Stadium. Seating Capacity: 2,000. Outfield Dimensions: LF—310, CF—390, RF—318.

COLUMBIA Lions

Conference: Ivy League (Gehrig).

Mailing Address: Dodge Physical Fitness Center, 3030 Broadway, New York, NY 10027. Website: www.gocolumbialions.com.

Head Coach: Paul Fernandes. Assistant Coaches: Grisha Davida, *Bryan Haley, Bob Koehler. Telephone: (212) 854-2543. ◆ Baseball SID: Darlene Camacho. Telephone: (212) 854-2535. FAX: (212) 854-8168.

CONNECTICUT Huskies

Conference: Big East.

Mailing Address: 2111 Hillside Road, Storrs, CT 06269. Website: www.uconnhuskies.com.

Head Coach: Jim Penders. Assistant Coach: *Dave Turgeon. Telephone: (860) 486-4089. ◆ Baseball SID: Courtney Walerius. Telephone: (860) 486-3531. FAX: (860) 486-5085.

Home Field: J.O. Christian Field. Seating Capacity: 2,000. Outfield Dimensions: LF—370, CF—405, RF—370. Press Box Telephone: Unavailable.

COPPIN STATE Eagles

Conference: Mid-Eastern Athletic.

Mailing Address: 2500 W. North Ave., Baltimore, MD 21216. Website: www.coppin.edu/athletics.

Head Coach: *Guy Robertson. Assistant Coaches: Ruffin Bell, Derrick DePriest, Patrick Rosko. Telephone: (410) 951-3740. ◆ Baseball SID: Kevin Paige. Telephone: (410) 951-3744. FAX: (410) 951-3718.

CORNELL Big Red

Conference: Ivy League (Rolfe).

Mailing Address: Teagle Hall, Campus Rd., Ithaca, NY 14853. Website: www.cornellbigred.com.

Head Coach: Tom Ford. Assistant Coaches: Scott Marsh, *Bill Walkenbach. Telephone: (607) 255-6604. ◆ Baseball SID: Eric Lawrence. Telephone: (607) 255-5627. FAX: (607) 255-2969.

CREIGHTON Blue Jays

Conference: Missouri Valley.

Mailing Address: 2500 California Plaza, Omaha, NE 68178. Website: www.gocreighton.com.

Head Coach: Ed Servais. Assistant Coaches: Spencer Allen, *Travis Wyckoff. Telephone: (402) 280-2483. ◆ Baseball SID: Brandon Holtz. Telephone: (402) 280-5801. FAX: (402) 280-2495.

Home Field: Creighton Sports Complex. Seating Capacity: 1,000. Outfield Dimensions: LF—332, CF—402, RF—332. Press Box Telephone: (402) 280-2495.

#DALLAS BAPTIST Patriots

Conference: Independent.

Mailing Address: 3000 Mountain Creek Pkwy., Dallas, TX 75211. Website: www.dbu.edu/athletics.

Head Coach: Eric Newman. Assistant Coaches: Nate Frieling, *Dan Heefner. Telephone: (214) 333-6957. ◆ Baseball SID: Ryan Ewin. Telephone: (214) 333-6987. FAX: (214) 333-5306.

DARTMOUTH Big Green

Conference: Ivy League (Rolfe).

Mailing Address: 6083 Alumni Gym, Hanover, NH 03755. Website: athletics.dartmouth.edu.

Head Coach: Bob Whalen. Assistant Coaches: *Tony Baldwin, Nicholas Enriquez. Telephone: (603) 646-2477. ◆ Baseball SID: Josh Kessler. Telephone: (603) 646-2468. FAX: (603) 646-3348.

DAVIDSON Wildcats

Conference: Southern.

Mailing Address: P.O. Box 7158, Davidson, NC 28035. Website: www.davidson.edu/athletics.

Head Coach: Dick Cooke. Assistant Coaches: Matt Hanson, *Chris Moore. Telephone: (704) 894-2368. ◆ Baseball SID: Rick Bender. Telephone: (704) 894-2123. FAX: (704) 894-2636.

DAYTON Flyers

Conference: Atlantic-10 (West).

Mailing Address: 300 College Park, Dayton, OH 45469. Website: www.daytonflyers.com.

Head Coach: *Tony Vittorio. Assistant Coaches: Terry Bell, Craig Bruce, Todd Linklater. Telephone: (937) 229-4456. ◆ Baseball SID: Bill Thomas. Telephone: (937) 229-4419. FAX: (937) 272-5599.

DELAWARE Fightin' Blue Hens

Conference: Colonial Athletic.

Mailing Address: Bob Carpenter Center, Newark, DE 19716. Website: www.udel.edu/sportsinfo

Head Coach: Jim Sherman. Assistant Coaches: Jim Fallers, Dan Hammer, *Greg Mamula. Telephone: (302) 831-8596. ◆ Baseball SID: John Kneisley. Telephone: (302) 831-2186. FAX: (302) 831-8653.

Home Field: Bob Hannah Stadium. Seating Capacity: 1,300. Outfield Dimensions: LF—330, CF—400, RF—330. Press Box Telephone: (302) 831-4122.

DELAWARE STATE Hornets

Conference: Mid-Eastern Athletic.

Mailing Address: 1200 N. DuPont Hwy., Dover, DE 19901. Website: www.dsc.edu/athletics.

Head Coach: J.P. Blandin. Assistant Coaches: Jimmy Conroy, Will Gardner, *Sean Moran. Telephone: (302) 857-6035. ◆ Baseball SID: Dennis Jones. Telephone: (302) 857-6068. FAX: (302) 857-6069.

DUKE Blue Devils

Conference: Atlantic Coast.

Mailing Address: P.O. Box 90555, Durham, NC 27708. Website: www.GoDuke.com.

Head Coach: Bill Hillier. Assistant Coaches: Marty Biggs, Bill Hillier Jr., John Yurkow. Telephone: (919) 684-2358. ◆ Baseball SID: Will Shapiro. Telephone: (919) 684-2668. FAX: (919) 684-2489.

Home Field: Jack Coombs Stadium. Seating Capacity: 1,500. Outfield Dimensions: LF—330, CF—400, RF—330. Press Box Telephone: (919) 684-6074.

DUQUESNE Dukes

Conference: Atlantic-10 (West).

Mailing Address: A.J. Palumbo Center, 600 Forbes Ave., Pittsburgh, PA 15282. Website: www.goduquesne.com.

Head Coach: *Mike Wilson. Assistant Coaches: Todd

Schiffhauer, Dan Schwartzbauer. **Telephone:** (412) 396-5245. ◆ **Baseball SID:** George Nieman. **Telephone:** (412) 396-5376. **FAX:** (412) 396-6210.

EAST CAROLINA Pirates
Conference: Conference USA.
Mailing Address: Ward Sports Medicine Building, Greenville, NC 27858. **Website:** www.ecupirates.com.
Head Coach: Randy Mazey. **Assistant Coaches:** Tommy Eason, *Allen Osborne, Ryan Riley. **Telephone:** (252) 328-4604. ◆ **Baseball SID:** Rob Dunning. **Telephone:** (252) 328-4522. **FAX:** (252) 328-4528.
Home Field: Clark-LeClair Field. **Seating Capacity:** 3,000. **Outfield Dimensions:** LF—320, CF—410, RF—320.

EAST TENNESSEE STATE Buccaneers
Conference: Southern.
Mailing Address: P.O. Box 70707, Johnson City, TN 37614. **Website:** www.ETSUBucs.com.
Head Coach: Tony Skole. **Assistant Coaches:** *Nate Goulet, Maynard McClarrinon. **Telephone:** (423) 439-4496. ◆ **Baseball SID:** Matt Snellings. **Telephone:** (423) 439-5263. **FAX:** (423) 439-6138.

EASTERN ILLINOIS Panthers
Conference: Ohio Valley.
Mailing Address: 600 Lincoln Ave., Charleston, IL 61920. **Website:** www.eiu.edu/panthers.
Head Coach: *Jim Schmitz. **Assistant Coach:** Sean Lyons. **Telephone:** (217) 581-2511. ◆ **Baseball SID:** Unavailable. **Telephone:** (217) 581-7480. **FAX:** (217) 581-6434.

EASTERN KENTUCKY Colonels
Conference: Ohio Valley.
Mailing Address: 115 Alumni Coliseum, Richmond, KY 40475. **Website:** www.ekusports.com.
Head Coach: Elvis Dominguez. **Assistant Coach:** *John Corbin, Brad Husz. **Telephone:** (859) 622-2128. ◆ **Baseball SID:** Joe Angolia. **Telephone:** (859) 622-1253. **FAX:** (859) 622-1230.

EASTERN MICHIGAN Eagles
Conference: Mid-American (West).
Mailing Address: 799 Hewitt Rd., Ypsilanti, MI 48197. **Website:** www.emich.edu/goeagles.
Head Coach: *Roger Coryell. **Assistant Coach:** Chris Hoiles. **Telephone:** (734) 487-0315. ◆ **Baseball SID:** Jay Sofen. **Telephone:** (734) 487-0317. **FAX:** (734) 485-3840.
Home Field: Oestrike Stadium. **Seating Capacity:** 2,500. **Outfield Dimensions:** LF—330, CF—390, RF—330. **Press Box Telephone:** (734) 481-9328.

ELON Phoonix
Conference: Southern.
Mailing Address: 100 Campus Dr., 2500 Campus Box, Elon College, NC 27244. **Website:** www.elon.edu/athletics.
Head Coach: Mike Kennedy. **Assistant Coaches:** *Austin Alexander, Robbie Huffstettler, Greg Starbuck. **Telephone:** (336) 278-6741. ◆ **Baseball SID:** Chris Rash. **Telephone:** (336) 278-6712. **FAX:** (336) 278-6768.
Home Field: Latham Park. **Seating Capacity:** 2,000. **Outfield Dimensions:** LF—317, CF—385, RF—328. **Press Box Telephone:** (336) 278-6788.

EVANSVILLE Purple Aces
Conference: Missouri Valley.
Mailing Address: 1800 Lincoln Ave., Evansville, IN 47722. **Website:** www.gopurpleaces.com.
Head Coach: Dave Schrage. **Assistant Coaches:** Tyler

Herbst, Kevin Koch, *Scott Lawler. **Telephone:** (812) 479-2059. ◆ **Baseball SID:** Tom Benson. **Telephone:** (812) 488-1152. **FAX:** (812) 479-2090.
Home Field: Braun Stadium. **Seating Capacity:** 1,200. **Outfield Dimensions:** LF—330, CF—400, RF—330. **Press Box Telephone:** (812) 479-2587.

FAIRFIELD Stags
Conference: Metro Atlantic.
Mailing Address: 1073 N. Benson Rd., Fairfield, CT 06430. **Website:** www.fairfieldstags.com.
Head Coach: John Slosar. **Assistant Coaches:** Patrick Hall, Dennis Whalen. **Telephone:** (203) 254-4000, ext. 2605. ◆ **Baseball SID:** Patrick Moran. **Telephone:** (203) 254-4000, ext. 2877. **FAX:** (203) 254-4117.

FAIRLEIGH DICKINSON Knights
Conference: Northeast.
Mailing Address: 1000 River Rd., Teaneck, NJ 07666. **Website:** www.fduknights.com.
Head Coach: *Jerry DeFabbia. **Assistant Coaches:** Dan Grey, Don Hahn, John Quirk. **Telephone:** (201) 692-2691. ◆ **Baseball SID:** Drew Brown. **Telephone:** (201) 692-2204. **FAX:** (201) 692-9361.

FLORIDA Gators
Conference: Southeastern (East).
Mailing Address: P.O. Box 14485, Gainesville, FL 32611. **Website:** www.gatorzone.com.
Head Coach: Pat McMahon. **Assistant Coaches:** Brian Fleetwood, *Ross Jones, Tim Parenton. **Telephone:** (352) 375-4683, ext. 4457. ◆ **Baseball SID:** John Hines. **Telephone:** (352) 375-4683, ext. 6130. **FAX:** (352) 375-4809.
Home Field: McKethan Stadium. **Seating Capacity:** 5,000. **Outfield Dimensions:** LF—329, CF—400, RF—325. **Press Box Telephone:** (352) 375-4683, ext. 4355.

FLORIDA A&M Rattlers
Conference: Mid-Eastern Athletic.
Mailing Address: 1500 Wahnish Way, Tallahassee, FL 32307. **Website:** www.thefamurattlers.com.
Head Coach: Joe Durant. **Assistant Coaches:** K.C. Carter, *Brett Richardson. **Telephone:** (850) 599-3202. ◆ **Baseball SID:** Ronnie Thompson. **Telephone:** (850) 599-3200. **FAX:** (850) 599-3206.

FLORIDA ATLANTIC Blue Wave
Conference: Atlantic Sun.
Mailing Address: 777 Glades Rd., Boca Raton, FL 33431. **Website:** www.fausports.com.
Head Coach: Kevin Cooney. **Assistant Coaches:** Tony Fossas, *John McCormack, George Roig. **Telephone:** (561) 297-3956. ◆ **Baseball SID:** Dawn Elston. **Tolophone:** (561) 297-3513. **FAX:** (561) 297-3499.
Home Field: FAU Field. **Seating Capacity:** 2,500. **Dimensions:** LF—330, CF—400, RF—330. **Press Box Telephone:** (561) 302-0461.

FLORIDA INTERNATIONAL Golden Panthers
Conference: Sun Belt.
Mailing Address: University Park, 11200 SW 8th St., Miami, FL 33199. **Website:** www.fiusports.com.
Head Coach: Danny Price. **Assistant Coaches:** *Tony Casas, Chris Holick, Lou Sanchez. **Telephone:** (305) 348-3166. ◆ **Baseball SID:** Danny Kambel. **Telephone:** (305) 348-2084. **FAX:** (305) 348-2963.
Home Field: University Park. **Seating Capacity:** 2,000. **Outfield Dimensions:** LF—325, CF—400, RF—325. **Press Box Telephone:** (786) 298-1478.

FLORIDA STATE Seminoles
Conference: Atlantic Coast.

Mailing Address: University Center D 107, Tallahassee, FL 32306. **Website:** www.seminoles.com.
Head Coach: Mike Martin. **Assistant Coaches:** Jerrod Brown, Mike Martin Jr., *Jamey Shouppe. **Telephone:** (850) 644-1073. ◆ **Baseball SID:** Elliott Finebloom. **Telephone:** (850) 644-5656. **FAX:** (850) 644-3820.
Home Field: Dick Howser Stadium. **Seating Capacity:** 6,700. **Outfield Dimensions:** LF—340, CF—400, RF—320. **Press Box Telephone:** (850) 644-1553.

FORDHAM Rams
Conference: Atlantic-10 (East).
Mailing Address: 441 E. Fordham Rd., Bronx, NY 10458. **Website:** www.fordhamsports.com.
Head Coach: Nick Restaino. **Assistant Coach:** Pat Carey. **Telephone:** (718) 817-4292. ◆ **Baseball SID:** Scott Kwiatkowski. **Telephone:** (718) 817-4240. **FAX:** (718) 817-4244.

FRESNO STATE Bulldogs
Conference: Western Athletic.
Mailing Address: 5305 N. Campus Dr., Room 153, Fresno, CA 93740. **Website:** www.gobulldogs.com.
Head Coach: Mike Batesole. **Assistant Coaches:** Matt Curtis, *Tim Montez, Chad Thornhill. **Telephone:** (559) 278-2178. ◆ **Baseball SID:** Roger Kirk. **Telephone:** (559) 278-2178. **FAX:** (559) 278-4689.
Home Field: Beiden Field. **Seating Capacity:** 6,575. **Outfield Dimensions:** LF—330, CF—400, RF—330. **Press Box Telephone:** (559) 278-7678.

FURMAN Paladins
Conference: Southern.
Mailing Address: 3300 Poinsett Hwy., Greenville, SC 29613. **Website:** www.furmanpaladins.com.
Head Coach: Ron Smith. **Assistant Coaches:** Jon Placko, Brent Shade. **Telephone:** (864) 294-2146. ◆ **Baseball SID:** Katie Parmelee. **Telephone:** (864) 294-2061. **FAX:** (864) 294-3061.

GARDNER-WEBB Runnin' Bulldogs
Conference: Atlantic Sun.
Mailing Address: P.O. Box 877, Boiling Springs, NC 28017. **Website:** www.gwusports.com.
Head Coach: Rusty Stroupe. **Assistant Coaches:** Danny Breece, Derek Hassell, *Dan Roszel. **Telephone:** (704) 406-4421. ◆ **Baseball SID:** Marc Rabb. **Telephone:** (704) 406-4355. **FAX:** (704) 406-4739.

GEORGE MASON Patriots
Conference: Colonial Athletic.
Mailing Address: 4400 University Dr., Fairfax, VA 22030. **Website:** www.gomason.com.
Head Coach: Bill Brown. **Assistant Coaches:** Ken Munoz, *Shawn Stiffler. **Telephone:** (703) 993-3282. ◆ **Baseball SID:** Richard Coco. **Telephone:** (703) 993-3264. **FAX:** (703) 993-3259.
Home Field: Hap Spuhler Field. **Seating Capacity:** 900. **Outfield Dimensions:** LF—320, CF—400, RF—320.

GEORGE WASHINGTON Colonials
Conference: Atlantic-10 (West).
Mailing Address: 600 22nd St. NW, Washington, DC 20052. **Website:** www.gwsports.com.
Head Coach: Steve Mrowka. **Assistant Coaches:** Brad Gooding, *Jim Mason, Darryl Morhardt. **Telephone:** (202) 994-7399. ◆ **Baseball SID:** Ted Leshinski. **Telephone:** (202) 994-0339. **FAX:** (202) 994-2713.
Home Field: Barcroft Field. **Seating Capacity:** 500. **Outfield Dimensions:** LF—325, CF—370, RF—325. **Press Box Telephone:** (703) 671-2151.

GEORGETOWN Hoyas
Conference: Big East.
Mailing Address: McDonough Arena, 37th & O Streets NW, Washington, DC 20057. **Website:** www.guhoyas.com.
Head Coach: Pete Wilk. **Assistant Coaches:** Matt Bok, *Mark Van Ameyde. **Telephone:** (202) 687-2462. ◆ **Baseball SID:** Dayna Johnson. **Telephone:** (202) 687-2492. **FAX:** (202) 687-2491.
Home Field: Shirley Povich Field. **Seating Capacity:** 1,500. **Outfield Dimensions:** LF—330, CF—375, RF—330.

GEORGIA Bulldogs
Conference: Southeastern (East).
Mailing Address: P.O. Box 1472, Athens, GA 30603. **Website:** www.georgiadogs.com.
Head Coach: David Perno. **Assistant Coaches:** Jason Eller, Don Norris, *Butch Thompson. **Telephone:** (706) 542-7971. ◆ **Baseball SID:** Christopher Lakos. **Telephone:** (706) 542-1621. **FAX:** (706) 542-7993.
Home Field: Foley Field. **Seating Capacity:** 3,291. **Outfield Dimensions:** LF—345, CF—404, RF—314. **Press Box Telephone:** (706) 542-6161.

GEORGIA SOUTHERN Eagles
Conference: Southern.
Mailing Address: P.O. Box 8085, Statesboro, GA 30460. **Website:** www.georgiasoutherneagles.com.
Head Coach: Rodney Hennon. **Assistant Coaches:** Brett Lewis, *Mike Tidick. **Telephone:** (912) 486-7360. ◆ **Baseball SID:** Mike Tidick. **Telephone:** (912) 681-5188. **FAX:** (912) 681-1366.
Home Field: J.I. Clements Stadium. **Seating Capacity:** 3,000. **Outfield Dimensions:** LF—325, CF—385, RF—325.

GEORGIA STATE Panthers
Conference: Atlantic Sun.
Mailing Address: 125 Decatur St., Suite 201, Atlanta, GA 30303. **Website:** www.georgiastatesports.com.
Head Coach: Mike Hurst. **Assistant Coaches:** Adrian Dorsey, Greg Frady, Michael Nelson. **Telephone:** (404) 244-5804. ◆ **Baseball SID:** Jon Newberry. **Telephone:** (404) 651-4629. **FAX:** (404) 651-3204.
Home Field: Panthersville Field. **Seating Capacity:** 1,000. **Outfield Dimensions:** LF—334, CF—385, RF—338.

GEORGIA TECH Yellow Jackets
Conference: Atlantic Coast.
Mailing Address: 150 Bobby Dodd Way, Atlanta, GA 30332. **Website:** www.ramblinwreck.com.
Head Coach: Danny Hall. **Assistant Coaches:** *Josh Holliday, Bobby Moranda, Victor Menocal. **Telephone:** (404) 894-5471. ◆ **Baseball SID:** Chris Capo. **Telephone:** (404) 894-5445. **FAX:** (404) 894-1248.
Home Field: Russ Chandler Stadium. **Seating Capacity:** 4,157. **Outfield Dimensions:** LF—328, CF—400, RF—334. **Press Box Telephone:** (404) 894-3167.

GONZAGA Bulldogs
Conference: West Coast.
Mailing Address: 502 E. Boone Ave., Spokane, WA 99258. **Website:** www.gozags.com.
Head Coach: Mark Machtolf. **Assistant Coaches:** *Scott Asan, Steve Bennett, Danny Evans. **Telephone:** (509) 323-4209. ◆ **Baseball SID:** Chris Loucks. **Telephone:** (509) 323-4227. **FAX:** (509) 323-5730.
Home Field: Avista Stadium. **Seating Capacity:** 7,800. **Outfield Dimensions:** LF—330, CF—400, RF—

330. **Press Box Telephone:** (509) 279-1005.

GRAMBLING STATE Tigers
Conference: Southwestern Athletic.
Mailing Address: P.O. Box 868, Grambling, LA 71245.
Website: www.gram.edu/sports.
Head Coach: James Randall. **Assistant Coach:** Channing Cornelius. **Telephone:** (318) 274-6121.
◆ **Baseball SID:** Roderick Mosley. **Telephone:** (318) 274-6281. **FAX:** (318) 274-2761.

HARTFORD Hawks
Conference: America East.
Mailing Address: 200 Bloomfield Ave., West Hartford, CT 06117. **Website:** www.HartfordHawks.com.
Head Coach: Jeff Calcaterra. **Assistant Coaches:** Al Furrow, Mike Susi. **Telephone:** (860) 768-4656.
◆ **Baseball SID:** Mike Vigneux. **Telephone:** (860) 768-4501. **FAX:** (860) 768-5047.

HARVARD Crimson
Conference: Ivy League (Rolfe).
Mailing Address: 65 N. Harvard St., Boston, MA 02163. **Website:** www.gocrimson.com.
Head Coach: Joe Walsh. **Assistant Coaches:** Gary Donovan, *Matt Hyde, Paul Sullivan. **Telephone:** (617) 495-2629. ◆ **Baseball SID:** Kevin Anderson. **Telephone:** (617) 495-2206. **FAX:** (617) 495-2130.

HAWAII Rainbows
Conference: Western Athletic.
Mailing Address: 1337 Lower Campus Rd., Honolulu, HI 96822. **Website:** www.hawaiiathletics.hawaii.edu.
Head Coach: Mike Trapasso. **Assistant Coaches:** Travis Janssen, *Chad Konishi, Keith Komeiji. **Telephone:** (808) 956-6247. ◆ **Baseball SID:** Pakalani Bello. **Telephone:** (808) 956-7506. **FAX:** (808) 956-4470.
Home Field: Les Murakami Stadium. **Seating Capacity:** 4,312. **Outfield Dimensions:** LF—325, CF—385, RF—325. **Press Box Telephone:** (808) 956-6253.

HAWAII-HILO Vulcans
Conference: Independent.
Mailing Address: 200 W. Kawili Street, Hilo, HI 96720. **Website:** vulcans.uhh.hawaii.edu.
Head Coach: *Joey Estrella. **Assistant Coaches:** Kevin Kane, Kal Miyataki, Kevin Yee. **Telephone:** (808) 974-7700. ◆ **Baseball SID:** Kelly Leong. **Telephone:** (808) 974-7606. **FAX:** (808) 974-7711.

HIGH POINT Panthers
Conference: Big South.
Mailing Address: 833 Montlieu Ave., High Point, NC 27262. **Website:** www.highpointpanthers.com.
Head Coach: *Sal Bando. **Assistant Coaches:** Phil Maier, Kal Sorensen. **Telephone:** (336) 841-9190.
◆ **Baseball SID:** Lee Owen. **Telephone:** (336) 841-4605. **FAX:** (336) 841-9276.

HOFSTRA Pride
Conference: Colonial Athletic.
Mailing Address: 230 Hofstra University PFC 230, Hempstead, NY 11549. **Website:** www.hofstra.edu/athletics.
Head Coach: Chris Dotolo. **Assistant Coaches:** Scott Coppola, Asa Grunenwald. **Telephone:** (516) 463-5065.
◆ **Baseball SID:** Sara Weber. **Telephone:** (516) 463-2907. **FAX:** (516) 463-5033.

HOLY CROSS Crusaders
Conference: Patriot.
Mailing Address: One College St., Worcester, MA 01610. **Website:** www.holycross.edu/athletics.

Head Coach: *Craig Najarian. **Assistant Coaches:** Scott Loiseau, Matt Weagle. **Telephone:** (508) 793-2753.
◆ **Baseball SID:** Brian Mallaghan. **Telephone:** (508) 793-2780. **FAX:** (508) 793-2309.

HOUSTON Cougars
Conference: Conference USA.
Mailing Address: 3100 Cullen Blvd., Houston, TX 77204. **Website:** www.uhcougars.com.
Head Coach: Rayner Noble. **Assistant Coaches:** Sean Allen, *Kirk Blount, Rommie Maxey. **Telephone:** (713) 743-9396. ◆ **Baseball SID:** Jeff Conrad. **Telephone:** (713) 743-9404. **FAX:** (713) 743-9411.
Home Field: Cougar Field. **Seating Capacity:** 3,500. **Outfield Dimensions:** LF—330, CF—390, RF—330. **Press Box Telephone:** (713) 743-0840.

ILLINOIS Fighting Illini
Conference: Big Ten.
Mailing Address: 1700 S. Fourth St., Champaign, IL 61820. **Website:** www.fightingillini.com.
Head Coach: Richard "Itch" Jones. **Assistant Coaches:** *Dan Hartleb, Eric Snider. **Telephone:** (217) 333-8605. ◆ **Baseball SID:** Derek Neal. **Telephone:** (217) 244-3707. **FAX:** (217) 333-5540.
Home Field: Illinois Field. **Seating Capacity:** 3,000. **Outfield Dimensions:** LF—330, CF—400, RF—330. **Press Box Telephone:** (217) 333-1227.

ILLINOIS-CHICAGO Flames
Conference: Horizon.
Mailing Address: 839 W. Roosevelt Rd., Chicago, IL 60608. **Website:** www.uicflames.com.
Head Coach: Mike Dee. **Assistant Coaches:** Nick Bridich, *Sean McDermott, Mike Nall. **Telephone:** (312) 996-8645. ◆ **Baseball SID:** Matt Brendich. **Telephone:** (312) 996-5881. **FAX:** (312) 996-5882.

ILLINOIS STATE Redbirds
Conference: Missouri Valley.
Mailing Address: Campus Box 7130, Normal, IL 61790. **Website:** www.redbirds.org.
Head Coach: Jim Brownlee. **Assistant Coaches:** *Tim Brownlee, Kyle Ehrhardt, Seth Kenny. **Telephone:** (309) 438-5151. ◆ **Baseball SID:** Aaron Johnston. **Telephone:** (309) 438-3598. **FAX:** (309) 438-5643.
Home Field: Redbird Field. **Seating Capacity:** 1,500. **Outfield Dimensions:** LF—330, CF—400, RF—330. **Press Box Telephone:** (309) 438-3504.

INDIANA Hoosiers
Conference: Big Ten.
Mailing Address: 1001 E. 17th St., Bloomington, IN 47408. **Website:** www.iuhoosiers.com.
Head Coach: Bob Morgan. **Assistant Coaches:** Clay Eason, Chris Moore, Ted Tom. **Telephone:** (812) 855-1680. ◆ **Baseball SID:** Jeff Keag. **Telephone:** (812) 855-6209. **FAX:** (812) 855-9401.
Home Field: Sembower Field. **Seating Capacity:** 3,500. **Outfield Dimensions:** LF—333, CF—385, RF—333. **Press Box Telephone:** (812) 855-4787.

INDIANA-PURDUE UNIVERSITY-FORT WAYNE Mastodons
Conference: Independent.
Mailing Address: 2101 E. Coliseum Blvd., Fort Wayne, IN 46805. **Website:** www.ipfw.edu/athletics.
Head Coach: Billy Gernon. **Assistant Coaches:** Blaine McFerrin, *Chad Newhard. **Telephone:** (260) 481-5480.
◆ **Baseball SID:** Rudy Yovich. **Telephone:** (260) 481-6646. **FAX:** (260) 481-6002.

INDIANA STATE Sycamores
Conference: Missouri Valley.
Mailing Address: Baseball Office, Indiana State University, Terre Haute, IN 47809. **Website:** www.ind-state.edu/athletics.
Head Coach: Bob Warn. **Assistant Coach:** *C.J. Keating. **Telephone:** (812) 237-4051. ◆ **Baseball SID:** Dan Gisel. **Telephone:** (812) 237-4160. **FAX:** (812) 237-4157.
Home Field: Sycamore Field. **Seating Capacity:** 2,500. **Outfield Dimensions:** LF—340, CF—402, RF—340.

IONA Gaels
Conference: Metro Atlantic.
Mailing Address: 715 North Ave., New Rochelle, NY 10801. **Website:** www.iona.edu/gaels.
Head Coach: Al Zoccolillo. **Assistant Coaches:** *Forrest Irwin. **Telephone:** (914) 633-2319. ◆ **Baseball SID:** Brian Beyrer. **Telephone:** (914) 633-2057. **FAX:** (914) 633-2072.

IOWA Hawkeyes
Conference: Big Ten.
Mailing Address: 232 Carver-Hawkeye Arena, Iowa City, IA 52242. **Website:** www.hawkeyesports.com.
Head Coach: Jack Dahm. **Assistant Coaches:** *Ryan Brownlee, Nick Zumsande. **Telephone:** (319) 335-9329. ◆ **Baseball SID:** Tony Wirt. **Telephone:** (319) 335-9411. **FAX:** (319) 335-9417.
Home Field: Duane Banks Field. **Seating Capacity:** 3,000. **Outfield Dimensions:** LF—330, CF—400, RF—330. **Press Box Telephone:** (319) 335-9520.

JACKSON STATE Tigers
Conference: Southwestern Athletic.
Mailing Address: 1400 John R. Lynch St., Jackson, MS 39217. **Website:** www.jsums.edu.
Head Coach: Mark Salter. **Assistant Coaches:** Frank Adams, *Omar Johnson. **Telephone:** (601) 979-3928. ◆ **Baseball SID:** Deidra Bell-Jones. **Telephone:** (601) 979-2273. **FAX:** (601) 979-2000.

JACKSONVILLE Dolphins
Conference: Atlantic Sun.
Mailing Address: 2800 University Blvd. N., Jacksonville, FL 32211. **Website:** www.judolphins.com.
Head Coach: Terry Alexander. **Assistant Coaches:** *Chris Hayes, Les Wright. **Telephone:** (904) 256-7412. ◆ **Baseball SID:** Josh Ellis. **Telephone:** (904) 256-7402. **FAX:** (904) 256-7424.
Home Field: Alexander Brest Stadium. **Seating Capacity:** 2,300. **Outfield Dimensions:** LF—340, CF—405, RF—340. **Press Box Telephone:** (904) 256-7588.

JACKSONVILLE STATE Gamecocks
Conference: Ohio Valley.
Mailing Address: 700 Pelham Road N., Jacksonville, AL 36265. **Website:** www.jsugamecocksports.com.
Head Coach: Jim Case. **Assistant Coaches:** Steve Gillispie, Jeremy Talbot. **Telephone:** (256) 782-5367. ◆ **Baseball SID:** Greg Seitz. **Telephone:** (256) 782-5279. **FAX:** (256) 782-5958.

JAMES MADISON Dukes
Conference: Colonial Athletic.
Mailing Address: MSC 2303 Godwin Hall, Harrisonburg, VA 22807. **Website:** www.jmusports.com.
Head Coach: Spanky McFarland. **Assistant Coaches:** Travis Ebaugh, *Jay Sullenger. **Telephone:** (540) 568-3932. ◆ **Baseball SID:** Curt Dudley. **Telephone:** (540) 568-6154. **FAX:** (540) 568-3703.

Home Field: Long Field/Mauck Stadium. **Seating Capacity:** 1,200. **Outfield Dimensions:** LF—340, CF—400, RF—320. **Press Box Telephone:** (540) 568-6545.

KANSAS Jayhawks
Conference: Big 12.
Mailing Address: Allen Fieldhouse, 1651 Naismith Dr., Lawrence, KS 66045. **Website:** www.kuathletics.com.
Head Coach: Ritch Price. **Assistant Coaches:** Steve Abney, *Ryan Graves. **Telephone:** (785) 864-7907. ◆ **Baseball SID:** Adam Quisenberry. **Telephone:** (785) 864-7314. **FAX:** (785) 864-7944.
Home Field: Hoglund Ballpark. **Seating Capacity:** 2,500. **Outfield Dimensions:** LF—330, CF—392, RF—330. **Press Box Telephone:** (785) 864-4037.

KANSAS STATE Wildcats
Conference: Big 12.
Mailing Address: 1800 College Ave., Manhattan, KS 66502. **Website:** www.k-statesports.com.
Head Coach: Brad Hill. **Assistant Coaches:** *Sean McCann, Tom Myers. **Telephone:** (785) 532-3926. ◆ **Baseball SID:** Kenny Lannou. **Telephone:** (785) 532-7708. **FAX:** (785) 532-6093.
Home Field: Tointon Stadium. **Seating Capacity:** 2,331. **Outfield Dimensions:** LF—340, CF—400, RF—325. **Press Box Telephone:** (785) 532-5801.

KENT STATE Golden Flashes
Conference: Mid-American (East).
Mailing Address: 234 Mac Center, Kent, OH 44242. **Website:** www.kentstatesports.com.
Head Coach: Scott Stricklin. **Assistant Coaches:** *Mike Birkbeck, Scott Daely, Ryan Glass. **Telephone:** (330) 672-8432. ◆ **Baseball SID:** Jason Tirotta. **Telephone:** (330) 672-8419. **FAX:** (330) 672-2112.
Home Field: Gene Michael Field. **Seating Capacity:** 2,000. **Outfield Dimensions:** LF—320, CF—415, RF—320.

KENTUCKY Wildcats
Conference: Southeastern (East).
Mailing Address: Memorial Coliseum, Room 23, Lexington, KY 40502. **Website:** www.ukathletics.com.
Head Coach: John Cohen. **Assistant Coaches:** Brad Bohannon, *Gary Henderson, Jan Weisberg. **Telephone:** (859) 257-8052. ◆ **Baseball SID:** Scott Dean. **Telephone:** (859) 257-3838. **FAX:** (859) 323-4310.
Home Field: Cliff Hagan Stadium. **Seating Capacity:** 3,000. **Outfield Dimensions:** LF—340, CF—390, RF—310. **Press Box Telephone:** (859) 257-8027.

LAFAYETTE Leopards
Conference: Patriot.
Mailing Address: Kirby Sports Center, Pierce and Hamilton Streets, Easton, PA 18042. **Website:** www.goleopards.com.
Head Coach: *Joe Kinney. **Assistant Coaches:** Gregg Durrah, Paul Englehardt, Scott Stewart. **Telephone:** (610) 330-5476. ◆ **Baseball SIDs:** Philip LaBella. **Telephone:** (610) 330-5122. **FAX:** (610) 330-5519.

LAMAR Cardinals
Conference: Southland.
Mailing Address: Box 10066, Beaumont, TX 77710. **Website:** www.lamarcardinals.com.
Head Coach: Jim Gilligan. **Assistant Coaches:** Scott Hatten, *Jim Ricklefsen. **Telephone:** (409) 880-8135. ◆ **Baseball SID:** Daucy Crizer. **Telephone:** (409) 880-8329. **FAX:** (409) 880-2323.
Home Field: Vincent-Beck Stadium. **Seating Capacity:** 3,500. **Outfield Dimensions:** LF—325, CF—

380, RF—325. **Press Box Telephone:** (409) 880-8327.

LA SALLE Explorers
Conference: Atlantic-10 (West).
Mailing Address: 1900 W. Olney Ave., Philadelphia, PA 19141. **Website:** www.goexplorers.com.
Head Coach: Lee Saverio. **Assistant Coaches:** John Duffy, Mike Lake. **Telephone:** (215) 951-1995. ◆ **Baseball SID:** Kale Beers. **Telephone:** (215) 951-1513. **FAX:** (215) 951-1694.

LEHIGH Mountain Hawks
Conference: Patriot.
Mailing Address: 641 Taylor St., Bethlehem, PA 18015. **Website:** www.lehighsports.com.
Head Coach: *Sean Leary. **Assistant Coaches:** Dennis Morgan, Josh Perich. **Telephone:** (610) 758-4315. ◆ **Baseball SID:** Jeff Tourial. **Telephone:** (610) 758-3158. **FAX:** (610) 758-6629.

LE MOYNE Dolphins
Conference: Metro Atlantic.
Mailing Address: 1419 Salt Springs Rd., Syracuse, NY 13214. **Website:** www.lemoyne.edu/athletics.
Head Coach: Steve Owens. **Assistant Coaches:** *Pete Hoy, Scott Landers, Bob Nandin. **Telephone:** (315) 445-4415. ◆ **Baseball SID:** Mike Donlin. **Telephone:** (315) 445-4412. **FAX:** (315) 445-4678.

LIBERTY Flames
Conference: Big South.
Mailing Address: 1971 University Blvd., Lynchburg, VA 24502. **Website:** www.libertyflames.com.
Head Coach: Matt Royer. **Assistant Coaches:** Reggie Reynolds, Randy Tomlin, Terry Weaver. **Telephone:** (434) 582-2103. ◆ **Baseball SID:** Ryan Bomberger. **Telephone:** (434) 582-2293. **FAX:** (434) 582-2076.
Home Field: Worthington Stadium. **Seating Capacity:** 1,000. **Outfield Dimensions:** LF—325, CF—390, RF—325. **Press Box Telephone:** (434) 582-2914.

LIPSCOMB Bisons
Conference: Atlantic Sun.
Mailing Address: 3901 Granny White Pike, Nashville, TN 37204. **Website:** www.lipscombsports.com.
Head Coach: Wynn Fletcher. **Assistant Coaches:** John Massey, *Cliff Terracuso. **Telephone:** (615) 279-5716. ◆ **Baseball SID:** Sherry Phillips. **Telephone:** (615) 279-5862. **FAX:** (615) 269-1806.

LONG BEACH STATE 49ers
Conference: Big West.
Mailing Address: 1250 Bellflower Blvd., Long Beach, CA 90840. **Website:** www.longbeachstate.com.
Head Coach: Mike Weathers. **Assistant Coaches:** Don Barbara, *Troy Buckley, Tim McConnell. **Telephone:** (562) 985-7548. ◆ **Baseball SID:** Niall Adler. **Telephone:** (562) 985-7565. **FAX:** (562) 985-1549.
Home Field: Blair Field. **Seating Capacity:** 3,000. **Outfield Dimensions:** LF—330, CF—400, RF—330. **Press Box Telephone:** (562) 433-8605.

LONG ISLAND Blackbirds
Conference: Northeast.
Mailing Address: One University Plaza, Brooklyn, NY 11201. **Website:** www.liu.edu/blackbirds.
Head Coach: Frank Giannone. **Assistant Coaches:** Chris Bagley, Mike Ryan. **Telephone:** (718) 488-1538. ◆ **Baseball SID:** Derek Crudele. **Telephone:** (718) 488-1307. **FAX:** (718) 488-3302.

LOUISIANA-LAFAYETTE Ragin' Cajuns
Conference: Sun Belt.

Mailing Address: 201 Reinhardt Dr., Lafayette, LA 70506. **Website:** www.ragincajuns.com.
Head Coach: Tony Robichaux. **Assistant Coaches:** Anthony Babineaux, Chris Domingue, *John Szefc. **Telephone:** (337) 482-6189. ◆ **Baseball SID:** Chris Yandle. **Telephone:** (337) 851-6332. **FAX:** (337) 482-6649.
Home Field: Moore Field. **Seating Capacity:** 3,755. **Outfield Dimensions:** LF—330, CF—400, RF—330. **Press Box Telephone:** (337) 482-2255.

LOUISIANA-MONROE Indians
Conference: Southland.
Mailing Address: 308 Stadium Dr., Monroe, LA 71209. **Website:** www.ulmathletics.com.
Head Coach: Brad Holland. **Assistant Coaches:** Britton Oubre, Britten Oubre, *Jeff Schexnaider. **Telephone:** (318) 342-3591. ◆ **Baseball SID:** Kiersten Coleman. **Telephone:** (318) 342-5463. **FAX:** (318) 342-5367.
Home Field: Indian Field. **Seating Capacity:** 3,000. **Outfield Dimensions:** LF—330, CF—400, RF—330. **Press Box Telephone:** (318) 342-5476.

LOUISIANA STATE Tigers
Conference: Southeastern (West).
Mailing Address: P.O. Box 25095, Baton Rouge, LA 70894. **Website:** www.LSUsports.net
Head Coach: Smoke Laval. **Assistant Coaches:** Jody Autery, *Turtle Thomas, Brady Wiederhold. **Telephone:** (225) 578-4148. ◆ **Baseball SID:** Bill Franques. **Telephone:** (225) 578-8226. **FAX:** (225) 578-1861.
Home Field: Alex Box Stadium. **Seating Capacity:** 7,760. **Outfield Dimensions:** LF—330, CF—405, RF—330. **Press Box Telephone:** (225) 578-4149.

LOUISIANA TECH Bulldogs
Conference: Western Athletic.
Mailing Address: P.O. Box 3146, Ruston, LA 71272. **Website:** www.latechsports.com.
Head Coach: Wade Simoneaux. **Assistant Coaches:** Fran Andermann, *Brian Rountree. **Telephone:** (318) 257-4111. ◆ **Baseball SID:** Robby Lockwood. **Telephone:** (318) 257-3144. **FAX:** (318) 257-3757.
Home Field: J.C. Love Field. **Seating Capacity:** 3,500. **Outfield Dimensions:** LF—325, CF—385, RF—315. **Press Box Telephone:** (318) 257-3144.

LOUISVILLE Cardinals
Conference: Conference USA.
Mailing Address: Athletics Department, University of Louisville, Louisville, KY 40292. **Website:** www.UofLsports.com.
Head Coach: Lelo Prado. **Assistant Coaches:** James McAuley, *Brian Mundorf, Bobby Perez. **Telephone:** (502) 852-0103. ◆ **Baseball SID:** Sean Moth. **Telephone:** (502) 852-2159. **FAX:** (502) 852-7401.
Home Field: Patterson Stadium. **Seating Capacity:** 2,500. **Outfield Dimensions:** LF—330, CF—402, RF—330.

LOYOLA MARYMOUNT Lions
Conference: West Coast.
Mailing Address: One LMU Drive, Los Angeles, CA 90045. **Website:** www.lmulions.com.
Head Coach: Frank Cruz. **Assistant Coaches:** Robbie Moen, *Jon Strauss. **Telephone:** (310) 338-2949. ◆ **Baseball SID:** Alissa Zito. **Telephone:** (310) 338-7638. **FAX:** (310) 338-2703.
Home Field: Page Stadium. **Seating Capacity:** 600. **Outfield Dimensions:** LF—326, CF—413, RF—330. **Press Box Telephone:** (310) 338-3046.

MAINE Black Bears
Conference: America East.
Mailing Address: 5747 Memorial Gym, Orono, ME 04469. **Website:** www.goblackbears.com.
Head Coach: Paul Kostacopoulos. **Assistant Coach:** *Scott Friedholm. **Telephone:** (207) 581-1090.
◆ **Baseball SID:** Laura Reed. **Telephone:** (207) 581-3646. **FAX:** (207) 581-3297.

MANHATTAN Jaspers
Conference: Metro Atlantic.
Mailing Address: 4513 Manhattan College Pkwy., Riverdale, NY 10471. **Website:** www.gojaspers.com.
Head Coach: Steve Trimper. **Assistant Coaches:** Kevin Leighton, *Tom Sowinski. **Telephone:** (718) 862-7486. ◆ **Baseball SID:** Mike Antonaccio. **Telephone:** (718) 862-7228. **FAX:** (718) 862-8020.

MARIST Red Foxes
Conference: Metro Atlantic.
Mailing Address: 3399 North Rd., Poughkeepsie, NY 12601. **Website:** www.GoRedFoxes.com.
Head Coach: Joe Raccuia. **Assistant Coaches:** *Brian Anderson, Chris Barry, Ryan Mau. **Telephone:** (845) 575-3699. ◆ **Baseball SID:** Jason Corriher. **Telephone:** (845) 575-3699. **FAX:** (845) 471-3322.

MARSHALL Thundering Herd
Conference: Mid-American (East).
Mailing Address: P.O. Box 1360, Huntington, WV 25715. **Website:** www.herdzone.com.
Head Coach: Dave Piepenbrink. **Assistant Coaches:** *Tom Carty, Jim Koerner, Tim Rice. **Telephone:** (304) 696-5277. ◆ **Baseball SID:** Bob Pristash. **Telephone:** (304) 696-4662. **FAX:** (304) 696-2325.

MARYLAND Terrapins
Conference: Atlantic Coast.
Mailing Address: Comcast Center, Terrapin Trail, College Park, MD 20742. **Website:** www.umterps.com.
Head Coach: Terry Rupp. **Assistant Coaches:** *Carmen Carcone, Ben Bachmann, Kyle George. **Telephone:** (301) 314-7114. ◆ **Baseball SID:** Dustin Hockensmith. **Telephone:** (301) 314-7064. **FAX:** (301) 314-9094.
Home Field: Shipley Field. **Seating Capacity:** 2,500. **Outfield Dimensions:** LF—320, CF—380, RF—325. **Press Box Telephone:** (301) 314-0379.

MARYLAND-BALTIMORE COUNTY Retrievers
Conference: America East.
Mailing Address: 1000 Hilltop Circle, Baltimore, MD 21250. **Website:** www.umbcretrievers.com.
Head Coach: *John Jancuska. **Assistant Coach:** Bob Mumma. **Telephone:** (410) 455-2239. ◆ **Baseball SID:** Andy Warner. **Telephone:** (410) 455-2639. **FAX:** (410) 455-3994.

MARYLAND-EASTERN SHORE Fighting Hawks
Conference: Mid-Eastern Athletic.
Mailing Address: William P. Hytche Athletic Center, Princess Anne, MD 21853. **Website:** www.umeshawks.com.
Head Coach: *Robert Rodriguez. **Assistant Coaches:** Ed Erisman, Bob Janeski, Derrick Mason. **Telephone:** (410) 651-8908. ◆ **Baseball SID:** Stan Bradley. **Telephone:** (410) 651-6499. **FAX:** (410) 651-7514.

MASSACHUSETTS Minutemen
Conference: Atlantic-10 (East).
Mailing Address: Baseball Office, 248 Boyden Building, Amherst, MA 01003. **Website:** www.umassathletics.com.
Head Coach: Mike Stone. **Assistant Coaches:** Dave Bettencourt, Jason Gappa, Ernie May. **Telephone:** (413)

545-3120. ◆ **Baseball SID:** John Sinnett. **Telephone:** (413) 545-2439. **FAX:** (413) 545-1556.

McNEESE STATE Cowboys
Conference: Southland.
Mailing Address: 700 E. McNeese., Lake Charles, LA 70607. **Website:** www.mcneese.edu/sports.
Head Coach: Chad Clement. **Assistant Coaches:** Ric Davis, Mike Trahan. **Telephone:** (337) 475-5484. ◆ **Baseball SID:** Louis Bonnette. **Telephone:** (337) 475-5207. **FAX:** (337) 475-5202.
Home Field: Cowboy Diamond. **Seating Capacity:** 2,000. **Outfield Dimensions:** LF—330, CF—400, RF—330. **Press Box Telephone:** (337) 475-8007.

MEMPHIS Tigers
Conference: Conference USA.
Mailing Address: 570 Normal, ADB Room 207, Memphis, TN 38152. **Website:** www.gotigersgo.com.
Head Coach: Daron Schoenrock. **Assistant Coaches:** *Mike Federico, Greg Olsen, Jerry Zulli. **Telephone:** (901) 678-4137. ◆ **Baseball SID:** Jason Redd. **Telephone:** (901) 678-4640. **FAX:** (901) 678-4134.
Home Field: Nat Buring Stadium. **Seating Capacity:** 2,000. **Outfield Dimensions:** LF—320, CF—380, RF—320. **Press Box Telephone:** (901) 678-1300.

MERCER Bears
Conference: Atlantic Sun.
Mailing Address: 1400 Coleman Ave., Macon, GA 31207. **Website:** www.mercerbears.com.
Head Coach: Craig Gibson. **Assistant Coach:** Jason Jackson, *Link Jarrett. **Telephone:** (478) 301-2396. ◆ **Baseball SID:** Brett Jarrett. **Telephone:** (478) 301-2735. **FAX:** (478) 301-5350.

MIAMI Hurricanes
Conference: Atlantic Coast.
Mailing Address: 5821 San Amaro Dr., Coral Gables, FL 33146. **Website:** www.hurricanesports.com.
Head Coach: Jim Morris. **Assistant Coaches:** J.D. Arteaga, *Gino DiMare, Joe Mercadante. **Telephone:** (305) 284-4171. ◆ **Baseball SID:** Evan Koch. **Telephone:** (305) 284-3244. **FAX:** (305) 284-2807.
Home Field: Mark Light Stadium. **Seating Capacity:** 5,000. **Outfield Dimensions:** LF—330, CF—400, RF—330. **Press Box Telephone:** (305) 284-5626.

MIAMI RedHawks
Conference: Mid-American (East).
Mailing Address: 120 Withrow Ct., Oxford, OH 45056. **Website:** www.MURedHawks.com.
Head Coach: Tracy Smith. **Assistant Coaches:** *Joe Kruzel, Tyson Neal, Fred Nori. **Telephone:** (513) 529-6631. ◆ **Baseball SID:** Jess Bechard. **Telephone:** (513) 529-1601. **FAX:** (513) 529-6729.
Home Field: McKie Field at Hayden Park. **Seating Capacity:** 1,500. **Outfield Dimensions:** LF—332, CF—400, RF—343. **Press Box Telephone:** (513) 529-4331.

MICHIGAN Wolverines
Conference: Big Ten.
Mailing Address: 1000 S. State St., Ann Arbor, MI 48109. **Website:** www.mgoblue.com.
Head Coach: Rich Maloney. **Assistant Coaches:** *Jake Boss Jr., Bob Keller, Scott Kingston. **Telephone:** (734) 647-4550. ◆ **Baseball SID:** Jim Schneider. **Telephone:** (734) 763-4423. **FAX:** (734) 647-1188.
Home Field: Ray Fisher Stadium. **Seating Capacity:** 4,000. **Outfield Dimensions:** LF—330, CF—400, RF—330. **Press Box Telephone:** (734) 647-1283.

MICHIGAN STATE Spartans
Conference: Big Ten.
Mailing Address: 304 Jenison Field House, East Lansing, MI 48824. **Website:** www.msuspartans.com.
Head Coach: Ted Mahan. **Assistant Coaches:** John Musachio, Dylan Putnam, *John Young. **Telephone:** (517) 355-4486. ◆ **Baseball SID:** Corey Miggins. **Telephone:** (517) 355-2271. **FAX:** (517) 353-9636.
Home Fields Kobs Field. **Seating Capacity:** 4,000. **Outfield Dimensions:** LF—340, CF—410, RF—305. **Press Box Telephone:** (517) 353-3009.

MIDDLE TENNESSEE STATE Blue Raiders
Conference: Sun Belt.
Mailing Address: 1301 E. Main St., Murfreesboro, TN 37132. **Website:** www.goblueraiders.com.
Head Coach: Steve Peterson. **Assistant Coaches:** Kevin Erminio, Andy Haines, *Jim McGuire. **Telephone:** (615) 898-2984. ◆ **Baseball SID:** Jo Jo Freeman. **Telephone:** (615) 898-5270. **FAX:** (615) 898-5626.
Home Field: Reese Smith Field. **Seating Capacity:** 2,600. **Outfield Dimensions:** LF—330, CF—390, RF—330. **Press Box Telephone:** (615) 898-2117.

MINNESOTA Golden Gophers
Conference: Big Ten.
Mailing Address: 244 Bierman Field Athletic Building, 516 15th Ave. SE, Minneapolis, MN 55455. **Website:** www.gophersports.com.
Head Coach: John Anderson. **Assistant Coaches:** *Rob Fornasiere, Todd Oakes, Lee Swenson. **Telephone:** (612) 625-0869. ◆ **Baseball SID:** Steve Geller. **Telephone:** (612) 624-9396. **FAX:** (612) 625-0359.
Home Fields (Seating Capacity): Siebert Field (1,100), Metrodome (48,678). **Outfield Dimensions:** Siebert Field/LF—330, CF—380, RF—330; Metrodome/LF—343, CF—408, RF—327. **Press Box Telephones:** Siebert Field/(612) 625-4031; Metrodome/(612) 627-4400.

MISSISSIPPI Rebels
Conference: Southeastern (West).
Mailing Address: P.O. Box 217, University, MS 38677. **Website:** www.OleMissSports.com.
Head Coach: Mike Bianco. **Assistant Coaches:** Kyle Bunn, Stuart Lake, *Dan McDonnell. **Telephone:** (662) 915-6643. ◆ **Baseball SID:** Rick Stupak. **Telephone:** (662) 915-7522. **FAX:** (662) 915-7006.
Home Field: Oxford-University Stadium/Swayze Field. **Seating Capacity:** 3,500. **Outfield Dimensions:** LF—330, CF—390, RF—330. **Press Box Telephone:** (662) 915-7858.

MISSISSIPPI STATE Bulldogs
Conference: Southeastern (West).
Mailing Address: P.O. Box 5327, Starkville, MS 39762. **Website:** www.mstateathletics.com.
Head Coach: Ron Polk. **Assistant Coaches:** Wade Hedges, Russ McNickle, Tommy Raffo. **Telephone:** (662) 325-3597. ◆ **Baseball SID:** Joe Dier. **Telephone:** (662) 325-8040. **FAX:** (662) 325-3654.
Home Field: Dudy Noble Field/Polk-DeMent Stadium. **Seating Capacity:** 15,000. **Outfield Dimensions:** LF—330, CF—390, RF—326. **Press Box Telephone:** (662) 325-3776.

MISSISSIPPI VALLEY STATE Delta Devils
Conference: Southwestern Athletic.
Mailing Address: 14000 Hwy. 82 W., No. 7246, Itta Bena, MS 38941. **Website:** www.mvsu.edu/athletics.html.
Head Coach: Doug Shanks. **Assistant Coaches:** *Jay Rayborn, Aaron Stevens. **Telephone:** (662) 254-3834.

◆ **Baseball SID:** Ralph Myers. **Telephone:** (662) 254-3011. **FAX:** (662) 254-3639.

MISSOURI Tigers
Conference: Big 12.
Mailing Address: 370 Hearnes Center, Columbia, MO 65211. **Website:** www.mutigers.com.
Head Coach: Tim Jamieson. **Assistant Coaches:** Kevin Cullen, *Evan Pratte, Tony Vitello. **Telephone:** (573) 884-0731. ◆ **Baseball SID:** Josh Murray. **Telephone:** (573) 884-3241. **FAX:** (573) 882-4720.
Home Field: Taylor Stadium at Simmons Field. **Seating Capacity:** 2,200. **Outfield Dimensions:** LF—340, CF—400, RF—340. **Press Box Telephone:** (573) 884-8912.

MONMOUTH Hawks
Conference: Northeast.
Mailing Address: 400 Cedar Ave., West Long Branch, NJ 07764. **Website:** www.monmouth.edu/athletics.
Head Coach: Dean Ehehalt. **Assistant Coaches:** *Jeff Barbalinardo, Dan McMurtry. **Telephone:** (732) 263-5186. ◆ **Baseball SID:** Chris Tobin. **Telephone:** (732) 263-5180. **FAX:** (732) 571-3535.

MOREHEAD STATE Eagles
Conference: Ohio Valley.
Mailing Address: Allen Field, Morehead State University, Morehead, KY 40351. **Website:** www.msueagles.com.
Head Coach: John Jarnagin. **Assistant Coaches:** Ryan Schmalz, *Rob Taylor. **Telephone:** (606) 783-2882. ◆ **Baseball SID:** Randy Stacy. **Telephone:** (606) 783-2500. **FAX:** (606) 783-2550.

MOUNT ST. MARY'S Mountaineers
Conference: Northeast.
Mailing Address: 16300 Old Emmitsburg Rd., Emmitsburg, MD 21727. **Website:** www.mountathletics.com.
Head Coach: Scott Thomson. **Assistant Coaches:** Steve Mott, Steve Thomson. **Telephone:** (301) 447-3806. ◆ **Baseball SID:** Mark Vandergrift. **Telephone:** (301) 447-5384. **FAX:** (301) 447-5300.

MURRAY STATE Thoroughbreds
Conference: Ohio Valley.
Mailing Address: 218 Stewart Stadium, Murray, KY 42071. **Website:** www.goracers.com.
Head Coach: Rob McDonald. **Assistant Coaches:** Justus Scott, Paul Wyczawski. **Telephone:** (270) 762-4892. ◆ **Baseball SID:** David Snow. **Telephone:** (270) 762-3351. **FAX:** (270) 762-6814.

NAVY Midshipmen
Conference: Patriot.
Mailing Address: 566 Brownson Rd., Annapolis, MD 21402. **Website:** www.navysports.com.
Head Coach: Steve Whitmyer. **Assistant Coach:** Dan Nellum. **Telephone:** (410) 293-5571. ◆ **Baseball SID:** Doug DeBiase. **Telephone:** (410) 293-8771. **FAX:** (410) 293-8954.

NEBRASKA Cornhuskers
Conference: Big 12.
Mailing Address: P.O. Box 880160, Lincoln, NE 68588. **Website:** www.huskers.com.
Head Coach: Mike Anderson. **Assistant Coaches:** Will Bolt, *Rob Childress, Andy Sawyers. **Telephone:** (402) 472-2269. ◆ **Baseball SID:** Shamus McKnight. **Telephone:** (402) 472-7772. **FAX:** (402) 472-2005.
Home Field: Hawks Field at Haymarket Park. **Seating Capacity:** 8,486. **Outfield Dimensions:** LF—335, CF—395, RF—325. **Press Box Telephone:** (402) 434-6861.

NEVADA Wolf Pack
Conference: Western Athletic.
Mailing Address: 1664 N. Virginia St., Reno, NV 89557. **Website:** www.nevadawolfpack.com.
Head Coach: Gary Powers. **Assistant Coaches:** Jarek Krukow, *Stan Stolte, Jay Uhlman. **Telephone:** (775) 784-6900, ext. 252. ◆ **Baseball SID:** Jack Kuestermeyer. **Telephone:** (775) 784-6900, ext. 244. **FAX:** (775) 784-4386.
Home Field: Peccole Park. **Seating Capacity:** 3,000. **Outfield Dimensions:** LF—340, CF—401, RF—340. **Press Box Telephone:** (775) 784-5815.

NEVADA-LAS VEGAS Rebels
Conference: Mountain West.
Mailing Address: 4505 Maryland Pkwy., Las Vegas, NV 89154. **Website:** www.unlvrebels.com.
Head Coach: Buddy Gouldsmith. **Assistant Coaches:** Chuck Hazzard, *Scott Malone, Nate Yeskie. **Telephone:** (702) 895-3499. ◆ **Baseball SID:** Bryan Haines. **Telephone:** (702) 895-3764. **FAX:** (702) 895-0989.
Home Field: Earl E. Wilson Stadium. **Seating Capacity:** 3,500. **Outfield Dimensions:** LF—335, CF—400, RF—335. **Press Box Telephone:** (702) 895-1595.

NEW MEXICO Lobos
Conference: Mountain West.
Mailing Address: Athletic Dept., MSC04 2680, 1 University of New Mexico, Albuquerque, NM 87131. **Website:** www.GoLobos.com.
Head Coach: Rich Alday. **Assistant Coaches:** Kris Didion, Ken Jacome, *Mark Martinez. **Telephone:** (505) 925-5720. ◆ **Baseball SID:** Ben Phlegar. **Telephone:** (505) 925-5533. **FAX:** (505) 925-5529.
Home Field: Isotopes Park. **Seating Capacity:** 11,124. **Outfield Dimensions:** LF—340, CF—400, RF—340. **Press Box Telephone:** (505) 222-4093.

NEW MEXICO STATE Aggies
Conference: Sun Belt.
Mailing Address: P.O. Box 30001, Las Cruces, NM 88003. **Website:** www.nmstatesports.com.
Head Coach: Rocky Ward. **Assistant Coaches:** Brad Dolejsi, John Michael Herrera, *Chad Wolff. **Telephone:** (505) 646-5813. ◆ **Baseball SID:** Garret Ward. **Telephone:** (505) 646-3269. **FAX:** (505) 646-2425.
Home Field: Presley Askew Field. **Seating Capacity:** 1,000. **Outfield Dimensions:** LF—340, CF—400, RF—340. **Press Box Telephone:** (505) 646-5700.

NEW ORLEANS Privateers
Conference: Sun Belt.
Mailing Address: Lakefront Arena, New Orleans, LA 70148. **Website:** www.unoprivateers.com.
Head Coach: Tom Walter. **Assistant Coaches:** Chuck Bartlett, Bill Cilento, *Dennis Healy. **Telephone:** (504) 280-6100. ◆ **Baseball SID:** Jack Duggan. **Telephone:** (504) 280-7027. **FAX:** (504) 280-7240.
Home Field: Maestri Field. **Seating Capacity:** 4,200. **Outfield Dimensions:** LF—330, CF—405, RF—330. **Press Box Telephone:** (504) 280-3874.

NEW YORK TECH Bears
Conference: Independent.
Mailing Address: P.O. Box 8000, Old Westbury, NY 11568. **Website:** www.nyit.edu/athletics.
Head Coach: Bob Hirschfield. **Assistant Coaches:** Tim Belz, *Mike Caulfield, Ray Giannelli. **Telephone:** (516) 686-7513. ◆ **Baseball SID:** Ben Arcuri. **Telephone:** (516) 686-7504. **FAX:** (516) 686-1219.

NIAGARA Purple Eagles
Conference: Metro Atlantic.

Mailing Address: P.O. Box 2009, Niagara University, NY 14109. **Website:** www.purpleeagles.com.
Head Coach: Chris Chernisky. **Assistant Coach:** Kyle Swiatocha. **Telephone:** (716) 286-8624. ◆ **Baseball SID:** Michele Schmidt. **Telephone:** (716) 286-8588. **FAX:** (716) 286-8582.

NICHOLLS STATE Colonels
Conference: Southland.
Mailing Address: P.O. Box 2032, Thibodaux, LA 70301. **Website:** www.colonelsports.com.
Head Coach: B.D. Parker. **Assistant Coaches:** Jake Carlson, *Gerald Cassard. **Telephone:** (985) 448-4808. ◆ **Baseball SID:** Bobby Galinsky. **Telephone:** (985) 448-4281. **FAX:** (985) 448-4924.
Home Field: Ray Didier Field. **Seating Capacity:** 1,000. **Outfield Dimensions:** LF—340, CF—410, RF—340. **Press Box Telephone:** (985) 448-4834.

NORFOLK STATE Spartans
Conference: Mid-Eastern Athletic.
Mailing Address: 700 Park Ave., Norfolk, VA 23504. **Website:** www.nsu.edu/athletics.
Head Coach: *Marty Miller. **Assistant Coaches:** Claudell Clark, Enrique Mendieta. **Telephone:** (757) 823-9539. ◆ **Baseball SID:** Matt Michalec. **Telephone:** (757) 823-2628. **FAX:** (757) 823-8218.

NORTH CAROLINA Tar Heels
Conference: Atlantic Coast.
Mailing Address: P.O. Box 2126, Chapel Hill, NC 27515. **Website:** www.tarheelblue.com.
Head Coach: Mike Fox. **Assistant Coaches:** *Chad Holbrook, Alex Marconi, Roger Williams. **Telephone:** (919) 962-2351. ◆ **Baseball SID:** John Martin. **Telephone:** (919) 962-0084. **FAX:** (919) 845-2309.
Home Field: Boshamer Stadium. **Seating Capacity:** 2,500. **Outfield Dimensions:** LF—335, CF—400, RF—335. **Press Box Telephone:** (919) 962-3509.

UNC ASHEVILLE Bulldogs
Conference: Big South.
Mailing Address: One University Heights, Asheville, NC 28804. **Website:** www.unca.edu/athletics.
Head Coach: Willie Stewart. **Assistant Coaches:** Eddie Guessford, Pete Jenkins, *Tim Perry. **Telephone:** (828) 251-6920. ◆ **Baseball SID:** Everett Hutto. **Telephone:** (828) 251-6931. **FAX:** (828) 251-6386.

UNC GREENSBORO Spartans
Conference: Southern.
Mailing Address: P.O. Box 26168, Greensboro, NC 27402. **Website:** www.uncgspartans.com.
Head Coach: Mike Gaski. **Assistant Coaches:** Ryan Gordon, *Mike Rodriguez, Mike Sollie. **Telephone:** (336) 334-3247. ◆ **Baseball SID:** Chris Jones. **Telephone:** (336) 334-5615. **FAX:** (336) 334-3182.
Home Field: UNCG Baseball Stadium. **Seating Capacity:** 3,500. **Outfield Dimensions:** LF—340, CF—405, RF—340. **Press Box Telephone:** (336) 334-5625.

UNC WILMINGTON Seahawks
Conference: Colonial Athletic.
Mailing Address: 601 S. College Rd., Wilmington, NC 28403. **Website:** www.uncwsports.com.
Head Coach: Mark Scalf. **Assistant Coaches:** Morgan Frazier, *Randy Hood, Scott Jackson. **Telephone:** (910) 962-3570. ◆ **Baseball SID:** Tom Riordan. **Telephone:** (910) 962-4099. **FAX:** (910) 962-3686.
Home Field: Brooks Field. **Seating Capacity:** 3,500. **Outfield Dimensions:** LF—340, CF—380, RF—340. **Press Box Telephone:** (910) 395-5141.

NORTH CAROLINA A&T Aggies

Conference: Mid-Eastern Athletic.
Mailing Address: 1601 E. Market St., Moore Gym, Greensboro, NC 27411. **Website:** www.ncat.edu/~athletic.
Head Coach: *Keith Shumate. **Assistant Coaches:** Arthur Davis, Rod Gorham. **Telephone:** (336) 334-7371. ◆ **Baseball SID:** Brian Holloway. **Telephone:** (336) 334-7141. **FAX:** (336) 334-7181.

NORTH CAROLINA STATE Wolfpack

Conference: Atlantic Coast.
Mailing Address: P.O. Box 8505, Raleigh, NC 27695. **Website:** www.gopack.com.
Head Coach: Elliott Avent. **Assistant Coaches:** Tony Guzzo, Chris Roberts, Jeff Waggoner. **Telephone:** (919) 515-3613. ◆ **Baseball SID:** Bruce Winkworth. **Telephone:** (919) 515-1182. **FAX:** (919) 515-2898.
Home Field: Doak Field. **Seating Capacity:** 2,500. **Outfield Dimensions:** LF—325, CF—400, RF—330.

#NORTH DAKOTA STATE Bison

Conference: Independent.
Mailing Address: P.O. Box 5600, University Station, Fargo, ND 58105. **Website:** www.gobison.com.
Head Coach: Mitch McLeod. **Assistant Coach:** Mike Skogen. **Telephone:** (701) 231-8853. ◆ **Baseball SID:** Ryan Perreault. **Telephone:** (701) 231-8022. **FAX:** (701) 866-8605.

NORTHEASTERN Huskies

Conference: America East.
Mailing Address: 219 Cabot Center, 360 Huntington Ave., Boston, MA 02115. **Website:** www.gonu.com.
Head Coach: Neil McPhee. **Assistant Coaches:** *Greg DiCenzo, Kevin Gately, Tim Troville. **Telephone:** (617) 373-3657. ◆ **Baseball SID:** Jon Litchfield. **Telephone:** (617) 373-3643. **FAX:** (617) 373-3152.

#NORTHERN COLORADO Bears

Conference: Independent.
Mailing Address: 251 Butler-Hancock Hall, Box 117, Greeley, CO 80639. **Website:** www.uncbears.com.
Head Coach: Kevin Smallcomb. **Assistant Coaches:** *Chris Forbes, Bruce Vaughn, Patrick Wiley. **Telephone:** (970) 351-1714. ◆ **Baseball SID:** Kyle Schwartz. **Telephone:** (970) 351-2522. **FAX:** (970) 351-1995.

NORTHERN ILLINOIS Huskies

Conference: Mid-American (West).
Mailing Address: 1525 W. Lincoln Hwy. Suite 209, DeKalb, IL 60115. **Website:** www.niuhuskies.com.
Head Coach: Ed Mathey. **Assistant Coaches:** Steve Joslyn, *Tim McDonough, Luke Sabers. **Telephone:** (815) 753-2225. ◆ **Baseball SID:** Dave Retier. **Telephone:** (815) 753-3706. **FAX:** (815) 753-9540.

NORTHERN IOWA Panthers

Conference: Missouri Valley.
Mailing Address: UNI-Dome NW Upper, Cedar Falls, IA 50614. **Website:** www.unipanthers.com.
Head Coach: Rick Heller. **Assistant Coaches:** *Dan Davis, Ryan Jacobs, Marty Sutherland. **Telephone:** (319) 273-6323. ◆ **Baseball SID:** Brandie Glasnapp. **Telephone:** (319) 273-5455. **FAX:** (319) 273-3602.
Home Field: Riverfront Stadium. **Seating Capacity:** 4,277. **Outfield Dimensions:** LF—335, CF—380, RF—335. **Press Box Telephone:** (319) 232-5633.

NORTHWESTERN Wildcats

Conference: Big Ten.
Mailing Address: 1501 Central St., Evanston, IL 60208. **Website:** www.nusports.com.
Head Coach: Paul Stevens. **Assistant Coaches:** Ron

Klein, *Tim Stoddard. **Telephone:** (847) 491-4652. ◆ **Baseball SID:** Aaron Bongle. **Telephone:** (847) 491-7503. **FAX:** (847) 491-8818.
Home Field: Rocky Miller Park. **Seating Capacity:** 1,000. **Outfield Dimensions:** LF—330, CF—400, RF—330. **Press Box Telephone:** (847) 491-4200.

NORTHWESTERN STATE Demons

Conference: Southland.
Mailing Address: Athletic Fieldhouse, Natchitoches, LA 71497. **Website:** www.nsudemons.com.
Head Coach: Mitch Gaspard. **Assistant Coaches:** *J.P. Davis, Jeff McCannon. **Telephone:** (318) 357-4139. ◆ **Baseball SID:** Matt Bonnette. **Telephone:** (318) 357-6467. **FAX:** (318) 357-4515.

NOTRE DAME Fighting Irish

Conference: Big East.
Mailing Address: 112 Joyce Center, Notre Dame, IN 46556. **Website:** www.und.com.
Head Coach: Paul Mainieri. **Assistant Coaches:** *David Grewe, Terry Rooney. **Telephone:** (574) 631-6366. ◆ **Baseball SID:** Pete LaFleur. **Telephone:** (574) 631-7516. **FAX:** (574) 631-7941.
Home Field: Frank Eck Stadium. **Seating Capacity:** 2,500. **Outfield Dimensions:** LF—331, CF—401, RF—331. **Press Box Telephone:** (574) 631-9018.

OAKLAND Golden Grizzlies

Conference: Mid-Continent.
Mailing Address: Athletic Center Building, Rochester, MI 48309. **Website:** www.ougrizzlies.com.
Head Coach: Mark Avery. **Assistant Coaches:** Ryan Freiburger, Chris Newell, Justin Robertson. **Telephone:** (248) 370-4159. ◆ **Baseball SID:** Rebecca Vick. **Telephone:** (248) 370-3123. **FAX:** (248) 370-4156.

OHIO Bobcats

Conference: Mid-American (East).
Mailing Address: Convocation Center, Richland Ave., Athens, OH 45701. **Website:** www.ohiobobcats.com.
Head Coach: *Joe Carbone. **Assistant Coaches:** Scott Malinowski, Bill Toadvine. **Telephone:** (740) 593-1180. ◆ **Baseball SID:** Jason Cunningham. **Telephone:** (740) 593-1837. **FAX:** (740) 597-1838.
Home Field: Bob Wren Stadium. **Seating Capacity:** 6,000. **Outfield Dimensions:** LF—340, CF—405, RF—340. **Press Box Telephone:** (740) 593-0526.

OHIO STATE Buckeyes

Conference: Big Ten.
Mailing Address: 410 Woody Hayes Dr., Columbus, OH 43210. **Website:** www.ohiostatebuckeyes.com.
Head Coach: Bob Todd. **Assistant Coaches:** Pat Bangston, *Greg Cypret, Eric Parker. **Telephone:** (614) 292-1075. ◆ **Baseball SID:** Todd Lamb. **Telephone:** (614) 688-0343. **FAX:** (614) 292-8547.
Home Field: Bill Davis Stadium. **Seating Capacity:** 4,450. **Outfield Dimensions:** LF—330, CF—400, RF—330. **Press Box Telephone:** (614) 292-0021.

OKLAHOMA Sooners

Conference: Big 12.
Mailing Address: 180 W. Brooks St., Room 2525, Norman, OK 73019. **Website:** www.soonersports.com.
Head Coach: Larry Cochell. **Assistant Coaches:** *Fred Corral, Sunny Golloway, Ryan Wade. **Telephone:** (405) 325-8354. ◆ **Baseball SID:** Craig Moran. **Telephone:** (405) 325-8372. **FAX:** (405) 325-7623.
Home Field: L. Dale Mitchell Park. **Seating Capacity:** 2,700. **Outfield Dimensions:** LF—335, CF—411, RF—335. **Press Box Telephone:** (405) 325-8363.

OKLAHOMA STATE Cowboys
Conference: Big 12.
Mailing Address: 220 OSU Athletics Center, Stillwater, OK 74078. **Website:** www.okstate.com.
Head Coach: Frank Anderson. **Assistant Coaches:** *Greg Evans, Robin Harriss, Billy Jones. **Telephone:** (405) 744-7141. ◆ **Baseball SID:** Thomas Samuel. **Telephone:** (405) 744-7853. **FAX:** (405) 744-7754.
Home Field: Allie P. Reynolds Stadium. **Seating Capacity:** 4,000. **Outfield Dimensions:** LF—390, CF—400, RF—385. **Press Box Telephone:** (405) 744-5757.

OLD DOMINION Monarchs
Conference: Colonial Athletic.
Mailing Address: Hampton Blvd., Norfolk, VA 23529. **Website:** www.odusports.com.
Head Coach: Jerry Meyers. **Assistant Coaches:** Eric Folmar, *Ryan Morris, Matt Reid. **Telephone:** (757) 683-4230. ◆ **Baseball SID:** Carol Hudson. **Telephone:** (757) 683-3372. **FAX:** (757) 683-3119.
Home Field: Bud Metheny Stadium. **Seating Capacity:** 2,500. **Outfield Dimensions:** LF—325, CF—395, RF—325. **Press Box Telephone:** (757) 683-5036.

ORAL ROBERTS Golden Eagles
Conference: Mid-Continent.
Mailing Address: 7777 S. Lewis Ave., Tulsa, OK 74171. **Website:** www.orugoldeneagles.com.
Head Coach: *Rob Walton. **Assistant Coaches:** Ryan Folmar, Ryan Neill, Todd Shelton. **Telephone:** (918) 495-7205. ◆ **Baseball SID:** Cris Belvin. **Telephone:** (918) 495-7094. **FAX:** (918) 495-7142.
Home Field: J.L. Johnson Stadium. **Seating Capacity:** 2,500. **Outfield Dimensions:** LF—330, CF—400, RF—330. **Press Box Telephone:** (918) 495-7165.

OREGON STATE Beavers
Conference: Pacific-10.
Mailing Address: Gill Coliseum, Room 127, Corvallis, OR 97331. **Website:** www.osubeavers.com.
Head Coach: Pat Casey. **Assistant Coaches:** Marty Lees, Troy Schader, *Dan Spencer. **Telephone:** (541) 737-2825. ◆ **Baseball SID:** Kip Carlson. **Telephone:** (541) 737-7472. **FAX:** (541) 737-3072.
Home Field: Goss Stadium at Coleman Field. **Seating Capacity:** 2,000. **Outfield Dimensions:** LF—330, CF—400, RF—330. **Press Box Telephone:** (541) 737-7475.

PACIFIC Tigers
Conference: Big West.
Mailing Address: 3601 Pacific Ave., Stockton, CA 95211. **Website** www.pacifictigers.com.
Head Coach: Ed Sprague. **Assistant Coaches:** Jim Brink, *Steve Pearse. **Telephone:** (209) 946-2709. ◆ **Baseball SID:** Glen Sisk. **Telephone:** (209) 946-2730. **FAX:** (209) 946-2757.
Home Field: Billy Hebert Field. **Seating Capacity:** 3,500. **Outfield Dimensions:** LF—325, CF—390, RF—330. **Press Box Telephone:** (209) 644-1917.

PENNSYLVANIA Quakers
Conference: Ivy League (Gehrig).
Mailing Address: 235 S. 33rd St., Philadelphia, PA 19104. **Website:** www.pennathletics.com.
Head Coach: *Bob Seddon. **Assistant Coaches:** Ralph Roesler, Bill Wagner. **Telephone:** (215) 898-6282. ◆ **Baseball SID:** Mat Kanan. **Telephone:** (215) 573-4125. **FAX:** (215) 898-1747.

PENN STATE Nittany Lions
Conference: Big Ten.
Mailing Address: 112 Bryce Jordan Center, University

Park, PA 16802. **Website:** www.GoPSUsports.com.
Head Coach: Robbie Wine. **Assistant Coaches:** Jason Bell, Jon Ramsey. **Telephone:** (814) 863-0230. ◆ **Baseball SID:** Bob Volkert. **Telephone:** (814) 865-1757. **FAX:** (814) 863-3165.
Home Field: Beaver Field. **Seating Capacity:** 1,000. **Outfield Dimensions:** LF—350, CF—405, RF—350. **Press Box Telephone:** (814) 865-2552.

PEPPERDINE Waves
Conference: West Coast.
Mailing Address: 24255 Pacific Coast Hwy., Malibu, CA 90263. **Website:** www.pepperdinesports.com.
Head Coach: Steve Rodriguez. **Assistant Coaches:** *Rick Hirtensteiner, Ari Jacobs, Sean Kenny. **Telephone:** (310) 506-4371. ◆ **Baseball SID:** Al Barba. **Telephone:** (310) 506-4455. **FAX:** (310) 506-4322.
Home Field: Eddy D. Field Stadium. **Seating Capacity:** 1,800. **Outfield Dimensions:** LF—330, CF—400, RF—330. **Press Box Telephone:** (310) 506-4598.

PITTSBURGH Panthers
Conference: Big East.
Mailing Address: 3719 Terrace St., Pittsburgh, PA 15213. **Website:** www.pittsburghpanthers.com.
Head Coach: Joe Jordano. **Assistant Coaches:** Joel Dombkowski, Dan Ninemire. **Telephone:** (412) 648-8202. ◆ **Baseball SID:** Burt Lauten. **Telephone:** (412) 648-8240. **FAX:** (412) 648-8248.
Home Field: Trees Field. **Seating Capacity:** 500. **Outfield Dimensions:** LF—302, CF—400, RF—328.

PORTLAND Pilots
Conference: West Coast.
Mailing Address: 5000 N. Willamette Blvd., Portland, OR 97203. **Website:** www.portlandpilots.com.
Head Coach: Chris Sperry. **Assistant Coaches:** Matt Hollod, *Gary Van Tol. **Telephone:** (503) 943-7707. ◆ **Baseball SID:** Jason Brough. **Telephone:** (503) 943-7439. **FAX:** (503) 943-7247.
Home Field: Joe Etzel Stadium. **Seating Capacity:** 1,500. **Outfield Dimensions:** LF—350, CF—390, RF—340. **Press Box Telephone:** (503) 943-7253.

PRAIRIE VIEW A&M Panthers
Conference: Southwestern Athletic.
Mailing Address: P.O. Box 97, Prairie View, TX 77446. **Website:** www.pvamu.edu/sports.
Head Coach: Michael Robertson. **Assistant Coach:** Waskyla Cullivan. **Telephone:** (936) 857-4290. ◆ **Baseball SID:** Keith Roy. **Telephone:** (936) 857-2114. **FAX:** (936) 857-2408.

PRINCETON Tigers
Conference: Ivy League (Gehrig).
Mailing Address: Jadwin Gymnasium, Princeton University, Princeton, NJ 08544. **Website:** www.goprincetontigers.com.
Head Coach: Scott Bradley. **Assistant Coaches:** *Lloyd Brewer, Jeremy Meccage, Pete Silletti. **Telephone:** (609) 258-5059. ◆ **Baseball SID:** Yariv Amir. **Telephone:** (609) 258-5701. **FAX:** (609) 258-2399.

PURDUE Boilermakers
Conference: Big Ten.
Mailing Address: Mollenkopf Athletic Center, 1225 Northwestern Ave., West Lafayette, IN 47907. **Website:** www.purduesports.com.
Head Coach: Doug Schreiber. **Assistant Coaches:** *Todd Murphy, Ryan Sawyers, Rob Smith. **Telephone:** (765) 494-3998. ◆ **Baseball SID:** Mark Leddy. **Telephone:** (765) 494-3281. **FAX:** (765) 494-5447.

Home Field: Lambert Field. **Seating Capacity:** 1,100. **Outfield Dimensions:** LF—340, CF—408, RF—340. **Press Box Telephone:** Unavailable.

QUINNIPIAC Braves

Conference: Northeast.
Mailing Address: 275 Mount Carmel Ave., Hamden, CT 06518. **Website:** www.quinnipiacbobcats.com.
Head Coach: Dan Gooley. **Assistant Coaches:** Dan Scarpa, Marc Stonaha, Joe Tonelli. **Telephone:** (203) 582-8966. ◆ **Baseball SID:** Tom Wilkins. **Telephone:** (203) 582-5387. **FAX:** (203) 582-5385.

RADFORD Highlanders

Conference: Big South.
Mailing Address: P.O. Box 6913, Radford, VA 24142. **Website:** www.radford.edu/athletics.
Head Coach: Lew Kent. **Assistant Coaches:** *Ryan Brittle, Chip Schaffne. **Telephone:** (540) 831-5881. ◆ **Baseball SID:** Andrew Dickerson. **Telephone:** (540) 831-5211. **FAX:** (540) 831-5556.

RHODE ISLAND Rams

Conference: Atlantic-10.
Mailing Address: 3 Keaney Rd., Suite One, Kingston, RI 02881. **Website:** www.gorhody.com.
Head Coach: Frank Leoni. **Assistant Coaches:** Stephen Breitbach, Jim Foster. **Telephone:** (401) 874-4550. ◆ **Baseball SID:** Mark Kwolek. **Telephone:** (401) 874-2409. **FAX:** (401) 874-5354.

RICE Owls

Conference: Western Athletic.
Mailing Address: 6100 Main St., Houston, TX 77005. **Website:** www.RiceOwls.com.
Head Coach: Wayne Graham. **Assistant Coaches:** Zane Curry, *David Pierce, Mike Taylor. **Telephone:** (713) 348-8864. ◆ **Baseball SID:** John Sullivan. **Telephone:** (713) 348-5636. **FAX:** (713) 348-6019.
Home Field: Reckling Park. **Seating Capacity:** 4,500. **Outfield Dimensions:** LF—330, CF—400, RF—330. **Press Box Telephone:** (713) 348-4931.

RICHMOND Spiders

Conference: Atlantic-10 (West).
Mailing Address: Baseball Office, Robins Center, Richmond, VA 23173. **Website:** www.richmondspiders.com.
Head Coach: Ron Atkins. **Assistant Coaches:** Jason Johnson, Mike Loyd, *Adam Taylor. **Telephone:** (804) 289-8391. ◆ **Baseball SID:** Scott Meyer. **Telephone:** (804) 289-6313. **FAX:** (804) 289-8820.
Home Field: Pitt Field. **Seating Capacity:** 600. **Outfield Dimensions:** LF—328, CF—390, RF—328. Press Box Telephone. (804) 289 8714.

RIDER Broncs

Conference: Metro Atlantic.
Mailing Address: 2083 Lawrenceville Rd., Lawrenceville, NJ 08648. **Website:** www.gobroncs.com.
Head Coach: Barry Davis. **Assistant Coaches:** Thomas Carr, Josh Copskey, Matt Wolski. **Telephone:** (609) 896-5055. ◆ **Baseball SID:** Bud Focht. **Telephone:** (609) 896-5138. **FAX:** (609) 896-0341.

RUTGERS Scarlet Knights

Conference: Big East.
Mailing Address: 83 Rockefeller Rd., Piscataway, NJ 08854. **Website:** www.scarletknights.com.
Head Coach: Fred Hill. **Assistant Coaches:** Jim Agnello, Rick Freeman, *Glen Gardner. **Telephone:** (732) 445-7833. ◆ **Baseball SID:** Pat McBride. **Telephone:** (732) 445-7884. **FAX:** (732) 445-3063.
Home Field: Class of '53 Baseball Complex. **Seating**

Capacity: 1,500. **Outfield Dimensions:** LF—330, CF—410, RF—325. **Press Box Telephone:** (732) 445-2776.

SACRAMENTO STATE Hornets

Conference: Independent.
Mailing Address: 6000 J St., Sacramento, CA 95819. **Website:** www.hornetsports.com.
Head Coach: John Smith. **Assistant Coaches:** Jim Barr, Rusty McLain. **Telephone:** (916) 278-7225. ◆ **Baseball SID:** Andria Wenzel. **Telephone:** (916) 278-6896. **FAX:** (916) 278-5429.

SACRED HEART Pioneers

Conference: Northeast.
Mailing Address: 5151 Park Ave., Fairfield, CT 06825. **Website:** www.sacredheartpioneers.com.
Head Coach: Nick Giaquinto. **Assistant Coaches:** Bob Andrews, *Seth Kaplan, Chuck Ristano. **Telephone:** (203) 365-7632. ◆ **Baseball SID:** Gene Gumbs. **Telephone:** (203) 396-8127. **FAX:** (203) 371-7889.

ST. BONAVENTURE Bonnies

Conference: Atlantic-10 (East).
Mailing Address: Reilly Center, St. Bonaventure, NY 14778. **Website:** www.gobonnies.com.
Head Coach: Larry Sudbrook. **Assistant Coach:** *Jonathan Myler. **Telephone:** (716) 375-2641. ◆ **Baseball SID:** Steve Mest. **Telephone:** (716) 375-2319. **FAX:** (716) 375-2380.

ST. FRANCIS Terriers

Conference: Northeast.
Mailing Address: 180 Remsen St., Brooklyn, NY 11201. **Website:** athletics.stfranciscollege.edu.
Head Coach: Frank Del George. **Assistant Coaches:** Robert Cruz, Tommy Weber. **Telephone:** (718) 489-5490. ◆ **Baseball SID:** Angela Manekas. **Telephone:** (718) 489-5369. **FAX:** (718) 797-2140.

ST. JOHN'S Red Storm

Conference: Big East.
Mailing Address: 8000 Utopia Pkwy., Queens, NY 11439. **Website:** www.redstormsports.com.
Head Coach: Ed Blankmeyer. **Assistant Coaches:** Scott Brown, *Mike Hampton. **Telephone:** (718) 990-6148. ◆ **Baseball SID:** Mex Carey. **Telephone:** (718) 990-1521. **FAX:** (718) 969-8468.
Home Field: The Ballpark at St. John's. **Seating Capacity:** 3,500. **Outfield Dimensions:** LF—325, CF—400, RF—325. **Press Box Telephone:** (718) 990-2725.

ST. JOSEPH'S Hawks

Conference: Atlantic-10 (East).
Mailing Address: 5600 City Ave., Philadelphia, PA 19131. **Website:** www.sjuhawks.com.
Head Coach: Shawn Pender. **Assistant Coaches:** Rich Coletta, Greg Manco, *Kevin Sharp. **Telephone:** (610) 660-1718. ◆ **Baseball SID:** Phil Denne. **Telephone:** (610) 660-1738. **FAX:** (610) 660-1724.

SAINT LOUIS Billikens

Conference: Conference USA.
Mailing Address: 3672 W. Pine Blvd., St. Louis, MO 63103. **Website:** www.slubillikens.com.
Head Coach: Bob Hughes. **Assistant Coach:** *Wes Sells. **Telephone:** (314) 977-3172. ◆ **Baseball SID:** Diana Koval. **Telephone:** (314) 977-3463. **FAX:** (314) 977-7193.
Home Field: Billiken Sports Center. **Seating Capacity:** 500. **Outfield Dimensions:** LF—330, CF—395, RF—330. **Press Box Telephone:** (314) 402-8655.

ST. MARY'S Gaels

Conference: West Coast.
Mailing Address: 1928 St. Mary's Rd., Moraga, CA 94575. **Website:** www.smcgaels.com.
Head Coach: Jedd Soto. **Assistant Coaches:** Steve Roberts, *Gabe Zappin. **Telephone:** (925) 631-4637. ◆ **Baseball SID:** Ryan Reggiani. **Telephone:** (925) 631-4402. **FAX:** (925) 631-6290.
Home Field: Louis Guisto Field. **Seating Capacity:** 500. **Outfield Dimensions:** LF—340, CF—390, RF—340.

ST. PETER'S Peacocks

Conference: Metro Atlantic.
Mailing Address: 2641 John F. Kennedy Blvd., Jersey City, NJ 07306. **Website:** www.spc.edu.
Head Coach: Derek England. **Assistant Coaches:** Marty Craft, *Charles Rozzi, Josh Piniero. **Telephone:** (201) 915-9459. ◆ **Baseball SID:** Tim Camp. **Telephone:** (201) 915-9101. **FAX:** (201) 915-9092.

SAM HOUSTON STATE Bearkats

Conference: Southland.
Mailing Address: P.O. Box 2268, Huntsville, TX 77341. **Website:** www.shsu.edu.
Head Coach: Chris Rupp. **Assistant Coach:** Phillip Ghutzman. **Telephone:** (936) 294-1731. ◆ **Baseball SID:** Paul Ridings. **Telephone:** (936) 294-1764. **FAX:** (936) 294-3538.

SAMFORD Bulldogs

Conference: Ohio Valley.
Mailing Address: 800 Lakeshore Dr., Birmingham, AL 35229. **Website:** www.samfordsports.com.
Head Coach: Casey Dunn. **Assistant Coaches:** *Tony David, Mick Fieldbinder, Shayne Kelley. **Telephone:** (205) 726-2134. ◆ **Baseball SID:** Joey Mullins. **Telephone:** (205) 726-2799. **FAX:** (205) 726-2545.

SAN DIEGO Toreros

Conference: West Coast.
Mailing Address: 5998 Alcala Park, San Diego, CA 92110. **Website:** usdtoreros.com.
Head Coach: Rich Hill. **Assistant Coaches:** *Mike Kramer, Eric Valenzuela. **Telephone:** (619) 260-5953. ◆ **Baseball SID:** Nick Mirkovich. **Telephone:** (619) 260-7930. **FAX:** (619) 260-2990.
Home Field: Cunningham Stadium. **Seating Capacity:** 1,500. **Outfield Dimensions:** LF—309, CF—395, RF—329. **Press Box Telephone:** (619) 260-8829.

SAN DIEGO STATE Aztecs

Conference: Western Athletic.
Mailing Address: Department of Athletics, San Diego State University, San Diego, CA 92182. **Website:** www.goaztecs.com.
Head Coach: Tony Gwynn. **Assistant Coaches:** *Rusty Filter, Anthony Johnson, Jay Martel. **Telephone:** (619) 594-6889. ◆ **Baseball SID:** Dave Kuhn. **Telephone:** (619) 594-5547. **FAX:** (619) 582-6541.
Home Field: Tony Gwynn Stadium. **Seating Capacity:** 3,000. **Outfield Dimensions:** LF—340, CF—410, RF—340. **Press Box Telephone:** (619) 594-4103.

SAN FRANCISCO Dons

Conference: West Coast.
Mailing Address: Memorial Gym, 2130 Fulton St., San Francisco, CA 94118. **Website:** www.usfdons.com.
Head Coach: Nino Giarratano. **Assistant Coaches:** Rigoberto Lopez, *Greg Moore, Troy Nakamura. **Telephone:** (415) 422-2934. ◆ **Baseball SID:** Ryan McCrary. **Telephone:** (415) 422-6162. **FAX:** (415) 422-2929.

Home Field: Benedetti Diamond. **Seating Capacity:** 1,000. **Outfield Dimensions:** LF—345, CF—415, RF—321. **Press Box Telephone:** (415) 422-2929.

SAN JOSE STATE Spartans

Conference: Western Athletic.
Mailing Address: One Washington Square, San Jose, CA 95192. **Website:** www.sjsuspartans.com.
Head Coach: Sam Piraro. **Assistant Coaches:** Jason Bugg, Dean Madsen, *Doug Thurman. **Telephone:** (408) 924-1255. ◆ **Baseball SID:** Neil Parry. **Telephone:** (408) 924-1217. **FAX:** (408) 924-1291.
Home Field: Municipal Stadium. **Seating Capacity:** 5,000. **Outfield Dimensions:** LF—330, CF—400, RF—330. **Press Box Telephone:** (408) 924-7276.

SANTA CLARA Broncos

Conference: West Coast.
Mailing Address: 500 El Camino Real, Santa Clara, CA 95053. **Website:** www.santaclarabroncos.com.
Head Coach: Mark O'Brien. **Assistant Coaches:** Matt Mueller, *Mike Oakland, Mike Zirelli. **Telephone:** (408) 554-4680. ◆ **Baseball SID:** Neila Matheny. **Telephone:** (408) 554-4670. **FAX:** (408) 554-6942.
Home Field: Buck Shaw Stadium. **Seating Capacity:** 6,800. **Outfield Dimensions:** LF—350, CF—400, RF—320. **Press Box Telephone:** Unavailable.

SAVANNAH STATE Tigers

Conference: Independent.
Mailing Address: 3219 College St., Savannah, GA 31404. **Website:** www.savstate.edu/athletics.
Head Coach: Jamie Rigdon. **Assistant Coaches:** Ricardo Castillo, Tim Paige, Chris Scesario. **Telephone:** (912) 356-2801. ◆ **Baseball SID:** Lee Pearson. **Telephone:** (912) 356-2446. **FAX:** (912) 353-3073.

SETON HALL Pirates

Conference: Big East.
Mailing Address: 400 S. Orange Ave., South Orange, NJ 07079. **Website:** www.shupirates.com.
Head Coach: Rob Sheppard. **Assistant Coaches:** Phil Cundari, Jim Duffy. **Telephone:** (973) 761-9557. ◆ **Baseball SID:** Jeff Mead. **Telephone:** (973) 761-9493. **FAX:** (973) 761-9061.
Home Field: Owen T. Carroll Field. **Seating Capacity:** 1,000. **Outfield Dimensions:** LF—320, CF—400, RF—320. **Press Box Telephone:** Unavailable.

SIENA Saints

Conference: Metro Atlantic.
Mailing Address: 515 Loudon Rd., Loudonville, NY 12211. **Website:** www.sienasaints.com.
Head Coach: Tony Rossi. **Assistant Coaches:** Tim Brown, *Casey Fahy, Paul Thompson. **Telephone:** (518) 786-5044. ◆ **Baseball SID:** Jason Rich. **Telephone:** (518) 783-2411. **FAX:** (518) 783-2992.

SOUTH ALABAMA Jaguars

Conference: Sun Belt.
Mailing Address: 1209 Mitchell Center, Mobile, AL 36688. **Website:** www.usajaguars.com.
Head Coach: Steve Kittrell. **Assistant Coaches:** George Hernandez, Ronnie Powell, *Scot Sealy. **Telephone:** (251) 460-6876. ◆ **Baseball SID:** Matt Smith. **Telephone:** (251) 460-7035. **FAX:** (251) 460-7297.
Home Field: Eddie Stanky Field. **Seating Capacity:** 3,500. **Outfield Dimensions:** LF—330, CF—400, RF—330. **Press Box Telephone:** (251) 460-7126.

SOUTH CAROLINA Gamecocks

Conference: Southeastern (East).

Mailing Address: 1300 Rosewood Dr., Columbia, SC 29209. **Website:** www.uscsports.com.
Head Coach: Ray Tanner. **Assistant Coaches:** Mark Calvi, Monte Lee, *Jim Toman. **Telephone:** (803) 777-0116. ◆ **Baseball SID:** Andrew Kitick. **Telephone:** (803) 777-5257. **FAX:** (803) 777-2967.
Home Field: Sarge Frye Field. **Seating Capacity:** 6,000. **Outfield Dimensions:** LF—320, CF—390, RF—320. **Press Box Telephone:** (803) 777-6648.

#SOUTH DAKOTA STATE Jackrabbits
Conference: Independent.
Mailing Address: Stanley J. Marshall HPER Center, SDSU Box 2820, Brookings, SD 57007. **Website:** www.sdstate.edu/athletics.
Head Coach: Reggie Christiansen. **Assistant Coaches:** Matt Duncan, Pat Holmes, *Chris Smart. **Telephone:** (605) 688-5027. ◆ **Baseball SID:** Ron Lenz. **Telephone:** (605) 688-4623. **FAX:** (605) 688-5999.

SOUTH FLORIDA Bulls
Conference: Conference USA.
Mailing Address: 4202 E. Fowler Ave., ATH 100, Tampa, FL 33620. **Website:** www.GoUSFBulls.com.
Head Coach: Eddie Cardieri. **Assistant Coaches:** Nelson North, Greg Parris, *Bryan Peters. **Telephone:** (813) 974-4023. ◆ **Baseball SID:** Paul Dodson. **Telephone:** (813) 974-4029. **FAX:** (813) 974-5328.
Home Field: Red McEwem Field. **Seating Capacity:** 1,500. **Outfield Dimensions:** LF—340, CF—400, RF—340. **Press Box Telephone:** (813) 974-3604.

SOUTHEAST MISSOURI STATE Indians
Conference: Ohio Valley.
Mailing Address: One University Plaza, Cape Girardeau, MO 63701. **Website:** www.gosoutheast.com.
Head Coach: Mark Hogan. **Assistant Coaches:** *Jeff Dodson, Scott Southard. **Telephone:** (573) 651-2645. ◆ **Baseball SID:** Patrick Clark. **Telephone:** (573) 651-2937. **FAX:** (573) 651-2810.

SOUTHEASTERN LOUISIANA Lions
Conference: Southland.
Mailing Address: SLU Station 10309, Hammond, LA 70402. **Website:** www.LionSports.net.
Head Coach: Dan Canevari. **Assistant Coaches:** *Graham Martin, John Stephenson, Luke Weatherford. **Telephone:** (985) 549-2253. ◆ **Baseball SID:** Matt Sullivan. **Telephone:** (985) 549-3774. **FAX:** (985) 549-3773.

SOUTHERN Jaguars
Conference: Southwestern Athletic.
Mailing Address: P.O. Box 10850, Baton Rouge, LA 70813. **Website:** www.subr.edu/baseball.
Head Coach: Roger Cador. **Assistant Coaches:** Fernando Puebla, *Barret Rey. **Telephone:** (225) 771-2513. ◆ **Baseball SID:** Kevin Manns. **Telephone:** (225) 771-4142. **FAX:** (225) 771-5671.

SOUTHERN CALIFORNIA Trojans
Conference: Pacific-10.
Mailing Address: Dedeaux Field Building, Los Angeles, CA 90089. **Website:** www.usctrojans.com.
Head Coach: Mike Gillespie. **Assistant Coaches:** Chad Kreuter, *Dave Lawn, Andy Nieto. **Telephone:** (213) 740-5762. ◆ **Baseball SID:** Jason Pommier. **Telephone:** (213) 740-3807. **FAX:** (213) 740-7584.
Home Field: Dedeaux Field. **Seating Capacity:** 2,500. **Outfield Dimensions:** LF—335, CF—395, RF—335. **Press Box Telephone:** (213) 748-3449.

SOUTHERN ILLINOIS Salukis
Conference: Missouri Valley.

Mailing Address: Room 118 Lingle Hall, Carbondale, IL 62901. **Website:** www.siusalukis.com.
Head Coach: Dan Callahan. **Assistant Coaches:** Tony Etnier, *Ken Henderson, Bryan Wolff. **Telephone:** (618) 453-2802. ◆ **Baseball SID:** Jeff Honza. **Telephone:** (618) 453-5470. **FAX:** (618) 453-2648.
Home Field: Abe Martin Field. **Seating Capacity:** 2,000. **Outfield Dimensions:** LF—340, CF—390, RF—340.

SOUTHERN MISSISSIPPI Golden Eagles
Conference: Conference USA.
Mailing Address: 118 College Dr. #5017, Hattiesburg, MS 39406. **Website:** www.southernmiss.com.
Head Coach: Corky Palmer. **Assistant Coaches:** Scott Berry, *Lane Burroughs, Josh Hoffpauir. **Telephone:** (601) 266-5194. ◆ **Baseball SID:** Mike Montoro. **Telephone:** (601) 266-5947. **FAX:** (601) 266-4507.
Home Field: Pete Taylor Park at Hill Denson Field. **Seating Capacity:** 3,678. **Outfield Dimensions:** LF—340, CF—400, RF—340. **Press Box Telephone:** (601) 266-5684.

SOUTHERN UTAH Thunderbirds
Conference: Mid-Continent.
Mailing Address: 351 W. University Blvd., Cedar City, UT 84720. **Website:** www.suu.edu/athletics.
Head Coach: *David Eldredge. **Assistant Coaches:** Marshall Phillips, Robert Stephens, Rick Wilding. **Telephone:** (435) 586-7932. ◆ **Baseball SID:** Steve Johnson. **Telephone:** (435) 586-7752. **FAX:** (435) 865-8037.

SOUTHWEST MISSOURI STATE Bears
Conference: Missouri Valley.
Mailing Address: 901 S. National Ave., Springfield, MO 65804. **Website:** www.smsbears.net.
Head Coach: Keith Guttin. **Assistant Coaches:** Sam Carel, *Paul Evans, Brent Thomas. **Telephone:** (417) 836-5242. ◆ **Baseball SID:** Jeff Williams. **Telephone:** (417) 836-5402. **FAX:** (417) 836-4868.
Home Field (Seating Capacity): Hammons Field (8,000). **Outfield Dimensions:** LF—315, CF—400, RF—330. **Press Box Telephone:** (417) 863-0395, ext. 3070.

STANFORD Cardinal
Conference: Pacific-10.
Mailing Address: Arrillaga Family Sports Center, 541 E. Campus Dr., Stanford, CA 94305. **Website:** www.gostanford.com.
Head Coach: Mark Marquess. **Assistant Coaches:** Tom Kunis, David Nakama, *Dean Stotz. **Telephone:** (650) 723-4528. ◆ **Baseball SID:** Kyle McRae. **Telephone:** (650) 725-2959. **FAX:** (650) 726-2067.
Home Field: Sunken Diamond. **Seating Capacity:** 4,000. **Outfield Dimensions:** LF—335, CF—400, RF—335. **Press Box Telephone:** (650) 723-4629.

STETSON Hatters
Conference: Atlantic Sun.
Mailing Address: 421 N. Woodland Blvd., DeLand, FL 32723. **Website:** www.stetson.edu/athletics.
Head Coach: Pete Dunn. **Assistant Coaches:** Mitch Markham, Frank Martello, *Garrett Quinn. **Telephone:** (386) 822-8106. ◆ **Baseball SID:** Jamie Bataille. **Telephone:** (386) 822-8130. **FAX:** (386) 822-8132.
Home Field: Melching Field at Conrad Park. **Seating Capacity:** 2,500. **Outfield Dimensions:** LF—335, CF—403, RF—335. **Press Box Telephone:** (386) 736-7360.

STONY BROOK Seawolves
Conference: America East.
Mailing Address: SBU Sports Complex, Stony Brook,

NY 11794. **Website:** www.goseawolves.org.
Head Coach: Matt Senk. **Assistant Coaches:** Tom Nielsen, *Gerry Sputo. **Telephone:** (631) 632-9226. ◆ **Baseball SID:** Matt Wrynn. **Telephone:** (631) 632-6312. **FAX:** (631) 632-8841.

TEMPLE Owls
Conference: Atlantic-10 (East).
Mailing Address: Vivacqua Hall, 4th Floor, 1700 N. Broad St., Philadelphia, PA 19122. **Website:** www.owl-sports.com.
Head Coach: Skip Wilson. **Assistant Coaches:** Toby Fisher, *John McCardle. **Telephone:** (215) 204-3146. ◆ **Baseball SID:** Kevin Bonner. **Telephone:** (215) 204-9149. **FAX:** (215) 204-7499.

TENNESSEE Volunteers
Conference: Southeastern (East).
Mailing Address: 1720 Volunteer Blvd., Knoxville, TN 37996. **Website:** www.utsports.com.
Head Coach: Rod Delmonico. **Assistant Coaches:** Mike Bell, Larry Simcox. **Telephone:** (865) 974-1223. ◆ **Baseball SID:** Tom Satkowiak. **Telephone:** (865) 974-1212. **FAX:** (865) 974-1269.
Home Field: Lindsey Nelson Stadium. **Seating Capacity:** 4,000. **Outfield Dimensions:** LF—335, CF—404, RF—330. **Press Box Telephone:** (865) 974-3376.

TENNESSEE-MARTIN Skyhawks
Conference: Ohio Valley.
Mailing Address: 1037 Elam Center, Martin, TN 38238. **Website:** www.utmsports.com.
Head Coach: *Bubba Cates. **Assistant Coach:** Jason Sullivan. **Telephone:** (731) 881-3500. ◆ **Baseball SID:** Joe Lofaro. **Telephone:** (731) 881-7632. **FAX:** (731) 881-7624.

TENNESSEE TECH Golden Eagles
Conference: Ohio Valley.
Mailing Address: P.O. Box 5057, Cookeville, TN 38505. **Website:** www.ttusports.com.
Head Coach: *Matt Bragga. **Assistant Coaches:** Craig Moore, Brian Owens. **Telephone:** (931) 372-3925. ◆ **Baseball SID:** Michelle Cunningham. **Telephone:** (931) 372-3293. **FAX:** (931) 372-6145.

TEXAS Longhorns
Conference: Big 12.
Mailing Address: P.O. Box 7399, Austin, TX 78713. **Website:** www.TexasSports.com.
Head Coach: Augie Garrido. **Assistant Coaches:** *Tommy Harmon, Tom Holliday, Greg Swindell. **Telephone:** (512) 471-5732. ◆ **Baseball SID:** Mike Forcucci. **Telephone:** (512) 471-6039. **FAX:** (512) 471-6040.
Home Field: Disch-Falk Field. **Seating Capacity:** 6,649. **Outfield Dimensions:** LF—340, CF—400, RF—325. **Press Box Telephone:** (512) 471-1146.

TEXAS-ARLINGTON Mavericks
Conference: Southland.
Mailing Address: 1309 W. Mitchell St., Arlington, TX 76013. **Website:** www.utamavs.edu.
Head Coach: Jeff Curtis. **Assistant Coaches:** Jay Sirianni, *Darin Thomas. **Telephone:** (817) 272-2060. ◆ **Baseball SID:** John Brush. **Telephone:** (817) 272-5706. **FAX:** (817) 272-2254.
Home Field: Clay Gould Ballpark. **Seating Capacity:** 1,600. **Outfield Dimensions:** LF—330, CF—400, RF—330. **Press Box Telephone:** (817) 462-4226.

TEXAS-PAN AMERICAN Broncs
Conference: Independent.
Mailing Address: 1201 W. University Dr., Edinburg, TX 78541. **Website:** www.utpabroncs.com.

Head Coach: *Willie Gawlik. **Assistant Coaches:** Justin Meccage, Kiki Trevino. **Telephone:** (956) 381-2235. ◆ **Baseball SID:** Joe Monaco. **Telephone:** (956) 381-2240. **FAX:** (956) 381-2398.

TEXAS-SAN ANTONIO Roadrunners
Conference: Southland.
Mailing Address: 6900 N. Loop 1604 W., San Antonio, TX 78249. **Website:** www.goutsa.com.
Head Coach: Sherman Corbett. **Assistant Coaches:** Jim Blair, *Jason Marshall. **Telephone:** (210) 458-4805. ◆ **Baseball SID:** Matt Schabert. **Telephone:** (210) 458-4930. **FAX:** (210) 458-4569.

TEXAS A&M Aggies
Conference: Big 12.
Mailing Address: P.O. Box 30017, College Station, TX 77843. **Website:** www.aggieathletics.com.
Head Coach: Mark Johnson. **Assistant Coaches:** *David Coleman, Jason Hutchins, Jim Lawler. **Telephone:** (979) 845-4810. ◆ **Baseball SID:** Chuck Glenewinkel. **Telephone:** (979) 845-3239. **FAX:** (979) 845-0564.
Home Field: Olsen Field. **Seating Capacity:** 7,053. **Outfield Dimensions:** LF—330, CF—400, RF—330. **Press Box Telephone:** (979) 458-3604.

TEXAS A&M-CORPUS CHRISTI Islanders
Conference: Independent.
Mailing Address: 6300 Ocean Dr., Corpus Christi, TX 78412. **Website:** www.goislanders.com.
Head Coach: Hector Salinas. **Assistant Coach:** Gene Salazar. **Telephone:** (361) 825-3252. **Baseball SID:** Aaron Ames. **Telephone:** (361) 825-3411. **FAX:** (361) 825-3218.

TEXAS CHRISTIAN Horned Frogs
Conference: Conference USA.
Mailing Address: TCU Box 297600, Fort Worth, TX 76129. **Website:** www.gofrogs.com.
Head Coach: Jim Schlossnagle. **Assistant Coaches:** Mike Dilley, Derek Matlock, Matt Siegel, *Todd Whitting. **Telephone:** (817) 257-5354. ◆ **Baseball SID:** Brandie Davidson. **Telephone:** (817) 257-7479. **FAX:** (817) 257-7964.
Home Field: Lupton Stadium. **Seating Capacity:** 1,500. **Outfield Dimensions:** LF—330, CF—400, RF—330. **Press Box Telephone:** (817) 257-7966.

TEXAS SOUTHERN Tigers
Conference: Southwestern Athletic.
Mailing Address: 3100 Cleburne St., Houston, TX 77004. **Website:** www.tsu.edu.
Head Coach: Candy Robinson. **Assistant Coach:** *Brian White. **Telephone:** (713) 313-7993. ◆ **Baseball SID:** Rodney Bush. **Telephone:** (713) 313-6829. **FAX:** (713) 313-1045.

TEXAS STATE Bobcats
Conference: Southland.
Mailing Address: 601 University Dr., San Marcos, TX 78666. **Website:** www.txstatebobcats.com.
Head Coach: Ty Harrington. **Assistant Coaches:** *Howard Bushong, Marcus Hendry. **Telephone:** (512) 245-7566. ◆ **Baseball SID:** Ron Mears. **Telephone:** (512) 245-2966. **FAX:** (512) 245-2967.
Home Field: Bobcat Field. **Seating Capacity:** 1,500. **Outfield Dimensions:** LF—325, CF—404, RF—325.

TEXAS TECH Red Raiders
Conference: Big 12.
Mailing Address: P.O. Box 43021, Lubbock, TX 79409. **Website:** www.texastech.com.

Head Coach: Larry Hays. **Assistant Coaches:** *Daren Hays, Travis Walden. **Telephone:** (806) 742-3355. ◆ **Baseball SID:** Blayne Beal. **Telephone:** (806) 742-2770. **FAX:** (806) 742-1970.
Home Field: Dan Law Field. **Seating Capacity:** 5,050. **Outfield Dimensions:** LF—330, CF—405, RF—330. **Press Box Telephone:** (806) 742-3688.

TOLEDO Rockets
Conference: Mid-American (West).
Mailing Address: 2801 W. Bancroft St., Toledo, OH 43606. **Website:** www.utrockets.com.
Head Coach: Cory Mee. **Assistant Coaches:** T.J. Brock, Matt Husted. **Telephone:** (419) 530-6263. ◆ **Baseball SID:** Brian DeBenedictis. **Telephone:** (419) 530-4919. **FAX:** (419) 530-4930.

TOWSON Tigers
Conference: Colonial Athletic.
Mailing Address: 8000 York Rd., Towson, MD 21252. **Website:** www.towsontigers.com.
Head Coach: Mike Gottlieb. **Assistant Coaches:** Mel Bacon, Paul Quaranta, *Scott Roane. **Telephone:** (410) 704-3775. ◆ **Baseball SID:** Dan O'Connell. **Telephone:** (410) 704-3102. **FAX:** (410) 704-3861.
Home Field: John Schuerholz Park. **Seating Capacity:** 1,500. **Outfield Dimensions:** LF—312, CF—424, RF—315. **Press Box Telephone:** (410) 704-5810.

TROY Trojans
Conference: Atlantic Sun.
Mailing Address: Davis Field House, 100 George Wallace Dr., Troy, AL 36082. **Website:** www.troytrojans.com.
Head Coach: Bobby Pierce. **Assistant Coaches:** Todd Lamberth, Michael Murphee, *Mark Smartt. **Telephone:** (334) 670-3489. ◆ **Baseball SID:** Ricky Hazel. **Telephone:** (334) 670-3832. **FAX:** (334) 670-5665.
Home Field: Riddle-Pace Field. **Seating Capacity:** 2,000. **Outfield Dimensions:** LF—322, CF—390, RF—308. **Press Box Telephone:** (334) 670-5701.

TULANE Green Wave
Conference: Conference USA.
Mailing Address: Wilson Center, Ben Weiner Drive, New Orleans, LA 70018. **Website:** www.tulanegreenwave.com.
Head Coach: Rick Jones. **Assistant Coaches:** Matthew Boggs, *Mark Kingston, Chad Sutter. **Telephone:** (504) 862-8238. ◆ **Baseball SID:** Richie Weaver. **Telephone:** (504) 314-7232. **FAX:** (504) 865-5512.
Home Field: Turchin Stadium. **Seating Capacity:** 3,600. **Outfield Dimensions:** LF—325, CF—400, RF—325. **Press Box Telephone:** (504) 862-8224.

UTAH Utes
Conference: Mountain West.
Mailing Address: 1825 E. South Campus Dr., Salt Lake City, UT 84112. **Website:** www.utahutes.com.
Head Coach: Bill Kinneberg. **Assistant Coaches:** *Bryan Conger, Todd Delnoce, Bill Groves. **Telephone:** (801) 581-3526. ◆ **Baseball SID:** Andy Seeley. **Telephone:** (801) 581-3771. **FAX:** (801) 581-4358.
Home Field: Franklin Covey Field. **Seating Capacity:** 15,000. **Outfield Dimensions:** LF—345, CF—400, RF—315.

#UTAH VALLEY STATE Wolverines
Conference: Independent.
Mailing Address: 800 W. University Parkway, Orem, UT 84058. **Website:** www.wolverinesports.net.
Head Coach: Steve Gardner. **Assistant Coaches:** Eric

Madsen, Nate Mathis, Aaron Tash. **Telephone:** (801) 863-8647. ◆ **Baseball SID:** Clint Burgi. **Telephone:** (801) 863-6231. **FAX:** (801) 863-8813.

VALPARAISO Crusaders
Conference: Mid-Continent.
Mailing Address: Athletic Recreation Center, Valparaiso, IN 46383. **Website:** www.valpo.edu/athletics.
Head Coach: Paul Twenge. **Assistant Coaches:** Brian O'Connor, John Olson, Mark Waite. **Telephone:** (219) 464-5239. ◆ **Baseball SID:** Bill Rogers. **Telephone:** (219) 464-6953. **FAX:** (219) 464-6953.

VANDERBILT Commodores
Conference: Southeastern (East).
Mailing Address: 2601 Jess Neely Dr., Nashville, TN 37212. **Website:** www.vucommodores.com.
Head Coach: Tim Corbin. **Assistant Coaches:** Blake Allen, *Erik Bakich, Derek Johnson. **Telephone:** (615) 322-4121. ◆ **Baseball SID:** Tammy Boclair. **Telephone:** (615) 322-4121. **FAX:** (615) 343-7064.
Home Field: Hawkins Field. **Seating Capacity:** 1,575. **Outfield Dimensions:** LF—310, CF—400, RF—330. **Press Box Telephone:** (615) 320-0436.

VERMONT Catamounts
Conference: America East.
Mailing Address: 226 Patrick Gym, Burlington, VT 05405. **Website:** www.uvmathletics.com.
Head Coach: Bill Currier. **Assistant Coaches:** Jim Carter, *Anthony DeCicco, Jason Spaulding. **Telephone:** (802) 656-7701. ◆ **Baseball SID:** Bruce Bosley. **Telephone:** (802) 656-1109. **FAX:** (802) 656-8328.

VILLANOVA Wildcats
Conference: Big East.
Mailing Address: Jake Nevin Field House, 800 Lancaster Ave., Villanova, PA 19085. **Website:** www.villanova.com.
Head Coach: Joe Godri. **Assistant Coaches:** *Rick Clagett, Rod Johnson, Doc Kennedy. **Telephone:** (610) 519-4529. ◆ **Baseball SID:** David Berman. **Telephone:** (610) 519-6460. **FAX:** (610) 519-7323.
Home Field: Villanova Ballpark at Plymouth Community Center. **Seating Capacity:** 750. **Outfield Dimensions:** LF—320, CF—405, RF—320.

VIRGINIA Cavaliers
Conference: Atlantic Coast.
Mailing Address: P.O. Box 400853, Charlottesville, VA 22904. **Website:** www.virginiasports.com.
Head Coach: Brian O'Connor. **Assistant Coaches:** Joe Hastings, Karl Kuhn, *Kevin McMullan. **Telephone:** (434) 982-5092. ◆ **Baseball SID:** Adam Jones. **Telephone:** (434) 982-5131. **FAX:** (434) 982-5525.
Home Field: Virginia Baseball Field. **Seating Capacity:** 2,000. **Outfield Dimensions:** LF—352, CF—408, RF—352. **Press Box Telephone:** (434) 295-9262.

VIRGINIA COMMONWEALTH Rams
Conference: Colonial Athletic.
Mailing Address: 1300 W. Broad St., Richmond, VA 23284. **Website:** www.vcurams.vcu.edu.
Head Coach: Paul Keyes. **Assistant Coaches:** Justin Clift, *Tim Haynes, Mark McQueen. **Telephone:** (804) 828-4820. ◆ **Baseball SID:** Niki DeSantis. **Telephone:** (804) 828-8818. **FAX:** (804) 828-9428.
Home Field: Petersburg Sports Complex. **Seating Capacity:** 2,000. **Press Box Telephone:** (804) 722-0141.

VIRGINIA MILITARY INSTITUTE Keydets
Conference: Big South.
Mailing Address: Baseball Office, Cameron Hall,

Lexington, VA 24450. **Website:** www.vmikeydets.com.
Head Coach: Marlin Ikenberry. **Assistant Coaches:** Chris Booth, Matt Kirby, *Andrew Slater. **Telephone:** (540) 464-7609. ◆ **Baseball SID:** Chris Kent. **Telephone:** (540) 464-7015. **FAX:** (540) 463-5033.

VIRGINIA TECH Hokies
Conference: Atlantic Coast.
Mailing Address: Room 210, Cassell Coliseum, Blacksburg, VA 24061. **Website:** www.hokiesports.com.
Head Coach: Chuck Hartman. **Assistant Coaches:** Adam Everman, Jon Hartness, *Jay Phillips. **Telephone:** (540) 231-3671. ◆ **Baseball SID:** Dave Smith. **Telephone:** (540) 231-6726. **FAX:** (540) 231-6984.
Home Field: English Field. **Seating Capacity:** 1,500. **Outfield Dimensions:** LF—330, CF—400, RF—330. **Press Box Telephone:** (540) 231-4013.

WAGNER Seahawks
Conference: Northeast.
Mailing Address: Spiro Sports Center, One Campus Rd., Staten Island, NY 10301. **Website:** www.wagner.edu/athletics.
Head Coach: *Joe Litterio. **Assistant Coach:** Jim Agnello, Jeff Toth. **Telephone:** (718) 390-3154. ◆ **Baseball SID:** Ben Shove. **Telephone:** (718) 390-3227. **FAX:** (718) 390-3347.

WAKE FOREST Demon Deacons
Conference: Atlantic Coast.
Mailing Address: P.O. Box 7426, Winston-Salem, NC 27109. **Website:** www.wakeforestsports.com.
Head Coach: Rick Rembielak. **Assistant Coaches:** Marshall Canosa, *Jon Palmieri, Chris Sinacori. **Telephone:** (336) 758-4208. ◆ **Baseball SID:** Michael Bertsch. **Telephone:** (336) 758-5640. **FAX:** (336) 758-5140.
Home Field: Hooks Stadium. **Seating Capacity:** 2,500. **Outfield Dimensions:** LF—340, CF—400, RF—315. **Press Box Telephone:** (336) 759-9711.

WASHINGTON Huskies
Conference: Pacific-10.
Mailing Address: Graves Bldg., Box 354070, Seattle, WA 98195. **Website:** www.gohuskies.com.
Head Coach: Ken Knutson. **Assistant Coaches:** Donny Harrel, *Joe Ross, Gregg Swenson. **Telephone:** (206) 616-4335. ◆ **Baseball SID:** Jeff Bechthold. **Telephone:** (206) 685-7910. **FAX:** (206) 543-5000.
Home Field: Husky Ballpark. **Seating Capacity:** 1,500. **Outfield Dimensions:** LF—327, CF—390, RF—317. **Press Box Telephone:** (206) 685-1994.

WASHINGTON STATE Cougars
Conference: Pacific-10.
Mailing Address: 195 Bohler Athletic Complex, Pullman, WA 99164. **Website:** www.wsucougars.com.
Head Coach: Donnie Marbut. **Assistant Coaches:** Ryan Brust, *Travis Jewett, Duggan Moran. **Telephone:** (509) 335-0211. ◆ **Baseball SID:** Ilsa Gramer. **Telephone:** (509) 335-4296. **FAX:** (509) 335-0267.
Home Field: Bailey-Brayton Field. **Seating Capacity:** 3,500. **Outfield Dimensions:** LF—330, CF—400, RF—375. **Press Box Telephone:** (509) 335-2684.

WEST VIRGINIA Mountaineers
Conference: Big East.
Mailing Address: P.O. Box 0877, Morgantown, WV 26507. **Website:** www.MSNSportsnet.com.
Head Coach: Greg Van Zant. **Assistant Coaches:** *Bruce Cameron, Andrew Leighton, Pat Sherald. **Telephone:** (304) 293-2300. ◆ **Baseball SID:** Scott Castleman. **Telephone:** (304) 293-2821. **FAX:** (304) 293-4105.

Home Field: Hawley Field. **Seating Capacity:** 1,500. **Outfield Dimensions:** LF—325, CF—390, RF—325. **Press Box Telephone:** (304) 293-5988.

WESTERN CAROLINA Catamounts
Conference: Southern.
Mailing Address: Ramsey Center, Cullowhee, NC 28723. **Website:** www.catamountsports.com.
Head Coach: Todd Raleigh. **Assistant Coaches:** Alan Beck, *Eric Filipek, Paul Menhart. **Telephone:** (828) 227-7338. ◆ **Baseball SID:** Mike Cawood. **Telephone:** (828) 227-2339. **FAX:** (828) 227-7688.
Home Field: Childress Field at Hennon Stadium. **Seating Capacity:** 1,500. **Outfield Dimensions:** LF—325, CF—390, RF—325. **Press Box Telephone:** (828) 227-7020.

WESTERN ILLINOIS Leathernecks
Conference: Mid-Continent.
Mailing Address: 204 Western Hall, 1 University Dr., Macomb, IL 61455. **Website:** www.wiuathletics.com.
Head Coach: *Stan Hyman. **Assistant Coaches:** Ryan Cougill, Justin Gordon, Brigham John, Greg Schaub. **Telephone:** (309) 298-1521. ◆ **Baseball SID:** Shana Daniels. **Telephone:** (309) 298-1133. **FAX:** (309) 298-3366.

WESTERN KENTUCKY Hilltoppers
Conference: Sun Belt.
Mailing Address: 1 Big Red Way, Bowling Green, KY 42101. **Website:** www.wkusports.com.
Head Coach: Joel Murrie. **Assistant Coaches:** Luis Rodriguez, Mike McLaury, *Dan Mosier. **Telephone:** (270) 745-6023. ◆ **Baseball SID:** Chris Glowacki. **Telephone:** (270) 745-4298. **FAX:** (270) 745-3444.
Home Field: Nick Denes Field. **Seating Capacity:** 1,050. **Outfield Dimensions:** LF—330, CF—400, RF—330. **Press Box Telephone:** (270) 745-6941.

WESTERN MICHIGAN Broncos
Conference: Mid-American (West).
Mailing Address: 1903 W. Michigan Ave., Kalamazoo, MI 49008. **Website:** www.wmubroncos.com.
Head Coach: Randy Ford. **Assistant Coach:** *Scott Demetral. **Telephone:** (269) 387-8160. ◆ **Baseball SID:** Paula Haughn. **Telephone:** (269) 387-4123. **FAX:** (269) 387-4139.

WICHITA STATE Shockers
Conference: Missouri Valley.
Mailing Address: 1845 Fairmount St., Campus Box 18, Wichita, KS 67260. **Website:** www.goshockers.com.
Head Coach: Gene Stephenson. **Assistant Coaches:** *Brent Kemnitz, Mike Stover, Jim Thomas. **Telephone:** (316) 978-3636. ◆ **Baseball SID:** Tami Cutler. **Telephone:** (316) 978-5559. **FAX:** (316) 978-3336.
Home Field: Tyler Field-Eck Stadium. **Seating Capacity:** 7,851. **Outfield Dimensions:** LF—330, CF—390, RF—330. **Press Box Telephone:** (316) 978-3390.

WILLIAM & MARY Tribe
Conference: Colonial Athletic.
Mailing Address: P.O. Box 399, Williamsburg, VA 23187. **Website:** www.tribeathletics.com.
Head Coach: Jim Farr. **Assistant Coaches:** Matt Kirby, *Ryan Wheeler. **Telephone:** (757) 221-3399. ◆ **Baseball SID:** Chris Poore. **Telephone:** (757) 221-3370. **FAX:** (757) 221-3412.
Home Field: Plumeri Park. **Seating Capacity:** 1,000. **Outfield Dimensions:** LF—315, CF—390, RF—315. **Press Box Telephone:** Unavailable.

WINTHROP Eagles
Conference: Big South.

Mailing Address: Winthrop Coliseum, Rock Hill, SC 29733. **Website:** www.winthropeagles.com.

Head Coach: Joe Hudak. **Assistant Coaches:** Kyle DiEduardo, *Scott Forbes, Stas Swerdzewski. **Telephone:** (803) 323-2129. ◆ **Baseball SID:** Mike Baur. **Telephone:** (803) 323-2129. **FAX:** (803) 323-2433.

Home Field: Winthrop Ballpark. **Seating Capacity:** 2,000. **Outfield Dimensions:** LF—325, CF—390, RF—325. **Press Box Telephone:** (803) 323-2155.

WISCONSIN-MILWAUKEE Panthers
Conference: Horizon.

Mailing Address: P.O. Box 413, Milwaukee, WI 53201. **Website:** www.uwmpanthers.com.

Head Coach: Jerry Augustine. **Assistant Coaches:** Cory Bigler, *Scott Doffek. **Telephone:** (414) 229-5670. ◆ **Baseball SID:** Bret Seymour. **Telephone:** (414) 229-4593. **FAX:** (414) 229-6759.

WOFFORD Terriers
Conference: Southern.

Mailing Address: 429 N. Church St., Spartanburg, SC 29303. **Website:** www.wofford.edu/athletics.

Head Coach: Steve Traylor. **Assistant Coaches:** Scott Brickman, *Brandon McKillop. **Telephone:** (864) 597-4126. ◆ **Baseball SID:** Mark Cohen. **Telephone:** (864) 597-4093. **FAX:** (864) 597-4129.

WRIGHT STATE Raiders
Conference: Horizon.

Mailing Address: 3640 Col. John Glenn Hwy., Dayton, OH 45435. **Website:** www.wsuraiders.com.

Head Coach: Rob Cooper. **Assistant Coaches:** Brennan Hall, *Greg Lovelady, Kurt Palmer. **Telephone:** (937) 775-2771. ◆ **Baseball SID:** Greg Campbell. **Telephone:** (937) 775-4687. **FAX:** (937) 775-2818.

XAVIER Musketeers
Conference: Atlantic-10 (West).

Mailing Address: 3800 Victory Pkwy., Cincinnati, OH 45207. **Website:** www.xavier.edu/athletics.

Head Coach: Dan Simonds. **Assistant Coaches:** *Scott Googins, J.D. Heilmann. **Telephone:** (513) 745-2890. ◆ **Baseball SID:** Jake Linder. **Telephone:** (513) 745-3388. **FAX:** (513) 745-2825.

YALE Bulldogs
Conference: Ivy League (Rolfe).

Mailing Address: P.O. Box 208216, New Haven, CT 06520. **Website:** www.yalebulldogs.com.

Head Coach: John Stuper. **Assistant Coaches:** *Bill Asermely, John Dorman, Glenn Lungarini. **Telephone:** (203) 432-1466. ◆ **Baseball SID:** Casey Hart. **Telephone:** (203) 432-1448. **FAX:** (203) 432-1454.

YOUNGSTOWN STATE Penguins
Conference: Horizon.

Mailing Address: One University Plaza, Youngstown, OH 44555. **Website:** www.ysusports.com.

Head Coach: Mike Florak. **Assistant Coaches:** Craig Antush, Jim Lipinski, *Kyle Sobecki. **Telephone:** (330) 941-3485. ◆ **Baseball SID:** John Vogel. **Telephone:** (330) 941-3192. **FAX:** (330) 941-3191.

SMALL COLLEGES

NCAA DIVISION II • NCAA DIVISION III • NAIA

- NCAA DIVISION II (II)
- NCAA DIVISION III (III)
- NAIA (A)
- NATIONAL CHRISTIAN COLLEGE (C)

School	Level	Mailing Address	Head Coach	Telephone
Abilene Christian U.	II	ACU Station, Box 27916, Abilene, TX 79699	Britt Bonneau	(325) 674-2325
Adelphi U.	II	One South Ave., Garden City, NY 11530	Dom Scala	(516) 877-4240
Adrian College	III	110 S. Madison St., Adrian, MI 49221	Craig Rainey	(517) 264-3977
Alabama-Huntsville, U. of	II	205 Spragins Hall, Huntsville, AL 35899	Lowell Mooneyham	(256) 824-2197
Albany State U.	II	504 College Dr., Albany, GA 31705	Edward Taylor	(229) 430-1829
Albertson College	A	2112 Cleveland Blvd., Caldwell, ID 83605	Shawn Humberger	(208) 459-5861
Albertus Magnus College	III	700 Prospect St., New Haven, CT 06511	Brian Leighton	(203) 773-8578
Albion College	III	611 E. Porter St., Albion, MI 49224	Scott Carden	(517) 629-0517
Albright College	III	PO Box 15234, Reading, PA 19612	Jeff Feiler	(610) 921-7678
Alderson-Broaddus	II	500 College Hill Rd., Philippi, WV 26416	Kit Laird	(304) 457-6265
Alice Lloyd College	A	100 Purpose Rd., Pippa Passes, KY 41844	Scott Cornett	(606) 368-6119
Allegheny College	III	520 N. Main St., Meadville, PA 16335	Mike Ferris	(814) 332-2830
Alma College	III	614 W. Superior St., Alma, MI 48801	John Leister	(989) 463-7265
Alvernia College	III	400 Saint Bernardine St., Reading, PA 19607	Yogi Lutz	(610) 796-8476
American Int'l Coll.	II	1000 State St., Springfield, MA 01109	Nick Callini	(413) 205-3574
Amherst College	III	PO Box 5000, Amherst, MA 01002	Bill Thurston	(413) 542-2284
Anderson College	II	316 Boulevard St., Anderson, SC 29621	Joe Miller	(864) 231-2013
Anderson U.	III	1100 E. 5th St., Anderson, IN 46012	Don Brandon	(765) 641-4488
Angelo State U.	II	2601 West Ave. N., San Angelo, TX 76909	Kevin Brooks	(325) 942-2091
Anna Maria College	III	50 Sunset Lane, Paxton, MA 01612	Mike Wilson	(508) 849-3446
Aquinas College	A	1607 Robinson Rd. SE, Grand Rapids, MI 49506	Doug Greenslate	(616) 632-2935
Arcadia University	III	450 S. Easton Rd., Glenside, PA 19038	Stan Exeter	(215) 572-2976
Arkansas Tech	II	1604 Coliseum Dr., Russellville, AR 72801	Billy Goss	(479) 968-0648
Arkansas-Monticello, U. of	II	UAM Box 3066, Monticello, AR 71656	Kevin Downing	(870) 460-1257
Armstrong Atlantic State U.	II	11935 Abercorn St., Savannah, GA 31419	Joe Roberts	(912) 921-5686
Asbury College	A	1 Macklem Dr., Wilmore, KY 40390	Joe Reed	(859) 858-3511
Ashland U.	II	916 King Rd., Ashland, OH 44805	John Schaly	(419) 289-5444
Assumption College	II	500 Salisbury St., Worcester, MA 01609	Jamie Pinzino	(508) 767-2232
Atlanta Christian College	C	2605 Ben Hill Rd., East Point, GA 30344	Alan Wilson	(404) 669-2059
Auburn U.-Montgomery	A	7301 Senators Dr., Montgomery, AL 36124	Q.V. Lowe	(334) 244-3237
Augsburg College	III	2211 Riverside Ave., Minneapolis, MN 55454	Keith Bateman	(612) 330-1395
Augusta State U.	II	2500 Walton Way #10, Augusta, GA 30904	Stanley Fish	(706) 731-7917
Augustana College	III	3500 5th Ave., Rock Island, IL 61201	Greg Wallace	(309) 794-7521
Augustana College	II	2001 S. Summit Ave, Sioux Falls, SD 57197	Jeff Holm	(605) 274-5541
Aurora U.	III	347 S. Gladstone Ave, Aurora, IL 60506	Shaun Neitzel	(630) 844-6515
Austin College	III	900 N. Grand Ave, Suite 6A, Sherman, TX 75090	Bruce Mauppin	(903) 813-2516
Averett University	III	420 W. Main St., Danville, VA 24541	Ed Fulton	(434) 791-5030
Avila U.	A	11901 Wornall Rd., Kansas City, MO 64145	Ryan Howard	(816) 501-3739
Azusa Pacific U.	A	901 E. Alosta Ave., Azusa, CA 91702	Paul Svagdis	(626) 815-6000
Babson College	III	Webster Center, Babson Park, MA 02457	Matt Noone	(781) 239-5823
Bacone College	A	2299 Old Bacone Rd., Muskogee, OK 74403	Dan Bowers	(918) 781-7237
Baker U.	A	PO Box 65, Baldwin City, KS 66006	Phil Hannon	(785) 594-8493
Baldwin-Wallace College	III	275 Eastland Rd., Berea, OH 44017	Bob Fisher	(440) 826-2182
Baptist Bible College	C	538 Venard Rd., Clarks Summit, PA 18411	Don Sintic	(570) 585-9322
Barber-Scotia College	A	145 Cabarrus Ave. West, Concord, NC 28025	Lane Mears	(704) 789-2960
Barry U.	II	11300 NE 2nd Ave., Miami Shores, FL 33161	Juan Ranero	(305) 899-3558
Barton College	II	401 Rountree St., Wilson, NC 27893	Todd Wilkinson	(252) 399-6552
Baruch College	III	55 Lexington Ave., New York, NY 10010	Miguel Iglesias	(616) 312-5052
Bates College	III	130 Central Ave., Lewiston, ME 04240	Craig Vandersea	(207) 786-6063
Becker College	III	964 Main St., Leicester, MA 01524	Walter Beede	(508) 791-9241
Belhaven College	A	1500 Peachtree St., Jackson, MS 39202	Hill Denson	(601) 968-8898
Bellarmine College	II	2001 Newburg Rd., Louisville, KY 40205	Deron Spink	(502) 452-8278
Bellevue U.	A	1000 Galvin Rd. S., Bellevue, NE 68005	Mike Evans	(402) 293-3782
Belmont Abbey College	III	100 Belmont-Mount Holly Rd., Belmont, NC 28012	Kermit Smith	(704) 825-6804
Beloit College	III	700 College St., Beloit, WI 53511	Dave DeGeorge	(608) 363-2039
Bemidji State U.	II	1500 Birchmont Dr. NE, Bemidji, MN 56601	Chris Brown	(218) 755-4620
Benedict College	II	1600 Harden St., Columbia, SC 29204	Derrick Johnson	(803) 733-7421
Benedictine College	A	1020 N. 2nd St., Atchison, KS 66002	Dan Griggs	(913) 367-5340
Benedictine U.	III	5700 College Rd., Lisle, IL 60532	John Ostrowski	(630) 829-6147
Bentley College	II	175 Forest St., Waltham, MA 02452	Bob DeFelice	(781) 891-2332
Berea College	A	CPO 2187, Berea, KY 40404	A. Maines	(859) 985-3423
Berry College	A	PO Box 495015, Mount Berry, GA 30149	David Beasley	(706) 236-1743

College	Div	Address	Coach	Phone
Bethany College	III	Hummel Fieldhouse, Bethany, WV 26032	Rick Carver	(304) 829-7246
Bethany College	A	800 Bethany Dr., Scotts Valley, CA 95066	Dennis Patton	(831) 438-3800
Bethany College	A	421 N. First, Lindsborg, KS 67456	Matt Tramel	(785) 227-3380
Bethel College	A	1001 McKinley Ave, Mishawaka, IN 46545	Seth Zartman	(574) 257-3287
Bethel U.	III	3900 Bethel Dr., St. Paul, MN 55112	Greg Indlecoffer	(651) 638-6143
Bethel College	A	325 Cherry Ave., McKenzie, TN 38201	Glenn Hayes	(731) 352-4206
Biola U.	A	13800 Biola Ave, La Mirada, CA 90639	John Verhoeven	(562) 944-0351
Blackburn College	III	700 College Ave., Carlinville, IL 62626	Mike Neal	(217) 854-3231
Bloomfield College	II	467 Franklin St., Bloomfield, NJ 07003	Matt Belford	(973) 748-9000
Bloomsburg U.	II	400 E. 2nd St., Bloomsburg, PA 17815	Matt Haney	(570) 389-4375
Bluefield College	A	3000 College Dr., Bluefield, VA 24605	Billy Berry	(276) 326-4545
Bluefield State College	II	219 Rock St., Bluefield, WV 24701	Geoff Hunter	(304) 327-4084
Bluffton College	III	1 University Dr., Bluffton, OH 45817	James Grandey	(419) 358-3292
Bowdoin College	III	9000 College Station, Brunswick, ME 04011	Michael Connolly	(207) 725-3751
Brandeis U.	III	Gosman Sports Center, MS 007, Waltham, MA 02454	Pete Varney	(781) 736-3639
Brescia U.	A	717 Frederica St., Owensboro, KY 42301	Jason Vittone	(270) 686-4207
Brevard College	A	400 N. Broad St., Brevard, NC 28712	Gil Payne	(828) 884-8273
Brewton Parker College	A	Hwy. 280, Mt. Vernon, GA 30445	Chad Parker	(912) 583-3177
Briar Cliff U.	A	PO Box 2100, Sioux City, IA 51104	Boyd Pitkin	(712) 279-5553
Bridgeport, U. of	II	120 Waldemere Ave., Bridgeport, CT 06601	John Anquillare	(203) 576-4229
Bridgewater College	III	402 E. College St., Bridgewater, VA 22812	Curt Kendall	(540) 828-5407
Bridgewater State College	III	200-325 Plymouth St., Bridgewater, MA 02325	Rick Smith	(508) 580-0711
British Columbia, U. of	A	6081 University Blvd., Vancouver, B.C. V6T 1Z1	Terry McKaig	(604) 822-4270
Bryan College	A	721 Bryan Dr., Dayton, TN 37321	Joel Johnson	(423) 775-7569
Bryant College	II	1150 Douglas Pike, Smithfield, RI 02917	Jon Sjogren	(401) 232-6397
Buena Vista U.	III	610 West 4th St., Storm Lake, IA 50588	Steve Eddie	(712) 749-2298
C.W. Post/Long Island U.	II	720 Northern Blvd., Brookville, NY 11548	Dick Vining	(516) 299-2938
Caldwell College	II	9 Ryerson Ave., Caldwell, NJ 07006	Chris Reardon	(973) 618-3462
UC San Diego	II	9500 Gilman Dr., La Jolla, CA 92093	Dan O'Brien	(858) 534-4211
Cal Poly Pomona	II	3801 West Temple Ave., Pomona, CA 91768	Mike Ashman	(909) 869-2829
Cal State Chico	II	1st & Orange Sts., Chico, CA 95929	Lindsay Meggs	(530) 898-4374
Cal State Dominguez Hills	II	1000 E. Victoria St., Carson, CA 90747	George Wing	(310) 243-3765
Cal State Hayward	III	25800 Carlos Bee Blvd., Hayward, CA 94542	Dirk Morrison	(510) 885-3046
Cal State Los Angeles	II	5151 State University Dr., Los Angeles, CA 90032	Dave Taylor	(323) 343-3093
Cal State San Bernardino	II	5500 University Pwy., San Bernardino, CA 92407	Don Parnell	(909) 880-5021
Cal State Stanislaus	II	801 W. Monte Vista Ave., Turlock, CA 95382	Kenny Leonesio	(209) 667-3272
Cal Tech	III	1200 E. California Blvd., Pasadena, CA 91125	John D'Auria	(626) 395-3263
California Baptist U.	A	8432 Magnolia Ave., Riverside, CA 92504	Gary Adcock	(951) 343-4382
California Lutheran U.	III	60 W. Olsen Rd., Thousand Oaks, CA 91360	Marty Slimak	(805) 493-3398
California U. (Pa.)	II	250 University Ave., California, PA 15419	Mike Conte	(724) 938-5837
Calumet College	A	2400 New York Ave., Whiting, IN 46394		(219) 473-4327
Calvin College	III	3195 Knight Way SE, Grand Rapids, MI 49546	Jim Timmer	(616) 526-6037
Cameron U.	II	2800 West Gore Blvd., Lawton, OK 73505	Todd Holland	(580) 581-2479
Campbellsville U.	A	1316 University Dr., Campbellsville, KY 42718	Beauford Sanders	(270) 789-5056
Capital U.	III	2199 E. Main St., Columbus, OH 43209	Greg Weyrich	(614) 236-6203
Cardinal Stritch U.	A	6801 N. Yates Rd., Milwaukee, WI 53217	Michael Zolecki	(414) 410-4519
Carleton College	III	One N. College St., Northfield, MN 55057	Bill Nelson	(507) 646-4051
Carroll College	III	100 N. East Ave, Waukesha, WI 53186	Steve Dannhoff	(262) 524-7105
Carson-Newman College	II	2130 Branner Ave., Jefferson City, TN 37760	Brent Achord	(865) 471-3465
Carthage College	III	2001 Alford Park Dr., Kenosha, WI 53140	Augie Schmidt	(262) 551-5935
Case Western Reserve U.	III	10900 Euclid Ave., Cleveland, OH 44106	Jerry Seimon	(216) 368-5379
Castleton State College	III	One Glennbrook Rd., Castleton, VT 05735	Ted Shipley	(802) 468-1491
Catawba College	II	2300 W. Innes St., Salisbury, NC 28144	Jim Gantt	(704) 637-4160
Catholic U.	III	3606 McCormack Rd. NE, Washington, DC 20064	Ross Natoli	(202) 319-6092
Cazenovia College	III	Liberty Street, Cazenovia, NY 13035	Peter Liddell	(315) 655-7141
Cedarville U.	A	251 N. Main St., Cedarville, OH 45314	Greg Hughes	(937) 766-3246
Centenary College	III	400 Jefferson St., Hackettstown, NJ 07840	Dave Sawicki	(908) 852-1400
Central Arkansas, U. of	II	314 Western Ave., Conway, AR 72032	Doug Clark	(501) 450-3407
Central Christian College	C	PO Box 1403, McPherson, KS 67460	Jared Hamilton	(620) 241-0723
Central College	III	812 University St., Pella, IA 50219	Adam Stevens	(641) 628-5396
Central Methodist U.	A	411 CMC Square, Fayette, MO 65248	Van Vanatta	(660) 248-6352
Central Missouri State U.	II	500 Washington St., Warrensburg, MO 64093	Darin Hendrickson	(660) 543-4800
Central Oklahoma, U. of	II	100 N. University Dr., Edmond, OK 73034	Wendell Simmons	(405) 974-2506
Central Washington U.	II	400 E. University Way, Ellensburg, WA 98926	Desi Storey	(509) 963-3018
Centre College	III	600 W. Walnut St., Danville, KY 40422	Mike Pritchard	(859) 238-5489
Chapman U.	III	One University Dr., Orange, CA 92866	Tom Tereschuk	(714) 997-6662
Charleston, U. of	II	2300 MacCorkle Ave. SE, Charleston, WV 25304	Tom Nozica	(304) 357-4823
Chicago, U. of	III	5530 S. Ellis Ave., Chicago, IL 60637	Brian Baldea	(773) 702-4643
Chowan College	III	200 Jones Dr., Murfreesboro, NC 27855	Aaron Carroll	(252) 398-6287
Christian Brothers U.	II	650 E. Parkway South, Memphis, TN 38104	Phil Goodwin	(901) 321-3375
Christopher Newport U.	III	1 University Place, Newport News, VA 23606	John Harvell	(757) 594-7054
Circleville Bible Coll.	C	PO Box 458, Circleville, OH 43113	Larry Olson	(740) 477-7761

College	Div	Address	Coach	Phone
Claflin U.	II	400 Magnolia St., Orangeburg, SC 29115	Brian Newsome	(803) 535-5295
Claremont-Mudd-Scripps Coll	III	500 E. 9th St., Claremont, CA 91711	Randy Town	(909) 607-3796
Clarion U.	II	Wood St./Tippin Gym, Room 112 Clarion, PA 16214	Scott Feldman	(814) 393-1651
Clark Atlanta U.	II	223 Brawley Dr., Atlanta, GA 30314	Chris Atwell	(404) 880-6648
Clark U.	III	950 Main St., Worcester, MA 01610	Jason Falcon	(508) 421-3832
Clarke College	III	1550 Clarke Dr., Dubuque, IA 52001	Eric Frese	(563) 588-6601
Clarkson U.	III	Box 5830, Alumni Gym, Potsdam, NY 13669	Jim Kane	(315) 268-3759
Clearwater Christian	C	3400 Gulf-to-Bay Blvd., Clearwater, FL 33759	Steve Milton	(727) 726-1153
Coe College	III	1220 First Ave. NE, Cedar Rapids, IA 52402	Steve Cook	(319) 399-8849
Coker College	II	300 E. College Ave., Hartsville, SC 29550	Dave Schmotzer	(843) 383-8105
Colby College	III	4900 Mayflower Hill, Waterville, ME 04901	Tom Dexter	(207) 859-4917
Colby-Sawyer College	III	541 Main St., New London, NH 03257	Jim Broughton	(603) 526-3607
Colorado School of Mines	II	1500 Illinois St., Golden, CO 80401	Mike Mulvaney	(303) 273-3367
Colorado State U.-Pueblo	II	2200 N. Bonforte Blvd., Pueblo, CO 81001	Stan Sanchez	(719) 549-2065
Columbia Union College	II	7600 Flower Ave., Takoma Park, MD 20912	Bruce Peifer	(301) 891-4481
Columbus State U.	II	4225 University Ave., Columbus, GA 31907	Greg Appleton	(706) 568-2444
Concord U.	II	Campus Box 77, Athens, WV 24712	Kevin Garrett	(304) 384-5340
Concordia College (Ala.)	C	1804 Green St., Selma, AL 36703	Frank Elliott	(334) 874-7143
Concordia College (Minn.)	III	901 8th Street S., Moorhead, MN 56562	Don Burgau	(218) 299-3209
Concordia College (N.Y.)	II	171 White Plains Rd., Bronxville, NY 10708	Bob Greiner	(914) 337-9300
Concordia U. (Calif.)	A	1530 Concordia West, Irvine, CA 92612	Tony Barbone	(949) 584-8002
Concordia U. (Ill.)	III	7400 W. Augusta St., River Forest, IL 60305	Spiro Lempesis	(708) 209-3125
Concordia U. (Mich.)	A	4090 Geddes Rd., Ann Arbor, MI 48105	Karl Kling	(734) 995-7343
Concordia U. (Minn.)	II	275 Syndicate St. N., St. Paul, MN 55104	Mark McKenzie	(651) 603-6208
Concordia U. (Neb.)	A	800 N. Columbia Ave, Seward, NE 68434	Jeremy Geidel	(402) 643-7347
Concordia U. (Ore.)	A	2811 NE Holman St., Portland, OR 97211	Rob Vance	(503) 280-8691
Concordia U. (Texas)	III	3400 I-35 North, Austin, TX 78705	Mike Gardner	(512) 486-1160
Concordia U. (Wis.)	III	12800 N. Lake Shore Dr., Mequon, WI 53097	Val Keiper	(262) 243-4266
Cornell College	III	600 1st Street W., Mount Vernon, IA 52314	Frank Fisher	(319) 895-4150
Cortland State	III	P.O. Box 2000, Cortland, NY 13045	Joe Brown	(607) 753-4950
Crichton College	A	255 N. Highland, Memphis, TN 38111	Junior Weaver	(901) 320-1706
Crown College	III	6425 County Road 30, St. Bonafacius, MN 55375	Kelly Spann	(952) 446-4146
Culver-Stockton College	A	One College Hill, Canton, MO 63435	Doug Bletcher	(573) 231-6374
Cumberland College	A	7526 College Station Dr., Williamsburg, KY 40769	Brad Shelton	(606) 539-4387
Cumberland U.	A	One Cumberland Sq., Lebanon, TN 37087	Woody Hunt	(615) 444-2562
Curry College	III	1071 Blue Hill Ave., Miller Gym, Milton, MA 02186	Dave Perdios	(617) 333-2055
D'Youville College	III	320 Porter Ave., Buffalo, NY 14201	Jeff Johnson	(716) 912-2717
Dakota State U.	A	820 N. Washington Ave, Madison, SD 57042	Pat Dolan	(605) 256-5235
Dakota Wesleyan U.	A	1200 W. University Ave, Mitchell, SD 57301	Adam Neisius	(605) 995-2853
Dallas, U. of	III	1845 E. Northgate Dr., Irving, TX 75062	Sam Blackmon	(972) 721-5117
Dana College	A	2848 College Dr., Blair, NE 68008	Chad Gorman	(402) 426-7913
Daniel Webster College	III	20 University Dr., Nashua, NH 03063	Jim Cardello	(603) 577-6497
Davis & Elkins College	II	100 Campus Dr., Elkins, WV 26241	Ryan Brisbin	(304) 637-1342
Defiance College	III	701 N. Clinton St., Defiance, OH 43512	Chad Donsbach	(419) 783-2341
Delaware Valley College	III	700 E. Butler Ave., Doylestown, PA 18901	Bob Altieri	(215) 489-2379
Delta State U.	II	DSU BOX A3, Cleveland, MS 38733	Mike Kinnison	(662) 846-4300
Denison U.	III	PO Box 111, Granville, OH 43023	Barry Craddock	(740) 587-6714
De Pauw U.	III	702 S. College Ave., Greencastle, IN 46135	Matt Walker	(765) 658-4939
DeSales U.	III	2755 Station Ave., Center Valley, PA 18034	Tim Nieman	(610) 282-1100
Dickinson College	III	PO Box 1773, Carlisle, PA 17013	Russell Wrenn	(717) 245-1982
Dickinson State U.	A	291 Campus Dr., Dickinson, ND 58601	Duane Monlux	(701) 483-2716
Doane College	A	1014 Boswell Ave., Crete, NE 68333	Jack Hudkins	(402) 826-8646
Dominican College	II	470 Western Hwy., Orangeburg, NY 10962	Rick Giannetti	(845) 398-3008
Dominican U.	III	7900 W. Division St., River Forest, IL 60305	Terry Casey	(708) 524-6542
Dordt College	A	498 4th Ave. NE, Sioux Center, IA 51250	Jeff Scholten	(712) 722-6232
Dowling College	II	150 Idle Hour Blvd., Oakdale, NY 11769	Chris Celano	(631) 244-3229
Drew U.	III	36 Madison Ave., Madison, NJ 07940	Vince Masco	(973) 408-3443
Dubuque, U. of	III	2000 University Ave., Dubuque, IA 52001	Shane Schmellsmidt	(563) 589-3124
Earlham College	III	801 National Rd. W., Richmond, IN 47374	Tom Parkevich	(765) 983-1237
East Central U.	II	1100 East 14th St., Ada, OK 74820	Ron Hill	(580) 436-4940
East Stroudsburg U.	II	Smith & Normal Streets, East Stroudsburg, PA 18301	Roger Barren	(570) 422-3353
East Texas Baptist U.	III	1209 N. Grove St., Marshall TX 75670	Robert Riggs	(903) 935-7963
Eastern U.	III	1300 Eagle Rd., St. Davids, PA 19087	Brian Burke	(610) 341-1582
Eastern Connecticut State U.	III	83 Windham St., Willimantic, CT 06226	Bill Holowaty	(860) 465-5185
Eastern Mennonite U.	III	1200 Park Rd., Harrisonburg, VA 22802	Rob Roeschley	(540) 432-4333
Eastern Nazarene College	III	23 East Elm Ave., Quincy, MA 02170	Todd Reid	(617) 745-3648
Eastern New Mexico U.	II	Greyhound Arena, Station 17, Portales, NM 88130	Phil Clabaugh	(505) 562-2889
Eastern Oregon U.	A	One University Blvd., La Grande, OR 97850	Wes McAllaster	(541) 962-3110
Eckerd College	II	4200 54th Ave. S., St. Petersburg, FL 33711	Bill Mathews	(727) 864-8253
Edgewood College	III	1000 Edgewood College Dr., Madison, WI 53711	Al Brisack	(608) 663-3289
Edward Waters College	A	1658 Kings Rd., Jacksonville, FL 32209	Carl Burden	(904) 470-8276

College	Div	Address	Contact	Phone
Elizabeth City State U.	II	Campus Box 900, Elizabeth City, NC 27909	Terrance Whittle	(252) 335-3392
Elizabethtown College	III	One Alpha Dr., Elizabethtown, PA 17022	Matt Jones	(717) 361-1463
Elmhurst College	III	190 Prospect Ave., Elmhurst, IL 60126	Clark Jones	(630) 617-3143
Elms College	III	291 Springfield St., Chicopee, MA 01013	Don LaValley	(413) 265-2433
Embry-Riddle U.	A	600 S. Clyde Morris Blvd., Daytona Beach, FL 32114	Greg Guilliams	(386) 323-5010
Emmanuel College	A	PO Box 129, Franklin Springs, GA 30639	Ryan Gray	(706) 245-2859
Emory & Henry College	III	King Athletic Center, Emory, VA 24327	Dewey Lusk	(276) 944-6855
Emory U.	III	600 Asbury Circle, Atlanta, GA 30322	Mike Twardoski	(404) 727-0877
Emporia State U.	II	12th & Commercial Streets, Emporia, KS 66801	Bob Fornelli	(620) 341-5930
Endicott College	III	376 Hale St., Beverly, MA 01915	Larry Hiser	(978) 232-2304
Erskine College	II	2 Washington St., Due West, SC 29639	Kevin Nichols	(864) 379-8777
Eureka College	III	300 E. College Ave., Eureka, IL 61530	Airren Nylin	(309) 467-6376
Evangel U.	A	1111 North Glenstone Ave, Springfield, MO 65802	Al Poland	(417) 865-2815
Fairleigh Dickinson U.-Florham	III	285 Madison Ave., Madison, NJ 07940	Doug Radziewicz	(973) 443-8826
Fairmont State College	II	1201 Locust Ave., Fairmont, WV 26554	Ray Bonnett	(304) 367-4146
Faulkner U.	A	5345 Atlanta Hwy., Montgomery, AL 36109	Brent Barker	(334) 386-7318
Felician College	II	262 S. Main St., Lodi, NJ 07644	Chris Langan	(201) 559-3509
Ferrum College	III	435 Ferrum Mountain Rd., Ferrum, VA 24088	Abe Naff	(540) 365-4488
Findlay, U. of	II	1000 N. Main St., Findlay, OH 45840	Troy Berry	(419) 434-6684
Finlandia U.	III	601 W. Quincy St., Hancock, MI 49930	Matt Farrell	(906) 487-7212
Fisher College	A	118 Beacon St., Boston, MA 02116	Scott Dulin	(617) 236-8877
Fisk U.	III	17 Avenue N., Nashville, TN 37208	Shannon Hill	(615) 329-8782
Fitchburg State College	III	160 Pearl St., Fitchburg, MA 01420	Pete Egbert	(978) 665-3726
Flagler College	A	74 King St., St. Augustine, FL 32084	Dave Barnett	(904) 819-6252
Florida Gulf Coast U.	II	10501 FGCU Blvd., South, Fort Myers, FL 33965	Dave Tollett	(239) 590-7051
Florida Memorial College	A	15800 NW 42nd Ave., Opa Locka, FL 33054	Robert Smith	(305) 626-3168
Florida Southern College	A	111 Lake Hollingsworth Dr., Lakeland, FL 33801	Pete Meyer	(863) 680-4264
Florida Tech	II	150 W. University Blvd., Melbourne, FL 32901	Paul Knight	(321) 674-8193
Fontbonne College	III	6800 Wydown St., St. Louis, MO 63105	Scott Cooper	(314) 719-8064
Fort Hays State U.	II	600 Park St., Hays, KS 67601	Matt Ranson	(785) 628-4357
Framingham State College	III	100 State St., Framingham, MA 01701	Mike Savno	(508) 626-4566
Francis Marion U.	II	PO Box 100547, Florence, SC 29501	Art Inabinet	(843) 661-1242
Franciscan U.	A	400 North Bluff Blvd., Clinton, IA 52732	Desi Druschel	(563) 242-4257
Franklin & Marshall College	III	PO Box 3003, Lancaster, PA 17604	Brett Boretti	(717) 358-4530
Franklin College	III	101 Branigin Blvd., Franklin, IN 46131	Lance Marshall	(317) 738-8136
Franklin Pierce College	II	20 College Rd., Rindge, NH 03461	Jayson King	(603) 899-4084
Fredonia State U.	III	Dods Hall, Fredonia, NY 14063	Matt Palisin	(716) 673-3743
Freed-Hardeman U.	A	158 E. Main St., Henderson, TN 38340	Pat McCarthy	(731) 989-6994
Friends U.	A	2100 W. University St., Wichita, KS 67213	Mark Carvalho	(316) 295-5769
Frostburg State U.	III	101 Braddock Rd, Frostburg, MD 21532	Chris McKnight	(301) 687-4273
Gallaudet U.	III	800 Florida Ave. NE, Washington, DC 20002	Jeff Salit	(202) 651-5601
Gannon U.	II	109 University Square, Erie, PA 16541	Rick Iacobucci	(814) 871-5846
Geneva College	A	3200 College Ave., Beaver Falls, PA 15010	Alan Sumner	(724) 847-6647
George Fox U.	III	414 N. Meridian St., Newberg, OR 97132	Pat Bailey	(503) 554-2914
Georgetown College	A	400 E. College St., Georgetown, KY 40324	Erik Hagen	(502) 863-8207
Georgia College & State U.	II	Campus Box 65, Milledgeville, GA 31061	Chris Calciano	(478) 445-5319
Georgia Southwestern	A	800 Wheatley St., Americus, GA 31709	Bryan McLain	(229) 931-2220
Gettysburg College	III	300 N. Washington St, Gettysburg, PA 17325	John Campo	(717) 337-6413
Gordon College	III	255 Grapevine Rd., Wenham, MA 01984	Joe Scarano	(978) 867-4116
Goshen College	A	1700 S. Main St., Goshen, IN 46526	Jayson Best	(574) 535-7495
Grace College	A	200 Seminary Dr., Winona Lake, IN 46590	Glenn Goldsmith	(574) 372-5100
Graceland U	A	One University Pl. Lamoni IA 50140	Brady McKillip	(641) 784-5351
Grand Canyon U.	II	PO Box 11097, Phoenix, AZ 85061	Dave Stapleton	(602) 589-2817
Grand Valley State U.	II	1 Campus Dr., Allendale, MI 49401	Steve Lyon	(616) 331-3584
Grand View College	A	1200 Grandview Ave., Des Moines, IA 50316	Lou Yacinich	(515) 263-2897
Greensboro College	III	815 W. Market St., Greensboro, NC 27401	Ken Carlyle	(336) 272-7102
Greenville College	III	315 E. College Ave., Greenville, IL 62246	Lynn Carlson	(618) 664-6623
Grinnell College	III	1118 10th Ave., Grinnell, IA 50112	Tim Hollibaugh	(641) 269-3822
Grove City College	III	200 Campus Dr., Grove City, PA 16127	Rob Skaricich	(724) 458-3836
Guilford College	III	5800 W. Friendly Ave., Greensboro, NC 27410	Gene Baker	(336) 316-2161
Gustavus Adolphus College	III	800 W. College Ave., St. Peter, MN 56082	Mike Carroll	(507) 933-6297
Gwynedd Mercy College	III	1325 Sumneytown Pike, Gwynedd Valley, PA 19437	Paul Murphy	(215) 641-5533
Hamilton College	III	198 College Hill Rd., Clinton, NY 13323	John Keady	(315) 859-4763
Hamline U.	III	1536 Hewitt Ave., St. Paul, MN 55104	Jason Verdugo	(651) 523-2035
Hampden-Sydney College	III	1 Kirby Field House Lane, Hampden-Sydney, VA 23943	Jeff Kinne	(434) 223-6981
Hannibal-LaGrange College	A	2800 Palmyra Rd., Hannibal, MO 63401	Clay Biggs	(573) 221-3675
Hanover College	II	PO Box 108, Hanover, IN 47243	Dick Naylor	(812) 866-7374
Hardin-Simmons U.	III	PO Box 16185, Abilene, TX 79698	Steve Coleman	(325) 670-1493
Harding U.	II	Box 12281, Searcy, AR 72149	Shane Fullerton	(501) 279-4344
Harris-Stowe State College	A	3026 Laclede Ave., St. Louis, MO 63103	Darren Munns	(314) 340-3530

Hartwick College	III	I Hartwick Dr., Oneonta, NY 13820	Doug Kimbler	(607) 431-4706
Hastings College	A	7th & Turner, Hastings, NE 68902	Jim Boeve	(402) 461-7468
Haverford College	III	370 Lancaster Ave., Haverford, PA 19041	Dave Beccaria	(610) 896-1172
Hawaii Pacific U.	II	1060 Bishop St., Honolulu, HI 96813	Allan Sato	(808) 543-8021
Heidelberg College	III	310 E. Market St., Tiffin, OH 44883	Matt Palm	(419) 448-2009
Henderson State U.	II	PO Box 7630, Arkadelphia, AR 71999	John Harvey	(870) 230-5071
Hendrix College	III	1600 Washington Ave., Conway, AR 72032	Lane Stahl	(501) 450-3898
Hilbert College	III	5200 S. Park Ave, Hamburg, NY 14075	Randy Cialone	(716) 649-7900
Hillsdale College	II	201 Oak St., Hillsdale, MI 49242	Paul Noce	(517) 607-3146
Hillsdale Freewill Baptist	C	3701 S. I-35, Moore, OK 73160	Ryan Wade	(405) 912-9038
Hiram College	III	PO Box 1777, Hiram, OH 44234	Howard Jenter	(330) 569-5348
Hope College	III	137 E. 12th St., Holland, MI 49422	Stu Fritz	(616) 395-7692
Houston Baptist U.	A	7502 Fondren Rd., Houston, TX 77074	Brian Huddleston	(281) 649-3332
Howard Payne U.	III	508 2nd St., Brownwood, TX 76801	Mike Kennemer	(325) 649-8117
Huntingdon College	III	1500 E. Fairview Ave, Montgomery, AL 36106	D.J. Conville	(334) 833-4252
Huntington College	A	2303 College Ave., Huntington, IN 46750	Mike Frame	(260) 359-4082
Huron U.	A	333 9th Street SW, Huron, SD 57350	Josue Prado	(605) 353-2010
Husson College	III	1 College Circle, Husson, ME 04401	John Winkin	(207) 941-7096
Huston-Tillotson College	A	900 Chicon St., Austin, TX 78702	Alvin Moore	(512) 505-3151
Illinois College	III	1101 W. College Ave., Jacksonville, IL 62650	Jay Eckhouse	(217) 245-3387
Illinois Tech	A	3300 S. Federal St., Chicago, IL 60616	John Fitzgerald	(312) 567-7128
Illinois Wesleyan U.	III	PO Box 2900, Bloomington, IL 61702	Dennis Martel	(309) 556-3335
Incarnate Word, U. of the	II	4301 Broadway St., San Antonio, TX 78209	Danny Heep	(210) 829-3822
Indiana Tech	A	1600 E. Washington Blvd., Fort Wayne, IN 46803	Steve Devine	(260) 422-5561
Indiana U. (Pa.)	II	107 Memorial Fieldhouse, Indiana, PA 15705	Tom Kennedy	(724) 357-7830
Indiana U.-Northwest	A	3400 Broadway, Gary, IN 46408	Tom Bainbridge	(219) 980-6945
Indiana U.-Southeast	A	4201 Grant Line Rd., New Albany, IN 47150	Joe Decker	(812) 941-2435
Indiana Wesleyan U.	A	4201 S. Washington St., Marion, IN 46953	Mark DeMichael	(765) 677-2324
Indianapolis, U. of	II	1400 E. Hanna Ave., Indianapolis, IN 46227	Gary Vaught	(317) 788-3414
Iowa Wesleyan College	A	601 N. Main St., Mount Pleasant, IA 52641	Matt Cloud	(319) 385-6349
Ithaca College	III	935 Danby Rd., Ithaca, NY 14850	George Valesente	(607) 274-3749
Jamestown College	A	PO Box 6088, Jamestown, ND 58405	Tom Hager	(701) 252-3467
Jarvis Christian College	A	PO Box 1470, Hawkins, TX 75765	Robert Thomas	(903) 769-5763
John Carroll U.	III	20700 N. Park Blvd., University Heights, OH 44118	Marc Thibeault	(216) 397-4660
John Jay College	III	899 10th Ave., New York, NY 10019	Dan Palumbo	(212) 237-8639
Johns Hopkins U.	III	3400 N. Charles St., Baltimore, MD 21218	Bob Babb	(410) 516-7485
Johnson & Wales U.	III	8 Abbott Park Pl., Providence, RI 02903	John LaRose	(401) 598-1609
Johnson Bible College	C	7900 Johnson Dr., Knoxville, TN 37998	Jack Barr	(865) 251-7762
Judson College	A	1151 N. State St., Elgin, IL 60123	Loren Torres	(847) 628-2523
Juniata College	III	1700 Moore St., Huntingdon, PA 16652	George Zanic	(814) 641-3515
Kalamazoo College	III	1200 Academy St., Kalamazoo, MI 49006	Steve Wideen	(269) 337-7287
Kansas Wesleyan U.	A	100 E. Claflin Ave, Salina, KS 67401	Tim Bellew	(785) 827-5541
Kean U.	III	1000 Morris Ave., Union, NJ 07083	Neil Ioviero	(908) 737-5452
Keene State College	III	229 Main St., Keene, NH 03435	Ken Howe	(603) 357-2809
Kennesaw State U.	II	1000 Chastain Rd. NW, Kennesaw, GA 30144	Mike Sansing	(770) 423-6264
Kentucky State U.	II	400 E. Main St., Frankfort, KY 40601	Elwood Johnson	(502) 597-6018
Kentucky Wesleyan College	II	PO Box 1039, Owensboro, KY 42302	Todd Lillpop	(270) 852-3342
Kenyon College	III	Athletic Dept., Duff Street, Gambier, OH 43022	Matt Burdette	(740) 427-5810
Keystone College	III	One College Green, La Plume, PA 18440	Jamie Shevchik	(570) 945-8234
King College	A	1350 King College Rd., Bristol, TN 37620	Craig Kleinmann	(423) 652-6017
King's College	III	133 N. River St., Wilkes-Barre, PA 18711	Jerry Greeley	(570) 208-5855
Knox College	III	2 E. South St., Galesburg, IL 61401	Jami Isaacson	(309) 341-7456
Kutztown U.	II	Keystone Hall, Kutztown, PA 19530	Chris Blum	(610) 683-4063
LaGrange College	III	601 Broad St., La Grange, GA 30240	Kevin Howard	(706) 880-8295
Lake Erie College	III	391 W. Washington St., Painesville, OH 44077	Ken Krsolovic	(440) 375-7470
Lakeland College	III	PO Box 359, Sheboygan, WI 53082	John Govek	(920) 565-1411
Lambuth U.	A	705 Lambuth Blvd., Jackson, TN 38301	Wayne Albury	(731) 425-3385
Lancaster Bible College	C	901 Eden Rd., Lancaster, PA 17608	Paul Lane	(717) 560-8267
Lander U.	II	CPO 6016, Greenwood, SC 29649	Mike McGuire	(864) 388-8961
Lane College	II	545 Lane Ave., Jackson, TN 38301	John Gore	(731) 426-7571
La Roche College	III	9000 Babcock Blvd., Pittsburgh, PA 15237	Rich Pasquale	(412) 536-1046
La Verne, U. of	III	1950 3rd St., La Verne, CA 91750	Scott Winterburn	(909) 593-3511
Lawrence U.	III	PO Box 599, Appleton, WI 54912	Korey Krueger	(920) 832-7346
Lebanon Valley College	III	101 N. College Ave., Annville, PA 17003	Keith Evans	(717) 867-6271
Lee U.	A	1120 N. Ocoee St., Cleveland, TN 37311	Dave Altopp	(423) 614-8445
Lehman College	III	250 Bedford Park Blvd. W., Bronx, NY 10468	John Mehling	(718) 960-7746
LeMoyne-Owen College	II	807 Walker Ave., Memphis, TN 38126	Willie Patterson	(901) 774-9090
Lenoir-Rhyne College	II	PO Box 7356, Hickory, NC 28603	Frank Pait	(828) 328-7136
LeTourneau U.	III	PO Box 7001, Longview, TX 75602	Bernie Martinez	(903) 233-3721

Lewis & Clark College	III	0615 SW Palatine Hill Rd., Portland, OR 97219	Reed Rainey	(503) 768-7059
Lewis U.	II	One University Pkwy, Romeoville, IL 60446	Irish O'Reilly	(815) 836-5255
Lewis-Clark State College	A	500 8th Ave., Lewiston, ID 83501	Ed Cheff	(208) 792-2272
Limestone College	II	1115 College Dr., Gaffney, SC 29340	Chico Lombardo	(864) 488-4565
Lincoln Christian College	C	100 Campus View Dr., Lincoln, IL 62656	Greg Lowes	(217) 732-3168
Lincoln Memorial U.	II	PO Box 2028, Harrogate, TN 37752	Jeff Sziksai	(423) 869-6345
Lincoln U.	II	820 Chestnut St., Jefferson City, MO 65102		(573) 681-5334
Lincoln U.	III	1570 Baltimore Pike, Lincoln University, PA 19352	Paul Johnson	(215) 990-3188
Lindenwood U.	A	209 S. Kings Highway, St. Charles, MO 63301	Brian Behrens	(636) 949-4185
Lindsey Wilson College	A	210 Lindsey Wilson St., Columbia, KY 42728	Mike Talley	(270) 384-8074
Linfield College	III	900 SE Baker St., McMinnville, OR 97128	Scott Carnahan	(503) 883-2229
Lock Haven U.	II	Thomas Fieldhouse, Lock Haven, PA 17745	Smokey Stover	(570) 893-2245
Longwood U.	II	201 High St., Farmville, VA 23909	Buddy Bolding	(434) 395-2352
Loras College	III	1450 Alta Vista St., Dubuque, IA 52004	Carl Tebon	(563) 588-7732
Louisiana College	III	1140 College Dr., Pineville, LA 71359	Mike Byrnes	(318) 487-7322
Loyola U.	A	6363 St. Charles Ave., New Orleans, LA 70118	Michael Beeman	(504) 864-7392
LSU-Shreveport	A	One University Place, Shreveport, LA 71115	Rocke Musgraves	(318) 798-4106
Lubbock Christian U.	A	5601 W. 19th St., Lubbock, TX 79407	Nathan Blackwood	(806) 720-7853
Luther College	III	700 College Dr., Decorah, IA 52101	Brian Gillogly	(563) 387-1590
Lynchburg College	III	1501 Lakeside Dr., Lynchburg, VA 24501	Percy Abell	(434) 544-8496
Lyndon State College	A	PO Box 919, Lyndonville, VT 05851	Ryan Farley	(802) 626-6224
Lynn U.	II	3601 N. Military Trail, Boca Raton, FL 33431	Rudy Garbalosa	(561) 237-7242
Lyon College	A	PO Box 2317, Batesville, AR 72503	Kirk Kelley	(870) 698-4337
Macalester College	III	1600 Grand Ave., St. Paul, MN 55105	Matt Parrington	(651) 696-6770
Mac Murray College	III	447 E. College Ave, Jacksonville, IL 62650	Kevin Vest	(217) 479-7153
Madonna U.	A	36600 Schoolcraft Rd., Livonia, MI 48150	Greg Haeger	(734) 432-5609
Maine-Farmington, U. of	III	111 South St., Farmington, ME 04938	Dick Meader	(207) 778-7148
Maine-Presque Isle, U. of	III	181 Main St., Presque Isle, ME 04769		(207) 768-9421
Malone College	A	515 25th St. NW, Canton, OH 44709	Tom Crank	(330) 471-8286
Manchester College	III	604 E. College Ave., North Manchester, IN 46962	Rick Espeset	(260) 982-5034
Manhattanville College	III	2900 Purchase St., Purchase, NY 10577	Jeff Caulfield	(914) 323-7284
Mansfield U.	II	Academy Street, Mansfield, PA 16933	Harry Hillson	(570) 662-4457
Maranatha Baptist College	III	745 W. Main St., Watertown, WI 53094	Phil Price	(920) 206-6190
Marian College	III	45 S. National Ave., Fond du Lac, WI 54935	Jason Bartelt	(920) 923-8090
Marian College	A	3200 Cold Spring Rd., Indianapolis, IN 46222	Kurt Guldner	(317) 955-6310
Marietta College	III	215 5th St., Marietta, OH 45750	Brian Brewer	(740) 376-4517
Mars Hill College	II	100 Athletic St., Mars Hill, NC 28754	Daniel Taylor	(828) 689-1173
Martin Luther College	III	1995 Luther Court, New Ulm, MN 56073	Drew Buck	(507) 354-8221
Martin Methodist College	A	433 W. Madison St., Pulaski, TN 38478	George Ogilvie	(931) 363-9827
Mary, U. of	A	7500 University Dr., Bismarck, ND 58504	Van Vanetta	(701) 355-8270
Mary Hardin-Baylor U.	III	900 College St., Belton, TX 76513	Micah Wells	(254) 295-4619
Mary Washington, U. of	III	1301 College Ave., Fredericksburg, VA 22401	Tom Sheridan	(540) 654-1882
Maryville College	III	502 E. Lamar Alexander Pkwy., Maryville, TN 37804	Eric Etchison	(865) 981-8283
Maryville U.-St. Louis	III	13550 Conway Rd., St. Louis, MO 63141	Mike Sigler	(314) 529-9555
Marywood U.	III	2300 Adams Ave., Scranton, PA 18509	Joe Ross	(570) 961-4724
Mass College of Liberal Arts	III	375 Church St., North Adams, MA 01247	Jeff Puleri	(413) 662-5403
Mass. Institute of Technology	III	120 Vassar St., Cambridge, MA 02139	Andy Barlow	(617) 258-7310
Mass Maritime Academy	III	101 Academy Dr., Buzzards Bay, MA 02532	Bob Corradi	(508) 830-5055
Mass-Boston Harbor, U. of	III	100 Morrissey Blvd., Boston, MA 02125	Mark Bettencourt	(617) 287-7817
Mass-Dartmouth, U. of	III	285 Old Wesport Rd., North Dartmouth, MA 02747	Robert Curran	(508) 999-8721
Mass-Lowell, U. of	II	1 University Ave, Costello Gym, Lowell, MA 01854	Ken Connerty	(978) 934-2344
Master's College, The	A	21726 Placerita Canyon Rd., Santa Clarita, CA 91321	Monte Brooks	(661) 259-3540
Mayville State U.	A	330 3rd St. NE, Mayville, ND 58257	Scott Berry	(701) 788-4771
McDaniel College	III	2 College Hill, Westminster, MD 21157	David Seibert	(410) 857-2583
McKendree College	A	701 College Rd., Lebanon, IL 62254	Jim Boehne	(618) 537-6906
McMurry U.	III	South 14th St. & Sayles Blvd., Abilene, TX 79697	Lee Driggers	(325) 793-4650
Medaille College	III	18 Agassiz Circle, Buffalo, NY 14214	Ron Nero	(716) 884-3281
Menlo College	III	1000 El Camino Real, Atherton, CA 94027	Ken Bowman	(650) 543-3932
Mercy College	II	555 Broadway, Dobbs Ferry, NY 10522	Billy Sullivan	(914) 674-7566
Mercyhurst College	II	501 E. 38th St., Erie, PA 16546	Joe Spano	(814) 824-2441
Merrimack College	II	315 Turnpike St., North Andover, MA 01845	Joe Sarno	(978) 837-5000
Mesa State College	II	1100 North Ave., Grand Junction, CO 81501	Chris Hanks	(970) 248-1891
Messiah College	III	One College Ave., Grantham, PA 17027	Frank Montgomery	(717) 766-2511
Methodist College	III	5400 Ramsey St., Fayetteville, NC 28311	Tom Austin	(910) 630-7176
Metropolitan State U.	II	PO Box 173362, Campus Box 9, Denver, CO 80217	Vince Porreco	(303) 556-3301
Mid-America Christian U.	C	3500 SW 119th St., Oklahoma City, OK 73170	Jason Blackwell	(405) 692-3138
Mid-America Nazarene U.	A	2030 E. College Way, Olathe, KS 66062	Todd Garrett	(913) 791-3462
Mid-Continent College	A	99 Powell Rd. E., Mayfield, KY 42066	William Russell	(270) 247-8521
Middlebury College	III	Memorial Fieldhouse, Middlebury, VT 05753	Bob Smith	(802) 443-5264
Midland Lutheran College	A	900 N. Clarkson St., Fremont, NE 68025	Jeff Field	(402) 941-6371
Miles College	II	5500 Myron Massey Blvd., Birmingham, AL 35208	Ken Hatcher	(205) 929-1617
Millersville U.	II	PO Box 1002, Millersville, PA 17551	Glenn Gallagher	(717) 871-2411

College		Address	Coach	Phone
Milligan College	A	PO Box 500, Milligan College, TN 37682	Danny Clark	(423) 461-8722
Millikin U.	III	1184 W. Main St., Decatur, IL 62522	Josh Manning	(217) 424-3608
Millsaps College	III	1701 N. State St., Jackson, MS 39210	Jim Page	(601) 974-1196
Milwaukee Engineering	III	1025 N. Broadway, Milwaukee, WI 53202	Len VandenBoom	(414) 277-7154
Minnesota-Crookston, U. of	II	Sports Center, Crookston, MN 56716	Steve Olson	(218) 281-8419
Minnesota-Duluth, U. of	II	1216 Ordean Court, Duluth, MN 55812	Scott Hanna	(218) 726-7563
Minnesota-Morris, U. of	II	E. 2nd St., Morris, MN 56267	Mark Fohl	(320) 589-6421
Minnesota State U.-Mankato	II	135 Myers Fieldhouse, Mankato, MN 56001	Dean Bowyer	(507) 389-2689
Minot State U.	A	500 University Ave. W., Minot, ND 58707	Dick Limke	(701) 858-4328
Misericordia College	III	301 Lake St., Dallas, PA 18612	Josh Tehonica	(570) 674-6471
Mississippi College	III	PO Box 4049, Clinton, MS 39058	Lee Kuyrkendall	(601) 925-3346
Missouri Baptist U.	A	1 College Park Dr., St. Louis, MO 63141	Eddie Uschold	(314) 392-2384
Missouri Southern State Coll.	II	3950 E. Newman Rd, Joplin, MO 64801	Warren Turner	(417) 625-9312
Missouri-Rolla, U. of	II	705 W. 10th St., Rolla, MO 65401	Todd DeGraffenreid	(573) 341-4191
Missouri-St. Louis, U. of	II	One University Blvd., St. Louis, MO 63121	Jim Brady	(314) 516-5647
Missouri Valley College	A	500 E. College St., Marshall, MO 65340	Dan Bowers	(660) 831-4113
Missouri Western State	II	4525 Downs Dr., St. Joseph, MO 64507	Buzz Verduzco	(816) 271-4484
Mobile, U. of	A	5735 College Pkwy, Mobile, AL 36663	Mike Jacobs	(251) 442-2228
Molloy College	II	1000 Hempstead Ave., Rockville Centre, NY 11570	Bernie Havern	(516) 256-2207
Monmouth College	III	700 E. Broadway, Monmouth, IL 61462	Roger Sander	(309) 457-2169
Montclair State U.	III	One Normal Ave., Montclair, NJ 07043	Norm Schoenig	(973) 655-5281
Montevallo, U. of	II	Station 6600, Montevallo, AL 35115	Greg Goff	(205) 665-6761
Montreat College	A	310 Gaither Circle, Montreat, NC 28757	Travis Little	(828) 669-8011
Moravian College	III	1200 Main St., Bethlehem, PA 18018	Ed Little	(610) 861-1536
Morehouse College	II	830 Westview Dr. SW, Atlanta, GA 30314	Andre Pattillo	(404) 215-2752
Morningside College	A	1501 Morningside Ave, Sioux City, IA 51106	Jim Scholten	(712) 274-5258
Morris College	A	100 W. College St., Sumter, SC 29150	Clarence Houck	(803) 934-3235
Mount Aloysius College	A	7373 Admiral Pearl Hwy., Cresson, PA 16630	Garrett Sidor	(814) 886-6339
Mount Marty College	A	1105 West 8th St., Yankton, SD 57078	Andy Bernatow	(605) 668-1601
Mount Mercy College	A	1330 Elmhurst Drive NE, Cedar Rapids, IA 52402	Justin Schulte	(319) 363-1323
Mount Olive College	II	634 Henderson St., Mount Olive, NC 28365	Carl Lancaster	(919) 658-7805
Mount St. Joseph College	III	5701 Delhi Rd., Cincinnati, OH 45233	Chuck Murray	(513) 244-4402
Mount St. Mary College	III	330 Powell Ave., Newburgh, NY 12550	Matt Dembinsky	(845) 569-3253
Mount Union College	III	1972 Clark Ave., Alliance, OH 44601	Paul Hesse	(330) 823-4878
Mount Vernon Nazarene Coll.	A	800 Martinsburg Rd., Mt. Vernon, OH 43050	Keith Veale	(740) 392-6868
Muhlenberg College	III	2400 W. Chew St., Allentown, PA 18104	Bob Macaluso	(484) 664-3684
Muskingum College	III	163 Stormont St., New Concord, OH 43762	Gregg Thompson	(740) 826-8318
Myers U.	A	112 Prospect Ave., Cleveland, OH 44115	Charles Cangeosi	(216) 696-9000
Nebraska-Kearney, U. of	II	Hwy 30 & 15th Ave., Kearney, NE 68849	Damon Day	(308) 865-8022
Nebraska-Omaha, U. of	II	6001 Dodge St., Omaha, NE 68182	Bob Herold	(402) 554-3388
Nebraska Wesleyan U.	III	5000 St. Paul Ave., Lincoln, NE 68504	Mark Mancuso	(402) 465-2171
Neumann College	III	One Neumann Dr., Aston, PA 19014	Len Schuler	(610) 358-4505
New England College	III	Clement Arena, 24 Bridge St., Henniker, NH 03242	Dave Decew	(603) 428-2447
New Haven, U. of	II	300 Boston Port Rd., West Haven, CT 06516	Frank Vieira	(203) 932-7018
New Jersey City U.	III	2039 Kennedy Blvd., Jersey City, NJ 07305	Ken Heaton	(201) 200-3079
New Jersey Tech	II	University Heights, Newark, NJ 07102	Brian Callahan	(973) 596-5827
New Jersey, College of	III	PO Box 7718, Ewing, NJ 08628	Rick Dell	(609) 771-2374
New Mexico Highlands U.	II	P.O. Box 9000, Las Vegas, NM 87701	Steve Jones	(505) 454-3587
Newberry College	II	2100 College St., Newberry, SC 29108	Tim Medlin	(803) 321-5162
Newman U.	A	3100 McCormick Ave., Wichita, KS 67213	Kevin Ulwelling	(316) 942-4291
Nichols College	III	PO Box 5000, Dudley, MA 01571	Brian Lambert	(508) 213-2363
North Alabama, U. of	II	Box 5072, Florence, AL 35632	Mike Lane	(256) 765-4615
North Carolina Wesleyan	III	3400 N. Wesleyan Blvd., Rocky Mount, NC 27804	Charlie Long	(252) 985-5219
North Carolina-Pembroke, U. of	II	PO Box 1510, Pembroke, NC 28372	Paul O'Neil	(910) 521-6810
North Central College	III	30 N. Brainard St., Naperville, IL 60540	Brian Michalak	(630) 637-5512
North Dakota, U. of	II	PO Box 9013, Grand Forks, ND 58202	Kelvin Ziegler	(701) 777-4038
North Florida, U. of	II	4567 St. Johns Bluff Rd. S., Jacksonville, FL 32224	Dusty Rhodes	(904) 620-1556
North Georgia College	A	130 College Ave., Dahlonega, GA 30597	Tom Cantrell	(706) 867-2754
North Greenville College	II	PO Box 1892, Tigerville, SC 29688	Tim Nihart	(864) 977-7156
North Park U.	III	3225 W. Foster Ave, Chicago, IL 60625	Steve Vanden Branden	(773) 244-5675
Northeastern State U.	II	600 N. Grand Ave., Tahlequah, OK 74464	Sergio Espinal	(918) 456-5511
Northern Kentucky U.	II	1 Nunn Drive, Highland Heights, KY 41099	Todd Asalon	(859) 572-6474
Northern State U.	II	1200 South Jay St., Aberdeen, SD 57401	Curt Fredrickson	(605) 626-7735
Northland College	III	1411 Ellis Ave., Ashland, WI 54806	Joel Barta	(715) 682-1387
Northwest Missouri State	II	800 University Dr., Maryville, MO 64468	Darin Loe	(660) 562-1352
Northwest Nazarene U.	II	623 Holly St., Nampa, ID 83686	Tim Onofrei	(208) 467-8351
Northwestern College	A	101 7th St. SW, Orange City, IA 51041	Dave Nonnemacher	(712) 707-7366
Northwestern College	III	3003 Snelling Ave. N., St. Paul, MN 55113	Dave Hieb	(651) 631-5345
Northwestern Okla. State	A	709 Oklahoma Blvd., Alva, OK 73717	Joe Phillips	(580) 327-8635
Northwood U.	A	2600 N. Military Tr., West Palm Beach, FL 33409	Rick Smoliak	(561) 478-5552
Northwood U.	II	4000 Whiting Drive, Midland, MI 48640	Joe DiBenedetto	(989) 837-4427
Northwood U.	A	1114 West FM 1382, Cedar Hill, TX 75104	Pat Malcheski	(972) 293-5439

College	Div	Address	Coach	Phone
Norwich U.	III	158 Harmon Dr., Northfield, VT 05663	Shawn McIntyre	(802) 485-2230
Notre Dame College	A	4545 College Rd., Cleveland, OH 44121	Craig Moro	(216) 373-5427
Nova Southeastern U.	II	3301 College Ave., Fort Lauderdale, FL 33314	Michael Mominey	(954) 262-8252
Nyack College	II	1 South Blvd., Nyack, NY 10960	Jason Beck	(845) 358-1710
Oakland City U.	II	143 Lucretia St., Oakland City, IN 47660	Ray Fletcher	(812) 749-1576
Oberlin College	III	200 Woodland Ave., Oberlin, OH 44074	Eric Lahetta	(440) 775-8502
Occidental College	III	1600 Campus Rd., Los Angeles, CA 90041	Denny Barrett	(323) 259-2683
Oglethorpe U.	III	4484 Peachtree Rd. NE, Atlanta, GA 30319	Bill Popp	(404) 364-8417
Ohio Dominican College	A	1216 Sunbury Rd., Columbus, OH 43219	Paul Page	(614) 251-4535
Ohio Northern U.	III	525 S. Main, Ada, OH 45810	Milan Rasic	(419) 772-2442
Ohio Valley College	II	1 Campus View Dr., Vienna, WV 26105	Chad Porter	(304) 865-6209
Ohio Wesleyan U.	III	61 S. Sandusky St., Delaware, OH 43015	Roger Ingles	(740) 368-3738
Oklahoma, U. of Science/Arts	A	1727 W. Alabama, Chickisha, OK 73018	L.J. Powell	(405) 574-1228
Oklahoma Baptist U.	A	500 W. University St., Shawnee, OK 74801	Bobby Cox	(405) 878-2139
Oklahoma City U.	A	2501 N. Blackwelder, Oklahoma City, OK 73106	Denny Crabaugh	(405) 521-5156
Oklahoma Wesleyan Coll.	A	2201 Silver Lake Rd., Bartlesville, OK 74006	Bengie Rodriguez	(918) 335-6848
Olivet College	III	320 S. Main St., Olivet, MI 49076	Carlton Hardy	(269) 749-4184
Olivet Nazarene U.	A	One University Ave., Bourbonnais, IL 60914	Elliot Johnson	(815) 939-5119
Oneonta State U.	III	Ravine Pkwy., Oneonta, NY 13820	Rick Ferchen	(607) 436-2661
Oregon Tech	A	3201 Campus Dr., Klamath Falls, OR 97601	Pete Whisler	(541) 885-1722
Ottawa U.	A	1001 South Cedar St., Ottawa, KS 66067	Jarrod Titus	(785) 242-5200
Otterbein College	III	160 Center St., Westerville, OH 43081	George Powell	(614) 823-3521
Ouachita Baptist U.	II	410 Ouachita St., Arkadelphia, AR 71998	Scott Norwood	(870) 245-4255
Ozarks, College of the	III	PO Box 17, Point Lookout, MO 65726	Patrick McGaha	(417) 334-6411
Ozarks, U. of the	III	415 N. College Ave., Clarksville, AR 72830	Jimmy Clark	(479) 979-1409
Pace U.	II	861 Bedford Rd., Pleasantville, NY 10570	Henry Manning	(914) 773-3413
Pacific Lutheran U.	III	12180 Park Ave. S., Tacoma, WA 98447	Geoff Loomis	(253) 535-8789
Pacific U.	III	2043 College Way, Forest Grove, OR 97116	Greg Bradley	(503) 359-2142
Paine College	II	1235 15th St., Augusta, GA 30901	Pete Cardenas	(706) 821-8228
Palm Beach Atlantic Coll.	II	901 S. Flagler Dr., West Palm Beach, FL 33416	Mike Lord	(561) 803-2523
Panhandle State U.	II	PO Box 430, Goodwell, OK 73939	Robert Rudel	(580) 349-1331
Park U.	A	8700 NW River Park Dr., Parkville, MO 64152	Cary Lundy	(816) 584-6746
Paul Quinn College	A	3837 Simpson Stuart Rd., Dallas, TX 75241	Don Cofer	(214) 801-1168
Penn State Behrend College	III	5091 Station Rd., Erie, PA 16563	Paul Benim	(814) 898-6322
Penn State-Allentown	III	8380 Mohr Lane, Fogelsville, PA 18051	Joe Smull	(610) 396-6151
Penn State-Altoona	III	3000 Ivyside Park, Altoona, PA 16601	Joe Piotti	(814) 949-5226
Penn State-Hazelton		76 University Dr., Hazelton, PA 18202	Tim Thompson	(570) 459-1869
Penn State-McKeesport		4000 University Dr., McKeesport, PA 15132	Mike Cherepko	(412) 675-9487
Peru State College	A	PO Box 10, Peru, NE 68421	Mark Bayliss	(402) 872-2443
Pfeiffer U.	II	PO Box 960, Misenheimer, NC 28109	Mark Hayes	(704) 463-1360
Philadelphia, U. of Sciences	II	600 S. 43rd St., Philadelphia, PA 19104	Frank Angelosi	(215) 595-8782
Philadelphia U.	II	421 Henry Ave., Philadelphia, PA 19144	Don Flynn	(215) 951-2630
Philadelphia Biblical U.	III	200 Manor Ave., Langhorne, PA 19047	Rich Sparling	(215) 702-4403
Piedmont College	III	165 Central Ave., Demorest, GA 30535	Jim Peeples	(706) 778-8500
Pikeville College	A	147 Sycamore St., Pikeville, KY 41501	Johnnie LeMaster	(606) 218-5370
Pittsburg State U.	II	1701 S. Broadway, Pittsburg, KS 66762	Steve Bever	(620) 232-7951
Pittsburgh-Bradford, U. of	III	300 Campus Dr., Bradford, PA 16701	Bret Butler	(814) 362-5093
Pittsburgh-Greensburg, U. of	III	1150 Mt. Pleasant Rd., Greensburg, PA 15601	Joe Hill	(724) 836-7185
Pittsburgh-Johnstown, U. of	II	450 Schoolhouse Rd., Johnstown, PA 15904	Todd Williams	(814) 269-5271
Plymouth State College	III	PE Center #32, Holderness Rd., Plymouth, NH 03264	Dennis McManus	(603) 535-2756
Point Loma Nazarene U.	A	3900 Lomaland Dr., San Diego, CA 92106	Jay Johnson	(619) 849-2765
Point Park College	A	201 Wood St., Pittsburgh, PA 15222	Al Liberi	(412) 392-3845
Polytechnic U.	III	0 Metro Tech Ctr., Brooklyn, NY 11201	Arty Williams	(718) 260-3453
Pomona-Pitzer College	III	220 E. 6th St., Claremont, CA 91711	Frank Pericolosi	(909) 621-8422
Presbyterian College	II	105 Ashland Ave., Clinton, SC 29325	Elton Pollock	(864) 833-8236
Presentation College	III	1500 N. Main, Aberdeen, SD 57401	Rick Kline	(605) 229-8406
Principia College	III	1 Maybeck Place, Elsah, IL 62028	Mike Barthelmess	(618) 374-5036
Puget Sound, U. of	III	1500 N. Warner St., Tacoma, WA 98416	Brian Billings	(253) 879-3365
Purdue U.-North Central	A	1401 U.S. Hwy. 421 S., Westville, IN 46391	Ryan Brown	(219) 785-5273
Queens College	II	65-30 Kissena Blvd., Flushing, NY 11367	Frank Battaglia	(718) 997-2781
Quincy U.	II	1800 College Ave., Quincy, IL 62301	Greg McVey	(217) 228-5268
Ramapo College	III	505 Ramapo Valley Rd., Mahwah, NJ 07430	Rich Martin	(201) 684-7674
Randolph-Macon College	III	PO Box 5005, Ashland, VA 23005	Gregg Waters	(804) 752-7303
Redlands, U. of	III	1200 E. Colton Ave., Redlands, CA 92373	Scott Laverty	(909) 793-2121
Reinhardt College	A	7300 Reinhardt College Cir., Waleska, GA 30183	Bill Popp	(770) 720-5568
Regis U.	II	Athletic Dept., Denver, CO 80221	Dan McDermott	(303) 458-3519
Rensselaer Poly Institute	III	110 8th St., Troy, NY 12180	Karl Steffen	(518) 276-6185
Rhode Island College	III	600 Mt. Pleasant Ave., Providence, RI 02908	Jay Grenier	(401) 456-8258
Rhodes College	III	2000 N. Parkway, Memphis, TN 38112	Jeff Cleathes	(901) 843-3456

College	Div	Address	Coach	Phone
Richard Stockton College	III	PO Box 195, Pomona, NJ 08240	Marty Kavanagh	(609) 626-6010
Rio Grande, U. of	A	218 N. College Ave, Rio Grande, OH 45674	Brad Warnimont	(740) 245-7486
Ripon College	III	300 Seward St., Ripon, WI 54971	Gordon Gillespie	(920) 748-8776
Rivier College	III	420 Main St., Nashua, NH 03060	Bill Maniotis	(603) 897-8681
Roanoke College	III	221 College Lane, Salem, VA 24153	Richard Morris	(540) 378-2338
Robert Morris College	A	401 S. State St., Chicago, IL 60605	Woody Urchak	(312) 935-6801
Rochester, U. of	III	Goergen Athletic Center, Rochester, NY 14627	Joe Reina	(585) 275-6027
Rochester College		800 W. Avon Rd., Rochester Hills, MI 48307	Virgil Smith	(248) 218-2135
Rochester Tech	III	51 Lomb Memorial Dr., Rochester, NY 14623	Rob Grow	(585) 475-2615
Rockford College	III	5050 E. State St., Rockford, IL 61108	Brian Nelson	(815) 394-5062
Rockhurst U.	II	1100 Rockhurst Rd., Kansas City, MO 64110	Gary Burns	(816) 501-4130
Roger Williams U.	III	1 Old Ferry Rd., Bristol, RI 02809	Derek Carlson	(401) 254-3163
Rollins College	II	1000 Holt Ave, Winter Park, FL 32789	Bob Rikeman	(407) 646-2328
Rose-Hulman Tech	III	5500 Wabash Ave., Terre Haute, IN 47803	Jeff Jenkins	(812) 877-8209
Rowan U.	III	201 Mullica Hill Rd., Glassboro, NJ 08028	John Cole	(856) 256-4687
Rust College	III	150 E. Rust Ave., Holly Springs, MS 38635	Avery Mason	(662) 252-4661
Rutgers U.-Camden	III	3rd & Linden Streets, Camden, NJ 08102	Keith Williams	(856) 225-2746
Rutgers U.-Newark	III	42 Warren St., Newark, NJ 07102	Mark Rizzi	(973) 353-5474
Saginaw Valley State	II	7400 Bay Rd., University Center, MI 48710	Walt Head	(989) 964-7334
St. Ambrose U.	A	518 W. Locust St., Davenport, IA 52803	Jim Callahan	(563) 333-6237
St. Andrews Presbyterian	II	1700 Dogwood Mile St., Laurinburg, NC 28352	Bobby Simmons	(910) 277-5426
St. Anselm College	II	100 St. Anselm Dr., Manchester, NH 03102	J.P. Pyne	(603) 656-6016
St. Augustine's College	II	1315 Oakwood Ave., Raleigh, NC 27610	Andy Wood	(919) 516-4711
St. Cloud State U.	II	720 4th Ave. S., St. Cloud, MN 56301	Denny Lorsung	(320) 308-3208
St. Edwards U.	II	3001 S. Congress Ave., Austin, TX 78704	Jerry Farber	(512) 448-8497
St. Francis, U. of	A	500 Wilcox St., Joliet, IL 60435	Tony Delgado	(815) 740-3406
St. Francis, U. of	A	2701 Spring St., Fort Wayne, IN 46808	Doug Coate	(260) 434-7414
St. Gregory's U.	A	1900 W. MacArthur Dr., Shawnee, OK 74804	Chris Pingry	(405) 878-5151
St. John Fisher College	III	3690 East Ave., Rochester, NY 14618	Dan Pepicelli	(585) 385-8419
St. John's U.	III	PO Box 7277, Collegeville, MN 56321	Jerry Haugen	(320) 363-2756
St. Joseph's College	II	PO Box 875, Rensselaer, IN 47978	Rick O'Dette	(219) 866-6399
St. Joseph's College	III	278 Whites Bridge Rd., Standish, ME 04084	Will Sanborn	(207) 893-6675
St. Joseph's College	III	155 W. Roe Blvd., Patchogue, NY 11772	Randy Caden	(631) 447-3349
St. Lawrence U.	III	Park Street, Canton, NY 13617	Tom Fay	(315) 229-5882
St. Leo U.	II	PO Box 6665, St. Leo, FL 33574	Ricky Ware	(352) 588-8227
St. Louis Christian College	C	1360 Grandview Dr., Florissant, MO 63033	Derrick Johnston	(314) 837-6777
St. Martin's College	II	5300 Pacific Ave. SE, Lacey, WA 98503	Joe Dominiak	(360) 438-4531
St. Mary, U. of	A	4100 S. 4th St., Leavenworth, KS 66048	Rob Miller	(913) 758-6160
St. Mary's College	III	18952 E. Fisher Rd., St. Mary's City, MD 20686	Lew Jenkins	(240) 895-4312
St. Mary's U.	III	700 Terrace Heights #47, Winona, MN 55987	Nick Whaley	(507) 457-1577
St. Mary's U.	II	1 Camino Santa Maria St., San Antonio, TX 78228	Charlie Migl	(210) 436-3034
St. Michael's College	II	One Winooski Park, Colchester, VT 05439	Perry Bove	(802) 654-2725
St. Norbert College	III	100 Grant St., De Pere, WI 54115	Tom Winske	(920) 403-3545
St. Olaf College	III	1520 St. Olaf Ave., Northfield, MN 55057	Matt McDonald	(507) 646-3638
St. Rose, College of	II	432 Western Ave., Albany, NY 12203	Bob Bellizzi	(518) 454-2041
St. Scholastica, College of	III	1200 Kenwood Ave., Duluth, MN 55811	John Baggs	(218) 723-6298
St. Thomas, U. of	III	2115 Summit Ave., St. Paul, MN 55105	Dennis Denning	(651) 962-5924
St. Thomas Aquinas	II	125 Route 340, Sparkill, NY 10976	Scott Muscat	(845) 398-4027
St. Thomas U.	A	16400 NW 32nd Ave., Miami, FL 33054	Manny Mantrana	(305) 628-6730
St. Vincent College	A	300 Fraser Purchase Rd., Latrobe, PA 15650	Mick Janosko	(724) 805-2396
St. Xavier U.	A	3700 W. 103rd St., Chicago, IL 60655	Mike Dooley	(773) 298-3103
Salem-International U.	II	223 W. Main St., Salem, WV 26426	Rich Leitch	(304) 782-5632
Salem State College	III	352 Lafayette St., Salem, MA 01970	Ken Perrone	(978) 542-6000
Salisbury U.	III	1101 Camden Ave., Salisbury, MD 21801	Doug Fleetwood	(410) 543-6034
Salve Regina U.	III	100 Ochre Point Ave., Newport, RI 02840	Steve Cirella	(401) 341-2267
San Francisco State U.	II	1600 Holloway Ave., San Francisco, CA 94132	Matt Markovich	(415) 338-1226
Savannah Art & Design	A	PO Box 3146, Savannah, GA 31402	Doug Wollenburg	(912) 525-4782
Schreiner U.	III	2100 Memorial Blvd., Kerrville, TX 78028	Joe Castillo	(830) 792-7292
Scranton, U. of	III	800 Linden St., Scranton, PA 18510	Mike Bertoletti	(570) 941-7440
Seton Hill U.	A	PO Box 287, Greensburg, PA 15601	Marc Marizzaldi	(724) 830-1169
Shaw U.	II	118 E. South St., Raleigh, NC 27601	Bobby Sanders	(919) 546-8278
Shawnee State U.	A	940 2nd St., Portsmouth, OH 45662	Tom Bergan	(740) 351-3537
Shenandoah U.	III	1460 University Dr., Winchester, VA 22601	Kevin Anderson	(540) 665-4531
Shepherd College	II	P.O. Box 3210, Shepherdstown, WV 25443	Wayne Riser	(304) 876-5472
Shippensburg U.	II	1871 Old Main Dr., Shippensburg, PA 17257	Bruce Peddie	(717) 477-1508
Shorter College	A	315 Shorter Ave., Rome, GA 30165	Matt Larry	(706) 233-7510
Siena Heights U.	A	1247 E. Siena Heights Dr., Adrian, MI 49221	John Kolasinski	(517) 264-7872
Simpson College	A	2211 College View Dr., Redding, CA 96003	Josh Gleason	(530) 226-2977
Simpson College	III	701 North C St., Indianola, IA 50125	John Sirianni	(515) 961-1620
Sioux Falls, U. of	A	1101 W. 22nd St., Sioux Falls, SD 57105	Luke Langenfeld	(605) 331-6638
Skidmore College	III	815 N. Broadway, Saratoga Springs, NY 12866	Ron Plourde	(518) 580-5380
Slippery Rock U.	II	1 Morrow Way, Slippery Rock, PA 19383	Jeff Messer	(724) 738-2813

Sonoma State U.	II	1801 E. Cotati Ave., Rohnert Park, CA 94928	John Goelz	(707) 664-2524
South Carolina-Aiken, U. of	II	471 University Parkway, Aiken, SC 29801	Kenny Thomas	(803) 641-3410
South Carolina-Upstate, U. of	II	800 University Way, Spartanburg, SC 29303	Matt Fincher	(864) 503-5135
South, U. of the	III	735 University Ave., Sewanee, TN 37383	Scott Baker	(931) 598-1455
Southeastern College	C	1000 Longfellow Blvd, Lakeland, FL 33801	Frank Yurchak	(863) 667-5039
Southeastern Oklahoma State	II	1405 N. 4th, PMB 4049, Durant, OK 74701	Mike Metheny	(580) 745-2478
Southern Arkansas U.	II	100 E. University St., Magnolia, AR 71753	Mike Godfrey	(870) 235-4127
Southern Connecticut State	II	125 Wintergreen Ave., New Haven, CT 06515	Tim Shea	(203) 392-6021
Southern Illinois U.-Edwardsville	II	SIUE Box 1027, Edwardsville, IL 62026	GaryCollins	(618) 650-2872
Southern Indiana, U. of	II	8600 University Blvd, Evansville, IN 47712	Mike Goedde	(812) 464-1943
Southern Maine, U. of	III	37 College Ave., Gorham, ME 04038	Ed Flaherty	(207) 780-5474
Southern Nazarene U.	A	6729 NW 39th Expy., Bethany, OK 73008	Scott Selby	(405) 491-6630
Southern New Hampshire U.	II	2500 N. River Rd., Manchester, NH 03106	Bruce Joyce	(603) 645-9637
Southern Tech	A	1100 S. Marietta Pkwy., Marietta, GA 30060	Matt Griffin	(678) 915-5445
Southern Vermont College	III	982 Mansion Dr., Bennington, VT 05201	Todd Downing	(802) 447-4628
Southern Virginia U.	A	1 College Hill Dr., Buena Vista, VA 24416	Jerry Schlegelmilch	(540) 261-8400
Southern Wesleyan U.	A	1 Wesleyan Dr., Central, SC 29630	Mike Gillespie	(864) 644-5035
Southwest, College of the	A	6610 N. Lovington Hwy., Hobbs, NM 88240	Mike Galvan	(505) 392-6561
Southwest Baptist U.	II	1600 University Ave., Bolivar, MO 65613	Sam Berg	(417) 328-1794
Southwest Minnesota State U.	II	1501 State St., Marshall, MN 56258	Paul Blanchard	(507) 537-7268
Southwestern Assemblies of God	A	1200 Sycamore, Waxahachie, TX 75165	Greg Hayes	(972) 937-4010
Southwestern Oklahoma State	II	100 Campus Dr., Weatherford, OK 73096	Charles Teasley	(580) 774-3263
Southwestern U.	III	1001 E. University, Georgetown, TX 78626	Jim Shelton	(512) 863-1254
Spalding U.	A	851 S. 4th St., Louisville, KY 40203	Kevin Kocks	(502) 452-2580
Spring Arbor College	A	106 E. Main St., Spring Arbor, MI 49283	Sam Riggleman	(517) 750-6713
Spring Hill College	A	4000 Dauphin St., Mobile, AL 36608	Frank Sims	(251) 380-3486
Springfield College	III	263 Alden St., Springfield, MA 01109	Mark Simeone	(413) 748-3274
Staten Island, College of	III	2800 Victory Blvd., Staten Island, NY 10314	Bill Cali	(718) 982-3171
Sterling College	A	125 W. Cooper, Sterling, KS 67579	Scott Norwood	(620) 278-4227
Stevens Tech	III	1 Castle Point on Hudson, Hoboken, NJ 07030	John Crane	(201) 216-8033
Stillman College	III	3600 Stillman Blvd., Tuscaloosa, AL 35401	Randal Jennings	(205) 366-8891
Stonehill College	II	320 Washington St., North Easton, MA 02357	Patrick Boen	(508) 565-1351
Suffolk U.	III	41 Temple St., Boston, MA 02114	Cary McConnell	(617) 573-8379
Sul Ross State U.	III	Box C-17, Hwy. 90 E., Alpine, TX 79832	Mike Pallanez	(432) 837-8231
SUNY Brockport	III	350 New Campus Dr., Brockport, NY 14420	Mark Rowland	(585) 395-5329
SUNY Farmingdale	III	2350 Broadhollow Rd., Farmingdale, NY 11735	Ken Rocco	(631) 420-2123
SUNY Maritime College	III	6 Pennyfield Ave., Bronx, NY 10465	Frank Menna	(718) 409-7331
SUNY New Paltz	III	75 S. Manheim Blvd., New Paltz, NY 12561	Mike Juhl	(845) 257-3915
SUNY Old Westbury	III	PO Box 210, Old Westbury, NY 11568	Hector Aristy	(516) 876-3241
SUNY Oswego	III	202 Laker Hall, Oswego, NY 13126	Frank Paino	(315) 312-2405
SUNY Plattsburg	III	101 Broad St., Plattsburg, NY 12901	Kris Doorey	(518) 564-4136
SUNY Institute of Technology	III	PO Box 3050, Utica, NY 13504	Kevin Edick	(315) 792-7523
Susquehanna U.	III	514 University Ave., Selinsgrove, PA 17870	Matt Karchner	(570) 372-4417
Swarthmore College	III	500 College Ave., Swarthmore, PA 19081	Frank Agovino	(610) 328-8216
Tabor College	A	400 S. Jefferson St., Hillsboro, KS 67063	John Sparks	(620) 947-3121
Tampa, U. of	II	401 W. Kennedy Blvd., Tampa, FL 33606	Joe Urso	(813) 253-6240
Tarleton State U.	II	Box T-80, Stephenville, TX 76402	Trey Felan	(254) 968-9528
Taylor U.	A	236 W. Reade Ave, Upland, IN 46989	Kyle Gould	(765) 998-4635
Teikyo-Post U.	II	800 Country Club Rd., Waterbury, CT 06723	Wayne Mazzoni	(203) 596-4533
Tennessee Temple U.	C	1815 Union Ave., Chattanooga, TN 37404	Bob Hall	(423) 493-4234
Tennessee Wesleyan College	A	40 Green St., Athens, TN 37371	Ashley Lawson	(423) 746-5277
Texas A&M-Kingsville	II	MSC 202, Kingsville, TX 78363	Russell Stockton	(361) 593-3487
Texas-Dallas, U. of	III	Box 830688 AB 10, Richardson, TX 75083	Shane Shewmake	(972) 883-2392
Texas-Tyler, U. of	III	PO Box 4500, Tyler, TX 75712	Reginald Coleman	(903) 593-8311
Texas Lutheran U.	III	1000 W. Court St., Seguin, TX 78155	Bill Miller	(830) 372-8124
Texas-Permian Basin, U. of	A	4901 E. University Blvd., Odessa, TX 79762	Eddie Tillenger	(432) 552-4677
Texas Wesleyan U.	A	1201 Wesleyan St., Fort Worth, TX 76105	Mike Jeffcoat	(817) 531-7547
Thiel College	III	75 College Ave., Greenville, PA 16125	Joe Schaly	(724) 589-2138
Thomas College	III	180 West River Rd., Waterville, ME 04901	Greg King	(207) 859-1208
Thomas U.	A	1501 Millpond Rd., Thomasville, GA 31792	Mike Lee	(229) 226-1621
Thomas More College	III	333 Thomas More Pkwy., Crestview Hills, KY 41017	Jeff Hetzer	(859) 344-3532
Tiffin U.	II	155 Miami St., Tiffin, OH 44883	Lonny Allen	(419) 448-3359
Toccoa Falls College	C	PO Box 800818, Toccoa Falls, GA 30598	Justin Pollock	(706) 886-6831
Transylvania U.	III	300 N. Broadway, Lexington, KY 40508	Shayne Stock	(859) 233-8699
Trevecca Nazarene U.	A	333 Murfreesboro Rd., Nashville, TN 37210	Jeff Forehand	(615) 248-1276
Tri-State U.	III	1 University Ave., Angola, IN 46703	Greg Perschke	(260) 665-4135
Trinity Christian College	C	6601 W. College Dr., Palos Heights, IL 60463	Matt Schans	(708) 239-4780
Trinity College	III	380 Summit St., Hartford, CT 06106	Bill Decker	(860) 297-2066
Trinity International U.	C	500 NE 1st Ave., Miami, FL 33132	Jud Damon	(305) 577-4600
Trinity International U.	A	2065 Half Day Rd., Deerfield, IL 60015	Mike Manes	(847) 317-7093
Trinity U.	III	1 Trinity Place, San Antonio, TX 78212	Tim Scannell	(210) 999-8287
Truman State U.	II	100 E. Normal St., Kirksville, MO 63501	Larry Scully	(660) 785-6003

College	Div	Address	Coach	Phone
Tufts U.	III	161 College Ave., Medford, MA 02155	John Casey	(617) 627-5218
Tusculum College	II	PO Box 5090, Greenville, TN 37743	Doug Jones	(423) 636-7322
Tuskegee U.	II	321 James Center, Tuskegee, AL 36088	Antonio Knight	(334) 727-8485
Union College	A	310 College St., Barbourville, KY 40906	Bart Osborne	(606) 546-1355
Union College	III	807 Union Ave., Schenectady, NY 12308	Jeremy Rivenburg	(518) 388-6000
Union U.	A	1050 Union University Dr., Jackson, TN 38305	Andy Rushing	(731) 661-5333
U.S. Coast Guard Academy	III	15 Mohegan Ave., New London, CT 06320	Pete Barry	(860) 701-6132
U.S. Merchant Marine Acad.	III	300 Steamboat Rd., Kings Point, NY 11024	Dennis Gagnon	(516) 773-5727
Upper Iowa U.	III	605 Washington, Fayette, IA 52142	Mark Danker	(563) 425-5290
Urbana U.	A	579 College Way, Urbana, OH 43078	Scott Spriggs	(937) 454-1377
Ursinus College	III	601 Main St., Collegeville, PA 19426	Brian Thomas	(610) 409-3611
Utica College	III	1600 Burnstone Rd., Utica, NY 13502	Don Guido	(315) 752-3378
Valdosta State U.	II	1500 N. Patterson St, Valdosta, GA 31698	Tommy Thomas	(229) 259-5562
Valley City State U.	A	101 College St. SW, Valley City, ND 58072	Cory Anderson	(701) 845-7413
Valley Forge Christian	C	1401 Charlestown Rd., Phoenixville, PA 19460	Roger Burke	(610) 917-1479
Vanguard U.	A	55 Fair Dr., Costa Mesa, CA 92626	Scott Mallernee	(714) 556-3610
Vassar College	III	124 Raymond Ave., Poughkeepsie, NY 12604	Chris Campassi	(845) 437-5344
Vermont Tech		Randolph Center, VT 05061	Aaron Hill	(802) 728-1382
Villa Julie College	III	1525 Greenspring Valley Rd., Stevenson, MD 21153	Jason Tawney	(443) 334-2334
Virginia Intermont	A	1013 Moore St., Bristol, VA 24201	Chris Holt	(276) 466-7945
Virginia State U.	II	PO Box 9058, Petersburg, VA 23806	Merrill Morgan	(804) 524-5816
Virginia Wesleyan College	III	1584 Wesleyan Dr., Norfolk, VA 23502	Nick Boothe	(757) 455-3348
Virginia-Wise, U. of	A	1 College Ave., Wise, VA 24293	Hank Banner	(276) 376-4504
Viterbo College	A	900 Viterbo Dr., La Crosse, WI 54601	Larry Lipker	(608) 796-3824
Voorhees College	A	PO Box 678, Voorhees Rd., Denmark, SC 29042	Adrian West	(803) 703-7142
Wabash College	III	301 West Wabash Ave., Crawfordsville, IN 47933	Tom Flynn	(765) 361-6209
Waldorf College	II	106 S. 6th St., Forest City, IA 50436	Brian Grunzke	(641) 585-8263
Walsh U.	A	2020 Easton St. NW, North Canton, OH 44720	Tim Mead	(330) 490-7013
Warner Southern College	A	13895 Hwy. 27, Lake Wales, FL 33853	Jeff Sikes	(863) 638-7259
Wartburg College	III	100 Wartburg Blvd., Waverly, IA 50677	Joel Holst	(319) 352-8532
Washburn U.	II	1700 SW College Ave., Topeka, KS 66621	Steve Anson	(785) 231-1010
Washington & Jefferson College	III	60 S. Lincoln St., Washington, PA 15301	Jeff Mountain	(724) 250-3306
Washington & Lee U.	III	P.O. Drawer 928, Lexington, VA 24450	Jeff Stickley	(540) 458-8680
Washington College	III	300 Washington Ave, Chestertown, MD 21620	Al Streelman	(410) 778-7239
Washington U.	III	Campus Box 1067, St. Louis, MO 63130	Ric Lessmann	(314) 935-5945
Wayland Baptist U.	A	1900 W.7th St., Plainview, TX 79072	Brad Bass	(806) 291-1132
Wayne State College	II	1111 Main St., Wayne, NE 68787	John Manganaro	(402) 375-7499
Wayne State U.	II	5101 Lodge Dr., Detroit, MI 48202	Jay Alexander	(313) 577-2749
Waynesburg College	III	51 W. College St., Waynesburg, PA 15370	Duane Lanzy	(724) 852-3229
Webber International U.	A	1201 N. Scenic Hwy. 27 South, Babson Park, FL 33827	Brad Niethammer	(863) 638-2951
Webster U.	III	470 E. Lockwood Ave, St. Louis, MO 63119	Marty Hunsucker	(314) 961-2660
Wentworth Tech	III	550 Huntington Ave., Boston, MA 02115	Steve Studley	(617) 989-4824
Wesley College	III	120 N. State St., Dover, DE 19901	Matt Addonizio	(302) 735-5939
Wesleyan U.	III	Freeman Athletic Center, Middletown, CT 06459	Mark Woodworth	(860) 685-2924
West Alabama, U. of	II	UWA Station 5, Livingston, AL 35470	Gary Rundles	(205) 652-3870
West Chester U.	II	Sturzebecker Center, West Chester, PA 19383	Mike Okulich	(610) 436-2152
West Florida, U. of	II	11000 University Pkwy., Pensacola, FL 32514	Jim Spooner	(850) 474-2488
West Georgia, State U. of	II	1600 Maple St., Carrollton, GA 30118	Doc Fowlkes	(770) 836-4622
West Liberty State College	II	Bartell Fieldhouse, West Liberty, WV 26074	Bo McConnaughy	(304) 336-8235
West Texas A&M U.	II	WTAMU Box 60049, Canyon, TX 79016	Mark Jones	(806) 651-2676
West Virginia State College	II	210 Fleming Hall, Institute, WV 25112	Cal Bailey	(304) 766-3238
West Virginia Tech	II	405 Fayette Pike, Route 61, Montgomery, WV 25136	Tim Epling	(304) 442-3831
West Virginia Wesleyan	II	59 College Ave., Buckhannon, WV 26201	Randy Tenney	(304) 473-8054
Western Baptist College	A	5000 Deer Park Drive SE, Salem, OR 97301	Paul Gale	(503) 589-8183
Western Connecticut State	III	181 White St., Danbury, CT 06810	John Susi	(203) 837-8608
Western New England College	III	1215 Wilbraham Rd., Springfield, MA 01119	Matt LaBranche	(413) 782-1792
Western Oregon U.	II	345 Monmouth Ave N., Monmouth, OR 97361	Terry Baumgartner	(503) 838-8448
Westfield State College	III	577 Western Ave., Westfield, MA 01086	Tom LoRicco	(413) 572-5633
Westminster College	III	501 Westminster Ave, Fulton, MO 65251	Scott Pritchard	(573) 592-5333
Westminster College	III	319 Market St., New Wilmington, PA 16172	Carmen Nocera	(724) 658-0701
Westmont College	A	955 La Paz Rd., Santa Barbara, CA 93108	Robert Crawford	(805) 565-6012
Wheaton College	III	501 East College Ave, Wheaton, IL 60187	Bobby Elder	(630) 752-7164
Wheaton College	III	26 E. Main St., Norton, MA 02766	Eric Podbelski	(508) 286-3394
Whitman College	III	345 Boyer Ave., Walla Walla, WA 99362	Casey Powell	(509) 527-4931
Whittier College	III	13406 E. Philadelphia St., Whittier, CA 90608	Mike Rizzo	(562) 907-4967
Whitworth College	III	300 W. Hawthorne Rd., Spokane, WA 99251	Keith Ward	(509) 777-4394
Widener U.	III	1 University Place, Chester, PA 19013	Steve Carcarey	(610) 499-4446
Wiley College	A	711 Wiley Ave., Marshall, TX 75670	Eddie Watson	(903) 927-3292
Wilkes U.	III	PO Box 111, Wilkes-Barre, PA 18703	Joe Folek	(570) 408-4056
Willamette U.	III	900 State St., Salem, OR 97301	Matt Allison	(503) 370-6011

William Carey Col	A	498 Tuscan Ave., Hattiesburg, MS 39401	Bobby Halford	(601) 318-6110
William Jewell Col	A	500 College Hill, Liberty, MO 64068	Mike Stockton	(816) 415-5962
William Paterson U.	III	300 Pompton Rd., Wayne, NJ 07470	Jeff Albies	(973) 720-2210
William Penn U.	A	201 Trueblood Ave., Oskaloosa, IA 52577	Mike Laird	(641) 673-1023
William Woods U.	A	1 University Drive, Fulton, MO 65251	Ryan Bay	(573) 592-1187
Williams Baptist College	A	PO Box 3387, College City, AR 72476	John Katrosh	(870) 759-4192
Williams College	III	22 Spring St., Williamstown, MA 01267	Dave Barnard	(413) 597-3026
Wilmington College	II	320 N. DuPont Highway, New Castle, DE 19720	Brian August	(302) 328-9435
Wilmington College	III	251 Ludovic St., Wilmington, OH 45177	Tony Haley	(937) 382-6661
Wingate U.	II	230 N. Camden Rd., Wingate, NC 28174	Bill Nash	(704) 233-8381
Winona State U.	II	PO Box 5838, Winona, MN 55987	Kyle Poock	(507) 457-2332
Wisconsin Lutheran College	III	8800 W. Bluemound Rd., Milwaukee, WI 53226	Brook Smith	(414) 443-8990
Wisconsin-La Crosse, U. of	III	1725 State St., La Crosse, WI 54601	Chris Schwarz	(608) 785-6540
Wisconsin-Oshkosh, U. of	III	800 Algoma Blvd., Oshkosh, WI 54901	Tom Lechnir	(920) 424-0374
Wisconsin-Parkside, U. of	II	900 Wood Rd., Kenosha, WI 53141	Tracy Archuleta	(262) 595-2317
Wisconsin-Platteville, U. of	III	1 University Plaza, Platteville, WI 53818	Jamie Sailors	(608) 342-1843
Wisconsin-Stevens Point, U. of	III	205 4th Ave., Stevens Point, WI 54481	Pat Bloom	(715) 346-4412
Wisconsin-Stout, U. of	III	241 Sports & Fitness Center, Menomonie, WI 54751	Craig Walter	(715) 232-1459
Wisconsin-Superior, U. of	III	1800 Grand Ave., Superior, WI 54880	Chris Vito	(715) 395-4671
Wisconsin-Whitewater, U. of	III	Schwager Drive, Whitewater, WI 53190	John Vodenlich	(262) 472-1420
Wittenberg U.	III	PO Box 720, Springfield, OH 45501	Jay Lewis	(937) 327-6494
Wooster, College of	III	1189 Beall Ave., Wooster, OH 44691	Tim Pettorini	(330) 263-2180
Worcester State College	III	486 Chandler St., Worcester, MA 01602	Dirk Baker	(508) 929-8852
Worcester Tech	III	100 Institute Rd., Worcester, MA 01609	Chris Robertson	(508) 831-5100
York College	A	1125 E. 8th St., York, NE 68467	Nick Harlan	(402) 363-5736
York College	III	Country Club Road, York, PA 17405	Paul Saikia	(717) 815-1245

JUNIOR COLLEGES

School	Address	Coach	Telephone
Abraham Baldwin College	ABAC 41, 2802 Moore Hwy, Tifton, GA 31793	Steve Janousek	(229) 386-3931
Adirondack CC	640 Bay Road, Queensbury, NY 12804	John Hayes	(518) 743-2269
Alabama Southern CC	2800 S. Alabama Ave., Monroeville, AL 36461	Mike Kandler	(251) 575-3156
Alfred State Col	Orvis Center, Alfred, NY 14802	Tom Kenney	(607) 587-4361
Allan Hancock Col	800 S. College Dr., Santa Maria, CA 93454	Chris Stevens	(805) 922-6966
Allegany College	12401 Willowbrook Rd., Cumberland, MD 21502	Steve Bazarnic	(301) 784-5265
Allegheny CCAC	808 Ridge Ave., Pittsburgh, PA 15212	Scott Downer	(412) 237-2503
Allegheny County CC -Boyce	595 Beatty Rd., Monroeville, PA 15146	Bill Holmes	(724) 325-6621
Allegheny County CC -South	1750 Clairton Rd., West Mifflin, PA 15122	Jeff Minick	(412) 469-6243
Allen County CC	1801 N. Cottonwood St., Iola, KS 66749	Val McLean	(620) 365-5116
Alvin CC	3110 Mustang Rd., Alvin, TX 77511	Bryan Alexander	(281) 756-3696
American River CC	4700 College Oak Dr., Sacramento, CA 95841	Doug Jumelet	(916) 484-8294
Ancilla College	9601 S. Union Rd., Donaldson, IN 46513	Gene Reese	(574) 936-8898
Andrew College	413 College St., Cuthbert, GA 39840	Scot Hemmings	(229) 732-5955
Angelina College	PO Box 1768, Lufkin, TX 75902	Jeff Livin	(936) 633-5367
Anne Arundel CC	101 College Parkway, Arnold, MD 21012	Mark Palmerino	(410) 777-2322
Anoka-Ramsey CC	11200 Mississippi Blvd. NW, Coon Rapids, MN 55433	Tom Yelle	(763) 422-3526
Antelope Valley Col	3041 W. Avenue K, Lancaster, CA 93536	Jeffrey Leonard	(661) 722-6440
Arapahoe CC	5900 S. Santa Fe Dr., Littleton, CO 80160	Mark Laschanzky	(303) 797-5853
Arizona Western College	PO Box 929, Yuma, AZ 85366	John Stratton	(928) 344-7535
Arkansas-Fort Smith	5210 Grand Ave., Fort Smith, AR 72913	Dale Harpenau	(479) 788-7597
Bakersfield College	1801 Panorama Dr., Bakersfield, CA 93305	Tim Painton	(661) 395-4261
Baltimore City CC	2901 Liberty Heights Ave, Baltimore, MD 21215	Lance Mauck	(410) 462-7752
Barstow CC	2700 Barstow Rd., Barstow, CA 92311	Mike Gorman	(760) 252-2411
Barton County CC	245 NE 30th Rd., Great Bend, KS 67530	Mike Warren	(620) 792-9378
Baton Rouge CC	5310 Florida Blvd., Baton Rouge, LA 70806	Charles Dawson	(225) 216-8200
Bellevue CC	3000 Landerholm Circle SE, Bellevue, WA 98007	Mark Yoshino	(425) 564-2356
Bergen CC	400 Paramus Rd., Paramus, NJ 07652	John Decker	(201) 447-7183
Bevill State CC- Fayette	2631 Temple Ave N., Fayette, AL 35555	Joey May	(205) 387-0511
Bevill State CC- Sumiton	PO Box 800, Sumiton, AL 35148	Ed Langham	(205) 648-3211
Big Bend CC	7662 Chanute St., Moses Lake, WA 98837	Don Lindgren	(509) 762-5351
Bishop State CC	351 N. Broad St., Mobile, AL 36603	Johnny Watkins	(251) 690-6436
Bismarck State CC	1500 Edwards Ave., Bismarck, ND 58506	Len Stanley	(701) 224-5736
Black Hawk College	6600 34th Ave., Moline, IL 61265	Arnie Chavera	(309) 796-5607
Blinn College	902 College Ave., Brenham, TX 77833	Brian Roper	(979) 830-4171
Blue Mountain CC	2411 NW Carden Ave., Pendleton, OR 97801	Brett Bryan	(541) 278-5900
Blue Ridge CC	180 Campus Dr., Flat Rock, NC 28731	Damon Towe	(828) 694-1778
Bossier Parish CC	2719 Airline Dr., Bossier City, LA 71111	Elliott Sampley	(318) 746-9851
Brevard CC	3865 N. Wickham Rd., Melbourne FL 32940	Ernie Rosseau	(321) 433-5601
Briarcliffe College	1055 Stewart Ave., Bethpage, NY 11714	Pete Alfero	(516) 918-3800

College	Address	Contact	Phone
Bronx CC	W. 181st & Washington, Bronx, NY 10453	Adolfo DeJesus	(718) 289-5274
Brookdale CC	765 Newman Springs Rd., Lincroft, NJ 07738	Johnny Johnson	(732) 224-2379
Brookhaven College	3939 Valley View Lane, Farmers Branch, TX 75244	Denny Dixon	(972) 860-4121
Broome CC	901 Front St., Binghamton, NY 13902	Brett Carter	(607) 778-5003
Broward CC	3501 College Ave., Davie, FL 33314	Bob Deutschman	(954) 201-6949
Brown Mackie CC	2106 S. Ninth, Salina, KS 67401	Steve Bartow	(785) 825-5422
Bucks County CC	275 Swamp Rd, Newton, PA 18940	Craig Scioscia	(215) 968-8451
Bunker Hill CC	250 New Rutherford Ave, Boston, MA 02129	Scott Blumsack	(617) 228-2088
Burlington County CC	601 Pemberton-Browns Mill Rd., Pemberton, NJ 08068	John Holt	(609) 929-7809
Butler County CC	901 S. Haverhill Rd., El Dorado, KS 67042	Steve Johnson	(316) 322-3201
Butler County CC	PO Box 1203, Butler, PA 16003	Tom Roper	(724) 287-8711
Butte College	3536 Butte Campus Dr., Oroville, CA 95965	Anthony Ferro	(530) 895-2521
Cabrillo College	6500 Soquel Dr., Aptos, CA 95003	Rich Weidinger	(831) 479-6594
Camden County College	PO Box 200, Blackwood, NJ 08012	Frank Angeloni	(856) 227-7200
Canada College	4200 Farm Hill Blvd., Redwood City, CA 94061	Tonny Lucca	(650) 306-3269
Canyons, College of the	26455 Rockwell Canyon Rd., Santa Clarita, CA 91355	Chris Cota	(661) 259-7800
Carl Albert State College	1507 S. McKenna St., Poteau, OK 74953	Mark Pollard	(918) 647-1376
Carl Sandburg College	2400 Tom L. Wilson Blvd., Galesburg, IL 61401	Justin Inskeep	(309) 341-5227
CCBC-Catonsville	800 S. Rolling Rd., Catonsville, MD 21228	Dan Blue	(410) 455-4419
CCBC-Dundalk	7200 Sollers Point Rd., Dundalk, MD 21222	Jason King	(410) 285-9714
CCBC-Essex	7201 Rossville Blvd., Baltimore, MD 21237	George Henderson	(410) 780-6346
Cecil CC	One Seahawk Dr., North East, MD 21901	Charlie O'Brien	(410) 287-1080
Cedar Valley College	3030 N. Dallas Ave., Lancaster, TX 75134	Kyle Koehler	(972) 860-8184
Central Alabama CC	1675 Cherokee Rd., Alexander City, AL 35010	Don Ingram	(256) 215-4320
Central Arizona College	8470 N. Overfield Rd., Coolidge, AZ 85228	Clint Myers	(520) 426-4336
Central Florida CC	3001 SW College Rd., Ocala, FL 34474	Marty Smith	(352) 873-5807
Central Lakes College	501 W. College Dr., Brainerd, MN 56401	Warren Mertens	(218) 855-8210
Centralia College	600 W. Locust St., Centralia, WA 98531	Bruce Pocklington	(360) 736-9391
Cerritos College	11110 East Alondra Blvd., Norwalk, CA 90650	Ken Gaylord	(562) 860-2890
Cerro Coso CC	3000 College Heights Blvd., Ridgecrest, CA 93555	Dick Adams	(760) 384-6386
Chabot College	25555 Hesperian Blvd., Hayward, CA 94545	Steve Friend	(510) 723-6935
Chaffey College	5885 Haven Ave., Rancho Cucamonga, CA 91739	Jeff Harlow	(909) 941-2345
Chandler-Gilbert CC	2626 E. Pecos Rd., Chandler, AZ 85225	Doyle Wilson	(480) 732-7364
Chattahoochee Valley CC	2602 College Dr., Phenix City, AL 36869	Adam Thomas	(334) 214-4880
Chattanooga State Tech CC	4501 Amnicola Hwy., Chattanooga, TN 37406	Greg Dennis	(423) 697-3397
Chemeketa CC	4000 Lancaster Dr. NE, Salem, OR 97309	John Doran	(503) 399-7953
Chesapeake College	1000 College Dr., PO Box 8, Wye Mills, MD 21679	Frank Szymanski	(410) 827-5828
Chipola JC	3094 Indian Circle, Marianna, FL 32446	Jeff Johnson	(850) 718-2299
Cisco JC	101 College Heights, Cisco, TX 76437	David White	(254) 442-5172
Clackamas CC	19600 S. Molalla Ave., Oregon City, OR 97045	Robin Robinson	(503) 657-6958
Clarendon College	PO Box 968, Clarendon, TX 79226	Cory Hall	(806) 874-3571
Clark State CC	570 E. Leffel Ln., Springfield, OH 45501	Tim Rigel	(937) 328-6027
Cleveland State CC	PO Box 3570, Cleveland, TN 37320	Mike Policastro	(423) 478-6219
Clinton CC	136 Clinton Point Dr., Plattsburgh, NY 12901	Tom Neale	(518) 562-4220
Cloud County CC	Box 1002, Concordia, KS 66901	Greg Brummett	(785) 243-1435
Coahoma JC	3240 Friars Point Rd., Clarksdale, MS 38614	Billy Fields	(662) 621-4232
Cochise County CC	4190 W. Hwy. 80, Douglas, AZ 85607	Todd Inglehart	(520) 417-4095
Coffeyville CC	400 W. 11th St., Coffeyville, KS 67337	Ryan McCune	(620) 252-7095
Colby CC	1255 S. Range Ave, Colby, KS 67701	Ryan Carter	(785) 462-3984
Colorado Northwestern CC	500 Kennedy Dr., Rangely, CO 81648	Dustin Colborn	(970) 675-3314
Columbia Basin CC	2600 N. 20th Ave., Pasco, WA 99301	Scott Rogers	(509) 547-0511
Columbia State CC	PO Box 1315, Columbia, TN 38402	Jim Painter	(931) 540-2632
Columbia-Greene CC	4400 Route 23, Hudson, NY 12534	Bob Godlewski	(518) 828-4181
Columbus State CC	550 E. Spring St., Columbus, OH 43215	Harry Caruso	(614) 287-2445
Compton CC	111 East Artesia Blvd., Compton, CA 90221	Shannon Williams	(310) 900-1600
Connecticut -Avery Point, U. of	1084 Shennescossett Rd., Groton, CT 06340	Roger Bidwell	(860) 405-9183
Connors State College	Rt. 1, Box 1000, Warner, OK 74469	Perry Keith	(918) 463-6218
Contra Costa College	2600 Mission Bell Dr., San Pablo, CA 94806	Marvin Webb	(510) 235-7800
Copiah-Lincoln JC	PO Box 649, Wesson, MS 39191	Keith Case	(601) 643-8318
Corning CC	1 Academic Dr., Corning, NY 14830	Brian Hill	(607) 962-9409
Cosumnes River CC	8401 Center Pkwy., Sacramento CA 95823	Tony Bloomfield	(916) 691-7397
Cowley County CC	125 S. 2nd St., Arkansas City, KS 67005	Dave Burroughs	(620) 441-5246
Crowder College	601 Laclede Ave., Neosho, MO 64850	Chip Durham	(417) 455-4526
Crowley's Ridge College	100 College Dr., Paragould, AR 72450	James Scott	(870) 236-6901
Cuesta College	PO Box 8106, San Luis Obispo, CA 93403	Bob Miller	(805) 546-3100
Cumberland County College	PO Box 1500, Vineland, NJ 08362	Dave Yorke	(856) 691-8600
Cuyahoga CC-West	11000 Pleasant Valley Rd., Parma, OH 44130	Brian Harrison	(216) 987-5459
Cypress College	9200 Valley View St., Cypress, CA 90630	Scott Pickler	(714) 826-7014
Dakota County Tech College	1300 145th St. E, Rosemount, MN 55068	Tim Huber	(952) 997-9577
Danville Area CC	2000 E. Main St., Danville, IL 61832	Tim Bunton	(217) 443-8807
Darton College	2400 Gillionville Rd., Albany, GA 31707	Glenn Eames	(229) 430-6788

Dawson CC	PO Box 421, Glendive, MT 59330	Brent Diegel	(406) 377-9450
Daytona Beach CC	1200 Int'l Speedway Rd., Daytona Beach, FL 32120	Tim Touma	(386) 506-4486
Dean College	99 Main St., Franklin, MA 02038	Kevin Burr	(508) 541-1814
De Anza College	21250 Stevens Creek Blvd., Cupertino, CA 95014	Scott Hertler	(408) 864-8741
Delaware County CC	901 S. Media Line Rd., Media, PA 19063	Paul Motta	(610) 353-8584
Delaware Tech & CC-Owens	PO Box 610, Route 18, Georgetown, DE 19947	Curtis Brock	(302) 855-1636
Delgado CC	615 City Park Ave., New Orleans, LA 70119	Joe Scheuermann	(504) 483-4381
Des Moines Area CC-Boone	1125 Hancock Dr., Boone, IA 50036	John Smith	(515) 433-5050
Desert, College of the	43500 Monterey Ave., Palm Desert, CA 92260	Lou McCollum	(760) 773-2585
Diablo Valley College	321 Golf Club Rd., Pleasant Hill, CA 94523	Carl Fraticelli	(925) 685-1230
Dixie State College	225 S. 700 E., St. George, UT 84770	Mike Littlewood	(435) 652-7530
Dodge City CC	2501 N. 14th Ave., Dodge City, KS 67801	Erick Wright	(620) 227-9347
DuPage, College of	425 Fawell Blvd., Glen Ellyn, IL 60137	Dan Kusinski	(630) 942-2734
Dutchess CC	53 Pendell Rd., Poughkeepsie, NY 12601	Joe DeRosa	(845) 431-8468
Dyersburg State CC	1510 Lake Rd., Dyersburg, TN 38024	Robert White	(731) 286-3259
East Central College	1964 Prairie Dell Rd., Union, MO 63084	Gale Wallis	(314) 583-5195
East Los Angeles College	1301 Avenida Cesar Chavez, Monterey Park, CA 91754	James Hines	(323) 265-8650
East Mississippi JC	PO Box 158, Scooba, MS 39358	Bill Baldner	(662) 476-5128
Eastern Arizona JC	615 N. Stadium Dr., Thatcher, AZ 85552	Jim Bagnall	(928) 428-8412
Eastern Oklahoma State	1301 W. Main St., Wilburton, OK 74578	Todd Shelton	(918) 465-2361
Eastern Utah, College of	451 E. 400 N., Price, UT 84501	Scott Madsen	(435) 613-5357
Eastfield College	3737 Motley Dr., Mesquite, TX 75150	Michael Martin	(972) 860-7642
Edmonds CC	20000 68th Ave. W., Lynnwood, WA 98036	Tighe Dickinson	(425) 640-1003
El Camino College	16007 Crenshaw Blvd., Torrance, CA 90506	Greg Bergeron	(310) 660-3679
El Paso CC	PO Box 20500, El Paso, TX 79998	Ken Jacome	(915) 831-6433
Elgin CC	1700 Spartan Dr., Elgin, IL 60123	Bill Angelo	(847) 214-7552
Ellsworth CC	1100 College Ave., Iowa Falls, IA 50126	Joel Lueken	(800) 322-9235
Enterprise-Ozark CC	PO Box 1300, Enterprise, AL 36331	Tim Hulsey	(334) 347-2623
Erie CC	21 Oak St., Buffalo, NY 14203	Joe Bauth	(716) 851-1220
Everett CC	2000 Tower St., Everett, WA 98201	Levi Lacey	(425) 388-9322
Faulkner State CC	1900 Hwy. 31 South, Minette, AL 36507	Wayne Larker	(251) 580-2160
Feather River College	570 Golden Eagle Ave., Quincy, CA 95971	Reed Peters	(530) 283-0202
Finger Lakes CC	4355 Lakeshore Dr., Canandaigua, NY 14424	Robert Lowden	(585) 394-3500
Florence-Darlington Tech	2715 W. Lucas St., Florence, SC 29501	Curtis Hudson	(843) 661-8291
Florida CC	11901 Beach Blvd., Jacksonville, FL 32246	Chris Blaquier	(904) 766-6752
Florida College	119 N. Glen Arven Ave., Temple Terrace, FL 33617	Rich Leggatt	(813) 899-6789
Fort Scott CC	2108 S. Horton St., Fort Scott, KS 66701	Chris Moddelmog	(620) 223-2700
Frank Phillips College	PO Box 5118, Borger, TX 79008	Guy Simmons	(806) 274-5961
Frederick CC	7932 Opossumtown Pike, Frederick, MD 21702	Rodney Bennett	(301) 846-2501
Fresno City College	1101 E. University Ave., Fresno, CA 93741	Ron Scott	(559) 237-8974
Fullerton College	321 E. Chapman Ave., Fullerton, CA 92832	Nick Fuscardo	(714) 992-7401
Fulton-Montgomery CC	2805 State Highway 67, Johnstown, NY 12095	Mike Mulligan	(518) 762-4651
Gadsden State CC	PO Box 227, Gadsden, AL 35902	Bill Lockridge	(256) 549-8311
Galveston College	4015 Avenue Q, Galveston, TX 77550	Javier Solis	(409) 944-1314
Garden City CC	801 Campus Dr., Garden City, KS 67846	Rick Sabath	(620) 276-9599
Garrett College	687 Mosser Rd., McHenry, MD 21541	Eric Hallenbeck	(301) 387-3055
Gateway CC	60 Sargent Dr., New Haven, CT 06511	Lance Lusisnan	(203) 285-3025
Gavilan College	5055 Santa Teresa Blvd., Gilroy, CA 95020	Neal Andrade	(408) 848-4916
Genesee CC	1 College Rd., Batavia, NY 14020	Barry Garigen	(585) 345-6898
George C. Wallace CC-Dothan	1141 Wallace Dr., Dothan, AL 36303	Mackey Sasser	(334) 556-2216
George C. Wallace CC-Selma	3000 Earl Goodwin Pkwy, Selma, AL 36702	Barry Dean	(334) 876-9292
Georgia Perimeter College	3251 Panthersville Rd., Decatur, GA 30034	Ted Wallen	(404) 244-5765
Glen Oaks CC	62240 Shimmel Rd., Centreville, MI 49032	Joel Mishler	(888) 994-7818
Glendale CC	6000 W. Olive Ave., Glendale, AZ 85302	David Grant	(623) 845-3046
Glendale College	1500 N. Verdugo Rd., Glendale, CA 91208	Chris Cicuto	(818) 551-5693
Globe Tech	291 Broadway, New York, NY 10007	Justin Timmerman	(212) 349-4330
Gloucester County College	1400 Tanyard Rd., Sewell, NJ 08080	Rob Valli	(856) 415-2213
Golden West College	15744 Golden West St., Huntington Beach, CA 92647	Roberto Villarreal	(714) 895-8260
Gordon College	419 College Dr., Barnesville, GA 30204	Travis McClanahan	(770) 358-5278
Grand Rapids CC	143 Bostwick Ave. NE, Grand Rapids, MI 49503	Mike Cupples	(616) 234-3990
Grays Harbor College	1620 Edward P. Smith Dr., Aberdeen, WA 98520	Shon Schreiber	(360) 538-4062
Grayson County College	6101 Grayson Dr., Denison, TX 75020	Tim Tadlock	(903) 463-8719
Green River CC	12401 SE 320th St., Auburn, WA 98092	Matt Acker	(253) 833-9111
Grossmont College	8800 Grossmont College Dr., El Cajon, CA 92020	Ed Olsen	(619) 644-7447
Gulf Coast CC	5230 W. Highway 98, Panama City, FL 32401	Darren Mazeroski	(850) 872-3830
Hagerstown CC	11400 Robinwood Dr., Hagerstown, MD 21742	Scott Jennings	(301) 790-2800
Harford CC	401 Thomas Run Rd., Bel Air, MD 21015	Bill Greenwell	(410) 836-4321
Harper College	1200 W. Algonquin Rd., Palatine, IL 60067	Vern Hasty	(847) 925-6969
Hartnell CC	156 Homestead Ave., Salinas, CA 93901	Dan Teresa	(831) 755-6840

College	Address	Contact	Phone
Henry Ford CC	5101 Evergreen Rd., Dearborn, MI 48128	Darnell Walker	(313) 845-9647
Herkimer County CC	100 Reservoir Rd., Herkimer, NY 13350	Jason Rathbin	(315) 866-0300
Hesston College	325 S. College Dr., Box 3000, Hesston, KS 67062	Art Mullet	(620) 327-8278
Hibbing CC	1515 E. 25th St., Hibbing, MN 55746	Mike Turnbull	(218) 262-6748
Highland CC	2998 W. Pearl City Rd., Freeport, IL 61032	Sam Knaack	(815) 599-3465
Highland CC	606 W. Main, Highland, KS 66035	Rick Eberly	(785) 442-6039
Hill College	PO Box 619, Hillsboro, TX 76645	Gary Benton	(254) 582-2555
Hillsborough CC	PO Box 30030, Tampa, FL 33630	Gary Calhoun	(813) 253-7311
Hinds CC	PO Box 1100, Raymond, MS 39154	Rick Clarke	(601) 857-3325
Hiwassee College	225 Hiwassee College Dr., Madisonville, TN 37354	Jerry Edwards	(423) 442-2001
Holmes CC	PO Box 369, Goodman, MS 39079	Kenny Dupont	(662) 472-9124
Holyoke CC	303 Homestead Ave., Holyoke, MA 01040	J.C. Fernandes	(413) 552-2161
Hostos CC	500 Grand Concourse, Bronx, NY 10451	Jose Martinez	(718) 518-6551
Howard College	1001 Birdwell Lane, Big Spring, TX 79720	Britt Smith	(432) 264-5044
Hudson Valley CC	80 Vandenburg Ave., Troy, NY 12180	Tom Reinisch	(518) 629-7328
Hutchinson CC	1300 N. Plum St., Hutchinson, KS 67501	Kyle Crookes	(620) 665-3441
Illinois Central College	One College Dr., East Peoria, IL 61635	Brett Kelley	(309) 694-5429
Illinois Valley CC	815 N. Orlando Smith St., Oglesby, IL 61348	Bob Koopmann	(815) 224-0471
Imperial Valley College	PO Box 158, Imperial, CA 92251	Jim Mecate	(760) 355-6341
Independence CC	PO Box 708, Independence, KS 67301	Jon Olsen	(620) 331-4100
Indians Hills CC	721 N. 1st St., Centerville, IA 52544	Cam Walker	(641) 683-5243
Indian River CC	3209 Virginia Ave., Fort Pierce, FL 34981	Mike Easom	(772) 462-4772
Iowa Central CC	330 Avenue M, Fort Dodge, IA 50501	Rick Pederson	(515) 576-0099
Iowa Lakes CC	300 S. 18th St., Estherville, IA 51334	Jason Nell	(712) 362-7915
Iowa Western CC	2700 College Rd., Council Bluffs, IA 51503	Marc Rardin	(712) 325-3331
Irvine Valley College	5500 Irvine Center Dr., Irvine, CA 92618	Kent Madole	(949) 451-5763
Itasca CC	1851 E. Hwy. 169, Grand Rapids, MN 55744	Justin Lamppa	(218) 327-4226
Itawamba CC	602 W. Hill St., Fulton, MS 38843	Rick Collier	(662) 862-8118
Jackson State CC	2046 N. Parkway, Jackson, TN 38301	Steve Cornelison	(731) 424-3520
Jamestown CC	525 Falconer St., Jamestown, NY 14701	Kerry Kellogg	(716) 665-5220
Jefferson CC	1220 Coffeen St., Watertown, NY 13601	Paul Alteri	(315) 786-2497
Jefferson College	1000 Viking Dr., Hillsboro, MO 63050	Dave Oster	(636) 789-3000
Jefferson Davis CC	PO Box 958, Brewton, AL 36427	Jim Morrill	(251) 809-1622
Jefferson State CC	2601 Carson Rd., Birmingham, AL 35215	Ben Short	(205) 856-7879
John A. Logan College	700 Logan College Rd., Carterville, IL 62918	Jerry Halstead	(618) 985-3741
Johnson County CC	12345 College Blvd., Overland Park, KS 66210	Kent Shelley	(913) 469-3820
John Wood CC	1301 S. 48th St., Quincy, IL 62301	Greg Wathen	(217) 641-4308
Joliet JC	1215 Houbolt Rd., Joliet, IL 60431	Wayne King	(815) 280-2210
Jones County JC	900 S. Court St., Ellisville, MS 39437	Bobby Glaze	(601) 477-4088
Kalamazoo Valley CC	PO Box 4070, Kalamazoo, MI 49003	Bernie Vallier	(269) 488-4393
Kankakee CC	PO Box 888, River Rd., Kankakee, IL 60901	Todd Post	(815) 802-8616
Kansas City CC	7250 State Ave., Kansas City, KS 66112	Steve Burleson	(913) 288-7150
Kaskaskia CC	27210 College Rd., Centralia, IL 62801	Brad Tuttle	(618) 545-3146
Kellogg CC	450 North Ave., Battle Creek, MI 49017	Russ Bortell	(269) 965-4151
Kingsborough CC	2001 Oriental Blvd., Brooklyn, NY 11235	Jim Ryan	(718) 368-5737
Kirkwood CC	6301 Kirkwood Blvd. SW, Cedar Rapids, IA 52406	John Lewis	(319) 398-4910
Kishwaukee CC	21193 Malta Rd., Malta, IL 60150	Josh Pethod	(815) 825-2086
Labette CC	200 S. 14th St., Parsons, KS 67357	Tom Hilton	(620) 820-1011
Lackawanna College	501 Vine St., Scranton, PA 18509	Chris Pensak	(570) 961-0700
Lake City CC	149 SE Vocational Pl., Lake City, FL 32025	Tom Clark	(386) 754-4363
Lake County, College of	19351 W. Washington St., Grayslake, IL 60030	Cory Domel	(847) 543-2477
Lake Land College	5001 Lake Land Blvd., Mattoon, IL 61938	Jim Jarrett	(217) 234-5336
Lake Michigan College	2755 E. Napier Ave., Benton Harbor, MI 49022	Keith Schreiber	(269) 927-8165
Lake-Sumter CC	9501 US Hwy. 441, Leesburg, FL 32788	Mike Matulia	(352) 323-3643
Lakeland CC	7700 Clocktower Dr., Kirtland, OH 44094	Howie Krause	(440) 525-7350
Lamar CC	2401 S. Main St., Lamar, CO 81052	Scott Crampton	(719) 336-1681
Lane CC	4000 E. 30th Ave., Eugene, OR 97405	Rob Strickland	(541) 463-5817
Laney College	900 Fallon St., Oakland, CA 94607	Francisco Zapata	(510) 464-3476
Lansing CC	PO Box 40010, Lansing, MI 48901	Frank Deak	(517) 483-1622
Laredo CC	West End, Washington St., Laredo, TX 78040	Chase Tidwell	(956) 721-5326
Lassen College	PO Box 3000, Susanville, CA 96130	Glen Yonan	(530) 251-8815
Lenoir CC	PO Box 188, Kinston, NC 28502	Lind Hartsell	(252) 233-6856
Lewis & Clark CC	5800 Godfrey Rd., Godfrey, IL 62035	Randy Martz	(618) 468-6230
Lincoln College	300 Keokuk St., Lincoln, IL 62656	Tony Thomas	(217) 732-3155
Lincoln Land CC	5250 Shepherd Rd., Springfield, IL 62794	Ron Riggle	(217) 786-2581
Lincoln Trail College	11220 State Hwy. 1, Robinson, IL 62454	Mitch Hannahs	(618) 544-5299
Linn-Benton CC	6500 Pacific Blvd. SW, Albany, OR 97321	Greg Hawk	(541) 917-4242
Lon Morris College	800 College Ave., Jacksonville, TX 75766	Josh Stewart	(903) 589-4076
Long Beach City College	4901 E. Carson St., Long Beach, CA 90808	Casey Crook	(562) 938-4242

College	Address	Contact	Phone
Longview CC	500 SW Longview Rd., Lee's Summit, MO 64081	Gary Haarmann	(816) 672-2440
Los Angeles City College	855 N. Vermont Ave., Los Angeles, CA 90029	Alec Adame	(323) 953-4000
Los Angeles Harbor College	1111 Figueroa Pl., Wilmington, CA 90744	Marco Alvillar	(310) 233-4140
Los Angeles Pierce College	6201 Winnetka Ave., Woodland Hills, CA 91371	Bob Lofrano	(818) 710-2823
Los Angeles Valley College	5800 Fulton Ave., Valley Glen, CA 91401	Glen Hefferman	(818) 947-2899
Los Medanos College	2700 E. Leland Rd., Pittsburg, CA 94565	Tony Dress	(925) 439-2185
Louisburg College	501 N. Main St., Louisburg, NC 27549	Billy Godwin	(919) 497-3249
Lower Columbia College	1600 Maple St., Longview, WA 98632	Kelly Smith	(360) 442-2870
LSU-Eunice	PO Box 1129, Eunice, LA 70535	Jeff Willis	(337) 550-1287
Lurleen B. Wallace State JC	PO Box 1418, Andalusia, AL 36420	Steve Helms	(334) 881-2203
Macomb CC	14500 E. 12 Mile Rd., Warren, MI 48088	Mike Kaczmarek	(586) 445-7119
Madison Area Tech	3550 Anderson St., Madison, WI 53704	Mike Davenport	(608) 246-6699
Manatee CC	5840 26th St. W, Bradenton, FL 34207	Tim Hill	(941) 752-5575
Manchester CC	1 Great Path MS No. 7, Manchester, CT 06045	Chris Strahowski	(860) 512-2612
Manhattan CC	199 Chambers St., New York, NY 10007	John Torres	(212) 220-8260
Maple Woods CC	2601 NE Barry Rd., Kansas City, MO 64156	Martin Kilgore	(816) 437-3175
Marin, College of	835 College Ave., Kentfield, CA 94904	Steve Berringer	(415) 485-9589
Marshalltown CC	3700 S. Center St., Marshalltown, IA 50158	Kevin Benzing	(641) 752-7106
Massachusetts Bay CC	50 Oakland St., Wellesley Hills, MA 02481	Bob Hanson	(508) 270-4065
Massasoit CC	1 Massasoit Blvd., Brockton, MA 02302	Tom Frizzell	(508) 588-9100
McCook CC	1205 E. 3rd St., McCook, NE 69001	Jeremy Jorgensen	(308) 345-6303
McHenry County College	8900 U.S. Hwy. 14, Crystal Lake, IL 60012	Kim Johnson	(815) 455-8580
McLennan CC	1400 College Dr., Waco, TX 76708	Pete Mejia	(254) 299-8326
Mendocino CC	1000 Hensley Creek Rd, Ukiah, CA 95482	Matt Gordon	(707) 468-3142
Merced College	3600 M St., Merced, CA 95348	Chris Pedretti	(209) 384-6028
Mercer County CC	1200 Old Trenton Rd., Trenton, NJ 08690	Kip Harrison	(609) 586-4800
Mercyhurst-North East	16 W. Division St., North East, PA 16428	Ryan Smith	(814) 725-6390
Meridian CC	910 Hwy. 19 N., Meridian MS 39307	Mike Federico	(601) 484-8699
Mesa CC	1833 W. Southern Ave., Mesa, AZ 85202	Tony Cirelli	(480) 461-7545
Mesabi Range College	1001 Chestnut St. W., Virginia, MN 55792	Brad Scott	(218) 749-7757
Miami-Dade CC	11011 SW 104 St., Miami, FL 33176	Steve Hertz	(305) 237-0730
Miami U.-Middletown	4200 E. University Blvd., Middletown, OH 45042	Kenneth Prichard	(513) 727-3273
Middle Georgia College	1100 2nd St. SE, Cochran, GA 31014	Craig Young	(478) 934-3044
Middlesex County College	2600 Woodbridge Ave., Edison, NJ 08818	Michael Lepore	(732) 906-4675
Midland College	3600 N. Garfield St., Midland, TX 79705	Steve Ramharter	(432) 685-5561
Miles CC	2715 Dickinson St., Miles City, MT 59301	Bob Bishop	(406) 874-6220
Milwaukee Area Tech	700 W. State St., Milwaukee, WI 53233	Tony Goodenough	(414) 297-7000
Mineral Area College	PO Box 1000., Park Hills, MO 63601	Jim Gerwitz	(573) 518-2197
Minn. State Comm & Tech	1414 College Way, Fergus Falls, MN 56357	Kent Bothwell	(218) 736-1618
Minn. West Comm. & Tech	1450 College Way, Worthington, MN 56187	Brian Iverson	(507) 372-3409
Minot State U.	105 Simrall Blvd., Bottineau, ND 58318	Jason Harris	(701) 228-5474
Mission College	3000 Mission College Blvd., Santa Clara, CA 95054	Todd Eagen	(408) 855-5366
Mississippi Delta CC	PO Box 668, Moorhead, MS 38761	Tony Hancock	(662) 246-6439
Mississippi Gulf Coast JC	Box 548, Perkinston, MS 39573	Cooper Farris	(601) 928-6224
Mitchell College	437 Pequot Ave., New London, CT 06320	Len Farquhar	(860) 701-5043
Modesto JC	435 College Ave., Modesto, CA 95350	Paul Aiello	(209) 575-6274
Mohawk Valley CC	1101 Sherman Dr., Utica, NY 13501	Dave Warren	(315) 792-5674
Monroe CC	1000 E. Henrietta Rd., Rochester, NY 14623	Skip Bailey	(585) 292-2831
Monterey Peninsula College	980 Fremont St., Monterey, CA 93940	Dan Phillips	(831) 646-4223
Montgomery College-Rockville	51 Mannakee St., Rockville, MD 20850	Tom Shaffer	(301) 251-7985
Montgomery-Germantown	20200 Observation Dr., Germantown, MD 20876	Tom Cassera	(301) 353-7727
Moorpark College	7075 Campus Rd., Moorpark, CA 93021	Mario Porto	(805) 378-1457
Moraine Valley CC	10900 S. 88th Ave., Palos Hills, IL 60465	Al Budding	(708) 974-5213
Morris, County College of	214 Center Grove Rd., Randolph, NJ 07869	Ed Moskal	(973) 328-5258
Morrisville State College	PO Box 901, Morrisville, NY 13408	Tim Byrnes	(315) 684-6072
Morton College	3801 S. Central Ave., Cicero, IL 60804	Tony Hubbard	(708) 656-8000
Motlow State CC	PO Box 8500, Lynchburg, TN 37352	Don Rhoton	(931) 393-1617
Mott CC	1401 E. Court St., Flint, MI 48503	Dan LaNoue	(810) 762-0419
Mount Hood CC	26000 SE Stark St., Gresham, OR 97030	Gabe Sandy	(503) 491-7352
Mount San Antonio College	1100 N. Grand Ave., Walnut, CA 91789	Stacy Parker	(909) 594-5611
Mount San Jacinto CC	1499 N. State St., San Jacinto, CA 92583	Steve Alonzo	(951) 487-6752
Murray State College	1 Murray Campus, Tishomingo, OK 73460	Mike McBrayer	(580) 371-2371
Muscatine CC	152 Colorado St., Muscatine, IA 52761	Rob Allison	(563) 288-6001
Muskegon CC	221 S. Quarterline Rd., Muskegon, MI 49442	Cap Pohlman	(231) 777-0381
Napa Valley College	2277 Napa-Vallejo Hwy., Napa, CA 94558	Bob Freschi	(707) 253-3232
Nassau CC	One Education Dr., Garden City, NY 11530	Larry Minor	(516) 572-7522
Navarro College	3200 W. 7th Ave., Corsicana, TX 75110	Skip Johnson	(903) 875-7487
Neosho County CC	800 W. 14th St., Chanute, KS 66720	Steve Murry	(620) 431-2820
New Hampshire Tech	31 College Dr., Concord, NH 03301	Tom Neal	(603) 271-7127
New Mexico JC	5317 N. Lovington Hwy., Hobbs, NM 88240	Ray Birmingham	(505) 392-5786
New Mexico Military Inst.	101 W. College Blvd., Roswell, NM 88201	Marty Zeller	(505) 624-8282

Niagara County CC	3111 Saunders Settlement Rd., Sanborn, NY 14132	Dave Nemi	(716) 614-6271
North Arkansas Tech	1515 Pioneer Dr., Harrison, AR 72601	Phil Wilson	(870) 391-3287
North Central Missouri College	1301 Main St., Trenton, MO 64683	Steve Richman	(660) 359-3948
North Central Texas College	1525 W. California St., Gainesville, TX 76240	Scott Harp	(940) 668-4285
North Florida CC	1000 Turner Davis Dr., Madison, FL 32340	Steve Givens	(850) 973-1609
North Hennepin CC	7411 85th Ave. N., Brooklyn Park, MN 55445		(763) 424-0800
North Iowa Area CC	500 College Dr., Mason City, IA 50401	Todd Rima	(641) 422-4281
North Lake CC	5001 N. MacArthur Blvd., Irving, TX 75038	Steve Cummings	(972) 273-3518
Northampton CC	3835 Green Pond Rd., Bethlehem, PA 18020	John Sweeney	(610) 861-5369
Northeast Mississippi CC	101 Cunningham Blvd., Booneville, MS 38829	Ray Scott	(662) 720-7352
Northeast Texas CC	PO Box 1307, Mount Pleasant, TX 75456	Chris Smith	(903) 572-1911
Northeastern JC	100 College Ave., Sterling, CO 80751	Bryan Shepherd	(970) 521-6641
Northeastern Oklahoma A&M	200 I Street NE, Miami, OK 74354	Roger Ward	(918) 540-6323
Northern Oklahoma-Enid	PO Box 2300, Enid, OK 73701	Raydon Leaton	(580) 548-2329
Northern Essex CC	100 Elliott St., Haverhill, MA 01830	Kerry Quinlan	(978) 556-3820
Northland Tech	1101 Highway 1 E., Thief River Falls, MN 56701	Guy Finstrom	(218) 681-0723
Northern Oklahoma College	PO Box 310, Tonkawa, OK 74653	Terry Ballard	(580) 628-6760
Northwest Mississippi CC	4975 Hwy. 51 N., Senatobia, MS 38668	Donny Castle	(662) 562-3422
Northwest Shoals CC	800 George Wallace Blvd., Muscle Shoals, AL 35661	David Langston	(256) 331-5462
Norwalk CC	188 Richards Ave., Norwalk, CT 06854	Mark Lambert	(203) 857-7155
Oakton CC	1600 E. Golf Rd., Des Plaines, IL 60016	Mike Pinto	(847) 635-1754
Ocean County College	PO Box 2001, Toms River, NJ 08754	Ernie Leta	(732) 255-0345
Odessa College	201 W. University Blvd., Odessa, TX 79764	Jon Wente	(432) 335-6874
Ohio State U. at Lima	4240 Campus Dr., Lima, OH 45804	Rob Livchak	(419) 995-8281
Ohlone College	43600 Mission Blvd., Fremont, CA 94539	Paul Moore	(510) 659-6056
Okaloosa-Walton CC	100 College Blvd., Niceville, FL 32578	Keith Griffin	(850) 729-5379
Olive-Harvey College	10001 S. Woodlawn Ave., Chicago, IL 60628	Mike Mayden	(773) 291-6365
Olney Central College	305 West St., Olney, IL 62450	Dennis Conley	(618) 395-7777
Olympic College	1600 Chester Ave., Bremerton, WA 98337	Michael Reese	(360) 475-7460
Onondaga CC	4941 Onondaga Rd., Syracuse, NY 13215	Joe Antonio	(315) 498-2492
Orange Coast College	2701 Fairview Rd., Costa Mesa, CA 92628	John Altobelli	(714) 432-5892
Orange County CC	115 South St., Middletown, NY 10940	Wayne Smith	(845) 341-4261
Otero JC	1802 Colorado Ave., La Junta, CO 81050	Mark Priegnitz	(719) 384-6833
Owens CC	PO Box 10000, Toledo, OH 43699	Bob Schultz	(567) 661-7973
Oxnard College	4000 S. Rose Ave., Oxnard, CA 93033	Jon Larson	(805) 986-5800
Palm Beach CC	4200 S. Congress Ave., Lake Worth, FL 33461	Craig Gero	(561) 868-3006
Palomar College	1140 W. Mission Rd., San Marcos, CA 92069	Bob Vetter	(760) 744-1150
Panola College	1109 W. Panola St., Carthage, TX 75633	Don Clinton	(903) 693-2062
Paris JC	2400 Clarksville St., Paris, TX 75460	Deron Clark	(903) 782-0218
Parkland College	2400 W. Bradley Ave., Champaign, IL 61820	Mitch Rosenthal	(217) 351-2297
Pasadena City College	1570 E. Colorado Blvd., Pasadena, CA 91106	Mike Scolinos	(626) 585-7789
Pasco-Hernando CC	10230 Ridge Rd., New Port Richey, FL 34654	Steve Winterling	(727) 816-3340
Pearl River CC	101 Hwy. 11 N., Poplarville, MS 39470	Jay Artigues	(601) 403-1326
Penn State-Abington	1600 Woodland Rd., Abington, PA 19001	Bobby Spratt	(215) 881-7440
Penn State-Beaver	100 University Dr., Monaca, PA 15061	John Bellaver	(724) 773-3826
Penn State-New Kensington	3550 7th Street Rd., New Kensington, PA 15068	Dave Montgomery	(724) 295-9544
Penn State-Wilkes-Barre	PO Box PSU, Lehman, PA 18627	Jack Monick	(570) 675-9262
Penn State-Worthington	120 Ridgeview Dr., Dunmore, PA 18512	Jeff Mallas	(570) 963-2611
Pennsyvania Tech	One College Ave., Williamsport, PA 17701	Michael Stanzione	(570) 327-4763
Pensacola JC	1000 College Blvd., Pensacola, FL 32504	Bill Hamilton	(850) 484-1304
Philadelphia, CC of	1700 Spring Garden St., Philadelphia, PA 19130		(215) 751-8964
Phoenix College	1202 W. Thomas Rd., Phoenix, AZ 85013	Ryan Reynolds	(602) 285-7293
Pierce College	9401 Farwest Dr. SW, Lakewood, WA 98498	Jason Picinich	(253) 964-6612
Pima CC	4905 B East Broadway Blvd., Tucson, AZ 85709	Edgar Soto	(520) 206-6005
Pitt CC	P.O. Drawer 7007, Greenville, NC 27835	Monte Little	(252) 321-4633
Polk CC	999 Avenue H NE, Winter Haven, FL 33881	Johnny Wiggs	(863) 297-1007
Porterville College	100 E. College Ave., Porterville, CA 93257	Bret Davis	(559) 791-2335
Potomac State College	101 Fort Ave., Keyser, WV 26726	Doug Little	(304) 788-6878
Prairie State College	202 S. Halstead St., Chicago Heights, IL 60411	Michael Pohlman	(708) 709-3950
Pratt CC	348 NE Hwy. 61, Pratt, KS 67124	Jeff Brewer	(620) 450-2154
Prince George's CC	301 Largo Rd., Largo, MD 20774	William Vaughan	(301) 322-0513
Queensborough CC	22205 56th Ave., Bayside, NY 11364	Craig Everett	(718) 631-6322
Quinsigamond CC	670 W. Boylston St., Worcester, MA 01606	Barry Glinski	(508) 854-4317
Ranger College	1100 College Circle, Ranger, TX 76470	Brent Leffingwell	(254) 647-3234
Raritan Valley CC	PO Box 3300, Route 28, Sommerville, NJ 08876	George Repetz	(908) 526-1200
Redlands CC	1300 S. Country Club Rd., El Reno, OK 73036	Matt Newgent	(405) 262-2552
Redwoods, College of the	7351 Tompkins Hill Rd., Eureka, CA 95501	Bob Brown	(707) 476-4239
Reedley College	Reed & Manning Ave, Reedley, CA 93654	Jack Hacker	(559) 638-0303
Rend Lake JC	468 N. Ken Gray Pkwy., Ina, IL 62846	Bob Simpson	(618) 437-5321

College	Address	Contact	Phone
Rhode Island, CC of	400 East Ave. Warwick, RI 02886	Jay Grenier	(401) 825-2114
Richland College	12800 Abrams Rd., Dallas, TX 75243	Bill Wharton	(972) 238-6261
Ridgewater College	2101 15th Ave. NW, Willmar, MN 56201	Dwight Kotila	(320) 231-7696
Rio Hondo College	3600 Workman Mill Rd., Whittier, CA 90601	Mike Salazar	(562) 692-0921
Riverland CC	1900 8th Ave. SW, Austin, MN 55912	Lee Brand	(507) 433-0543
Riverside CC	4800 Magnolia Ave., Riverside, CA 92506	Dennis Rogers	(909) 222-8333
Roane State CC	276 Patton Lane, Harriman, TN 37748	Larry Works	(865) 882-4583
Rochester Tech CC	851 30th Ave. SE, Rochester, MN 55904	Brian LaPlante	(507) 285-7106
Rockingham CC	PO Box 38, Wentworth, NC 27375	John Barrow	(336) 342-4261
Rock Valley College	3301 N. Mulford Rd., Rockford, IL 61114	Jeremy Warren	(815) 921-3802
Rockland CC	145 College Rd., Suffern, NY 10901	Patrick Carey	(845) 574-4452
Rose State College	6420 SE 15th St., Midwest City, OK 73110	Lloyd Cummings	(405) 733-7350
Roxbury CC	1234 Columbus Ave., Roxbury Crossing, MA 02120		(617) 541-2477
Sacramento City College	3835 Freeport Blvd., Sacramento, CA 95822	Andy McKay	(916) 558-2684
Saddleback CC	28000 Marguerite Pkwy., Mission Viejo, CA 92692	Jack Hodges	(949) 582-4642
St. Catharine College	2735 Bardstown Rd., St. Catharine, KY 40061	Luther Bramblet	(859) 336-5082
St. Charles CC	4601 Mid Rivers Mall Dr., St. Peters, MO 63376	Chris Gober	(636) 922-8211
St. Clair County CC	323 Erie St., Port Huron, MI 48060	Rick Smith	(810) 989-5671
St. Johns River CC	5001 St. Johns Ave., Palatka, FL 32177	Sam Rick	(386) 312-4162
St. Louis CC-Florissant Valley	3400 Pershall Rd., St. Louis, MO 63135	Donnie Hillerman	(314) 595-4587
St. Louis CC-Forest Park	5600 Oakland Ave., St. Louis, MO 63110	Royce Tippett	(314) 644-9688
St. Louis CC-Meramec	11333 Big Bend Rd., St. Louis, MO 63122	Joe Swiderski	(314) 984-7786
St. Petersburg CC	2465 Drew St., St. Petersburg, FL 33765	Dave Pano	(727) 791-2662
Salem CC	460 Hollywood Ave., Carney's Point, NJ 08069	Ron Palmer	(856) 351-2695
Salt Lake CC	4600 S. Redwood Rd., Salt Lake City, UT 84130	Bill Groves	(801) 957-4083
San Bernardino Valley JC	701 S. Mt. Vernon Ave., San Bernardino, CA 92410	Bill Mierzwik	(909) 384-8643
San Diego City College	1313 12th Ave., San Diego, CA 92101	Chris Brown	(619) 388-3705
San Diego Mesa College	7250 Mesa College Dr., San Diego, CA 92111	Kevin Hazlett	(619) 388-5804
San Francisco, City College of	50 Phelan Ave., San Francisco, CA 94112	John Vanoncini	(415) 239-3811
San Jacinto College-North	5800 Uvalde Rd., Houston, TX 77049	Tom Arrington	(281) 459-7613
San Joaquin Delta College	5151 Pacific Ave., Stockton, CA 95207	Jim Yanko	(209) 954-5198
San Jose City College	2100 Moorpark Ave., San Jose, CA 95128	Doug Robb	(408) 298-2181
San Mateo, College of	1700 W. Hillsdale Blvd., San Mateo, CA 94402	Doug Williams	(650) 358-6875
Santa Ana College	1530 W. 17th St., Santa Ana, CA 92706	Don Sneddon	(714) 564-6911
Santa Barbara City College	721 Cliff Dr., Santa Barbara, CA 93109	Teddy Warrecker	(805) 965-0581
Santa Fe CC	3000 NW 83rd St., Gainesville, FL 32606	Harry Tholen	(352) 395-5536
Santa Rosa JC	1501 Mendocino Ave., Santa Rosa, CA 95401	Damon Neidlinger	(707) 527-4389
Sauk Valley CC	173 State Route 2, Dixon, IL 61021	Terry Cox	(815) 288-5511
Schenectady County CC	78 Washington Ave., Schenectady, NY 12305	Tim Andi	(518) 381-1356
Scottsdale CC	9000 E. Chaparral Rd., Scottsdale, AZ 85256	Ed Yeager	(480) 423-6616
Seminole CC	100 Weldon Blvd., Sanford, FL 32773	Mike Nicholson	(407) 328-2148
Seminole State College	2701 Boren Blvd., Seminole, OK 74868	Eric Myers	(405) 382-9201
Sequoias, College of the	915 S. Mooney Blvd., Visalia, CA 93277	Jody Allen	(559) 737-6196
Seward County CC	1801 N. Kansas, Liberal, KS 67901	Galen McSpadden	(620) 629-2730
Shasta College	PO Box 496006, Redding, CA 96049	Brad Rupert	(530) 225-4919
Shawnee CC	8364 Shawnee College Rd., Ullin, IL 62992	Greg Sheppard	(618) 634-3245
Shelton State	9500 Old Greensboro Rd., Tuscaloosa, AL 35405	Bobby Sprowl	(205) 391-2918
Shoreline CC	16101 Greenwood Ave. N., Seattle, WA 98133	Steve Seki	(206) 546-4740
Sierra College	5000 Rocklin Rd., Rocklin, CA 95677	Rob Willson	(916) 781-0580
Sinclair CC	444 W. 3rd St., Dayton, OH 45402	Mike Goldschmidt	(937) 512-2353
Siskiyous, College of the	800 College Ave., Weed, CA 96094	Steve Neel	(530) 938-5231
Skagit Valley College	2405 E. College Way, Mount Vernon, WA 98273	Kevin Matthews	(360) 416-7780
Skyline College	3300 College Dr., San Bruno, CA 94066	Dino Nomicos	(650) 738-4197
Snead State CC	220 N. Walnut St., Boaz, AL 35957	Gerry Ledbetter	(256) 593-5120
Solano CC	4000 Suisun Valley Rd., Suisun City, CA 94534	Scott Stover	(707) 863-7822
South Carolina-Salkehatchie	PO Box 617, Allendale, SC 29810	Joe Baxter	(803) 584-3446
South Florida CC	600 W. College Dr., Avon Park, FL 33825	Rick Hitt	(863) 453-6661
South Georgia College	100 W. College Park Dr., Douglas, GA 31533	Scott Sims	(912) 389-4252
South Mountain CC	7050 S. 24th St., Phoenix, AZ 85040	Todd Eastin	(602) 243-8245
South Suburban College	15800 S. State St., South Holland, IL 60473	Steve Ruzich	(708) 596-2000
Southeastern CC	PO Box 151, Whiteville, NC 28472	Sheridan Wine	(910) 642-7141
Southeastern CC	1500 W. Agency Rd., West Burlington, IA 52655	Lonnie Winston	(319) 752-2731
Southeastern Illinois College	3575 College Rd., Harrisburg, IL 62946	Paul McSparrin	(618) 252-5400
Southern Idaho, College of	315 Falls Ave., Twin Falls, ID 83303	Boomer Walker	(208) 732-6285
Southern Maine CC	2 Fort Rd., South Portland, ME 04106	Philip Desjardins	(207) 839-6563
Southern Maryland, Col of	PO Box 910, La Plata, MD 20646	Joe Blandford	(301) 934-2251
Southern Nevada, CC of	700 College Dr., Henderson, NV 89015	Tim Chambers	(702) 651-3013
Southern Union State CC	PO Box 1000, Wadley, AL 36726	Joe Jordan	(256) 395-2211
Southwest Mississippi CC	2000 College Drive, Summit, MS 39666	Butch Holmes	(601) 276-2000
Southwest Tennessee CC	PO Box 780, Memphis, TN 38101	Johnny Ray	(901) 333-5145
Southwestern CC	1501 W. Townline Rd., Creston, IA 50801	Andy Osborne	(641) 782-1459
Southwestern College	900 Otay Lakes Rd., Chula Vista, CA 91910	Jerry Bartow	(619) 482-6370

Southwestern Illinois College	2500 Carlyle Ave., Belleville, IL 62221	Neil Fiala	(618) 222-5371
Southwestern Oregon CC	1988 Newmark Ave., Coos Bay, OR 97420	Corky Franklin	(541) 888-7348
Spartanburg Methodist JC	1000 Powell Mill Rd., Spartanburg, SC 29301	Tim Wallace	(864) 587-4237
Spokane Falls CC	3410 W. Fort George Wright Dr., Spokane, WA 99224	David Keller	(509) 533-3390
Spoon River College	23235 N. County Rd 22, Canton, IL 61520	Joe Moore	(309) 649-6303
Springfield College	1500 N. 5th St., Springfield, IL 62702	Steve Torricelli	(217) 525-1420
Suffolk CC-Grant	Crooked Hill Road, Brentwood, NY 11717	Robert Molinaro	(631) 851-6706
Suffolk County CC-Selden	533 College Rd., Selden, NY 11784	Eric Brown	(631) 732-2929
Sullivan County CC	112 College Rd., Loch Sheldrake, NY 12759	Jason Mitterwager	(845) 434-5750
SUNY Cobleskill	Route 7, Cobleskill, NY 12043	Shawn Noel	(518) 255-5209
SUNY Morrisville	PO Box 901, Morrisville, NY 13408	Carl Lohman	(315) 684-6199
Surry CC	630 S. Main St., Dobson, NC 27017	Mark Tucker	(336) 386-3217
Sussex County CC	1 College Hill Rd., Newton, NJ 07860	Todd Poltersdorf	(973) 300-2252
Tacoma CC	6501 S. 19th St., Tacoma, WA 98466	Michael Naughton	(253) 405-4994
Taft College	29 Emmons Park Dr., Taft, CA 93268	Tony Thompson	(661) 763-7740
Tallahassee CC	444 Appleyard Dr., Tallahassee, FL 32304	Mike McLeod	(850) 201-8588
Temple College	2600 S. First St., Temple, TX 76504	Craig McMurtry	(254) 298-8524
Texarkana College	2500 N. Robison Rd., Texarkana, TX 75599	James Mansinger	(903) 832-5565
Texas-Brownsville, U. of	80 Fort Brown, Brownsville, TX 78520	Eliseo Herrera	(956) 544-8293
Three Rivers CC	2080 Three Rivers Blvd., Poplar Bluff, MO 63901	Stacey Burkey	(573) 840-9611
Treasure Valley CC	650 College Blvd., Ontario, OR 97914	Russ Wright	(503) 889-6493
Trinidad State JC	600 Prospect St., Trinidad, CO 81082	Scott Douglas	(719) 846-5544
Triton College	2000 N. 5th Ave., River Grove, IL 60171	Spencer Allen	(708) 456-0300
Truett McConnell College	100 Alumni Dr., Cleveland, GA 30528	Jim Waits	(706) 865-2134
Tyler JC	PO Box 9020, Tyler, TX 75711	Jon Groth	(903) 510-2320
Ulster County CC	Cottekill Road, Stone Ridge, NY 12484	Ryan Snair	(845) 687-5278
Union County College	1033 Springfield Ave., Cranford, NJ 07016	Mark Domashinski	(908) 709-7093
Ventura College	4667 Telegraph Rd., Ventura, CA 93003	Don Adams	(805) 654-6400
Vermilion CC	1900 E. Camp St., Ely, MN 55731	Ray Podominick	(218) 365-7276
Vernon College	4400 College Dr., Vernon, TX 76384	Kevin Lallmann	(940) 552-6291
Victor Valley CC	18422 Bear Valley Rd., Victorville, CA 92392	Nate Lambdin	(760) 245-4271
Vincennes University	1002 N. 1st St., Vincennes, IN 47591	Jerry Blemker	(812) 888-4511
Volunteer State CC	1480 Nashville Pike, Gallatin, TN 37066	Jeff Smith	(615) 230-3448
Wabash Valley College	2200 College Dr., Mount Carmel, IL 62863	Rob Fournier	(618) 262-8641
Walla Walla CC	500 Tausick Way, Walla Walla, WA 99362	Mike Cummins	(509) 527-4494
Wallace State CC Hanceville	PO Box 2000, Hanceville, AL 35077	Randy Putman	(256) 352-8247
Walters State CC	500 S. Davy Crockett Pkwy., Morristown, TN 37813	Ken Campbell	(423) 585-6770
Waubonsee College	Route 47 at Waubonsee Dr., Sugar Grove, IL 60554	Dave Randall	(630) 466-2527
Waukesha County Tech	800 Main St., Pewaukee, WI 53072	Roy Jeske	(262) 691-5545
Wenatchee Valley CC	1300 5th St., Wenatchee, WA 98801	Bob Duda	(509) 682-6886
Weatherford College	225 College Park Dr., Weatherford, TX 76086	Jeff Lightfoot	(817) 598-0412
West Hills College	300 W. Cherry Lane, Coalinga, CA 93210	Paul Hodsdon	(559) 934-2458
West Valley College	14000 Fruitvale Ave., Saratoga, CA 95070	Mike Perez	(408) 741-2176
Westchester CC	75 Grasslands Rd., Valhalla, NY 10595	Robert Gerbassi	(914) 606-7895
Western Nebraska CC	1601 E. 27th St., Scottsbluff, NE 69361	Mike Jones	(308) 635-6198
Western Nevada CC	2201 W. College Pkwy., Carson City, NV 89703	D.J. Whittemore	(775) 445-3250
Western Oklahoma State	2801 N. Main St., Altus, OK 73521	Kurt Russell	(580) 477-7800
Western Texas College	6200 S. College Ave., Snyder, TX 79549	Billy Hefflinger	(325) 573-8511
Western Wisconsin Tech	304 North Sixth St., La Crosse, WI 54602	Mitch Baker	(608) 785-9442
Westmoreland County CC	400 Armbrust Rd., Youngwood, PA 15697	Mike Draghi	(724) 925-4129
Wharton County JC	911 E. Boling Hwy., Wharton, TX 77488	Bob Nottebart	(979) 532-6369
Wilkes CC	PO Box 120, Wilkesboro, NC 28697	Cam Heustess	(336) 838-6189
Williamson Free School	106 S. New Middletown Rd., Media, PA 19063	Sal Intelisano	(610) 566-1776
Williston State College	PO Box 1326, Williston, ND 58802	Kelly Heller	(701) 744-4242
Wisconsin, U. of-Barron	1800 College Dr., Rice Lake, WI 54868	Brad Randle	(715) 234-8176
Yakima Valley CC	PO Box 22520, Yakima, WA 98907		(509) 574-4724
Yavapai College	1100 E. Sheldon St., Prescott, AZ 86301	Sky Smeltzer	(928) 776-2292
Young Harris College	1 College St., Young Harris, GA 30582	Rick Robinson	(706) 379-4311
Yuba CC	2088 N. Beale Rd., Marysville, CA 95901	Tim Gloyd	(530) 634-7725

AMATEUR

INTERNATIONAL

INTERNATIONAL OLYMPIC COMMITTEE
Mailing Address: Chateau de Vidy, 1007 Lausanne, Switzerland. **Telephone:** (41-21) 621-6111. **FAX:** (41-21) 621-6216. **Website:** www.olympic.org.
President: Jacques Rogge. **Director, Communications:** Giselle Davies.
Games of the XXIX Olympiad: Aug. 8-24, 2008, at Beijing, China.

U.S. OLYMPIC COMMITTEE
Mailing Address: One Olympic Plaza, Colorado Springs, CO 80909. **Telephone:** (719) 866-4500. **FAX:** (719) 866-4654.
Chief Executive Officer: Jim Scherr. **Chief Communications Officer:** Darryl Seibel.

INTERNATIONAL BASEBALL FEDERATION
Mailing Address: Avenue de Mon-Repos 24, Case Postale 6099, 1002 Lausanne 5, Switzerland **Telephone:** (41-21) 318-8240. **FAX:** (41-21) 318-8241. **E-Mail Address:** ibaf@baseball.ch. **Website:** www.baseball.ch.
Year Founded: 1938.
Number of Affiliated National Federations: 113.
President: Aldo Notari (Italy). **Secretary General:** Eduardo De Bello (Panama). **Treasurer:** Frans van Aalen (Netherlands). **First Vice President:** Eiichiro Yamamoto (Japan). **Second Vice President:** Rodolfo Puente (Cuba). **Third Vice President:** Miguel Pozueta (Spain). **Members, At Large:** Mark Alexander (South Africa), Petr Ditrich (Czech Republic), Paul Seiler (United States).
    Continental Vice Presidents: Africa—Ishola Williams (Nigeria). America—Hector Pereyra (Dominican Republic). Asia—Tom C.H. Peng (Taiwan). Europe—Alexander Ratner (Russia). Oceania—Mark Peters (Australia).
    Executive Director: Miquel Ortin. **Communications Manager:** Enzo Di Gesu.

2005 Events
XVI World Children's Baseball Fair	Taipei, Taiwan, August
XII World Youth Championship	Monterrey, Mexico, Aug. 19-30
XXXVI World Cup	Amsterdam, Netherlands, Sept. 3-17

CONTINENTAL ASSOCIATIONS

CONFEDERATION PAN AMERICANA DE BEISBOL (COPABE)
Mailing Address: Calle 3, Francisco Filos, Vista Hermosa Edificio 74 Primer Alto, Local No. 2, Panama City, Panama. **Telephone:** (507) 2361-5677. **FAX:** (507) 261-5215. **E-Mail Address:** copabe@sinfo.net.
President: Eduardo De Bello (Panama). **Executive Director:** Jose Calazan (Panama).

2005 Events
*AA Pan Am Championship (17-18)	Date/site unavailable

AFRICAN BASEBALL/SOFTBALL ASSOCIATION
Mailing Address: Paiko Road, Changaga, Minna, Niger State, PMB 150, Nigeria. **Telephone:** (234-66) 224-555, (234-66) 224-711. **FAX:** (234-66) 224-555. **E-Mail Address:** absasec@yahoo.com.
President: Ishola Williams (Nigeria). **Executive Director:** Friday Ichide (Nigeria).

BASEBALL FEDERATION OF ASIA
Mailing Address: Mainichi Palaceside Bldg., 1-1-1, Hitotsubahi, Chiyoda-ku, Tokyo 100, Japan. **Telephone:** (81-3) 320-11155, (81-3) 321-36776. **FAX:** (81-3) 320-10707.
President: Eiichiro Yamamoto (Japan).

EUROPEAN BASEBALL CONFEDERATION
Mailing Address: Avenue de Mon-Repos 24, Case postale 131, 1000 Lausanne 5, Switzerland. **Telephone:** (32-3) 219-0440. **FAX:** (32-3) 772 7727. **E-Mail Address:** info@baseballeurope.com. **Website:** baseballeurope.com
President: Aldo Notari (Italy).

BASEBALL CONFEDERATION OF OCEANIA
Mailing Address: 48 Partridge Way, Mooroolbark, Victoria 3138, Australia. **Telephone:** (61-3) 9727-1779. **FAX:** (61-3) 9727-5959. **E-Mail Address:** chetg@ozemail.com.au
President: Mark Peters (Australia).
Friendship Series: Aug. 9-18 at Beijing, China.

ORGANIZATIONS

INTERNATIONAL GOODWILL SERIES, INC.
Mailing Address: P.O. Box 213, Santa Rosa, CA 95402. **Telephone:** (707) 975-7894. **FAX:** (707) 525-0214. **E-Mail Address:** rwilliams@goodwillseries.org. **Website:** www.goodwillseries.org.
President, Goodwill Series, Inc.: Bob Williams.
15th International Friendship Series (18 and Under): June 13 at Beijing, China; (16 and Under): Aug. 8 at Beijing, China.
11th Annual Australia Goodwill Series I: Dec. 15 at Adelaide, Canberra and Perth, Australia.

INTERNATIONAL SPORTS GROUP
Mailing Address: 142 Shadowood Dr., Pleasant Hill, CA 94523. **Telephone:** (925) 798-4591. **FAX:** (925) 680-1182. **E-Mail Address:** ISGbaseball@aol.com.
President: Jim Jones. **Vice President:** Tom O'Connell. **Secretary/Treasurer:** Randy Town.

NATIONAL

USA BASEBALL

Mailing Address, Corporate Headquarters: P.O. Box 1131, Durham, NC 27702. **Office Address:** 403 Blackwell St. Durham, NC 27701 **Telephone:** (919) 474-8721. **FAX:** (919) 474-8822. **E-Mail Address:** info@usabaseball.com. **Website:** www.usabaseball.com.

President: Mike Gaski. **Secretary General:** Jack Kelly. **Vice President, Treasurer:** Abraham Key. **Vice President, Administration:** Jerry Kindall. **Vice President, Secretary:** Elliott Hopkins. **General Counsel:** Lindsay Burbage.

Executive Director, Chief Executive Officer: Paul Seiler. **Director, National Teams:** Eric Campbell. **Director, National Teams:** Ray Darwin. **Assistant Director, National Teams:** Jeff Singer. **Director, Finance:** Miki Partridge. **Director, Marketing/Licensing:** David Perkins. **Director, Communications:** Dave Fanucchi.

National Members: Amateur Athletic Union (AAU), American Amateur Baseball Congress (AABC), American Baseball Coaches Association (ABCA), American Legion Baseball, Babe Ruth Baseball, Dixie Baseball, Little League Baseball, National Amateur Baseball Federation (NABF), National Association of Intercollegiate Athletics (NAIA), National Baseball Congress (NBC), National Collegiate Athletic Association (NCAA), National Federation of State High School Athletic Associations, National High School Baseball Coaches Association, National Junior College Athletic Association (NJCAA), Police Athletic League (PAL), PONY Baseball, T-Ball USA, United State Specialty Sports Association (USSSA), YMCAs of the USA.

2005 Events
Team USA—Professional Level

XXXVI World Cup .... Amsterdam, Netherlands, Sept. 3-17
2008 Olympics/Americas Regional Pre-Qualifier .... El Salvador, dates unavailable

Team USA—Collegiate Level

National Team Trials .... Raleigh, NC, June 26-30
USA/Japan Collegiate Series .... Japan, July 8-12
Friendship Series .... Taiwan, July 15-19

Team USA—Junior Level (18 and under)

Tournament of Stars .... Joplin, MO, June 20-27
National Team Trials .... Date/site unavailable
*COPABE Pan-Am Championship .... Date/site unavailable
*Qualifying tournament for 2006 World Junior Championship

Team USA—Youth Level (16 and under)

Junior Olympic Championship—West .... Peoria/Surprise, AZ, June 17-25
Junior Olympic Championship—East .... Jupiter, FL, June 17-25
National Team Trials .... Site unavailable, Aug. 6-17
IBAF AA World Championship .... Monterrey, Mexico Aug. 19-30

BASEBALL CANADA

Mailing Address: 2212 Gladwin Cres., Suite A7, Ottawa, Ontario K1B 5N1. **Telephone:** (613) 748-5606. **FAX:** (613) 748-5767. **E-mail Address:** info@baseball.ca. **Website:** www.baseball.ca.

Director General: Jim Baba. **Head Coach/Director, National Teams:** Greg Hamilton. **Manager, Baseball Operations:** Andre Lachance. **Manager, Media/Public Relations:** Matt Charbonneau.

2005 Events

Baseball Canada Cup (17 and under) .... Medicine Hat, Alberta, Aug. 18-21
2008 Olympics/Americas Regional Pre-Qualifier .... El Salvador, dates unavailable

AMERICAN BASEBALL FOUNDATION

Mailing Address: 1313 13th St. S., Birmingham, AL 35205. **Telephone:** (205) 550 4205. **FAX:** (205) 918-0800. **E-Mail Address:** abf@asmi.org. **Website:** www.americanbaseball.org.

Executive Director: David Osinski.

NATIONAL BASEBALL CONGRESS

Mailing Address: P.O. Box 1420, Wichita, KS 67201. **Telephone:** (316) 267-3372. **FAX:** (316) 267-3382. **Year Founded:** 1931.

President: Robert Rich Jr.

General Manager: Eric Edelstein. **Assistant GM, Director of Baseball/Stadium Operations:** Josh Robertson. **Tournament Director:** Jerry Taylor. **Marketing Manager:** Matt Rogers.

2005 NBC World Series (Collegiate, ex-professional, unlimited age): July 31-Aug. 14 at Wichita, KS (Lawrence Dumont Stadium).

ATHLETES IN ACTION

Mailing Address: 651 Taylor Dr., Xenia, OH 45385. **Telephone:** (937) 352-1000. **FAX:** (937) 352-1245. **E-Mail Address:** baseball@ai.com. **Website:** www.aiabaseball.org.

Director, AIA Baseball: Jason Lester (AIA-Texas). **General Managers, AIA Teams:** Chris Beck (AIA-Alaska), John McLaughlin (AIA-Latin America). **Director, Operations (AIA-Texas):** Eddie Lang.

SUMMER COLLEGE
LEAGUES

NATIONAL ALLIANCE OF COLLEGE SUMMER BASEBALL
Telephone: (704) 896-9100. **E-Mail Address:** jcarter@standpointtech.com.
Executive Director: Paul Galop (Cape Cod League). **Assistant Executive Directors:** Robert Pertsas (Atlantic Collegiate League), David Biery (Valley League). **Secretary:** Jeff Carter (Southern Collegiate League).
NCAA Sanctioned Leagues: Atlantic Collegiate League, Cape Cod League, Central Illinois Collegiate League, Great Lakes League, New England Collegiate League, New York Collegiate League, Southern Collegiate League, Valley League.

SUMMER COLLEGIATE BASEBALL ASSOCIATION
Mailing Address: 4900 Waters Edge Sr., Suite 201, Raleigh, NC 27606. **Telephone:** (919) 852-1960. **E-Mail Address:** info@summercollegiatebaseball.com. **Website:** www.summercollegiatebaseball.com.
Affiliated Leagues: Coastal Plain League, Northwoods League, Texas Collegiate League.

ALASKA BASEBALL LEAGUE
Mailing Address: P.O. Box 240061, Anchorage, AK 99524. **Telephone:** (907) 283-6186. **FAX:** (907) 274-3628.
Year Founded: 1974 (reunited, 1998).
President: Don Dennis (Alaska Goldpanners). **First Vice President/Marketing:** Ron Lucia (Peninsula Oilers). **VP/Secretary:** Lefty Van Brunt (Anchorage Glacier Pilots). **VP, Rules/Membership:** Pete Christopher (Mat-Su Miners). **VP, Umpiring:** Dennis Mattingly (Anchorage Bucs).
Division Structure: None.
Regular Season: 35 league games. **2005 Opening Date:** June 8. **Closing Date:** July 31.
All-Star Game: None.
Playoff Format: None. Top team from regular season qualifies for National Baseball Congress World Series in Wichita, Kan.
Roster Limit: 22, plus exemption for Alaska residents.
Player Eligibility Rule: Players with college eligibility, except drafted seniors.

ALASKA GOLDPANNERS
Mailing Address: P.O. Box 71154, Fairbanks, AK 99707. **Telephone:** (907) 451-0095, (619) 561-4581. **FAX:** (907) 456-6429. **E-Mail Address:** addennis@cox.net. **Website:** www.goldpanners.com.
General Manager: Don Dennis. **Head Coach:** Ed Cheff (Lewis-Clark State, Idaho, College).

ANCHORAGE BUCS
Mailing Address: P.O. Box 240061, Anchorage, AK 99524. **Telephone:** (907) 561-2827. **FAX:** (907) 561-2920. **E-Mail Address:** admin@anchoragebucs.com. **Website:** www.anchoragebucs.com.
General Manager: Dennis Mattingly. **Head Coach:** Matt Priess (U. of California).

ANCHORAGE GLACIER PILOTS
Mailing Address: 207 E. Northern Lights Blvd., Suite 105, Anchorage, AK 99503. **Telephone:** (907) 274-3627. **FAX:** (907) 274-3628. **E-Mail Address:** gpilots@alaska.net. **Website:** www.glacierpilots.com.
General Manager: Lefty Van Brunt. **Head Coach:** Andy McKay (Sacramento CC).

ATHLETES IN ACTION-ALASKA
Mailing Address: 651 Taylor Dr., Xenia, OH 45385. **Telephone:** (937) 352-1237. **FAX:** (937) 352-1245. **E-Mail Address:** chris.beck@aia.com. **Website:** www.aia baseball.org.
General Manager: Chris Beck. **Head Coach:** Brad Bass.

MAT-SU MINERS
Mailing Address: P.O. Box 2690, Palmer, AK 99645. **Telephone:** (907) 746-4914. **FAX:** (907) 746-5068. **E-Mail Address:** generalmanager@matsuminers.org. **Website:** www.matsuminers.org.
General Manager: Pete Christopher. **Head Coach:** Matt Tramel (Bethany, Kan., College).

PENINSULA OILERS
Mailing Address: 601 S. Main St., Kenai, AK 99611. **Telephone:** (907) 283-7133. **FAX:** (907) 283-3390. **E-Mail Address:** gm@oilersbaseball.com. **Website:** www.oilersbaseball.com.
General Manager: Ron Lucia. **Head Coach:** Mike Coutts.

ATLANTIC COLLEGIATE LEAGUE
Mailing Address: 43-18 209 St., Bayside, NY 11361. **Telephone:** (917) 882-5240. **E-Mail Address:** metronycadets@aol.cm. **Website:** www.acbl-online.com.
Year Founded: 1967.
Commissioner: Robert Pertsas. **President:** Tom Bonekemper. **Secretary/Treasurer:** Melinda Lavanco.
Division Structure: Wolff—Jersey Pilots, Kutztown Rockies, Lehigh Valley Catz, Quakertown Blazers. **Kaiser**—Long Island Collegians, Metro New York Cadets, New York Generals, Stamford Robins.
Regular Season: 40 games. **2005 Opening Date:** June 4. **Closing Date:** Aug. 15.
All-Star Game: July 18 at New York (Ardsley, N.Y.).
Playoff Format: Top two teams in each division meet in best-of-3 semifinals. Winners meet in one-game championship.
Roster Limit: 23 (college-eligible players only).

JERSEY PILOTS
Mailing Address: 401 Timber Dr., Berkeley Heights, NJ 07922. **Telephone:** (908) 464-8042. **E-Mail Address:** jerseypilots1@aol.com.
President/General Manager: Ben Smookler. **Head Coach:** Ray Ciecisz.

KUTZTOWN ROCKIES
Mailing Address: 429 Baldy Rd., Kutztown, PA 19530. **Telephone:** (610) 683-5273. **E-Mail Address:** Yeaks1@juno.com.
President/General Manager: Jon Yeakel. **Head Coach:** Unavailable.

LEHIGH VALLEY CATZ
Mailing Address: 103 Logan Dr., Easton, PA 18045. **Telephone:** (610) 533-9349. **E-Mail Address:** valleycatz@hotmail.com. **Website:** www.lvcatz.com.

Owner/President: Tommy Lisinicchia. General Manager: Pat O'Connell. Head Coach: Adrian Yaguez.

LONG ISLAND COLLEGIANS

Mailing Address: 431 Centre Island Rd., Oyster Bay, NY 11771. Telephone: (516) 686-7513. FAX: (516) 626-0750.

Owner/General Manager: Bob Hirschfield. Head Coach: Lou Petrucci.

METRO NEW YORK CADETS

Mailing Address: 220-55 46th St., 11-X Bayside, NY 11361. Telephone: (917) 82-5904. FAX: (718) 225-5695. E-Mail Address: metronycadets@aol.com.

Owner: Gus Antico. General Manager/Head Coach: Charles Papetti.

NEW YORK GENERALS

Mailing Address: 123 Euclid Ave., Ardsley, NY 10502. Telephone/FAX: (914) 693-4542. E-Mail Address: apoloto@aol.com.

Owner/General Manager: Nick DiSciullo. Head Coach: Unavailable.

QUAKERTOWN BLAZERS

Mailing Address: 510 Buttonwood St., Perkasie, PA 18944. Telephone: (215) 257-2645.

General Manager: Todd Zartman. Head Coach: Dennis Robison.

STAMFORD ROBINS

Mailing Address: P.O. Box 113254, Stamford, CT 06911. Telephone: (212) 522-5543, (203) 981-7516. E-Mail Address: coachwolff@aol.com, michaelhalo3131@aol.com.

General Manager: Rick Wolff. Scouting Liaison: Mike D'Angelo. Head Coach: Dan Gray.

CALIFORNIA COLLEGIATE LEAGUE

Mailing Address: 4299 Carpinteria Ave., Suite 201, Carpinteria, CA 93013. Telephone: (805) 684-0657. FAX: (805) 684-8596. E-Mail Address: pintard@sbforesters.org.

Year Founded: 1993.
President: Bill Pintard.
Member Clubs: Salinas Packers, San Luis Obispo Blues, Santa Barbara Foresters, Monterey Bay Sox.
Division Structure: None.
Regular Season: 40 games. 2005 Opening Date: June 1. Closing Date: Aug. 5.
Playoff Format: League champion advances to National Baseball Congress World Series in Wichita, Kan.
Roster Limit: 33.

CAL RIPKEN SR. COLLEGIATE BASEBALL LEAGUE

Mailing Address: 103 North Adams St., Rockville, MD 20850. E-Mail Address: info@ripkensrcollegebaseball.org. Website: www.ripkensrcollegebaseball.org

Year Founded: 2005.
Commissioner: William Spencer.
Division Structure: None
Regular Season: 40 games. 2005 Opening Date: June 10. Closing Date: Aug. 2.
All-Star Game: July 18 at Ripken Stadium in Aberdeen, Md.
Playoff Format: Top five teams meet in double-elimination tournament, Aug. 4-9.
Roster Limit: 27 (college-eligible players only).

BETHESDA BIG TRAIN

Mailing Address: P.O. Box 30306, Bethesda, MD

20824. Telephone: (301) 983-1006. FAX: (301) 652-0691. E-Mail Address: alex@bigtrain.org. Website: www.bigtrain.org.

President: Bruce Adams. General Manager: Alex Thompson. Head Coach: Sal Colangelo.

COLLEGE PARK BOMBERS

Mailing Address: 5033 56th Ave., Hyattsville, MD 20781. Telephone: (301) 674-7362. FAX: (301) 927-6997. E-Mail Address: bovello2@aol.com. Website: www.leaguelineup.com/marylandbombers.

President: Peter Shapiro. General Manager: Gene Bovello. Assistant GM: Jeff Finkelstein.
Head Coach: Tom Cassera.

MARYLAND ORIOLES

Mailing Address: 6451 St. Phillips Rd., Linthicum, MD 21090. Telephone: (410) 850-5714. E-Mail Address: daalbany22@cablespeed.com.

President: Dave Caplan. General Manager/Manager: Dean Albany.

MARYLAND REDBIRDS

Mailing Address: 10819 Sandringham Rd., Cockeysville, MD 21030. Telephone: (410) 823-3399, ext. 118. FAX: (410) 823-4144. E-Mail Address: redbird1@hotmail.com.

President: Joe DiBlasi. General Manager/Manager: Mark Russo. Head Coach: Pat Nagle.

ROCKVILLE EXPRESS

Mailing Address: 469 Winding Rose Dr., Rockville, MD 20850. Telephone: (301) 279-6780. FAX: (240) 465-0296. E-Mail Address: jhmport@aol.com.

President: John Pflieger. General Manager: Jim Adams. Head Coach: Tom Shaffer.

SILVER SPRING-TAKOMA THUNDERBOLTS

Mailing Address: 906 Glaizewood Ct., Takoma Park, MD 20912. Telephone: (301) 270-0598. E-Mail Address: EFSharp@juno.com. Website: www.tbolts.org

President/General Manager: Richard O'Connor. Head Coach: Bobby St. Pierre.

CAPE COD LEAGUE

Mailing Address: P.O. Box 266, Harwich Port, MA 02646. Telephone: (508) 432-6909. E-Mail Address: info@capecodbaseball.org. Website: www.capecodbaseball.org.

Year Founded: 1885.
Commissioner: Paul Galop. President: Judy Walden Scarafile. Vice Presidents: Phil Edwards, Peter Ford, Jim Higgins.
Deputy Commissioners: Dick Sullivan, Sol Yas. Treasurer: Steve Wilson. Director, Public Relations/Broadcast Media: John Garner. Director, Communications: Jim McGonigle. Director, Publications: Lou Barnicle. Official Photographer: Jan Volk.
Division Structure: East—Brewster, Chatham, Harwich, Orleans, Yarmouth-Dennis. West—Bourne, Cotuit, Falmouth, Hyannis, Wareham.
Regular Season: 44 games. 2005 Opening Date: June 16. Closing Date: Aug. 7.
All-Star Game: July 30 at Hyannis.
Playoff Format: Top two teams in each division meet in best-of-3 semifinals. Winners meet in best-of-3 series for league championship.
Roster Limit: 23 (college-eligible players only).

BOURNE BRAVES

Mailing Address: P.O. Box 895, Monument Beach, MA 02553. Telephone: (508) 888-5080. FAX: (508) 833-

9250. **E-Mail Address:** lynn.ladetto@verizon.net. **Website:** www.bournebraves.org.
President: Lynn Ladetto. **General Manager:** Michael Carrier.
Head Coach: Harvey Shapiro.

BREWSTER WHITE CAPS
Mailing Address: P.O. Box 2349, Brewster, MA 02631. **Telephone:** (617) 835-7130. **FAX:** (781) 934-0506. **E-Mail Address:** contact@brewsterwhitecaps.com, dpmfs@aol.com. **Website:** www. brewsterwhitecaps.com.
President: Hester Grue. **General Manager:** Dave Porter.
Head Coach: Bob Macaluso (Muhlenberg, Pa., College).

CHATHAM A's
Mailing Address: P.O. Box 428, Chatham, MA 02633. **Telephone:** (508) 945-3841. **FAX:** (508) 945-4787. **E-Mail Address:** cthoms@comcast.net. **Website:** www.chathamas.com.
President: Peter Troy. **General Manager:** Charles Thoms.
Head Coach: John Schiffner (Plainville, Conn., HS).

COTUIT KETTLEERS
Mailing Address: P.O. Box 411, Cotuit, MA 02635. **Telephone:** (508) 428-3358. **FAX:** (508) 420-5584. **E-Mail Address:** info@kettleers.org. **Website:** www.kettleers.org.
President: Martha Johnson. **General Manager:** Bruce Murphy.
Head Coach: Mike Roberts.

FALMOUTH COMMODORES
Mailing Address: 33 Wintergreen Rd., Mashpee, MA 02649. **Telephone:** (508) 477-5724. **FAX:** (508) 862-6011. **E-Mail Address:** chuckhs@comcast.net. **Website:** www.falcommodores.org.
President: Gerry Reily. **General Manager:** Chuck Sturtevant.
Head Coach: Jeff Trundy (The Gunnery School, Conn.).

HARWICH MARINERS
Mailing Address: P.O. Box 201, Harwich Port, MA 02646. **Telephone:** (508) 432-2000. **FAX:** (508) 432-5357. **Website:** www.harwichmariners.org. **E-Mail Address:** mehendy@comcast.net.
President: Mary Henderson. **General Manager:** Mike DeAnzeris.
Head Coach: Steve Englert (Boston College).

HYANNIS METS
Mailing Address: P.O. Box 852, Hyannis, MA 02601. **Telephone:** (508) 420-0962. **FAX:** (508) 428-8199. **E-Mail Address:** jhowitt932@comcast.net. **Website:** www.hyannismets.org.
President: Geoff Converse. **General Manager:** John Howitt.
Head Coach: Greg King (Thomas, Maine, College).

ORLEANS CARDINALS
Mailing Address: P.O. Box 504, Orleans, MA 02653. **Telephone/FAX:** (508) 255-0793. **FAX:** (508) 255-2237. **Website:** www.orleanscardinals.com.
President: Bob Korn. **General Manager:** Sue Horton.
Head Coach: Kelly Nicholson (Loyola HS, Los Angeles).

WAREHAM GATEMEN
Mailing Address: 71 Towhee Rd., Wareham, MA 02571. **Telephone:** (508) 295-3956. **FAX:** (508) 295-8821. **Website:** www.gatemen.org.
President, General Manager: John Wylde.

Head Coach: Cooper Farris (Mississippi Gulf Coast CC).

YARMOUTH-DENNIS RED SOX
Mailing Address: P.O. Box 814, South Yarmouth, MA 02664. **Telephone:** (508) 394-9387. **FAX:** (508) 398-2239. **E-Mail Address:** jf.martin@verizon.net. **Website:** ydredsox.org.
President: Bob Mayo. **General Manager:** Jim Martin.
Head Coach: Scott Pickler (Cypress, Calif., CC).

CENTRAL ILLINOIS COLLEGIATE LEAGUE
Mailing Address: 1137 Acacia Lane, Chatham, IL 62629. **Telephone:** (217) 483-5673. **FAX:** (217) 786-2788. **E-Mail Address:** commissioner@ciclbaseball.com. **Website:** www.ciclbaseball.com.
Year Founded: 1963.
Commissioner: Ron Riggle. **President:** Duffy Bass. **Administrative Assistant:** Mike Woods.
Division Structure: None.
Regular Season: 44 games. **2005 Opening Date:** June 14. **Closing Date:** Aug. 14.
All-Star Game: July 13 at DuPage.
Playoff Format: Top four teams meet in best-of-3 series. Winners meet in best-of-3 series for league championship.
Roster Limit: 24 (college-eligible players only).

DANVILLE DANS
Mailing Address: 138 E. Raymond, Danville, IL 61832. **Telephone:** (217) 446-5521. **FAX:** (217) 442-2137. **E-Mail Address:** jc@soltec.net. **Website:** www.soltec.net/dansbaseball.
General Manager: Rick Kurth. **Assistant GM:** Jeanie Cooke. **Head Coach:** Jamie Sailors.

DUBOIS COUNTY BOMBERS
Mailing Address: P.O. Box 332, Huntingburg, IN 47542. **Telephone:** (812) 683-3700. **E-Mail Address:** actjac@hotmail.com.
General Manager: Jack Tracz. **Head Coach:** Chris Erwin.

DUPAGE DRAGONS
Mailing Address: P.O. Box 3076, Lisle, IL 60532. **Telephone:** (630) 241-2255. **FAX:** (708) 784-1468. **E-Mail Address:** mike@madisongroupltd.com. **Website:** www.dupagedragons.com.
General Manager: Mike Thiessen. **Head Coach:** Bobby Sherrard.

EAST PEORIA SCRAPPERS
Mailing Address: 111 Highpoint Rd., Normal, IL 61761. **Telephone:** (309) 862-9118. **FAX:** (309) 747-4055. **E-Mail Address:** nmetzger@gridcom.net. **Website:** www.eastpeoriascrappers.com.
General Manager: Ray Berta. **Head Coach:** Nate Metzger.

GALESBURG PIONEERS
Mailing Address: P.O. Box 1387, Galesburg, IL 61402. **Telephone:** (309) 345-3683. **FAX:** (309) 343-2311. **E-Mail Address:** rsensabaugh@ci.galesburg.il.us.
General Manager: Roger Sensabaugh. **Head Coach:** Brian Unger.

QUINCY GEMS
Mailing Address: 300 Civic Center Plaza, Quincy, IL 62301. **Telephone:** (217) 223-1000. **FAX:** (217) 223-1330. **E-Mail Address:** jjansen@quincygems.com. **Website:** www.quincygems.com.
Executive Director: Jeff Jansen. **Head Coach:** Luke Sabers.

SPRINGFIELD RIFLES

Mailing Address: 100 Cartwright, Springfield, IL 62704. **Telephone:** (217) 698-9591. **FAX:** (217) 698-9891. **E-Mail Address:** sqular@aol.com.

General Manager: Larry Squires. **Head Coach:** Eric Weaver.

TWIN CITY STARS

Mailing Address: 907 N. School St., Normal, IL 61761. **Telephone:** (309) 452-3317. **FAX:** (217) 452-0377. **E-Mail Address:** duffybass@aol.com.

General Manager: Duffy Bass. **Head Coach:** Josh Manning.

CLARK GRIFFITH COLLEGIATE LEAGUE

Mailing Address: 10915 Howland Dr., Reston, VA 20191-4903

Telephone: (703) 860-0946. **FAX:** (703) 860-0143. **E-Mail Address:** fannanfj@erols.com. **Website:** www.clark-griffithbaseball.com.

Year Founded: 1945.

Executive Vice President: Frank Fannan. **Treasurer:** Tom Dellinger. **Media Director:** Ben Trittipoe. **VP/Rules Enforcement:** Byron Zeigler.

Regular Season: 36 games (split schedule). **2005 Opening Date:** June 3. **Closing Date:** July 29.

Playoff Format: Winners of each half meet in best-of-5 series (no championship series if same team wins both halves).

Roster Limit: 25 (college-eligible players only).

FAUQUIER GATORS

Mailing Address: 345 Winchester St., Warrenton, VA 20189. **Telephone:** (540) 347-0194. **FAX:** (540) 347-5199. **E-Mail Address:** hootbil@aol.com. **Website:** www.fauquiergators.com.

President: Steve Athey. **General Manager:** Sam Johnson. **Head Coach:** Paul Koch.

HERNDON BRAVES

Mailing Address: P.O. Box 962, Herndon, VA 20170. **Telephone:**
(703) 973-4444. **FAX:** (703) 783-1319. **E-Mail Address:** herndonbraves@cox.net. **Website:** www.herndonbraves.com.

President: Lisa Lombardozzi. **General Manager/Head Coach:** Chuck Faris.

RESTON HAWKS

Mailing Address: 12606 Magna Carta Rd., Herndon, VA 20171. **Telephone:** (703) 860-4780. **FAX:** (703) 860-0143. **E-Mail Address:** fannanfj@erols.com. **Website:** Unavailable.

General Manager: Frank Fannan. **Head Coach:** Kevin Kawecki.

VIENNA SENATORS

Mailing Address: 2727 Hidden Rd., Vienna, VA 22081. **Telephone:** (703)
247-3065. **FAX:** (703) 247-3070. **E-Mail Address:** cburr17@hotmail.com. **Website:** www.senatorbaseball.org.

President: Bill McGillicuddy. **General Manager:** Billy Emerson. **Head Coach:** Chris Burr.

COASTAL PLAIN LEAGUE

Mailing Address: 4900 Waters Edge Dr., Suite 201, Raleigh, NC 27606. **Telephone:** (919) 852-1960. **FAX:** (919) 852-1973. **Website:** www.coastalplain.com.

Year Founded: 1997.

Chairman/Chief Executive Officer: Jerry Petitt. **President:** Pete Bock. **Director, Media Relations:** Justin

Sellers. **Director, Administration:** Erin Callahan.

Division Structure: North—Edenton, Martinsville, Outer Banks, Peninsula, Petersburg. **South**—Fayetteville, Florence, New Bern, Wilmington, Wilson. **West**—Asheboro, Gastonia, Spartanburg, Thomasville.

Regular Season: 56 games (split schedule). **2005 Opening Date:** June 2. **Closing Date:** Aug. 10.

All-Star Game: July 19 at Wilson.

Playoff Format: Eight-team modified double-elimination tournament, at Fayetteville, Aug. 12-14.

Roster Limit: 22 (college-eligible players only).

ASHEBORO COPPERHEADS

Mailing Address: P.O. Box 4006, Asheboro, NC 27204. **Telephone:** (336) 460-7018. **FAX:** (336) 629-2651. **E-Mail Address:** info@teamcopperhead.com. **Website:** www.copperheadsbaseball.com.

Co-General Managers: Aaron Pugh, William Davis. **Head Coach:** Matt Boykin (Appalachian State U.).

EDENTON STEAMERS

Mailing Address: P.O. Box 86, Edenton, NC 27932. **Telephone:** (252) 482-4080. **FAX:** (252) 482-1717. **E-Mail Address:** edentonsteamers@hotmail.com. **Website:** www.edentonsteamers.com.

General Manager: Tim Schuster. **Head Coach:** Joel Tremblay (Wayne State, Mich., College).

FAYETTEVILLE SWAMPDOGS

Mailing Address: P.O. Box 64691, Fayetteville, NC 28306. **Telephone:** (910) 426-5900. **FAX:** (910) 426-3544. **E-Mail Address:** info@fayettevilleswampdogs.com. **Website:** www.fayettevilleswampdogs.com.

Owner: Lew Handelsman. **General Manager:** Steve Belcher. **Head Coach/Director of Operations:** Darrell Handelsman.

FLORENCE REDWOLVES

Mailing Address: P.O. Box 809, Florence, SC 29503. **Telephone:** (843) 629-0700. **FAX:** (843) 629-0703. **E-Mail Address:** Jamie@florenceredwolves.com. **Website:** www.florenceredwolves.com.

President: Kevin Barth. **General Manager:** Jamie Young. **Head Coach:** Scott Brickman (Wofford, N.C., College).

GASTONIA GRIZZLIES

Mailing Address: P.O. Box 177, Gastonia, NC 28053. **Telephone:** (704) 866-8622. **FAX:** (704) 864-6122. **E-Mail Address:** jthompson@gastoniagrizzlies.com. **Website:** www.gastonia-grizzlies.com.

President: Ken Silver. **Chief Executive Officer:** Jack Thompson. **General Manager:** Justin Rawlings. **Head Coach:** Chris Wiley (Louisburg, N.C., JC).

MARTINSVILLE MUSTANGS

Mailing Address: P.O. Box 1112, Martinsville, VA 24114. **Telephone:** (276) 403-5386. **FAX:** (276) 403-5387. **E-Mail Address:** dgibson@ci.martinsville.va.us. **Website:** www.martinsvillemustangs.com.

Owner: City of Martinsville. **General Manager:** Doug Gibson. **Head Coach:** Rob Watt (Mount Olive, N.C., College).

NEW BERN RIVER RATS

Mailing Address: 1311 N. Craven St., New Bern, NC 28560. **Telephone:** (252) 670-2633. **FAX:** (252) 637-2721. **E-Mail Address:** newbernriverrats@yahoo.com. **Website:** www.newbernriverrats.com.

President: Sabrina Bengel. **General Manager:** Buddy Bengel. **Head Coach:** Darin Vaughan (Central Missouri State U.).

OUTER BANKS DAREDEVILS
Mailing Address: 1014 Jefferson Ave., Newport News, VA 23607. **Telephone:** (252) 202-1842. **FAX:** (757) 244-3557. **E-Mail Address:** obxdaredevils@yahoo.com. **Website:** www.outerbanksdaredevils.com
Owner: Warren Spivey. **General Manager:** Joe McGowan. **Head Coach:** Mike Loyd (U. of Richmond).

PENINSULA PILOTS
Mailing Address: P.O. Box 7376, Hampton, VA 23666. **Telephone:** (757) 245-2222. **FAX:** (757) 245-8030. **E-Mail Address:** hank@peninsulapilots.com.
Website: www.peninsulapilots.com.
Owner: Henry Morgan. **General Manager:** Hank Morgan. **Head Coach:** Ryan Wheeler (College of William & Mary).

PETERSBURG GENERALS
Mailing Address: 1981 Midway Ave., Petersburg, VA 23804. **Telephone:** (804) 722-0141. **FAX:** (804) 733-7370. **E-Mail Address:** pbgenerals@aol.com. **Website:** www.petersburgsports.com/generals.
President: Larry Toombs. **General Manager:** Jeremy Toombs. **Head Coach:** Eric Coleman (San Diego Mesa JC).

SPARTANBURG STINGERS
Mailing Address: P.O. Box 5493, Spartanburg, SC 29304. **Telephone:** (864) 591-2250. **FAX:** (864) 591-2131. **E-Mail Address:** kferris@spartanburgstingers.com. **Website:** www.spartanburgstingers.com.
Owner: Ken Silver. **Chief Operating Officer:** Jack Thompson. **General Manager:** Kevin Ferris. **Head Coach:** Garrett Baron (U. of Albany).

THOMASVILLE HI-TOMS
Mailing Address: P.O. Box 3035, Thomasville, NC 27360. **Telephone:** (336) 472-8667. **FAX:** (336) 472-7198. **E-Mail Address:** info@hitoms.com. **Website:** www.hitoms.com
President: Greg Suire. **General Manager:** Jared Schjei. **Head Coach:** Josh Jordan (Fort Hays State, Kan.).

WILMINGTON SHARKS
Mailing Address: P.O. Box 15233, Wilmington, NC 28412. **Telephone:** (910) 343-5621. **FAX:** (910) 343-8932. **E-Mail Address:** info@wilmingtonsharks.com. **Website:** www.wilmingtonsharks.com.
President: Jim Morrison. **General Manager:** Amanda Yerdon. **Head Coach:** Cliff Godwin (Vanderbilt U.).

WILSON TOBS
Mailing Address: P.O. Box 633, Wilson, NC 27894. **Telephone:** (252) 291-8627. **FAX:** (252) 291-1224. **E-Mail Address:** wilsontobs@earthlink.net. **Website:** www.wilsontobs.com.
President: Greg Turnage. **General Manager:** Mike Edwards. **Head Coach:** Chris Cook (Lander, S.C., U.).

FLORIDA COLLEGIATE SUMMER LEAGUE
Mailing Address: 152 Lincoln Ave., Winter Park FL 32789. **Telephone:** (407) 694-6511 **FAX:** (407) 628-8535. **E-Mail Address:** rsitz@floridaleague.com.
Year Founded: 2004.
President: Sara Whiting. **Commissioner:** Sal Lombardo. **Treasurer:** Mike Whiting. **Director:** Ian Nathanson. **League General Manager:** Rob Sitz. **Public Relations:** Jen Lowndes. **Head Statistician:** Brian Smith.
Division Structure: None.
Regular Season: 30 games. **2005 Opening Date:** June 6. **Closing Date:** July 27.
All-Star Game: July 17 at Sanford.

Playoff Format: Six team, modified double-elimination tournament, July 28-31.
Roster Limit: 22 (college-eligible players only).

DAYTONA BEACH BARRACUDAS
Mailing Address: 152 Lincoln Ave., Winter Park FL 32789. **Telephone:** (386) 295-8461. **E-Mail Address:** DaytonaGM@floridaleague.com. **Website:** www.floridaleague.com/daytona.html.
Head Coach: Pat Leach (Daytona Beach, Fla., CC).

ORLANDO SHOCKERS
Mailing Address: 152 Lincoln Ave., Winter Park FL 32789. **Telephone:** (615) 566-6015. **E-Mail Address:** OrlandoGM@floridaleague.com. **Website:** www.floridaleague.com/orlando.html.
Chairman: Joe Russell. **Head Coach:** Randy Stegall (Cumberland, Tenn., U.)

SANFORD RIVER BATS
Mailing Address: 152 Lincoln Ave., Winter Park FL 32789. **Telephone:** (407)927-5957. **E-Mail Address:** SanfordGM@floridaleague.com. **Website:** www.floridaleague.com/sanford.html.
Chairman: Dan Ping. **Head Coach:** Ricky Plante (Seminole, Fla., CC).

WINTER PARK DIAMOND DAWGS
Mailing Address: 152 Lincoln Ave., Winter Park FL 32789. **Telephone:** (407)797-8582 **E-Mail Address:** WinterParkGM@floridaleague.com. **Website:** www.floridaleague.com/winterpark.html.
Chairman: Sean Connolly. **Head Coach:** Derek Wolfe (U. of Central Florida).

WINTER HAVEN WART HOGS
Mailing Address: 152 Lincoln Ave., Winter Park FL 32789. **Telephone:** (407) 222-6405. **E-Mail Address:** WinterHavenGM@floridaleague.com. **Website:** www.floridaleague.com/winterhaven.html.
Head Coach: Jim Murphy (Osceola HS, Kissimmee Fla.).

ZEPHYRHILLS SNAPPERS
Mailing Address: 152 Lincoln Ave., Winter Park FL 32789. **Telephone:** (407) 310-2532. **E-Mail Address:** ZephyrhillsGM@floridaleague.com. **Website:** www.floridaleague.com/zephyrhills.html.
General Manager: Lou Giella. **Head Coach:** Chad Sommers (St. Leo, Fla., U.)

FLORIDA COLLEGIATE INSTRUCTIONAL LEAGUE
Mailing Address: IMG Academies/Bollettieri Campus, 5500 34th St. W., Bradenton, FL 34210. **Telephone:** (941) 727-0303. **FAX:** (941) 727-2962. **E-Mail Address:** tpluto@gte.net. **Website:** www.zonebaseball.com.
Year Founded: 2001.
President: Tom Pluto. **Secretary:** Flody Suarez.
Regular Season: 36 games (split schedule). **2005 Opening Date:** June 15. **Closing Date:** July 31.
All-Star Game: July 10 at Bradenton, FL (McKechnie Stadium).
Playoff Format: One-game playoff between first- and second-half winners.
Roster Limit: Open. **Player Eligibility Rule:** (college-eligible players only).

GREAT LAKES LEAGUE
Mailing Address: 133 W. Winter St., Delaware, OH 43015. **Telephone:** (740) 368-3527. **FAX:** (740) 368-3999. **E-Mail Address:** kalance@owu.edu. **Website:**

www.greatlakesleague.org.
Year Founded: 1986.
President, Commissioner: Kim Lance.
Division Structure: None.
Regular Season: 42 games. **2005 Opening Date:** June 11. **Closing Date:** Aug. 6.
All-Star Game: July 17 at Athens, OH.
Playoff Format: Top six teams meet in double-elimination tournament.
Roster Limit: 27 (college-eligible players only).

COLUMBUS ALL-AMERICANS
Mailing Address: 3800 Municipal Way, Hilliard, OH 43026. **Telephone:** (614) 876-7361, ext. 500.
General Manager: Rodney Garnett. **Head Coach:** Brian Mannino.

DELAWARE COWS
Mailing Address: 3800 Criswell Dr., Columbus, OH 43220. **Telephone:** (614) 771-7070. **FAX:** (614) 771-7078.
General Manager/Head Coach: Bruce Heine.

GRAND LAKE MARINERS
Mailing Address: 717 W. Walnut St., Coldwater, OH 45828. **Telephone:** (419) 678-3607. **FAX:** (419) 586-4735.
General Manager: Wayne Miller. **Head Coach:** Mike Stafford.

INDIANAPOLIS SERVANTS
Mailing Address: 8888 Fitness Lane, Fishers, IN 46038. **Telephone:** (317) 842-2555. **FAX:** (317) 558-1162.
General Manager/Coach: Greg Lymberopoulos.

LAKE ERIE MONARCHS
Mailing Address: 26670 Glenwood Rd., Perrysburg, OH 43551. **Telephone:** (734) 626-1166.
General Manager: Jim DeSana. **Head Coach:** Dave Sontag.

LIMA LOCOS
Mailing Address: 3700 S. Dixie Hwy., Lima, OH 45806. **Telephone:** (419) 991-4296. **FAX:** (419) 999-4586.
General Manager: Barry Ruben. **Head Coach:** Robert Livchak.

PITTSBURGH PANDAS
Mailing Address: 118 Hetherton Dr., Pittsburgh, PA 15237. **Telephone:** (412) 759-4444. **FAX:** (412) 366-2064.
General Manager: Frank Gilbert. **Head Coach:** John Bellaver.

SOUTHERN OHIO COPPERHEADS
Mailing Address: Grover E 146, Ohio University, Athens, OH 45701. **Telephone:** (740) 593-4666. **FAX:** (740) 0539.
General Manager: Andrew Kreutzer. **Head Coach:** Brad Bohannon.

STARK COUNTY TERRIERS
Mailing Address: 1019 35th St. NW, Canton, OH 44709. **Telephone:** (330) 492-9220. **FAX:** (330) 492-9236.
General Manager: Greg Trbovich. **Head Coach:** Joe Gilhousen.

JAYHAWK LEAGUE
Mailing Address: 5 Adams Place, Halstead, KS 67056. **Telephone:** (316) 755-2361. **FAX:** (316) 755-1285.
Year Founded: 1976.
Commissioner: Bob Considine. **President:** J.D. Schneider. **Vice President:** Curt Bieber. **Public Relations/Statistician:** Gary Karr. **Secretary:** Christi Billups.
Regular Season: 40 games. **2005 Opening Date:**

June 10. **Closing Date:** July 29.
Playoff Format: Top two teams qualify for National Baseball Congress World Series.
Roster Limit: 30 to begin season; 25 at midseason.

EL DORADO BRONCOS
Mailing Address: 865 Fabrique, Wichita, KS 67218. **Telephone:** (316) 687-2309. **FAX:** (316) 942-2009. **Website:** www.eldoradobroncos.org.
General Manager: J.D. Schneider.

HAYS LARKS
Mailing Address: 1207 Felton Dr., Hays, KS 67601. **Telephone:** (785) 625-3486. **FAX:** (785) 625-8542. **E-Mail address:** cbieber@waffle-crete.com.
General Manager: Curt Bieber. **Manager:** Frank Leo.

JOPLIN SLASHERS
Mailing Address: 807 2nd Ave., Monett, MO 65708. **Telephone:** (417) 235-3193.
General Manager: Scott Wright.

LIBERAL BEEJAYS
Mailing Address: P.O. Box 793, Liberal, KS 67901. **Telephone:** (620) 624-1904. **FAX:** (620) 624-1906.
General Manager: Kim Snell.

NEVADA GRIFFONS
Mailing Address: 200 S. Alma, Nevada, MO 64772. **Telephone:** (417) 667-8308. **FAX:** (417) 667-8108.
General Manager: Jason Meisenheimer.

WICHITA TWINS
Mailing Address: 1245 N. Pine Grove, Wichita, KS 67212. **Telephone:** (316) 667-1104.
General Manager: Jeff Wells.

MOUNTAIN COLLEGIATE BASEBALL LEAGUE
E-Mail Address: info@mcbl.net, mark@mcbl.net. **Website:** www.mcbl.net.
Year Founded: 2005.
Commissioner: Mark Knudson. **Directors:** Kurt Colicchio, Ron Kailey, Ray Klesh.
Regular Season: 48 games. **Opening Date:** June 7. **Closing Date:** Aug. 13.
Playoff Format: Top two teams meet in best-of-3 series.
Roster limit: 25 (college-eligible players only).

CHEYENNE GRIZZLIES
Telephone: (307) 631-7337. **E-Mail Address:** rkaide@aol.com. **Website:** www.cheyennegrizzlies.com.
Owner/General Manager: Ron Kailey. **Head Coach:** Chris Smart (South Dakota State U).

FORT COLLINS FOXES
Telephone: (970) 225-9564. **E-Mail Address:** kcolicchio@msn.com. **Website:** www.fortcollinsfoxes.com.
Owner/General Manager: Kurt Colicchio. **Head Coach:** Paul Svagdis (Azusa Pacific, Calif., U.).

GREELEY GRAYS
Telephone: (303) 870-2523. **E-Mail Address:** rklesh@earthlink.net. **Website:** www.greeleygrays.com.
Owner/General Manager: Ray Klesh. **Head Coach:** Sam Blackmon (U. of Dallas).

LARAMIE COLTS
Website: www.laramiecolts.com.
Owner: Kurt Colicchio. **General Manager:** Unavailable. **Head Coach:** Brad Averitte (Texas Wesleyan U.).

NEW ENGLAND COLLEGIATE LEAGUE
Mailing Address: 515 Hawthorne Lane, Windsor, CT

06905. **Website:** www.necbl.com.
Year Founded: 1993.
President: Fay Vincent Jr. **Executive Vice President:** Joel Cooney. **Commissioner:** Kevin MacIlvane. **Deputy Commissioner:** Mario Tiani. **Treasurer:** Ed Slegeski. **Secretary:** Rich Rossiter.
Division Structure: North—Concord, Holyoke, Keene, Mill City, Sanford, Vermont. **South**—Berkshire, Danbury, Manchester, Newport, North Adams, Torrington.
Regular Season: 42 games. **2005 Opening Date:** June 7. **Closing Date:** July 31.
All-Star Game: July 24 at Newport.
Playoff Format: Top four teams in each division meet in best-of-3 quarterfinals; winners meet in best-of-3 semifinals. Winners meet in best-of-3 final for league championship.
Roster Limit: 25 (college-eligible players only).

BERKSHIRE DUKES
Mailing Address: P.O. Box 2021, Hinsdale, MA 01235. **Telephone:** (413) 655-8077. **FAX:** (413) 655-8635. **Website:** www.berkshiredukes.com.
President: Dan Duquette. **General Manager:** Kent Qualls. **Head Coach:** Steve Alonzo.

CONCORD QUARRY DOGS
Mailing Address: P.O. Box 404, Concord, NH 03302. **Telephone:** (603) 224-3333, ext. 612. **E-Mail Address:** info@quarrydogs.org. **Website:** www.quarrydogs.org
President: Tom Fredenburg. **General Manager:** Unavailable. **Head Coach:** Ken Connerty (U. of Massachusetts-Lowell).

DANBURY WESTERNERS
Mailing Address: 5 Old Hayrake Rd., Danbury, CT 06811. **Telephone:** (203) 313-3024. **FAX:** (203) 792-6177. **Website:** www.danburywesterners.com. **Website:** westerners1@aol.com.
General Manager: Terry Whalen. **Head Coach:** Rusty Goslin.

HOLYOKE GIANTS
Mailing Address: P.O. Box 1427 Holyoke, MA 01040. **Telephone:** (860) 593-1388. **Website:** www.holyokegiants.com. **E-Mail Address:** pj@holyokegiants.com.
President: Clinton Moffie. **General Manager:** P.P. Moynihan. **Head Coach:** Joel Southern.

KEENE SWAMP BATS
Mailing Address: 31 W. Surry Rd., Keene, NH 03431. **Telephone:** (603) 357-2578. **FAX:** (603) 354-7842.
General Manager: Vicki Bacon. **Head Coach:** Mike Sweeney (Amherst, Mass., College).

MANCHESTER SILKWORMS
Mailing Address: 16 West St., Manchester, CT 06040. **Telephone:** (860) 559-3126. **FAX:** (860) 432-1665. **Website:** www.manchestersilkworms.org
General Manager: Ed Slegeski. **Head Coach:** Anthony DeCicco (U. of Vermont).

MILL CITY ALL-AMERICANS
Mailing Address: P.O. Box 2228, Lowell, MA 01851. **Telephone:** (978) 454-5058. **FAX:** (978) 251-1211. **E-Mail Address:** info@millcityallamericans.com.
General Manager: Harry Ayotte. **Head Coach:** Chip Forrest.

NEWPORT GULLS
Mailing Address: P.O. Box 777, Newport, RI 02840. **Telephone:** (401) 845-6832. **Website:** www.newport-gulls.com

President/General Manager: Chuck Paiva. **Assistant GM:** Chris Patsos. **Head Coach:** Tommy Atkinson.

NORTH ADAMS STEEPLECATS
Mailing Address: P.O. Box 540, North Adams, MA 01247. **Telephone:** (413) 652-1031. **Website:** www.steeplecats.com
General Manager: Sean McGrath. **Head Coach:** Marc Pavao.

SANFORD MAINERS
Mailing Address: 924 Main St., Sanford, ME 04073. **Telephone:** (207) 324-0010. **FAX:** (207) 324-2227.
General Manager: Neil Olson. **Head Coach:** Greg Mamula (U. of Delaware).

TORRINGTON TWISTERS
Mailing Address: 4 Blinkoff Ct., Torrington, CT 06790. **Telephone/FAX:** (860) 482-0450.
General Manager: Kirk Fredriksson. **Head Coach:** Gregg Hunt.

VERMONT MOUNTAINEERS
Mailing Address: P.O. Box 586, Montpelier, VT 05602. **Telephone:** (802) 223-5224.
President: Ed Walbridge. **General Manager:** Brian Gallagher. **Head Coach:** John Russo.

NEW YORK COLLEGIATE LEAGUE
Summer Address: 28 Dunbridge Heights, Fairport, NY 14450. **Winter Address:** P.O. Box 2516, Tarpon Springs, FL 34688. **Telephone:** Florida—(585) 223-2328, New York—(727) 942-9120.
Year Founded: 1986.
Commissioner: Dave Chamberlain. **President:** Al Visingard. **Vice Chairman/Publicity:** Brian Spagnola. **Treasurer:** Dan Russo. **Secretary:** Ted Ford.
Member Clubs: Alfred A's, Alleghany County Nitros, Amsterdam Mohawks, Geneva Redwings, Genesee Valley River Bats, Glens Falls Golden Eagles, Hornell Dodgers, Mohawk Valley Cobras, Plattsburgh Thunder, Saratoga Phillies, Watertown Wizards, Wayne County Raptors.
Regular Season: 48 games. **2005 Opening Date:** June 10. **Closing Date:** Aug. 7.
All-Star Game: July 10 at Newark, N.Y.
Playoff Format: Top four teams meet in best-of-3 series. Winners meet in best-of-3 series for league championship.
Roster Limit: 25 (college-eligible players only).

NORTHWOODS LEAGUE
Office Address: 4000 4th St. SW, Rochester, MN 55902. **Telephone:** (507) 536-4579. **FAX:** (507) 536-4579. **E-Mail Address:** nwl@chartermi.net. **Website:** www.northwoodsleague.com.
Year Founded: 1994.
President: Dick Radatz Jr. **Director, Operations:** Rick Lindau.
Division Structure: North—Alexandria, Brainerd, Duluth, Mankato, St. Cloud, Thunder Bay. **South**—Eau Claire, La Crosse, Madison, Rochester, Waterloo, Wisconsin.
Regular Season: 68 games (split schedule). **2005 Opening Date:** June 1. **Closing Date:** Aug. 20.
All-Star Game: July 13 at Alexandria.
Playoff Format: First-half and second-half division winners meet in best-of-3 series. Winners meet in best-of-3 series for league championship.
Roster Limit: 26 (college-eligible players only).

ALEXANDRIA BEETLES

Mailing Address: 418 Third Ave. E., Alexandria, MN 56308. **Telephone:** (320) 763-8151. **FAX:** (320) 763-8152. **E-Mail Address:** beetles@alexandriabeetles.com. **Website:** www.alexandriabeetles.com.

General Manager: Ron Voz. **Head Coach:** Mike Rodriguez (UNC Greensboro).

BRAINERD BLUE THUNDER

Mailing Address: P.O. Box 1028, Brainerd, MN 56401. **Telephone:** (218) 828-2825. **FAX:** (218) 828-7857. **E-Mail Address:** Unavailable. **Website:** www.brainerdbluethunder.com.

General Manager: Skip Marr. **Head Coach:** Steve Abney (Kansas U.).

DULUTH HUSKIES

Mailing Address: 207 W. Superior St., Suite 206, Holiday Center Mall, Duluth, MN 55802. **Telephone:** (218) 786-9909. **FAX:** (218) 786-9001. **E-Mail Address:** huskies@duluthhuskies.com. **Website:** www.duluth-huskies.com.

General Manager: Craig Smith. **Head Coach:** Dave Parra.

EAU CLAIRE EXPRESS

Mailing Address: 108 E. Grand Ave., Eau Claire, WI 54701. **Telephone:** (715) 839-7788. **FAX:** (715) 839-7676. **E-Mail Address:** info@eauclaireexpress.com. **Website:** www.eauclaireexpress.com.

General Manager: Bill Rowlett. **Head Coach:** Dale Varsho.

LA CROSSE LOGGERS

Mailing Address: 1223 Caledonia St., La Crosse, WI 54603. **Telephone:** (608) 796-9553. **FAX:** (608) 796-9032. **E-Mail Address:** info@lacrosseloggers.com. **Website:** www.lacrosseloggers.com.

General Manager: Chris Goodell. **Head Coach:** Adam Sadler (Kirkwood, Iowa, CC).

MADISON MALLARDS

Mailing Address: 2920 N. Sherman Ave., Madison, WI 53704. **Telephone:** (608) 246-4277. **FAX:** (608) 246-4163. **E-Mail Address:** vern@mallardsbaseball.com. **Website:** www.mallardsbaseball.com.

General Manager: Vern Stenman. **Head Coach:** C.J. Thieleke (Madison Area Tech, Wis., JC).

MANKATO MOONDOGS

Mailing Address: 310 Belle Ave., Suite L-8, Mankato, MN 56001. **Telephone:** (507) 625-7047. **FAX:** (507) 625-7059. **E-Mail Address:** office@mankatomoondogs.com. **Website:** www.mankatomoondogs.com.

General Manager: Kyle Mrozek. **Head Coach:** Rob Huffstetler (Elon U.).

ROCHESTER HONKERS

Office Address: Mayo Field, 403 E. Center St., Rochester, MN 55904. **Mailing Address:** P.O. Box 482, Rochester, MN 55903. **Telephone:** (507) 289-1170. **FAX:** (507) 289-1866. **E-Mail Address:** honkers@rochesterhonkers.com. **Website:** www.rochesterhonkers.com.

General Manager: Dan Litzinger. **Head Coach:** Greg Labbe (U. of North Florida).

ST. CLOUD RIVER BATS

Office Address: Dick Putz Field, 5001 8th St. N., St. Cloud, MN 56303. **Mailing Address:** P.O. Box 5059, St. Cloud, MN 56302. **Telephone:** (320) 240-9798. **FAX:** (320) 255-5228. **E-Mail Address:** info@riverbats.com. **Website:** www.riverbats.com.

General Manager: Marc Jerzak. **Head Coach:** Jim Stoeckel.

THUNDER BAY BORDER CATS

Office Address: Port Arthur Stadium, 425 Winnipeg Ave., Thunder Bay, ON P7B 6P7. **Mailing Address:** P.O. Box 29105, Thunder Bay, ON P7B 6P9. **Telephone:** (807) 766-2287. **FAX:** (807) 345-8299. **E-Mail Address:** baseball@tbaytel.net.

General Manager: Unavailable. **Head Coach:** Chad Miller (Viterbo, Wis., College).

WATERLOO BUCKS

Office Address: Riverfront Stadium, 850 Park Rd., Waterloo, IA 50703. **Mailing Address:** P.O. Box 4124, Waterloo, IA 50704. **Telephone:** (319) 232-0500. **FAX:** (319) 232-0700. **E-Mail Address:** olson@waterloobucks.com. **Website:** www.waterloobucks.com.

General Manager: Jon Olson. **Head Coach:** Jason Shockey (Iowa Western CC).

WISCONSIN WOODCHUCKS

Office Address: Athletic Park, 300 Third St., L4, Wausau, WI 54402. **Telephone:** (715) 845-5055. **FAX:** (715) 845-5015. **E-Mail Address:** info@woodchucks.com. **Website:** www.woodchucks.com.

General Manager: Matt Brklacich. **Head Coach:** Darin Everson.

PACIFIC INTERNATIONAL LEAGUE

Mailing Address: 504 Yale Ave. N., Seattle, WA 98109. **Telephone:** (206) 623-8844. **FAX:** (206) 623-8361. **E-Mail Address:** spotter@potterprinting.com. **Website:** www.pacificinternationalleague.com.

Year Founded: 1992

President: Steve Konek. **Commissioner:** Seth Dawson. **Secretary:** Steve Potter. **Treasurer:** Mark Dow.

Member Clubs: Everett (Wash.) Merchants, Kirkland (Wash.) Kodiaks, Langley (B.C.) Blaze, Mount Vernon (Wash.), Portland (Ore.) Kings, Seattle Studs.

Regular Season: 24 league games. **2005 Opening Date:** June 3. **Closing Date:** July 26.

Playoff Format: Regular-season winner earns automatic berth in National Baseball Congress World Series.

Roster Limit: 30; 25 eligible for games (players must be at least 18 years old).

SOUTHERN COLLEGIATE BASEBALL LEAGUE

Mailing Address: 9300 Fairway Ridge Rd., Charlotte, NC 28277.

Telephone: (704) 847-5075. **FAX:** (704) 847-1455. **E-Mail Address:** SCBLCommissioner@aol.com. **Website:** www.oobl.org.

Year Founded: 1999.

Commissioner: Bill Capps. **President:** Jeff Carter. **Vice President:** Brian Swords. **Treasurer:** Steve Cunningham.

Division Structure: **North**—Carolina Copperheads, Kernersville, Lenoir, Rowan, Tennessee. **South**—Asheville, Athens, Carolina Chaos, Rock Hill, Spartanburg.

Regular Season: 45 games. **2005 Opening Date:** June 1. **Closing Date:** Aug. 5.

All Star Game: July 13, site unavailable.

Playoff Format: First-half division winners meet second-half division winners in best-of-3 series. Winners meet in best-of-3 series for league championship.

Roster Limit: 30 (College-eligible players only).

ASHEVILLE REDBIRDS

Mailing Address: P.O. Box 1515, Johnson City, TN

37605. **Telephone:** (423) 854-9282, (423) 914-0621. **FAX:** (423) 854-9594. **E-Mail Address:** EntSport@aol.com.

Owner/General Manager: Lyn Jeffers. **Head Coach:** Chris Mayes.

ATHENS PIRATE KINGS

Mailing Address: P.O. Box 462, Nicholson, GA 30565. **Telephone:** (706) 354-6789, (706) 296-4054. **E-Mail Address:** bpark@nbank.net. **Website:** www.eteamz.com/athenspirates.

Owner/General Manager: Bill Park. **Head Coach:** Bo Bray.

CAROLINA CHAOS

Mailing Address: 142 Orchard Dr., Liberty, SC 29657. **Telephone:** (864) 843-3232, (864) 901-4331. **E-Mail Address:** brian_swords@carolinachaos.com. **Website:** www.carolinachaos.com.

Owner/General Manager: Brian Swords. **Associate Head Coach:** Scott Whitlock.

CAROLINA COPPERHEADS

Mailing Address: P.O. Box 928, Cornelius, NC 28031. **Telephone:** (704) 892-1041, (704) 564-9211. **E-Mail Address:** jcarter@standpointtech.com. **Website:** www.Copperheadsports.org. **General Manager:** Jeff Carter. **Head Coach:** David Darwin.

KERNERSVILLE BULLDOGS

Mailing Address: 7057 Avenbury Circle, Kernersville, NC 27284. **Telephone:** (336) 993-8195, (336) 462-9058. **FAX:** (888) 777-5412. **Website:** www.kernersvillebulldogs.com.

Owner/General Manager: Art Wedemeyer. **Head Coach:** Dale Ijames.

LENOIR OILERS

Mailing Address: 4524 Oakhill School Rd., Lenoir, NC 28645. **Telephone:** (828) 496-7566, (828) 217-2116. **E-Mail Address:** buckdeal@charter.net, ·Freddie@dedola.com. **Website:** www.lenoiroilers.com. **President:** Buck Deal. **General Manager:** Freddie Davis. **Head Coach:** Chris Johnson.

ROCK HILL SOX

Mailing Address: 1443 Wedgefield Dr., Rock Hill, SC 29732. **Telephone:** (803) 366-2207, (803) 517-6626. **FAX:** (803) 980-7438. **E-Mail Address:** Ltrem1214@cs.com. **General Manager:** Larry Tremitiere. **Head Coach:** Stas Swerdzewski.

ROWAN PIRATES

Mailing Address: 9300 Fairway Ridge Rd., Charlotte, NC 28277. **Telephone:** (704) 847-5075, (704) 621-0940. **FAX:** (704) 847-1455. **E-Mail Address:** RowanPirates@aol.com.

Owner/General Manager: Bill Capps. **Head Coach:** Ray Greene.

SPARTANBURG CRICKETS

Mailing Address: P.O. Box 1429, Cowpens, SC 29330. **Telephone:** (864) 463-6667, (864) 266-3727. **E-Mail Address:** cricketsbb@bellsouth.net.

Owner/General Manager: Steve Cunningham. **Head Coach:** Mike Cunningham.

TENNESSEE THUNDER

Mailing Address: P.O. Box 1515, Johnson City, TN 37605. **Telephone:** (423) 854-9282, (423) 914-0621. **FAX:** (423) 854-9594. **E-Mail Address:** EntSport@aol.com. **Website:** www.TNThunder.org.

Owner/General Manager: Lyn Jeffers. **Head Coach:**

Glenn Davis.

TEXAS COLLEGIATE LEAGUE

Mailing Address: 210 West 6th St., Suite 1206, Fort Worth, TX 76102. **Telephone:** (817) 339-9367. **FAX:** (817) 339-9309. **E-Mail Address:** info@texascollegiate-league.com. **Website:** www.texascollegiateleague.com. **Year Founded:** 2004.

Chairman: Gerald Haddock. **Commissioner/Chief Operating Officer:** John Blake. **President:** Wayne Poage. **Vice President, Baseball Operations:** Darren Hall. **Director, Sponsor and Team Services:** Misti Winn. **Supervisor, Umpires:** John Ausmus.

Division Structure: Rogers Hornsby—Denton, Graham, Mineral Wells, Weatherford. **Tris Speaker**—Coppell, Euless, Highland Park, McKinney.

Regular Season: 48 games. **2005 Opening Date:** June 4. **Closing Date:** July 31.

All-Star Game: July 11 at McKinney.

Playoff Format: Top two teams in each division meet in best-of-3 division series. Winners meet in best-of-3 series for league championship.

Roster Limit: 28 (College-eligible players only).

COPPELL COPPERHEADS

Mailing Address: 509 West Bethel Rd., Suite 100, Coppell, TX 75019. **Telephone:** (972) 745-2929. **FAX:** (972) 745-0063. **E-Mail Address:** info@tclcopperheads.com. **Website:** www.tclcopperheads.com.

President: Steve Pratt. **Vice President, Baseball Operations:** Don English. **Head Coach:** Jack Giese.

DENTON OUTLAWS

Mailing Address: 1201 E. McKinney, Denton, TX 76209. **Telephone:** (940) 465-0845. **FAX:** (972) 250-1343. **E-Mail Address:** info@tcloutlaws.com. **Website:** www.tcloutlaws.com.

Owner: Jim Leslie. **Director of Player Personnel:** Sam Carpenter. **General Manager:** John Hampton. **Head Coach:** Derek Matlock (Texas Christian U.).

EULESS LONESTARS

Mailing Address: 1245 S. Main St., Suite 100, Grapevine, TX 76051. **Telephone:** (817) 354-0673. **FAX:** (817) 633-5729. **E-Mail Address:** info@tcllonestars.com. **Website:** www.tcllonestars.com.

President: Stacey Hollinger. **General Manager:** Scott Livingstone. **Head Coach:** Bob Townsend (UC Santa Barbara).

GRAHAM ROUGHNECKS

Mailing Address: 1346 Corvadura, Graham, TX 76450. **Telephone:** (940) 521-9898, (800) 256-4844. **FAX:** (940) 549-1346, (940) 549-6391. **E-Mail Address:** info@tclroughnecks.com. **Website:** www.tclroughnecks.com.

Owner: Frank Beaman. **General Manager:** Lisa McCool. **Head Coach:** K.J. Ellis (Hill, Texas, JC).

HIGHLAND PARK BLUE SOX

Mailing Address: P.O. Box 750116, Dallas, TX 75275. **Telephone:** (972) 567-6109. **FAX:** (214) 756-8278. **E-Mail Address:** info@tclbluesox.com. **Website:** www.tclbluesox.com.

Managing Partner: Paul Rogers. **General Manager:** Doug Conner. **Associate General Manager:** Christi Baker. **Head Coach:** Sam Carel (Southwest Missouri State U.).

McKINNEY MARSHALS

Mailing Address: The Ballfields at Craig Ranch, 6151 Alma Rd., McKinney, TX 75070. **Telephone:** (972) 747-

8248. **FAX:** (972) 747-9231. **E-Mail Address:** info@tclmarshals.com. **Website:** www.tclmarshals.com.
Owner: David Craig. **Owner/President:** Mike Henneman. **Executive Vice President:** Ray Ricchi. **General Manager:** Shayne Currin.
Head Coach: Kyle Hope (Richardson, Texas, HS).

MINERAL WELLS STEAM
Mailing Address: P.O. Box 606, Mineral Wells, TX 76068. **Telephone:** (940) 325-8500. **FAX:** (940) 328-0850. **E-Mail Address:** info@tclsteam.com. **Website:** www.tclsteam.com.
Owner: Athletes in Action. **General Manager:** Jason Lester. **Head Coach:** Unavailable.

WEATHERFORD WRANGLERS
Mailing Address: P.O. Box 2108, Weatherford, TX 76086. **Telephone:** (817) 771-8882. **FAX:** (817) 447-8637. **E-Mail Address:** info@tclwranglers.com. **Website:** www.tclwranglers.com.
Managing Partners: Jim Reeves, Randy Galloway. **Head Coach:** Jeff Lightfoot (Weatherford, Texas, JC).

VALLEY LEAGUE
Mailing Address: 58 Bethel Green Rd., Staunton, VA 24401. **Telephone:** (540) 885-8901. **FAX:** (540) 885-2068. **E-Mail Addresses:** davidb@fisherautoparts.com, kevin.warner@emu.edu. **Website:** www.valleyleague-baseball.com.
Year Founded: 1961.
President: David Biery. **Executive Vice President:** Todd Thompson. **Sports Information Director:** Kevin Warner.
Division Structure: North—Front Royal, Haymarket, Luray, New Market, Winchester. **South**—Covington, Harrisonburg, Staunton, Waynesboro, Woodstock.
Regular Season: 44 games. **2005 Opening Date:** June 3. **Closing Date:** July 26.
All-Star Game: July 10 at Winchester.
Playoff Format: Top four teams in each division meet in best-of-3 intra-divisional semifinal and final series. Winners meet in best-of-5 series for Jim Lineweaver Trophy.
Roster Limit: 28 (college eligible players only).

COVINGTON LUMBERJACKS
Mailing Address: P.O. Box 171, Low Moor, VA 24457. **Telephone/FAX:** (540) 863-5225. **E-Mail Address:** jacks@jacksbaseball.com **Website:** www.jacksbaseball.com.
Owners: Clyde Helmintoller, Jason Helmintoller. **Head Coach:** Brian Kraft (Oklahoma City U.).

FRONT ROYAL CARDINALS
Mailing Address: P.O. Box 995, Front Royal, VA 22630. **Telephone:** (540) 636-1892. **FAX:** (540) 635-6498. **E-Mail Address:** sminkeen@shentel.net. **Website:** www.frcardinalbaseball.com.
President: Linda Keen. **Head Coach:** Chad Oxendine (Coastal Carolina)

HARRISONBURG TURKS
Mailing Address: 1489 S. Main St., Harrisonburg, VA 22801. **Telephone/FAX:** (540) 434-5919. **E-Mail Address:** hbgturks@vaix.net. **Website:** www.harrisonburgturks.com.
General Manager/Head Coach: Bob Wease. **Operations Manager:** Teresa Wease. **Public Relations:** Curt Dudley.

HAYMARKET BATTLE CATS
Mailing Address: P.O. Box 95, Haymarket, VA 20168.

Telephone: (703) 768-5588. **Website:** www.haymarket-battlecats.com.
General Manager: Pat Malone. **Head Coach:** Harry Mayhew.

LURAY WRANGLERS
Mailing Address: 1203 E. Main St., Luray, VA 22835. **Telephone:** (540) 743-3338. **E-Mail Addresses:** luray-wranglers@hotmail.com, gmoyer@shentel.net.
President: Bill Turner. **General Manager:** Greg Moyer. **Head Coach:** Mike Bocock.

NEW MARKET REBELS
Mailing Address: P.O. Box 902, New Market, VA 22844. **Telephone:** (540) 740-4247, (540) 740-8569. **E-Mail Address:** nmrebels@shentel.net. **Website:** www.rebelsbaseballonline.com.
General Manager: Bruce Alger. **Executive Vice President:** Jim Weissenborn. **Head Coach:** Blaine Brown (Slippery Rock, Pa., College).

STAUNTON BRAVES
Mailing Address: 14 Shannon Place, Staunton, VA 24401. **Telephone:** (540) 886-0987. **FAX:** (540) 886-0905. **E-Mail Address:** sbraves@hotmail.com. **Website:** www.stauntonbraves.com.
General Manager: Steve Cox. **Director, Operations:** Kay Snyder. **Head Coach:** Lawrence Nesselrodt (West Virginia State U.).

WAYNESBORO GENERALS
Mailing Address: P.O. Box 615, Waynesboro, VA 22980. **Telephone:** (540) 949-0370, (540) 942-2474. **FAX:** (540) 949-0653. **E-Mail Address:** jim_critzer@hotmail.com. **Website:** www.waynesborogenerals.com.
Owner: Jim Critzer. **President:** Rennie Dobbins. **General Manager:** Dale Coffey. **Assistant GM:** Jim Stohlmann. **Head Coach:** Derek McDaniel.

WINCHESTER ROYALS
Mailing Address: P.O. Box 2485, Winchester, VA 22604. **Telephone:** (540) 667-9227, (540) 662-4466. **FAX:** (540) 662-3299. **E-Mail Addresses:** tgt@shentel.net, jimphill@shentel.net. **Website:** www.winchesterroyals.com.
President: Jim Shipp. **Vice President:** Jim Phillips. **Public Relations:** Mark Sawyer. **Baseball Operations:** Brian Burke. **Head Coach:** Kevin Anderson (Shenandoah, Va., U.)

WOODSTOCK RIVER BANDITS
Mailing Address: 2115 Battlefield Run Ct., Richmond, VA 23231. **Telephone:** (804) 795-5128. **FAX:** (804) 226-8706. **E-Mail Addresses:** woodstockriverbandits@yahoo.com **Website:** www.woodstockriverbandits.org.
President: Stu Richardson. **Vice President:** Glenn Berger. **General Manager:** Jerry Walters. **Assistant GM:** Harry Combs. **Head Coach:** Ricky Ware (St. Leo, Fla., U.).

WEST COAST COLLEGIATE LEAGUE
Mailing Address: 610 N. Mission St., Suite C-3, Wenatchee, WA 98801. **Telephone:** (509) 888-9378. **Website:** www.wccbl.com.
Year Founded: 2005.
Commissioner: Jim Dietz. **President:** Tony Larson. **Vice President:** Dan Segel.
Division Structure: None.
Regular Season: 36 league games. **2005 Opening Date:** June 14. **Closing Date:** Aug. 14.
Playoff Format: Top two teams meet in best-of-3 series.

Roster Limit: 25 (college-eligible players only).

ALOHA KNIGHTS

Mailing Address: P.O. Box 40212, Portland, OR 97240. **Telephone:** (503) 219-9919. **E-Mail Address:** info@alohaknights.com. **Website:** www.alohaknights.com.

President/General Manager: Dan Segel. **Head Coach:** Dale Stebbins (Mt. Hood, Ore., CC).

BELLINGHAM BELLS

Mailing Address: 1732 Iowa St., Bellingham, WA 98226. **Telephone:** (360) 527-1035. **E-Mail Address:** info@bellinghambells.com. **Website:** www.bellinghambells.com.

President/General Manager: Tony Larson. **Head Coach:** Sean Linville.

BEND ELKS

Mailing Address: P.O. Box 9009, Bend, OR 97708. **Telephone:** (541) 312-9259. **E-Mail Address:** richardsj@bendcable.com. **Website:** www.bendelks.com.

Owner/General Manager: Jim Richards. **Business Manager:** Elise Michaels. **Head Coach:** Rob Strickland (Lane, Ore., CC).

KELOWNA FALCONS

Mailing Address: 201-1014 Glenmore Dr., Kelowna, B.C., Canada V1Y 4P2. **Telephone:** (250) 763-4100. **E-Mail Address:** kelownafalcons@aol.com. **Website:** www.kelownafalcons.com.

Owner: Dan Nonis. **General Manager:** Bill Featherstone. **Business Manager:** Mark Nonis. **Head Coach:** Brian Hoop (Charleston Southern).

KITSAP BLUE JACKETS

Mailing Address: P.O. Box 68, Silverdale, WA 98383. **Telephone:** (360) 692-5566. **E-Mail Address:** rick@tscnet.com. **Website:** www.kitsapbluejackets.

Managing Partner/General Manager: Rick Smith. **Business Manager:** Wynne Littman. **Head Coach:** Matt Acker (Green River, Wash., CC).

SPOKANE RIVERHAWKS

Mailing Address: E. 303 Pacific, Spokane, WA 99202. **Telephone:** (509) 747-4991. **E-Mail Address:** mmccoy@spokaneriverhhawks.com. **Website:** www.spokaneriverhawks.com.

Owner: Bill Hogeboom. **General Manager:** Dave Keller. **Business Manager:** Matt McCoy. **Head Coach:** Kevin Stocker.

WENATCHEE APPLESOX

Mailing Address: P.O. Box 5100, Wenatchee, WA 98807. **Telephone:** (509) 665-6900. **E-Mail Address:** sales@applesox.com. **Website:** www.applesox.com.

Owner/General Manager: Jim Corcoran. **Head Coach:** Ed Knaggs.

HIGH SCHOOL/ YOUTH

HIGH SCHOOL
BASEBALL

NATIONAL FEDERATION OF STATE HIGH SCHOOL ASSOCIATIONS
Mailing Address: P.O. Box 690, Indianapolis, IN 46206. **Telephone:** (317) 972-6900. **FAX:** (317) 822-5700. **E-Mail Address:** baseball@nfhs.org. **Website:** www.nfhs.org.
Executive Director: Robert Kanaby. **Chief Operating Officer:** Bob Gardner. **Assistant Director/Baseball Rules Editor:** Elliot Hopkins. **Director, Publications/Communications:** Bruce Howard.

NATIONAL HIGH SCHOOL BASEBALL COACHES ASSOCIATION
Mailing Address: P.O. Box 12843, Tempe, AZ 85284. **Telephone:** (602) 615-0571. **FAX:** (480) 838-7133. **E-Mail Address:** rdavini@cox.net. **Website:** www.baseballcoaches.org.
Executive Director: Ron Davini. **President:** Stan McKeever, La Cueva HS, Albuquerque, NM. **First Vice President:** Frank Carey, North Reading HS, Reading, MA. **Second Vice President:** Craig Anderson, Pine Island HS, Zumbrota, MN. **2005 National Convention:** Dec. 1-4 at Louisville, KY.

GATORADE CIRCLE OF CHAMPIONS
(National High School Player of the Year Award)
Mailing Address: The Gatorade Company, 321 N. Clark St., Suite 24-3, Chicago, IL 60610. **Telephone:** (312) 821-3593. **Website:** www.gatorade.com.
Mailing Address, Scholastic Coach and Athletic Director: 557 Broadway, New York, NY 10012. **Telephone:** (212) 343-6131. **FAX:** (212) 343-6376. **E-Mail Address:** mwallace@scholastic.com. **Website:** coachad.com. **Publisher:** Bruce Weber. **Marketing Manager:** Mike Wallace.

NATIONAL TOURNAMENTS

In-Season
BASEBALL AT THE BEACH
Mailing Address: P.O. Box 1717, Georgetown, SC 29442. **Telephone:** (843) 546-3020. **FAX:** (843) 527-1816.
Tournament Director: Jim Owens.
2005 Tournament: March 3-5 at Myrtle Beach, SC (Coastal Federal Stadium/Myrtle Beach High School, 8 teams).

BATTLE AT THE RIDGE
Mailing Address: Miami Southridge HS, 19355 SW 114th Ave., Miami, FL 33157. **Telephone:** (305)-238-6110. **FAX:** 305-253-4456. **E-Mail Address:** edoskow@miamisouthridge.com.
Tournament Director: Ed Doskow.
2005 Tournament: March 21-24 (8 teams).

FIRST BANK CLASSIC
Mailing Address: 8708 Savannah Ave., Lubbock, TX 79424. **Telephone:** (806) 535-4505. **FAX:** 806-794-5306. **E-Mail Address:** scottgwinn@cox.net.
Tournament Director: Scott Gwinn.
2005 Tournament: March 10-12 (16 teams).

HORIZON CLEATS NATIONAL INVITATIONAL
Mailing Address: Horizon High School, 5601 E. Greenway Rd., Scottsdale, AZ 85254. **Telephone:** (602) 867-9003.
Tournament Director: Eric Kibler.
2005 Tournament: March 21-24 (16 teams).

INTERNATIONAL PAPER CLASSIC
Mailing Address: 4775 Johnson Rd., Georgetown, SC 29440. **Telephone:** (843) 527-9606, (843) 546-3807. **FAX:** (843) 546-8521. **Website:** www.ipclassic.com.
Tournament Director: Alicia Johnson.
2005 Tournament: March 3-6 (8 teams).

LIONS INVITATIONAL
Mailing Address: 3502 Lark St., San Diego CA 92103. **Telephone:** (619) 602-8650. **FAX:** (619) 239-3539. **E-Mail Address:** peter.gallagher@sdcourt.ca.gov.
Tournament Director: Peter Gallagher.
2005 Tournament: March 21-24 (80 teams).

MARCH MADNESS
Mailing Address: Westminster Academy, 5601 N. Federal Hwy., Fort Lauderdale, FL 33308. **Telephone:** (954) 735-1841. **FAX:** (954) 334- 6160. **E-Mail Address:** hofball11@aol.com.
Tournament Director: Rich Hofman.
2005 Tournament: March 15-18 (16 teams).

MIDLAND TOURNAMENT OF CHAMPIONS
Mailing Address: Midland High School, 906 W. Illinois Ave., Midland, TX 79701. **Telephone:** (432) 689-1337.
Tournament Director: Barry Russell.
2005 Tournament: March 3-5 (8 teams).

TOYO TIRES NATIONAL CLASSIC
Mailing Address: P.O. Box 338, Placentia, CA 92870. **Telephone:** (714) 993-2838. **FAX:** (714) 993-5350. **E-Mail Address:** placentiamustang@aol.com. **Website:** national-classic.com
Tournament Director: Todd Rogers.
2005 Tournament: March 26-31 at Cal State Fullerton (16 teams).

USA CLASSIC
Mailing Address: 5900 Walnut Grove Rd., Memphis, TN 38120. **Telephone:** (901) 872-8326. **FAX:** (901) 681-9443. **Website:** www.usabaseballstadium.org.
Tournament Organizers: John Daigle, Buster Kelso.
2005 Tournament: April 6-9 at USA Baseball Stadium, Millington, TN (16 teams).

WEST COAST CLASSIC
Mailing Address: 5000 Mitty Way, San Jose, CA 95129. **Telephone:** (408) 342-4273. **E-Mail Address:** hutton@mitty.com.
Tournament Director: Bill Hutton.
2005 Tournament: March 29-31 at Archbishop Mitty HS, San Jose, CA (16 teams).

WESTMINSTER NATIONAL CLASSIC
Mailing Address: Westminster Academy, 5601 N. Federal Hwy., Fort Lauderdale, FL 33308. **Telephone:** (954) 735-1841. **FAX:** (954) 334-6160.
Tournament Director: Rich Hofman.

2005 Tournament: March 29-April 1 (16 teams). Postseason

SUNBELT BASEBALL CLASSIC SERIES
Mailing Address: 505 North Blvd., Edmond, OK 73034. **Telephone:** (405) 348-3839. (918)-744-6254. **FAX:** (405) 340-7538.
Chairman: Gordon Morgan. **Director:** John Schwartz.
2005 Senior Series: Norman, OK, June 20-26. (8 teams: Arizona, California, Florida, Georgia, Maryland, Ohio, Oklahoma, Texas).
2005 Junior Series: McAlester and Hartshorne, OK, June 8-15 (10 teams: Arizona, California, Canada, Georgia, Mississippi, Missouri, Oklahoma Blue, Oklahoma Gold, Tennessee, Texas).
2005 Sophomore Series: Edmond, OK, June 2-5 (4 teams: Oklahoma, Tennessee, Texas, Missouri).

ALL-STAR GAMES

AFLAC HIGH SCHOOL ALL-AMERICA CLASSIC
Mailing Address: 10 S. Adams St., Rockville, MD 20850. **Telephone:** (301) 762-7894. **FAX:** (301) 762-1491.
Event Organizer: Sports America, Inc. **President, Chief Executive Officer:** Robert Geoghan.
2005 Game: High School Class of 2006, East vs. West, Aberdeen, MD, Aug. 10-13.

ALL-AMERICAN BASEBALL GAME
Mailing Address: 224 Stiger St., Hackettstown, NJ 07840. **Telephone:** (908) 684-5410. **FAX:** (908) 684-5415.
Event Organizer: SportsLink, Inc. **President, Chief Executive Officer:** Rich McGuinness.
2005 Game: Unavailable.

TALENT
SHOWCASES

PROFESSIONAL BASEBALL SCOUTING COMBINES

AREA CODE GAMES
Mailing Address: 23954 Madison St., Torrance, CA 90254. **Telephone:** (310) 791-1142, ex. 4424. **E-Mail Address:** andrew@studentsports.com. **Website:** www.areacodebaseball.org.
Event Organizer: Andrew Drennen, managing editor, Student Sports Baseball.
2005 Area Code Games: Aug. 6-10 at Long Beach, CA (Blair Field).

EAST COAST PROFESSIONAL BASEBALL SHOWCASE
Mailing Address: 601 S. College Rd., Wilmington, NC 28403. **Telephone:** (910) 962-3570.
Facility Directors: Mark Scalf, Randy Hood, Scott Jackson.
2005 Showcase: Aug. 1-4 at Wilmington, NC (UNC Wilmington).

HIGH SCHOOL SHOWCASE EVENTS

ALL-AMERICAN BASEBALL TALENT SHOWCASES
Mailing Address: 6 Bicentennial Ct., Erial, NJ 08081. **Telephone:** (856) 354-0201. **FAX:** (856) 354-0818. **E-Mail Address:** hitdoctor@thehitdoctor.com **Website:** thehitdoctor.com.
National Director: Joe Barth.

ARIZONA FALL CLASSIC
Mailing Address: 6102 W. Maui Lane, Glendale, AZ 85306 **Telephone:** (602) 978-2929. **FAX:** (602) 439-4494. **E-Mail Address:** azbaseballted@msn.com. **Website:** www.fallclassic.com.
Directors: Ted Heid, Tracy Heid.

2005 Events

Four Corner Classic (Open, 16 & under) .... Peoria, AZ, June 3-5
Senior Fall Classic (HS seniors) .... Peoria, AZ, Oct. 14-16
Junior Fall Classic (HS juniors/sophomores) .... Peoria, AZ, Oct. 21-23
International Classic (Open) .... Peoria, AZ, Oct. 28-30

BASEBALL FACTORY
Office Address: 9176 Red Branch Rd., Suite M, Columbia, MD 21045. **Telephone:** (800) 641-4487, (410) 715-5080. **FAX:** (410) 715-1975. **E-Mail Address:** info@baseballfactory.com. **Website:** www.baseballfactory.com.
Chief Executive Officer: Steve Sclafani. **President:** Rob Naddelman. **Senior Vice President, Baseball Operations:** Steve Bernhardt.
BATS Program: Year-round, various locations.

BLUE-GREY CLASSIC
Mailing Address: Pro-Motion Sports, 83 E. Bluff Rd., Ashland, MA 01721. **Telephone:** (508) 881-2782. **E-Mail Address:** gus@impactprospects.com. **Website:** www.impactprospects.com
Director: Gus Bell.
2005 Showcases: Pre-Draft Evaluation—May 22 at Tampa, FL (Progress Energy Park). Classic I—July 18-20 at Jacksonville, FL (Jacksonville U.). Pro-Time—July 29-31 at Clearwater, FL (Phillies minor league complex). Classic

II—Aug. 5-7 at Murfreesboro, TN (Middle Tennessee State U.) Classic III—Aug. 9-11 at Winston-Salem, NC (Wake Forest U.). Classic IV—Aug. 15-17 at Williamsburg, VA (College of William & Mary). Classic VI—Aug. 20-22 at Conway, SC (Coastal Carolina U.).

DOYLE BASEBALL SELECT SHOWCASES

Mailing Address: P.O. Box 9156, Winter Haven, FL 33883. **Telephone:** (863) 439-1000. **FAX:** (863) 439-7086. **E-Mail Address:** doyleinfo@doylebaseball.com. **Website:** www.doylebaseball.com.
President: Denny Doyle. **Director, Satellite School:** Rick Siebert.

IMPACT BASEBALL

Mailing Address: P.O. Box 47, Sedalia, NC 27342. **Telephone:** Unavailable. **E-Mail Address:** andypartin@aol.com. **Website:** www.impactbaseball.com.
Operator: Andy Partin.
2005 Showcases: June 6-7 at Durham, NC (Duke U.); June 27-28 at Columbia, SC (U. of South Carolina); Aug. 5-7 at Chapel Hill, NC (U. of North Carolina).

MID-AMERICA FIVE STAR BASEBALL SHOWCASE

Mailing Address—Cincinnati: Champions Baseball Academy, 510 E. Business Way, Cincinnati, OH 45241. **Telephone:** (513) 247-9511. **FAX:** (513) 247-0040. **Mailing Address—Louisville:** Champions Baseball Academy, 10701 Plantside Dr., Louisville, KY 40299. **Telephone:** (502) 261-9200. **FAX:** (502) 261-9278. **E-Mail Address:** champ8@aol.com. **Website:** championsbaseball.com.
President: John Marshall.
2005 Showcases: July 11-14 at Louisville, KY (Louisville Slugger Field); July 27-30 at Cincinnati, OH.

PACIFIC NORTHWEST CHAMPIONSHIP

Mailing Address: 11706 24th Ave. East, Unit A, Tacoma, WA 98445. **Telephone:** (253) 536-8001. **E-Mail Address:** mckay@baseballnorthwest.com. **Tournament Organizer:** Jeff McKay.
2005 Events: Aug. 26-29 at Tacoma, OR (Cheney Stadium). **Oregon Prospect Games:** June 20-21 at Corvallis, OR (Oregon State U.). **Washington Prospect Games:** East—July 18-19 at Spokane, WA (Avista Stadium). West—June 27-28, site unavailable. **Idaho Selection Games:** July 11-12, site unavailable.

PERFECT GAME USA

Mailing Address: 1203 Rockford Road SW, Cedar Rapids, IA 52404. **Telephone:** (319) 298-2923, (800) 447-9362. **FAX:** (319) 298-2924. **E-Mail Address:** pgjerry@qwest.net. **Website:** www.perfectgame.org.
President, Director: Jerry Ford. **National Supervisors:** Andy Ford, Jason Gerst, Tyson Kimm. **International Supervisor:** Kentaro Yasutake. **National Coordinators:** Jim Arp, Taylor McCollough.
Scouting Director, World Wood Bat Association: David Rawnsley.
Area Scouts: Kirk Gardner (Midwest), Mike Manning (Northeast), Bugs Moran (Southeast), Sandy Shofner (South). **Director, Instruction:** Jim VanScoyac.
Director, Public Relations: Andrea Bachman. **Marketing Director:** Frank Fulton.
Business Manager: Don Walser. **Office Manager:** Betty Ford. **Website Manager:** Tim Barcz. **Merchandise Director:** Tom Jackson. **National Softball Director:** Wendi Krejca.
2005 Events: Spring Top Prospect Showcase: April 30-May 1 at Cedar Rapids, IA. **National Pre Draft Showcase:** Date unavailable at Cedar Rapids, IA. **Sunshine East Showcase:** June 11-12 at Ft. Myers, FL. **Sunshine South Showcase:** June 11-12 at Dallas, TX. **Sunshine West Showcase:** June 11-12 at San Diego, CA. **Academic Showcase:** June 13-14 at Ft. Myers, FL. **Unsigned Seniors Showcase:** June 13-14 at Ft. Myers, FL. **National Showcase:** June 17-19, site unavailable. **WWBA National Championship (15 and under/summer):** June 29-July 3 at Marietta, GA. **WWBA National Championship (16 and under/summer):** July 19-24 at Marietta, GA. **WWBA National Championship (17 and under/summer):** July 5-10 at Marietta, GA. **WWBA National Championship (18 and under/summer):** July 11-17 at Marietta, GA. **South Top Prospect Showcase:** July 25-27 at Waco, TX. **South Underclass Showcase:** July 29-31 at Waco, TX. **Atlantic Coast Top Prospect Showcase:** Date unavailable at Chapel Hill, NC. **PG Baltimore Showcase:** Aug. 11-12 at Aberdeen, MD. **Atlantic Coast Underclass Showcase:** Aug. 12-14 at Durham, NC. **Northeast Underclass Showcase:** Aug. 15-17 at Wareham, MA. **Midwest Underclass Showcase:** Aug. 16-17 at Dayton, OH. **Ohio Valley Top Prospect Showcase:** Aug. 19-20 at Dayton, OH. **Northeast Top Prospect Showcase:** Aug. 19-21 at Wareham, MA. **WWBA Fall Championship (Florida Qualifier):** Aug. 26-28 at Ft. Myers, FL. **WWBA Fall Championship (Southeast Qualifier):** Sept. 16-18 at Marietta, GA. **Midwest Top Prospect Showcase:** Sept. 24-25 at Cedar Rapids, IA. **National Open Top Prospect Showcase:** Oct. 1-2 at Ft. Myers, FL. **WWBA Underclass Fall Championship:** Oct 7-10 at Ft. Myers, FL. **WWBA Fall Championship:** Oct. 28-31 at Jupiter, FL. **WWBA Thanksgiving Day Tournament:** Nov. 25-27 at Orange County, CA. **National Underclass Showcase:** Dec. 28-30 at Ft. Myers, FL. **World Showcase:** Jan. 7-8, 2006, at Fort Myers, FL.

PREMIER BASEBALL

Mailing Address: 2411 Teal Ave., Sarasota, FL 34237. **Telephone:** (941) 371-0989. **FAX:** (941) 371-0917.
Camp Directors: John Crumbley, Rich Hofman, Clyde Metcalf.

SELECTFEST BASEBALL

Mailing Address: 60 Franklin Pl., Morris Plains, NJ 07950. **Telephone:** (973) 539-4781. **E-Mail Address:** selectfest@optonline.net.
Camp Directors: Brian Fleury, Bruce Shatel.
2005 Showcase: June 24-25 at Piscataway, NJ (Rutgers U.).

TEAM ONE SHOWCASES

Mailing Address: P.O. Box 8843, Cincinnati, OH 45208. **Telephone:** (859) 466-8326. **E-Mail Address:**

TeamOneBB@aol.com. **Website:** www.teamonebaseball.com.
President, Team One Sports: Jeff Spelman.
2005 Team One Showcases: Dates unavailable.

TOP 96 INVITATIONAL SHOWCASE

Mailing Address: P.O. Box 5481, Wayland, MA 01778. **Telephone:** (508) 651-0165. **E-Mail Address:** kennethp50@comcast.net. **Website:** www.top96.com.
Showcase Organizers: Dave Callum, Doug Henson, Ken Hill.
2005 Showcases: June 3 at San Jose, CA; June 10 at Douglas, GA; June 17 at Mishawaka, IN; June 24 at Springfield, OH; July 13 at Detroit; July 15 at Rochester, NY; July 15 at St. Paul, MN; July 21 at Elizabethtown, PA; Aug. 5 at Winter Park, FL; Aug. 12 at Lowell, MA; Aug. 19 at Stamford, CT; Aug. 20 at Greenwood, SC; Aug. 21 at Waterbury, CT; Aug. 27 at Bethesda, MD; Sept. 16 at Phoenix; Oct. 1 at Los Angeles.

COLLEGE PROSPECT DEVELOPMENT CAMPS

COLLEGE SELECT SHOWCASE

Mailing Address: P.O. Box 783, Manchester, CT 06040. **Telephone:** (800) 782-3672. **E-Mail Address:** TRhit@msn.com. **Website:** www.collegeselect.org.
Consulting Director: Tom Rizzi.
2005 Showcases: July 18-20 at Norwich, CT; Aug. 15-17 at Binghamton, NY.

TOP GUNS SHOWCASE

Mailing Address: 7890 N. Franklin Rd., Suite 2, Coeur d'Alene, ID 83815. **Telephone/FAX:** (208) 762-1100. **E-Mail Address:** topgunsbss@hotmail.com. **Website:** www.topgunsbaseball.com.
President: Larry Rook. **National Director, Field Operations:** Gary Ward. **Assistant Director, National Scouting:** Nick Rook. **Scouting/Field Operations:** Cody Rook, Jason Rook.
2005 National Development Camp: June 28-30 at Las Vegas, NV (U. of Nevada-Las Vegas). **Regional Development Camps:** Nov. 25- 27 at Orlando, FL (U. of Central Florida); Nov. 25-27 at Arlington, TX (U. of Texas-Arlington).

SCOUTING SERVICES/HIGH SCHOOL, COLLEGE

BASEBALL FACTORY

Office Address: 9176 Red Branch Rd., Suite M, Columbia, MD 21045. **Telephone:** (800) 641-4487, (410) 715-5080. **FAX:** (410) 715-1975. **E-Mail Address:** info@baseballfactory.com. **Website:** www.baseballfactory.com.
Chief Executive Officer: Steve Sclafani. **President:** Rob Naddelman. **Senior Vice President, Baseball Operations:** Steve Bernhardt.

PROSPECTS PLUS

(A Joint Venture of Baseball America and Perfect Game USA)
Mailing Address: Baseball America, P.O. Box 2089, Durham, NC 27702. **Telephone:** (800) 845-2726. **FAX:** (919) 682-2880. **E-Mail Addresses:** alanmatthews@baseballamerica.com; jerry@perfectgame.org. **Website:** www.baseballamerica.com; www.perfectgame.org
Editors, Baseball America: Alan Matthews, Allan Simpson. **Director, Perfect Game USA:** Jerry Ford.

SKILLSHOW, INC.

Mailing Address: 290 King of Prussia Rd., Suite 102, Radnor, PA 19087. **Telephone:** (610) 687-9072. **FAX:** (610) 687-9629. **E-Mail Address:** info@skillshow.com. **Website:** www.skillshow.com.
Chief Executive Officer: Tom Koerick Jr. **President/Director, Sales:** Tom Koerick Sr.

TEAM ONE SHOWCASES

Mailing Address: P.O. Box 8843, Cincinnati, OH 45208. **Telephone:** (859) 466-8326. **E-Mail Address:** TeamOneBB@aol.com. **Website:** www.teamonebaseball.com.
President, Team One Sports: Jeff Spelman.

YOUTH
BASEBALL

ALL AMERICAN AMATEUR BASEBALL ASSOCIATION (AAABA)

Mailing Address: 331 Parkway Dr., Zanesville, OH 43701. **Telephone:** (740) 453-8531. **FAX:** (740) 453-3978. **E-Mail Address:** clw@aol.com. **Website:** www.aaaba.com.
Year Founded: 1944.
President: George Arcurio. **Executive Director/Secretary:** Bob Wolfe.
2005 National Tournament (21 and under): Aug. 8-13 at Johnstown, PA (16 teams). **AAABA Regionals:** Aug. 1-4 at Altoona, PA, Schenectady, NY and Zanesville, OH.

AMATEUR ATHLETIC UNION OF THE UNITED STATES, INC. (AAU)

Mailing Address: P.O. Box 10000, Lake Buena Vista, FL 32803. **Telephone:** (407) 934-7200. **FAX:** (407) 934-7242. **E-Mail Address:** jeremy@aausports.org. **Website:** www.aaubaseball.org.
Year Founded: 1982.
Senior Sports Manager/Baseball: Jeremy Bullock.

DIVISION I
Age Classifications, National Championships

8 and under	Concord, NC, July 17-23
9 and under	*Orlando, July 8-16
10 and under (46/60 foot)	Des Moines, IA, July 17-23
10 and under (48/65 foot)	Charlotte, NC, July 17-23
11 and under (46/60 foot)	Des Moines, IA, July 17-23
11 and under (50/70 foot)	*Orlando, July 15-23
12 and under (50/70 foot)	Burnsville/Lakeville, MN, July 23-30
13 and under (54/80 foot)	Burlington, NC, July 17-23
13 and under (60/90 foot)	Myrtle Beach, SC, July 22-30
14 and under (60/90 foot)	Sarasota, FL, July 22-30
15 and under	Roanoke, VA, July 22-30
Junior Olympics (16 and under)	New Orleans, July 28-Aug. 6
17 and under	Louisville, KY, July 15-23
18 and under/19 and under	*Orlando, July 8-16

DIVISION II
Age Classifications, National Championships

14 and under (60/90 foot)	*Orlando, July 22-30
15 and under	*Orlando, July 15-23
16 and under	*Orlando, July 15-23

Age Classifications, Regional National Championships
NORTHEAST

10 and under (46/60 foot)	Voorhees, NJ, July 18-22
10 and under (48/65 foot)	Blackwood, NJ, July 18-22
11 and under (50/70 foot)	Reading, PA, July 11-15
12 and under (50/70 foot)	Salisbury, MD, July 25-29
13 and under (60/90 foot)	Allentown, PA, July 11-15

SOUTHEAST

10 and under (46/60 foot)	Kinston, NC, July 17-22
10 and under (48/65 foot)	Charlotte, NC, July 17-22
11 and under (50/70 foot)	*Orlando, July 15-22
12 and under (50/70 foot)	Concord, NC, July 17-22
13 and under (60/90 foot)	Myrtle Beach, SC, July 22-30

CENTRAL

10 and under (46/60 foot)	Des Moines, IA, July 17-22
10 and under (48/65 foot)	Des Moines, IA, July 17-22
11 and under (50/70 foot)	Burnsville/Lakeside, MN, July 23-29
12 and under (50/70 foot)	Burnsville/Lakeside, MN, July 23-29
13 and under (60/90 foot)	Des Moines, IA, July 17-22

NORTHWEST

10 and under (46/60 foot)	Unavailable
10 and under (48/65 foot)	Unavailable
11 and under (50/70 foot)	Unavailable
12 and under (50/70 foot)	Unavailable
13 and under (60/90 foot)	Unavailable

SOUTHWEST

10 and under (48/65 foot)	Unavailable
10 and under (46/60 foot)	Unavailable
11 and under (50/70 foot)	Unavailable
12 and under (50/70 foot)	Unavailable
13 and under (54/80 foot)	Unavailable

Age Classifications, Super National Championships

10 and under (46/60 foot)	Cherry Hill, NJ, Sept. 2-5
10 and under (48/65 foot)	Charlotte, NC, Sept. 2-5
11 and under (50/70 foot)	Concord, NC, Sept. 2-5
12 and under (50/70 foot)	Charlotte, NC, Sept. 2-5
13 and under (60/90 foot)	Cherry Hill, NJ, Sept. 2-5

Age Classifications, West Coast Nationals

10 and under (46/60 foot)	Portland, OR/Vancouver, WA, Sept. 1-5
10 and under (48/65 foot)	Portland, OR/Vancouver, WA, Sept. 1-5
11 and under (50/70 foot)	Portland, OR/Vancouver, WA, Sept. 1-5
12 and under (50/70 foot)	Portland, OR/Vancouver, WA, Sept. 1-5

International Championships

10 and under (46/60 foot)	*Orlando, June 10-16
12 and under (50/70 foot)	*Orlando, June 10-16

Wood Bat Nationals

8-18 and under	Winter Haven, FL, Sept. 3-6

Winter Nationals

8-18 and under	Tampa, Dec. 27-30

*Disney's Wide World of Sports Complex, Lake Buena Vista.

AMERICAN AMATEUR BASEBALL CONGRESS (AABC)

National Headquarters: 100 West Broadway, Farmington, NM 87401. **Telephone:** (505) 327-3120. **FAX:** (505) 327-3132. **E-Mail Address:** mikedimond@aabc.us. **Website:** www.aabc.us.
   Year Founded: 1935.
   President: Mike Dimond.

Age Classifications, World Series

Roberto Clemente (8 and under)	McDonough, GA, July 21-24
Willie Mays (9)	Tulsa, OK, July 28-31
Willie Mays (10 and under)	Catano, PR, July 28-31
Pee Wee Reese (11)	Brooklyn, NY, Aug. 4-7
Pee Wee Reese (12 and under)	Toa Baja, PR, Aug. 4-7
Sandy Koufax (13)	Battle Creek, MI, July 27-31
Sandy Koufax (14 and under)	Rockford, IL, July 28-31
Mickey Mantle (15)	Owasso, OK, July 30-Aug. 3
Mickey Mantle (16 and under)	McKinney, TX, Aug. 3-7
Connie Mack (18 and under)	Farmington, NM, Aug. 6-12
Stan Musial (unlimited)	Battle Creek, MI, Aug. 12-15

AMERICAN AMATEUR YOUTH BASEBALL ALLIANCE

Mailing Address: 3851 Iris Lane, Bonne Terre, MO 63628. **Telephone:** (573) 518-0319. **FAX:** (314) 822-4974. **E-Mail Address:** clwjr28@aol.com. **Website:** www.aayba.com.
   President, Baseball Operations: Carroll Wood.

Age Classifications, Open World Series

10 and under	St. Louis, July 10-17
11 and under	St. Louis, July 10-17
12 and under	St. Louis, July 24-31
13 and under	St. Louis, July 24-31
14 and under	St. Louis, July 10-17

AMERICAN LEGION BASEBALL

National Headquarters: National Americanism Commission, P.O. Box 1055, Indianapolis, IN 46206. **Telephone:** (317) 630-1213. **FAX:** (317) 630-1369. **E-Mail Address:** acy@legion.org. **Website:** www.baseball.legion.org.
   Year Founded: 1925.
   Program Coordinator: Jim Quinlan.
   2005 World Series (19 and under): Aug. 19-23 at Fitzgerald Stadium, Rapid City, SD (8 teams). **Mailing Address:** 632 Crestview Dr., Rapid City, SD 57702. **Telephone:** (605) 343-0040. **E-Mail Address:** kheater7@aol.com. **Website:** www.alws2005.org. **Chairman:** Kevin Huether.
   2005 Regional Tournaments (Aug. 11-15, 8 teams): **Northeast**—West Warwick, RI; **Mid-Atlantic**—Brooklawn, NJ; **Southeast**—Dothan, AL; **Mid-South**—Pine Bluff, AR; **Great Lakes**—Moline, IL; **Central Plains**—Mandan, ND; **Northwest**—Yakima, WA; **Western**—Las Vegas, NV.

BABE RUTH BASEBALL

International Headquarters: 1770 Brunswick Pike, P.O. Box 5000, Trenton, NJ 08638. **Telephone:** (609) 695-1434.

FAX: (609) 695-2505. **Website:** www.baberuthleague.org.
Year Founded: 1951.
President, Chief Executive Officer: Ron Tellefsen.
Executive Vice President/Chief Financial Officer: Rosemary Schoellkopf. **Vice President, Operations/Marketing:** Joe Smiegocki. **Vice President, Planning/Development:** Debra Horn. **Commissioners:** Robert Faherty, Steven Tellefsen. **Executive Director, Special Events:** David Frolich.

Age Classifications, World Series

10 and under	Russellville, AR, Aug. 6-13
Cal Ripken (11-12)	Aberdeen, MD, Aug. 13-21
13	Jamestown, NY, Aug. 20-27
14	Quincy, MA, Aug. 19-27
13-15	Abbeville, LA, Aug. 13-20
16	Weimar, TX, Aug. 6-13
16-18	Newark, OH, Aug. 13-20

CONTINENTAL AMATEUR BASEBALL ASSOCIATION (CABA)

Mailing Address: 82 University St., Westerville, OH 43081. **Telephone:** (740) 382-4620. **E-Mail Address:** rtremaine@cababaseball.com. **Website:** www.cababaseball.com.
Year Founded: 1984.
Commissioner: John Mocny. **President:** Carl Williams. **Executive Director:** Roger Tremaine.

Age Classifications, Ultimate World Series

9 and under	Charles City, IA, July 29-Aug. 6
10 and under	Lynwood, IL, July 25-31
11 and under	Marion, OH, July 22-30
12 and under	Cincinnati, July 22-30
13 and under	Knoxville, TN, July 23-30
14 and under (54/80 foot)	Dublin, OH, July 22-30
14 and under/East (60/90 foot)	Guaynabo, PR, July 29-Aug. 7
14 and under/West (60/90 foot)	San Clemente, CA, July 15-23
15 and under	Crystal Lake, IL, July 29-Aug. 7
16 and under	Marietta, GA, July 30-Aug. 7
High school age	Euclid, OH, July 23-29
18 and under	Miami, July 15-22
18 and under (Wood Bat)	Charleston, SC, July 23-31
College age (Wood Bat)	Elgin, IL, July 23-31

Age Classifications, Quality World Series

9 and under	San Clemente, CA, July 15-23
10 and under	San Clemente, CA, July 15-23
11 and under	Jackson, TN, July 22-31
12 and under	Mentor/Painesville, OH, July 22-31
13 and under	St. Clair Shores, MI, July 22-30
14 and under	Mentor/Painesville, OH, July 22-31
15 and under	Nashville, TN, July 29-Aug. 7
16 and under	St. Clair Shores, MI, July 22-30

Age Classifications, Open World Series

9 and under/Southeast	Miami, June 30-July 5
10 and under/Southeast	Miami, June 30-July 5
10 and under/Great Plains	St. Clair Shores, MI, July 22-30
11 and under/Great Plains	St. Clair Shores, MI, July 22-30
12 and under/Southeast	Miami, June 30-July 5
12 and under/Great Plains	St. Clair Shores, MI, July 22-30
13 and under/Southeast	Miami, June 30-July 5
13 and under/Midwest	Lynwood, IL, July 25-31
13 and under/Northwest	Blaine, WA, Aug. 4-9
14 and under/Midwest	Lynwood, IL, July 25-31
14 and under/Great Plains	St. Clair Shores, MI, July 22-30
15 and under/Southeast	Miami, July 15-22
15 and under/Great Plains	St. Clair Shores, MI, July 22-30
16 and under/Northwest	Bellevue, WA, July 21-29

DIXIE BASEBALL, INC.

Mailing Address: P.O. Box 877, Marshall, TX 75671. **Telephone:** (903) 927-2255. **FAX:** (903) 927-1846. **Website:** www.dixie.org.
Year Founded: 1955.
Executive Director: Jim Quigley, 24 Pipes Loop, Covington, LA 70435. Telephone: (985) 893-1290. **Office Manager:** Rhonda Skelton.

Age Classifications, World Series

Dixie Youth (9-10)	Auburn, AL, Aug. 7-13

Dixie Youth (12 and under) .... Auburn, AL, Aug. 7-13
Junior Dixie Boys (13) .... Muscle Shoals, AL, Aug. 6-11
Dixie Boys (13-14) .... Muscle Shoals, AL, Aug. 6-11
Dixie Pre-Majors (15-16) .... Ponchatoula, LA, Aug. 6-11
Dixie Majors (15-18) .... Laurel, MS, Aug. 6-11

DIZZY DEAN BASEBALL, INC.
Mailing Address: P.O. Box 856, Hernando, MS 38632. **Telephone:** (662) 429-4365, (850) 455-8827.
Year Founded: 1962.
Commissioner: Danny Phillips. **Treasurer/Administrator:** D.B. Stewart.

Age Classifications, World Series
6 and under .... Forsyth, GA, July 15-20
7 and under .... Henry County, GA, July 14-19
8 and under .... Southaven, MS, July 22-27
9 and under .... Southaven, MS, July 22-27
10 and under .... Moody, AL, July 15-20
11 and under .... Rossville, GA, July 15-20
12 and under .... Moody, AL, July 15-20
13 and under .... Southaven, MS, July 22-27
14 and under .... Southaven, MS, July 22-27
Junior (15-16) .... Southaven, MS, July 22-27
Senior (17-18) .... Southaven, MS, July 22-27
High school .... Starkville, MS, July 14-19

HAP DUMONT YOUTH BASEBALL
(A Division of the National Baseball Congress)
Mailing Address: P.O. Box 771352, Wichita, KS 67277. **Telephone:** (316) 721-1779. **FAX:** (316) 721-8054. **E-Mail
Address:** hapdumontbball@yahoo.com. **Website:** hapdumontbaseball.com.
Year Founded: 1974.
National Chairman: Jerry Crowell.

LITTLE LEAGUE BASEBALL, INC.
International Headquarters: P.O. Box 3485, Williamsport, PA 17701. **Telephone:** (570) 326-1921. **FAX:** (570) 326-
1074. **Website:** www.littleleague.org.
Year Founded: 1939.
Chairman: Timothy Hughes.
President/Chief Executive Officer: Steve Keener. **Director, Media Relations/Communications:** Lance Van Auken.
Director, Publications: Scott Miller. **Director, Special Projects:** Scott Rosenberg.

Age Classifications, World Series
Little League (11-12) .... Williamsport, PA, Aug. 19-28
Junior League (13-14) .... Taylor, MI, Aug. 14-20
Senior League (14-16) .... Bangor, ME, Aug. 14-20
Big League (16-18) .... Easley, SC, July 30-Aug. 6

NATIONAL AMATEUR BASEBALL FEDERATION (NABF)
Mailing Address: P.O. Box 705, Bowie, MD 20718. **Telephone:** (301) 464-5460. **FAX:** (301) 352-0214. **E-Mail
Address:** nabf1914@aol.com. **Website:** www.nabf.com.
Year Founded: 1914.
Executive Director: Charles Blackburn. **Special Events Coordinator, NABF Classics:** Michael Felton.

Age Classifications, World Series
Sophomore (14 and under) .... Joplin, MO, July 14-18
Junior (16 and under) .... Northville, MI, July 27-31
High School (17 and under) .... Greensboro, NC, July 20-24
Senior (18 and under) .... Jackson, MS, Aug. 3-7
College (22 and under) .... Toledo, OH, Aug. 3-7
Major (unlimited) .... Louisville, KY, Aug. 17-21

NABF Classics (Invitational)
10 and under .... Southaven, MS, July 3-7
11 and under .... Southaven, MS, July 3-7
12 and under .... Hopkinsville, KY, July 12-16
13 and under (54/80 foot) .... Southaven, MS, July 3-7
13 and under (60/90 foot) .... Southaven, MS, July 3-7
15 and under .... Nashville, July 19-23

NATIONAL ASSOCIATION OF POLICE ATHLETIC LEAGUES
Mailing Address: 618 U.S. Highway 1, Suite 201, North Palm Beach, FL 33408. **Telephone:** (561) 844-1823. **FAX:**
(561) 863-6120. **E-Mail Address:** copnkid@nationalpal.org. **Website:** www.nationalpal.org.
Year Founded: 1914.
Executive Director: Bob Still. **National Program Manager:** Eric Widness.

12 and under .... Unavailable

PONY BASEBALL, INC.

International Headquarters: P.O. Box 225, Washington, PA 15301. **Telephone:** (724) 225-1060. **FAX:** (724) 225-9852. **E-Mail Address:** info@pony.org. **Website:** www.pony.org.
Year Founded: 1951.
President: Abraham Key. **Director, Baseball Operations:** Don Clawson.

Age Classifications, World Series

Shetland (5-6)	No National Tournament
Pinto (7-8)	No National Tournament
Mustang (9-10)	Irving, TX, Aug. 3-6
Bronco (11-12)	Monterey, CA, Aug. 4-9
Pony (13)	Chino Hills, CA, July 29-Aug. 1
Pony (13-14)	Washington, PA, Aug. 13-20
Colt (15-16)	Lafayette, IN, Aug. 3-10
Palomino (17-18)	Santa Clara, CA, Aug. 5-8

REVIVING BASEBALL IN INNER CITIES (RBI)

Mailing Address: 245 Park Ave., New York, NY 10167. **Telephone:** (212) 931-7897. **FAX:** (212) 949-5695.
Year Founded: 1989.
Founder: John Young. **Vice President, Community Affairs:** Thomas Brasuell.

Age Classifications, World Series

Junior Boys (13-15)	Pittsburgh, Aug. 3-11
Senior Boys (16-18)	Pittsburgh, Aug. 3-11

SUPER SERIES BASEBALL OF AMERICA

National Headquarters: 4036 East Grandview St., Mesa, AZ 85205. **Telephone:** (480) 664-2998. **FAX:** (480) 664-2997. **E-Mail Address:** info@superseriesbaseball.com. **Website:** www.superseriesbaseball.com.
President: Mark Mathew.

Age Classifications, National Championships
NATIONAL DIVISION

9 and under	DeSoto, TX, July 17-24
10 and under	Broken Arrow, OK, July 9-16
11 and under	O'Fallon, MO, July 16-23
12 and under	Collierville, TN, July 9-16
13 and under	Longmont, CO, July 9-16
14 and under (54/80 foot)	Mesquite, TX, July 23-30
14 and under (60/90 foot)	Peoria, AZ, July 9-16
15 and under	Broken Arrow, OK, July 23-30
16 and under	Peoria, AZ, July 23-30
17 and under	Peoria, AZ, July 16-23
18 and under	Peoria, AZ, July 23-30

AMERICAN DIVISION

8 and under (coach pitch)	DeSoto, TX, July 17-24
9 and under	Liberty, MO, July 9-16
10 and under	Broken Arrow, OK, July 9-16
11 and under	Sherwood, AR, July 22-29
12 and under	Collierville, TN, July 23-30
13 and under	Tulsa, OK, July 16-23
14 and under (54/80 foot)	Liberty, MO, July 23-30
14 and under (60/90 foot)	Peoria, AZ, July 9-16

MINORS DIVISION

8 and under (machine pitch)	Oklahoma City, July 9-16
9 and under	Liberty, MO, July 9-16
10 and under	Broken Arrow, OK, July 9-16
11 and under	O'Fallon, MO, July 16-23
12 and under	Collierville, TN, July 9-16
13 and under	Longmont, CO, July 9-16
14 and under (54/80 foot)	Liberty, MO, July 23-30
14 and under (60/90 foot)	Peoria, AZ, July 10-17

T-BALL USA ASSOCIATION, INC.

Office Address: 2499 Main St., Stratford, CT 06615. **Telephone:** (203) 381-1449. **FAX:** (203) 381-1440. **E-Mail Address:** teeballusa@aol.com. **Website:** www.teeballusa.org.
Year Founded: 1993.
President: Bing Broido. **Executive Vice President:** Lois Richards.

TRIPLE CROWN SPORTS

Mailing Address: 3930 Automation Way, Fort Collins, CO 80525. **Telephone:** (970) 223-6644. **FAX:** (970) 223-

3636. **Websites:** www.triplecrownsports.com.
Director, Baseball Operations: Sean Hardy.

Age Classifications, National Championships

10, 13, 15 World Series	Steamboat Springs, CO, July 19-24
8, 9, 12, 14 World Series	Steamboat Springs, CO, July 26-31
8, 9, 10, 11, 12, 14, 16, 18 Regionals	Myrtle Beach, SC, Aug. 1-5
13, 15 Regionals	Myrtle Beach, SC, Aug. 3-7
8, 9, 11, 13, 15, 16 Fall Nationals	Henderson, NV, Sept. 16-18
10, 12, 14, 18 Fall Nationals	Henderson, NV, Sept. 23-25
10,12,14,15,18 Fall Nationals	St. Augustine, FL. Oct. 14-16
8, 9,11,13, 16 Fall Nationals	St. Augustine, FL, Oct. 21-23

U.S. AMATEUR BASEBALL ASSOCIATION (USABA)
Mailing Address: 7101 Lake Ballinger Way, Edmonds, WA 98026. **Telephone/FAX:** (425) 776-7130. **E-Mail Address:** usaba@usaba.com. **Website:** www.usaba.com.
Year Founded: 1969.
Executive Director: Al Rutledge. **Secretary:** Roberta Engelhart.

Age Classifications, World Series

11 and under	Unavailable
12 and under	Unavailable
13 and under	Sonora, CA, July 16-23
14 and under	Pasco, WA, Aug. 1-7
15 and under	Hoquiam, WA, July 29-Aug. 6
16 and under	Richland, WA, Aug. 6-14
17 and under	Unavailable
18 and under	Kennewick, WA, Aug. 14-21

U.S. AMATEUR BASEBALL FEDERATION (USABF)
Mailing Address: 911 Stonegate Court, Chula Vista, CA 91913. **Telephone:** (619) 934-2551. **FAX:** (619) 271-6659. **E-Mail Address:** usabf@cox.net. **Website:** www.usabf.com.
Year Founded: 1997.
Senior Chief Executive Officer/President: Tim Halbig.

Age Classifications, World Series

10 and under	San Diego, July 25-31
11 and under	San Diego, July 25-31
12 and under	San Diego, July 25-31
13 and under	San Diego, July 25-31
14 and under	San Diego, Aug. 5-14
15 and under	San Diego, Aug. 5-14
16 and under	San Diego, Aug. 5-14
18 and under	San Diego, Aug. 5-14
Open	San Diego, July 27-31

UNITED STATES SPECIALTY SPORTS ASSOCIATION (USSSA)
Executive Vice President, Baseball: Rick Fortuna, 6324 N. Chatham Ave., No. 136, Kansas City, MO 64151. **Telephone:** (816) 587-4545. **FAX:** (816) 587-4549. **E-Mail Address:** linda@kcsports.org. **Website:** kcsports.org.
Year Founded: (1965)/Baseball (1996).

Age Classifications, National Championships

7 and under (coach pitch)	Sulphur, LA, July 11-17
7 and under (machine pitch)	Edmond, OK, July 11-17
8 and under (coach pitch)	Sulphur, LA, July 11-17
8 and under (machine pitch)	Edmond, OK, July 11-17
0 and under (machine pitch)	Thompson, GA, July 11-17
8 and under/West	Chino Hills, CA, July 26-31
8 and under/Central	Kansas City, MO, July 11-17
8 and under/East	Atlanta, July 12-17
9 and under	St. Louis, July 17-24

Age Classifications, Major National Championships

10 and under	Henderson, NV, July 17-24
11 and under	Statesboro, GA, July 25-31
11 and under	Omaha, July 25-31
12 and under	Statesboro, GA, July 25-31
12 and under	Omaha, July 25-31
13 and under	Statesboro, GA, July 25-31
13 and under	Omaha, July 25-31
14 and under	Statesboro, GA, July 25-31
14 and under	Omaha, July 25-31
15 and under/Freshman	Orlando/Kissimmee, FL, July 24-31
16 and under/Sophomore	Knoxville, TN, July 17-24

17 and under/Junior .... Edmond, OK, July 17-24
18 and under/Senior .... Orlando/Kissimmee, FL, July 17-24

Age Classifications, AAA National Championships

10 and under .... Southaven, MS, July 10-17
11 and under .... Overland Park, KS, July 10-17
12 and under .... Hutchinson, KS, July 10-17
13 and under .... Canton, MI, July 17-24
14 and under (54/80 foot) .... Tulsa, OK, July 10-17
14 and under (60/90 foot) .... Kingsport, TN, July 23-30
15 and under/Freshman .... Orlando/Kissimmee, FL, July 24-31
16 and under/Sophomore .... Knoxville, TN, July 17-24
17 and under/Junior .... Edmond, OK, July 17-24
18 and under/Senior .... Orlando/Kissimmee, FL, July 17-24

USA JUNIOR OLYMPIC BASEBALL CHAMPIONSHIP

Mailing Address: USA Baseball, 403 Blackwell St., Durham, NC 27701. **Telephone:** (919) 474-8721. **FAX:** (919) 474-8822. **E-Mail Address:** jeffsinger@usabaseball.com. **Website:** www.usabaseball.com.
Assistant Director, Baseball Operations: Jeff Singer.

Age Classifications, Championships

16 and under/West (72 teams) .... Peoria/Surprise, AZ, June 17-25
16 and under/East (72 teams) .... Jupiter, FL, June 17-25

WORLD WOOD BAT ASSOCIATION
(A Division of Perfect Game USA)

Mailing Address: 1203 Rockford Road SW, Cedar Rapids, IA 52404. **Telephone**: (319) 298-2923, (800) 447-9362. **FAX**: (319) 298-2924. **Website**: www.worldwoodbat.com.
League Commisioner: Jerry Ford. **League President:** Andy Ford. **National Director:** Greg Legg. **Scouting Director:** David Rawnsley.

Age Classifications, World Series

2008 graduates/15 and under .... Marietta, GA, June 29-July 4
2007 graduates/16 and under .... Marietta, GA, July 19-24
2006 graduates/17 and under .... Marietta, GA, July 5-10
2005 graduates/18 and under .... Marietta, GA, July 11-17
Fall Championship (underclassmen) .... Fort Myers, FL, Oct. 7-10
Fall Championship (high school) .... Jupiter, FL, Oct. 28-31

YOUTH BASEBALL TOURNAMENT CENTERS

BASEBALL USA

Mailing Address: 2626 W. Sam Houston Pkwy. N., Houston, TX 77043. **Telephone:** (713) 690-5055. **FAX:** (713) 690-9448. **E-Mail Address:** info@baseballusa.com. **Website:** www.baseballusa.com.
President: Charlie Maiorana. **Tournament Director:** Steve Olson. **Building Manager, Accounting:** Ken Ahrens. **Director, Marketing/Development:** Trip Couch. **League Baseball:** Chuck Deci. **Pro Shop Manager:** Don Lewis.
Activities: Camps, baseball/softball spring and fall leagues, instruction, indoor cage and field rentals, youth tournaments, World Series events, corporate days, summer college league, pro shop.

CALIFORNIA COMPETITIVE YOUTH BASEBALL

Mailing Address: P.O. Box 338, Placentia, CA 92870. **Telephone:** (714) 993-2838. **FAX:** (714) 961-6078. **E-Mail Address:** ccybnet@aol.com.
Tournament Director: Todd Rogers.
2005 Tournament (ages 10-16): Aug. 6-13 at Fullerton, CA.

COCOA EXPO SPORTS CENTER

Mailing Address: 500 Friday Rd., Cocoa, FL 32926. **Telephone:** (321) 639-3976. **FAX:** (321) 639-0598. **E-Mail Address:** athleticdirector@cocoaexpo.com. **Website:** www.cocoaexpo.com.
Executive Director: Jeff Biddle.
Activities: Spring training program, instructional camps, team training camps, youth tournaments.
2005 Events/Tournaments (ages 10-18): First Pitch Festival, June 3-5. Cocoa Expo Internationale, June 28-July 3. Cocoa Expo Summer Classic, Aug. 2-7. Labor Day Challenge, Sept. 2-5. Cocoa Expo Fall Classic, Oct. 14-16.

COOPERSTOWN BASEBALL WORLD

Mailing Address: P.O. Box 398, Bergenfield, NJ 07621. **Telephone:** (888) 229-8750. **FAX:** (888) 229-8720. **E-Mail Address:** cbw@cooperstownbaseballworld.com.
Complex Address: Cooperstown Baseball World, SUNY-Oneonta, Ravine Parkway, Oneonta, NY 13820.
President/Chairman: Eddie Einhorn. **Vice President:** Debra Sirianni. **Senior Coordinator, Special Events:** Jennifer Einhorn.
2005 Invitational Tournaments: 12 and under, 13 and under, 15 and under: June 25-July 1. 12 and under, 13 and under, 14 and under: July 2-8, July 9-15, July 16-22, July 23-29, July 30-Aug. 5. 12 and under, 13 and under: Aug. 6-Aug. 12.

COOPERSTOWN DREAMS PARK

Mailing Address: 101 E. Fisher St., 3rd Floor, Salisbury, NC 28144. **Telephone:** (704) 630-0050. **FAX:** (704) 630-

0737. **E-Mail Address:** info@cooperstowndreamspark.com. **Website:** www.cooperstowndreamspark.com.
   Complex Address: 4450 State Highway 28, Cooperstown, NY 13807.
   Chief Executive Officer: Lou Presutti. **Program Director:** Phil Kehr.
   2005 Invitational Tournaments (80 teams per week): 10 and under—June 18-24; 12 and under—June 25-July 1, July 2-8, July 9-15, July 16-22, July 23-29, July 30-Aug. 5, Aug. 6-12, Aug. 13-19, Aug. 20-26.
   2005 National American Tournament of Champions: 12 and under—Aug. 27-Sept. 2.

DISNEY'S WIDE WORLD OF SPORTS
   Mailing Address: P.O. Box 10000, Lake Buena Vista, FL 32830. **Telephone:** (407) 938-3802. **FAX:** (407) 938-3442.
   E-Mail Address: wdw.sports.baseball@disney.com. **Website:** www.disneyworldsports.com.
   Manager, Sports Events: Kevin Reynolds. **Sports Manager:** Brian Fling. **Tournament Director:** Al Schlazer. **Sales Manager, Baseball:** Rick Morris. **Sports Sales Coordinator, Baseball:** Kirk Stanley.
   2005 Events/Tournaments: Disney's Sun & Surf Baseball Bash (8 and under coach pitch, 10 and under, 11, 12, 14, 16, 18), May 27-30. **Disney's Salute to Baseball Festival** (8 and under coach pitch, 10 and under, 11, 12, 14, 16, 18), July 2-8. **Disney's Turn Back the Clock Weekend** (8 and under coach pitch, 10 and under, 11, 12, 14, 16, 18), Sept. 1-5. **Disney's Sunshine Showdown** (8 and under coach pitch, 10 and under, 11, 12, 14, 16, 18), Oct. 8-10. **Disney's New Year's Baseball Classic** (10 and under, 11, 12, 14, 16, 18), Dec. 28-Jan. 1, 2006.

KC SPORTS TOURNAMENTS
   Mailing Address: KC Sports, 6324 N. Chatham Ave., No. 136, Kansas City, MO 64151. **Telephone:** (816) 587-4545. **FAX:** (816) 587-4549. **E-Mail Addresses:** rick@kcsports.org, wally@kcsports.org, linda@kcsports.org. **Website:** www.kcsports.org.
   Activities: Youth tournaments (ages 6-18).
   Tournament Organizers: Rick Fortuna, Wally Fortuna, Linda Hottovy.
   U.S. AMATEUR BASEBALL FEDERATION (USABF)
   Mailing Address: 911 Stonegate Court, Chula Vista, CA 91913. **Telephone:** (619) 934-2551. **FAX:** (619) 271-6659.
   E-Mail Address: usabf@cox.net. **Website:** www.usabf.com.
   Senior Chief Executive Officer/President: Tim Halbig.

INSTRUCTIONAL SCHOOLS/PRIVATE CAMPS

ACADEMY OF PRO PLAYERS
   Mailing Address: 317 Midland Ave., Garfield, NJ 07026. **Telephone:** (973) 772-3355. **FAX:** (973) 772-4839. **Website:** www.academypro.com.
   Camp Director: Lar Gilligan.

ALDRETE BASEBALL ACADEMY
   Office Address: P.O. Box 4048, Monterey, CA 93942. **Telephone:** (831) 884-0400. **FAX:** (831) 884-0800. **E-Mail Address:** aldretebaseball@aol.com. **Website:** www.aldretebaseball.com.
   Camp Director: Rich Aldrete.

ALL-STAR BASEBALL ACADEMY
   Mailing Addresses: 650 Parkway Blvd., Broomall, PA 19008; 52 Penn Oaks Dr., West Chester, PA 19382. **Telephone:** (610) 355-2411, (610) 399-8050. **FAX:** (610) 355-2414. **E-Mail Address:** info@allstarbaseballacademy.com. **Website:** www.allstarbaseballacademy.com.
   Directors: Mike Manning, Chris Madonna.

THE BASEBALL ACADEMY
   Mailing Address: IMG Academies, 5500 34th St. W., Bradenton, FL 34210.
   Telephone: (941) 727-0303. **FAX:** (941) 727-2962. **E-Mail Address:** netsales@imgworld.com. **Website:** www.imgacademies.com.
   Camp Director, Baseball: Ken Bolek.

BUCKY DENT BASEBALL SCHOOL
   Mailing Address: 490 Dotterel Rd., Delray Beach, FL 33444. **Telephone:** (561) 265-0280. **FAX:** (561) 278-6679. **E-Mail Address:** staff@dentbaseball.com. **Website:** www.dentbaseball.com.
   Vice President: Larry Hoskin.

DOYLE BASEBALL SCHOOL
   Mailing Address: P.O. Box 9156, Winter Haven, FL 33883. **Telephone:** (863) 439-1000. **FAX:** (863) 439-7086. **E-Mail Address:** doyleinfo@doylebaseball.com. **Website:** www.doylebaseball.com.
   President: Denny Doyle. **Chief Executive Officer:**
Blake Doyle. **Director, Satellite School:** Rick Siebert.

FROZEN ROPES TRAINING CENTERS
   Mailing Address: 12 Elkay Dr., Chester, NY 10918. **Telephone:** (877) 846-5699. **FAX:** (845) 469-6742. **E-Mail Address:** specialevents@frozenropes.com. **Website:** www.frozenropes.com.
   Corporate Director: Tony Abbatine. **Camp Director:** Dan Hummel.

MARK CRESSE BASEBALL SCHOOL
   Mailing Address: 1188 N. Grove St., Suite C, Anaheim, CA 92806. **Telephone:** (714) 892-6145. **FAX:** (714) 892-1881. **E-Mail Address:** info@markcresse.com. **Website:** www.markcresse.com.
   Owner/Founder: Mark Cresse. **Executive Director:** Jeff Courvoisier.

MICKEY OWEN BASEBALL SCHOOL
   Mailing Address: P.O. Box 88, Miller, MO 65707. **Telephone:** (800) 999-8369, (417) 882-2799. **FAX:** (417) 889-6978. **E-Mail Address:** info@mickeyowen.com. **Website:** www.mickeyowen.com.
   President: Ken Rizzo. **Camp Director:** Bobby Doe. **Clinician:** Joe Fowler. **Advisor:** Howie Bedell.

NORTH CAROLINA BASEBALL ACADEMY
   Mailing Address: 1137 Pleasant Ridge Rd., Greensboro, NC 27409. **Telephone:** (336) 931-1118. **E-Mail Address:** ncba@att.net. **Website:** www.ncbaseball.com.
   Owner/Director: Scott Bankhead. **Assistant Director:** Matt Schirm. **Academy Director:** Tommy Jackson.

PENNSYLVANIA DIAMOND BUCKS BASEBALL CAMP
   Mailing Address: 2320 Whitetail Court, Hellertown, PA 18055. **Telephone:** (610) 838-1219, (610) 442-6998. **E-Mail Address:** jciganick@moravian.edu.
   Camp Director: Chuck Ciganick.

PERFECT GAME USA

Mailing Address: 1203 Rockford Rd. SW, Cedar Rapids, IA 52404. **Telephone:** (319) 298-2923. **FAX:** (319) 298-2924. **E-Mail Address:** staff@perfectgame.org. **Website:** www.perfectgame.org.

President, Director: Jerry Ford. **National Supervisor:** Andy Ford. **Director, Instruction:** Jim VanScoyac.

PROFESSIONAL BASEBALL INSTRUCTION

Mailing Address: 107 Pleasant Ave., Upper Saddle River, NJ 07458. **Telephone:** (800) 282-4638 (NY/NJ), (877) 448-2220 (rest of U.S.). **FAX:** (201) 760-8820. **E-Mail Address:** info@baseballclinics.com. **Website:** www.baseballclinics.com.

President: Doug Cinnella.

RIPKEN BASEBALL CAMPS

Mailing Address: 1427 Clarkview Rd., Suite 100, Baltimore, MD 21209. **Telephone:** (800) 486-0850. **E-Mail Address:** information@ripkenbaseball.com. **Website:** www.ripkenbaseball.com.

Director, Operations: Bill Ripken.

ROOKIES BASEBALL INSTRUCTION, LLC

Mailing Address: 376 Hollywood Ave., Suite 209, Fairfield, NJ 07004. **Telephone:** (973) 808-7222. **FAX:** (973) 882-9311. **E-Mail Address:** info@rookiesbaseball.com. **Website:** www.rookiesbaseball.com.

Founders: Pat Byrnes, Joe Huffman.

SAN DIEGO SCHOOL OF BASEBALL

Mailing Address: P.O. Box 1492, La Mesa, CA 91944. **Telephone:** (619) 491-4000. **FAX:** (619) 469-5572. **E-Mail Address:** sdsbb@aol.com. **Website:** www.sandiego schoolofbaseball.com.

Chief Executive Officer: Bob Cluck. **Vice Presidents:** Dave Smith, Alan Trammell, Reggie Waller. **Consultants:** Steve Finley, Luis Gonzalez.

SHO-ME BASEBALL CAMP

Mailing Address: P.O. Box 2270, Branson West, MO 65737. **Telephone:** (800) 993-2267, (417) 338-5838. **FAX:** (417) 338-2610. **E-Mail Address:** info@shome-baseball.com. **Website:** www.shomebaseball.com.

Camp Director: Christopher Schroeder. **Head of Instruction:** Dick Birmingham.

SOUTHWEST PROFESSIONAL BASEBALL SCHOOL

Mailing Address: 462 S. Gilbert Rd., Mesa, AZ 85204. **Telephone:** (888) 830-8031. **FAX:** (480) 830-7455. **E-Mail Address:** leonard@swpbs.com. **Website:** www.swpbs.com

Camp Directors: Leonard Garcia, Joe Maddon.

UTAH BASEBALL ACADEMY

Mailing Address: 389 West 10000 South, South Jordan, UT 84095. **Telephone:** (801) 561-1700. **FAX:** (801) 571-5965. **E-Mail Address:** info@utahbaseballacademy.com. **Website:** www.utahbaseballacademy.com.

COLLEGE CAMPS

Almost all of the elite college baseball programs have summer/holiday instructional camps. Please consult the college section, Pages 305-325 for listings.

SENIOR
LEAGUES

MEN'S SENIOR BASEBALL LEAGUE
(28 and Over, 38 and Over)

Mailing Address: One Huntington Quadrangle, Suite 3N07, Mellville, NY 11747. **Telephone:** (631) 753-6725. **FAX:** (631) 753-4031.

President: Steve Sigler. **Vice President:** Gary D'Ambrisi.

E-Mail Address: info@msblnational.com. **Website:** www.msblnational.com.

2005 World Series: Oct. 16-Nov. 5, Phoenix, AZ (28-plus, 38-plus, 48-plus, 58-plus, father/son divisions). **Fall Classic:** Nov. 3-12, Clearwater, FL (28-plus, 38-plus, 47-plus).

MEN'S ADULT BASEBALL LEAGUE
(18 and Over)

Mailing Address: One Huntington Quadrangle, Suite 3N07, Mellville, NY 11747. **Telephone:** (631) 753-6725. **FAX:** (631) 753-4031.

E-Mail Address: info@msblnational.com. **Website:** www.msblnational.com.

President: Steve Sigler. **Vice President:** Gary D'Ambrisi.

2005 World Series: Oct. 19-23, Phoenix, AZ (four divisions). **Fall Classic:** Nov. 4-7, Clearwater, FL.

NATIONAL ADULT BASEBALL ASSOCIATION

Mailing Address: 3609 S. Wadsworth Blvd., Suite 135, Lakewood, CO 80235. **Telephone:** (800) 621-6479. **FAX:** (303) 639-6605. **E-Mail:** nabanational@aol.com. **Website:** www.dugout.org.

President: Shane Fugita.

2005 Events. Memorial Day Tournaments: 18 and over, 30 and over, 40 and over, 50 and over—May 28-30, Las Vegas, NV; 18 and over, 28 and over, 38 and over, May 28-30, Atlantic City, NJ. **Hall of Fame Tournament:** 18 and over, 28 and over, July 1-4, Cooperstown, NY. **Mile High Classic:** 18 and over, 28 and over, 38 and over, July 2-4, Denver, CO. **NABA World Championship Series:** 18 and over, 28 and over, 38 and over, 48 and over, Oct. 4-15, Phoenix, AZ. **NABA Over 50 Baseball National Fun Tournament:** 48 and over, 58 and over, Oct. 23-29, Las Vegas, NV.

ROY HOBBS BASEBALL
Open (28-over), Veterans (38-over), Masters (48-over),

Legends (55-over), Classics (60-over), Women's open

Mailing Address: 2048 Akron Peninsula Rd., Akron, OH 44313. **Telephone:** (330) 923-3400. **FAX:** (330) 923-1967.

E-Mail Address: rhbb@royhobbs.com. **Website:** www.royhobbs.com.

President: Tom Giffen. **Vice President:** Ellen Giffen.

2005 World Series (all in Fort Myers, FL): Oct. 22-29—Open Division; Oct. 29-Nov. 5—Veterans Division; Nov. 5-9—Women's Division; Nov. 5-12—Masters Division; Nov. 12-16—Father-Son Division; Nov. 12-19—Legends Division, Classics Division, Seniors Division.

AMATEUR ATHLETIC UNION WOMEN'S BASEBALL
Open Division (16 and over)

Mailing Address: 2048 Akron Peninsula Rd., Akron, OH 44313. **Telephone:** (330) 923-3400. **FAX:** (330) 923-1967.

E-Mail Address: uswb@royhobbs.com. **Website:** www.uswb.org.

National Women's Baseball Chairman: Tom Giffen. **Vice Chairman:** Chris Hill. **Youth Chairman:** John Kovach.

Committee Members: Adriane Adler, Tina Beining, Tom Giffen, Chris Hill, Cherie Leatherwood, John Kovach.

2005 National Championship: Nov. 5-9 at Fort Myers, FL.

FANTASY CAMPS

LOS ANGELES DODGERS ADULT BASEBALL CAMP

Mailing Address: Dodgertown, P.O. Box 2887, Vero Beach, FL 32961. **Telephone:** (772) 569-4900, (800) 334-7529. **FAX:** (772) 299-6708. **E-Mail Address:** nancyg@ladodgers.com. **Website:** www.ladabc.com.

Camp Administrator: Nancy Gollnick.

RANDY HUNDLEY'S FANTASY BASEBALL CAMPS

Mailing Address: 128 S Northwest Hwy., Palatine, IL 60067. **Telephone/FAX:** (847) 991-9595. **E-Mail:** rhundley@home.com. **Website:** www.cubsfantasycamps.com.

Camp Coordinator: Barb Kozuh.

PHILLIES ADULT PHANTASY BASEBALL CAMP

Mailing Address: 750 E. Haverford Rd., Bryn Mawr, PA 19010. **Telephone:** (610) 520-3400. **E-Mail:** clandosky@esfcamps.com **Website:** www.philliesacademy.com.

Camp Coordinator: Kurt Funk.

AGENT
DIRECTORY

SERVICE
DIRECTORY

INDEX

AGENT DIRECTORY

Advance Athletic Representation
Michael Moline
P.O. Box 2578
Agoura Hills CA 91376
818-889-3933

Arias & Associates International
Mike Arias, Chip Oliver
6701 Center Drive West Suite 1400
Los Angeles, CA 90045
800-475-2570
fax 310-670-1231
aaiclients.com

Barry Axelrod, APC
2236 Encinitas Blvd. Suite A
Encinitas CA 92024
760-753-0088
fax 760-436-7399
baxy@msn.com

Baseball Management International
Jesse Frescas Jr.
P.O. Box 1286
La Quinta CA 92253
760-771-5109
fax 760-771-5143
jfrescas@dc.rr.com

Bouza, Klein and Goosenberg
Joseph Klein
David Goosenberg
950 S. Flower St. #100
Los Angeles CA 90015
213-488-0675
fax 213-488-1316
jklein@bkglaw.com

David S. Abramson Esq.
Verrill Dana, LLP
One Portland Square
Portland, Maine 04112-0586
207-774-4000
fax 207-774-7499
dabramson@sportslaw.com
dabramson@verilldana.com

DRM Brothers Sports Management Group
William S. Rose, Brian Doyle, Todd Middlebrooks, Esq.
31 Compass Lane
Ft. Lauderdale FL 33308
954-609-1505
fax 954-267-0336
ltdnyy@aol.com
drmsportsmgmt.com

Focus Management, Inc.
Frank A. Blandino
204 Towne Centre Drive
Hillsborough NJ 08844
908-217-3226
fax 908-281-0596
fablaw@earthlink.net

Garden City Sports Council
Glenn Kempa, CPA
David M. Namm, Esq. (Of Counsel)
P.O. Box 7477
Wantagh NY 11793
800-581-7177
fax 516-935-6295
glennkempa@aol.com

Golden Gate Sports Firm
Miles McAfee PhD
Marcus Leazer,
Miles E. McAfee, Esq
7677 Oakport Street
Suite 1050
Oakland CA 94621
510-567-1390
fax 510-567-1395
goldengatesports1.com
milesmcafee@aol.com

Iglesias Sports Management
Juan C. Iglesias
Fernando Iglesias, Esq.
2655 LeJeune Rd.
Ste. 532
Coral Gables FL 33134
305-446-9960
fax 305-446-9980

Jennings Taylor Wheeler & Haley, P.C.
David L. Taylor, Esq.
Charles T. Jennings, Esq.
Quinn A. Moore
11711 North Pennsylvania St.
Suite 250
Carmel IN 46032
317-575-7979
fax 317-575-7977
indbulls@sbcglobal.net

Jet Sports Management
B.B. Abbott
Hank Sargent
Corporate Headquarters:
3514 West Obispo Street
Tampa FL 33629
813-902-9511
fax 813-902-0900
www.jetssportsmanagement.com
bbabbott@jetsportsmanagement.com
sarge@jetsportsmanagement.com

KDN Sports Inc.
Don Nomura
Stuart Odori
900 Wilshire Blvd.
Suite 1114
Los Angeles CA 90017
213-488-6430
fax 213-488-6436

King & King LLC
Stanley O. King, Esq
231 South Broad Street
Woodbury NJ 08096
856-845-3001
fax 856-845-3079
stan@kingslaw.com

McDowell & Associates
Jim McDowell
Craig Wallenbrock
10061 Riverside Drive #870
Toluca Lake CA 91602
818-597-9948
fax 818-597-3212
jimmcdowell@sbcglobal.net

Mighty Warriors of Rhode Island
Jose Delarosa
2 Norwich Drive
Johnston RI 02919
800-436-3182
fax 401-383-7335
dkdelarosa@aol.com

Monaco Law Office
610 Newport Center Dr.
Suite 450
Newport Beach CA 92660
949-719-2669
fax 949-719-2607
randell@monacolawoffice.com

Northstar Sports Management
Barry Praver
105 Angelfish Lane
Jupiter FL 33477
561-775-6313
fax 561-775-7633
northstarsports@aol.com

Optimum Sports
Steve Pierce, Lisa Pierce
6539 East Dreyfus
Scottsdale AZ 85284
480-991-1830/480-221-6885
fax 480-991-2762
optimumsportsla@aol.com

Peter E. Greenberg & Associates
Peter E. Greenberg, Esq
Edward L. Greenberg, Esq
Chris Lible
200 Madison Avenue Suite 2225
New York NY 10016
212-334-6880
fax 212-334-6895

Platinum Sports and Enterainment Management LLC
Nick Brockmeyer
123 N. 5th St.
St. Charles MO 63301
636-946-0960
fax 636-946-0283
psemagents.com
nbrockmeyer@psemagents.com

Pro Agents, Inc.
David P. Pepe
Billy Martin, Jr.
90 Woodbridge Center Drive
Suite 901
Woodbridge NJ 07095
800-795-3454
fax 732-726-6688
pepeda@wilentz.com

Professional Sports Management Group
Alan Meersand, Adam Karon,
Miguel Rodriguez
2100 N. Sepulveda Blvd.
Suite 23
Manhattan Beach CA 90266
310-546-3400
fax 310-546-4046
meersand@aol.com

Pro Star Management Inc.
Joe Bick
1600 Scripps Center
312 Walnut Street
Cincinnati OH 45202
513-762-7676
fax 513-721-4628
prostar@fuse.net

Prospex Sports Management, Inc.
Edwin K. Setlik, Amber E. Simons
721 Enterprise Drive Suite 201
Oak Brook IL 60523
800-899-9159
fax 630-472-0562
ambersimons12@hotmail.com

ProSport Management, Inc.
James K. Krivacs
1831 N. Belcher Road, G-3
Clearwater FL 33765
727-791-7556
fax 727-791-1489
vkrivacs@tampabay.rr.com

Pro-Talent Inc.
3753 North Western Ave.
Chicago IL 60618
773-583-3411
fax 773-583-4277
protalentchicago@aol.com

RMG Sports Management
Robert Garber, Esq., Brent Laurvick,
Robert Lisanti
115 South Vine St. Suite 1E
Hinsdale IL 60521
630-986-2500
fax 630-986-0171

Reich, Katz and Landis Baseball Group
Thomas M. Reich, Adam Katz
Craig Landis
One Altoona Place
Pittsburgh PA 15228
412-391-2626
fax 412-391-2613

Reynolds Sports Management
Larry Reynolds
Patrick Murphy, Esq
Matt Kinzer
3880 Lemon Street Suite 200
Riverside CA 92501
951-784-6333
fax 951-784-1451
reynoldssports@aol.com

Riverfront Sports Management
Brian M. Goldberg
4300 Carew Tower
441 Vine Street
Cincinnati OH 45202
513-721-3111
fax 513-721-3077

Santa Barbara Management
Dan Wise
8700 E. Vista Bonita STE 204
Scottsdale AZ 85255
480-575-8100
fax 480-575-9214
santabarbaramanagement.com

SKA Sports and Entertainment
Steve Greenberg
Steve Goldstein
499 North Canon Drive 3rd Floor
Beverly Hills CA 90210
310-551-0381
fax 310-551-0386
skasports@aol.com

Sosnick Cobbe Sports
Paul Cobbe, Matt Sosnick
1601 North California Blvd.
Suite 150
Walnut Creek CA 94596
650-697-7070
fax 650-697-7004
mattsoz@aol.com
paulcobbe@msn.com

Sports Management Group Worldwide, Inc.
Dominick A. Pilli, President
10560 Main Street, Suite 308
Fairfax VA 22030
703-273-4640
fax 703-273-1733
sportsmgt.net
dpilli@bwwonline.com

The Show
Andrew J. Mongelluzzi, Esq
Kevin Christman
30750 US 19 N
Palm Harbor FL 34683
727-789-2019
thesho.net
andrew@thesho.net

The Sparta Group
Michael Nicotera
Gene Casaleggio
140 Littleton Rd Suite 100
Parsippany NJ 07054
973-335-0550
fax 973-335-2148
frontdesk@thespartagroup.com

Turner-Gary Sports, Inc.
Jim Turner, Rex Gary, Chris Wimmer
101 S. Hanley Road Sutie 1065
St. Louis MO 63105
314-863-6611
fax 314-863-9911

West Coast Sports Management LLC
Bill Shupper, Len Strelitz,
Jim Lentine
369 South Fairoaks
Pasadena CA 91105
626-844-1861
fax 626-844-1863
proballfirm.com
bills@proballfirm.com

SERVICE DIRECTORY

401K/RETIREMENT

A.G. Edwards
Gina Garner, AAMS Financial
Consultant
150 John F. Kennedy Pkwy
Short Hills NJ 07078
973-467-3404
fax 973-467-9743
gina.garner@agedwards.com

ACCESSORIES

The College House/CH Sports
1400 Chamberlayne Ave.
Richmond, VA 23222
800-888-7606
fax 804-643-4408
chsport.com
chouse601@aol.com

ACCOUNTING

Resnick Amsterdam Leshner P.C.
653 Skippack Pike Suite 300
Blue Bell PA 19422
215-628-8080
fax 215-628-4952
www.ral-cpa.com
sr@ral-cpa.com

APPAREL

All-Pro Sports
16919 Ventura Blvd.
Encino CA 91316
818-981-5264
fax 818-981-3020
allprosportshoes.com
allprosports@socal.rr.com

Minor Leagues, Major Dreams
P.O. Box 6098
Anaheim CA 92816
800-345-2421
fax 714-939-0655
minorleagues.com
mlmd@minorleagues.com

**My First Baseball Game
T-Shirt Kit**
14 Bond St. Suite 125
Great Neck NY 11021
516-466-0614
fax 516-466-0614
myfirstbaseballgamekit.com
bradley@sgsproducts.com

Ropes Baseball Apparel
P.O. Box 521
Southbury CT 06488
203-267-1823
fax 203-267-1825
ropesbaseball.com
dfraddy@ropesbaseball.com

ARTWORK

Low and Inside, LLC
2022 N. Ferry Street Suite 3100
Minneapolis MN 55303
763-797-0777
fax 763-767-5510
lowandinside.com
creative@lowandinside.com

BACKPACKS

Grand River Company
16580 Harbor BL. #C
Fountain Valley CA 92708
714-839-8788
fax 714-839-9889
grandriverco.com
sales@grandriverco.com

BACKSTOPS

L.A. Steelcraft Products, Inc.
1975 N. Lincoln Ave.
Pasadena CA 91109
800-371-2438
fax 626-798-1482
lasteelcraft.com
info@lasteelcraft.com

BANNERS/FLAGS

Olympus Flag and Banner
9000 West Heather Ave.
Milwaukee WI 53224
414-355-2010
fax 414-355-1931
olympus-flag.com
sales@olympus-flag.com

BASES

C&H Baseball, Inc.
2215 60th Drive East
Bradenton FL 34203
941-727-1533
fax 941-727-0588
chbaseball.com

L.A. Steelcraft Products, Inc.
1975 N. Lincoln Ave.
Pasadena CA 91109
800-371-2438
fax 626-798-1482
lasteelcraft.com
info@lasteelcraft.com

BASEBALLS

**Brett Brothers Sports
International**
East 9514 Montgomery St. Bldg #25
Spokane WA 99206
509-891-6435
fax 509-891-4156
brettbros.com
brettbats@aol.com

BASEBALL CARDS

Grandstand Cards
22647 Ventura Bl. #192
Woodland Hills CA 91364
818-992-5642
fax 818-348-9122
jscards1@pacbell.net

The Topps Company, Inc
1 Whitehall Street
New York NY 10004
212-376-0300
fax 212-376-0634
topps.com

BATS

Akadema
317 Midland Avenue
Garfield NJ 07026
973-772-7669
fax 973-772-4839
akademapro.com
akademapro@akademapro.com

Atlantic Bat Company
P.O. Box 2027
Hamilton, MA 01982
978-468-9947
fax 978-468-9947
AtlanticBat.com
michelle@atlanticbats.com

**Brett Brothers Sports
International**
East 9514 Montgomery St. Bldg #25
Spokane WA 99206
509-891-6435
fax 509-891-4156
brettbros.com
brettbats@aol.com

BWP
Rd. 1 Box 409A
Brookville, PA 15825
814-849-0089
fax 814-849-8584
bwpbats.com
sales@bwpbats.com

D-Bat
1400 Preston Rd. Suite 110
Plano TX 75093
888-398-3393
fax 972-398-1001
batsales@dbatinc.com

Hoosier Bat Co.
4511 Evans Ave.
Valparaiso IN 46383
800-228-3787
fax 219-465-0877
hoosierbat.com
baseball@netnitco.net

MetalWood Bats, LLC
P.O. Box 167-301F
Roosevelt Blvd.
Eleanor WV 25070
866-982-2287
304-586-3755
metalwoodbats.com
info@metalwoodbats.com

Old Hickory Bat Company
1735 Hwy 31 W
Goodlettsville TN 37072
866-PROBATS
phone/fax (615) 285-0588
oldhickorybats.com
mail@oldhickorybats.com

Phoenix Bat Company
7801 Corporate Blvd. Suite E
Plain City OH 43064
877-598-BATS
614-851-9448
phoenixbats.com

**The Original Maple Bat
Company**
202 Rochester Street
Ottawa, ON K1R 7M6
(613) 724-2421
(613) 725-3299
sambat.com
bats@sambat.com

Zinger -X Professional Bats
939 W. Center A
Lindon UT 84042
801-372-1117
fax 801-226-5448
zingerx.com

BATTING CAGES

C&H Baseball, Inc.
2215 60th Drive East
Bradenton FL 34203
941-727-1533
fax 941-727-0588
chbaseball.com

**Douglas Sport Nets and
Equipment**
3441 South 11th Avenue
Eldridge Iowa 52748
800-553-8907
fax 800-443-8907
douglas-sports.com
sales@douglas-sports.com

Lanier Batting Cages
206 S. Three Notch
Andalusia AL 36420
800-716-9189
fax 334-222-3323
alaweb.com/~battingcages
battingcages@alaweb.com

Miller Net Company Inc.
P.O. Box 18787
Memphis TN 38181
800-423-6603/901-744-3804
901-743-6580
millernets.com
miller@millernets.com

National Batting Cages, Inc.
P.O. Box 250
Forest Grove OR 97116-0250
800-547-8800
fax 503-357-3727
nationalbattingcages.com
sales@nationalbattingcages.com

Russell Batting Cages
2045 Hickory Road
Birmingham AL 35216
888-722-2243
russellbattingcages.com

Vantage Products International
7895 Stage Hills Blvd. Suite 105
Memphis TN 38133
800-244-4457
fax 800-321-5882
jwb@vpisports.com

BATTING GLOVES

Akadema
317 Midland Avenue
Garfield NJ 07026
973-772-7669
fax 973-772-4839
akademapro.com
akademapro@akademapro.com

All-Pro Sports
16919 Ventura Blvd.
Encino CA 91316
818-981-5264
fax 818-981-3020
allprosportshoes.com
allprosports@socal.rr.com

BUSINESS CONSULTING

**Resnick Amsterdam
Leshner P.C.**
653 Skippack Pike Suite 300
Blue Bell PA 19422
215-628-8080
fax 215-628-4952
www.ral-cpa.com
sr@ral-cpa.com

CLEATS/FOOTWEAR

All-Pro Sports
16919 Ventura Blvd.
Encino CA 91316
818-981-5264
fax 818-981-3020
allprosportshoes.com
allprosports@socal.rr.com

CAMPS/SCHOOLS

Mickey Owen Baseball School
P.O. Box 4504
Springfield MO 65808
417-882-2799
fax 417-889-6978
mickeyowen.com
ken@mickeyowen.com

Sho-Me Baseball Camp
P.O. Box 2270
Branson West MO 65737
800-993-2287
fax 417-338-2610
shomebaseball.com

The Baseball Academy
5500 34t St. West
Bradenton FL 34210
800-872-6425
fax 941-752-2531
imgacademies.com
netsales@imgworld.com

**Professional Baseball
Instruction**
107 Pleasant Avenue
Upper Saddle River NJ 07458
877-448-2220
fax 201-760-8820
baseballclinics.com
info@baseballclinics.com

CAPS/HEADWEAR

Capco Sportswear
5945 Shiloh Road
Alpharetta GA 30005
800-381-3331
fax 800-525-2613
kccaps.com
alans@kccaps.com

Minor Leagues, Major Dreams
P.O. Box 6098
Anaheim CA 92816
800-345-2421
fax 714-939-0655
minorleagues.com
mlmd@minorleagues.com

Ropes Baseball Apparel
P.O. Box 521
Southbury CT 06488
203-267-1823
fax 203-267-1825
ropesbaseball.com
dfraddy@ropesbaseball.com

COMPUTERS

**Retail Pro-BHD Information
Systems**
3205 Ramos Circle
Sacramento CA 95827
800-377-7776
fax 916-368-1411
bigharydog.com
karenp@bighairydog.com

CONCESSIONS

Houston's Peanuts
P.O. Box 160
Dublin NC 28332
800-334-8383
fax 910-862-8076
houstonspeanuts.com
peanutprocessors@carolina.net

CUP HOLDERS

Caddy Products
72-064 Adelaid Street
Thousand Palms, CA 92276
800-845-0591
760-343-7598
caddyproducts.com
sales@caddyproducts.com

See our ad on Page 9

ENTERTAINMENT

BirdZerk!
P.O. Box 36061
Louisville KY 40233
800-219-0899
502-458-4020
fax 502-458-0867
birdzerk.com
johnny@birdzerk.com

Gameops.com
P.O. Box 770440
Lakewood OH 44107
866-gameops
fax 978-418-0058
gameops.com
info@gameops.com

Street Characters Inc.
#2 2828 18st. NE
Calgary AB T2E 7B1
888-627-2687
fax 403-250-3846
mascots.com
sales@mascots.com

ZOOperstars!
P.O. Box 36061
Louisville KY 40233
800-219-0899
502-458-4020
fax 502-458-0867
zooperstars.com
johnny@zooperstars.com

FIELD CONSTRUCTION/ RENOVATION

Alpine Services, Inc.
5313 Brookeville Rd.
Gaithersburg MD 20882
301-963-8833
fax 301-963-7901
alpineservices.com
asi@alpineservices.com

Sports Turf Managers Association
805 New Hampshire Ste E
Lawrence KS 66044
800-323-3875
fax 800-366-2977
sportsturfmanager.com
stminfo@sportsturfmanager.com

FIELD COVERS/TARPS

C&H Baseball, Inc.
2215 60th Drive East
Bradenton FL 34203
941-727-1533
fax 941-727-0588
chbaseball.com

Covermaster Inc.
100 Westmore Dr. 11-D
Rexdale ON CA M9V5C3
800-387-5808
fax 416-742-6837
covermaster.com
info@covermaster.com

Colorado Lining
28043 FM 1485 East
New Caney, TX 77357
281-689-8000
fax 281-689-8006
www.coloradolining.com

See our ad on Page 25

Douglas Sport Nets and Equipment
3441 South 11th Avenue
Eldridge Iowa 52748
800-553-8907
fax 800-443-8907
douglas-sports.com
sales@douglas-sports.com

Vantage Products International
7895 Stage Hills Blvd. Suite 105
Memphis TN 38133
800-244-4457
fax 800-321-5882
jwb@vpisports.com

FIELD WALL PADDING

C&H Baseball, Inc.
2215 60th Drive East
Bradenton FL 34203
941-727-1533
fax 941-727-0588
chbaseball.com

Covermaster Inc.
100 Westmore Dr. 11-D
Rexdale ON CA M9V5C3
800-387-5808
fax 416-742-6837
covermaster.com
info@covermaster.com

Promats, Inc.
P.O. Box 508
Fort Collins CO 80522
800-678-6287
fax 970-482-7740
promats.com
info@promats.com

FINANCIAL SERVICES

A.G. Edwards
Gina Garner, AAMS Financial
Consultant
150 John F. Kennedy Pkwy
Short Hills NJ 07078
973-467-3404
fax 973-467-9743
gina.garner@agedwards.com

FIREWORKS

Bay Fireworks, Inc.
110 Route 110 Suite 102
Huntington Station, NY 11746
631-549-0900 ext. 105
fax 631-549-3151
bayfireworks.com

Fireworks Productions Inc.
P.O. Box 294
Maryland Line MD 21105
800-765-2264
fax 410-357-0187
fireworksproductionsinc.com
larry@fireworksproductions.com

S Vitale Pyrotechnic Industries Inc. Pyrotecnico
P.O. Box 149
302 Wilson Road
New Castle PA 16103
800-854-4705
fax 724-652-1288
pyrotecnico.com
svitale@pyrotecnico.com

Zambelli Fireworks International
P.O. Box 1463
New Castle PA 16103
800-245-0397
fax 724-658-8318
zambellifireworks.com
zambelli@zambellifireworks.com

FOOD SERVICE

Concession Solutions Inc.
16022-26th Ave. NE
Shoreline WA 98155
206-440-9203
206-440-9213
concessionsolutions.com
theresa@concessionsolutions.com

GLOVES

Akadema
317 Midland Avenue
Garfield NJ 07026
973-772-7669
fax 973-772-4839
akademapro.com
akademapro@akademapro.com

All-Pro Sports
16919 Ventura Blvd.
Encino CA 91316
818-981-5264
fax 818-981-3020
allprosportshoes.com
allprosports@socal.rr.com

HUMAN RESOURCE SERVICES

WorkInSports.com
7335 E. Acoma Drive Suite 200
Scottsdale AZ 85260
480-905-7221
fax 480-905-7231
workinsports.com
info@workinsports.com

INFLATABLES

Inflatable Images
2880 Interstate Parkway
Brunswick OH 44212
800-783-5717 ext 134
fax 330-273-3212
inflatableimages.com
m.yates@scherba.com

Rainbow Symphony, Inc.
6860 Canby Ave. #120
Reseda CA 91335
818-708-8400/800-821-5122
fax 818-708-8470
rainbowsymphony.com
mark@rainbowsymphony.com

INSURANCE

K & K Insurance Group, Inc.
P.O. Box 2338
Fort Wayne IN 46801
800-441-3994
fax 260-459-5120
kandkinsurance.com

See our ad after Page 224

Gagliardi Insurance Services, Inc.
284 Digital Drive
Morgan Hill CA 95037
408-414-8100
fax 408-414-8199
insuranceforsports.com
ngagliardi@insuranceforsports.com

See our ad on Page 5

INSURANCE, LIFE

A.G. Edwards
Gina Garner, AAMS Financial
Consultant
150 John F. Kennedy Pkwy
Short Hills NJ 07078
973-467-3404
fax 973-467-9743
gina.garner@agedwards.com

GRAPHIC DESIGN

Low and Inside, LLC
2022 N. Ferry Street Suite 3100
Minneapolis MN 55303
763-797-0777
fax 763-767-5510
lowandinside.com
creative@lowandinside.com

LIGHTING

Musco Lighting
100 1st Avenue West
Oskaloosa IA 52577
800-825-6020
fax 641-673-4740
musco.com
rick.sneed@musco.com

MARKETING SOFTWARE

eBrandedSolutions/SponsorshipPRO +
1954 Airport Road Ste 207
Atlanta GA 30341
678-720-0700
fax 678-720-0704
sponsorshippro.com
sales@sponsorshippro.com

MASCOTS

Olympus Flag and Banner
9000 West Heather Ave.
Milwaukee WI 53224
414-355-2010
fax 414-355-1931
olympus-flag.com
sales@olympus-flag.com

Scollon Productions, Inc.
P.O. Box 486
White Rock SC 29177
803-345-3922 x48
fax 803-345-9313
scollon.com
rick@scollon.com

MUSIC/SOUND EFFECTS

Action Sports Media-Game Opps Commander
4380 SW Macadam Suite 540
Portland OR 97239
800-346-8037/503-797-9746
fax: 503-736-5066
gameopscommander.com
john.jackson@actionsportsmedia.com

Sound and Video Creations
2820 Azalea Place
Nashville, TN 37204
clickeffects.com
fran2nz@aol.com

See our ad on Page 17

NETTING/POSTS

C&H Baseball, Inc.
2215 60th Drive East
Bradenton FL 34203
941-727-1533
fax 941-727-0588
chbaseball.com

Douglas Sport Nets and Equipment
3441 South 11th Avenue
Eldridge Iowa 52748
800-553-8907
fax 800-443-8907
douglas-sports.com
sales@douglas-sports.com

Vantage Products International
7895 Stage Hills Blvd. Suite 105
Memphis TN 38133
800-244-4457
fax 800-321-5882
jwb@vpisports.com

PITCHING MACHINES

BATA
2910 Norman Strasse Unit 102
San Marcos CA 92069
760-597-9501
fax 760-597-9502
batabaseball.com
batabaseball@sbcglobal.net

C&H Baseball, Inc.
2215 60th Drive East
Bradenton FL 34203
941-727-1533
fax 941-727-0588
chbaseball.com

Master Pitching Machines
4200 Northeast Birmingham Road
Kansas City MO 64117
800-878-8228
masterpitch.com

Vantage Products International
7895 Stage Hills Blvd. Suite 105
Memphis TN 38133
800-244-4457
fax 800-321-5882
jwb@vpisports.com

PITCHING TOES

All-Pro Sports
16919 Ventura Blvd.
Encino CA 91316
818-981-5264
fax 818-981-3020
allprosportshoes.com
allprosports@socal.rr.com

PRINTING

Low and Inside, LLC
2022 N. Ferry Street Suite 3100
Minneapolis MN 55303
763-797-0777
fax 763-767-5510
lowandinside.com
creative@lowandinside.com

GameCard Enterprises
1409 East Blvd.
Charlotte NC 28203
704-370-7755
rostercard.com
info@rostercard.com

MultiAd Sports
1720 W. Detweiller Dr.
Peoria IL 61615
800-348-6485
fax 309-682-8378
multiad.com/sports
bjeske@multiad.com

Ticketcraft
1390 Jerusalem Ave.
Merrick NY 11566
800-645-4944
fax 516-538-4860
ticketcraft.com
tickets@ticketcraft.com

PLAYING FIELD PRODUCTS

C&H Baseball, Inc.
2215 60th Drive East
Bradenton FL 34203
941-727-1533
fax 941-727-0588
chbaseball.com

Diamond Pro TXI
1341 West Mockingbird Lane
Dallas TX 75247
800-228-2987
fax 800-640-6735
diamondpro.com

L.A. Steelcraft Products, Inc.
1975 N. Lincoln Ave.
Pasadena CA 91109
800-371-2438
fax 626-798-1482
lasteelcraft.com
info@lasteelcraft.com

Midwest Athletic Surfaces
1125 West State St.
Marshfield WI 54449
715-384-7027
fax 715-384-7027
webpages.charter.net/warningtrack
warningtrack@charter.net

Stabilizer Solutions, Inc.
205 S. 28th Street
Phoenix AZ 85134
604-225-5900
fax 602-225-5902
stabilizersolutions.com
info@stabilizersolutions.com

Promats, Inc.
P.O. Box 508
Fort Collins CO 80522
800-678-6287
fax 970-482-7740
promats.com
info@promats.com

PROMOTIONAL ITEMS

Action Sports America
5263 Placentia Pkwy
Las Vegas NV 89118
610-832-7500
fax 781-846-0262
actionsportsamerica.com
fun@giantjersey.com

Barton Enterprises/Classic Balloons
1416 Upfield Drive
Carrollton TX 75006
800-338-4606
fax 972-242-7333
classic-balloon.com
robinp@classic-balloon.com

Funkirides
2808 McKinney Ave. Ste 313
Dallas TX 75204
214-707-8993
fax 866-547-7516
funkirides.com
kegan@fivetool.net

Gameops.com
P.O. Box 770440
Lakewood OH 44107
866-gameops
fax 978-418-0058
gameops.com
info@gameops.com

Grand River Company
16580 Harbor BL. #C
Fountain Valley CA 92708
714-839-8788
fax 714-839-9889
grandriverco.com
sales@grandriverco.com

My First Baseball Game T-Shirt Kit
14 Bond St. Suite 125
Great Neck NY 11021
516-466-0614
fax 516-466-0614
myfirstbaseballgamekit.com
bradley@sgsproducts.com

O2-Cool Water Misting Fans
1415 N. Dayton St.
Chicago IL 60622
312-951-6700
fax 312-951-6707
o2-cool.com
sales@o2cool.com

Phoenix Sports Inc.
301 Boren Ave. North
Seattle WA 98109
800-776-9229
fax 800-776-4422
phoesports@aol.com

Rainbow Symphony, Inc.
6860 Canby Ave. #120
Reseda CA 91335
818-708-8400/800-821-5122
fax 818-708-8470
rainbowsymphony.com
mark@rainbowsymphony.com

Rico Industries Inc./Tag Express
1712 South Michigan Ave.
Chicago IL 60616
800-423-5856
fax 312-427-0190
ricoinc.com
jimz@ricoinc.com

Street Characters Inc.
#2 2828 18st. NE
Calgary AB T2E 7B1
888-627-2687
fax 403-250-3846
mascots.com
sales@mascots.com

PENNANTS, FOAM FINGERS & NOVELTY

Rico Industries Inc./Tag Express
1712 South Michigan Ave.
Chicago IL 60616
800-423-5856
fax 312-427-0190
ricoinc.com
jimz@ricoinc.com

POINT-OF-SALE SYSTEMS

Retail Pro-BHD Information Systems
3205 Ramos Circle
Sacramento CA 95827
800-377-7776
fax 916-368-1411
bigharydog.com
karenp@bighairydog.com

PUBLICATIONS

GameCard Enterprises
1409 East Blvd.
Charlotte NC 28203
704-370-7755
rostercard.com
info@rostercard.com

RADAR EQUIPMENT

Applied Concepts/ Stalker Radar
2609 Technology Drive
Plano TX 75074-7467
800-Stalker
Stalkerradar.com
See our ad on Page 21

SCOREBOARDS

All American Scoreboards
401 So. Main St.
Pardeeville WI 53954
800-356-8146
fax 608-429-9216
allamericanscoreboards.com
scoreboards@everbrite.com

Eversan Inc.
34 Main Street
Whitesboro NY 13492
800-383-6060
fax 315-736-4058
eversan.com
sales@eversan.com

SEATING

L.A. Steelcraft Products, Inc.
1975 N. Lincoln Ave.
Pasadena CA 91109
800-371-2438
fax 626-798-1482
lasteelcraft.com
info@lasteelcraft.com

Southern Bleacher Company
P.O. Box ONE
Graham TX 76450
800-433-0912
fax 940-549-1365
southernbleacher.com
info@southernbleacher.com

Sturdisteel Company
PO Box 2655
Waco, TX 76702
800-433-3116
254-666-4472
www.sturdisteel.com
rgroppe@sturdisteel.com
See our ad on Page 19

Vantage Products International
7895 Stage Hills Blvd. Suite 105
Memphis TN 38133
800-244-4457
fax 800-321-5882
jwb@vpisports.com

SOFTWARE

E Solutions
400 North Tampa Street 16th Floor
Tampa, FL 33602
888-840-4999
813-342-2123
esnet.com
mmorizio@esnet.com

See our
ad after
Page 32

Retail Pro-BHD Information Systems
3205 Ramos Circle
Sacramento CA 95827
800-377-7776
fax 916-368-1411
bigharydog.com
karenp@bighairydog.com

SOUVENIRS

Grand River Company
16580 Harbor BL. #C
Fountain Valley CA 92708
714-839-8788
fax 714-839-9889
grandriverco.com
sales@grandriverco.com

SPORTING GOODS

All-Pro Sports
16919 Ventura Blvd.
Encino CA 91316
818-981-5264
fax 818-981-3020
allprosportsshoes.com
allprosports@socal.rr.com

Frank's Sport Shop
430 East Tremont Avenue
New York, NY 10457
718-299-9628
718-583-1652
frankssportshop.com

See our
ad after
Page 128

JugheadSports
107 Pleasant Avenue
Upper Saddle River NJ 07458
877-448-2220
fax 201-760-8820
jugheadsports.com
info@baseballclinics.com

SPORTS MEDICINE

Cho-Pat
P.O. Box 293
Hainesport NJ 08036
800-221-1601
fax 609-261-7593
cho-pat.com
sales@cho-pat.com

STADIUM ARCHITECTS

360 Architecture
1801 McGee St. Suite 200
Kansas City MO 64108
816-472-3360
fax 816-531-3388
360architects.com
clamberth@360architects.com

Jack L. Gordon Architects
345 Seventh Avenue
New York NY 10001
212-279-0550
fax 212-279-4015
jlgordon.com
jlga@jlgordon.com

STADIUM DISPLAY SYSTEMS

BARCO
1651 N. 1000 West
Logan UT 84321
435-753-2224
barcosports.com

See our ad
on Inside
Back Cover

STATISTICAL SERVICES

Baseball Info Solutions
528 North New Street
Bethlehem PA 18018
610-814-0107
fax 610-814-0166
baseballinfosolutions.com
info@baseballinfosolutions.com

More Than ERA
11038 Hildreth Ct.
Camarillo CA 93012
805-491-3379
fax 805-491-2229
morethanera.com

TICKETS

Etix.com
5171 Glenwood Ave.
Raleigh NC 27612
919-782-5010
etix.com
steve@etix.com
ben@etix.com

Ticketcraft
1390 Jerusalem Ave.
Merrick NY 11566
800-645-4944
fax 516-538-4860
ticketcraft.com
tickets@ticketcraft.com

TICKETING SOFTWARE

ShoWare by VisionOne
6781 N. Palm Suite 120
Fresno CA 93704
559-432-8000
fax 559-431-5082
showare.com
showare@v-1.com

TRAVEL

Broach Baseball Tours
5821 Fairview Rd. Suite 118
Charlotte NC 28209
Baseballtoursusa.com
Broachtour@aol.com

TRAVEL, TEAM

World Sports International Sports Tours
P.O. Box 661624
Los Angeles CA 90495
800-496-8687
fax 310-314-8872
worldsport-tours.com

UNIFORMS

A.I.S.
2202 Anderson St.
Vernon CA 90058
800-666-2733
fax 323-582-2831
aisuniforms.com
info@aisuniforms.com

WASTE RECEPTACLES

Witt Industries
4454 Steel Place
Cincinnati OH 45209
800-543-7417
stadiumseries.com
products@witt.com

WINDSCREENS

C&H Baseball, Inc.
2215 60th Drive East
Bradenton FL 34203
941-727-1533
fax 941-727-0588
chbaseball.com

Douglas Sport Nets and Equipment
3441 South 11th Avenue
Eldridge Iowa 52748
800-553-8907
fax 800-443-8907
douglas-sports.com
sales@douglas-sports.com

OT Sports
172 Boone Street
Burlington NC 27215
800-988-6285 x208
fax 336-227-3765
otsports.com
sales@otsports.com

2005 DIRECTORY
INDEX

MAJOR LEAGUE TEAMS
AMERICAN LEAGUE

Page	Club	Phone	FAX
36	Anaheim Angels	714-940-2000	714-940-2001
42	Baltimore Orioles	410-685-9800	410-547-6272
44	Boston Red Sox	617-267-9440	617-375-0944
48	Chicago White Sox	312-674-1000	312-674-5116
52	Cleveland Indians	216-420-4200	216-420-4396
56	Detroit Tigers	313-471-2000	313-471-2138
62	Kansas City Royals	816-921-8000	816-921-1366
68	Minnesota Twins	612-375-1366	612-375-7480
72	New York Yankees	718-293-4300	718-293-8431
74	Oakland Athletics	510-638-4900	510-562-1633
86	Seattle Mariners	206-346-4000	206-346-4400
88	Tampa Bay Devil Rays	727-825-3137	727-825-3111
90	Texas Rangers	817-273-5222	817-273-5110
92	Toronto Blue Jays	416-341-1000	416-341-1250

NATIONAL LEAGUE

Page	Club	Phone	FAX
38	Arizona Diamondbacks	602-462-6500	602-462-6599
40	Atlanta Braves	404-522-7630	404-614-1392
46	Chicago Cubs	773-404-2827	773-404-4129
50	Cincinnati Reds	513-765-7000	513-765-7342
54	Colorado Rockies	303-292-0200	303-312-2116
58	Florida Marlins	305-626-7400	305-626-7428
60	Houston Astros	713-259-8000	713-259-8981
64	Los Angeles Dodgers	323-224-1500	323-224-1269
66	Milwaukee Brewers	414-902-4400	414-902-4053
74	New York Mets	718-507-6387	718-507-6395
76	Philadelphia Phillies	215-463-6000	215-389-3050
78	Pittsburgh Pirates	412-323-5000	412-325-4412
80	St. Louis Cardinals	314-421-3060	314-425-0640
82	San Diego Padres	619-795-5000	619-795-5035
84	San Francisco Giants	415-972-2000	415-947-2800
94	Washington Nationals	514-253-3434	514-253-8282

MINOR LEAGUE TEAMS

Page	Club	League	Phone	FAX
203	Aberdeen	NY-P	410-297-9292	410-297-6653
153	Akron	Eastern	330-253-5151	330-253-3300
144	Albuquerque	PCL	505-924-2255	505-242-8899
153	Altoona	Eastern	814-943-5400	814-943-9132
166	Arkansas	Texas	501-664-1555	501-664-1834
195	Asheville	SAL	828-258-0428	828-258-0320
203	Auburn	NY-P	315-255-2489	315-255-2675
195	Augusta	SAL	706-736-7889	706-736-1122
171	Bakersfield	Cal	661-716-4487	661-322-8199
203	Batavia	NY-P	585-343-5454	585-343-5620
188	Beloit	Midwest	608-362-2272	608-362-0418
220	Billings	Pioneer	406-252-1241	406-252-2968
154	Binghamton	Eastern	607-723-6387	607-723-7779
160	Birmingham	Southern	205-988-3200	205-988-9698
215	Bluefield	Appy	276-326-1326	276-326-1318
210	Boise	Northwest	208-322-5000	208-322-6846
154	Bowie	Eastern	301-805-6000	301-464-4911
182	Brevard County	FSL	321-633-9200	321-633-9210
215	Bristol	Appy	540-645-7275	540-669-7686
204	Brooklyn	NY-P	718-449-8497	718-449-6368
136	Buffalo	IL	716-846-2000	716-852-6530
188	Burlington, IA	Midwest	319-754-5705	319-754-5882
215	Burlington, NC	Appy	336-222-0223	336-226-2498
195	Capital City	SAL	803-256-4110	803-256-4338
160	Carolina	Southern	919-269-2287	919-269-4910
220	Casper	Pioneer	307-232-1111	307-265-7867
188	Cedar Rapids	Midwest	319-363-3887	319-363-5631

195	Charleston	SAL	843-723-7241	843-723-2641
136	Charlotte	IL	704-357-8071	704-329-2155
160	Chattanooga	Southern	423-267-2208	423-267-4258
182	Clearwater	FSL	727-712-4300	727-712-4498
189	Clinton	Midwest	563-242-0727	563-242-1433
144	Colorado Springs	PCL	719-597-1449	719-597-2491
196	Columbus, GA	SAL	706-571-8866	706-571-9984
137	Columbus, OH	IL	614-462-5250	614-462-3271
166	Corpus Christi	Texas	361-561-4665	361-561-4666
216	Danville	Appy	434-797-3792	434-797-3799
189	Dayton	Midwest	937-228-2287	937-228-2284
182	Daytona	FSL	386-257-3172	386-257-3382
196	Delmarva	SAL	410-219-3112	410-219-9164
183	Dunedin	FSL	727-733-9302	727-734-7661
137	Durham	IL	919-687-6500	919-687-6560
216	Elizabethton	Appy	423-547-6440	423-547-6442
155	Erie	Eastern	814-456-1300	814-456-7520
210	Eugene	Northwest	541-342-5367	541-342-6089
210	Everett	Northwest	425-258-3673	425-258-3675
183	Fort Myers	FSL	239-768-4210	239-768-4211
190	Fort Wayne	Midwest	260-482-6400	260-471-4678
177	Frederick	Carolina	301-662-0013	301-662-0018
145	Fresno	PCL	559-320-4487	559-264-0795
166	Frisco	Texas	972-731-9200	972-731-7455
220	Great Falls	Pioneer	406-452-5311	406-454-0811
197	Greensboro	SAL	336-268-2255	336-273-7350
217	Greeneville	Appy	423-638-0411	423-638-9450
197	Greenville	SAL	864-424-1510	—
197	Hagerstown	SAL	301-791-6266	301-791-6066
155	Harrisburg	Eastern	717-231-4444	717-231-4445
221	Helena	Pioneer	406-495-0500	406-495-0900
198	Hickory	SAL	828-322-3000	828-322-6137
171	High Desert	Cal	760-246-6287	760-246-3197
204	Hudson Valley	NY-P	845-838-0094	845-838-0014
161	Huntsville	Southern	256-882-2562	256-880-0801
221	Idaho Falls	Pioneer	208-522-8363	208-522-9858
138	Indianapolis	IL	317-269-3542	317-269-3541
171	Inland Empire	Cal	909-888-9922	909-888-5251
145	Iowa	PCL	515-243-6111	515-243-5152
161	Jacksonville	Southern	904-358-2846	904-358-2845
205	Jamestown	NY-P	716-664-0915	716-664-4175
217	Johnson City	Appy	423-461-4866	423-461-4864
184	Jupiter	FSL	561-775-1818	561-691-6886
190	Kane County	Midwest	630-232-8811	630-232-8815
198	Kannapolis	SAL	704-932-3267	704-938-7040
217	Kingsport	Appy	423-378-3744	423-392-8538
177	Kinston	Carolina	252-527-9111	252-527-0498
199	Lake County	SAL	440-975-8085	440-975-8958
172	Lake Elsinore	Cal	951-245-4487	951-245-0305
184	Lakeland	FSL	863-686-8075	863-688-9589
199	Lakewood	SAL	732-901-7000	732-901-3967
172	Lancaster	Cal	661-726-5400	661-726-5406
191	Lansing	Midwest	517-485-4500	517-485-4518
146	Las Vegas	PCL	702-386-7200	702-386-7214
200	Lexington	SAL	859-252-0747	859-252-0747
138	Louisville	IL	502-212-2287	502-515-2255
205	Lowell	NY-P	978-459-2255	978-459-1674
177	Lynchburg	Carolina	434-528-1144	434-846-0768
205	Mahoning Valley	NY-P	330-505-0000	330-505-9696
146	Memphis	PCL	901-721-6000	901-842-1222
167	Midland	Texas	432-520-2255	432-520-8326
162	Mississippi	Southern	601-932-8788	601-936-3567
222	Missoula	Pioneer	406-543-3300	406-543-9463
162	Mobile	Southern	251-479-2327	251-476-1147
173	Modesto	Cal	209-572-4487	209-572-4490
163	Montgomery	Southern	334-323-2255	334-323-2225
178	Myrtle Beach	Carolina	843-918-6002	843-918-6001
147	Nashville	PCL	615-242-4371	615-256-5684
155	New Britain	Eastern	860-224-8383	860-225-6267
156	New Hampshire	Eastern	603-641-2005	603-641-2055
206	New Jersey	NY-P	973-579-7500	973-579-7502
147	New Orleans	PCL	504-734-5155	504-734-5118
139	Norfolk	IL	757-622-2222	757-624-9090

156	Norwich	Eastern	860-887-7962	860-886-5996
222	Ogden	Pioneer	801-393-2400	801-393-2473
148	Oklahoma	PCL	405-218-1000	405-218-1001
148	Omaha	PCL	402-734-2550	402-734-7166
206	Oneonta	NY-P	607-432-6326	607-432-1965
222	Orem	Pioneer	801-377-2255	801-377-2345
139	Ottawa	IL	613-747-5969	613-747-0003
185	Palm Beach	FSL	561-775-1818	561-691-6886
140	Pawtucket	IL	401-724-7300	401-724-2140
191	Peoria	Midwest	309-680-4000	309-680-4080
157	Portland, ME	Eastern	207-874-9300	207-780-0317
149	Portland, OR	PCL	503-553-5400	503-553-5405
178	Potomac	Carolina	703-590-2311	703-590-5716
218	Princeton	Appy	304-487-2000	304-487-8762
218	Pulaski	Appy	540-980-1070	540-980-1850
191	Quad Cities	Midwest	563-324-3000	563-324-3109
173	Rancho Cucamonga	Cal	909-481-5000	909-481-5005
157	Reading	Eastern	610-375-8469	610-373-5868
140	Richmond	IL	804-359-4444	804-359-0731
141	Rochester	IL	585-454-1001	585-454-1056
201	Rome	SAL	706-368-9388	706-368-6525
149	Round Rock	PCL	512-255-2255	512-255-1558
150	Sacramento	PCL	916-376-4700	916-376-4710
185	St. Lucie	FSL	772-871-2100	772-878-9802
179	Salem	Carolina	540-389-3333	540-389-9710
211	Salem-Keizer	Northwest	503-390-2225	503-390-2227
150	Salt Lake	PCL	801-325-2273	801-485-6818
167	San Antonio	Texas	210-675-7275	210-670-0001
174	San Jose	Cal	408-297-1435	408-297-1453
185	Sarasota	FSL	941-365-4460	941-365-4217
201	Savannah	SAL	912-351-9150	912-352-9722
141	Scranton/Wilkes-Barre	IL	570-969-2255	570-963-6564
192	South Bend	Midwest	574-235-9988	574-235-9950
192	Southwest Michigan	Midwest	269-660-2287	269-660-2288
211	Spokane	Northwest	509-535-2922	509-534-5368
168	Springfield	Texas	417-863-2143	417-863-0388
207	Staten Island	NY-P	718-720-9265	718-273-5763
174	Stockton	Cal	209-644-1900	209-644-1931
142	Syracuse	IL	315-474-7833	315-474-2658
151	Tacoma	PCL	253-752-7707	253-752-7135
186	Tampa	FSL	813-875-7753	813-673-3174
163	Tennessee	Southern	865-286-2300	865-523-9913
142	Toledo	IL	419-725-4367	419-725-4368
158	Trenton	Eastern	609-394-3300	609-394-9666
207	Tri-City, NY	NY-P	518-629-2287	518-629-2299
212	Tri-City, WA	Northwest	509-544-8789	509-547-9570
151	Tucson	PCL	520-434-1021	520-889-9477
168	Tulsa	Texas	918-744-5998	918-747-3267
212	Vancouver	Northwest	604-872-5232	604-872-1714
208	Vermont	NY-P	802-655-4200	802-655-5660
186	Vero Beach	FSL	772-569-4900	772-567-0819
175	Visalia	Cal	559-625-0480	559-739-7732
193	West Michigan	Midwest	616-784-4131	616-784-4911
164	West Tenn	Southern	731-988-5299	731-988-5246
201	West Virginia	SAL	304-344-2287	304-344-0083
169	Wichita	Texas	316-267-3372	316-267-3382
208	Williamsport	NY-P	570-326-3389	570-326-3494
179	Wilmington	Carolina	302-888-2015	302-888-2032
180	Winston-Salem	Carolina	336-759-2233	336-759-2042
193	Wisconsin	Midwest	920-733-4152	920-733-8032
212	Yakima	Northwest	509-457-5151	509-457-9909

Phone and FAX numbers for minor league offices can be found on page 129.

INDEPENDENT LEAGUE TEAMS

Page	Club	League	Phone	FAX
269	Atlantic City	Atlantic	609-344-8873	609-344-7010
264	Bangor	Can-Am	207-947-1900	207-947-9900
260	Bridgeport	Atlantic	203-345-4800	203-345-4830
264	Brockton	Can-Am	508-559-7000	508-587-2802
275	Calgary	Northern	403-277-2255	—
261	Camden	Atlantic	856-963-2600	856-963-8534
270	Chillicothe	Frontier	740-773-8326	740-773-8338

267	Coastal Bend	Central	361-387-8585	361-387-3535
267	Edinburg	Central	956-289-8800	956-289-8833
275	Edmonton	Northern	780-423-2255	780-423-3112
264	Elmira	Can-Am	607-734-1270	607-734-0891
267	El Paso	Central	915-755-2000	915-757-0671
271	Evansville	Frontier	812-435-8686	812-435-8688
275	Fargo-Moorhead	Northern	701-235-6161	701-297-9247
271	Florence	Frontier	859-594-4487	859-647-4639
268	Fort Worth	Central	817-226-2287	817-534-4620
276	Gary Southshore	Northern	219-882-2255	219-882-2259
271	Gateway	Frontier	618-337-3000	618-332-3625
268	Jackson	Central	601-362-2294	601-362-9577
276	Joliet	Northern	815-726-2255	815-726-9223
272	Kalamazoo	Frontier	269-388-8326	269-388-8333
277	Kansas City	Northern	913-328-2255	913-685-5652
261	Lancaster	Atlantic	717-509-4487	717-509-4456
277	Lincoln	Northern	402-474-2255	402-474-2254
262	Long Island	Atlantic	631-940-3825	631-940-3800
272	Mid-Missouri	Frontier	573-256-4004	573-256-4003
262	Nashua	Atlantic	603-883-2255	603-883-0880
265	New Haven County	Can-Am	203-777-5636	203-777-4369
265	New Jersey	Can-Am	973-746-7434	973-655-8021
262	Newark	Atlantic	973-848-1000	973-621-0095
265	North Shore	Can-Am	781-592-0007	781-592-0004
272	Ohio Valley	Frontier	—	—
269	Pensacola	Central	850-934-8444	850-934-8744
266	Quebec	Can-Am	418-521-2255	418-521-2266
272	Richmond, IN	Frontier	765-935-7529	765-962-7047
273	River City	Frontier	636-240-2287	636-240-7313
273	Rockford	Frontier	815-964-2255	815-964-2462
277	St. Paul	Northern	651-644-3517	651-644-1627
269	San Angelo	Central	915-942-6587	915-947-9480
278	Schaumburg	Northern	877-891-2255	847-891-6441
269	Shreveport	Central	318-636-5555	318-636-5670
278	Sioux City	Northern	712-277-9467	712-277-9406
278	Sioux Falls	Northern	605-333-0179	605-333-0139
263	Somerset	Atlantic	908-252-0700	908-252-0776
273	Washington	Frontier	724-250-9555	724-250-2333
274	Windy City	Frontier	708-489-2255	708-489-2999
279	Winnipeg	Northern	204-982-2273	204-982-2274
266	Worcester	Can-Am	508-792-2288	508-926-3662

INDEPENDENT LEAGUE OFFICES

Page	League	Phone	FAX
260	Atlantic League	856-541-9400	856-541-9410
262	Central League	919-956-8150	919-683-2693
263	Canadian-American League	919-401-8150	919-401-8152
270	Frontier League	740-452-7400	740-452-2999
279	Golden League	925-226-2889	925-226-2891
274	Northern League	817-378-9898	817-378-9805

OTHER ORGANIZATIONS

Page	Organization	Phone	FAX
128	AAU Women's Baseball	330-923-3400	330-923-1967
119	ABC Sports Radio	212-456-5185	—
118	ABC Sports	212-456-4878	212-456-2877
373	Academy of Pro Players	973-772-3355	973-772-4839
363	AFLAC High School Classic	301-762-7894	301-762-1491
348	African Baseball/Softball Assoc.	234-66-224-711	234-66-224-555
350	Alaska Baseball League	907-283-6186	907-274-3628
373	Aldrete Baseball Academy	831-884-0400	831-884-0800
366	All-American Amateur Baseball Association	740-453-8351	740-453-3978
363	All-American Baseball Talent Showcases	856-354-0201	856-354-0818
373	All-Star Baseball Academy	610-355-2411	610-355-2414
366	Amateur Athletic Union	407-934-7200	407-934-7242
375	Amateur Athletic Union Women's Baseball	330-923-3400	330-923-1967
367	American Amateur Baseball Congress	505-327-3120	505-327-3132
367	American Amateur Youth Baseball Alliance	573-518-0319	314-822-4974
300	American Baseball Coaches Association	989-775-3300	989-775-3600
349	American Baseball Foundation	205-558-4235	205-918-0800
367	American Legion Baseball	317-630-1213	317-630-1369
363	Area Code Games	856-354-0201	856-354-0818
363	Arizona Fall Classic	602-978-2929	602-439-4494

Page	Organization	Phone	Fax
297	Arizona Fall League	480-496-6700	480-496-6384
119	Associated Press	212-621-1630	212-621-1639
127	Association of Professional Baseball Players	714-935-9993	714-935-0431
349	Athletes In Action	937-352-1000	937-352-1245
121	Athlon Sports Baseball	615-327-0747	615-327-1149
350	Atlantic Collegiate League	917-882-5240	-
367	Babe Ruth Baseball	609-695-1434	609-695-2505
125	Babe Ruth Birthplace/Orioles Museum	410-727-1539	410-727-1652
373	The Baseball Academy	941-727-0303	941-727-2962
121	Baseball America	919-682-9635	919-682-2880
127	Baseball Assistance Team	212-931-7822	212-949-5433
362	Baseball At The Beach	843-546-3020	843-527-1816
349	Baseball Canada	613-748-5606	613-748-5767
127	Baseball Chapel	609-391-6444	—
348	Baseball Confederation of Oceania	61-3-9727-1779	61-3-9727-5959
121	Baseball Digest	847-491-6440	847-491-6203
363	The Baseball Encyclopedia	212-633-3516	212-633-3327
363	Baseball Factory	410-715-5080	410-715-1975
348	Baseball Federation of Asia	81-3-320-11155	81-3-320-10707
127	Baseball Trade Show	727-822-6937	727-825-3785
372	Baseball USA	713-690-5055	713-690-9448
120	Baseball Writers Association of America	718-767-2582	718-767-2583
362	Battle at the Ridge	843-546-3020	843-527-1816
122	Beckett Publications	800-840-3137	972-991-8930
119	Bloomberg Sports News	609-750-4691	609-897-8397
363	Blue-Grey Classic	508-881-2782	—
373	Bucky Dent Baseball School	561-265-0280	561-278-6679
118	CBS Sports	212-975-5230	212-975-4063
348	COPABE	507-2361-5977	507-261-5215
351	California Collegiate League	805-684-0657	805-684-8596
299	California CC Commision on Athletics	916-444-1600	916-444-2616
372	California Competitive Youth Baseball	714-993-2838	714-961-6078
351	Cal Ripken Sr. Collegiate Baseball League	—	
126	Canadian Baseball Hall of Fame	519-284-1838	519-284-1234
120	Canadian Press	416-364-0321	416-364-0207
347	Cape Cod League	508-432-6909	—
295	Caribbean Baseball Confederation	809-562-4737	809-565-4654
352	Central Illinois Collegiate League	217-483-5673	217-786-2788
290	China Baseball Association	86-10-8582-6002	86-10-8582-5994
291	Chinese Professional Baseball League	886-2-2577-6992	886-2-2577-2606
122	Citadel Media	888-979-0979	206-728-7744
353	Clark Griffith League	703-860-0946	703-860-0143
353	Coastal Plain League	919-852-1960	919-852-1973
372	Cocoa Expo Sports Center	321-639-3976	321-639-0598
365	College Select Baseball Showcase	800-782-3672	—
121	Collegiate Baseball	520-623-4530	520-624-5501
368	Continental Amateur Baseball Association	740-382-4620	—
372	Cooperstown Baseball World	888-229-8750	888-229-8720
372	Cooperstown Dreams Park	704-630-0050	704-630-0737
372	Disney's Wide World of Sports	407-938-3802	407-938-3442
368	Dixie Baseball, Inc.	903-927-2255	903-927-1846
369	Dizzy Dean Baseball	662-429-4365	—
289	Dominican Summer League	809-532-3619	—
295	Dominican Winter League	809-567-6371	809-567-5720
128	Donruss/Playoff Trading Cards	817-903-0300	817-983-0400
364	Doyle Baseball Select Showcases	863-439-1000	863-439-7086
292	Dutch Major League	31-30-607-6070	31-30-294-3043
117	ESPN/ESPN2-TV	860-766-2000	860-766-2213
120	ESPN The Magazine	212-515-1000	212-515-1290
119	ESPN Radio	860-766-2000	860-589-5523
363	East Coast Professional Baseball Showcase	910-962-3570	—
117	Elias Sports Bureau	212-869-1530	212-354-0980
348	European Baseball Confederation	32-3-219-0440	32-3-772-7727
126	Field of Dreams Movie Site	888-875-8404	319-875-7253
362	First Bank HS Classic	806-535-4505	806-794-5306
128	Fleer/Skybox Trading Cards	800-343-6816	856-231-0383
354	Florida Collegiate Instructional League	941-727-0303	941-727-2962
354	Florida Collegiate Summer League	407-694-6511	407-628-8535
118	FOX Sports	212-556-2500	212-354-6902
118	FOX Sports Net	310-369-1000	310-969-6049
373	Frozen Ropes Training Centers	877-846-5699	845-469-6742
362	Gatorade Circle of Champions	312-821-3593	—
128	Grandstand Cards	818-992-5642	818-348-9122

354	Great Lakes League	740-368-3527	740-368-3999
369	Hap Dumont Youth Baseball	316-721-1779	316-721-8054
125	Harry Wendelstedt Umpire School	386-672-4879	386-672-3212
362	Horizon National High School Invitational	602-867-9003	
364	Impact Baseball Showcase	—	—
122	Indians Ink	440-953-2200	440-953-2202
125	Inside Edge Scouting	800-858-3343	508-526-6145
348	International Baseball Federation	41-21-318-8240	41-21-318-8241
348	International Olympic Committee	41-21-621-6111	41-21-621-6216
362	International Paper Classic	843-527-9606	843-546-3807
348	International Sports Group	925-798-4591	925-680-1182
292	Italian Serie A/1	39-06-36858376	39-06-36858201
290	Japan League	03-3502-0022	03-3502-0140
355	Jayhawk League	316-755-2361	316-755-1285
125	Jim Evans Academy of Professional Umpiring	512-335-5959	512-335-5411
121	Junior Baseball Magazine	818-710-1234	818-710-1877
372	KC Sports Tournaments	816-587-4545	816-587-4549
289	Korea Baseball Organization	02-3460-4643	02-3460-4649
122	Krause Publications	715-445-4612	715-445-4087
126	Legends of the Game Baseball Museum	817-273-5600	
369	Little League Baseball, Inc.	570-326-1921	570-326-1074
126	Little League Baseball Museum	570-326-3607	570-326-2267
362	Lions High School Invitational	619-602-8650	619-239-3539
375	Los Angeles Dodgers Fantasy Camp	800-334-7529	772-229-6708
126	Louisville Slugger Museum	502-588-7228	502-585-1179
117	MLB Advanced Media (MLB.com)	212-485-3444	212-485-3456
119	MLB.com Radio	212-485-3444	212-485-3456
33	MLB Commissioner's Office	212-931-7800	—
33	MLB International	212-931-7500	212-949-5795
127	MLB Players Alumni Association	719-477-1870	719-477-1875
124	MLB Players Association	212-826-0808	212-752-4378
33	MLB Productions	212-931-7777	212-931-7788
124	Major League Scouting Bureau	909-980-1881	909-980-7794
362	March Madness High School Tournament	954-735-1841	954-334-6160
373	Mark Cresse Baseball School	714-892-6145	714-892-1881
375	Men's Adult Baseball League	631-753-6725	631-753-4031
375	Men's Senior Baseball League	631-753-6725	631-753-4031
288	Mexican League	555-557-1007	555-395-2454
295	Mexican Pacific League	667-761-25-70	667-761-25-71
373	Mickey Owen Baseball School	800-999-8369	417-889-6978
364	Mid-America Five Star Showcase	513-247-9511	513-247-0040
358	Midwest Prospects Showcase	405-942-5455	405-942-3012
129	Minor League Baseball	727-822-6937	727-821-5819
127	Minor League Baseball Alumni Association	727-477-6937	727-825-3785
355	Mountain Collegiate Baseball League	—	—
128	Multi-Ad Sports	800-348-6485	309-692-8378
126	Museum of Minor League Baseball	901-722-0207	901-527-1642
299	NAIA	913-791-0044	913-791-9555
118	NBC Sports	212-664-2014	212-664-6365
299	NCAA	317-917-6857	317-917-6826
299	NJCAA	719-590-9788	719-590-7324
128	National Adult Baseball Association	800-621-6479	303-639-6605
350	National Alliance of Collegiate Summer Baseball	704-896-9100	—
369	National Amateur Baseball Federation	301-464-5460	301-352-0214
349	National Baseball Congress	316-267-3372	316-267-3382
126	National Baseball Hall of Fame	607-547-7200	607-547-2044
120	National Collegiate Baseball Writers	214-753-0102	214-753-0145
362	National Federation of State High School Association	317-972-6900	317-822-5700
362	National High School Baseball Coaches Association	602-615-0571	480-838-7133
126	Negro Leagues Baseball Museum	816-221-1920	816-221-8424
355	New England Collegiate League	—	—
356	New York Collegiate League	585-223-2328	
126	Nolan Ryan Foundation and Exhibit Center	281-388-1134	281-388-1135
373	North Carolina Baseball Academy	336-931-1118	—
356	Northwoods League	507-536-4579	507-289-1866
122	Outside Pitch (Orioles)	410-234-8888	410-234-1029
357	Pacific International League	206-623-8844	602-623-8361
364	Pacific Northwest Championship	253-536-8001	—
373	Pennsylvania Diamond Bucks Camp	610-838-1219	—
364	Perfect Game USA	800-447-9362	319-298-2924
375	Phillies Adult Phantasy Camp	610-520-3400	—
369	Police Athletic Leagues	561-844-1823	561-863-6120
370	PONY Baseball, Inc.	724-225-1060	724-225-9852

364	Premier Baseball	941-371-0989	941-371-0917
125	Professional Baseball Athletic Trainers Society	404-875-4000	404-892-8560
128	Professional Baseball Employment Opportunities	866-937-7236	727-821-5819
374	Professional Baseball Instruction	877-448-2220	201-760-8820
124	Professional Baseball Scouts Foundation	310-858-1935	310-246-4862
125	Professional Baseball Umpire Corp.	727-822-6937	727-821-5819
125	Prospects Plus/The Scouting Report	800-845-2726	919-682-2880
296	Puerto Rican League	787-765-6285	787-767-3028
370	RBI	212-931-7897	212-949-5695
375	Randy Hundley's Fantasy Baseball Camps	847-991-9595	847-991-9595
122	Reds Report	614-486-2202	614-486-3650
374	Ripken Baseball Camps	800-486-0850	—
118	Rogers SportsNet	416-332-5600	416-332-5767
370	Roy Hobbs Baseball	330-923-3400	330-923-1967
127	SABR	216-575-0500	216-575-0502
374	San Diego School of Baseball	619-491-4000	619-469-5572
124	Scout of the Year Foundation	561-798-5897	561-798-4644
364	Selectfest Baseball	973-539-4781	—
374	Sho-Me Baseball Camp	800-993-2267	417-338-5838
125	Skillshow, Inc.	610-687-9072	610-687-9629
357	Southern Collegiate League	704-847-5075	704-847-1455
374	Southwest Professional Baseball School	888-830-8031	480-830-7455
121	The Sports Encyclopedia: Baseball	212-764-5151	—
120	The Sporting News	314-997-7111	314-997-0765
121	Sporting News Baseball Yearbook	314-997-7111	314-997-0765
119	Sporting News Radio Network	847-509-1661	847-509-1677
119	Sports Byline USA	415-434-8300	415-391-2569
120	SportsTicker	201-309-1200	201-860-9742
120	Sports Illustrated	212-522-1212	212-522-4543
121	Sports Illustrated for Kids	212-522-1212	212-522-0120
118	The Sports Network	416-332-5000	416-332-7658
121	Spring Training Baseball Yearbook	919-967-2420	919-967-6294
117	STATS, Inc.	847-583-2100	847-470-9160
121	Street and Smith's Baseball Yearbook	704-973-1575	704-973-1576
120	Street and Smith's Sports Business Journal	704-973-1400	704-973-1401
350	Summer Collegiate Baseball Association	919-852-1960	—
363	Sunbelt High School Baseball Classic Series	405-348-3839	405-340-7538
370	Super Series Baseball of America	480-664-2998	480-664-2997
370	T-Ball USA Association, Inc.	203-381-1449	203-381-1440
118	TBS	404-827-1700	404-827-1593
365	Team One Showcases	859-466-8326	—
127	Ted Williams Museum/Hitters Hall of Fame	352-527-6566	352-527-4163
358	Texas Collegiate League	807-339-9367	817-339-9309
365	Top 96 Showcase	508-651-0165	—
365	Top Guns Showcase	208-762-1100	—
128	Topps	212-376-0300	212-376-0573
121	Total Baseball	416-466-0418	416-466-9530
362	Toyo Tires National Classic	714-993-2838	714-993-5350
370	Triple Crown Sports	970-223-6644	970-223-3636
128	Upper Deck	800-873-7332	760-929-6548
371	US Amateur Baseball Association	425-776-7130	—
371	US Amateur Baseball Federation	619-934-2551	619-271-6659
371	US Specialty Sports Association	816-587-4545	816-587-4549
349	USA Baseball	919-474-8721	919-474-8822
362	USA HS Classic	901-072-0020	001-681-9443
372	USA Junior Olympic BB Championship	919-474-8721	919-474-8822
371	USSSA	816-587-4545	816-587-4549
348	US Olympic Committee	719-866-4500	719-866-4654
120	USA Today	703-854-5954	703-854-2072
120	USA Today Sports Weekly	703-854-6319	703-854-2034
374	Utah Baseball Academy	801-561-1700	801-561-5965
359	Valley League	540-885-8901	540-885-2068
289	Venezuelan Summer League	58-241-824-0321	58-241-824-0705
296	Venezuelan Winter League	58-212-761-4932	58-212-761-7661
122	Vine Line (Cubs)	773-404-2827	773-404-4129
118	WGN	773-528-2311	773-528-6050
362	West Coast Classic	408-252-6670	—
359	West Coast Collegiate League	509-888-9378	—
362	Westminster National High School Classic	954-735-1841	954-735-6160
125	World Umpires Association	920-969-1580	920-969-1892
372	World Wood Bat Association	319-298-2923	319-298-2924
119	XM Satellite Radio	202-380-4000	202-280-4500
122	Yankees Magazine	800-986-2657	—